ONTARIO
CIVIL
PRACTICE
1997

ONTARIO CIVIL PRACTICE 1997

by

PROFESSOR GARRY D. WATSON, Q.C.

and

MICHAEL McGOWAN
of the Ontario Bar

Contributing Editors

John T. Porter

and

Justin W. de Vries
of the Ontario Bar

CARSWELL
Thomson Professional Publishing

ISBN 0-459-56091-3
ISBN 0-459-56092-1 (Student)

The paper used in this publication meets the minimum requirements of the American National Standard for Information Sciences — Permanence of Paper for Printed Library Materials, ANSI Z39, 48-1984.

This work reproduces official English language versions of Ontario statutes and/or regulations. As this material also exists in official French language form, the reader is advised that reference to the official French language version may be warranted in appropriate circumstances.

CARSWELL
Thomson Professional Publishing

One Corporate Plaza, 2075 Kennedy Road, Scarborough, Ontario M1T 3V4
Customer Service:
Toronto 1-416-609-3800
Elsewhere in Canada/U.S. 1-800-387-5164
Fax 1-416-298-5094

To

Lucille W. McGowan, Paula A. Barran and M.E. Sullivan, Q.C.

and

The Late Walter B. Williston, Q.C.,
A. Foster Rodger, Q.C., The Honourable
John Morden and The Honourable Marvin Catzman —
all teachers who had a grateful professor for a student

TABLE OF CONTENTS

PREFACE

This is the eighth edition of the *Ontario Civil Practice*. This edition follows the same general format and organization as the last edition however a new softcover companion volume titled *Ontario Civil Practice: Forms, Case Management Guide and Special Materials* has been created.

A few months ago we conducted a survey of our readers' views concerning last year's decision to move the Forms out of the main work and into a softcover companion volume. That decision was made to protect the portability of the main work which was being threatened by the growth of materials, particularly the voluminous estate rules and forms introduced last year.

We wish to thank the hundreds of readers who responded to the survey. There was a strong consensus that portability of the book was very important and since the Forms materials were rarely required in court, publishing the Forms separately was widely welcomed. Many lawyers found it helpful to be able to give the Forms volume to their secretary or clerk.

We are therefore continuing and expanding the companion volume now titled *Ontario Civil Practice: Forms, Case Management Guide and Special Materials*. We have transferred the texts of the *Judicial Review Procedure Act*, the *Statutory Powers Procedure Act* and related case digests from the main work to the companion volume. We have also republished the case management guide and the class action materials in the companion volume. Finally, in response to the readers' requests we have included the text of the Small Claims Court Rules in the companion volume.

The net result is that the main work now contains materials which (a) are of general application throughout the province and (b) are likely to be needed in court. The softcover companion volume contains (a) general materials which are rarely needed in court (*e.g.* the Forms) or (b) specialized materials which either relate to specific geographic areas (*e.g.* the case management rules for Toronto, Essex and Algoma) or to a specialized practice area (*e.g.* class actions, administrative law cases, and Small Claims Court cases).

Over 200 new case digests have been added. The commentary has been revised where appropriate and this year's Annual Survey, page ciii, summarizes the major developments in the law of civil procedure since the last edition.

We have included all appropriate cases decided to approximately April 1996. Where the citation for the full text report of a particular case was not available at press time, we have provided a Weekly Digest of Civil Procedure (W.D.C.P.) citation. Such cases will soon be reported in Carswell's Practice Cases, probably at about Volumes 43 and 44 (3rd series).

Any amendments to the Rules of Civil Procedure and the *Courts of Justice Act* or other major developments occurring before the next edition of this work will be dealt with in supplements which will be sent to subscribers and which may be inserted in a pocket inside the back cover. Some assembly is required! — the self-adhesive pocket will be provided with the first supplement but must be attached to the inside back cover by the reader.

We thank our colleagues at Carswell, most particularly Sheila McLeish, for their support, hard work and efficiency.

June 1996

GDW
MM

TABLES OF CONCORDANCE

Following are four concordance tables. The first two relate to the *Courts of Justice Act, 1984*, S.O. 1984, c. 11, as it existed before the 1989 amendments, the *Courts of Justice Act* as it existed after the 1989 amendments and the *Courts of Justice Act*, R.S.O. 1990, c. C.43, as amended. The final two tables trace the interrelationship between the provisions of the Rules of Civil Procedure, O. Reg. 560/84 as amended to 1992 and the Rules of Civil Procedure, R.R.O. 1990, Reg. 194, as amended.

For tables relating the *Courts of Justice Act* to the *Judicature Act* and the Rules of Civil Procedure to the former Rules of Practice, see Holmested and Watson, *Ontario Civil Procedure*.

COURTS OF JUSTICE ACT 1984/1989/1990

The following table shows the interrelationship of the *Courts of Justice Act, 1984*, S.O. 1984, c. 11, including minor amendments up to 1988 (referred to as "C.J.A. 84"), the *Courts of Justice Act* with all amendments including the *Courts of Justice Amendment Acts, 1989* (referred to as "C.J.A. 89") and the *Courts of Justice Act*, R.S.O. 1990, c. C.43, as amended (referred to as "C.J.A. 90"). The 1989 amendments were extensive and there was a general renumbering of the sections in Parts I, II, III and IV of the Act. For additional tables relating the C.J.A. 84, C.J.A. 89 and C.J.A. 90 to the *Judicature Act* as it existed in 1984, see Holmested and Watson, *Ontario Civil Procedure*.

C.J.A. 84	C.J.A. 89	C.J.A. 90
1	1	1
2(1)	2, 10	2, 11
2(2)	2(1), 10(1)	2(1), 11(1)
3(1)	3(1)	3(1)
3(2)	5(2), (3)	5(2), (3)
3(3)	—	—
3(4)	6(1)	6(1)
3(5)	6(3)	6(3)
4(1)	11(1)	12(1)
4(2)	52(1), (2)	53(1), (2)
4(3)	13(4)	14(4)
5	17	18
6(1), (2)	3(4), 11(2), 39	3(3), 12(2), 40
6(3)	3(5), 6(3), 11(3), 39	3(4), 6(3), 12(3), 40
7	—	—
8	4(2), 12(2)	4(2), 13(2)
9(1)	12(1)	13(1)
9(2)	4(1)	4(1)
10	51	—
11	—	—
12	—	—
13(1)	—	—
13(2)	16	17

C.J.A. 84	C.J.A. 89	C.J.A. 90
14(1), (2)	13(1), 15	14(1), 16
14(3)	15	16
15(1)	18(1)	19(1)
15(2)	18(2), (3)	19(2), (3)
16	20	21
17(1)	6(1)	6(1)
17(2)	6(2), (3)	6(2), (3)
18(1)	7(1)	7(1)
18(2)	—	—
18(3)	7(2)-(5)	7(2)-(5)
18(4)	7	7
18(5)	5(1)	5(1)
19	8	8
20(1)	—	—
20(2)	—	—
20(3), (4)	52(1), 101(2)	53(1), 87(2)
20(5), (7)	52(3)-(5)	53(3), (4)
20(8)-(10)	—	—
20(11)	101(3)	87(3)
21(1), (2)	—	—
21(3)	—	—
22	101a	88
23	—	—
24	—	—
25	—	—
26	—	—
27	—	—
28	—	—
29	—	—
30	—	—
31	—	—
32	—	—
33	—	—
34	—	—
35	—	—
36(1)-(3)	—	—
36(4)	18(4)	19(4)
36(5)	—	—
37(1)	—	—
37(2)	—	—
38	53	—
39	54	—
40(1), (2)	55(1), (2)	—
40(3)	—	—
40(4)	55(3)	—
41	56	—
42	57	—
43	—	—
44	58	—
45	59	—
46(1), (2)	60(1), (2)	—
46(3)	—	—
46(4)	60(4)	—

C.J.A. 84	C.J.A. 89	C.J.A. 90
47	61	62
48	—	—
49	62	63
50	—	—
51	63	64
52	41(1), (2)	42(1), (2)
53	42	43
54	43(9)	44(9)
55	—	—
56	—	—
57	—	—
58	47	48
59	48	49
60	—	—
61	—	—
62	153a	146
63(1)	41(3)	42(3)
63(2)-(4)	—	—
63(5)	35(1)	36(1)
63(6)	—	—
63(7)	35(4)	36(4)
64	—	—
65	44(4)	45(4)
66(1)	—	—
66(2)	38(1)	39(1)
67(1)	37(1)	38(1)
67(2)	37(3)	38(3)
68(1)	—	—
68(2)	38(2)	39(2)
69	37(2)	38(2)
70	—	—
71	—	—
72	40	41
73(1), (2)	—	—
73(3)	69(3)	70(3)
74(1)	—	—
74(2)	38(1)	39(1)
75(1)	37(2), (3)	38(2), (3)
75a	—	—
76	—	—
77	—	—
78(1)	22(1)	23(1)
78(2)	—	—
78(3)	24	25
79	25	26
80	26	27
81	27	28
82	29	—
83	30	31
84	22(2), (3)	23(2), (3)
85	—	—
86	—	—
87(1)	52(1)	53(1)

C.J.A. 84	C.J.A. 89	C.J.A. 90
87(2)-(4)	52(3)-(5)	53(3), (4)
88	50	—
89	64	65
90	65	66
91	91	71
92	91a	72
93	93(1)	76(1)
94	94	77
95	95	78
96	96	80
97	97	81
98	98	82
99	99	83
100	100	84
101(1)-(3)	—	—
101(4)	95a	79
102	102	89
103	103	90
104(1)-(3)	—	—
104(4)	104(4)	91
105	105	92
106	106	93
107	107	94
108	108	95
109	109	96
110	110	97
111	111	98
112	112	99
113	113	100
114	114	101
115	115	102
116(1)-(7)	116(1)-(7)	103(1)-(7)
116(8), (9)	116(8), (9)	*
117	117	104
118	118	105
119	119	106
120(1)-(3)	120(1)-(3)	107(1)-(4)
120(4)-(6)	—	—
121	121	108
122	122	109
123	123	110
124	124	111
125	125	112
126	126	113
127	127	114
128	128	115
129	129	116
130	130	117
131	131	121
132	132	122
133	133	123

* Not contained in R.S.O. 1990, but still in force (see R.S.O. 1990, Vol. 12, Schedule C).

C.J.A. 84	C.J.A. 89	C.J.A. 90
134	134	124
135	135	125
136(1)	136 sch. 1	126 sch. 1
136(2)-(4)	136(1), (2)	126(1), (2)
136(5)-(11)	136(3)-(9)	126(3)-(9)
137	137	127
138(1)-(3)	138(1)-(3)	128(1)-(4)
138(4)	138(4)	*
139(1)-(5)	139(1)-(5)	129(1)-(5)
139(6)	139(6)	*
140	140	130
141	141	131
142	142	132
143	143	133
144	144	134
145	145	135
146	146	136
147	147	137
148	148	138
149	149	139
150	150	140
151	151	142
152	152	143
153	153	145
154	154	147
155	155	148
156	156	*
157	157	—
158	158	*
159	159	—
159a	159a	150
160	160a	—

* Not contained in R.S.O. 1990, but still in force (see R.S.O. 1990, Vol. 12, Schedule C).

COURTS OF JUSTICE ACT 1990/1989/1984

The following table shows the interrelationship of the *Courts of Justice Act*, R.S.O. 1990, c. C.43, as amended (referred to as "C.J.A. 1990"), the *Courts of Justice Act, 1984*, S.O. 1984, c. 11, with all amendments including the *Courts of Justice Amendment Acts, 1989* (referred to as "C.J.A. 89) and the *Courts of Justice Act, 1984* including minor amendments up to 1988 (referred to as "C.J.A. 84"). The 1989 amendments were extensive and there was a general renumbering of the sections in Parts I, II, III and IV of the Act. For additional tables relating the C.J.A. 84, C.J.A. 89 and C.J.A. 90 to the *Judicature Act* as it existed in 1984, see Holmested and Watson, *Ontario Civil Procedure*.

C.J.A. 90	*C.J.A. 89*	*C.J.A. 84*
1	1	1
2	2	2
3(1)	3(1)	3(1)
3(2)	3(2)	—
3(3), (4)	3(4), (5)	6(1), (3)
4	4	8, 9(2)
5	5	3(2), 18(5)
6	6	17(1), (2)
7	7	18(1), (3)
8	8	19
9	8a	—
10	9	—
11	10	2(1)
12	11	4(1), 6(1), (3)
13	12	8, 9(1)
14	13	4(3), 14(2)
15	14	—
16	15	14(1)
17	16	13(2)
18(1), (2)	17(1)	5
18(3)	17(2)	5
19	18	15(1), (2), 36(4)
20	19	—
21	20	16
21.1	—	—
21.2	—	—
21.3	—	—
21.4	—	—
21.5	—	—
21.6	—	—
21.7	—	—
21.8	—	—
21.9	—	—
21.10	—	—
21.11	—	—
21.12	—	—
21.13	—	—
21.14	—	—
21.15	—	—

C.J.A. 90	*C.J.A. 89*	*C.J.A. 84*
22(1), (2)	21(1)	—
22(3)	21(2)	—
23	22	78(1), 84
24	23	—
25	24	78(3)
26	25	79
27	26	80
28	27	81
29	28	—
31	30	83
32	31(1), (2)	—
33	—	—
33.1	—	—
34	33	—
35	34	—
36	35	63(5), (7)
37	36	—
38	37	67, 69, 75(1)
39	38	66(2), 68(2), 74(2)
40	39(1), (2)	6
41	40	72
42	41	52, 63(1)
43	—	—
44	—	—
45	—	—
46	42	53
47	43	54
48	44	65
49	46, 47	57
50	—	—
51	—	—
51.1	—	—
51.2	—	—
51.3	—	—
51.4	—	—
51.5	—	—
51.6	—	—
51.7	—	—
51.8	45	56
51.9	—	—
51.10	—	—
51.11	—	—
51.12	—	—
51.13	50	88
52	51	10
53	52	4(2), 20(4)-(7), 87(1)-(4)
65(1), (2)	64(1)	89
65(3)-(6)	64(2)-(5)	89
66	65	90
67(1), (2)	66(1)	—
67(3)-(6)	66(2)-(5)	—
68	67	—
69(1), (2)	68(1)	—

C.J.A. 90	C.J.A. 89	C.J.A. 84
69(3)-(6)	68(2)-(5)	—
70	69	73(3)
71	91	91
72(1), (2)	91a(1)	92
72(3)	91a(2)	92
73(1), (2)	92(1)	—
73(3), (4)	92(2), (3)	—
74	92a	—
75	92b	—
76	93	93
77	94	94
78	95	95
79	95a	101(4)
80	96	96
81	97	—
82	98	98
83	99	99
84	100	100
85	100a	—
86	100b	—
87	101	20(3), (11)
87.1	—	—
88	101a	22
89	102	102
90	103	103
91	104(4)	104
92	105	105
93	106	106
94	107	107
95	108	108
96	109	109
97	110	110
98	111	111
99	112	112
100	113	113
101	114	114
102	115	115
103	116(1)-(7)	116(1)-(7)
104	117	117
105	118	118
106	119	119
107(1), (2)	120(1), (2)	120(1), (2)
107(3)	120(2a)	—
107(4)-(7)	120(3)-(6)	—
108	121	121
109	122	122
110	123	123
111	124	124
112	125(1)-(4)	125
113	126	126
114	127	127
115	128	128
116	129	129

C.J.A. 90	C.J.A. 89	C.J.A. 84
117	130	130
118	130a	—
119	130b	—
120	130c	—
121	131	131
122	132	132
123	133	133
124	134	134
125	135	135
126	136	136
127	137	137
128(1)	138(1)	138
128(2)	138(1a)	—
128(3)	138(2)	138
128(4)	138(3)	138
129	139(1)-(5)	139
130	140	140
131	141	141
132	142	142
133	143	143
134	144	144
135	145	145
136	146	146
137	147	147
138	148	148
139	149	149
140	150	150
141	150a	—
142	151	151
143	152	152
144	152a	—
145	153	153
146	153a	62
147	154	154
148	155	155
149	—	—
150	159a	159a
151	160c	—
Schedule	—	—

1984 RULES/1990 RULES

The following table relates the Rules of Civil Procedure, O. Reg. 560/84, as amended to 1992 (referred to as "1984 Rule") to the Rules of Civil Procedure, R.R.O. 1990, Reg. 194, as amended (referred to as "1990 Rule"). For those wishing to go back further in time, the prior history can be traced by referring to the Rules of Practice and Procedure historical concordance table in Holmested and Gale, *Ontario Judicature Act and Rules of Practice.*

1984 Rule	1990 Rule	1984 Rule	1990 Rule	1984 Rule	1990 Rule
1.01(1)	1.01(1)	2.02	2.02	(5)	(5)
(2)	(2)	2.03	2.03	(6)	(6)
(3)	(3)	3.01(1)	3.01(1)	4.08	4.08
1.02(1)	1.02(1)	(2)	(2)	4.09(1)	4.09(1)
(2)	(2)	3.02(1)	3.02(1)	(2)	(2)
(3)	(3)	(2)	(2)	(3)	(3)
(4)	(4)	(3)	(3)	(4)	(4)
1.03 *1*	1.03 "action"	(4)	(4)	(5)	(5)
2	"appellant"	3.03(1)	3.03(1)	(6)	(6)
3	"appellate court"	(2)	(2)	(7)	(7)
4	"applicant"	4.01(1)	4.01(1)	(8)	(8)
5	"application"	(2)	(2)	(9)	(9)
6	"county"	4.02(1)	4.02(1)	(10)	(10)
7	"court"	(2)	(2)	(11)	(11)
8	"defendant"	(3)(a)	(3)(a)	4.10(1)	4.10(1)
9	"deliver"	(3)(b)	(3)(b)	(2)	(2)
10	"disability"	(3)(ba)	(3)(c)	4.11	4.11
11	"discovery"	(3)(c)	(3)(d)	5.01(1)	5.01(1)
12	"hearing"	(3)(d)	(3)(e)	(2)	(2)
13	"holiday"	(3)(e)	(3)(f)	(3)	(3)
14	"judge"	4.03	4.03	5.02(1)	5.02(1)
15	"judgment"	4.04	4.04	(2)	(2)
17	"motion"	4.05(1)	4.05(1)	5.03(1)	5.03(1)
18	"moving party"	(2)	(2)	(2)	(2)
19	"order"	(3)	(3)	(3)	(3)
20	"originating process"	(4)	(4)	(4)	(4)
21	"plaintiff"	(5)	(5)	(5)	(5)
22	"proceeding"	(6)	(6)	(6)	(6)
23	"referee"	4.06(1)	4.06(1)	5.04(1)	5.04(1)
24	"registrar"	(2)	(2)	(2)	(2)
25	"respondent"	(3)	(3)	(3)	(3)
26	"responding party"	(4)	(4)	5.05	5.05
26a	"solicitor's office"	(5)	(5)	6.01(1)	6.01(1)
27	"statute"	(6)	(6)	(2)	(2)
1.04(1)	1.04(1)	(7)	(7)	6.02	6.02
(2)	(2)	(8)	(8)	7.01(1)	7.01(1)
(3)	(3)	(9)	(9)	(2)	(2)
1.05	1.05	4.07(1)	4.07(1)	7.02(1)	7.02(1)
1.06	1.06	(2)	(2)	(2)	
2.01(1)	2.01(1)	(3)	(3)	7.03(1)	7.03(1)
(2)	(2)	(4)	(4)	(2)	(2)

1984 Rule	1990 Rule	1984 Rule	1990 Rule	1984 Rule	1990 Rule
(3)	(3)	(6)	(6)	15.04(1)	15.04(1)
(4)	(4)	(7)	(7)	(2)	(2)
(5)	(5)	10.01(1)	10.01(1)	(3)	(3)
(6)	(6)	(2)	(2)	(4)	(4)
(7)	(7)	(3)	(3)	(5)	(5)
(8)	(8)	(4)	(4)	15.05	15.05
(9)	(9)	10.02	10.02	15.06	15.06
(10)	(10)	10.03	10.03	16.01(1)	16.01(1)
7.04	7.04(1)	11.01	11.01	(2)	(2)
7.05(1)	7.05(1)	11.02(1)	11.02(1)	(3)	(3)
(2)	(2)	(2)	(2)	(4)	(4)
(3)	(3)	11.03	11.03	16.02(1)	16.02(1)
7.06(1)	7.06(1)	12.01	12.01	(2)	(2)
(2)	(2)	12.02	12.02	16.03(1)	16.03(1)
7.07(1)	7.07(1)	13.01(1)	13.01(1)	(2)	(2)
(2)	(2)	(2)	(2)	(3)	(3)
7.08(1)	7.08(1)	13.02	13.02	(4)	(4)
(2)	(2)	13.03(1)	13.03(1)	(5)	(5)
(3)	(3)	(2)	(2)	(6)	(6)
(4)	—	14.01(1)	14.01(1)	16.04(1)	16.04(1)
(5)	(4)	(2)	(2)	(2)	(2)
(6)	(5)	(3)	(3)	(3)	(3)
7.09(1)	7.09(1)	(4)	(4)	16.05(1)	16.05(1)
(2)	(2)	14.02	14.02	(2)	(2)
8.01(1)	8.01(1)	14.03(1)	14.03(1)	(3)	(3)
(2)	(2)	(2)	(2)	(3a)	(3.1)
8.02	8.02	(3)	(3)	(3b)	(3.2)
8.03(1)	8.03(1)	(4)	(4)	16.06(1)	16.06(1)
(2)	(2)	(5)	(5)	(2)	(2)
8.04	8.04	14.04	14.04	16.07	16.07
8.05(1)	8.05(1)	14.05(1)	14.05(1)	16.08	16.08
(2)	(2)	(2)	(2)	16.09(1)	16.09(1)
(3)	(3)	(3)	(3)	(2)	(2)
8.06(1)	8.06(1)	14.06(1)	14.06(1)	(3)	(3)
(2)	(2)	(2)	(2)	(4)	(4)
(3)	(3)	(3)	(3)	(5)	(5)
8.07(1)	8.07(1)	14.07(1)	14.07(1)	17.01	17.01
(2)	(2)	(2)	(2)	17.02	17.02
9.01(1)	9.01(1)	14.08(1)	14.08(1)	17.03(1)	17.03(1)
(2)(a)	(2)(a)	(2)	(2)	(2)	(2)
(2)(aa)	(2)(b)	14.09	14.09	17.04(1)	17.04(1)
(2)(b)	(2)(c)	14.10(1)	14.10(1)	(2)	(2)
(2)(c)	(2)(d)	(2)	(2)	17.05(1)	17.05(1)
(2)(d)	(2)(e)	15.01(1)	15.01(1)	(2)	(2)
(3)	(3)	(2)	(2)	3)	(3)
(4)	(4)	(3)	(3)	(4)	(4)
9.02(1)	9.02(1)	15.02(1)	15.02(1)	17.06(1)	17.06(1)
(2)	(2)	(2)	(2)	(2)	(2)
9.03(1)	9.03(1)	(3)	(3)	(3)	(3)
(2)	(2)	(4)	(4)	(4)	(4)
(3)	(3)	15.03(1)	15.03(1)	18.01	18.01
(4)	(4)	(2)	(2)	18.02(1)	18.02(1)
(5)	(5)	(3)	(3)	(2)	(2)

1984 Rule	1990 Rule	1984 Rule	1990 Rule	1984 Rule	1990 Rule
(3)	(3)	(2)	(2)	(5)	(5)
19.01(1)	19.01(1)	22.02	22.02	(6)	(6)
(2)	(2)	22.03(1)	22.03(1)	25.08(1)	25.08(1)
(3)	(3)	(2)	(2)	(2)	(2)
(4)	(4)	22.04	22.04	(3)	(3)
(5)	(5)	22.05(1)	22.05(1)	(4)	(4)
19.02(1)	19.02(1)	(2)	(2)	25.09(1)	25.09(1)
(2)	(2)	23.01(1)	23.01(1)	(2)	(2)
(3)	(3)	(2)	(2)	25.10	25.10
19.03(1)	19.03(1)	23.02	23.02	25.11	25.11
(2)	(2)	23.03	23.03	26.01	26.01
19.04(1)	19.04(1)	23.04(1)	23.04(1)	26.02	26.02
(2)	(2)	(2)	(2)	26.03(1)	26.03(1)
(3)	(3)	23.05	23.05	(2)	(2)
(4)	(4)	23.06(1)	23.06(1)	(3)	(3)
(5)	(5)	(2)	(2)	26.04(1)	26.04(1)
(6)	(6)	23.07	23.07	(2)	(2)
19.05(1)	19.05(1)	24.01	24.01	(3)	(3)
(2)	(2)	24.02	24.02	26.05(1)	26.05(1)
(3)	(3)	24.03	24.03	(2)	(2)
(4)	(4)	24.04	24.04	26.06	26.06
19.07	19.06	24.05(1)	24.05(1)	27.01(1)	27.01(1)
19.08	19.07	(2)	(2)	(2)	(2)
19.09(1)	19.08(1)	24.06	24.06	27.02	27.02
(2)	(2)	25.01(1)	25.01(1)	27.03	27.03
(3)	(3)	(2)	(2)	27.04(1)	27.04(1)
19.10	19.09	(3)	(3)	(2)	(2)
20.01(1)	20.01(1)	(4)	(4)	(3)	(3)
(2)	(2)	(5)	(5)	27.05(1)	27.05(1)
(3)	(3)	25.02	25.02	(2)	(2)
20.02	20.02	25.03(1)	25.03(1)	(3)	(3)
20.03	20.03	(2)	(2)	27.06	27.06
20.04(1)	20.04(1)	(3)	(3)	27.07(1)	27.07(1)
(2)	(2)	25.04(1)	25.04(1)	(2)	(2)
(3)	(3)	(2)	(2)	27.08(1)	27.08(1)
(4)	(4)	(3)	(3)	(2)	(2)
(5)	(5)	(4)	(4)	27.09(1)	27.09(1)
20.05(1)	20.05(1)	(5)	(5)	(2)	(2)
(2)	(2)	(6)	(6)	(3)	(3)
(3)	(3)	25.05	25.05	27.10	27.10
(4)	(4)	25.06(1)	25.06(1)	28.01(1)	28.01(1)
(5)	(5)	(2)	(2)	(2)	(2)
20.06(1)	20.06(1)	(3)	(3)	28.02	28.02
(2)	(2)	(4)	(4)	28.03	28.03
20.07	20.07	(5)	(5)	28.04(1)	28.04(1)
20.08	20.08	(6)	(6)	(2)	(2)
20.09	20.09	(7)	(7)	28.05(1)	28.05(1)
21.01(1)	21.01(1)	(8)	(8)	(2)	(2)
(2)	(2)	(9)	(9)	28.06(1)	28.06(1)
(3)	(3)	25.07(1)	25.07(1)	(2)	(2)
21.02	21.02	(2)	(2)	(3)	(3)
21.03	21.03	(3)	(3)	(4)	(4)
22.01(1)	22.01(1)	(4)	(4)	(5)	(5)

1984 Rule	1990 Rule	1984 Rule	1990 Rule	1984 Rule	1990 Rule
28.07	28.07	(2)	(2)	33.04(1)	33.04(1)
28.08	28.08	(3)	(3)	(2)	(2)
28.09	28.09	(4)	(4)	33.05	33.05
28.10	28.10	30.11	30.11	33.06(1)	33.06(1)
28.11	28.11	31.01	31.01	(2)	(2)
29.01	29.01	31.02(1)	31.02(1)	33.07	33.07
29.02(1)	29.02(1), (1.1), (1.2)	(2)	(2)	33.08	33.08
(2)	(2)	31.03(1)	31.03(1)	34.01	34.01
(3)	(3)	(2)	(2)	34.02	34.02
29.03	29.03	(3)	(3)	34.03	34.03
29.04	29.04	(4)	(4)	34.04(1)	34.04(1)
29.05(1)	29.05(1)	(5)	(5)	(2)	(2)
(2)	(2)	(6)	(6)	(3)	(3)
(3)	(3)	(7)	(7)	(4)	(4)
(4)	(4)	(8)	(8)	(5)	(5)
(5)	(5)	(9)	(9)	(6)	(6)
29.06	29.06	31.04(1)	31.04(1)	(7)	(7)
29.07	29.07	(2)	(2)	(8)	(8)
29.08(1)	29.08(1)	(3)	(3)	34.04a	34.04.1
(2)	(2)	31.05	31.05	34.05(1)	34.05(1)
29.09	29.09	31.06(1)	31.06(1)	(2)	(2)
29.10	29.10	(2)	(2)	34.06	34.06
29.11(1)	29.11(1)	(3)	(3)	34.07(1)	34.07(1)
(2)	(2)	(4)	(4)	(2)	(2)
(3)	(3)	(4a)	(5)	(3)	(3)
29.12	29.12	(5)	(6)	(4)	(4)
29.13	29.13	31.07(1)	31.07(1)	(5)	(5)
30.01(1)	30.01(1)	(2)	(2)	(6)	(6)
(2)	(2)	31.08	31.08	(7)	(7)
30.02(1)	30.02(1)	31.09(1)	31.09(1)	34.08(1)	34.08(1)
(2)	(2)	(2)	(2)	(2)	(2)
(3)	(3)	(3)	(3)	34.09(1)	34.09(1)
(4)	(4)	31.10(1)	31.10(1)	(2)	(2)
30.03(1)	30.03(1)	(2)	(2)	34.10(1)	34.10(1)
(2)	(2)	(3)	(3)	(2)	(2)
(3)	(3)	(4)	(4)	(3)	(3)
(4)	(4)	(5)	(5)	(4)	(4)
(5)	(5)	31.11(1)	31.11(1)	34.11(1)	34.11(1)
30.04(1)	30.04(1)	(2)	(2)	(2)	(2)
(2)	(2)	(3)	(3)	(3)	(3)
(3)	(3)	(4)	(4)	(4)	(4)
(4)	(4)	(5)	(5)	(5)	(5)
(5)	(5)	(6)	(6)	34.12(1)	34.12(1)
(6)	(6)	(7)	(7)	(2)	(2)
(7)	(7)	(8)	(8)	(3)	(3)
(8)	(8)	32.01(1)	32.01(1)	34.13	34.13
30.05	30.05	(2)	(2)	34.14(1)	34.14(1)
30.06	30.06	(3)	(3)	(2)	(2)
30.07	30.07	(4)	(4)	34.15(1)	34.15(1)
30.08(1)	30.08(1)	33.01	33.01	(2)	(2)
(2)	(2)	33.02(1)	33.02(1)	34.16	34.16
30.09	30.09	(2)	(2)	34.17(1)	34.17(1)
30.10(1)	30.10(1)	33.03	33.03	(2)	(2)

1984 Rule	1990 Rule	1984 Rule	1990 Rule	1984 Rule	1990 Rule
(3)	(3)	37.10(1)	37.10(1)	(2)	(2)
34.18(1)	34.18(1)	(3)	(2)	(3)	(3)
(2)	(2)	(4)	(3)	38.13	38.12
(2a)	(3)	(5)	(4)	39.01(1)	39.01(1)
(3)	(4)	(6)	(5)	(2)	(2)
34.19(1)	34.19(1)	(7)	(6)	(3)	(3)
(2)	(2)	37.11(1)	37.11(1)	(4)	(4)
35.01	35.01	(2)	(2)	(5)	(5)
35.02(1)	35.02(1)	37.12	37.12	(6)	(6)
(2)	(2)	37.13(1)	37.13(1)	39.02(1)	39.02(1)
35.03	35.03	(2)	(2)	(2)	(2)
35.04(1)	35.04(1)	(3)	(3)	(3)	(3)
(2)	(2)	37.14(1)	37.14(1)	(4)	(4)
(3)	(3)	(2)	(2)	39.03(1)	39.03(1)
(4)	(4)	(3)	(3)	(2)	(2)
35.05	35.05	(4)	(4)	(2a)	(3)
35.06	35.06	(4a)	(5)	(3)	(4)
36.01(1)	36.01(1)	(5)	(6)	(4)	(5)
(2)	(2)	37.15(1)	37.15(1)	39.04	39.04
(3)	(3)	(2)	(2)	40.01	40.01
36.02(1)	36.02(1)	37.16	37.16	40.02(1)	40.02(1)
(2)	(2)	37.17	37.17	(2)	(2)
36.03	36.03	38.01(1)	38.01(1)	(3)	(3)
36.04(1)	36.04(1)	(2)	(2)	(4)	(4)
(2)	(2)	38.03	38.02	40.03	40.03
(3)	(3)	38.04(1)	38.03(1)	41.01	41.01
(4)	(4)	(1a)	(1.1)	41.02	41.02
(5)	(5)	(2)	(2)	41.03	41.03
(6)	(6)	(3)	(3)	41.04	41.04
(7)	(7)	(4)	(4)	41.05	41.05
37.01	37.01	38.05	38.04	41.06	41.06
37.02(1)	37.02(1)	38.06	38.05	42.01(1)	42.01(1)
(3)	(2)	38.07(1)	38.06(1)	(2)	(2)
37.03(1)	37.03(1)	(2)	(2)	(3)	(3)
(2)	(2)	(3)	(3)	(4)	(4)
(3)	(3)	(4)	(4)	42.02(1)	42.02(1)
(5)	(4)	38.08(1)	38.07(1)	(2)	(2)
(6)	(5)	(2)	(2)	43.01	43.01
37.04	37.04	(3)	(3)	43.02	43.02
37.05(1)	37.05(1)	38.09(1)	38.08(1)	43.03(1)	43.03(1)
(2)	(2)	(2)	(2)	(2)	(2)
37.06	37.06	(3)	(3)	(3)	(3)
37.07(1)	37.07(1)	(4)	(4)	43.04(1)	43.04(1)
(2)	(2)	38.10(1)	38.09(1)	(2)	(2)
(3)	(3)	(1a)	(2)	(3)	(3)
(4)	(4)	(2)	(3)	43.05(1)	43.05(1)
(5)	(5)	(3)	(4)	(1)(a)	(1) "property"
(6)	(6)	(4)	(5)	(1)(b)	(1) "writ of execution"
37.08(1)	37.08(1)	(5)	(6)	(2)	(2)
(2)	(2)	38.11(1)	38.10(1)	(3)	(3)
37.09(1)	37.09(1)	(2)	(2)	(4)	(4)
(2)	(2)	(3)	(3)	(5)	(5)
(3)	(3)	38.12(1)	38.11(1)		

1984 Rule	1990 Rule	1984 Rule	1990 Rule	1984 Rule	1990 Rule
(6)	(6)	48.07	48.07	50.03	50.03
(7)	(7)	48.08(1)	48.08(1)	50.04	50.04
44.01(1)	44.01(1)	(2)	(2)	50.05	50.05
(2)	(2)	48.09	48.09	50.06	50.06
44.02	44.02	48.10	48.10	50.07	50.07
44.03(1)	44.03(1)	48.11	48.11	50.08	50.08
(2)	(2)	48.12	48.12	51.01	51.01
44.04(1)	44.04(1)	48.13	48.13	51.02(1)	51.02(1)
(2)	(2)	48.14(1)	48.14(1)	(2)	(2)
(3)	(3)	(2)	(2)	51.03(1)	51.03(1)
44.05	44.05	(3)	(3)	(2)	(2)
44.06	44.06	(4)	(4)	(3)	(3)
44.07(1)	44.07(1)	(5)	(5)	51.04	51.04
(2)	(2)	(6)	(6)	51.05	51.05
(3)	(3)	(7)	(7)	51.06(1)	51.06(1)
(4)	(4)	(8)	(8)	(2)	(2)
44.08	44.08	(9)	(9)	52.01(1)	52.01(1)
45.01(1)	45.01(1)	(10)	(10)	(2)	(2)
(2)	(2)	(11)	(11)	(3)	(3)
45.02	45.02	49.01(a)	49.01 "defendant"	52.02	52.02
45.03(1)	45.03(1)	(b)	"plaintiff"	52.03(1)	52.03(1)
(2)	(2)	49.02(1)	49.02(1)	(2)	(2)
(3)	(3)	(2)	(2)	(3)	(3)
46.01(1)	46.01(1)	49.03	49.03	(4)	(4)
(2)	(2)	49.04(1)	49.04(1)	(5)	(5)
(3)	(3)	(2)	(2)	(6)	(6)
46.02	46.02	(3)	(3)	(7)	(7)
46.03(1)	46.03(1)	(4)	(4)	(8)	(8)
(2)	(2)	49.05	49.05	(9)	(9)
47.01	47.01	49.06(1)	49.06(1)	(10)	(10)
47.02(1)	47.02(1)	(2)	(2)	(11)	(11)
(2)	(2)	(3)	(3)	52.04(1)	52.04(1)
(3)	(3)	49.07(1)	49.07(1)	(2)	(2)
48.01	48.01	(2)	(2)	(3)	(3)
48.02(1)	48.02(1)	(3)	(3)	(4)	(4)
(2)	(2)	(4)	(4)	52.05	52.05
(3)	(3)	(5)	(5)	52.06(1)	52.06(1)
(4)	(4)	(6)	(6)	(2)	(2)
(5)	(5)	(7)	(7)	(3)	(3)
48.03(1)	48.03(1)	49.08	49.08	(4)	(4)
(2)(a)	(2)(a)	49.09	49.09	52.07(1)	52.07(1)
(2)(b)	(2)(b)	49.10(1)	49.10(1)	(2)	(2)
(2)(c)	(2)(c)	(2)	(2)	(3)	(3)
(2)(ca)	(2)(d)	(3)	(3)	(4)	(4)
(2)(d)	(2)(e)	49.11	49.11	52.08(1)	52.08(1)
(2)(e)	(2)(f)	49.12(1)	49.12(1)	(2)	(2)
48.04(1)	48.04(1)	(2)	(2)	52.09	52.09
(2)	(2)	(3)	(3)	52.10	52.10
48.05(1)	48.05(1)	49.13	49.13	53.01(1)	53.01(1)
(2)	(2)	49.14	49.14	(2)	(2)
48.06(1)	48.06(1)	50.01	50.01	(3)	(3)
(2)	(2)	50.02(1)	50.02(1)	(4)	(4)
(3)	(3)	(2)	(2)	(5)	(5)

1984 Rule	1990 Rule	1984 Rule	1990 Rule	1984 Rule	1990 Rule
(6)	(6)	(4)	(4)	56.01(1)	56.01(1)
53.02(1)	53.02(1)	(5)	(5)	(2)	(2)
(2)	(2)	(6)	(6)	56.02	56.02
(3)	—	(7)	(7)	56.03(1)	56.03(1)
53.03(1)	53.03(1)	(8)	(8)	(2)	(2)
(2)	(2)	(9)	(9)	56.04	56.04
53.04(1)	53.04(1)	(10)	(10)	56.05	56.05
(2)	(2)	(11)	(11)	56.06	56.06
(3)	(3)	(12)	(12)	56.07	56.07
(4)	(4)	(13)	(13)	56.08	56.08
(5)	(5)	(14)	(14)	56.09	56.09
(6)	(6)	(14a)	(14.1)	57.01(1)	57.01(1)
(7)	(7)	(14b)	(14.2)	(2)	(2)
(8)	(8)	(15)	(15)	(3)	(3)
53.05	53.05	(16)	(16)	(4)	(4)
53.06	53.06	(17)	(17)	57.02(1)	57.02(1)
53.07(1)	53.07(1)	(18)	(18)	(2)	(2)
(2)	(2)	(19)	(19)	57.03(1)	57.03(1)
(3)	(3)	(20)	(20)	(2)	(2)
(4)	(4)	(21)	(21)	(3)	(3)
53.08	53.08	(22)	(22)	57.04	57.04
53.09	53.09	55.03(1)	55.03(1)	57.05(1)	57.05(1)
53.10	53.10	(2)	(2)	(2)	(2)
54.01	54.01	(3)	(3)	(3)	(3)
54.02(1)	54.02(1)	(4)	(4)	(4)	(4)
(2)	(2)	55.04(1)	55.04(1)	57.06(1)	57.06(1)
54.03(1)	54.03(1)	(2)	(2)	(2)	(2)
(2)	—	(3)	(3)	57.07(1)	57.07(1)
(3)	(2)	(4)	(4)	(2)	(2)
(4)	(3)	(5)	(5)	(3)	(3)
54.04(1)	54.04(1)	(6)	(6)	58.01	58.01
(2)	(2)	55.05(1)	55.05(1)	58.02(1)	58.02(1)
(3)	(3)	(2)	(2)	(2)	(2)
54.05(1)	54.05(1)	(3)	(3)	58.03(1)	58.03(1)
(2)	(2)	(4)	(4)	(2)	(2)
(3)	(3)	(5)	(5)	58.04(1)	58.04(1)
54.06	54.06	55.06(1)	55.06(1)	(2)	(2)
54.07(1)	54.07(1)	(2)	(2)	(3)	(3)
(2)	(2)	(3)	(3)	(4)	(4)
54.08(1)	54.08(1)	(4)	(4)	58.06(1)	58.05(1)
(2)	(2)	(5)	(5)	(2)	(2)
54.09(1)	54.09(1)	(6)	(6)	(3)	(3)
(2)	(2)	(7)	(7)	(4)	(4)
(3)	(3)	(8)	(8)	(5)	(5)
(4)	(4)	(9)	(9)	(6)	(6)
(5)	(5)	(10)	(10)	58.07(1)	58.06(1)
54.10	54.10	(11)	(11)	(2)	(2)
55.01(1)	55.01(1)	(12)	(12)	58.08	58.07
(2)	(2)	(13)	(13)	58.09(1)	58.08(1)
(3)	(3)	(14)	(14)	(2)	(2)
55.02(1)	55.02(1)	(15)	(15)	58.10	58.09
(2)	(2)	55.07(1)	55.07(1)	58.11(1)	58.10(1)
(3)	(3)	(2)	(2)	(2)	(2)

1984 Rule	1990 Rule	1984 Rule	1990 Rule	1984 Rule	1990 Rule
(3)	(3)	(2)	(2)	(2)	(2)
(4)	(4)	60.07(1)	60.07(1)	(3)	(3)
58.12	58.11	(2)	(2)	(4)	(4)
58.13(1)	58.12(1)	(3)	(3)	(5)	(5)
(2)	(2)	(4)	(4)	(6)	(6)
(3)	(3)	(5)	(5)	(7)	(7)
(4)	(4)	(6)	(6)	(8)	(8)
(5)	(5)	(7)	(7)	(9)	(9)
59.01	59.01	(8)	(8)	(10)	(10)
59.02(1)	59.02(1)	(9)	(9)	60.12	60.12
(2)	(2)	(10)	(10)	60.13(1)	60.13(1)
59.03(1)	59.03(1)	(10a)	(11)	(2)	(2)
(2)	—	(11)	(12)	(3)	(3)
(3)	(3)	(12)	(13)	(4)	(4)
(4)	(4)	(13)	(14)	60.14(1)	60.14(1)
(5)	(5)	(14)	(15)	(2)	(2)
(6)	(6)	(15)	(16)	60.15(1)	60.15(1)
(7)	(7)	(16)	(17)	(2)	(2)
(8)	(8)	(17)	(18)	(3)	(3)
59.04(1)	59.04(1)	(18)	(19)	60.16(1)	60.16(1)
(2)	(2)	(19)	(20)	(2)	(2)
(3)	(3)	(20)	(21)	(3)	(3)
(3a)	(4)	(21)	(22)	60.17	60.17
(4)	(5)	(22)	(23)	60.18(1)	60.18(1)
(5)	(6)	(23)	(24)	(2)	(2)
(5a)	(7)	60.08(1)	60.08(1)	(3)	(3)
(6)	(8)	(2)	(2)	(4)	(4)
(7)	(9)	(3)	(3)	(5)	(5)
(8)	(10)	(4)	(4)	(6)	(6)
(9)	(11)	(5)	(5)	(7)	(7)
(10)	(12)	(6)	(6)	60.19(1)	60.19(1)
(11)	(13)	(7)	(7)	(2)	(2)
(12)	(14)	(8)	(8)	61.01	61.01
(13)	(15)	(9)	(9)	61.02	61.02
(14)	(16)	(10)	(10)	61.03(1)	61.03(1), 61.03.1(3)
59.05(1)	59.05(1)	(11)	(11)	(2)	61.03(2), 61.03.1(4)-(6)
(2)	(2)	(12)	(12)		
(3)	(3)	(13)	(13)	(2a)	61.03(3), 61.03.1(7)-(10)
(4)	(4)	(14)	(14)		
(5)	(5)	(15)	(15)	(3)	(4)
(6)	(6)	(16)	(16)	(3a)	61.03(5), 61.03.1(15)
59.06(1)	59.06(1)	(17)	(17)		
(2)	(2)	(18)	(18)	(4)	(6)
59.07	59.07	(19)	(19)	61.04(1)	61.04(1)
60.01(a)	60.01 "creditor"	(20)	(20)	(3)	(2)
(b)	"debtor"	60.09(1)	60.09(1)	(4)	(3)
60.02(1)	60.02(1)	(2)	(2)	(5)	(4)
(2)	(2)	(3)	(3)	61.05(1)	61.05(1)
60.03	60.03	(4)	(4)	(2)	(2)
60.04(1)	60.04(1)	60.10(1)	60.10(1)	(3)	(3)
(2)	(2)	(2)	(2)	(4)	(4)
60.05	60.05	(3)	(3)	(5)	(5)
60.06(1)	60.06(1)	60.11(1)	60.11(1)	(6)	(6)

1984 Rule	1990 Rule	1984 Rule	1990 Rule	1984 Rule	1990 Rule
(7)	(7)	(10)	(10)	(5)	(5)
(8)	(8)	62.02(1)	62.02(1)	(6)	(6)
61.05a(1)	61.06(1)	(3)	(2)	(7)	(7)
(2)	(2)	(4)	(3)	(8)	(8)
61.06(1)	61.07(1)	(5)	(4)	(9)	(9)
(2)	(2)	(5a)	(5)	(10)	(10)
(3)	(3)	(6)	(6)	(11)	(11)
61.07(1)	61.08(1)	(7)	(7)	(12)	(12)
(2)	(2)	(8)	(8)	(13)	(13)
(3)	(3)	63.01(1)	63.01(1)	(14)	(14)
61.08(1)	61.09(1)	(2)	(3)	64.05(1)	64.05(1)
(2)	(2)	(3)	(5)	(2)	(2)
(3)(a)	(3)(a)	63.02(1)	63.02(1)	(3)	(3)
(3)(aa)	(3)(b)	(2)	(3)	(4)	(4)
(3)(b)	(3)(c)	(3)	(4)	(5)	(5)
(4)	(4)	63.03(1)	63.03(1)	(6)	(6)
(5)	(5)	(2)	(2)	(7)	(7)
61.09(1)	61.10(1)	(3)	(3)	(8)	(8)
(2)	(2)	(4)	(4)	(9)	(9)
61.10	61.11	(5)	(5)	(10)	(10)
61.11(1)	61.12(1)	(6)	(6)	64.06(1)	64.06(1)
(2)	(2)	64.01	64.01	(2)	(2)
(3)	(3)	64.02	64.02	(3)	(3)
(4)	(4)	64.03(1)	64.03(1)	(4)	(4)
61.12(1)	61.13(1)	(2)	(2)	(5)	(5)
(2)	(2)	(3)	(3)	(6)	(6)
(3)	(3)	(4)	(4)	(7)	(7)
(4)	(4)	(5)	(5)	(8)	(8)
(5)	(5)	(6)	(6)	(9)	(9)
(6)	(6)	(7)	(7)	(10)	(10)
(7)	(7)	(8)	(8)	(11)	(11)
(8)	(8)	(9)	(9)	(12)	(12)
61.13(1)	61.14(1)	(10)	(10)	(13)	(13)
(2)	(2)	(11)	(11)	(14)	(14)
(3)	(3)	(12)	(12)	(15)	(15)
61.14(1)	61.15(1)	(13)	(13)	(16)	(16)
(2)	(2)	(14)	(14)	(17)	(17)
61.15(1)	61.16(1)	(15)	(15)	(18)	(18)
(2)	(2)	(16)	(16)	(19)	(19)
(3)	(3)	(17)	(17)	(20)	(20)
(4)	(4)	(18)	(18)	(21)	(21)
(5)	(5)	(19)	(19)	(22)	(22)
(6)	(6)	(20)	(20)	(23)	(23)
62.01(1)	62.01(1)	(21)	(21)	(24)	(24)
(1a)	—	(22)	(22)	(25)	(25)
(2)	(2)	(23)	(23)	(26)	(26)
(3)	(3)	(24)	(24)	(27)	(27)
(4)	(4)	(25)	(25)	65.01(1)	65.01(1)
(5)	(5)	(26)	(26)	(2)	(2)
(6)	(6)	64.04(1)	64.04(1)	(3)	(3)
(7)	(7)	(2)	(2)	65.02(1)	65.02(1)
(8)	(8)	(3)	(3)	(2)	(2)
(9)	(9)	(4)	(4)	(3)	(3)

1984 Rule	1990 Rule	1984 Rule	1990 Rule	1984 Rule	1990 Rule
66.01(1)	66.01(1)	70.08	69.08	70.19(1)	69.19(1)
(2)	(2)	70.09(1)	69.09(1)	(2)	(2)
66.02	66.02	(2)	(2)	(3)	(3)
66.03	66.03	(3)	(3)	(4)	(4)
67.01	67.01	(4)	(4)	(5)	(5)
67.02(1)	67.02(1)	(5)	(5)	(6)	(6)
(2)	(2)	(6)	(6)	(7)	(7)
(3)	(3)	(7)	(7)	(7a)	(8)
67.03(1)	67.03(1)	70.10(1)	69.10(1)	(8)	(9)
(2)	(2)	(2)	(2)	(9)	(10)
(3)	(3)	(3)	(3)	(10)	(11)
(4)	(4)	70.11(1)	69.11(1)	(11)	(12)
68.01(1)	68.01(1)	(2)	(2)	70.20(1)	69.20(1)
(2)	(2)	70.12(1)	69.12(1)	(2)	(2)
68.02(1)	68.02(1)	(2)	(2)	(3)	(3)
(2)	(2)	(3)	(3)	(4)	(4)
68.03	68.03	(4)	(4)	70.21(1)	69.21(1)
68.04(1)	68.04(1)	(5)	(5)	(2)	(2)
(2)	(2)	70.13	69.13	(3)	(3)
(3)	(3)	70.14(1)	69.14(1)	(4)	(4)
(4)	(4)	(2)	(2)	70.22	69.22
(5)	(5)	(3)	(3)	70.23	69.23
(6)	(6)	(4)	(4)	70.24(1)	69.24(1)
(7)	(7)	(5)	(5)	(2)	(2)
(8)	(8)	(6)	(6)	(3)	(3)
(9)	(9)	(7)	(7)	(4)	(4)
68.05(1)	68.05(1)	(8)	(8)	(5)	(5)
(2)	(2)	(9)	(9)	(6)	(6)
68.06(1)	68.06(1)	(10)	(10)	(7)	(7)
(2)	(2)	(11)	(11)	(8)	(8)
(3)	(3)	(12)	(12)	(9)	(9)
(4)	(4)	(13)	(13)	(10)	(10)
70.01	69.01	(14)	(14)	(11)	(11)
70.02	69.02	(15)	(15)	(12)	(12)
70.03(1)	69.03(1)	70.15(1)	69.15(1)	(13)	(13)
(2)	(2)	(2)	(2)	70.25(1)	69.25(1)
(3)	(3)	(3)	(3)	(2)	(2)
(4)	(4)	(4)	(4)	70.26	69.26
(5)	(5)	(5)	(5)	70.27	69.27
(6)	(6)	(6)	(6)	71.01	70.01
(7)	(7)	70.16(1)	69.16(1)	71.02	70.02
70.04(1)	69.04(1)	(2)	(2)	71.03(1)	70.03(1)
(2)	(2)	(3)	(3)	(2)	(2)
(3)	(3)	(4)	(4)	71.04(1)	70.04(1)
(4)	(4)	(5)	(5)	(2)	(2)
(5)	(5)	(6)	(6)	(3)	(3)
(6)	(6)	(7)	(7)	(4)	(4)
70.05	69.05	(8)	(8)	(5)	(5)
70.06(1)	69.06(1)	(9)	(9)	(6)	(6)
(2)	(2)	70.17(1)	69.17(1)	(7)	(7)
70.07(1)	69.07(1)	(2)	(2)	(8)	(8)
(2)	(2)	(3)	(3)	(9)	(9)
(3)	(3)	70.18	69.18	(10)	(10)

1984 Rule	1990 Rule	1984 Rule	1990 Rule	1984 Rule	1990 Rule
71.05(1)	70.05(1)	(7)	(7)	(4)	(4)
(2)	(2)	(8)	(8)	(5)	(5)
(3)	(3)	72.01	71.01	(6)	(6)
71.05a	70.06	72.02(1)	71.02(1)	(7)	(7)
71.06	70.07	(2)	(2)	(8)	(8)
71.07	70.08	(3)	(3)	(9)	(9)
71.08(1)	70.09(1)	(4)	(4)	(10)	(10)
(2)	(2)	(5)	(5)	(11)	(11)
71.09(1)	70.10(1)	(6)	(6)	(12)	(12)
(2)	(2)	(7)	(7)	(13)	(13)
(3)	(3)	72.03	71.03	(14)	(14)
(4)	(4)	73.01	72.01	73.04(1)	72.04(1)
(5)	(5)	73.02(1)	72.02(1)	(2)	(2)
(6)	(6)	(1a)	(2)	(3)	(3)
71.09a	70.10.1	(2)	(3)	73.05(1)	72.05(1)
71.10	70.11	(3)	(4)	(2)	(2)
71.11	70.12	(3a)	(5)	(3)	(3)
71.12	70.13	(4)	(6)	74.01	73.01
71.13(1)	70.14(1)	(5)	(7)	74.02(1)	73.02(1)
(2)	(2)	(6)	(8)	(2)	(2)
(3)	(3)	(7)	(9)	(3)	(3)
(4)	(4)	73.03(1)	72.03(1)	(4)	(4)
(5)	(5)	(2)	(2)	74.03	73.03
(6)	(6)	(3)	(3)		

1990 RULES/1984 RULES

The following table relates the Rules of Civil Procedure, R.R.O. 1990, Reg. 194, as amended (referred to as "1990 Rule"), to the Rules of Civil Procedure, O. Reg. 560/84, as amended to 1992 (referred to as "1984 Rule"). For those wishing to go back further in time, the prior history can be traced by referring to the Rules of Practice and Procedure historical concordance table in Holmested and Gale, *Ontario Judicature Act and Rules of Practice*.

1990 Rule	1984 Rule	1990 Rule	1984 Rule	1990 Rule	1984 Rule
1.01(1)	1.01(1)	2.02	2.02	(4)	(4)
(2)	(2)	2.03	2.03	(5)	(5)
(3)	(3)	3.01(1)	3.01(1)	(6)	(6)
1.02(1)	1.02(1)	(2)	(2)	4.08	4.08
(2)	(2)	3.02(1)	3.02(1)	4.09(1)	4.09(1)
(3)	(3)	(2)	(2)	(2)	(2)
(4)	(4)	(3)	(3)	(3)	(3)
1.03 "action"	1.03 1	(4)	(4)	(4)	(4)
"appellant"	2	3.03(1)	3.03(1)	(5)	(5)
"appellate court"	3	(2)	(2)	(6)	(6)
"applicant"	4	4.01(1)	4.01(1)	(7)	(7)
"application"	5	(2)	(2)	(8)	(8)
"county"	6	4.02(1)	4.02(1)	(9)	(9)
"court"	7	(2)	(2)	(10)	(10)
"defendant"	8	(3)(a)	(3)(a)	(11)	(11)
"deliver"	9	(3)(b)	(3)(b)	4.10(1)	4.10(1)
"disability"	10	(3)(c)	(3)(ba)	(2)	(2)
"discovery"	11	(3)(d)	(3)(c)	4.11	4.11
"hearing'	12	(3)(e)	(3)(d)	5.01(1)	5.01(1)
"holiday"	13	(3)(f)	(3)(e)	(2)	(2)
"judge"	14	(4)		(3)	(3)
"judgment"	15	4.03	4.03	5.02(1)	5.02(1)
"motion"	17	4.04	4.04	(2)	(2)
"moving party"	18	4.05(1)	4.05(1)	5.03(1)	5.03(1)
"order"	19	(2)	(2)	(2)	(2)
"originating process"	20	(3)	(3)	(3)	(3)
"plaintiff"	21	(4)	(4)	(4)	(4)
"proceeding"	22	(5)	(5)	(5)	(5)
"referee"	23	(6)	(6)	(6)	(6)
"registrar"	24	4.06(1)	4.06(1)	5.04(1)	5.04(1)
"respondent"	25	(2)	(2)	(2)	(2)
"responding party"	26	(3)	(3)	(3)	(3)
"solicitor's office"	26a	(4)	(4)	5.05	5.05
"statute"	27	(5)	(5)	6.01(1)	6.01(1)
1.04(1)	1.04(1)	(6)	(6)	(2)	(2)
(2)	(2)	(7)	(7)	6.02	6.02
(3)	(3)	(8)	(8)	7.01(1)	7.01(1)
1.05	1.05	(9)	(9)	(2)	
1.06	1.06	4.07(1)	4.07(1)	(3)	
2.01(1)	2.01(1)	(2)	(2)	(4)	
(2)	(2)	(3)	(3)	7.02(1)	7.02(1)

1990 Rule	1984 Rule	1990 Rule	1984 Rule	1990 Rule	1984 Rule
(3)	(3)	(2)	(2)	25.04(1)	25.04(1)
(4)	(4)	(3)	(3)	(2)	(2)
(5)	(5)	(4)	(4)	(3)	(3)
17.01	17.01	(5)	(5)	(4)	(4)
17.02	17.02	20.05(1)	20.05(1)	(5)	(5)
17.03(1)	17.03(1)	(2)	(2)	(6)	(6)
(2)	(2)	(3)	(3)	25.05	25.05
17.04(1)	17.04(1)	(4)	(4)	25.06(1)	25.06(1)
(2)	(2)	(5)	(5)	(2)	(2)
17.05(1)	17.05(1)	20.06(1)	20.06(1)	(3)	(3)
(2)	(2)	(2)	(2)	(4)	(4)
(3)	(3)	20.07	20.07	(5)	(5)
(4)	(4)	20.08	20.08	(6)	(6)
17.06(1)	17.06(1)	20.09	20.09	(7)	(7)
(2)	(2)	21.01(1)	21.01(1)	(8)	(8)
(3)	(3)	(2)	(2)	(9)	(9)
(4)	(4)	(3)	(3)	25.07(1)	25.07(1)
18.01	18.01	21.02	21.02	(2)	(2)
18.02(1)	18.02(1)	21.03	21.03	(3)	(3)
(2)	(2)	22.01(1)	22.01(1)	(4)	(4)
(3)	(3)	(2)	(2)	(5)	(5)
19.01(1)	19.01(1)	22.02	22.02	(6)	(6)
(2)	(2)	22.03(1)	22.03(1)	25.08(1)	25.08(1)
(3)	(3)	(2)	(2)	(2)	(2)
(4)	(4)	22.04	22.04	(3)	(3)
(5)	(5)	22.05(1)	22.05(1)	(4)	(4)
19.02(1)	19.02(1)	(2)	(2)	25.09(1)	25.09(1)
(2)	(2)	23.01(1)	23.01(1)	(2)	(2)
(3)	(3)	(2)	(2)	25.10	25.10
19.03(1)	19.03(1)	23.02	23.02	25.11	25.11
(2)	(2)	23.03	23.03	26.01	26.01
19.04(1)	19.04(1)	23.04(1)	23.04(1)	26.02	26.02
(2)	(2)	(2)	(2)	26.03(1)	26.03(1)
(3)	(3)	23.05	23.05	(2)	(2)
(4)	(4)	23.06(1)	23.06(1)	(3)	(3)
(5)	(5)	(2)	(2)	26.04(1)	26.04(1)
(6)	(6)	23.07	23.07	(2)	(2)
19.05(1)	19.05(1)	24.01	24.01	(3)	(3)
(2)	(2)	24.02	24.02	26.05(1)	26.05(1)
(3)	(3)	24.03	24.03	(2)	(2)
(4)	(4)	24.04	24.04	26.06	26.06
19.06	19.07	24.05(1)	24.05(1)	27.01(1)	27.01(1)
19.07	19.08	(2)	(2)	(2)	(2)
19.08(1)	19.09(1)	24.06	24.06	27.02	27.02
(2)	(2)	25.01(1)	25.01(1)	27.03	27.03
(3)	(3)	(2)	(2)	27.04(1)	27.04(1)
19.09	19.10	(3)	(3)	(2)	(2)
20.01(1)	20.01(1)	(4)	(4)	(3)	(3)
(2)	(2)	(5)	(5)	27.05(1)	27.05(1)
(3)	(3)	25.02	25.02	(2)	(2)
20.02	20.02	25.03(1)	25.03(1)	(3)	(3)
20.03	20.03	(2)	(2)	27.06	27.06
20.04(1)	20.04(1)	(3)	(3)	27.07(1)	27.07(1)

1990 Rule	1984 Rule	1990 Rule	1984 Rule	1990 Rule	1984 Rule
(2)	(2)	30.03(1)	30.03(1)	(6)	(5)
27.08(1)	27.08(1)	(2)	(2)	31.07(1)	31.07(1)
(2)	(2)	(3)	(3)	(2)	(2)
27.09(1)	27.09(1)	(4)	(4)	31.08	31.08
(2)	(2)	(5)	(5)	31.09(1)	31.09(1)
(3)	(3)	30.04(1)	30.04(1)	(2)	(2)
27.10	27.10	(2)	(2)	(3)	(3)
28.01(1)	28.01(1)	(3)	(3)	31.10(1)	31.10(1)
(2)	(2)	(4)	(4)	(2)	(2)
28.02	28.02	(5)	(5)	(3)	(3)
28.03	28.03	(6)	(6)	(4)	(4)
28.04(1)	28.04(1)	(7)	(7)	(5)	(5)
(2)	(2)	(8)	(8)	31.11(1)	31.11(1)
28.05(1)	28.05(1)	30.05	30.05	(2)	(2)
(2)	(2)	30.06	30.06	(3)	(3)
28.06(1)	28.06(1)	30.07	30.07	(4)	(4)
(2)	(2)	30.08(1)	30.08(1)	(5)	(5)
(3)	(3)	(2)	(2)	(6)	(6)
(4)	(4)	30.09	30.09	(7)	(7)
(5)	(5)	30.10(1)	30.10(1)	(8)	(8)
28.07	28.07	(2)	(2)	32.01(1)	32.01(1)
28.08	28.08	(3)	(3)	(2)	(2)
28.09	28.09	(4)	(4)	(3)	(3)
28.10	28.10	30.11	30.11	(4)	(4)
28.11	28.11	30.1(1)		33.01	33.01
29.01	29.01	(2)		33.02(1)	33.02(1)
29.02(1)	29.02(1)	(3)		(2)	(2)
(2)	(2)	(4)		33.03	33.03
(3)	(3)	(5)		33.04(1)	33.04(1)
29.03	29.03	(6)		(2)	(2)
29.04	29.04	(7)		33.05	33.05
29.05(1)	29.05(1)	(8)		33.06(1)	33.06(1)
(2)	(2)	31.01	31.01	(2)	(2)
(3)	(3)	31.02(1)	31.02(1)	33.07	33.07
(4)	(4)	(2)	(2)	33.08	33.08
(5)	(5)	31.03(1)	31.03(1)	34.01	34.01
29.06	29.06	(2)	(2)	34.02	34.02
29.07	29.07	(3)	(3)	34.03	34.03
29.08(1)	29.08(1)	(4)	(4)	34.04(1)	34.04(1)
(2)	(2)	(5)	(5)	(2)	(2)
29.09	29.09	(6)	(6)	(3)	(3)
29.10	29.10	(7)	(7)	(4)	(4)
29.11(1)	29.11(1)	(8)	(8)	(5)	(5)
(2)	(2)	(9)	(9)	(6)	(6)
(3)	(3)	31.04(1)	31.04(1)	(7)	(7)
29.12	29.12	(2)	(2)	(8)	(8)
29.13	29.13	(3)	(3)	34.04.1	34.04a
30.01(1)	30.01(1)	31.05	31.05	34.05(1)	34.05(1)
(2)	(2)	31.06(1)	31.06(1)	(2)	(2)
30.02(1)	30.02(1)	(2)	(2)	34.06	34.06
(2)	(2)	(3)	(3)	34.07(1)	34.07(1)
(3)	(3)	(4)	(4)	(2)	(2)
(4)	(4)	(5)	(4a)	(3)	(3)

1990 Rule	1984 Rule	1990 Rule	1984 Rule	1990 Rule	1984 Rule
(4)	(4)	(3)	(3)	(2)	(2)
(5)	(5)	(4)	(4)	38.02	38.03
(6)	(6)	(5)	(5)	38.03(1)	38.04(1)
(7)	(7)	(6)	(6)	(1.1)	(1a)
34.08(1)	34.08(1)	(7)	(7)	(2)	(2)
(2)	(2)	37.01	37.01	(3)	(3)
34.09(1)	34.09(1)	37.02(1)	37.02(1)	(4)	(4)
(2)	(2)	(2)	(3)	38.04	38.05
34.10(1)	34.10(1)	37.03(1)	37.03(1)	38.05	38.06
(2)	(2)	(2)	(2)	38.06(1)	38.07(1)
(3)	(3)	(3)	(3)	(2)	(2)
(4)	(4)	(4)	(5)	(3)	(3)
34.11(1)	34.11(1)	(5)	(6)	(4)	
(2)	(2)	37.04	37.04	38.07(1)	38.08(1)
(3)	(3)	37.05(1)	37.05(1)	(2)	(2)
(4)	(4)	(2)	(2)	(3)	(3)
(5)	(5)	37.06	37.06	(4)	(4)
34.12(1)	34.12(1)	37.07(1)	37.07(1)	38.08(1)	38.09(1)
(2)	(2)	(2)	(2)	(2)	(2)
(3)	(3)	(3)	(3)	(3)	(3)
34.13	34.13	(4)	(4)	(4)	(4)
34.14(1)	34.14(1)	(5)	(5)	38.09(1)	38.10(1)
(2)	(2)	(6)	(6)	(2)	(1a)
34.15(1)	34.15(1)	37.08(1)	37.08(1)	(3)	(2)
(2)	(2)	(2)	(2)	(4)	(3)
34.16	34.16	37.09(1)	37.09(1)	(5)	(4)
34.17(1)	34.17(1)	(2)	(2)	(6)	(5)
(2)	(2)	(3)	(3)	(7)	
(3)	(3)	37.10(1)	37.10(1)	(8)	
34.18(1)	34.18(1)	(2)	(3)	38.10(1)	38.11(1)
(2)	(2)	(3)	(4)	(2)	(2)
(3)	(2a)	(4)	(5)	(3)	(3)
(4)	(3)	(5)	(6)	(4)	
34.19(1)	34.19(1)	(6)	(7)	38.11(1)	38.12(1)
(2)	(2)	37.11(1)	37.11(1)	(2)	(2)
35.01	35.01	(2)	(2)	(3)	(3)
35.02(1)	35.02(1)	37.12	37.12	38.12	38.13
(2)	(2)	37.12.1	—	39.01(1)	39.01(1)
35.03	35.03	37.13(1)	37.13(1)	(2)	(2)
35.04(1)	35.04(1)	(2)	(2)	(3)	(3)
(2)	(2)	(3)	(3)	(4)	(4)
(3)	(3)	(4)		(5)	(5)
(4)	(4)	37.14(1)	37.14(1)	(6)	(6)
35.05	35.05	(2)	(2)	39.02(1)	39.02(1)
35.06	35.06	(3)	(3)	(2)	(2)
36.01(1)	36.01(1)	(4)	(4)	(3)	(3)
(2)	(2)	(5)	(4a)	(4)	(4)
(3)	(3)	(6)	(5)	39.03(1)	39.03(1)
36.02(1)	36.02(1)	37.15(1)	37.15(1)	(2)	(2)
(2)	(2)	(2)	(2)	(3)	(2a)
36.03	36.03	37.16	37.16	(4)	(3)
36.04(1)	36.04(1)	37.17	37.17	(5)	(4)
(2)	(2)	38.01(1)	38.01(1)	39.04	39.04

1990 Rule	1984 Rule	1990 Rule	1984 Rule	1990 Rule	1984 Rule
40.01	40.01	45.02	45.02	(9)	(9)
40.02(1)	40.02(1)	45.03(1)	45.03(1)	(10)	(10)
(2)	(2)	(2)	(2)	(11)	(11)
(3)	(3)	(3)	(3)	49.01 "defendant"	49.01(a)
(4)	(4)	46.01(1)	46.01(1)	"plaintiff"	(b)
40.03	40.03	(2)	(2)	49.02(1)	49.02(1)
41.01	41.01	(3)	(3)	(2)	(2)
41.02	41.02	46.02	46.02	49.03	49.03
41.03	41.03	46.03(1)	46.03(1)	49.04(1)	49.04(1)
41.04	41.04	(2)	(2)	(2)	(2)
41.05	41.05	47.01	47.01	(3)	(3)
41.06	41.06	47.02(1)	47.02(1)	(4)	(4)
42.01(1)	42.01(1)	(2)	(2)	49.05	49.05
(2)	(2)	(3)	(3)	49.06(1)	49.06(1)
(3)	(3)	48.01	48.01	(2)	(2)
(4)	(4)	48.02(1)	48.02(1)	(3)	(3)
42.02(1)	42.02(1)	(2)	(2)	49.07(1)	49.07(1)
(2)	(2)	(3)	(3)	(2)	(2)
43.01	43.01	(4)	(4)	(3)	(3)
43.02	43.02	(5)	(5)	(4)	(4)
43.03(1)	43.03(1)	48.03(1)	48.03(1)	(5)	(5)
(2)	(2)	(2)(a)	(2)(a)	(6)	(6)
(3)	(3)	(2)(b)	(2)(b)	(7)	(7)
43.04(1)	43.04(1)	(2)(c)	(2)(c)	49.08	49.08
(2)	(2)	(2)(d)	(2)(ca)	49.09	49.09
(3)	(3)	(2)(e)	(2)(d)	49.10(1)	49.10(1)
43.05(1)"property"	43.05(1)(a)	(2)(f)	(2)(e)	(2)	(2)
(1)"writ of execution"	(1)(b)	48.04(1)	48.04(1)	(3)	(3)
(2)	(2)	(2)	(2)	49.11	49.11
(3)	(3)	48.05(1)	48.05(1)	49.12(1)	49.12(1)
(4)	(4)	(2)	(2)	(2)	(2)
(5)	(5)	(3)	(3)	(3)	(3)
(6)	(6)	48.06(1)	48.06(1)	49.13	49.13
(7)	(7)	(2)	(2)	49.14	49.14
44.01(1)	44.01(1)	(3)	(3)	50.01	50.01
(2)	(2)	48.07	48.07	50.02(1)	50.02(1)
44.02	44.02	48.08(1)	48.08(1)	(2)	(2)
44.03(1)	44.03(1)	(2)	(2)	50.03	50.03
(2)	(2)	48.09	48.09	50.04	50.04
44.04(1)	44.04(1)	48.10	48.10	50.05	50.05
(2)	(2)	48.11	48.11	50.06	50.06
(3)	(3)	48.12	48.12	50.07	50.07
44.05	44.05	48.13	48.13	50.08	50.08
44.06	44.06	48.14(1)	48.14(1)	51.01	51.01
44.07(1)	44.07(1)	(2)	(2)	51.02(1)	51.02(1)
(2)	(2)	(3)	(3)	(2)	(2)
(3)	(3)	(4)	(4)	51.03(1)	51.03(1)
(4)	(4)	(4.0.1)	—	(2)	(2)
44.08	44.08	(4.1)	—	(3)	(3)
45.01(1)	45.01(1)	(5)	(5)	51.04	51.04
(2)	(2)	(6)	(6)	51.05	51.05
		(7)	(7)	51.06(1)	51.06(1)
		(8)	(8)	(2)	(2)

1990 Rule	1984 Rule	1990 Rule	1984 Rule	1990 Rule	1984 Rule
(3)	(3)	53.06	53.06	(18)	(18)
52.01(1)	52.01(1)	53.07(1)	53.07(1)	(19)	(19)
(2)	(2)	(2)	(2)	(20)	(20)
(3)	(3)	(3)	(3)	(21)	(21)
52.02	52.02	(4)	(4)	(22)	(22)
52.03(1)	52.03(1)	53.08	53.08	55.03(1)	55.03(1)
(2)	(2)	53.09	53.09	(2)	(2)
(3)	(3)	53.10	53.10	(3)	(3)
(4)	(4)	54.01	54.01	(4)	(4)
(5)	(5)	54.02(1)	54.02(1)	55.04(1)	55.04(1)
(6)	(6)	(2)	(2)	(2)	(2)
(7)	(7)	54.03(1)	54.03(1)	(3)	(3)
(8)	(8)	(2)	(3)	(4)	(4)
(9)	(9)	(3)	(4)	(5)	(5)
(10)	(10)	54.04(1)	54.04(1)	(6)	(6)
(11)	(11)	(2)	(2)	55.05(1)	55.05(1)
52.04(1)	52.04(1)	(3)	(3)	(2)	(2)
(2)	(2)	54.05(1)	54.05(1)	(3)	(3)
(3)	(3)	(2)	(2)	(4)	(4)
(4)	(4)	(3)	(3)	(5)	(5)
52.05	52.05	54.06	54.06	55.06(1)	55.06(1)
52.06(1)	52.06(1)	54.07(1)	54.07(1)	(2)	(2)
(2)	(2)	(2)	(2)	(3)	(3)
(3)	(3)	54.08(1)	54.08(1)	(4)	(4)
(4)	(4)	(2)	(2)	(5)	(5)
52.07(1)	52.07(1)	54.09(1)	54.09(1)	(6)	(6)
(2)	(2)	(2)	(2)	(7)	(7)
(3)	(3)	(3)	(3)	(8)	(8)
(4)	(4)	(4)	(4)	(9)	(9)
52.08(1)	52.08(1)	(5)	(5)	(10)	(10)
(2)	(2)	54.10	54.10	(11)	(11)
52.09	52.09	55.01(1)	55.01(1)	(12)	(12)
52.10	52.10	(2)	(2)	(13)	(13)
53.01(1)	53.01(1)	(3)	(3)	(14)	(14)
(2)	(2)	55.02(1)	55.02(1)	(15)	(15)
(3)	(3)	(2)	(2)	55.07(1)	55.07(1)
(4)	(4)	(3)	(3)	(2)	(2)
(5)	(5)	(4)	(4)	56.01(1)	56.01(1)
(6)	(6)	(5)	(5)	(2)	(2)
53.02(1)	53.02(1)	(6)	(6)	56.02	56.02
(2)	(2)	(7)	(7)	56.03(1)	56.03(1)
(3)	(3)	(8)	(8)	(2)	(2)
53.03(1)	53.03(1)	(9)	(9)	56.04	56.04
(2)	(2)	(10)	(10)	56.05	56.05
53.04(1)	53.04(1)	(11)	(11)	56.06	56.06
(2)	(2)	(12)	(12)	56.07	56.07
(3)	(3)	(13)	(13)	56.08	56.08
(4)	(4)	(14)	(14)	56.09	56.09
(5)	(5)	(14.1)	(14a)	57.01(1)	57.01(1)
(6)	(6)	(14.2)	(14b)	(2)	(2)
(7)	(7)	(15)	(15)	(3)	(3)
(8)	(8)	(16)	(16)	(4)	(4)
53.05	53.05	(17)	(17)	57.02(1)	57.02(1)

1990 Rule	1984 Rule	1990 Rule	1984 Rule	1990 Rule	1984 Rule
60.15(1)	60.15(1)	(7)	(7)	(9)	(9)
(2)	(2)	(8)	(8)	(10)	(10)
(3)	(3)	61.06(1)	61.05a(1)	62.02(1)	62.02(1)
60.16(1)	60.16(1)	(2)	(2)	(2)	(3)
(2)	(2)	61.07(1)	61.06(1)	(3)	(4)
(3)	(3)	(2)	(2)	(4)	(5)
60.17	60.17	(3)	(3)	(5)	(5a)
60.18(1)	60.18(1)	61.08(1)	61.07(1)	(6)	(6)
(2)	(2)	(2)	(2)	(7)	(7)
(3)	(3)	(3)	(3)	(8)	(8)
(4)	(4)	61.09(1)	61.08(1)	63.01(1)	63.01(1)
(5)	(5)	(2)	(2)	(2)	—
(6)	(6)	(3)(a)	(3)(a)	(3)	(2)
(7)	(7)	(3)(b)	(3)(aa)	(4)	—
60.19(1)	60.19(1)	(3)(c)	(3)(b)	(5)	(3)
(2)	(2)	(4)	(4)	63.02(1)	63.02(1)
61.01	61.01	(5)	(5)	(2)	—
61.02	61.02	61.10(1)	61.09(1)	(3)	(2)
61.03(1)	61.03(1)	(2)	(2)	(4)	(3)
(2)	(2)	61.11	61.10	63.03(1)	63.03(1)
(3)	(3)	61.12(1)	61.11(1)	(2)	(2)
(4)	(4)	(2)	(2)	(3)	(3)
(5)	(5)	(3)	(3)	(4)	(4)
(6)	(6)	(3.1)	(3)	(5)	(5)
(7)		(4)	(4)	(6)	(6)
(8)		61.13(1)	61.12(1)	64.01	64.01
(9)		(2)	(2)	64.02	64.02
61.03.1(1)		(2.1)		64.03(1)	64.03(1)
(2)		(3)	(3)	(2)	(2)
(3)	61.03(1)	(4)	(4)	(3)	(3)
(4)	61.03(2)	(5)	(5)	(4)	(4)
(5)	61.03(2)	(6)	(6)	(5)	(5)
(6)	61.03(2)	(7)	(7)	(6)	(6)
(7)	61.03(2a)	(8)	(8)	(7)	(7)
(8)	61.03(2a)	61.14(1)	61.13(1)	(8)	(8)
(9)	61.03(2a)	(2)	(2)	(9)	(9)
(10)		(3)	(3)	(10)	(10)
(11)		61.15(1)	61.14(1)	(11)	(11)
(12)		(2)	(2)	(12)	(12)
(13)		61.16(1)	61.15(1)	(13)	(13)
(14)		(2)	(2)	(14)	(14)
(15)	61.03(3a)	(3)	(3)	(15)	(15)
(16)		(4)	(4)	(16)	(16)
61.04(1)	61.04(1)	(5)	(5)	(17)	(17)
(2)	(3)	(6)	(6)	(18)	(18)
(3)	(4)	62.01(1)	62.01(1)	(19)	(19)
(4)	(5)	(2)	(2)	(20)	(20)
61.05(1)	61.05(1)	(3)	(3)	(21)	(21)
(2)	(2)	(4)	(4)	(22)	(22)
(3)	(3)	(5)	(5)	(23)	(23)
(4)	(4)	(6)	(6)	(24)	(24)
(5)	(5)	(7)	(7)	(25)	(25)
(6)	(6)	(8)	(8)	(26)	(26)

1990 Rule	1984 Rule	1990 Rule	1984 Rule	1990 Rule	1984 Rule
64.04(1)	64.04(1)	(3)	(3)	69.06(1)	70.06(1)
(2)	(2)	65.02(1)	65.02(1)	(2)	(2)
(3)	(3)	(2)	(2)	69.07(1)	70.07(1)
(4)	(4)	(3)	(3)	(2)	(2)
(5)	(5)	66.01(1)	66.01(1)	(3)	(3)
(6)	(6)	(2)	(2)	69.08	70.08
(7)	(7)	66.02	66.02	69.09(1)	70.09(1)
(8)	(8)	66.03	66.03	(2)	(2)
(9)	(9)	67.01	67.01	(3)	(3)
(10)	(10)	67.02(1)	67.02(1)	(4)	(4)
(11)	(11)	(2)	(2)	(5)	(5)
(12)	(12)	(3)	(3)	(6)	(6)
(13)	(13)	67.03(1)	67.03(1)	(7)	(7)
(14)	(14)	(2)	(2)	69.10(1)	70.10(1)
64.05(1)	64.05(1)	(3)	(3)	(2)	(2)
(2)	(2)	(4)	(4)	(3)	(3)
(3)	(3)	68.01(1)	68.01(1)	69.11(1)	70.11(1)
(4)	(4)	(2)	(2)	(2)	(2)
(5)	(5)	68.02(1)	68.02(1)	69.12(1)	70.12(1)
(6)	(6)	(2)	(2)	(2)	(2)
(7)	(7)	68.03	68.03	(3)	(3)
(8)	(8)	68.04(1)	68.04(1)	(4)	(4)
(9)	(9)	(2)	(2)	(5)	(5)
(10)	(10)	(3)	(3)	69.13	70.13
64.06(1)	64.06(1)	(4)	(4)	69.14(1)	70.14(1)
(2)	(2)	(5)	(5)	(2)	(2)
(3)	(3)	(6)	(6)	(3)	(3)
(4)	(4)	(7)	(7)	(4)	(4)
(5)	(5)	(8)	(8)	(5)	(5)
(6)	(6)	(9)	(9)	(6)	(6)
(7)	(7)	68.05(1)	68.05(1)	(7)	(7)
(8)	(8)	(2)	(2)	(8)	(8)
(9)	(9)	68.06(1)	68.06(1)	(9)	(9)
(10)	(10)	(2)	(2)	(10)	(10)
(11)	(11)	(3)	(3)	(11)	(11)
(12)	(12)	(4)	(4)	(12)	(12)
(13)	(13)	69.01	70.01	(13)	(13)
(14)	(14)	69.02	70.02	(14)	(14)
(15)	(15)	69.03(1)	70.03(1)	(15)	(15)
(16)	(16)	(2)	(2)	69.15(1)	70.15(1)
(17)	(17)	(3)	(3)	(2)	(2)
(18)	(18)	(4)	(4)	(3)	(3)
(19)	(19)	(5)	(5)	(4)	(4)
(20)	(20)	(6)	(6)	(5)	(5)
(21)	(21)	(7)	(7)	(6)	(6)
(22)	(22)	(8)	(8)	69.16(1)	70.16(1)
(23)	(23)	69.04(1)	70.04(1)	(2)	(2)
(24)	(24)	(2)	(2)	(3)	(3)
(25)	(25)	(3)	(3)	(4)	(4)
(26)	(26)	(4)	(4)	(5)	(5)
(27)	(27)	(5)	(5)	(6)	(6)
65.01(1)	65.01(1)	(6)	(6)	(7)	(7)
(2)	(2)	69.05	70.05	(8)	(8)

1990 Rule	1984 Rule	1990 Rule	1984 Rule	1990 Rule	1984 Rule
(9)	(9)	(6)	(6)	(4)	(4)
69.17(1)	70.17(1)	(7)	(7)	(5)	(5)
(2)	(2)	(8)	(8)	(6)	(6)
(3)	(3)	(9)	(9)	(7)	(7)
69.18	70.18	(10)	(10)	(8)	(8)
69.19(1)	70.19(1)	70.05(1)	71.05(1)	(9)	(9)
(2)	(2)	(2)	(2)	(10)	(10)
(3)	(3)	(3)	(3)	(11)	(11)
(4)	(4)	70.06	71.05a	(12)	(12)
(5)	(5)	70.07	71.06	(13)	(13)
(6)	(6)	70.08	71.07	(14)	(14)
(7)	(7)	70.09(1)	71.08(1)	72.04(1)	73.04(1)
(8)	(8)	(2)	(2)	(2)	(2)
(9)	(9)	70.10(1)	71.09(1)	(3)	(3)
(10)	(10)	(2)	(2)	72.05(1)	73.05(1)
(11)	(11)	(3)	(3)	(2)	(2)
(12)	(12)	(4)	(4)	(3)	(3)
69.20(1)	70.20(1)	(5)	(5)	73.01	74.01
(2)	(2)	(6)	(6)	73.02(1)	74.02(1)
(3)	(3)	70.10.1	71.09a	(2)	(2)
(4)	(4)	70.11	71.10	(3)	(3)
69.21(1)	70.21(1)	70.12	71.11	(4)	(4)
(2)	(2)	70.13	71.12	73.03	74.03
(3)	(3)	70.14(1)	71.13(1)	74.01	
(4)	(4)	(2)	(2)	74.02	
69.22	70.22	(3)	(3)	74.03	
69.23	70.23	(4)	(4)	74.04	
69.24(1)	70.24(1)	(5)	(5)	74.05	
(2)	(2)	(6)	(6)	74.06	
(3)	(3)	(7)	(7)	74.07	
(4)	(4)	(8)	(8)	74.08	
(5)	(5)	71.01	72.01	74.09	
(6)	(6)	71.02(1)	72.02(1)	74.10	
(7)	(7)	(2)	(2)	74.11	
(8)	(8)	(3)	(3)	74.12	
(9)	(9)	(4)	(4)	74.13	
(10)	(10)	(5)	(5)	74.14	
(11)	(11)	(6)	(6)	74.15	
(12)	(12)	(7)	(7)	74.16	
(13)	(13)	71.03	72.03	74.17	
69.25(1)	70.25(1)	72.01	73.01	74.18	
(2)	(2)	72.02(1)	73.02(1)	75.01	
69.26	70.26	(2)	(1a)	75.02	
69.27	70.27	(2)	(2)	75.03	
70.01	71.01	(3)	(3)	75.05	
70.02	71.02	(4)	(3a)	75.06	
70.03(1)	71.03(1)	(5)	(4)	75.07	
(2)	(2)	(6)	(5)	75.07.1	
70.04(1)	71.04(1)	(7)	(6)	75.08	
(2)	(2)	(8)	(7)	75.09	
(3)	(3)	(9)	73.03(1)	76.01	
(4)	(4)	72.03(1)	(2)	76.02	
(5)	(5)	(2)	(3)	76.03	
		(3)			

1990 Rule	1984 Rule	1990 Rule	1984 Rule	1990 Rule	1984 Rule
76.04		76.07		76.10	
76.05		76.08		76.11	
76.06		76.09			

TABLE OF CASES

TABLE OF CASES

ANNUAL SURVEY OF RECENT DEVELOPMENTS IN CIVIL PROCEDURE

TABLE OF CONTENTS

SURVEY

A. CASE LAW DEVELOPMENTS

This section highlights certain recent case law developments. It does not attempt to refer to all of the new cases added to the body of this work in this edition; only some of those decisions with significance are discussed here.

Certificate of Pending Litigation: Section 103

It is well established that, since the statements contained in a certificate of pending litigation are absolutely privileged (see *Tersigni v. Fagan*, [1950] O.W.N. 94 (C.A.)), an action for slander of title cannot be maintained insofar as it is based on statements contained in the certificate of pending litigation. This was confirmed in *Geo. Cluthe Manufacturing Co. v. ZTW Properties Inc.* (1995), 23 O.R. (3d) 370 (Div. Ct.), but the court there held that no privilege attached to the registration of a certificate of pending litigation against lands not covered by the order granting leave to issue the certificate and that such registration constituted slander of title. In *Charleston Partners, L.P. v. Dickenson* (1996), 7 W.D.C.P. (2d) 166 (Ont. Gen. Div.), the court granted summary judgment against a party who had registered a certificate of pending litigation without a reasonable claim to an interest in the lands (in an action based upon s. 103(4) of the *Courts of Justice Act*) and quantified the damages that related to the legal costs incurred. However, the issue of exemplary or punitive damages could not be determined on a motion for summary judgment.

Stay of Proceedings: Section 106

The court's discretion to stay a civil action pending a criminal trial arising out of the same facts is to be exercised only in extraordinary or exceptional circumstances and the applicable test requires the moving party to demonstrate, not just that a continuation of the proceedings will compel him to break his silence, but that in some extraordinary way the right to a fair trial will be detrimentally affected. In *Bour v. Manraj* (1995), 24 O.R. (3d) 279 (Ont. Gen. Div.), Madam Justice Chapnik held this test was satisfied. The defendant's criminal preliminary inquiry was in progress, though adjourned, and the solicitor for the plaintiffs in the civil action was on the list of Crown witnesses in the criminal proceeding. If the examinations for discovery in the civil action were to proceed the defendant would be compelled to submit to interrogation under oath by counsel who was a witness for the Crown in the defendant's own criminal trial. This, she held, represented an extraordinary circumstance which might prejudice B's right to a fair trial in the criminal proceedings. Moreover, if the discovery were to proceed as scheduled the order excluding witnesses from the courtroom in the preliminary inquiry would be emasculated and the overall result would be insufficient separation of the criminal and civil proceedings.

In *Gillis v. Eagleson* (1995), 23 O.R. (3d) 164 (Gen. Div.) the defendant demonstrated that his right to a fair criminal trial in the United States would be prejudiced by civil discovery or trial testimony in Ontario, and the court granted a nine-month stay of the Ontario action.

Prejudgment Interest: Sections 128 – 130

In *Bifolchi v. Sherar (Litigation Administrator of)* (1995), 25 O.R. (3d) 637 (Gen. Div.), the court held it could not vary prejudgment interest under former s. 140 of the Act and could not take into consideration the generosity of the amounts awarded by the jury, the late date that the plaintiff was sent to medical experts or the undue delay in bringing the matter on for trial. In *Canada (Attorney General) v. Bitove Corp.* (1996), 7 W.D.C.P. (2d) 164 (Ont. Gen. Div.), the court used the statutory prescribed rate of interest, declining to apply a contractual interest provision where to apply it would have been unjust. In *Emery v. Royal Oak Mines Inc.* (1995), 26 O.R. (3d) 216 (Gen. Div.), the court refused to apply the average rate of interest over the material time, rather than the prescribed statutory rate; the difference was only 2.7 per cent which was not sufficient to warrant departure from the statutory rate. In *120 Adelaide Leaseholds Inc. v. Thomson, Rogers* (1995), 38 C.P.C. (3d) 69 (Ont. Gen. Div.) the court exercised its discretion and altered the prejudgment rate where the prescribed rate was significantly higher than the average of the rates over the period in issue.

Joinder of Claims and Parties: Rule 5

While rule 5.05 gives the court power to order separate hearings where there is a joinder of multiple claims or parties, it is generally recognized that the court should be slow to grant such relief since it results in a multiplicity of proceedings. In *Lippert v. Lippert* (1995), 24 O.R. (3d) 249 (Gen. Div.), the court, however, exercised the power. In that case, parents and their infant children sued for personal injuries alleged to be caused by carbon monoxide poisoning from a furnace installed in the house in which they were living. The adults' injuries could be determined now, but the children's injuries could not be determined for several more years. The court ordered that the issues of liability and the adults' damages be tried now and that the children's damage issues be severed and tried later.

Class Proceedings: Rule 12

Survey of class actions commenced to date. What types of cases have been commenced to date under the *Class Proceedings Act* and how many? Determining with completeness and accuracy what cases have been commenced under the *Class Proceedings Act* is virtually impossible, since there is no central repository of such information. The best we have been able to do is to track those class proceedings which have been reported or which come up on Quick Law, to consult with the judge in Toronto who is specially assigned to deal with class proceedings and to rely upon information obtained by networking with others interested in class proceedings. This quite imprecise process, which is almost certainly not exhaustive, indicates there have been somewhere in the order of 40 proceedings commenced under the legislation so far. These cases are listed below in several fairly rough categories. (Except where indicated the actual status of these cases is unknown; we have given citations, title of the proceeding and file numbers only when known.)

Product liability/Mass torts cases. Bendall v. McGhan Medical Corp. (1993), 14 O.R. (3d) 734 (Gen. Div.) (a class action commenced on behalf of women who had received silicone gel breast implants; certified as a class proceeding); *Norman v. Dow Chemical Co.*, 20582/95 (London action) (another breast implant case; no motion to certify to date); *Serwaczek v. Medical Engineering Corp*, 17629/94 (another breast implant class action; certified on consent for the purposes of settlement; the case has been settled; it is a companion case to a Quebec class action against the same defendant); *Neuman v. Medical Engineering Corp.* (1994), 17 O.R. (3d) 524 (Gen. Div.) (another breast implant case; the action is now apparently defunct, having been superseded by the preceding action); *Burke v. American Heyer-Schultz Corp.* (January 31, 1994, Doc. 15981/93) (Ont. Gen. Div.) (striking out a breast implant class action as statute-barred; the decision is currently under appeal); *Sutherland v. Canadian Red Cross Society* (1994), 17 O.R. (3d) 645 (Gen. Div.) (a class action to recover damages for people who had contracted HIV as a result of receiving contaminated blood and blood products; certification refused); *Nantais v. Telectronics Proprietary (Canada) Ltd.* (1995), 25 O.R. (3d) 331 (Gen. Div.) (a class action by recipients of allegedly defective heart pacemakers; certification granted), leave to appeal refused 25 O.R. (3d) 331 at 347 (Gen. Div.); *Godi v. Toronto Transit Commission* (Doc. 95 CU 89529) (Ont. Gen. Div.) (action on behalf of persons injured in a subway collision); *Campbell v. WCI Canada Inc.*, 18784/94 (a consumer class action by purchasers of household dryers who allege that the dryers were defective); *Ontario New Home Warranty Program v. Chevron Chemical Co.*, 22484/96 (a class action on behalf of an estimated 10,000 homeowners alleged to have suffered damages to their homes as a result of the installation of defective plastic furnace venting systems); *Managan v. Inco Ltd.*, C-1923/96 (a class action claiming personal injury damages allegedly suffered as a result of the release of toxic gases from the defendant's Sudbury plant).

Group defamation. *Elliott v. C.B.C.* (1993), 16 O.R. (3d) 677 (Gen. Div.); *McCann v. Ottawa Sun* (1993), 16 O.R. (3d) 672 (Gen. Div.) (both striking out claims for group defamation as not maintainable); *Kenora (Town) Police Services Bd. v. Savino*, [1995] O.J. No. 486 (refusing to strike a defamation action brought on behalf of police).

Contract cases. *Abdool v. Anaheim Management Ltd.* (1995), 21 O.R. (3d) 453 (Div. Ct.) (a class action by investors in a condominium scheme; certification denied); *Peppiatt v. Nicol* (1993), 16 O.R. (3d) 133 (Gen. Div.) (a class action commenced on behalf of equity members of a golf club against the developer of the project; certified; subsequently, (1996), 27 O.R. (3d) 462 (Gen. Div.), decertification was refused but substantial subclassing was ordered); *Smith v. Canadian Tire Acceptance Ltd.* (1994), 19 O.R. (3d) 610 (Gen. Div.) (a class action by credit card holders alleging improper calculation of interest charges; dismissed on a motion for summary judgment brought prior to a motion for certification); *Garland v. Consumers' Gas Co.* (1995), 22 O.R. (3d) 451 (Gen. Div.) (a consumer class action for damages alleging illegal calculation of interest rates dismissed on a motion for summary judgment brought prior to a motion for certification; under appeal), 22 O.R. (3d) 767 (disposition as to costs); *Krauter v. Hydro Electric Power Commission of the City of London*, 17838/94 (London action), *Krauter v. Union Gas Ltd*, 17837/94 (London Action) and *Pichette v. Toronto Hydro* (all are similar actions to *Garland*); *Ewing v. Francisco Petroleum Enterprises Inc.*, [1994] O.J. No. 1852 (an application for an accounting respecting oil well operations; certified); *Lewicki v. Bettman*, 2083/94 (a class action on behalf of all ticket holders to a hockey game cancelled because of the NHL strike by a ticket holder who had been given two tickets and had been offered a refund; action struck out by Divisional Court as failing to disclose a cause of action and as an abuse of process); *Rosedale Motors Inc. v. PetroCanada Inc.*, 94-CQ-53786 CP (a class action by service station owners against a franchiser oil company); *Windisman v. Toronto College Park Ltd.*, Sharp J., February 13, 1996 (Ont. Gen. Div.) (a class action by owners of condominiums against the developer for interest on moneys paid as deposits; certified; also certified as a defendant class action was a counterclaim brought by the developer against the condominium owners; the judgment cited is a determination of the merits of the action in favour of the plaintiff class); *Hooker v. Nuden*, 2644/95 (an action by purchasers of vinyl siding against installers, the solicitor involved in related mortgage transactions and the mortgagee finance company); *Chan v. Red Lobster* (Doc. 96-CU- 98081) (a consumer class action alleging false advertising that food is cooked only in pure vegetable oil).

Corporate disputes. *Maxwell v. MLG Ventures Ltd.*, (April 27, 1995), Doc. 95-CQ-60022 (Ont. Gen. Div.) (a class action by former shareholders who had sold shares based on alleged misrepresentations in an offering circular; certified; reportedly a settlement has been reached); *Rogers Broadcasting Ltd. v. Alexander* (1994), 25 C.P.C. (3d) 159 (Ont. Gen. Div. [Commercial List]) (where a corporation applied under the *CBCA* to fix the fair value of shares of dissenting shareholders to a proposed amalgamation, a dissenting shareholder made a counter-application seeking damages for oppression and certification of a class proceeding on behalf of all minority shareholders alleging that the amalgamation and subsequent privatization was effected in a manner which was oppressive and unfairly prejudicial to the minority; certification denied). *Millgate Financial Corp. v. BF Realty Holdings*, [1994] O.J. No. 1968 (a class action by corporate debenture holders).

Pension cases. Cooper Industries (Can.) Inc. v. Babin, B173/95 and *Cooper Industries (Can.) Inc v. Adam*, B172/95 (applications by employer/pension plan administrator against a defendant class of beneficiaries to implement a settlement of a dispute as to entitlement to pension plan surplus; certified and settlement approved by court); *Rivett v. Hospitals of Ontario Pension Plan*, [1995] O.J. No. 3270 (Gen. Div.) (an action by a class of beneficiaries to determine pension entitlements; case was certified and then summary judgment granted dismissing the action).

Miscellaneous. Loomis v. Ontario (Ministry of Agriculture and Food) (1994), 16 O.R. (3d) 188 (Div. Ct.) (a class action by students in a community college who had enrolled in a program which was subsequently cancelled by the provincial government prior to the beginning of the school year; reported on the point of refusing an interlocutory interim declaration against the Crown in the absence of deliberate flaunting of established law); *Nash v. CIBC Trust Corp.*, 94-CQ-58919-CP and *Nash v. Ontario*, 94-CQ-56218 (actions by investors against a trust company and the government re investments in syndicated mortgages); *Stamos v. Belanger*, [1994] O.J. No. 2205 (an internal trade union dispute; the plaintiffs, members of a voluntary unincorporated association were certified); *Edwards v. Law Society of Upper Canada*, [1995] O.J. No 2900 (Gen. Div.) (an action alleging negligence by the LSUC in failing to detect the misuse of lawyers' trust accounts in connection with a scheme to sell gold bars); *Adler v. Law Society of Upper Canada*, 95-MU-12831 (an application for a declaration that the Law Society and the Ontario Government where in breach of their statutory obligations to pay outstanding legal aid bills; decision taken not to seek certification and underlying dispute settled); *Warner Chapel Music v. Toronto Life*, 94-CU-77943 (action for failure to pay music royalties); *J – v. A.G. Ontario* (an action brought to strike down on grounds of discrimination the practice of deducting $100 from the welfare cheques of immigrants whose sponsors default).

Recent cases. The case of *Nantais v. Telectronics Proprietary (Can.) Ltd.* (1995), 25 O.R. (3d) 331 (Gen. Div.), leave to appeal refused (1995), 25 O.R. (3d) 331 at 347 (Gen. Div.), is of interest for two reasons — it resulted in the certification of a mass tort case and the court sanctioned the certification of a national class. The action, against defendants who manufactured and marketed leads for pacemakers, was brought on behalf of persons who had been implanted with pacemakers, the leads of which had a fracture rate of between 16 and 25 per cent. The plaintiffs sought certification of an action against the defendants for damages for improper design, manufacture inspection and marketing of the leads. All the claims were in negligence, strict liability or breach of a common law warranty of fitness and no cause of action in contract was asserted. (It was estimated that some 1,125 Canadians were implanted with the lead, and some 700 of them resided in Ontario.) Recognizing that the damage claims of the different plaintiffs may be different, plaintiffs' counsel proposed certification only for determination of the issue of the liability of the defendants.

At first instance, Brockenshire J. observed that since the individual lead recipients did not contract with the defendants, and had no knowledge of the cause of the lead failures, and did not contribute to it, nothing could be gained by discovery of them. Moreover, attempting proof of liability of the defendants would require extensive and expensive medical, scientific and legal work. Also, there might well be a risk of inconsistent verdicts if liability had to be tried more than once. He concluded that satisfaction of the policy goals of access to justice and judicial economy could, in this situation, best be achieved through a class action. He was referred to, but rejected, a line of U.S. authorities showing a consistent reluctance to certify mass torts in products liability cases on the ground that individual issues would so outnumber common issues that nothing should be gained.

In *Abdool v. Ahaheim Management Ltd.* (1995), 21 O.R. (3d) 453 (Div. Ct.), Moldaver J. had reasoned that while the legislature did not incorporate a "predominant" issue test in s. 5 of the Act, it did not intend that individual issues should be completely ignored. Otherwise, there would be no need for s. 6 of the Act and where more than one of the five grounds mentioned in s. 6 are present the court may deny certification. Faced in *Nantais* with an argument based on Moldaver J.'s s. 6 analysis, Brockenshire J. swept it aside on several grounds — Moldaver J.'s analysis was not essential to the decision, he was not convinced it was correct, and in any event it did not apply to the facts before him since only one of the five factors referred to in s. 6 — individual damage assessments — existed in this case. He concluded that the defendants did not raise any issues that should prevent certification; on the contrary, he was persuaded that in this case a class proceeding on liability was a fair, efficient and manageable method of advancing the claim. He further rejected a defence contention that the proposed representative plaintiffs, and the majority of the proposed class whose leads had not failed, had no cause of action, because their only damage claim was for fear of a future problem, and that for policy reasons the courts will not permit a claim for damages for simple fear. He concluded that these allegations as to damages were not patently ridiculous or incapable of proof, and the defendants had not demonstrated that it was plain and obvious beyond doubt that the plaintiffs could not succeed. (He observed the proposed class was analogous to women implanted with faulty breast implants or persons negligently rendered HIV positive.)

Brockenshire J. also concluded that it was appropriate to certify a national class. He noted that the United States Supreme Court has concluded that certification of a national class was appropriate in *Phillips Petroleum Co. v. Shutes* (1985), 105 S.Ct. 2965. He observed that although the Supreme Court of Canada has not yet addressed the issue, the decisions and reasoning in *Morguard Investments Ltd. v. De Savoye*, [1990] 3 S.C.R. 1077 and *Hunt v. T & N plc*, [1993] 4 S.C.R. 289, might support a similar conclusion in the Canadian context. He noted that a national class had been certified in *Bendall v. McGhan* (the breast implant case) (1993), 16 C.P.C. (3d) 156 (Ont. Gen. Div.). He was unmoved by the fact that the recently enacted British Columbia *Class Proceedings Act* (Bill 16-1995) specifically requires non-residents to opt in to a British Columbia class action. He also observed that if the class members outside of Ontario were free to sue despite a class judgment in Ontario, how are the defendants any worse off than if the class was limited to residents of Ontario? If these class members later argue that they were not bound by a decision, the defendant would be in no different position than if those persons simply opted out now. Moreover, he queried whether the problem surrounding the certification of a national class was really relevant to the present action; it seemed to him to be something to be resolved in another action (by a non-resident class member) before another court in another jurisdiction.

Zuber J. dismissed the defendants' motion for leave to appeal to the Divisional Court from the judgment certifying the class proceeding, and the national class, on the ground that there was no good reason to doubt the correctness of the order made by Brockenshire J. He rejected an argument that the proposed representative plaintiffs were not representative of the class. The defendants had argued that the two representative plaintiffs, both of whose leads had not failed, could not represent those whose leads had failed. Zuber J. concluded that if the plaintiffs' case on liability has merit, the wrong was done when the faulty lead was implanted. He also rejected the defence argument that in this case there was a multitude of issues, *e.g.*, that the leads were distributed to many different hospitals, implanted by many different doctors into the bodies of a wide variety of patients. In his view, none of these factual variations diminished the fact that the primary issue was whether or not the defendants were negligent in the manufacture, design and distribution of the leads and this issue was central to the claims of all members of the class. He also concluded that a class proceeding was the preferable procedure, indeed this was the kind of case for which the *Class Proceedings Act* was designed. The financial burden of the litigation would consume almost all of the proceeds of the judgment of any single plaintiff and if the class action was refused the defendants would likely be insulated from any of the claims because of financial consequences alone. Not only was a class proceeding preferable, it was the only procedure whereby members of the class would have any real access to the courts.

Zuber J. also upheld the certification of a national class. He rejected the notion that this involved Ontario imposing jurisdiction on non-residents, since non-residents were free to opt out as the same manner as those inside Ontario. Whether the result reached in Ontario would bind members of the class in other provinces who remained passive and did not opt out remained to be seen, and he observed that the law of *res judicata* may have to adapt itself to the class proceeding concept. The defendants argued that a court attempting to try a national class proceeding would face a multiplicity of laws from all of the provinces which would confuse the matter. Zuber J. rejected this as being largely speculative since it had not been shown that there was any difference in the law respecting products liability or negligence among the common law provinces or indeed on this matter with the law of the Province of Quebec. If problems arose with regard to differing applicable law, or if class actions were commenced in other provinces, this could be dealt with by adjusting or redefining the class.

Nantais is also important for two points that were decided at a subsequent hearing, *i.e.*, what types of contingent fee arrangements may class counsel enter into and, having entered into a contingent fee arrangement, what impact does this have upon the liability of the defendant to pay party and party costs to the plaintiff? In the second *Nantais* decision (19/3/96, court file 95-GD-31789, Windsor) the plaintiff sought the costs of two motions, the motion for certification and an earlier motion, challenging service out of the jurisdiction, the plaintiff having been successful on both motions. In opposition to the costs motion, the defendant took the position (a) that the contingent fee arrangement entered into by plaintiff's counsel was illegal, and (b) since costs are intended to indemnify a party for the costs that party must pay to his/her own counsel, since the plaintiffs had entered into a contingent fee arrangement they were not liable to pay any costs per se to their solicitors and in the absence of any such liability they had no right to claim indemnification through costs against the defendant. In addition, the defendant argued that costs are normally not payable until the conclusion of litigation, that it is only in exceptional circumstances that costs are ordered payable forthwith on a motion and on that ground the plaintiff's motion should be denied. Brockenshire J. rejected each of the defendant's arguments. In so doing he made decisions which are extremely important in terms of furthering the development of class actions.

Plaintiff's counsel had entered into a fee agreement with the representative plaintiffs which had become binding on all class members through having been approved by the court. The essence of the agreement was that if the plaintiffs were successful counsel would receive a fixed sum of $5,000 per implanted class member plus all party-party costs, together with any disbursements not recovered as party and party costs. (Recall in the first *Nantais* decision it had been estimated that there were some 1,125 class members Canada-wide, representing a contingent fee of some $5,626,000.) The defendant argued that the only contingency fee arrangement permitted or sanctioned by the *Class Proceedings Act* was the "multiplier" agreement provided for in s. 33(3)–(9). Rejecting the defendant's argument, the court concluded that the special provisions relating to "multipliers" for hourly rates did not prevent other arrangements authorized under s. 32(1)(c), *i.e.*, payment by means of a lump sum as was the case in *Nantais*. Moreover, the court concluded that s. 33(1), in sanctioning agreement for payment only in the event of success, despite other statutes, sanctions all kinds of fee arrangements contingent upon success, and not just hourly rate multipliers. Although the court did not specifically so state, this would include percentage contingent fees. The general wisdom to date had been that percentage contingent fees were not available under the Act and that non-lump sum fees were restricted to fees calculated by the "multiplier" approach.

It is worth noting that the Ontario Law Reform Commission in its draft Act (s. 42(3), see *Report on Class Actions (1982)*) had proscribed *percentage* contingent fees, but this provision did not find its way into the *Class Proceedings Act*. As the *Class Proceedings Act* provisions are drafted, Brockenshire J.'s conclusion that contingency fee agreements are not limited to those calculated under the "multiplier" seems to be clearly correct.

On the issue of the plaintiff's ability under a contingency fee arrangement to recover party and party costs, the court acknowledged the general principle that where plaintiffs have no liability for costs they have no right to claim indemnification from the opposing party. But the court distinguished the leading cases establishing that principle which were all cases involving salaried solicitors who agreed, in exchange for salary, to have no right to claim for costs against the client. In the instant case the situation was "completely different". Without the contingency fee agreement the representative parties would have been entitled to claim costs and by their contingency agreement they assigned this "property right" to their counsel. This led the court to grant the order sought by the plaintiff, *i.e.*, that the contingency fee agreement did not affect their right to recover costs of motions generally and the costs of the motions presently before the court.

This decision is very significant. The defendants had unsuccessfully argued that costs are not awarded to a party to permit that party to participate in the litigation — costs are not to be used as a funding mechanism. The court rejected this argument on the basis that there was no evidence before the court of costs being sought to finance further participation; plaintiff's counsel simply stated an entitlement to costs, not a need of costs to fund the litigation. Notwithstanding that reasoning, the undoubted effect of the court's rulings — that party and party costs are recoverable notwithstanding a contingency fee and that the court should in class actions follow the standard practice in Ontario of fixing costs at the end of a motion — is to provide plaintiff's counsel in class actions (who have fee arrangements similar to those entered into in *Nantais*) with a significant source of interim cash flow where their ultimate remuneration is only to come with success in actions. It also undermines the defence tactic of running up costs to starve out the plaintiff or plaintiff's counsel, a tactic which could proliferate if the risk of costs awards to plaintiffs were removed. In his decision Brockenshire J. did not quantify the costs recoverable — they were directed to be fixed or assessed at a later date — but plaintiff's counsel claimed slightly more than $293,000 and $158,000 (inclusive of disbursements) in respect of the two motions.

It is unclear what to make of the decision in *Peppiatt v. Royal Bank of Canada* (1996), 27 O.R. (3d) 462 (Gen. Div.), *i.e.*, whether it was correctly decided. The case involved an action for damages for breach of contract, breach of trust, negligence, misrepresentation and breach of fiduciary duty against the promoters of a residence and golf club development, and their banker. This action had been certified earlier by Chilcott J. as a class proceeding: (1993), 16 O.R. (3d) 133 (Gen. Div.). Subsequently, the bank, after learning more about the case through discovery of the representative plaintiffs, moved for an order to decertify the proceedings, or to create a host of sub-classes, or for an order that each member of the class deliver an affidavit of documents and attend to be examined for discovery at his or her own expense.

The original certification had been granted essentially on the basis of an allegation that misrepresentations had been made in a membership information package provided to potential purchasers. It has now emerged that at least some 74 members/purchasers had applied for membership before the package had been issued. Further differences between the situations of the class members had also emerged, *e.g.*, some members had letters of credit which made reference to "in trust" and others did not; some, but not all, members had been plaintiffs in an injunction proceeding which had resulted in consent for the developer to draw on the letters of credit; some, but not all, members had received investment advice from the bank; some members had sat on a board of governors that approved construction costs; some members had acquired their membership by transfer from another member. On the basis of these differences amongst the class members the bank sought the relief outlined above. Chilcott J. spent little time considering the relief of decertification or that all class members should be subject to being examined for discovery, but did grant an order for the establishment of some six different sub-classes with the intent that a representative of each sub-class be made available for examination for discovery by the defendant bank. With respect, it appears Chilcott J. misunderstood or ignored the purpose of sub-classing. In *Peppiatt* it would have been preferable to have dealt directly with the underlying issue raised by the defendant — who beyond the existing class representative should be examined for discovery — and avoid an analysis based upon sub-classing.

Sections 5(2) and 8(2) of the *Class Proceedings Act* indicate that a sub-class is a group of class members who "have claims or defences that raise common issues not shared by all the class members". Moreover, the creation of a formal sub-class is only required where "the protection of the interests of the sub-class members requires that they be separately represented" (s. 5(2) and s. 8(2)). The result then is that there are two elements which are key in the creation of sub-classes — common issues and the need for separate representation.

The "common issues" requirement is not met by establishing sub-classes on the basis of who will or will not win on a particular issue (which seems to be what was done in *Peppiatt*). Whether the defendants had made misrepresentations was an issue common to all of the class members and is a matter which will need to be resolved at the common issues stage of the adjudication and does not necessitate sub-classing. The question of whether or not class members *relied upon* any misrepresentations (which will involve the issue of whether they ever received the document in which the misrepresentations were made) is not a common issue and need not be resolved at the common issues stage of the adjudication. Further these questions do not concern issues "such that the protection of the interests of the sub-class members requires that they be separately represented". In most cases the class representative will be perfectly able to protect the interests of a sub-class and the creation of formal sub-classes with separate representatives will simply complicate the case. This is particularly so in factually complex cases where there may be many combinations and permutations of common issues. The routine creation of sub-classes for every combination and permutation will simply create procedural complications and could lead to severe practical problems *e.g.* what if no willing representative is available for a particular sub-class. It should be kept in mind that sub-classing was not devised to benefit defendants; it is for the protection of members of the plaintiff class.

In terms of discovery rights there is no doubt that the practical result of Chilcott J.'s decision is correct. The defendant was allowed to discover a small cross-section of class members and will know the case it has to meet at trial. The defendant was not allowed to discover all class members, which would clearly have been too much discovery, nor was it restricted to the representative plaintiff alone which would have been too little discovery in the circumstances. However this balanced result would better have been achieved under s. 15(3), which sets out the factors to be considered for allowing discovery of class members, without the ongoing complications of creating formal sub-classes. Indeed, the s. 15(3)(c) factor is the presence of sub-classes — presence of a formal sub-class created under the "protection" rationale of s. 5(2) and s. 8(2) would mean that the sub-class representative would be discoverable as of right under s. 15(1) and would militate against leave to discover additional class members under s. 15(3); whereas lack of formal sub-classes might militate in favour of granting leave if there were crucial factual issues which could not be satisfied through discovery of the representative plaintiff alone.

New B.C. legislation. British Columbia has now joined Ontario and Quebec by adopting class action legislation. The *Class Proceedings Act* (S.B.C. 1995, c. 21) came into force on August 1, 1995. The British Columbia legislation is based upon its Ontario counterpart and on most questions of policy and, in many cases, its drafting tracks the Ontario legislation. However, there are differences and at least in some areas these are significant. The Act directly addresses the question of non-resident class members; the class representative must be a resident of British Columbia and an opt-in regime is established for non-resident class members. The Ontario legislation, while requiring that a class proceeding be the "preferable procedure for the resolution of the common issues", leaves at large the question of how that is to be determined. The British Columbia legislation, however, goes on to list a number of factors to be considered by the court on this issue (drawn from the Ontario Law Reform Commission's *Report on Class Actions (1982)*). Quebec, but not Ontario, permits entities such as non-profit corporations and associations to act as class representatives. On this issue British Columbia has followed the Quebec model. While the Ontario legislation adopts the position that any part of a damage award that remains undistributed should be returned to the defendant, the British Columbia legislation provides for *cy-pres*-like distribution of these funds (as was recommended by the Ontario Law Reform Commission).

Finally, again following the Ontario Law Reform Commission, the British Columbia legislation adopts a different costs rule than its Ontario counterpart. Under the Ontario legislation the court may order costs against losing class representatives where the proceeding was not a test case, did not raise a novel point of law or did not involve a matter of public interest. Under the British Columbia there is a basic no-costs rule, *i.e.*, neither party is liable for costs except where it has been found guilty of vexatious, frivolous or abusive conduct. Since theoretically the residual liability of class representatives for costs in Ontario is likely a deterrent to the bringing of class actions in this province, it will be interesting to see whether the British Columbia no-cost rule encourages more class action activity in that province.

Intervention: Rule 13

In *Thomson v. Thomson Estate* (1995), 26 O.R. (3d) 250 (Gen. Div.), an insurer's putative subrogated claim was included in the plaintiff's statement of claim. Subsequently, a conflict developed and the insurer was granted leave to intervene where the insurer would play a limited role in the litigation and would not advance the position adverse in interest to the plaintiff. Subsequently, leave to appeal this decision was granted on the ground that there was doubt as to its correctness and the issue raised — the right of an insurer with a subrogated interest to intervene in cases of litigation involving its insured — was a matter of general importance. However, subsequent to the granting of leave the matter was settled: see (1995), 27 O.R. (3d) 415 (Gen. Div.).

Service out of Ontario: Rule 17

In the 1996 Annual Survey of Recent Developments in Civil Procedure the holding of the majority of the Court of Appeal in *Frymer v. Brettschneider* (1994), 19 O.R. (3d) 60, that in cases of service *ex juris* the burden is on the plaintiff to justify the choice of the domestic forum where it is challenged as being inconvenient, was sharply criticized. It was criticized on the ground, *inter alia*, that it was difficult to reconcile with the statements made by Sopinka J. on this issue on *Amchem Products Inc. v. British Columbia (Workers' Compensation Board)*, [1993] 1 S.C.R. 897, and in any event Arbour J.A. offered no cogent reasons for distinguishing Sopinka J.'s statements. In *Fidelity Management & Research Co. v. Gulf Canada Resources Ltd.* (1995), 25 O.R. (3d) 548 (Gen. Div. [Commercial List]), R. A. Blair J. revisited this burden issue, although in a slightly different context to *Frymer*. In *Frymer* both parties had been served out of the jurisdiction. By contrast, in *Fidelity Management* some parties had been served within the jurisdiction and other defendants were served out of the jurisdiction under rule 17.02(o) on the grounds that they were necessary or proper parties to a proceedings properly brought against another person served in Ontario. The defendants served *ex juris* sought a stay of proceeding on the grounds that Ontario was not the convenient forum and Blair J. held that in these circumstances the onus was on the *defendant* disputing jurisdiction to satisfy the court that there is clearly another jurisdiction which is the more appropriate forum. This conclusion, he felt, was consistent with *Amchem* and is not inconsistent with the decision in *Frymer* where the court was not only called upon to deal with a situation where the plaintiff had chosen a forum "as of right" against some of the defendants. In his reasoning there is perhaps a hint that he was more comfortable with the decision in *Amchem* than that in *Frymer*.

Enforcement of foreign judgments. In *United States of America v. Ivy* (1995), 26 O.R. (3d) 533, Sharpe J., in a lengthy and well-reasoned judgment, considered the issue of whether the "real and substantial connection" test laid down by the Supreme Court of Canada in *Morguard Investments Ltd. v. De Savoye*, [1990] 3 S.C.R. 1077, as the test for the enforcement of sister province judgments, also applies to the enforcement of foreign judgments. He concluded that it did. His starting point was that *Morguard* dealt specifically with the recognition and enforcement of a judgment of the courts of one province by the courts of another province. While there is no doubt that considerations relating specifically to Canadian federalism played an important role in the Supreme Court's decision in *Morguard*, principles of broader application were also at work. He concluded that (as already held by MacPherson J. in *Arrowmaster Inc. v. Unique Forming Ltd.* (1993), 17 O.R. (3d) 407 (Gen. Div.), and by the British Columbia Court of Appeal in *Moses v. Shore Boat Builders Ltd.* (1993), 106 D.L.R. (4th) 654), the Supreme Court intended the *Morguard* rule to apply to the judgments of the courts of the United States and other foreign courts with legal regimes based upon principles compatible with Canadian concepts of justice.

At issue in the case was a Michigan default judgment, in favour of the United States Government, dealing with environmental clean-up costs in respect of a waste disposal site owned and operated by the defendants who were Ontario residents. Sharpe J. had little difficulty in concluding that the real and substantial connection test was met in this case since the defendants engaged in the waste disposal business in Michigan and the cause of action arose within the jurisdiction of the Michigan court. As a result the plaintiffs succeeded in obtaining a summary judgment enforcing the Michigan judgment (which was for (U.S.) $4.5 million).

The case also illustrates the matters which will become the focus of such enforcement litigation once the real and substantial connection test is satisfied (as it often will be). The defendants raised, unsuccessfully, the arguments that the Michigan judgments were based on "penal", "revenue", or "public" laws and that accordingly the enforcement should be refused. An argument that the judgments should not be enforced because they were obtained in a manner which violated the principles of natural justice was also rejected, although this ground for refusing enforcement was recognized by the court. Finally, Sharpe J. rejected an argument that enforcement should be refused on the grounds that it would be contrary to public policy for this court to enforce the judgments. He noted, citing the Ontario Court of Appeal and Professor J-G. Castel, that while the public policy defence exists in theory, it has been rarely applied and seldom invoked and has been construed narrowly; Canadian courts will generally apply foreign law even though the result may be contrary to domestic law; care must be exercised in relying upon public policy as a ground for refusing enforcement; it is not enough to deny recognition of the claim that the local law on the same point differs from the foreign law — fundamental values must be at stake.

On its facts *Ivy* was a fairly easy and uncontroversial case. The Ontario residents had been actively involved in business in Michigan, the proceedings against them were fair by any standards and they were being asked to pay environmental clean-up costs for which they would have been liable under similar circumstances in Ontario. What the judgment in *Ivy* does not tell us is how the court will deal with much more troubling circumstances, *i.e.*, enormous damage awards by largely uncontrolled juries applying standards of damage assessments widely different from those applied by Canadian courts. However, there is little in Sharpe J.'s brief discussion of the public policy exception to give Canadian residents who run afoul of such U.S. juries much comfort.

Default Proceedings: Rule 19

In *Tomazio v. Rutale* (1995), 26 O.R. (3d) 191 (Gen. Div.), Borins J. held that a master lacks jurisdiction to sign a default judgment in respect of a claim for which a registrar has not been given the power to sign a default judgment. A motion before a master under rule 19.04(3) is to obtain a default judgment where the registrar should have signed it. It is only a judge, under rule 19.05(1), who is given jurisdiction to grant a default judgment where the registrar has no power to sign a default judgment. In this case, on the plaintiff's claim for unliquidated damages, the master exceeded his jurisdiction when he assessed the plaintiff's damages and granted judgment accordingly. The default judgment having been obtained in an irregular manner the defendant was entitled to have it set aside as of right and without the imposition of terms, other than costs.

Esprit de Corp. (1980) Ltd. v. Papadimitriou (1995), 23 O.R. (3d) 733 (Gen. Div.), held that where a plaintiff had obtained default judgment against the corporate defendant it could not later move to set aside the default judgment in order to pursue its action against the individual defendants; having made its election to proceed against the corporate defendant it was not now open to the plaintiff to proceed against the individual defendants. (A notice of appeal has been filed in this case.)

Summary Judgment: Rule 20

In *Royal Bank of Canada v. Feldman* (1995), 23 O.R. (3d) 798 (Gen. Div.), on the plaintiff's motion for summary judgment, the master had before him the defendant's affidavit and the transcript of her examination for discovery in which she stated that she did not know, or could not be sure, whether it was her signature on certain documents and on a certificate of independent legal advice. The master dismissed the motion for summary judgment, stating that he could not resolve the issue of credibility. On appeal, Borins J. held that the master had erred in assuming that *any issue* with respect to credibility constitutes a genuine issue for trial. The court is precluded from granting summary judgment only when what is said to be an issue of credibility is a genuine issue of credibility: *Irving Ungerman Ltd. v. Galanis* (1991), 4 O.R. (3d) 545 (C.A.). Considered in the context of all of the evidence, the defendant's evidence was so disingenuous as not to constitute a genuine issue for trial. In *Innovative Automation Inc. v. Candea Inc.* (1995), 24 O.R. (3d) 639 (Gen. Div.), the plaintiff brought a motion for summary judgment after the exchange of pleadings. After the exchange of affidavits and after cross-examination on the affidavit it became apparent to the plaintiff that the motion would not succeed and it sought to abandon its summary judgment motion without paying the defendant's costs pursuant to rule 20.06. Belleghem J. held that the defendant should be entitled to its costs thrown away because of the bringing of the motion, on a solicitor and client basis. The test under the rule was whether or not the bringing of the motion for summary judgment was reasonable and here the pleadings had patently disclosed a factually based action which would likely involve issues of credibility and hence, at the time the pleadings were exchanged, it was obvious that there was a triable issue and that the motion had little or no chance of success.

Determination of Issue Before Trial: Rule 21

Res judicata and issue estoppel. There has been confusion in recent court decisions regarding the use of criminal convictions (or rulings made in criminal proceedings) in subsequent civil proceedings. Because invariably the parties in the two proceedings are different, issue estoppel, if interpreted as requiring mutuality or the same parties — as it typically is in Canada — is inapplicable. The courts have resolved the matter by adopting two principles.

The first principle applies where a party wishes to use the prior conviction defensively as did the insurance company in *Demeter v. British Pacific Life Insurance Co.* (1983), 43 O.R. (2d) 33, affirmed (1984), 48 O.R. (2d) 266 (C.A.). In that case, abuse of process (operating here just like issue estoppel) was applied to prevent the plaintiff, a convicted murderer, from attacking his criminal conviction by means of an action on his victim's life insurance policy; the action was completely dismissed as an abuse of process.

The second principle applies where a party seeks to use the determination in the prior criminal case affirmatively (akin to offensive non-mutual issue estoppel) by relying on the earlier findings in support of a civil action. In this context the courts have generally adopted the principle that the prior criminal conviction is admissible as *prima facie* evidence, subject to rebuttal by the defendant/accused. (For discussion of both non-mutual issue estoppel and abuse of process see G. Watson, "Duplicative Litigation: Issue Estoppel, Abuse of Process and the Death of Mutuality" (1990), 69 Can. Bar Rev. 623.)

The judgment in *Canadian Tire Corp. v. Summers* (1995), 23 O.R. (3d) 106 (Gen. Div.), is unclear both as to the nature of the prior criminal conviction and the current civil action, but apparently the plaintiff was seeking to recover moneys in respect of which the defendant, R.S., had already been convicted of some offence (theft? embezzlement?). In the civil proceeding the plaintiff sought an order that the defendant be estopped from calling any evidence in relation to the finding made against him in the criminal proceeding. In a somewhat confusing judgment the court concluded, relying on *Demeter*, that the six convictions of R.S. were admissible at trial as *"prima facie* proof" of his conviction on the charges and it "would be an abuse of process for any of the defendants to be permitted to adduce evidence and argue against those convictions". The judge, Wilkins J., did not explain the conflict between his use of *"prima facie"* proof and his further holding that the defendants were not to be permitted to call *any* evidence regarding the convictions. The reason is that he got the relevant principles mixed up. *Demeter* was not the relevant authority because it dealt with a different situation — one where the convicted person seeks to bring a civil action (as plaintiff) — in an attempt to relitigate the criminal conviction. In such circumstances the prior conviction prohibits the action because it constitutes an abuse of process. But in the type of case before Wilkins J. (one akin to offensive non-mutual issue estoppel) the existing Ontario authorities adopt the position that the previous conviction is *prima facie* evidence, subject to rebuttal; see *Q. v. Minto Management Ltd.* (1984) 46 O.R. (2d) 756 (H.C.); *Re Del Core and Ont. College of Pharmacists* (1985), 51 O.R. (2d) 1 (C.A.); *Taylor v. Baribeau* (1985), 51 O.R. (2d) 541 (Div. Ct.). The use of the phrase *"prima facie evidence"* in these cases is indicative of the fact that the *prima facie* evidence is subject to rebuttal by the defendant at the trial.

It has been argued elsewhere (see Watson, above) that for most criminal convictions the *"prima facie* evidence, subject to rebuttal" approach makes no sense and that in the "offensive" situation the plaintiff should be permitted to use the criminal conviction as an issue estoppel, *i.e.*, binding on the defendant/accused to the same extent as issue estoppel, notwithstanding the difference in parties (because, and provided that, the defendant had a full and fair opportunity to defend himself in the criminal proceeding). In other words, the result achieved by Wilkins J. in *Canadian Tire* appears to be correct, but does not deal with the conflicting Ontario authorities.

The English decision of Jacob J. in *Brinks Limited v. Abu-Saleh*, [1995] 4 All E.R. 65 (Ch.D.), represents a much sounder approach to the issue faced in *Canadian Tire*. It also provides a rationale that brings the *"prima facie* evidence, subject to rebuttal" rule more in line with normal issue estoppel principles. The facts of the case were essentially similar to *Canadian Tire*. It was an action by Brinks to recover millions of pounds which were the proceeds of gold thefts for which the defendants had been convicted, and the plaintiff moved for summary judgment against the defendants based on their convictions. Jacob J. had to work with the English *Criminal Evidence Act* 1968 which enshrines the *prima facie* evidence rule, providing that in a civil proceeding where a person's conviction is proven "he shall be taken to have committed that offence unless the contrary is proved". What is meant by the phrases "unless the contrary is proved" or "subject to rebuttal" has to date been unclear, but appeared to leave open the possibility of the defendant/accused being free to relitigate the issue of his conviction. Not so, held Jacob J. in granting summary judgment. The only evidence admissible to ''prove the contrary'' is essentially the type of evidence that would be admissible where a true issue estoppel applies, *i.e.*, the defendant is required to show that new evidence, not called at the criminal trial but to be called at the civil trial, would raise a fair and reasonable probability of his having a real or *bona fide* defence to the claim that would entirely change the aspect of the case.

Persaud v. Donaldson (1995) 25 O.R. (3d) 270 (Gen. Div.), represents another instance where the court arrived at the correct decision on an issue estoppel point involving a criminal proceeding, but the reasoning is wanting. P. had been charged with possession of stolen property following a police search of his house. At the preliminary inquiry the judge held that the information to obtain the search warrant was deficient, that the search amounted to a warrantless search, which was *prima facie* unreasonable, and that P.'s rights under s. 8 of the *Charter* were violated. The illegally obtained evidence was excluded and P. was acquitted. P. then brought a civil action against the police involved to recover damages for the *Charter* violation, and in the civil proceeding contended that there was an issue estoppel as to the question of the unreasonableness of the search since it had been determined in the criminal proceeding and the civil court was bound by that finding. Chilcott J. rejected this argument and held there was no issue estoppel because the requirement that the parties be the same was not met. In the circumstances of this case, even dropping the same parties requirement should not lead to issue estoppel applying. This was a situation where offensive non-mutual issue estoppel, even if accepted as a permissible doctrine, would not help the plaintiff. The reason is that for the doctrine to apply the person against whom it is to be used must have had their day in court on the issue and had a full and fair opportunity to litigate the issue and lost. This was not so in *Persaud* because the defendants — the police officers involved in the investigation — had never litigated the issue. The Crown had, but not the police officers. It is fundamental to the application of offensive non-mutual issue estoppel that the person against whom it is to be pleaded has had their day in court and this was not so in *Persaud*.

Pleadings: Rule 25

New common law libel privilege to report on court documents. All litigation lawyers are, or should be, concerned as to what it is that they can say or publish regarding allegations or statements made in court documents. Prior to the decision in *Hill v. Church of Scientology of Toronto*, [1995] 2 S.C.R. 1130, the common law defamation privilege for reporting on judicial proceedings applied only when the reporting was about proceedings in open court; it did not extend to documents filed with the court which had not been referred to or read in open court. In *Hill* the Supreme Court significantly expanded this privilege. Michael Doody in a case comment ''New Common Law Libel Privilege to Report on Court Documents: *Hill v. Church of Scientology of Toronto*'' (1996) 18 Advocates' Q. 251, states that the new rule enunciated by the court, based on the protection of the *Charter* value of freedom of expression under s. 2(b), is as follows:

(1) there is a common law privilege which protects those who report on pleadings in court documents which are filed (or are about to be filed) before trial; and

(2) if the publisher is acting in a manner other than attempting to present a fair and accurate report of the proceedings, then the court may deny the privilege protection if the publisher does not make a further investigation into the accuracy of the facts alleged in the proceedings.

However, the new extended privilege by no means gives counsel carte blanche to publish the contents of court documents filed or about to be filed, as was demonstrated by the actual decision in *Hill*. The Church's lawyer, standing on the steps of Osgoode Hall, read out to media representatives a notice which the Church was about to file in court seeking a judicial determination that the plaintiff Hill was in contempt of court because of the Church's claim that he had violated a court order. The court decided that this reading by the lawyer of the court document, which he was about to file, was a report on a privileged occasion to the public. However, the court also decided that the lawyer's conduct caused his statements to fall outside the protection of this privilege. Unfortunately, the circumstances which will lead to privilege being lost are unclear from the court's decision. The court referred to the lawyer's actions as describing Hill's conduct in the "worst possible light", at a time when "he should have been aware of the Scientology investigation pertaining to access to the sealed documents", and without investigating himself or waiting for the Scientology investigation to be completed. This conduct the court described as "high-handed and careless" and held that, since he was a lawyer, and indeed an experienced lawyer, this imposed on him some special duty above non-lawyers to further investigate the facts in this case before he reported them to other people.

In his comment, above, Michael Doody also raises questions as to whether the qualified privilege enunciated in *Hill* may require qualification to the implied undertaking rule enunciated in *Goodman v. Rossi* (1995), 24 O.R. (3d) 359 (C.A.), and now embodied in Rule 30.1 Deemed Undertaking.

Amendment of Pleadings: Rule 26

In *Whiten v. Pilot Insurance Co.* (1996), 7 W.D.C.P. (2d) 105 (Ont. Gen. Div.), the court permitted an amendment to increase the amount claimed to equal the $1 million punitive damage award made by the jury. The Divisional Court in *Myers v. Metropolitan Toronto (Municipality) Police Force* (1995), 37 C.P.C. (3d) 349, held, where the trial judge allowed the plaintiff to amend its pleadings but ordered the plaintiff to pay the cost of the wasted trial day on a solicitor-client basis within 15 days, that the trial judge acted reasonably in not taking into account the plaintiff's claim of impecuniosity and it would, generally, only interfere with the trial judge's discretion to award costs in limited circumstances. In *Hales Contracting Inc. v. Towlan-Hewitson Construction Ltd.* (1996), 7 W.D.C.P. (2d) 151 (Ont. Gen. Div.), leave to appeal granted 7 W.D.C.P. (2d) 187, the court granted the plaintiff's motion, brought on the eve of trial, to add a claim for punitive and exemplary damages but ordered the plaintiff to pay certain consequential costs. The Court of Appeal in *Haikola v. Arasenau* (January 19, 1996), Doc. CA C15469, reversed an order that refused an amendment two weeks before trial to increase the amount claimed where the defendant had failed to demonstrate prejudice. In *Transamerica Life Insurance Co. of Canada v. Canada Life Assurance Co.* (1995), 25 O.R. (3d) 106 (Gen. Div.) (motion for leave to appeal to Div. Court filed), where the defendants failed to establish that they would suffer prejudice, the court allowed the plaintiff to file a fresh statement of claim based on information it had obtained during the examination for discovery of the defendants.

Discovery of Documents: Rule 30

Waiver of privilege. In *Woodglen & Co. v. Owens* (1995), 24 O.R. (3d) 261 (Gen. Div.), certain privileged documents were ordered produced where the plaintiffs had put in issue the nature of the legal advice they had received, and therefore were deemed to have waived the solicitor and client privilege. In *Agrico Canada Ltd. v. Northgate Insurance Brokers Inc.* (1994), 35 C.P.C. (3d) 370 (Ont. Gen. Div.), it was held that where a document which was clearly prepared in contemplation of litigation had been inadvertently or accidentally disclosed the defendant could deliver a fresh affidavit of documents and assert privilege over the document.

Production from non-parties. The decision of the Court of Appeal in *Ontario (Attorney General) v. Ballard Estate* (1995), 26 O.R. (3d) 39, is an important one on the production of documents from non-parties. On the plaintiff's motion under rule 30.10 for production of documents in the hands of non-parties to the action, the motion judge found that the documents were relevant to material issues in the litigation. However, on the issue of whether it would be unfair to require the plaintiffs to proceed to trial without having discovery of those documents (as provided in the rule) he held that the most important factor in determining the factor of unfairness is whether the evidence sought to be produced is "crucial" to the action and since he found that the documents sought to be produced were not "crucial and vital" to the central issues in the action he dismissed the plaintiff's motion. On the appeal the Court of Appeal held that by requiring the documents to be "vital" or "crucial" the motion judge had imposed a higher standard of materiality than was contemplated by the rule and effectively neutered the fairness assessment demanded by rule 30.10(1)(b). The importance of the documents is only one factor to be considered in making the determination required by this rule. In deciding whether to order production in the circumstances of this case the court indicated the factors to be considered should include: the importance of the documents in the litigation; whether production at the discovery stage of the process as opposed to production at trial was necessary to avoid unfairness to the plaintiff; whether the discovery of the defendants with respect to the issues to which the documents were relevant was adequate and if not, whether responsibility for that inadequacy rests with the defendants; the position of the non-parties with respect to production; the availability of the documents or their informational equivalent from some other source which was accessible to the plaintiff; and the relationship of the non-parties for whom production was sought to the litigation and the parties to the litigation. The court observed that non-parties who have an interest in the subject matter of the litigation and whose interests are allied with the party opposing production should be more susceptible to a production order than a true "stranger" to the litigation.

Offer to Settle: Rule 49

In *Johnson & Johnson Inc. v. Bristol-Myers Squibb Canada Inc.* (January 23, 1996), Doc. Toronto 94-CQ-58779 (Ont. Gen. Div.), it was held that a proposal to settle a motion need not be in writing to form the basis for a solicitor and client costs award. However, in *Veilleux v. Ranger* (1995), 25 O.R. (3d) 759 (Gen. Div.), it was held that an oral offer, since it was incapable of being served pursuant to rule 49.02, could not attract costs consequences.

In *Diefenbacher v. Young* (1995), 22 O.R. (3d) 641 (C.A.), it was held that where a plaintiff serves two offers to settle during the course of a law suit and the second offer is lower than the first and is silent about the first offer, the second offer withdraws the first offer by implication. The situation is similar where a defendant makes two offers, the second of which is higher than the first and is silent about the first offer.

In *Schmieder v. Singh* (February 20, 1996), Doc. 67472/91Q, 91-CQ-4785 (Ont. Gen. Div.), several parties had entered into a "Mary Carter" agreement designed to maximise the liability of certain parties and reduce the exposure of another party. The court did not require the amounts involved to be disclosed.

In *Fatal v. Burton* (1995), 24 O.R. (3d) 234 (Gen. Div.), a defendant made an offer to a co-defendant to divide liability 75 per cent-25 per cent and the co-defendant was found 100 per cent liable at trial. The court awarded the first defendant party and party costs of the crossclaim to the date of the offer and solicitor and client costs thereafter. In *McCullough v. Bursey* (1995), 25 O.R. (3d) 655 (Gen. Div.), the plaintiff agreed to dismiss his action against B, but defendant C (who had cross-claimed against defendant B) refused to agree. In the result defendant C was ordered to pay the costs of defendant B on a solicitor and client scale.

Evidence at Trial: Rule 53

In *Whiten v. Pilot Insurance Co.* (1996), 27 O.R. (3d) 479 (Gen. Div.), counsel for the plaintiff served a notice of intention to call the defendant F as a witness under rule 53.07. When the defendant failed to undertake to call F the plaintiff proceeded to call F as part of the plaintiff's case and, relying on rule 53.07(3), was permitted to cross-examine him. Counsel for the defendant then sought to cross-examine F and put leading questions to him. Matlow J. ruled that counsel for the defendant was not entitled to cross-examine F. It would make no sense to interpret rule 53.07 so as to confer on counsel for the defendant an advantage that he would not otherwise have had, namely, the right to cross-examine F, as a reward for failing to call F himself or to give the undertaking.

Costs: Rule 57

Judge Dan Ferguson held in *Harnden v. Kosir* (1995), 26 O.R. (3d) 588 (Gen. Div.), that there is no rigid principle that false testimony cannot justify costs on a solicitor and client scale and the concept that perjury should be remedied by the criminal law is not an appropriate basis for refusing solicitor and client costs. Perjury in civil cases seldom results in criminal prosecution and consequently, parties could commit perjury with impunity if a trial judge imposed no sanction. In this case, where the defendant had based his whole case on false evidence, an award of solicitor and client costs was appropriate.

In *Goulin v. Goulin* (1995), 26 O.R. (3d) 472 (Gen. Div.), it was held that the principle that solicitor and client costs may be awarded where there had been reprehensible, scandalous or outrageous conduct on the part of one of the parties is not limited to trials or judicial hearings. The principle is a general application, and early discontinuance should not result in absolution. In this case there had been no proper basis for allegations of fraud, dishonesty and wrongdoing made against the defendant and on the plaintiff's discontinuance of the action it was proper to award costs against the plaintiff on a solicitor and client basis.

Security for Costs of Appeal: rule 61.06

In *Schmidt v. Toronto-Dominion Bank* (1995), 24 O.R. (3d) 1 (C.A.), and *McKee v. Di Battista, Gambin Developments Ltd.* (1995), 22 O.R. (3d) 700 (C.A.), it was held that in order to obtain an order for security for costs it is necessary that the appeal appears to be frivolous or vexatious, and it need not be established that the appeal is frivolous or vexatious. See also R. Malen, Case Comment: "Security for Costs on Appeal" (1996), 18 Advocates' Q. 247.

B. AMENDMENTS TO THE RULES

The following is a summary of the effect of all but the most minor Rule amendments made since the last Annual Survey. Although there have been a large number of rule amendments, most are not of great significance. The really major amendments are the introduction of two new Rules, *i.e.*, Rule 30.1 Deemed Undertaking and Rule 76 Simplified Procedure. (For an extended analysis of these and all other Rule amendments, see Holmested & Watson, *Ontario Civil Procedure*, Volume 5 under the tab "Appendix of Amendments".)

Rule 4.02(4): Inclusion of Fax Numbers in Court Documents

This new subrule requires that every document served or filed in a proceeding must bear the fax number, if any, of the person serving or filing it and the fax number, if known, of the recipient of the document.

Rule 15.03(4) and (5): Solicitor's Lien

These two new subrules provide a procedure for obtaining a speedy determination of whether the party's former solicitor is entitled to a lien on the party's file and the terms, if any, by which it may be discharged.

Rule 25.06(8): Pleading Nature of Act or Condition of Mind — Malice and Intent

Prior to its amendment this rule required full particulars of fraud, misrepresentation or breach of trust, but provided that malice, intent or knowledge may be alleged as a fact without pleading the circumstances from which it may be inferred. The rule has now been amended to require particulars of malice and intent to be pleaded.

Rule 30.1: Deemed Undertaking

This new Rule largely codifies the law relating to implied undertaking established as part of the law of Ontario by the decision in *Goodman v. Rossi* (1995), 24 O.R. (3d) 359 (C.A.). See the Highlights to this Rule in the main body of the work for an analysis of the Rule.

Rule 39.04: Evidence by Examination for Discovery

Prior to this amendment, rule 39.04 provided that on the hearing of a motion the transcript of an examination for discovery may be used in the same manner as at trial. The rule was amended to resolve the issue of whether a party may use its own examination for discovery on a motion, as was held in *Peirson* v. *Bent* (1993), 13 O.R. (3d) 429 (Gen. Div.) (a party may use its own discovery evidence on a motion for summary judgment); contrast *Clark* v. *Tiger Brand Knitting Co.* (1986), 10 C.P.C. (2d) 288 (Ont. H.C.) (holding that a party could not use its own examination for discovery) and *313473 Ont. Ltd.* v. *Lornal Const. Ltd. (No. 2)* (1976), 13 O.R. (2d) 585 (H.C.) (holding a party could use the transcript of its own examination for discovery in support of a motion to amend its pleading). The new rule resolves this issue by providing that a party's own examination for discovery cannot be used, unless the parties consent to its use.

Rule 59.05(5): Entry of Court of Appeal Orders

Prior to this amendment, the Rules required orders of the Court of Appeal had to be entered in the office of the registrar in which the action or application was commenced *and also* in the office of the local registrar at Toronto. As a result of the amendment, rather than being entered in the office of the local registrar at Toronto, they are now to be entered in the office of the registrar of the Court of Appeal. This amendment merely codifies what has been happening to date on an *ad hoc* arrangement.

Rule 60.08 (6.1): Notice of Garnishment

Prior to this amendment it was not crystal clear from rule 60.08 as to whether a single notice of garnishment could be used for more than one debtor and for more than one garnishee, although court staff acted on the assumption that a notice of garnishment could name only one debtor and one garnishee. The new amendment specifically so provides. The administration of the garnishment process would become extremely complicated and many problems would arise for court staff, sheriffs and garnishees if a notice of garnishment could name more than one debtor or more than one garnishee.

Rule 60.18(7): Service on the Debtor of a Notice of Examination in Aid of Execution

The purpose of this amendment is to make it clear that a party examined in aid of execution must be served personally, or by an alternative to personal service, and that *service on the party's solicitor is unavailable*. The reason for the amendment is that it is often unclear whether a party's solicitor continues to act after judgment. In the past, some solicitors have been served with an examination in aid of execution and this has caused them difficulty and expense as they tried to get in touch with their former clients.

Rule 61.03: Motion for Leave to Appeal to Divisional Court

Formerly rule 61.03 dealt with all motions for leave to appeal to "an appellate court" *i.e.* the Divisional Court and the Court of the Appeal. Now rule 61.03.1, originally introduced for a one-year trial period and amended to become permanent (see below), regulates motions for leave to appeal to the Court of Appeal, which are to be made in writing. As amended, rule 61.03 now provides that it governs only motions for leave to appeal to the Divisional Court (rule 61.03(1)), which — unlike leave motions in the Court of Appeal — are not to be made in writing. Minor consequential amendments have been made to subrules 61.03(3) and (4). The amendments to rule 61.03(2) require that the motion record include a copy of any order or decision (and the reasons, if any, therefore) that was the subject of the hearing before the court or tribunal from which leave to appeal is sought. Parallel amendments were made by this regulation to rule 61.10(1) concerning the contents of appeal books (see below).

Rule 61.03.1: Motion for Leave to Appeal to the Court of Appeal to be in Writing

The former (experimental) rule 61.03.1, providing for motions for leave to appeal to the Court of Appeal to be made in writing, was, by its own terms, revoked on April 1, 1996. This experiment was monitored, including questionnaires to counsel involved in motions under the experimental procedure. Based on the data collected from the questionnaire it was determined that the experiment had been successful. The new rule 61.03.1

establishes the motion for leave to appeal to the Court of Appeal in writing as a permanent procedure and makes some minor modifications to the prior practice, *i.e.*, the moving party may serve a reply factum; the contents of factums are expanded; provision is made for the filing of books of authorities; the time for filing of responding party's material has been extended to 25 days and it is specifically provided that a motion shall be submitted to the court for consideration 36 days after service of the moving party's motion record, etc. or on the filing of the moving party's reply factum, if any, whichever is earlier.

Rule 61.03(7)–(9): Leave to Appeal Order as to Costs Where Cost Appeal Joined With Appeal as of Right

The *Courts of Justice Act*, s.133(b), provides that where there is an appeal only as to costs that are in the discretion of the court that made the order for costs, no appeal lies without leave of the court to which the appeal is to be taken. Perhaps somewhat curiously, the jurisprudence is to the effect that where there is an appeal both on the merits and also as to the disposition of costs, and the appeal on the merits fails, then the appellate court has no jurisdiction to hear the appeal as to costs unless leave to appeal is granted: *Cameron v. Julien*, [1957] O.W.N. 430 (C.A.). Some litigators, unaware of this law, did not seek leave to appeal as to costs when their appeal on the merits is as of right (while other litigators had been applying, in advance of the hearing of the appeal, to the motions court for leave in these circumstances). The Court of Appeal responded to this situation in an *ad hoc* way by allowing a motion for leave during the hearing of an appeal. The amendment now clarifies the situation and provides that where a party seeks to join an appeal as to costs under s.133(b) with an appeal as of right, the request for leave to appeal is to be included in the notice of appeal as part of the relief sought and leave to appeal shall be sought from the panel of the appellate court hearing the appeal as of right, *i.e.*, it is unnecessary to make a prior motion to the motions court for leave to appeal the costs order. The rule is drafted in such a way as to also apply to a cross-appeal as to costs under s.133(b).

Rule 61.10(1): Appeal Books

This amendment simply ensures that where the appeal is a second appeal, *e.g.* on appeal to the Court of Appeal from a decision of the Divisional Court, the second appellate court will have before it the order and reasons for decision that were before the first appellate court.

Rules 61.11 and 61.12(3): Time Estimates for Argument to be Included in Factums

These amendments require counsel to provide an estimate of the length of time for his or her oral argument on an appeal: see rules 61.11(1)(e) and 61.12(3)(e). The Court of Appeal requested that counsel be required to provide an estimate of the duration of their argument and include the estimate as part of the factum to help the court in scheduling appeals and keeping to the schedule to the benefit of all concerned.

Rule 61.13(2.1) and 61.13(3)(b): Dismissal for Delay of Appeals from Summary Judgments

The Court of Appeal requested this amendment because the general provisions of rule 61.13 relating to a dismissal of an appeal for delay were not tailored to deal with appeals from a summary judgment. After a summary judgment has been granted, there is little reason for delay in perfecting the appeal (there is no need to order transcripts because they will already be part of the record for the hearing of the motion for summary judgment) and there is rarely a need for counsel to come to an agreement about the material for the Appeal Book. Hence it was appropriate to introduce a special rule to encourage the more expeditious perfection of these appeals and the new rule 61.13(2.1) does this. This amendment requires a minor consequential amendment to rule 61.13(3)(b).

Rule 61.13(6) and (7): Dismissal of Motion for Leave to Appeal for Delay

Rule 61.13(6) enables the responding party to move to have an appeal dismissed for delay as soon as the moving party fails to file its material in a timely manner. However, prior to this amendment, rule 61.13(7) provided the Registrar could not commence steps to have the motion dismissed for delay until 6 months had passed. Now, as a result of the amendment to rule 61.13(7), the Registrar may dismiss a motion for leave for delay if the moving party has not filed its motion record, etc., within 60 days after filing of the notice for motion for leave to appeal. Minor amendments have also been made to rule 61.13(6) because of the differentiation now made between leave motions to the Divisional Court (see rule 61.03) and leave motions to the Court of Appeal (rule 61.03.1).

Rule 63.02(2): Stay Pending Appeal by Order — Expiry of Trial Court Stay

This amendment simply removes practical problems that existed under this rule as formerly drafted. In circumstances where an automatic stay pending appeal is unavailable, rule 63.02 provides that a stay may be obtained by order and the order may either be obtained from the trial court or the appeal court. Where a stay was granted by the trial court, rule 63.02(2) formerly provided that such a stay expired, *inter alia*, when a notice of motion for leave to appeal was delivered. This provision was obviously extremely inconvenient because, in order to maintain the stay in place, the appellant would have to move in the appellate court either immediately before delivering the notice of motion for leave to appeal, or immediately after delivering it. The rule has now simply been redrafted so that delivering a notice of motion for leave to appeal no longer terminates a stay granted by the trial court.

Rules 64.03 and 64.04: Filing of Request for Sale or Request to Redeem

These amendments involve changes to four subrules i.e., 64.03(6), 64.03(17), 64.03(18)(b) and 64.04(5). Prior to these amendments each of these provisions provided only for the *filing* of either a request for sale or a request to redeem. By contrast, rule 64.03(19) requires a subsequent encumbrancer added on a reference in a foreclosure action who wishes a sale to *serve on the plaintiff and file with proof of service a request for sale*. Under the amended provisions, before their amendment, the plaintiff would only find out about the request by searching court files. The Civil Rules Committee felt that to bring about consistency and to facilitate the plaintiff's carriage of the action it would be preferable to amend these provisions to provide that the plaintiff be served with a copy of the request to redeem or the request for sale in all cases.

Rule 74.18: Service on Application to Pass Accounts in Non-Contentious Estate Proceedings

This new subrule gives the Public Guardian and Trustee or the Children's Lawyer, when representing a person with an interest in an estate, the right to service of the same documents as the estate beneficiaries.

Rule 76: Simplified Procedure

This is an entirely new procedure applicable to cases where the plaintiff's claim is for $25,000 or less. For an extensive analysis of the Rule see the Highlights at the beginning of Rule 76 in the main body of the work.

PROCEDURAL CHARTS

TABLE OF CONTENTS

Additional charts are located under the relevant Rule. These are as follows:

Non-Resident Examination Chart (Rule 34)
Cost Consequences of Offer to Settle Pictogram (Rule 49)
Stay Pending Appeal Status Chart (Rule 63)
Summaries of Procedure for Case Management are located in the Companion Volume.

SUMMARIES OF PROCEDURE

The following procedural summaries outline the various steps to be taken in respect of different proceedings or aspects of proceedings. (They were formerly located under the relevant rules and are now located here in one place for the convenience of the reader.)

A. SUMMARY OF PROCEDURE IN AN ACTION

(Major steps only are included, not necessarily in chronological order, and only up to trial. Case management effects are not shown.) See p. cxlvi, below, for cases subject to Rule 76 (Simplified Procedure).

Who Does It	What To Do	When
Plaintiff and registrar	**Issue statement of claim** (Form 14A or 14B); rules 14.01, 14.03.	Within limitation period.
	Alternatively, if there is not sufficient time to prepare a statement of claim, issue a notice of action (Form 14C) in which case a statement of claim (Form 14D) must be filed: rule 14.03.	Within 30 days after the notice of action is issued.
Plaintiff	**Serve statement of claim:** rule 14.08. If action commenced by a notice of action, the notice of action and statement of claim must be served together.	Within 6 months after the statement of claim or notice of action is issued.
Defendant	**Deliver statement of defence** (Form 18A): rule 18.01. Alternatively, the defendant may deliver a notice of intent to defend (Form 18B) within the time prescribed for delivery of a statement of defence and gain an additional 10 days in which to deliver a statement of defence: rule 18.02.	Within 20, 40, or 60 days of being served, depending on where defendant was served: see rule 18.01. However a defendant may deliver a statement of defence at any time until noted in default: rules 18.01, 19.01(5).
Defendant	**Counterclaim by defendant** (Form 27A or 27B) is to be included in the same document as statement of defence: rule 27.02.	See time for delivery of statement of defence, above, and rules 27.04(1) and 18.01.

Who Does It	What To Do	When
	If a person not already a party to the main action is made a defendant to the counterclaim, the statement of defence and counterclaim must be issued before it is served. (As to subsequent pleadings in the counterclaim, see rules 27.05-27.07).	To be issued within the time prescribed for delivery of statement of defence or subsequently with leave (rule 27.03) and served within 30 days after it is issued, or any time before defendant is noted in default or subsequently with leave: rule 27.04(2).
Defendant	**Crossclaim by defendant against a co-defendant** (Form 28A) is to be included in the same document as the statement of defence: rule 28.02. (As to subsequent pleadings in the crossclaim, see rules 28.05-28.08).	Statement of defence and crossclaim is to be delivered within the time for delivery of the statement of defence, see above, or subsequently with leave: rules 28.04 and 18.01.
Defendant	**Third party claim by defendant** requires the issuing of a third party claim (Form 29A): rules 29.01 and 29.02. (As to subsequent pleadings in a third party claim, see rules 29.03-29.07.)	To be issued within 10 days of the time prescribed by rule 18.01 for delivery of statement of defence or at any time before defendant is noted in default or subsequently with leave: rule 29.02(1). To be served within 30 days after being issued: rule 29.02(2).
Plaintiff	**Note the defendant in default** if defendant fails to deliver a statement of defence in time: rule 19.01(1). Plaintiff may then sign judgment (rule 19.04), or move for judgment (rule 19.05), whichever is appropriate.	See times for delivery of statement of defence, above, and rule 18.01.
Plaintiff or defendant	**Deliver a jury notice** (Form 47A) where a jury trial is desired and s. 108 of the *Courts of Justice Act* or another statute does not prohibit jury trial: rule 47.01.	At any time before the close of pleadings (as to which see rule 25.05).

Who Does It	What To Do	When
Plaintiff or defendant	**Motion for summary judgment** may be made where it appears there is no genuine issue for trial with respect to the claim or defence, or the only genuine issue is as to the amount due, a question of law or the only claim is for an accounting: rule 20.04. Note that if the moving party obtains no relief he or she will be ordered to pay solicitor and client costs forthwith, unless the making of the motion was reasonable: rule 20.06(1). See Summary of the Procedure on a Motion.	Plaintiff may move after defendant has delivered a statement of defence or served a notice of motion: rule 20.01(1). With leave, plaintiff may serve the motion with the statement of claim: rule 20.01(2). A defendant may move after delivery of statement of defence: rule 20.01(3).
Plaintiff and defendant	**Serve affidavit of documents** (Form 30A or 30B) on every other party to the action: rule 30.03(1).	Within 10 days after close of pleadings: rules 30.03(1), 25.05.
Plaintiff and defendant	**Serve notice of examination for discovery of parties adverse in interest** (Form 34A), rule 34.04, and give notice of the examination to every other party: rule 34.05. Unless agreed otherwise, no party may serve a notice until he or she has served an affidavit of documents.	A person seeking to examine a plaintiff must have delivered a statement of defence. A defendant may be examined only after delivery of a statement of defence or he or she has been noted in default: rule 31.04. The person to be examined and every other party is to be given not less than 2 days notice of the examination: rule 34.05.
	Alternatively a party may serve written questions (Form 35A) on the person to be examined and on every other party: rules 35.01, 31.02.	Same time frame, for initiating the examination as for oral examination for discovery, see above and rule 31.04.
Plaintiff or defendant	**Medical examination.** If relevant, obtain order for, or consent to, medical examination: see *Courts of Justice Act,* s. 105 and Rule 33.	At any time before the party seeking examination sets the action down or consents to the action being placed on a trial list: see rule 48.04.

Who Does It	What To Do	When
Plaintiff and defendant	**Disclose information obtained subsequent to examination for discovery** when necessary to correct or complete answers given on an examination for discovery: see generally rule 31.09, and also rule 30.07 re documents.	Forthwith after discovering answers were or are incorrect or incomplete: rules 31.09(1), 48.04(2)(b).
Plaintiff or defendant	**Motion for leave to examine a non-party for discovery** where appropriate or necessary: see rule 31.10.	Should be brought after examination for discovery of parties and after attempts have been made to obtain the information from the person sought to be examined: see the requirements of rule 31.10(2)(a).
Plaintiff or defendant	**Set the action down for trial** by serving and filing with proof of service a trial record: rule 48.02(1) and (2).	After the close of pleadings by any party who is not in default and who is ready for trial. As to the consequences of setting down or consenting to the action being placed in the trial list, see rule 48.04.
Registrar	**Place on trial list:** rule 48.06. As to the consequences of an action being placed on the trial list, see rule 48.07.	60 days after the action was set down or immediately after the filing of the consent of all parties other than the one who set the action down unless outside Toronto the notice is received less than 10 days before the commencement of the next sitting: rule 48.06.
Party filing trial record	**Requisition court file,** including trial record, to be sent to court at place of trial, if trial is to take place other than where the action was commenced: rule 48.02(5).	No time limit (but it would seem reasonable to do this at the time of filing the notice of listing for trial).

Who Does It	What To Do	When
Registrar	**Serve status notice.** Form 48C is to be served on all solicitors of record in any action in which a statement of defence has been filed and the action has not been placed on a trial list or terminated by other means within 2 years from the filing of the statement of defence: rule 48.14. As to the response required by the parties, dismissal by the registrar and the power of court on the status hearing, see rule 48.14.	Two years after filing of statement of defence.
Plaintiff or defendant	**Give notice abandoning claim of privilege** in respect of any document to be used at trial for other than impeachment purposes: if not done in a timely manner the document may not be used except with leave: rules 30.09, 53.08. See also the similar obligation imposed by rule 31.07 re information refused on examination for discovery.	Not later than 10 days after the action is set down for trial.
Plaintiff or defendant	**Serve an offer to settle** (Form 49A), rule 49.02, with a view to either settling the action or obtaining the more favourable cost consequences provided in rule 49.10.	At any time, but the offer must be made at least 7 days before the trial commences to obtain the cost consequences: rule 49.03.
Every party	**Inform court of settlement** by advising registrar and confirming in writing: rule 48.12.	When the action is settled.
Judge or parties	**Pre-trial conference.** A judge may on his own initiative or at the request of a party direct the solicitors and parties to appear for a pre-trial conference: rule 50.01.	When the action has been placed on a trial list: rule 51.01.

Who Does It	What To Do	When
Plaintiff or defendant	**Serve a request to admit** (Form 51A) the truth of a fact or the authenticity of any document on any other party: rule 51.02.	At any time: rules 51.02(1), 48.04(2)(c).
Party served with request to admit	**Serve a response to the request to admit** (Form 51B) since failure to make a specific response leads to a deemed admission of the facts or the authenticity of the document referred to in the request: rule 51.03.	To be served within 20 days after request is served: rule 51.03.
Plaintiff and defendant	**Serve expert's report** on other parties for each expert to be called as a witness: rule 53.03(1). Unless this is done an expert may not testify, except with leave: rules 53.03(1), 53.08.	Not less than 10 days before the commencement of the trial: rule 53.03(1).
Plaintiff and defendant	**Serve summons to witnesses** (Form 53A) to secure their attendance at trial: rule 53.04. As to calling an adverse party, who may be cross-examined by the party calling him or her, see rule 53.07.	No time limit.

B. SUMMARY OF PROCEDURE ON AN APPLICATION

(Excluding applications for judicial review to the Divisional Court, as to which see below, applications on the Commercial List, as to which see the Commercial List Practice Direction, and applications made without notice.)

Who Does It	What To Do	When
Applicant	**Obtain hearing date.** Subject to any practice direction, the hearing may be on any day a judge is scheduled to hear applications: rule 38.03(2). If the hearing will be more than two hours long, a hearing date is to be obtained from the registrar: rule 38.03(3). (If urgent, see rule 38.03(3.1).)	Before notice of application is served.

Who Does It	What To Do	When
Applicant	**Issue notice of application** (Form 14E): rules 14.01, 38.05. This does not apply to applications for a certificate of appointment of an estate trustee under Rule 74: rule 14.01(2.1).	Before it is served: rule 38.05.
Applicant	**Serve notice of application** together with the **affidavits** on which the application is founded: rules 38.06 and 39.01(2).	At least 10 days before the date of hearing: if served outside Ontario, it is to be served at least 20 days before the hearing: rule 38.06(3).
Respondent	**Deliver a notice of appearance** (Form 38A): rule 38.07.	Forthwith after being served with the notice of application. Until it is delivered a respondent may not file material, examine a witness or cross-examine on an affidavit etc. (see rule 38.03(3)) except re a motion to set aside service outside Ontario.
Applicant or respondent	**Affidavits in opposition or reply** are to be served and filed with proof of service in the court office at the place of hearing: rule 39.01(3). Instead of being filed separately, these affidavits may be included in the party's application record: see rule 38.09(5). See below re serving affidavits before cross-examining.	Not later than 2:00 p.m. on the day before the hearing.
Applicant or respondent	**Examination of witness before the hearing.** Any party may do so for the purpose of having a transcript available for use at the hearing: rule 39.03. The examining party must proceed with reasonable diligence.	Not later than 2 days notice of the time and place of examination must be given to the person to be examined and to all parties: rule 34.05.

Who Does It	What To Do	When
Applicant or respondent	**Cross-examination on affidavits.** A party who wishes to cross-examine on affidavits served by an opponent must proceed with reasonable diligence and must first serve every affidavit on which he or she intends to rely and conduct all examinations under rule 39.03: rule 39.02.	Not less than 2 days notice of the time and place of examination must be given to the person to be examined and to all parties: rule 34.05.
Applicant or respondent	**Transcripts.** Any party who intends to refer to a transcript on the hearing is to file a copy of the transcript in the court office at the place of hearing: rule 34.18(2).	Not later than 2:00 p.m. on the day before the hearing.
Applicant	**Application record and factum** are to be served and filed with proof of service in the court office at the place of hearing: rule 38.09(1).	To be served at least 3 days before the hearing and filed not later than 2:00 p.m. on the day before the hearing: rule 38.09(1).
Respondent	**Respondent's application record (if any) and factum** are to be served and filed with proof of service in the court office at the place of hearing: rule 38.09(3).	Not later than 2:00 p.m. on the day before the hearing.

C. SUMMARY OF PROCEDURE ON AN APPLICATION FOR JUDICIAL REVIEW IN THE DIVISIONAL COURT

(For the procedure on an application for judicial review to a judge of the General Division under s. 6(2) of the *Judicial Review Procedure Act*, see the Summary of the Procedure on an Application.)

Who Does It	What To Do	When
Applicant	**Issue notice of application for judicial review** (Form 68A): rule 68.01. The notice must state that the application is to be heard on a date to be fixed by the registrar at the place of hearing (rule 68.03) and must include the address of the court office in the place where the application is to be heard: rule 4.02(2)(d).	Before it is served.

Who Does It	What To Do	When
Local registrar	**Transferring papers to Divisional Court office.** Where the application is commenced other than at a regional centre, a copy of the notice of application and any material filed in support of the application are to be transferred to the court office at the regional centre where the application is to be heard, and all further documents are to be filed there: rules 68.01(2), 4.05(3).	Forthwith after commencement of the application: rule 68.01(2).
Applicant	**Serve notice of application** together with the **affidavits** on which the application is founded: rules 38.06 and 39.01(2).	At least 10 days before the date of hearing; if served outside Ontario, it is to be served at least 20 days before the hearing: rule 38.06(3).
Respondent	**Deliver a notice of appearance** (Form 38A): rule 38.07.	Forthwith after being served with the notice of application. Until it is delivered a respondent may not file material, examine a witness or cross-examine etc. (see rule 38.03(3)) except re a motion to set aside service outside Ontario.
Applicant or respondent	**Affidavits in opposition or reply** are to be served (see rules 39.01(3), 39.02(1)) and filed as part of the applicant's application record: rule 68.04(2)(c). See below re serving affidavits before cross-examining.	To be filed as part of the applicant's application record, see below.
Applicant or respondent	**Examination of witness before the hearing.** Any party may do so for the purpose of having a transcript available for use at the hearing: rule 39.03.	Not less than 2 days notice of the time and place of examination must be given to the person to be examined and to all parties: rule 34.05.

Who Does It	What To Do	When
Applicant or respondent	**Cross-examination on affidavits.** A party who wishes to cross-examine on affidavits served by an opponent must proceed with reasonable diligence and must first serve every affidavit on which he or she intends to rely (rule 39.02) and complete any examination under rule 39.03.	Not less than 2 days notice of the time and place of examination must be given to the person to be examined and to all parties: rule 34.05.
Applicant	**Applicant's application record and factum** is to be served and filed with proof of service: rule 68.04(1). Three copies are to be filed (rule 68.04(7)), together with three copies of any transcript intended to be referred to: rule 68.04(9).	Where a record of the tribunal's proceedings is required, within 30 days after the record is filed with the registrar. Where no record is required, within 30 days after the application is commenced.
Applicant	**Certificate of perfection** is to be filed with the applicant's application record: rule 68.05(1).	With the applicant's application record.
Registrar	**Notice of listing for hearing** (Form 68B) is to be mailed after the application has been placed on a list for hearing: rule 68.05(2).	When the certificate of perfection has been filed: rule 68.05(2).
Respondent	**Respondent's application record and factum** are to be served and filed with proof of service: rule 68.04(4). Three copies are to be filed (rule 68.04(7)), together with three copies of any transcript intended to be referred to: rule 68.04(9).	Within 30 days after service of the applicant's application record and factum.

D. SUMMARY OF PROCEDURE ON A MOTION

(Not including motions in matters on the Commercial List, as to which see the Commercial List Practice Direction, motions in an appellate court, motions without oral argument, as to which see rule 37.12.1, or motions made without notice.)

Who Does It	What To Do	When
Moving party	**Place of hearing.** Determine by reference to rule 37.03 where the motion is to be brought. Determine by reference to rule 37.04 to whom it is to be made.	Before preparing the notice of motion.
Moving party	**Hearing date.** Subject to any practice direction, the hearing may be on any day a judge or master is scheduled to hear motions: rule 37.05)(1). If the hearing will be more than two hours long, obtain a hearing date from the registrar: rule 37.05(2). (If urgent, see rule 37.05(3).)	Before the notice of motion is served.
Moving party	**Serve notice of motion** together with the **affidavits** on which the motion is founded: rules 37.07 and 39.01(2).	At least 3 days before the hearing date: rule 37.07(6).
Moving party	**File notice of motion** with proof of service in the court office at the place of hearing: rule 37.08. Instead of being filed separately, the notice of motion may be filed as part of the motion record: see rule 37.10(4).	At least 2 days before the hearing date.
Moving or responding party	**Affidavits in opposition or reply** are to be served and filed with proof of service in the court office at the place of hearing: rule 39.01(3). Instead of being filed separately, these affidavits may be included in the party's motion record: see rule 37.10(4). See below re serving affidavits before cross-examining.	Not later than 2:00 p.m. on the day before the hearing.

Who Does It	What To Do	When
Moving or responding party	**Examination of witness before the hearing.** Any party may do so for the purpose of having a transcript available for use at the hearing: rule 39.03. The examining party must proceed with reasonable diligence.	Not less than 2 days notice at the time and place of examination must be given to the person to be examined and to all parties: rule 34.05.
Moving or responding party	**Cross-examination on affidavits.** A party who wishes to cross-examine on an affidavit served by an opponent must proceed with reasonable diligence and must first serve every affidavit on which he or she intends to rely and conduct all examinations under rule 39.03: rule 39.02.	Not less than 2 days notice at the time and place of examination must be given to the person to be examined and to all parties: rule 34.05.
Moving or responding party	**Transcripts.** Any party who intends to refer to a transcript on the hearing is to file a copy of the transcript in the court office at the place of hearing: rule 34.18(2).	Not later than 2:00 p.m. on the day before the hearing.
Moving or responding party	**Requisition court file.** Usually the court file is not to be placed before the officer hearing the motion unless he or she requests it or a party requisitions it: rule 37.10(1), (2). A party may, if desired, requisition the transmission of documents to the place of hearing: rule 4.10.	In time to have the documents physically delivered to the place of hearing not later than 2:00 p.m. on the day before the hearing.
Moving party	**Motion record.** To be served and filed with proof of service in the court office at the place of hearing.	At least 2 days before the hearing: rule 37.10(1), as amended.
Responding party	**Responding party's motion record.** Where a motion record has been served, a responding party's motion record may be served and filed with proof of service in the court office at the place of hearing: rule 37.10(3).	Not later than 2:00 p.m. on the day before the hearing.

Who Does It	What To Do	When
Moving or responding party	**Factum.** On any motion a party may serve a factum and file it with proof of service in the court office at the place of hearing: rule 37.10(6). On the following motions factums are required: summary judgment (rule 20.03); determination of an issue before trial (rule 21.03); special case (rule 22.02); discharge of certificate of pending litigation (rule 42.02); motion for leave to appeal (rule 62.02).	Not later than 2:00 p.m. on the day before the hearing.

E. SUMMARY OF PROCEDURE IN A DIVORCE ACTION

(Major steps only are included and not necessarily in chronological order.)

Who Does It	What To Do	When
Petitioner	**File marriage certificate** (rule 69.03)**, and a financial statement** (Form 69K) if the petition contains a claim for support or division of property (rule 69.14(1)) or a waiver of financial statements, as to which see rule 69.14(3).	Before a petition is issued: rules 69.03(2), 69.14.
Petitioner and registrar	**Issue divorce petition** (Form 69A or 69B): rules 14.01, 14.04, 69.03.	After filing the above.
Petitioner	**Serve divorce petition:** rule 69.04.	Within 6 months after it is issued: rule 69.05.
Respondent	**Deliver an answer** (Form 69D): rule 69.07(1). Alternatively, the respondent may deliver a notice of intent to defend (Form 69J) within the time prescribed for delivering an answer and gain an additional 10 days to deliver an answer: rule 69.07(2) and (3).	Within 20, 40, 60 days depending on where the defendant was served: rule 69.07(1). However, a respondent may deliver an answer at any time until noted in default: rules 69.07(1), 19.01(5).
Respondent	**Counterpetition by respondent** (Form 69F or 69G) is to be included in the same document as the answer: rule 69.09.	See time for delivery of answer, above, and rules 69.10, 69.07.

Who Does It	What To Do	When
	If a person not already a party to the main action is made a respondent to the counterpetition, the answer and counterpetition must be issued before it is served. (As to subsequent pleadings in the counterpetition, see rules 69.12-69.13.)	To be issued within the time provided for delivery of answer or any time before the respondent is noted in default or subsequently with leave: rule 69.09(6).
Petitioner	**Note respondent in default,** if respondent fails to deliver an answer in time: rules 19.01(1), 69.01, 69.19(1). A petitioner may then make a motion for judgment: rules 19.05(1), 69.19.	See times for delivery of answer, above, and rule 69.07.
Petitioner or counterpetitioner	**Motion for interim relief** may be brought under rule 69.15. See Summary of Procedure on a Motion.	
Children's Lawyer	**Serve any Children's Lawyer's report** and any supporting affidavit, and file with proof of service: rule 69.16(5).	Within 60 days after service of notice of intention to investigate and report: rule 69.16(5).
	See the Summary of Procedure in an Action, re affidavit of documents, request to inspect documents, notice of examination for discovery, medical examination, disclosing information obtained subsequently to discovery, examination of a non-party for discovery, notice of status hearing, giving notice abandoning a claim for privilege, serving an offer to settle, and the pre-trial conference.	
Petitioner or respondent	**Setting down for trial.** For defended actions see Summary of Procedure in an Action (Re undefended actions, see rule 69.19.)	
Petitioner and respondent	**Serve request to admit.**	(See Summary of Procedure in an Action.)
	Serve response to request to admit.	
	Serve expert's report.	
	Serve summons to witness.	

Who Does It	What To Do	When
Petitioner and respondent	**File support deduction order information form (Form 70A.1):** rules 69.27, 70.10.1.	With the material for the hearing of a motion for judgment, interim support and trial.
Registrar	**Certificate respecting prior pending petitions** is to be attached to the trial or motion record: rule 69.18. **Trial or motion for judgment.**	Before action can be tried.
Registrar	**Certificate of divorce** may be issued on the requisition of either party rule 69.22.	After the divorce has taken effect.
Petitioner or respondent	**Variation of final order for corollary relief** may be obtained by application: rule 69.24. (See Summary of Procedure on an Application.)	After final order is made.

F. SUMMARY OF PROCEDURE FOR SETTLING, SIGNING AND ENTERING ORDERS

Who Does It	What To Do
Judge or officer making order	**Endorsement.** The court, judge or officer making the order is to endorse the order on the appeal book, record, notice of motion or notice of application unless the circumstances make it impractical to do so, except in an appellate court where written reasons are delivered. In any other court where written reasons are delivered, the endorsement may consist of a reference to the reasons: rule 59.02.
Any party affected by the order	**Preparation of draft formal order** (Form 59A, 59B or 59C) which is then to be sent to all other parties represented at the hearing for approval as to form: rule 59.03.
Party who prepared draft order	**Submission of order for signing.** Unless the court, judge or officer who made the order has signed it, it is to be submitted to the appropriate registrar (as to which see rule 59.04(1)) for his or her signature. Where the form of draft order has been approved by all parties represented at the hearing, the party who prepared the draft order is to file the approvals and a copy of the order, and leave the order with the registrar for signing: rule 59.04(5). (Where an approval as to the form of the draft order is not received within reasonable time, see below, "appointment to settle unapproved order before registrar".)

Who Does It	**What To Do**
	Where approval as to form is not required the draft order may be left with the registrar: rule 59.04(6).
Registrar	**Signing order.** Where the registrar is satisfied that the order is in proper form he or she shall sign the order and return it to the party who left it to be signed: rule 59.04(8).
	Where the registrar is not satisfied that the order is in proper form, he or she shall return it to the party who left it to be signed: rule 59.04(9).
Party who left order to be signed	**Resubmission of order for signing.** Where the registrar has returned the order unsigned as not in proper form, the party who left it to be signed may submit the order in proper form and, if required by the registrar, file the approval of the parties to the order in that form, together with a copy of the order: rule 59.04(9)(a). Alternatively, the party who left the order to be signed may obtain an appointment to have the order settled by the court, judge or officer who made it and serve notice of appointment on all other parties who were represented at the hearing: rule 59.04(9)(b).
Any party	**Appointment to settle unapproved order before registrar.** If approval of the form of draft order is not received within a reasonable time, a party may obtain an appointment to have the order settled by the registrar or, where the registrar considers it necessary, by the court, judge or officer that made it, and notice of the appointment shall be served on all other parties represented at the hearing: rule 59.04(10). In a case of urgency, the order may be settled and signed by the court, judge or officer that made it without the approval of any of the parties who were represented at the hearing: rule 59.04(11).
Objecting party	**Appointment to settle disputed order before judge or officer.** If an objection is taken to the proper form of order in the course of its settlement by the registrar, the objecting party may obtain an appointment with the court, judge or officer who made the order to settle that part of the order objected to, and notice of the appointment shall be served on all parties represented at the hearing: see rule 59.04(12)-(16).
Party who had order signed and registrar	**Entry of the order.** Immediately after the order is signed the party having the order signed shall give to the registrar the original and a sufficient number of copies for the purposes of entering and filing it: rule 59.05(1). The registrar shall then enter the order, and place a copy in the court file, as provided in rule 59.05(2)-(6).
Party who obtained relief under the order	**Satisfaction of order.** A party may acknowledge satisfaction of an order and the document, signed by a witness, may be filed and entered in the court office where the order was entered: rule 59.07.

G. SUMMARY OF PROCEDURE ON AN APPEAL TO AN APPELLATE COURT

(Appeals to the Court of Appeal for Ontario or to the Divisional Court — Rule 61)

Who Does It	What To Do	When
Appellant	**Stay pending appeal.** The general rule is that there is an automatic stay of any order for the payment of money, except a support order, upon delivery of the notice of appeal: rule 63.01. There is no automatic stay for orders granting non-monetary relief. Moreover, where leave to appeal is required there will be no immediate automatic stay because a notice of appeal cannot be delivered until leave to appeal is granted. Therefore, if desired, and no automatic stay is available, move for a stay under rule 63.02.	Can be as early as the time of the making of the order to be appealed: see rule 63.02.
Appellant	**Seek leave to appeal, if required** (a) by motion to a judge: rule 62.02.	Serve notice of motion within 7 days after date of the order sought to be appealed: rule 62.02, and see also rules 37.07(6) and 37.08(1).
	(b) by motion to the appellate court: rule 61.03. Motions for leave to appeal to the Court of Appeal shall be made in writing: rule 61.03.1.	Serve notice of motion within 15 days after date of order or decision sought to be appealed, unless a statute provides otherwise, and file with proof of service within 5 days after service.
Appellant	**Serve notice of appeal** (Form 61A) and **appellant's certificate of evidence** (Form 61C): rule 61.04.	Within 30 days after date of order appealed from unless a statute or the Rules provide otherwise (rule 61.04(1)) or within 7 days of the granting of leave to appeal where leave required: rules 61.03(6) and 62.02(8). In a divorce action a notice of appeal must be filed within 30 days of the date of judgment: *Divorce Act* (Canada), s. 21.
Appellant	**File notice of appeal** with proof of service: rule 61.04(4).	Within 10 days after it is served: rule 61.04(4).

Who Does It	What To Do	When
Respondent	**Serve respondent's certificate of evidence** (Form 61D): rule 61.05(2).	Within 15 days after service of appellant's certificate.
	or	
	Make an agreement as to documents and evidence: rule 61.05(4).	Within 30 days after service of notice of appeal.
Respondent	**Serve notice of cross-appeal** (Form 61E), if cross-appealing, and then file notice of cross-appeal with proof of service: rule 61.07.	Serve within 15 days after service of notice of appeal and file within 10 days after service.
Respondent	**Move for security for costs of appeal** if appropriate: rule 61.06.	On at least 3 days notice to the appellant: rules 61.16(1) and 37.07(6).
Appellant	**File proof of ordering transcript of evidence:** rule 61.05(5).	Within 30 days after filing notice of appeal.
Court reporter	**Give written notice to parties and registrar when evidence transcribed:** rule 61.05(7).	Forthwith.
Appellant	**Perfect the appeal** by (a) causing the record and original exhibits to be forwarded to the registrar, (b) serving and filing with proof of service the appeal book, the transcript of evidence and the appellant's factum, (c) filing with the registrar a certificate of perfection: rule 61.09.	If no transcript is required, within 30 days of filing notice of appeal; if a transcript is required, within 30 days after receiving notice that the evidence has been transcribed: rule 61.09(1).
Registrar	**Notice of listing for hearing** (Form 61G) is to be mailed after the appeal has been placed on the list of cases to be heard: rule 61.09(5).	When appeal perfected.
Respondent	**Move to dismiss for delay** if the appellant does not file proof that the necessary transcripts have been ordered or fails to perfect the appeal: rule 61.13(1).	On 10 days notice to the appellant.

Who Does It	What To Do	When
Respondent	**Respondent's factum** is to be served and filed with proof of service and is to include a factum as appellant by cross-appeal if there is a cross-appeal : rule 61.12.	Within 30 days after service of the appeal book, transcript of evidence and appellant's factum.
Appellant	**Deliver factum as respondent to the cross-appeal,** if there is a cross-appeal: rule 61.12(4)(b).	Within 10 days after service of the respondent's factum: rule 61.12(4)(b).

H. SUMMARY OF PROCEDURE ON AN APPEAL FROM AN INTERLOCUTORY ORDER

(The following is the procedure on an appeal to a judge of the General Division provided in rule 62.01. As to what appeals are covered by that rule, see rule 62.01(1).)

Who Does It	What To Do	When
Appellant	**Serve notice of appeal** (Form 62A): rule 62.01(2).	Within 7 days after the date of the order or certificate appealed from: rule 62.01(2).
Appellant	**File notice of appeal** in court office at the place where the appeal is to be heard: rule 62.01(5). Re place of hearing, see rule 62.01(6).	Not later than 3 days before the hearing date: rule 62.01(5).
Appellant	**Serve appeal record and factum** and file it, with proof of service, in the court office at the place where the appeal is to be heard: rule 62.01(7).	Not later than 3 days before the hearing date: rule 62.01(7).
Respondent	**Serve any further material and factum** and file, with proof of service, in the court office at the place where the appeal is to be heard: rule 62.01(8).	Not later than 2:00 p.m. on the day before the hearing: rule 62.01(8).

I. SUMMARY OF PROCEDURE FOR AN ACTION UNDER RULE 76 (SIMPLIFIED PROCEDURE)

This summary of procedure charge shows the major changes between the steps in an ordinary action and the steps in the simplified procedure for an action under Rule 76. Generally, this simplified procedure is mandatory for claims involving $25,000 or less and optional for other claims: rule 76.02(1), (2), and (8). This summary does not detail the steps which are the same as those in an ordinary action and which are not affected by Rule 76. In that regard see the Summary of Procedure in an Action at p. cxxvii. This summary does not deal with changing to or from the simplified procedure (as to which see rule 76.03) or undefended actions.

Who Does It	What To Do	When
Plaintiff	**Issue statement of claim** indicating simplified procedure is being used: rule 76.02(3).	Before expiry of limitation period.
Defendant	**Object to use of simplified procedure** if appropriate: rule 76.02(4).	When statement of defence is delivered.
Plaintiff	**Abandon excess claim** or revert to ordinary procedure, whichever is appropriate: rule 76.02(5) and (7).	When reply is delivered.
All parties	**Disclose witness list** (rule 76.04(1)) and certify witness disclosure obligation has been explained to deponent (rule 76.04(3)). An undisclosed witness may not testify at trial without leave: rule 76.04(2).	When affidavit of documents is delivered.
All parties	**Forego examinations** for discovery, cross-examinations on affidavits, and examinations under rule 39.03: rule 76.05.	Always.
All solicitors	**Conduct settlement conference** by meeting or by telephone call: rule 76.07(1).	Within 60 days after close of pleadings.
Any party	**May move for summary judgment:** rule 76.06. Procedure is abbreviated.	After close of pleadings.
Any party	**May move for summary trial:** rule 76.06. See *Summary of Procedure for a Summary Trial* below.	After close of pleadings.

Who Does It	What To Do	When
Any party	**Set down for trial** by delivering a notice of readiness for pre-trial conference (Form 76A) with a solicitor's certificate there has been a settlement conference; rule 76.08(1) and (2).	After settlement conference.
Registrar	**Place on trial list:** rule 76.09.	When notice of readiness for pre-trial conference is filed.
All parties	**File pre-trial materials:** rule 76.07(2). No pre-trial memorandum is required but copies of the affidavits of documents, medical reports and any other necessary materials must be filed: rule 76.07(2).	At least 5 days before pre-trial.
Pre-trial judge	**Fix trial date:** rule 76.07(3).	At pre-trial conference.
Party who set action down for trial	**Deliver trial record:** rule 76.08(3).	At least 10 days before trial.

J. SUMMARY OF PROCEDURE FOR A SUMMARY TRIAL

This summary of procedure chart shows the major steps in a motion for summary trial under Rule 76. The procedural options are complicated and the reader should review the text of the rule carefully to apply it to a particular case.

Who Does It	What To Do	When
Moving party	**Serve notice of motion** and affidavits for summary trial: rule 76.06(1).	After close of pleadings.
Moving party	**File notice of motion** but *not* affidavits: rule 76.06(3).	Immediately.
Registrar	**Fix trial date:** rule 76.06(2).	For at least 50 days after notice of motion served.
Responding party	**Convert motion** for summary trial to motion for summary judgment if appropriate by delivering notice: rule 76.06(4).	Within 30 days after moving party's material served.

Who Does It	What To Do	When
Responding party	*Serve* **affidavits** for summary trial but do not **file**: rule 76.06(8). Must set out specific facts: rule 76.06(10). Adverse inference possible if affidavits are on information and belief: rule 76.06(11).	Within 30 days after moving party's material served.
Moving party	**Abandon motion for summary judgment** if appropriate by delivering notice of abandonment: rule 76.06(5). the costs may not exceed $200: rule 76.06(6).	After responding party converts motion and serves its affidavits.
All parties	**Forego cross-examinations** on affidavits: rule 76.05.	Until trial.
Moving party	**Deliver motion record**: rule 76.06(12). Contents are specified by rule 76.06(13).	At least 5 days before trial date.
All parties	**Give notice of intention to cross-examine** on affidavit: rule 76.06(17). Party who filed afidavit must arrange for deponent to attend trial: rule 76.06(17).	At least 10 days before trial date.
Judge and parties	**Conduct summary trial:** rule 76.06(16). Affidavits replace examinations-in-chief, a party's aggregate cross-examinations are limited to 50 minutes, re-examination of a witness is limited to 10 minutes, and oral argument is limited to 45 minutes per party.	On trial date.

APPEAL ROUTE CHARTS

USE OF APPEAL ROUTE CHARTS

The applicability of the charts set out below depends on whether the order under appeal is "final" or "interlocutory". The basic test in that regard is whether the order finally disposes of a party's rights — see the cases collected under rule 62.01. Where there are sequential appeals, different charts may apply at different stages. For example, if a master dismisses a motion for summary judgment for $30,000 then the order is "interlocutory" and the Interlocutory Order chart applies and indicates the appeal is to a judge. If the appeal is allowed and judgment granted for $30,000 then that order is "final" and the Final Order chart applies and indicates a further appeal is available to the Court of Appeal.

Where there are several appeals in the same proceeding pending simultaneously to different courts, they may be combined and heard by the highest court involved: *Courts of Justice Act*, ss. 6(2), 19(2).

The following appeals are provided for in the *Courts of Justice Act*, but are not depicted in the charts: an appeal lies to the Court of Appeal from an order of a judge granting an injunction in a labour dispute (s. 102(10)); certain orders of the Provincial Division may be appealed to the General Division (s. 40). There are, of course, many statutes other than the *Courts of Justice Act* giving rights of appeal, particularly to the Divisional Court. The charts do not purport to give a complete picture of the Ontario appellate structure.

The use of a solid arrow in the charts indicates an appeal as of right. A broken arrow indicates leave to appeal is required.

APPEAL ROUTES FOR INTERLOCUTORY ORDERS

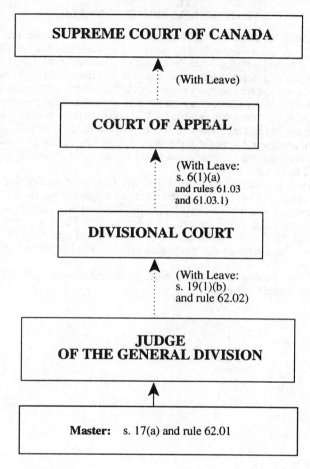

SUPREME COURT OF CANADA

(With Leave)

COURT OF APPEAL

(With Leave:
s. 6(1)(a)
and rules 61.03
and 61.03.1)

DIVISIONAL COURT

(With Leave:
s. 19(1)(b)
and rule 62.02)

**JUDGE
OF THE GENERAL DIVISION**

Master: s. 17(a) and rule 62.01

APPEAL ROUTES FOR FINAL ORDERS

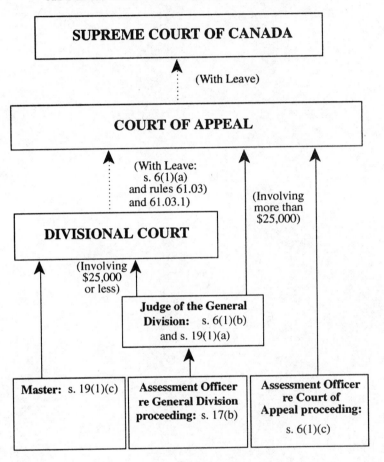

SUPREME COURT OF CANADA

(With Leave)

COURT OF APPEAL

(With Leave:
s. 6(1)(a)
and rules 61.03)
and 61.03.1)

(Involving
more than
$25,000)

DIVISIONAL COURT

(Involving
$25,000
or less)

Judge of the General
Division: s. 6(1)(b)
and s. 19(1)(a)

Master: s. 19(1)(c)

Assessment Officer
re General Division
proceeding: s. 17(b)

Assessment Officer
re Court of
Appeal proceeding:
s. 6(1)(c)

PART 1

COURTS OF JUSTICE ACT

COURTS OF JUSTICE ACT

R.S.O. 1990, c. C.43

[am. 1991 (Vol. 2), c. 46; O. Reg. 922/93; 1994, c. 12; 1994, c. 27, s. 43]

SUMMARY OF CONTENTS

1

COURTS OF JUSTICE ACT

INTRODUCTION TO THE COURTS OF JUSTICE ACT

The *Courts of Justice Act* has gone through three major phases.

The first phase was the passage of the original Act in 1984. That Act replaced the former *Judicature Act* and consolidated all Acts relating to the courts of Ontario (other than the surrogate courts), brought about significant changes in court structure (*e.g.*, it amalgamated all of the county and district courts into one province-wide District Court) and consolidated and reformed the law relating to court proceedings. It did all this in the context of the (then) new Rules of Civil Procedure which were drafted together with the Act as part of an integrated package, and both came into force at the same time. (For a comprehensive description of the changes brought about by the original Act, see the Introduction to the *Courts of Justice Act* in the 1985-1990 editions of Watson and McGowan, *Ontario Supreme and District Court Practice.*)

While minor amendments were made to the Act between 1984 and 1989, the second major phase began when the Act was substantially rewritten by the *Courts of Justice Amendment Acts, 1989* (Bills 2 and 81, S.O. 1989, cc. 55 and 70), to bring about court reform (including the merger of the former Supreme and District Courts in the new Ontario Court (General Division)) and the regionalization of the administration of the courts. (For a description of the changes brought about by these amendments, see the Annual Survey of Recent Developments in Civil Procedure in the 1990 edition of Watson and McGowan, *Ontario Civil Practice.*)

The Ministry of the Attorney General prepared commentary regarding the *Courts of Justice Act, 1984* and the *Courts of Justice Amendment Acts, 1989*, for the Ministry's own use and guidance during the legislative process. The Authors gratefully acknowledge the permission of the Ministry to use these commentaries. The commentaries, which are reproduced under each pertinent section of the current *Courts of Justice Act*, are accompanied by an indication of the particular statute for which they were prepared: "Original Act" refers to the *Courts of Justice Act, 1984*, S.O. 1984, c. 11; "Bill 2" refers to the *Courts of Justice Amendment Act, 1989*, S.O. 1989, c. 55; and "Bill 81" refers to the *Courts of Justice Amendment Act, 1989*, S.O. 1989, c. 70. In a few instances, the commentary used is the Explanatory Note which accompanied other amending legislation when in Bill form and this has been indicated. The Authors have made minor revisions required by context.

The third phase came with the Revised Statutes of Ontario 1990 — the *Courts of Justice Act* was substantially renumbered and there were minor revisions to certain sections. References to sections in the Ministry Commentary have been revised accordingly and placed in square brackets. See the Tables of Concordance (CONC.) for the interrelationship of the three versions of the *Courts of Justice Act*.

The following sections of the *Courts of Justice Act, 1984*, though not contained in the *Courts of Justice Act* as it appears in the R.S.O. 1990, are still in force (see Table of Unconsolidated and Unrepealed Acts, R.S.O. 1990, Vol. 12, Schedule C): 116(8) and (9); 138(4); 139(6); 156; 158. Those provisions have been reproduced in Authors' Comments under the pertinent current provisions.

Section 1

Definitions

1. In this Act,

"action" means a civil proceeding that is not an application and includes a proceeding commenced by,

(a) claim,

(b) statement of claim,

(c) notice of action,

(d) counterclaim,

(e) crossclaim,

(f) third or subsequent party claim, or

(g) divorce petition or counterpetition;

"application" means a civil proceeding that is commenced by notice of application or by application;

"defendant" means a person against whom an action is commenced;

"hearing" includes a trial;

"motion" means a motion in a proceeding or an intended proceeding;

"order" includes a judgment or decree;

"plaintiff" means a person who commences an action;

"region" means a region prescribed under section 74.

Ministry Comment

1989 Amendments

Bill 2

The new s. 1 of the *Courts of Justice Act* makes several minor changes in the definition section of the Act:

1. The references to specifically named courts in the definitions of "action" and "application" have been deleted as unnecessary.

2. A definition of "region" has been added. The new Act divides the province into regions, each of which will have a regional management structure for the courts. Each region will have regional senior judges responsible for the assignment of judicial duties. There will also be regional courts management committees, made up of representatives of the judiciary, the Ministry of the Attorney General, the bar and the public to monitor the operation of the courts in the region.

3. The definition "Rules of Civil Procedure" has been deleted. References to these specific rules have been replaced by references to "rules of court". Part IV of the new Act provides for several sets of rules, depending on the nature of the proceedings.

Cases

Snee v. Prashad (1983), 31 C.P.C. 60 (Ont. H.C.).

"Defendant" includes a third party.

A.G. Ont. v. Palmer, 28 O.R. (2d) 35, 15 C.P.C. 125, 108 D.L.R. (3d) 349, [1980] I.L.R. 1-1196 (C.A.).

A counterclaim is an "action" for the purposes of the limitation period in the *Public Authorities Protection Act*.

Hoffman v. Longworth, 17 O.R. (2d) 47, 4 C.P.C. 134, [1978] I.L.R. 1-929 (C.A.).

By virtue of the *Interpretation Act*, s. 6, the definitions contained in the Act apply to the Rules, unless a contrary intention appears.

PART I
COURT OF APPEAL FOR ONTARIO

Section 2

Court of Appeal
2.—(1) The Court of Appeal for Ontario is continued as a superior court of record under the name Court of Appeal for Ontario in English and Cour d'appel de l'Ontario in French.

Idem
(2) The Court of Appeal has the jurisdiction conferred on it by this or any other Act, and in the exercise of its jurisdiction has all the powers historically exercised by the Court of Appeal for Ontario.

Ministry Comment

1989 Amendments

Bill 2

The new Act re-enacts the portion of s. 2 of the 1984 Act that deals with the Court of Appeal. Under the new Act, there will be no court called the Supreme Court of Ontario. The Court of Appeal will be a separate court.

There are other modifications from s. 2(1) of the 1984 Act. The new provision deletes as unnecessary the reference to the court having civil and criminal jurisdiction. Specific federal and provincial statutes will give the Court of Appeal civil and criminal jurisdiction (see, for example, s. 6 of the new Act).

The language of subsection (2) of the new Act should also be contrasted with the corresponding language for the Ontario Court (General Division). Under s. [11(2)], the Ontario Court (General Division) has all the "jurisdiction power and authority" historically exercised in England and Ontario. Subsection (2) provides that, "in exercising its jurisdiction", [by courts of common law and equity] the Court of Appeal has the same power and authority. It is intended that the jurisdiction of the Court of Appeal will be set out in legislation. The jurisdiction of the Ontario Court (General Division), however, is primarily established by the common law.

Bill 81

This amendment [to subsection (2)] has been requested by the Court of Appeal. The provision in Bill 2 was based on the 1984 Act provision (s. 2) that applied to both the Court of Appeal and the High Court of Justice. However, its language was inappropriate for the Court of Appeal because that court is one of purely statutory jurisdiction and it should not have all of the inherent jurisdiction of courts of common law and equity. Accordingly, the amendment reflects the statutory nature of the jurisdiction and gives the court in the exercise of its jurisdiction the necessary incidental powers historically exercised by the Court of Appeal for Ontario. The language of this provision was worked out while Bill 2 was in committee.

Section 3

Composition of court
3.—(1) The Court of Appeal shall consist of,
(a) the Chief Justice of Ontario, who shall be president of the court;
(b) the Associate Chief Justice of Ontario; and
(c) fourteen other judges.

Idem

(2) The Lieutenant Governor in Council may by regulation increase the number of judges of the Court of Appeal who are in addition to the Chief Justice and the Associate Chief Justice.

Additional judges

(3) There shall be such additional offices of judge of the Court of Appeal as are from time to time required, to be held by Chief Justices of Ontario and Associate Chief Justices of Ontario who have elected under the *Judges Act* (Canada) to perform only the duties of a judge of the Court of Appeal.

Supernumerary judges

(4) There shall be such additional offices of supernumerary judge of the Court of Appeal as are from time to time required, to be held by judges of the Court of Appeal who have elected under the *Judges Act* (Canada) to hold office only as a supernumerary judge of the court.

Ministry Comment

1989 Amendments

Bill 2

Subsections (1) [and (2)] replace s. 3(1) of the 1984 Act. Under the new Act, the number of judges of the Court of Appeal may be changed by regulation.

Subsection [(3)] is derived from s. 6(1) of the 1984 Act. There is no change in substance. The changes in language are solely for the purpose of consistency with other provisions of the Act (see ss. [3(4), 12(2) and 12(3)]). Subsection [(3)] is intended to mesh with s. 32 of the federal *Judges Act*.

Subsection [(4)] re-enacts that part of s. 6(3) of the 1984 Act that dealt with the Court of Appeal. Subsection [(4)] is intended to mesh with s. 29 of the federal *Judges Act*.

Bill 81

The amendments to s. 3 were requested by the Court of Appeal. Until the enactment of Bill 2, the number of judges of the Court of Appeal was set by the statute itself. Bill 2 provided for the setting of the number by regulation so as to avoid having to come to the Legislature each time a judge was added to the Court of Appeal. This approach was adopted in 1984 in the *Courts of Justice Act* for the High Court of Justice (s. 4, originally enacted in 1981 in an amendment to the old *Judicature Act*) and for the District Court (s. 26, derived from the old *County Courts Act*). The Court of Appeal requested that any decision to decrease the size of the court, rather than increase, be a matter for the Legislature, and the Government agreed.

Section 4

Assignment of judges from General Division

4.—(1) The Chief Justice of Ontario, with the concurrence of the Chief Justice of the Ontario Court, may assign a judge of the Ontario Court (General Division) to perform the work of a judge of the Court of Appeal.

General Division judges

(2) A judge of the General Division is, by virtue of his or her office, a judge of the Court of Appeal and has all the jurisdiction, power and authority of a judge of the Court of Appeal.

Ministry Comment

1989 Amendments

Bill 2

Subsection (1) is derived from s. 9(2) of the 1984 Act. There is no change in substance. Changes in language reflect the new names of the courts and consistency with other provisions (see s. [13(1)]).

Subsection (2) re-enacts that part of s. 8 of the 1984 Act that makes superior trial court judges *ex officio* judges of the Court of Appeal.

Section 5

Powers and duties of Chief Justice
5.—(1) The Chief Justice of Ontario has general supervision and direction over the sittings of the Court of Appeal and the assignment of the judicial duties of the court.

Absence of Chief Justice
(2) If the Chief Justice of Ontario is absent from Ontario or is for any reason unable to act, his or her powers and duties shall be exercised and performed by the Associate Chief Justice of Ontario.

Absence of Associate Chief Justice
(3) If the Chief Justice of Ontario and the Associate Chief Justice of Ontario are both absent from Ontario or for any reason unable to act, the powers and duties of the Chief Justice shall be exercised and performed by a judge of the Court of Appeal designated by the Chief Justice or Associate Chief Justice.

Ministry Comment

1989 Amendments

Bill 2

Subsection (1) is the same as s. 18(5) of the 1984 Act.

Subsections (2) and (3) replace s. 3(2) of the 1984 Act. Subsection (2) allows the Associate Chief Justice to exercise all the powers of the Chief Justice if the Chief Justice is absent or unable to act. Under subsection (3), if both the Chief Justice and the Associate Chief Justice are absent or unable to act, the powers of the Chief Justice may be exercised by any judge designated by the Chief Justice or Associate Chief Justice.

Section 6

Court of Appeal jurisdiction
6.—(1) An appeal lies to the Court of Appeal from,
(a) an order of the Divisional Court, on a question that is not a question of fact alone, with leave of the Court of Appeal as provided in the rules of court;
(b) a final order of a judge of the Ontario Court (General Division), except an order referred to in clause 19(1)(a) or an order from which an appeal lies to the Divisional Court under another Act;
(c) a certificate of assessment of costs issued in a proceeding in the Court of Appeal, on an issue in respect of which an objection was served under the rules of court.

Combining of appeals from other courts
(2) The Court of Appeal has jurisdiction to hear and determine an appeal that lies to the Divisional Court or the Ontario Court (General Division) if an appeal in the same proceeding lies to and is taken to the Court of Appeal.

Idem
(3) The Court of Appeal may, on motion, transfer an appeal that has already been commenced in the Divisional Court or the Ontario Court (General Division) to the Court of Appeal for the purpose of subsection (2). [am. 1994, c. 12, s. 1]

Ministry Comment

1989 Amendments

Bill 2

Clauses (1)(a) and (b) re-enact s. 17(1)(a) and (b) of the 1984 Act with necessary terminology changes. Clause (1)(c) of the 1984 Act has been deleted, since judges will be exercising the jurisdiction formerly exercised by local judges.

The new clause (1)(c) is intended to cover that part of s. 13(2)(c) of the 1984 Act that dealt with costs in a proceeding in the Court of Appeal.

Subsections (2) and (3) re-enact the substance of s. 17(2) of the 1984 Act. Changes in language are intended solely to improve readability.

1995 Amendments

Section 6(1)(a) of the Act is amended to specify that when a statute requires leave for an appeal to the Court of Appeal, it is the Court of Appeal that grants or refuses leave.

Section 6(1)(b) of the Act is amended to make it clear that a provision for an appeal to Divisional Court in another statute, rather than to the Court of Appeal, prevails over the general provisions for appeals in the *Courts of Justice Act*.

Cases

Appeals from Divisional Court — s. 6(1)(a)

Re Ebsco Invts. Ltd. and Ebsco Subscription Services Ltd. (1976), 11 O.R. (2d) 305, 25 C.P.R. (2d) 200, 66 D.L.R. (3d) 47 (C.A.).

Similarity of corporate names is a question of fact.

Sault Dock Co. v. Sault Ste. Marie, [1973] 2 O.R. 479, 34 D.L.R. (3d) 327 (C.A.).

Before granting leave to appeal from an appellate decision of the Divisional Court, the court should be satisfied that there are questions of public interest involving interpretation of statutes, by-laws, agreements of public importance, or general rules of law, and the appellant should also demonstrate an arguable case.

Re United Glass and Ceramic Wkrs. and Dom. Glass Ltd., [1973] 2 O.R. 763, 35 D.L.R. (3d) 247 (C.A.).

Sault Dock distinguished on the ground that there the Divisional Court was exercising appellate jurisdiction: leave to appeal will be granted more readily where the Divisional Court was exercising original jurisdiction.

Re Can. Metal Co. and Heap (1975), 7 O.R. (2d) 185, 54 D.L.R. (3d) 641 (C.A.).

Leave may be granted on any question that is not a question of fact alone and the order need not be final.

Whether Order is Final or Interlocutory

See cases collected under Rule 62.

Miscellaneous

Hudson's Bay Co. v. Canada (Director of Investigation and Research) (1992), 10 O.R. (3d) 89, 42 C.P.R. (3d) 448, 58 O.A.C. 7 (C.A.), leave to appeal to Supreme Court of Canada refused (1993), 15 O.R. (3d) xvi (note), 50 C.P.R. (3d) v (note), 67 O.A.C. 158 (note).

There is no appeal from the *ex parte* issuance of a search warrant pursuant to the *Competition Act.*

R. v. Church of Scientology; R. v. Zaharia (1986), 6 C.P.C. (2d) 113, 25 C.C.C. (3d) 149, 13 O.A.C. 17 (C.A.).

Although the Court of Appeal is a statutory court, it possesses ancillary jurisdiction to make orders to prevent frustration of appeals to it. Such jurisdiction may be exercised by a panel of the court but not by a single judge in chambers.

Re Herman and Dep. A.G. Can. (1979), 26 O.R. (2d) 520, 13 C.P.C. 363, 103 D.L.R. (3d) 491, 79 D.T.C. 5372 (C.A.).

There is no right of appeal from an order of a High Court judge pursuant to s. 232 of the *Income Tax Act* concerning whether certain documents are privileged.

Section 7

Composition of court for hearings
7.—(1) A proceeding in the Court of Appeal shall be heard and determined by not fewer than three judges sitting together, and always by an uneven number of judges.

Idem, motions
(2) A motion in the Court of Appeal and an appeal under clause 6(1)(c) shall be heard and determined by one judge.

Idem
(3) Subsection (2) does not apply to a motion for leave to appeal, a motion to quash an appeal or any other motion that is specified by the rules of court.

Idem
(4) A judge assigned to hear and determine a motion may adjourn the motion to a panel of the Court of Appeal.

Idem
(5) A panel of the Court of Appeal may, on motion, set aside or vary the decision of a judge who hears and determines a motion.

Ministry Comment

1989 Amendments

Bill 2

Subsection (1) re-enacts the substance of s. 18(1) of the 1984 Act. The "unless otherwise provided" has been deleted as unnecessary, since a specific provision like s. 7(2) will prevail over the general principle in s. 7(1).

Subsection (2) of the 1984 Act has been deleted in light of changes made in the 1985 *Divorce Act.* Appeals in divorce proceedings now take the same routes as appeals in other civil proceedings.

Subsections (2) to (5) re-enact the substance of s. 18(3) of the 1984 Act. The splitting of s. 18(3) into four subsections is intended to improve readability. Subsection (2) also indicates that an appeal under s. 6(1)(c) from a certificate of assessment of costs issued in a proceeding in the Court of Appeal will be heard by one judge of the Court of Appeal.

Section 18(4) of the 1984 Act has been deleted. Under s. 5(1), the Chief Justice may assign any judge to preside over a panel of the Court of Appeal.

Cases

Lafraniere v. Kelly (1985), 6 C.P.C. (2d) 243 (Ont. C.A.).

A single judge of the Court of Appeal does not have jurisdiction to give judgment in terms of minutes of settlement.

Section 8

References to Court of Appeal

8.—(1) The Lieutenant Governor in Council may refer any question to the Court of Appeal for hearing and consideration.

Opinion of court

(2) The court shall certify its opinion to the Lieutenant Governor in Council, accompanied by a statement of the reasons for it, and any judge who differs from the opinion may certify his or her opinion and reasons in the same manner.

Submissions by Attorney General

(3) On the hearing of the question, the Attorney General of Ontario is entitled to make submissions to the court.

Idem

(4) The Attorney General of Canada shall be notified and is entitled to make submissions to the court if the question relates to the constitutional validity or constitutional applicability of an Act, or of a regulation or by-law made under an Act, of the Parliament of Canada or the Legislature.

Notice

(5) The court may direct that any person interested, or any one or more persons as representatives of a class of persons interested, be notified of the hearing and be entitled to make submissions to the court.

Appointment of counsel

(6) If an interest affected is not represented by counsel, the court may request counsel to argue on behalf of the interest and the reasonable expenses of counsel shall be paid by the Treasurer of Ontario.

Appeal

(7) The opinion of the court shall be deemed to be a judgment of the court and an appeal lies from it as from a judgment in an action.

Ministry Comment

1989 Amendments

Bill 2

Section 8 re-enacts the substance of s. 19 of the old Act.

Section 9

Meeting of judges
9.—(1) The judges of the Court of Appeal shall meet at least once in each year, on a day fixed by the Chief Justice of Ontario, in order to consider this Act, the rules of court and the administration of justice generally.

Idem
(2) The judges shall report their recommendations to the Attorney General.

Ministry Comment

1989 Amendments

Bill 81

This provision, requested by the Court of Appeal, is the exact counterpart of s. 51, which applies to the Ontario Court of Justice.

PART II
ONTARIO COURT OF JUSTICE

Section 10

Ontario Court
10.—(1) The Ontario Court of Justice is continued under the name Ontario Court of Justice in English and Cour de justice de l'Ontario in French.

Divisions
(2) The Ontario Court shall consist of two divisions, the General Division and the Provincial Division.

Ministry Comment

1989 Amendments

Bill 2

Section [10] is a new provision which establishes the Ontario Court of Justice, consisting of two divisions, the General Division and the Provincial Division.

ONTARIO COURT (GENERAL DIVISION)

Section 11

General Division
11.—(1) The Ontario Court (General Division) is continued as a superior court of record under the name Ontario Court (General Division) in English and Cour de l'Ontario (Division générale) in French.

Idem
(2) The General Division has all the jurisdiction, power and authority historically exercised by courts of common law and equity in England and Ontario.

Ministry Comment

1989 Amendments

Bill 2

Subsection (1) merges the High Court, the District Court and the surrogate courts into a superior court called the Ontario Court (General Division).

Subsection (2) repeats the portion of s. 2(1) of the 1984 Act necessary to give the General Division all the jurisdiction, power and authority historically exercised by courts of common law and equity in England and Ontario. As in the case of the Court of Appeal (see s. 2), the reference in the 1984 Act to the court having civil and criminal jurisdiction has been deleted as unnecessary.

Cases

R. v. Consolidated Fastfrate Transport Inc. (1995), 22 O.R. (3d) 172, 95 C.C.C. (3d) 457 (Gen. Div.).

The court has inherent jurisdiction to fashion an appropriate remedy where one otherwise would not exist.

Reza v. Canada (1993), 11 O.R. (3d) 65, 9 Admin. L.R. (2d) 121, 11 C.R.R. (2d) 213, 98 D.L.R. (4th) 88, 58 O.A.C. 377 (C.A.), reversed on other grounds [1994] 2 S.C.R. 394, 18 O.R. (3d) 640n, 22 Admin. L.R. (2d) 79, 24 Imm. L.R. (2d) 117, 116 D.L.R. (4th) 61, 167 N.R. 282, 72 O.A.C. 348.

Where a constitutional remedy is sought in good faith before a provincial superior court, that court should not decline jurisdiction simply because the identical remedy could be pursued in Federal Court.

Godley v. Coles (1988), 39 C.P.C. (2d) 162 (Ont. Dist. Ct.).

Where the plaintiff claims damages regarding both movable and immovable foreign property, an Ontario court may entertain the action notwithstanding *British South Africa Co. v. Companhis de Mocambique*, [1893] A.C. 602.

E. v. Eve, [1986] 2 S.C.R. 388, 13 C.P.C. (2d) 6 (*sub nom. Re Eve*), 8 C.H.R.R. D/3773, 31 D.L.R. (4th) 1, 71 N.R. 1, 61 Nfld. & P.E.I.R. 273, 185 A.P.R. 273.

The scope of the court's *parens patriae* jurisdiction is unlimited, but the discretion to exercise it is not unlimited: it is to be exercised with great caution, for the benefit of the person in need of protection and not for the benefit of others. Lengthy discussion of a court's *parens patriae* jurisdiction.

Re Wah Shing T.V. and Partners Ltd. Partnership and Chinavision Can. Corp. (1984), 48 O.R. (2d) 166, 2 C.P.R. (3d) 53, 13 D.L.R. (4th) 52 (H.C.), leave to appeal to Ont. Div. Ct. granted and injunction stayed 48 O.R. (2d) 166 at 189, 2 C.P.R. (3d) 53 at 76.

At first instance it was held that the Supreme Court had jurisdiction to restrain the respondent from broadcasting under a licence granted by the C.R.T.C. pending the hearing of a judicial review application and an appeal of that grant by the Federal Court. However, on a subsequent motion for leave to appeal, the injunction was stayed and leave granted on the basis that the Supreme Court lacked jurisdiction to restrain a successful applicant before the C.R.T.C.

Danard v. Can. (1984), 49 O.R. (2d) 23, 3 C.P.R. (3d) 538, 14 D.L.R. (4th) 124, 7 O.A.C. 148 (C.A.).

It was held that the plaintiffs' claim against the Federal Crown alleging wrongful issue of letters patent must be brought in the Federal Court, while their action in respect of the land in question must be brought in the Supreme Court of Ontario. Compelling the plaintiffs to sue in two separate courts does not deprive them of a fair hearing in accordance with the principles of fundamental justice, s. 2(e) of the *Canadian Bill of Rights*.

Gardner v. Ont., 45 O.R. (2d) 760, [1984] 3 C.N.L.R. 72, 7 D.L.R. (4th) 464 (H.C.).

Where the plaintiffs commenced an action against the Crown in right of the province in the provincial superior court, and a separate action against the Crown in right of Canada in the Federal Court, it was held that this was the only possible route available as each Crown had to be sued in that particular court.

80 Wellesley St. East Ltd. v. Fundy Bay Builders Ltd., [1972] 2 O.R. 280, 25 D.L.R. (3d) 386 (C.A.).

As a superior court of general jurisdiction, the Supreme Court of Ontario has all the powers that are necessary to do justice between the parties. Except where provided specifically to the contrary, the court's jurisdiction is unlimited and unrestricted in substantive law in civil matters.

Giffen v. Simonton (1920), 47 O.L.R. 49 (H.C.).

The High Court has jurisdiction to try the validity of wills whether or not probate has been granted.

A.G. Can. v. Rapanos Bros. Ltd. (1980), 29 O.R. (2d) 92, 16 C.P.C. 143, 112 D.L.R. (3d) 169 (H.C.).

The Ontario courts were held to be without jurisdiction to entertain claims against the federal Crown arising out of a contract by way of counterclaim, although jurisdiction exists to deal with the defence by way of set-off.

Reference Re Constitutional Validity of S. 11 of The Judicature Amendment Act, 1970 (No. 4), [1971] 2 O.R. 521, 3 R.F.L. 292, 18 D.L.R. (3d) 385 (C.A.).

Discussion of the power of the Legislature to determine the powers and jurisdiction of judges and local judges.

Section 12

Composition of General Division

12.—(1) The General Division consists of,
(a) the Chief Justice of the Ontario Court of Justice, who shall be president of the Ontario Court of Justice;
(b) the Associate Chief Justice of the Ontario Court of Justice;
(c) the Associate Chief Justice (Family Court) of the Ontario Court of Justice;
[Clause (1)(c) does not come into force until a day to be named by proclamation of the Lieutenant Governor; before a proclamation is issued naming the day on which clause (1)(c) comes into force, the Attorney General shall consult with the Chief Justice of the Ontario Court on the timing of the proclamation (1994, c. 12, s. 2(1.1), (1.2))]
(d) a regional senior judge of the General Division for each region;
(e) a senior judge of the General Division for the Unified Family Court; and
[Clause (1)(e) is repealed on a day to be named by proclamation of the Lieutenant Governor (1994, c. 12, s. 2(1.3))]
(f) such number of judges of the General Division as is fixed under clause 53(1)(a).

Additional judges

(2) There shall be such additional offices of judge of the General Division as are from time to time required, to be held by Chief Justices of the Ontario Court, Associate Chief Justices of the Ontario Court and regional senior judges of the General Division who have elected under the *Judges Act* (Canada) to perform only the duties of a judge of the Ontario Court.

Supernumerary judges

(3) **There shall be such additional offices of supernumerary judge of the General Division as are from time to time required, to be held by judges of the General Division who have elected under the** *Judges Act* **(Canada) to hold office only as a supernumerary judge of that division. [am. 1994, c. 12, s. 2]**

Ministry Comment

1989 Amendments

Bill 2

Subsection (1) replaces s. 4(1) of the 1984 Act. The composition of the General Division reflects the new regional structure of the courts. There will be one Chief Justice of the Ontario Court and, for each region, a regional senior judge. There will be no associate chief judge.

In order to provide a complete list, subsection (1) specifically mentions the senior judge for the Unified Family Court as a member of the General Division.

Subsection (2) is derived from s. 6(2) of the 1984 Act. The provision is intended to mesh with s. 32 of the federal *Judges Act*. The federal government will be asked to amend s. 32 to make clear that the election permitted by that section is also available to regional senior judges.

Subsection (3) re-enacts that part of. s. 6(3) of the 1984 Act that deals with the superior trial court. This provision is intended to mesh with s. 29 of the federal *Judges Act*.

Bill 81

[This is] the first of numerous amendments to Bill 2 consequent on the creation of the office of the Associate Chief Justice of the Ontario Court. This new office was created at the specific request of the federal Minister of Justice. The numerous duties imposed on the chief justice under federal and provincial legislation made it, in the federal minister's view, in the interest of the administration of justice to create an associate position.

The new clause [(1)(b)] creates the office itself.

The new subsection (2) is a consequential amendment.

The following regulation was made pursuant to the *Courts of Justice Act.*

O. Reg. 233/95
[am. O. Reg. 368/95]

NUMBER OF JUDGES

1. In addition to the Chief Justice of the Ontario Court of Justice, the Associate Chief Justice of the Ontario Court of Justice, the regional senior judges and the Senior Judge for the Unified Family Court, there shall be 206 judges of the Ontario Court (General Division), of whom eight shall be appointed to be members of the Family Court.

2. Each time one of the five judges of the General Division assigned to the Unified Family Court on June 30, 1993 leaves office,

(a) the number of judges of the General Division to be appointed to be members of the Family Court shall be increased by one; and

(b) the total number of judges of the General Division is not affected.

2.1. The number of judges of the Court of Appeal who are in addition to the Chief Justice and the Associate Chief Justice is increased from 14 to 16.

3. Ontario Regulation 74/95 is revoked.

Section 13

Assignment of judges from Court of Appeal

13.—(1) The Chief Justice of Ontario, with the concurrence of the Chief Justice of the Ontario Court, may assign a judge of the Court of Appeal to perform the work of a judge of the General Division.

Court of Appeal judges

(2) A judge of the Court of Appeal is, by virtue of his or her office, a judge of the General Division and has all the jurisdiction, power and authority of a judge of the General Division.

Ministry Comment

1989 Amendments

Bill 2

Subsection (1) replaces s. 9(1) of the 1984 Act. The new provision requires the concurrence of both the Chief Justice of Ontario and the Chief Judge of the Ontario Court. The new provision does not restrict Court of Appeal judges to work in Toronto.

Subsection (2) re-enacts that part of s. 8 of the 1984 Act that made judges of the Court of Appeal *ex officio* judges of the superior trial court.

Section 14

Powers and duties of Chief Justice of Ontario Court

14.—(1) The Chief Justice of the Ontario Court shall direct and supervise the sittings of the Ontario Court (General Division) and the assignment of its judicial duties.

Regional senior judges, General Division

(2) A regional senior judge of the General Division shall, subject to the authority of the Chief Justice of the Ontario Court, exercise the powers and perform the duties of the Chief Justice in respect of the General Division in his or her region.

Delegation

(3) A regional senior judge of the General Division may delegate to a judge of the General Division in his or her region the authority to exercise specified functions.

Absence of Chief Justice of Ontario Court

(4) If the Chief Justice of the Ontario Court is absent from Ontario or is for any reason unable to act, his or her powers and duties shall be exercised and performed by the associate chief justice designated by the Chief Justice.

Absence of regional senior judge of General Division

(5) The powers and duties of a regional senior judge of the General Division who is absent from Ontario or is for any reason unable to act shall be exercised and performed by a judge of the General Division designated by the Chief Justice of the Ontario Court.

Meetings with regional senior judges

(6) The Chief Justice of the Ontario Court may hold meetings with the associate chief justices and regional senior judges of the General Division in order to consider

any matters concerning sittings of the General Division and the assignment of its judicial duties. [am. 1994, c. 12, s. 3]

Ministry Comment

1989 Amendments

Bill 2

Subsection (1) replaces s. 14(2) of the 1984 Act. The 1984 Act made the assignment of judicial duties a collective responsibility of all judges of the High Court, with the Chief Justice's power restricted to making necessary readjustments or re-assignments. The new provision makes clear that overall responsibility for the assignment of judicial duties in the Ontario Court (General Division) rests with the Chief Justice of the Ontario Court.

Subsection (2) indicates that, in each region, the assignment of judicial duties is the responsibility of the regional senior judge, subject to the authority of the Chief Justice.

Subsection (3) permits a regional senior judge to delegate specified functions to other judges. For example, a regional senior judge might wish to delegate responsibility for the assignment of judicial duties in a particular geographic area within the region. Or, a regional senior judge might wish to delegate responsibility for the assignment of all family law duties.

Subsection (4) replaces s. 4(3) of the 1984 Act. The new provision permits the Chief Justice of the Ontario Court to designate a particular senior regional judge to act in his or her place when the Chief Justice is unable to act.

Subsection (5) gives the Chief Justice authority to designate a judge to act in the place of a regional senior judge who is absent or unable to act.

Bill 81

These amendments [insertion of subsection (4) and amendment to subsection (6)] are consequential on the creation of the office of Associate Chief Justice of the Ontario Court.

Section 15

Judges assigned to regions

15.—(1) The Chief Justice of the Ontario Court shall assign every judge of the General Division to a region and may re-assign a judge from one region to another.

At least one judge in each county

(2) There shall be at least one judge of the General Division assigned to each county and district.

High Court and District Court judges

(3) No judge of the General Division who was a judge of the High Court of Justice or the District Court of Ontario before the 1st day of September, 1990 shall be assigned without his or her consent to a region other than the region in which he or she resided immediately before that day.

Idem

(4) Subsections (1) to (3) do not prevent the temporary assignment of a judge to a location anywhere in Ontario.

Ministry Comment

1989 Amendments

Bill 2

Subsection (1) is a new provision that reflects the regionalization of the courts. Every judge of the General Division will be assigned to a region.

Subsection (2) guarantees that at least one judge of the General Division will be assigned to each county and district. A similar guarantee was provided in respect of the District Court by s. 27(2) of the old Act.

Subsection (3) assures former judges of the High Court and District Court that they will not be assigned without their consent to a region other than the region where they resided before the merger of their courts.

Subsection (4) makes clear that the other provisions of the section do not prevent a judge from being temporarily assigned to a location anywhere in the province.

Section 16

Composition of court for hearings
16. A proceeding in the General Division shall be heard and determined by one judge of the General Division.

Ministry Comment

1989 Amendments

Bill 2

Section [16] replaces s. 14(1) of the 1984 Act. The "unless otherwise provided" language of the old provision has been deleted as unnecessary, since a specific provision will prevail over the general provision in s. [16]. It should also be pointed out that, eventually, all motions in the General Division will be heard by judges (see s. [87]).

Cases

Children's Aid Society of Peel (Region) v. K. (D.) (1993), 13 C.P.C. (3d) 402 (Ont. Prov. Div.).
A litigant has no standing to apply for an order that a particular judge hear a particular case.

Ellis-Don Ltd. v. Ontario (Labour Relations Board) (1992), 93 C.L.L.C. 14,024, 98 D.L.R. (4th) 762, [1993] O.L.R.B. Rep. 80, 64 O.A.C. 321 (Div. Ct.).
1. The mere fact that a judge has expressed views on questions which have legal connotations prior to appointment to the Bench is not a ground for disqualification where the judge is subsequently considering those issues in a case.

2. The court dismissed a motion to disqualify, on the basis of apprehended bias, a member of the panel of the Divisional Court from hearing the matter because he was a former chairman of the respondent board.

Ontario (Attorney General) v. Paul Magder Furs Ltd. (1989), 42 C.P.C. (2d) 221 (Ont. H.C.).
On a motion to disqualify a judge on the grounds of an apprehension of bias, the test is whether there was a likelihood of real bias or a reasonable apprehension of bias.

Jonas v. Jonas Estate (1987), 16 C.P.C. (2d) 198 (Ont. Dist. Ct.).
The court refused to order that the trial be heard by the judge who had conducted a related reference. Counsel cannot choose the judge they would like to conduct a trial.

Section 17

Appeals to General Division
17. An appeal lies to the General Division from,
(a) an interlocutory order of a master;

(b) a certificate of assessment of costs issued in a proceeding in the General Division, on an issue in respect of which an objection was served under the rules of court.

Ministry Comment

1989 Amendments

Bill 2

Section [17] is derived from s. 13(2) of the 1984 Act. The reference to the *Divorce Act* has been deleted, since changes to the *Divorce Act* in 1985 now mean that appeals in divorce proceedings follow the same routes as appeals in other civil proceedings. Section 13(2)(b) of the 1984 Act has been deleted, since the office of "local judge" will not exist in the Ontario Court (General Division).

Cross-Reference: As to the distinction between final and interlocutory orders, see the cases collected under Rule 62. See s. 40 concerning appeals from the Provincial Division to the General Division in the absence of any other provision.

Cases

Wil-Can Electronics Canada Ltd. v. Ontario (Solicitor General) (1993), 4 W.D.C.P. (2d) 190 (Ont. Gen. Div.).

The fact that a judge was critical of the Ontario Provincial Police on a prior occasion did not disqualify the judge from hearing an unrelated case in which the OPP was a defendant.

Anthes Equipment Ltd. v. Wilhelm Layher GmbH (1986), 53 O.R. (2d) 435, 6 C.P.C. (2d) 252 (H.C.).

A judge sitting in Weekly Court has jurisdiction to hear matters usually heard by judges temporarily assigned to the Divisional Court sitting singly, and *vice versa.* The same judge may therefore dispose of an appeal from a master whether the order on appeal is interlocutory or final.

DIVISIONAL COURT

Section 18

Divisional Court
18.—(1) The branch of the General Division known as the Divisional Court is continued under the name Divisional Court in English and Cour divisionnaire in French.

Same
(2) The Divisional Court consists of the Chief Justice of the Ontario Court, who is president of the Divisional Court, the associate chief justices and such other judges as the Chief Justice designates from time to time.

Jurisdiction of judges
(3) Every judge of the General Division is also a judge of the Divisional Court. [am. 1994, c. 12, s. 5]

Ministry Comment

  1989 Amendments

  Bill 2

  Section [18] re-enacts s. 5 of the 1984 Act, with the necessary changes in terminology.

Cases

  Re Royal Trust Corp. of Can. and Roughley (1979), 27 O.R. (2d) 318, 10 R.P.R. 250 (Div. Ct.). Where a panel of the Court of Appeal heard an appeal falling within the jurisdiction of the Divisional Court, the members of the panel were retroactively designated as members of the Divisional Court.

Section 19

Divisional Court jurisdiction

19.—(1) An appeal lies to the Divisional Court from,

(a) a final order of a judge of the General Division,

    (i) for a single payment of not more than $25,000, exclusive of costs,

    (ii) for periodic payments that amount to not more than $25,000, exclusive of costs, in the twelve months commencing on the date the first payment is due under the order,

    (iii) dismissing a claim for an amount that is not more than the amount set out in subclause (i) or (ii), or

    (iv) dismissing a claim for an amount that is more than the amount set out in subclause (i) or (ii) and in respect of which the judge or jury indicates that if the claim had been allowed the amount awarded would have been not more than the amount set out in subclause (i) or (ii);

(b) an interlocutory order of a judge of the General Division, with leave as provided in the rules of court;

(c) a final order of a master.

Combining of appeals from General Division

(2) The Divisional Court has jurisdiction to hear and determine an appeal that lies to the General Division if an appeal in the same proceeding lies to and is taken to the Divisional Court.

Idem

(3) The Divisional Court may, on motion, transfer an appeal that has already been commenced in the General Division to the Divisional Court for the purpose of subsection (2).

Appeal from interlocutory orders

(4) No appeal lies from an interlocutory order of a judge of the General Division made on an appeal from an interlocutory order of the Provincial Division. [am. 1994, c. 12, s. 6]

Ministry Comment

  1989 Amendments

  Bill 2

  Subsection (1) is derived from s. 15(1) of the 1984 Act. The reference to the *Divorce Act* has been deleted as unnecessary. References to local judges have also been deleted.

Subsections (2) and (3) re-enact the substance of s. 15(2) of the 1984 Act. Changes in language are intended only to make the provision more readable.

Subsection (4) re-enacts the substance of s. 36(4) of the 1984 Act.

1995 Amendments

Section 19(1)(a)(iv) of the Act is amended to make it clear that civil jury verdicts are treated the same as judges' dismissals, for purposes of an appeal to Divisional Court.

Cross-Reference: As to the distinction between final and interlocutory orders, see the cases collected under Rule 62. See s. 31 regarding appeals from final orders of the Small Claims Court.

Cases

Appellate Jurisdiction

Medis Health & Pharmaceutical Services Inc. v. Belrose (1994), 17 O.R. (3d) 265, 23 C.P.C. (3d) 273, 72 O.A.C. 161 (C.A.).

Where a damage award is less than $25,000 but prejudgment interest brings the total above $25,000, the appeal lies to the Court of Appeal rather than the Divisional Court.

Hrab v. Hrab (1992), 88 D.L.R. (4th) 525, 54 O.A.C. 194 (Div. Ct.).

A motion to set aside an order respecting costs made on a motion for leave to appeal interlocutory orders does not lie to the Divisional Court, as the judge hearing the motion for leave to appeal has no jurisdiction to make the order as a judge of the Divisional Court.

Canejo v. Jencik (1991), 49 C.P.C. (2d) 294, 74 D.L.R. (4th) 317, 41 O.A.C. 158 (Div. Ct.).

Where judgment was granted with a reference to assess damages and it was clear that the damages would exceed $25,000, an appeal from the judgment was required to be heard by the Court of Appeal, not the Divisional Court.

Goh v. M.H. Ingle & Associates Ins. Brokers Ltd. (1988), 29 C.P.C. (2d) 276, 1 R.P.R. (2d) 309, 31 O.A.C. 79 (Div. Ct.).

The Divisional Court jurisdiction over an appeal depends on the amount of the judgment appealed from, not the amount sought on a cross-appeal.

Piscione v. Poston (1986), 12 C.P.C. (2d) 154 (Ont. H.C.).

The court transferred the appeal of an interlocutory order to the Divisional Court, where there was another appeal in the same proceeding pending before the Divisional Court.

Yorkville North Development Ltd. v. North York (City) (1988), 64 O.R. (2d) 225, 48 R.P.R. 225, 29 O.A.C. 110 (C.A.).

A provision of the *Planning Act* that an order was final was held to prevail over the predecessor of this provision.

Non-Appellate Jurisdiction

Koumoudouros v. Mun. of Metro. Toronto (1982), 37 O.R. (2d) 656, 29 C.P.C. 99, 67 C.C.C. (2d) 193, 136 D.L.R. (3d) 373 (H.C.).

An application for judicial review pursuant to s. 24 of the *Canadian Charter of Rights and Freedoms* should be to the Divisional Court.

Re Can. Wkrs. Union and Frankel Structural Steel Ltd. (1976), 12 O.R. (2d) 560, 76 C.L.L.C. 14,010 (H.C.).

The Divisional Court has jurisdiction to commit for contempt not in the face of the court.

Re C.F.R.B. Ltd. and A.G. Can. (No. 1), [1973] 1 O.R. 57, 9 C.C.C. (2d) 320, 30 D.L.R. (3d) 257 (Div. Ct.).

The Divisional Court does not have jurisdiction to prohibit criminal proceedings; the Criminal Appeal Rules apply and any such application should be made to a Supreme Court judge.

Section 20

Place for hearing appeals

20.—(1) An appeal to the Divisional Court shall be heard in the region where the hearing or other process that led to the decision appealed from took place, unlessthe parties agree otherwise or the Chief Justice of the Ontario Court orders otherwise because it is necessary to do so in the interests of justice.

Other proceedings in any region

(2) Any other proceeding in the Divisional Court may be brought in any region. [am. 1994, c. 12, s. 7]

Ministry Comment

1989 Amendments

Bill 2

Section [20] is a new provision that requires the Divisional Court to hear proceedings in every region.

1995 Amendments

Section 20(1) of the Act is amended to provide that Divisional Court appeals take place in the region where the hearing or other process that led to the decision took place, instead of where the decision was made. The section is also amended to allow the Chief Justice to move the appeal where necessary in the interests of justice.

Section 21

Composition of court for hearings

21.—(1) A proceeding in the Divisional Court shall be heard and determined by three judges sitting together.

Idem

(2) A proceeding in the Divisional Court may be heard and determined by one judge where the proceeding,

(a) is an appeal under clause 19(1)(c);

(b) is an appeal under section 31 from a provincial judge or a deputy judge presiding over the Small Claims Court; or

(c) is in a matter that the Chief Justice of the Ontario Court or a judge designated by the Chief Justice is satisfied, from the nature of the issues involved and the necessity for expedition, can and ought to be heard and determined by one judge.

Idem, motions

(3) A motion in the Divisional Court shall be heard and determined by one judge, unless otherwise provided by the rules of court.

Idem

(4) A judge assigned to hear and determine a motion may adjourn it to a panel of the Divisional Court.

Idem

(5) A panel of the Divisional Court may, on motion, set aside or vary the decision of a judge who hears and determines a motion.

Ministry Comment

1989 Amendments

Bill 2

Subsection (1) is derived from s. 16(1) of the 1984 Act. The "unless otherwise provided" language has been deleted as unnecessary, since a specific provision will prevail over the general principle in subsection (1).

Subsection (2) is derived from s. 16(2) of the 1984 Act. Clause (2)(b) indicates that an appeal from the Small Claims Court will only be heard by one judge when the appeal is from a provincial judge or a deputy judge. If the Small Claims Court is presided over by a judge of the General Division, three judges of the Divisional Court will hear the appeal.

Subsections (3) to (5) re-enact the substance of s. 16(3) of the 1984 Act. The old provision has been split into three subsections to improve readability.

Subsection (4) of the 1984 Act has been deleted as unnecessary. Under s. [14(1)] of the new Act, the Chief Judge of the Ontario Court supervises the sittings of the General Division, including the Divisional Court. In addition, under s. [20] of the new Act, sittings of the Divisional Court will be held in every region.

PRACTICE DIRECTION

Divisional Court

Re: PROCEEDINGS TO BE HEARD BY A SINGLE JUDGE

1. The following proceedings in Divisional Court are directed for a hearing before one judge of the Divisional Court:

(1) Appeals under ss. 19(1)(c) and 31 of the *Courts of Justice Act* and motions to quash such appeals.

(2) Applications for leave to appeal and requests for interim relief.

THE FOLLOWING PROVISIONS APPLY ONLY TO THE TORONTO REGION:

Matters to be Heard by One Judge

2. In the Toronto Region only, the following proceedings are directed to be brought in Divisional Court for a hearing before a single judge of that court sitting as a General Division judge:

(a) Motions under rule 62.02 for leave to appeal to the interlocutory order of a General Division judge;

(b) Applications for judicial review under s. 6(2) of the *Judicial Review Procedure Act.*

The notice of motion under rule 62.02 and the notice of application under s. 6(2), together with all other materials, will be filed with the Divisional Court office at Osgoode Hall.

Confirmation of Hearing Date

The number of Toronto Divisional Court motions have increased dramatically since application for leave to appeal and applications under s. 6(2) of the *Judicial Review Procedure Act* have been heard in Divisional Court motions by Divisional Court judges sitting in their capacity as judges of the General Division.

To bring more order into the scheduling of Divisional Court motions in Toronto, the practice now followed in Toronto in General Division motions and in family law matters will be applied to Divisional Court motions, applications, and appeals before a single judge.

In the case of appeals to a single judge, motions for leave to appeal and other motions incidental to appeals or applications, counsel should contact the Divisional Court office by telephone, (416) 327-6202, to arrange a hearing date. In all three-judge proceedings, a hearing date must be obtained from the Registrar by telephone, (416) 327-5036.

Notwithstanding that a matter is set down for a hearing, and unless otherwise ordered by a judge, the papers will not be forwarded to the presiding judge and, unless otherwise ordered, the matter will not be heard on the date scheduled unless counsel for the moving party or applicant, *by 4:30 p.m. two days prior to the scheduled hearing date*, files all necessary material and confirms that the motion or application is to proceed as scheduled.

Counsel for the moving party or applicant may confirm the hearing date by delivery of the attached form to the Divisional Court office at Osgoode Hall or by fax transmission to (416) 327-5549.

The presiding judge will generally exercise her/his discretion to decline to hear a matter without a factum.

It is the responsibility of counsel to see that the material is filed as directed. Divisional Court staff will no longer telephone counsel to remind them of the time requirements.

Counsel are reminded that all motions for leave to appeal must include, in the motion record, a copy of the signed and entered order from which leave to appeal is sought.

Time Limits on Argument

Counsel will generally limit argument on motions and leave applications to 15 minutes each. Where more time is needed, counsel will advise the Registrar at the time the appointment is given, of the estimated time requested.

When an application under s. 6(2) of the *Judicial Review Procedure Act* or an appeal under ss. 19(1)(c) and 21(2) of the *Courts of Justice Act* will require more than one hour for hearing, counsel should advise the Registrar of their best estimate when the appointment is given.

Application and Commencement

This practice direction applies only to motions, applications, and appeals before a single judge. It does not apply to matters to be heard by a Divisional Court panel.

This Practice Direction comes into force December 5, 1994 and replaces the Practice Direction dated the 4th of January, 1985, signed by G.T. Evans, Chief Justice of the High Court.

Dated September 13, 1994.

[Sgd.] Archie Campbell
The Honourable Archie Campbell
Regional Senior Justice

[Sgd.] Roy McMurtry
The Honourable
Roy McMurtry
Chief Justice of the Ontario Court

Cases

Standard Industries Ltd. v. Regional Assessment Commissioner, Region No. 13 (1993), 15
   C.P.C. (3d) 19, 61 O.A.C. 386 (Div. Ct.).

The decision of a single judge designated under s. 21(2) to hear an application for leave to
appeal from the Ontario Municipal Board is not reviewable by a panel of the Divisional Court
under s. 21(5). A proceeding heard under s. 21(2) is not a "motion". Section 21(5) applies only
to motions under s. 21(3) or (4).

Overseas Missionary Fellowship v. 578369 Ontario Ltd. (1990), 73 O.R. (2d) 73, 38 O.A.C.
   278 (C.A.).

An appeal from a single judge of the Divisional Court lies only to a full panel of that court and
not to the Court of Appeal with leave.

Anthes Equipment Ltd. v. Wilhelm Layher GmbH (1986), 53 O.R. (2d) 435, 6 C.P.C. (2d) 252
   (H.C.).

A judge of the High Court does not lose his or her jurisdiction as a judge of the Divisional Court
simply because he or she is sitting in one courtroom rather than another. Where an appeal which
should be brought before a judge of the Divisional Court sitting singly is brought incorrectly
before a judge in Weekly Court, or *vice versa*, the judge should hear the appeal in his or her
other capacity so that the parties are not shuttled back and forth between courts.

FAMILY COURT

Section 21.1

Family Court
**21.1.—(1) There shall be a branch of the Ontario Court (General Division)
known as the Family Court in English and Cour de la famille in French.**

Unified Family Court
**(2) The Unified Family Court is amalgamated with and continued as part of the
Family Court.**

Same
**(3) The Family Court has the jurisdiction conferred on it by this or any other
Act.**

Jurisdiction
**(4) The Family Court has jurisdiction in The Regional Municipality of Hamil-
ton-Wentworth and in the additional areas named in accordance with subsection (5).**

Proclamation
**(5) The Lieutenant Governor in Council may, by proclamation, name additional
areas in which the Family Court has jurisdiction. [en. 1994, c. 12, s. 8]**

   [*By proclamation dated May 19, 1995, the following areas are designated as
   areas in which the Family Court has jurisdiction effective August 1, 1995:*

   the County of Frontenac;

   the County of Lennox and Addington;

   the County of Middlesex; and

   the County of Simcoe

including *(for greater certainty) every municipality situated in those counties, whether or not the municipality forms part of the county for municipal purposes.*]

Ministry Comment

1995 Amendments

Introduction

Jurisdiction over family law throughout most of Ontario is split between two levels of court. The Ontario Court (General Division), whose judges are appointed by the federal government under section 96 of the *Constitution Act*, presides over divorce, division of property, child and spousal support and custody of and access to children. General Division judges tend to be generalists, hearing civil and criminal matters in addition to family cases. Few federal judges would consider themselves family law specialists.

Provincially appointed judges of the Ontario Court (Provincial Division) tend to specialize in either criminal or family law. In some smaller communities a judge will preside in both fields. Recently, more generalists have been appointed in order to provide greater judge power flexibility to regional senior judges. The Provincial Division has family law jurisdiction over support, custody, access, adoption, child protection and the *Young Offenders Act*. As provincial appointees with powers limited by section 96 they have no jurisdiction in divorce or division of property cases. (See appendix A for a sketch of Ontario family court jurisdiction at the present time.)

Only in the Unified Family Court of Hamilton-Wentworth is all family law jurisdiction consolidated in the hands of specialist judges who have both section 96 appointments and provincial judge powers. UFC Hamilton began as a federal-provincial pilot project in 1977 and was made a permanent court under Ontario's *Courts of Justice Act* in 1984. Despite the virtually unanimous opinion among judges, lawyers, community service providers and government officials that is a success, the UFC has not been extended to other Ontario jurisdictions until now.

Unified courts exist in Newfoundland (St. John's), Prince Edward Island (whole province), New Brunswick (whole province), Manitoba (whole province) and Saskatchewan (Saskatoon), all at the superior court level. British Columbia recently implemented a two tier family court giving jurisdiction to its superior court but using provincial judges to hear motions. Everywhere else in Canada, family jurisdiction is split much as in Ontario; the superior court has exclusive property and divorce jurisdiction; the provincial court has exclusive child welfare and youth court functions; and both have support, custody and access jurisdiction.

The existing family court hierarchy in Ontario is at the root of several serious problems such as unnecessary cost and delay to litigants and to government and loss of public respect for the justice system. Ontarians are not getting a satisfactory level of court service in family law matters because of the two tier structure. It is these problems and their negative consequences for litigants, judges and the public which have led to the call for a unified family court in Ontario since 1974.

Specialist Family Judges

Specialization can be informal (as exists in the Provincial Division as it is currently organized) or formally institutionalized as it was in the former Provincial Court with its criminal, family and civil divisions prior to the September 1, 1990 court reforms. Formal specialization need not be exclusive; that is, a judge need not be restricted to one area of specialization or sit until retirement on the same type of cases.

There is widespread support among lawyers and judges for specialization for a number of reasons. Society is complex, and so is the law; consequently, most lawyers are forced to specialize in order to provide good service. Specialized judicial positions will attract high calibre candidates. In addition, specialist judges are faster at disposing of cases as they don't need education on basic concepts.

Section 96 of the Constitution Act

Section 96 of the *Constitution Act*, as interpreted by the courts, precludes provincial judges from exercising any jurisdiction that is "broadly conformable" to a jurisdiction exercised at Confederation by superior court judges. The limits of provincial judges' jurisdiction have been tested repeatedly in the courts. Recent jurisprudence indicates that provincial judges can not be given power to divide property in family law or to award possession of the matrimonial home. The power to grant a divorce is also exclusively that of the section 96 judges of the Ontario Court (General Division).

Summary of UFC Provisions (sections 21.1 to 21.15)

There is a need for immediate action to remedy the problems with family court jurisdiction that now exist. Those problems were identified in the early 1970's, and unification was proposed as the solution in 1974 in Ontario. There has been general agreement across the country on unification at the section 96 court level for at least ten years. There is great pressure from a mobilized and united bar to move to expand the Hamilton model.

The present bill amends the *Courts of Justice Act* to allow for the creation of a unified family court throughout the province. Subject to a formal agreement with the federal Minister of Justice, a specialized court with full family law jurisdiction (including young offenders cases), called the Family Court, will be created early in 1994. Initially the court will be limited to Hamilton-Wentworth (site of the existing unified family court) and two or three other sites. The court will expand gradually to cover the entire province according to a timetable to be agreed with the federal Department of Justice.

The bill provides for the court to be a distinct part of the Ontario Court (General Division), which is the superior trial court of the province. The Family Court will have its own associate chief justice, appointed when the court is of sufficient size to warrant it and after the federal government amends its *Judges Act* to allow for the position. In the interim, the incumbent senior judge of the unified family court will act as head of the court.

The bill also provides for the court to be staffed by General Division judges appointed under section 96 of the *Constitution Act* by the federal government to be full time members of the Family Court. The appointment process includes the involvement of Ontario's Judicial Appointments Advisory Committee in a manner to be agreed with the federal Department of Justice.

Family Court judges are to be appointed on the understanding that they would spend all of their time in family law, but in exceptional circumstances, at the request of the General Division's chief justice and with the concurrence of the Associate Chief Justice (Family Court), a family judge could be assigned to other work in the General Division. Further, by agreement of the Chief Justice and Associate Chief Justice (Family Court), General Division judges with the appropriate interest and expertise would be assigned to family work in the new court on a regular basis to do family law work now being done in the General Division.

The Ministry of the Attorney General will seek the cooperation of the federal government in reappointing all qualified provincial family judges as section 96 judges and in ensuring access to Family Court services and judges in all locations where the Provincial Division offers those services now.

Those provincial judges who are not reappointed by the federal government to be section 96 judges will be assigned to Ontario Court (Provincial Division) criminal or family cases or possibly to cases in the family court (to the extent of their constitutional jurisdiction).

The bill provides that each community that has a unified family court will have a statutory community liaison committee, consisting of judges, lawyers, court administrators and members of the public, to deal with matters affecting the general operations of the court. Each community will also have a statutory community resources committee, representing the same four constituencies and social service agencies, to develop links between the court and community resources and to identify needed resources and develop strategies for putting them in place in the community.

The Attorney General will negotiate the necessary arrangements with the federal Minister of Justice. The federal minister has been very supportive of Ontario's efforts.

Section 21.2

Composition of Family Court
21.2.—(1) The Family Court consists of,
(a) the Chief Justice of the Ontario Court, who shall be president of the Family Court;
(b) the Associate Chief Justice (Family Court);
(c) the senior judge of the General Division for the Unified Family Court;
(d) the five judges and one supernumerary judge of the General Division assigned to the Unified Family Court on June 30, 1993;
(e) the judges of the General Division appointed to be members of the Family Court, the number of whom is fixed by regulation under clause 53(1)(a.1);
(f) the judges of the General Division assigned to the Family Court by the Chief Justice from time to time.

Supernumerary judges
(2) There shall be such additional offices of supernumerary judge of the General Division and member of the Family Court as are from time to time required, to be held by judges referred to in clauses (1)(d) and (e) who have elected under the *Judges Act* (Canada) to hold office only as supernumerary judges.

Jurisdiction of judges
(3) Every judge of the General Division is also a judge of the Family Court.

Coming into force of cl. (1)(b)
(4) Clause (1)(b) does not come into force until a day to be named by proclamation of the Lieutenant Governor.

Consultation
(5) Before a proclamation is issued naming the day on which clause (1)(b) comes into force, the Attorney General shall consult with the Chief Justice of the Ontario Court on the timing of the proclamation.

Repeal of cl. (1)(c)
(6) Clause (1)(c) is repealed on a day to be named by proclamation of the Lieutenant Governor. [en. 1994, c. 12, s. 8]

Ministry Comment

1995 Amendments

See above, s. 21.1.

Section 21.3

Transitional measure
21.3.—(1) As a transitional measure, the Chief Judge of the Provincial Division, with the concurrence of the Associate Chief Justice (Family Court), may assign a judge of the Provincial Division who was appointed to that division before January 1, 1994 to perform the work of a judge of the Family Court that is within the constitutional jurisdiction of a provincial judge. [Proclaimed in force August 1, 1995]

Coming into force of subs. (1)
(2) Subsection (1) does not come into force until a day to be named by proclamation of the Lieutenant Governor.

Repeal of subs. (1)
(3) Subsection (1) is repealed on a day to be named by proclamation of the Lieutenant Governor. [en. 1994, c. 12, s. 8]

Ministry Comment

1995 Amendments

     See above, s. 21.1.

Section 21.4

Provincial Division matters
21.4.—(1) The Lieutenant Governor in Council may authorize a judge of the General Division assigned to the Family Court under clause 21.2(1)(f) to exercise the jurisdiction of a judge of the Provincial Division.

Authorization required
(2) A judge assigned to the Family Court under clause 21.2(1)(f) shall not preside over the Family Court before receiving the authorization referred to in subsection (1). [en. 1994, c. 12, s. 8]

Ministry Comment

1995 Amendments

     See above, s. 21.1.

Section 21.5

Powers and duties of Associate Chief Justice (Family Court)
21.5.—(1) The Associate Chief Justice (Family Court) shall direct and supervise the sittings of the Family Court and the assignment of its judicial duties.

Absence of Associate Chief Justice (Family Court)
(2) If the Associate Chief Justice (Family Court) is absent from Ontario or is for any reason unable to act, his or her powers and duties shall be exercised and performed by a judge of the Family Court designated by the Associate Chief Justice (Family Court).

Senior judge
(3) Until the first Associate Chief Justice (Family Court) is appointed, the senior judge of the General Division for the Unified Family Court shall direct and supervise the sittings of the Family Court and the assignment of its judicial duties and has, for the purpose, the same powers and duties that a regional senior judge of the General Division has in respect of the General Division in his or her region, and the powers of the Associate Chief Justice (Family Court) referred to in subsection 21.3(1), section 21.6, subsections 21.13(2) and 21.14(2) and clauses 67(2)(f) and (l).

Repeal of subs. (3)
(4) Subsection (3) is repealed on a day to be named by proclamation of the Lieutenant Governor. [en. 1994, c. 12, s. 8]

Ministry Comment

> *1995 Amendments*
>
> > See above, s. 21.1.

Section 21.6

Judges assigned to region
21.6.—(1) The Associate Chief Justice (Family Court) shall assign every judge of the Family Court to a region and may re-assign a judge from one region to another.

Temporary assignments
(2) Subsection (1) does not prevent the temporary assignment of a judge to a location anywhere in Ontario. [en. 1994, c. 12, s. 8]

Ministry Comment

> *1995 Amendments*
>
> > See above, s. 21.1.

Section 21.7

Composition of court for hearings
21.7. A proceeding in the Family Court shall be heard and determined by one judge, sitting without a jury. [en. 1994, c. 12, s. 8]

Ministry Comment

> *1995 Amendments*
>
> > See above, s. 21.1.

Section 21.8

Proceedings in Family Court
21.8.—(1) In the parts of Ontario where the Family Court has jurisdiction, proceedings referred to in the Schedule to this section, except appeals and prosecutions, shall be commenced, heard and determined in the Family Court.

Motions for interlocutory relief
(2) A motion for interim or other interlocutory relief in a proceeding referred to in the Schedule that is required or permitted by the rules or an order of a court to be heard and determined in a part of Ontario where the Family Court has jurisdiction shall be heard and determined in the Family Court.

Same
(3) A motion for interim or other interlocutory relief in a proceeding referred to in the Schedule that is required or permitted by the rules or an order of the Family Court to be heard and determined in a part of Ontario where the Family Court does not have jurisdiction shall be heard and determined in the court that would have had jurisdiction if the proceeding had been commenced in that part of Ontario.

SCHEDULE

1. **Proceedings under the following statutory provisions:**
    Change of Name Act
    Child and Family Services Act, Parts III, VI and VII
    Children's Law Reform Act, except sections 59 and 60
    Divorce Act (Canada)
    Family Law Act, except Part V
    Family Support Plan Act
    Marriage Act, sections 6 and 9
    Reciprocal Enforcement of Support Orders Act
2. **Proceedings for the interpretation, enforcement or variation of a marriage contract, cohabitation agreement, separation agreement or paternity agreement.**
3. **Proceedings for relief by way of constructive or resulting trust or a monetary award as compensation for unjust enrichment between persons who have cohabited.**
4. **Proceedings for annulment of a marriage or for a declaration of validity or invalidity of a marriage. [en. 1994, c. 12, s. 8]**

Ministry Comment

1995 Amendments

See above, s. 21.1.

Section 21.9

Other jurisdiction
21.9. Where a proceeding referred to in the Schedule to section 21.8 is commenced in the Family Court and is combined with a related matter that is in the judge's jurisdiction but is not referred to in the Schedule, the court may, with leave of the judge, hear and determine the combined matters. [en. 1994, c. 12, s. 8]

Ministry Comment

1995 Amendments

See above, s. 21.1.

Section 21.10

Orders of predecessor court
21.10.—(1) The Family Court may hear and determine an application under an Act to discharge, vary or suspend an order made by the Provincial Court (Family Division), the Ontario Court (Provincial Division), the Ontario Court (General Division) or the Unified Family Court.

Same
(2) The Family Court may enforce orders made by the Provincial Court (Family Division), the Ontario Court (Provincial Division), the Ontario Court (General Division) or the Unified Family Court. [en. 1994, c. 12, s. 8]

Ministry Comment

1995 Amendments

See above, s. 21.1.

Section 21.11

Place where proceeding commenced
21.11.—(1) Proceedings referred to in the Schedule to section 21.8 may be commenced in the Family Court if the applicant or the respondent resides in a part of Ontario where the Family Court has jurisdiction.

Custody and access
(2) An application under Part III of the *Children's Law Reform Act* in respect of a child who ordinarily resides in a part of Ontario where the Family Court has jurisdiction may be commenced in the Family Court in that part of Ontario.

Transfer to other court
(3) A judge presiding over the Family Court may, on motion, order that a proceeding commenced in the Family Court be transferred to the appropriate court in a place where the Family Court does not have jurisdiction if, in the judge's opinion, the preponderance of convenience favours having the matter dealt with by that court in that place.

Transfer from other court
(4) A judge of a court having jurisdiction in a proceeding referred to in the Schedule to section 21.8 in an area where the Family Court does not have jurisdiction may, on motion, order that the proceeding be transferred to the Family Court in a particular place if, in the judge's opinion, the preponderance of convenience favours having the matter dealt with by that court in that place.

Directions
(5) A judge making an order under subsection (3) or (4) may give such directions for the transfer as are considered just. [en. 1994, c. 12, s. 8]

Ministry Comment

1995 Amendments

See above, s. 21.1.

Section 21.12

Criminal jurisdiction
21.12.—(1) A judge presiding over the Family Court has all the powers of a judge sitting in the Ontario Court (Provincial Division) for the purposes of proceedings under the Criminal Code *(Canada)*.

Same
(2) A judge presiding over the Family Court shall be deemed to be a judge of the Provincial Division,
    (a) for the purpose of dealing with young persons as defined in the *Provincial Offences Act*; and

(b) for the purpose of prosecutions under Part III (Child Protection) and Part VII (Adoption) of the *Child and Family Services Act*, the *Children's Law Reform Act*, the *Education Act*, the *Family Law Act*, the *Family Support Plan Act* and the *Minors' Protection Act*.

Same

(3) The Family Court is a youth court for the purpose of the *Young Offenders Act* (Canada). [en. 1994, c. 12, s. 8]

Ministry Comment

1995 Amendments

See above, s. 21.1.

Section 21.13

Community liaison committee
21.13.—(1) There shall be a community liaison committee for every upper-tier municipality, as defined in the *Ontario Unconditional Grants Act*, in the parts of Ontario where the Family Court has jurisdiction.

Composition
(2) A community liaison committee consists of judges, lawyers, persons employed in court administration and other residents of the community, appointed by the Associate Chief Justice (Family Court) or by a person whom he or she designates for the purpose.

Function
(3) A community liaison committee shall consider matters affecting the general operations of the court in the municipality and make recommendations to the appropriate authorities. [en. 1994, c. 12, s. 8]

Ministry Comment

1995 Amendments

See above, s. 21.1.

Section 21.14

Community resources committee
21.14.—(1) There shall be a community resources committee for every upper-tier municipality, as defined in the *Ontario Unconditional Grants Act*, in the parts of Ontario where the Family Court has jurisdiction.

Composition
(2) A community resources committee consists of judges, lawyers, members of social service agencies, persons employed in court administration and other residents of the community, appointed by the Associate Chief Justice (Family Court) or by a person whom he or she designates for the purpose.

Function
(3) A community resources committee shall develop links between the court and social service resources available in the community, identify needed resources and develop strategies for putting them in place. [en. 1994, c. 12, s. 8]

Ministry Comment

1995 Amendments

See above, s. 21.1.

Section 21.15

Dispute resolution service
21.15. A service for the resolution of disputes by alternatives to litigation may be established, maintained and operated as part of the Family Court. [en. 1994, c. 12, s. 8]

Ministry Comment

1995 Amendments

See above, s. 21.1.

SMALL CLAIMS COURT

Section 22

Small Claims Court
22.—(1) The Small Claims Court is continued as a branch of the General Division under the name Small Claims Court in English and Cour des petites créances in French.

Idem
(2) The Small Claims Court consists of the Chief Justice of the Ontario Court who shall be president of the court and such other judges of the General Division as the Chief Justice designates from time to time.

Jurisdiction of judges
(3) Every judge of the General Division is also a judge of the Small Claims Court.

Ministry Comment

1989 Amendments

Bill 2

Section [22] converts the Provincial Court (Civil Division) into a branch of the General Division. It will maintain a separate identity as the Small Claims Court.

Section 23

Jurisdiction

23.—(1) The Small Claims Court,

(a) has jurisdiction in any action for the payment of money where the amount claimed does not exceed the prescribed amount exclusive of interest and costs; and

(b) has jurisdiction in any action for the recovery of possession of personal property where the value of the property does not exceed the prescribed amount.

Transfer from General Division

(2) An action in the General Division may be transferred to the Small Claims Court by the local registrar of the General Division on requisition with the consent of all parties filed before the trial commences if,

(a) the only claim is for the payment of money or the recovery of possession of personal property; and

(b) the claim is within the jurisdiction of the Small Claims Court.

Idem

(3) An action transferred to the Small Claims Court shall be titled and continued as if it had been commenced in that court.

Authors' Comment

Pursuant to s. 23 the monetary jurisdiction of the Small Claims Court is prescribed by regulation. By O. Reg. 92/93 (in force April 1, 1993) the monetary jurisdiction of the Small Claims Court was increased to six thousand ($6,000) dollars. The relevant provision of the regulation provides as follows:

1.–(1) The maximum amount of a claim in the Small Claims Court is $6,000.

(2) The maximum amount of a claim over which a deputy judge may preside is $6,000.

Except where there are related claims in different courts (see s. 107) it would appear that the only mechanism for transferring a General Division action to the Small Claims Court (to take advantage of the increased monetary jurisdiction of the Small Claims Court) is that provided by s. 23(2) and note that it requires the consent of "all parties". This would still seem to be the correct interpretation of the section, notwithstanding the decision in *Shoppers Trust Co. v. Mann Taxi Management Ltd.*, below.

With the increased jurisdiction of the Small Claims Court, rule 57.05 (costs where action brought in wrong court) must be kept in mind. Rule 57.05(1) provides that if a plaintiff recovers an amount within the monetary jurisdiction of the Small Claims Court, the court may order that the plaintiff shall not recover any costs.

Ministry Comment

1989 Amendments

Bill 2

Subsection (1) is derived from s. 78(1) and (2) of the 1984 Act. In future, the monetary limit of the Small Claims Court will be prescribed by regulation. This will facilitate more regular increases in jurisdiction to reflect changes in the value of money. Section 78(1)(c) of the 1984

Act has been deleted as unnecessary. If another statute gives the Small Claims Court a function, there is no need for an additional provision in the *Courts of Justice Act.*

Subsections (2) and (3) are derived from s. 84 of the 1984 Act. There is no change in substance.

Cases

Shoppers Trust Co. v. Mann Taxi Management Ltd. (1993), 16 O.R. (3d) 192, 19 C.P.C. (3d) 7 (Gen. Div.).

Notwithstanding that s. 25(2) requires the consent of the parties for a transfer by the registrar to the Small Claims Court, a judge has inherent jurisdiction to make such a transfer without consent of the parties.

Graves v. Avis Rent A Car System Inc. (1993), 21 C.P.C. (3d) 391 (Ont. Gen. Div.).

The court transferred an action to the Small Claims Court notwithstanding the objection of the defendant.

Murday v. Schmidt (1992), 8 O.R. (3d) 231, 6 C.P.C. (3d) 389 (Gen. Div.).

The non-uniform monetary jurisdiction for the Small Claims Court in various regions of Ontario does not violate the *Charter of Rights.*

Naffouj v. D.E. Wilson Management Co. (1991), 5 O.R. (3d) 424 (Small Cl. Ct.).

Ontario's regulation setting the Small Claims Court monetary jurisdiction at $3,000 in Toronto and $1,000 elsewhere offends the *Charter of Rights* and is of no force or effect. The monetary limit is $3,000 throughout Ontario.

Moore v. Cdn. Newspapers Co. (1989), 69 O.R. (2d) 262, 60 D.L.R. (4th) 113 (Div. Ct.).

The Small Claims Court does not have jurisdiction to grant equitable relief.

Ontario (A.G.) v. Pembina Exploration Can. Ltd., [1989] 1 S.C.R. 206, 57 D.L.R. (4th) 710, 92 N.R. 137, 33 O.A.C. 321.

The Small Claims Court has jurisdiction to deal with a claim with respect to damages sustained by a ship's net in provincial inland waters.

Section 24

Composition of court for hearings

24.—(1) A proceeding in the Small Claims Court shall be heard and determined by one judge of the General Division.

Provincial judge or deputy judge may preside

(2) A proceeding in the Small Claims Court may also be heard and determined by,

(a) a provincial judge who was assigned to the Provincial Court (Civil Division) immediately before the 1st day of September, 1990,

(b) a deputy judge appointed under section 32, or

(c) *a Small Claims Court referee, if all parties to the proceeding consent to have the proceeding heard and determined by a Small Claims Court referee [Clause (c) not yet in force].*

Where deputy judge not to preside

(3) A deputy judge shall not hear and determine an action,

(a) for the payment of money in excess of the prescribed amount; or

(b) for the recovery of possession of personal property exceeding the prescribed amount in value. [am. 1994, c. 12, s. 9]

Ministry Comment

1989 Amendments

Bill 2

Subsection (1) is derived from that part of s. 77(2) and (3) of the 1984 Act that indicated that one judge or deputy judge presided over the Small Claims Court.

Subsection (2) is derived from that part of s. 77(3) of the 1984 Act that restricted the monetary jurisdiction of deputy judges. In future, this restriction will be prescribed by regulation, so it can be adjusted more regularly to reflect changes in the value of money.

Section 25

Summary hearings

25. The Small Claims Court shall hear and determine in a summary way all questions of law and fact and may make such order as is considered just and agreeable to good conscience.

Ministry Comment

1989 Amendments

Bill 2

Section [25] re-enacts s. 78(3) of the 1984 Act.

Section 26

Representation

26. A party may be represented in a proceeding in the Small Claims Court by counsel or an agent but the court may exclude from a hearing anyone, other than a lawyer qualified to practise in Ontario, appearing as an agent on behalf of a party if it finds that such person is not competent properly to represent the party or does not understand and comply at the hearing with the duties and responsibilities of an advocate. [am. 1994, c. 12, s. 10]

Ministry Comment

1989 Amendments

Bill 2

Section [26] re-enacts s. 79 of the 1984 Act.

Section 27

Evidence

27.—(1) Subject to subsections (3) and (4), the Small Claims Court may admit as evidence at a hearing and act upon any oral testimony and any document or other thing so long as the evidence is relevant to the subject-matter of the proceeding, but the court may exclude anything unduly repetitious.

Idem

(2) Subsection (1) applies whether or not the evidence is given or proven under oath or affirmation or admissible as evidence in any other court.

Idem
(3) Nothing is admissible in evidence at a hearing,
(a) that would be inadmissible by reason of any privilege under the law of evidence; or
(b) that is inadmissible by any Act.

Conflicts
(4) Nothing in subsection (1) overrides the provisions of any Act expressly limiting the extent to or purposes for which any oral testimony, documents or things may be admitted or used in evidence in any proceeding.

Copies
(5) A copy of a document or any other thing may be admitted as evidence at a hearing if the presiding judge is satisfied as to its authenticity.

Ministry Comment

1989 Amendments

Bill 2

Section [27] is derived from s. 80 of the 1984 Act. There is no change in substance.

Cases

Central Burner Service Inc. v. Texaco Can. Inc. (1989), 36 O.A.C. 239 (Div. Ct.).
The Small Claims Court may decide cases on the basis of hearsay evidence.

Section 28

Instalment orders
28. The Small Claims Court may order the times and the proportions in which money payable under an order of the court shall be paid.

Ministry Comment

1989 Amendments

Bill 2

Section [28] re-enacts s. 81 of the 1984 Act.

Section 29

Limit on costs
29. An award of costs in the Small Claims Court, other than disbursements, shall not exceed 15 per cent of the amount claimed or the value of the property sought to be recovered unless the court considers it necessary in the interests of justice to penalize a party, counsel or agent for unreasonable behaviour in the proceeding.

Ministry Comment

1989 Amendments

Bill 2

Rules 20.02, 20.03, and 20.04 of the Rules of the Provincial Court (Civil Division) now deal with the issue of costs in the Small Claims Court. Rule 20.02 permits the court to allow a successful party an amount not exceeding $30 for preparation and filing of pleadings. Rule 20.03 permits the court to allow an amount not exceeding $300 as a counsel fee at trial where the amount claimed exceeds $500. Rule 20.04 provides that, where a successful party is not represented, the amount claimed exceeds $500 and the court is satisfied that the proceeding has been unduly complicated or prolonged by an unsuccessful party, the court may order that unsuccessful party to pay the successful party an amount not exceeding $300 as compensation for inconvenience and expense.

Section [29] enacts a new provision dealing with costs in the Small Claims Court. It establishes a sliding scale for costs other than disbursements. These costs shall not exceed 15% of the amount claimed or the value of the property sought to be recovered unless the court considers it necessary in the interest of justice to penalize a party, counsel or agent for unreasonable behaviour in the proceeding. For example, in an action claiming $1,000, costs other than disbursements should not exceed $150. In an action claiming $5,000, costs other than disbursements should not exceed $750.

Section 30

30. [Repealed 1994, c. 12, s. 11]

Section 31

Appeals
31. An appeal lies to the Divisional Court from a final order of the Small Claims Court in an action,

(a) for the payment of money in excess of $500, excluding costs; or

(b) for the recovery of possession of personal property exceeding $500 in value.

Ministry Comment

1989 Amendments

Bill 2

Section [31] re-enacts s. 83 of the 1984 Act.

Section 32

Deputy judges
32.—(1) A regional senior judge of the General Division may, with the approval of the Attorney General, appoint a lawyer to act as a deputy judge of the Small Claims Court for a term of three years.

Idem
(2) A regional senior judge of the General Division may renew the appointment of a deputy judge for one or more three-year terms. [am. 1994, c. 12, s. 12]

Section 33

Deputy Judges Council
33.—(1) A council known as the Deputy Judges Council in English and as Conseil des juges suppléants in French is established.

Composition
(2) The Deputy Judges Council is composed of,

(a) the Chief Justice of the Ontario Court, or another judge of the General Division designated by the Chief Justice;

(b) a regional senior judge of the General Division, appointed by the Chief Justice;

(c) a judge of the General Division, appointed by the Chief Justice;

(d) a provincial judge who was assigned to the Provincial Court (Civil Division) immediately before September 1, 1990, or a deputy judge, appointed by the Chief Justice;

(e) three persons who are neither judges nor lawyers, appointed by the Lieutenant Governor in Council on the Attorney General's recommendation.

Criteria

(3) In the appointment of members under clause (2)(e), the importance of reflecting, in the composition of the Council as a whole, Ontario's linguistic duality and the diversity of its population and ensuring overall gender balance shall be recognized.

Chair

(4) The Chief Justice of the Ontario Court, or his or her designate, shall chair the meetings of the Deputy Judges Council.

Same

(5) The chair is entitled to vote, and may cast a second deciding vote if there is a tie.

Functions

(6) The functions of the Deputy Judges Council are,

(a) to review and approve standards of conduct for deputy judges as established by the Chief Justice;

(b) to review and approve a plan for the continuing education of deputy judges as established by the Chief Justice; and

(c) to make recommendations on matters affecting deputy judges. [re-en. 1994, c. 12, s. 13]

Ministry Comment

1995 Amendments

A new section 33 is added to establish a disciplinary body, called the Deputy Judges Council, to deal with complaints about Small Claims Court judges. (Deputy judges are lawyers who act as part time judges of the Small Claims Court).

Section 33.1

Complaint

33.1.—(1) Any person may make a complaint alleging misconduct by a deputy judge, by writing to the judge of the General Division designated by the regional senior judge in the region where the deputy judge sits.

Dismissal

(2) The judge shall review the complaint and may dismiss it without further investigation if, in his or her opinion, it falls outside the jurisdiction of the regional senior judge, is frivolous or an abuse of process, or concerns a minor matter to which an appropriate response has already been given.

Notice of dismissal

(3) The judge shall notify the regional senior judge, the complainant and the deputy judge in writing of a dismissal under subsection (3), giving brief reasons for it.

Committee

(4) If the complaint is not dismissed, the judge shall refer it to a committee consisting of three persons chosen by the regional senior judge.

Same

(5) The three persons shall be a judge of the General Division, a deputy judge and a person who is neither a judge nor a lawyer, all of whom reside or work in the region where the deputy judge who is the subject of the complaint sits.

Investigation

(6) The committee shall investigate the complaint in the manner it considers appropriate, and the complainant and deputy judge shall be given an opportunity to make representations to the committee, in writing or, at the committee's option, orally.

Recommendation

(7) The committee shall make a report to the regional senior judge, recommending a disposition in accordance with subsections (8), (9) and (10).

Disposition

(8) The regional senior judge may dismiss the complaint, with or without a finding that it is unfounded, or, if he or she concludes that the deputy judge's conduct presents grounds for imposing a sanction, may,

(a) warn the deputy judge;

(b) reprimand the deputy judge;

(c) order the deputy judge to apologize to the complainant or to any other person;

(d) order that the deputy judge take specified measures, such as receiving education or treatment, as a condition of continuing to sit as a deputy judge;

(e) suspend the deputy judge for a period of up to 30 days;

(f) inform the deputy judge that his or her appointment will not be renewed under subsection 32(2);

(g) direct that no judicial duties or only specified judicial duties be assigned to the deputy judge; or

(h) remove the deputy judge from office.

Same

(9) The regional senior judge may adopt any combination of the dispositions set out in clauses (8)(a) to (g).

Disability

(10) If the regional senior judge finds that the deputy judge is unable, because of a disability, to perform the essential duties of the office, but would be able to perform them if his or her needs were accommodated, the regional senior judge shall order that the deputy judge's needs be accommodated to the extent necessary to enable him or her to perform those duties.

Application of subs. (10)
(11) Subsection (10) applies if,
(a) the effect of the disability on the deputy judge's performance of the essential duties of the office was a factor in the complaint; and
(b) the regional senior judge dismisses the complaint or makes a disposition under clauses (8)(a), (b), (c), (d), (e) or (g).

Undue hardship
(12) Subsection (10) does not apply if the regional senior judge is satisfied that making an order would impose undue hardship on the person responsible for accommodating the judge's needs, considering the cost, outside sources of funding, if any, and health and safety requirements, if any.

Opportunity to participate
(13) The regional senior judge shall not make an order under subsection (10) against a person without ensuring that the person has had an opportunity to participate and make submissions.

Crown bound
(14) An order made under subsection (10) binds the Crown.

Compensation
(15) The regional senior judge shall consider whether the deputy judge should be compensated for all or part of his or her costs for legal services incurred in connection with all the steps taken under this section in relation to the complaint.

Recommendation
(16) If the regional senior judge is of the opinion that the deputy judge should be compensated, he or she shall make a recommendation to the Attorney General to that effect, indicating the amount of compensation.

Same
(17) If the complaint is dismissed with a finding that it is unfounded, the regional senior judge shall recommend to the Attorney General that the deputy judge be compensated for his or her costs for legal services and shall indicate the amount of compensation.

Maximum
(18) The amount of compensation recommended under subsection (16) or (17) shall be based on a rate for legal services that does not exceed the maximum rate normally paid by the Government of Ontario for similar legal services.

Payment
(19) The Attorney General shall pay compensation to the judge in accordance with the recommendation.

Non-application of SPPA
(20) The *Statutory Powers Procedure Act* does not apply to a judge, regional senior judge or member of a committee acting under this section.

Personal liability
(21) No action or other proceeding for damages shall be instituted against a judge, regional senior judge or member of a committee for any act done in good faith

in the execution or intended execution of the person's duty under this section. [en. 1994, c. 12, s. 13]

PROVINCIAL DIVISION

Section 34

Provincial Division

34. The Ontario Court (Provincial Division) is continued as a court of record under the name Ontario Court (Provincial Division) in English and Cour de l'Ontario (Division provinciale) in French.

Ministry Comment

1989 Amendments

Bill 2

Section [34] fuses the Provincial Court (Criminal Division), Provincial Court (Family Division) and the Provincial Offences Court into one court named the Ontario Court (Provincial Division).

Authors' Comment

Subsection 158 of the *Courts of Justice Act, 1984* is an unconsolidated and unrepealed transition provision which states as follows:

Former Chief Judge, etc.

158.–(1) A provincial judge who was a Chief Judge, Associate Chief Judge or senior judge of the Provincial Court (Criminal Division), the Provincial Court (Family Division) or the Provincial Court (Civil Division) immediately before this section comes into force shall continue to hold the office of provincial judge, is entitled to retain the title of Chief Judge, Associate Chief Judge or senior judge, as the case may be, and is entitled to an annual salary equal to the greater of,

(a) the current annual salary of a provincial judge; or

(b) the annual salary the judge received immediately before this section comes into force.

Former Senior Master

(2) A master who was the Senior Master immediately before this section comes into force shall continue to hold the office of master, is entitled to retain the title of Senior Master and is entitled to an annual salary equal to the greater of,

(a) the current annual salary of a master; or

(b) the annual salary the master received immediately before this section comes into force. [am. 1989, c. 55, s. 29].

Section 35

Composition of Provincial Division

35. The Provincial Division shall consist of,

(a) the Chief Judge of the Provincial Division appointed under subsection 42(3), who shall be president of the Provincial Division;

(a.1) the Associate Chief Judge and the Associate Chief Judge—Co-ordinator of Justices of the Peace of the Provincial Division appointed under subsections 42(4) and (5);

(b) a regional senior judge of the Provincial Division appointed under subsection 42(6) for each region;

(c) such provincial judges as are appointed under subsection 42(1); and

(d) such provincial judges as were assigned to the Provincial Court (Criminal Division) or the Provincial Court (Family Division) on the 31st day of December, 1989. [am. 1994, c. 12, s. 14]

Ministry Comment

1989 Amendments

Bill 2

Section [35] sets out the composition of the Ontario Court (Provincial Division)). The Provincial Division will consist of the Chief Judge of the Provincial Division, a regional senior judge for each region and all other provincial judges. There will be no associate chief judge.

Bill 81

[Section 35(d)] was requested by the judges of the Provincial Court. It makes it clear that incumbent Provincial Judges assigned to the Criminal Division or Family Division are members of the new Ontario Court (Provincial Division) without the necessity for any reappointment.

Section 36

Powers and duties of Chief Judge of Provincial Division
36.—(1) The Chief Judge of the Provincial Division shall direct and supervise the sittings of the Provincial Division and the assignment of its judicial duties.

Regional senior judges, Provincial Division
(2) A regional senior judge of the Provincial Division shall, subject to the authority of the Chief Judge of the Provincial Division, exercise the powers and perform the duties of the Chief Judge of the Provincial Division in his or her region.

Delegation
(3) A regional senior judge of the Provincial Division may delegate to a judge of the Provincial Division in his or her region the authority to exercise specified functions.

Absence of Chief Judge of Provincial Division
(4) If the Chief Judge of the Provincial Division is absent from Ontario or is for any reason unable to act, his or her powers and duties shall be exercised and performed by an associate chief judge of the Provincial Division designated by the Chief Judge of the Provincial Division.

Absence of regional senior judge of Provincial Division
(5) The powers and duties of a regional senior judge of the Provincial Division who is absent from Ontario or is for any reason unable to act shall be exercised and performed by a judge of the Provincial Division designated by the Chief Judge of the Provincial Division.

Meetings with regional senior judges
(6) The Chief Judge of the Provincial Division may hold meetings with the regional senior judges of the Provincial Division in order to consider any matters concerning sittings of the Provincial Division and the assignment of its judicial duties. [am. 1994, c. 12, s. 15]

Ministry Comment

1989 Amendments

Bill 2

Subsection (1) replaces s. 63(5) of the 1984 Act.
Subsection (2) sets out the powers of the new office of regional senior judge.
Subsection (3) permits a regional senior judge of the Provincial Division to delegate some of his or her functions to another judge. As is the case under s. [14(3)], these functions may be defined, for example, with reference to a geographic area or to subject matter.
Subsection (4) replaces s. 63(7) of the 1984 Act. If the Chief Judge of the Provincial Division is absent or unable to act, his or her power shall be exercised by a regional senior judge designated by the Chief Judge.
Subsection (5) is a new provision that permits a Chief Judge of the Provincial Division to designate a judge to act in the place of a regional senior judge who is absent or unable to act.

Section 37

Judges assigned to regions
37.—(1) The Chief Judge of the Ontario Court (Provincial Division) shall assign every provincial judge to a region and may re-assign a judge from one region to another.

Idem
(2) Subsection (1) does not prevent the temporary assignment of a provincial judge to a location anywhere in Ontario.

Ministry Comment

1989 Amendments

Bill 2

Under subsection (1), every provincial judge will be assigned to a region as part of the regionalization of the courts. Subsection (2) makes clear that assignment to a particular region does not prevent temporary assignments anywhere in the province.

Section 38

Criminal jurisdiction
38.—(1) A provincial judge has the power and authority of two or more justices of the peace when sitting in the Provincial Division and shall exercise the powers and perform the duties that any Act of the Parliament of Canada confers on a provincial court judge when sitting in the Provincial Division.

Provincial offences and family jurisdiction
(2) The Provincial Division shall perform any function assigned to it by or under the *Provincial Offences Act*, the *Family Law Act*, the *Children's Law Reform Act*, the *Child and Family Services Act* or any other Act.

Youth court jurisdiction
(3) The Provincial Division is a youth court for the purposes of the *Young Offenders Act* (Canada).

Ministry Comment

1989 Amendments

Bill 2

Subsection (1) is derived from s. 67(1) of the 1984 Act. The subsection is intended to mesh with the definition of "provincial court judge" in s. 2 of the federal *Criminal Code*. When sitting in the Provincial Division, a provincial judge has the power and authority of two or more justices of the peace. This permits the provincial judge to exercise the authority given to provincial court judges under the *Criminal Code*. Any other jurisdiction given by federal statutes to provincial court judges will be exercised in Ontario by provincial judges sitting in the Provincial Division.

Subsection (2) combines in the Provincial Division the jurisdiction formerly referred to in s. 69 and s. 75(1)(a) and (c) of the 1984 Act.

Subsection (3) replaces s. 67(2) and s. 75(1)(b) of the 1984 Act. Jurisdiction over all young offenders will be combined in the Provincial Division.

Section 39

Judge to preside
39.—(1) A proceeding in the Provincial Division shall be heard and determined by one judge of the Provincial Division.

Justice of the peace may preside
(2) A justice of the peace may preside over the Provincial Division in a proceeding under the *Provincial Offences Act*.

Ministry Comment

1989 Amendments

Bill 2

Subsection (1) is derived from ss. 66(2) and 74(2) of the 1984 Act. Changes in language are made for consistency with s. [16] of the new Act.

Subsection (2) re-enacts that part of s. 68(2) of the 1984 Act that permits justices of the peace to preside over provincial offence proceedings.

Section 40

Appeals
40.—(1) If no provision is made concerning an appeal from an order of the Provincial Division, an appeal lies to the General Division.

Exception
(2) Subsection (1) does not apply to a proceeding under the *Criminal Code* (Canada) or the *Provincial Offences Act*.

Ministry Comment

1989 Amendments

Bill 2

Section [40] is intended to re-enact the substance of s. 75a of the 1984 Act. The purpose of subsection (2) is to restrict the application of the provision to family law proceedings in the Provincial Division.

Section 41

Penalty for disturbance outside courtroom
41. Any person who knowingly disturbs or interferes with a proceeding in the Provincial Division without reasonable justification while outside the courtroom is guilty of an offence and on conviction is liable to a fine of not more than $1,000 or to imprisonment for a term of not more than thirty days, or to both.

Ministry Comment

1989 Amendments

Bill 2

Section [41] is derived from s. 72 of the 1984 Act. The old provision applied only to the Provincial Offences Court but, since the Provincial Division does not have common law authority to punish contempt out of the face of the court, s. [41] is made applicable to all proceedings in the Provincial Division.

PROVINCIAL JUDGES

Section 42

Appointment of provincial judges
42.—(1) The Lieutenant Governor in Council, on the recommendation of the Attorney General, may appoint such provincial judges as are considered necessary.

Qualification
(2) No person shall be appointed as a provincial judge unless he or she has been a member of the bar of one of the provinces or territories of Canada for at least ten years or, for an aggregate of at least ten years, has been a member of such a bar or served as a judge anywhere in Canada after being a member of such a bar.

Chief Judge
(3) The Lieutenant Governor in Council may appoint a provincial judge as Chief Judge of the Ontario Court (Provincial Division).

Associate chief judges
(4) The Lieutenant Governor in Council may appoint two provincial judges as associate chief judges of the Ontario Court (Provincial Division).

Same
(5) One of the associate chief judges shall be appointed to the office of Associate Chief Judge—Co-ordinator of Justices of the Peace, which is created for the purposes of the *Justices of the Peace Act*.

Regional senior judges
(6) The Lieutenant Governor in Council may appoint a provincial judge to be the regional senior judge of the Provincial Division for each region.

Terms of office
(7) The Chief Judge and associate chief judges each hold office for six years, and regional senior judges each hold office for three years.

Reappointment
(8) The Chief Judge and associate chief judges shall not be reappointed.

Same
(9) A regional senior judge may be reappointed once, for a further three years, on the Chief Judge's recommendation; if the Chief Judge so recommends, the Lieutenant Governor in Council shall reappoint the regional senior judge.

Salary at end of term
(10) A Chief Judge, associate chief judge or regional senior judge whose term expires continues to be a provincial judge and is entitled to receive the greater of the current annual salary of a provincial judge and the annual salary he or she received immediately before the expiry.

Transition
(11) The following applies to the Chief Judge and regional senior judges who are in office on the day section 16 of the *Courts of Justice Statute Law Amendment Act, 1994* comes into force:
1. The Chief Judge holds office for six years from the time of his or her appointment. If a successor has not yet been appointed on the day the term expires, the Chief Judge continues in office until a successor is appointed, but shall not hold office for more than seven years in any event.
2. A regional senior judge holds office for five years from the time of his or her appointment, and may be reappointed once, for a further three years, on the Chief Judge's recommendation. If the Chief Judge so recommends, the Lieutenant Governor in Council shall reappoint the regional senior judge. [am. 1994, c. 12, s. 16]

Ministry Comment

1989 Amendments

Bill 2

Subsections (1) and (2) re-enact s. 52 of the 1984 Act.
Subsection (3) replaces s. 63(1) to (4) of the 1984 Act. One chief judge will be responsible for the Provincial Division.
Subsection (4) is a new provision permitting the appointment of regional senior judges.
Subsections (5) to (8) are new provisions. They provide that the Chief Judge and regional senior judges of the Provincial Division hold those offices for fixed terms of five years (subject to automatic extension up to seven years if a successor is not appointed). When the fixed term of office expires, the Chief Judge or regional senior judge continues to hold the office of provincial judge and is guaranteed that there will be no reduction in his or her salary. To avoid any perception of possible interference with independence, a Chief Judge or regional senior judge shall not be appointed to the same position after his or her term of office expires.

Bill 81

This [amendment to subsection (8)] clarifies that the "same position" referred to in the original provision in Bill 2 meant, in the case of a regional senior judge, the position of regional senior judge in any of the eight regions and not just the position in the particular region where the regional senior judge had just completed a term of office.

1995 Amendments

The Act is amended to create 2 positions of associate chief judge of the Ontario Court (Provincial Division) (section 42(4)). One of the positions will be called Associate Chief Judge — Co-ordinator of Justices of the Peace (section 42(5)). When the term of office of the current Co-ordinator of Justices of the Peace expires, his functions will be assumed by the Associate Chief Judge — Co-ordinator of Justices of the Peace. (Amendments to *Justices of the Peace Act*, sections 50-56 of the bill).

The term of office of the Chief Judge is extended to 6 years, with the current chief only (not future chiefs) being allowed to remain in office up to 7 years if not replaced. The Act is amended to allow the Chief Judge to have any or all of the existing 8 regional senior judges renewed for a further 3 year term; shorten the term of future regional senior judges to 3 years, with power in the Chief Judge to have any or all of them renewed for a further 3 years; and remove the provision allowing a regional senior judge to remain in office up to 7 years (section 42(7)-(11)).

Section 43

Judicial Appointments Advisory Committee

43.—(1) A committee known as the Judicial Appointments Advisory Committee in English and as Comité consultatif sur les nominations à la magistrature in French is established.

Composition

(2) The Committee is composed of,

(a) two provincial judges, appointed by the Chief Judge of the Provincial Division;

(b) three lawyers, one appointed by The Law Society of Upper Canada, one by the Canadian Bar Association—Ontario and one by the County and District Law Presidents' Association;

(c) seven persons who are neither judges nor lawyers, appointed by the Attorney General;

(d) a member of the Judicial Council, appointed by it.

Criteria

(3) In the appointment of members under clauses (2)(b) and (c), the importance of reflecting, in the composition of the Committee as a whole, Ontario's linguistic duality and the diversity of its population and ensuring overall gender balance shall be recognized.

Term of office

(4) The members hold office for three-year terms and may be reappointed.

Staggered terms

(5) Despite subsection (4), the following applies to the first appointments made under subsection (2):

1. One of the provincial judges holds office for a two-year term.

2. The lawyer appointed by the Canadian Bar Association—Ontario holds office for a two-year term and the lawyer appointed by the County and District Law Presidents' Association holds office for a one-year term.

3. Two of the persons who are neither judges nor lawyers hold office for two-year terms and two hold office for one-year terms.

Chair
(6) The Attorney General shall designate one of the members to chair the Committee for a three-year term.

Term of office
(7) The same person may serve as chair for two or more terms.

Function
(8) The function of the Committee is to make recommendations to the Attorney General for the appointment of provincial judges.

Manner of operating
(9) The Committee shall perform its function in the following manner:

1. When a judicial vacancy occurs and the Attorney General asks the Committee to make a recommendation, it shall advertise the vacancy and review all applications.

2. For every judicial vacancy with respect to which a recommendation is requested, the Committee shall give the Attorney General a ranked list of at least two candidates whom it recommends, with brief supporting reasons.

3. The Committee shall conduct the advertising and review process in accordance with criteria established by the Committee, including assessment of the professional excellence, community awareness and personal characteristics of candidates and recognition of the desirability of reflecting the diversity of Ontario society in judicial appointments.

4. The Committee may make recommendations from among candidates interviewed within the preceding year, if there is not enough time for a fresh advertising and review process.

Qualification
(10) A candidate shall not be considered by the Committee unless he or she has been a member of the bar of one of the provinces or territories of Canada for at least ten years or, for an aggregate of at least ten years, has been a member of such a bar or served as a judge anywhere in Canada after being a member of such a bar.

Recommendation by Attorney General
(11) The Attorney General shall recommend to the Lieutenant Governor in Council for appointment to fill a judicial vacancy only a candidate who has been recommended for that vacancy by the Committee under this section.

Rejection of list
(12) The Attorney General may reject the Committee's recommendations and require it to provide a fresh list.

Annual report
(13) The Committee shall submit to the Attorney General an annual report of its activities.

Tabling

(14) The Attorney General shall submit the annual report to the Lieutenant Governor in Council and shall then table the report in the Assembly.

Ministry Comment

1995 Amendments

Introduction

The bill entrenches in legislation the Judicial Appointments Advisory Committee (JAAC), a public dominated advisory committee to select the candidates to be appointed as provincial judges. See section 43 of the Act, added by section 16 of the bill.

This process was developed in response to public and lawyer concerns about provincial judicial appointments. Public scrutiny of the courts and judges has increased as concern has grown about crime and the burdens on the criminal justice system. Another concern relates to the pre-1988 appointment process; there was the perception that the pre-1988 appointment process was susceptible of use for patronage, and was not designed to select candidates on the basis of their potential to be the best judges. Furthermore, there is general pressure for openness, accountability and fairness in government. A related concern is that the old appointment process did not promote change in the demographic make up of the judiciary.

The bill responds to these concerns by entrenching the current JAAC process in legislation. This process has been developed over the last 5 years and it is generally applauded by lawyers and the general public. This reform guarantees the continued existence of the improved system, which has greatly increased public confidence in the provincial judiciary and the process by which it is selected. (See the Final Report and Recommendations of the Judicial Appointments Advisory Committee (June, 1992), previously distributed to all members of the Legislative Assembly.)

Mandate of the Committee (section 43(8) and (9))

The development of general and specific criteria for appointment to the bench was one of the important challenges for the JAAC pilot project. The criteria provide a statement about how society views the function of a judge. The JAAC statement that Ontario judges ought to display ''an absence of pomposity and authoritarian tendencies and respect the essential dignity of all persons'', when written down and used as a measure of all candidates, forms part of a valuable code to direct the work of the committee. Most responses to the consultation on the pilot project were content with the criteria for appointment developed during the pilot project.

The bill requires JAAC to develop criteria for judicial appointment. The criteria must be based on the following factors: professional excellence; community awareness; personal characteristics; and recognition of the desirability of reflecting the diversity of Ontario society in judicial appointments.

In addition, the bill entrenches JAAC's role as a nominating committee. Under the legislation, responsibility for developing and maintaining the process for advertising and reviewing all applications is conferred on JAAC.

Selection Process (section 43(9))

During the course of the pilot project the committee developed a process to attract and screen applicants. The method of advertising vacancies, the application forms, and the reviewing/interview process have generally met with approval.

The bill requires the committee to provide the Attorney General with a ranked list of at least two candidates, ranked in order of recommendation, for each judicial vacancy. Recommendations are made from a pool of candidates interviewed by the committee within the preceding year if time does not permit new interviews and the committee feels it could recommend from among those candidates. The Attorney General must appoint from the ranked list of candidates nominated by the committee. However, the Attorney General may reject the entire list and request a new list of names.

The bill provides that JAAC is the only body to review and recommend candidates for appointment. The bill also makes one member of the Judicial Council a member of the committee.

Composition of the Committee (section 43(2)-(6))

The Ontario committee is the first to have a non-lawyer majority in Canada. In the United States, most committees have a majority of non-lawyers. Non-lawyers bring new insights which those closely connected to the justice system may not have. For this reason, the bill provides for a majority of public members on the committee.

The committee must be large enough to be representative but not so large that it is not functional. The bill sets the total number of members at 13; the members of JAAC are comprised of the following: one member from the Judicial Council, two judges, three lawyers and seven public members.

The chair of the committee during the project was selected by the Attorney General from among the public members. The existing JAAC recommends that it be possible for any of the members (not only a non-lawyer) to be the chair. The bill implements the recommendation of the committee.

Selection of Committee Members

Committee members are selected in the following manner: judicial representatives are selected by the Chief Judge of the Provincial Division; lawyer representatives are selected by the Canadian Bar Association — Ontario and the County and District Law Presidents Association; the Judicial Council representative is selected by the Judicial Council; the public representatives are selected by the Attorney General.

The Attorney General and the lawyers' associations appointing to JAAC are required, in naming their members of JAAC, to recognize the importance of reflecting Ontario's linguistic duality and the diversity of its population, and of ensuring gender balance, in the composition of the committee as a whole.

Part Time Provincial Judges (section 44)

Chief Judge Linden and others have recommended consideration of the use on a part time basis of judges who have just retired, or who will soon retire, as a temporary, flexible expedient to deal with backlogs or fluctuating case loads. Others have suggested that the government should consider regular part time status for provincial judges, just as now exists for civil servants. The bill allows for a judge to go on part time service (or to increase or decrease the judge's percentage of full time service) at any time, at the option of the judge and with the concurrence of the Chief Judge.

The bill permits the Chief Judge to call on a retired judge for part time (daily rate) service (not exceeding 50% of full time in a year) with the approval of the Attorney General. This provision avoids the need for the full process of a new appointment for calling a retired judge back into service once he or she has left office.

Miscellaneous Technical Provisions

The bill also includes a number of provisions relating to technical matters. It requires the Judicial Appointments Advisory Committee to submit an annual report of its activities to the Attorney General (section 43(13)), who must table the report in the Legislature (section 43(14)). Secondly, the eligibility requirement of 10 years membership in the bar is amended to include time served as a judge in any province or territory (section 42(2)). Finally, the ability to opt for part time service is made available (section 87.1) to full time Small Claims court judges) (they are provincial judges) and to masters of the Ontario Court (General Division) (section 87(3)).

Section 44

Full and part-time service
44.—(1) A provincial judge may, at his or her option and with the Chief Judge's consent, change from full-time to part-time service or the reverse, or increase or decrease the amount of part-time service.

Part-time judges
(2) The Chief Judge, with the Attorney General's consent, may designate a former provincial judge who has retired from office to serve as a provincial judge on a part-time basis, not to exceed 50 per cent of full-time service in a calendar year.

Same
(3) A person designated under subsection (2) is a provincial judge and a member of the Provincial Division.

Same
(4) A judge who is serving on a part-time basis under subsection (1) or (2) shall not engage in any other remunerative occupation. [re-en. 1994, c. 12, s. 16]

Ministry Comment

1995 Amendments

See s. 43, above.

Section 45

Application for order that needs be accommodated
45.—(1) A provincial judge who believes that he or she is unable, because of a disability, to perform the essential duties of the office unless his or her needs are accommodated may apply to the Judicial Council for an order under subsection (2).

Duty of Judicial Council
(2) If the Judicial Council finds that the judge is unable, because of a disability, to perform the essential duties of the office unless his or her needs are accommodated, it shall order that the judge's needs be accommodated to the extent necessary to enable him or her to perform those duties.

Undue hardship
(3) Subsection (2) does not apply if the Judicial Council is satisfied that making an order would impose undue hardship on the person responsible for accommodating the judge's needs, considering the cost, outside sources of funding, if any, and health and safety requirements, if any.

Guidelines and rules of procedure
(4) In dealing with applications under this section, the Judicial Council shall follow its guidelines and rules of procedure established under subsection 51.1(1).

Opportunity to participate
(5) The Judicial Council shall not make an order under subsection (2) against a person without ensuring that the person has had an opportunity to participate and make submissions.

Crown bound
(6) The order binds the Crown. [re-en. 1994, c. 12, s. 16]

Section 46

Outside activities
46.—(1) A provincial judge may act as commissioner, arbitrator, adjudicator, referee, conciliator or mediator only if expressly authorized by an Act of the Parliament of Canada or the Legislature or appointed or authorized by the Governor in Council or Lieutenant Governor in Council.

Same
(2) A judge who, before January 1, 1985, had the consent of the Attorney General to act as an arbitrator or conciliator may continue to do so.

Remuneration
(3) A judge acting under subsection (1) shall not receive remuneration but shall be reimbursed for reasonable travelling and other expenses incurred while so acting. [re-en. 1994, c. 12, s. 16]

Section 47

Retirement
47.—(1) Every provincial judge shall retire upon attaining the age of sixty-five years.

Same
(2) Despite subsection (1), a judge appointed as a full-time magistrate, judge of a juvenile and family court or master before December 2, 1968 shall retire upon attaining the age of seventy years.

Continuation of judges in office
(3) A judge who has attained retirement age may, subject to the annual approval of the Chief Judge of the Provincial Division, continue in office as a full-time or part-time judge until he or she attains the age of seventy-five years.

Same, regional senior judges
(4) A regional senior judge of the Provincial Division who is in office at the time of attaining retirement age may, subject to the annual approval of the Chief Judge, continue in that office until his or her term (including any renewal under subsection 42(9)) expires, or until he or she attains the age of seventy-five years, whichever comes first.

Same, Chief Judge and associate chief judges
(5) A Chief Judge or associate chief judge of the Provincial Division who is in office at the time of attaining retirement age may, subject to the annual approval of the Judicial Council, continue in that office until his or her term expires, or until he or she attains the age of seventy-five years, whichever comes first.

Same
(6) If the Judicial Council does not approve a Chief Judge's or associate chief judge's continuation in that office under subsection (5), his or her continuation in

the office of provincial judge is subject to the approval of the Judicial Council and not as set out in subsection (3).

Criteria
(7) Decisions under subsections (3), (4), (5) and (6) shall be made in accordance with criteria developed by the Chief Judge and approved by the Judicial Council.

Transition
(8) If the date of retirement under subsections (1) to (5) falls earlier in the calendar year than the day section 16 of the *Courts of Justice Statute Law Amendment Act, 1994* comes into force and the annual approval is outstanding on that day, the judge's continuation in office shall be dealt with in accordance with section 44 of this Act as it read immediately before that day. [re-en. 1994, c. 12, s. 16]

Section 48

Resignation of judge
48.—(1) A provincial judge may at any time resign from his or her office by delivering a signed letter of resignation to the Attorney General.

Resignation as Chief Judge, etc.
(2) A Chief Judge, an associate chief judge or a regional senior judge may, before the expiry of his or her term of office under section 42, elect to hold the office of a provincial judge only, by delivering a signed letter to that effect to the Attorney General.

Former Co-ordinator of Justices of the Peace
(3) The former Co-ordinator of Justices of the Peace holds the office of a provincial judge, and is entitled to an annual salary equal to the greater of the current annual salary of a provincial judge or the annual salary he or she received immediately before ceasing to be Co-ordinator.

Effective date
(4) A resignation or election under this section takes effect on the day the letter is delivered to the Attorney General or, if the letter specifies a later day, on that day.

Repeal
(5) [*Subsection (3) was repealed and replaced by the current subsection (3) on September 1, 1995.*] [re-en. 1994, c. 12, s. 16]

Ministry Comment

1989 Amendments

Bill 2

Subsection (1) is derived from s. 55 of the 1984 Act. Under the new provision, the letter of resignation is delivered to the Attorney General, instead of the Lieutenant Governor. This is intended to avoid delays in the processing of the resignation.

Subsection (2) is derived from s. 65 of the 1984 Act. The new provision permits a Chief Judge or regional senior judge to make the election at any time. It is not necessary for the judge to have been in office for five years. The former provision was modelled on s. 32 of the federal *Judges Act*. It had the effect of limiting the circumstances in which the judge's pension would be based on the salary of a chief judge to situations where the judge had served as chief judge for five years or ceased to hold office as a judge at the same time that he or she ceased to hold office as chief judge (see also s. 43(2) of the federal *Judges Act*). This limitation can be provided for by an amendment to the provincial judges' pension regulation (O. Reg. 332/84), without restricting the availability of the election to situations where the judge has held office for at least five years.

Subsection (4) makes clear that the resignation or election takes effect on the day the letter is delivered to the Attorney General or, if the judge specifies a later day, on that day. The effective date is entirely within the control of the judge. There is no need for the resignation or election to be "accepted" by the Attorney General.

ONTARIO JUDICIAL COUNCIL

Section 49

Judicial Council
49.—(1) The Ontario Judicial Council is continued under the name Ontario Judicial Council in English and Conseil de la magistrature de l'Ontario in French.

Composition
(2) The Judicial Council is composed of,
(a) the Chief Justice of Ontario, or another judge of the Court of Appeal designated by the Chief Justice;
(b) the Chief Judge of the Provincial Division, or another judge of that division designated by the Chief Judge, and the Associate Chief Judge of the Provincial Division;
(c) a regional senior judge of the Provincial Division, appointed by the Lieutenant Governor in Council on the Attorney General's recommendation;
(d) two judges of the Provincial Division, appointed by the Chief Judge;
(e) the Treasurer of The Law Society of Upper Canada, or another bencher of the Law Society who is a lawyer, designated by the Treasurer;
(f) a lawyer who is not a bencher of The Law Society of Upper Canada, appointed by the Law Society;
(g) four persons who are neither judges nor lawyers, appointed by the Lieutenant Governor in Council on the Attorney General's recommendation.

Temporary members
(3) The Chief Judge of the Provincial Division may appoint a judge of that division to be a temporary member of the Judicial Council in the place of another provincial judge, for the purposes of dealing with a complaint, if the requirements of subsections (13), (15), (17), (19) and (20) cannot otherwise be met.

Criteria
(4) In the appointment of members under clauses (2)(d), (f) and (g), the importance of reflecting, in the composition of the Judicial Council as a whole, Ontario's linguistic duality and the diversity of its population and ensuring overall gender balance shall be recognized.

Term of office
(5) The regional senior judge who is appointed under clause (2)(c) remains a member of the Judicial Council until he or she ceases to hold office as a regional senior judge.

Term of office

(6) The members who are appointed under clauses (2)(d), (f) and (g) hold office for four-year terms and shall not be reappointed.

Staggered terms

(7) Despite subsection (6), one of the members first appointed under clause (2)(d) and two of the members first appointed under clause (2)(g) shall be appointed to hold office for six-year terms.

Chair

(8) The Chief Justice of Ontario, or another judge of the Court of Appeal designated by the Chief Justice, shall chair the meetings and hearings of the Judicial Council that deal with complaints against particular judges and its meetings held for the purposes of section 45 and subsection 47(5).

Same

(9) The Chief Judge of the Provincial Division, or another judge of that division designated by the Chief Judge, shall chair all other meetings and hearings of the Judicial Council.

Same

(10) The chair is entitled to vote, and may cast a second deciding vote if there is a tie.

Open and closed hearings and meetings

(11) The Judicial Council's hearings and meetings under sections 51.6 and 51.7 shall be open to the public, unless subsection 51.6(7) applies; its other hearings and meetings may be conducted in private, unless this Act provides otherwise.

Vacancies

(12) Where a vacancy occurs among the members appointed under clause (2)(d), (f) or (g), a new member similarly qualified may be appointed for the remainder of the term.

Quorum

(13) The following quorum rules apply, subject to subsections (15) and (17):
1. Eight members, including the chair, consistute a quorum.
2. At least half the members present must be judges and at least four must be persons who are not judges.

Review panels

(14) The Judicial Council may establish a panel for the purpose of dealing with a complaint under subsection 51.4(17) or (18) or subsection 51.5(8) or (10) and considering the question of compensation under section 51.7, and the panel has all the powers of the Judicial Council for that purpose.

Same

(15) The following rules apply to a panel established under subsection (14):
1. The panel shall consist of two provincial judges other than the Chief Judge, a lawyer and a person who is neither a judge nor a lawyer.
2. One of the judges, as designated by the Judicial Council, shall chair the panel.
3. Four members constitute a quorum.

Hearing panels
(16) The Judicial Council may establish a panel for the purpose of holding a hearing under section 51.6 and considering the question of compensation under section 51.7, and the panel has all the powers of the Judicial Council for that purpose.

Same
(17) The following rules apply to a panel established under subsection (16):
1. Half the members of the panel, including the chair, must be judges, and half must be persons who are not judges.
2. At least one member must be a person who is neither a judge nor a lawyer.
3. The Chief Justice of Ontario, or another judge of the Court of Appeal designated by the Chief Justice, shall chair the panel.
4. Subject to paragraphs 1, 2 and 3, the Judicial Council may determine the size and composition of the panel.
5. All the members of the panel constitute a quorum.

Chair
(18) The chair of a panel established under subsection (14) or (16) is entitled to vote, and may cast a second deciding vote if there is a tie.

Participation in stages of process
(19) The members of the subcommittee that investigated a complaint shall not,
(a) deal with the complaint under subsection 51.4(17) or (18) or subsection 51.5(8) or (10); or
(b) participate in a hearing of the complaint under section 51.6.

Same
(20) The members of the Judicial Council who dealt with a complaint under subsection 51.4(17) or (18) or subsection 51.5(8) or (10) shall not participate in a hearing of the complaint under section 51.6.

Expert assistance
(21) The Judicial Council may engage persons, including counsel, to assist it.

Support services
(22) The Judicial Council shall provide support services, including initial orientation and continuing education, to enable its members to participate effectively, devoting particular attention to the needs of the members who are neither judges nor lawyers and administering a part of its budget for support services separately for that purpose.

Same
(23) The Judicial Council shall administer a part of its budget for support services separately for the purpose of accommodating the needs of any members who have disabilities.

Confidential records
(24) The Judicial Council or a subcommittee may order that any information or documents relating to a mediation or a Council meeting or hearing that was not held in public are confidential and shall not be disclosed or made public.

Same
(25) Subsection (24) applies whether the information or documents are in the possession of the Judicial Council, the Attorney General or any other person.

Exceptions

(26) Subsection (24) does not apply to information and documents,
(a) that this Act requires the Judicial Council to disclose; or
(b) that have not been treated as confidential and were not prepared exclusively for the purposes of the mediation or Council meeting or hearing.

Personal liability

(27) No action or other proceeding for damages shall be instituted against the Judicial Council, any of its members or employees or any person acting under its authority for any act done in good faith in the execution or intended execution of the Council's or person's duty.

Remuneration

(28) The members who are appointed under clause (2)(g) are entitled to receive the daily remuneration that is fixed by the Lieutenant Governor in Council. [re-en. 1994, c. 12, s. 16]

Ministry Comment

1989 Amendments

Bill 2

Subsection [(1), (2)] is derived from s. 57(1) of the 1984 Act. The name of the Judicial Council for Provincial Judges is changed to the Ontario Judicial Council. The judges on the new Council are changed to reflect the judges who will occupy the senior judicial positions in the revised court structure.

Section 57(2) of the 1984 Act is not re-enacted. In the revised court structure, the Chief Judge of the Ontario Court supervises the duties of masters and the Chief Judge is a member of the Judicial Council.

Subsections [(3) to (5)] re-enact s. 57(3) to (5).

Subsection [(6)] provides that investigations commenced by the Judicial Council before the new legislation comes into force will be continued by the individuals who made up the Council under the 1984 Act.

1995 Amendments

Sections 49 to 51.11 of the *Courts of Justice Statute Law Amendment Act*, 1993 introduce changes to the composition, powers and procedures of the Ontario Judicial Council.

Background

The Ontario Judicial Council is the body established by the *Courts of Justice Act* to investigate complaints against provincial judges. Provincial judges work in the courts which handle the overwhelming majority of criminal and more than half of the family law matters in the province.

The Present System

The *Courts of Justice Act* currently establishes a Judicial Council composed of the Chief Justice of Ontario and three other federally-appointed judges, the Chief Judge of the Provincial Division, the Treasurer of the Law Society of Upper Canada and two persons appointed by the Lieutenant Governor in Council.

Complaints made against provincial judges are investigated by the Council in private. The Council has no sanction powers of its own; it can only refer a complaint to the Chief Judge or recommend that a public inquiry be conducted in order to determine whether the judge should be removed from office.

Where an inquiry is recommended Cabinet appoints a General Division (federally appointed) judge to conduct the inquiry. There have been seven such inquiries established in Ontario to date (one dealing with two judges). If the inquiry judge finds that the conduct of the judge warrants removal, a recommendation to that effect is laid before the Legislative Assembly which makes the final decision.

The existing process for handling complaints against these judges has been criticized by some members of the public and the media, on the following grounds:

- insufficient public input into complaints decisions
- Council not representative of Ontario society as a whole
- decisions are made behind closed doors
- Council powerless to deal with misconduct unless it is serious enough to justify removal from the bench
- judicial education should be mandatory

In addition, the provincial judges themselves have expressed concern that the Council has proportionately too few provincial judges, and that the complaints process is unfair.

The Proposed New System

Fundamental to any consideration of the complaints process is the principle of judicial independence. In order to be a fair and impartial judge of disputes in our courts, many of which involve the government as one of the parties, judges must be free from improper pressures from government and members of the public that would jeopardize this impartiality. The core issues of discipline, education, standards for conduct and performance evaluations are reserved for the judges themselves. However, the government can provide appropriate powers and structures to facilitate the exercise of these responsibilities.

The proposed changes to the existing law are designed to achieve the following goals while respecting judicial independence:

1) to create a more open, accessible, effective and accountable complaints process
2) to increase the confidence of the public, and of the judiciary, in the fairness of the complaints process
3) to support and encourage the development of standards for judicial conduct and a program for judicial performance evaluations and to require the development of a program for judicial education

Composition (sections 49(2) to 49(12))

The new Council will be comprised as follows:

- the Chief Justice of Ontario (or designate)
- the Chief Judge (or designate) and the Associate Chief Judge of the Provincial Division
- a regional senior judge appointed by the Lieutenant Governor in Council on the recommendation of the Attorney General
- two additional provincial judges appointed by the Chief Judge
- the Treasurer of the Law Society of Upper Canada (or designate) and another lawyer appointed by the Law Society
- four persons, neither judges nor lawyers, who are appointed by the Lieutenant Governor in Council on the recommendation of the Attorney General

The Chair may cast an extra vote in the event of a tie. The larger number of public members on the Council will enhance public input into the handling of complaints about the judiciary. However, the majority of Council votes will continue to be exercised by judges, as required by the Constitution. Quorum rules are proposed to ensure the appropriate balance of members (subsections 49(13), (15) and (17)).

The Chief Justice, a federally appointed judge, will chair all proceedings dealing with complaints against specific judges, except for review panel meetings which will be chaired by a provincial judge designated by the Judicial Council. The Chief Judge will chair all other meetings of the Council (subsections 49(8) and (9)).

In appointing the 2 provincial judges, the lawyer and the public members, the importance of reflecting Ontario's linguistic duality and the diversity of its population and of ensuring overall gender balance will be recognized (section 49(4)).

Services and Access (subsections 49(22), (23) and section 51)

Support services, including initial orientation and ongoing training, will be made available to all Council members, with an emphasis on meeting the needs of the public members.

The Council will publish information about itself, and the justice system, and will arrange for assistance to the public in the drafting of complaints to the Council. Province-wide free telephone access will also be provided. The Council will be required to produce an annual report of its activities. The needs of persons with disabilities are to be accommodated to enhance access to the complaints process.

Complaints Process (subsection 49(11) and sections 51.3-51.8)

A rotating subcommittee of Council members, comprised always of a provincial judge other than the Chief Judge and a public member, will screen the complaints made to the Council. The subcommittee will screen out complaints which are either outside the jurisdiction of the Council (for example matters for appeal or complaints about federal judges) or are frivolous or an abuse of process. All other complaints will be investigated.

Once the investigation is completed, the subcommittee may, by unanimous vote, dismiss the complaint or refer it to the Chief Judge for informal resolution or to mediation. In all other cases, the complaint must be referred to the Council for a determination of the route the complaint is to take. Mediation will only be available where appropriate given the nature of the allegations (subsection 51.5(3)).

The Council (review panel) will review, and may replace, all decisions of the subcommittee. Subcommittee members who participated in the screening of a complaint will not participate in a review panel or Council hearing of that complaint. Review panel members will not participate in a hearing of that complaint.

Most Council hearings will be open to the public. In exceptional circumstances, where the Council determines in accordance with published criteria that the value of an open hearing is outweighed by the value of privacy, the hearings may be closed. The identity of the judge, after a closed hearing, will only be disclosed in exceptional circumstances determined by the Council. In certain circumstances, the Council will also have the power to prohibit the publication of information that would identify the identity of a complainant or of a judge. The *Statutory Powers Procedure Act* (with the exception of a few provisions) will apply to complaints hearings.

The Council may require the Attorney General to compensate the judge for legal costs incurred in connection with an investigation and hearing.

Proceedings other than hearings to consider complaints against specific judges will not be required to be held in public.

The referral of the complaint to a judicial inquiry will be eliminated. Instead, the Council itself will hold hearings to determine whether a recommendation should be made to the Legislative Assembly that the judge be removed from office.

For the first time, the Council will be empowered to impose a range of dispositions, in addition to recommending removal from the bench, in response to a complaint. It will be able to warn or reprimand the judge, order an apology, impose measures (for example receiving treatment) as conditions of continuing to sit as a judge, and to suspend the judge, with pay for any period, or without pay (but with benefits) for up to 30 days. The Council will also have the power to order that the needs of a judge with a disability be accommodated, subject to undue hardship. These dispositions, which may be adopted alone or in combination, will permit the Council to respond appropriately to misconduct, and to help prevent conduct which might give rise to new complaints.

A judge may also apply for an accommodation order in the absence of a complaint (section 45).

Judicial Education, Standards for Judicial Conduct and Performance Evaluations (sections 51.9, 51.10 and 51.11)

The Chief Judge will be given new powers to support and enhance the personal and professional development of judges.

The Chief Judge may establish and make public standards for judicial conduct, subject to the approval of the Judicial Council. These standards will give the public an accurate expectation of the conduct that can be expected of judges, and will provide guidance to judges.

The Chief Judge may also implement a judicial performance evaluation program, subject to Council approval.

The Chief Judge is required to implement and make public a plan for continuing judicial education.

Confidential records, including judicial performance evaluations, will be protected from disclosure under the *Freedom of Information and Protection of Privacy Act.*

Continuation of Judges After Retirement (section 47)

The Chief Judge will now be responsible for annually approving the continuation of judges in office between the ages of 65 and 75, except in the case of his own renewal or that of the associate chiefs. At present, the Judicial Council itself must consider renewals for each judge between the ages of 70 and 75 on a yearly basis. All decisions as to renewal will be made in accordance with criteria developed by the Chief Judge and approved by the Judicial Council.

Section 50

Complaint against Chief Judge
50.—(1) If the Chief Judge is the subject of a complaint,
(a) the Chief Justice of Ontario shall appoint another judge of the Provincial Division to be a member of the Judicial Council instead of the Chief Judge, until the complaint is finally disposed of;
(b) the associate chief judge appointed under clause 49(2)(b) shall chair meetings and hearings of the Council instead of the Chief Judge, and make appointments under subsection 49(3) instead of the Chief Judge, until the complaint is finally disposed of; and
(c) any reference of the complaint that would otherwise be made to the Chief Judge under clause 51.4(13)(b) or 51.4(18)(c), subclause 51.5(8)(b)(ii) or clause 51.5(10)(b) shall be made to the Chief Justice of the Ontario Court instead of to the Chief Judge.

Suspension of Chief Judge
(2) If the Chief Judge is suspended under subsection 51.4(12),
(a) complaints that would otherwise be referred to the Chief Judge under clauses 51.4(13)(b) and 51.4(18)(c), subclause 51.5(8)(b)(ii) and clause 51.5(10)(b) shall be referred to the associate chief judge appointed under clause 49(2)(b), until the complaint is finally disposed of; and
(b) annual approvals that would otherwise be granted or refused by the Chief Judge shall be granted or refused by that associate chief judge, until the complaint is finally disposed of.

Complaint against associate chief judge or regional senior judge
(3) If the associate chief judge appointed under clause 49(2)(b) or the regional senior judge appointed under clause 49(2)(c) is the subject of a complaint, the Chief Judge shall appoint another judge of the Provincial Division to be a member of the

Judicial Council instead of the associate chief judge or regional senior judge, as the case may be, until the complaint is finally disposed of. [re-en. 1994, c. 12, s. 16]

Ministry Comment

1995 Amendments

See above, s. 49.

Section 51

Provision of information to public

51.—(1) The Judicial Council shall provide, in courthouses and elsewhere, information about itself and about the justice system, including information about how members of the public may obtain assistance in making complaints.

Same

(2) In providing information, the Judicial Council shall emphasize the elimination of cultural and linguistic barriers and the accommodation of the needs of persons with disabilities.

Assistance to public

(3) Where necessary, the Judicial Council shall arrange for the provision of assistance to members of the public in the preparation of documents for making complaints.

Telephone access

(4) The Judicial Council shall provide province-wide free telephone access, including telephone access for the deaf, to information about itself and its role in the justice system.

Persons with disabilities

(5) To enable persons with disabilities to participate effectively in the complaints process, the Judicial Council shall ensure that their needs are accommodated, at the Council's expense, unless it would impose undue hardship on the Council to do so, considering the cost, outside sources of funding, if any, and health and safety requirements, if any.

Annual report

(6) After the end of each year, the Judicial Council shall make an annual report to the Attorney General on its affairs, in English and French, including, with respect to all complaints received or dealt with during the year, a summary of the complaint, the findings and a statement of the disposition, but the report shall not include information that might identify the judge or the complainant.

Tabling

(7) The Attorney General shall submit the annual report to the Lieutenant Governor in Council and shall then table the report in the Assembly. [re-en. 1994, c. 12, s. 16]

Ministry Comment

1995 Amendments

See above, s. 49.

Section 51.1

Rules
51.1—(1) The Judicial Council shall establish and make public rules governing its own procedures, including the following:
1. Guidelines and rules of procedure for the purpose of section 45.
2. Guidelines and rules of procedure for the purpose of subsection 51.4(21).
3. Guidelines and rules of procedure for the purpose of subsection 51.4(22).
4. If applicable, criteria for the purpose of subsection 51.5(2).
5. If applicable, guidelines and rules of procedure for the purpose of subsection 51.5(13).
6. Rules of procedure for the purpose of subsection 51.6(3).
7. Criteria for the purpose of subsection 51.6(7).
8. Criteria for the purpose of subsection 51.6(8).
9. Criteria for the purpose of subsection 51.6(10).

Regulations Act
(2) The *Regulations Act* does not apply to rules, guidelines or criteria established by the Judicial Council.

Sections 28, 29 and 33 of SPPA
(3) Sections 28, 29 and 33 of the *Statutory Powers Procedure Act* do not apply to the Judicial Council. [en. 1994, c. 12, s. 16]

Ministry Comment

1995 Amendments

See above, s. 49.

Section 51.2

Use of official languages of courts
51.2.—(1) The information provided under subsections 51(1), (3) and (4) and the matters made public under subsection 51.1(1) shall be made available in English and French.

Same
(2) Complaints against provincial judges may be made in English or French.

Same
(3) A hearing under section 51.6 shall be conducted in English, but a complainant or witness who speaks French or a judge who is the subject of a complaint and who speaks French is entitled, on request,
(a) to be given, before the hearing, French translations of documents that are written in English and are to be considered at the hearing;
(b) to be provided with the assistance of an interpreter at the hearing; and
(c) to be provided with simultaneous interpretation into French of the English portions of the hearing.

Same
(4) Subsection (3) also applies to mediations conducted under section 51.5 and to the Judicial Council's consideration of the question of compensation under section 51.7, if subsection 51.7(2) applies.

Bilingual hearing or mediation
(5) The Judicial Council may direct that a hearing or mediation to which subsection (3) applies be conducted bilingually, if the Council is of the opinion that it can be properly conducted in that manner.

Part of hearing or mediation
(6) A directive under subsection (5) may apply to a part of the hearing or mediation, and in that case subsections (7) and (8) apply with necessary modifications.

Same
(7) In a bilingual hearing or mediation,
(a) oral evidence and submissions may be given or made in English or French, and shall be recorded in the language in which they are given or made;
(b) documents may be filed in either language;
(c) in the case of a mediation, discussions may take place in either language;
(d) the reasons for a decision or the mediator's report, as the case may be, may be written in either language.

Same
(8) In a bilingual hearing or mediation, if the complainant or the judge who is the subject of the complaint does not speak both languages, he or she is entitled, on request, to have simultaneous interpretation of any evidence, submissions or discussions spoken in the other language and translation of any document filed or reasons or report written in the other language. [en. 1994, c. 12, s. 16]

Ministry Comment

1995 Amendments

See above, s. 49.

Section 51.3

Complaints
51.3.—(1) Any person may make a complaint to the Judicial Council alleging misconduct by a provincial judge.

Same
(2) If an allegation of misconduct against a provincial judge is made to a member of the Judicial Council, it shall be treated as a complaint made to the Judicial Council.

Same
(3) If an allegation of misconduct against a provincial judge is made to any other judge or to the Attorney General, the other judge, or the Attorney General, as the case may be, shall provide the person making the allegation with information about the Judicial Council's role in the justice system and about how a complaint may be made, and shall refer the person to the Judicial Council.

Carriage of matter
(4) Once a complaint has been made to the Judicial Council, the Council has carriage of the matter.

Information re complaint
(5) At any person's request, the Judicial Council may confirm or deny that a particular complaint has been made to it. [en. 1994, c. 12, s. 16]

Ministry Comment

   1995 Amendments

     See above, s. 49.

Section 51.4

   Review by subcommittee
   51.4.—(1) A complaint received by the Judicial Council shall be reviewed by a subcommittee of the Council consisting of a provincial judge other than the Chief Judge and a person who is neither a judge nor a lawyer.

   Rotation of members
   (2) The eligible members of the Judicial Council shall all serve on the subcommittee on a rotating basis.

   Dismissal
   (3) The subcommittee shall dismiss the complaint without further investigation if, in the subcommittee's opinion, it falls outside the Judicial Council's jurisdiction or is frivolous or an abuse of process.

   Investigations
   (4) If the complaint is not dismissed under subsection (3), the subcommittee shall conduct such investigation as it considers appropriate.

   Expert assistance
   (5) The subcommittee may engage persons, including counsel, to assist it in its investigation.

   Investigation private
   (6) The investigation shall be conducted in private.

   Non-application of SPPA
   (7) The *Statutory Powers Procedure Act* does not apply to the subcommittee's activities.

   Interim recommendations
   (8) The subcommittee may recommend to a regional senior judge the suspension, with pay, of the judge who is the subject of the complaint, or the judge's reassignment to a different location, until the complaint is finally disposed of.

   Same
   (9) The recommendation shall be made to the regional senior judge appointed for the region to which the judge is assigned, unless that regional senior judge is a member of the Judicial Council, in which case the recommendation shall be made to another regional senior judge.

   Powers of regional senior judge
   (10) The regional senior judge may suspend or reassign the judge as the subcommittee recommends.

   Discretion
   (11) The regional senior judge's discretion to accept or reject the subcommittee's recommendation is not subject to the direction and supervision of the Chief Judge.

Exception: Complaints against certain judges

(12) If the complaint is against the Chief Judge, an associate chief judge or the regional senior judge who is a member of the Judicial Council, any recommendation under subsection (8) in connection with the complaint shall be made to the Chief Justice of the Ontario Court, who may suspend or reassign the judge as the subcommittee recommends.

Subcommittee's decision

(13) When its investigation is complete, the subcommittee shall,

(a) dismiss the complaint;

(b) refer the complaint to the Chief Judge;

(c) refer the complaint to a mediator in accordance with section 51.5; or

(d) refer the complaint to the Judicial Council, with or without recommending that it hold a hearing under section 51.6.

Same

(14) The subcommittee may dismiss the complaint or refer it to the Chief Judge or to a mediator only if both members agree; otherwise, the complaint shall be referred to the Judicial Council.

Conditions, reference to Chief Judge

(15) The subcommittee may, if the judge who is the subject of the complaint agrees, impose conditions on a decision to refer the complaint to the Chief Judge.

Report

(16) The subcommittee shall report to the Judicial Council, without identifying the complainant or the judge who is the subject of the complaint, its disposition of any complaint that is dismissed or referred to the Chief Judge or to a mediator.

Power of Judicial Council

(17) The Judicial Council shall consider the report, in private, and may approve the subcommittee's disposition or may require the subcommittee to refer the complaint to the Council.

Same

(18) The Judicial Council shall consider, in private, every complaint referred to it by the subcommittee, and may,

(a) hold a hearing under section 51.6;

(b) dismiss the complaint;

(c) refer the complaint to the Chief Judge, with or without imposing conditions as referred to in subsection (15); or

(d) refer the complaint to a mediator in accordance with section 51.5.

Non-application of SPPA

(19) The *Statutory Powers Procedure Act* does not apply to the Judicial Council's activities under subsections (17) and (18).

Notice to judge and complainant

(20) After making its decision under subsection (17) or (18), the Judicial Council shall communicate it to the judge and the complainant, giving brief reasons in the case of a dismissal.

Guidelines and rules of procedure

(21) In conducting investigations, in making recommendations under subsection (8) and in making decisions under subsections (13) and (15), the subcommittee shall follow the Judicial Council's guidelines and rules of procedure established under subsection 51.1(1).

Same

(22) In considering reports and complaints and making decisions under subsections (17) and (18), the Judicial Council shall follow its guidelines and rules of procedure established under subsection 51.1(1). [en. 1994, c. 12, s. 16]

Ministry Comment

1995 Amendments

See above, s. 49.

Section 51.5

Mediation

51.5.—(1) The Judicial Council may establish a mediation process for complainants and for judges who are the subject of complaints.

Criteria

(2) If the Judicial Council establishes a mediation process, it must also establish criteria to exclude from the process complaints that are inappropriate for mediation.

Same

(3) Without limiting the generality of subsection (2), the criteria must ensure that complaints are excluded from the mediation process in the following circumstances:

1. There is a significant power imbalance between the complainant and the judge, or there is such a significant disparity between the complainant's and the judge's accounts of the event with which the complaint is concerned that mediation would be unworkable.

2. The complaint involves an allegation of sexual misconduct or an allegation of discrimination or harassment because of a prohibited ground of discrimination or harassment referred to in any provision of the *Human Rights Code*.

3. The public interest requires a hearing of the complaint.

Legal advice

(4) A complaint may be referred to a mediator only if the complainant and the judge consent to the referral, are able to obtain independent legal advice and have had an opportunity to do so.

Trained mediator

(5) The mediator shall be a person who has been trained in mediation and who is not a judge, and if the mediation is conducted by two or more persons acting together, at least one of them must meet those requirements.

Impartiality

(6) The mediator shall be impartial.

Exclusion

(7) No member of the subcommittee that investigated the complaint and no member of the Judicial Council who dealt with the complaint under subsection 51.4(17) or (18) shall participate in the mediation.

Review by Council

(8) The mediator shall report the results of the mediation, without identifying the complainant or the judge who is the subject of the complaint, to the Judicial Council, which shall review the report, in private, and may,

(a) approve the disposition of the complaint; or

(b) if the mediation does not result in a disposition or if the Council is of the opinion that the disposition is not in the public interest,

(i) dismiss the complaint,

(ii) refer the complaint to the Chief Judge, with or without imposing conditions as referred to in subsection 51.4(15), or

(iii) hold a hearing under section 51.6.

Report

(9) If the Judicial Council approves the disposition of the complaint, it may make the results of the mediation public, providing a summary of the complaint but not identifying the complainant or the judge.

Referral to Council

(10) At any time during or after the mediation, the complainant or the judge may refer the complaint to the Judicial Council, which shall consider the matter, in private, and may,

(a) dismiss the complaint;

(b) refer the complaint to the Chief Judge, with or without imposing conditions as referred to in subsection 51.4(15); or

(c) hold a hearing under section 51.6.

Non-application of SPPA

(11) The *Statutory Powers Procedure Act* does not apply to the Judicial Council's activities under subsections (8) and (10).

Notice to judge and complainant

(12) After making its decision under subsection (8) or (10), the Judicial Council shall communicate it to the judge and the complainant, giving brief reasons in the case of a dismissal.

Guidelines and rules of procedure

(13) In reviewing reports, considering matters and making decisions under subsections (8) and (10), the Judicial Council shall follow its guidelines and rules of procedure established under subsection 51.1(1). [en. 1994, c. 12, s. 16]

Ministry Comment

1995 Amendments

See above, s. 49.

Section 51.6

Adjudication by Council

51.6.—(1) When the Judicial Council decides to hold a hearing, it shall do so in accordance with this section.

Application of SPPA

(2) The *Statutory Powers Procedure Act*, except section 4 and subsection 9(1), applies to the hearing.

Rules of procedure

(3) The Judicial Council's rules of procedure established under subsection 51.1(1) apply to the hearing.

Communication re subject-matter of hearing

(4) The members of the Judicial Council participating in the hearing shall not communicate directly or indirectly in relation to the subject-matter of the hearing with any party, counsel, agent or other person, unless all the parties and their counsel or agents receive notice and have an opportunity to participate.

Exception

(5) Subsection (4) does not preclude the Judicial Council from engaging counsel to assist it in accordance with subsection 49(21), and in that case the nature of the advice given by counsel shall be communicated to the parties so that they may make submissions as to the law.

Parties

(6) The Judicial Council shall determine who are the parties to the hearing.

Exception, closed hearing

(7) In exceptional circumstances, if the Judicial Council determines, in accordance with the criteria established under subsection 51.1(1), that the desirability of holding open hearings is outweighed by the desirability of maintaining confidentiality, it may hold all or part of the hearing in private.

Disclosure in exceptional circumstances

(8) If the hearing was held in private, the Judicial Council shall, unless it determines in accordance with the criteria established under subsection 51.1(1) that there are exceptional circumstances, order that the judge's name not be disclosed or made public.

Orders prohibiting publication

(9) If the complaint involves allegations of sexual misconduct or sexual harassment, the Judicial Council shall, at the request of a complainant or of another witness who testifies to having been the victim of similar conduct by the judge, prohibit the publication of information that might identify the complainant or witness, as the case may be.

Publication ban

(10) In exceptional circumstances and in accordance with the criteria established under subsection 51.1(1), the Judicial Council may make an order prohibiting, pending the disposition of a complaint, the publication of information that might identify the judge who is the subject of the complaint.

Dispositions

(11) After completing the hearing, the Judicial Council may dismiss the complaint, with or without a finding that is unfounded or, if it finds that there has been misconduct by the judge, may,

(a) warn the judge;

(b) reprimand the judge;

(c) order the judge to apologize to the complainant or to any other person;

(d) order that the judge take specified measures, such as receiving education or treatment, as a condition of continuing to sit as a judge;

(e) suspend the judge with pay, for any period;

(f) suspend the judge without pay, but with benefits, for a period up to thirty days; or

(g) recommend to the Attorney General that the judge be removed from office in accordance with section 51.8.

Same

(12) The Judicial Council may adopt any combination of the dispositions set out in clauses (11)(a) to (f).

Disability

(13) If the Judicial Council finds that the judge is unable, because of a disability, to perform the essential duties of the office, but would be able to perform them if his or her needs were accommodated, the Council shall order that the judge's needs be accommodated to the extent necessary to enable him or her to perform those duties.

Application of subs. (13)

(14) Subsection (13) applies if,

(a) the effect of the disability on the judge's performance of the essential duties of the office was a factor in the complaint; and

(b) the Judicial Council dismisses the complaint or makes a disposition under clauses (11) (a) to (f).

Undue hardship

(15) Subsection (13) does not apply if the Judicial Council is satisfied that making an order would impose undue hardship on the person responsible for accommodating the judge's needs, considering the cost, outside sources of funding, if any, and health and safety requirements, if any.

Opportunity to participate

(16) The Judicial Council shall not make an order under subsection (13) against a person without ensuring that the person has had an opportunity to participate and make submissions.

Crown bound

(17) An order made under subsection (13) binds the Crown.

Report to Attorney General

(18) The Judicial Council may make a report to the Attorney General about the complaint, investigation, hearing and disposition, subject to any order made under subsection 49(24), and the Attorney General may make the report public if of the opinion that this would be in the public interest.

Non-identification of persons
(19) The following persons shall not be identified in the report:
1. A complainant or witness at whose request an order was made under subsection (9).
2. The judge, if the hearing was conducted in private, unless the Judicial Council orders that the judge's name be disclosed.

Continuing publication ban
(20) If an order was made under subsection (10) and the Judicial Council dismisses the complaint with a finding that it was unfounded, the judge shall not be identified in the report without his or her consent and the Council shall order that information that relates to the complaint and might identify the judge shall never be made public without his or her consent. [en. 1994, c. 12, s. 16]

Ministry Comment

1995 Amendments

See above, s. 49.

Section 51.7

Compensation
51.7.—(1) When the Judicial Council has dealt with a complaint against a provincial judge, it shall consider whether the judge should be compensated for his or her costs for legal services incurred in connection with all the steps taken under sections 51.4, 51.5 and 51.6 and this section in relation to the complaint.

Consideration of question combined with hearing
(2) If the Judicial Council holds a hearing into the complaint, its consideration of the question of compensation shall be combined with the hearing.

Public or private consideration of question
(3) The Judicial Council's consideration of the question of compensation shall take place in public if there was a public hearing into the complaint, and otherwise shall take place in private.

Recommendation
(4) If the Judicial Council is of the opinion that the judge should be compensated, it shall make a recommendation to the Attorney General to that effect, indicating the amount of compensation.

Same
(5) If the complaint is dismissed after a hearing, the Judicial Council shall recommend to the Attorney General that the judge be compensated for his or her costs for legal services and shall indicate the amount.

Disclosure of name
(6) The Judicial Council's recommendation to the Attorney General shall name the judge, but the Attorney General shall not disclose the name unless there was a public hearing into the complaint or the Council has otherwise made the judge's name public.

Amount of compensation
(7) The amount of compensation recommended under subsection (4) or (5) may relate to all or part of the judge's costs for legal services, and shall be based on a rate for legal services that does not exceed the maximum rate normally paid by the Government of Ontario for similar services.

Payment
(8) The Attorney General shall pay compensation to the judge in accordance with the recommendation. [en. 1994, c. 12, s. 16]

Ministry Comment

1995 Amendments

See above, s. 49.

Section 51.8

Removal for cause
51.8.—(1) A provincial judge may be removed from office only if,
(a) a complaint about the judge has been made to the Judicial Council; and
(b) the Judicial Council, after a hearing under section 51.6, recommends to the Attorney General that the judge be removed on the ground that he or she has become incapacitated or disabled from the due execution of his or her office by reason of,
(i) inability, because of a disability, to perform the essential duties of his or her office (if an order to accommodate the judge's needs would not remedy the inability or could not be made because it would impose undue hardship on the person responsible for meeting those needs, or was made but did not remedy the inability),
(ii) conduct that is incompatible with the due execution of his or her office, or
(iii) failure to perform the duties of his or her office.

Tabling of recommendation
(2) The Attorney General shall table the recommendation in the Assembly if it is in session or, if not, within fifteen days after the commencement of the next session.

Order for removal
(3) An order removing a provincial judge from office under this section may be made by the Lieutenant Governor on the address of the Assembly.

Application
(4) This section applies to provincial judges who have not yet attained retirement age and to provincial judges whose continuation in office after attaining retirement age has been approved under subsection 47 (3), (4) or (5).

Transition
(5) A complaint against a provincial judge that is made to the Judicial Council before the day section 16 of the *Courts of Justice Statute Law Amendment Act, 1994* comes into force, and considered at a meeting of the Judicial Council before that day, shall be dealt with by the Judicial Council as it was constituted immediately before

that day and in accordance with section 49 of this Act as it read immediately before that day. [en. 1994, c. 12, s. 16]

Ministry Comment

1995 Amendments

See above, s. 49.

Section 51.9

Standards of conduct
51.9.—(1) The Chief Judge of the Provincial Division may establish standards of conduct for provincial judges, including a plan for bringing the standards into effect, and may implement the standards and plan when they have been reviewed and approved by the Judicial Council.

Duty of Chief Judge
(2) The Chief Judge shall ensure that the standards of conduct are made available to the public, in English and French, when they have been approved by the Judicial Council.

Goals
(3) The following are among the goals that the Chief Judge may seek to achieve by implementing standards of conduct for judges:
    1. Recognizing the independence of the judiciary.
    2. Maintaining the high quality of the justice system and ensuring the efficient administration of justice.
    3. Enhancing equality and a sense of inclusiveness in the justice system.
    4. Ensuring that judges' conduct is consistent with the respect accorded to them.
    5. Emphasizing the need to ensure the professional and personal development of judges and the growth of their social awareness through continuing education.
[en. 1994, c. 12, s. 16]

Ministry Comment

1995 Amendments

See above, s. 49.

Section 51.10

Continuing education
51.10.—(1) The Chief Judge of the Provincial Division shall establish a plan for the continuing education of provincial judges, and shall implement the plan when it has been reviewed and approved by the Judicial Council.

Duty of Chief Judge
(2) The Chief Judge shall ensure that the plan for continuing education is made available to the public, in English and French, when it has been approved by the Judicial Council.

Goals
(3) Continuing education of judges has the following goals:
1. Maintaining and developing professional competence.
2. Maintaining and developing social awareness.
3. Encouraging personal growth. [en. 1994, c. 12, s. 16]

Ministry Comment

1995 Amendments

See above, s. 49.

Section 51.11

Performance evaluation
51.11.—(1) The Chief Judge of the Provincial Division may establish a program of performance evaluation for provincial judges, and may implement the program when it has been reviewed and approved by the Judicial Council.

Duty of Chief Judge
(2) The Chief Judge shall make the existence of the program of performance evaluation public when it has been approved by the Judicial Council.

Goals
(3) The following are among the goals that the Chief Judge may seek to achieve by establishing a program of performance evaluation for judges:
1. Enhancing the performance of individual judges and of judges in general.
2. Identifying continuing education needs.
3. Assisting in the assignment of judges.
4. Identifying potential for professional development.

Scope of evaluation
(4) In a judge's performance evaluation, a decision made in a particular case shall not be considered.

Confidentiality
(5) A judge's performance evaluation is confidential and shall be disclosed only to the judge, his or her regional senior judge, and the person or persons conducting the evaluation.

Inadmissibility, exception
(6) A judge's performance evaluation shall not be admitted in evidence before the Judicial Council or any court or other tribunal unless the judge consents.

Application of subss. (5), (6)
(7) Subsections (5) and (6) apply to everything contained in a judge's performance evaluation and to all information collected in connection with the evaluation. [en. 1994, c. 12, s. 16]

Ministry Comment

1995 Amendments

See above, s. 49.

Section 51.12

Consultation
51.12. In establishing standards of conduct under section 51.9, a plan for continuing education under section 51.10 and a program of performance evaluation under section 51.11, the Chief Judge of the Provincial Division shall consult with judges of that division and with such other persons as he or she considers appropriate. [en. 1994, c. 12, s. 16]

Ministry Comment

1995 Amendments

See above, s. 49.

PROVINCIAL JUDGES

Section 51.13

Provincial Judges Remuneration Commission
51.13.—(1) The committee known as the Provincial Judges Remuneration Commission in English and as Commission de rémunération des juges provinciaux in French is continued.

Composition and functions
(2) The composition and functions of the Commission are set out in Appendix A of the framework agreement set out in the Schedule to this Act.

Framework agreement
(3) The framework agreement forms part of this Act. [en. 1994, c. 12, s. 16]

Ministry Comment

1989 Amendments

Bill 2

Subsections (1) and (2) are derived from s. 88(1) of the 1984 Act. Subsection (1) changes the name of the Ontario Provincial Courts Committee to the Provincial Judges Remuneration Committee. The name change is made necessary by the fact that there will no longer be a court called the Provincial Court.

Paragraph 1 of subsection (2) is drafted differently from s. 88(1)(a) of the 1984 Act, in the event that the provincial judges wish to organize their associations differently.

Subsections (3) to (5) re-enact s. 88(2) to (4) of the 1984 Act.

MISCELLANEOUS

Section 52

Meeting of General Division judges
52.—(1) The judges of the Ontario Court (General Division) shall meet at least once in each year, on a day fixed by the Chief Justice of the Ontario Court, in order to consider this Act, the rules of court and the administration of justice generally.

Same, Family Court

(2) The judges of the Family Court of the Ontario Court (General Division) shall meet at least once in each year, on a day fixed by the Associate Chief Justice (Family Court), in order to consider this Act, the rules of court and the administration of justice generally.

Same, Provincial Division

(2.1) The judges of the Ontario Court (Provincial Division) shall meet at least once in each year, on a day fixed by the Chief Judge of that division, in order to consider this Act, the rules of court and the administration of justice generally.

Same, regional senior judges

(2.2) The regional senior judges of the General Division shall meet at least once in each year with the Chief Justice and the associate chief justices of that division, on a day fixed by the Chief Justice, in order to consider this Act, the rules of court and the administration of justice generally.

Idem

(3) The regional senior judges of the Provincial Division shall meet at least once in each year with the Chief Judge of the Provincial Division, on a day fixed by the Chief Judge, in order to consider this Act, the rules of court and the administration of justice generally.

Regional meeting of judges

(4) The judges of the Ontario Court of Justice in each region shall meet at least once in each year, on a day fixed by the regional senior judge of the General Division, in order to consider this Act, the rules of court and the administration of justice in the region generally.

Report of recommendations

(5) The judges meeting under this section shall report their recommendations to the Attorney General. [am. 1994, c. 12, s. 17]

Ministry Comment

1989 Amendments

Bill 2

Subsections (1) and (2) are derived from s. 10 of the 1984 Act. The new provision applies to all judges of the Ontario Court.

Subsections [(4) and (5)] also require regional meetings of the Ontario Court judges. Section 27(3) of the old Act required regional meetings of the District Court judges.

The provisions in s. [52] requiring meetings mesh with s. 41(1) of the federal *Judges Act*, which guarantees the payment of travelling expenses to federally appointed judges who attend meetings they are expressly authorized by law to attend.

Bill 81

These amendments [the repeal of the original subsections (2) and (4) and the addition of subsections (2), (3) and (5)], requested by the judiciary, provide for meetings at least annually of the chiefs and regional senior judges of each division of the Ontario Court.

Section 53

> *Regulations*
> 53.—(1) The Lieutenant Governor in Council may make regulations,
> (a) fixing the number of judges of the General Division who are in addition to the Chief Justice, the associate chief justices, the regional senior judges and the Senior Judge for the Unified Family Court;
> (a.1) fixing the number of judges of the General Division who are members of the Family Court and are in addition to the Chief Justice, the Associate Chief Justice (Family Court) and the Senior Judge for the Unified Family Court;
> [On a day to be named by proclamation of the Lieutenant Governor, clauses 53(1)(a) and (a.1) of the Act are repealed and the following substituted (1994, c. 12, s. 18(2))]
> (a) fixing the number of judges of the General Division who are in addition to the Chief Justice, the associate chief justices and the regional senior judges;
> (a.1) fixing the number of judges of the General Division who are members of the Family Court and are in addition to the Chief Justice and the Associate Chief Justice (Family Court);
> (b) [Repealed 1994, c. 12, s. 18]
> (c) [Repealed 1994, c. 12, s. 18]
> (d) prescribing territorial divisions for the Small Claims Court;
> (e) prescribing the maximum amount of a claim in the Small Claims Court for the purposes of subsection 23(1);
> (f) prescribing the maximum amount of a claim over which a deputy judge may preside for the purposes of subsection 24(3);
> (g) [Repealed 1994, c. 12, s. 18]
> (h) [Repealed 1994, c. 12, s. 18]
> (i) prescribing for each region the minimum number of judges of the General Division and of the Provincial Division who are to be assigned to that region;
> (j) prescribing for each region the minimum number of judges of the General Division who are members of the Family Court and to be assigned to that region.
>
> *Idem*
> (2) A reduction in the number of judges of the General Division under clause (1)(a) does not affect appointments existing at the time of the reduction.
> (3) [Repealed 1994, c. 12, s. 18]
>
> *Application of regulations*
> (4) A regulation made under subsection (1) may be general or particular in its application. [am. 1994, c. 12, s. 18]

Ministry Comment

1989 Amendments

Bill 2

Section [53] collects in one provision the various regulation-making powers relating to the Ontario Court of Justice.

Clause (1)(a) is derived from the first part of s. 4(2) of the 1984 Act.

Clauses (1)(b) and (c) are derived from ss. 20(4)(a) and (b) and 87(1)(b) and (c) of the 1984 Act. The language at the end of ss. 20(4)(b) and 87(1)(c) concerning the transfer or other disposition of benefits to which public servants who are appointed as judges were entitled at the time of their appointment has been deleted as unnecessary. There are no such regulations at the present time.

Clause (1)(d) is derived from s. 87(1)(e) of the 1984 Act.

Clauses (1)(e) and (f) are new provisions.

Clause (1)(g) is derived from s. 87(1)(g) of the 1984 Act.

Clause (1)(h) is a new provision allowing the Lieutenant Governor in Council to prescribe for each region the minimum number of judges of the General Division and of the Provincial Division who must be assigned to that region.

Section 87(1)(a), (d), (f) and (h) of the 1984 Act have been deleted as unnecessary.

Subsection (2) is derived from the last part of s. 4(2) of the 1984 Act.

Subsections [(3) to (4)] re-enact s. 87(2) to (4) of the 1984 Act.

Sections 54-64

54-64. [Repealed 1994, c. 12, s. 19]

PART IV
RULES OF COURT

Section 65

Civil Rules Committee

65.—(1) The committee known as the Civil Rules Committee is continued under the name Civil Rules Committee in English and Comité des régles en matière civile in French.

Composition

(2) The Civil Rules Committee shall be composed of,

(a) the Chief Justice and Associate Chief Justice of Ontario;

(a.1) the Chief Justice and associate chief justices of the Ontario Court;

(a.2) the Chief Judge of the Ontario Court (Provincial Division) or, at his or her designation, an associate chief judge;

(b) two judges of the Court of Appeal, who shall be appointed by the Chief Justice of Ontario;

(c) eight judges of the Ontario Court (General Division), who shall be appointed by the Chief Justice of the Ontario Court;

(d) one judge who was assigned to the Provincial Court (Civil Division) on the 1st day of October, 1989, who shall be appointed by the Chief Justice of the Ontario Court;

(e) the Attorney General or a person designated by the Attorney General;

(f) one law officer of the Crown, who shall be appointed by the Attorney General;

(g) two persons employed in the administration of the courts, who shall be appointed by the Attorney General;

(h) four lawyers, who shall be appointed by The Law Society of Upper Canada;

(i) one lawyer, who shall be appointed by the Chief Justice of Ontario;

(j) four lawyers, who shall be appointed by the Chief Justice of the Ontario Court.

Idem

(3) The Chief Justice of Ontario shall preside over the Civil Rules Committee but, if the Chief Justice of Ontario is absent or so requests, another member designated by the Chief Justice of Ontario shall preside.

Tenure of office
(4) Each of the members of the Civil Rules Committee appointed under clauses (2)(b), (c), (f), (g), (h), (i) and (j) shall hold office for a period of three years and is eligible for reappointment.

Vacancies
(5) Where a vacancy occurs among the members appointed under clause (2)(b), (c), (f), (g), (h), (i) or (j), a new member similarly qualified may be appointed for the remainder of the unexpired term.

Quorum
(6) One-third of the members of the Civil Rules Committee constitutes a quorum. [am. 1994, c. 12, s. 20]

Ministry Comment

1989 Amendments

Bill 2

Subsection [(1), (2)] is derived from s. 89(1) of the 1984 Act. The new Act establishes three separate rules committees. The Civil Rules Committee will make rules of court applicable to civil proceedings. The membership of the Civil Rules Committee is similar to the membership of the previous Rules Committee of the Supreme and District Courts.

Subsection [(3)] replaces s. 89(2) and (3) of the 1984 Act. The new provision permits the Chief Justice of Ontario to designate any member of the Civil Rules Committee to preside over the Committee.

Subsections [(4) and (5)] replace s. 89(4) and (5) of the 1984 Act.

Subsection [(6)] is derived from s. 89(6) of the 1984 Act.

Bill 81

The amended clause [(2)(a)] is consequential on the creation of the office of Associate Chief Justice of the Ontario Court.

The amendments to clauses [(2)(b) and (c)] result from a request by the Court of Appeal to have greater representation on the Civil Rules Committee.

The new clause [(2)(d)] gives effect to a request by the judiciary to have a judge with Small Claims Court experience on the Civil Rules Committee, which is responsible for making rules for the Small Claims Court.

The amendment to subsection [(6)] reduces the quorum of meetings of the committee from a majority to one third. This will make it easier to assemble a meeting if rule changes are needed urgently.

Section 66

Civil Rules
66.—(1) Subject to the approval of the Lieutenant Governor in Council, the Civil Rules Committee may make rules for the Court of Appeal and the Ontario Court (General Division) in relation to the practice and procedure of those courts in all civil proceedings, including family law proceedings.

Idem
(2) The Civil Rules Committee may make rules for the courts described in subsection (1), even though they alter or conform to the substantive law, in relation to,

(a) conduct of proceedings in the courts;

(b) joinder of claims and parties, settlement of claims by or against persons under disability, whether or not a proceeding has been commenced in respect of the claim, the binding effect of orders and representation of parties;

(c) commencement of proceedings, representation of parties by solicitors and service of process in or outside Ontario;

(d) disposition of proceedings without a hearing and its effect and authorizing the Court of Appeal to determine in the first instance a special case arising in a proceeding commenced in the Ontario Court (General Division);

(e) pleadings;

(f) discovery and other forms of disclosure before hearing, including their scope and the admissibility and use of that discovery and disclosure in a proceeding;

(g) examination of witnesses in or out of court;

(h) jurisdiction of masters, including the conferral on masters of any jurisdiction of the Ontario Court (General Division), including jurisdiction under an Act, but not including the trial of actions or jurisdiction conferred by an Act on a judge;

(i) jurisdiction and duties of officers;

(j) motions and applications, including the hearing of motions in the absence of the public and prohibiting a party from making motions and applications without leave;

(k) preservation of rights of parties pending the outcome of litigation, including sale, recovery of possession or preservation of property;

(l) interpleader;

(m) preparation for trial and offers to settle and their legal consequences;

(n) the mode and conduct of trials;

(o) the appointment by the court of independent experts, their remuneration and the admissibility and use of their reports;

(p) the discount rate to be used in determining the amount of an award in respect of future pecuniary damages;

(q) references of proceedings or issues in a proceeding and the powers of a person conducting a reference;

(r) costs of proceedings, including security for costs and a solicitor's liability for or disentitlement to costs;

(s) enforcement of orders and process or obligations under the rules;

(t) the time for and procedure on appeals and stays pending appeal;

(u) payment into and out of court;

(v) the method of calculating the amount to be included in an award of damages to offset any liability for income tax on income from investment of the award;

(w) the prejudgment interest rate with respect to the rate of interest on damages for non-pecuniary loss;

(x) any matter that is referred to in an Act as provided for by rules of court.

Idem

(3) Nothing in subsection (1) or (2) authorizes the making of rules that conflict with an Act, but rules may be made under subsections (1) and (2) supplementing the provisions of an Act in respect of practice and procedure.

Idem

(4) Rules made under clauses (2)(p), (v) and (w) shall be reviewed at least once in every four-year period. [am. 1994, c. 12, s. 21]

Ministry Comment

1989 Amendments

Bill 2

Subsections (1) and (2) are derived from s. 90(1) of the 1984 Act. Under subsection (1), the Civil Rules Committee will make rules in relation to the practice and procedure of the Court of Appeal and the Ontario Court (General Division) in all civil proceedings. The reference to the Ontario Court (General Division) includes the Divisional Court and the Small Claims Court, since they are branches of the General Division.

The list in subsection (2) is the same as the list in s. 90(1) of the 1984 Act, except that s. 90(1)(h) and the portion of s. 90(1)(j) dealing with hours of business for court offices have been deleted as unnecessary.

Subsection (3) re-enacts s. 90(2) of the 1984 Act.

1995 Amendments

Sections 66(2)(w) and 128(2) of the Act are amended to remove references to "discount rate" and substitute references to the prejudgment interest rate.

Section 66(2)(j) of the Act is amended to clarify the authority of the Civil Rules Committee to make rules allowing applications to be dealt with in writing, without counsel appearing.

Cases

Unical Properties v. 784688 Ontario Ltd. (1990), 75 O.R. (2d) 284, 45 C.P.C. (2d) 288, 73 D.L.R. (4th) 761 (Gen. Div.).

This section does not give the Rules Committee the right to alter the common law relating to partnerships. Any change in the substantive law made by rules must be to such portions of the common law as relate to issues such as evidence, practice or procedure.

K Mart Can. Ltd./K Mart Can. Ltée v. Millmink Developments Ltd., 10 C.P.C. (2d) 109, [1986] I.L.R. 1-2102 (Ont. Master), affirmed 56 O.R. (2d) 422, 11 C.P.C. (2d) 243, 24 C.C.L.I. 139, 31 D.L.R. (4th) 135, [1986] I.L.R. 1-2114 (H.C.).

This section, insofar as it delegates to the Rules Committee the power to alter the substantive law, is not *ultra vires*.

Section 67

Family Rules Committee
67.—(1) The committee known as the Family Rules Committee is continued under the name Family Rules Committee in English and Comité des Règles en matière de droit de la famille in French.

Composition
(2) The Family Rules Committee is composed of,
(a) the Chief Justice and Associate Chief Justice of Ontario;
(b) the Chief Justice and associate chief justices of the Ontario Court;
(c) the Chief Judge of the Ontario Court (Provincial Division) or, at his or her designation, an associate chief judge;
(d) one judge of the Court of Appeal, who shall be appointed by the Chief Justice of Ontario;
(e) two judges of the General Division, who shall be appointed by the Chief Justice of the Ontario Court;

(f) two judges of the Family Court, the General Division, or the Provincial Division, who shall be appointed by the Associate Chief Justice (Family Court);

(g) two judges of the Provincial Division, who shall be appointed by the Chief Judge of that division;

(h) the Attorney General or a person designated by the Attorney General;

(i) one law officer of the Crown, who shall be appointed by the Attorney General;

(j) two persons employed in the administration of the courts, who shall be appointed by the Attorney General;

(k) four lawyers, who shall be appointed by The Law Society of Upper Canada;

(l) two lawyers, who shall be appointed by the Associate Chief Justice (Family Court); and

(m) two lawyers, who shall be appointed by the Chief Judge of the Provincial Division.

Idem

(3) The Chief Justice of Ontario shall preside over the Family Rules Committee but, if the Chief Justice of Ontario is absent or so requests, another member designated by the Chief Justice shall preside.

Tenure of office

(4) Each of the members of the Family Rules Committee appointed under clauses (2)(c), (d), (e), (g), (h), (i), (j) and (k) shall hold office for a period of three years and is eligible for reappointment.

Vacancies

(5) Where a vacancy occurs among the members appointed under clause (2)(c), (d), (e), (g), (h), (i), (j) or (k), a new member similarly qualified may be appointed for the remainder of the unexpired term.

Quorum

(6) One-third of the members of the Family Rules Committee constitutes a quorum. [am. 1994, c. 12, s. 22]

Ministry Comment

1989 Amendments

Bill 2

Subsection [(1), (2)] establishes a new rules committee called the Family Rules Committee. Subsections [(3) to (6)] are similar to s. [65(3) to (6)].

Bill 81

The amendment to subsection [(6)] reduces the quorum of the Family Rules Committee from a majority to one third, in order to facilitate the holding of meetings to deal with urgent rule changes.

Section 68

Family Rules

68.—(1) Subject to the approval of the Lieutenant Governor in Council, the Family Rules Committee may make rules for the Court of Appeal, the Ontario Court

(General Division) and the Ontario Court (Provincial Division) in relation to the practice and procedure of those courts in proceedings under statutory provisions set out in the Schedule to Part III (Unified Family Court), except proceedings under the *Young Offenders Act* (Canada).

Idem
(2) Subsections 66(2) and (3) apply with necessary modifications to the Family Rules Committee making rules for the courts described in subsection (1).

May modify civil rules
(3) The rules made by the Family Rules Committee may adopt, modify or exclude the rules made by the Civil Rules Committee.

Rules for Young Offenders Act
(4) Subject to the approval of the Lieutenant Governor in Council, the Family Rules Committee may prepare rules for the purpose of section 68 of the *Young Offenders Act* (Canada) for consideration by the Ontario Court (Provincial Division).

Ministry Comment

1989 Amendments

Bill 2

Under subsection (1), the Family Rules Committee may make rules for the Court of Appeal, the Ontario Court (General Division) and the Ontario Court (Provincial Division) in relation to the practice and procedure of those courts in family law proceedings.

Under subsection (2), the specific powers of the Civil Rules Committee apply with necessary modifications to the Family Rules Committee.

Under subsection (3), the rules made by the Family Rules Committee may adopt, modify or exclude the rules made by the Civil Rules Committee.

Under subsection (4), the Family Rules Committee may prepare rules for the purpose of s. 68 of the federal *Young Offenders Act* for consideration by the Ontario Court (Provincial Division). Section 6 of that Act permits every youth court to establish rules of court to, among other things, regulate the practice and procedure in the court.

Section 69

Criminal Rules Committee
69.—(1) The committee known as the Criminal Rules Committee is continued under the name Criminal Rules Committee in English and Comité des règles en matière criminelle in French.

Idem
(2) The Criminal Rules Committee shall be composed of,
(a) the Chief Justice and Associate Chief Justice of Ontario, the Chief Justice and Associate Chief Justice of the Ontario Court and the Chief Judge and associate chief judges of the Ontario Court (Provincial Division);
(b) one judge of the Court of Appeal, who shall be appointed by the Chief Justice of Ontario;
(c) three judges of the Ontario Court (General Division), who shall be appointed by the Chief Justice of the Ontario Court;
(d) four judges of the Ontario Court (Provincial Division), who shall be appointed by the Chief Judge of the Ontario Court (Provincial Division);

(e) [Repealed 1994, c. 12, s. 23 (effective September 1, 1995)];

(f) the Attorney General or a person designated by the Attorney General;

(g) one law officer of the Crown, who shall be appointed by the Attorney General;

(h) four Crown attorneys, deputy Crown attorneys or assistant Crown attorneys, who shall be appointed by the Attorney General;

(i) two persons employed in court administration, who shall be appointed by the Attorney General;

(j) two lawyers, who shall be appointed by The Law Society of Upper Canada;

(k) one lawyer, who shall be appointed by the Chief Justice of Ontario;

(l) one lawyer, who shall be appointed by the Chief Justice of the Ontario Court; and

(m) two lawyers, who shall be appointed by the Chief Judge of the Provincial Division.

Idem

(3) The Chief Justice of Ontario shall preside over the Criminal Rules Committee but, if the Chief Justice of Ontario is absent or so requests, another member designated by the Chief Justice of Ontario shall preside.

Tenure of office

(4) Each of the members of the Criminal Rules Committee appointed under clauses (2)(b), (c), (d), (e), (g), (h), (i), (j), (k), (l) and (m) shall hold office for a period of three years and is eligible for reappointment.

Vacancies

(5) Where a vacancy occurs among the members appointed under clause (2)(b), (c), (d), (e), (g), (h), (i), (j), (k), (l) or (m), a new member similarly qualified may be appointed for the remainder of the unexpired term.

Quorum

(6) One-third of the members of the Criminal Rules Committee constitutes a quorum. [am. 1994, c. 12, s. 23]

Ministry Comment

1989 Amendments

Bill 2

Subsection [(2)] establishes a new rules committee called the Criminal Rules Committee. Subsections [(3) to (6)] are similar to s. [65(3) to (6)].

Bill 81

The amendment to subsection [(6)] reduces the quorum of the Criminal Rules Committee from a majority to one third, in order to facilitate the holding of meetings to deal with urgent rule changes.

Section 70

Criminal rules

70.—(1) At the request of the Court of Appeal, the Ontario Court (General Division) or the Ontario Court (Provincial Division), the Criminal Rules Committee may prepare rules for the purposes of section 482 of the *Criminal Code* (Canada) for consideration by the relevant court.

Provincial offences rules
(2) Subject to the approval of the Lieutenant Governor in Council, the Criminal Rules Committee may make rules for the Court of Appeal, the Ontario Court (General Division) and the Ontario Court (Provincial Division) in relation to the practice and procedure of those courts in proceedings under the *Provincial Offences Act.*

Idem
(3) The Criminal Rules Committee may make rules under subsection (2),
(a) regulating any matters relating to the practice and procedure of proceedings under the *Provincial Offences Act*;
(b) prescribing forms;
(c) regulating the duties of the employees of the courts;
(d) prescribing and regulating the procedures under any Act that confers jurisdiction under the *Provincial Offences Act* on the Ontario Court (Provincial Division) or a judge or justice of the peace sitting in it;
(e) prescribing any matter relating to proceedings under the *Provincial Offences Act* that is referred to in an Act as provided for by the rules of court. [am. 1994, c. 12, s. 24]

Ministry Comment

1989 Amendments

Bill 2

Subsection (1) permits the Criminal Rules Committee to prepare rules for the purposes of s. 482 of the *Criminal Code* for consideration by the Court of Appeal, the Ontario Court (General Division) and the Ontario Court (Provincial Division). Section 482 of the *Criminal Code* gives rule-making powers to every superior court of criminal jurisdiction, every court of appeal and every court of criminal jurisdiction.

Subsections (2) and (3) give the Criminal Rules Committee power to make rules for the Court of Appeal, the Ontario Court (General Division) and the Ontario Court (Provincial Division) in relation to the practice and procedure of those courts in proceedings under the *Provincial Offences Act.* These provisions replace s. 73 of the 1984 Act, as well as s. 123 of the *Provincial Offences Act.*

1995 Amendments

Section 70 of the Act is amended to deal with legal objections to its wording by removing the requirements of Lieutenant Governor in Council approval of criminal rules and to expressly recognize that the Criminal Rules Committee may deal with criminal rules only at the request of a court.

PART V

COURTS ADMINISTRATION

Section 71

Attorney General's administrative responsibility
71. The Attorney General shall superintend all matters connected with the administration of the courts, other than matters that are assigned by law to the judiciary.

Ministry Comment

Original Act

This provision expresses the Attorney General's responsibility for the administration of the courts. It represents a specific aspect of the Attorney General's responsibilities under s. 5(c) of the *Ministry of the Attorney General Act*.

Cases

Smiley v. Smiley (1983), 39 C.P.C. 309 (Ont. H.C.).

Whether or not directives issued by the Attorney General are valid and binding is to be determined on an individual basis depending on whether they are "judicial" or "administrative".

Section 72

Ontario Courts Advisory Council

72.—(1) The council known as the Ontario Courts Advisory Council is continued under the name Ontario Courts Advisory Council in English and Conseil consultatif des tribunaux de l'Ontario in French.

Same
(2) The Ontario Courts Advisory Council is composed of,

(a) the Chief Justice of Ontario, who shall preside, and the Associate Chief Justice of Ontario;

(b) the Chief Justice and the associate chief justices of the Ontario Court;

(c) the Chief Judge and the associate chief judges of the Ontario Court (Provincial Division);

(d) the regional senior judges of the General Division and of the Provincial Division;

(e) the senior judge for the Unified Family Court; and

(f) the Co-ordinator of Justices of the Peace. [Clause 72(2)(e) of the Act is repealed on a day to be named by proclamation of the Lieutenant Governor (1994, c. 12, s. 25(2)). Clause 72(2)(f) of the Act is repealed on September 1, 1995 (1994, c. 12, s. 25(3)).]

Mandate
(3) The Ontario Courts Advisory Council shall meet to consider any matter relating to the administration of the courts that is referred to it by the Attorney General or that it considers appropriate on its own initiative, and shall make recommendations on the matter to the Attorney General and to its members. [am. 1994, c. 12, s. 25]

Ministry Comment

1989 Amendments

Bill 81

At the request of the chiefs of the existing courts, the Ontario Courts Advisory Council, originally dropped by Bill 2, has been restored. It has also been expanded to include the regional senior judges, the senior judge for the Unified Family Court and the Coordinator of Justices of the Peace.

Section 73

Ontario Courts Management Advisory Committee

73.—(1) The committee known as the Ontario Courts Management Advisory Committee is continued under the name Ontario Courts Management Advisory Committee in English and Comité consultatif de gestion des tribunaux de l'Ontario in French.

Same

(2) The Ontario Courts Management Advisory Committee is composed of,

(a) the Chief Justice and Associate Chief Justice of Ontario, the Chief Justice and associate chief justices of the Ontario Court, and the Chief Judge and associate chief judges of the Ontario Court (Provincial Division);

(b) the Attorney General, the Deputy Attorney General, the Assistant Deputy Attorney General responsible for courts administration, the Assistant Deputy Attorney General responsible for criminal law and two other public servants chosen by the Attorney General;

(c) three lawyers appointed by The Law Society of Upper Canada and three lawyers appointed by the County and District Law Presidents' Association; and

(d) not more than six other persons, appointed by the Attorney General with the concurrence of the judges mentioned in clause (a) and the lawyers appointed under clause (c).

Who presides

(3) The following persons shall preside over meetings of the Committee, by rotation at intervals fixed by the Committee:

1. A judge mentioned in clause (2)(a), selected by the judges mentioned in that clause.

2. The Attorney General, or a person mentioned in clause (2)(b) and designated by the Attorney General.

3. A lawyer appointed under clause (2)(c), selected by the lawyers appointed under that clause.

4. A person appointed under clause (2)(d), selected by the persons appointed under that clause.

Function of Committee

(4) The function of the Committee is to consider and recommend to the relevant bodies or authorities policies and procedures to promote the better administration of justice and the effective use of human and other resources in the public interest. [am. 1994, c. 12, s. 26]

Ministry Comment

1989 Amendments

Bill 2

Section 92 of the 1984 Act gives statutory recognition to the Ontario Courts Advisory Council, a body consisting of the senior judges of all the courts. The new s. [73] replaces this provision with a provision creating the Ontario Courts Management Advisory Committee. The Committee, which will consist of the senior judicial officers in the province and representatives of the Ministry of the Attorney General, the legal profession and the public, will monitor the operation of the courts and recommend policies and procedures to promote the better administration of justice and the effective use of human and other resources.

Section 74

Regions
74.—(1) Ontario is divided into the regions prescribed under subsection (2), for administrative purposes related to the administration of justice in the province.

Regulations
(2) The Lieutenant Governor in Council may make regulations prescribing regions for the purpose of this Act and prescribing the municipality in each region where the offices of the regional senior judges, the regional director of courts administration and the regional director of Crown attorneys are to be located. [am. 1994, c. 12, s. 27]

Ministry Comment

1989 Amendments

Bill 2

Section [74] is a new provision that permits Ontario to be divided, for judicial purposes, into regions prescribed by regulation. These regions will replace the territorial divisions now established for judicial purposes by s. 1 of the *Territorial Division Act*.

The new division of Ontario for judicial purposes may have some effect on the place of trial in criminal proceedings. The common law rule is that criminal proceedings should be tried in the territorial division where the offence occurred. If the case of *R. v. Simons* (1976), 30 C.C.C. (2d) 162 (Ont. C.A.) is still the law of Ontario, the existing *Territorial Division Act* has the effect of requiring most proceedings to be tried in the county or district where the offence occurred. The re-division of Ontario for judicial purposes in s. [74] would have the effect of permitting criminal proceedings to be tried anywhere in the region where the offence occurred. While no significant change in practice is expected, this greater flexibility will permit some cases in the busier counties to be heard in less busy nearby locations. It should be noted that, with the creation of the province-wide District Court of Ontario and Provincial Court (Criminal Division) by the 1984 *Courts of Justice Act*, the law as stated in *R. v. Simons* may have changed. It may be that the existing law already permits criminal proceedings to be brought anywhere in the province (see *Re Falkner and the Queen* (1978), 40 C.C.C. (2d) 117 (B.C. C.A.)).

There are still a variety of statutory provisions or rules of court that require certain kinds of proceedings to be heard in a particular county or district. For example, s. 113 of the *Landlord and Tenant Act* requires an application for a writ of possession to be made in the county or district where the premises are situate. These proceedings will continue to be heard in those counties and districts (see also [s. 151]).

Bill 81

This amendment [to subsection (2)] adds to the regulation making power concerning regions the power to prescribe where the regional centre will be for the regional senior judges, the regional director of courts administration and the regional director of Crown attorneys.

1995 Amendments

Section 74 of the Act is amended to provide that the regions created in the regulations under the Act are administrative only and that Ontario is a single jurisdictional unit.

Cross-Reference: See R.R.O. 1990, Reg. 186 and Map of Regions.

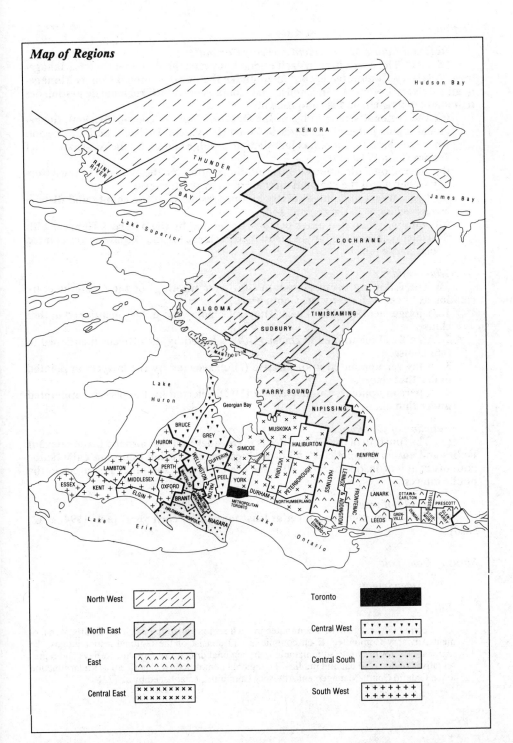

Map of Regions

Section 75

Regional Courts Management Advisory Committee

75.—(1) The committee in each region known as the Regional Courts Management Advisory Committee is continued under the name Regional Courts Management Advisory Committee in English and Comité consultatif régional de gestion des tribunaux in French, and is composed of,

(a) the regional senior judge of the Ontario Court (General Division), the regional senior judge of the Ontario Court (Provincial Division) and, in a region where the Family Court has jurisdiction, a judge chosen by the Associate Chief Justice (Family Court);

(b) the regional director of courts administration for the Ministry of the Attorney General and the regional director of Crown attorneys;

(c) two lawyers appointed jointly by the presidents of the county and district law associations in the region; and

(d) not more than two other persons, appointed by the Attorney General with the concurrence of the judges mentioned in clause (a) and the lawyers appointed under clause (c).

Who presides

(2) The following persons shall preside over meetings of the Committee, by rotation at intervals fixed by the Committee:

1. A judge mentioned in clause (1)(a), selected by the judges mentioned in that clause.

2. An official mentioned in clause (1)(b), selected by the officials mentioned in that clause.

3. A lawyer appointed under clause (1)(c), selected by the lawyers appointed under that clause.

4. A person appointed under clause (1)(d), selected by the persons appointed under that clause.

Function of Committee

(3) The function of the Committee is to consider and recommend to the relevant bodies and authorities policies and procedures for the region to promote the better administration of justice and the effective use of human and other resources in the public interest.

Frequency of meetings

(4) The Committee shall meet at least four times each year. [am. 1994, c. 12, s. 28]

Ministry Comment

1989 Amendments

Bill 2

Section [75] establishes a committee in each region called the Regional Courts Management Advisory Committee. Each committee will consist of the regional senior judges, the regional director of courts administration, the regional director of Crown attorneys and representatives of the local bar and public. The regional committees will perform a similar function to the Ontario Courts Management Advisory Committee established by s. [73].

Bill 81

At the request of the Unified Family Court judges, the amendment [to clause (1)(a)] adds their senior judge to the Regional Courts Management Advisory Committee.

Section 76

Powers of chief or regional senior judge

76.—(1) The powers and duties of a judge who has authority to supervise and direct the sittings and the assignment of the judicial duties of his or her court include the following:

1. Determining the sittings of the court.
2. Assigning judges to the sittings.
3. Assigning cases and other judicial duties to individual judges.
4. Determining the sitting schedules and places of sittings for individual judges.
5. Determining the total annual, monthly and weekly workload of individual judges.
6. Preparing trial lists and assigning courtrooms, to the extent necessary to control the determination of who is assigned to hear particular cases.

Powers in respect of masters

(2) Subsection (1) applies with necessary modifications in respect of supervising and directing the sittings and assigning the judicial duties of masters.

Ministry Comment

1989 Amendments

Bill 2

Section [76] is intended to spell out more comprehensively the powers of judges who have authority to supervise sittings and assign judicial duties. The new provision incorporates the powers set out in s. 93 of the 1984 Act.

Bill 81

At the request of the judiciary, the amendment [to para. 3 of subsection (1)] makes it clear that a judicial manager has a right to assign not only cases, but also other judicial duties.

Cases

General Host Corp. v. Chemalloy Minerals Ltd., [1972] 3 O.R. 142, 27 D.L.R. (3d) 561 (H.C.). Discussion of use of court facilities by unofficial court reporters.

Section 77

Appointment of court officers and staff

77.—(1) Registrars, sheriffs, court clerks, assessment officers and any other administrative officers and employees that are considered necessary for the administration of the courts in Ontario may be appointed under the *Public Service Act*.

Exercise of powers of registrar, sheriff, etc.

(2) A power or duty given to a registrar, sheriff, court clerk, bailiff, assessment officer, Small Claims Court referee or official examiner under an Act, regulation or

rule of court may be exercised or performed by a person or class of persons to whom the power or duty has been assigned by the Deputy Attorney General or a person designated by the Deputy Attorney General.

Idem

(3) Subsection (2) applies in respect of an Act, regulation or rule of court made under the authority of the Legislature or of the Parliament of Canada. [am. 1994, c. 12, s. 29]

Ministry Comment

1989 Amendments

Bill 2

Section 94 of the 1984 Act permits employees of the courts to be appointed under the *Public Service Act*. However, there were some officials who were appointed by the Lieutenant Governor in Council. Sections 21, 37 and 48 and s. 86(1) to (3) of the 1984 Act provided for the appointment by the Lieutenant Governor in Council of various registrars and court clerks. Under ss. 103(1) and 104(1) of the 1984 Act, many of these officials were also assessment officers and official examiners. The *Sheriffs Act* also provided for sheriffs to be appointed by the Lieutenant Governor in Council. In future, it is intended that all these officials will be appointed under s. 94 of the 1984 Act as public servants.

Two new subsections are added to s. [77] to permit designated court officials to continue to perform the functions of registrars, sheriffs, court clerks, bailiffs, assessment officers and official examiners. Subsection (2) indicates that, where a power or duty is given to one of these officials, it may be exercised or performed by any person or class of persons designated by the Deputy Attorney General. In practice, the power to make these designations will be delegated to the senior courts administration officials in the Ministry of the Attorney General.

The new subsection (3) makes clear that the ability to designate court employees to perform functions given to registrars and other officials also applies to functions given by federal law.

Bill 81

The amended subsection (1) lists the principal administrative officers of the courts specifically, as the other statutory provisions creating these officers have been repealed by Bills 2 and 3.

The amended subsection (2) adds a reference to the bailiffs of the Small Claims Court, as these officers have duties assigned by the rules of that court and a reorganization of the duties of the officers of the Small Claims Court may take place in the coming year as the jurisdiction of the court is increased.

1995 Amendments

Section 77(2) of the Act is amended to allow the powers and duties of a Small Claims Court referee to be assigned to employees by the Deputy Attorney General or his/her designee.

Section 78

Direction of court staff

78.—(1) In matters that are assigned by law to the judiciary, registrars, court clerks, court reporters, interpreters and other court staff shall act at the direction of the chief justice or chief judge of the court.

Idem

(2) Court personnel referred to in subsection (1) who are assigned to and present in a courtroom shall act at the direction of the presiding judge or master while the court is in session.

Ministry Comment

Original Act

This provision requires court staff assigned to and present in the courtroom to act at the direction of the presiding judge or master while the court is in session.

Section 79

Destruction of documents
79. Documents and other material that are no longer required in a court office shall be disposed of in accordance with the directions of the Deputy Attorney General, subject to the approval of,
(a) in the Court of Appeal, the Chief Justice of Ontario;
(b) in the Ontario Court (General Division), the Chief Justice of the Ontario Court;
(c) in the Ontario Court (Provincial Division), the Chief Judge of the Provincial Division;
(d) in the Unified Family Court, the Senior Judge for the Unified Family Court.

Ministry Comment

1989 Amendments

Bill 2

Section [79] replaces s. 101(4) of the 1984 Act.

PART VI
JUDGES AND OFFICERS

Section 80

Oath of office
80. Every judge or officer of a court in Ontario, including a deputy judge of the Small Claims Court, shall, before entering on the duties of office, take and sign the following oath or affirmation in either the English or French language:

I solemnly swear (affirm) that I will faithfully, impartially and to the best of my skill and knowledge execute the duties of .... So help me God.
(Omit this line in an affirmation)

[am. 1994, c. 12, s. 30]

Ministry Comment

1995 Amendments

Section 80 of the Act is amended to include a requirement that Small Claims Court deputy judges take an oath of office to act impartially.

Section 81

Persona designata abolished.
81. Where an adjudicative function is given by an Act to a judge or officer of a court in Ontario, the jurisdiction shall be deemed to be given to the court.

Ministry Comment

Original Act

Provincial statutes often gave jurisdiction to "a judge of the county or district court" or "a judge of the Supreme Court", instead of simply referring to "the court". This form of language arose particularly frequently in statutes that can be traced to the latter part of the 19th century. Over the years, provisions giving jurisdiction to "a judge" instead of "a court" generated a great deal of litigation on the issue of whether the judge was to act as the court or as a *persona designata*. In many cases, it was decided that the judge was acting as *persona designata*.

Where a judge acted as *persona designata*, several consequences followed. Since the judge was not acting as the court, the rules of court did not apply, the powers of the court did not apply and no appeal could be taken. These consequences resulted in considerable confusion. Some of the most serious drawbacks of the *persona designata* concept were dealt with in the *Judges' Orders Enforcement Act*, R.S.O. 1980, c. 222. That Act provided for enforcement of the orders of a judge acting as *persona designata*, for the judge to have jurisdiction to award costs, and for an appeal from the judge's order. However, the Act left many other issues unresolved.

The concept of judges acting as *persona designata* had been severely criticized. In recent years, a series of Supreme Court of Canada decisions dramatically altered the law of *persona designata*: *Herman v. Dep. A.G. Can.*, [1979] 1 S.C.R. 729, 5 C.R. (3d) 242, [1978] C.T.C. 744, 78 D.T.C. 6456, 91 D.L.R. (3d) 3, 23 N.R. 235; *Re Residential Tenancies Act, Ont.*, [1981] 1 S.C.R. 714, 123 D.L.R. (3d) 554, 37 N.R. 158; *Min. of Indian Affairs and Northern Development v. Ranville*, [1982] 2 S.C.R. 518, [1983] 1 C.N.L.R. 12, 139 D.L.R. (3d) 1, [1983] R.D.J. 16, 44 N.R. 616. These cases established the principle that a judge will be acting as *persona designata* only if there is an express provision to that effect. This test effectively abolished the concept of *persona designata*. To eliminate any lingering doubts, s. [81] of the *Courts of Justice Act* provides that, where an adjudicative function is given by statute to a judge or officer of a court, the jurisdiction shall be deemed to be given to the court.

Section 82

Liability of judges

82. Every judge of a court in Ontario including a judge presiding in the Small Claims Court and a deputy judge of that court and every master has the same immunity from liability as a judge of the Ontario Court (General Division). [am. 1994, c. 12, s. 32]

Ministry Comment

1995 Amendments

Section 82 of the Act is amended to clarify that Small Claims Court judges and deputy judges have the same immunity as any other judge.

Section 83

Compensation for statutory duties

83.—(1) Every judge who was a judge of the Supreme Court or of the District Court before the 1st day of September, 1990 shall be paid out of the Consolidated Revenue Fund the annual sum of $3,000, payable quarterly, as compensation for the services the judge is called on to render by any Act of the Legislature in addition to his or her ordinary duties.

Supernumerary judges
(2) No payment shall be made under subsection (1) to a judge who becomes a supernumerary judge after this subsection comes into force. [am. 1991 (Vol. 2), c. 46, s. 1].

Ministry Comment

1989 Amendments

Bill 2

The 1984 s. 99 provided that every judge of the Supreme Court and of the District Court would be paid $3,000 annually by the province for services the judge is called on to render in addition to his or her ordinary duties. Section 57(2) of the federal *Judges Act* permits these payments, although it indicates that these payments cannot be made for acting on a commission or on an inquiry. In 1983, the federal Commission on Judges' Salaries and Benefits recommended that the four provinces which make these payments be asked to discontinue them. The new s. [83] will continue the $3,000 payments to judges who were judges of the Supreme Court or District Court, but no payments will be made to future appointees.

Section 84

Extra-judicial services
84.—(1) A judge of the Court of Appeal or the Ontario Court (General Division) may act as a conciliator, arbitrator or referee or on a commission of inquiry under an Act of the Legislature or under an agreement made under any such Act.

Remuneration
(2) A judge acting under subsection (1) shall not receive any remuneration but shall be reimbursed for reasonable travelling and other expenses incurred while so acting.

Ministry Comment

1989 Amendments

Bill 2

Section [84] meshes with s. 56(1)(b) of the federal *Judges Act*. The amendment [to subsection (1)] reflects the new names of the federally appointed courts.

Section 85

Judges' gowns
85. The Lieutenant Governor in Council may make regulations respecting the form of the gown to be worn in court by all judges appointed after the 1st day of September, 1990.

Ministry Comment

1989 Amendments

Bill 2

Section [85] is a new provision that permits the Lieutenant Governor in Council to prescribe the form of the gown to be worn in court by judges appointed after the section comes into force.

To reduce the hierarchial distinctions between the courts, it is intended that one type of gown will be worn by all judges. The section, however, does permit judges appointed before the selection comes into force to continue to wear the variety of gowns now in use.

Section 86

How certain judges to be addressed

86.—(1) Every judge of the Ontario Court (General Division) and the Unified Family Court may be addressed as "Your Honour" or as "(*Mr. or Madam*) Justice (*naming the judge*)" in English or as "Votre Honneur" ou "(M. ou Mme) le/la Juge (*nom de juge*)" in French.

Idem

(2) A judge appointed to the High Court of Justice before the 1st day of September, 1990 may elect to be addressed according to the practice in existence before that day.

Subs. (1) amended

(3) On a day to be named by proclamation of the Lieutenant Governor, subsection (1) is amended by striking out "Ontario Court (General Division)" in the first and second lines and substituting "Ontario Court of Justice".

Subs. (1) amended

(4) On a day to be named by proclamation of the Lieutenant Governor, subsection (1) is amended by striking out "and the Unified Family Court" in the second and third lines. [am. 1994, c. 12, s. 33]

Ministry Comment

1989 Amendments

Bill 2

Subsection (1) provides that every judge of the Ontario Court of Justice and the Unified Family Court may be addressed as "Your Honour" or as "Mr. or Madam Justice   ".

Subsection (2) permits judges appointed to the High Court before the section comes into force to elect to be addressed as "My Lord", "My Lady", "Mr. Justice   " or "Madam Justice   ".

Bill 81

The effect of the amendment [addition of subsection (3)] is to permit all judges of the Ontario Court General Division and Provincial Division to be called "Mr. Justice" or "Mme. Justice" on a date to be named by proclamation.

Section 87

Masters

87.—(1) Every person who was a master of the Supreme Court before the 1st day of September, 1990 is a master of the Ontario Court (General Division).

Jurisdiction

(2) Every master has the jurisdiction conferred by the rules of court in proceedings in the General Division.

Application of ss. 44 to 51.12
(3) Sections 44 to 51.12 apply to masters, with necessary modifications, in the same manner as to provincial judges.

Exception
(4) The power of the Chief Judge of the Provincial Division referred to in subsections 44(1) and (2) shall be exercised by the Chief Justice of the Ontario Court with respect to masters.

Same
(5) The right of a master to continue in office under subsection 47(3) is subject to the approval of the Chief Justice of the Ontario Court, who shall make the decision according to criteria developed by himself or herself and approved by the Judicial Council.

Same
(6) When the Judicial Council deals with a complaint against a master, the following special provisions apply:
  1. One of the members of the Judicial Council who is a provincial judge shall be replaced by a master. The Chief Judge of the Provincial Division shall determine which judge is to be replaced and the Chief Justice of the Ontario Court shall designate the master who is to replace the judge.
  2. Complaints shall be referred to the Chief Justice of the Ontario Court rather than to the Chief Judge of the Provincial Division.
  3. Subcommittee recommendations with respect to interim suspension shall be made to the appropriate regional senior judge of the General Division, to whom subsections 51.4(10) and (11) apply with necessary modifications.

Same
(7) Section 51.9, which deals with standards of conduct for provincial judges, section 51.10, which deals with their continuing education, and section 51.11, which deals with evaluation of their performance, apply to masters only if the Chief Justice of the Ontario Court consents.

Compensation
(8) Masters shall receive the same salaries, pension benefits, other benefits and allowances as provincial judges receive under the framework agreement set out in the Schedule to this Act. [am. 1994, c. 12, s. 34]

Ministry Comment

1989 Amendments

Bill 2

Subsection (1) replaces s. 20(1) and (2) of the 1984 Act. No new masters will be appointed. Existing masters will continue to perform their functions but, ultimately, all judicial duties of the masters will be performed by judges of the Ontario Court (General Division).

Subsection (2) is derived from s. 20(3) of the 1984 Act.

Subsection (3) is derived from s. 20(11) of the 1984 Act.

Section 20(8) to (10) of the 1984 Act, which deal with the office of Senior Master, are not re-enacted. In future, supervision and direction over the sittings of the masters and the assignment of their judicial duties will be the responsibility of the Chief Judge of the Ontario Court and the regional senior judges of the Ontario Court (General Division) (see s. 13(1) and (2)).

Section 87.1

Small Claims Court judges
87.1.—(1) This section applies to provincial judges who were assigned to the Provincial Court (Civil Division) immediately before September 1, 1990.

Full and part-time service
(2) The power of the Chief Judge of the Provincial Division referred to in subsections 44(1) and (2) shall be exercised by the Chief Justice of the Ontario Court with respect to provincial judges to whom this section applies.

Continuation in office
(3) The right of a provincial judge to whom this section applies to continue in office under subsection 47(3) is subject to the approval of the Chief Justice of the Ontario Court, who shall make the decision according to criteria developed by himself or herself and approved by the Judicial Council.

Complaints
(4) When the Judicial Council deals with a complaint against a provincial judge to whom this section applies, the following special provisions apply:
1. One of the members of the Judicial Council who is a provincial judge shall be replaced by a provincial judge who was assigned to the Provincial Court (Civil Division) immediately before September 1, 1990. The Chief Judge of the Provincial Division shall determine which judge is to be replaced and the Chief Justice of the Ontario Court shall designate the judge who is to replace that judge.
2. Complaints shall be referred to the Chief Justice of the Ontario Court rather than to the Chief Judge of the Provincial Division.
3. Subcommittee recommendations with respect to interim suspension shall be made to the appropriate regional senior judge of the General Division, to whom subsections 51.4(10) and (11) apply with necessary modifications.

Application of ss. 51.9, 51.10, 51.11
(5) Section 51.9, which deals with standards of conduct for provincial judges, section 51.10, which deals with their continuing education, and section 51.11, which deals with evaluation of their performance, apply to provincial judges to whom this section applies only if the Chief Justice of the Ontario Court consents. [en. 1994, c. 12, s. 35]

Section 88

Regulations
88. The Lieutenant Governor in Council may make regulations,
(a) prescribing the officer or employee to whom money paid into the Ontario Court (General Division) shall be paid and providing for the vesting of that money and any securities in which that money is invested in that officer or employee;
(b) governing the management and investment of money paid into a court;
(c) providing for the payment of interest on money paid into a court and fixing the rate of interest so paid;
(d) prescribing the officer or employee in whose name mortgages and other securities taken under an order of the Ontario Court (General Division) and

instruments taken as security in respect of a proceeding in the Ontario Court
(General Division) shall be taken;

(e) respecting the deposit of the mortgages, securities and instruments and the
duty or obligation, if any, in respect of them of the officer or employee in whose
name they are taken.

Ministry Comment

1989 Amendments

*[Authors' Note: Bill 2 originally contained two sections — 101a and 101b — dealing with the
payment of money in and out of court. Bill 81 repealed both of these sections and introduced a
new s. [88]. The Ministry Comment from both Bills is reproduced here.]*

Bill 2

Section 101a is derived from s. 22 of the 1984 Act. The name of the Accountant is changed
to the Accountant of the Ontario Court.

Section 22(1) and (2) of the 1984 Act have been deleted. There is no need to continue the
Accountant as a corporation sole. In future, the Accountant will be appointed under s. [76] of
the *Courts of Justice Act* as a public servant.

Section 101b re-enacts s. 23 of the 1984 Act.

Bill 81

The amendments provide for the making of regulations dealing with the payment of money
into and out of court and the investment of that money. Regulations rather than statutory
provisions permit greater flexibility as reorganization of the offices of the courts occurs over
the coming months.

Section 89

Children's Lawyer

**89.—(1) The Lieutenant Governor in Council, on the recommendation of the
Attorney General, may appoint a Children's Lawyer for Ontario.**

Qualification

**(2) No person shall be appointed as Children's Lawyer unless he or she has been
a member of the bar of one of the provinces or territories of Canada for at least ten
years or, for an aggregate of at least ten years, has been a member of such a bar or
served as a judge anywhere in Canada after being a member of such a bar.**

Duties

**(3) Where required to do so by an Act or the rules of court, the Children's
Lawyer shall act as litigation guardian of a minor or other person who is a party to
a proceeding.**

Same

**(3.1) At the request of a court, the [Children's Lawyer] may act as the legal
representative of a minor or other person who is not a party to a proceeding.**

Costs

**(4) The same costs as are payable to litigation guardians are payable to the
Children's Lawyer and costs recovered by the Children's Lawyer shall be paid into
the Consolidated Revenue Fund.**

Security for costs

(5) The Children's Lawyer shall not be required to give security for costs in any proceeding.

Mortgages held by Accountant

(6) Where a person for whom the Children's Lawyer has acted is interested in a mortgage held by the Accountant of the Ontario Court, the Children's Lawyer shall take reasonable care to ensure that,

(a) money payable on the mortgage is promptly paid;

(b) the mortgaged property is kept properly insured; and

(c) taxes on the mortgaged property are promptly paid.

Payment into court

(7) Money received by the Children's Lawyer on behalf of a person for whom he or she acts shall, unless the court orders otherwise, be paid into court to the credit of the person entitled.

Assessment of costs

(8) Where the amount payable into court under subsection (7) is to be ascertained by the deduction of unassessed costs from a fund, the Children's Lawyer may require the costs to be assessed forthwith.

Audit

(9) The Provincial Auditor shall examine and report on the accounts and financial transactions of the Children's Lawyer. [am. 1994, c. 12, s. 37; c. 27, s. 43]

Ministry Comment

Original Act

Subsection (3) is intended to restate, in the terminology of the new Act and Rules, the provisions of s. 109(2) of the *Judicature Act.*

Subsection (6) is derived from former Rule 724, which will not appear in the new Rules.

Subsection (7) is derived from former Rule 737(2), which will not appear in the new Rules.

Subsection (8) is derived from former Rule 737(6), which will not appear in the new Rules.

1989 Amendments

Bill 2

The amendment to subsection (3) replaces a reference to the Rules of Civil Procedure with a reference to rules of court. Under Part IV it is conceivable that both the rules made by the Civil Rules Committee and the rules made by the Family Rules Committee will require the Official Guardian to act as litigation guardian.

1995 Amendments

Section 89 of the Act is amended to state the qualifications for appointment as Children's Lawyer in the same way as the qualifications for appointment as a provincial judge and to give the Children's Lawyer the power to decline to act as litigation guardian of a minor who is not party to a case. [*Authors' Comment:* "Children's Lawyer" is the new name for the former "Official Guardian".]

Cases

Re Knoch (1979), 25 O.R. (2d) 312, 9 R.F.L. (2d) 395 (H.C.).

Discussion of basis of appointment of Official Guardian.

Section 90

Assessment officers
90.—(1) The Lieutenant Governor in Council, on the recommendation of the Attorney General, may appoint assessment officers.

Idem
(2) Every master is an assessment officer.

Jurisdiction
(3) Every assessment officer has jurisdiction to assess costs in a proceeding in any court.

Appeal from assessment of costs before tribunal
(4) Where costs of a proceeding before a tribunal other than a court are to be assessed by an assessment officer,
    (a) the rules of court governing the procedure on an assessment of costs apply with necessary modifications; and
    (b) an appeal lies to the Ontario Court (General Division) from a certificate of assessment of the costs if an objection was served in respect of the issue appealed in accordance with the rules of court.

Ministry Comment

Original Act

Taxing officers were formerly appointed under s. 83 of the *Judicature Act*, a general provision dealing with the appointment of officers of the Supreme Court. Subsection (1) gives specific statutory recognition to this office. It provides that the Registrar of the Supreme Court, each master, local registrar and deputy local registrar, and the clerk of the Unified Family Court is an assessment officer. The new Act and Rules replace the term "taxing officer" with the more modern term "assessment officer".

Subsection (4) is a new provision that is intended to provide an appeal from decisions of an assessment officer in a proceeding outside the Supreme Court or the District Court. For example, the Ontario Energy Board and the Ontario Municipal Board both have authority to refer assessments of costs to assessment officers.

1989 Amendments

Bill 2

Subsection (1) is derived from s. 103(2) of the 1984 Act.
Subsection (2) is derived from s. 103(1) of the 1984 Act. The other officials mentioned in the former provision will be able to perform duties as assessment officers under the new s. 94(2).
Subsection (3) makes clear that assessment officers may assess costs in a proceeding in any court. A similar provision now exists for official examiners in s. [91].
Subsection (4) re-enacts s. 103(4) of the 1984 Act.

Section 91

Officers of court
91. Every official examiner and deputy official examiner is an officer of every court in Ontario.

Ministry Comment

1989 Amendments

Bill 2

The repeal of s. 104(1) of the 1984 Act is permitted by the new s. [77(2)], which will permit the officials referred to in subsection (1) to continue to act as official examiners.

The amendment to subsection (2) is consequential on the repeal of subsection (1).

Bill 81

The repeal of subsections (2) and (3) gives effect to a policy decision to phase out the office of official examiner. The incumbent official examiners who are not registrars will continue to hold their office and carry out their duties until they retire. Registrars will continue to offer the service of official examiner for the time being, as long as there is a need. It is expected that private court reporting services will compete for the business of out of court examinations and will eventually supplant all of the official examiners.

Cases

Pond v. Regional Assess. Comm., Region No. 9 (1985), 52 O.R. (2d) 165, 5 C.P.C. (2d) 224, 31 M.P.L.R. 89 (H.C.).

Discussion of status of special examiner.

Avery v. Avery, [1954] O.W.N. 364 (H.C.).

An official examiner may file a certificate rather than an affidavit on a motion. Discussion of the powers of an official examiner.

Smith v. Walnut Dairy Ltd., [1945] O.W.N. 801 (H.C.).

The official examiner's office is not a public court and he has a discretion as to who may be present at an examination.

Section 92

Administration of oaths

92. Every officer of a court has, for the purposes of any matter before him or her, power to administer oaths and affirmations and to examine parties and witnesses.

Section 93

Money held by officer of court

93. Money or property vested in or held by an officer of a court shall be deemed to be vested in the officer in trust for Her Majesty, subject to being disposed of in accordance with any Act, rule of court or order.

Section 94

Disposition of court fees

94.—(1) All fees payable to a salaried officer of a court in respect of a proceeding in the court shall be paid into the Consolidated Revenue Fund.

Exception

(2) Subsection (1) does not apply to fees payable to court reporters under the *Administration of Justice Act*.

PART VII
COURT PROCEEDINGS

Section 95

Application of Part
95.—(1) This Part applies to civil proceedings in courts of Ontario.

Application to criminal proceedings
(2) Sections 109 (constitutional questions) and 123 (giving decisions), section 125 and subsection 126(5) (language of proceedings) and sections 132 (judge sitting on appeal), 136 (prohibition against photography at court hearing) and 146 (where procedures not provided) also apply to proceedings under the *Criminal Code* (Canada), except in so far as they are inconsistent with that Act.

Application to provincial offences
(3) Sections 109 (constitutional questions), 125, 126 (language of proceedings), 132 (judge sitting on appeal), 136 (prohibition against photography at court hearings), 144 (arrest and committal warrants enforceable by police) and 146 (where procedures not provided) also apply to proceedings under the *Provincial Offences Act* and, for the purpose, a reference in one of those sections to a judge includes a justice of the peace presiding in the Ontario Court (Provincial Division).

Ministry Comment

1989 Amendments

Bill 2

Section [95] indicates that Part [VII] of the *Courts of Justice Act*, applies to civil proceedings in all courts. Under subsection (2), certain provisions in that Part are also applicable to proceedings under the *Criminal Code.*, The amendment to subsection (2) indicates that the new s. [146] will apply to *Criminal Code*, proceedings.

Subsection (3) provides that certain provisions in Part [VII] apply to proceedings under the *Provincial Offences Act.*, The amendment to subsection (3) makes clear that the new s. [146] also applies to provincial offences proceedings. The amendment also changes a reference to the Provincial Offences Court to be a reference to the Ontario Court (Provincial Division).

COMMON LAW AND EQUITY

Section 96

Rules of law and equity
96.—(1) Courts shall administer concurrently all rules of equity and the common law.

Rules of equity to prevail
(2) Where a rule of equity conflicts with a rule of the common law, the rule of equity prevails.

Jurisdiction for equitable relief
(3) Only the Court of Appeal and the Ontario Court (General Division), exclusive of the Small Claims Court, may grant equitable relief, unless otherwise provided. [am. 1994, c. 12, s. 37]

Ministry Comment

Original Act

This section revises the statutory provisions dealing with law and equity. It is similar in some respects to s. 49 of the English *Supreme Court Act 1981*, 1981 (U.K.), c. 54. The section is intended to simplify the old provisions dealing with law and equity.

Subsection (1) replaces paras. 1, 3, 4, 5 and 7 of s. 18 of the *Judicature Act.* These paragraphs stated that courts shall recognize all claims and defences, whether arising under the common law or equity, asserted by both plaintiffs and defendants. This is implicit in the statement that courts shall administer concurrently all rules of equity and the common law.

1995 Amendments

Sections 96(3) and 97 of the Act are amended to make it clear that the Small Claims Court cannot give equitable relief or a declaratory judgment.

Cases

Ontario (Director of Family Support Plan) v. Freyseng (1994), 18 O.R. (3d) 361, 4 R.F.L. (4th) 454 (Prov. Div.), affirmed 21 O.R. (3d) 642 (C.A.).

The Ontario Court (Provincial Division) does not have jurisdiction to grant equitable relief, including a claim for equitable set-off.

LeMesurier v. Andrus (1986), 54 O.R. (2d) 1, 38 R.P.R. 183, 25 D.L.R. (4th) 424, 12 O.A.C. 299 (C.A.), leave to appeal to S.C.C. refused 63 O.R. (2d) x, 74 N.R. 239, 21 O.A.C. 239n.

Where specific performance with an abatement is available the plaintiff must equally be entitled to the common law remedy of damages with an abatement for a deficiency in title.

McGee (Irwin) v. Irwin (1986), 8 C.P.C. (2d) 86, 50 R.F.L. (2d) 65 (Ont. Fam. Ct.).

This section confers jurisdiction on the Provincial Court (Family Division) to apply equitable rules although it does not grant jurisdiction to give equitable remedies.

Section 97

Declaratory orders

97. The Court of Appeal and the Ontario Court (General Division), exclusive of the Small Claims Court, may make binding declarations of right whether or not any consequential relief is or could be claimed. [am. 1994, c. 12, s. 39]

Ministry Comment

1995 Amendments

Sections 96(3) and 97 of the Act are amended to make it clear that the Small Claims Court cannot give equitable relief or a declaratory judgment.

Cases

Aroland First Nation v. Ontario (1996), 7 W.D.C.P. (2d) 138 (Ont. Gen. Div.).

The court has jurisdiction to grant an interim declaration against the Crown. Such a declaration should generally be made only where there is evidence of a deliberate flouting of established law by a governmental authority.

T1T2 Ltd. Partnership v. Canada (1995), 23 O.R. (3d) 81, 38 C.P.C. (3d) 167, additional reasons 38 C.P.C. (3d) 167 at 180 (Gen. Div.), affirmed 24 O.R. (3d) 546, 38 C.P.C. (3d) 183 (C.A.).

The court granted a declaration on a motion for partial summary judgment. Discussion of the availability of declaratory relief.

Loomis v. Ontario (Minister of Agriculture & Food) (1993), 16 O.R. (3d) 188, 22 C.P.C. (3d) 396, 108 D.L.R. (4th) 330 (Div. Ct.).

As a general rule, an interlocutory or interim declaration should not be granted against the Crown, absent evidence of deliberate flouting of established law.

McConnell v. Rabin (1986), 13 C.P.C. (2d) 184 (Ont. H.C.).

A claim for declaratory relief regarding breach of a regulation was struck out under rule 21.01(1) where no consequential relief was sought and the declaration would serve no useful purpose.

MacRae v. Lecompte (1983), 32 C.P.C. 78, 143 D.L.R. (3d) 219 (Ont. H.C.).

Discussion of availability of declaratory relief.

Grys v. Sewell, [1972] 1 O.R. 733 (Master).

A declaratory judgment is a judicial act and ought not to be made merely on the consent of the parties.

London (City) v. Talbot Square Ltd. (1978), 22 O.R. (2d) 21, 93 D.L.R. (3d) 364 (Div. Ct.).

The court may not make an interlocutory declaration for the simple reason that a declaration is in its nature final.

Royal Securities Corp. v. Montreal Trust Co., [1967] 1 O.R. 137, 59 D.L.R. (2d) 666, affirmed [1967] 2 O.R. 200, 63 D.L.R. (2d) 15 (C.A.).

The agent of the payee of a promissory note was held to have sufficient interest in the matter to be entitled to seek a declaration of validity.

Re Oil, Chemical & Atomic Wkrs. Int. Union and Polymer Corp., [1966] 1 O.R. 774, 55 D.L.R. (2d) 198 (H.C.).

A declaration was refused because under the former Rules a declaratory judgment was not available on an originating motion. *Accord: Re Casterton* (1978), 23 O.R. (2d) 24, 13 C.P.C. 192, 94 D.L.R. (3d) 290 (H.C.); *Collins v. Collins* (1981), 32 O.R. (2d) 358, 21 C.P.C. 148, 122 D.L.R. (3d) 141 (H.C.); but see *R. v. Bales*, [1971] 2 O.R. 305, 17 D.L.R. (3d) 641 (H.C.). [*But see now rule 14.05(3)(h) — Authors.*]

Greenlees v. A.G. Can., [1946] O.R. 90, [1946] 1 D.L.R. 550 (C.A.).

Actions seeking declarations which indirectly affect the Crown are permissible.

Section 98

Relief against penalties

98. A court may grant relief against penalties and forfeitures, on such terms as to compensation or otherwise as are considered just.

Cases

Evenchick v. Cancorp Financial Services Ltd. (1991), 3 O.R. (3d) 441, amended 3 O.R. (3d) xii, 50 C.P.C. (2d) 261, 2 B.L.R. (2d) 123, 5 C.B.R. (3d) 191 (Gen. Div.).

The court granted relief from forfeiture of securities where their value far exceeded the indebtedness which they secured and the intervention of the Ministry of Financial Services contributed to the default.

Sheikh v. Sheffield Homes Ltd. (1989), 73 O.R. (2d) 348, 10 R.P.R. (2d) 253 (H.C.).

The court granted relief from forfeiture where a tenant defaulted in a rental payment as a result of a bank error.

Liscumb v. Provenzano (1985), 51 O.R. (2d) 129, 40 R.P.R. 31 (H.C.), affirmed (1986), 55 O.R. (2d) 404 (C.A.).

This section gives the court broad jurisdiction to relieve against forfeiture, and that jurisdiction is in no way restricted to preclude relief from forfeiture of interests in land. Discussion of appropriate questions to consider in determining when relief should be granted.

Section 99

Damages in substitution for injunction or specific performance
99. A court that has jurisdiction to grant an injunction or order specific performance may award damages in addition to, or in substitution for, the injunction or specific performance.

Cases

Duchman v. Oakland Dairy Co., 63 O.L.R. 111, [1929] 1 D.L.R. 9 (C.A.).

The court has a discretion to award damages in lieu of an injunction which should be exercised according to the rule in *Shelfer v. City of London Electric Lighting Co.*, [1895] 1 Ch. 287, and the justice of the case.

Section 100

Vesting orders
100. A court may by order vest in any person an interest in real or personal property that the court has authority to order be disposed of, encumbered or conveyed.

Cases

Ont. Housing Corp. v. Ong (1987), 58 O.R. (2d) 125, 15 C.P.C. (2d) 279 (H.C.), affirmed (1988), 63 O.R. (2d) 799, 26 C.P.C. (2d) 139 (C.A.).

After setting aside a final order of foreclosure the court made a vesting order in favour of the innocent purchasers who acquired the subject property from the mortgagee.

INTERLOCUTORY ORDERS

Section 101

Injunctions and receivers
101.—(1) In the Ontario Court (General Division), an interlocutory injunction or mandatory order may be granted or a receiver or receiver and manager may be appointed by an interlocutory order, where it appears to a judge of the court to be just or convenient to do so.

Terms
(2) An order under subsection (1) may include such terms as are considered just. [am. 1994, c. 12, s. 40]

Ministry Comment

Original Act

This section is derived from s. 19(1) of the *Judicature Act*. The provision specifically mentions the power to appoint a receiver and manager. The concluding words of the former subsection, dealing with waste and trespass, have been deleted as redundant. Injunctions are available to restrain any unlawful act.

Cross-Reference: See Rule 40 for cases on interlocutory injunctions and mandatory orders. See Rule 41 for cases on the appointment of receivers. See Rule 45 for cases on "Anton Piller" orders.

Section 102

"labour dispute" defined

102.—(1) In this section, "labour dispute" means a dispute or difference concerning terms, tenure or conditions of employment or concerning the association or representation of persons in negotiating, fixing, maintaining, changing or seeking to arrange terms or conditions of employment, regardless of whether the disputants stand in the proximate relation of employer and employee.

Notice

(2) Subject to subsection (8), no injunction to restrain a person from an act in connection with a labour dispute shall be granted without notice.

Steps before injunction proceeding

(3) In a motion or proceeding for an injunction to restrain a person from an act in connection with a labour dispute, the court must be satisfied that reasonable efforts to obtain police assistance, protection and action to prevent or remove any alleged danger of damage to property, injury to persons, obstruction of or interference with lawful entry or exit from the premises in question or breach of the peace have been unsuccessful.

Evidence

(4) Subject to subsection (8), affidavit evidence in support of a motion for an injunction to restrain a person from an act in connection with a labour dispute shall be confined to statements of facts within the knowledge of the deponent, but any party may by notice to the party filing such affidavit, and payment of the proper attendance money, require the attendance of the deponent to be cross-examined at the hearing.

Interim injunction

(5) An interim injunction to restrain a person from an act in connection with a labour dispute may be granted for a period of not longer than four days.

Notice

(6) Subject to subsection (8), at least two days notice of a motion for an interim injunction to restrain a person from any act in connection with a labour dispute shall be given to the responding party and to any other person affected thereby but not named in the notice of motion.

Idem

(7) Notice required by subsection (6) to persons other than the responding party may be given,

(a) where such persons are members of a labour organization, by personal service on an officer or agent of the labour organization; and

(b) where such persons are not members of a labour organization, by posting the notice in a conspicuous place at the location of the activity sought to be restrained where it can be read by any persons affected,

and service and posting under this subsection shall be deemed to be sufficient notice to all such persons.

Interim injunction without notice

(8) Where notice as required by subsection (6) is not given, the court may grant an interim injunction where,

(a) the case is otherwise a proper one for the granting of an interim injunction;

(b) notice as required by subsection (6) could not be given because the delay necessary to do so would result in irreparable damage or injury, a breach of the peace or an interruption in an essential public service;

(c) reasonable notification, by telephone or otherwise, has been given to the persons to be affected or, where any of such persons are members of a labour organization, to an officer of that labour organization or to the person authorized under section 89 of the *Labour Relations Act* to accept service of process under that Act on behalf of that labour organization or trade union, or where it is shown that such notice could not have been given; and

(d) proof of all material facts for the purpose of clauses (a), (b) and (c) is established by oral evidence.

Misrepresentation as contempt of court

(9) The misrepresentation of any fact or the withholding of any qualifying relevant matter, directly or indirectly, in a proceeding for an injunction under this section, constitutes a contempt of court.

Appeal

(10) An appeal from an order under this section lies to the Court of Appeal without leave.

Ministry Comment

Original Act

This section is derived from s. 20 of the *Judicature Act*. Slight changes in language have been made to conform with the terminology of the new Act and Rules.

Cases

Meaning of "Labour Dispute" — s. 102(1)

Trudel & Sons Roofing Ltd. v. Canadian Union of Shinglers & Allied Workers (1994), 28 C.P.C. (3d) 160 (Ont. Gen. Div.).

A non-union employer's application for an interlocutory injunction restraining picketing was granted where there was not a labour dispute within the meaning of s. 102, the applicant was not related to the struck employers, and the applicant was working at its own distinct sites.

C.P. Ltd. v. Weatherbee; C.P. Ltd. v. Pullman (1979), 26 O.R. (2d) 776 at 777, (*sub nom. C.P. Ltd. v. B.R.A.C., Loc. 2302*) 80 C.L.L.C. 14,001, 103 D.L.R. (3d) 739 at 740, affirmed 26 O.R. (2d) 776 at 784, 14 C.P.C. 225, 103 D.L.R. (3d) 739 at 747 (C.A.).

A "labour dispute" was held to exist between the plaintiff and the employees of one of its subsidiaries where there was a close physical proximity and a continuing functional relationship between the companies.

Sasso Disposal Ltd. v. Webster (1975), 10 O.R. (2d) 304, 63 D.L.R. (3d) 108 (H.C.).

A "labour dispute" exists between persons engaged in a lawful strike and a corporation which supplies workers to perform work normally done by the strikers.

Tatham Co. v. Blackburn (1975), 9 O.R. (2d) 570, 61 D.L.R. (3d) 210 (H.C.).

An injunction preventing employees of a municipality from picketing at the site of a bridge being built for the municipality by the applicant is in relation to a "labour dispute" and may be obtained only by complying with this section.

Neumann & Young Ltd. v. O'Rourke (1974), 6 O.R. (2d) 388, 75 C.L.L.C. 14,288, 53 D.L.R. (3d) 11 (H.C.).

Strikers picketing a warehouse where their employer stores goods are not engaged in a "labour dispute".

Al Sugar Contracting & Excavating Ltd. v. Collver (1974), 5 O.R. (2d) 466, 50 D.L.R. (3d) 533 (H.C.).

Consideration of meaning of "labour dispute".

Dominion Auto Transit Co. v. Cowle (1974), 4 O.R. (2d) 261, 47 D.L.R. (3d) 641 (H.C.).

An injunction was granted to prohibit strikers from picketing a company in order to prevent that company from carrying on its business with the company being struck. No "labour dispute" existed between the strikers and the first-mentioned company.

Secondary Picketing and Ex Parte Orders — s. 102(2)

Darrigo's Grape Juice Ltd. v. Masterson, [1971] 3 O.R. 772, 21 D.L.R. (3d) 660 (H.C.).

The prerequisites for injunctions in labour disputes set out in this provision do not apply in cases of "secondary picketing".

CTV Television Network Ltd. v. Kostenuk, [1972] 2 O.R. 653, 26 D.L.R. (3d) 385, affirmed [1972] 3 O.R. 338, 28 D.L.R. (3d) 180 (C.A.).

An injunction to restrain secondary picketing may be obtained *ex parte*.

Ford Motor Co. of Can. v. McDermott (1978), 20 O.R. (2d) 160, 87 D.L.R. (3d) 109 (H.C.).

An interim injunction was granted *ex parte* to restrain secondary picketing since the plaintiff was neutral to the controversy which provoked the picketing and was not involved in a "labour dispute" with the defendants.

Ford Motor Co. of Can. v. Browning (1978), 20 O.R. (2d) 14, 86 D.L.R. (3d) 579 (H.C.).

An interim injunction was granted *ex parte* to restrain secondary picketing since no "labour dispute" existed between the applicant and the respondents.

Commonwealth Holiday Inns of Can. Ltd. v. Sundy (1974), 2 O.R. (2d) 601, 74 C.L.L.C. 14,225, 43 D.L.R. (3d) 641 (H.C.).

Picketing of a motel wherein an employer has set up temporary offices is an act "in connection with a labour dispute" and is not "secondary picketing".

Inglis Ltd. v. Rao (1974), 2 O.R. (2d) 525 (H.C.).

Where an employer operates two plants and the employees of one plant are engaged in a lawful strike, their picketing of the other plant is an act "in connection with a labour dispute".

Domtar Chemicals Ltd. v. Leddy (No. 2) (1973), 1 O.R. (2d) 367, 40 D.L.R. (3d) 351 (H.C.).

Where an employer has two completely unrelated operations, picketing of one operation by striking employees of the other is secondary picketing.

Nedco Ltd. v. Nichols, [1973] 3 O.R. 944, 38 D.L.R. (3d) 664 (H.C.).

An application for an injunction restraining picketing was refused where the applicant was a closely related subsidiary of the employer.

Refrigeration Supplies Co. v. Ellis, [1971] 1 O.R. 190, 14 D.L.R. (3d) 682 (H.C.).

Where a struck company moved part of its operation to the premises of an affiliate, picketing of such premises was held to be primary picketing rather than secondary picketing.

Evidence of Efforts to Control Unlawful Conduct — s. 102(3), (4)

Blackstone Industrial Products Ltd. v. Parsons (1979), 23 O.R. (2d) 529 (H.C.).

An injunction may be granted only in those cases where the unlawful conduct or threatened unlawful conduct cannot reasonably be controlled by the police.

Windsor Bd. of Education v. Ont. Secondary School Teachers' Federation (1974), 7 O.R. (2d) 26, 75 C.L.L.C. 14,297, 54 D.L.R. (3d) 190 (H.C.).

General statements in an affidavit that police action was unsuccessful are not sufficient; particulars must be given.

Texpack Ltd. v. Rowley, [1972] 2 O.R. 93, 24 D.L.R. (3d) 675 (C.A.).

The respondent has the right to cross-examine *viva voce* on the question of reasonable efforts to obtain police assistance and the lack of success thereof.

Charterways Transportation Ltd. v. Alexander (1975), 9 O.R. (2d) 198, 60 D.L.R. (3d) 40 (H.C.).

The court held that an applicant seeking an injunction against picketing in a labour dispute must comply with the requirements of this section notwithstanding that the strike in question is unlawful.

Notice Requirements — s. 102(7)

International Alliance of Theatrical Stage Employees v. C.B.C., [1972] 1 O.R. 161, 22 D.L.R. (3d) 413 (H.C.).

A motion was allowed to proceed where the applicant established that if damage was going to result from the situation it would occur before the motion could be heard in the normal course.

MCA Can. Ltd. v. Lavictoire (1975), 10 O.R. (2d) 309 (H.C.).

Discussion of notice requirements respecting an interim injunction in a labour dispute.

Appeal to Court of Appeal — s. 102(10)

C.P. Ltd. v. Weatherbee; C.P. Ltd. v. Pullman (1979), 26 O.R. (2d) 776 at 777, (*sub nom. C.P. Ltd. v. B.R.A.C., Loc. 2302*) 80 C.L.L.C. 14,001, 103 D.L.R. (3d) 739 at 740, affirmed 26 O.R. (2d) 776 at 784, 14 C.P.C. 225, 103 D.L.R. (3d) 739 at 747 (C.A.).

The Court of Appeal refused to entertain appeals from orders dismissing applications for interlocutory injunctions where the strike giving rise to the matter was settled prior to the appeal.

Labour Injunctions — Miscellaneous

Queen's University at Kingston v. C.U.P.E., Local 229 (1994), 28 C.P.C. (3d) 64, 94 C.L.L.C. 14,030 (Ont. Gen. Div.), affirmed 95 C.L.L.C. 210-105, 120 D.L.R. (4th) 717, 76 O.A.C. 356 (C.A.)

The court had the authority to issue an injunction restraining picketing where there was a "labour dispute" within the meaning of s. 102, and the applicant had met the requirements of s. 102(3) and s. 101.

683481 Ontario Ltd. v. Beattie (1990), 44 C.P.C. (2d) 121, 90 C.L.L.C. 14,041, 73 D.L.R. (4th) 346 (Ont. H.C.).

The court refused to enjoin secondary picketing where the picketing was peaceful, and the plaintiff had entered into extraordinary warehousing arrangements with the subject employer in an apparent attempt to permit the employer to avoid the impact of a legal strike.

Gravel & Lake Services Ltd. v. I.W.A., Local 2693 (1989), 37 C.P.C. (2d) 292 (Ont. Dist. Ct.).

The court refused to grant an injunction where it appeared that the parties were engaged in a "labour dispute" and the requirements of s. [102] had not been met.

Clarkay Environmental Services Ltd. v. Martin (1987), 23 C.P.C. (2d) 79 (Ont. H.C.).

The court dissolved an interim injunction granted under s. [101] where a labour dispute was involved and the injunction ought to have proceeded under s. [102].

Ont. Hydro v. Johnson (1985), 1 C.P.C. (2d) 234 (Ont. H.C.).

The court granted an interlocutory injunction in similar terms to an interim order granted under s. [102(8)]. Evidence that no labour incidents occurred between the making of the interim order and the hearing of the motion for an interlocutory order is not sufficient to prevent the making of the interlocutory order.

A.G. Ont. v. C.U.P.E. (1981), 31 O.R. (2d) 618, 20 C.P.C. 208, 119 D.L.R. (3d) 428 (H.C.).

An injunction was granted preventing hospital workers from continuing a strike, the court holding that this section did not apply to an application by the Attorney General to prevent breach of a statutory prohibition against such a strike.

Bulk-Life Systems Ltd. v. Warehousemen & Miscellaneous Drivers' Union (1975), 10 O.R. (2d) 612, 75 C.L.L.C. 14,306, 64 D.L.R. (3d) 208 (H.C.).

An injunction was granted limiting picketing but not enjoining it where strikers engaged in acts of vandalism, threats, obstructions and assaults.

Consumers Glass Co. v. Melling (1973), 1 O.R. (2d) 335 (H.C.).

A trade union has status to appear by counsel in injunction proceedings to restrain activities relating to a labour dispute.

Section 103

Certificate of pending litigation
103.—(1) The commencement of a proceeding in which an interest in land is in question is not notice of the proceeding to a person who is not a party until a certificate of pending litigation is issued by the court and the certificate is registered in the proper land registry office under subsection (2).

Registration
(2) Where a certificate of pending litigation is issued under subsection (1) it may be registered whether the land is registered under the *Land Titles Act* or the *Registry Act.*

Exception
(3) Subsections (1) and (2) do not apply to a proceeding for foreclosure or sale on a registered mortgage or to enforce a lien under the *Construction Lien Act.*

Liability where no reasonable claim
(4) A party who registers a certificate under subsection (2) without a reasonable claim to an interest in the land is liable for any damages sustained by any person as a result of its registration.

Recovery of damages

(5) The liability for damages under subsection (4) and the amount thereof may be determined in the proceeding in respect of which the certificate was registered or in a separate proceeding.

Order discharging certificate

(6) The court may make an order discharging a certificate,

(a) where the party at whose instance it was issued,

(i) claims a sum of money in place of or as an alternative to the interest in the land claimed,

(ii) does not have a reasonable claim to the interest in the land claimed, or

(iii) does not prosecute the proceeding with reasonable diligence;

(b) where the interests of the party at whose instance it was issued can be adequately protected by another form of security; or

(c) on any other ground that is considered just,

and the court may, in making the order, impose such terms as to the giving of security or otherwise as the court considers just.

Effect

(7) Where a certificate is discharged, any person may deal with the land as fully as if the certificate had not been registered.

Ministry Comment

Original Act

This section is derived from ss. 38 and 39 of the *Judicature Act.* Subsection (2) is a new provision intended to make clear that, when a certificate of pending litigation is issued in respect of land registered under the *Land Titles Act,* the certificate itself will be registered on title. It will no longer be necessary to obtain a caution from the land registrar.

Authors' Comment

Subsections 116(8) and (9) of the *Courts of Justice Act, 1984* are unconsolidated and unrepealed transition provisions which state as follows:

Application of section

(8) Subsections (1) to (7) apply with necessary modifications to a certificate of caution under section 38 of the *Judicature Act,* being chapter 223 of the Revised Statutes of Ontario, 1980, registered after the 24th day of November, 1977 and before this Act comes into force.

Idem

(9) Subsections (1), (2), (3), (6) and (7) apply with necessary modifications to a certificate or caution under section 38 of the *Judicature Act* registered before the 25th day of November, 1977.

Cross-Reference: See also Rule 42.

Cases

Authors' Note on Organization of Cases

Cases relevant to this provision have been organized as follows:

Availability of Certificate
Discharge of Certificate — Standard to be Applied
Discharge of Certificate — Procedural Matters
Discharge of Certificate — Examples Where Discharge Granted
Discharge of Certificate — Examples Where Discharge Refused
Liability for Improper Use of Certificate — s. 103(4)
Certificate of Pending Litigation — Miscellaneous

Availability of Certificate (See also cases re Discharge, below.)

Nuforest Watson Bancorp v. Prenor Trust Co. of Canada (1994), 21 O.R. (3d) 328 (Gen. Div.).
A certificate of pending litigation was allowed against a mortgage to protect a claim for a constructive trust.

Chilian v. Augdome Corp. (1991), 2 O.R. (3d) 696, 49 C.P.C. (2d) 1, 78 D.L.R. (4th) 129, 44
    O.A.C. 263 (C.A.).
Entitlement to a certificate of pending litigation does not necessarily require that the interest in the land in question be claimed directly by the plaintiff for itself. It is sufficient that an interest in land is otherwise in question.

Gelakis v. Giouroukos (1989), 34 C.P.C. (2d) 223, 4 R.P.R. (2d) 301 (Ont. H.C.), affirmed 39
    C.P.C. (2d) 96 (Ont. H.C.).
The plaintiffs were granted a certificate on a second motion, where the first certificate had been discharged for failure to comply with rule 39.01(6). There had been no hearing on the merits in the first motion, the property was unique, and the balance of convenience favoured the plaintiff.

McMurdo v. McMurdo Estate (1988), 26 C.P.C. (2d) 20, 13 R.F.L. (3d) 317 (Ont. Master).
A spouse's right to possession of a matrimonial home under the *Family Law Act* is not an interest in land and a certificate will not be granted in that regard.

Davidson v. Hyundai Auto Canada Inc. (1987), 59 O.R. (2d) 789 (Ont. Master).
A breach of fiduciary duty can give rise to an equitable interest in land and an order for restitution thereof, and so will support a claim for a certificate of pending litigation, which the court granted on terms.

Homebuilder Inc. v. Man-Sonic Industries Inc. (1987), 22 C.P.C. (2d) 39, 14 C.I.P.R. 229, 28
    C.L.R. 18 (Ont. Master).
The test on a motion for leave to issue a certificate made on notice to the defendants is the same as the test on a motion to discharge a certificate.

Keeton v. Cain (1986), 57 O.R. (2d) 380, 14 C.P.C. (2d) 150 (H.C.).
An action to set aside an alleged fraudulent conveyance brings into question an "interest in land" and justifies issuing a certificate of pending litigation.

Namasco Ltd. v. Globe Equipment Sales and Rentals (1983) Ltd. (1985), 2 C.P.C. (2d) 242
    (Ont. H.C.).
The phrase "interest in land" does not include the interest of a person whose personal property has become affixed to the defendant's real property and no certificate will be issued in that regard.

515924 Ont. Ltd. v. Greymac Trust Co. (1984), 45 C.P.C. 80, 33 R.P.R. 89 (Ont. H.C.)
(application for leave to appeal dismissed without written reasons on October 12, 1984).
A certificate should not be issued to prevent the exercise of a power of sale under a mortgage which is a valid mortgage accepted as such.

Rauf v. Rauf (1983), 34 C.P.C. 262 (Ont. Master).
A family law plaintiff seeking an unequal division of a matrimonial home was refused a certificate of pending litigation. It may however be appropriate to obtain an order requiring the defendant spouse not to dissipate the asset.

Reznik v. Coolmur Properties Ltd. (1982), 25 R.P.R. 43 (Ont. H.C.).

A contractual provision that the agreement is personal to the parties will prevent the purchaser from obtaining a certificate against the land.

Lieba Ins. v. Start (1982), 30 C.P.C. 111 (Ont. Master).

A plaintiff whose status as a "creditor" was in dispute in a pending action was granted a certificate of pending litigation in a subsequent action to set aside a fraudulent conveyance where the defendant transferor was the defendant in the earlier action.

Bank of Montreal v. Ewing (1982), 35 O.R. (2d) 225, 135 D.L.R. (3d) 382 (Div. Ct.).

The court permitted a plaintiff, conducting an action to set aside an alleged fraudulent conveyance pursuant to leave given under s. 20 of the *Bankruptcy Act*, to obtain a certificate of pending litigation.

Reicher v. Reicher (1980), 19 C.P.C. 228, 20 R.F.L. (2d) 213 (Ont. Div. Ct.).

A certificate can be obtained in a divorce action where a claim under the *Family Law Reform Act* is made for an interest in land.

Peppe's Pizza Factory Ltd. v. Stacey (1979), 27 O.R. (2d) 41, 14 C.P.C. 235, 11 R.P.R. 246, 105 D.L.R. (3d) 120 (H.C.).

A certificate of pending litigation was permitted where the plaintiff claimed a leasehold interest.

Freedman v. Lawrence (1978), 18 O.R. (2d) 423, 6 C.P.C. 24, 82 D.L.R. (3d) 747 (H.C.).

The assignee of an interest in a partnership is entitled to a share of the partnership assets and a certificate of pending litigation is proper in an action for a declaration of ownership of a share of partnership lands.

Hirji v. Khimani (1978), 19 O.R. (2d) 750, 6 C.P.C. 29 (H.C.).

A certificate of pending litigation was permitted where the claim was for an interest in a mortgage.

Bowbriar Investments Inc. v. Wellesley Community Homes Inc. (1977), 24 R.P.R. 241 (Ont. H.C.).

A plaintiff who has obtained a certificate may be required to elect between the alternative remedies of specific performance with an abatement or return of the deposit. If the claim for specific performance is abandoned the certificate will be discharged upon posting of security by the defendant.

Kentish v. Karasy (1976), 14 O.R. (2d) 519 (H.C.).

Leave will be refused where the plaintiff delays unduly in bringing the motion.

Wood v. Wood (1974), 14 R.F.L. 138 (Ont. H.C.).

A spouse's claim for possession of the matrimonial home entitles him to a certificate of pending litigation. In this case the certificate was vacated on terms.

Dileo v. Ginell, [1968] 2 O.R. 32 (Master).

Failure to claim an interest in the land in the originating process is a fatal defect.

Discharge of Certificate — Standard to be Applied

931473 Ontario Ltd. v. Coldwell Banker Canada Inc. (1992), 5 C.P.C. (3d) 238, additional reasons 5 C.P.C. (3d) 271 (Ont. Gen. Div.).

The governing test — that the court must exercise its discretion in equity and look at all the relevant matters between the parties in determining whether a certificate should be vacated — applies generally and not only in special or unusual cases.

Waxman v. Waxman (1991), 2 W.D.C.P. (2d) 88, leave to appeal refused 2 W.D.C.P. (2d) 208, additional reasons 2 W.D.C.P. (2d) 226 (Ont. Gen. Div.).

On a motion to discharge, the court will consider whether there is a reasonable claim to an interest in the land, examine the equities, including the eight factors in *572383 Ontario Inc. v. Dhunna, infra*, and then exercise its discretion.

572383 Ontario Inc. v. Dhunna (1987), 24 C.P.C. (2d) 287 (Ont. Master).

In considering whether to discharge a certificate of pending litigation the court will examine: (1) whether the plaintiff is a shell corporation, (2) whether the land is unique, (3) the intent of the parties in acquiring the land, (4) whether there is an alternative claim for damages, (5) the ease or difficulty in calculating damages, (6) whether damages would be a satisfactory remedy, (7) the presence or absence of a willing purchaser, and (8) the harm to each party if the certificate is or is not removed with or without security.

Sandhu v. Braebury Homes Corp. (1986), 8 C.P.C. (2d) 22, 39 R.P.R. 10 (Ont. H.C.).

In considering discharging the certificate the judge must exercise his discretion in equity and look at all relevant matters between the parties. The test is not simply whether there is a triable issue with respect to a decree of specific performance.

Graywood Developments Ltd. v. Campeau Corp. (1985), 8 C.P.C. (2d) 58 (Ont. Master).

Section 116 does not alter the standard to be applied on a motion to discharge a certificate of pending litigation from that applied under the *Judicature Act* notwithstanding changes in the language used in the statute.

Stanko v. Sorko (1985), 38 R.P.R. 100 (Ont. H.C.).

Discharge may be granted when damages are claimed even if the action is not frivolous or vexatious.

Kingsberg Developments Ltd. v. K Mart Can. Ltd. (1982), 40 O.R. (2d) 348, 27 R.P.R. 184 (H.C.).

Where a plaintiff seeking specific performance of an agreement to purchase land has failed to indicate the amount of abatement sought and provide the defendant with an opportunity to close the transaction in escrow, a certificate will not be maintained because the right to specific performance has been foregone.

Freedman v. Lawrence (1978), 18 O.R. (2d) 423, 6 C.P.C. 24, 82 D.L.R. (3d) 747 (H.C.).

A certificate of pending litigation will not be vacated unless the action is clearly shown to be an abuse of process or the plaintiff cannot possibly succeed in obtaining an interest in the land.

Clock Investments Ltd. v. Hardwood Estates Ltd. (1977), 16 O.R. (2d) 671, 79 D.L.R. (3d) 129 (Div. Ct.).

The court has an equitable discretion in unusual cases to discharge a certificate even where it has not been shown that the action cannot possibly succeed or is an abuse of process. Whether the property is held for investment purposes is not the governing principle, but merely one of the relevant factors to be weighed in exercising this discretion.

Galinski v. Jurashek (1976), 1 C.P.C. 68 (Ont. H.C.).

To obtain an order vacating a certificate, there must be clear proof that the action is an abuse of process, or that the plaintiff cannot obtain an interest in land.

Discharge of Certificate — Procedural Matters

791715 Ontario Inc. v. Robinson (1989), 72 O.R. (2d) 337, 49 C.P.C. (2d) 158 (Master), affirmed (1990), 72 O.R. (2d) 237n, 49 C.P.C. (2d) 158n (H.C.).

A certificate was discharged where for five months there had been no reasonable efforts to serve the order granting the certificate or to prosecute the action.

Gordon v. Lawrence Avenue Group Ltd. (1988), 65 O.R. (2d) 545, 1 R.P.R. (2d) 48 (H.C.).

A certificate should not be discharged where the failure to promptly serve the order granting it was due to inadvertence.

Holden Corp. v. Gingerfield Properties Ltd. (1988), 26 C.P.C. (2d) 211 (Ont. Master), appeal quashed 65 O.R. (2d) 454, 30 C.P.C. (2d) 302 (H.C.).

A party may bring more than one motion to vacate a certificate of pending litigation, but on a further motion the party must provide substantial new evidence of an overwhelming nature.

Cimaroli v. Pugliese (1988), 25 C.P.C. (2d) 10 (Ont. H.C.), leave to appeal to Ont. Div. Ct. refused 12 W.D.C.P. 123.

The certificate will be discharged for non-disclosure of material facts if the existence of a contractual provision prohibiting registration of a certificate is not drawn to the attention of the court hearing the *ex parte* motion to grant the certificate.

Young v. 503708 Ont. Ltd. (1986), 10 C.P.C. (2d) 156 (Ont. Master).

A master has jurisdiction to hear a motion to discharge a certificate of pending litigation.

Chan v. Kingsberg Property Invts. Ltd. (1983), 35 C.P.C. 236 (Ont. H.C.).

On a motion to vacate a certificate of pending litigation the judge may require the plaintiff to be cross-examined on his affidavit filed in support of the original motion to obtain the certificate.

463308 Ont. Ltd. v. Elviston Const. Ltd. (1981), 22 C.P.C. 288, leave to appeal granted 30 C.P.C. 151 (Ont. H.C.).

Cross-examination on an affidavit filed in support of an *ex parte* motion for a certificate of pending litigation was not permitted for use on motion to discharge the certificate.

Sas v. Solomon (1978), 20 O.R. (2d) 603 (Master).

On a motion to discharge, the moving party is entitled to cross-examine on the affidavit supporting the motion made to obtain the certificate.

313473 Ont. Ltd. v. Lornal Const. Ltd. (1976), 18 O.R. (2d) 374 (Div. Ct.).

An order dismissing a motion to vacate a certificate of pending litigation is interlocutory for purposes of an appeal.

Discharge of Certificate — Examples Where Discharge Granted

561895 Ontario Ltd. v. Metropolitan Trust Co. of Canada, (1994), 34 C.P.C. (3d) 251 (Ont. Gen. Div.).

The court discharged a certificate where, *inter alia,* the plaintiff delayed six years in seeking the certificate and it would have interfered with the sale of the property.

Vettese v. Fleming (1992), 8 C.P.C. (3d) 237 (Ont. Gen. Div.).

The court granted a certificate of pending litigation in this action to set aside a fraudulent conveyance even though the plaintiff had no interest in the land and was not yet a judgment creditor. The plaintiff had shown a *prima facie* case.

Queen's Court Developments Ltd. v. Duquette (1989), 36 C.P.C. (2d) 297 (Ont. H.C.).

The court vacated a certificate of pending litigation on equitable grounds where the underlying sale had been subject to severance. The plaintiff elected to have its own solicitor make the severance application on behalf of both parties, and the plaintiff's failure to appeal the severance decision had eliminated the possibility of an early resolution of the problem.

Memphis Holdings v. Plastics Land Partnership (1989), 35 C.P.C. (2d) 177, 4 R.P.R. (2d) 169 (Ont. H.C.).

The court discharged a certificate of pending litigation where the plaintiffs failed to show a sufficient interest in the land and were mainly concerned that the land be available for judgment.

Orangeville Raceway (Ont.) Inc. v. Frieberg (1988), 63 O.R. (2d) 658, 12 R.F.L. (3d) 180 (H.C.).

The court refused to issue the certificate where, although neither party merited the equitable assistance of the court, the balance of convenience favoured the defendant.

Eastwalsh Homes Ltd. v. Anatal Development Corp. (1988), 29 C.P.C. (2d) 266, additional reasons 17 W.D.C.P. 58 (Ont. H.C.).

The court vacated a certificate regarding investment property registered against an entire parcel of which only part was involved in the action.

Allen v. Hennessey (1988), 29 C.P.C. (2d) 209 (Ont. Master), leave to appeal to Ont. H.C. and Div. Ct. refused 30 C.P.C. (2d) lv.

The master discharged a certificate in a fraudulent conveyance action where he could not find or infer the necessary fraudulent intent.

St. Thomas Subdividers v. 639373 Ont. Ltd. (1988), 29 C.P.C. (2d) 1, 3 R.P.R. (2d) 56 (H.C.), leave to appeal to Ont. Div. Ct. refused 29 C.P.C. (2d) xlv.

The court discharged a certificate where the agreement of purchase and sale expressly did not create an interest in the land until the closing date.

Aztec Investments Ltd. v. Wynston (1988), 64 O.R. (2d) 733, 27 C.P.C. (2d) 238 (Master).

Where there had been a lack of disclosure on the original motion and the investment property was scheduled to be sold at substantial profit, a certificate of pending litigation was discharged on terms that the proceeds of sale be paid into court.

Reuel v. Thomas (1988), 27 C.P.C. (2d) 101 (Ont. Dist. Ct.).

Where a vendor had title to some but not all of the property to be conveyed, which problem might be remedied, the vendor was given 90 days to resolve the title problems and the certificate was discharged on terms, including payment into court of a disputed abatement.

Kakeway v. Canada (1988), 64 O.R. (2d) 52, 26 C.P.C. (2d) 25 (H.C.).

The court refused to permit a certificate of pending litigation regarding an Indian land claim.

Homebuilder Inc. v. Man-Sonic Industries Inc. (1987), 22 C.P.C. (2d) 39, 14 C.I.P.R. 229, 28 C.L.R. 18 (Ont. Master).

A certificate of pending litigation was not allowed where it was clear that the plaintiff would have difficulty proving its claim, and the plaintiff had claimed a sum of money in place of or as an alternative to the interest in the land. The interests of the plaintiff could adequately be protected by another form of security.

Baluster Investments Ltd. v. Iona Corp. (1987), 21 C.P.C. (2d) 114 (Ont. Master), affirmed 21 C.P.C. (2d) xlvii (Ont. H.C.).

A certificate was discharged on payment of security where damages were claimed in the alternative in the action, which would fully compensate the plaintiff.

Greenbaum v. 619908 Ont. Ltd. (1986), 11 C.P.C. (2d) 26 (Ont. H.C.).

A certificate of pending litigation was discharged on terms where its continuation would constitute a breach of the development agreement between the defendant-builder and the land-owner and would jeopardize financing arrangements.

Rocovitis v. Argerys Estate (1986), 9 C.P.C. (2d) 62 (Ont. Master), affirmed (1988), 63 O.R. (2d) 755, 26 C.P.C. (2d) 302, 28 E.T.R. 191, 27 O.A.C. 300 (Div. Ct.).

The court discharged a certificate registered against land owned by the beneficiary under a will where the plaintiff's claim against the testator had not been reduced to judgment within three years of the testator's death. The plaintiff's unliquidated claim for damages was not a "debt" within the meaning of the *Estates Administration Act*.

Pete & Marty's (Front) Ltd. v. Market Block Toronto Properties Ltd. (1985), 5 C.P.C. (2d) 97, 37 R.P.R. 157 (Ont. H.C.).

The court discharged a certificate where the plaintiff's claim for damages would be a satisfactory alternative to the plaintiff's claim for specific performance and the plaintiff had no assets. The defendant was not required to establish that the plaintiff had no reasonable claim to an interest in the land.

Bernhard v. United Merchandising Enterprises Ltd. (1984), 47 O.R. (2d) 520 (H.C.).

A third chargee of land who had brought an action to set aside a sale or for damages on the ground that the sale was grossly undervalued obtained a caution. It was vacated because, having failed to offer to redeem, he could not possibly obtain an interest in land.

Davidson v. Horvat (1984), 45 C.P.C. 203 (Ont. H.C.).

The court vacated a certificate registered against the defendant corporation's lands where the plaintiff's claim was based on an alleged agreement with the other defendants to incorporate a company to acquire the property. The corporate veil should not be lifted in such circumstances in order to give individuals an interest in land which they do not have directly.

T.D. Bank v. Zukerman (1982), 40 O.R. (2d) 724, 33 C.P.C. 300 (H.C.).

Where there was no allegation of fraud or underhanded dealings, and the plaintiff bank presumably knew at the outset that the land was taken in one of the defendants' wife's name, the court vacated the certificate in this action which, *inter alia*, sought a declaration that the defendants had an interest in the land.

Cedarville Scrap Iron & Metals (1968) Ltd. v. Deeks (1981), 25 C.P.C. 190 (Ont. H.C.).

Delay in serving the originating process for reasons of convenience or strategy, after registering a certificate of pending litigation against a defendant's land, is an abuse of process and will result in an order vacating the certificate.

Arnett v. Menke (1979), 11 C.P.C. 263 (Ont. H.C.).

A certificate was set aside where (1) the action was not proceeded with expeditiously, (2) the equities were strongly in favour of the applicant, (3) the action for specific performance could never succeed.

J & P Goldfluss Ltd. v. 306569 Ont. Ltd. (1977), 4 C.P.C. 296 (Ont. H.C.).

A plaintiff suing for the return of his deposit is entitled to a certificate of pending litigation. However, the certificate will be vacated where there has been serious non-disclosure in the affidavit material upon which the certificate was obtained.

Heron Bay Invts. Ltd. v. Peel-Elder Devs. Ltd. (1976), 2 C.P.C. 338 (Ont. H.C.).

A certificate of pending litigation was vacated where the land involved was purchased as an investment and any loss of profits could be compensated for in damages.

Finkle v. Marway Dev. Enterprises Ltd. (1976), 3 C.P.C. 35 (Ont. H.C.).

A certificate was vacated because the land sale contract was merely oral and no sufficient acts of part performance were alleged.

Lai Kim Tsai v. Kwong Hei Wong (1976), 1 C.P.C. 71 (Ont. H.C.).

Where the claim was frivolous and had not been prosecuted in good faith, the certificate was ordered vacated upon payment into court of security.

Discharge of Certificate — Examples Where Discharge Refused

Mirrow Homes Ltd. v. Filice (1989), 44 C.P.C. (2d) 204 (Ont. H.C.).

A certificate of pending litigaiton was reinstated on appeal where a delay in proceeding could be explained, and there was a strong *prima facie* case. Furthermore, the master had erred in law by making a determination of credibility on affidavit evidence with respect to issues that went to the root of the triable issue.

Petrela v. Denney (1989), 38 C.P.C. (2d) 107 (Ont. Dist. Ct.).

A court granted a certificate of pending litigation where the plaintiff submitted a written offer to purchase and alleged an oral acceptance.

Corsi v. di Cecco (1988), 32 C.P.C. (2d) 310 (Ont. H.C.).

The master found triable issues, and implicitly found the plaintiff had a reasonable claim to the land. However, the master had ordered the certificate discharged. On appeal, the court reinstated the certificate as the master must have misapplied the legal tests.

777829 Ont. Ltd. v. 616070 Ont. Inc. (1988), 67 O.R. (2d) 72, 32 C.P.C. (2d) 38 at 46, 2 R.P.R. (2d) 54 (H.C.).

The court permitted a certificate to remain on title pending a sale and imposed terms in that regard.

Royal Bank v. Muzzi (1987), 22 C.P.C. (2d) 66, additional reasons 22 C.P.C. (2d) 66 at 71 (Ont. Master).

A certificate of pending litigation was permitted to stand where a creditor claimed that the proceeds from a fraudulent conveyance had been invested by the transferor in the property in question. However, the certificate of pending litigation should be discharged upon payment into court of the amount in issue.

Holden Corp. v. Gingerfield Properties Ltd. (1987), 59 O.R. (2d) 304, 25 C.P.C. (2d) 225 (H.C.), leave to appeal to Ont. Div. Ct. refused 25 C.P.C. (2d) 225n.

Section 116(6)(a)(i) is not to be interpreted to mean that the court should discharge the certificate simply because there is an alternative claim for damages. The court refused to discharge the certificate provided the plaintiff executed a postponement agreement regarding an unsevered portion of the subject lands to which the plaintiff did not have a claim.

608853 Ont. Inc. v. Tiveron (1986), 9 C.P.C. (2d) 75 (Ont. Master).

The master declined to discharge a certificate of pending litigation where the law might permit the plaintiff to succeed in its claim for specific performance of an agreement to purchase the subject property with an abatement of the purchase price and notwithstanding an alternative claim for damages.

Graywood Developments Ltd. v. Campeau Corp. (1985), 8 C.P.C. (2d) 58 (Ont. Master).

The court refused to discharge the certificate notwithstanding the land claimed was an unsevered portion of a larger parcel and had no precise legal description or boundaries. The certificate was registered against the entire parcel and the plaintiff executed a postponement document subordinating the certificate to a mortgage to permit advances by the mortgagee.

McEwen v. 341595 Ont. Ltd. (1984), 34 R.P.R. 258 (Ont. H.C.).

Discharge of the certificate on the ground the plaintiff delayed in prosecuting an action for specific performance was refused where the delay was justified by ongoing settlement negotiations.

Jones v. Jones (1982), 32 C.P.C. 105 (Ont. Master).

The court refused to vacate a certificate of pending litigation obtained in a divorce action by a wife alleging property had been fraudulently transferred by her husband to his corporation to defeat her.

Notarfonzo v. Goodman (1981), 24 C.P.C. 127 (Ont. H.C.).

Although the plaintiff's case appeared weak, a certificate of pending litigation was not vacated where a triable issue was raised.

Moehring v. Ivankovic (1981), 20 C.P.C. 285 (Ont. H.C.).

An application to vacate a certificate of pending litigation was refused where the plaintiff claimed an interest in a corporation, the only substantial asset of which was the subject land.

Hirji v. Khimani (1978), 19 O.R. (2d) 750, 6 C.P.C. 29 (H.C.).

A mortgage constitutes an interest in land and where a mortgage is the subject matter of litigation and a certificate of pending litigation has been registered, such certificate should not be vacated notwithstanding that the title to the property is not in dispute.

Laprairie v. Laprairie (1976), 29 R.F.L. 207 (Ont. H.C.).

The court refused to vacate a certificate of pending litigation regarding a claim by one spouse for a declaration that he had a half interest in the matrimonial home which was registered in the name of the other spouse.

Liability for Improper Use of Certificate — s. 103(4)

Charleston Partners, L.P. v. Dickenson (1996), 7 W.D.C.P. (2d) 166 (Ont. Gen. Div.).

The court granted summary judgment against a party who had registered a certificate of pending litigation without a reasonable claim to an interest in the lands and quantified those damages relating to the legal costs incurred. The issue of exemplary or punitive damages could not be determined on a motion for summary judgment.

Geo. Cluthe Manufacturing Co. v. ZTW Properties (1995), 23 O.R. (3d) 370, 39 C.P.C. (3d) 322, 81 O.A.C. 141 (Div. Ct.), leave to appeal to Ont. C.A. refused 39 C.P.C. (3d) 322n.

The court held that registration of a certificate of pending litigation against lands not covered by the order granting leave to issue the certificate was slander of title.

Chilian v. Augdome Corp. (1991), 2 O.R. (3d) 696, 49 C.P.C. (2d) 1, 78 D.L.R. (4th) 129, 44 O.A.C. 263 (C.A.).

The claim to an interest in land refers to the claim made in the proceeding whether or not it belongs directly to the party at whose instance the certificate was issued.

Pete & Marty's (Front) Ltd. v. Market Block Toronto Properties Ltd. (1985), 5 C.P.C. (2d) 97, 37 R.P.R. 157 (Ont. H.C.).

A certificate of pending litigation is absolutely privileged and cannot form the basis of a claim for slander of title.

Micro Carpets Ltd. v. De Souza Dev. Ltd. (1980), 29 O.R. (2d) 77, 19 C.P.C. 118, 112 D.L.R. (3d) 178 (H.C.).

No cause of action is conferred by this provision against a solicitor acting *qua* solicitor.

Certificate of Pending Litigation — Miscellaneous

Rinaldis v. Landmark Development (North Bay) Ltd. (1995), 23 O.R. (3d) 564, 21 C.L.R. (2d) 137, 32 C.B.R. (3d) 291, 124 D.L.R. (4th) 279 (Div. Ct.).

Where a trustee in bankruptcy registered a certificate of pending litigation with respect to a fraudulent conveyance of property, the court held that the trustee had priority over construction lien claimants who had registered their liens after the certificate.

Paquette v. Smith (1989), 70 O.R. (2d) 449 (H.C.).

The court held that the issue of whether written evidence of a broker could constitute a "note or memorandum" in compliance with the *Statute of Frauds* created a sufficient triable issue to warrant the reinstatement of a vacated certificate.

Holden Corp. v. Gingerfield Properties Ltd. (1988), 65 O.R. (2d) 454, 30 C.P.C. (2d) 302 (H.C.).

The court has no authority to impose terms where a certificate of pending litigation is not discharged.

Rushville Construction Ltd. v. 572321 Ontario Inc. (1987), 21 C.P.C. (2d) 156 (Ont. H.C.).

The court granted a mandatory order requiring the plaintiff to remove from title the registration of a notice of agreement of purchase and sale and the renewal thereof where a certificate of pending litigation flowing from the same agreement had been ordered discharged and the plaintiff's rights of appeal from that order had been exhausted.

Zevest Development Corp. v. K Mart Can. Ltd. (1986), 16 C.P.C. (2d) 301 (Ont. H.C.).

A plaintiff who failed to appeal an interlocutory order, vacating a certificate of pending litigation on the basis of a finding that no valid agreement existed and that the plaintiff therefore had no interest in the property, was held to be estopped from relitigating the issue of the existence of a valid contract at trial.

Doucette v. Doucette (1974), 4 O.R. (2d) 278, 47 D.L.R. (3d) 658 (H.C.).

A pre-existing equitable interest is not affected by the registration of a certificate of pending litigation.

Section 104

Interim order for recovery of personal property

104.—(1) In an action in which the recovery of possession of personal property is claimed and it is alleged that the property,

    (a) was unlawfully taken from the possession of the plaintiff; or

    (b) is unlawfully detained by the defendant,

the court, on motion, may make an interim order for recovery of possession of the property.

Damages

(2) A person who obtains possession of personal property by obtaining or setting aside an interim order under subsection (1) is liable for any loss suffered by the person ultimately found to be entitled to possession of the property.

Ministry Comment

Original Act

Subsection (1) is derived from s. 2 of the *Replevin Act.*

Subsection (2) is a new provision making a person who obtains an interim order for possession of personal property liable for any loss suffered if it ultimately turns out that he or she was not entitled to the property.

Cross-Reference: For cases regarding interim recovery of personal property, see Rule 44.

Section 105

"health practitioner" defined

105.—(1) In this section, "health practitioner" means a person licensed to practise medicine or dentistry in Ontario or any other jurisdiction, a psychologist registered under the *Psychologists Registration Act* or a person certified or registered as a psychologist by another jurisdiction.

Order for physical or mental examination

(2) Where the physical or mental condition of a party to a proceeding is in question, the court, on motion, may order the party to undergo a physical or mental examination by one or more health practitioners.

Idem
(3) Where the question of a party's physical or mental condition is first raised by another party, an order under this section shall not be made unless the allegation is relevant to a material issue in the proceeding and there is good reason to believe that there is substance to the allegation.

Further examinations
(4) The court may, on motion, order further physical or mental examinations.

Examiner may ask questions
(5) Where an order is made under this section, the party examined shall answer the questions of the examining health practitioner relevant to the examination and the answers given are admissible in evidence.

Ministry Comment

Original Act

This section replaces the provisions of s. 77 of the *Judicature Act*, which dealt with medical examinations. Subsection (1) is derived from s. 77(7) of the *Judicature Act*. It makes clear that examinations may be conducted by practitioners licensed outside Ontario.

Subsection (2) is derived from s. 77(1) of the *Judicature Act*. The new provision is not limited to proceedings in respect of bodily injury. Since the new provision is not limited to personal injury actions, subs. (3) has been included to protect a party whose physical or mental condition has been put in issue by another party.

1989 Amendments

Bill 2

Section [105] of the Act permits a court to order a physical or mental examination of a party. The new subsection (1) adds registered psychologists to the list of persons who may conduct these examinations. This reflects the jurisprudence under the existing provision (see *Ontario (A.G.) v. CEC Construction* (1986), 57 O.R. (2d) 782 (H.C.)).

The amendments to subsections (2) and (5) are consequential on the new subsection (1).

Cross-Reference: For cases regarding medical examinations, see Rule 33.

Section 106

Stay of proceedings
106. A court, on its own initiative or on motion by any person, whether or not a party, may stay any proceeding in the court on such terms as are considered just.

Ministry Comment

Original Act

This section is derived from para. 6 of s. 18 of the *Judicature Act*. It also replaces s. 24 of the *Judicature Act*.

Cases (See also cases under rule 17.06 and rule 21.01(3).)

Stay of Proceedings — Jurisdiction

Bonaventure Systems Inc. v. Royal Bank (1987), 57 O.R. (2d) 270, 16 C.P.C. (2d) 32, 32 D.L.R. (4th) 721, 18 O.A.C. 112 (Div. Ct.).

The master has jurisdiction to stay a proceeding.

Empire-Universal Films Ltd. v. Rank, [1947] O.R. 775 (H.C.).

This section merely confers a statutory right that had been previously considered inherent in the jurisdiction of the court.

Stay of Proceedings — Pending Determination of Criminal Proceedings

Bour v. Manraj (1995), 24 O.R. (3d) 279 (Gen. Div.).

The court stayed a civil proceeding pending determination of a related criminal proceeding. Generally, such a stay is appropriate only where the defendant's right to a fair trial would be detrimentally affected in some extraordinary way.

Gillis v. Eagleson (1995), 23 O.R. (3d) 164, 37 C.P.C. (3d) 252 (Gen. Div.).

Where the defendant demonstrated that his right to a fair criminal trial in the United States would be prejudiced by civil discovery or trial testimony in Ontario, the court granted a nine-month stay of the Ontario action.

Belanger v. Caughell (1995), 22 O.R. (3d) 741 (Gen. Div.).

The court refused to stay a civil action based on alleged sexual assault pending completion of related criminal proceedings. The court may have been prepared to restrict the use of the defendant's discovery evidence but was requested not to do so by the defendant.

Forbes v. Thurlow (1993), 23 C.P.C. (3d) 107 (Ont. Gen. Div.).

The court refused to stay a civil action pending determination of a related criminal case, but did order the civil file sealed.

Buxbaum v. Buxbaum (1988), 29 C.P.C. (2d) 161 (Ont. H.C.).

An order staying the civil action until all criminal proceedings were completed was too wide, and therefore grossly unfair, and was varied. Discretion to stay should be exercised only in extraordinary or exceptional cases and only as required.

Event Sales Inc. v. Rommco Group Inc. (1987), 17 C.P.C. (2d) 318 (Ont. Master).

The master refused to exercise his jurisdiction to stay a civil action where the prejudice alleged was exposure to the discovery process before the conclusion of related criminal proceedings.

Seaway Trust Co. v. Kilderkin Investments Ltd. (1986), 55 O.R. (2d) 545, 11 C.P.C. (2d) 140, 29 D.L.R. (4th) 456 (H.C.).

A court should exercise its discretion to stay an action only in extraordinary and exceptional circumstances, and the exposure of a criminally accused person in a civil action is not sufficient.

Stickney v. Trusz (1973), 2 O.R. (2d) 469, 25 C.R.N.S. 257, 16 C.C.C. (2d) 25, 45 D.L.R. (3d) 275, affirmed 3 O.R. (2d) 538, 28 C.R.N.S. 125, 17 C.C.C. (2d) 478, 46 D.L.R. (3d) 80, which was affirmed 3 O.R. (2d) at 539, 28 C.R.N.S. at 126, 17 C.C.C. (2d) at 480, 46 D.L.R. (3d) at 82 (C.A.).

In order to have an action stayed pending the resolution of related criminal proceedings, the applicant must show some specific or particular way in which he would be prejudiced in his criminal trial.

Terra Communications Ltd. v. Communicomp Data Ltd. (1973), 1 O.R. (2d) 682 (H.C.).

An application to stay the action pending resolution of a related criminal proceeding was denied where no prejudice to the defence of the criminal proceeding was shown.

Archer-Shee v. Anderson, [1968] 1 O.R. 294 (H.C.).

An action was stayed pending the resolution of criminal proceedings where it appeared the action had been commenced in order to obtain damaging statements from the defendant.

Stay of Proceedings Based on Convenience of Forum

Amchem Products Inc. v. British Columbia (Workers' Compensation Board), [1993] 1 S.C.R. 897, 14 C.P.C. (3d) 1, 77 B.C.L.R. (2d) 62, [1993] 3 W.W.R. 441, 23 B.C.A.C 1, 102 D.L.R. (4th) 96, 150 N.R. 321, 39 W.A.C. 1.

The test for *forum non conveniens* is that there must be some other forum more convenient and appropriate for the pursuit of the action and for securing the ends of justice. There is no reason why the loss of juridical advantage in principle should be treated as a separate and distinct condition rather than being weighed with the other factors which are considered in identifying the appropriate forum. The burden of proof on a motion to stay should not depend upon whether the defendant was served within the jurisdiction or outside the jurisdiction. Whether the burden of proof should be on the plaintiff in *ex juris* cases depends on the rule that permits service out of the jurisdiction. If it requires that service out of the jurisdiction be justified by the plaintiff, whether on a motion for an order or in defending service *ex juris* where no order is required, then the rule must govern. In any event the burden of proof should not play a significant role in this matter as it only applies in cases in which the judge cannot come to a determinative decision on the basis of the materials presented by the parties.

S.P.N.M. de Bonth v. Revenue Properties Co. (1996), 7 W.D.C.P. (2d) 150 (Ont. Gen. Div.).

The court stayed this action where the defendants established that British Columbia was a clearly more appropriate forum.

Dudnik v. Canada (Canadian Radio-Television & Telecommunications Commission) (1995), 41 C.P.C. (3d) 336, 61 C.B.R. (3d) 129 (Ont. Gen. Div.).

The court stayed a proceeding where, although the Ontario Court of Justice and the Federal Court of Canada had concurrent jurisdiction, the Federal Court of Canada was the more convenient forum.

Mannai Properties (Jersey) Ltd. v. Horsham Corp. (1994), 36 C.P.C. (3d) 235 (Ont. Gen. Div.).

The defendant's motion to permanently stay an action on the grounds that Ontario was *forum non conveniens* was allowed where there was no real connection between Ontario and the issues in the litigation.

Lehndorff Management Ltd. v. Gentra Canada Investments Inc. (1994), 34 C.P.C. (3d) 354 (Ont. Gen. Div.).

The court refused to stay an Ontario action pending disposition of a related Alberta action where it was not established that Alberta was a more convenient forum.

Métis National Council Secretariat Inc. v. Evans (1994), 33 C.P.C. (3d) 395 (Ont. Gen. Div.).

The court stayed an action which had little connection with Ontario.

SDI Simulation Group Inc. v. Chameleon Technologies Inc. (1994), 34 C.P.C. (3d) 346 (Ont. Gen. Div.).

The court stayed an action which had virtually no connection with Ontario and awarded solicitor and client costs against the plaintiff.

Bank Van Parijs en de Nederlanden Belgie N.W. v. Cabri (1993), 19 C.P.C. (3d) 362 (Ont. Gen. Div.).

The defendant's motion for a stay of proceedings was granted where Belgium was the forum that had the most real and substantial connection with the law suit and the plaintiff would not be deprived of any personal or juridical advantage by litigating there.

Sterling Software International (Canada) Inc. v. Software Recording Corp. of America (1993), 12 O.R. (3d) 694, 17 C.P.C. (3d) 116, 47 C.P.R. (3d) 420 (Gen. Div.).

The court stayed an Ontario action pending determination of a related Texas action. The subject contract had been negotiated in Texas and was governed by Texas law and the Texas action had been commenced first. Texas was the most convenient forum. The defendants had given undertakings obviating the need for interlocutory relief in Ontario.

Abus KG v. Secord Inc. (1992), 8 C.P.C. (3d) 343 (Ont. Gen. Div.).

The court permitted a German plaintiff to sue in Ontario rather than Germany where the case had a connection to Ontario and the claim was not statute-barred in Ontario but was barred in Germany.

Galtaco Redlaw Castings Corp. v. Brunswick Industrial Supply Co. (1989), 69 O.R. (2d) 478, 36 C.P.C. (2d) 225 (H.C.), leave to appeal to Ont. Div. Ct. refused 17 W.D.C.P. 349.

When determining whether to stay an action as between competing jurisdictions, the moving party must show that there is another forum, with amenable jurisdiction, in which justice could be done at substantially less inconvenience or expense. The moving party must also show that the foreign jurisdiction is the convenient forum, and that it has the most real and substantial connection with the law suit. If this is shown, the responding party must demonstrate that the stay would deprive it of a legitimate personal or juridical advantage.

Pace v. Synetics Inc. (1983), 41 O.R. (2d) 267, 34 C.P.C. 1, 145 D.L.R. (3d) 749 (H.C.).

The court refused to stay an action on the basis of *forum conveniens* where the defendant had assets in Ontario and prosecution of the action elsewhere would deny the plaintiff the legitimate advantage of execution after judgment. An action should not be stayed if it would deprive the plaintiff of a legitimate juridical advantage.

BP Can. Holdings Ltd. v. Westmin Resources Ltd. (1983), 32 C.P.C. 300 (Ont. H.C.).

In order to obtain a stay of proceedings on the basis of *forum non conveniens* the defendant must establish that: (1) there is another forum to whose jurisdiction the defendant is amenable in which justice can be done at substantially less inconvenience and expense; and (2) a stay would not deprive the plaintiffs of a legitimate personal or juridical advantage which would be available in Ontario.

Stay of Proceedings — Pending Arbitration

Jaffasweet Juices Ltd. v. Michael J. Firestone & Associates (1996), 7 W.D.C.P. (2d) 148 (Ont. Gen. Div.).

The court refused to stay the action where the dispute did not appear to fall within the arbitration clause and, even if it did, the claim was not appropriate for arbitration.

ABN Amro Bank Canada v. Krupp Mak Machinenbau GmbH (1994), 21 O.R. (3d) 511 (Gen. Div.).

The court refused to stay an action and refer the dispute to arbitration where the moving party had made no timely request for arbitration and where the responding party was not a party to the arbitration agreement.

T1T2 Ltd. Partnership v. Canada (1994), 23 O.R. (3d) 66, 35 C.P.C. (3d) 353, 19 B.L.R. (2d) 72 (Gen. Div.).

The court refused to grant a stay based on a contractual arbitration provision where on proper interpretation the arbitration provision did not apply to the dispute being litigated.

Alton Developments Inc. v. Millcroft Inn Ltd. (1992), 17 C.P.C. (3d) 334 (Ont. Gen. Div.).

Where the subject contract provided for arbitration the court stayed the action and discharged a certificate of pending litigation notwithstanding that the defendant accepted service of the statement of claim.

Ontario Hydro v. Denison Mines Ltd. (June 3, 1992), Doc. B54/92 (Ont. Gen. Div.).

The court stayed an action where the contract between the parties provided for arbitration. Pursuant to the *Arbitration Act* the court must, with a narrow set of exceptions, stay law suits concerning matters which have been submitted to arbitration by contract.

Mind Star Toys Inc. v. Samsung Co. (1992), 9 O.R. (3d) 374, 6 C.P.C. (3d) 241 (Gen. Div.).

The court stayed an action where the subject contract provided for arbitration and the *International Commercial Arbitration Act*, R.S.O. 1990, c. I.19, applied.

Scotia Realty Ltd. v. Olympia & York SP Corp. (1992), 9 O.R. (3d) 414, 9 C.P.C. (3d) 339 (Gen. Div.).

The court stayed this proceeding pending arbitration. Discussion of the *Arbitration Act, 1991*, S.O. 1991, c. 17, which indicates the court ought not to jealously guard its jurisdiction against encroachment by arbitration.

International Semi-Tech Microelectronics Inc. v. Provigo Inc. (1990), 75 O.R. (2d) 724 (Gen. Div.).

The court refused to stay proceedings pending arbitration where the dispute was not within the ambit of the arbitration provision.

Metropolitan Toronto Housing Authority v. York University (1988), 28 C.P.C. (2d) 225 (Ont. Dist. Ct.).

The jurisdiction of the court was not ousted by an arbitration agreement where the court determined that the plaintiff would not receive substantial justice if the matter were to remain in the course of arbitration. The court therefore refused to grant the defendant a stay of the plaintiff's action.

Crowder v. Webcor Electronics (Can.) Inc. (1987), 17 C.P.C. (2d) 282 (Ont. Dist. Ct.).

The court refused to stay an action based on an arbitration clause contained in the contract where the issues involved mixed fact and law and the interpretation of the contract.

Allergan Inc. v. Bausch & Lomb Can. Inc. (1986), 13 C.P.C. (2d) 48 (Ont. Dist. Ct.).

The court refused to stay proceedings by reason of concurrent arbitrations in progress where the action was not covered by the parties' agreement or the *Arbitrations Act* and where to do so would complicate a relatively simple matter.

Brewer v. Maple Leaf Gardens Ltd. (1985), 3 C.P.C. (2d) 239 (Ont. H.C.).

The court stayed an action where arbitration proceedings had been commenced pursuant to a contract between the parties.

Strauss v. Hazelton Lanes Ltd. (1984), 39 C.P.C. 13 (Ont. H.C.).

An action was stayed pursuant to the *Arbitrations Act*, where the issues were within the purview of an arbitration clause between the parties and capable of being decided by the arbitrators and there was no reason the parties should not abide by their contractual commitment to arbitrate.

M. Loeb Ltd. v. Harzena Holdings Ltd. (1980), 18 C.P.C. 245 (Ont. H.C.).

Discussion of principles to be followed in determining whether an action should be stayed pending arbitration.

Singh v. Air India (1976), 14 O.R. (2d) 525, leave to appeal to Div. Ct. refused 14 O.R. (2d) 525 at 529n (H.C.).

An action for an injunction was stayed pursuant to s. 7 of the *Arbitrations Act*, R.S.O. 1970, c. 25.

Stay of Proceedings Based on Exclusive Jurisdiction Clause

Ash v. Corp. of Lloyd's (1992), 9 O.R. (3d) 755, 7 C.P.C. (3d) 364, 94 D.L.R. (4th) 378, 60 O.A.C. 241, additional reasons 9 O.R. (3d) 755 at 761, 7 C.P.C. (3d) 372, 95 D.L.R. (4th) 766, 60 O.A.C. 241 at 261 (C.A.), leave to appeal to Supreme Court of Canada refused 10 O.R. (3d) xv (note), 94 D.L.R. (4th) vii, 59 O.A.C. 160 (note).

A mere allegation of fraud does not make a contract void *ab initio* and vitiate the choice of jurisdiction clause in the contract.

Fairfield v. Low (1990), 71 O.R. (2d) 599, 44 C.P.C. (2d) 65, 28 C.P.R. (3d) 289 (H.C.).

Where parties have agreed upon jurisdiction in a contract which is the subject matter of a dispute, and where it is not unconscionable or against public policy, the court will give effect to the agreement unless it is shown that the interests of the parties and the interest of justice favour another jurisdiction.

Stay of Proceedings — Examples

White v. Bay-Shep Restaurant & Tavern Ltd. (1995), 16 C.C.E.L. (2d) 57 (Ont. Gen. Div.).

The court refused to stay a wrongful dismissal action pending determination of a related Ontario Human Rights Commission complaint.

Hedley v. Air Canada (1994), 23 C.P.C. (3d) 352 (Ont. Gen. Div.).

The court stayed an action for malicious prosecution pending the determination of an action for fraud.

Osmosis Waste Systems Ltd. v. Guardian Insurance Co. of Canada, 12 O.R. (3d) 786, 17 C.C.L.I. (2d) 162, [1993] I.L.R. 1-2952 (Gen. Div.).

The court stayed an action brought in Ontario by a plaintiff who sought recovery under an insurance policy for a loss by theft which occurred in British Columbia. British Columbia had the most real and substantial connection with the law suit, in that it was where the loss by theft arose and where the majority of the witnesses resided. The fact that both parties carried on business in Ontario was not determinative.

Kidder (Litigation Guardian of) v. Peel Memorial Hospital (1993), 12 O.R. (3d) 477 (Gen. Div.).

The court stayed the action for three years where the plaintiff was four years of age and more time was required to assess prospective injuries arising from the subject accident.

Campeau v. Olympia & York Developments Ltd. (1992), 14 C.P.C. (3d) 339, 14 C.B.R. (3d) 303 (Ont. Gen. Div.).

The court refused to lift a stay granted under s. 11 of the *Companies' Creditors Arrangement Act* and allow the plaintiff's action to proceed. The balance of convenience was in favour of maintaining a stay, and there was no prejudice to the plaintiffs.

Canadian Express Ltd. v. Blair (1992), 11 O.R. (3d) 221, 13 C.P.C. (3d) 375 (Gen. Div.).

The power to stay should be exercised sparingly and in the clearest of cases. The party seeking the stay must show that (1) the continuance of the action would work an injustice because it is oppressive, vexatious or an abuse of the process of the court; and (2) the stay would not cause an injustice to the other party.

Wright v. Rank City Wall Canada Ltd. (1990), 72 O.R. (2d) 44, 41 C.P.C. (2d) 38 (Master), affirmed 74 O.R. (2d) 224 (H.C.).

The court will exercise its jurisdiction to stay under this provision in the context of what is really a motion to dismiss for want of prosecution, but the occasions on which it will do so will inevitably be rare and the onus on the defendant to show inordinate or inexcusable delay and prejudice will be a heavy one.

Great-West Life Assurance Co. v. Continental Ins. Co. (1988), 65 O.R. (2d) 785, 30 C.P.C. (2d) 128, 35 C.C.L.I. 73 (H.C.).

Where the plaintiff had commenced an action in Ontario in order to preserve a limitation period pending the determination of an appeal in California, the plaintiff's motion to stay its Ontario action was dismissed. One of the defendants wanted the Ontario action to proceed, and the plaintiff had failed to show that there was something oppressive, vexatious or abusive in the continuance of its Ontario action.

Tremblay Estate v. Demers (1988), 66 O.R. (2d) 323, 30 C.P.C. (2d) 257 (H.C.).

The court stayed an application in Ontario where an action had been commenced previously in Quebec and Quebec was the convenient forum.

Manufacturers Life Ins. Co. v. Guarantee Co. of North America, 62 O.R. (2d) 147, 22 C.P.C. (2d) 176, 27 C.C.L.I. 1, [1987] I.L.R. 1-2254 (H.C.).

Where a plaintiff had instituted several actions in different jurisdictions, it was not permitted to stay the Ontario action while it tested the waters in other jurisdictions that might be more favourable to its cause.

General Dynamics Corp. v. Veliotis (1987), 21 C.P.C. (2d) 85 (Ont. Master), affirmed 61 O.R. (2d) 111, 21 C.P.C. (2d) 169, 23 O.A.C. 339 (Div. Ct.), leave to appeal to Ont. C.A. refused 21 C.P.C. (2d) 169n.

A motion by a non-party to intervene in litigation, claiming interest in the subject-matter, or to stay the litigation pending the trial of a foreign action was dismissed where the non-party had been aware of the material facts for several years and the litigation for many months before moving.

Can. Systems Group (EST) Ltd. v. Allendale Mutual Ins. Co. (1982), 29 C.P.C. 60, 137 D.L.R. (3d) 287, affirmed 41 O.R. (2d) 135, 33 C.P.C. 210, 145 D.L.R. (3d) 266 (Div. Ct.).

The court stayed this action under a business interruption policy in order to avoid inconsistent findings, where there were hundreds of other actions pending arising out of the same incident, all before a single judge.

Plibrico (Can.) Ltd. v. Suncor Inc. (1982), 35 O.R. (2d) 781, 27 C.P.C. 5 (H.C.).

Where most or all of the witnesses were in Alberta and the plaintiff in this Ontario action could assert its claim in a subsequent action commenced in Alberta by the defendant, the Ontario action was stayed.

Provencher v. Temelini (1982), 35 O.R. (2d) 645, 27 C.P.C. 9 (H.C.).

A subrogated action for property damage was stayed where there was a prior personal injury action arising out of the same action, the defendant having consented to amending the latter action to advance the property damage claim.

Gold v. Gold (1980), 27 C.P.C. 168 (Ont. Co. Ct.).

The court stayed an action for arrears of support where the same relief was available in a second action for custody and support.

OHIP v. Lourie (1980), 29 O.R. (2d) 346, 16 C.P.C. 228, 112 D.L.R. (3d) 727 (H.C.).

Where the plaintiffs had already commenced an action, a subsequent subrogated action by OHIP was stayed.

Benet v. GEC Can. Ltd. (1980), 31 O.R. (2d) 49, 18 C.P.C. 197, 81 C.L.L.C. 14,075, 118 D.L.R. (3d) 87 (H.C.).

An action for wrongful dismissal and discrimination was stayed pending the determination of proceedings by a Board of Inquiry under the *Ontario Human Rights Code*.

MacIntosh v. Gzowski (1979), 27 O.R. (2d) 151, 15 C.P.C. 14, 105 D.L.R. (3d) 721 (C.A.).

Where a plaintiff elected to claim benefits under the *Workmen's Compensation Act*, his action against the wrongdoer was stayed.

Proctor v. Proctor (1979), 26 O.R. (2d) 394, 15 C.P.C. 1, 103 D.L.R. (3d) 538, affirmed 16
  C.P.C. 220, 14 R.F.L. (2d) 385, 112 D.L.R. (3d) 370, 3 Fam. L. Rev. 135 (C.A.).

The court stayed a proceeding until the plaintiff submitted to a form of discovery not required
by the rules of court, where to deny the defendant the information sought would be contrary to
the interests of justice.

Re Abitibi Paper Co. and R. (1979), 24 O.R. (2d) 742, 47 C.C.C. (2d) 487, 8 C.E.L.R. 98, 99
  D.L.R. (3d) 333 (C.A.).

The court enforced an agreement not to prosecute by staying the proceedings.

Anderson v. Thomas, [1935] O.W.N. 228, [1935] 3 D.L.R. 286 (H.C.).

The court refused to interfere with the choice of Ontario as the forum by staying the action
notwithstanding that the parties were non-residents.

Section 107

Consolidation of proceedings in different courts
**107.—(1) Where two or more proceedings are pending in two or more different
courts, and the proceedings,**
  (a) have a question of law or fact in common;
  **(b) claim relief arising out of the same transaction or occurrence or series of
  transactions or occurrences; or**
  (c) for any other reason ought to be the subject of an order under this section,
an order may, on motion, be made,
  **(d) transferring any of the proceedings to another court and requiring the
  proceedings to be consolidated, or to be heard at the same time, or one immediately after the other; or**
  (e) requiring any of the proceedings to be,
    (i) stayed until after the determination of any other of them, or
    (ii) asserted by way of counterclaim in any other of them.

Transfer from Small Claims Court
**(2) A proceeding in the Small Claims Court shall not be transferred under
clause (1)(d) to the Ontario Court (General Division) without the consent of the
plaintiff in the proceeding in the Small Claims Court.**

Idem
**(3) A proceeding in the Small Claims Court shall not be required under sub-
clause (1)(e)(ii) to be asserted by way of counterclaim in a proceeding in the Ontario
Court (General Division) without the consent of the plaintiff in the proceeding in the
Small Claims Court.**

Motions
(4) The motion shall be made to a judge of the Ontario Court (General Division).

Directions
**(5) An order under subsection (1) may impose such terms and give such direc-
tions as are considered just, including dispensing with service of a notice of readiness
or listing for trial and abridging the time for placing an action on the trial list.**

Transfer
**(6) A proceeding that is transferred to another court under clause (1)(d) shall
be titled in the court to which it is transferred and shall be continued as if it had been
commenced in that court.**

Discretion at hearing
(7) Where an order has been made that proceedings be heard either at the same time or one immediately after the other, the judge presiding at the hearing nevertheless has discretion to order otherwise.

Ministry Comment

Original Act

This is a provision that deals with the consolidation of two or more proceedings that are pending in two or more different courts. It is similar to a provision in the Rules that deals with the consolidation of two or more proceedings that are pending in the same court. These provisions could be used, for example, when a single incident results in a number of separate court proceedings. Since many of the issues will be the same in all the proceedings, it may be convenient to consolidate the proceedings.

Cross-Reference: See Rule 6 for consolidation of cases.

PROCEDURAL MATTERS

Section 108

Jury trials
108.—(1) In an action in the Ontario Court (General Division) that is not in the Small Claims Court, a party may require that the issues of fact be tried or the damages assessed, or both, by a jury, unless otherwise provided.

Trials without jury
(2) The issues of fact and the assessment of damages in an action shall be tried without a jury in respect of a claim for any of the following kinds of relief:
1. Injunction or mandatory order.
2. Partition or sale of real property.
3. Relief under Part I, II or III of the *Family Law Act* or under the *Children's Law Reform Act.*
4. Dissolution of a partnership or taking of partnership or other accounts.
5. Foreclosure or redemption of a mortgage.
6. Sale and distribution of the proceeds of property subject to any lien or charge.
7. Execution of a trust.
8. Rectification, setting aside or cancellation of a deed or other written instrument.
9. Specific performance of a contract.
10. Declaratory relief.
11. Other equitable relief.
12. Relief against a municipality.

Idem
(3) On motion, the court may order that issues of fact be tried or damages assessed, or both, without a jury.

Composition of jury
(4) Where a proceeding is tried with a jury, the jury shall be composed of six persons selected in accordance with the *Juries Act.*

Verdicts or questions

(5) Where a proceeding is tried with a jury,

(a) the judge may require the jury to give a general verdict or to answer specific questions, subject to section 15 of the *Libel and Slander Act*; and

(b) judgment may be entered in accordance with the verdict or the answers to the questions.

Idem

(6) It is sufficient if five of the jurors agree on the verdict or the answer to a question, and where more than one question is submitted, it is not necessary that the same five jurors agree to every answer.

Discharge of juror at trial

(7) The judge presiding at a trial may discharge a juror on the ground of illness, hardship, partiality or other sufficient cause.

Continuation with five jurors

(8) Where a juror dies or is discharged, the judge may direct that the trial proceed with five jurors, in which case the verdict or answers to questions must be unanimous.

Specifying negligent acts

(9) Where a proceeding to which subsection 193(1) of the *Highway Traffic Act* applies is tried with a jury, the judge may direct the jury to specify negligent acts or omissions that caused the damages or injuries in respect of which the proceeding is brought.

Malicious prosecution

(10) In an action for malicious prosecution, the trier of fact shall determine whether or not there was reasonable and probable cause for instituting the prosecution.

Ministry Comment

Original Act

Subsection (1) replaces s. 59 of the *Judicature Act*. It states the general principle that most actions in the Ontario Court excluding the Small Claims Court may be tried with a jury. The Act does not make jury trials mandatory for actions of libel, slander, malicious arrest, malicious prosecution, and false imprisonment. Like other actions, these actions may be tried with a jury if a jury notice is served under the Rules.

Subsection (2) prohibits jury trials against municipalities, in the same way that s. 15 of the *Proceedings Against the Crown Act*, R.S.O. 1980, c. 393, prohibits jury trials against the provincial government.

Subsection (3) makes clear that a judge may order that an action be tried without a jury.

Subsection (4) is a new provision intended to serve as a bridge between subss. (2) and (3), which deal with the circumstances in which proceedings are tried without a jury, and the remaining provisions of the section, which deal with proceedings tried with a jury.

Clause (5)(a) is derived from s. 64 and s. 65(1) of the *Judicature Act*. There appears to be no difference between a special verdict and the giving of answers to specific questions. Therefore, the new provision does not mention special verdicts. At common law, a jury could give a general verdict even if the judge requested a special verdict. The new provision, like s. 64(1) of the *Judicature Act*, permits the judge to require answers to specific questions. Section 15 of the *Libel and Slander Act*, R.S.O. 1980, c. 237, permits a jury to give a general verdict notwithstanding that the judge addressed specific questions to them. This specific provision will continue to prevail over the provisions of s. 121(5)(a) of the *Courts of Justice Act.*

Clause (5)(b) is derived from s. 65(3) of the *Judicature Act.* Subsection (6) is derived from s. 62 of the *Judicature Act.* Subsections (7) and (8) are derived from s. 63 of the *Judicature Act.*

Subsection (9) is derived from s. 65(2) of the *Judicature Act.* This provision is necessary to overrule the decision of the Supreme Court of Canada in *Beach v. Healey,* [1943] S.C.R. 272, [1943] 2 D.L.R. 665.

Subsection (10) replaces s. 66 of the *Judicature Act.* The new provision alters the law, as recommended by the Uniform Law Conference of Canada in s. 187 of the *Uniform Evidence Act,* so that the trier of fact determines whether there was reasonable and probable cause for instituting the prosecution.

1989 Amendments

Bill 2

Section [108(2)] of the 1984 Act was derived from s. 60(4) of the *Judicature Act,* which provided that the right to have issues of fact tried or damages assessed by a jury did not apply "to causes, matters or issues over the subject of which the Court of Chancery had exclusive jurisdiction before the commencement of *The Administration of Justice Act of 1873*". Section [108(2)] was intended to indicate more clearly the substance of the *Judicature Act* provision. However, s. [108(2)] inadvertently changed one aspect of the law. It had formerly been possible, in an action claiming some equitable (*i.e.* Court of Chancery) relief, to have issues of fact related to a claim for other relief tried by a jury. For example, if an action claimed damages for breach of contract and an injunction, it was possible to have the damages assessed by a jury. However, under the language of s. [108(2)], a claim in an action for any of the enumerated types of relief appeared to prevent a jury from hearing any issues of fact, even if they were issues that did not relate to the claim for equitable relief. The 1989 amendment to subsection (2) was intended to restore the law to the situation where a jury is only prohibited in respect of the claim for one of the enumerated kinds of relief; a jury could still determine the issues of fact with respect to other claims in the action.

Cases (For further cases regarding jury trials, see Rule 47.)

Jury Trials — Generally

Re McKellar Estate (1995), 7 E.T.R. (2d) 299 (Ont. Div. Ct.), leave to appeal to Ont. C.A. refused (July 17, 1995), Doc. CA M15861.

The court refused to direct that certain issues in this estate matter be tried by a jury. Discussion of the discretion to order jury trials under s. 8 of the *Estates Act.*

Trials Without Jury — s. 108(2)

Davidson v. Rachlin (1994), 36 C.P.C. (3d) 226 (Ont. Master).

A claim for relief against a municipality may not be tried by a jury but a claim against a co-defendant who is not a municipality may be tried by a jury.

Crupi v. Royal Ottawa Hospital (1986), 12 C.P.C. (2d) 207 (Ont. Dist. Ct.).

Section [108(2)] of the *Courts of Justice Act* does not violate the equality rights contained in s. 15 of the *Charter of Rights and Freedoms.*

Composition of Jury — s. 108(4)

Hrup v. Cipollone (1994), 19 O.R. (3d) 715, 33 C.P.C. (3d) 275, 117 D.L.R. (4th) 440, 73 O.A.C. 269 (C.A.).

Defendants, including those adverse in interest, have an aggregate of only four peremptory challenges of jurors.

Melfi v. Palozzi, [1971] 2 O.R. 395, 18 D.L.R. (3d) 62 (C.A.).

A jury verdict was set aside where the judge had failed to instruct the jury that at least five of its members must agree on the verdict.

Letourneau v. Ottawa Bronson Const. Ltd., [1970] 1 O.R. 24, 7 D.L.R. (3d) 403 (C.A.).

A trial should not be commenced with a five-person jury; if a juror is discharged before the trial, he should be replaced.

Questions for Jury and Jury Verdicts — s. 108(5)

Rose v. Sabourin (1994), 31 C.P.C. (3d) 309, 118 D.L.R. (4th) 729 (Ont. Gen. Div.).

Once a jury verdict is recorded and the jury discharged, the jury may not be recalled to reconsider the verdict except to rectify errors made in the transmission or recording of the verdict.

Maliewski v. Pastushok (No. 2), [1966] 1 O.R. 612, 54 D.L.R. (2d) 482 (C.A.).

Questions of fact put to the jury may relate to both liability and damages.

St. Amour v. Ottawa Transportation Comm., [1957] O.W.N. 367 (C.A.).

Where a jury finds a defendant negligent but is unable to give any particulars of such negligence, the action should be dismissed rather than ordering a new trial.

Judd v. Frost, [1957] O.W.N. 539 (C.A.).

Where inconsistencies appear on the face of the jury's answers, the judge should send them back to clarify the answers. The trial judge allowed the jury to be polled although this practice was questioned by the Court of Appeal.

Walkinshaw v. Drew, [1936] O.W.N. 539, 67 C.C.C. 152, [1936] 4 D.L.R. 685 (C.A.).

Libel actions are governed by the provisions of the *Libel and Slander Act*.

Discharge of Juror — s. 108(7)

Harris (Litigation Guardian of) v. Lambton (County) Roman Catholic School Board (1994), 39 C.P.C. (3d) 396 (Ont. Gen. Div.).

Where a juror was discharged after it was discovered during the trial that he was serving a jail sentence on the weekend, the court declared a mistrial and adjourned the action to the next jury settings.

Section 109

Notice of constitutional question
109.—(1) Notice of a constitutional question shall be served on the Attorney General of Canada and the Attorney General of Ontario in the following circumstances:

1. The constitutional validity or constitutional applicability of an Act of the Parliament of Canada or the Legislature, of a regulation or by-law made under such an Act or of a rule of common law is in question.

2. A remedy is claimed under subsection 24(1) of the *Canadian Charter of Rights and Freedoms* in relation to an act or omission of the Government of Canada or the Government of Ontario.

Failure to give notice
(2) If a party fails to give notice in accordance with this section, the Act, regulation, by-law or rule of common law shall not be adjudged to be invalid or inapplicable, or the remedy shall not be granted, as the case may be.

Form of notice
(2.1) The notice shall be in the form provided for by the rules of court or, in the case of a proceeding before a board or tribunal, in a substantially similar form.

Time of notice
(2.2) The notice shall be served as soon as the circumstances requiring it become known and, in any event, at least fifteen days before the day on which the question is to be argued, unless the court orders otherwise.

Notice of appeal
(3) Where the Attorney General of Canada and the Attorney General of Ontario are entitled to notice under subsection (1), they are entitled to notice of any appeal in respect of the constitutional question.

Right of Attorneys General to be heard
(4) Where the Attorney General of Canada or the Attorney General of Ontario is entitled to notice under this section, he or she is entitled to adduce evidence and make submissions to the court in respect of the constitutional question.

Right of Attorneys General to appeal
(5) Where the Attorney General of Canada or the Attorney General of Ontario makes submissions under subsection (4), he or she shall be deemed to be a party to the proceedings for the purpose of any appeal in respect of the constitutional question.

Boards and tribunals
(6) This section applies to proceedings before boards and tribunals as well as to court proceedings. [am. 1994, c. 12, s. 42]

Ministry Comment

Original Act

Subsection (1) is derived from s. 35(1) of the *Judicature Act*. The new provision requires notice whenever the constitutional applicability of a statute, as well as the constitutional validity of a statute, is questioned.

Subsection (2) replaces s. 35(2) and (3) of the *Judicature Act*. The rules of court provide a form (*e.g.* Form 4F of the Rules of Civil Procedure) for the notice which gives more detail concerning the content of the notice. The new subsection also extends the period of notice from six days to ten days, subject to the court permitting a different period.

Subsection (3) is a new provision intended to make clear that the Attorney General of Canada and the Attorney General of Ontario are entitled to notice of any appeal in respect of a constitutional issue.

1995 Amendments

Section 109 of the Act is amended to require notice to the Attorney General of a constitutional issue,

(a) arising before a board or tribunal, if notice would have to be given if the issue arose before a court;
(b) involving a claim for a remedy under section 24(1) of the Charter in relation to a government action, omission or policy; and
(c) involving a Charter challenge to a rule of common law.

The section is also amended to require that notice be given at the earliest time that it becomes known that a constitutional question will be raised, and to guarantee that the Attorney General will have at least 15 days to prepare for the argument of the question, subject to the court's (or tribunal's) power to shorten the minimum period in appropriate cases.

Cross-Reference: See also rule 4.11 and Form 4F.

Cases

Christian Horizons v. Ontario Human Rights Commission (1993), 14 O.R. (3d) 374, 60 O.A.C. 395 (Div. Ct.).

Although the parties had agreed not to raise *Charter* issues on an Ontario Human Rights Commission hearing, on appeal the court disregarded the agreement, and permitted a party to intervene for the purpose of raising the *Charter* issue. It is not open to parties to determine that a statute is to be interpreted without reference to the *Charter*.

Ontario (Workers' Compensation Board) v. Mandelbaum, Spergel Inc. (1993), 12 O.R. (3d) 385, 18 C.B.R. (3d) 22, 46 C.C.E.L. 136, 15 C.R.R. (2d) 97, 100 D.L.R. (4th) 742, 61 O.A.C. 361 (C.A.).

An inadvertent failure to give notice to the Attorney General of a constitutional question did not render the decision at first instance a nullity, as the constitutional question had been fully argued in the lower court and the Attorney General was unable to show any prejudice.

A.G. Ont. v. A.G. Can., [1931] O.R. 5, 55 C.C.C. 346, [1931] 2 D.L.R. 297 (H.C.).

The Ontario court has jurisdiction to make a declaration as to the validity of any statute of Ontario or of Canada which purports to have force in Ontario if the Attorneys General of both jurisdictions are parties to the action.

Currie v. Harris Lithographic Co. (1917), 40 O.L.R. 290, reversed on other grounds 41 O.L.R. 475, 41 D.L.R. 227, which was reversed (*sub nom. Great West Saddlery Co. v. R.*) [1921] 2 A.C. 91, [1921] 1 W.W.R. 1034, 58 D.L.R. 1 (P.C.).

The Attorney General for Ontario can maintain an action for a declaration as to the constitutional validity of a provincial statute.

Section 110

Proceeding in wrong forum

110.—(1) Where a proceeding or a step in a proceeding is brought or taken before the wrong court, judge or officer, it may be transferred or adjourned to the proper court, judge or officer.

Continuation of proceeding

(2) A proceeding that is transferred to another court under subsection (1) shall be titled in the court to which it is transferred and shall be continued as if it had been commenced in that court.

Ministry Comment

Original Act

This is a new provision that permits a proceeding, or a step in a proceeding, brought or taken before the wrong court, judge or officer, to be transferred or adjourned to the proper court, judge or officer. Without this provision, a person who mistakenly chooses the wrong forum may find that he has missed a time period and is too late to start again.

Cases

Tawfik v. Baker (1992), 10 O.R. (3d) 569, 10 C.P.C. (3d) 239 (Gen. Div.).

The court has an inherent jurisdiction to transfer an action from a lower court to a superior court. Accordingly, where the plaintiff's claim was brought in Small Claims Court, but the value of the claim exceeded its jurisdiction, the court acted within its authority in transferring the action to the Ontario Court of Justice (General Division).

Dunnington v. 656956 Ontario Ltd. (1991), 9 O.R. (3d) 124, 6 C.P.C. (3d) 298, 89 D.L.R. (4th) 607, 54 O.A.C. 345 (Div. Ct.).

The court has a discretion whether to adjourn the case to the proper forum. Where an appeal is brought to the wrong court, that court should consider (1) whether the appellant has a meritorious appeal, (2) whether the respondent will suffer undue prejudice by delay, and (3) whether the appellant moved expeditiously once the jurisdiction was disputed. In this case, the Divisional Court refused to transfer an appeal to the Court of Appeal.

Castle v. Toronto Harbour Commrs. (1987), 20 C.P.C. (2d) 266 (Ont. Prov. Ct.).

The Provincial Court (Civil Division) does not have jurisdiction in an action for negligence occurring on navigable inland waters.

Dumas v. Dumas (1985), 49 C.P.C. 140 (Ont. Master).

A motion beyond jurisdiction of a master was adjourned to be heard by a judge.

Re Zurich Ins. Co. and Torbay Dining Ltd.; Re C.I.B.C. (1985), 49 C.P.C. 26 (Ont. Master).

An application wrongly brought before a master was transferred to be heard by a judge.

Section 111

Set off

111.—(1) In an action for payment of a debt, the defendant may, by way of defence, claim the right to set off against the plaintiff's claim a debt owed by the plaintiff to the defendant.

Idem

(2) Mutual debts may be set off against each other, even if they are of a different nature.

Judgment for defendant

(3) Where, on a defence of set off, a larger sum is found to be due from the plaintiff to the defendant than is found to be due from the defendant to the plaintiff, the defendant is entitled to judgment for the balance.

Ministry Comment

Original Act

Subsection (1) is derived from s. 134 of the *Judicature Act.* The new provision is intended to make clear that the set-off is claimed by way of defence, not by way of counterclaim. Subsection (2) is derived from s. 135(1) of the *Judicature Act.* It also provides that a set-off may be claimed in respect of debts that are owed in different capacities, a matter that was dealt with in part by s. 134 of the *Judicature Act.*

The language in s. 135(1) of the *Judicature Act,* dealing with penalties, as well as s. 135(2), has been deleted as unnecessary. Penalties are unenforceable because of the law of equity, not because of s. 135.

1989 Amendments

Bill 2

Section 124(2) of the 1984 Act was derived from s. 135(1) of the *Judicature Act.* The former provision did not contain a reference to setting off debts owed in a personal capacity against debts owed in another capacity. The presence of this language in s. [111(2)] of the existing Act would seem to permit, for example, a debt owed by a person in his or her own personal capacity to be set off against a debt owing to that person in his or her capacity as executor of an estate. This was clearly not a logical result. The new subsection (2) is intended to return to the concept originally provided for in s. 135(1) of the *Judicature Act.*

Cases

Mercantile Bank of Canada v. Leon's Furniture Ltd. (1992), 11 O.R. (3d) 713, 18 C.B.R. (3d) 72, 98 D.L.R. (4th) 449, 62 O.A.C. 187 (C.A.).

A claim for set-off may be asserted in response to a claim by a bank holding security taken under s. 178 of the *Bank Act* (Canada). There is no clear or express language in the *Bank Act* which would preclude the application of equitable set-off.

Agway Metals Inc. v. Dufferin Roofing Ltd. (1991), 46 C.P.C. (2d) 133 (Ont. Gen. Div.).

Legal set-off has two conditions: first, that both obligations be debts and, second, that such debts be mutual cross-obligations. The debts must be liquidated sums or money demands which can be ascertained with certainty. Equitable set-off applies to two obligations which are so closely bound up that it would be unconscionable not to permit set-off and can apply to non-debt obligations such as unliquidated claims.

Mercantile Bank of Can. v. Leon's Furniture Ltd. (1989), 67 O.R. (2d) 454, 42 B.L.R. 1 (H.C.).

A bank was subject to the equities between its customer and a third party manufacturer when collecting its customer's accounts, and accordingly the manufacturer was allowed to set off certain items against the bank's claim in accordance with its understanding with the bank's customer.

H.D. Madden & Associates Inc. v. Brendan Wood, Tutsch & Partners Inc. (1989), 33 C.P.C. (2d) 263 (Ont. Dist. Ct.).

Unlike set-off at law, equitable set-off does not require mutual debts but only opposing claims which flow from the same transaction or relationship between the parties.

Haick v. Smith (1988), 27 C.P.C. (2d) 193 (Ont. Master).

The defence of equitable set-off does not apply to claims based on a bill of exchange.

Davis v. Spectrix Microsystems Inc. (1987), 63 O.R. (2d) 151, 23 C.P.C. (2d) 120 (Master), affirmed (1988), 69 O.R. (2d) 639n, 32 C.P.C. (2d) 312 (Div. Ct.).

For a claim to be an equitable set-off it has to arise out of the same transaction as the contract on which the plaintiff is suing; a claim for unliquidated damages cannot be a set-off of mutual debts as contemplated by s. [111].

McGee (Irwin) v. Irwin (1986), 8 C.P.C. (2d) 86, 50 R.F.L. (2d) 65 (Ont. Fam. Ct.).

A husband was entitled to an equitable set-off of the amount of a debt owed by the wife from a support payment that he owed to the wife, although the debt and the support payment were unconnected transactions.

Iraco Ltd. v. Staiman Steel Ltd. (1986), 54 O.R. (2d) 488, 8 C.P.C. (2d) 293, 27 D.L.R. (4th) 69 (H.C.), affirmed (1987), 62 O.R. (2d) 129n, 45 D.L.R. (4th) 158 (C.A.).

A counterclaim for unliquidated damages with respect to a partial failure of consideration and breach of warranty of the quality of goods was no defence to an action on a bill of exchange between immediate parties; the law of equitable set-off does not apply to bills of exchange.

Hattori Overseas (Hong Kong) Ltd. v. Phillip Cox Agency Inc. (1985), 2 C.P.C. (2d) 257 (Ont. Div. Ct.).

A claim for unliquidated damages may be set off against a claim for liquidated damages provided the opposing claims arise out of the same transaction or relationship between the parties and raise an equity in favour of the defendant.

Re L.S.U.C. and Merker (1985), 49 O.R. (2d) 345, 54 C.B.R. (N.S.) 153 (*sub nom. Re Merker*) (H.C.).

Money owing by a bankrupt solicitor to the Law Society's compensation fund was set off against an account owing to the solicitor under the Legal Aid Plan.

Can. Southern Ry. Co. v. Michigan Central Railroad Co. (1983), 45 O.R. (2d) 257, 39 C.P.C. 18, 6 D.L.R. (4th) 324 (H.C.), leave to appeal to Ont. C.A. refused 39 C.P.C. 18n.

Where a dividend was declared following a corporate reorganization, the company alleged "abuse of majority position" against its former director. It was held that the plaintiff's claim could be set off against the dividend payable to the former directors.

Mabri Const. Ltd. v. Thomas C. Assaly Corp. (1974), 6 O.R. (2d) 178 (H.C.).

The defendant's claim for damages for breach of contract was required to be asserted by way of counterclaim rather than set-off.

Langdon v. Traders Finance Corp., [1966] 1 O.R. 655, 8 C.B.R. (N.S.) 294, 55 D.L.R. (2d) 12 (C.A.).

The court does not have a discretion to refuse a request to enforce a valid set-off.

Section 112

Investigation and report of Children's Lawyer

112.—(1) In a proceeding under the *Divorce Act* (Canada) or the *Children's Law Reform Act* in which a question concerning custody of or access to a child is before the court, the Children's Lawyer may cause an investigation to be made and may report and make recommendations to the court on all matters concerning custody of or access to the child and the child's support and education.

Idem

(2) The Children's Lawyer may act under subsection (1) on his or her own initiative, at the request of a court or at the request of any person.

Report as evidence

(3) An affidavit of the person making the investigation, verifying the report as to facts that are within the person's knowledge and setting out the source of the person's information and belief as to other facts, with the report attached as an exhibit thereto, shall be served on the parties and filed and on being filed shall form part of the evidence at the hearing of the proceeding.

Attendance on report

(4) Where a party to the proceeding disputes the facts set out in the report, the Children's Lawyer shall if directed by the court, and may when not so directed, attend the hearing on behalf of the child and cause the person who made the investigation to attend as a witness. [am. 1994, c. 27, s. 43]

Ministry Comment

Bill 161, 1987 (Explanatory Note)

The Official Guardian's report will no longer be automatic in all divorce proceedings involving children. Instead, whenever a question concerning custody of or access to a child is before the court in proceedings under the *Divorce Act, 1985* (Canada) or the *Children's Law Reform Act*, the Official Guardian will be empowered to investigate and report to the court on matters affecting the child. The Official Guardian will determine which cases will be investigated and the nature and extent of the investigation. [*Authors' Comment:* "Children's Lawyer" is the new name for "Official Guardian".]

Cross-Reference: See also rules 69.16 and 70.06.

Section 113

Agreement preventing third party claim or crossclaim
113. Rules of court permitting a defendant to make a third party claim or crossclaim apply despite any agreement that provides that no action may be brought until after judgment against the defendant.

Ministry Comment

Original Act

This is a new provision intended to implement a recommendation of the Morden Subcommittee. They recommended that a defendant should be permitted to make a third party claim against his or her insurer, notwithstanding that the contract of insurance contains a "no action" clause that prevents the defendant from taking action against the insurer until judgment is obtained against the defendant. Without this provision, a defendant must suffer judgment and expose his or her property to execution before an action can even be commenced against the insurer based on the insurer's contractual liability to indemnify the defendant.

Section 114

Agreement as to place of hearing
114. Where a party moves to change the place of hearing in a proceeding, an agreement as to the place of hearing is not binding, but may be taken into account.

Ministry Comment

Original Act

This section is derived from s. 61 of the *Judicature Act*. The new section states that, although an agreement as to the place of hearing is not binding if a motion to change the place of hearing is made, the agreement may be taken into account on the motion.

Section 115

Security
115. Where a person is required to give security in respect of a proceeding in a court, a bond of a guarantee company to which the *Guarantee Companies Securities Act* applies is sufficient, unless the court orders otherwise.

Ministry Comment

Original Act

This section replaces s. 76 of the *Judicature Act*. The regulations under the *Guarantee Companies Securities Act*, list the companies that are permitted to give security in court proceedings.

Section 116

Periodic payment and review of damages

116.—(1) In a proceeding where damages are claimed for personal injuries or under Part V of the *Family Law Act* for loss resulting from the injury to or death of a person, the court,

(a) if all affected parties consent, may order the defendant to pay all or part of the award for damages periodically on such terms as the court considers just; and

(b) if the plaintiff requests that an amount be included in the award to compensate for income tax payable on the award, shall order the defendant to pay all or part of the award periodically on such terms as the court considers just.

No order

(2) An order under clause (1)(b) shall not be made if the parties otherwise consent or if the court is of the opinion that the order would not be in the best interest of the plaintiff, having regard to all the circumstances of the case.

Best interests

(3) In considering the best interests of the plaintiff, the court shall take into account,

(a) whether the defendant has sufficient means to fund an adequate scheme of periodic payments;

(b) whether the plaintiff has a plan or a method of payment that is better able to meet the interests of the plaintiff than periodic payments by the defendant; and

(c) whether a scheme of periodic payments is practicable having regard to all the circumstances of the case.

Future review

(4) In an order made under this section, the court may, with the consent of all the affected parties, order that the award be subject to future review and revision in such circumstances and on such terms as the court considers just.

Amount to offset liability for income tax

(5) If the court does not make an order for periodic payment under subsection (1), it shall make an award for damages that shall include an amount to offset liability for income tax on income from investment of the award.

Ministry Comment

1989 Amendments

Bill 69 (Explanatory Note)

Section [116] of the 1984 Act provides for periodic (structured) payments if all parties consent and for a review and revision of an order for such payments. The section is rewritten retaining the current concepts while providing structured payments to be imposed where the plaintiff requests a gross up to compensate for income tax payable.

Authors' Comment

The amendments to this section (and to the other sections referred to below) were part of the package of reforms implementing certain recommendations of the

Osborne Report respecting personal injury actions and the Ontario Law Reform Commission's 1987 *Report on Compensation for Personal Injuries and Death*, brought about by S.O. 1989, c. 67 (Bill 69), in force December 14, 1989. (For an analysis of the impact of that Act, see the Annual Survey of Recent Developments in Civil Procedure in the 1990 edition of Watson and McGowan, *Ontario Civil Practice.*)

The transition provision of that Act (s. 8) is relatively complex and creates a difficulty because it appears not to be comprehensive. (For the full text of this provision see the "Transition Guide" supplement to Watson and McGowan, *Ontario Supreme and District Court Practice 1990*, p. 24.) The transition provision provides that the amendments to s. [116] (periodic payments), s. [127(1)] (definition of pre-judgment interest rate), s. [128(1)-(3)] (prejudgment interest), and s. [130] (discretion of court re interest) "apply to causes of action arising after the 23rd day of October, 1989". By contrast, the amendments to s. [118] (guidance and submissions to jury re damages), s. [119] (court on appeal may substitute own damage award), s. [120] (advance payments) and s. [128(4)(e)] (exclusions re prejudgment interest) apply to:

(a) actions commenced but not settled or adjudicated upon before this Act comes into force; and

(b) causes of action arising after this Act comes into force.

The provision applying to causes of action arising after October 23, 1989, causes no difficulty (assuming the date on which the cause of action arose can be determined). The difficulty is with regard to the other transition provision. Since it applies (in effect) to actions pending on December 14, 1989, and to causes of action arising on or after December 14, 1989, this transition provision is silent with regard to an important (and sizeable) class of claims: *i.e.*, those commenced on or *after* December 14, 1989, based on causes of action arising *before* December 14, 1989. In policy terms there seems no reason why such claims should not be covered by the new regime, given that the new regime applies to actions *pending* on December 14, 1989. However, the statute does not so provide and it is arguable that such claims are covered by the former law.

There is one further difficulty that arises from the drafting (although it is of less significance). It is arguable that s. [120] (advance payments) does not apply to applications, since the provision speaks of a "defendant" and a "plaintiff" which terms are defined in s. 1 to apply only to parties to an action. While it would seem desirable that advance payments be permitted in applications, it would appear that a respondent who makes an advance payment to an applicant will not necessarily be able to rely on s. [120].

As explained above, the new s. [116] (periodic payment and review of damages) applies only to causes of action arising after October 23, 1989. Hence, causes of action arising on or before October 23, 1989, are governed by the former s. 129 which provided as follows:

Periodic payment and review of damages
129. In a proceeding where damages are claimed,
(a) for personal injuries; or
(b) under Part V of the *Family Law Reform Act*, for loss resulting from the injury to or death of a person,
the court may, with the consent of all affected parties,

(c) order the defendant to pay all or part of the award for damages periodically on such terms as the court considers just;

(d) order that the award for damages be subject to future review and revision in such circumstances and on such terms as the court considers just.

Cases

Wilson v. Martinello (1995), 23 O.R. (3d) 417, 37 C.P.C. (3d) 325, 125 D.L.R. (4th) 240, 81 O.A.C. 24 (C.A.).

Where the plaintiff requested a gross-up for income taxes and a management fee in a lump sum award for pecuniary loss, the court was obliged under s. 116 to structure the award unless the plaintiff could satisfy the court that a structured award was not in the plaintiff's best interest considering the factors set out in s. 116(3)(a), (b), (c). The court upheld the award for income tax gross-up, but not the management fee.

Wilson v. Martinello (1993), 29 C.P.C. (3d) 18 (Ont. Gen. Div.).

The court held it was premature to rule early in the trial whether an order for periodic payments was in the best interests of the plaintiffs.

Kenyeres (Litigation Guardian of) v. Cullimore (1992), 13 C.P.C. (3d) 385 (Ont. Gen. Div.), affirmed (March 7, 1994), Doc. CA C12531/92 (Ont. C.A.).

Where the parties in a personal injury action consented to a periodic payments scheme but could not agree on the terms, the court set the terms.

Kendall (Litigation Guardian of) v. Kindl Estate (1992), 10 C.P.C. (3d) 24 (Ont. Gen. Div.).

The court may not order an unwilling defendant to enter into a structured settlement. The court's *parens patriae* jurisdiction does not provide jurisdiction to do so for a minor plaintiff.

Section 117

Assessment of damages

117. Where damages are to be assessed in respect of,

(a) a continuing cause of action;

(b) repeated breaches of a recurring obligation; or

(c) intermittent breaches of a continuing obligation,

the damages, including damages for breaches occurring after the commencement of the proceeding, shall be assessed down to the time of the assessment.

Ministry Comment

Original Act

This section is derived from former Rule 259, which does not appear in the new Rules.

Cases

East Middlesex Dist. High School Bd. v. London Bd. of Educ., [1965] 2 O.R. 51, 49 D.L.R. (2d) 586, affirmed [1967] S.C.R. 49, 59 D.L.R. (2d) 213.

Damages may be assessed to the time of assessment without prejudice to a later action for subsequent damages.

Section 118

Guidance and submissions
118. In an action for damages for personal injury, the court may give guidance to the jury on the amount of damages and the parties may make submissions to the jury on the amount of damages.

Ministry Comment

1989 Amendments

Bill 69 (Explanatory Note)

The new s. [118] of the Act allows trial judges in jury cases to express an opinion to the jury as to the range of compensation.

Authors' Comment

As to the operative date of this provision, see the Authors' Comment following s. 116.

Cases

Roy v. Watson (1993), 19 C.P.C. (3d) 352 (Ont. Gen. Div.).
Counsel may refer to the amount of damages in their opening addresses to the jury.

Caron v. Chodan Estate (1993), 58 O.A.C. 173 (C.A.).
The Ontario Court of Appeal ordered a new trial on the issue of damages where during the course of the plaintiff's address to the jury, counsel had suggested an inappropriate range of damages and had drawn the jury's attention to the limits of the available insurance coverage.

Baurose v. Hart (1990), 44 C.P.C. (2d) 283 (Ont. Gen. Div.).
In a non-castastrophic personal injury case, it was held to be inappropriate for counsel to advise the jury of the limit for general damages for non-pecuniary loss set by the Supreme Court of Canada.

Section 119

Power of court on appeal
119. On an appeal from an award for damages for personal injury, the court may, if it considers it just, substitute its own assessment of the damages.

Ministry Comment

1989 Amendments

Bill 69 (Explanatory Note)

The new s. [119] allows an appeal court to substitute its assessment of damages for that of a jury.

Authors' Comment

As to the operative date of this provision, see the Authors' Comment following s. 116.

Section 120

Advance payments

120.—(1) If a defendant makes a payment to a plaintiff who is or alleges to be entitled to recover from the defendant, the payment constitutes, to the extent of the payment, a release by the plaintiff or the plaintiff's personal representative of any claim that the plaintiff or the plaintiff's personal representative or any person claiming through or under the plaintiff or by virtue of Part V of the *Family Law Act*, may have against the defendant.

Idem

(2) Nothing in this section precludes the defendant making the payment from demanding, as a condition precedent to such payment, a release from the plaintiff or the plaintiff's personal representative or any other person to the extent of such payment.

Payment to be taken into account

(3) The court shall adjudicate upon the matter first without reference to the payment but, in giving judgment, the payment shall be taken into account and the plaintiff shall only be entitled to judgment for the net amount, if any.

Disclosure

(4) The fact of any payment shall not be disclosed to the judge or jury until after judgment but shall be disclosed before formal entry thereof.

Ministry Comment

1989 Amendments

Bill 69 (Explanatory Note)

The new s. 120 permits payments to a plaintiff without prejudice to the defendant either as an admission of liability or otherwise.

Authors' Comment

As to the operative date of this provision, see the Authors' Comment following s. 116.

Cases

Ecuimates v. Rix (1993), 27 C.P.C. (3d) 301 (Ont. Gen. Div.).

As a payment made by the defendants as a term of an adjournment was not an advance payment, the plaintiff was not required to return the money when his action was dismissed.

Downey v. Maes (1992), 8 O.R. (3d) 440 (Gen. Div.).

A defendant who has made an advance payment is entitled to have that sum applied first to the principal sum of the judgment, with the surplus, if any, to be applied to accrued prejudgment interest.

Section 121

Foreign money obligations

121.—(1) Subject to subsections (3) and (4), where a person obtains an order to enforce an obligation in a foreign currency, the order shall require payment of an

amount in Canadian currency sufficient to purchase the amount of the obligation in the foreign currency at a bank in Ontario listed in Schedule I to the *Bank Act (Canada)* at the close of business on the first day on which the bank quotes a Canadian dollar rate for purchase of the foreign currency before the day payment of the obligation is received by the creditor.

Multiple payments
(2) **Where more than one payment is made under an order referred to in subsection (1), the rate of conversion shall be the rate determined as provided in subsection (1) for each payment.**

Discretion of court
(3) **Subject to subsection (4), where, in a proceeding to enforce an obligation in a foreign currency, the court is satisfied that conversion of the amount of the obligation to Canadian currency as provided in subsection (1) would be inequitable to any party, the order may require payment of an amount in Canadian currency sufficient to purchase the amount of the obligation in the foreign currency at a bank in Ontario on such other day as the court considers equitable in the circumstances.**

Other obligations that include conversion
(4) **Where an obligation enforceable in Ontario provides for a manner of conversion to Canadian currency of an amount in a foreign currency, the court shall give effect to the manner of conversion in the obligation.**

Enforcement by seizure or garnishment
(5) **Where a writ of seizure and sale or notice of garnishment is issued under an order to enforce an obligation in a foreign currency, the day the sheriff, bailiff or clerk of the court receives money under the writ or notice shall be deemed, for the purposes of this section and any obligation referred to in subsection (4), to be the day payment is received by the creditor.**

Authors' Comment

The purpose of this provision is to provide a flexible mechanism for the enforcement of foreign currency obligations and to protect parties from fluctuations in exchange rates.

The effect of the section is that where a judgment debtor wishes to voluntarily discharge the judgment, he or she simply provides the judgment creditor with the amount of Canadian funds which would have been required to purchase the necessary amount of foreign currency on the previous trading day (see s. 121(1)).

In the case of execution under the judgment, where the sheriff receives an amount of Canadian funds, he or she simply determines the amount of foreign currency the Canadian funds would have purchased on the day prior to receipt and credits that amount to the judgment debt.

The section contemplates that the judgment will express the judgment debt as "the amount in Canadian currency necessary to purchase" the foreign currency amount on the appropriate conversion date. Conversion is deferred until recovery is made under the judgment.

A contractual provision regarding conversion of currency will override the mechanism provided by this section: s. 121(4).

This section is also intended to apply to actions in Ontario based on foreign judgments. If the foreign judgment provides for conversion to Canadian currency, subs. (4) applies.

Section 122

Actions for accounting
122.—(1) Where an action for an accounting could have been brought against a person, the action may be brought against the person's personal representative.

Idem
(2) An action for an accounting may be brought by a joint tenant or tenant in common, or his or her personal representative, against a co-tenant for receiving more than the co-tenant's just share.

Section 123

Giving decisions — Definitions
123.—(1) In this section,
"chief judge" means a person having authority to assign duties to the judge;
"judge" includes a master.

Decision after retirement, etc.
(2) A judge may, within ninety days of,
(a) reaching retirement age;
(b) resigning; or
(c) being appointed to another court,
give a decision or participate in the giving of a decision in any matter previously tried or heard before the judge.

Inability to give decision; panel of judges
(3) Where a judge has commenced a hearing together with other judges and,
(a) dies before the decision is given;
(b) is for any reason unable to participate in the giving of the decision; or
(c) does not participate in the giving of the decision under subsection (2),
the remaining judges may complete the hearing and give the decision of the court but, if the remaining judges are equally divided, a party may make a motion to the chief judge for an order that the matter be reheard.

Inability to give decision; sitting alone
(4) Where a judge has commenced hearing a matter sitting alone and,
(a) dies without giving a decision;
(b) is for any reason unable to make a decision; or
(c) does not give a decision under subsection (2),
a party may make a motion to the chief judge for an order that the matter be reheard.

Failure to give decision
(5) Where a judge has heard a matter and fails to give a decision,
(a) in the case of a judgment, within six months; or
(b) in any other case, within three months,
the chief judge may extend the time in which the decision may be given and, if necessary, relieve the judge of his or her other duties until the decision is given.

Continued failure
(6) Where time has been extended under subsection (5) but the judge fails to give the decision within that time, unless the chief judge grants a further extension,

(a) the chief judge shall report the failure and the surrounding circumstances to the appropriate judicial council; and

(b) a party may make a motion to the chief judge for an order that the matter be reheard.

Rehearing
(7) Where an order is made under subsection (3), (4) or (6) for the rehearing of a matter, the chief judge may,

(a) dispose of the costs of the original hearing or refer the question of those costs to the judge or judges presiding at the rehearing;

(b) direct that the rehearing be conducted on the transcript of evidence taken at the original hearing, subject to the discretion of the court at the rehearing to recall a witness or require further evidence; and

(c) give such other directions as are considered just.

Ministry Comment

Original Act

This section deals with the giving of decisions by a judge who retires or resigns and with the situation where a rehearing is required. Subsection (1) defines the persons to whom the section applies.

Subsection (2) is derived from ss. 11(1), 11(2) and 42(5) of the *Judicature Act*, s. 19 of the *County Judges Act* and s. 13 of the *Unified Family Court Act*. The time in which the decision can be given has been extended from eight weeks to ninety days.

Subsection (3) is derived from s. 11(3) of the *Judicature Act*. It also permits a rehearing if the remaining judges are equally divided.

Subsection (4) is derived from s. 30(1) of the *County Courts Act*. The new provision extends to judges of all courts, not just District Court judges.

Subsections (5) and (6) are intended to deal with delayed decisions.

1989 Amendments

Bill 2

The amendment to clause (1)(a) is intended to permit any judge with authority to assign judicial duties (including the regional senior judges) the power to perform the "chief judge's" powers under the section.

Cases

Johnston v. Stewart (1994), 28 C.P.C. (3d) 20, 116 D.L.R. (4th) 180 (Ont. Gen. Div.).

Where a trial judge had written extensively on a case, but had died prior to a judgment being released, the court held that the judge's writings did not constitute a "decision" within the meaning of s. 123(4), as all of the issues of fact and law were not the subject of a disposition.

Crocker v. Sipus (1992), 9 O.R. (3d) 713, 11 C.P.C. (3d) 127, 41 R.F.L. (3d) 19, 95 D.L.R. (4th) 360, 57 O.A.C. 310 (C.A.).

The filing of a notice of appeal after the disposition of a case has been announced does not bar the consideration on appeal of subsequent reasons for decision.

Guastelluccia v. Scott (1978), 20 O.R. (2d) 241, 87 D.L.R. (3d) 423 (C.A.).

Where a judge considering a reserved case concludes that the plaintiff may be entitled to succeed on a cause of action which has not been pleaded, he should recall counsel so that the pleadings may be amended and additional evidence given.

Wm. Unser Ltd. v. Toronto, [1954] O.W.N. 263, [1954] 2 D.L.R. 364 (C.A.).

It is improper for a trial judge to deliver supplementary reasons for decision following reversal of his judgment by the Court of Appeal.

Section 124

Service on Sunday

124. No document shall be served and no order shall be executed on Sunday, except with leave of the court.

Ministry Comment

Original Act

This section is derived from s. 132 of the *Judicature Act*. The new provision permits documents to be served on Sunday if leave of the court is obtained. For example, there may be occasions where an urgent motion for an interim injunction must be made to stop an activity that is planned to take place on a Sunday. If the order is not obtained until late Saturday, it should still be possible to serve the order on Sunday. The new section also implements the Ontario Law Reform Commission recommendation that "the Lord's Day" be replaced by "Sunday": *Report on Sunday Observance Legislation* (1970), p. 367.

LANGUAGE

Section 125

Official languages of the courts

125.—(1) The official languages of the courts of Ontario are English and French.

Proceedings in English unless otherwise provided

(2) Except as otherwise provided with respect to the use of the French language,
(a) hearings in courts shall be conducted in the English language and evidence adduced in a language other than English shall be interpreted into the English language; and
(b) documents filed in courts shall be in the English language or shall be accompanied by a translation of the document into the English language certified by affidavit of the translator.

Ministry Comment

Original Act

Subsection (1) states that the official languages of the courts in Ontario are English and French. Although subs. (2) provides that most proceedings are conducted in English, s. 136 provides very significant rights to litigants who speak French.

Subsection (2) is derived from s. 130(1) of the *Judicature Act*. The section is intended to state more clearly the existing practice of the courts. For example, documentary evidence that is not in the English language may be filed if it is accompanied by a translation of the document into the English language.

Cases

Metropolitan Toronto (Municipality) v. Barrett (1991), 2 C.P.C. (3d) 129 (Ont. Prov. Div.).

In a bilingual trial under s. [125] and s. [126] of the *Courts of Justice Act*, each party may lead evidence and make submissions in the official language of its choice and receive the assistance of an interpreter. There is no requirement that a bilingual prosecutor be assigned to the case.

Trumble v. Kapuskasing (Town) (1986), 57 O.R. (2d) 139 at 155, 14 C.P.C. (2d) 66, 34 D.L.R. (4th) 545 at 560 (H.C.).

Where a respondent to an application delivered two affidavits written in French, the court ruled that the costs of the translation should be borne by the court.

Section 126

Bilingual proceedings
126.—(1) A party to a proceeding who speaks French has the right to require that it be conducted as a bilingual proceeding.

Idem
(2) The following rules apply to a proceeding that is conducted as a bilingual proceeding:

1. The hearings that the party specifies shall be presided over by a judge or officer who speaks English and French.
2. If a hearing that the party has specified is held before a judge and jury in an area named in Schedule 1, the jury shall consist of persons who speak English and French.
3. If a hearing that the party has specified is held without a jury, or with a jury in an area named in Schedule 1, evidence given and submissions made in English or French shall be received, recorded and transcribed in the language in which they are given.
4. Any other part of the hearing may be conducted in French if, in the opinion of the presiding judge or officer, it can be so conducted.
5. Oral evidence given in English or French at an examination out of court shall be received, recorded and transcribed in the language in which it is given.
6. In an area named in Schedule 2, a party may file pleadings and other documents written in French.
7. Elsewhere in Ontario, a party may file pleadings and other documents written in French if the other parties consent.
8. The reasons for a decision may be written in English or French.
9. On the request of a party or counsel who speaks English or French but not both, the court shall provide interpretation of anything given orally in the other language at hearings referred to in paragraphs 2 and 3 and at examinations out of court, and translation of reasons for a decision written in the other language.

Prosecutions
(2.1) When a prosecution under the *Provincial Offences Act* by the Crown in right of Ontario is being conducted as a bilingual proceeding, the prosecutor assigned to the case must be a person who speaks English and French.

Appeals
(3) When an appeal is taken in a proceeding that is being conducted as a bilingual proceeding, a party who speaks French has the right to require that the

appeal be heard by a judge or judges who speak English and French; in that case subsection (2) applies to the appeal, with necessary modifications.

Documents

(4) A document filed by a party before a hearing in a proceeding in the Family Court of the Ontario Court (General Division), the Ontario Court (Provincial Division) or the Small Claims Court may be written in French.

Process

(5) A process issued in or giving rise to a criminal proceeding or a proceeding in the Family Court of the Ontario Court (General Division) or the Ontario Court (Provincial Division) may be written in French.

Translation

(6) On a party's request, the court shall provide translation into English or French of a document or process referred to in subsection (4) or (5) that is written in the other language.

Interpretation

(7) At a hearing to which paragraph 3 of subsection (2) does not apply, if a party acting in person makes submissions in French or a witness gives oral evidence in French, the court shall provide interpretation of the submissions or evidence into English.

Parties who are not natural persons

(8) A corporation, partnership or sole proprietorship may exercise the rights conferred by this section in the same way as a natural person, unless the court orders otherwise.

Regulations

(9) The Lieutenant Governor in Council may make regulations,

(a) prescribing procedures for the purpose of this section;

(b) adding areas to Schedule 1 or 2. [am. 1994, c. 12, s. 43]

SCHEDULE 1
BILINGUAL JURIES

Paragraphs 2 and 3 of subsection 126(2)

The following counties:
   Essex
   Kent
   Prescott and Russell
   Renfrew
   Simcoe
   Stormont, Dundas and Glengarry

The following territorial districts:
   Algoma
   Cochrane
   Kenora
   Nipissing
   Sudbury

Thunder Bay
Timiskaming

The area of the County of Welland as it existed on December 31, 1969.
The Regional Municipality of Hamilton-Wentworth.
The Regional Municipality of Ottawa-Carleton.
The Regional Municipality of Peel.
The Regional Municipality of Sudbury.
The Municipality of Metropolitan Toronto.

[am. O. Reg. 922/93, s. 1; 1994, c. 12, s. 43]

SCHEDULE 2
BILINGUAL DOCUMENTS

Paragraph 6 of subsection 126(2)

The following counties:
Essex
Kent
Prescott and Russell
Renfrew
Simcoe
Stormont, Dundas and Glengarry

The following territorial districts:
Algoma
Cochrane
Kenora
Nipissing
Sudbury
Thunder Bay
Timiskaming

The area of the County of Welland as it existed on December 31, 1969.
The Regional Municipality of Hamilton-Wentworth.
The Regional Municipality of Ottawa-Carleton.
The Regional Municipality of Peel.
The Regional Municipality of Sudbury.
The Municipality of Metropolitan Toronto.

[am. O. Reg. 922/93, s. 2; 1994, c. 12, s. 43]

Ministry Comment

1989 Amendments

Bill 62 (Explanatory Note)

Section [126] of the *Courts of Justice Act, 1984*, which deals with the use of French in the courts is re-enacted. The following are the major changes:
1. The concept of the "designated court" is no longer necessary because trials before bilingual judges have been available in all courts throughout Ontario since January, 1987.
2. Parties are entitled to have a bilingual judge or officer preside over all the hearings in a proceeding (for example, procedural motions, pre-trial hearings, hearings to assess costs), not just the trial.

3. In the following areas, parties are entitled as of right to file pleadings and other documents written in French:

Counties of Essex, Prescott and Russell, and Stormont, Dundas and Glengarry

Judicial Districts of Niagara South, Ottawa-Carleton and York

Territorial Districts of Cochrane and Sudbury

(Other areas may be added to the list by regulation.) In areas where French documents may be filed as of right, the courts will not be required to provide translations. However, the courts will continue to translate documents filed before hearings in the Provincial [Division].

The following regulation was made pursuant to the *Courts of Justice Act.*

R.R.O. 1990, Regulation 185
[am. O. Reg. 681/92]

BILINGUAL PROCEEDINGS

1. In this Regulation,

"consecutive", when used in reference to interpretation, means given during periodic pauses in the material being interpreted so as to be heard by every person present;

"electronic simultaneous", when used in reference to interpretation, means given concurrently with the material being interpreted and communicated by an electronic amplification and distribution system so as to be heard by every person present who uses an individual electronic apparatus for the purpose;

"whispered", when used in reference to interpretation, means given concurrently with the material being interpreted so as to be heard only by the persons in the interpreter's immediate vicinity.

2.—(1) A party may exercise a right under subsection 126(1) of the Act (bilingual proceedings),

(a) in a proceeding in any court, by filing a requisition in Form 1 with the clerk or local registrar where the proceeding was commenced, within the time limits prescribed by subsection (2);

(b) in a proceeding in the Unified Family Court, the Ontario Court (Provincial Division) or the Small Claims Court by,

(i) making an oral statement to the court during an appearance in the proceeding, or

(ii) filing a written statement with the clerk where the proceeding was commenced,

within the time limits prescribed by subsection (2);

(c) in a proceeding in the Ontario Court (Provincial Division), by filing the party's application or answer in the French language; and

(d) in a proceeding in the Ontario Court (Provincial Division), by filing the party's claim or defence in the French language.

(2) The requisition or statement referred to in clause (1)(a) or (b) shall be filed or made, as the case may be,

(a) in the case of an action in the Ontario Court (General Division), before the action is set down for trial;

(b) in the case of an action in the Small Claims Court, before the notice of trial is sent;

(c) in the case of an application made by the party, at the time the application is commenced;

(d) in the case of a proceeding in the Ontario Court (Provincial Division),

(i) if a summons is served on the defendant under Part I or III of the *Provincial Offences Act*, at the time the trial date is set, and

(ii) if an offence notice is served on the defendant under Part I of that Act, at the time the offence notice is delivered to the court; and

(iii) if a parking infraction notice is served on the defendant under Part II of that Act, at the time the parking infraction notice is delivered to the place specified in the notice; and

(e) in all other cases, at least seven days before the hearing,

or subsequently with leave of the court.

(3) A party who files a requisition under clause (1)(a) in a proceeding in the Ontario Court (General Division) shall forthwith serve a copy of the requisition on every other party to the proceeding.

(4) In a proceeding in the Unified Family Court, the Ontario Court (Provincial Division) or the Small Claims Court, where a party files a requisition under clause (1)(a) or makes or files a statement under clause (1)(b), the clerk shall forthwith notify every other party to the proceeding of the requisition or statement, by ordinary mail.

(5) In the Ontario Court (Provincial Division), a statement to be filed under subclause (1)(b)(ii) may be written directly on the party's offence notice or parking infraction notice.

3.—(1) A party may exercise a right under subsection 126(3) of the Act (hearing of appeal before bilingual judge or judges) by filing a requisition (Form 1) with the registrar or clerk of the court to which the appeal is taken,
   (a) if the party is the appellant, at the time the notice of appeal is filed; and
   (b) if the party is the respondent, within ten days after the notice of appeal is served,
or subsequently with leave of the court.

(2) A party who files a requisition under subsection (1) shall forthwith serve a copy of it on every other party to the appeal.

4. In a proceeding in which a party has exercised a right under subsection 126(1) of the Act, every party who seeks an appointment for an examination to be conducted before or after the hearing shall advise the examiner in writing at the time of making the appointment that the examination is governed by paragraph 5 of subsection 126(2) of the Act, and in that case the examiner shall ensure that a court reporter and an interpreter who speak both the English and French languages are available for the examination.

5. In a proceeding in which a party has exercised a right under subsection 126(1) of the Act, a transcript of oral evidence shall include any consecutive or electronic simultaneous interpretation into the English or French language that is provided but need not include whispered interpretation.

6. A party who,
   (a) acts in person and intends to make submissions to the court in the French language; or
   (b) intends to call a witness who will give oral evidence in the French language,
at a hearing to which subsection 126(7) of the Act applies (interpretation at English trial), shall advise the court of the fact in writing at least ten days before the hearing, or subsequently with leave of the court.

7.—(1) Oral interpretation provided by the court under paragraph 9 of subsection 126(2) of the Act shall be consecutive unless the provision of electronic simultaneous interpretation is authorized under subsection (2) or (3).

(2) The Deputy Attorney General may, at a party's request made at least thirty days before the hearing, authorize the provision of electronic simultaneous interpretation if satisfied that the special circumstances of the case justify the expense.

(3) Where a party's request under subsection (2) is refused and the court is satisfied that the provision of electronic simultaneous interpretation is essential to the proper administration of justice, the court may authorize the provision of electronic simultaneous interpretation.

(4) Subsections (1), (2) and (3) do not apply to a prosecution in the Ontario Court (Provincial Division).

(5) In a prosecution in the Ontario Court (Provincial Division),
   (a) where the prosecution is conducted by an agent of the Attorney General, oral interpretation provided by the court under paragraph 9 of subsection 126(2) of the Act shall be whispered interpretation provided for the defendant only, unless the defendant expressly requests that the whole proceeding be interpreted, and in that case consecutive interpretation shall be provided; and
   (b) where the prosecution is not conducted by an agent of the Attorney General, consecutive interpretation shall be provided.

8.—(1) In a proceeding in which a party has exercised a right under subsection 126(1) of the Act, a witness who speaks neither the English nor the French language shall be questioned only in the one of those two languages that the judge determines is understood by all counsel, and the witness' testimony shall be interpreted only into that language.

(2) Where a party does not understand the language in which a witness is being questioned under subsection (1), the court shall provide whispered interpretation of the witness' questions and answers for that party only.

9. In a proceeding in the Ontario Court (Provincial Division) in which a party has exercised a right under subsection 126(1) of the Act, if an agent of the Attorney General conducts the prosecution each witness may choose whether he or she wishes to be questioned in the English or French language.

Form 1

Courts of Justice Act

REQUISITION — BILINGUAL PROCEEDING

(Court file no.)

(Court)

(Title of proceeding)

REQUISITION

(Name of party), a party who speaks the French language, requires that:

1. The hearing be conducted before a judge or a judge and jurors who speak both the English and French languages.

2. The hearing of the appeal be conducted before a judge or judges who speak both the English and French languages.

(choose 1 or 2)

(Date)

(Name, address and telephone
number of solicitor or party
filing requisition)

INTEREST AND COSTS

Section 127

Definitions
127.—(1) In this section and in sections 128 and 129,
"bank rate" means the bank rate established by the Bank of Canada as the minimum rate at which the Bank of Canada makes short-term advances to the banks listed in Schedule I to the *Bank Act (Canada)*;
"date of the order" means the date the order is made, even if the order is not entered or enforceable on that date, or that the order is varied on appeal, and in the case of an order directing a reference, the date the report on the reference is confirmed;
"postjudgment interest rate" means the bank rate at the end of the first day of the last month of the quarter preceding the quarter in which the date of the order falls, rounded to the next higher whole number where the bank rate includes a fraction, plus 1 per cent;
"prejudgment interest rate" means the bank rate at the end of the first day of the last month of the quarter preceding the quarter in which the proceeding was commenced, rounded to the nearest tenth of a percentage point;

"quarter" means the three-month period ending with the 31st day of March, 30th day of June, 30th day of September or 31st day of December.

Calculation and publication of interest

(2) After the first day of the last month of each quarter, a person designated by the Deputy Attorney General shall forthwith,

(a) determine the prejudgment and postjudgment interest rate for the next quarter; and

(b) publish in *The Ontario Gazette* a table showing the rate determined under clause (a) for the next quarter and for all the previous quarters during the preceding ten years.

Ministry Comment

Original Act

This section and the three sections that follow replace ss. 36 and 37 of the *Judicature Act*, which dealt with prejudgment and postjudgment interest. The new Act bases its interest provisions on the bank rate, instead of on the prime rate. Difficulties were encountered using the prime rate because the *Bank of Canada Review* is not published until some time after the prime rates are set. The bank rate, however, can be determined immediately.

Clause (1)(b) defines "date of the order", a term that is used throughout the interest sections. It is intended to make clear that the relevant date for the purpose of calculating prejudgment and postjudgment interest is the date the order is made, notwithstanding that it is not entered or enforceable on that date or that the order is varied on appeal. The definition also provides that the relevant date for determining interest rates when a reference is ordered is the date the report on the reference is confirmed, since that is the date that the exact amount owing will become known.

Clause (1)(c) fixes the postjudgment interest rate for each quarter. The rate will be equal to the bank rate at the end of the first day of the last month of the quarter preceding the date of the order, rounded to a whole number if the bank rate includes a fraction, plus one per cent. This means that the postjudgment interest rate will always be a whole number, which will make calculations with the rate easier. The postjudgment interest rate will be between one and two points above the bank rate, and will average 1.5 points above the bank rate. This approximates the prime rate. A similar calculation is made in clause (1)(d) for the prejudgment interest rate.

Subsection (2) requires the Registrar of the Supreme Court to determine the prejudgment and postjudgment interest rates for each quarter. He must also publish the rates in *The Ontario Gazette*. For convenience, the *Gazette* will also contain the rates determined under this subsection (*i.e.* those rates determined after the *Courts of Justice Act* comes into force) for the ten-year period preceding publication.

1989 Amendments

Bill 69 (Explanatory Note)

[The definition of "prejudgment interest rate"] is amended so that the prejudgment interest rate is the bank rate rounded up or down to the nearest tenth of a percentage point.

Bill 2

The amendment to subsection (2) replaces a reference to the Registrar of the Supreme Court with a reference to a person designated by the Deputy Attorney General. With the restructuring of the courts, the title "Registrar of the Supreme Court" will not continue. The ability to designate who will perform functions of the Registrar of the Supreme Court is consistent with the new s. [77(2)].

Authors' Comment

As to the operative date of this provision see the Authors' Comment following s. 116. It appears that causes of action arising on or before October 23, 1989, are governed by the former s. 137(1)(d) which stated:

(d) "prejudgment interest rate" means the bank rate at the end of the first day of the last month of the quarter preceding the quarter in which the proceeding was commenced, rounded to the next higher whole number where the bank rate includes a fraction, plus 1 per cent;

As a result of the amendment to s. [127(1) "prejudgment interest rate"] the prejudgment and postjudgment interest rates are now to be calculated differently. Hence, pursuant to s. 127(2), two interest rates will need to be calculated and published.

Two interest rate tables follow. Table 1 is the relevant table for postjudgment interest (see s. 127(1) "postjudgment interest rate") and for the prejudgment interest applying to causes of action arising on or before October 23, 1989. Table 2 shows prejudgment interest rates calculated under the amended s. 127(1) "prejudgment interest rate" in respect of causes of action arising after October 23, 1989.

Using the tables. To determine the relevant interest rate, refer to the column for the quarter (1) in which the date of the order falls, re postjudgment interest — Table 1, or (2) in which the proceeding was commenced, re prejudgment interest — Table 2. (This follows because, by reason of the language of section 127(2), the figures that appear in the tables for each quarter were fixed during the preceding quarter for the next quarter. Consequently, if an action was commenced in May 1991 (*i.e.* during the second quarter) the relevant prejudgment interest rate is 10% as shown in Table 2 for the second quarter of 1991 because the figure of 10% was fixed and determined under s. 127(2), pursuant to s. 127(1), at the end of the first day of March, 1991.)

TABLE 1

**POSTJUDGMENT INTEREST RATES (AND PREJUDGMENT
INTEREST RATES FOR CAUSES OF ACTION ARISING
ON OR BEFORE OCTOBER 23, 1989)**

SOURCE: *THE ONTARIO GAZETTE*

	1st Quarter	2nd Quarter	3rd Quarter	4th Quarter
1985	12	13	11	11
1986	11	13	10	10
1987	10	9	10	11
1988	10	10	11	12
1989	13	13	14	14
1990	14	15	15	14
1991	14	11	11	10
1992	9	9	8	7
1993	10	8	7	6
1994	6	6	8	7
1995	8	10	9	8
1996	8	7		

This table shows the postjudgment interest rates for orders made in the quarters indicated. This table also shows the prejudgment interest rates for actions commenced in the quarters indicated in respect of causes of action arising on or before October 23, 1989.

TABLE 2

**PREJUDGMENT INTEREST RATES
(Re CAUSES OF ACTION ARISING AFTER OCTOBER 23, 1989)**

SOURCE: *THE ONTARIO GAZETTE*

	1st Quarter	2nd Quarter	3rd Quarter	4th Quarter
1989	—	—	—	12.4
1990	12.5	13.5	13.9	12.9
1991	12.3	10.0	9.1	8.8
1992	7.7	7.5	6.3	5.1
1993	8.3	6.1	5.1	5.0
1994	4.3	4.1	6.6	5.6
1995	6.0	8.0	7.6	6.6
1996	6.1	5.6		

This table shows the prejudgment interest rates for actions commenced in the quarters indicated in respect of causes of action arising after October 23, 1989.

Section 128

Prejudgment interest

128.—(1) A person who is entitled to an order for the payment of money is entitled to claim and have included in the order an award of interest thereon at the prejudgment interest rate, calculated from the date the cause of action arose to the date of the order.

Exception for non-pecuniary loss on personal injury

(2) Despite subsection (1), the rate of interest on damages for non-pecuniary loss in an action for personal injury shall be the rate determined by the rules of court under clause 66(2)(w).

Special damages

(3) If the order includes an amount for past pecuniary loss, the interest calculated under subsection (1) shall be calculated on the total past pecuniary loss at the end of each six-month period and at the date of the order.

Exclusion

(4) Interest shall not be awarded under subsection (1),

(a) on exemplary or punitive damages;

(b) on interest accruing under this section;

(c) on an award of costs in the proceeding;

(d) on that part of the order that represents pecuniary loss arising after the date of the order and that is identified by a finding of the court;

(e) with respect to the amount of any advance payment that has been made towards settlement of the claim, for the period after the advance payment has been made;

(f) where the order is made on consent, except by consent of the debtor; or

(g) where interest is payable by a right other than under this section. [am. 1994, c. 12, s. 44]

Ministry Comment

Original Act

This section is derived from s. 36(3), (4) and (5) of the *Judicature Act*.

Subsection (4) provides that this section does not apply to proceedings commenced before the section comes into force. Those proceedings will continue to be governed by the old provisions of the *Judicature Act*.

1989 Amendments

Bill 69 (Explanatory Note)

Subsections [(1) and (2)] of the Act provide for the payment of prejudgment interest. This subsection is amended to remove the distinction as to whether the claim is for a liquidated or an unliquidated amount. Subsection [(3)] has been reworded to clarify the meaning. Subsection [(4)] sets out when prejudgment interest is not to be paid. The new clause is self-explanatory.

Authors' Comment

As to the operative date of this provision see the Authors' Comment following s. 116.

It appears that causes of action arising on or before October 23, 1989, are governed by the former s. 138 which stated:

Prejudgment interest
138.—(1) A person who is entitled to an order for the payment of money is entitled to claim and have included in the order an award of interest thereon at the prejudgment interest rate, calculated,
    (a) where the order is made on a liquidated claim, from the date the cause of action arose to the date of the order; or
    (b) where the order is made on an unliquidated claim, from the date the person entitled gave notice in writing of his claim to the person liable therefor to the date of the order.

Special damages
    (2) Where the order includes an amount for special damages, the interest calculated under subsection (1) shall be calculated on the balance of special damages incurred as totalled at the end of each six-month period following the notice in writing referred in in clause (1)(b) and at the date of the order.

Exclusion
    (3) Interest shall not be awarded under subsection (1),
    (a) on exemplary or punitive damages;
    (b) on interest accruing under this section;
    (c) on an award of costs in the proceeding;
    (d) on that part of the order that represents pecuniary loss arising after the date of the order and that is identified by a finding of the court;
    (e) where the order is made on consent, except by consent of the debtor; or
    (f) where interest is payable by a right other than under this section.

Application
    (4) Where a proceeding is commenced before this section comes into force, this section does not apply and section 36 of the *Judicature Act*, being chapter 223 of the Revised Statutes of Ontario, 1980, continues to apply, notwithstanding section 187.

Prejudgment interest in proceedings commenced before January 1, 1985 is governed by s. 36 of the *Judicature Act*, R.S.O. 1980, c. 223. The text of that provision and a table of interest rates are reproduced in the 1985-1990 editions of Watson and McGowan, *Ontario Supreme and District Court Practice* following the text of s. 138 of the *Courts of Justice Act, 1984*.

Cross-Reference: See also cases under s. 130. Regarding the rate of interest referred to in s. 128(2), see rule 53.10.

Cases

Prejudgment Interest — Miscellaneous

Diefenbacher v. Young (1995), 22 O.R. (3d) 641, 123 D.L.R. (4th) 641, 80 O.A.C. 216 (C.A.). In a claim for division of assets under the *Partnership Act*, the interest rate prescribed by that Act, not by the *Courts of Justice Act*, applies.

Tait v. Roden (1994), 20 O.R. (3d) 20 (Gen. Div.).

Prejudgment interest on damages for libel should be calculated under s. 128(1). Damages for libel are not analogous to "damages for non-pecuniary loss" under rule 53.10.

Kalla v. Wolkowicz (1994), 26 C.P.C. (3d) 131 (Ont. Gen. Div.).

The court held that the cause of action arose before October 23, 1989, and that prejudgment interest was governed by s. 138 of the *Courts of Justice Act, 1984*, not s. 128 of the *Courts of Justice Act*, R.S.O. 1990.

Merit Clothing Corp. v. Abiti by Michael Luisi Ltd. (1992), 8 C.P.C. (3d) 39, 92 D.L.R. (4th) 168 (Ont. Gen. Div.).

Where the purported contractual interest rate offended the *Interest Act*, R.S.C. 1985, c. I-18, the court awarded prejudgment interest at five per cent pursuant to that Act. The *Interest Act* is constitutionally paramount over the prejudgment interest provisions of the *Courts of Justice Act*.

Gregoric v. Gregoric (1991), 4 O.R. (3d) 604 (Gen. Div.).

An award of prejudgment interest was denied in this family law proceeding, where the claim on which the petitioner succeeded was asserted three years after the action was commenced. That party had also failed to demand financial disclosure at the time of entering into a separation agreement which complicated the proceeding.

Claiborne Industries Ltd. v. National Bank of Can. (1989), 69 O.R. (2d) 65, 59 D.L.R. (4th) 533, 34 O.A.C. 241 (C.A.).

The court can award compound interest, apart from the statute, for wrongful detention of money.

Chatham Motors Ltd. v. Fidelity & Casualty Ins. Co. of New York (1986), 53 O.R. (2d) 581, 7 C.P.C. (2d) 251 (H.C.), varied on other grounds (1988), 63 O.R. (2d) 205, 27 C.P.C. (2d) 31 (C.A.).

In addition to statutory provisions allowing prejudgment interest, the court has a discretion to award interest on equitable principles where a wrongdoer deprives the plaintiff of money which it needs for use in its business.

Hope Estate v. Co-operators Ins. Assn., 53 O.R. (2d) 208, 16 C.C.L.I. 145, 24 D.L.R. (4th) 78, [1986] I.L.R. 1-2015 (Div. Ct.).

An arbitrator under the *Arbitrations Act* has the power to award prejudgment interest.

Public Trustee v. Mortimer (1985), 49 O.R. (2d) 741, 18 E.T.R. 219, 16 D.L.R. (4th) 404 (H.C.).

In an action against a solicitor and his partners for the loss caused by the solicitor's theft of clients' money, interest was not calculated under this section because the liability therefor arose by virtue of the *Partnerships Act* and because the solicitor was a trustee.

Borland v. Muttersbach (1985), 49 O.R. (2d) 165, 8 C.C.L.I. 232 (*sub nom. Borland v. Muttersbach; Barchuk v. Muttersbach; Borland v. Zurich Ins. Co.; Borland v. Allstate Ins. Co. of Can.*), 15 D.L.R. (4th) 486, [1985] I.L.R. 1-1851 (*sub nom. Borland v. Muttersback/ Muttersbach*), supplementary reasons at 8 C.C.L.I. 264, [1985] I.L.R. 1-1939 (H.C.), reversed in part on other grounds 53 O.R. (2d) 129, 16 C.C.L.I. 177, 23 D.L.R. (4th) 664, [1986] I.L.R. 1-2003, supplementary reasons at 17 C.C.L.I. xxxix (C.A.).

Rather than using the formula set out in s. 138(2), it is a common practice to award interest on special damages at one-half the rate otherwise applicable.

Re Weiss Air Sales Ltd. (Trustee) and Bank of Montreal (1982), 35 O.R. (2d) 344, 40 C.B.R. (N.S.) 139, 134 D.L.R. (3d) 706 (S.C.), affirmed 39 O.R. (2d) 800, 44 C.B.R. (N.S.) 143, 140 D.L.R. (3d) 576 (C.A.).

A claim to prejudgment interest was not barred by the failure to specifically claim interest for six years after service of originating process.

James v. Peter Hennan Ltd. (1981), 32 O.R. (2d) 480, 21 C.P.C. 243, 122 D.L.R. (3d) 734 (H.C.).

Accident benefits received are to be deducted from the award before calculating prejudgment interest.

Stelmaszynski v. Hi-Fi Express Inc. (1979), 25 O.R. (2d) 661, 14 C.P.C. 1 (H.C.).

A claim for statutory rather than contractual prejudgment interest should not state a specific rate.

Section 129

Postjudgment interest
129.—(1) Money owing under an order, including costs to be assessed or costs fixed by the court, bears interest at the postjudgment interest rate, calculated from the date of the order.

Interest on periodic payments
(2) Where an order provides for periodic payments, each payment in default shall bear interest only from the date of default.

Interest on orders originating outside Ontario
(3) Where an order is based on an order given outside Ontario or an order of a court outside Ontario is filed with a court in Ontario for the purpose of enforcement, money owing under the order bears interest at the rate, if any, applicable to the order given outside Ontario by the law of the place where it was given.

Costs assessed without order
(4) Where costs are assessed without an order, the costs bear interest at the postjudgment interest rate in the same manner as if an order were made for the payment of costs on the date the person to whom the costs are payable became entitled to the costs.

Other provision for interest
(5) Interest shall not be awarded under this section where interest is payable by a right other than under this section.

Ministry Comment

Original Act
Subsection (1) is derived from s. 37(1) of the *Judicature Act*. The new provision makes clear that postjudgment interest runs on costs from the date of the order.

Subsection (2) clarifies the calculation of postjudgment interest on orders that provide for periodic payments.

Subsection (3) is a new provision intended to clarify the application of postjudgment interest to orders based on orders made outside Ontario, and to orders made outside Ontario but filed in Ontario for enforcement (*e.g.* under the *Reciprocal Enforcement of Maintenance Orders Act, 1982*, S.O. 1982, c. 9).

Subsection (4) is a new subsection that clarifies the application of postjudgment interest to costs assessed without an order. The new subsection is also intended to fit with provisions in the new Rule that, in some cases, permit costs to be assessed without an order.

Subsection (5) is a new provision that corresponds to a similar provision in the prejudgment interest section. If the parties have agreed on the interest, the agreement will prevail.

Subsection (6) provides that this section does not apply to orders made before it comes into force. Those orders will continue to be dealt with under s. 37 of the *Judicature Act*.

Authors' Comment

Subsection 139(6) of the *Courts of Justice Act, 1984* is an unconsolidated and unrepealed transition provision which states as follows:

> *Application*
> (6) Where an order for the payment of money is made before this section comes into force, this section does not apply and section 37 of the *Judicature Act*, being chapter 223 of the Revised Statutes of Ontario, 1980, continues to apply, notwithstanding section 187.

Cases

Walker v. CFTO Ltd. (1994), 24 C.P.C. (3d) 280 (Ont. Master).

Postjudgment interest on the assessed costs of the trial was allowed from the date of the judgment awarding costs, despite a subsequent appeal and a second trial in relation to some issues. The Court of Appeal had specifically ordered that the first trial judge's award of costs remain in force, and the plaintiff was successful in the second trial.

Placentile v. Fabris (1993), 14 C.P.C. (3d) 210 (Ont. Gen. Div.).

The court held that postjudgment interest on costs commenced one month after the issuance of reasons for decision regarding costs.

First City Capital Ltd. v. Hall (1989), 67 O.R. (2d) 12 at 19 (H.C.).

The court declined to award a high rate of postjudgment interest where neither postjudgment interest nor the specific rate were included in the prayer for relief.

Kidd Creek Mines Ltd. v. Northern & Central Gas Corp. (1988), 66 O.R. (2d) 11, 29 C.P.C. (2d) 257, 53 D.L.R. (4th) 123, 30 O.A.C. 146 (C.A.).

The postjudgment interest provision is not merely procedural but gives a substantive right to interest.

L.M. Rosen Realty Ltd. v. D'Amore (1988), 29 C.P.C. (2d) 106 (Ont. H.C.).

A motion to vary a judgment by altering the rate of postjudgment interest on the ground that interest rates had declined thereafter was dismissed.

Sporn v. Herman (1987), 63 O.R. (2d) 95 (Master).

Postjudgment interest is calculated on the total judgment obtained, including the applicable prejudgment interest.

Kimpe v. Union Gas Ltd. (1985), 51 O.R. (2d) 112, 2 C.P.C. (2d) 168, 19 D.L.R. (4th) 176, 33 L.C.R. 1, 10 O.A.C. 382 (Div. Ct.).

Postjudgment interest does not accrue on costs awarded by the Ontario Energy Board.

Erco Industs. Ltd. v. Allendale Mut. Ins. Co. (No. 2) (1984), 48 O.R. (2d) 17, (*sub nom. Erco Industs. Ltd. v. Allendale Mut. Ins. Co. (No. 4)*) 46 C.P.C. 100 (H.C.).

Where the trial judge determined the question of costs some time after releasing his decision on the merits of the action, postjudgment interest was held to run from the time the defendant could determine the amount of money properly payable. In this case the defendant could not know whether there was a net amount payable by it until the costs issues were determined.

Houser v. West Lincoln (1984), 46 O.R. (2d) 703 (H.C.).

Where the Court of Appeal varied the trial judge's judgment which gave the plaintiff his entitlement to trial costs, interest on costs was still to be computed from the date of the trial judgment.

Metro. Toronto v. Poole Const. Ltd. (1982), 43 O.R. (2d) 358, 40 C.P.C. 20, additional reasons 43 O.R. (2d) 358 at 360, 40 C.P.C. 20 at 23 (H.C.).

The rate of interest to be applied on an award of costs by the Court of Appeal is the rate prevailing at the date when that court's order is made.

Billes v. Parkin Partnership Architects Planners (1983), 40 O.R. (2d) 525, 31 C.P.C. 198, 143 D.L.R. (3d) 55 (C.A.).

An award under the *Arbitrations Act* bears interest from the date of the award at the same rate as a judgment debt.

Imperial Roadways Ltd. v. C.P. Ltd. (1982), 28 C.P.C. 151, 134 D.L.R. (3d) 149, affirmed 146 D.L.R. (3d) 191 (Ont. C.A.).

The trial judge amended his judgment to indicate that it was to bear postjudgment interest after disposition of an appeal.

McNabb v. MacKeand (1981), 33 O.R. (2d) 51, 21 C.P.C. 90, 123 D.L.R. (3d) 188 (H.C.).

Where a Court of Appeal order increases the damages award but is silent as to interest, prejudgment interest is payable on the increased award up to the date of the trial judgment and postjudgment interest thereafter.

National Trust Co. v. Speakman (1978), 8 C.P.C. 44, 3 E.T.R. 193 (Ont. H.C.).

Interest was awarded on a consent judgment from the date after the judgment on which notice of such a claim was made where the defendant had failed to pay due to an alleged lack of authority.

Crone v. Orion Ins. Co., [1966] 1 O.R. 221, 53 D.L.R. (2d) 98, affirmed [1967] S.C.R. 157, [1967] I.L.R. 1-179, 60 D.L.R. (2d) 630.

Postjudgment interest is included in "the amount of the judgment" for purposes of the *Insurance Act*, s. 106(1).

Section 130

Discretion of court

130.—(1) The court may, where it considers it just to do so, in respect of the whole or any part of the amount on which interest is payable under section 128 or 129,

  (a) disallow interest under either section;
  (b) allow interest at a rate higher or lower than that provided in either section;
  (c) allow interest for a period other than that provided in either section.

Idem

(2) For the purpose of subsection (1), the court shall take into account,
  (a) changes in market interest rates;
  (b) the circumstances of the case;
  (c) the fact that an advance payment was made;
  (d) the circumstances of medical disclosure by the plaintiff;
  (e) the amount claimed and the amount recovered in the proceeding;
  (f) the conduct of any party that tended to shorten or to lengthen unnecessarily the duration of the proceeding; and
  (g) any other relevant consideration.

Ministry Comment

1989 Amendments

Bill 69 (Explanatory Note)

Section [130] of the 1984 Act gave the court a discretion in allowing interest. The revised section sets out matters for the court to consider when considering interest payments.

Cross-Reference: See s. 119 as to the power of the court on appeal to substitute its own assessment of damages.

Authors' Comment

As to the operative date of this provision, see the Authors' Comment following s. 116. It appears that causes of action arising on or before October 23, 1989, are governed by the former s. 140 which stated:

> *Discretion of court*
> 140. The court may, where it considers it just to do so, having regard to changes in market interest rates, the circumstances of the case, the conduct of the proceeding or any other relevant consideration,
> (a) disallow interest under section 138 or 139;
> (b) allow interest at a rate higher or lower than that provided in section 138 or 139;
> (c) allow interest for a period other than that provided in section 138 or 139, in respect of the whole or any part of the amount on which interest is payable under section 138 or 139.

Cases

Exercise of Discretion re Prejudgment Interest — General

Bifolchi v. Sherar (Litigation Administrator) (1995), 25 O.R. (3d) 637 (Gen. Div.).

The court held that it could not vary prejudgment interest under former s. 140 of the Act and could not take into consideration the generosity of the amounts awarded by the jury, the late date the plaintiff was sent to medical experts or the undue delay in bringing the matter on for trial.

Hill v. Church of Scientology of Toronto (1994), 18 O.R. (3d) 385, 20 C.C.L.T. (2d) 129, 114 D.L.R. (4th) 1, 71 O.A.C. 161 (C.A.), affirmed [1995] 2 S.C.R. 1130, 24 O.R. (3d) 865 (note), 25 C.C.L.T. (2d) 89, 30 C.R.R. (2d) 189, 126 D.L.R. (4th) 129, 184 N.R. 1, 84 O.A.C. 1.

Although a successful plaintiff has a *prima facie* right to receive prejudgment interest, where counsel for the defendants accommodated counsel for the plaintiff by allowing him time to participate in a Royal Commission, it was unfair to charge the defendant with prejudgment interest during the corresponding period.

Oakville Storage & Forwarders Ltd. v. Canadian National Railway Co. (1991), 5 O.R. (3d) 1 (*sub nom. Armak Chemicals Ltd. v. Canadian National Railway Co.*), 4 C.P.C. (3d) 280, 84 D.L.R. (4th) 326, 52 O.A.C. 188 (C.A.), leave to appeal to Supreme Court of Canada refused (1992), 6 O.R. (3d) xiii (note), 86 D.L.R. (4th) viii (note), 137 N.R. 238 (note), 55 O.A.C. 320 (note).

An award of prejudgment interest is to compensate for loss of use of money and ought not to be used as a penalty for misconduct.

Sawadski v. Heil (1991), 2 C.P.C. (3d) 101, 33 M.V.R. (2d) 82, 86 D.L.R. (4th) 364, 52 O.A.C. 127 (C.A.).

The court has a broader jurisdiction under the *Courts of Justice Act, 1984*, S.O. 1984, c. 11, s. 140, than under the *Judicature Act*, R.S.O. 1980, c. 223, s. 36, to reduce prejudgment interest on account of delay by the plaintiff.

Graham v. Rourke (1990), 75 O.R. (2d) 622, 74 D.L.R. (4th) 1, 40 O.A.C. 301 (C.A.), affirmed on reconsideration 75 O.R. (2d) 622 at 644 (C.A.).

The trial judge may consider the conduct of the proceedings, including the conduct of the parties, when determining the rate of prejudgment interest but prejudgment interest must be viewed as part of the compensation package and cannot become a means of punishing or rewarding a party.

Brinkos v. Brinkos (1989), 69 O.R. (2d) 798, 61 D.L.R. (4th) 766, additional reasons 69 O.R. (2d) 798 at 800, 61 D.L.R. (4th) 766 at 768 (C.A.).

Prejudgment interest was awarded at the rate earned on the account holding the funds from which the judgment was to be paid.

Oakville Storage & Forwarders Ltd. v. C.N.R. (1987), 27 C.P.C. (2d) 56 (Ont. H.C.).

The court exercised its discretion and awarded prejudgment interest commencing on the date the defendant could reasonably be expected to evaluate the commercial reasonableness of the claim against it.

Moore v. Moore (1987), 21 C.P.C. (2d) 191 (Ont. H.C.).

The court denied prejudgment interest on a divorce judgment where the wife had had exclusive possession of the matrimonial home since separation and had received interim support.

Irvington Holdings Ltd. v. Black (1987), 58 O.R. (2d) 449, 14 C.P.C. (2d) 229, 35 D.L.R. (4th) 641 at 676, 20 O.A.C. 390 (C.A.).

A successful plaintiff should not be deprived of prejudgment interest on the grounds the case was novel or complex or because the defendant, though liable, acted in good faith. Interest should not be used either as a reward or a penalty, but should reflect the value of money wrongfully withheld from the plaintiff.

Arthur J. Fish Ltd. v. Moore (1985), 53 O.R. (2d) 65, 8 C.P.C. (2d) 77 (*sub nom. Arthur J. Fish Ltd. v. Superstructure Door Co. of Can. (Trustee of)*), 17 C.L.R. 137, 23 D.L.R. (4th) 424, 13 O.A.C. 117 (Div. Ct.).

Difficulty in determining the amount of recovery by the plaintiff is not a valid ground to disallow prejudgment interest.

Borland v. Muttersbach (1985), 49 O.R. (2d) 165, 8 C.C.L.I. 232 (*sub nom. Borland v. Muttersbach; Barchuk v. Muttersbach; Borland v. Zurich Ins. Co.; Borland v. Allstate Ins. Co. of Can.*), 15 D.L.R. (4th) 486, [1985] I.L.R. 1-1851 (*sub nom. Borland v. Muttersback/ Muttersbach*), supplementary reasons at 8 C.C.L.I. 264, [1985] I.L.R. 1-1939 (H.C.), reversed in part on other grounds 53 O.R. (2d) 129, 16 C.C.L.I. 177, 23 D.L.R. (4th) 664 [1986] I.L.R. 1-2003, supplementary reasons at 17 C.C.L.I. xxxix (C.A.).

The court rejected the argument that prejudgment interest on non-pecuniary damages should be reduced because such damages were in respect of future as well as past losses: to do so would be to discourage advance payment by defendants and would be contrary to the policy of s. 138.

McWhinnie v. Scott (1985), 5 C.P.C. (2d) 245 (Ont. Dist. Ct.).

Where the plaintiff's claim for loss of income was reformulated after the pre-trial conference and thereby substantially increased the claim and caused the trial to be delayed, the court awarded prejudgment interest on the full amount but only to the date the trial would have concluded if there had been no delay. The interest rate used was half the normal rate following the treatment of accumulating special damages in *Anderson v. Booth* (Ont. C.A., June 6, 1983, unreported).

Longview Forming Ltd. v. Valentine Devs. Ltd.; Valentine Devs. Ltd. v. York Steel Const. Ltd. (1984), 42 C.P.C. 37, 6 C.L.R. 213 (Ont. Master).

In exercising its discretion regarding prejudgment interest in this construction lien action, the court took into account the fact that the plaintiff had lost considerably due to the restriction on costs to no more than 25 per cent of recovery and had by statute little choice as to when to commence the action, and that the defendant had received funds from a supplier, substantially through the plaintiff's efforts, but did not pass them on to the plaintiff.

Dugdale v. Boissneau (1983), 41 O.R. (2d) 152 (C.A.).

The prevailing principle is that prejudgment interest is to be allowed from the time of written notice of an unliquidated claim. Failure of the plaintiff to deliver his medical reports and inability of the defendant to conclude his medical investigations prior to receipt of notice is insufficient reason to reduce the interest payable.

Brock v. Cole (1983), 40 O.R. (2d) 97, 31 C.P.C. 184, 13 E.T.R. 235, 142 D.L.R. (3d) 461 (C.A.).

Compound interest was awarded in this case where the defendant solicitors dealt with the plaintiff's money in breach of trust and had wrongfully detained the plaintiff's money.

Mason v. Peters (1982), 39 O.R. (2d) 27, 22 C.C.L.T. 21, 139 D.L.R. (3d) 104 (C.A.), leave to appeal to Supreme Court of Canada refused 46 N.R. 538.

The court ought not to refuse prejudgment interest merely because a novel claim is advanced.

Landry v. Cameron, 20 C.P.C. 204, [1981] I.L.R. 1-1338 (Ont. C.A.).

Prejudgment interest was awarded on the general damages recovered at trial from the date of notice.

Bank of Montreal v. Inco Ltd. (1979), 24 O.R. (2d) 710, (*sub nom. Bank of Montreal v. Inco Ltd; Conveyor Belt Maintenance Service Ltd. v. Inco Ltd.; Laurentian Elec. Ltd. v. Blezard Piping & Welded Products Ltd.*) 10 C.P.C. 205 (Ont. H.C.).

Interest was not awarded against a defendant who withheld funds from the plaintiff only because of competing claimants and who obtained an interpleader order.

Astro Tire & Rubber Co. v. Western Assur. Co., 24 O.R. (2d) 268, 97 D.L.R. (3d) 515, [1979] I.L.R. 1-1098 (C.A.).

Interest should be awarded unless there are special circumstances justifying departure from the usual practice.

H.G. Winton Ltd. v. One Medical Place Ltd., [1968] 2 O.R. 384, 69 D.L.R. (2d) 383 (C.A.).

The court refused to deprive a successful plaintiff of prejudgment interest merely because of its dishonesty and evasiveness.

Exercise of Discretion re Prejudgment Interest — Rate of Interest

Canada (Attorney General) v. Bitove Corp. (1996), 7 W.D.C.P. (2d) 164 (Ont. Gen. Div. [Commercial List]).

The court used the prescribed rate of interest rather than apply a contractual interest provision where to do so would have been unjust.

Emery v. Royal Oak Mines Inc. (1995), 26 O.R. (3d) 216, 15 C.C.E.L. (2d) 49 (Gen. Div.).

The court refused to apply the average rate of interest over the material time rather than the prescribed statutory rate. The difference was only 2.7 per cent which was not sufficient to warrant departure from the statutory rate.

120 Adelaide Leaseholds Inc. v. Thomson, Rogers (1995), 38 C.P.C. (3d) 69 (Ont. Gen. Div.).

The court exercised its discretion to alter the prejudgment interest rate where the prescribed rate was significantly higher than the average of the rates over the period in issue.

Niagara Air Bus Inc. v. Camerman (1991), 3 O.R. (3d) 108, 5 B.L.R. (2d) 227, 80 D.L.R. (4th) 611, 49 O.A.C. 7 (C.A.), leave to appeal to Supreme Court of Canada refused (1992), 7 O.R. (3d) xii (note), 87 D.L.R. (4th) vii, 138 N.R. 413 (note), 56 O.A.C. 79 (note).

Although prior to maturity of the subject debt the interest rate to which the plaintiff was entitled was limited to 5 per cent by s. 4 of the *Interest Act*, thereafter the loan was not governed by that section and the court exercised its discretion by allowing interest at the rate contemplated by the loan documents.

Zamonsky v. Soundair Corp. (1987), 19 C.P.C. (2d) 202 (Ont. H.C.), reversed in part on other grounds (1989), 44 C.P.C. (2d) 102 (Ont. C.A.).

The court fixed interest at 13 per cent where it considered the prime rate of 21.25 per cent excessive.

Ross Steel Fabricators & Contractors v. Loaring Construction Co. (1986), 15 C.P.C. (2d) 27 (Ont. H.C.).

The court awarded prejudgment interest at a rate equivalent to the borrowing rate of the plaintiff but refused to award equitable interest.

Spencer v. Rosati (1985), 50 O.R. (2d) 661, 1 C.P.C. (2d) 301, 9 O.A.C. 119 (C.A.).

Where the *prima facie* interest rate applicable was 16.5 per cent and the average rate was 15.2 per cent and the trial judge awarded interest at 12 per cent, the court of appeal increased the rate to 15.2 per cent. The rate applied ought not to depend upon the plaintiff's degree of sophistication as an investor.

McCann v. B & M Renovating (1983), 34 C.P.C. 188 (Ont. H.C.).

Where interest rates fluctuated dramatically prior to judgment, the court exercised its discretion and awarded prejudgment interest based on the average rate.

Sipco Oil Ltd. v. D'Amore Const. (Windsor) Ltd. (1981), 21 C.P.C. 313 (Ont. Master).

Where interest rates had risen since the institution of the action, the court exercised its discretion to increase the rate awarded.

Airtemp Corp. v. Chrysler Airtemp Can. Ltd. (1980), 11 B.L.R. 47, 16 C.P.C. 163, affirmed 31 O.R. (2d) 481, 23 C.P.C. 322, 121 D.L.R. (3d) 236 (Div. Ct.).

A claim for interest based on the cost of borrowing was held to be proper.

Exercise of Discretion re Prejudgment Interest — Wrongful Dismissal Cases

Chang v. Simplex Textiles Ltd. (1985), 6 C.C.E.L. 247, 7 O.A.C. 137 (C.A.).

In this wrongful dismissal action, prejudgment interest was awarded from the date the plaintiff was dismissed from employment and not from the date the plaintiff gave notice in writing of his claim. While the claim was not liquidated, it related to moneys that the plaintiff would have received had there been no breach by the defendant, and this disposition respecting interest was more just than the basic rule provided in s. [128(1)].

Blackburn v. Coyle Motors Ltd. (1983), 44 O.R. (2d) 690, 3 C.C.E.L. 1 (H.C.).

In an action for wrongful dismissal, prejudgment interest was awarded on the entire damage award from the date of the wrongful dismissal, without any reduction for the fact that plaintiff's salary would have been paid in instalments. *Rushton v. Lake Ontario Steel Co., infra*, not followed.

Rushton v. Lake Ontario Steel Co. (1980), 29 O.R. (2d) 68, 16 C.P.C. 191, 112 D.L.R. (3d) 144 (H.C.).

In a wrongful dismissal action, prejudgment interest was awarded on a month-to-month basis as the salary would have been received.

Exercise of Discretion re Postjudgment Interest

Eastwalsh Homes Ltd. v. Anatal Development Corp. (1995), 26 O.R. (3d) 528 (Gen. Div.).

The court refused to reduce the postjudgment interest rate where, *inter alia*, the issue was not litigated in an appeal to the Court of Appeal concerning the judgment.

Moog v. Moog (1984), 39 R.F.L. (2d) 15 (Ont. H.C.), varied on other grounds (1985), 50 O.R. (2d) 113, 44 R.F.L. (2d) 301, 17 D.L.R. (4th) 172, 8 O.A.C. 200 (C.A.).

The onus is on the party seeking an order under this section to show that it would be just to grant the order.

Section 131

Costs

131.—(1) Subject to the provisions of an Act or rules of court, the costs of and incidental to a proceeding or a step in a proceeding are in the discretion of the court, and the court may determine by whom and to what extent the costs shall be paid.

Crown costs

(2) In a proceeding to which Her Majesty is a party, costs awarded to Her Majesty shall not be disallowed or reduced on assessment merely because they relate to a lawyer who is a salaried officer of the Crown, and costs recovered on behalf of Her Majesty shall be paid into the Consolidated Revenue Fund. [am. 1994, c. 12, s. 45]

Cross-Reference: See also Rule 57.

Cases

General

Garson v. Braithwaite (1994), 34 C.P.C. (3d) 87 (Ont. Gen. Div.).

The court may not award costs to a party who is represented by an agent who is neither a student-at-law nor a clerk operating under the supervision of a solicitor.

Organ v. Barnett (1992), 11 O.R. (3d) 210 (Gen. Div.).

The court will award interim costs of a proceeding only in very exceptional cases.

Hill v. Hill (1988), 63 O.R. (2d) 618, 27 C.P.C. (2d) 319 (H.C.).

The court has inherent jurisdiction to award interim costs and disbursements in proceedings subject to the *Courts of Justice Act*, unless there is a specific statutory provision to the contrary.

Bruce (Twp.) v. Thornburn (1986), 57 O.R. (2d) 77, 17 O.A.C. 127 (Div. Ct.).

The court reversed an order awarding costs to a representative class in advance and regardless of the outcome of an action, where no specific provisions or established exception removed that discretion from the trial judge.

Krigstin v. Samuel (1982), 31 C.P.C. 41 (Ont. H.C.).

The Supreme Court has an inherent jurisdiction to deal with the taxation of accounts for solicitor's work done in proceedings in that court.

Orr v. Positano (1978), 6 C.P.C. 276 (Ont. Dist. Ct.).

The court had no power to order a witness to pay a portion of the costs of the action.

Can. Metal Co. v. C.B.C. (1976), 2 C.P.C. 53, varied 14 O.R. (2d) 115, 2 C.P.C. 58 (H.C.).

A Crown agency is entitled to receive costs awarded even though it is represented by salaried counsel.

Re Kingston Enterprises Ltd. and Min. of Municipal Affairs, [1970] 2 O.R. 463, [1970] 3 O.R. 360, 12 D.L.R. (3d) 516 (H.C.).

Full costs were allowed where a Minister of the Crown successfully resisted an application for *certiorari* notwithstanding that he was represented by salaried counsel.

APPEALS

Section 132

Judge not to hear appeal from own decision
132. A judge shall not sit as a member of a court hearing an appeal from his or her own decision.

Section 133

Leave to appeal required
133. No appeal lies without leave of the court to which the appeal is to be taken,
(a) from an order made with the consent of the parties; or
(b) where the appeal is only as to costs that are in the discretion of the court that made the order for costs.

Authors' Comment

This section derives from s. 27 of the *Judicature Act* which formerly prohibited appeals from consent orders (now they may be appealed with leave) and required leave of the judge appealed from to appeal a costs order (now leave of the court appealed to is required).

Cases

Leave to Appeal Costs Order — s. 133(b)

Fekete v. 415585 Ltd. (1988), 64 O.R. (2d) 542, 27 C.P.C. (2d) 108, additional reasons 64 O.R. (2d) 542 at 552, 30 C.P.C. (2d) 10 at 11 (H.C.).

Where the master awarded costs against a solicitor personally without appearing to afford the solicitor a real opportunity to oppose liability, the court held that leave to appeal was not necessary.

Ray Kennedy Const. Ltd. v. Moore Park Homes Ltd. (1975), 10 O.R. (2d) 127 (Div. Ct.).

No leave is required to appeal an award of costs on the grounds the court lacked jurisdiction to make such an award. *Accord: Alexanian v. Dolinski* (1973), 2 O.R. (2d) 609, 43 D.L.R. (3d) 649 (C.A.); *Rockwell Devs. Ltd. v. Newtonbrook Plaza Ltd.*, [1972] 3 O.R. 199, 27 D.L.R. (3d) 651 (C.A.).

Bondy v. Bondy (1978), 6 C.P.C. 117, 4 R.F.L. (2d) 285 (Ont. H.C.).

Leave to appeal an order of costs was granted where costs had been awarded to the petitioner at trial although the respondent had been successful on the actual issues involved.

Cameron v. Julien, [1957] O.W.N. 430, 9 D.L.R. (2d) 460 (C.A.).

Leave is required to appeal with respect to costs even where an appeal is launched on other points.

Axelrod v. Beth Jacob of Kitchener, [1943] O.W.N. 80, [1943] 2 D.L.R. 115 (H.C.).

Leave to appeal on the question of costs should be granted only sparingly and in the most obvious cases.

Section 134

Powers on appeal

134.—(1) Unless otherwise provided, a court to which an appeal is taken may,

(a) make any order or decision that ought to or could have been made by the court or tribunal appealed from;

(b) order a new trial;

(c) make any other order or decision that is considered just.

Interim orders

(2) On motion, a court to which an appeal is taken may make any interim order that is considered just to prevent prejudice to a party pending the appeal.

Power to quash

(3) On motion, a court to which an appeal is taken may, in a proper case, quash the appeal.

Determination of fact

(4) Unless otherwise provided, a court to which an appeal is taken may, in a proper case,

(a) draw inferences of fact from the evidence, except that no inference shall be drawn that is inconsistent with a finding that has not been set aside;

(b) receive further evidence by affidavit, transcript of oral examination, oral examination before the court or in such other manner as the court directs; and

(c) direct a reference or the trial of an issue,

to enable the court to determine the appeal.

Scope of decisions

(5) The powers conferred by this section may be exercised even if the appeal is as to part only of an order or decision, and may be exercised in favour of a party even though the party did not appeal.

New trial

(6) A court to which an appeal is taken shall not direct a new trial unless some substantial wrong or miscarriage of justice has occurred.

Idem

(7) Where some substantial wrong or miscarriage of justice has occurred but it affects only part of an order or decision or some of the parties, a new trial may be ordered in respect of only that part or those parties.

Ministry Comment

Original Act

Subsection (2) is a new provision intended to permit the appeal court to prevent prejudice pending the appeal.

Subsection (3) is intended to allow a court to quash an appeal in a proper case. See s. 51 of the *Judicature Act*, R.S.O. 1897, c. 51. See also *Pigott v. Pigott*, [1969] 2 O.R. 427 (C.A.).

Authors' Comment

As to the power of the court on appeal to substitute its own assessment of damages, see s. 119.

Cases

Authors' Note on Organization of Cases

Cases relevant to this provision have been organized as follows:

Setting Aside Jury Verdicts
Lack of Reasons for Decision by Lower Court
Interim Orders Pending Appeal — s. 134(2)
Quashing Appeals for Mootness — s. 134(3)
Quashing Appeals for Being Devoid of Merit — s. 134(3)
Setting Aside Findings of Fact — s. 134(4)(a)
Introduction of Further Evidence on Appeal — s. 134(4)(b)
Ordering New Trial — Generally
Ordering New Trial — Misdirection of Law
Ordering New Trial — Denial of Opportunity to be Heard
Powers on Appeal — General — s. 134(1)(a)
Disposition of Appeal on Grounds Not Pressed at Trial

Setting Aside Jury Verdicts

Farrugia v. Springer (1992), 9 C.P.C. (3d) 55, 36 M.V.R. (2d) 84 (Ont. C.A.).

The Court of Appeal reversed a jury finding that the plaintiff was 70 per cent at fault due to contributory negligence.

Graham v. Hodgkinson (1983), 40 O.R. (2d) 697 (C.A.), leave to appeal to Supreme Court of
    Canada refused 51 N.R. 398.

The court set aside a jury verdict, directed the defendant be found liable and directed a new trial to assess damages. Discussion of circumstances where a jury verdict will be set aside.

McNichol v. Ardiel (1978), 22 O.R. (2d) 324, 10 C.P.C. 148, 93 D.L.R. (3d) 335 (C.A.).

The Court of Appeal set aside the verdict of a jury in a slander case as perverse and directed judgment for the plaintiff.

Delbrocco v. Johnstone, [1962] O.R. 337, 32 D.L.R. (2d) 259 (C.A.).

The court will rarely interfere with the verdict of a jury based on evidence from jury members as to what may have transpired during the course of their deliberations.

McCulloch v. Ottawa Transportation Comm., [1954] O.W.N. 203, [1954] 2 D.L.R. 443 (C.A.).

The court received affidavits of jurors showing that a clerical error had been made by the foreman.

Vertulia v. Kratz, [1956] O.R. 884, 6 D.L.R. (2d) 8 (C.A.).

The Court of Appeal set aside a jury verdict and, because it was so wholly unsupported by the evidence, dismissed the action rather than order a new trial.

Lack of Reasons for Decision by Lower Court

Avco Financial Services Realty Ltd. v. Lagace (1985), 5 C.P.C. (2d) 40 (Ont. C.A.).

Lack of written reasons is not in itself a ground to set aside the order under appeal. The appellate court must determine whether written reasons of the lower court are necessary to make an appellate decision.

Wagman v. Blue Mountain Resorts Ltd. (1984), 47 C.P.C. 53 (Ont. H.C.).

Where a judge or officer gives no reasons for his decision in a discretionary matter, the appeal court must hear the matter *de novo*.

Copenhagen Handelsbank A/S. v. Peter Makos Furs Ltd. (1984), 46 C.P.C. 21, 28 B.L.R. 26 (Ont. H.C.).

Where the court of first instance on a complicated matter gives reasons that are of no assistance to the appellate tribunal, the appeal should be heard as though there had been no contrary decision in the court below.

Savin v. McKay (1984), 44 C.P.C. 192 (Ont. Div. Ct.).

A trial judge should specify the reasons for findings of credibility, but in the circumstances of this case, failure to do so did not amount to reversible error.

426873 Ont. Ltd. v. Windermere on the Thames Ltd. (1984), 45 C.P.C. 215 (Ont. Div. Ct.).

Lack of reasons for granting summary judgment is not necessarily fatal on appeal; it is for each appellate court to determine whether it requires the reasons of the lower court to deal effectively with the appeal.

Koschman v. Hay (1977), 17 O.R. (2d) 557, 6 C.P.C. 243, 4 C.C.L.T. 47, 80 D.L.R. (3d) 766 (C.A.).

A new trial was ordered because the trial judge did not give reasons for judgment. The parties are entitled to the findings of the trial judge on disputed evidence and an appellate court cannot properly exercise its function without them.

Wright v. Ruckstuhl, [1955] O.W.N. 32, [1955] 2 D.L.R. 77 (C.A.).

A new trial was ordered where the judge gave no reasons for judgment and the Court of Appeal was therefore unable to determine matters of credibility. Discussion of desirability of trial judge giving reasons for judgment.

Interim Orders Pending Appeal — s. 134(2)

Peel (Regional Municipality) v. Great Atlantic & Pacific Co. of Can. (1990), 74 O.R. (2d) 161, 44 C.P.C. (2d) 109, 40 O.A.C. 117 (C.A.).

The court refused to grant an interim stay of an order pending appeal where there would be no prejudice to the moving party if the stay was not granted and the balance of hardship was not in its favour.

Kennedy v. Kennedy (1985), 45 R.F.L. (2d) 109 (Ont. C.A.).

The court ordered a party to this family law proceeding to lodge certain assets with the court pending appeal where it appeared likely he would otherwise dispose of the assets.

Kaye v. Kaye (No. 2) (1975), 8 O.R. (2d) 86, 21 R.F.L. 57, 57 D.L.R. (3d) 182 (C.A.).

The Court of Appeal and a judge of that court have jurisdiction to award interim alimony pending an appeal from a judgment dismissing a claim for alimony.

Quashing Appeals for Mootness — s. 134(3)

Borowski v. Canada (A.G.), [1989] 1 S.C.R. 342, 33 C.P.C. (2d) 105, [1989] 3 W.W.R. 97, 47 C.C.C. (3d) 1, 38 C.R.R. 232, 57 D.L.R. (4th) 231, 92 N.R. 110, 75 Sask. R. 82.

Where at the time of hearing of an appeal the issues have became moot, the court has a discretion to determine the appeal and should consider (1) the adversarial context of the case; (2) the judicial economy of hearing the case; and (3) the court's law-making function.

C.P. Ltd. v. Weatherbee; C.P. Ltd. v. Pullman (1979), 26 O.R. (2d) 776 at 784, 14 C.P.C. 225, 103 D.L.R. (3d) 739 at 747 (C.A.).

The court has a long-standing practice to exercise its discretion against entertaining appeals which have become moot and are of no immediate consequence between the parties.

Marek v. Cieslak (1975), 6 O.R. (2d) 343 (C.A.).

Where the death of a party renders an appeal moot, the appeal will be quashed.

Drewery v. Century City Devs. Ltd. (No. 2) (1974), 6 O.R. (2d) 299, 52 D.L.R. (3d) 523 (C.A.).

Where a statutory amendment puts an end to all arguable legal points in an appeal, the appeal should be dismissed.

CTV Television Network Ltd. v. Kostenuk, [1972] 3 O.R. 338, 28 D.L.R. (3d) 180 (C.A.).

Where an appeal from an interim injunction was launched after the injunction had become spent, the court dismissed the appeal without dealing with the merits of the case.

Re Assessment Comm. of Brantford and Veres; Re Assessment Comm. of Brantford and Castle, [1970] 3 O.R. 626 (C.A.).

The court refused to entertain appeals in which the parties' only interests were hypothetical.

Pigott v. Pigott, [1969] 2 O.R. 427 (C.A.).

Where a party acts to take advantage of a judgment and subsequently attempts to appeal from it, the appeal will be quashed.

Quashing Appeals for Being Devoid of Merit — s. 134(3)

Schmidt v. Toronto Dominion Bank (1995), 24 O.R. (3d) 1, 37 C.P.C. (3d) 383, 82 O.A.C. 233 (C.A.).

A motion to quash an appeal as devoid of merit will not be granted where it would require lengthy consideration of the trial record, etc.

Lesyork Holdings Ltd. v. Munden Acres Ltd. (1976), 13 O.R. (2d) 430, 1 C.P.C. 261 (C.A.).

If an appeal is manifestly devoid of merit, it may properly be quashed on a motion to quash. *Accord, Oatway v. Canadian Wheat Board*, [1945] S.C.R. 204, [1945] 2 D.L.R. 145.

Setting Aside Findings of Fact — s. 134(4)(a)

General Signal Ltd. v. Magnum Express Ltd. (1995), 79 O.A.C. 287 (Div. Ct.).

The court held that an appellate court should only interfere with the findings and conclusion of a trial judge where there was a palpable and overriding error which affected the trial judge's assessment of the facts.

Lensen v. Lensen, [1987] 2 S.C.R. 672, 23 C.P.C. (2d) 33, [1988] 1 W.W.R. 481, 44 D.L.R. (4th) 1, 79 N.R. 334, 64 Sask. R. 6.

A finding of fact by a trial judge based on credibility of witnesses may not be set aside by an appellate court unless the trial judge made a palpable and overriding error which affected his or her assessment of the facts.

Re Barath and Bacsek (1975), 11 O.R. (2d) 531, 25 R.F.L. 218, 66 D.L.R. (3d) 595 (Div. Ct.).

An appellate court may reverse findings of fact made by a trial judge.

Industrial Tanning Co. v. Reliable Leather Sportwear Ltd., [1953] O.W.N. 921, [1953] 4 D.L.R. 522, affirmed [1955] 2 D.L.R. 284 (S.C.C.).

Discussion of circumstances in which an appellate court will reverse the findings of the trial judge.

Jeffs v. Matheson, [1951] O.R. 743 (C.A.).

An appellate court may reverse a finding of fact by a trial judge based on inferences which are incorrect and unsupported by the evidence.

Introduction of Further Evidence on Appeal — s. 134(4)(b)

Snelgrove v. Steinberg Inc. (1995), 85 O.A.C. 365 (C.A.).

The court allowed the appellant's request to hear three itms that were not normally part of an appeal record where the items were not "fresh evidence" in the accepted sense but were all necessary to understand the position that the plaintiff found herself in at trial.

Sengmueller v. Sengmueller (1994), 17 O.R. (3d) 208, 25 C.P.C. (3d) 61, 2 R.F.L. (4th) 232, 111 D.L.R. (4th) 19, 69 O.A.C. 312 (C.A.).

The court admitted fresh evidence which did not exist at the time of trial where the evidence was necessary to deal fairly with the issues on appeal.

Keuhl v. Beachburg (Village) (1990), 1 O.R. (3d) 154, 45 C.P.C. (2d) 225, 75 D.L.R. (4th) 193, *(sub nom. Keuhl v. Renfrew (County))* 42 O.A.C. 387 (C.A.).

On appeal from an order under Rule 21 dismissing an action due to the expiry of a limitation period, the appellant was permitted to file an affidavit indicating the plaintiff was of unsound mind at a material time.

Hallum v. Cdn. Memorial Chiropractic College (1989), 70 O.R. (2d) 119 (H.C.).

Even where an appeal on an interlocutory matter is heard *de novo* the parties have no right to introduce further evidence. The court has a discretion to admit or refuse further evidence.

Jackson v. Inglis (1985), 50 C.P.C. 126, 7 O.A.C. 377 (C.A.).

The court permitted additional evidence regarding the plaintiff's loss of future earnings to resolve uncertainty regarding that aspect of the case.

Re Paige; Kope v. Buyers (1984), 47 C.P.C. 216 (Ont. Div. Ct.).

Where the respondent alleged on appeal that documents relied on by the appellant at trial were forgeries, the court adjourned the appeal to permit the respondent to file affidavit evidence and bring a motion for leave to call *viva voce* evidence.

Cook v. Mounce (1979), 26 O.R. (2d) 129, 12 C.P.C. 5, 104 D.L.R. (3d) 635 (Div. Ct.).

New evidence should not be admitted on appeal unless: (1) it is apparently credible; (2) if admitted it would probably have an important influence on the result; and (3) it could not have been obtained by reasonable diligence at the time of the original hearing.

Re Houston and Cirmar Holdings Ltd. (No. 1) (1977), 17 O.R. (2d) 254, 79 D.L.R. (3d) 766 (Div. Ct.).

An appellate court is more willing to hear fresh evidence in an appeal from an administrative tribunal than in an appeal from a lower court.

Whitehall Dev. Corp. v. Walker (1977), 17 O.R. (2d) 241, 4 C.P.C. 97 (C.A.).

The Court of Appeal refused to accept new evidence which could have been obtained by reasonable diligence prior to judgment being granted.

Mercer v. Sijan; Sijan v. R. (1976), 14 O.R. (2d) 12, 1 C.P.C. 281, 72 D.L.R. (3d) 464 (C.A.).

New evidence will be admitted on appeal where it was not ascertainable before the end of the trial with reasonable diligence, it is wholly credible, and it is practically conclusive of an issue in the action. In this fatal accident case evidence of the deceased's spouse remarriage was admitted.

Nash v. Glickman (1975), 7 O.R. (2d) 711 (C.A.).

When seeking leave to introduce new evidence on appeal, it is improper to file the material for which leave is sought before the application for leave has been heard.

Buchanan v. Oliver Plumbing & Heating Ltd., [1959] O.R. 238, 18 D.L.R. (2d) 575 (C.A.).

Where two actions are tried together the court may use evidence from one action in the other.

Ordering New Trial — Generally

Snelgrove v. Steinberg Inc. (1995), 85 O.A.C. 365 (C.A.).

The court ordered a new trial where the defendant had not given the plaintiff proper discovery. The breaches were flagrant and continuing and resulted in substantial prejudice to the plaintiff.

Shoppers Mortgage & Loan Corp. v. Health First Wellington Square Ltd. (1995), 23 O.R. (3d) 362, 38 C.P.C. (3d) 8, 124 D.L.R. (4th) 440, 80 O.A.C. 346, additional reasons 25 O.R. (3d) 95, 38 C.P.C. (3d) 18, 124 D.L.R. (4th) 440 at 448 (C.A.).

Where the trial judge's numerous interventions and prejudgment of issues destroyed the appearance of fairness and impartiality, the court ordered a new trial.

Reed v. Parkside Management Ltd. (1995), 81 O.A.C. 156 (C.A.).

Where the defendant's explanation fell far short of establishing that there was no negligence on its part and no jury reviewing the evidence as a whole and acting judicially could have reached the conclusion that the defendant was not negligent, the court ordered a new trial.

Cyanamid of Canada Ltd. v. Bigelow Liptak of Canada Ltd. (1992), 99 D.L.R. (4th)118, 60 O.A.C. 69 (C.A.).

The Court of Appeal ordered a new trial where the trial judge in his reasons for judgment had failed to deal with strong, clear and uncontradicted evidence which, if accepted, would have resulted in the plaintiff succeeding.

Gibson v. Toth (1990), 44 C.P.C. (2d) 137 (Ont. Div. Ct.).

A new trial was ordered where the trial judge had refused to permit the introduction of a specialist's evidence because of the plaintiff's failure to serve a report pursuant to s. 52(3) of the *Evidence Act*, and because the trial judge had refused to permit a physiotherapist to give evidence. The plaintiff had been unable to serve a report because the specialist had refused to provide one, and the evidence of the physiotherapist might have been relevant.

Arland v. Taylor, [1955] O.R. 131, [1955] 3 D.L.R. 358 (C.A.).

The court laid down the following general propositions: a new trial should not be ordered unless the interests of justice plainly require it; an appellant cannot ask for a new trial as of right because of a misdirection or other error to which no objection was made at trial; a new trial will not be granted because of a misdirection or error unless it caused some substantial wrong; and, a new trial should not be granted because of a non-direction in the charge to the jury if the appellant failed to request that such direction be made.

Colautti Construction Ltd. v. Ottawa (City) (1984), 46 O.R. (2d) 236, 7 C.L.R. 264, 9 D.L.R. (4th) 265, 5 O.A.C. 741 (C.A.).

A new trial was necessary in the absence of critical findings of fact by the trial judge.

Serrurier v. Ottawa (1983), 42 O.R. (2d) 321, 36 C.P.C. 144, 148 D.L.R. (3d) 655 (C.A.).

A new trial was ordered where the trial judge, having permitted evidence to be given through an interpreter, commented unfavourably on the use of the interpreter in making a finding as to credibility.

Ayerst, McKenna & Harrison Inc. v. Apotex Inc. (1983), 41 O.R. (2d) 366, 146 D.L.R. (3d) 93 (C.A.).

A new trial was ordered by reason of the failure to permit the plaintiff to present critical reply evidence coupled with the judge's antipathy towards the plaintiff shown throughout the trial.

Dominion Readers' Service Ltd. v. Brant (1982), 41 O.R. (2d) 1, 30 C.P.C. 266, 140 D.L.R. (3d) 283 (C.A.).

A new trial on the basis of counsel's failure to inform the defendant of a fixed trial date was refused.

Robson v. McDonnell (1980), 19 C.P.C. 239 (Ont. C.A.).

Where the verdict of the jury is perverse and the trial judge reduces the award to below the amount claimed by the plaintiff, the defendant is entitled to a new trial.

Baker v. Hutchinson (1976), 13 O.R. (2d) 591, 1 C.P.C. 291 (C.A.).

A new trial will be ordered where the opportunity of putting the full case before the court was denied.

Lefniski Const. Ltd. v. Katz (1976), 1 C.P.C. 177 (Ont. Div. Ct.).

Where a plaintiff was taken by surprise by a change in the testimony of one of the defendants, and was misled by the pleadings, a new trial was ordered.

Ordering New Trial — Misdirection of Law

Findlay v. Diver (1992), 7 O.R. (3d) 48, 35 M.V.R. (2d) 150, 54 O.A.C. 7 (C.A.).

A new trial was ordered where the charge to the jury did not properly explain contributory negligence.

Angelopoulos v. Machen (1992), 7 O.R. (3d) 45, 36 M.V.R. (2d) 198, 54 O.A.C. 153 (C.A.).

A new trial was ordered where the charge to the jury did not properly explain the defendant's onus of proof.

Vieczorek v. Piersma (1987), 58 O.R. (2d) 583, 16 C.P.C. (2d) 62, 36 D.L.R. (4th) 136, 18 O.A.C. 308 (C.A.).

The failure of the trial judge to outline in his charge to the jury the positions of the plaintiffs and defendants with respect to differing medical opinions is sufficient to require a new trial. In this case the charge was also defective in not properly instructing the jury they could draw an adverse inference from the failure of the plaintiffs to lead evidence from certain treating physicians.

Fink v. McMaster (1987), 58 O.R. (2d) 401, 16 C.P.C. (2d) 163, 35 D.L.R. (4th) 638, 18 O.A.C. 399 (C.A.).

A new trial on the issue of liability was ordered where the trial judge had misdirected the jury that a finding of even one per cent fault against a defendant would on the basis of vicarious liability make that defendant responsible for the total damages occasioned by the fault of the other defendants.

Tsalamatas v. Wawanesa Mutual Ins. Co., 31 C.P.C. 257, (sub nom. *Tsalamatas v. Wawanesa Mutual Ins. Co. (No. 2))* 141 D.L.R. (3d) 322, [1983] I.L.R. 1-1603 (Ont. C.A.).

A party will not be granted a new trial on the ground of non-direction in the judge's charge to the jury where, having opportunity to do so, no objection was taken at trial.

Katsiroumbas v. Dasilva (1982), 132 D.L.R. (3d) 696 (Ont. C.A.).

A new trial was ordered where the charge was unnecessarily long and repetitious and there were several recharges, leading to apparent confusion of the jury which may have affected the verdict.

McNeil v. Fingard, [1945] O.R. 396, [1945] 3 D.L.R. 358 (C.A.).

A misdirection in law is not *per se* a ground upon which a new trial will be ordered. It must also appear that a substantial wrong or miscarriage has resulted. It is necessary to fully and carefully consider the verdict, together with the whole charge and evidence.

Temple v. Ottawa Drug Co., [1946] O.W.N. 295 (C.A.).

An appellant who seeks a new trial on the ground of misdirection must at least establish a doubt in the mind of the court as to whether the misdirection caused a substantial wrong or miscarriage.

Ordering New Trial — Denial of Opportunity to Be Heard

Children's Aid Society of Metropolitan Toronto v. A. (M.) (1993), 14 C.P.C. (3d) 214, 99 D.L.R.
(4th) 715 (Ont. Gen. Div.).

A new trial was ordered where the trial judge reached a decision before giving counsel an
opportunity to make submissions.

Dicker v. Femson Holdings Ltd. (1991), 49 C.P.C. (2d) 188 (Ont. C.A.).

A trial judge may on occasion require argument on an issue by issue basis but ought never
deliver judgment in issue by issue instalments, rather judgment should be reserved until completion of all argument.

Canadian Express Ltd. v. Blair (1991), 6 O.R. (3d) 212, 5 C.P.C. (3d) 161, 53 O.A.C. 397 (Div.
Ct.).

A party may appeal only from an order, not from the related reasons for decision. Even where
the reasoning may prejudice a party in another proceeding, there is no appeal; the prejudice
should be dealt with in the other proceeding.

Gellie v. Naylor (1986), 55 O.R. (2d) 400, 9 C.P.C. (2d) 123, 28 D.L.R. (4th) 762, 15 O.A.C.
129 (C.A.).

A new trial was ordered where the trial judge had deprived the plaintiff of the right to address
the jury last.

Carrier v. Cameron (1985), 6 C.P.C. (2d) 208, 11 O.A.C. 369 (Div. Ct.).

The court refused to order a new trial where a Small Claims Court judge had denied the plaintiff
an opportunity to argue the case but no substantial wrong or miscarriage of justice resulted.

A.H. Al-Sagar & Bros. Engineering Project Co. v. Al-Jabouri (1984), 47 C.P.C. 33 (Ont. H.C.).

Where the master did not permit counsel to make submissions on a material issue, the motion
was referred back for rehearing.

Moyes v. Tovell (1976), 2 C.P.C. 1 (Ont. Div. Ct.).

Where a party has engaged in practically continuous argument throughout trial, a judgment
rendered without argument after the evidence does not constitute a denial of the right to present
argument.

Flynn v. Saunders, [1947] O.W.N. 975 (C.A.).

The failure to hear counsel before dismissing the jury was regarded as an omission or irregularity
which did not result in a substantial wrong or miscarriage of justice.

Felker v. Felker, [1946] O.W.N. 368 (C.A.).

Where the trial judge pronounces judgment before according counsel the right to present
argument a new trial should be ordered.

Powers on Appeal — General — s. 134(1)(a)

Olympia & York v. Royal Trust Co. (1993), 14 O.R. (3d) 1, 9 B.L.R. (2d) 221, 19 C.B.R. (3d)
1, 103 D.L.R. (4th) 129, 64 O.A.C. 324 (C.A.), leave to appeal to Supreme Court of Canada
refused (1994), 17 O.R. (3d) xvix (note), 12 B.L.R. (2d) 324n, 25 C.B.R. (3d) 217n, 110
D.L.R. (4th) vii (note), 174 N.R. 160n, 72 O.A.C. 238n.

Where the trial judge's decision did not turn on the exercise of a discretion but, rather on the
application of legal principles to facts with respect to which there was no material dispute, the
scope of appellate review was not narrow.

Capsule Investments Ltd. v. Heck (1993), 12 O.R. (3d) 225, 103 D.L.R. (4th) 556, 62 O.A.C. 196 (C.A.), leave to appeal to Supreme Court of Canada refused 14 O.R. (3d) xv (note), 103 D.L.R. (4th) vi (note), 160 N.R. 314 (note), 65 O.A.C. 239 (note).

There must be a palpable and overriding error in factual matters before the Court of Appeal will interfere with a judge's confirmation of a report on a reference.

People First of Ontario v. Ontario (Coroner) (1992), 54 O.A.C. 182 (C.A.).

On an appeal from an order dismissing an application for judicial review of a coroner's inquest, the applicant moved for a stay of the inquest pending the hearing of the appeal. The court found that it had jurisdiction to make the order sought, but in the result dismissed the motion.

Harzuz Holdings Ltd. v. Confederation Life Ins. Co. (1989), 34 C.P.C. (2d) 312 (Ont. C.A.).

An established precedent which has become the basis for commercial affairs should not be overruled unless it is clearly in error and there is real necessity to do so.

Silver v. Silver (1986), 54 O.R. (2d) 591, 49 R.F.L. (2d) 148, 13 O.A.C. 16 (C.A.).

In an appeal from a judgment dividing family assets and awarding maintenance, an appellate body is entitled to interfere only where the decision exceeds the generous ambit within which reasonable disagreement is possible.

R. v. Church of Scientology of Toronto; R. v. Zaharia (1985), 5 C.P.C. (2d) 92 (Ont. C.A.).

A single judge of the Court of Appeal held that he lacked jurisdiction to continue an interim order of the lower court that certain documents be sealed. The matter was referred to a panel of the court.

Mulroy v. Aqua Scene (1982), 36 O.R. (2d) 653 (C.A.).

An appeal court must use this statutory power and obligation in a generally supervisory fashion over damage awards as over other matters but cannot substitute a figure of its own merely because it would have awarded a different figure if it had tried the case at first instance.

Rotenberg v. York (1976), 13 O.R. (2d) 101, 1 C.P.C. 85, (*sub nom. Re Rotenberg and York (No. 2)*) 9 L.C.R. 289 (C.A.).

This provision does not allow the Court of Appeal to make an order that the trial judge could not make.

Rawson v. Kasman, [1956] O.W.N. 359, 3 D.L.R. (2d) 376 (C.A.).

The Court of Appeal may not substitute its assessment of damages for an assessment made by a jury but may do so with respect to an assessment made by a trial judge.

Marleen Invts. Ltd. v. McBride (1979), 23 O.R. (2d) 125, 27 Chitty's L.J. 69 (H.C.).

An appellate court will not interfere with the exercise of the discretion of the master unless it is clearly wrong.

Schiowitz v. I.O.S. Ltd., [1972] 3 O.R. 262, 28 D.L.R. (3d) 40 (C.A.).

An appeal on the merits of an action does not entitle the appellate court to review interlocutory matters for which no leave to appeal has been given.

Coniagas Reduction Co. v. H.E.P.C. of Ont., [1932] O.R. 463, [1932] 3 D.L.R. 360 (C.A.).

The power conferred by this provision is discretionary, not obligatory. The power should not be exercised against the trial judge's order as to costs where the order was not made the subject of appeal.

Disposition of Appeal on Grounds Not Pressed at Trial

Scarborough Golf & Country Club v. Scarborough (City) (1988), 66 O.R. (2d) 257, 41 M.P.L.R. 1, 1 R.P.R. (2d) 225, 54 D.L.R. (4th) 1, 31 O.A.C. 260 (C.A.).

On appeal, the court refused to entertain argument on an issue which had not been pleaded or argued at trial.

National Trust Co. v. Bouckhuyt (1987), 59 O.R. (2d) 556, 21 C.P.C. (2d) 226, 38 B.L.R. 77, 7 P.P.S.A.C. 273, 46 R.P.R. 221, 43 D.L.R. (4th) 543, 23 O.A.C. 40 (C.A.).

An appeal should not be decided on the basis of a ground raised for the first time in the appeal court unless the appellant shows beyond doubt that all facts bearing on that ground are in the record and that the respondent is not prejudiced by inability to adduce evidence on the new issue.

Shaver Hosp. for Chest Diseases v. Slesar (1979), 27 O.R. (2d) 383, 15 C.P.C. 97, 106 D.L.R. (3d) 377 (C.A.), leave to appeal to Supreme Court of Canada adjourned 27 O.R. (2d) 383n, 106 D.L.R. (3d) 377n.

A technical defence raised in the pleadings but virtually abandoned at trial will not be considered on appeal where not all relevant evidence bearing on it was introduced.

Canadiana Towers Ltd. v. Fawcett (1978), 21 O.R. (2d) 545, 90 D.L.R. (3d) 758 (C.A.), leave to appeal to Supreme Court of Canada refused 26 N.R. 241.

An appellate court will act on arguments not raised or pleaded at trial only if it is satisfied that all the facts relevant to the new argument are before it.

Legault v. Chapleau Realties & Enterprises Ltd. (1976), 1 C.P.C. 220 (Ont. C.A.).

Leave may be granted on an appeal to amend a pleading where the related evidence was fully disclosed at trial, there is no surprise, and there is no injustice not compensable in costs.

PUBLIC ACCESS

Section 135

Public hearings
135.—(1) Subject to subsection (2) and rules of court, all court hearings shall be open to the public.

Exception
(2) The court may order the public to be excluded from a hearing where the possibility of serious harm or injustice to any person justifies a departure from the general principle that court hearings should be open to the public.

Disclosure of information
(3) Where a proceeding is heard in the absence of the public, disclosure of information relating to the proceeding is not contempt of court unless the court expressly prohibited the disclosure of the information.

Ministry Comment

Original Act

Subsections (1) and (2) are derived from ss. 82 and 117 of the *Judicature Act.* Subsection (1) is a more direct enunciation of the principle that court hearings should generally be open to the public. Subsection (2) is believed to represent a more realistic test for excluding the public than the "public decency and morals" test in s. 82 of the former Act.

Subsection (3) is a new provision designed to reinforce the principle that the public is entitled to be informed about proceedings in courts.

Cross-Reference: See s. 137 regarding access to court files.

Cases

McCreadie v. Rivard (1995), 6 W.D.C.P. (2d) 453 (Ont. Gen. Div.).

The court refused to order an *in camera* hearing and the sealing of the court file in this commercial case. There is a strong public policy in favour of openness of court proceedings.

Ontario (Solicitor General) v. Ontario (Assistant Information & Privacy Commissioner) (1993), 12 Admin. L.R. (2d) 300, 102 D.L.R. (4th) 602, 64 O.A.C. 60 (Div. Ct.), reversed on other grounds 18 Admin. L.R. (2d) 50, 107 D.L.R. (4th) 454, 68 O.A.C. 317 (C.A.), leave to appeal to Supreme Court of Canada refused (1994), 20 Admin. L.R. (2d) 145n.

Except in the most exceptional circumstances, proceedings before the courts must be open to the public.

Orpin v. College of Physicians & Surgeons (Ont.) (1988), 25 C.P.C. (2d) 19, 25 O.A.C. 235 (Div. Ct.).

The court refused to ban publication of the name of a physician found by the college to be guilty of misconduct pending appeal. There is a powerful presumption that the public has a right to know what transpires in its courts of law.

Re Clark (1982), 26 C.P.C. 238 (Ont. Div. Ct.).

The court had no authority to ban *ex post facto* the publication of what transpired in public proceedings before it.

Section 136

Prohibition against photography, etc., at court hearing
136.—(1) Subject to subsections (2) and (3), no person shall,
(a) take or attempt to take a photograph, motion picture, audio recording or other record capable of producing visual or aural representations by electronic means or otherwise,
  (i) at a court hearing,
  (ii) of any person entering or leaving the room in which a court hearing is to be or has been convened, or
  (iii) of any person in the building in which a court hearing is to be or has been convened where there is reasonable ground for believing that the person is there for the purpose of attending or leaving the hearing; or
(b) publish, broadcast, reproduce or otherwise disseminate a photograph, motion picture, audio recording or record taken in contravention of clause (a); or
(c) broadcast or reproduce an audio recording made as described in clause (2)(b).

Exceptions
(2) Nothing in subsection (1),
(a) prohibits a person from unobtrusively making handwritten notes or sketches at a court hearing; or
(b) prohibits a solicitor, a party acting in person or a journalist from unobtrusively making an audio recording at a court hearing, in the manner that has been approved by the judge, for the sole purpose of supplementing or replacing handwritten notes.

Exceptions
(3) Subsection (1) does not apply to a photograph, motion picture, audio recording or record made with authorization of the judge,

(a) where required for the presentation of evidence or the making of a record or for any other purpose of the court hearing;

(b) in connection with any investitive, naturalization, ceremonial or other similar proceeding; or

(c) with the consent of the parties and witnesses, for such educational or instructional purposes as the judge approves.

Offence

(4) Every person who contravenes this section is guilty of an offence and on conviction is liable to a fine of not more than $25,000 or to imprisonment for a term of not more than six months, or to both.

Ministry Comment

Original Act

This section is derived from s. 67 of the *Judicature Act*. The section has been expanded to prohibit unauthorized audio recordings of court proceedings. Otherwise, the slight changes in language do not change the meaning or scope of the section.

Subsection (2) is included to clarify the law respecting the taking of notes and sketches. On a strict interpretation of subs. (1), a sketch could be held to be a "record capable of producing visual . . . representations". Clause 2(a) clarifies that this is not the intention.

Clause 2(b) permits the making of audio recordings by a solicitor or party acting in person if used only as a substitute for notes.

Section 137

Documents public

137.—(1) On payment of the prescribed fee, a person is entitled to see any document filed in a civil proceeding in a court, unless an Act or an order of the court provides otherwise.

Sealing documents

(2) A court may order that any document filed in a civil proceeding before it be treated as confidential, sealed and not form part of the public record.

Court lists public

(3) On payment of the prescribed fee, a person is entitled to see any list maintained by a court of civil proceedings commenced or judgments entered.

Copies

(4) On payment of the prescribed fee, a person is entitled to a copy of any document the person is entitled to see.

Ministry Comment

Original Act

Subsection (1) is derived from s. 129(4) of the *Judicature Act*. The new provision permits any person to see documents filed in civil proceedings in courts, not just "persons affected". The new section makes s. 129(2) of the *Judicature Act* unnecessary.

Subsection (2) provides authority for a court to order that certain documents be kept confidential.

Cross-Reference: See rule 4.03 regarding obtaining certified copies of documents and see s. 135 regarding hearings being open to the public.

Cases

RBC Dominion Securities Inc. v. Horne (1995), 37 C.P.C. (3d) 95 (Ont. Gen. Div.).

On motion of a newspaper the court set aside an order sealing the court file.

887574 Ontario Inc. v. Pizza Pizza Ltd. (1994), 35 C.P.C. (3d) 323 (Ont. Gen. Div. [Commercial List]), leave to appeal to Ont. C.A. refused (June 7, 1995), Doc. CA M15773.

The court refused to seal the court file in a proceeding arising from an arbitration which had been conducted privately.

Publow v. Wilson (1994), 36 C.P.C. (3d) 33, 9 C.C.E.L. (2d) 22, 59 C.P.R. (3d) 294 (Ont. Gen. Div.).

The court refused to grant a broad confidentiality order in this wrongful dismissal case notwithstanding the defendant's position that disclosure of its financial condition would cause severe harm.

Symons v. United Church of Canada (1993), 16 O.R. (3d) 379, 68 O.A.C. 141 (Div. Ct.).

An individual who had complained of sexual misconduct on the part of three ministers was subsequently named as a party to an action brought by the same ministers. The complainant brought an application for a publication ban respecting her identity, but the application was dismissed. The Ontario Divisional Court granted leave to appeal. There was good reason to doubt the correctness of the original order, since it appeared that the motion judge had not addressed the established policy objective of encouraging victims to come forward.

Canada Mortgage & Housing Corp. v. Andres (1993), 24 C.P.C. (3d) 16 (Ont. Gen. Div.).

The court ordered that copies of discovery transcripts were to be sealed, where the deponent feared that the information given on discovery might be used against her in an outstanding criminal prosecution. Although her evidence would be protected by the *Canada Evidence Act*, the Ontario *Evidence Act*, and the *Charter of Rights and Freedoms*, the information which she would give might assist the Crown in obtaining further evidence against her in the criminal prosecution.

Forbes v. Thurlow (1993), 23 C.P.C. (3d) 107 (Ont. Gen. Div.).

The court ordered the file sealed pending determination of a related criminal case.

MDS Health Group Ltd. v. Canada (A.G.) (1993), 15 O.R. (3d) 630, 20 C.P.C. (3d) 137 (Gen. Div.).

Where publicity was not likely to destroy the subject-matter of the action itself but only to upset the marketplace, the court refused to order that the proposed action proceed under a pseudonym and that the court record be sealed.

National Bank of Canada v. Melnitzer (1991), 5 O.R. (3d) 234, 2 C.P.C. (3d) 106, 84 D.L.R. (4th) 315 (Gen. Div.).

Section [137] of the *Courts of Justice Act* does not violate the *Charter of Rights and Freedoms*.

R. (T.) v. D. (R.A.) (1989), 37 C.P.C. (2d) 122 (Ont. Master).

The court refused to seal the court file in a paternity action where there was insufficient evidence to support the allegation that the defendant would suffer harm if the contents of the court file became public knowledge.

A. (J.) v. Can. Life Assurance Co. (1989), 35 C.P.C. (2d) 1 (Ont. Master), affirmed 35 C.P.C. (2d) 5 (Ont. H.C.), leave to appeal to Ont. Div. Ct. granted 70 O.R. (2d) 27, 35 C.P.C. (2d) 6.

The court declined to seal the court file of an action by two AIDS victims notwithstanding the consent of the parties and a prior order permitting the plaintiffs to use pseudonyms.

S. (P.) v. C. (D.) (1987), 22 C.P.C. (2d) 225, additional reasons 22 C.P.C. (2d) 225 at 231 (Ont. H.C.).

The public record is only to be sealed in the clearest of cases and on the clearest of material.

Sorbara v. Sorbara (1987), 59 O.R. (2d) 153, 15 C.P.C. (2d) 4 (Master).

The court refused to order the court file sealed in this divorce proceeding where the affidavit supporting the motion was made by the solicitor rather than the client and did not provide specifics as to the probable damage to the moving party.

McCormick v. Newman (1986), 15 C.P.C. (2d) 1 (Ont. Master).

The court refused to seal the court file of an action which had been settled notwithstanding allegations of possible embarrassment and financial harm to the moving party. The potential harm was little different than that many defendants suffer when they become embroiled in litigation.

Haessler-DeWay Ltd. v. Color Tech. Inc. (1985), 49 C.P.C. 156, 4 C.I.P.R. 77, 5 C.P.R. (3d) 191 (Ont. Dist. Ct.).

The court ordered documents regarding a secret manufacturing process to be treated as confidential, to be sealed and not to form part of the public record.

Howes v. Accountant of Ont. S.C. (1985), 49 O.R. (2d) 121, 47 C.P.C. 252, 18 E.T.R. 249 (H.C.).

The Order Book kept by the Accountant of the Supreme Court of Ontario is not available for public inspection.

B. v. P. (1982), 35 O.R. (2d) 325 (Ont. Master).

In a paternity suit, the court exercised its inherent discretion to order the file sealed until commencement of trial to protect the privacy of the defendant.

MISCELLANEOUS

Section 138

Multiplicity of proceedings
138. As far as possible, multiplicity of legal proceedings shall be avoided.

Cross-Reference: See cases under rule 21.01(3)(c).

Cases

Bourne v. Saunby (1993), 23 C.P.C. (3d) 333, 49 M.V.R. (2d) 65 (Ont. Gen. Div.).

The court refused to sever the issues of liability and damages in a case arising out of a collision between an automobile and a train.

Wellington Insurance Co. v. Beaudin (1992), 8 C.P.C. (3d) 165, 11 C.C.L.I. (2d) 129 (Ont. Gen. Div.).

The court refused to permit an insurer to prosecute an action for property damage in the name of its insured where the insured had commenced an action for personal injury and was prepared to amend that claim to include property damage. Both claims should be asserted in the same action. The fact that the insurer had denied the insured's claim for accident benefits did not justify a separate action.

Section 139

Joint liability not affected by judgment or release
139.—(1) Where two or more persons are jointly liable in respect of the same cause of action, a judgment against or release of one of them does not preclude judgment against any other in the same or a separate proceeding.

Two proceedings in respect of same damage
(2) Where a person who has suffered damage brings two or more proceedings in respect of the damage, the person is not entitled to costs in any of the proceedings, except the first proceeding in which judgment is obtained, unless the court is of the opinion that there were reasonable grounds for bringing more than one proceeding.

Ministry Comment

Original Act

This provision abolishes the rule that judgment against, or a release of, a person who is jointly liable prevents judgment from being obtained against any other joint wrongdoer. The provision makes it unnecessary for the new Rules to incorporate the joint liability provisions of former Rules 54 and 65.

Subsection (2) is a complementary provision intended to discourage unnecessary proceedings.

Cross-Reference: See rule 19.07 regarding default judgment.

Cases

Westar Aluminum & Glass Ltd. v. Brenner (1993), 17 C.P.C. (3d) 228 (Ont. Gen. Div.).

Where the plaintiff obtained a default judgment against one of several defendants on a contract which did not entail joint liability, the plaintiff lost its right to pursue the other defendant and the action was dismissed in that regard.

CFGM 1320 Radio Broadcasting Ltd. v. Doyle (1987), 17 C.P.C. (2d) 65 (Ont. Dist. Ct.).

Section [139(1)] does not apply in cases involving alternative liability. The plaintiff was not entitled to judgment against the defendant agent when judgment had already been obtained against the principal.

Royal Bank v. Metcalfe (1985), 3 C.P.C. (2d) 228 (Ont. Dist. Ct.).

The term ''cause of action'' refers to the entire set of facts that gives rise to an enforceable claim.

Section 140

Vexatious proceedings
140.—(1) Where a judge of the Ontario Court (General Division) is satisfied, on application, that a person has persistently and without reasonable grounds,
    (a) instituted vexatious proceedings in any court; or
    (b) conducted a proceeding in any court in a vexatious manner,
the judge may order that,
    (c) no further proceeding be instituted by the person in any court; or
    (d) a proceeding previously instituted by the person in any court not be continued,
except by leave of a judge of the Ontario Court (General Division).

Attorney General
(2) An application under subsection (1) shall be made only with the consent of the Attorney General, and the Attorney General is entitled to be heard on the application.

Application for leave to proceed
(3) Where a person against whom an order under subsection (1) has been made seeks leave to institute or continue a proceeding, the person shall do so by way of an application in the Ontario Court (General Division).

Leave to proceed
(4) Where an application for leave is made under subsection (3),
(a) leave shall be granted only if the court is satisfied that the proceeding sought to be instituted or continued is not an abuse of process and that there are reasonable grounds for the proceeding;
(b) the person making the application for leave may seek the recission of the order made under subsection (1) but may not seek any other relief on the application;
(c) the court may rescind the order made under subsection (1);
(d) the Attorney General is entitled to be heard on the application; and
(e) no appeal lies from a refusal to grant relief to the applicant.

Abuse of process
(5) Nothing in this section limits the authority of a court to stay or dismiss a proceeding as an abuse of process or on any other ground.

Ministry Comment

Original Act

This section is derived from the *Vexatious Proceedings Act*. Subsection (1) expands the grounds on which an order may be made against a vexatious litigant to include conducting a proceeding in a vexatious manner. In *Foy v. Foy (No. 2)* (1979), 26 O.R. (2d) 220, (*sub nom. Foy v. Foy*) 12 C.P.C. 188, 102 D.L.R. (3d) 342, a majority of the Court of Appeal held that, although one of the parties had brought "a myriad of interlocutory proceedings", the language of the existing Act was not broad enough to permit an order to be made on that basis. The new provision is intended to overcome that problem.

Subsection (2) is derived from s. 1(2) of the *Vexatious Proceedings Act*.

Subsection (3) indicates how a person against whom an order has been made may seek leave to institute or continue a proceeding.

Clause (4)(a) is derived from the concluding words of s. 1(1) of the *Vexatious Proceedings Act*.

Clauses (4)(b), (c), (d) and (e) are new provisions. Clause (b) is intended to prevent a person against whom an order has been made from harassing others by instituting applications for leave that also claim other relief. The only other relief permitted by clause (b) is an order rescinding the original order. The rescission order would be made under clause (c). Clause (d) permits the Attorney General to appear on the application for leave. Clause (e) prevents a vexatious litigant from endlessly appealing a refusal to grant leave.

Subsection (5) preserves the authority of the courts to stay or dismiss a proceeding as an abuse of process.

Cases

Mascan Corp. v. French (1988), 64 O.R. (2d) 1, 49 D.L.R. (4th) 434, 26 O.A.C. 326 (C.A.).
The court may consider all proceedings whether original, interlocutory or by way of appeal. The language used in s. [140(1)(b)] overrules *Foy v. Foy (No. 2)* (1979), 26 O.R. (2d) 220, 12 C.P.C. 188, 102 D.L.R. (3d) 342 (C.A.).

Lang Michener Lash Johnston v. Fabian (1987), 59 O.R. (2d) 353, 16 C.P.C. (2d) 93, 37 D.L.R. (4th) 685 (H.C.).

The court ordered the respondents not to institute new proceedings without leave of a judge. Discussion of principles applicable to s. [140] of the *Courts of Justice Act.*

Mascan Corp. v. French (1986), 8 C.P.C. (2d) 187 (Ont. H.C.), affirmed (1988), 64 O.R. (2d) 1, 49 D.L.R. (4th) 434, 26 O.A.C. 326 (C.A.).

The court ordered that the respondent commence no further proceedings against the applicant except by leave of a judge of the High Court.

L.S.U.C. v. Zikov (1984), 47 C.P.C. 42 (Ont. H.C.).

The court made an order that the defendant institute no further actions without leave.

Section 141

Civil orders directed to sheriffs

141.—(1) Unless the Act provides otherwise, orders of a court arising out of a civil proceeding and enforceable in Ontario shall be directed to a sheriff for enforcement.

Police to assist sheriff

(2) A sheriff who believes that the execution of an order may give rise to a breach of the peace may require a police officer to accompany the sheriff and assist in the execution of the order.

Ministry Comment

Bill 2

Section [141] puts into the *Courts of Justice Act* the provisions of s. 2 of the *Sheriffs Act,* as amended by Bill 187.

Section 142

Protection for acting under court order

142. A person is not liable for any act done in good faith in accordance with an order or process of a court in Ontario.

Section 143

Enforcement of bonds and recognizances

143.—(1) A bond or recognizance arising out of a civil proceeding may be enforced in the same manner as an order for the payment of money by leave of a judge on motion by the Attorney General or any other person entitled to enforcement.

Enforcement of fines for contempt

(2) A fine for contempt of court may be enforced by the Attorney General in the same manner as an order for the payment of money or in any other manner permitted by law.

Enforcement by sheriff

(3) The sheriff to whom a writ obtained under subsection (1) or (2) is directed shall proceed immediately to carry out the writ without a direction to enforce.

Section 143.1

No garnishment of certain amounts

143.1 **No benefit, allowance or assistance paid under the *Family Benefits Act* or the *General Welfare Assistance Act* may be garnished by a creditor of the person to whom it is payable.**

Deemed protection

(2) **Subsection (1) applies even if the amount has been paid into the person's account at a financial institution.**

Section 144

Orders enforceable by police

144. **Warrants of committal, warrants for arrest and any other orders requiring persons to be apprehended or taken into custody shall be directed to police officers for enforcement.**

Ministry Comment

1989 Amendments

Bill 187 (Explanatory Note)

This amendment is complementary to the re-enactment of s. 2 of the *Sheriffs Act*, and makes it clear that . . . orders for arrest in civil proceedings are to be enforced by the police and not by sheriffs. These are exceptions to the general rule found in proposed s. 2 of the *Sheriffs Act*.

Section 145

Consul as official representative

145. **Where a person who is ordinarily resident in a foreign country is entitled to money or property that is in the hands of a court or an executor or administrator, and if the foreign country has a consul in Canada who is authorized to act as the person's official representative, the money or property may be paid or delivered to the consul.**

Section 146

Where procedures not provided

146. **Jurisdiction conferred on a court, a judge or a justice of the peace shall, in the absence of express provision for procedures for its exercise in any Act, regulation or rule, be exercised in any manner consistent with the due administration of justice.**

Ministry Comment

1989 Amendments

Bill 2

Section [146] is derived from s. 62 of the 1984 Act. The new provision is applicable to all courts and judges, not just the Provincial Division and provincial judges.

Section 147

Seal of court
147.—(1) The courts shall have such seals as are approved by the Attorney General.

Idem
(2) Every document issued out of a court in a civil proceeding shall bear the seal of the court.

Section 148

Jurisdiction of Federal Court
148. The Federal Court of Canada has jurisdiction,
(a) in controversies between Canada and Ontario;
(b) in controversies between Ontario and any other province in which an enactment similar to this section is in force,
in accordance with section 19 of the *Federal Court Act* (Canada).

PART VIII

MISCELLANEOUS

Section 149

Documents
149.—(1) A document filed in court that refers to the Unified Family Court is not for that reason invalid and shall be deemed to refer to the Family Court of the Ontario Court (General Division).

Repeal
(2) Subsection (1) is repealed on January 1, 1996. [re-en. 1994, c. 12, s. 47]

Section 150

Renewal of writs of execution issued before January 1, 1985
150. A writ of execution that was issued before the 1st day of January, 1985 may be renewed in the same manner and with the same effect as a writ of execution issued on or after that day.

Section 151

References to counties for judicial purposes
151.—(1) A reference in this Act or any other Act, rule or regulation to a county or district for judicial purposes is deemed to be a reference to the corresponding area that, for municipal or territorial purposes, comprises the county, district, union of counties or regional, district or metropolitan municipality.

Separated municipalities
(2) For the purpose of subsection (1), every city, town and other municipality is united to and forms part of the county in which it is situate.

Exceptions

(3) Subsection (1) is subject to the following:

1. A reference in an Act or regulation to a county or district for judicial purposes is, in the case of The Regional Municipality of Haldimand-Norfolk, deemed to be a reference to the following areas:

    i. All the area of the County of Haldimand as it existed on the 31st day of March, 1974.

    ii. All the area of the County of Norfolk as it existed on the 31st day of March, 1974.

2. A reference in an Act or regulation to a county or district for judicial purposes is, in the case of The Regional Municipality of Niagara, deemed to be a reference to the following areas:

    i. All the area of the County of Lincoln as it existed on the 31st day of December, 1969.

    ii. All the area of the County of Welland as it existed on the 31st day of December, 1969.

3. A reference in an Act or regulation to a county or district for judicial purposes is, in the case of The Regional Municipality of Sudbury and the Territorial District of Sudbury, deemed to be a reference to all the area in The Regional Municipality of Sudbury and in the Territorial District of Sudbury.

4. A reference in an Act or regulation to a county or district for judicial purposes is, in the case of an area described below, deemed to be a reference to all the area in the areas described below:

    i. All the area in the County of Victoria.

    ii. All the area in the County of Haliburton.

    iii. All the area in any part of the townships of Sherborne, McClintock, Livingstone, Lawrence and Nightingale located in Algonquin Park, so long as the part remains part of Algonquin Park.

SCHEDULE

APPENDIX A OF FRAMEWORK AGREEMENT

BETWEEN:

Her Majesty the Queen in right of the Province of Ontario represented by the Chair of Management Board

(''the Minister'')

and

the Judges of the Ontario Court (Provincial Division) and the former Provincial Court (Civil Division) represented by the respective Presidents of The Ontario Judges Association, The Ontario Family Law Judges Association, and the Ontario Provincial Court (Civil Division) Judges' Association

(''the Judges'')

These are the terms to which the Minister and the Judges agree:

DEFINITIONS

1. In this agreement,

(a) "Commission" means the Provincial Judges' Remuneration Commission;

(b) "Crown" means Her Majesty the Queen in right of the Province of Ontario;

(c) "judges' associations" means the associations representing the Judges of the Ontario Court (Provincial Division) and the former Provincial Court (Civil Division);

(d) "parties" means the Crown and the judges' associations.

INTRODUCTION

2. The purpose of this agreement is to establish a framework for the regulation of certain aspects of the relationship between the executive branch of the government and the Judges, including a binding process for the determination of Judges' compensation. It is intended that both the process of decision-making and the decisions made by the Commission shall contribute to securing and maintaining the independence of the Provincial Judges. Further, the agreement is intended to promote co-operation between the executive branch of the government and the judiciary and the efforts of both to develop a justice system which is both efficient and effective, while ensuring the dispensation of independent and impartial justice.

3. It is the intention of the parties that the binding process created by this document will take effect with respect to the 1995 Provincial Judges Remuneration Commission, and thereafter.

4. The Minister or the Judges may designate one or more persons to act on their behalf under this agreement.

COMMISSION AND APPOINTMENTS

5. The parties agree that the Provincial Judges Remuneration Commission is continued.

6. The parties agree that the Commission shall consist of the following three members:

1. One appointed jointly by the associations representing provincial judges.

2. One appointed by the Lieutenant Governor in Council.

3. One, who shall head the Commission, appointed jointly by the parties referred to in paragraphs 1 and 2.

7. The parties agree that the members of the Commission shall serve for a term of three years beginning on the first day of July in the year their inquiry under paragraph 13 is to be conducted.

8. The parties agree that the term of office of the persons who are members of the Commission on May 1, 1991 shall expire on June 30, 1995.

9. The parties agree that the members of the Commission may be reappointed when their term of office expires.

10. The parties agree that if a vacancy occurs on the Commission, a replacement may be appointed for the unexpired part of the term.

11. The parties agree that judges and public servants, as defined in the Public Service Act, shall not be members of the Commission.

12. The parties agree that the members of the Commission shall be paid the remuneration fixed by the Management Board of Cabinet and, subject to Management Board's approval, the reasonable expenses actually incurred in carrying out their duties.

SCOPE

13. The parties agree that in 1995, and in every third year after 1995, the Commission shall conduct an inquiry respecting:

(a) the appropriate base level of salaries,

(b) the appropriate design and level of pension benefits, and

(c) the appropriate level of and kind of benefits and allowances of provincial judges.

14. The parties agree that in addition to the inquiry referred to in paragraph 13, the Commission may, in its discretion, conduct any further inquiries into any matter relating to salary levels, allowances and benefits of provincial judges that are mutually agreed by the judges and the Government of Ontario.

15. The parties agree that the Commission whose term begins on July 1, 1995 and all subsequent Commissions shall begin their inquiry under paragraph 13 immediately after their term begins and shall, on or before the thirty-first day of December in the year the inquiry began, present recommendations and a report to the Chair of the Management Board of Cabinet.

16. The parties agree that the Commission shall make an annual report of its activities to the Chair of Management Board and the Chair shall table the report in the Legislature.

POWERS AND PROCEDURES

17. The parties agree that the Commission may retain support services and professional services, including the services of counsel, as it considers necessary, subject to the approval of the Management Board.

18. The parties agree that the representatives of the Judges and the Lieutenant Governor in Council may confer prior to, during or following the conduct of an inquiry and may file such agreements with the Commission as they may be advised.

19. The parties agree that the Commission may participate in joint working committees with the judges and the government on specific items related to the inquiry of the Commission mentioned in paragraphs 13 and 14.

20. The parties agree that in conducting its inquiries, the Commission shall consider written and oral submissions made by provincial judges' associations and by the Government of Ontario.

21. The parties agree that the following rules govern the presentation to the Commission of submissions by provincial judges' associations and by the Government of Ontario, and their consideration by the Commission:

1. Each judges' association is entitled to receive advance disclosure of written submissions by the Government of Ontario and is entitled to make a written submission in reply.

2. The Government of Ontario is likewise entitled to receive advance disclosure of written submissions by provincial judges' associations and is entitled to make a written submission in reply.

3. When a representative of the Government of Ontario or of a judges' association makes an oral submission, the Commission may exclude from the hearing all persons except representatives of the Government of Ontario and of the judges' associations.

4. The representatives of the Government of Ontario and of the judges' associations are entitled to reply to each other's oral submissions.

5. If people have been excluded from the hearing under paragraph 3, the submissions of the Government of Ontario and of the judges' associations shall not be made public except to the extent that they are mentioned in the Commission's report.

22. The parties agree that the Commission may hold hearings, and may consider written and oral submissions from other interested persons and groups.

23. The parties agree that the Government of Ontario and the provincial judges' associations are entitled to be present when other persons make oral submissions to the Commission and are entitled to receive copies of other persons' written submissions.

24. In connection with, and for the purposes of, any inquiry, the Commission or any member thereof has the powers of a commission under the Public Inquiries Act.

CRITERIA

25. The parties agree that the Commission in making its recommendation on provincial judges' compensation shall give every consideration to, but not limited to, the following criteria, recognizing the purposes of this agreement as set out in paragraph 2:
 (a) the laws of Ontario,
 (b) the need to provide fair and reasonable compensation for judges in light of prevailing economic conditions in the province and the overall state of the provincial economy,
 (c) the growth or decline in real per capita income,
 (d) the parameters set by any joint working committees established by the parties,
 (e) that the Government may not reduce the salaries, pensions or benefits of Judges, individually or collectively, without infringing the principle of judicial independence,
 (f) any other factor which it considers relevant to the matters in issue.

REPORT

26. The parties agree that they may jointly submit a letter to the Commission requesting that it attempt, in the course of its deliberations under paragraph 13, to produce a unanimous report, but in the event that the Commission cannot deliver a majority report, the Report of the Chair shall be the Report of the Commission for the purpose of paragraphs 13 and 14.

BINDING AND IMPLEMENTATION

27. The recommendations of the Commission under paragraph 13, except those related to pensions, shall come into effect on the first day of April in the year following the year the Commission began its inquiry, except in the case of salary recommendations which shall come into effect on the first of April in the year in which the Commission began its inquiry and shall have the same force and effect as if enacted by the Legislature and are in substitution for the provisions of any schedule made pursuant to this Agreement and shall be implemented by the Lieutenant Governor in Council by order-in-council within sixty days of the delivery of the Commission's report pursuant to paragraph 15.

28. The parties agree that the Commission may, within thirty days, upon application by the Crown or the judges' associations made within ten days after the delivery of its recommendations and report pursuant to paragraph 15, subject to affording the Crown and the judges' associations the opportunity to make representations thereupon to the Commission, amend, alter or vary its recommendations and report where it is shown to the satisfaction of the Commission that it has failed to deal with any matter properly arising from the inquiry under paragraph 13 or that an error relating to a matter properly under paragraph 13 is apparent on the report, and such decision is final and binding on the Crown and the judges' associations, except those related to pensions.

29. Where a difference arises between the Crown and the judges' associations relating to the implementation of recommendations properly within the scope of issues set out in paragraph 13, except those related to pensions, the difference shall be referred to the Commission and, subject to affording the Crown and the judges' associations the opportunity to make representation thereupon to the Commission, its decision is final and binding on the Crown and the judges' associations.

30. The parties agree that the recommendations with respect to pensions, or any reconsideration under paragraph 28 of a matter relating to pensions, shall be presented to the Management Board of Cabinet for consideration.

31. The parties agree the recommendations and report of the Commission following a discretionary inquiry pursuant to paragraph 14 shall be presented to the Chair of Management Board of Cabinet.

32. The parties agree that the recommendations of the Commission in consequence of an inquiry pursuant to paragraph 14 shall be given every consideration by Management Board of Cabinet, but shall not have the same force and effect as recommendations referred to in paragraph 13.

33. The parties agree that if the Management Board of Cabinet endorses recommendations referenced in paragraph 30 or 31, or some variation of those recommendations, the Chair of Management Board shall make every effort to implement them at the earliest possible date, following subsequent approval from Cabinet.

DISPUTES

34. The parties agree that if disputes arise as to whether a recommendation is properly the subject of an inquiry referenced in paragraph 13, or whether the recommendation falls within the parameters of paragraph 27 or 30, or with respect to the process, either party may require the Commission to consider the matter further.

35. The parties agree that requests by either party, made under paragraph 34, shall be presented to the Commission for consideration within one month of the presentation of the report to the Chair of Management Board.

36. The parties agree that the Commission, upon receiving notice from either party as set out in paragraph 34, shall present to the Chair of Management Board a decision with respect to the said matter, within one month of receiving such notice.

37. The parties may, during the course of the Commission's inquiry set out in paragraph 34, present either written or oral positions to the Commission for consideration on the said matter, which shall be disclosed to either party.

38. The parties agree that the decision of the Commission, as set out in paragraph 36, shall be given every consideration and very great weight by the Management Board of Cabinet.

39. Neither party can utilize the dispute clauses to limit, or to narrow, the scope of the Commission's review as set out under paragraph 13, or the binding effect of recommendations within its scope as set out under paragraphs 27 and 28.

40. The parties agree that in the event that an item(s) is referred to the Commission under paragraph 34, the Minister will proceed to implement the other recommendations of the Commission as set out in paragraphs 27, 28 and 33, except where the matter in dispute under paragraph 34 directly impacts the remaining items.

REVIEW

41. The parties agree that either party may, at any time, request the other party to meet and discuss improvements to the process.

42. The parties agree that any amendments agreed to by the parties in paragraph 41 shall have the same force and effect as if enacted by the Legislature and are in substitution for the provisions of this Act or any schedule made pursuant to this Act.

COMMUNICATION

43. The parties agree that all provincial judges should be made aware of any changes to their compensation package as a result of recommendations of the Commission.

44. The parties agree that all provincial judges should receive updated copies of legislation, regulations or schedules as necessary, related to compensation changes.

SALARIES AND INDEXING

45. The parties agree that effective on the first day of April in every year after 1995, the annual salaries for full-time provincial judges shall be adjusted as follows:

1. Determine the Industrial Aggregate for the twelve-month period that most recently precedes the first day of April of the year for which the salaries are to be calculated.

2. Determine the Industrial Aggregate for the twelve-month period immediately preceding the period referred to in paragraph 1.

3. Calculate the percentage that the Industrial Aggregate under paragraph 1 is of the Industrial Aggregate under paragraph 2.

4. If the percentage calculated under paragraph 3 exceeds 100 per cent, the salaries are to be calculated by multiplying the appropriate salaries for the year preceding the year for which the salaries are to be calculated by the lesser of that percentage and 107 per cent.

5. If the percentage calculated under paragraph 3 does not exceed 100 per cent, the salaries shall remain unchanged.

46. In paragraph 45, "Industrial Aggregate" for a twelve-month period is the average for the twelve-month period of the weekly wages and salaries of the Industrial Aggregate in Canada as published by Statistics Canada under the authority of the Statistics Act (Canada).

47. The salaries, allowances and benefits of provincial judges shall be paid out of the Consolidated Revenue Fund.

ADDITIONAL PROVISIONS

48. This agreement shall be binding upon and enure to the benefit of the parties hereto and their respective successors and assigns.

APPENDIX B OF FRAMEWORK AGREEMENT

JUDICIAL SALARIES

Date	Formula
April 1, 1991	$124,250
April 1, 1992	0%
April 1, 1993	AIW*
April 1, 1994	AIW*

* Note: See paragraph 45 of Appendix "A". [en. 1994, c. 12, s. 48]

PART 2

RULES, FORMS AND TARIFFS

RULES OF CIVIL PROCEDURE

R.R.O. 1990, Regulation 194

[am. O. Regs. 219/91; 396/91; 73/92; 175/92; 535/92; 770/92; 212/93; 465/93; 466/93; 766/93; 351/94; 484/94; 739/94; 740/94; 69/95; 70/95; 377/95; 533/95; 534/95; 60/96; 61/96; 175/96]

SUMMARY OF CONTENTS

[For detailed Table of Contents, see page 199]

TABLE OF CONTENTS

GENERAL MATTERS

RULES OF CIVIL PROCEDURE

INTRODUCTION TO THE RULES OF CIVIL PROCEDURE

The Rules of Civil Procedure came into force in 1985 replacing the former Rules of Practice. The Rules of Civil Procedure were drafted together with the *Courts of Justice Act* as part of an integrated package, and both came into force at the same time. The Rules brought about a myriad of changes in Ontario civil procedure. (For a comprehensive description of the major changes from the former practice, see the "Introduction to the Rules of Civil Procedure" in the 1985-1990 editions of Watson and McGowan, *Ontario Supreme and District Court Practice.*)

Since their original passage, there have been numerous amendments to the Rules of Civil Procedure. The pervasive amendments consequent upon the restructuring of Ontario courts brought about by the *Courts of Justice Amendment Acts, 1989* are described in the Annual Survey of Recent Developments in Civil Procedure in the 1990 edition of Watson and McGowan, *Ontario Civil Practice.*

The Revised Regulations of Ontario, 1990 (which came into force November 16, 1992) substantially renumbered the Rules to accommodate amendments to the Rules which had been passed since they were originally enacted in 1984. Also, there were some changes in the language of the Rules to effect grammatical changes, to further the goal of gender neutral language or to achieve greater uniformity.

GENERAL MATTERS

RULE 1　CITATION, APPLICATION AND INTERPRETATION

Highlights

 Application. The Rules of Civil Procedure apply to all civil proceedings in the Ontario Court (General Division) and the Court of Appeal except Small Claims Court proceedings, proceedings under the *Estates Act*, or where a statute provides otherwise: rule 1.02(1). Subject to two exceptions, the Rules apply to all proceedings whenever commenced, though the court has power to order that proceedings commenced under the old Rules be continued under those Rules: rule 1.02(2), (4).

 Proceedings commenced in Toronto, the District of Algoma or the County of Essex are or may be subject to case management rules. The Algoma, Essex and Toronto Case Management Rules with accompanying commentary are reproduced in the companion volume, *Forms, Case Management and Special Materials*. Where there is a conflict between the Rules of Civil Procedure and the case management rules, the case management rules prevail: Algoma Civil Case Management Rule 1(2), Essex Civil Case Management Rule 2, Toronto Civil Case Management Rule 1.01(3) and Toronto Family Case Management Rule 1.01(2).

 Interpretation. Rule 1.04(1) is an important provision requiring that the Rules be "liberally construed to secure the just, most expeditious and least expensive determination of every civil proceeding on its merits". It has been applied in numerous cases including, for example, *Clancy v. Fransky* (1985), 52 O.R. (2d) 793, 5 C.P.C. (2d) 209, 21 E.T.R. 85, 12 O.A.C. 208 (Div.Ct.); *Fedorczenko v. Jamieson* (1986), 56 O.R. (2d) 252, 14 C.P.C. (2d) 299 (H.C.); and *Abco Box & Carton Co. v. Dafoe & Dafoe Inc.* (1987), 20 C.P.C. (2d) 128, 65 C.B.R. (N.S.) 292 (Ont. Dist. Ct.).

 Basic concepts and terminology are defined in the lengthy definition provision in rule 1.03: the most important include "action", "application", "motion", "proceeding", "originating process", "court" and "judge".

 The court is given a general power to impose terms in the making of any order: rule 1.05. The prescribed forms are to be used where applicable and with such variations as the circumstances require: rule 1.06.

 Former Rules: Rules 1-3, 817.

CITATION

Short Title

1.01(1)　These rules may be cited as the Rules of Civil Procedure.

Subdivision

(2)　In these rules,

(a)　all the provisions identified by the same number to the left of the decimal point comprise a Rule (for example, Rule 1, which consists of rules 1.01 to l.06);

(b)　a provision identified by a number with a decimal point is a rule (for example, rule 1.01); and

(c)　a rule may be subdivided into,

    (i) **subrules (for example, subrule 1.01(2)),**
    (ii) **clauses (for example, clause 1.01(2)(c) or 2.02(a)),**
    (iii) **subclauses (for example, subclause 1.01(2)(c)(iii) or 7.01(c)(i)),**
    (iv) **paragraphs (for example, paragraph 1 of subrule 52.07(1)), and**
    (v) **definitions (for example, the definition of "action" in rule 1.03).**

Alternative Method of Referring to Rules

    (3) In a proceeding in a court, it is sufficient to refer to a rule or subdivision of a rule as "rule" followed by the number of the rule, subrule, clause, subclause or paragraph (for example, rule 1.01, rule 1.01(2), rule 1.01(2)(c), rule 1.01(2)(c)(iii) or rule 52.07(1) 1).

APPLICATION OF RULES

Court of Appeal and Ontario Court (General Division)

    1.02(1) These rules apply to all civil proceedings in the Court of Appeal and in the Ontario Court (General Division), subject to the following exceptions:

    1. They do not apply to proceedings in the Small Claims Court, which are governed by Regulation 201 of Revised Regulations of Ontario, 1990.

    2. [Revoked O. Reg. 484/94, s. 1]

    3. They do not apply if a statute provides for a different procedure.

Transitional Provisions

    (2) These rules apply to a proceeding, whenever commenced, unless the court makes an order under subsection 156(3) of the *Courts of Justice Act, 1984*.

    (3) Despite subrule (2), rule 48.14 (status hearing in actions) applies only to actions in which a statement of defence is filed after these rules come into force.

    (4) Despite subrule (2), on the assessment of costs of a proceeding under rule 58.01, the assessment officer shall, unless the court orders otherwise, assess and allow,

    (a) for services rendered and disbursements incurred before these rules [came] into force, solicitors' fees and disbursements in accordance with the Tariffs in force immediately before these rules came into force; and

    (b) for services rendered and disbursements incurred after these rules came into force, solicitors' fees and disbursements in accordance with the Tariffs to these rules. [am. O. Reg. 484/94, s. 1]

Authors' Comment

    Subsection 156 of the *Courts of Justice Act, 1984* is an unconsolidated and unrepealed transition provision which states as follows:

Application to all proceedings

    156.—(1) This Act applies to all proceedings, whether commenced before or after this Act comes into force, subject to subsections (2) and (3) and except as otherwise provided.

Exception
(2) Where a notice of appeal is delivered before this Act comes into force, the appeal shall be heard and determined by the court that had jurisdiction over the appeal before this Act comes into force.

Exception
(3) Where a proceeding is commenced before this Act comes into force, on motion, the court in which the proceeding was commenced may order, subject to such terms as are considered just and subject to variation by further order, that the proceeding or a step in the proceeding be conducted under the Acts and rules of court that governed the matter immediately before this Act comes into force or may make any other order that is considered just.

Application of Rules — Generally

Ont. Securities Comm. v. Electra Invts. (Can.) Ltd. (1983), 44 O.R. (2d) 61, 38 C.P.C. 57 (C.A.).
The Rules apply to applications brought pursuant to specific statutory provisions.

Johnson v. Milton (No. 1) (1981), 34 O.R. (2d) 289, 24 C.P.C. 205 (H.C.).
The Rules were held to apply to an application to quash by-laws pursuant to the *Municipal Act.*

Re Cessland Corp. and Fort Norman Explorations Inc. (1979), 25 O.R. (2d) 69, 100 D.L.R. (3d) 378 (H.C.).
A practice direction is for the better administration of the court and does not affect the rights and obligations of the parties.

Application of Rules — Transitional Provisions — rule 1.02(2), (3), (4)

Cocomile Estate v. Cocomile Estate (1988), 33 C.P.C. (2d) 61 (Ont. Master).
The court ordered that a specially endorsed writ of summons be treated as a notice of action and extended the time to file the statement of claim notwithstanding a lengthy delay in prosecuting the action.

Atchison v. Dennis (1985), 7 C.P.C. (2d) 13 (Ont. Dist. Ct.).
The court validated service of a writ of summons issued under the old Rules and statement of claim filed under the new Rules notwithstanding that the statement of claim was filed and both documents were served more than six months after the new Rules came into force.

Divitaris v. Divitar Manufacturing Ltd. (1985), 50 O.R. (2d) 786 (H.C.).
The court dismissed a motion to amend a writ of summons issued under the old Rules, since the new Rules do not contemplate commencing a proceeding by writ and the moving party did not bring a motion under s. 156(3) of the *Courts of Justice Act, 1984* to permit the proceeding to be continued under the old Act and Rules.

Seaway Trust Co. v. Feldman (1985), 4 C.P.C. (2d) 62 (Ont. H.C.).
On a motion under s. 156(3) of the *Courts of Justice Act, 1984* the moving party had an onus to demonstrate that some practical difficulty had arisen and that it had suffered some special prejudice as a result of the rule change, or some compelling reason to warrant a departure from the Rules of Civil Procedure which were to govern all actions whenever commenced. The court reversed a decision of the master continuing the old summary judgment procedure in this case.

Medwin v. DeHavilland Aircraft of Can. Ltd. (1985), 50 C.P.C. 240 (Ont. Master).
Where examinations for discovery were conducted prior to the Rules of Civil Procedure coming into force, the court ordered that the Rules of Practice should apply to a motion to compel answers to certain refused questions. However, all parties were permitted to deliver written interrogatories to obtain the information contemplated by rule 31.06(2), (3) and (4).

Drake v. Kellmann, 50 O.R. (2d) 45, 49 C.P.C. 260, [1985] I.L.R. 1-1903 (H.C.).
The court ordered the defendant to produce an insurance policy pursuant to rule 30.02(3) notwithstanding the plaintiff had delivered a certificate of readiness and set the action down for trial prior to January 1, 1985.

First City Dev. Corp. v. Avenue Properties Ltd. (1985), 50 C.P.C. 189 (Ont. Master).
The court ordered that the old Rules apply to a motion to set aside a default judgment where the motion had originally been returnable prior to January 1, 1985 and where application of the new Rules would deprive the defendant of an argument in favour of setting aside the judgment.

Marshall v. Hoffman (1985), 48 O.R. (2d) 701, 47 C.P.C. 7 (Master).
Where one party had been examined for discovery under the former Rules of Practice, the court ordered that the old Rules should also apply to the oral examination of the other party subject to both parties being at liberty to conduct written examinations to obtain the information contemplated by rule 31.06(2), (3) and (4).

Mutual Life Assur. Co. of Can. v. Windsor Westchester at the Lake Ltd. (1985), 47 C.P.C. 12 (Ont. Master).
The court ordered that the former Rules of Practice apply to a motion for judgment on a specially endorsed writ, which motion had been scheduled to be heard while the old Rules were in force but adjourned at the instance of the defendants.

Application of Rules — Case Management Rules

Covello v. Brydon Motors (Propane) Repair Ltd. (1993), 19 C.P.C. (3d) 118 (Ont. Gen. Div.).
Where a statement of claim is selected for case management and it subsequently appears that amendments are necessary, counsel should amend the existing statement of claim rather than issuing a new one.

Opoku v. Pruitt (1993), 14 O.R. (3d) 107 (Gen. Div.).
A case management judge has jurisdiction to hear an application to set aside an order of the registrar dismissing an action under the Toronto Civil Case Management Rules. In the result, the application was dismissed as there had been a series of defaults of serious proportions over a substantial length of time.

Hribar v. Snop (1992), 14 C.P.C. (3d) 349 (Ont. Gen. Div.).
In a case under the Toronto Family Case Management Rules, the case management judge has sole jurisdiction until trial, but the Rules of Civil Procedure apply thereafter. Accordingly, where a default judgment has been obtained, enforcement proceedings do not have to be brought before the case management judge.

O'Donnell v. Xanthopoulos (1992), 11 O.R. (3d) 724, 12 C.P.C. (3d) 210 (Gen. Div.).
A motion to cure a default was granted where the defendants were served only a day or two later than required by the Case Management Rules; there was no serious delay in bringing a motion and the plaintiff had a triable case.

DEFINITIONS

1.03 In these rules, unless the context requires otherwise,
"action" means a proceeding that is not an application and includes a proceeding commenced by,

    (a) statement of claim,
    (b) notice of action,
    (c) counterclaim,
    (d) crossclaim,
    (e) third or subsequent party claim, or
    (f) divorce petition or counterpetition;

"appellant" means a person who brings an appeal;

"appellate court" means the Court of Appeal or the Divisional Court, as the circumstances require;

"applicant" means a person who makes an application;

"application" means a proceeding commenced by notice of application;

"county" includes a district or a regional, district or metropolitan municipality;

"court" means the court in which a proceeding is pending and, in the case of a proceeding in the Ontario Court (General Division), includes a master having jurisdiction to hear motions under Rule 37;

"defendant" means a person against whom an action is commenced;

"deliver" means serve and file with proof of service, and "delivery" has a corresponding meaning;

"disability", where used in respect of a person or party, means that the person or party is,

    (a) a minor,
    (b) mentally incapable within the meaning of section 6 or 45 of the *Substitute Decisions Act, 1992* in respect of an issue in the proceeding, whether the person or party has a guardian or not, or
    (c) an absentee within the meaning of the *Absentees Act*;

"discovery" means discovery of documents, examination for discovery, inspection of property and medical examination of a party as provided under Rules 30 to 33;

"hearing" means the hearing of an application, motion, reference, appeal or assessment of costs, or a trial;

"holiday" means,

    (a) any Saturday or Sunday,
    (b) New Year's Day,
    (c) Good Friday,
    (d) Easter Monday,
    (e) Victoria Day,
    (f) Canada Day,
    (g) Civic Holiday,
    (h) Labour Day,
    (i) Thanksgiving Day,
    (j) Remembrance Day,
    (k) Christmas Day,
    (l) Boxing Day, and

    (m) any special holiday proclaimed by the Governor General or the Lieutenant Governor,

and where New Year's Day, Canada Day or Remembrance Day falls on a Saturday or Sunday, the following Monday is a holiday, and where Christmas Day falls on a Saturday or Sunday, the following Monday and Tuesday are holidays, and where Christmas Day falls on a Friday, the following Monday is a holiday;

"judge" means a judge of the court;

"judgment" means a decision that finally disposes of an application or action on its merits and includes a judgment entered in consequence of the default of a party;

"motion" means a motion in a proceeding or an intended proceeding;

"moving party" means a person who makes a motion;

"order" includes a judgment;

"originating process" means a document whose issuing commences a proceeding under these rules, and includes,

    (a) a statement of claim,

    (b) a notice of action,

    (c) a petition,

    (d) a notice of application,

    (d.1) an application for a certificate of appointment of an estate trustee,

    (e) a counterclaim against a person who is not already a party to the main action,

    (f) a third or subsequent party claim, and

    (g) a counterpetition against a person who is not already a party to the main action,

but does not include a counterclaim or counterpetition that is only against persons who are parties to the main action, a crossclaim, or a notice of motion;

"plaintiff" means a person who commences an action;

"proceeding" means an action or application;

"referee" means the person to whom a reference in a proceeding is directed;

"registrar" means the Registrar of the Divisional Court or Court of Appeal, or a local registrar of the Ontario Court (General Division), as the circumstances require;

"respondent" means a person against whom an application is made or an appeal or a divorce action is brought, as the circumstances require;

"responding party" means a person against whom a motion is made;

"solicitor's office" means the office of the solicitor of record as set out in the last document filed by him or her;

"statute" includes a statute passed by the Parliament of Canada.

[am. O. Regs. 535/92, s. 2; 484/94, s. 2; 69/95, s. 1]

Definitions - Generally

Hoffman v. Longworth, 17 O.R. (2d) 47, 4 C.P.C. 134, [1978] I.L.R. 1-929 (C.A.).

The definitions in the *Judicature Act* were held to apply to the Rules unless a contrary intention appeared.

"Deliver"

DeForest v. Saunders, [1960] O.W.N. 111 (H.C.).

A party will not be permitted to use his own unexplained delay in filing a document to his advantage.

"Holiday"

Young v. Mississauga (City) (1993), 16 O.R. (3d) 409, 24 C.P.C. (3d) 202, 18 M.P.L.R. (2d) 138, 108 D.L.R. (4th) 90 (Gen. Div.).

In determining whether notice of a slip and fall injury was given on a timely basis to the defendant municipality, the court held that the definition of "holiday" which was contained in the Rules of Civil Procedure should be used instead of the definition contained in the *Interpretation Act,* as the notice requirement related to a legal matter. As the Rules of Civil Procedure define Saturday as a holiday, the plaintiff's notice was effective.

Kapularic v. Longphee (1990), 42 C.P.C. (2d) 313 (Ont. H.C.).

Where the last day for issuing a claim or notice of action fell on a Saturday, the limitation period prescribed by the *Highway Traffic Act* was extended by the *Interpretation Act* to the next day that was not a holiday.

"Proceeding"

Rauscher v. Roltford Developments Ltd. (1989), 69 O.R. (2d) 749 (H.C.).

"Proceeding" includes a motion for the purpose of Rule 6.

Maple Leaf Racquet Court Inc. v. Beaver Engineering Ltd. (1987), 60 O.R. (2d) 626 (Master).

"Proceeding" does not include an appeal for the purpose of rule 56.01.

Crown Trust Co. v. Rosenberg (1986), 60 O.R. (2d) 87, 22 C.P.C. (2d) 131, 67 C.B.R. (N.S.) 320n, 39 D.L.R. (4th) 526 (H.C.).

"Proceeding" does not include a motion for the purpose of Rule 13.

"Responding Party"

Greymac Trust Co. v. Burnett (1987), 59 O.R. (2d) 50, 16 C.P.C. (2d) 75 (H.C.).

"Responding party" includes a party or person who will be affected by the order sought.

G.C. Rentals & Enterprises Ltd. v. Giamnarino (1986), 9 C.P.C. (2d) 10 (Ont. H.C.).

A "responding party" is any person against whom a motion is made and need not be a party to the litigation.

INTERPRETATION

General Principle

1.04(1) These rules shall be liberally construed to secure the just, most expeditious and least expensive determination of every civil proceeding on its merits.

Matters Not Provided For
   (2) **Where matters are not provided for in these rules, the practice shall be determined by analogy to them.**

Party Acting in Person
   (3) **Where a party to a proceeding is not represented by a solicitor but acts in person in accordance with subrule 15.01(2) or (3), anything these rules require or permit a solicitor to do shall be done by the party.**

General Principle - rule 1.04(1)

Re Sam Richman Invts. (London) Ltd. and Riedel (1974), 6 O.R. (2d) 335, 52 D.L.R. (3d) 655
   (Div. Ct.).
Subheadings may be used to assist in interpretation where a provision is doubtful or ambiguous.

Matters Not Provided For - rule 1.04(2)

Bayliss v. Wren Lake Estates Ltd. (1991), 49 C.P.C. (2d) 274 (Ont. Gen. Div.).
Where a statute provided for a right of appeal but did not state the appeal period, the court applied the Rules of Civil Procedure concerning both the length of the period and its extension.

Reekie v. Messervey [1990] 1 S.C.R. 219, 39 C.P.C. (2d) 1, 43 B.C.L.R. (2d) 145, [1990] 3
   W.W.R. 673, 66 D.L.R. (4th) 765, 108 N.R. 170.
The Supreme Court of Canada relied upon an analogous rule to give effect to substantive rights notwithstanding a deficiency in the Rules.

Crombie v. R., 52 O.L.R. 72, [1923] 2 D.L.R. 542 (C.A.).
The predecessor of this provision was held to rescind all former rules and abrogate the earlier practice. The court is in consequence governed exclusively by the language of the Rules themselves, interpreted according to the general rules of statutory interpretation.

Kemp v. Beattie, 63 O.L.R. 176, [1929] 1 D.L.R. 55 (H.C.).
The Rules are a complete code of procedure, either by special provisions or by analogy. The English practice no longer governs.

Andreacchi v. Perruccio, [1972] 1 O.R. 508 (C.A.).
This provision is to be applied only in matters of minor importance.

ORDERS ON TERMS

   1.05 When making an order under these rules the court may impose such terms and give such directions as are just.

Authors' Note

One possible term of an order is that a party give security by way of bond. For a listing of approved guarantee companies issuing performance bonds, see the Authors' Note following rule 44.04.

Bradbury v. Traise (1986), 12 C.P.C. (2d) 261 (Ont. Dist. Ct.).
The court has jurisdiction to impose directions when dismissing a motion.

Jordan v. McKenzie (1985), 3 C.P.C. (2d) 220 (Ont. H.C.).
The court included a term in a judgment requiring the successful plaintiff to transfer certain shares to the defendant after payment of the judgment in order to avoid further litigation.

FORMS

1.06 The forms prescribed in these rules shall be used where applicable and with such variations as the circumstances require.

Queensway Lincoln Mercury Sales (1980) Ltd. v. 409918 Ont. Ltd. (1981), 34 O.R. (2d) 568, 25 C.P.C. 186 (H.C.).

The Forms are guides only, and reasonable conformity to them is sufficient.

PRACTICE DIRECTIONS

Court of Appeal
1.07(1) A practice direction, notice or guide for proceedings in the Court of Appeal shall be signed by the Chief Justice of Ontario, filed with the secretary of the Civil Rules Committee and published in the *Ontario Reports*.

General Division
(2) A practice direction, notice or guide for proceedings in the Ontario Court (General Division) shall be signed or countersigned by the Chief Justice of the Ontario Court, filed with the secretary of the Civil Rules Committee and published in the *Ontario Reports*.

Effective Date
(3) A practice direction, notice or guide shall not come into effect before being published in the *Ontario Reports*, unless the relevant chief justice is of the opinion that it is necessary to bring it into effect before that time, in which case it shall so indicate and shall state the date on which it comes into effect. [en. O. Reg. 770/92, s. 2]

RULE 2   NON-COMPLIANCE WITH THE RULES

Highlights

Rule 2.01 deals with the effect of non-compliance with the Rules and is broader than its predecessors. It states that a failure to comply with the Rules is an irregularity and does not render the proceeding a nullity. It further provides that the court may grant all necessary amendments and, in very limited circumstances, set aside a proceeding. (There are supplementary provisions to this rule, dealing expressly with procedural defects in estate litigation, in rule 9.03.)

Rule 2.03 gives the court power to dispense with compliance with any rule at any time but "only where and as necessary in the interest of justice". This is to relieve against overly rigid application of the Rules where that would be inappropriate. In addition to this general power, many individual rules provide that they apply "unless the court orders otherwise": see *e.g.* rule 37.09(3).

A motion attacking irregularity in the proceeding is to be made promptly and before taking a further step in the proceeding, but the court may relieve against this requirement by granting leave: rule 2.02.

Former Rules: Rules 185-187.

EFFECT OF NON-COMPLIANCE

2.01(1) A failure to comply with these rules is an irregularity and does not render a proceeding or a step, document or order in a proceeding a nullity, and the court,

(a) may grant all necessary amendments or other relief, on such terms as are just, to secure the just determination of the real matters in dispute; or

(b) only where and as necessary in the interest of justice, may set aside the proceeding or a step, document or order in the proceeding in whole or in part.

(2) The court shall not set aside an originating process on the ground that the proceeding should have been commenced by an originating process other than the one employed.

General (See also cases under rules 5.04, 14.06 and 26.01.)

Beaver Engineering Ltd. v. Swedlove (1994), 17 O.R. (3d) 355, 25 C.P.C. (3d) 392, 13 C.L.R. (2d) 54, 111 D.L.R. (4th) 750 (Div. Ct.).

Where a construction lien case was not formally set down for trial within the time required by the *Construction Lien Act* because the local practice of the court did not conform to the Rules of Civil Procedure, the court cured the defect pursuant to Rule 2.

O'Donnell v. Xanthopoulos (1992), 11 O.R. (3d) 724, 12 C.P.C. (3d) 210 (Gen. Div.).

A motion to cure a default was granted where the defendants were served only a day or two later than required by the Case Management Rules; there was not serious delay in bringing a motion and the plaintiff had a triable case.

Giles v. Arnold Palmer Motors Inc. (1991), 5 O.R. (3d) 536 (Gen. Div.).

The court held that service on a Pennsylvanian defendant was proper notwithstanding that the plaintiff's committee did not obtain permission from the court to commence the action.

Bieler v. Bieler (1986), 10 C.P.C. (2d) 226 (Ont. Master).

An application to vary a judgment was reconstituted as a notice of motion.

Re Harper (1981), 34 O.R. (2d) 491, 39 C.B.R. (N.S.) 23, 1 P.P.S.A.C. 36, 126 D.L.R. (3d) 327 (S.C.).

The court permitted a party to file an affidavit to prove a fact omitted by a slip.

Pub. Trustee v. Guar. Trust Co. of Can., [1980] 2 S.C.R. 931, 19 C.P.C. 157, 7 E.T.R. 287, 115 D.L.R. (3d) 513, 33 N.R. 271.

An action by a plaintiff against itself in its representative capacity was an irregularity cured by the substitution of the Public Trustee in its stead.

Re Solicitor (1978), 7 C.P.C. 240 (Ont. H.C.).

An order of a County Court judge referring a solicitor's bill for taxation was treated as one by a local judge pursuant to the predecessor of this provision.

Re Huffmon and Breese (1974), 3 O.R. (2d) 416 (H.C.).

Where a judgment is given in favour of the estate of a deceased rather than in favour of his administratrix, leave to amend the name should be given.

Patterson v. Schuett, [1947] O.W.N. 1013 (H.C.).

An amendment to a pleading made in an improper form and without authority was cured.

Caines v. Cumpsen, [1946] O.W.N. 739 (H.C.).

An action commenced by an infant plaintiff without a next friend was held to be an irregularity which could be corrected.

Muldoon v. Simcoe Public Utilities Comm., [1945] O.W.N. 863 (H.C.).

The failure to make an amendment within the time ordered is an irregularity which may be relieved against.

Limitation Periods (See also cases under rules 5.04, 14.06 and 26.01.)

Gordon v. Deputy Minister of National Revenue (Customs & Excise) (1990), 44 C.P.C. (2d) 129 (Ont. Dist. Ct.).

A notice of application under the *Customs Tariff Act* was sent to the court and the respondent by registered mail within the applicable limitation period, but the notice was never issued or filed by the court. These were irregularities, and as the respondent had received timely notice of the proceeding, the application was deemed to have been issued *nunc pro tunc* from the date it was received by the court.

Tummillo v. Prouty (1990), 42 C.P.C. (2d) 308 (Ont. Dist. Ct.).

Where, as a result of a delay by the court office, a statement of claim was issued after the relevant limitation period had expired, the court ordered the issuance date of the statement of claim to be amended *nunc pro tunc*.

Algoma Dist. Medical Group v. Southam Press (Ont.) Ltd. (1978), 19 O.R. (2d) 153, 5 C.P.C. 197, 84 D.L.R. (3d) 595 (H.C.).

Where a defamation action was mistakenly commenced in District Court within the relevant limitation period, it was held that an action commenced outside the limitation period in Supreme Court was not statute-barred.

Adomaitis v. Parkin, [1973] 1 O.R. 105 (Master).

Where defendants were found to be improperly joined, but the relevant limitation periods had expired, the plaintiff was permitted to deliver fresh statements of claim and proceed with two separate actions.

ATTACKING IRREGULARITY

2.02 A motion to attack a proceeding or a step, document or order in a proceeding for irregularity shall not be made, except with leave of the court,
(a) after the expiry of a reasonable time after the moving party knows or ought reasonably to have known of the irregularity; or
(b) if the moving party has taken any further step in the proceeding after obtaining knowledge of the irregularity.

Time for Motion

O'Donnell v. Xanthopoulos (1992), 11 O.R. (3d) 724, 12 C.P.C. (3d) 210 (Gen. Div.).
Delay in attacking an irregularity is not a bar to the motion where the moving party did not have timely knowledge of the irregularity.

Bajzat v. Bajzat (1991), 35 R.F.L. (3d) 59, 52 O.A.C. 25, additional reasons [1992] W.D.F.L. 022 (Div. Ct.).
A party objecting to an irregularity respecting a motion should raise the objection at the first return date of the motion, or at least provide notice of the objection at that time.

MacKenzie v. Wood Gundy Inc. (1989), 35 C.P.C. (2d) 272 (Ont. H.C.).
A delay of five or six months in bringing a motion to strike out pleadings is too long and will bar the motion.

Matters Not Affected By Further Steps

Stankovic v. Leighton (1988), 28 C.P.C. (2d) 155 (Ont. H.C.).
Serving a demand for particulars is not a fresh step barring a motion to strike out the statement of claim.

Steiner v. Lindzon (1976), 14 O.R. (2d) 122, 1 C.P.C. 237 (H.C.).
An application for particulars is probably not foreclosed by taking a fresh step.

Malkowicz v. Ciemiega, [1957] O.W.N. 532 (M.C.).
Improper joinder is not cured by the taking of a fresh step.

Stylecraft Dress Co. v. Gotlin, [1946] O.W.N. 114 (H.C.).
A motion for security for costs can be made at any time in the proceedings (and is not a fresh step).

Patterson v. Proprietary Mines Ltd., [1945] O.W.N. 237 (M.C.).
A motion for particulars is normally a fresh step, but where the motion is both to strike out and for particulars, the applicant may secure relief upon the motion to strike out.

Bruce v. John Northway & Son Ltd., [1962] O.W.N. 150 (M.C.).
Steps taken after the service of a notice of motion attacking an irregularity do not cure the irregularity.

Effect of Certain Steps

Sports Mgmt. Ltd. v. Nedomansky (1982), 28 C.P.C. 223 (Ont. Master).
A motion for consolidation was held to be a further step precluding attack on an irregularity.

G.C.C. Ltd. v. Thunder Bay (1981), 32 O.R. (2d) 111, 20 C.P.C. 276 (H.C.).
Although the motion was made over two years after the irregularity, a party was held not to have waived the irregularity.

Strezeszewski v. Mackenzie (1980), 20 C.P.C. 9 (Ont. Master).
A step taken inadvertently may not constitute a waiver of an irregularity.

T. & D. Contracting Co. v. J.M. Const. Ltd. (1978), 7 C.P.C. 278n (Ont. H.C.).
Arranging an examination for discovery is a fresh step.

Terminal Warehouses Ltd. v. J.H. Lock & Sons Ltd., [1956] O.W.N. 581 (Master).
The court dismissed an attack on the statement of claim made seven months after discovery.

Guaranty Trust Co. of Can. v. Celenza, [1967] 2 O.R. 236 (H.C.).
Filing a request to redeem is a fresh step.

Taylor v. Burrow (1980), 16 C.P.C. 109 (Ont. Co. Ct.).
The delivery of a statement of defence was not a bar to an application to strike out paragraphs of the statement of claim on a determination of a question of law.

Gregory v. Andwell Theatres Ltd., [1945] O.W.N. 106 (Master).
Acceptance of service by a solicitor is not a fresh step.

Bickerton v. Caughell, [1946] O.W.N. 841 (Master).
A plaintiff's demand for particulars of a counterclaim is not a fresh step.

Heffering v. Heffering, [1944] O.W.N. 53 (Master).
A motion for particulars and interim alimony is not a fresh step.

COURT MAY DISPENSE WITH COMPLIANCE

2.03 The court may, only where and as necessary in the interest of justice, dispense with compliance with any rule at any time.

Stamper v. Finnigan (1983), 47 N.B.R. (2d) 252, 124 A.P.R. 252 (Q.B.).
A corresponding New Brunswick rule was invoked to relieve a plaintiff of the obligation to pay attendance money and compensation to non-parties being examined for discovery with leave of the court.

RULE 3   TIME

Highlights

This Rule regulates the computation and the extension or abridgment of time under the Rules and when proceedings may be heard.

In contrast to the former practice, a common method of computing time is now prescribed, whether or not the terms "clear days" or "at least" are used: rule 3.01(1)(a). Holidays are not to be counted where a period of less than seven days is prescribed (rule 3.01(1)(b)).

The general power of the court to extend or abridge time limits (rule 3.02) is the basis for the court to extend the time for serving a statement of claim. With the abolition of the writ of summons, the concept of originating process being "in effect for" a specified period and the requirement of "renewal" have disappeared. The Rules simply require the statement of claim to be served within six months after it is issued (rule 14.08) and rule 3.02 gives the court power to extend that time and any other time-limit prescribed by a rule or order.

The concept of court vacation no longer exists and has been replaced by a prohibition on the holding of trials over Christmas, unless all parties consent or the court orders otherwise: rule 3.03(1). The waiting period before the court may proceed to hear a motion in the absence of the opposite party is fifteen minutes: rule 3.03(2). Rule 3.04 (court office hours) has been revoked and that matter is now dealt with by regulation.

Case management. Case management time requirements are governed by the case management rules in place for Toronto, Algoma and Essex and are much less flexible than those set by the Rules of Civil Procedure. The Case Management Rules are reproduced in the companion volume, *Forms, Case Management Guide and Special Materials.*

Former Rules: Rules 174-179.

COMPUTATION

3.01(1) In the computation of time under these rules or an order, except where a contrary intention appears,

(a) where there is a reference to a number of days between two events, they shall be counted by excluding the day on which the first event happens and including the day on which the second event happens, even if they are described as clear days or the words "at least" are used;

(b) where a period of less than seven days is prescribed, holidays shall not be counted;

(c) where the time for doing an act under these rules expires on a holiday, the act may be done on the next day that is not a holiday; and

(d) service of a document, other than an originating process, made after 4 p.m. or at any time on a holiday shall be deemed to have been made on the next day that is not a holiday.

(2) Where a time of day is mentioned in these rules or in any document in a proceeding, the time referred to shall be taken as the time observed locally.

Scarcello v. Whalley (1992), 10 C.P.C. (3d) 19 (Ont. Gen. Div.).

Where an offer to settle was served on September 13 and the trial commenced on September 20, the offer was made "at least seven days" before the commencement of the hearing within the meaning of rules 3.01 and 49.10.

Kenora-Patricia Child & Family Services v. S. (R.) (1989), 33 C.P.C. (2d) 295 (Ont. Dist. Ct.).

"Month" means a calendar month.

Zhilka v. Turney, [1955] O.R. 213, [1955] 4 D.L.R. 280, affirmed [1956] O.W.N. 369, 3 D.L.R. (2d) 5 (C.A.).

A judicial act is deemed to have occurred on the first moment of the day on which it was done. The issuance of an originating process is not a judicial act and the court may consider the actual time at which it occurred.

Graham v. Dept. of Health and Markdale, [1939] O.W.N. 313 (Master).

The period of time for service of an originating process is inclusive of the day of its issue, and service on the anniversary of the day of its issue is too late.

Re Gow and Downer, [1935] O.R. 397, [1935] O.W.N. 322, [1935] 3 D.L.R. 607 (C.A.).

The predecessor of rule 3.01(1)(b) did not apply where the period was fixed by statute.

EXTENSION OR ABRIDGMENT

General Powers of Court

3.02(1) Subject to subrule (3), the court may by order extend or abridge any time prescribed by these rules or an order, on such terms as are just.

(2) A motion for an order extending time may be made before or after the expiration of the time prescribed.

Times in Appeals

(3) An order under subrule (1) extending or abridging a time prescribed by these rules and relating to an appeal to an appellate court may be made only by a judge of the appellate court.

Consent in Writing

(4) A time prescribed by these rules for serving, filing or delivering a document may be extended or abridged by consent in writing.

Cross-Reference: See rule 14.03 for cases extending the time for filing a statement of claim where a notice of action has been issued. See rule 47.02 for cases regarding extension of time to deliver a jury notice.

Extension of Time — General

Buleychuk v. Danson (1992), 8 O.R. (3d) 762, 7 C.P.C. (3d) 232, 55 O.A.C. 162 (Div. Ct.).

In determining whether to extend the time for service of an originating process, the court should consider whether such extension will advance the just resolution of the dispute without prejudice or unfairness to the parties. If there is no prejudice, the extension should be granted notwithstanding the expiry of the limitation period.

Davoulgian v. Windsor (City) (1987), 23 C.P.C. (2d) 299, 37 M.P.L.R. 54 (Ont. Dist. Ct.), affirmed (1990), 41 C.P.C. (2d) 230 (Ont. H.C.).

Notwithstanding rule 2.01, the plaintiff has an onus to demonstrate that the defendant will not be prejudiced by an order extending time for service of the originating process.

De Pasquale v. Rodrigo (1985), 53 O.R. (2d) 123, 7 C.P.C. (2d) 86, 31 M.P.L.R. 99 (Dist. Ct.).
This rule does not permit extension of time limits imposed by statute.

Demeter v. Occidental Ins. Co. (1975), 11 O.R. (2d) 369 (Master).
Time for delivering a pleading was extended where the publicity arising from this civil action
might have prejudiced the plaintiff in a criminal proceeding and where there was no prejudice
to the opposing party.

Berndt v. Berndt, [1945] O.W.N. 664 (Master).
The time for moving against an *ex parte* order was extended as there was good reason for the
defendant's delay.

Extension of Time for Service — Practice

Weir v. Maillet (1983), 34 C.P.C. 194 (Ont. Div. Ct.).
On a motion to set aside an *ex parte* order extending the time for service of an originating
process, the court should consider whether the master who made the order exercised his
discretion properly, not whether the court hearing the motion to set aside would have exercised
its discretion similarly.

Last v. La Communauté des Soeurs de Charité de la Providence (1974), 6 O.R. (2d) 650 (H.C.).
Where an application to extend time for service is refused, a second application may only be
brought on new grounds.

Buim v. Sherritt, [1972] 2 O.R. 268 (Master).
Failure to account for delay in the materials filed in support of an application to extend time is
fatal.

Courtemanche v. Germain (1973), 1 O.R. (2d) 12 (Master).
Where a defendant dies after the issuance of an originating process, a subsequent order extending
the time for service made prior to an order to continue is a mere irregularity capable of being
corrected.

Laurin v. Foldesi (1979), 23 O.R. (2d) 321, 10 C.P.C. 144 (C.A.).
It is desirable but not mandatory that the defendant be served with notice of a motion to extend
the time for service of an originating process.

Re Gold (1975), 8 O.R. (2d) 694, 22 R.F.L. 280, 59 D.L.R. (3d) 58 (Surr. Ct.).
Service of notice of application to extend the time for an application under the *Dependants'
Relief Act,* R.S.O. 1970, c. 126, on the solicitors of the executor, combined with knowledge of
the application on the part of the executor, is sufficient.

Bateman v. Stasyszyn (1979), 25 O.R. (2d) 247 (H.C.).
Although an order extending the time for service of an originating process may have been
incorrect, a motion to set it aside was dismissed where there had been a two-year delay in
bringing the motion.

Cruickshanks v. Hickman, [1959] O.R. 414 (H.C.).
An order extending the time for service may not be attacked after the defendant takes a fresh
step.

Extension of Time for Service — General

Aliferis v. Parfeniuk (1985), 1 C.P.C. (2d) 41, 9 O.A.C. 215 (C.A.).
The plaintiff has an onus to establish that the defendant will not be prejudiced by an order
extending the time for service. Expiry of a limitation period creates a presumption of prejudice.
In this case relief was granted where, *inter alia,* the defendant's insurer knew of the nature of
the claim and completed much of its investigation within the limitation period.

Nugent v. Crook (1969), 40 O.R. (2d) 110 (C.A.).

Time for service of an originating process should be extended only where delay was caused by a solicitor's inadvertence or slip or some other reasonable cause, the plaintiff had been lulled into a false sense of security by the defendant's conduct, or the defendant suffered no prejudice by the delay.

Syms v. Wojtaniak (1977), 18 O.R. (2d) 369, 4 C.P.C. 278 (C.A.).

An unexplained delay of eleven months before applying to renew the originating process, and a further unexplained lapse of almost six months before effecting service, are significant factors in refusing to renew the originating process.

Strezeszewski v. Mackenzie (1980), 20 C.P.C. 9 (Ont. Master).

Discussion of the factors involved in an application to extend time for service of an originating process.

Davis v. Chubey, [1960] O.W.N. 88 (H.C.).

In order to obtain an order extending the time for service of an originating process the plaintiff must establish inability to serve the defendant after diligent efforts to do so.

Extension of Time for Service — Cases Granting Extension

Ulisch-Plunkett (Litigation Guardian of) v. Zwick Estate (1995), 85 O.A.C. 288 (Div. Ct.).

The court extended the time for service of the statement of claim where the limitation period had not expired.

Smith v. Toronto General Hospital (1994), 26 C.P.C. (3d) 99 (Ont. Gen. Div.).

The court validated service of the statement of claim 21 months after it had been issued where the defendant was not prejudiced.

Samuel, Son & Co. v. Tonolli Canada Ltd. (1994), 18 O.R. (3d) 81, 25 C.P.C. (3d) 235 (Gen. Div.).

Where a notice of action had been issued but there had been no timely delivery of the statement of claim, the court extended the time for service on terms that the defendant could raise the limitation period as a defence. It was unclear when the limitation period expired.

Wildbore v. Kangasaho (1993), 15 O.R. (3d) 380, 19 C.P.C. (3d) 129, 48 M.V.R. (2d) 153 (Gen. Div.).

Time for service was extended where the delay had been caused by the plaintiff's solicitor and there was no prejudice to the defendant.

Ford v. Ronholm (1993), 16 C.P.C. (3d) 257 (Ont. Gen. Div.).

The plaintiffs were granted leave to deliver a statement of claim more than two years after a notice of action had been issued. Although the applicable limitation period had expired in the interim, the only prejudice to the defendant was the loss of a technical limitation defence. The defendant had received prompt notice of the accident in issue, and the plaintiffs' solicitor had delivered medical information which had resulted in advance payments being made.

Anness v. Alvaro (1992), 14 C.P.C. (3d) 222 (Ont. Gen. Div.).

The court extended the time to serve the statement of claim by about two and a half years where a solicitor purportedly acting for the defendant had promised to accept service and where the defendant's insurer had early notice of the claim. There was no prejudice to the defendant.

Ledo v. Atchison (1992), 9 O.R. (3d) 126 (Master).

On a motion to extend time for service of a statement of claim, the overriding consideration is prejudice to the defendant. There was no prejudice where the defendant was aware of the nature of the claims being made.

Dubois v. Robinson Estate (1992), 7 O.R. (3d) 142 (Gen. Div.).

In proper circumstances, a statement of claim can be renewed. The plaintiff's solicitor was dilatory but the defendants had full particulars, and knew the case they had to meet well before the limitation period expired.

St. Lawrence Cement Inc. v. Wakeham & Sons Ltd. (1987), 62 O.R. (2d) 724, 23 C.P.C. (2d) 236 (Master).

Where the plaintiff commenced an action by notice of action but failed to file its statement of claim within 30 days as required by rule 14.03(3) and serve both documents within 6 months as required by rule 14.08, the court made an order extending time with a term that the defendant be entitled to raise a defence that for purposes of any limitation periods the action was commenced on the date of filing of the statement of claim.

Waites v. Alltemp Products Co. (1987), 19 C.P.C. (2d) 185 (Ont. Dist. Ct.).

The court extended the time for service of a notice of action and statement of claim where the plaintiffs advanced sufficient reason to excuse non-delivery of the documents and showed that the defendants suffered no prejudice.

Wardell v. Mohr (1986), 13 C.P.C. (2d) 79 (Ont. H.C.).

The court extended time for service where the originating process was served on time but inadvertently on the wrong one of two people having the same name, the action was prosecuted diligently, the defendants' solicitors knew of the mistake but said nothing, and no prejudice resulted.

Atchison v. Dennis (1985), 7 C.P.C. (2d) 13 (Ont. Dist. Ct.).

The court validated service of a writ of summons issued under the old Rules and statement of claim filed under the new Rules notwithstanding that the statement of claim was filed and both documents were served more than six months after the new Rules came into force. The defendant's insurer had investigated the claim.

Strazisar v. Can. Universal Ins. Co. (1981), 21 C.P.C. 51 (Ont. Co. Ct.).

The court extended time for service where the defendant had been fully informed as to the plaintiff's injuries and had not been prejudiced.

Riederer v. Sestokas (1980), 18 C.P.C. 139 (Ont. Master).

Time for service was extended where the solicitor for the plaintiff was lulled into a false sense of security by the chief claims examiner of the insurer of the defendant.

Laurin v. Foldesi (1979), 23 O.R. (2d) 321, 10 C.P.C. 144 (C.A.).

Where the defendant has knowledge that an action has been commenced against him, an application to extend the time for service of the originating process which has been brought in a timely fashion should be granted.

Robertson v. T.T.C. (1978), 7 C.P.C. 178 (Ont. C.A.).

Where the defendant was aware that the action was pending and not abandoned, the court made an order extending time for service.

Dewar v. Carson (1977), 15 O.R. (2d) 686, 3 C.P.C. 334 (C.A.).

Time for service was extended where one defendant had died before the action began, the defendants knew of the claim, serious negotiations had taken place, and the plaintiff had been advised that the defendant who had been served was the executor.

McCluckie v. McMillan (1973), 2 O.R. (2d) 56, 41 D.L.R. (3d) 701 (Div. Ct.).

Time for service of an originating process was extended where the plaintiff had delayed service to obtain evidence and the originating process had been given to a bailiff for service one month before the expiration of time for service.

Willson v. Federated Mutual Ins. Co., [1962] O.W.N. 193 (H.C.).

The court has a broad discretion to extend the time for service of an originating process even after the limitation period has expired.

Hawkins v. Cox, [1960] O.W.N. 530 (H.C.).

The court extended the time for service of an originating process where the defendant had been evading service.

Brown v. Humble, [1959] O.R. 586, 21 D.L.R. (2d) 38 (C.A.).

The court extended the time for service of an originating process notwithstanding the expiration of a limitation period.

Extension of Time for Service — Cases Refusing Extension

Rosevear v. Breitenstein (1993), 15 O.R. (3d) 615, 19 C.P.C. (3d) 157 (Gen. Div.).

The court refused to extend the time to serve the statement of claim where the limitation period had expired and the defendants were prejudiced.

Gaudet v. Levy (1983), 35 C.P.C. 161 (Ont. Div. Ct.).

The court refused to extend the time for service of an originating process where the plaintiff had made a deliberate decision not to proceed with the action. A long delay is, by itself, prejudice to the defendant.

Power v. Anderson, [1971] 2 O.R. 739 (H.C.).

An order renewing an originating process was refused where there had been a delay of more than seven years.

Arnett v. Menke (1979), 11 C.P.C. 263 (Ont. H.C.).

Time for service was not extended where no attempts were made to serve within time and the defendant had no knowledge of the action for four years.

Merrick v. Woods, [1972] 1 O.R. 701 (H.C.).

The court refused to renew an originating process where service thereof had been delayed for almost three years following the expiry of the relevant limitation period.

Macko v. Remus (1977), 6 C.P.C. 173 (Ont. Master).

In a medical malpractice case, time for service of originating process was not extended where the defendant was first made aware of the claim two and a half years after the event and the relevant limitation period had expired.

Ward v. Registrar of Motor Vehicles, [1969] 1 O.R. 787 (Master).

An order renewing an originating process was set aside where it was served almost two years after the expiry of the limitation period and the defendant had no prior notice of the claim.

Mathews v. Wilkes, [1960] O.W.N. 336, 24 D.L.R. (2d) 426, affirmed [1961] O.W.N. 76n, 28 D.L.R. (2d) 776 (C.A.).

The court refused to extend the time for service of an originating process where the delay was unjustified and caused serious prejudice.

Amer. Motors (Can.) Ltd. v. Renwick (1976), 1 C.P.C. 153 (Ont. Co. Ct.).

After expiry of the time for service of originating process and a limitation period, the court declined to grant an extension of time for service where one defendant had no notice of the claim and the other may have concluded that the plaintiff had abandoned its claim.

Appeals — Extension of Time — rule 3.02(3)

Walden v. Walden, [1996] W.D.F.L. 612 (Ont. C.A.).

The court refused to extend the time for appeal where, *inter alia*, there had been a six-month delay, the appellant's intention was questionable, and the merit of the appeal was dubious.

Frey v. MacDonald (1989), 33 C.P.C. (2d) 13 (Ont. C.A.).

The appeal period will be extended if required by the "justice of the case" notwithstanding the lack of an intention to appeal within the appeal period or an explanation for the delay.

Massen v. Massen (1987), 22 C.P.C. (2d) 49 (Ont. Div. Ct.), affirmed 22 C.P.C. (2d) 49n (Ont. Div. Ct.).

The time for filing a notice of appeal was extended by almost 15 months where the appeal had reasonable merit and the defendant moved expeditiously once he became aware of the terms of the judgment against him. A motion to amend the defendant's pleadings was reserved to the court hearing the appeal.

Sutton v. Sutton (1985), 45 R.F.L. (2d) 148 (Ont. C.A.).

The court extended the time for a cross-appeal in this custody proceeding notwithstanding lack of intention to appeal within the appeal period.

Joynson v. Williams (1984), 44 C.P.C. 203 (Ont. H.C.).

After reviewing the merits of an appeal, the court refused to extend the time for service of a notice of appeal, even though service was late only because it was done by mail rather than personally.

Miller Mfg. & Dev. Co. v. Alden (1979), 13 C.P.C. 63 (Ont. C.A.).

Where there was no arguable question of law and the applicant failed for more than a year to take steps to perfect an appeal, the court refused to grant an extension of time for filing the notice of appeal.

Re Meridian Property Management and Fournier, [1973] 2 O.R. 322 (H.C.).

A judge should not extend time for an appeal to the Divisional Court unless he is functioning at the time as a judge of that court.

Re Blackwell, [1962] O.R. 832, 34 D.L.R. (2d) 369 (C.A.).

The court refused a three-year extension of the time for appeal notwithstanding that the decision at first instance had been overruled by the Court of Appeal in a subsequent case.

R. v. Toronto Magistrates; Ex parte Tank Truck Transport Ltd., [1960] O.W.N. 549, (*sub nom. R. v. Telegram Publishing Co.*) 129 C.C.C. 209 (H.C.).

In order to obtain an extension of the time limited for an appeal the applicant must show that he had a *bona fide* intention to appeal within the prescribed time and that the extension is necessary in the interests of justice.

Re Blair and Weston, [1959] O.W.N. 368 (C.A.).

The court refused to extend the time for appeal where the applicant had had no intention to appeal within the time limited for so doing and failed to show an arguable point of law to be dealt with on the appeal.

Sinclair v. Ridout, [1955] O.W.N. 633 (C.A.).

Time to appeal was extended where justice required it notwithstanding that no intention to appeal had been formed during the prescribed period.

Can. Wool Co. v. Brampton Knitting Mills, [1954] O.W.N. 867 (C.A.).

In order to obtain an extension of time to appeal the applicant should show that he had a *bona fide* intention to appeal before the time expired.

WHEN PROCEEDINGS MAY BE HEARD

Hearings Throughout the Year

3.03(1) Proceedings may be heard throughout the year, except that from December 24th to the following January 6th no trial of an action shall be held unless all parties consent in writing or the court orders otherwise.

In Absence of Opposite Party

(2) No motion, reference, examination, assessment of costs or other matter, except a motion made without notice, shall proceed before a judge, master or other officer in the absence of the opposite party until fifteen minutes after the time fixed for it. [am. O. Reg. 770/92, s. 3]

RULE 4   COURT DOCUMENTS

Highlights

This Rule regulates the format and contents of court documents.

The paper required by rule 4.01 is regular $8\frac{1}{2} \times 11$ inch letter-size paper expressed in millimetres: it is not "metric letter size" which is, in fact, 210×257 millimetres. The term "title of the proceeding" has replaced the former "style of cause" (rule 4.02(1)). Provision is made for the registrar to issue certified copies of documents in the court file (rule 4.03), but no provision is now made for the issuing of "duplicate" copies.

Every document filed by a party must include the telephone number of the solicitor or of a party acting in person, both in the body of the document and on the backsheet: rule 4.02(2) and (3). The documents should also include any pertinent fax numbers: rule 4.02(4). Any document, other than one that is to be issued (*e.g.* originating process or order), may be filed by mail: rule 4.05(1) and (4). The general rule is that all documents are to be filed in the office where the proceeding was commenced (rule 4.05(2)), but where a motion or application is to be heard at some other place the papers to be used on the hearing are to be filed in the court office at the place of hearing: rules 4.05(3), 34.18, 37.08 and 37.10.

Colour coded binding requirements in rule 4.07 are as follows: light blue back-sheets for records for motions, applications, trials and appeals; light grey backsheets for transcripts for motions, applications or trials; buff front and back covers for appeal books; red front and back covers for transcripts for appeals; white front and back covers for appellants', applicants' and moving parties' factums and case books; and green front and back covers for respondents' or responding parties' factums and case books.

Affidavits. The general rule is that affidavits shall be confined to facts within the personal knowledge of the deponent "or to other evidence that the deponent could give if testifying as a witness in court" except as otherwise provided: rule 4.06(2). Rule 39.01(5) provides an exception: on applications, information and belief is permitted with respect to uncontested facts. On motions generally affidavits may contain information and belief provided the source of the information and the fact of the belief are specified: rule 39.01(4). However, where the motion is one for summary judgment, adverse inferences may be drawn if an affidavit on information and belief is used rather than one of a person having personal knowledge of the contested facts: rule 20.02. On a motion for a contempt order, the requirement as to the content of affidavits is the same as on an application — rule 60.11(3).

A request to the registrar to carry out a duty under the Rules is by the filing of a "requisition" rather than the former "*praecipe*": rule 4.08. A procedure is provided for a party to requisition the transmission of court documents where they are required at another location: rule 4.10.

Recent amendments. Effective October 2, 1995, rule 4.02(4) requires that documents include the fax number of the person serving or filing a document and of the person upon whom it is served.

Former Rules: Rules 12, 142, 190-199, 237, 290-295, 298, 760-763.

FORMAT

Standards

4.01(1) Every document in a proceeding shall meet the following standards:

1. The text shall be printed, typewritten, written or reproduced legibly, with double spaces between the lines and a margin of approximately 40 millimetres on the left-hand side.
2. The characters used shall be of at least 12 point or 10 pitch size.
3. Good quality white paper or good quality near white recycled paper 216 millimetres by 279 millimetres shall be used.

One Side or Both

(2) The text may appear on one side or on both sides of the paper. [re-en. O. Reg. 396/91, s. 2; am. O. Regs. 535/92, s. 3; 212/93, s. 2; 465/93, s. 1]

CONTENTS

General Heading

4.02(1) Every document in a proceeding shall have a heading in accordance with (Form 4A (actions) or 4B (applications)) that sets out,

(a) the name of the court and the court file number; and

(b) the title of the proceeding in accordance with rule 14.06 (action or application) or subrule 69.03(3) (divorce action), but in a document other than an originating process, pleading, record, order or report, where there are more than two parties to the proceeding, a short title showing the names of the first party on each side followed by the words "and others" may be used.

(1.1) Clause (1)(b) does not apply to documents in proceedings under Rules 74 and 75.

Body of Document

(2) Every document in a proceeding shall contain,

(a) the title of the document;

(b) its date;

(c) where the document is filed by a party and not issued by a registrar or is an originating process, the name, address and telephone number of the solicitor filing the document or, where a party acts in person, his or her name, address for service and telephone number; and

(d) where the document is issued by a registrar, the address of the court office in which the proceeding was commenced or, in the case of an application to the Divisional Court, the address of the court office in the place where the application is to be heard.

Backsheet

(3) Every document in a proceeding shall have a backsheet in accordance with (Form 4C) that sets out,

(a) the short title of the proceeding;

(b) the name of the court and the court file number;

(c) in the case of an affidavit, the deponent's name and the date when he or she swore it;

(d) the location of the court office in which the proceeding was commenced;

(e) the title of the document; and

(f) the name, address and telephone number of the solicitor serving or filing the document or, where a party acts in person, his or her name, address for service and telephone number. [am. O. Reg. 484/94, s. 3]

Fax Numbers

(4) Every document in a proceeding that is served or filed shall contain the fax number, if any, of the person serving or filing it and the fax number, if known, of the person on whom it is served or to be served. [am. O. Regs. 484/94, s. 3; 377/95, s. 1]

CERTIFIED COPIES OF COURT DOCUMENTS

4.03 On the requisition of a person entitled to see a document in the court file under section 137 of the *Courts of Justice Act* and on payment of the prescribed fee the registrar shall issue a certified copy of the document.

NOTICE TO BE IN WRITING

4.04 Where these rules require notice to be given, it shall be given in writing.

ISSUING AND FILING OF DOCUMENTS

Issuing Documents

4.05(1) A document may be issued only on personal attendance in the court office by the party seeking to issue it or by someone on the party's behalf.

Place of Filing

(2) All documents required to be filed in a proceeding shall be filed in the court office in which the proceeding was commenced, except where they are filed in the course of a hearing or where these rules provide otherwise.

(3) An affidavit, transcript, record or factum to be used on the hearing of a motion or application shall be filed in the court office in the place where the hearing is to be held.

Filing by Leaving in Court Office or by Mail

(4) Any document, other than one that is to be issued, may be filed by leaving it in the proper court office or mailing it to the proper court office, accompanied by the prescribed fee.

Date of Filing where Filed by Mail

(5) Where a document is filed by mail, the date of the filing stamp of the court office on the document shall be deemed to be the date of its filing, unless the court orders otherwise.

Where Document Filed by Mail not Received

(6) Where a court office has no record of the receipt of a document alleged to have been filed by mail, the document shall be deemed not to have been filed, unless the court orders otherwise.

AFFIDAVITS

Format

4.06(1) An affidavit used in a proceeding shall,

(a) be in (Form 4D);

(b) be expressed in the first person;

(c) state the full name of the deponent and, if the deponent is a party or a solicitor, officer, director, member or employee of a party, shall state that fact;

(d) be divided into paragraphs, numbered consecutively, with each paragraph being confined as far as possible to a particular statement of fact; and

(e) be signed by the deponent and sworn or affirmed before a person authorized to administer oaths or affirmations.

Contents

(2) An affidavit shall be confined to the statement of facts within the personal knowledge of the deponent or to other evidence that the deponent could give if testifying as a witness in court, except where these rules provide otherwise.

Exhibits

(3) An exhibit that is referred to in an affidavit shall be marked as such by the person taking the affidavit and where the exhibit,

(a) is referred to as being attached to the affidavit, it shall be attached to and filed with the affidavit;

(b) is referred to as being produced and shown to the deponent, it shall not be attached to the affidavit or filed with it, but shall be left with the registrar for the use of the court, and on the disposition of the matter in respect of which the affidavit was filed, the exhibit shall be returned to the solicitor or party who filed the affidavit, unless the court orders otherwise; and

(c) is a document, a copy shall be served with the affidavit, unless it is impractical to do so.

By Two or More Deponents

(4) Where an affidavit is made by two or more deponents, there shall be a separate jurat for each deponent, unless all the deponents make the affidavit before the same person at the same time, in which case one jurat containing the words "Sworn (or affirmed) by the above-named deponents" may be used.

For a Corporation

(5) Where these rules require an affidavit to be made by a party and the party is a corporation, the affidavit may be made for the corporation by an officer, director or employee of the corporation.

For a Partnership

(6) Where these rules require an affidavit to be made by a party and the party is a partnership, the affidavit may be made for the partnership by a member or employee of the partnership.

By an Illiterate or Blind Person

(7) Where it appears to a person taking an affidavit that the deponent is illiterate or blind, the person shall certify in the jurat that the affidavit was read in his or her presence to the deponent, that the deponent appeared to understand it, and that the deponent signed the affidavit or placed his or her mark on it in the presence of the person taking the affidavit.

By a Person who does not Understand the Language

(8) Where it appears to a person taking an affidavit that the deponent does not understand the language used in the affidavit, the person shall certify in the jurat that the affidavit was interpreted to the deponent in the person's presence by a named interpreter who took an oath or made an affirmation before him or her to interpret the affidavit correctly.

Alterations

(9) Any interlineation, erasure or other alteration in an affidavit shall be initialled by the person taking the affidavit and, unless so initialled, the affidavit shall not be used without leave of the presiding judge or officer.

BINDING OF DOCUMENTS

Records

4.07(1) Records for motions, applications, trials and appeals shall have a light blue backsheet.

Transcripts

(2) Transcripts of evidence for use on a motion or application or at trial shall have a light grey backsheet.

Appeal Books

(3) Appeal books shall be bound front and back in buff covers.

Transcripts on Appeal

(4) Transcripts of evidence for use in an appeal shall be bound front and back in red covers, except where the transcript forms part of the appeal book or record and, where there is more than one volume of transcripts, the volumes shall be clearly numbered.

Factums and Case Books

(5) A factum or case book filed by an applicant, moving party or appellant shall be bound front and back in white covers, and a factum or case book of a respondent or responding party shall be bound front and back in green covers.

Cover Stock

(6) Backsheets and covers shall be of 176g/m2 cover stock. [re-en. O. Reg. 219/91, s. 2; am. O. Reg. 770/92, s. 4]

REQUISITION

4.08 Where a party is entitled to require the registrar to carry out a duty under these rules, the party may do so by filing a requisition (Form 4E) and paying the prescribed fee, if any.

TRANSCRIPTS

Paper Size

4.09(1) Evidence shall be transcribed on paper 216 millimetres by 279 millimetres in size with a margin 25 millimetres wide on the left side delimited by a vertical line.

Heading

(2) The name of the court or, in the case of an examiner, the examiner's name, title and location shall be stated on a single line no more than 15 millimetres from the top of the first page.

Standards

(3) The text shall be typewritten on thirty-two lines numbered in the margin at every fifth line.

(4) Headings, such as swearing of a witness, direct examination and cross-examination, shall be capitalized and separated from the preceding text by the space of a numbered line, and the number of lines of text on the page may be reduced by one for each heading that appears on the page.

(5) Every question shall commence on a new line and shall begin with the designation "Q.", followed, within 10 millimetres, by the question.

(6) Every answer shall commence on a new line and shall begin with the designation "A.", followed, within 10 millimetres, by the answer.

(7) The first line of a question or answer shall be indented 35 millimetres from the margin and shall be 130 millimetres in length.

(8) In a transcript of evidence taken in court, every line of a question or answer, other than the first line, shall begin at the margin and shall be 165 millimetres in length.

(9) In a transcript of evidence taken out of court, every line of a question or answer, other than the first line, shall begin 15 millimetres from the margin and shall be 150 millimetres in length, and questions shall be numbered consecutively by means of a number placed in the 15 millimetres to the right of the margin.

(10) Lines of text other than questions and answers shall be indented 35 millimetres from the margin and shall be 130 millimetres in length.

(11) Every transcript of evidence taken in court or out of court shall have,

(a) a cover page setting out,
    (i) the court,
    (ii) the title of the proceeding,
    (iii) the nature of the hearing or examination,
    (iv) the place and date of the hearing or examination,
    (v) the name of the presiding judge or officer, and
    (vi) the names of counsel; and
(b) a table of contents setting out,
    (i) the name of each witness with the page number at which the examination, cross-examination and re-examination of the witness commence,
    (ii) the page number at which the charge to the jury, the objections to the charge and the re-charge commence,
    (iii) the page number at which the reasons for judgment commence,
    (iv) a list of the exhibits with the page number at which they were made exhibits, and
    (v) at the foot of the page, the date the transcript was ordered, the date it was completed and the date the parties were notified of its completion.

TRANSMISSION OF DOCUMENTS

4.10(1) Where documents filed with the court or exhibits in the custody of an officer are required for use at another location, the registrar shall send them to the registrar at the other location on a party's requisition, on payment of the prescribed fee.

(2) Documents or exhibits that have been filed at or sent to a location other than where the proceeding was commenced for a hearing at that location shall be sent by the registrar, after the completion of the hearing, to the registrar at the court office where the proceeding was commenced.

NOTICE OF CONSTITUTIONAL QUESTION

4.11 The notice of constitutional question referred to in section 109 of the *Courts of Justice Act* shall be in (Form 4F).

PARTIES AND JOINDER

RULE 5   JOINDER OF CLAIMS AND PARTIES

Highlights

This Rule regulates the joinder of claims and parties in both actions and applications. The joinder rules are extremely liberal, but it is provided that if multiple joinder may "unduly complicate or delay the hearing or cause undue prejudice to a party" the court may relieve against joinder: rule 5.05. For the most part this Rule codifies the practice that existed under the former Rules, but generally it is more liberal as to the joinder of both multiple plaintiffs and multiple defendants.

Joinder of multiple plaintiffs. Rule 5.02(1) is broader than the former provision in that clauses (a) and (b) are each independent grounds for joinder: under the former provision both requirements had to be satisfied. Clause (c) is a new and independent ground for joinder.

Joinder of multiple defendants. Rule 5.02(2) is also broader and more permissive in favouring multiple joinder. While clause (d) is new as a rule, it codified existing practice (see, *e.g., O'Sullivan v. Kidney* (1975), 7 O.R. (2d) 518 (H.C.)). Clause (e) is also new but is in keeping with the prior case law (see *e.g., Canadian Steel Corp. v. Standard Litho. Co.,* [1933] O.R. 624, [1933] 3 D.L.R. 394 (C.A.); *Thomas W. Sayle Transport Ltd. v. Rivers,* [1955] O.W.N. 321, affirmed [1955] O.W.N. at 323 (H.C.)).

Necessary parties. Much of rule 5.03 is new but it basically codified pre-existing, and rarely invoked, case law.

Reconstituting action. Rule 5.04(2) is a broadly framed provision continuing the court's powers to add, delete or substitute parties or correct the name of a party. The rule is subject to common law restrictions regarding adding parties after the expiry of a limitation period. However, it may be possible to add parties after expiry if there are "special circumstances" as discussed in *Basarsky v. Quinlan,* [1972] S.C.R. 380, [1972] 1 W.W.R. 303, 24 D.L.R. (3d) 720, or if the requirements of s. 2(8) of the *Family Law Act* are met in cases governed by that statute (*e.g. Gatterbauer v. Ballast Holdings Ltd.* (1986), 55 O.R. (2d) 91, 9 C.P.C. (2d) 273, 15 O.A.C. 299 (Div. Ct.).

Rule 13.01 (leave to intervene as added party) authorizes orders to be made adding a person as a party to the proceeding on his or her own motion.

Relief against joinder. The powers given to the court by rule 5.05(c) and (d) were new. The latter clause permits the court to achieve a different result than that arrived at in *Pryshlack v. Urbancic* (1975), 10 O.R. (2d) 263, 63 D.L.R. (3d) 67 (H.C.); see G.D. Watson, "Joinder of Defendants Sued in the Alternative: Solicitors as Co-Defendants" (1981), 2 Advocates' Q. 365.

Former Rules: Rules 66-73, 90, 136.

JOINDER OF CLAIMS

5.01(1) A plaintiff or applicant may in the same proceeding join any claims the plaintiff or applicant has against an opposite party.

(2) A plaintiff or applicant may sue in different capacities and a defendant or respondent may be sued in different capacities in the same proceeding.

(3) Where there is more than one defendant or respondent, it is not necessary for each to have an interest in all the relief claimed or in each claim included in the proceeding.

Cross-Reference: See also cases under rule 5.05 (relief against joinder).

Joinder of Claims — Generally

Mohan v. Philmar Lumber (Markham) Ltd. (1991), 50 C.P.C. (2d) 164, 39 C.C.E.L. 211 (Ont. Gen. Div.).

A claim for damages for wrongful dismissal which was asserted as part of an oppression remedy application was struck out, as such claims were properly the subject of an action.

Dobud v. Herbertz (1985), 50 C.P.C. 283 (Ont. Dist. Ct.).

Leave was refused to an existing plaintiff to add a new claim where the defendant did not know of the facts relating to the claim within the limitation period and would have been prejudiced by the amendment.

Brisbois v. Nehaul (1984), 47 C.P.C. 39 (Ont. Master).

The court permitted a claim for aggravated damages in an action under Part V of the *Family Law Reform Act.*

A.G. Ont. v. Tiberius Productions Inc. (1984), 46 O.R. (2d) 152, 44 C.P.C. 14, 8 D.L.R. (4th) 479 (H.C.).

The court struck out a claim for punitive damages in an action for breach of a commercial contract.

Hartwick v. MacIntyre (1982), 35 O.R. (2d) 119, 25 C.P.C. 54, 26 R.F.L. (2d) 11, 131 D.L.R. (3d) 333 (C.A.).

An injured person cannot advance a claim on behalf of the statutory beneficiaries under Part V of the *Family Law Reform Act.*

Someplace Else Restaurant Ltd. v. Calendar Magazines Ltd. (1979), 27 O.R. (2d) 760, 15 C.P.C. 160, 107 D.L.R. (3d) 636 (H.C.).

The court permitted the joinder of claims for damages for injurious falsehood, libel, wrongful interference with economic rights, and negligence, leaving it to the trial judge to separate the trials of the various issues.

Vulcan Indust. Packaging Ltd. v. C.B.C. (1979), 23 O.R. (2d) 213, 13 C.P.C. 156, 94 D.L.R. (3d) 729 (Master).

Claims for damages for libel and slander of goods were joined in this case.

Rose Park Wellesley Invts. Ltd. v. Sewell, [1973] 1 O.R. 102 (Master).

A claim for breach of contract may be joined with a claim for conspiracy.

Joinder of Claims — Wrongful Dismissal Actions

Foley v. Signtech Inc. (1988), 66 O.R. (2d) 729, 31 C.P.C. (2d) 216, 55 D.L.R. (4th) 152 (H.C.).

A claim for wrongful dismissal may be joined with a claim for defamation.

Makkar v. Scarborough (1985), 48 C.P.C. 141 (Ont. H.C.).

The court struck out a claim for injurious falsehood in this wrongful dismissal case.

Dudziak v. Boots Drug Stores (Can.) Ltd. (1983), 40 C.P.C. 140, 3 C.C.E.L. 130 (Ont. Master).
A claim for false imprisonment was permitted to be joined with a wrongful dismissal claim. A claim for loss of reputation cannot be asserted in a wrongful dismissal action. A claim for mental distress must arise out of the lack of notice rather than the dismissal and be in the contemplation of the parties at the time of entering into the contract.

Elkind v. Elks Stores Ltd. (1983), 36 C.P.C. 242 (Ont. H.C.).
There is no inflexible rule that claims for wrongful dismissal and libel cannot be joined. In the circumstances of this case, where the claims were against difference defendants, the claims were severed.

O'Brien v. Curtis Indust. of Can. Ltd. (1983), 34 C.P.C. 266 (Ont. Master)
The court permitted a claim for assault to be joined with a claim for wrongful dismissal.

Johnston v. Muskoka Lakes Golf & Country Club Ltd. (1983), 40 O.R. (2d) 762, 33 C.P.C. 239 (H.C.).
The court permitted joinder of a claim for loss of reputation with a claim for wrongful dismissal.

Tellier v. Bank of Montreal (1982), 32 C.P.C. 17 (Ont. Master)
The court permitted joinder of a claim for inducing breach of contract with a claim for wrongful dismissal.

Kelly v. Amer. Airlines Inc. (1981), 32 O.R. (2d) 626 (H.C.).
The court refused to permit the plaintiff to join a claim for defamation with a claim for wrongful dismissal.

Smith v. Oster Lane Group Ltd. (1980), 28 O.R. (2d) 564, 110 D.L.R. (3d) 760 (H.C.).
A claim for loss of reputation was struck out in an action for wrongful dismissal.

Delmotte v. John Labatt Ltd. (1978), 22 O.R. (2d) 90, 92 D.L.R. (3d) 259 (H.C.).
The court refused to strike out a claim for mental distress in a wrongful dismissal action.

McMinn v. Oakville (1978), 19 O.R. (2d) 366, 85 D.L.R. (3d) 131 (H.C.).
A claim for damages for loss of reputation is not proper in an action for wrongful dismissal.

Overholt v. Williams, [1957] O.W.N. 501, 9 D.L.R. (2d) 384 (H.C.)
Plaintiffs were permitted to join a claim for wrongful dismissal with a claim for damages for loss of benefits under a trust to which they were entitled by virtue of their employment.

JOINDER OF PARTIES

Multiple Plaintiffs or Applicants

5.02(1) Two or more persons who are represented by the same solicitor of record may join as plaintiffs or applicants in the same proceeding where,

(a) they assert, whether jointly, severally or in the alternative, any claims to relief arising out of the same transaction or occurrence, or series of transactions or occurrences;

(b) a common question of law or fact may arise in the proceeding; or

(c) it appears that their joining in the same proceeding may promote the convenient administration of justice.

Multiple Defendants or Respondents

(2) Two or more persons may be joined as defendants or respondents where,

(a) there are asserted against them, whether jointly, severally or in the alternative, any claims to relief arising out of the same transaction or occurrence, or series of transactions or occurrences;

(b) a common question of law or fact may arise in the proceeding;

(c) there is doubt as to the person or persons from whom the plaintiff or applicant is entitled to relief;

(d) damage or loss has been caused to the same plaintiff or applicant by more than one person, whether or not there is any factual connection between the several claims apart from the involvement of the plaintiff or applicant, and there is doubt as to the person or persons from whom the plaintiff or applicant is entitled to relief or the respective amounts for which each may be liable; or

(e) it appears that their being joined in the same proceeding may promote the convenient administration of justice.

Cross-Reference: See also cases under rule 5.05 (relief against joinder).

Joinder of Parties — General

Clough v. Greyhound Leasing & Financial of Can. Ltd. (1979), 26 O.R. (2d) 590, 103 D.L.R. (3d) 565 (H.C.).

The fundamental rule is that, as far as possible, all matters in controversy between the parties should be determined in one proceeding.

Gracey v. Thomson Newspapers Corp. (1991), 4 O.R. (3d) 180, 82 D.L.R. (4th) 244 (Gen. Div.).

The joinder of two defamation claims against two sets of defendants was permitted where the occurrences were closely connected in time and subject matter, and common questions of law and fact arose with respect to the alleged statements.

Shell Can. Ltd. v. Phillips (1983), 42 C.P.C. 80 (Ont. H.C.).

A discharged bankrupt is neither a necessary nor a proper party to an action brought to set aside conveyances pre-dating the bankruptcy as being fraudulent and void.

MacRae v. Lecompte (1983), 32 C.P.C. 78, 143 D.L.R. (3d) 219 (H.C.).

It is improper to join a party for the sole purpose of discovery when the same discovery may be had of existing parties; however, if the discovery sought is not available from existing parties, such joinder may be permissible.

Ottawa Separate School Trustees v. Que. Bank (1917), 39 O.L.R. 118, 35 D.L.R. 134 (H.C.).

Discussion of the principles and rationale of joinder of parties, joinder of claims, and consolidation of actions.

Joinder of Parties — Multiple Plaintiffs

Krolo v. Nixon (1985), 50 O.R. (2d) 285, 1 C.P.C. (2d) 295 (H.C.).

A minor whose bicycle had collided with a motor vehicle commenced an action against the driver and owner and also against his parents for lack of care and supervision. The minor's brother asserted a claim under s. 60 of the *Family Law Reform Act* on behalf of family members including the parents. In the circumstances the court permitted the parents to discontinue their *Family Law Reform Act* claim as against themselves only. The parents were permitted to retain separate counsel to present their claim for damages against the driver and owner of the vehicle.

Ryan v. Hoover (1984), 45 O.R. (2d) 216, 40 C.P.C. 261 (Master).

After an action had been commenced by one firm of solicitors on behalf of all plaintiffs, one of the plaintiffs was permitted to change solicitors and deliver her own pleading with the court making an order as to the further method of proceeding.

Sugden v. Metro. Toronto Police Commrs. Bd. (1978), 19 O.R. (2d) 669 (H.C.).

A collective bargaining agent was held not be to a proper party to a class action by some of the members it represented against their employer where none of the relief claimed related to the collective bargaining agreement.

Agnew v. Sault Ste. Marie Bd. of Educ. (1976), 2 C.P.C. 273 (Ont. H.C.).

Joinder was permitted where 365 plaintiffs in similar circumstances sued on their individual contracts with the defendant.

Bath v. Birnstihl (1975), 11 O.R (2d) 770 (H.C.).

An action by several participants in two tours against the tour promoters and travel agents was held to be proper since there were common questions of law and fact and the claims arose out of the same series of transactions or occurrences.

McManus v. Sulpher, [1966] 1 O.R. 672 (H.C.).

Claims by two plaintiffs regarding publication of two defamatory statements, each regarding only one plaintiff, may not be joined.

Joinder of Parties — Standing of Plaintiff to Sue

(See also cases under rule 21.03 (Capacity to Bring Action).)

Joinder of Parties — Multiple Defendants

Rade v. Rade (1983), 45 C.P.C. 186 (Ont. Div. Ct.).

The court permitted the plaintiff to sue her former solicitors in contract and negligence before first establishing that she suffered a loss as a result of the conduct of the other defendants, but stayed prosecution of the claim against the solicitors as being premature.

Sacchetti v. Kramaric (1983), 36 C.P.C. 247 (Ont. H.C.).

An automobile insurer cannot be added as a party defendant to an action against a motorist allegedly insured by that insurer.

Waterloo Ins. Co. v. Zurbrigg, 43 O.R. (2d) 219, 3 C.C.L.I. 94, 37 C.P.C. 264, [1983] I.L.R. 1-1707 (C.A.).

A motor vehicle insurer, faced with a potential claim under the uninsured motorist coverage, cannot be added as a party defendant in an action by its insured against the alleged uninsured motorist. *Riosa v. Marko, infra,* disapproved.

Riosa v. Marko, 39 O.R. (2d) 661, 34 C.P.C. 34, 140 D.L.R. (3d) 314, [1983] I.L.R. 1-1593 (Div. Ct.).

The plaintiff's insurer, which had issued an underinsured motorist endorsement, was added as a party defendant where the original defendant appeared to have insufficient policy limits.

Brett v. Fleet (1980), 30 O.R. (2d) 397, 16 C.P.C. 155, 116 D.L.R. (3d) 516 (H.C.).

Where the plaintiff sought indemnity from the defendant for a debt due the bank, the bank was added as a party defendant to avoid a multiplicity of proceedings and to bind the bank.

Thames Steel Const. Ltd. v. Portman (1980), 28 O.R. (2d) 445, 15 C.P.C. 308, 111 D.L.R. (3d) 460 (Div. Ct.).

If alternative claims arise out of the same transaction or series of transactions and involve a common question of fact or law, the governing principle is the balance of convenience. The fact that the claim against certain defendants, in this case solicitors, may be unnecessary if the plaintiff succeeds against the main defendants is only one consideration.

Krezanowski v. Scarborough, [1961] O.W.N. 315 (Master).

A person who could be made a third party should not be added as a defendant unless the plaintiff consents.

Thomas W. Sayle Transport Ltd. v. Rivers, [1955] O.W.N. 321, affirmed [1955] O.W.N. at 323 (H.C.).

Where damage to a motor vehicle was caused by two separate accidents, the court permitted the plaintiff to sue both defendants in a single proceeding.

JOINDER OF NECESSARY PARTIES

General Rule
5.03(1) Every person whose presence is necessary to enable the court to adjudicate effectively and completely on the issues in a proceeding shall be joined as a party to the proceeding.

Claim by Person Jointly Entitled
(2) A plaintiff or applicant who claims relief to which any other person is jointly entitled with the plaintiff or applicant shall join, as a party to the proceeding, each person so entitled.

Claim by Assignee of Chose in Action
(3) In a proceeding by the assignee of a debt or other chose in action, the assignor shall be joined as a party unless,
(a) the assignment is absolute and not by way of charge only; and
(b) notice in writing has been given to the person liable in respect of the debt or chose in action that it has been assigned to the assignee.

Power of Court to Add Parties
(4) The court may order that any person who ought to have been joined as a party or whose presence as a party is necessary to enable the court to adjudicate effectively and completely on the issues in the proceeding shall be added as a party.

Party Added As Defendant or Respondent
(5) A person who is required to be joined as a party under subrule (1), (2) or (3) and who does not consent to be joined as a plaintiff or applicant shall be made a defendant or respondent.

Relief Against Joinder of Party
(6) The court may by order relieve against the requirement of joinder under this rule.

Necessary Parties — General

Lovric v. Federation Insurance Co. of Can. (1989), 71 O.R. (2d) 403, 42 C.C.L.I. 29 (Dist. Ct.).
Where a necessary party refused to join an action as a plaintiff, he was added as a defendant.

Morandan Investments Ltd. v. Spohn (1987), 58 O.R. (2d) 621, 16 C.P.C. (2d) 252 (Dist. Ct.).
A trustee acting as mortgagee is a necessary party in an action on the covenant against the mortgagor. The court set aside a default judgment where the trustee had not been made a party plaintiff.

Re Holley (1986), 54 O.R. (2d) 225, 59 C.B.R. (N.S.) 17, 12 C.C.E.L. 161, 26 D.L.R. (4th) 230, 14 O.A.C. 65 (C.A.).
The trustee in bankruptcy of a plaintiff can be added as a party in order to enable the court to effectively adjudicate upon the question of the plaintiff's status to bring the action.

Donaldson v. Piron (1984), 44 O.R. (2d) 487, 41 C.P.C. 92, 4 D.L.R. (4th) 568 (H.C.).
In an action pursuant to s. 60 of the *Family Law Reform Act,* it is necessary to plead the names of all statutory beneficiaries and, where known, the nature of their claims. Where it is uncertain whether a claim will be asserted, the pleading should say so.

Fidelity Trust Co. v. Durocher (1980), 30 O.R. (2d) 59, 15 R.P.R. 195 (H.C.).
Where mortgaged premises have been leased to a tenant and the mortgagee sues for possession, it is generally not necessary to join the mortgagor as a defendant.

Township of Bastard and Burgess(S) v. Johnston (1974), 5 O.R. (2d) 191 (Co. Ct.).
An action by a municipality for a declaration that certain lands were a public highway was held to be improperly constituted because the Attorney General was not a party.

Rose Park Wellesley Invts. Ltd. v. Sewell, [1973] 1 O.R. 102 (Master).
Not all participants to a conspiracy need be joined in an action based on that tort.

Necessary Parties — Persons Jointly Entitled

Sheridan v. Sharpe Instruments Ltd., [1962] O.W.N. 210 (Master).
Ontario practice does not require the plaintiff to offer an indemnity for costs before adding a jointly entitled person as a party defendant.

Necessary Parties — Assignors

Canadian Acceptance Corp. Ltd. v. Southcott, [1972] 2 O.R. 163 (Master).
The assignor of a conditional sales contract is a necessary party to an action thereunder where no notice has been given as required by the *Conveyancing and Law of Property Act,* R.S.O. 1970, c. 85, s. 54.

Union Gas Co. of Can. Ltd. v. Brown, [1970] 1 O.R. 715, 9 D.L.R. (3d) 337 (C.A.).
A purported assignor of a cause of action was added as a plaintiff *nunc pro tunc.*

Canning v. Avigdor, [1961] O.W.N. 59 (C.A.).
An assignor may be added notwithstanding the expiry of the limitation period.

Allux Ltd. v. McKenna, [1962] O.W.N. 258 (Div. Ct.).
Where a legal assignment of a legal *chose in action* has been made, the assignor loses his status to sue.

Graner v. Ins. Co. of N. Amer., [1959] O.W.N. 150 (H.C.).

An assignee of part only of a *chose in action* is not entitled to sue in his own name; the assignor is a necessary party.

MISJOINDER, NON-JOINDER AND PARTIES INCORRECTLY NAMED

Proceedings not to be Defeated

5.04(1) No proceeding shall be defeated by reason of the misjoinder or non-joinder of any party and the court may, in a proceeding, determine the issues in dispute so far as they affect the rights of the parties to the proceeding and pronounce judgment without prejudice to the rights of all persons who are not parties.

Adding, Deleting or Substituting Parties

(2) At any stage of a proceeding the court may by order add, delete or substitute a party or correct the name of a party incorrectly named, on such terms as are just, unless prejudice would result that could not be compensated for by costs or an adjournment.

Adding Plaintiff or Applicant

(3) No person shall be added as plaintiff or applicant unless the person's consent is filed.

Adding, etc., Parties – General

Seaway Trust Co. v. Markle (1988), 25 C.P.C. (2d) 64 (Ont. Master).

On a motion to add a party the court should not consider the factual and evidentiary merits of the proposed new claims by or against the added party.

Rakowski v. Mount Sinai Hospital (1987), 59 O.R. (2d) 349, 16 C.P.C. (2d) 103 (Master).

Where a plaintiff is unaware of the true identities of certain defendants and names them as "John Doe" and "Jane Doe", the court may later substitute the correct names if a person having knowledge of the facts would be aware of their true identities by reading the statement of claim.

Rodrigues v. Madill (1985), 3 C.P.C. (2d) 1 (Ont. Master).

Questions regarding the merits of a proposed claim against a new party are proper in cross-examining on an affidavit in support of a motion to add the new party.

Jarrett v. Kay (1985), 50 C.P.C. 157 (Ont. Master), affirmed 50 C.P.C. lv (Ont. H.C.).

The Crown is subject to the same principles regarding correction of names as any other party. "The Ministry of Transportation and Communications" was amended to "Her Majesty the Queen in right of the Province of Ontario, represented by the Minister of Transportation and Communications for the Province of Ontario".

Bardot Realty v. Kelner (1982), 31 C.P.C. 111, affirmed 31 C.P.C. 111 at 118 (Ont. H.C.).

Only in the case of a misnomer will a party plaintiff be added *nunc pro tunc*.

Turgeon v. Border Supply (Emo) Ltd. (1977), 16 O.R. (2d) 43, 3 C.P.C. 233 (Div. Ct.).

A new plaintiff will not be substituted where the original plaintiff has no cause of action.

Coulson v. Secure Holdings Ltd. (1976), 1 C.P.C. 168 (Ont. C.A.).

Judgment does not deprive the court of jurisdiction to add parties. In the circumstances of this lease, the *in rem* judgment was set aside and the applicants were added as parties.

Dill v. Alves, [1968] 1 O.R. 58, 65 D.L.R. (2d) 416 (C.A.).

A plaintiff seeking to add or substitute a new party should pay the costs of the motion and costs thrown away as a condition precedent to the amendment.

Di Guilio v. Boland, [1963] 1 O.R. 113 (C.A.).

Where leave is given to add a party on filing his consent, an application to the registrar is also necessary to physically amend the style of cause.

Lett v. Draper Dobie & Co., [1957] O.W.N. 265 (Master).

A motion to add a party should be made on notice to all parties previously served with the originating process and, if it appears likely that a present party will contest the motion, notice should also be given to the proposed party so that all objections can be disposed of at one time.

Boland v. Bear Exploration Ltd., [1949] O.W.N. 503 (H.C.).

When an action against the present-named defendant cannot proceed, the court must not add new defendants.

Lee v. Hepburn, [1946] O.W.N. 918 (Master).

The master has no power to strike out the name of a defendant who claims to be improperly joined where the adjudication of the matter affects the substantive rights of the plaintiff and goes to the root of his claim.

McCartney v. Morison, [1945] O.W.N. 24 (Master).

An order adding or striking out parties may be made at any stage of the proceedings except in the case of applications made under the *Negligence Act,* which requires that the application should not be made until after the defence has been filed.

Adding, etc., Parties – Examples

Kelly v. Royal Insurance Co. of Canada (1993), 15 C.P.C. (3d) 386 (Ont. Gen. Div.).

In an action for non-repair of a highway the court refused to substitute "The Municipality of Metropolitan Toronto" for the originally named defendant "The Corporation of the City of Toronto".

206084 Ontario Ltd. v. Sun Alliance Insurance Co. (1992), 9 O.R. (3d) 462 (Gen. Div.).

The style of cause was amended to correct a transposition error in the name of the plaintiff numbered company.

Baddeley v. Baddeley (1989), 71 O.R. (2d) 318, 65 D.L.R. (4th) 130 (H.C.).

In a wife's application for support the court upheld the master's addition, on motion by the respondent husband, of the wife's adult son as a respondent who might also have support obligations.

Fusco v. Yofi Creations Ltd. (1987), 60 O.R. (2d) 287 (Master).

A plaintiff's motion to add the defendants was not permitted after the action had been ordered listed for trial at a status hearing. The addition of the defendants would create further delays, and therefore the motion would not be permitted unless the status hearing order was set aside or extended.

Manultape Inc. v. Arvak Ltd. (1985), 7 C.P.C. (2d) 44 (Ont. H.C.).

Where the plaintiff corporation had ceased to exist prior to commencement of the action as a result of a merger, the court substituted a successor corporation as plaintiff.

Muraca v. INA Ins. Co. of Can., 49 O.R. (2d) 32, 48 C.P.C. 100, 10 C.C.L.I. 264, 30 M.V.R. 243, [1985] I.L.R. 1-1857 (H.C.).

In an action on an uninsured motorist endorsement the defendant's motion to have the owner and driver of a motor vehicle involved in a collision with the plaintiff's vehicle added as a party defendant was allowed. Such an order was appropriate so that the driver would be bound by the results of the action between the plaintiff and the insurer.

Bernard v. Kendall (1984), 48 C.P.C. 60 (Ont. Co. Ct.).

The injured person's business partner was added as a plaintiff in this dog bite case to assert a claim for business loss.

Safadi v. Dowling, 45 O.R. (2d) 300, 42 C.P.C. 51, [1984] I.L.R. 1-1773 (Master) (under appeal to Divisional Court).

In this motor vehicle action the plaintiff sued the tortfeasor and the uninsured motorist coverage insurer. The insurer sought to add an alleged "real" owner of the vehicle in order to establish that it was insured. The master dismissed the motion as being premature, since the availability of another policy was not to be determined in the pending action, at least at that stage.

Grimshaw v. Grimshaw (1983), 32 C.P.C. 11 (Ont. H.C.).

The court permitted amendment of the style of cause to delete the plaintiff in her capacity as administratrix of an estate and to add her child and herself as litigation guardian for the child.

Werner v. Henegen (1982), 30 C.P.C. 144 (Ont. Master).

In an action against a solicitor for damage to the plaintiff's house, alleging his failure to arrange appropriate insurance and inspection of the house, a motion by the solicitor to add the builder and the builder's president as parties defendant was denied.

Arnett v. Menke (1979), 11 C.P.C. 263 (Ont. H.C.).

In a specific performance action, the court set aside an order adding a purchaser in good faith and his mortgagee where the plaintiff had made no attempts at service for over four years.

Bray v. Bray (1979), 9 C.P.C. 241 (Ont. H.C.).

An execution creditor was added as a party to an application by the debtor's wife under s. 7 of the *Family Law Reform Act* having the sole purpose of ensuring that certain assets were unavailable to creditors.

Tycoos Devs. Ltd. v. Cookstown Estates Ltd. (1973), 2 O.R. (2d) 574, 43 D.L.R. (3d) 518, affirmed 3 O.R. (2d) 466n, 45 D.L.R. (3d) 682 (C.A.).

A shareholder of a defendant corporation, who seeks to show that the contract giving rise to the cause of an action against the company was *ultra vires* the company, should not be added as a party defendant but rather should proceed under s. 16(2) of the *Business Corporations Act,* R.S.O. 1970, c. 53.

Bank of Montreal v. Bay Bus Terminal (North Bay) Ltd., [1964] 2 O.R. 425, 45 D.L.R. (2d) 705 (C.A.).

Where a party was added during the course of an appeal, a new trial was ordered so that findings of fact binding on the added party could be made.

A.G. Ont. v. Palmer (1977), 15 O.R. (2d) 670, 3 C.P.C. 214 (H.C.).

Failure to name the Crown correctly is an irregularity only.

Collins v. Haliburton, Kawartha Pine Ridge Dist. Health Unit (No. 2), [1972] 3 O.R. 643, 29 D.L.R. (3d) 151 (H.C.).

Where the plaintiff improperly named a district health unit as defendant, the court permitted a correction to name the board of health of the district health unit as defendant.

Adding etc. Parties – After Limitation Period – Family Law Act Actions

Nasouski v. Potentier (1994), 35 C.P.C. (3d) 16, 76 O.A.C. 349 (Div. Ct.).

Where the limitation period under the *Family Law Act* had expired, the court held that the plaintiff had not satisfied the onus of proving on a balance of probabilities that special circumstances existed and dismissed the plaintiff's motion to add a plaintiff.

Wildbore v. Kangasaho (1993), 15 O.R. (3d) 380, 19 C.P.C. (3d) 129, 48 M.V.R. (2d) 153 (Gen. Div.).

Where a minor suffers injuries, the limitation period for both the minor's claims and any derivative *Family Law Act* claims begins to run on the minor's eighteenth birthday.

Deaville v. Boegeman (1984), 48 O.R. (2d) 725, 47 C.P.C. 285, 30 M.V.R. 227, 14 D.L.R. (4th) 81, 6 O.A.C. 297 (C.A.).

Limitation periods were not enacted to be ignored. The expiry of a limitation period creates a presumption of prejudice to the defendant. The court refused to add a claimant under s. 60 of the *Family Law Reform Act* after the expiry of the limitation period.

Vilela Estate v. Amber Foods Ltd. (1991), 5 O.R. (3d) 124, 3 C.P.C. (3d) 28 (Gen. Div.).

The court permitted a minor to be added as a party plaintiff where there was no deliberate delay by the plaintiffs and no special prejudice to the defendants.

Giladi v. Areias (1990), 72 O.R. (2d) 461 (Master).

Where no special circumstances were present, the court refused to add the derivative claims of a spouse and two adult children under the *Family Law Act* to an action after the expiry of the limitation period.

Coplen Estate v. Bauman Estate (1989), 71 O.R. (2d) 308, 44 C.P.C. (2d) 85, 64 D.L.R. (4th) 750, 36 O.A.C. 321 (C.A.).

The court refused to add a party to an action after the applicable limitation period had expired, merely because one of the plaintiffs was a minor. The minor plaintiff could not maintain a representative action on behalf of the adult plaintiffs in the circumstances and there were no special circumstances warranting an extension of the limitation period.

Bosch (Litigation Guardian of) v. Brown (1989), 40 C.P.C. (2d) 133 (Ont. H.C.).

The court permitted an amendment to a statement of claim to add the derivative claims of infants under the *Family Law Reform Act*, as the provisions of s. 47 of the *Limitations Act* applied.

Linstead v. Taylor (1989), 37 C.P.C. (2d) 151 (Ont. Div. Ct.).

The court permitted the addition of *Family Law Act* claimants, including an infant *en ventre sa mere* at the time of the subject motor vehicle accident, notwithstanding that more than two years had passed since the accident.

Miller v. Robertson (1988), 27 C.P.C. (2d) 247 (Ont. H.C.).

The court refused to permit the addition of a *Family Law Reform Act* claim after the expiry of the limitation period, even though the relevant diagnosis had recently changed, where to do so would prejudice the defendants.

Mullan v. Perry (1988), 26 C.P.C. (2d) 128 (Ont. Master).

An infant plaintiff was not permitted to amend his statement of claim to add a claim on behalf of his parents under the *Family Law Act* where there were no special circumstances. The motion was made almost four years after the limitation period expired and about six years after the accident itself.

Chedour v. Newmarket (Town) (1988), 63 O.R. (2d) 680, 25 C.P.C. (2d) 126, 27 O.A.C. 179 (Div. Ct.).

The court granted leave to add *Family Law Act* plaintiffs where the defendant knew before the expiry of the limitation period that the plaintiff had sustained very severe injuries and had a family. These and other special circumstances outweighed any prejudice of the loss of the limitation period defence.

Hemmerich v. Olinskie (1987), 63 O.R. (2d) 383, 33 C.P.C. (2d) 307, 47 D.L.R. (4th) 480 (C.A.).

Where a plaintiff sought to add a defendant outside the limitation period and the defendant had already been added as a third party in another action arising from the same occurrence, the court permitted the addition, leaving the difficult question of law as to whether or not the claim was statute-barred to be decided by the trial judge.

Rosso v. Bozzo (1987), 63 O.R. (2d) 192 (Master).

On a motion to add *Family Law Act* claimants after expiry of the limitation periods, infant claimants were added, but the court held that adult claimants should not be added unless the defendant had reason to know of the claims.

Pole v. Hendery (1987), 61 O.R. (2d) 486, 21 C.P.C. (2d) 109, 43 D.L.R. (4th) 150, 23 O.A.C. 238 (C.A.).

The relationship founding a claim under s. 60 of the *Family Law Reform Act* must be in existence at the time of the tortious conduct. The court held that a common-law husband who married the injured plaintiff after the accident could not thereby "marry into" a s. 60 claim.

Duchesne v. Vallee (1987), 19 C.P.C. (2d) 233 (Ont. Master).

The court added *Family Law Reform Act* claimants as plaintiffs in this motor vehicle action some three years after expiry of the limitation period, holding that there was no substantial prejudice to the defendant and special circumstances were shown as required.

Macaulay v. Anderson (1987), 59 O.R. (2d) 295, 16 C.P.C. (2d) 271, 38 D.L.R. (4th) 153, 20 O.A.C. 386 (Div. Ct.).

The court permitted the addition of plaintiffs under the *Family Law Reform Act*.

MacIsaac v. Smith (1987), 58 O.R. (2d) 289, 19 C.P.C. (2d) 56, 39 C.C.L.T. 239, 35 D.L.R. (4th) 451, 20 O.A.C. 241 (Div. Ct.).

The court refused to add an infant who was conceived and born after the accident which was the subject-matter of this case as a party plaintiff under the *Family Law Reform Act*. A claimant under s. 60 of the *Family Law Reform Act* must fall within the statutorily delimited relationship at the time the principal cause of action arose.

Gatterbauer v. Ballast Holdings Ltd. (1986), 55 O.R. (2d) 91, 9 C.P.C. (2d) 273, 15 O.A.C. 299 (Div. Ct.).

In seeking an extension of time to bring a derivative *Family Law Reform Act* claim after expiry of the limitation period, "special circumstances" need not be shown where the main action was in time and loss of the benefit of the limitation period alone does not meet the test of "substantial hardship to the defendant".

Fagan v. Emery Investments Ltd. (1986), 54 O.R. (2d) 615, 8 C.P.C. (2d) 101, 27 D.L.R. (4th) 257, 15 O.A.C. 231 (C.A.).

The court extended the time to bring an action under s. 60 of the *Family Law Reform Act* where the plaintiff's solicitor missed the limitation period due to settlement negotiations. The delay occurred in good faith and the presumption of prejudice to the defendant was rebutted.

Starecki v. Henriques (1985), 6 C.P.C. (2d) 71 (Ont. Master).

A motion to extend the limitation period prescribed in s. 60(4) of the *Family Law Reform Act* should not be granted where the requirements set out in s. 2(5) of that Act have not been met. Where the material fails to show that the proposed claimants have suffered any loss and there is no material to show that the failure to add the claims resulted from a solicitor's negligence or inadvertence, the extensions should not be granted.

Cooper v. Lewis (1985), 6 C.P.C. (2d) 184 (Ont. Master).

The court extended the limitation period under the *Family Law Reform Act* where information about the claim had been provided to the defendant prior to the expiry of the limitation period and the delay had not been incurred in bad faith.

Glykis v. Pardy (1985), 5 C.P.C. (2d) 147 (Ont. Master).

The court permitted an amendment to assert claims under the *Family Law Reform Act* where the substance of the claim did not occur until after the expiry of the limitation period and where there was no prejudice to the defendants other than being deprived of the limitation defence.

Lucas v. Cernigoj (Cernigot) (1985), 2 C.P.C. (2d) 294 (Ont. H.C.).

The court dismissed a motion to add a party plaintiff to assert a claim under the *Family Law Reform Act* three years after the expiry of the limitation period where there were no "special circumstances" in favour of the plaintiff.

Woolford v. Lockhart (1985), 2 C.P.C. (2d) 16 (Ont. H.C.).

The court refused leave to assert a derivative claim under the *Family Law Reform Act* which had not been made before expiry of the limitation period due to the negligence of the plaintiff's former solicitor.

MacIntosh v. Bowles (1985), 50 O.R. (2d) 287 (H.C.).

An amendment was permitted adding plaintiffs after the limitation period where the defendants had learned on discovery facts which could give rise to a claim under the *Family Law Reform Act* and the defendants were unable to show any prejudice.

Hudson v. Rumola (1985), 1 C.P.C. (2d) 29 (Ont. H.C.).

The court added a defendant after the expiration of a limitation period where it was alleged he had participated in deceit or fraud to prevent the plaintiffs from discovering their cause of action against him.

Mirecki v. Lubiana (1984), 46 C.P.C. 170, 29 M.V.R. 248 (Ont. H.C.).

In a motion to add a plaintiff under Part V of the *Family Law Reform Act* after the expiry of the limitation period, the onus is on the defendant to establish substantial prejudice or hardship. [*But see Deaville v. Boegeman, supra — Authors.*]

Moffett v. Farnsworth (1984), 47 O.R. (2d) 620, 44 C.P.C. 229, 12 D.L.R. (4th) 101, 6 O.A.C. 241 (Div. Ct.).

Discussion of test to be applied on motion to add a person as a party plaintiff for the purpose of asserting a claim under the *Family Law Reform Act* after expiration of the limitation period.

Seghers v. Double A Farms Ltd. (1984), 46 O.R. (2d) 258, 43 C.P.C. 193, 9 D.L.R. (4th) 273 (H.C.).

Leave was granted to add a further claimant under the *Family Law Reform Act* after expiry of the limitation period where a claim under that Act was made within the limitation period.

Martin v. Wright (1984), 45 O.R. (2d) 317, 43 C.P.C. 95, 6 D.L.R. (4th) 335 (H.C.).

The limitation period for claims under the *Family Law Reform Act* was extended and the statement of claim amended to advance such claims in this action.

Newton v. Serre (1984), 45 O.R. (2d) 314, 42 C.P.C. 284, 6 D.L.R. (4th) 320, affirmed 48 O.R.
   (2d) 704, 14 D.L.R. (4th) 608 (C.A.).

An amendment to add a claim by relatives under the *Family Law Reform Act* was refused where
the defendant had no knowledge of the claim until after the expiry of the limitation period.

Roeder v. Collins (1984), 44 O.R. (2d) 626, 40 C.P.C. 318, 5 D.L.R. (4th) 500 (H.C.).

The plaintiff's wife was not added as a party after expiry of a limitation period where a long
period passed before bringing the motion, there had been nothing known to the defendant to
indicate a relative's potential claim and liability had been admitted. Without any affidavit
material being required, it is obvious that if a defendant was of the opinion it was facing possible
additional claims its conduct in defending the action would have been different.

Goulais v. Pepin; Williams v. Bidner; Duic v. Dominion Stores Ltd.; Sakr v. Paul (1984), 39
   C.P.C. 189 (Ont. H.C.).

Discussion of principles applicable to adding claimants under s. 60 of the *Family Law Reform
Act* after expiry of a limitation period.

Lambkin v. Chapeskie (1983), 37 C.P.C. 158 (Ont. Co. Ct.).

On a motion seeking leave to add the plaintiff's spouse as a party plaintiff to assert a claim
under Part V of the *Family Law Reform Act*, following expiry of a limitation period the onus is
on the defendant to show prejudice. Mere failure to apprise the defendant of the additional
claim before the limitation period has expired is of itself insufficient.

Kyrzwernhart v. Soaring Assn. of Can. (1983), 34 C.P.C. 325 (Ont. Master).

The court permitted the addition of a plaintiff asserting a claim under s. 60 of the *Family Law
Reform Act* notwithstanding the expiry of the relevant limitation period.

Juda v. Patterson (1982), 39 O.R. (2d) 737, 141 D.L.R. (3d) 327 (H.C.).

The court added the plaintiff's spouse as a party plaintiff after the expiry of a limitation period
to claim damages under the *Family Law Reform Act.*

Ward v. Wetton (1983), 33 C.P.C. 11 (Ont. Master).

After the limitation period had expired, an amendment was granted to permit a *Family Law
Reform Act* claim to be advanced by the plaintiff's wife.

Vasiliou v. Liston (1982), 29 C.P.C. 239, affirmed 29 C.P.C. 239 at 246 (Ont. H.C.).

The court permitted an amendment to add a party plaintiff in order to advance a claim pursuant
to Part V of the *Family Law Reform Act* after expiry of the limitation period and delivery of a
certificate of readiness in this action.

Osborne v. Foldesi (1985), 48 C.P.C. 188 (Ont. Dist. Ct.).

The court refused to add a plaintiff under s. 60 of the *Family Law Reform Act* after the expiry
of the limitation period where to do so would expose the defendant to a claim in excess of the
limits of his insurance policy.

Adding, etc., Parties – After Limitation Period – Generally

Eneroil Co. v. Hunter Enterprises (Orillia) Ltd. (1995), 6 W.D.C.P. (2d) 438 (Ont. Gen. Div.).

The court added two corporate plaintiffs as parties where the corporations had been dissolved
but were revived for the purpose of being added as parties.

Knudsen v. Holmes (1995), 22 O.R. (3d) 160, (*sub nom. Knudsen v. Knudsen*) 27 C.C.L.I. (2d)
   225, 11 M.V.R. (3d) 226, additional reasons 22 O.R. (3d) 160 at 166, 27 C.C.L.I. (2d)
   232, 11 M.V.R. (3d) 226n (Gen. Div.).

The court refused to add a party defendant after expiry of the limitation period where there were
no "special circumstances". Absence of prejudice to the defendant does not equate to the
presence of "special circumstances".

Di Re v. Chow (1993), 27 C.P.C. (3d) 291 (Ont. Master).

Where the involvement of the Superintendent of Insurance was tenuous and the limitation period had expired, the court refused to add the Superintendent as a defendant.

Patrick Harrison & Co. v. Devran Petroleum Ltd. (1993), 22 C.P.C. (3d) 285 (Ont. Gen. Div.).

The court refused to add parties defendant where the relevant limitation period had expired.

Ryan v. Singh (1993), 19 C.P.C. (3d) 41, 18 C.C.L.I. (2d) 174 (Ont. Gen. Div.).

In order to add a new party after the expiry of a limitation period special circumstances must exist. That is a matter to be determined on the facts of each case.

Eugene v. Metropolitan Toronto (Municipality) (1993), 18 C.P.C. (3d) 70, 15 M.P.L.R. (2d) 98, 63 O.A.C. 164 (Div. Ct.).

A plaintiff was permitted to add a municipality as a party defendant after the expiry of the applicable limitation period. There were special circumstances present as the plaintiff had originally given the municipality proper written notice of the claim, and the city's adjusters had provided the plaintiff's solicitors with incorrect information about the site of the accident.

MacKinlay (Litigation Guardian of) v. Matthews (1993), 12 O.R. (3d) 700, 18 C.P.C. (3d) 43, 14 M.P.L.R. (2d) 224, 44 M.V.R. (2d) 100, 61 O.A.C. 233 (Div. Ct.).

The plaintiff was permitted to amend a statement of claim by adding a municipality as a party defendant after the expiry of the three-month limitation period contained in s. 284 of the *Municipal Act*, where the plaintiff was a mental incompetent.

Swiderski v. Broy Engineering Ltd. (1992), 11 O.R. (3d) 594, 16 C.P.C. (3d) 46, 40 M.V.R. (2d) 228, 60 O.A.C. 260 (Div. Ct.).

The plaintiffs' motion to add defendants after the expiry of the two-year limitation period in the *Highway Traffic Act* was dismissed where there were not sufficient special circumstances present to support the amendment.

Tran v. Tejada (1992), 10 C.P.C. (3d) 392 (Ont. Gen. Div.).

In an action arising out of a motor vehicle accident, the court allowed the minor plaintiffs' motion to add their parents as defendants to the action. Although the relevant limitation period had expired, there were special circumstances present.

Martin v. Listowel Memorial Hospital (1992), 9 O.R. (3d) 65, 9 C.P.C. (3d) 183, 93 D.L.R. (4th) 452, 56 O.A.C. 337 (C.A.), leave to appeal to Supreme Court of Canada refused (1993), 19 C.P.C. (3d) 23 (note), 105 D.L.R. (4th) vi (note).

The limitation period in s. 17 of the *Health Disciplines Act* does not begin to run against an infant plaintiff until his or her majority, whether or not a litigation guardian is appointed. The limitation period for the derivative claims of family members is co-terminus.

Swain v. Lake of the Woods District Hospital (1992), 9 O.R. (3d) 74, 9 C.P.C. (3d) 169, 93 D.L.R. (4th) 440, 56 O.A.C. 327 (C.A.), leave to appeal to Supreme Court of Canada refused (1993), 19 C.P.C. (3d) 25 (note).

Generally a claim on behalf of the estate of a deceased minor should be brought within two years of the death pursuant to s. 38(3) of the *Trustee Act*, R.S.O. 1990, c. L.15. In this case "special circumstances" existed to permit that claim and the derivative claims of family members to be brought after that time.

Toner (Litigation Guardian of) v. Toner Estate (1992), 8 C.P.C. (3d) 366, 88 D.L.R. (4th) 295 (Ont. Gen. Div.), affirmed (1993), 13 O.R. (3d) 617, 45 N.V.R. (2d) 94, 104 D.L.R. (4th) 32, 64 O.A.C. 50 (Div. Ct.).

The court extended the limitation period under the *Highway Traffic Act* regarding the claims of minors where the defendants and their insurers had fully investigated the matter before the expiry of the limitation period and where the minors were entitled to an extension of time for their *Family Law Act* claims. These were special circumstances as discussed in *Basarsky v. Quinlan*, [1972] S.C.R. 380, [1972] 1 W.W.R. 303, 24 D.L.R. (3d) 720.

Gracey v. Thomson Newspapers Corp. (1991), 4 O.R. (3d) 180, 1 C.P.C. (3d) 21, 82 D.L.R. (4th) 244 (Gen. Div.).

The plaintiff was permitted to add the CBC as a party to an action after the expiry of the three-month limitation period in the *Libel and Slander Act* where the CBC had knowledge of the plaintiff's intent to sue within the limitation period since it had actually been sued in the Federal Court within the limitation period.

Lawson v. Hospital for Sick Children (1990), 74 O.R. (2d) 11, 44 C.P.C. (2d) 146, 4 C.C.L.T. (2d) 303, 71 D.L.R. (4th) 557, 40 O.A.C. 56 (Div. Ct.).

Section 47 of the *Limitations Act* gives absolute protection to a minor, which is not lost by the appointment of a litigation guardian; accordingly, an infant plaintiff was permitted to add physicians as defendants notwithstanding the expiry of the one-year period provided for in s. 17 of the *Health Disciplines Act*, R.S.O. 1980, c. 196.

Shachar v. Bailey (1989), 67 O.R. (2d) 726, 33 C.P.C. (2d) 223, 16 M.V.R. (2d) 295 (Master), affirmed 67 O.R. (2d) 732, 34 C.P.C. (2d) 195 (H.C.).

The court added a plaintiff to assert a claim for personal injuries where the defendants were aware of the claim before the expiry of the limitation period and the proposed plaintiff had been omitted through an error.

Uzun v. General Accident Assurance Co. of Canada (1988), 2 O.R. (3d) 557 (C.A.), leave to appeal to Supreme Court of Canada refused (1989), 2 O.R. (3d) 557n, 101 N.R. 160 (note).

The court permitted a party to be added as a defendant to a personal injury action after the expiry of the applicable limitation period. Special circumstances warranting the joinder were present as the defendant had knowledge of the accident and the nature of the injuries suffered by the plaintiff.

Moreau v. Northwestern General Hospital (1988), 65 O.R. (2d) 128, 27 C.P.C. (2d) 164 (Master).

Where a plaintiff in a malpractice action failed to point an adequate "litigation finger" at the male physician sued as "Dr. Richard Roe", the court refused an amendment to substitute the correct physician after the expiry of the limitation period. In the circumstances, this was not a "misnomer".

Jones v. Martin (1988), 24 C.P.C. (2d) 239 (Ont. H.C.).

The court corrected a misnomer of the defendant after expiry of the limitation period where the defendant originally named was a deceased person unconnected with the subject accident but the correct insurer had been notified.

Branche v. MacArthur (1986), 56 O.R. (2d) 71, 11 C.P.C. (2d) 8, 30 D.L.R. (4th) 301, 16 O.A.C. 306 (Div. Ct.).

Parties who alleged the expiry of limitation periods were nevertheless added as defendants to an action; the issue of the limitation periods should be determined at trial and not upon interlocutory motion.

Ingram Estate v. Imperial Life Assurance Co. of Can. (1986), 54 O.R. (2d) 762 (H.C.).

A party was permitted to be added as a plaintiff outside the relevant limitation period where it had been a defendant to the action from the outset of the action and there were special circumstances to warrant adding it as a plaintiff despite the expiry of the limitation period.

Dukoff v. Toronto Gen. Hospital (1986), 54 O.R. (2d) 58, 8 C.P.C. (2d) 93 (H.C.).

The court refused to substitute the names of certain defendants for the fictitious names John Doe and Jane Doe used in the title of proceeding, since the limitation period had expired and the requested change was more than correcting a misnomer. *Jackson v. Bubela* (1972), 28 D.L.R. (3d) 500 (B.C. C.A.) distinguished.

Ostroff v. Phoenix Continental Management Ltd. (1986), 8 C.P.C. (2d) 208 (Ont. H.C.).

The court amended the title of proceeding to replace ''Phoenix Continental Management Ltd.'' with ''Continental Insurance Company'' where the error arose from incorrect information supplied by the office of the defendant's counsel and the defendant was not prejudiced.

Duval v. Acker (1986), 8 C.P.C. (2d) 313 (Ont. H.C.).

The court dismissed a motion to add a party defendant after the expiry of the limitation period where the plaintiff could have obtained information implicating the proposed defendant if an investigation had been conducted at an earlier time.

Branche v. MacArthur (1985), 6 C.P.C. (2d) 142 (Ont. Master), reversed in part on other grounds (1986), 56 O.R. (2d) 71, 11 C.P.C. (2d) 8, 30 D.L.R. (4th) 301, 16 O.A.C. 306 (Div. Ct.).

Deception may be a special circumstance permitting the addition of a defendant after the expiry of a limitation period; however, the deception must be at least partially that of the proposed defendant. The onus to establish that is on the plaintiff.

Chatelois v. Western Gen. Mutual Ins. Co. (1985), 5 C.P.C. (2d) 316, 14 C.C.L.I. 18 (Ont. Master).

The court added a party plaintiff in this fire insurance action notwithstanding the defendant's contention that the proposed plaintiff was not an insured under the policy and that the limitation period had expired. Those defences could be raised at trial.

227223 Earth Moving Ltd. v. Parviz Haddad Associates Ltd. (1985), 4 C.P.C. (2d) 107 (Ont. Master).

Where the relevant limitation period has expired and the plaintiff therefore cannot succeed, the proposed defendant ought not be added. It is not necessary for the proposed defendant to file material to show prejudice, as the prejudice is patent.

Ray v. Snider (1985), 50 C.P.C. 140 (Ont. Master).

Where the plaintiff sued a corporation, ''Snider Pumps Inc.'', rather than a partnership, ''Snider Pumps'', the court refused a motion to add the partners as parties defendant after expiry of the limitation period. It was not a case of misnomer; the plaintiff's solicitors made a choice as to who to sue. However, the partners were added as third parties.

Barsalou v. Wolf (1985), 48 C.P.C. 294 (Ont. H.C.).

A hotel which had served the defendant driver a considerable quantity of alcohol was added as a defendant after the expiry of the limitation period in the *Highway Traffic Act*. That limitation period does not apply to the claim against the hotel.

East York v. Geos Co. (1984), 46 O.R. (2d) 375, 43 C.P.C. 307 (H.C.).

Where the facts concerning the applicability of the limitation period and the court's discretion to extend it were not available, and the proposed defendants did not oppose being added so long as their right to plead the limitation period was preserved, an order to that effect was made.

Schmidt v. Janitsch, 45 O.R. (2d) 11, 40 C.P.C. 334, 4 C.C.L.I. 63, [1984] I.L.R. 1-1743 (H.C.).

In an action for damages caused by an unidentified motor vehicle, the court refused to add an insurer as a party defendant more than two years after the accident since the limitation period had expired.

Mucsi v. Ackroyd (1983), 37 C.P.C. 165 (Ont. H.C.).

After the expiry of a limitation period, the court refused to grant leave to amend the style of cause so as to permit the plaintiff to sue a different police officer having the same last name.

Sousa v. Drew (1983), 37 C.P.C. 171 (Ont. Co. Ct.).

Where four days after the expiry of the limitation period the defendants were notified of the inadvertence in not naming a party plaintiff, of whose claim the defendants were aware, the court granted leave to add the party plaintiff.

OHIP v. D. & M. Transport Ltd. (1981), 34 O.R. (2d) 611, 25 C.P.C. 123, 128 D.L.R. (3d) 644 (H.C.).

An injured person is entitled to be added as a party plaintiff in a subrogated action commenced by OHIP notwithstanding the expiry of a limitation period.

Hydro Mississauga v. Clarke (1976), 2 C.P.C. 334 (Ont. Co. Ct.).

The plaintiff was permitted an amendment to indicate its proper legal name after the expiry of a limitation period.

Witco Chemical Co. v. Oakville, [1975] 1 S.C.R. 273, 43 D.L.R. (3d) 413, 1 N.R. 453.

An action was commenced in the name of a corporation which had amalgamated. An amendment to change the name of the plaintiff to that of the amalgamated corporation was permitted notwithstanding the expiry of a limitation period.

Ladouceur v. Howarth, [1974] S.C.R. 1111, 41 D.L.R. (3d) 416.

In the circumstances, the naming of the wrong person as plaintiff was a misnomer which could be corrected notwithstanding the expiry of a limitation period.

Bryson v. Kerr (1976), 13 O.R. (2d) 672, 2 C.P.C. 46 (Div. Ct.).

Legislation increasing a limitation period applies to causes of action not barred at the date the amendment becomes effective.

Re Palermo Bakery Ltd. and Dom. of Can. Gen. Ins. Co. (1976), 12 O.R. (2d) 50 (H.C.).

A new plaintiff was added notwithstanding the expiration of a limitation period where the defendant was fully aware of the facts.

Ont. Hosp. Services Comm. v. Barsoski, [1973] 3 O.R. 721, 38 D.L.R. (3d) 67 (C.A.).

Under the special statutory provisions applicable to the Hospital Services Commission, an infant insured may be added to an action brought by the Commission in its own name under its right of subrogation notwithstanding the expiry of a limitation period, but a parent of the infant cannot be added to assert a claim in his or her own right.

Accaputo v. Simanovskis, [1973] 3 O.R. 368 (H.C.).

The husband of the plaintiff was added as a co-plaintiff after the expiry of a limitation period for the purpose of claiming medical expenses etc. incurred on behalf of his wife.

Armour v. Stackhouse, [1973] 1 O.R. 432 (H.C.).

The plaintiff in a motor vehicle case was permitted to add a claim for indemnification for moneys paid in settlement of a claim by a third person notwithstanding the expiry of a limitation period.

Chretien v. Herrman, [1969] 2 O.R. 339 (C.A.).

The court may correct the name of a party notwithstanding the expiration of a limitation period.

Crozier v. O'Connor, [1960] O.W.N. 352 (C.A.).

The court added a party plaintiff after the expiry of the limitation period but refused to make the joinder *nunc pro tunc.*

Durham v. West, [1959] O.W.N. 169 (C.A.).

The general principle is that the court should allow an amendment if the resisting party has not been misled or substantially injured by the error. The name of a school board was substituted for the names of the trustees thereof.

Greig v. T.T.C., [1958] O.W.N. 480 (C.A.).

The new party is added as of the date of the order; the expiry of a limitation period prior to that date is a defence.

McEvoy v. Gen. Security Ins. Co. of Can., 29 O.R. (2d) 461, 16 C.P.C. 312, 113 D.L.R. (3d) 457, [1981] I.L.R. 1-1331 (H.C.).

Where the limitation period had expired, mortgagees were not permitted to be added as parties plaintiff to an action commenced by mortgagors against the insurer of premises destroyed by fire.

Ranco v. Till (1978), 21 O.R. (2d) 112, 8 C.P.C. 214, 89 D.L.R. (3d) 565 (Co. Ct.).

Where the plaintiff commenced his action against only one of two possible tortfeasors and the limitation period had expired, he was not permitted to substitute the new party for the existing party.

Arnold Lumber Ltd. v. Vodouris, [1968] 2 O.R. 478 (Master).

A defendant will not be added in a mechanics' lien action after the expiry of the limitation period.

Bd. of Commrs. of Police of London v. Western Freight Lines Ltd., [1962] O.R. 948, 34 D.L.R. (2d) 689 (C.A.).

The court refused to substitute "The Corporation of the Township of London" as plaintiff after the expiry of the limitation period.

Adding, etc., Parties – Interested or Affected Persons

Cases dealing with this subject are gathered under rule 13.01.

RELIEF AGAINST JOINDER

5.05 Where it appears that the joinder of multiple claims or parties in the same proceeding may unduly complicate or delay the hearing or cause undue prejudice to a party, the court may,

(a) order separate hearings;

(b) require one or more of the claims to be asserted, if at all, in another proceeding;

(c) order that a party be compensated by costs for having to attend, or be relieved from attending, any part of a hearing in which the party has no interest;

(d) stay the proceeding against a defendant or respondent, pending the hearing of the proceeding against another defendant or respondent, on condition that the party against whom the proceeding is stayed is bound by the findings made at the hearing against the other defendant or respondent; or

(e) make such other order as is just.

Cross-reference: See rule 27.09 regarding relief against joinder of counterclaims, rule 28.10 regarding relief against joinder of crossclaims and rule 29.09 regarding relief against joinder of third party claims.

Relief Against Joinder – Generally

Symons Gen. Ins. Co. v. Can. Union Ins. Co. (1985), 50 C.P.C. 75 (Ont. Master).

A plaintiff seeking an order that a third party claim be asserted in a separate action must give notice to the third parties as well as the defendant. The motion should not be brought until it is possible to determine which third parties will defend the third party claim and which, if any, wish to defend the main action.

Federation Ins. Co. v. Piscione, [1964] 2 O.R. 404 (H.C.).

The modern trend is to permit all issues between the parties to be dealt with in one action.

Rotenberg v. Rosenberg, [1964] 1 O.R. 160, affirmed [1964] 1 O.R. 160 at 162n (H.C.).

Defamation actions, which are very technical, should not generally be tried with other claims.

Relief Against Joinder – Examples Granting Relief

Lippert v. Lippert (1995), 24 O.R. (3d) 249 (Gen. Div.), leave to appeal granted (June 28, 1995), Doc. Kitchener 16/88 (Ont. Gen. Div.).

Where a family had sustained injuries and the adults' injuries could be determined now but the children's injuries could not be determined for several more years, the court ordered that the liability issue and the adults' damage issues be tried now and the children's damage issues be severed and tried later.

Walker v. Wiensczyk (1984), 42 C.P.C. 310 (Ont. Master).

The master severed claims against an uninsured motorist and the underinsured motorist coverage insurer.

Priene Ltd. v. Metro. Toronto Condominium Corp. No. 539 (1983), 38 C.P.C. 100 (Ont. Master).

The court required a counterclaim against the plaintiff's counsel to be asserted in a separate proceeding, if at all, where trial with the main action would have deprived the plaintiff of the counsel of his choice who had particular expertise in the subject-matter of the action.

Samuel v. Klein (1976), 14 O.R. (2d) 389, 3 C.P.C. 21 (H.C.).

The court struck out two defendants where the cause of action alleged against them depended on the plaintiff's failure against three other defendants.

Heider v. Levine, [1955] O.W.N. 936 (Master).

The court required a claim for breach of contract and a claim for indecent assault to be asserted in separate actions.

Relief Against Joinder – Examples Refusing Relief

Schulenberg v. Schulenberg (1987), 59 O.R. (2d) 798, 17 C.P.C. (2d) 252 (Master).

The court refused to sever a claim for divorce from the corollary issues.

Gibson v. Bagnall (No. 2) (1979), 24 O.R. (2d) 567, 98 D.L.R. (3d) 760, 3 L. Med. Q. 139 (H.C.).

The court refused to sever claims against a medical practitioner for negligence, breach of contract, and battery.

Bath v. Birnstihl (1975), 11 O.R. (2d) 770 (H.C.).

The court declined to order separate trials on an interlocutory application, being of the opinion that the trial judge could better give directions relieving the inconvenience of numerous parties.

RULE 6　CONSOLIDATION OR HEARING TOGETHER

Highlights

This Rule empowers the court to order consolidation or the hearing of proceedings together. The former Rules spoke only of consolidation of actions and made no mention of the more common practice of ordering the trial of actions together or one after the other. The new Rule expressly draws all of these procedures together as available remedies where there is a multiplicity of related proceedings. Moreover, it is not limited to actions and authorizes the consolidation or hearing together of applications. For Rule 6 to operate, all the proceedings have to be in one court. However, s. 107 of the *Courts of Justice Act* permits the exercise of consolidation and related powers where the proceedings are in different courts.

The general policies underlying the Rule — avoiding multiplicity of proceedings and promoting expeditious and inexpensive determination of proceedings — are reflected in s. 138 of the *Courts of Justice Act* and rule 1.04(1) respectively.

Former Rules: Rule 319.

WHERE ORDER MAY BE MADE

6.01(1) Where two or more proceedings are pending in the court and it appears to the court that,

(a) they have a question of law or fact in common;

(b) the relief claimed in them arises out of the same transaction or occurrence or series of transactions or occurrences; or

(c) for any other reason an order ought to be made under this rule, the court may order that,

(d) the proceedings be consolidated, or heard at the same time or one immediately after the other; or

(e) any of the proceedings be,

(i) stayed until after the determination of any other of them, or

(ii) asserted by way of counterclaim in any other of them.

(2) In the order, the court may give such directions as are just to avoid unnecessary costs or delay and, for that purpose, the court may dispense with service of a notice of listing for trial and abridge the time for placing an action on the trial list.

Consolidation or Hearing Together – General Principles

Rauscher v. Roltford Developments Ltd. (1989), 69 O.R. (2d) 749 (H.C.).

The court can order motions to be heard together by virtue of rule 6.01, since "proceeding" includes motions, or, alternatively, under its inherent jurisdiction.

Bain v. Schudel (1988), 67 O.R. (2d) 221, 31 C.P.C. (2d) 134, 15 M.V.R. (2d) 117 (H.C.).

Where the plaintiff commences two actions regarding separate accidents which caused overlapping injuries, the two actions should be tried together so damages may be assessed properly.

Toronto v. B.A. Oil Co.; Toronto Harbour Commrs. v. B.A. Oil Co., [1946] O.W.N. 398 (Master).

The purpose of consolidation is to save expense and avoid multiplicity of pleadings and proceedings. Where two actions are ready for trial, that purpose is defeated; however, if the evidence will be the same or similar in each, they should be tried together.

Flitney v. Howard, [1958] O.R. 701, 15 D.L.R. (2d) 534 (C.A.).

A motion for consolidation should be made at as early a stage as possible.

Husband Transport Ltd. v. T.T.C.; Black v. Husband Transport Ltd., [1956] O.W.N. 133 (Master).

The master should not attempt to determine which of two actions to be tried together should proceed first; that question should be left to the trial judge.

McKenzie v. Cramer; Hickey v. McKenzie; Britney v. McKenzie, [1947] O.R. 196, [1947] 3 D.L.R. 232 (H.C.).

Where the parties in separate actions arising out of the same occurrence are different, consolidation should not be permitted.

J. Hollinger & Co. v. Toronto-Peterborough Transport Co., [1945] O.W.N. 289, 291 (Master).

In deciding whether or not actions should be consolidated, an important factor is who shall have carriage of the proceedings.

Golberg v. Gardner; Smuckler v. Gardner, [1944] O.W.N. 292, [1944] 2 D.L.R. 733 (H.C.).

The court may order consolidation notwithstanding that neither party applies for such an order.

Consolidation or Hearing Together – Differing Modes of Trial

Brown v. Buckley Cartage Ltd. (1993), 13 O.R. (3d) 375, 17 C.P.C. (3d) 325 (Master).

Where only one of two actions being consolidated had a jury notice, the court ordered that the liability issues in both claims and the damage issues in the jury claim be determined by a jury but the damage issues in the non-jury claim be determined by the trial judge.

Matear v. Catling (1993), 13 O.R. (3d) 280 (Gen. Div.).

Where the defendant did not deliver a jury notice but later sought to consolidate the action with related actions where jury notices had been served, it was held to be inappropriate to subject the unwilling plaintiff in the first action to a jury trial.

Marin v. Salituro (1986), 7 C.P.C. (2d) 237 (Ont. Dist. Ct.).

Where the plaintiff sustained injuries in two motor vehicle accidents and had commenced separate actions the court struck out a jury notice in one action and ordered trial together with the second action.

Toronto Star Ltd. v. C.B.C. (1975), 11 O.R. (2d) 289 (Master).

A defamation action against the Crown, which must be tried by a judge alone, may not be fully consolidated with an ordinary defamation action, which must be tried by a judge and jury, but the same judge may preside in both actions.

Rintoul v. Dominion Stores Ltd.; Rintoul v. X-Ray and Radium Indust. Ltd., [1955] O.W.N. 114 (H.C.).

The court struck out a jury notice and ordered a change of place of trial of one action and made an order for the trial of two actions together.

Bennett v. Stutt; Ayling v. Stutt, [1944] O.W.N. 698 (H.C.).

Two actions ought not be consolidated where a jury notice has been served in one but not in the other.

Consolidation or Hearing Together – Examples

Baglione v. Menegon (1994), 29 C.P.C. (3d) 208 (Ont. Gen. Div.).

A wife's adverse reaction to her husband's accident was not enough to have her own personal injury action stemming from an earlier separate accident postponed and tried together with her husband's action.

Tusa v. Walsh (1994), 23 C.P.C. (3d) 178 (Ont. Gen. Div.).

Where two actions were ordered to be tried together, the court permitted the defendants in the first action to participate in the discovery of the defendants in the second action.

Jaffe v. Miller (1991), 3 O.R. (3d) 680 (Master).

Two actions were ordered consolidated although the defendant being sued personally in one action was plaintiff in the other action in his capacity as trustee in bankruptcy.

Reichmann v. Toronto Life Publishing Co. (1988), 31 C.P.C. (2d) 54 (Ont. H.C.).

The court refused to order the trial of two defamation actions together where, although there were common issues, there would be prejudice to the defendants from the increase in complexity and cumulative effect of the two trials on the jury.

Beck v. Beck (1986), 56 O.R. (2d) 205, 11 C.P.C. (2d) 171, 30 D.L.R. (4th) 591 (H.C.).

The court refused to consolidate two actions based on the same automobile accident where to do so would deprive a plaintiff claiming personal injury damages of a right to claim on behalf of statutory beneficiaries under the *Family Law Reform Act*.

Cranberry Lake Dev. Ltd. v. Bank of Montreal; Bank of Montreal v. Graat (1984), 45 C.P.C. 208 (Ont. H.C.).

The court refused to order consolidation or trial together since to do so would deprive the bank of its right to cross-examine on the affidavit of merits and to move for judgment in the second action, there were different parties and issues, and the bank would be delayed.

Gorin v. Ho; Gorin v. Stewart & Cass (1982), 31 C.P.C. 316 (Ont. H.C.).

A medical malpractice action and action against the plaintiff's former solicitors for negligence in prosecuting the malpractice claim were ordered to be tried together in this case.

Stewart v. Stewart (1980), 30 O.R. (2d) 63, 116 D.L.R. (3d) 383 (Master).

Where two cross divorce petitions were issued within one hour, the first was given precedence and leave was given to amend the second to be a counterpetition.

Whiteoak Lincoln Mercury Sales Ltd. v. C.P. Ltd. (1982), 30 C.P.C. 136 (Ont. H.C.).

Some 389 actions arising out of the Mississauga train derailment were ordered to be tried together, with certain test cases going forward to dispose of the liability issues.

Arrow Transit Lines Ltd. v. Tank Truck Transport Ltd.; Joyce v. Tank Truck Transport Ltd., [1968] 1 O.R. 154, 65 D.L.R. (2d) 683 (H.C.).

Where conflicts between an insured and an insurer resulted in two actions on the same facts, the court refused to dismiss one of the actions and instead directed trial together.

Nadas v. Royal Bank of Can. (1978), 8 C.P.C. 50 (Ont. H.C.).

Actions were consolidated where the issues in the second action could be dealt with by way of counterclaim in the first action.

Re Pajelle Invts. Ltd. and Booth (No. 2) (1975), 7 O.R. (2d) 229 (Co. Ct.).

An application for consolidation of applications under the *Landlord and Tenant Act*, R.S.O. 1970, c. 236, was refused where it appeared each case would require separate arguments, the request for consolidation was not brought at an early stage, and there was a possibility that a decision in one case might reduce the length of the other cases.

Bender v. Raper; Bender v. Atcheson, [1954] O.W.N. 93 (H.C.).

Where a plaintiff commences several actions, the latest of which asserts a cause of action which accrued after the first actions were commenced, consolidation should not be ordered, but the actions should be put on the trial list together.

Avery v. Homewood Sanitarium of Guelph, Ont. Ltd., [1953] O.W.N. 901 (H.C.).
The court postponed the trial of one action where other related actions were not ready for trial.

Hall v. Wilson; Bengle v. Wilson; Henson v. Wilson, [1951] O.W.N. 228 (H.C.).
An order for consolidation of three actions was refused where, *inter alia,* the three plaintiffs could not agree on a common solicitor.

Consolidation or Hearing Together – Procedure

Tusa v. Walsh (1994), 23 C.P.C. (3d) 178 (Ont. Gen. Div.).
Where two actions were ordered to be tried together, the court permitted the defendants in the first action to participate in the discovery of the defendants in the second action.

DISCRETION OF PRESIDING JUDGE

6.02 Where the court has made an order that proceedings be heard either at the same time or one immediately after the other, the judge presiding at the hearing nevertheless has discretion to order otherwise.

RULE 7   PARTIES UNDER DISABILITY

Highlights

Thxis Rule regulates the bringing of proceedings by or against parties under disability. Its central requirement is that persons under disability must be represented by a litigation guardian (except where the party under disability is a respondent to an application under the *Substitute Decisions Act, 1992*: rule 7.01(2)).

Rule 7 introduced new terminology. "Party under disability" is used as a general term to include minors, mental incompetents and absentees: see the definition in rule 1.03. The term "litigation guardian" for a plaintiff, or a defendant, replaced "next friend" and "guardian *ad litem*", respectively.

The 1995 amendments to Rule 7, consequential on the coming into force of the *Substitute Decisions Act, 1992*, S.O. 1992, c. 30, also changed the terminology by removing references to "mentally incompetent" and substituting "mentally incapable" and by removing "committee" and substituting "litigation guardian" instead: rule 7.01(3). Other legislation changed the name of the former "Official Guardian" to "Children's Lawyer" and renamed the former "Public Trustee" as the "Public Guardian and Trustee". These name changes were incorporated throughout Rule 7.

A litigation guardian for a plaintiff may act without court appointment, but he or she must first file an affidavit to the effect that, *inter alia*, he or she consents, has retained a solicitor, has no interest adverse to the party under disability and has been informed of his or her possible liability for costs: rule 7.02(2). Rule 7.02 creates a presumptive right for a mentally incapable person's guardian or attorney under a power of attorney to act as litigation guardian, so long as the guardian or attorney has the authority to act by the terms of his or her appointment as guardian or attorney.

A litigation guardian for a defendant must be appointed by the court, and the procedure to be followed on a motion for appointment by either a non-party or the plaintiff is spelled out: rule 7.03. However, a defendant's guardian or attorney under a power of attorney has a presumptive right to act as litigation guardian without obtaining a court order, so long as the guardian or attorney has the authority to act by the terms of his or her appointment as guardian or attorney. The guardian or attorney must file an affidavit with the court before acting: rule 7.03(2.2).

Unless there is some other proper person willing to act as litigation guardian, the court is to appoint the Children's Lawyer or the Public Guardian and Trustee, and the Rule specifies the area of responsibility of each of these officers. The Children's Lawyer is to be appointed where the disabled person is a minor, the Public Guardian and Trustee is to be appointed in cases of mental incapacity, and where the person suffers both disabilities, either may be appointed: rule 7.04.

Rule 7.04 as amended in 1995 deals with who represents disabled parties and non-parties (such as children or estate beneficiaries whose interests need representation). Parties and non-parties alike may have a litigation guardian, except that non-party children will be represented by the Children's Lawyer, or some other proper person, acting as "legal representative" rather than a litigation guardian. This results from a 1995 amendment to s. 89 of the *Courts of Justice Act*, which governs the Children's Lawyer.

Rule 7.05(3) provides that a litigation guardian, other than the Children's Lawyer or Public Guardian and Trustee, must act by a solicitor and may not act in person: see also rule 15.01(1). A party under disability may not be noted in default except by leave of a judge to be obtained on notice to the Children's Lawyer or the Public Guardian and Trustee: rules 7.07 and 19.01(4). Similar principles apply to the discontinuance of an action by or against a party under disability (rule 23.01) and to the dismissal for delay of an action brought by a party under disability: rules 24.02 and 48.14(7).

Rule 7.08 largely codifies the common law rules as to the requirement of court approval of settlements involving persons under disability and spells out the mechanics of obtaining such approval. Rule 7.08(5) provides that the involvement of the Children's Lawyer (or the Public Guardian and Trustee) is not automatic, but is to be residual and only at the direction of the judge approving the settlement.

Former Rules: Rules 18-22, 92-100.

REPRESENTATION BY LITIGATION GUARDIAN

Party under Disability

7.01(1) Unless the court orders or a statute provides otherwise, a proceeding shall be commenced, continued or defended on behalf of a party under disability by a litigation guardian.

Substitute Decisions Act Applications

(2) Despite subrule (1), an application under the *Substitute Decisions Act, 1992* may be commenced, continued and defended without the appointment of a litigation guardian for the respondent in respect of whom the application is made, unless the court orders otherwise.

Previously Appointed Committees

(3) A committee named by order or statute before April 3, 1995 is the litigation guardian of the person in respect of whom the committee was named, and shall be referred to as the litigation guardian for all purposes.

(4) Subrule (3) also applies to the Public Guardian and Trustee acting under an order made under subsection 72(1) or (2) of the *Mental Health Act* as it read before April 3, 1995. [am. O. Regs. 69/95, s. 2; 377/95, s. 2]

General

Bilek v. Constitution Insurance (1990), 49 C.P.C. (2d) 304 (Ont. Dist. Ct.).

The court dismissed a motion by the defendant that a litigation guardian be appointed for the plaintiff on the basis that the plaintiff lacked mental capacity. The court is very cautious in reaching a conclusion which would deprive the plaintiff of the final say in the conduct of the litigation.

Lawson v. Hospital for Sick Children (1990), 74 O.R. (2d) 11, 44 C.P.C. (2d) 146, 4 C.C.L.T. (2d) 303, 71 D.L.R. (4th) 557, 40 O.A.C. 56 (Div. Ct.).

Section 47 of the *Limitations Act* gives absolute protection to a minor, which is not lost by the appointment of a litigation guardian; accordingly, an infant plaintiff was permitted to add physicians as defendants notwithstanding the expiry of the one-year period provided for in s. 17 of the *Health Disciplines Act*, R.S.O. 1980, c. 196.

Martin v. Listowel Memorial Hospital (1989), 34 C.P.C. (2d) 303, additional reasons 34 C.P.C. (2d) 303 at 311 (Ont. H.C.), affirmed (1992), 9 O.R. (3d) 65, 9 C.P.C. (3d) 183, 93 D.L.R. (4th) 452, 56 O.A.C. 337 (C.A.), leave to appeal to Supreme Court of Canada refused (1993), 19 C.P.C. (3d) 23 (note), 105 D.L.R. (4th) vi (note).

Appointment of a litigation guardian for a minor does not trigger the running of limitation periods against the minor.

Brosseau v. C.A.S. of Sudbury Inc. (1986), 7 C.P.C. (2d) 312 (Ont. H.C.).

A minor having a *bona fide* cause of action is a privileged suitor. The minor and the Official Guardian acting on his behalf should not be visited with the sins of previous next friends or litigation guardians. The court refused to dismiss an action for delay although fourteen years had passed after commencement of the action.

Medhurst v. Medhurst (1984), 46 O.R. (2d) 263, 38 R.F.L. (2d) 225, 9 D.L.R. (4th) 252 (H.C.).

A litigation guardian can only act for a person, and an unborn child is not a person.

Barnes v. Kirk, [1968] 2 O.R. 213 (C.A.).

The onus of establishing incompetence rests on the party alleging it.

Oates v. Patriquin, [1958] O.W.N. 89 (Master).

Where an infant who commences a proceeding by a litigation guardian subsequently becomes a mental incompetent not so found, a new litigation guardian is not required.

Late Appointment of Litigation Guardian

Crossett v. Labraceur, [1958] O.W.N. 29 (H.C.).

Failure to appoint a litigation guardian is an irregularity which can be cured even after the expiry of the limitation period.

Kozaruk v. Kozaruk, [1953] O.W.N. 265 (H.C.).

Where, in giving evidence at trial, a party demonstrates she is mentally incompetent, a litigation guardian may be appointed.

Gauthier v. Gauthier, [1947] O.W.N. 1053 (H.C.).

Where, during the course of a trial, a party was discovered to be a minor, a litigation guardian was appointed.

Effect of Judgment Where No Litigation Guardian Appointed

Re Haskell and Letourneau (1979), 25 O.R. (2d) 139, 1 F.L.R.A.C. 306, 100 D.L.R. (3d) 329, (Co. Ct.).

Where there was no objection until after trial that a minor had no litigation guardian, the court held that the action was validly constituted.

Augustine v. Carlaw (1976), 1 C.P.C. 149 (Ont. H.C.).

Where it appears that a successful plaintiff is mentally incompetent, the court may direct that the judgment be paid into court pending an application under the *Mental Incompetency Act*.

Re Hrivnak, [1963] 2 O.R. 729, 40 D.L.R. (2d) 953 (H.C.).

Where a party was a minor when certain litigation was commenced, and no litigation guardian had been appointed, the court held that the outcome of such litigation was binding on such party only to the extent it benefited her, notwithstanding that she had attained her majority before the conclusion of the litigation.

MacBeth v. Curran, [1948] O.R. 444, [1948] 3 D.L.R. 85 (H.C.).

A judgment in a tort action may be binding upon a minor even where there was no litigation guardian, unless proceedings are taken to set aside the judgment.

LITIGATION GUARDIAN FOR PLAINTIFF OR APPLICANT

Court Appointment Unnecessary

7.02(1) Any person who is not under disability may act, without being appointed by the court, as litigation guardian for a plaintiff or applicant who is under disability, subject to subrule (1.1).

Mentally Incapable Person or Absentee

(1.1) Unless the court orders otherwise, where a plaintiff or applicant,

(a) is mentally incapable and has a guardian with authority to act as litigation guardian in the proceeding, the guardian shall act as litigation guardian;

(b) is mentally incapable and does not have a guardian with authority to act as litigation guardian in the proceeding, but has an attorney under a power of attorney with that authority, the attorney shall act as litigation guardian;

(c) is an absentee and a committee of his or her estate has been appointed under the *Absentees Act*, the committee shall act as litigation guardian;

(d) is a person in respect of whom an order was made under subsection 72(1) or (2) of the *Mental Health Act* as it read before April 3, 1995, the Public Guardian and Trustee shall act as litigation guardian.

Affidavit to be Filed

(2) No person except the Children's Lawyer or the Public Guardian and Trustee shall act as litigation guardian for a plaintiff or applicant who is under disability until the person has filed an affidavit in which the person,

(a) consents to act as litigation guardian in the proceeding;

(b) confirms that he or she has given written authority to a named solicitor to act in the proceeding;

(b.1) provides evidence concerning the nature and extent of the disability;

(b.2) in the case of a minor, states the minor's birth date;

(c) states whether he or she and the person under disability are ordinarily resident in Ontario;

(d) sets out his or her relationship, if any, to the person under disability;

(e) states that he or she has no interest in the proceeding adverse to that of the person under disability; and

(f) acknowledges that he or she has been informed of his or her liability to pay personally any costs awarded against him or her or against the person under disability. [am. O. Reg. 69/95, s. 3]

Adverse Interest — rule 7.02(2)(e)

Carter v. Booth, [1956] O.W.N. 812 (C.A.).

The litigation guardian of an infant plaintiff was added as a third party under the *Negligence Act*.

Liability of Litigation Guardian for Costs — rule 7.02(2)(f)

Lament v. Kirkpatrick, [1962] O.W.N. 8 (Master).

The litigation guardian of a plaintiff under disability is responsible for costs irrespective of the type of disability.

Rooney v. Jasinski, [1952] O.R. 869, [1953] 1 D.L.R. 225 (C.A.).

Where costs are incurred *bona fide* and for the benefit of the party under disability, the party may be liable to indemnify the litigation guardian.

LITIGATION GUARDIAN FOR DEFENDANT OR RESPONDENT

Generally must be Appointed by Court

7.03(1) No person shall act as a litigation guardian for a defendant or respondent who is under disability until appointed by the court, except as provided in subrule (2), (2.1) or (3).

Where Minor Interested in Estate or Trust

(2) Where a proceeding is against a minor in respect of the minor's interest in an estate or trust, the Children's Lawyer shall act as the litigation guardian of the minor defendant or respondent, unless the court orders otherwise.

Mentally Incapable Person or Absentee

(2.1) Unless the court orders otherwise, where a proceeding is against,

(a) a mentally incapable person who has a guardian with authority to act as litigation guardian in the proceeding, the guardian shall act as litigation guardian;

(b) a mentally incapable person who does not have a guardian with authority to act as litigation guardian in the proceeding but has an attorney under a power of attorney with that authority, the attorney shall act as litigation guardian;

(c) an absentee, and a committee of his or her estate has been appointed under the *Absentees Act*, the committee shall act as litigation guardian;

(d) a person in respect of whom an order has been made under subsection 72(1) or (2) of the *Mental Health Act* as it read before April 3, 1995, the Public Guardian and Trustee shall act as litigation guardian.

Affidavit by guardian or attorney

(2.2) A person who has authority under subrule (2.1) to act as litigation guardian shall, before acting in that capacity in a proceeding, file an affidavit containing the information referred to in subrule (10).

Defending Counterclaim

(3) A litigation guardian for a plaintiff may defend a counterclaim without being appointed by the court.

Motion by Person Seeking to be Litigation Guardian

(4) A person who seeks to be the litigation guardian of a defendant or respondent under disability shall move to be appointed by the court before acting as litigation guardian.

Motion by Plaintiff or Applicant to Appoint Litigation Guardian

(5) Where a defendant or respondent under disability has been served with an originating process and no motion has been made under subrule (4) for the appointment of a litigation guardian, a plaintiff or applicant, before taking any further step in the proceeding, shall move for an order appointing a litigation guardian for the party under disability.

(6) At least ten days before moving for the appointment of a litigation guardian, a plaintiff or applicant shall serve a request for appointment of

litigation guardian (Form 7A) on the party under disability personally or by an alternative to personal service under rule 16.03.

(7) The request may be served on the party under disability with the originating process.

(8) A motion for the appointment of a litigation guardian may be made without notice to the party under disability.

(9) A plaintiff or applicant who moves to appoint the Children's Lawyer or the Public Guardian and Trustee as the litigation guardian shall serve the notice of motion and the material required by subrule (10) on the Children's Lawyer or the Public Guardian and Trustee.

Evidence on Motion to Appoint

(10) A person who moves for the appointment of a litigation guardian shall provide evidence on the motion concerning,

(a) the nature of the proceeding;

(b) the date on which the cause of action arose and the date on which the proceeding was commenced;

(c) service on the party under disability of the originating process and the request for appointment of litigation guardian;

(d) the nature and extent of the disability;

(e) in the case of a minor, the minor's birth date;

(f) whether the person under disability ordinarily resides in Ontario; and

except where the proposed litigation guardian is the Children's Lawyer or the Public Guardian and Trustee, evidence,

(g) concerning the relationship, if any, of the proposed litigation guardian to the party under disability;

(h) whether the proposed litigation guardian ordinarily resides in Ontario;

(i) that the proposed litigation guardian,

(i) consents to act as litigation guardian in the proceeding;

(ii) is a proper person to be appointed;

(iii) has no interest in the proceeding adverse to that of the party under disability; and

(iv) acknowledges having been informed that he or she may incur costs that may not be recovered from another party. [am. O. Reg. 69/95, ss. 4, 19, 20]

Morgan v. Mowat, [1951] O.W.N. 748 (Master).

The appointment of a litigation guardian is within the jurisdiction of the master.

REPRESENTATION OF PERSONS UNDER DISABILITY

7.04(1) Unless there is some other proper person willing and able to act as litigation guardian for a party under disability, the court shall appoint,

(a) the Children's Lawyer, if the party is a minor;

(b) the Public Guardian and Trustee, if the party is mentally incapable within the meaning of section 6 or 45 of the *Substitute Decisions Act, 1992* in respect of an issue in the proceeding and there is no guardian or attorney under a power of attorney with authority to act as litigation guardian;

(c) either of them, if clauses (a) and (b) both apply to the party.

Legal representation for minor who is not a party

(2) Where, in the opinion of the court, the interests of a minor who is not a party require separate representation in a proceeding, the court may request and may by order authorize the Children's Lawyer, or some other proper person who is willing and able to act, to act as the person's legal representative.

Litigation guardian for incapable person who is not a party

(3) Where, in the opinion of the court, the interests of a mentally incapable person who is not a minor and not a party require separate representation in a proceeding, the court may appoint as the mentally incapable person's litigation guardian the Public Guardian and Trustee or some other proper person who is willing and able to act. [am. O. Reg. 69/95, s. 5]

Kryzanowski (Litigation Guardian of) v. F.W. Woolworth Co. (1993), 18 C.P.C. (3d) 367 (Ont. Gen. Div.).

The court appointed the Official Guardian as litigation guardian of two infant third parties, although they were in the care of the Children's Aid Society at the time the motion was heard. The incident in issue had occurred prior to the Children's Aid Society becoming involved with the children, and for valid reasons the mother was not acting as litigation guardian.

Fairbairn v. Gouldby, [1962] O.W.N. 103 (Master).

Where two infants were adverse in interest, the Official Guardian was appointed as litigation guardian for one and the Public Trustee as litigation guardian for the other.

Gilman v. Allingham, [1962] O.W.N. 247 (Co. Ct.).

The Official Guardian was appointed, over his objection, as litigation guardian.

POWERS AND DUTIES OF LITIGATION GUARDIAN

7.05(1) Where a party is under disability, anything that a party in a proceeding is required or authorized to do may be done by the party's litigation guardian.

(2) A litigation guardian shall diligently attend to the interests of the person under disability and take all steps necessary for the protection of those interests, including the commencement and conduct of a counterclaim, crossclaim or third party claim.

(3) A litigation guardian other than the Children's Lawyer or the Public Guardian and Trustee shall be represented by a solicitor and shall instruct the solicitor in the conduct of the proceeding. [am. O. Reg. 69/95, ss. 18, 19, 20]

Poulin v. Nadon, [1950] O.R. 219, [1950] 2 D.L.R. 303 (C.A.).
Discussion of status of litigation guardian.

REMOVAL OR SUBSTITUTION OF LITIGATION GUARDIAN

7.06(1) Where, in the course of a proceeding,

(a) a minor for whom a litigation guardian has been acting reaches the age of majority, the minor or the litigation guardian may, on filing an affidavit stating that the minor has reached the age of majority, obtain from the registrar an order to continue (Form 7B) authorizing the minor to continue the proceeding without the litigation guardian;

(b) a party under any other disability for whom a litigation guardian has been acting ceases to be under disability, the party or the litigation guardian may move without notice for an order to continue the proceeding without the litigation guardian,

and the order shall be served forthwith on every other party and on the litigation guardian.

(2) Where it appears to the court that a litigation guardian is not acting in the best interests of the party under disability, the court may substitute the Children's Lawyer, the Public Guardian and Trustee or any other person as litigation guardian. [am. O. Reg. 69/95, ss. 18, 19, 20]

Saccon (Litigation Guardian of) v. Sisson (1992), 9 C.P.C. (3d) 383 (Ont. Gen. Div.).
The Official Guardian was substituted as litigation guardian for minor plaintiffs where their mother, who had acted as litigation guardian, would not post security for costs.

Marchewka (Litigation Guardian of) v. Machtinger (1991), 9 C.P.C. (3d) 320 (Ont. Master).
The court removed a litigation guardian who had a conflict of interest and substituted the Public Trustee.

Panzavecchia v. Piche, [1972] 2 O.R. 811, 26 D.L.R. (2d) 690 (H.C.).
A litigation guardian was removed and replaced by the Official Guardian where he refused to accept a settlement recommended by counsel and found reasonable by the court.

NOTING PARTY UNDER DISABILITY IN DEFAULT

7.07(1) A party under disability may not be noted in default under rule 19.01 without leave of a judge.

(2) Notice of a motion for leave under subrule (1) shall be served,

(a) on the litigation guardian of the party under disability; and

(b) on the Children's Lawyer, unless,

> **(i) the Public Guardian and Trustee is the litigation guardian, or**

> **(ii) a judge orders otherwise. [am. O. Reg. 69/95, ss. 18, 19, 20]**

APPROVAL OF SETTLEMENT

Settlement Requires Judge's Approval

7.08(1) No settlement of a claim made by or against a person under disability, whether or not a proceeding has been commenced in respect of the claim, is binding on the person without the approval of a judge.

(2) Judgment may not be obtained on consent in favour of or against a party under disability without the approval of a judge.

Where no Proceeding Commenced

(3) Where an agreement for the settlement of a claim made by or against a person under disability is reached before a proceeding is commenced in respect of the claim, approval of a judge shall be obtained on an application.

Material Required for Approval

(4) On a motion or application for the approval of a judge under this rule, there shall be served and filed with the notice of motion or notice of application,

 (a) an affidavit of the litigation guardian setting out the material facts and the reasons supporting the proposed settlement and the position of the litigation guardian in respect of the settlement;

 (b) an affidavit of the solicitor acting for the litigation guardian setting out the solicitor's position in respect of the proposed settlement;

 (c) where the person under disability is a minor who is over the age of sixteen years, the minor's consent in writing, unless the judge orders otherwise; and

 (d) a copy of the proposed minutes of settlement.

Notice to Children's Lawyer or Public Guardian and Trustee

(5) On a motion or application for the approval of a judge under this rule, the judge may direct that the material referred to in subrule (4) be served on the Children's Lawyer or on the Public Guardian and Trustee as the litigation guardian of the party under disability and may direct the Children's Lawyer or the Public Guardian and Trustee, as the case may be, to make an oral or written report stating any objections he or she has to the proposed settlement and making recommendations, with reasons, in connection with the proposed settlement. [am. O. Reg. 69/95, ss. 18, 19, 20]

Examples of Settlements Approved or Refused — rule 7.08(1)

Kay v. Coffin (1991), 49 C.P.C. (2d) 278, [1991] 2 C.T.C. 154, 91 D.T.C. 5350, [1991] I.L.R.
 1-2749 (Ont. Gen. Div.).

The court approved a "structured" settlement involving a self-insurer. Discussion of requirements of structured settlements.

Helston v. Air Canada (1986), 4 W.D.C.P. 12 (Ont. H.C.).

The court refused to approve a settlement structured through annuities issued by a United States insurer.

Carter v. Junkin, 47 O.R. (2d) 427, 7 C.C.L.I. 217, 11 D.L.R. (4th) 545, [1984] I.L.R. 1-1815,
 6 O.A.C. 310 (Div. Ct.).

Where an insurer offered to make a payment into court in respect of a claim by an infant, and the judge accepted this on the condition that the insurer make up the difference between prejudgment interest and interest earned on the payment into court, the judge was able to require the additional payment, as he had the power to grant and refuse leave with regard to the best interests of the child.

Steeves v. Fitzsimmons (1975), 11 O.R. (2d) 387, 66 D.L.R. (3d) 203 (H.C.).

The court approved a settlement on behalf of an infant which provided that, should handicaps or learning disabilities be perceived within a prescribed period, an application could be brought re-opening the matter.

Stevens v. Howitt, [1969] 1 O.R. 761, 4 D.L.R. (3d) 50 (H.C.).

An agreement by a parent to indemnify a potential defendant for all subsequent claims made by his child is void as against public policy.

Hurd v. Dumont, [1955] O.W.N. 568 (H.C.).

A settlement should provide either that solicitor and client costs are fixed at a specified amount or that the full amount of the settlement be paid into court and costs on a solicitor and client basis be paid out after taxation.

Approval of Solicitor's Fees

Kenyeres (Litigation Guardian of) v. Cullimore (1992), 13 C.P.C. (3d) 385 (Ont. Gen. Div.), affirmed (March 7, 1994), Doc. No. CA C12531/92 (Ont. C.A.).

The court permitted counsel for a successful minor plaintiff to recover solicitor and client fees above the party and party costs recoverable from the defendant.

Stribbell v. Bhalla (1990), 73 O.R. (2d) 748, 42 C.P.C. (2d) 161 (H.C.).

Where the parents consented, the trial judge permitted counsel for a successful minor plaintiff to recover out of the judgment proceeds costs in excess of the usual party and party scale. Justice requires that deserving actions be prosecuted by competent counsel, and competent counsel are entitled to be paid a reasonable fee for the value of the work done.

Material Required for Approval — rule 7.08(4)

Poulin v. Nadon, [1950] O.R. 219, [1950] 2 D.L.R. 303 (C.A.).

A settlement will be approved only if it is for the benefit of the person under disability; the court may require extensive evidence to establish that fact. The proceedings to obtain approval should be made part of the record.

Andreacchi v. Perruccio, [1973] 2 O.R. 543 (H.C.).

The court should hear *viva voce* evidence or be furnished with acceptable affidavit evidence as to both the issues of damages and liability. Useful discussion of other aspects of settlement with a party under disability.

Approval of Settlements — Miscellaneous

Kendall (Litigation Guardian of) v. Kindl Estate (1992), 10 C.P.C. (3d) 24 (Ont. Gen. Div.).

The court may not order an unwilling defendant to enter into a structured settlement. The court's *parens patriae* jurisdiction does not provide jurisdiction to do so for a minor plaintiff.

Tepperman v. Rosenberg (1985), 48 C.P.C. 317 (Ont. H.C.).

The court refused to set aside an infant settlement where the court which originally approved the settlement had ample evidence before it to decide whether the settlement was in the best interest of the infant.

Hamilton v. Maryland Casualty Co., [1973] 2 O.R. at 786, 35 D.L.R. (3d) at 342, [1972] I.L.R. 1-476, affirmed [1973] 2 O.R. 791, 35 D.L.R. (3d) 342, [1973] I.L.R. 1-561 (C.A.).

Where a settlement regarding injuries to an infant was made without approval of the court, but an action was subsequently commenced following the expiry of a limitation period, the action was held to be statute-barred.

Re Yates, [1955] O.W.N. 481 (H.C.).

The Official Guardian was permitted to withdraw his approval of a settlement where, before the settlement had been confirmed by the court, the law applicable to the case was clarified in another action.

MONEY TO BE PAID INTO COURT

7.09(1) Any money payable to a person under disability under an order or a settlement shall be paid into court, unless a judge orders otherwise.

(2) Any money paid to the Children's Lawyer on behalf of a person under disability shall be paid into court, unless a judge orders otherwise. [am. O. Reg. 69/95, s. 19]

RULE 8   PARTNERSHIPS AND SOLE PROPRIETORSHIPS

Highlights

This Rule governs proceedings by or against a partnership using the firm name or by or against a sole proprietorship using a business name.

It is no longer a prerequisite to a proceeding using the firm name of a partnership that the partnership be carrying on business in Ontario. Under the former practice, all persons sued as partners in the firm name were required to enter individual appearances. Now, rule 8.02 requires partners to deliver a common defence in the name of the firm, and a person who admits he or she was a partner may defend separately only with leave. A person who denies he or she was a partner may defend separately, but if the person does so, he or she becomes a separate party to the proceeding: rule 8.04.

Where a partnership is sued in the firm name, service on the firm is made by leaving the originating process with a partner or a person who appears to be in control of management of the principal place of business: rule 16.02(1)(m). A judgment obtained against a firm based on such service is enforceable only against the property of the partnership: rule 8.06(1).

If the plaintiff or applicant seeks a judgment enforceable against partners personally, the plaintiff or applicant should serve each partner he or she seeks to make personally liable with the originating process and a notice to the alleged partner: rule 8.03(1). If a person so served is determined to be a partner then a judgment against the partnership in the firm name may also be enforced against him or her: rule 8.06(2). Alternatively, after obtaining judgment against a partnership in the firm name, the plaintiff or applicant may move for leave to enforce the judgment against the person alleged to be a partner: rule 8.06(3). By rule 8.05, disclosure may be had of the names and addresses of the partners of a plaintiff or defendant firm.

A major change in respect of sole proprietorships is that, in addition to being sued in a business name, they may now sue using a business name: rule 8.07.

Former Rules: Rules 14, 102-110.

PARTNERSHIPS

8.01(1) A proceeding by or against two or more persons as partners may be commenced using the firm name of the partnership.

(2) Subrule (1) extends to a proceeding between partnerships having one or more partners in common. [am. O. Reg. 535/92, s. 4]

872928 Ontario Ltd. v. Gallery Pictures Inc. (1990), 75 O.R. (2d) 273 (Gen. Div.).

A limited partnership can sue and be sued in its own name. Although the general partner controls the affairs of the limited partnership, the general partner cannot institute proceedings in its own name or on behalf of the limited partnership.

Unical Properties v. 784688 Ontario Ltd. (1990), 75 O.R. (2d) 284, 45 C.P.C. (2d) 288, 73 D.L.R. (4th) 761 (Gen. Div.).

Notwithstanding rule 8.01(2), one partner cannot sue another partner in the partnership name.

Dye and Durham v. Redfern Const. Co., [1962] O.R. 1025, 35 D.L.R. (2d) 102 (H.C.).

The firm name may be used in an action by the partnership notwithstanding that the composition of the partnership changed between the time the cause of action arose and the time the action was commenced.

Minnesota Mining and Mfg. Co. v. Dahm, [1957] O.W.N. 100 (H.C.).
If a firm is named as a party, the members of the firm should not be named individually.

Green & Co. v. Cukier, [1949] O.W.N. 619, [1949] 4 D.L.R. 729 (C.A.).
Consideration of effects of the death of a partner in a plaintiff firm.

British Products Unlimited v. Tenenbaum, [1949] O.W.N. 240 (Master).
Where a partnership is duly registered and a declaration is filed showing some of the partners to be infants, the partners may sue in the firm name without the need for the infant partners to be represented by litigation guardians.

Consumer's Soybean Mills Inc. v. Sullivan, [1947] O.W.N. 478 (Master).
A plaintiff may sue using the firm name or using "A and B carrying on business as C". In either case, it is proper to counterclaim in the name of A and B as individuals.

DEFENCE

8.02 Where a proceeding is commenced against a partnership using the firm name, the partnership's defence shall be delivered in the firm name and no person who admits having been a partner at any material time may defend the proceeding separately, except with leave of the court.

133/135 King East Inc. v. Wood Wilkings Ltd. (1983), 43 O.R. (2d) 698, 39 C.P.C. 49 (Master).
A general partner was required to appear in his own name, but the limited partners were not.

NOTICE TO ALLEGED PARTNER WHERE ENFORCEMENT SOUGHT AGAINST PARTNER

8.03 (1) In a proceeding against a partnership using the firm name, where a plaintiff or applicant seeks an order that will be enforceable personally against a person as a partner, the plaintiff or applicant may serve the person with the originating process, together with a notice to alleged partner (Form 8A) stating that the person was a partner at a material time specified in the notice.

(2) A person served as provided in subrule (1) shall be deemed to have been a partner at the material time, unless the person defends the proceeding separately denying that he or she was a partner at the material time.

PERSON DEFENDING SEPARATELY

8.04 A person becomes a party to a proceeding as a defendant or respondent, and the title of the proceeding shall be amended accordingly, if the person defends a proceeding separately,
(a) denying having been a partner at the material time; or
(b) with leave of the court under rule 8.02.

DISCLOSURE OF PARTNERS

8.05(1) Where a proceeding is commenced by or against a partnership using the firm name, any other party may serve a notice requiring the part-

nership to disclose forthwith the names and addresses of all the partners constituting the partnership at a time specified in the notice and, where the present address of a partner is unknown, the partnership shall disclose the last known address of that partner.

(2) Where a partnership fails to comply with a notice under subrule (1), its claim may be dismissed or the proceeding stayed or its defence may be struck out.

(3) Where the name of a partner is disclosed pursuant to a notice under subrule (1) and the partner has not been served as provided in rule 8.03, the partner may be so served within fifteen days after the name is disclosed.

ENFORCEMENT OF ORDER

Against Partnership Property

8.06(1) An order against a partnership using the firm name may be enforced against the property of the partnership.

Against Person Served as Alleged Partner

(2) An order against a partnership using the firm name may also be enforced, where the order or a subsequent order so provides, against any person who was served as provided in rule 8.03 and who,

(a) under that rule, is deemed to have been a partner;

(b) has admitted having been a partner; or

(c) has been adjudged to have been a partner,

at the material time.

Against Person not Served as Alleged Partner

(3) Where, after an order has been made against a partnership using the firm name, the party obtaining it claims to be entitled to enforce it against any person alleged to be a partner other than a person who was served as provided in rule 8.03, the party may move before a judge for leave to do so, and the judge may grant leave if the liability of the person as a partner is not disputed or, if disputed, after the liability has been determined in such manner as the judge directs.

SOLE PROPRIETORSHIPS

8.07(1) Where a person carries on business in a business name other than his or her own name, a proceeding may be commenced by or against the person using the business name.

(2) Rules 8.01 to 8.06 apply, with necessary modifications, to a proceeding by or against a sole proprietor using a business name, as though the sole proprietor were a partner and the business name were the firm name of a partnership.

Towne & Countrye Pet Village v. Silver (1986), 58 O.R. (2d) 287, 14 C.P.C. (2d) 271 (Div. Ct.), leave to appeal to Ont. C.A. refused (1987), 26 C.P.C. (2d) 1.

Rule 8.07(1) does not have retrospective effect. An action commenced by a corporation in its business name prior to January 1, 1985, is a nullity.

S. Reichmann & Sons Ltd. v. The Ambassador, [1967] 1 O.R. 440, affirmed [1967] 1 O.R. 444n (H.C.).

Where a limited company operates under a business style, a judgment against the company in the name of the business style may be enforced against the property of the company.

RULE 9   ESTATES AND TRUSTS

Highlights

Rule 9 deals with three aspects of the subject of parties in proceedings brought by and against an estate or trust.

Rule 9.01(1) sets forth the general rule that in proceedings by or against an estate or trust the appropriate representative may sue or be sued without joining the persons beneficially entitled. Subrule (2) codifies the situations in which it would be inappropriate for the representatives alone to be parties and where the persons beneficially entitled must be joined. Subrule (4) is broader than the former provision in that it empowers the court to order, not only that any beneficiary be joined, but also "any . . . creditor or other interested person".

Rule 9.02 deals with the situation where it is sought to sue an estate and there is no personal representative. It provides that in such circumstances the court may on motion appoint a "litigation administrator" to represent the estate for the purpose of a proceeding. This procedure replaces the "administrator *ad litem*" provisions formerly contained in the *Trustee Act*, R.S.O. 1980, c. 512, s. 38(5) and (6).

Rule 9.03 contains a series of new remedial provisions to overcome a body of pre-existing case law holding that, in a variety of situations, the improper constituting of proceedings against an estate made the proceedings a nullity. The rule is a specific application or an extension of the general principle found in rule 2.01. Subrule (3) replaces and is broader than the former *Trustee Act*, s. 38(3) and (4).

Former Rules: Rule 74.

PROCEEDINGS BY OR AGAINST EXECUTOR, ADMINISTRATOR OR TRUSTEE

General Rule

9.01(1) A proceeding may be brought by or against an executor, administrator or trustee as representing an estate or trust and its beneficiaries without joining the beneficiaries as parties.

Exceptions

(2) Subrule (1) does not apply to a proceeding,

(a) to establish or contest the validity of a will;

(b) for the interpretation of a will;

(c) to remove or replace an executor, administrator or trustee;

(d) against an executor, administrator or trustee for fraud or misconduct; or

(e) for the administration of an estate or the execution of a trust by the court.

Executor, Administrator or Trustee Refusing to be Joined

(3) Where a proceeding is commenced by executors, administrators or trustees, any executor, administrator or trustee who does not consent to be joined as a plaintiff or applicant shall be made a defendant or respondent.

Beneficiaries and Others Added by Order

(4) The court may order that any beneficiary, creditor or other interested person be made a party to a proceeding by or against an executor, administrator or trustee.

Robinson v. Pakiela, [1956] O.W.N. 244 (Master).

Where an executor defendant in a foreclosure action was unable and unwilling to redeem, the court allowed a beneficiary to be made a party for the purpose of redemption.

Kamins v. Geller, [1949] O.W.N. 597 (Master).

The court added the administrator *pendente lite* of the estate of the deceased whose will was being contested in the surrogate court, but refused to add the principal beneficiary under the will as all beneficiaries were adequately represented by the administrator.

PROCEEDING AGAINST ESTATE THAT HAS NO EXECUTOR OR ADMINISTRATOR

9.02(1) Where it is sought to commence or continue a proceeding against the estate of a deceased person who has no executor or administrator, the court on motion may appoint a litigation administrator to represent the estate for the purposes of the proceeding.

(2) An order in a proceeding to which a litigation administrator is a party binds or benefits the estate of the deceased person, but has no effect on the litigation administrator in a personal capacity, unless a judge orders otherwise.

REMEDIAL PROVISIONS

Proceeding Commenced before Probate or Administration

9.03(1) Where a proceeding is commenced by or against a person as executor or administrator before a grant of probate or administration has been made and the person subsequently receives a grant of probate or administration, the proceeding shall be deemed to have been properly constituted from its commencement.

Proceeding Brought by or against Estate

(2) A proceeding commenced by or against the estate of a deceased person,

    (a) by naming "the estate of A.B., deceased", "the personal representative of A.B., deceased" or any similar designation; or

    (b) in which the wrong person is named as the personal representative,

shall not be treated as a nullity, but the court may order that the proceeding be continued by or against the proper executor or administrator of the deceased or against a litigation administrator appointed for the purpose of the proceeding, and the title of the proceeding shall be amended accordingly.

Proceeding Commenced in the Name of or against a Deceased Person

(3) A proceeding commenced in the name of or against a person who has died before its commencement shall not be treated as a nullity, but the

court may order that the proceeding be continued by or against the executor or administrator or a litigation administrator appointed for the purpose of the proceeding and the title of the proceeding shall be amended accordingly.

Where There is an Executor or Administrator and a Litigation Administrator has been Appointed

(4) **Where it appears that a deceased person for whom a litigation administrator has been appointed had an executor or administrator at the time of the appointment, the proceeding shall not be treated as a nullity, but the court may order that the proceeding be continued against the executor or administrator and the title of the proceeding shall be amended accordingly.**

General Power

(5) **A proceeding by or against a deceased person or an estate shall not be treated as a nullity because it was not properly constituted, but the court may order that the proceeding be reconstituted by analogy to the provisions of this rule.**

Stay of Proceeding until Properly Constituted

(6) **No further step in a proceeding referred to in subrule (2), (3), (4) or (5) shall be taken until it is properly constituted and, unless it is properly constituted within a reasonable time, the court may dismiss the proceeding or make such other order as is just.**

Terms May be Imposed

(7) **On making an order under this rule, the court may impose such terms as are just, including a term that an executor or an administrator shall not be personally liable in respect of any part of the estate of a deceased person that the executor or administrator has distributed or otherwise dealt with in good faith while not aware that a proceeding had been commenced against the deceased person or the estate.**

Raiz v. Vaserbakh (1986), 9 C.P.C. (2d) 141, 22 E.T.R. 252 (Ont. Dist. Ct.).

The court refused to appoint a litigation administrator to bring an action regarding injuries suffered by the deceased in a motor vehicle accident. The proposed litigation guardian should instead seek letters of administration. The court is cautious in granting authority to prosecute an action without the burden of administering the estate and being answerable therefor.

Clancy v. Fransky (1985), 52 O.R. (2d) 793, 5 C.P.C. (2d) 209, 21 E.T.R. 85, 12 O.A.C. 208 (Div. Ct.).

Relief was granted under rule 9.03(1) in an action commenced prior to the Rules of Civil Procedure coming into force.

Gibson v. Oliver (1983), 32 C.P.C. 5, 13 E.T.R. 97 (Ont. H.C.).

A counterclaim against the spouse of a deceased person who was neither executrix nor administratrix of the deceased's estate was dismissed as a nullity.

Morin v. Hawker (1978), 19 O.R. (2d) 648, 86 D.L.R. (3d) 156 (H.C.).

An action commenced by a litigation administrator which ought to have been commenced by a personal representative is not a nullity.

Gray v. Saunders (1975), 10 O.R. (2d) 776 (Co. Ct.).

Where an originating process names a deceased person as defendant, the date of commencement of the action for limitation period purposes is the date of filing of the originating process, not the date the originating process is validated under the *Trustee Act*, R.S.O. 1970, c. 470, s. 38 [*now rule 9.03(3) - Authors*].

Smith v. Smith (1973), 3 O.R. (2d) 231 (H.C.).

Commencement of an action against an estate is an irregularity which can be corrected notwithstanding the expiry of a limitation period.

RULE 10   REPRESENTATION ORDER

Highlights

Situations can arise where the outcome of litigation (of the type described in rule 10.01) may have an impact on persons who are not before the court and who cannot be brought into the litigation because they are unborn or unascertained, or because they cannot be readily found or served. The former Rules dealt with this problem by providing that in certain circumstances the court could appoint someone to represent these absent persons. Those Rules further provided that in some situations the persons so represented were bound by the judgment and in other situations the represented persons were bound, except where the judgment was obtained by fraud or non-disclosure. Rule 10 deals with the underlying problem in the same way, but the circumstances in which the court may make a representation order are broadened: see rule 10.01. In addition, the Rule gives the court a more general power to determine when represented persons will not be bound by the resulting judgment: see rule 10.03.

Former Rules: Rules 76-79, 91.

REPRESENTATION OF AN INTERESTED PERSON WHO CANNOT BE ASCERTAINED

Proceedings in which Order May be Made

10.01(1) In a proceeding concerning,

(a) the interpretation of a deed, will, contract or other instrument, or the interpretation of a statute, order in council, regulation or municipal by-law or resolution;

(b) the determination of a question arising in the administration of an estate or trust;

(c) the approval of a sale, purchase, settlement or other transaction;

(d) the approval of an arrangement under the *Variation of Trusts Act*;

(e) the administration of the estate of a deceased person; or

(f) any other matter where it appears necessary or desirable to make an order under this subrule,

a judge may by order appoint one or more persons to represent any person or class of persons who are unborn or unascertained or who have a present, future, contingent or unascertained interest in or may be affected by the proceeding and who cannot be readily ascertained, found or served.

Order Binds Represented Persons

(2) Where an appointment is made under subrule (1), an order in the proceeding is binding on a person or class so represented, subject to rule 10.03.

Settlement Affecting Persons who are not Parties

(3) Where in a proceeding referred to in subrule (1) a settlement is proposed and some of the persons interested in the settlement are not parties to the proceeding, but,

(a) those persons are represented by a person appointed under subrule (1) who assents to the settlement; or

(b) there are other persons having the same interest who are parties to the proceeding and assent to the settlement,
the judge, if satisfied that the settlement will be for the benefit of the interested persons who are not parties and that to require service on them would cause undue expense or delay, may approve the settlement on behalf of those persons.

(4) A settlement approved under subrule (3) binds the interested persons who are not parties, subject to rule 10.03.

Toronto Fire Department Pensioners' Assn. v. Fitzsimmons (1995), 40 C.P.C. (3d) 298 (Ont. Gen. Div.).
A motion for a representation order pursuant to rule 10.01(a) and (b) was dismissed where the applicant corporation was not an appropriate representative in the circumstances of the case.

Bruce (Twp.) v. Thornburn (1986), 57 O.R. (2d) 77, 17 O.A.C. 127 (Div. Ct.).
A representation order under rule 10.01 was reversed on appeal where no attempt was made to determine the essential characteristics of the members of the class and to limit the class to persons having those characteristics. The class was inappropriately broad.

REPRESENTATION OF A DECEASED PERSON

10.02 Where it appears to a judge that the estate of a deceased person has an interest in a matter in question in the proceeding and there is no executor or administrator of the estate, the judge may order that the proceeding continue in the absence of a person representing the estate of the deceased person or may by order appoint a person to represent the estate for the purposes of the proceeding, and an order in the proceeding binds the estate of the deceased person, subject to rule 10.03, as if the executor or administrator of the estate of that person had been a party to the proceeding.

Hanton v. White, [1956] O.W.N. 775 (Master).
An executor named in a will which had not yet been probated was held to be a personal representative of the deceased.

McKillop v. McKillop, [1944] O.W.N. 733 (H.C.).
It is improper to appoint a person as a personal representative without his consent.

Re Martin and McAuley, [1947] O.W.N. 270 (H.C.).
Discussion of correct procedure where the most suitable personal representative refuses to act.

RELIEF FROM BINDING EFFECT OF ORDER

10.03 Where a person or an estate is bound by reason of a representation order made under subrule 10.01(1) or rule 10.02, an approval under subrule 10.01(3) or an order that the proceeding continue made under rule 10.02, a judge may order in the same or a subsequent proceeding that the person or estate not be bound where the judge is satisfied that,

(a) the order or approval was obtained by fraud or non-disclosure of material facts;

(b) the interests of the person or estate were different from those represented at the hearing; or

(c) for some other sufficient reason the order or approval should be set aside.

RULE 11 TRANSFER OR TRANSMISSION OF INTEREST

Highlights

Rule 11 provides the procedure for the continuation of proceedings where a transfer or transmission of interest or liability of a party has occurred, *e.g.* through death, assignment or bankruptcy. The necessary "order to continue" the proceedings can be obtained on requisition from a registrar without notice and must then be served on all parties. The form of order (Form 11A) provides that the title of the continued proceeding is to show only the name of the new party and not the name of the former party.

Former Rules: Rules 299-305.

EFFECT OF TRANSFER OR TRANSMISSION

11.01 Where at any stage of a proceeding the interest or liability of a party is transferred or transmitted to another person by assignment, bankruptcy, death or other means, the proceeding shall be stayed until an order to continue the proceeding by or against the other person has been obtained.

Income Trust Co. v. Kelleher (1996), 26 O.R. (3d) 641 (Gen. Div.).
The purpose of Rule 11 is to overcome the common law rule that a right of action, whether in contract or tort, died with the claimant.

ORDER TO CONTINUE

11.02(1) Where a transfer or transmission of the interest or liability of a party takes place while a proceeding is pending, any interested person may, on filing an affidavit verifying the transfer or transmission of interest or liability, obtain on requisition from the registrar an order to continue (Form 11A), without notice to any other party.

(2) An order to continue shall be served forthwith on every other party.

Transmission of Interest by Death of Party

Etkin v. Ont. (1984), 40 C.P.C. 227 (Ont. Master).
Where the plaintiff died, her claim under the *Family Law Reform Act* for loss of care and guidance did not survive and her personal representative was not permitted to continue the action.

Wilson v. Morrow (1977), 17 O.R. (2d) 298, 4 C.P.C. 172, 2 E.T.R. 34 (H.C.).
Consideration of situation where the plaintiffs obtained a revivor order prior to judgment but failed to seek the substitution of the names of the executors for that of the deceased defendant until after judgment.

Matyus v. Papp (1973), 1 O.R. (2d) 54 (Master).
Where a plaintiff died after the issuance of an originating process but before service thereof, service was set aside.

Courtemanche v. Germain (1973), 1 O.R. (2d) 12 (Master).
Where a defendant dies after the issuance of an originating process, a subsequent order extending the time for service made prior to an order to continue is a mere irregularity capable of being corrected.

Thrush v. Read, [1949] O.R. 757 (H.C.).

The death of a party while judgment is reserved does not normally affect the rights of the parties.

Lunn v. Barber, [1948] O.W.N. 213 (Master).

In an action for payment of promissory notes made in a foreign jurisdiction, the court held that the foreign administratrix may continue an action originally commenced by the deceased without taking out ancilliary letters of administration in Ontario.

Tansill v. King, [1947] O.W.N. 807 (Master).

A foreign executor cannot sue in Ontario for the recovery of moneys due the testator's estate without first obtaining probate in Ontario.

Transmission of Interest by Assignment

Sydlo Inc. v. Mixing Equipment Co. (No. 3) (1987), 18 C.P.C. (2d) 79, 22 O.A.C. 231 (*sub nom. Love v. Mixing Equipment Co.*) (Div. Ct.).

An order to continue based on an assignment of the cause of action by a corporation to an individual for the purpose of avoiding an order requiring the corporation to post security for costs was held to be an abuse of process. The court permitted the order to continue to stand provided the plaintiff posted security for costs.

De Courcy v. Di Tursi Const. Ltd., [1964] 1 O.R. 15 (Master).

Where an interest in property which is the subject-matter of the litigation is transferred after the action is commenced, the transferee should be added by an order to continue rather than being added as an original party.

Roscar Invt. Ltd. v. Selkirk, [1960] O.W.N. 465 (Master).

Where an interest has been the subject of several assignments, orders to continue are not necessary in respect of intermediate assignors.

Transmission of Interest by Bankruptcy

Hall-Chem Inc. v. Vulcan Packaging Inc. (1994), 21 O.R. (3d) 89, 28 C.B.R. (3d) 161, 120 D.L.R. (4th) 552, 75 O.A.C. 74 (C.A.).

Where an appellant whose claim was dismissed at first instance makes an assignment in bankruptcy while the appeal is pending, the trustee in bankruptcy should comply with Rule 11.

Re Barton, [1970] 3 O.R. 624, 14 C.B.R. (N.S.) 125 (S.C.).

Discussion of appropriate order where the defendant becomes bankrupt.

Transmission of Interest — Miscellaneous

International Display & Lighting Group Ltd. v. R.A.E. Industrial Electronics Ltd. (1993), 15 C.P.C. (3d) 165 (Ont. Gen. Div.).

It is not necessary to revive a dissolved Ontario corporation to prosecute an action on behalf of the corporation; however, it is necessary to do so to enforce any judgment obtained.

Courtemanche v. Germain (1973), 1 O.R. (2d) 12 (Master).

Failure to amend the style of cause appropriately is a mere irregularity.

Boland v. McTaggart, [1961] O.W.N. 109 (Master).

A copy of the order to continue must be served on all parties.

Transmission of Interest - Time for Order

Easco Aluminum Corp. v. Jolub Const. Ltd. (1982), 31 C.P.C. 102 (Ont. Div. Ct.).

This provision does not contemplate the addition of a party after the action has been tried and completed.

FAILURE TO OBTAIN ORDER TO CONTINUE ACTION

11.03 Where a transfer or transmission of the interest of a plaintiff takes place while an action is pending and no order to continue is obtained within a reasonable time, a defendant may move to have the action dismissed for delay, and rules 24.02 to 24.05 apply, with necessary modifications.

Loblaw Cos. v. Lido Industrial Products Ltd. (1993), 19 C.P.C. (3d) 183 (Ont. Gen. Div.).

An order to continue may be granted *nunc pro tunc*.

RULE 12   CLASS PROCEEDINGS AND OTHER REPRESENTATIVE PROCEEDINGS

Highlights

Until January 1, 1993, class actions in Ontario were available on an extremely limited basis pursuant to former Rule 12 (which essentially reproduced Rule 75 of the former Rules of Practice). On that date the situation changed dramatically with the introduction of Ontario's new class proceedings legislation, consisting of two Acts — the *Class Proceedings Act, 1992*, S.O. 1992, c. 6, which establishes the procedure for class proceedings, and the *Law Society Amendment Act (Class Proceedings Funding), 1992*, S.O. 1992, c. 7, which provides a funding mechanism for class actions. In addition, a regulation has been made under the latter Act (O. Reg. 771/92) and the Class Proceedings Committee has issued its Practice Direction #1 (February 22, 1993) and Practice Direction #2 (September 20, 1995).

At the same time as the new class proceedings legislation came into effect, the former Rule 12 (Representative Proceedings) was revoked and a new Rule 12 enacted. The procedure to be followed in class proceedings is to be found partly in the *Class Proceedings Act, 1992* and partly in the Rules generally. (Section 35 of the Act expressly provides that the "rules of court apply to class proceedings".) Hence, it is not the function of the new Rule 12 to provide any comprehensive procedure applicable to class proceedings, but rather to provide supplementary provisions applicable to class proceedings and to rationalize the operation of the Rules of Civil Procedure generally to the conduct of class proceedings.

Practice directions. The Class Proceedings Committee's Practice Directions #1 and #2 are reproduced below.

Related case law. Briefs of cases under the *Class Proceedings Act* are reproduced following rule 12.05.

Recent amendments. An amendment to rule 76.01(1) makes it clear that the new Simplified Procedure under Rule 76 does not apply to class actions.

Cross-Reference: For the text of the *Class Proceedings Act* and the *Law Society Amendment Act* and further commentary, see the companion volume, *Forms, Case Management Guide and Special Materials.*

CLASS PROCEEDINGS COMMITTEE
PRACTICE DIRECTION #1

Purpose of the Class Proceedings Committee

1. The Class Proceedings Committee (the "Committee") has been established under the *Law Society Amendment Act (Class Proceedings Funding), 1992*, S.O. 1992, c. 7, to determine whether plaintiffs in class proceedings should receive financial support from the Class Proceedings Fund (the "Fund") and the amount of such support.

How to Contact the Committee

2. The Committee's address is Suite 2210, 20 Queen Street West, Toronto, M5H 3R3, and its telephone number is 595-1425. [*Authors' Note:* the Committee's fax number is 598-1526.]

How to Prepare an Application

3. Section 3 of O. Reg. 771/92 sets out the materials required to be included in the first application. The Committee requests that the materials be bound into a Class Proceeding Funding Application Record with tab numbers corresponding to the paragraph numbers of

subsection 3(1) of the regulation. If considered helpful, material under a numbered tab may be subdivided under tabs bearing the number and a letter (e.g. Tabs 5a, 5b, etc.).

4. With respect to Tab 11 (corresponding to paragraph 11 of s. 3(1)), the Committee is interested in knowing the amount, if any, of funds the applicant has or expects to raise to supplement any funding granted by the Committee taking into account the nature of the case and the circumstances of the plaintiff.

5. The first application record should also contain:

(a) a tab (Tab 16) containing a list of the individual lawyers expected to participate in the prosecution of the case, a description of their experience and qualifications, a statement whether a contingency fee agreement has been entered into under s. 33 of the *Class Proceedings Act, 1992*, and an estimate of the aggregate number of hours the applicant's solicitors expect to and are prepared to devote to the case;

(b) a tab (Tab 17) containing material addressing the issue of th defendant's ability to pay any judgment and comply with any non-monetary relief which may ultimately be granted against it, and if it appears the defendant will not be able to pay or comply, explaining why financial support should nevertheless be granted;

(c) a tab (Tab 18) containing the plan or draft plan which has been or is intended to be filed pursuant to s. 5(1)(e)(ii) of the *Class Proceedings Act, 1992*;

(d) a tab (Tab 19) containing a budget regarding disbursements expected to be required up to and including trial; and

(e) a final tab (Tab 20) containing an Executive Summary concerning the application.

6. The materials for subsequent applications, if any, should be bound into a First (*or as the case may be*) Supplementary Class Proceeding Funding Application Record, should not duplicate the contents of any previous record, should be organized under tabs continuing the numbering sequence of the immediately preceding record, and should contain:

(a) tabs containing whatever materials the applicant thinks necessary;

(b) a tab containing copies of any pleadings filed and orders made by the court in the proceedings which have not already been included in a previous record;

(c) a tab containing a concise report on the status of the class proceeding including an estimated timetable;

(d) a tab containing written submissions concerning the application; and

(e) a final tab containing an Executive Summary.

7. Paragraph 5 of subsection 3(1) of O. Reg. 771/92 requires a copy of the pleadings be included in the application. It should be noted that this includes the statement of defence. The Committee will not consider an application regarding an action to be complete unless the statement of defence is included (or the defendant has been noted in default). Where the defendant does not deliver a statement of defence but rather brings a motion of any kind, it is sufficient to include a copy of the motion record in lieu of the statement of defence. Where the court proceeding has been commenced by Notice of Application, it is sufficient to include a copy of the respondent's Notice of Appearance and any other materials filed with the court by the respondent.

Confidentiality

8. Subsection 3(1) of O. Reg. 771/92 requires certain confidential documents or information, including legal opinions, to be included in the application. The Committee expects and encourages full and frank disclosure and will protect the confidentiality of such materials except as may be compelled by law. When information is disclosed by the Committee in the course of giving a direction to the Board of Trustees of The Law Foundation of Ontario (the "Board"), and when information is disclosed by the Committee in the course of its annual report to the

Law Foundation, and in the event reasons for decision are issued by the Committee, disclosure of specific confidential information will be avoided.

How to Submit an Application

9. Six fully legible copies of the record should be mailed, couriered or hand delivered to the Committee's office. It is the applicant's responsibility to ensure proper delivery; however, the Secretary will acknowledge receipt of all records in writing.

How Applications will be Considered

10. With respect to the applicant's first application, after a complete application is received the Committee will advise the applicant's solicitor of the time and place of the Committee's meeting to consider the application. It is expected the meetings will be held at the Committee's office approximately once per month and may occur in either an afternoon or an evening session. The Committee will meet *in camera* with the applicant and the applicant's solicitor. The applicant's solicitor may make oral submissions not exceeding 20 minutes. The Committee will then discuss the application with the applicant and the applicant's solicitor. The Committee will reserve its decision and advise the applicant of its decision in writing in due course. Applications by conference call may be arranged if appropriate in the circumstances. The Committee's meetings will not be open to the public.

11. With respect to subsequent applications, the applicant may make written submissions as described in paragraph 6 but may not make oral submissions unless leave to do so is granted in special circumstances on written application for that purpose or on the Committee's own motion. The Committee will advise the applicant of its decision in writing in due course.

How Funding is Received

12. In the event an application is granted in whole or in part the Committee will provide a written direction to the Board to make payments to the applicant's solicitor. A copy of the direction will be provided to the applicant's solicitor. The Board, not the Committee, is responsible for disbursing the funds and the requirements of O. Reg. 771/92 should be considered in that regard. The Board's address is Suite 2210, 20 Queen Street West, Toronto, M5H 3R3, telephone number is 598-1550, and fax number is 598-1526.

If Funding is Refused

13. Where an application is refused, the applicant may re-apply if so desired in which case paragraphs 6 and 11 govern.

Levy Against Awards and Settlement Funds

14. If an applicant is financially supported by the Committee and the class proceeding is successful, the amount advanced to the plaintiff from the Fund plus 10% of the settlement funds or monetary award is to be paid to the Fund. Pursuant to rule 12.05 of the Rules of Civil Procedure payment of this levy will be addressed in the order approving the settlement or in the judgment.

Applications for Defendant's Costs

15. Applications regarding payments of defendant's costs are made to the Board, not to the Committee.

Dated the 22nd day of February 1993.

> Anne Molloy,
> Chair
> Class Proceedings Committee

CLASS PROCEEDINGS COMMITTEE
PRACTICE DIRECTION #2

Defendants' Submissions Regarding Funding Applications

1. An application for funding brought by a representative plaintiff (the "Plaintiff") under s. 59.3 of the *Law Society Amendment Act (Class Proceedings Funding) 1992* S.O. 1992, c. 7 is not an adversarial proceeding and the Act does not provide the defendant in the class proceeding (the "Defendant") with a right to oppose the application. However the Class Proceedings Committee (the "Committee") does have a broad discretion under s. 59.3(4)(e) to consider any matter relevant to the application for funding and is at liberty to seek information from any available source including the Defendant.

Plaintiff's Consent Required

2. The Committee may ask the Plaintiff to consent to the Committee requesting the Defendant to provide written submissions subject to certain safeguards to protect the Plaintiff and the funding process.

3. Without the express consent of the Plaintiff the Committee will never:
(a) request submissions from a Defendant;
(b) review unsolicited submissions from a Defendant; or
(c) confirm or deny to a Defendant that the Plaintiff has submitted an application.

Acknowledgment and Undertaking

4. If the Plaintiff consents to the Committee requesting written submissions from a Defendant, the Committee will request the Defendant to file the submissions together with a written Acknowledgment and Undertaking directed to both the Committee and the Plaintiff agreeing to specific conditions which the Committee considers appropriate in the circumstances and which may include the following:
(a) An acknowledgment that the Defendant will not be entitled to make oral submissions to the Committee;
(b) An acknowledgment that the Defendant will not be entitled to any information about, or materials from, the Plaintiff's application;
(c) An acknowledgment that the Defendant's written submissions will not be treated as confidential, a copy of the Defendant's submissions will be provided to the Plaintiff for response, and the Defendant will not be informed of the Plaintiff's response or be given a right of reply;
(d) An undertaking that, in consideration of the delay in the determination of the Plaintiff's application for funding which may result from the Defendant's submissions, the Defendant will consent to any extensions of time for the certification motion, or any other steps in the class proceeding, requested by the Plaintiff until the Committee has either granted or refused the Plaintiff's application;

(e) An undertaking that, in consideration of the extra expense to the Plaintiff which may result from responding to the Defendant's submissions, the Defendant will consent to the discontinuance of the class proceeding without costs in the event the Plaintiff's application for funding is refused and the Plaintiff subsequently seeks leave from the court to discontinue the class proceeding; and

(f) An acknowledgment that the committee's request for written submissions from the Defendant, and the Defendant's filing of written submissions, do not confer any rights whatsoever on the Defendant, such as, without limitation, the right to a copy of the Committee's reasons for decision or the right to apply for judicial review of the Committee's decision.

Form of Defendant's Written Submissions

5. The Defendant's written submissions may include any materials it considers relevant and should be organized appropriately and bound into a Class Proceeding Funding Defendant's Record (the "Defendant's Record"). Six copies of the Defendant's Record should be provided to the Committee at Suite 2210, 20 Queen Street West, Toronto, M5H 3R3 together with proof of service of one copy on the solicitors for the Plaintiff.

Communication of Decision

6. In a case where the Defendant is requested to file, and does file, written submissions, the Committee shall advise the Defendant of the Committee's decision whether to grant or deny funding but the Committee will not disclose to the Defendant any reasons for decision or the amount of any funding granted. In the event the Committee adjourns or temporarily stays the Plaintiff's application for the purpose of permitting the Plaintiff to take certain steps or provide certain information, or for any other reason, the Committee will not advise the Defendant of such adjournment or temporary stay or the reason therefor.

Dated this 20th day of September 1995.

Michael McGowan,
Chair
Class Proceedings Committee

DEFINITIONS

12.01 In rules 12.02 to 12.06,
"Act" means the *Class Proceedings Act, 1992*;
"Foundation" means The Law Foundation of Ontario;
"Fund" means the Class Proceedings Fund of the Foundation. [re-en. O. Reg. 770/92, s. 5; am O. Reg. 465/93, s. 2]

TITLE OF PROCEEDING

12.02(1) In a proceeding commenced under subsection 2(1) of the Act, the title of the proceeding shall include, after the names of the parties, "Proceeding under the *Class Proceedings Act, 1992*".

(2) In a proceeding referred to in section 3 or 4 of the Act, the notice of motion for an order certifying the proceeding, the order certifying it and all

subsequent documents shall include, after the names of the parties, "Proceeding under the *Class Proceedings Act, 1992*". [re-en. O. Reg. 770/92, s. 5]

DISCOVERY OF CLASS MEMBERS

12.03(1) For the purpose of subrule 31.11(1) (reading in examination), a class member who is examined for discovery under subsection 15(2) of the Act is examined in addition to the party.

(2) Rule 31.10 (discovery of non-parties) and clause 34.15(1)(b) (sanctions for default or misconduct) do not apply when a class member is examined for discovery under subsection 15(2) of the Act. [en. O. Reg. 770/92, s. 5]

COSTS

Application of rule

12.04(1) This rule applies to class proceedings in which the plaintiff or applicant has received financial support from the Fund.

Rights of Foundation

(2) No order for costs or assessment of costs shall be made unless the Foundation has had notice and an opportunity to present evidence and make submissions in respect of the costs.

(3) The Foundation is a party for the purpose of an appeal in relation to costs.

Failure to Accept Defendant's Offer

(4) Subrule 49.10(2) (costs consequences) does not apply. [en. O. Reg. 770/92, s. 5]

CONTENTS OF JUDGMENTS AND ORDERS

12.05(1) A judgment in a class proceeding or an order approving a settlement, discontinuance or abandonment of a class proceeding under section 29 of the Act shall contain directions with respect to,

(a) the distribution of amounts awarded under section 24 or 25 of the Act, and the costs of distribution;

(b) the payment of amounts owing under an enforceable agreement made under section 32 of the Act between a solicitor and a representative party;

(c) the payment of the costs of the proceeding; and

(d) the payment of any levy in favour of the Fund under clause 59.5(1)(g) of the *Law Society Act..*

(2) An order certifying two or more proceedings as a class proceeding under section 3 of the Act or decertifying a class proceeding under section 10 of the Act shall contain directions with respect to pleadings and other procedural matters. [en. O. Reg. 770/92, s. 5]

[The cases in Part 1 were decided under the Class Proceedings Act, 1992. References in the headings are to sections of that Act — Authors.]

Authors' Note on Organization of Cases

Cases relevant to class proceedings have been organized as follows:

Interpretation of Act — s. 1

Abdool v. Anaheim Management Ltd. (1993), 15 O.R. (3d) 39, 16 C.P.C. (3d) 141 (Gen. Div.), affirmed (1995), 21 O.R. (3d) 453, 31 C.P.C. (3d) 197, 121 D.L.R. (4th) 496, 78 O.A.C. 377 (Div. Ct.).

This Act is remedial and should be given a broad, purposive interpretation.

Bendall v. McGhan Medical Corp. (1993), 14 O.R. (3d) 734, 16 C.P.C. (3d) 156, 106 D.L.R. (4th) 339 (Gen. Div.).

1. The three major goals of this Act are judicial economy, increased access to the courts, and modification of behaviour of actual or potential wrongdoers.
2. Cases under Rule 23 of the U.S. Federal Rules of Civil Procedure are helpful; however, in some ways the U.S. Rule is more restrictive than this Act.

Disposition of Certification Motions

Nantais v. Telectronics Proprietary (Canada) Ltd. (1995), 25 O.R. (3d) 331, 40 C.P.C. (3d) 245, 127 D.L.R. (4th) 552 (Gen. Div.), leave to appeal refused 25 O.R. (3d) 331 at 347, 40 C.P.C. (3d) 263, 129 D.L.R. (4th) 110 (Gen. Div.).

The court certified a class action on behalf of the recipients of allegedly defective pacemakers.

Maxwell v. MLG Ventures Ltd. (1995), 7 C.C.L.S. 155 (Ont. Gen. Div.).

The court certified a class action by former shareholders who had sold shares based on alleged misrepresentations in an offering circular.

Abdool v. Anaheim Management Ltd. (1995), 21 O.R. (3d) 453, 31 C.P.C. (3d) 197, 121 D.L.R. (4th) 496, 78 O.A.C. 377 (Div. Ct.).

The court refused to certify a class action by condominium investors where there were numerous individual issues, individual discovery of class members was likely, and the class members' claims were individually viable. The goals of the *Class Proceedings Act* are (1) access to justice, (2) judicial economy, and (3) modification of behaviour.

Rogers Broadcasting Ltd. v. Alexander (1994), 25 C.P.C. (3d) 159, 4 C.C.L.S. 227 (Ont. Gen. Div. [Commercial List]).

Where a corporation applied under the *Canada business Corporations Act* to fix the fair value of shares of shareholders who dissented to a proposed amalgamation, a dissenting shareholder made a counter-application seeking damages for oppression and certification of a class proceeding on behalf of all minority shareholders contending that the amalgamation and subsequent privatization was effected in a manner which was oppressive and unfairly prejudicial to the minority. In refusing certification it was held that (1) since the non-dissenting minority shareholders had made no complaint about oppression and unfairness it would be wrong to include them in any class; (2) since there was little evidence of oppression or unfairness except with regard to the representative plaintiff, oppression was not a common issue; and (3) even if there was a common issue the preferable procedure to resolve the claims of the dissenting shareholders was to proceed with the valuation pursuant to s. 190(15) of the *CBCA* as there was no judicial economy to be gained by a class proceeding where a mechanism was in place for valuation under the *CBCA*.

Sutherland v. Canadian Red Cross Society (1994), 17 O.R. (3d) 645, 21 C.P.C. (3d) 137, 112 D.L.R. (4th) 504 (Gen. Div.).

Certification was refused in a proposed class action to recover damages for people who had contracted HIV as a result of receiving contaminated blood and blood products. Certification was refused on the ground that (1) the claims of the class members did not raise common issues; (2) a class action was not the preferable procedure to resolve the controversy; (3) a multitude of disparate third party claims would make the proceeding unduly complicated and unmanageable; and (4) the named plaintiff was not an adequate representative plaintiff for the class.

Peppiatt v. Nicol (1993), 16 O.R. (3d) 133, 20 CP.C. (3d) 272 (Gen. Div.).

A class action commenced on behalf of the equity members of a golf club was certified where the representative plaintiffs had no conflict of interest, had been widely selected, had retained experienced counsel, and had demonstrated a willingness and ability to act. Without certification, a large number of members would be denied access to the legal system.

Bendall v. McGhan Medical Corp. (1993), 14 O.R. (3d) 734, 16 C.P.C. (3d) 156, 106 D.L.R. (4th) 339 (Gen. Div.).

A class action commenced on behalf of persons who had received silicone gel breast implants was certified as a class proceeding. A large number of women would not be able to access the judicial system except by way of class action, and the cost of individual litigation would be prohibitive. A class action would avoid that problem because of the system of regulated contingent fees.

Certification of Class Proceedings — Generally

Peppiatt v. Nicol (1993), 16 O.R. (3d) 133, 20 C.P.C. (3d) 272 (Gen. Div.).

If the court should err in determining a certification motion, it should do so on the side of protecting people who have a right of access to the courts.

Bendall v. McGhan Medical Corp. (1993), 14 O.R. (3d) 734, 16 C.P.C. (3d) 156, 106 D.L.R. (4th) 339 (Gen. Div.).

1. In case of doubt, the court should err on the side of granting certification and protecting people who have a right of access to the courts.
2. Certification is a fluid, flexible procedural process. It is conditional and is always subject to decertification.

Certificate of Class Proceedings — Affidavits and Cross-examinations

Edwards v. Law Society of Upper Canada (1995), 40 C.P.C. (3d) 316 (Ont. Gen. Div.).

A motion to strike out affidavits filed in support of a motion for certification of an action as a class proceeding was allowed where the affidavits: (1) contained the reasons for judgment in a quasi-criminal proceeding; and (2) included an exhibit for which privilege was claimed and evidence as to information and belief where the source was counsel who was attempting to shield himself from cross-examination.

Certification of Class Proceedings — Miscellaneous

Sutherland v. Canadian Red Cross Society (1994), 17 O.R. (3d) 645, 21 C.P.C. (3d) 137, 112 D.L.R. (4th) 504 (Gen. Div.).

The court declined to rule on an argument that the action was statute-barred where no separate motion was brought under Rule 21 in that regard. A certification motion includes affidavit evidence which may be inappropriate to mix with a Rule 21 motion.

Certification of Class Proceedings — Disclosing a Cause of Action — s. 5(1)(a)

Peppiatt v. Nicol (1993), 16 O.R. (3d) 133, 20 C.P.C. (3d) 272 (Gen. Div.).

As under Rule 21, the test for disclosing a cause of action is whether it is plain and obvious to the court the claim could not succeed.

Abdool v. Anaheim Management Ltd. (1993), 15 O.R. (3d) 39, 16 C.P.C. (3d) 141 (Gen. Div.), affirmed (1995), 21 O.R. (3d) 453, 31 C.P.C. (3d) 197, 121 D.L.R. (4th) 496, 78 O.A.C. 377 (Div. Ct.).

This Act does not create an explicit test to determine the existence of a cause of action, however cases under Rule 21 are helpful in that regard. No evidence should be referred to to determine whether a cause of action exists.

Bendall v. McGhan Medical Corp. (1993), 14 O.R. (3d) 734, 16 C.P.C. (3d) 156, 106 D.L.R. (4th) 339 Gen. Div.).

In cases involving multiple plaintiffs and defendants it is not necessary that each plaintiff have a cause of action against each defendant so long as each defendant has a cause of action asserted against it by at least one plaintiff.

Certification of Class Proceedings — Existence of Identifiable Class — s. 5(1)(b)

Nantais v. Telectronics Proprietary (Canada) Ltd. (1995), 25 O.R. (3d) 331, 40 C.P.C. (3d) 245, 127 D.L.R. (4th) 552 (Gen. Div.), leave to appeal refused 25 O.R. (3d) 331 at 347, 40 C.P.C. (3d) 263, 129 D.L.R. (4th) 110 (Gen. Div.).

A nation wide class was certified. For the reasons given in *Morguard Investments Ltd. v. De Savoye*, [1990] 3 S.C.R. 1077, and to accomplish the goals of the *Class Proceedings Act*, it is eminently sensible that the question of liability be determined as far as possible once and for all for all Canadians.

Peppiatt v. Nicol (1993), 16 O.R. (3d) 133, 20 C.P.C. (3d) 272 (Gen. Div.).

It is not necessary that the precise numbers or identities of the class members be known if it is clear there is an identifiable class of more than two persons.

Bendall v. McGhan Medical Corp. (1993), 14 O.R. (3d) 734, 16 C.P.C. (3d) 156, 106 D.L.R. (4th) 339 (Gen. Div.).

This court granted certification notwithstanding that only two class members had been specifically identified where there were potentialy many more class members not yet identified. If it developed that there were only a handful of class members that court could consider decertification.

Certification of Class Proceedings — Common Issues — s. 5(1)(c)

Maxwell v. MLG Ventures Ltd. (1995), 7 C.C.L.S. 155 (Ont. Gen. Div.).

Where there were clearly common issues regarding misrepresentations to shareholders in an offering circular, individual issues concerning whether some class members had actual knowledge of the matters not disclosed in the offering circular could be dealt with by way of affidavits from class members stating whether they had such knowledge.

Abdool v. Anaheim Management Ltd. (1995), 21 O.R. (3d) 453, 31 C.P.C. (3d) 197, 121 D.L.R. (4th) 496, 78 O.A.C. 377 (Div. Ct.).

In *obiter* the court stated that notwithstanding the mandatory language of s. 5(1) of the *Class Proceedings Act* the court has a discretion not to certify a proceeding which meets all of the requirements of s. 5(1). The court may consider the individual issues involved in the litigation, the purposes of the Act, and the rights of the parties.

Rogers Broadcasting Ltd. v. Alexander (1994), 25 C.P.C. (3d) 159, 4 C.C.L.S. 227 (Ont. Gen. Div. [Commercial List]).

The court held that conduct which allegedly oppressed minority shareholders contrary to the *Canada Business Corporations Act* did not constitute a common issue.

Sutherland v. Canadian Red Cross Society (1994), 17 O.R. (3d) 645, 21 C.P.C. (3d) 137, 112 D.L.R. (4th) 504 (Gen. Div.).

It is not necessary that all common issues be cast in stone at the certification stage provided it is clear some common issue exists. Without a common issue there can be no certification.

Bendall v. McGhan Medical Corp. (1993), 14 O.R. (3d) 734, 16 C.P.C. (3d) 156, 106 D.L.R. (4th) 339 (Gen. Div.).

Unlike Rule 23 of the U.S. Federal Rules of Civil Procedure, this Act does not require that the common issues predominate over the individual issues.

Certification of Class Proceedings — Preferable Procedure — s. 5(1)(d)

Maxwell v. MLG Ventures Ltd. (1995), 7 C.C.L.S. 155 (Ont. Gen. Div.).

The possibility of individual issues constituting a defence to the claims of some class members did not mean that a class action was not the preferable procedure. The individual issues could be resolved by class members filing affidavits.

Abdool v. Anaheim Management Ltd. (1995), 21 O.R. (3d) 453, 31 C.P.C. (3d) 197, 121 D.L.R. (4th) 496, 78 O.A.C. 377 (Div. Ct.).

In considering whether a class action is the preferable procedure the court should examine the three major goals of the Act namely (1) access to justice, (2) judicial economy, and (3) modification of behaviour. The court held that a class action was not the preferable procedure where none of these goals would be advanced by certification.

Rogers Broadcasting Ltd. v. Alexander (1994), 25 C.P.C. (3d) 159, 4 C.C.L.S. 227 (Ont. Gen. Div. [Commercial List]).

A class proceeding is not the "preferable procedure" to resolve the claims of dissenting shareholders who have a right to participate in a valuation procedure under s. 190(15) of the *Canada Business Corporations Act*.

Certification of Class Proceedings — Fair and Adequate Representation — s. 5(1)(e)(i)

Maxwell v. MLG Ventures Ltd. (1995), 7 C.C.L.S. 155 (Ont. Gen. Div.).

Lack of a complete knowledge of issues involved in the class proceeding did not mean that the representative plaintiff could not adequately represent the class. The representative had adequate knowledge and was clearly able to instruct counsel.

Abdool v. Anaheim Management Ltd. (1995), 21 O.R. (3d) 453, 31 C.P.C. (3d) 197, 121 D.L.R. (4th) 496, 78 O.A.C. 377 (Div. Ct.).

The class representative need not be typical of class members provided he or she has no conflict of interest and will fairly and adequately advance the class claims.

Sutherland v. Canadian Red Cross Society (1994), 17 O.R. (3d) 645, 21 C.P.C. (3d) 137, 112 D.L.R. (4th) 504 (Gen. Div.).

In *obiter* the court held the plaintiff was not a representative plaintiff because she did not have the characteristics of some of the class members. [*The Act does not require that a representative plaintiff represent all of the characteristics of the class. The key issue under s. 5(1)(e) is whether the plaintiff properly represents the interests of the class. — Authors.*]

Certification of Class Proceedings — Litigation Plan — s. 5(1)(e)(ii)

Maxwell v. MLG Ventures Ltd. (1995), 7 C.C.L.S. 155 (Ont. Gen. Div.).

The failure of the litigation plan to address several details could be corrected and did not prevent certification.

Peppiatt v. Nicol (1993), 16 O.R. (3d) 133, 20 C.P.C. (3d) 272 (Gen. Div.).

The plaintiff's plan may be expanded or fine-tuned as the action progresses.

Certification of Class Proceedings — Conflicts of Interest — s. 5(1)(e)(iii)

Maxwell v. MLG Ventures Ltd. (1995), 7 C.C.L.S. 155 (Ont. Gen. Div.).

The fact that class counsel had previously acted in a somewhat related matter did not put class counsel in a conflict and in any event could not possibly taint the representative plaintiff.

Certification of Class Proceedings — Subclasses — s. 5(2)

Peppiatt v. Royal Bank (1996), 7 W.D.C.P. (2d) 94 (Ont. Gen. Div.).

Where significant factual variations among the members of the class arose after certification as a class action, the court dismissed the defendant's motion to decertify the case and instead ordered the creation of subclasses to deal with the factual variations.

Bendall v. McGhan Medical Corp. (1993), 14 O.R. (3d) 734, 16 C.P.C. (3d) 156, 106 D.L.R. (4th) 339 (Gen. Div.).

Subclasses can be created after certification as the need arises.

Certification of Class Proceedings — Size of Class — s. 5(3)

Peppiatt v. Nicol (1993), 16 O.R. (3d) 133, 20 C.P.C. (3d) 272 (Gen. Div.).

It is not necessary that the precise numbers or identities of the class members be known if it is clear that there is an identifiable class of more than two persons.

Bendall v. McGhan Medical Corp. (1993), 14 O.R. (3d) 734, 16 C.P.C. (3d) 156, 106 D.L.R. (4th) 339 (Gen. Div.).

The court granted certification notwithstanding that only two class members had been specifically identified where there were potentially many more class members not yet identified. If it developed that there were only a handful of class members the court could consider decertification.

Certification of Class Proceedings — Adjournments — s. 5(4)

Abdool v. Anaheim Management (1993), 15 O.R. (3d) 39, 16 C.P.C. (3d) 141 (Gen. Div.), affirmed (1995), 21 O.R. (3d) 453, 31 C.P.C. (3d) 197, 121 D.L.R. (4th) 496, 78 O.A.C. 377 (Div. Ct.).

The court offered the plaintiff an opportunity for an adjournment where the defendant attacked the adequacy of the plaintiff's pleading.

Certain Matters not Bar to Certification — s. 6

Nantais v. Telectronics Proprietary (Canada) Ltd. (1995), 25 O.R. (3d) 331, 40 C.P.C. (3d) 245, 127 D.L.R. (4th) 552 (Gen. Div.), leave to appeal refused 25 O.R. (3d) 331 at 347, 40 C.P.C. (3d) 263, 129 D.L.R. (4th) 110 (Gen. Div.).

The interpretation of s. 6 in *Abdool v. Anaheim* may be incorrect. The word "any" in the opening of s. 6 should be interpreted as "any one or more" not "any one".

Abdool v. Anaheim Management Ltd. (1995), 21 O.R. (3d) 453, 31 C.P.C. (3d) 197, 121 D.L.R. (4th) 496, 78 O.A.C. 377 (Div. Ct.).

Where more than one of the five grounds mentioned in s. 6 are present the court may deny certification.

Opting out — s. 9

Nantais v. Telectronics Proprietary (Canada) Ltd. (1995), 25 O.R. (3d) 331, 40 C.P.C. (3d) 245, 127 D.L.R. (4th) 552 (Gen. Div.), leave to appeal refused, 25 O.R. (3d) 331 at 347, 40 C.P.C. (3d) 263, 129 D.L.R. (4th) 110 (Gen. Div.).

Where a list of names and addresses of class members was easily available, the court set a 90-day deadline for opting out.

Decertification — s. 10

Peppiatt v. Royal Bank (1996), 7 W.D.C.P. (2d) 94 (Ont. Gen. Div.).

Where significant factual variations among the members of the class arose after certification as a class action, the court dismissed the defendant's motion to decertify the case and instead ordered the creation of subclasses to deal with the factual variations.

Bendall v. McGhan Medical Corp. (1993), 14 O.R. (3d) 734, 16 C.P.C. (3d) 156, 106 D.L.R. (4th) 339 (Gen. Div.).

1. Certification is a fluid, flexible procedure process. It is conditional and is always subject to decertification.
2. The court granted certification notwithstanding that only two class members had been specifically identified where there were potentially many more class members not yet identified. If it developed that there were only a handful of class members the court could consider decertification.

Discovery — s. 15

Peppiatt v. Royal Bank (1996), 7 W.D.C.P. (2d) 94 (Ont. Gen. Div.).

The court refused to permit discovery of all class members but did permit discovery of subclass representatives.

Notice of Certification — s. 17

Maxwell v. MLG Ventures Ltd. (1995), 7 C.C.L.S. 155 (Ont. Gen. Div.).

Where individual issues necessitated affidavits from class members and made discovery of class members a possibility, the court required the notice to state that affidavits would be required and discuss possible discovery costs.

Costs of Class Proceedings — s. 31

Elliott v. Canadian Broadcasting Corp. (1995), 25 O.R. (3d) 302, 38 C.P.C. (3d) 332, 62 C.P.R. (3d) 19, 125 D.L.R. (4th) 534, 82 O.A.C. 115 (C.A.), leave to appeal to Supreme Court of Canada refused (March 7, 1996), Doc. 24895.

Although an order striking out the statement of claim in a class action was upheld on appeal, each party was ordered to bear its own costs of the original motion and the appeal as the case involved novel and complex questions of law.

Garland v. Consumers' Gas Co. (1995), 22 O.R. (3d) 767, 17 B.L.R. (2d) 239n (Gen. Div.).

The court refused to award costs to a successful defendant where the case was a test case, raised a novel point of law, and involved a matter of public interest.

Smith v. Canadian Tire Acceptance Ltd. (1995), 22 O.R. (3d) 433, 36 C.P.C. (3d) 175 (Gen. Div.), affirmed 26 O.R. (3d) 94, 40 C.P.C. (3d) 129.

The court awarded solicitor and client costs against an individual and organization who raised funds, purportedly to fund the class action, by holding out to the public that they could receive a share of the proceeds of the law suit, *e.g.* up to $64,500 for a $100 investment.

Abdool v. Anaheim Management Ltd. (1995), 21 O.R. (3d) 453, 31 C.P.C. (3d) 197, 121 D.L.R. (4th) 496, 78 O.A.C. 377 (Div. Ct.).

Class members are not liable for costs except with respect to the determination of their own individual claims.

Fee Agreements — ss. 32 and 33

Nantais v. Telectronics Propriety (Canada) Ltd. (19/3/96, court file 95-GD-31789, Windsor).

1. The fact that the plaintiff's solicitor has a contingent fee arrangement with the plaintiff is no defence to an award of party and party costs against the defendant. A flexible approach should be taken to problems arising from contingency fee arrangements, if only to facilitate access to the courts for more Canadians. Anything less would be to preserve the court's facilities for the wealthy and powerful.
2. All kinds of fee arrangements contingent upon success are permitted. The multiplier method referred to in s. 33(4) is simply one method authorized by use of the word "otherwise" in s. 32(1)(c).

Motions — s. 35

Chippewas of Sarnia Band v. Canada (Attorney General) (1996), 7 W.D.C.P. (2d) 172 (Ont. Gen. Div.).

It is for the Chief Justice or the Regional Senior Judge of the region where the case will be tried to decide whether a judge should be designated pursuant to rule 37.15(1) to hear motions in a class action. If a judge is so designated, rule 37.03 regarding venue for motions does not apply.

Funding of Class Proceedings by the Class Proceedings Committee

Edwards v. Law Society of Upper Canada (1994), 36 C.P.C. (3d) 116 (Ont. Class Proceedings Committee).

Discussion of funding of class actions by the Class Proceedings Committee. The merits of the case is the most important consideration. To obtain funding the applicant should generally have a strong arguable case on the merits.

Class Actions — Pleadings

Maxwell v. MLG Ventures Ltd. (1995), 40 C.P.C. (3d) 304 (Ont. Gen. Div.).

The plaintiff in a certified action was not permitted to amend the statement of claim where the proposed amendments fundamentally changed the nature of the action originally certified. Other amendments which did not change the nature of the action were allowed.

Newman v. Medical Engineering Corp. (1994), 17 O.R. (3d) 524, 23 C.P.C. (3d) 348 (Gen. Div.).

Where one judge was already seized of a class proceeding and a second judge made an *ex parte* order amending the pleading, the court granted leave to appeal to the Divisional Court.

Class Actions — Security for Costs

Sutherland v. Canadian Red Cross Society (1994), 25 C.P.C. (3d) 118 (Ont. Gen. Div.).

The court dismissed a motion for security for costs in a class action where, although the plaintiffs resided outside Ontario, they undertook to seek funding from the Class Proceedings Committee. If funding were granted, the Class Proceedings Fund would become responsible for defence costs.

[The following cases were decided prior to the enactment of the Class Proceedings Act, 1992. In view of that Act, and the new Rule 12, cases decided under the former practice should be read with great care — Authors.]

Class Actions — Generally

Re 433616 Ontario Inc. (Receiver of) (1992), 7 O.R. (3d) 670 (Gen. Div.).

Assignment of individual claims to a trustee was allowed although neither the test for a representative action under Rule 12 nor the common law principles allowing a representative action were met. In the circumstances the assignments did not constitute champerty or maintenance and a single action would not be as cumbersome as numerous separate actions.

Clow Darling Ltd. v. Big Trout Lake Band (1989), 70 O.R. (2d) 56, [1990] 4 C.N.L.R. 7 (Dist. Ct.).

An Indian band has legal status to sue or be sued in its own name, and therefore a representation order was unnecessary.

Butler v. Regional Assessment Commr., Assessment Region No. 9 (1982), 39 O.R. (2d) 365, 19 M.P.L.R. 233, 139 D.L.R. (3d) 158, affirmed 143 D.L.R. (3d) 573 (Div. Ct.).

A class action must meet the following requirements: the class must be properly defined; all members must have a common interest; there must be a wrong common to all; damage suffered must be the same to all except in amount; the relief sought must be beneficial to all; and none of the members of the class may have an interest antagonistic to the other members.

General Motors of Can. Ltd. v. Naken (1983), 32 C.P.C. 138, 144 D.L.R. (3d) 385, 46 N.R. 139 (S.C.C.).

Lengthy discussion of principles regarding class actions. The court dismissed an action brought on behalf of purchasers of allegedly defective motor vehicles.

Farnham v. Fingold, [1973] 2 O.R. 132, 33 D.L.R. (3d) 156 (C.A.).

A class action will not necessarily be dismissed because it sounds in damages.

Murphy v. Webbwood Mobile Home Estates Ltd. (1978), 19 O.R. (2d) 300, 6 C.P.C. 124 (H.C.).

The permissibility of a class action is a fundamental question which should be determined at a preliminary stage. A class action by tenants against a landlord for overpayments in respect of water and taxes was not permitted.

Olsen v. Cleveland, [1973] 3 O.R. 427 (H.C.).

Where the plaintiff fails to set out his status in the statement of claim, the statement of claim will be struck out and the action stayed until the status is clarified.

Abraham v. Prosoccer Ltd. (1980), 31 O.R. (2d) 475, 18 C.P.C. 237, 119 D.L.R. (3d) 167 (H.C.).

A party who had shown no interest in pursuing a shareholders' class action up to the time the action was settled by the named plaintiff was refused leave to substitute himself for the named plaintiff who wished to discontinue the action.

Harrison v. Sinclair, [1945] O.W.N. 399 (Master).

Where the persons to be authorized to defend have the control of a fund to which the plaintiff may be entitled to resort in satisfaction of his claim, those persons may be appointed to represent the general membership in defending the fund.

Class Actions by and Against Trade Unions

Wilkes v. Teichmann (1985), 50 C.P.C. 151 (Ont. C.A.), leave to appeal to Supreme Court of Canada refused 11 O.A.C. 144.

The court permitted an action against seven named individual defendants as representatives of members of a union local.

Dionisio v. Allain (1985), 50 C.P.C. 11, 85 C.L.L.C. 14,021 (Ont. H.C.).

The members of a local of a labour union were permitted to bring a class action regarding conspiracy to induce breach of contract and certain damages which would not require separate assessment for each member of the class.

Canning v. Governing Council of Univ. of Toronto (1984), 48 O.R. (2d) 360, 46 C.P.C. 165 (H.C.).

The court struck out a class action brought on behalf of foreign students where each member of the class had to establish reliance on representations of the defendant and the damages sustained may be different for each member.

Seafarers Int. Union of Can. v. Lawrence (1979), 24 O.R. (2d) 257, 13 C.P.C. 281, 97 D.L.R. (3d) 324 (C.A.), leave to appeal to Supreme Court of Canada refused 24 O.R. (2d) 257n, 97 D.L.R. (3d) 324n.

A class action for defamation of a union cannot be maintained. Each member of the union must be able to bring a separate personal action and the defences and measure of damages must be the same. A derivative action is not available where the union cannot bring an action itself.

Northdown Drywall & Const. Ltd. v. Austin Co. (1975), 8 O.R. (2d) 691, 59 D.L.R. (3d) 55 (Div. Ct.).

A class action is not a proper procedure for members of a trade union to claim for loss of wages and loss of opportunity to work.

Drohan v. Sangamo Co., [1972] 3 O.R. 399 (H.C.).

A class action was permitted to be brought by members of a union and former employees against an employer claiming a declaration that a pension agreement was valid and an injunction requiring performance of its provisions.

Class Actions by Condominium Corporations

Loader v. Rose Park Wellesley Invts. Ltd. (1980), 29 O.R. (2d) 381, 17 C.P.C. 150, 114 D.L.R. (3d) 105 (H.C.).

The *Condominium Act* precludes a class action by unit owners with respect to the common elements. A class action alleging damage to the units cannot be maintained where individual assessments would be required.

York Condominium Corp. No. 228 v. Tenen Invts. Ltd. (1977), 17 O.R. (2d) 579, 6 C.P.C. 185 (H.C.).

The court refused to strike out a class action on behalf of unit owners of a condominium in respect of the common elements and common funds.

York Condominium Corp. No. 104 v. Halliwell Terrace Ltd. (1975), 12 O.R. (2d) 46 (H.C.).

The determination of the propriety of a class action was left to the trial judge rather than being decided on an interlocutory motion.

Frontenac Condominium Corp. No. 1 v. Macciocchi & Sons Ltd. (1974), 3 O.R. (2d) 331, 45 D.L.R. (3d) 347, reversed on other grounds 11 O.R. (2d) 649, 67 D.L.R. (3d) 199 (C.A.).

A condominium corporation may bring an action in its own name; a class action is not necessary.

Examples — Class Actions Permitted

Lucyk v. Shipp Corp. (1991), 4 O.R. (3d) 684 (Gen. Div.).

The criteria of a properly constituted class action were met where the exact amount of the total claim being made against the respondent was known, and the same mathematical formula was used to calculate the claim of each member of the class.

Radelja v. Cdn. General Ins. Co. (1988), 29 C.C.L.I. 168 (Ont. Dist. Ct.).

The court permitted an action under s. 226(1) of the *Insurance Act*, R.S.O. 1980, c. 218, which provided a right of action against a motor vehicle insurer by judgment creditors of the insured, to be reconstituted as a class action notwithstanding the expiry of a limitation period.

A.G. Ont. v. Bear Island Foundation; Potts v. A.G. Ont., 49 O.R. (2d) 353, [1985] 1 C.N.L.R. 1, 15 D.L.R. (4th) 321 (H.C.).

In an action to assert a claim to aboriginal rights, standing was granted to the chief and other band members to sue as representing themselves and the membership of the entire band.

Hewitt v. Simcoe County Bd. of Education (1981), 16 M.P.L.R. 265, 131 D.L.R. (3d) 92 (Ont. H.C.).

A ratepayer may sue in his own name on behalf of the other ratepayers to enjoin an *ultra vires* action of a municipality or other such authority.

Sugden v. Metro. Toronto Police Commrs. Bd. (1978), 19 O.R. (2d) 669 (H.C.).

Two policemen were permitted to maintain a class action for a declaration that they and certain other members of their force retained their former ranks following a reorganization of the force; the consent of all members of the class was not necessary.

Cobbold v. Time Can. Ltd. (1976), 13 O.R. (2d) 567, 1 C.P.C. 274, 71 D.L.R. (3d) 629 (H.C.).

A class action claiming specific relief or, alternatively, damages is proper notwithstanding that the damages of the various members of the class may differ.

Westinghouse Can. Ltd. v. Buchar (1975), 9 O.R. (2d) 137, 20 C.B.R. (N.S.) 246, 59 D.L.R. (3d) 641 (C.A.).

Where a debtor has fraudulently transferred property and the transferee has resold the property, an action by the creditors to seize the proceeds should be brought as a class action.

Farnham v. Fingold, [1973] 2 O.R. 132, 33 D.L.R. (3d) 156 (C.A.).

A class action was permitted to be brought by shareholders of a company against the controlling shareholders in respect of a premium paid for the sale of the controlling block of shares.

Korman's Electric Ltd. v. Schultes, [1970] 2 O.R. 548, 11 D.L.R. (3d) 425 (H.C.).

A class action under the *Fraudulent Conveyances Act*, R.S.O. 1960, c. 154, was permitted notwithstanding that the class was comprised of both unsecured creditors and a mechanics' lien claimant.

Examples — Class Actions Refused

Sherman v. Drabinsky (1990), 74 O.R. (2d) 596, 43 C.P.C. (2d) 55, additional reasons (October 1, 1990) Doc. No. Toronto 11486/82 (H.C.), affirmed (1994), 20 O.R. (3d) 228 (C.A.).

A representative action based in part on misrepresentation was not appropriate where the reliance of each plaintiff would vary from one individual to the next.

Stark v. Toronto Sun Publishing Corp. (1983), 42 O.R. (2d) 791, 36 C.P.C. 287 (H.C.).

This class action for defamation on behalf of all members of an unincorporated association was dismissed in the absence of an indication in the pleadings of identification on the part of the plaintiffs in the minds of the public with the association.

Dehler v. Ottawa Civic Hosp. (1979), 25 O.R. (2d) 748, 14 C.P.C. 4, 101 D.L.R. (3d) 686, 3 L. Med. Q. 141, affirmed 29 O.R. (2d) 677, 117 D.L.R. (3d) 512 (C.A.).

A class action on behalf of "those unborn persons or that class of unborn persons whose lives may be terminated by abortion in the defendant hospitals" was struck out.

Judge v. Muslim Soc. of Toronto Inc., [1973] 2 O.R. 45 (H.C.).

An action by the plaintiffs "on behalf of themselves and all members and adherents of the Jami' Mosque of Toronto" was dismissed, *inter alia*, because the class was too vaguely defined.

Murphy v. Webbwood Mobile Home Estates Ltd. (1978), 19 O.R. (2d) 300, 6 C.P.C. 124 (H.C.).

A claim on behalf of an individual and all other persons who were tenants of a mobile home park, alleging overcharging with respect to water charges paid by each, was not properly a class action.

Stephenson v. Air Canada (1979), 26 O.R. (2d) 369, 14 C.P.C. 40, 103 D.L.R. (3d) 148 (H.C.).

A class action on behalf of all persons whose flights were cancelled by the defendant was dismissed since, *inter alia*, the damages suffered by each member of the class differed.

Winchell v. Del Zotto (1976), 1 C.P.C. 338 (Ont. H.C.).

A class action should not be dismissed simply because it sounds in damages. Where there were derivative and personal claims inextricably woven together, and no leave under the *Business Corporations Act* was obtained, the statement of claim was struck out.

LEAVE TO APPEAL

Leave to be Obtained from Another Judge

12.06(1) Leave to appeal to the Divisional Court under subsection 30(2), (9), (10) or (11) of the Act shall be obtained from a judge other than the judge who made the order.

Certification Order — Grounds

(2) Leave to appeal from an order under subsection 30(2) of the Act shall be granted only on the grounds provided in subrule 62.02(4).

Order Awarding $3,000 or less or Dismissing Claim — Grounds

(3) Leave to appeal from an order under subsection 30(9), (10) or (11) of the Act shall not be granted unless,

(a) there has been a miscarriage of justice; or

(b) the order may be used as a precedent in determining the rights of other class members or the defendant in the proceeding under section 24 or 25 of the Act and there is good reason to doubt the correctness of the order.

Procedure

(4) Subrules 62.02(2), (3), (5), (6), (7) and (8) (procedure on motion for leave to appeal) apply to the motion for leave to appeal. [en. O. Reg. 465/93, s. 2]

PROCEEDING AGAINST REPRESENTATIVE DEFENDANT

12.07 Where numerous persons have the same interest, one or more of them may defend a proceeding on behalf or for the benefit of all, or may be authorized by the court to do so. [en. O. Reg. 465/93, s. 2]

Darcy v. Wheeler (1995), 25 O.R. (3d) 412, 95 C.L.L.C. 210-042 (Gen. Div.).

Where an action against a union president in her personal capacity was essentially a collective one, the court held that a representative order was necessary naming a defendant or defendants to act on behalf of the union.

RULE 13   INTERVENTION

Highlights

Rule 13 permits the court to grant leave to a non-party to intervene in a proceeding, and it provides for two distinct forms of intervention.

First, under rule 13.01, a non-party may seek leave on his or her own motion to intervene in a proceeding *as a party*, on the ground that he or she has an interest in the subject-matter of the proceeding or its outcome. This rule envisages that such intervention may lead to the intervenor becoming involved in the fact-finding process.

Second, rule 13.02 provides for a person to intervene in a proceeding *as a friend of the court* for the purpose of rendering assistance to the court by way of argument, without becoming a party. Intervention of this second kind may result from an invitation by the court or a motion for leave by the intervenor.

Rule 13.03 provides for intervention before the Divisional Court or the Court of Appeal.

Certainly, in its scope, Rule 13 is new. It creates a broad power and cases decided before the rule came into force are not binding: *United Parcel Service Can. Ltd. v. Ontario (Highway Transport Board)* (1989), 44 C.P.C. (2d) 213, 41 Admin. L.R. 97, 36 O.A.C. 249 (Div. Ct.). In particular, permitting intervention in *Charter* cases is becoming more common. On intervention generally, see Muldoon, *Law of Intervention: Status and Practice* (1989).

Former Rules: Rule 504a.

LEAVE TO INTERVENE AS ADDED PARTY

13.01(1) A person who is not a party to a proceeding may move for leave to intervene as an added party if the person claims,

(a) an interest in the subject matter of the proceeding;

(b) that the person may be adversely affected by a judgment in the proceeding; or

(c) that there exists between the person and one or more of the parties to the proceeding a question of law or fact in common with one or more of the questions in issue in the proceeding.

(2) On the motion, the court shall consider whether the intervention will unduly delay or prejudice the determination of the rights of the parties to the proceeding and the court may add the person as a party to the proceeding and may make such order as is just.

LEAVE TO INTERVENE AS FRIEND OF THE COURT

13.02 Any person may, with leave of a judge or at the invitation of the presiding judge or master, and without becoming a party to the proceeding, intervene as a friend of the court for the purpose of rendering assistance to the court by way of argument.

LEAVE TO INTERVENE IN DIVISIONAL COURT OR COURT OF APPEAL

13.03(1) Leave to intervene in the Divisional Court as an added party or as a friend of the court may be granted by a panel of the court, the Chief

Justice or Associate Chief Justice of the Ontario Court or a judge designated by either of them.
    (2) Leave to intervene as an added party or as a friend of the court in the Court of Appeal may be granted by a panel of the court, the Chief Justice of Ontario or the Associate Chief Justice of Ontario.

[In view of rule 13.01 which is new, the cases under the former practice should be read with great care — Authors.]

Intervention Generally

Peel (Regional Municipality) v. Great Atlantic and Pacific Co. of Canada (1990), 74 O.R. (2d) 164, 45 C.P.C. (2d) 1, 46 Admin. L.R. 1, 2 C.R.R. (3d) 327 (C.A.).

On a motion for intervenor status the matters to be considered are: (1) the nature of the case; (2) the issues that arise and (3) the likelihood of the moving party being able to make a useful contribution to the resolution of the appeal without causing injustice to the immediate parties.

Adler v. Ontario (1992), 8 O.R. (3d) 200, 7 C.P.C. (3d) 180, 88 D.L.R. (4th) 632 (Gen. Div.).

Leave to intervene is more readily granted in constitutional cases than in ordinary cases.

John Doe v. Ontario (Information & Privacy Commissioner) (1991), 7 C.P.C. (3d) 33, 87 D.L.R. (4th) 348, 53 O.A.C. 236, additional reasons (1992), 7 C.P.C. (3d) 33 at 38, 53 O.A.C. 236 at 239 (Div. Ct.).

There is greater latitude for intervention in public interest cases than in private cases. Factors to be considered are (1) the nature of the case; (2) the issues which will arise; and (3) the likelihood that the applicant will make a useful contribution without causing injustice to the parties.

United Parcel Service Can. Ltd. v. Ontario (Highway Transport Bd.) (1989), 44 C.P.C. (2d) 213, 41 Admin. L.R. 97, 36 O.A.C. 249 (Div. Ct.).

Rule 13.01 creates a broad power to add parties and cases decided before the rule came into force are not binding.

General Dynamics Corp. v. Veliotis (1987), 61 O.R. (2d) 111, 21 C.P.C. (2d) 169, 23 O.A.C. 339 (Div. Ct.), leave to appeal to Ont. C.A. refused 21 C.P.C. (2d) 169n.

Rule 13 does not contemplate the addition of a person as an intervenor for the purpose of making claims over against existing parties, but solely to permit a person to protect an interest that might be adversely affected by a judgment in the proceedings. No intervention is permitted if undue prejudice or delay will result.

Re Schofield and Min. of Consumer and Commercial Relations (1980), 28 O.R. (2d) 764, 19 C.P.C. 245, 112 D.L.R. (3d) 132 (C.A.).

That the decision in an action may be used as a precedent in another pending action between other parties is not a sufficient "interest" to support intervention.

Re Damien and Ont. Human Rights Comm. (1976), 12 O.R. (2d) 262 (Div. Ct.).

A person whose rights will be directly affected by the acts of the court should normally be permitted to be a party to the proceeding and may be given status to argue a preliminary jurisdictional question.

Re Clark and A.G. Can. (1977), 17 O.R. (2d) 593, 34 C.P.R. (2d) 91, 81 D.L.R. (3d) 33 (H.C.).

Discussion of circumstances in which intervention is allowed.

Wallin v. Wallin, [1973] 2 O.R. 870, 13 R.F.L. 305 (H.C.).

The Official Guardian may always have the ear of the court if infants are concerned.

Allstate Ins. Co. v. Coutu, [1959] O.W.N. 202, [1959] I.L.R. 1-334 (H.C.).

The court refused to add defendants at their own request where they lacked a definite and present interest in the subject-matter of the action.

Flewelling v. Smith, [1947] O.W.N. 469 (Master).

A plaintiff should not be compelled to sue anyone whom he does not want to sue and an outsider to an action cannot be added as defendant in order to see that the action is properly and aggressively defended.

Intervention — Examples

M. v. H. (1994), 20 O.R. (3d) 70 (Gen. Div.).

While leave to intervene may be granted regarding a motion it was refused in this private family law matter where a constitutional issue was to be argued relating to the definition of "spouse" in the *Family Law Act* and the moving parties failed to satisfy the onus on them to demonstrate that the court's ability to determine the constitutional question would be enhanced by their intervention.

Ontario (Attorney General) v. Ballard Estate (1994), 36 C.P.C. (2d) 213 (Gen. Div. [Commercial List]).

The court permitted security holders who asserted a transaction was oppressive to intervene in a proceeding attacking the same transaction under the *Charitable Gifts Act.*

Aiken v. Keppel (Township) (1993), 15 O.R. (3d) 620 (Gen. Div.).

The court refused to order a stay of proceedings and instead ordered that the moving parties be added as parties and designated as intervenors where they were necessary parties.

B. (R.) v. Children's Aid Society of Metropolitan Toronto (1992), 10 O.R. (3d) 321, 42 R.F.L. (3d) 36, 96 D.L.R. (4th) 45, *(sub nom. Re Sheena)* 58 O.A.C. 93 (C.A.), affirmed [1995] 1 S.C.R. 315, 21 O.R. (3d) 479 (note), 9 R.F.L. (4th) 157, 26 C.R.R. (2d) 202, 122 D.L.R. (4th) 1, 176 N.R. 161, 78 O.A.C. 1.

On appeal, the court upheld an order requiring the Attorney General, as intervenor, to pay the costs of the unsuccessful litigants in wardship proceedings. Although there was no misconduct, state action had precipitated the proceedings, religious beliefs were in issue, and the matter was of province-wide importance.

Adler v. Ontario (1992), 8 O.R. (3d) 200, 7 C.P.C. (3d) 180, 88 D.L.R. (4th) 632 (Gen. Div.).

Intervenor status was granted to certain parties in an application relating to the non-funding of Jewish day schools by the province, where those parties could make a useful contribution without causing injustice to the immediate participants.

David v. Pilot Insurance Co. (1991), 49 C.P.C. (2d) 282 (Ont. Gen. Div.).

The court awarded costs of this action jointly against the plaintiff and an intervenor under Rule 13.

Metropolitan Toronto Housing Authority v. Arsenault (1990), 44 C.P.C. (2d) 152 (Ont. Dist. Ct.).

The court does not have a discretion to allow the intervention of parties in an application pursuant to s. 113 of the *Landlord and Tenant Act*, as that statute has its own self-contained code of procedure.

France (Republic) v. De Havilland Aircraft of Can. Ltd. (1989), 40 C.P.C. (2d) 105, 50 C.C.C. (3d) 167 (Ont. H.C.), reversed on other grounds (1991), 3 O.R. (3d) 705, 1 C.P.C. (3d) 76, 65 C.C.C. (3d) 449, 49 O.A.C. 283 (C.A.).

A party was permitted to intervene on a motion to review an order commissioning the taking of evidence pursuant to letters rogatory. The party had a clear interest in the matter, as he was the subject of the criminal proceedings for which the evidence was requested.

Crown Trust Co. v. Rosenberg (No. 1) (1987), 60 O.R. (2d) 87 at 114, 22 C.P.C. (2d) 115 (H.C.).

A party was not permitted to intervene in a motion brought by a court-appointed receiver to approve the sale of properties where it only stood to lose a potential economic advantage. The loss of a potential economic advantage is not a legal or proprietary right.

Hansen v. Royal Ins. Co. (1985), 52 O.R. (2d) 755, 14 C.C.L.I. 161, 23 D.L.R. (4th) 29 (H.C.), affirmed (1986), 58 O.R. (2d) 52, 35 D.L.R. (4th) 480 (Div. Ct.).

A tavern owner named as a defendant in a personal injury action was permitted to be added as a party in an action brought by the plaintiff with respect to no-fault benefits.

Re Ont. Energy Board Act (1985), 51 O.R. (2d) 333, 2 C.P.C. (2d) 226, 15 Admin. L.R. 86 at 115, 19 D.L.R. (4th) 753, 11 O.A.C. 26 (Div. Ct.), leave to appeal to Ont. C.A. refused 15 Admin. L.R. 86 at 122n.

On an application to determine the jurisdiction of an administrative tribunal to award costs in advance of the hearing, the Divisional Court gave leave to intervene to two organizations frequently interested in matters before the tribunal in question.

Haal Securities Ltd. v. Goldhar; Revenue Properties Co. v. Haal Securities Ltd. (1985), 6 C.P.C. (2d) 225 (Ont. Master).

The court added a corporation as a party to a motion by a shareholder for leave to commence a derivative action in the name of the corporation pursuant to the *Business Corporations Act.*

Friction Division Products Inc. v. E.I. Du Pont de Nemours & Co. (1985), 51 O.R. (2d) 244, 6 C.P.R. (3d) 66 (H.C.).

On a proceeding to enforce letters of request, leave to intervene as an added party was granted where the applicant showed a "legitimate commercial interest" which could be adversely affected by the decision.

Hamilton-Wentworth v. Hamilton-Wentworth Save the Valley Committee Inc. (1985), 51 O.R. (2d) 23, 2 C.P.C. (2d) 117, 15 Admin. L.R. 86, 19 D.L.R. (4th) 356, 11 O.A.C. 8, 17 O.M.B.R. 411, additional reasons 51 O.R. (2d) 23 at 43, 2 C.P.C. (2d) 117 at 144, 15 Admin. L.R. 86 at 120, 19 D.L.R. (4th) 356 at 377, 17 O.M.B.R. 411 at 440 (Div. Ct.), leave to appeal to Ont. C.A. refused 17 O.M.B.R. 511.

The court permitted persons who would be profoundly affected by the court's decision to intervene as friends of the court.

Rubin v. Torlease Properties Ltd. (1985), 1 W.D.C.P. 178 (Ont. Master).

A party to a contract was permitted to intervene in an application between other parties to the same contract regarding interpretations of the contract notwithstanding the applicants did not seek any relief against the proposed intervenor.

Pershadsingh v. Pershadsingh (1984), 46 C.P.C. 143 (Ont. Master).

The court refused to add the existing parties' son as a party defendant in this family law action where his rights under a certain trust were not in issue. A party should not be added merely to hold a watching brief.

Income Invts. (Wentworth) Ltd. v. Elmore (1978), 8 C.P.C. 235 (Ont. H.C.).

The Attorney General was permitted to bring an application for an interlocutory injunction, although he had no interest in the relevant lands, where the respondent was in violation of an undertaking and there was an order against him under the *Vexatious Proceedings Act.*

Intervention by Insurers

Thomson v. Thomson Estate (1995), 26 O.R. (3d) 250 (Gen. Div.), leave to appeal granted 27 O.R. (3d) 415 (case was subsequently settled).

Where an insurer's putative subrogated claim was included in the plaintiff's statement of claim but a conflict developed subsequently, the insurer was granted leave to intervene under rule 13.01. The insurer would play a limited role in the litigation and would not advance a position adverse in interest to the plaintiff.

Amondsen v. Hunter (1995), 36 C.P.C. (3d) 55 (Ont. Gen. Div.).

An insurer who had denied coverage to a defendant was allowed to intervene and oppose a motion for judgment brought by the plaintiff.

Peixeiro v. Haberman (1994), 20 O.R. (3d) 666, 36 C.P.C. (3d) 388, 25 C.C.L.I. (2d) 6 (Gen. Div.).

The court refused leave for an insurer to intervene where it had no direct financial interest in the litigation but an adverse precedent might indirectly affect its insured in future litigation.

Robinson v. Eagle, 39 C.C.L.I. 195, [1989] I.L.R. 1-2438 (Ont. Dist. Ct.).

Where a minor plaintiff sued her grandparents for injuries caused by a fall and on discovery one grandparent gave evidence which contradicted a statement given to the adjuster for the grandparents' insurer, the court permitted the insurer to intervene as a party defendant.

Porretta v. Stock (1988), 67 O.R. (2d) 628, 32 C.P.C. (2d) 10, 20 M.V.R. (2d) 308, [1989] I.L.R. 1-2404 (H.C.), affirmed (1989), 67 O.R. (2d) 736, 35 C.P.C. (2d) 93 (C.A.).

An insurer which may be liable for its insureds' injuries pursuant to the underinsured motorist provisions of the policy may not intervene in an action by the insureds against the underinsured tortfeasor. *Power v. Hastings, infra*, not followed.

Hutchinson v. Clarke (1988), 67 O.R. (2d) 621, 32 C.P.C. (2d) 1 (H.C.).

An insurer which may be liable for its insured's injuries pursuant to the underinsured motorist provisions of the policy may intervene in an action by the insured against the underinsured tortfeasor. *Power v. Hastings, infra*, applied.

Power v. Hastings (County) (1986), 28 C.P.C. (2d) 107 (Ont. H.C.).

A plaintiff's S.E.F. 42 insurer was permitted to add itself as a defendant in an action brought by the plaintiff against an uninsured defendant.

Intervention by Municipalities and Ratepayers

Vachliotis v. Exodus Link Corp. (1987), 23 C.P.C. (2d) 72 (Ont. Master).

A municipality was permitted to intervene as an added party in an action involving the interpretation of a by-law in which success by the plaintiff might prompt a claim by the defendant against the municipality for improperly issuing a building permit.

Johnston v. Milton (No. 1) (1981), 34 O.R. (2d) 289, 24 C.P.C. 205 (H.C.).

Where there was a reasonable possibility that the legal rights of a Regional Municipality might be affected by an application to quash by-laws of a town, the Regional Municipality was added as a party respondent to the application.

Re Ronark Devs. and Hamilton (1974), 4 O.R. (2d) 195, affirmed 5 O.R. (2d) 136n (C.A.).

A ratepayers' organization is not a proper party to an application for judicial review in the nature of *mandamus* brought by a developer to compel a municipality to issue a building permit.

Re Starr and Puslinch (1976), 12 O.R. (2d) 40 (Div. Ct.).

The court retains a discretion to refuse to add a party even where the determination of the litigation may directly affect the parties' legal rights or economic interests.

Re Orangeville Highlands Ltd. and Mono (1975), 5 O.R. (2d) 266 (Div. Ct.).

An application by a municipality to be added to a *mandamus* proceeding against a neighbouring municipality was refused.

McDonald's Restaurants of Can. Ltd. v. Etobicoke (1977), 5 C.P.C. 55 (Ont. Div. Ct.).

A ratepayer will not be added as a party to a building permit application where his interests are already adequately represented.

Intervention on Appeal — rule 13.03

Stroh v. Millers Cove Resources Inc. (1995), 85 O.A.C. 26 (Div. Ct.).

Where certain shareholders had ample opportunity to enter an oppression remedy proceeding early on but chose not to do so until the eve of the appeal, the court dismissed their motion to intervene.

Peel (Regional Municipality) v. Great Atlantic & Pacific Co. of Canada (1990), 74 O.R. (2d) 164, 45 C.P.C. (2d) 1, 46 Admin. L.R. 1, 2 C.R.R. (2d) 327 (C.A.).

The Chief Justice permitted intervention as a friend of the court but on terms that (1) the intervenor take the record as it was and not adduce further evidence, (2) the intervenor would not seek costs but costs might be awarded against it, and (3) the intervenor deliver its factums promptly.

Wotherspoon v. C.P. Ltd.; Pope v. C.P. Ltd. (1981), 20 C.P.C. 72 (Ont. C.A.).

An application for leave to intervene in an appeal was granted on terms as to what could be argued and the staying of the intervenor's pending action. The intervenor was refused leave to adduce further evidence. A term of the intervention order was that the intervenor could not seek costs in the appeal but could be subject to them.

Halton Community Credit Union Ltd. v. ICL Computers Ltd. (1985), 3 C.P.C. (2d) 252 (Ont. C.A.).

An intervenor to an appeal takes the record as it exists subject to his right to seek leave to adduce new evidence on the appeal.

Halton Community Credit Union Ltd. v. ICL Computers Can. Ltd. (1985), 47 C.P.C. 162 (Ont. C.A.).

A solicitor whose alleged negligence permitted a default judgment to go against the defendant was permitted to intervene on the appeal from an order dismissing a motion to set aside the judgment. $3,000 security for costs was required.

Ont. Securities Comm. v. Electra Invts. (Can.) Ltd. (1983), 44 O.R. (2d) 61, 38 C.P.C. 57 (C.A.).

The court permitted shareholders of a target corporation in a takeover bid to be added as a parties respondent in an application brought to enforce provisions of the *Securities Act.*

Intervention on Motions

Aroland First Nation v. Ontario (1996), 7 W.D.C.P. (2d) 138 (Ont. Gen. Div.).

The court has jurisdiction to add a party to an intended action where a motion has been brought under rule 37.17.

M. v. H. (1994), 20 O.R. (3d) 70, 33 C.P.C. (3d) 337, 9 R.F.L. (4th) 94 (Gen. Div.).

In a proper case leave to intervene on a Rule 21 motion may be granted.

Ontario (Attorney General) v. Dieleman (1993), 16 O.R. (3d) 32, 108 D.L.R. (4th) 458 (Gen. Div.).

In an action in which the Attorney General of Ontario sought an injunction restraining the defendants from engaging in anti-abortion protest activities, the court refused to grant intervenor status to a non-profit civil liberties association where it did not have a real, substantial and identifiable interest in the subject-matter of the proceedings, it did not have a distinct and important perspective, and it was not a well-recognized group with special expertise and a broad identifiable membership base.

Reichmann v. Toronto Life Publishing Co. (1989), 36 C.P.C. (2d) 176 (Ont. H.C.).

Intervention by a non-party in interlocutory proceedings should only be permitted where there is the most pressing and urgent necessity.

Crown Trust Co. v. Rosenberg (1986), 60 O.R. (2d) 87, 22 C.P.C. (2d) 131, 67 C.B.R. (N.S.) 320, 39 D.L.R. (4th) 526 (H.C.).

Intervention is not permitted on a motion, as it is not a "proceeding".

COMMENCEMENT OF PROCEEDINGS

RULE 14　ORIGINATING PROCESS

Highlights

This is the basic Rule regulating the commencement of proceedings. The Rules provide for two types of civil proceedings — actions and applications. Generally, all civil proceedings are commenced by the issuing of an "originating process" (a term which is defined: see rule 1.03), but there are minor exceptions to this principle in respect of certain counterclaims, etc. (see below): rule 14.01.

Actions. The writ of summons has been abolished and the normal method of commencing an action is by issuing a "statement of claim": rule 14.03(1). However, where there is insufficient time to prepare a statement of claim, an action may be commenced by the issuing of a "notice of action" (rule 14.03(2)), but where this is done a statement of claim must be filed within 30 days: rule 14.03(3).

The statement of claim (or the notice of action and statement of claim) is to be served within six months of the date on which it was issued: rule 14.08. No specific provision is made for "renewal" of the statement of claim, because the new Rules do not retain the concept of the originating process "being in force" for a specified period or of "expiring". If service is not carried out within the six-month period, the time for service may be extended by the court using the general power to extend time: rule 3.02.

Under the new Rules the specially endorsed writ procedure has been replaced by a generally available summary judgment procedure (see Rule 20). However, in default of defence a plaintiff may sign default judgment in the same types of cases where it could have been signed or obtained on motion under the former Rules: rule 19.04.

Divorce actions are commenced by the issuing of a "petition": rule 14.04.

With respect to actions which are "engrafted" on an existing action (*i.e.*, counterclaims, counterpetitions, crossclaims and third party claims), an originating process must be issued only if new parties are being added. In the case of a crossclaim (which will always be between existing co-defendants, see rule 28.01), or a counterclaim or counterpetition that is only against persons who are already parties to the main action, no originating process need be issued: rule 14.01(2). However, in the case of a third party claim (which will always be against a person who is not a party to the main action, see rule 29.01) or a counterclaim or counterpetition against a person who is not already a party to the main action, the appropriate originating process must be issued: see rule 29.02 (third party claim), rule 27.04 (counterclaim), rule 69.09(6) (counterpetition).

Applications. Applications are commenced by a "notice of application" (rule 14.05(1)) which must be issued before it is served: rule 14.01(1).

The general rule is still that all proceedings shall be by action unless a statute or the Rules provide otherwise (rule 14.02). The situations in which proceedings may be taken by application are listed in rule 14.05 and are considerably expanded: rule 14.05(3). Indeed, it is now provided that proceedings may be taken by way of application in any case "where it is unlikely that there will be any material facts in dispute" (rule 14.05(3)(h)) and where a remedy is sought under the *Charter* : rule 14.05(3)(g.1). While proceeding by application is generally speedier, doing so where there are arguably material facts in dispute may lead the respondent to challenge the use of the procedure, resulting in the proceeding being converted into an action by the directing of a trial under rule 38.10(1)(b). In some circumstances it will be a speedier procedure to commence an action and for the plaintiff to proceed to bring a motion for summary judgment under Rule 20.

Rule 14.05(3) states that a proceeding may be brought by application, *inter alia*, "where these rules authorize the commencement of a proceeding by application". The following are examples of proceedings authorized by the Rules to be brought by application: for the approval of a settlement involving parties under disability reached before commencement of a proceeding (rule 7.08(3)), for an interpleader order (rules 43.03(1), 43.05(7), 60.13(4)), for the administration of an estate, etc. (rule 65.01(1)), for the approval of the sale, etc. of a minor's property (rule 67.01), for the variation of a final order for corollary relief in a divorce action (rule 69.24(1)), for registration of a United Kingdom judgment (rule 73.02).

Special notices of application are provided for judicial review applications (Rule 68, Form 68A) and for applications for registration of United Kingdom judgments (Form 73A). The procedure and evidence on applications are regulated by Rules 38 and 39, respectively. Rule 38.06(3) requires a notice of application to be served at least ten days before the hearing of the application, and at least twenty days before the hearing if served outside Ontario.

Miscellaneous. The term "title of the proceeding" replaces the former "style of cause": see rule 14.06. Rule 14.10 provides a straightforward procedure whereby a defendant who pays a money claim (and the amount claimed for costs) within the time for delivering a defence may on a motion have the action dismissed. Rule 14.01(4) provides that a party may rely on a fact which occurs after the commencement of a proceeding even if it gives rise to a new claim or defence.

Recent amendments. Rule 14.03.1 was added at the same time as the Rule 76 Simplified Procedure was introduced.

Summary of procedure. For a summary of the procedure in an action, see Procedural Charts (CHARTS).

Former Rules: Rules 4-11, 32-33, 192, 607-612, 787.

HOW PROCEEDINGS COMMENCED

By Issuing Originating Process
14.01(1) All civil proceedings shall be commenced by the issuing of an originating process by the registrar of the court in which the proceeding is to be commenced, except where a statute provides otherwise and as provided in subrules (2) and (2.1).

Exceptions
(2) A counterclaim or counterpetition that is only against persons who are already parties to the main action, and a crossclaim, shall be commenced by the delivery of the pleading containing the counterclaim, counterpetition or crossclaim, and the pleading need not be issued.

(2.1) An application for a certificate of appointment of estate trustee under Rule 74 need not be issued.

Where Leave Required

(3) **Where leave to commence a proceeding is required, it shall be obtained by motion.**

Relying on Subsequent Fact

(4) **A party may rely on a fact that occurs after the commencement of a proceeding, even though the fact gives rise to a new claim or defence, and, if necessary, may move to amend an originating process or pleading to allege the fact. [am. O. Reg. 484/94, s. 4]**

Toronto Harbour Commissioners v. Disero (1991), 5 O.R. (3d) 585 (Gen. Div.).

At common law, leave of the court must be sought in order to pursue a derivative action on behalf of a corporation. Indemnification as to reasonable costs is within the discretion of the court.

Clarkson v. Lukovich (1986), 54 O.R. (2d) 609, 2 R.F.L. (3d) 392, 28 D.L.R. (4th) 277 (H.C.), varied on other grounds (1988), 14 R.F.L. (3d) 436 (C.A.).

While rule 14.01(4) allows new facts that raise new claims and defences, it does not purport to eliminate defences. It does not take away rights once they have accrued.

PROCEEDINGS BY ACTION AS GENERAL RULE

14.02 Every proceeding in the court shall be by action, except where a statute or these rules provide otherwise.

ACTIONS — BY STATEMENT OF CLAIM OR NOTICE OF ACTION

Statement of Claim

14.03(1) The originating process for the commencement of an action is a statement of claim (Form 14A (general) or 14B (mortgage actions)), except as provided by,

(a) **subrule (2) (notice of action);**

(b) **rule 14.04 (divorce petition);**

(c) **rule 27.03 (counterclaim against person not already a party);**

(d) **subrule 29.02(1) (third party claim); and**

(e) **rule 29.11 (fourth and subsequent party claims).**

Notice of Action

(2) **Where there is insufficient time to prepare a statement of claim, an action other than a divorce action may be commenced by the issuing of a notice of action (Form 14C) that contains a short statement of the nature of the claim.**

(3) **Where a notice of action is used, the plaintiff shall file a statement of claim (Form 14D) within thirty days after the notice of action is issued, and no statement of claim shall be filed thereafter except with the written consent of the defendant or with leave of the court obtained on notice to the defendant.**

(4) **The notice of action shall not be served separately from the statement of claim.**

Statement of Claim may Alter or Extend Claim

(5) In an action commenced by the issuing of a notice of action, the statement of claim may alter or extend the claim stated in the notice of action.

Cross-Reference: See also rule 3.02 and cases thereunder re extension of time for service.

Notice of Action

Saieva v. Schmitt (1990), 45 C.P.C. (2d) 48 (Ont. Gen. Div.).
The court permitted the late filing of the statement of claim under rule 14.03(3) notwithstanding the expiry of the limitation period. There was no actual prejudice to the defendant.

Earnslaw Ltd. v. Schmalfeld (1989), 33 C.P.C. (2d) 268 (Ont. Dist. Ct.).
The court extended the time to file the statement of claim but ordered that for purposes of any limitation period the action be deemed to be commenced when the statement of claim was filed, not when the notice of action was filed.

G.R.H. & Associates Ltd. v. Turner (1987), 25 C.P.C. (2d) 156 (Ont. Master).
The test on a motion to extend the time to file a statement of claim under rule 14.03(3) is the same as the test to extend time for service of an originating process under rule 14.08 or former Rule 8.

Angelopoulos v. Angelopoulos (1986), 55 O.R. (2d) 101, 9 C.P.C. (2d) 285, additional reasons 55 O.R. (2d) 101 at 110, 9 C.P.C. (2d) 285 at 296 (H.C.).
Failure to file a statement of claim within 30 days after the issuance of a notice of action does not affect orders made in the meantime.

Cairns v. Grigg, [1945] O.W.N. 497 (Master).
The endorsement on an originating process must be sufficient to enable the defendant to identify the relationship or occurrence with respect to which he is being sued. An endorsement reading "damages for negligence" does not comply with this requirement and will be struck out with leave to amend.

Notice of Action — Extending Claims — rule 14.03(5)

McKinlay Transport Ltd. v. Motor Transport Industrial Relations Bureau of Ont. (Inc.) (1988), 65 O.R. (2d) 23, 26 C.P.C. (2d) 309 (H.C.), leave to appeal to Ont. Div. Ct. refused 41 C.P.C. (2d) 316.
The plaintiff's failure to use the word "conspiracy" in the endorsement on a writ of summons did not bar the introduction of such allegations in the statement of claim, where the factual situation giving rise to the claim was fully described in the original endorsement.

ORDINARY AND SIMPLIFIED PROCEDURE

14.03.1(1) The simplified procedure set out in Rule 76 shall be used in actions to which subrule 76.02(1) applies, and may be used in other actions in accordance with subrule 76.02(2); otherwise, the ordinary procedure set out in these Rules shall be used in all proceedings. [en. O. Reg. 533/95, s. 1 (revoked by subs. (2) on March 11, 2000)]

DIVORCE ACTIONS — BY PETITION

14.04 The originating process for the commencement of a divorce action is a petition for divorce (Form 69A or 69B), except as provided by subrule 69.09(6) (counterpetition against person not already a party (Form 69G)).

APPLICATIONS — BY NOTICE OF APPLICATION

Notice of Application

**14.05(1) The originating process for the commencement of an applica-
tion is a notice of application (Form 14E, 68A, 73A, 74.44 or 75.5).**

Application under Statute

**(2) A proceeding may be commenced by an application to the Ontario
Court (General Division) or to a judge of that court, if a statute so authorizes.**

Application under Rules

**(3) A proceeding may be brought by application where these rules
authorize the commencement of a proceeding by application or where the
relief claimed is,**

> **(a) the opinion, advice or direction of the court on a question affecting
> the rights of a person in respect of the administration of the estate of a
> deceased person or the execution of a trust;**
>
> **(b) an order directing executors, administrators or trustees to do or
> abstain from doing any particular act in respect of an estate or trust for
> which they are responsible;**
>
> **(c) the removal or replacement of one or more executors, administra-
> tors or trustees, or the fixing of their compensation;**
>
> **(d) the determination of rights that depend on the interpretation of a
> deed, will, contract or other instrument, or on the interpretation of a
> statute, order in council, regulation or municipal by-law or resolution;**
>
> **(e) the declaration of an interest in or charge on land, including the
> nature and extent of the interest or charge or the boundaries of the land,
> or the settling of the priority of interests or charges;**
>
> **(f) the approval of an arrangement or compromise or the approval of
> a purchase, sale, mortgage, lease or variation of trust;**
>
> **(g) an injunction, mandatory order or declaration or the appointment
> of a receiver or other consequential relief when ancillary to relief claimed
> in a proceeding properly commenced by a notice of application;**
>
> **(g.1) for a remedy under the *Canadian Charter of Rights and Freedoms*;
> or**
>
> **(h) in respect of any matter where it is unlikely that there will be any
> material facts in dispute. [am. O. Regs. 396/91, s. 3; 484/94, s. 5]**

Applications — Generally

McKay Estate v. Love (1991), 6 O.R. (3d) 511, 44 E.T.R. 181 (Gen. Div.), affirmed 6 O.R. (3d)
    511 at 519, 44 E.T.R. 190, 52 O.A.C. 159, additional reasons 14 C.P.C. (3d) 371 (C.A.).

Paragraph (h) of rule 14.05(3) is not a condition to the hearing of any matter under the preceding
paragraphs. The court has power to hear an application under paragraphs (a) - (g) even if there
are material facts in dispute, though it may still decline to direct the trial of an issue.

Re Forestell and Niagara College of Applied Arts and Technology (1981), 33 O.R. (2d) 282
    (H.C.).

Where the form of the notice of application did not follow the correct form, the court dismissed
the application.

Collins v. Collins (1981), 32 O.R. (2d) 358, 21 C.P.C. 148, 122 D.L.R. (3d) 141 (H.C.).

Declaratory relief cannot be sought by way of originating application. [*But see rule 14.05(3)(h)* — *Authors.*]

Stafford v. Can. Motor Cycle Assn. (1978), 22 O.R. (2d) 58 (H.C.).

Where a proceeding does not fall within an enumerated class of cases in which an originating application is appropriate and does not depend upon undisputed facts, an originating application should not be brought.

Re Northview Const. Co. and Jonbar Const. Co., [1971] 1 O.R. 369, 15 D.L.R. (3d) 399 (Co. Ct.).

The court refused to determine a question brought by notice of application where there was a substantial dispute of fact; an action was said to be appropriate.

R. v. York Twp.; Ex parte 125 Varsity Rd. Ltd., [1960] O.R. 238, 23 D.L.R. (2d) 465 (C.A.).

The court refused to grant substantive relief of a nature normally available by action to parties to an originating application who were joined so that they would be bound by the decision of the court on another point.

Inc. Synod of Diocese of Huron v. Ferguson (1924), 56 O.L.R. 161 (H.C.).

A successful plaintiff was deprived of costs where a matter which could have been disposed of by originating application was asserted by action.

Application Permitted by Statute — rule 14.05(2)

Schreter v. Gasmac Inc. (1991), 7 O.R. (3d) 608, 10 C.P.C. (3d) 74, 6 B.L.R. (2d) 71, 41 C.P.R. (3d) 494, 89 D.L.R. (4th) 365, additional reasons 10 C.P.C. (3d) 92, 6 B.L.R. (2d) 71 at 89, 41 C.P.R. (3d) 509, 89 D.L.R. (4th) 380 (Gen. Div.).

A foreign arbitral award is enforced by way of application.

Chilian v. Augdome Corp. (1991), 2 O.R. (3d) 696, 49 C.P.C. (2d) 1, 78 D.L.R. (4th) 129, 44 O.A.C. 263 (C.A.).

Where a statute merely enables a person to "apply" to a court for specified relief, the law does not mandate one particular form of proceeding — application or action. Where one form of proceeding would be more appropriate, the defendant's remedy is in costs or an order staying the proceeding on the ground that it is an abuse of process. *Muljadi v. O'Brien, infra*, approved. *Title Estate v. Harris, infra*, not followed.

Muljadi v. O'Brien (1990), 75 O.R. (2d) 270 (Gen. Div.).

Relief under the oppression remedy provisions of s. 247 of the *Business Corporations Act* may be sought by action or application.

Renegade Capital Corp. v. Hees International Bancorp Inc. (1990), 73 O.R. (2d) 311 (H.C.).

The court stayed an application for an order under the *Securities Act* and required the matter to proceed as an action where there were complex and disputed questions of fact, issues of credibility, and a requirement for oral evidence.

Title Estate v. Harris (1990), 72 O.R. (2d) 468, 68 D.L.R. (4th) 619 (H.C.).

Portions of a statement of claim claiming oppression remedies under the *Business Corporations Act* were struck out; that statute required the proceeding to be taken by way of an application.

Niagara Air Bus Inc. v. Camerman (1989), 69 O.R. (2d) 717, 37 C.P.C. (2d) 267 (H.C.).

An application brought to determine interest rates in promissory notes was proper since it was, in the circumstances, authorized by statute and depended on the interpretation of a contract; but the trial of issue was ordered to determine a dispute as to the facts.

Energy Probe v. Canada (A.G.) (1989), 68 O.R. (2d) 449, 35 C.P.C. (2d) 201, 37 Admin. L.R.
    1, 3 C.E.L.R. (N.S.) 262, 40 C.R.R. 303, 58 D.L.R. (4th) 513, 33 O.A.C. 39 (C.A.), leave
    to appeal to Supreme Court of Canada refused 102 N.R. 399, 37 O.A.C. 160n.

Where a *Charter* challenge had been commenced by application, it was held that, even if the
application was justified under the rule, it could be more conveniently dealt with at trial since
there were certain differences as to factual matters and if s. 1 of the *Charter* became material,
the trial court would be much better equipped to balance the evidence of justification. Therefore
the application was to be treated for all purposes as an action.

Johnson v. Ontario (1985), 50 O.R. (2d) 30, 49 C.P.C. 132, 13 C.R.R. 331 (*sub nom. Johnson
    v. R.*), 16 D.L.R. (4th) 441 (H.C.).

As the *Charter of Rights and Freedoms* is a statute of Canada within the meaning of rule 1.03,
an application pursuant to s. 24(1) of the Charter to have a statute declared unconstitutional
may be brought pursuant to rule 14.05(2). However, because whether or not an infringement of
rights is reasonable and can be demonstrably justified in a free and democratic society will
almost always involve a question of fact, the application may not be made pursuant to rule
14.05(3)(h).

Sparling v. Royal Trustco Ltd. (1984), 45 O.R. (2d) 484, 24 B.L.R. 145, 6 D.L.R. (4th) 682, 1
    O.A.C. 279 (C.A.), affirmed [1986] 2 S.C.R. 537, 70 N.R. 203, 18 O.A.C. 156.

In respect of a proceeding by the Director under the *Canada Business Corporations Act* for
failure to disclose all the material facts in a takeover bid, s. 241 of the Act permits an application
to be made. However, this is not mandatory and here it was appropriate to proceed by action.

Durham Condominium Corp. No. 56 v. 472287 Ont. Inc. (1982), 31 C.P.C. 29, 26 R.P.R. 195,
    affirmed 31 C.P.C. 29 at 33, 26 R.P.R. 201 (Ont. C.A.).

A County Court proceeding under s. 49(1) of the *Condominium Act* must be by action, not by
application. It may be brought by application in the Supreme Court.

Re Nat. Auto Radiator Mfg. Co. and Warner (1981), 20 C.P.C. 196 (Ont. H.C.).

A motion to quash an originating application seeking an order that the applicant was entitled to
be paid for her shares as a dissenting shareholder under the *Canada Business Corporations Act*
was refused.

Applications re Estate and Trust Matters — rule 14.05(3)(a), (b), (c)

Canada Trust Co. v. Ontario (Human Rights Commission) (1990), 74 O.R. (2d) 481, 38 E.T.R.
    1, 12 C.H.R.R. D/184, 69 D.L.R. (4th) 321, (*sub non. Re Leonard Foundation Trust*) 37
    O.A.C. 191 (C.A.).

A trustee applied to the court to seek advice and directions as to the issue of whether a charitable
trust contravened the Ontario *Human Rights Code*, before the Ontario Human Rights Commission had investigated the complaint. It was held that the issue was a pure question of law, the
necessary remedy would have to be sought eventually from a court and the administration of
trusts was within the inherent jurisdiction of superior courts. Accordingly, the court had jurisdiction to decide the question before any determination by the commission.

Page Estate v. Sachs (1990), 72 O.R. (2d) 409, 37 E.T.R. 226 (H.C.).

Where a testator died in Quebec owning certain lands situate in Ontario, an Ontario court had
jurisdiction to hear an application for advice and directions in the administration of the estate
since the estate owned land within the province.

Re Sun Life Assur. Co. of Can. and Johnsen, 48 C.P.C. 113, [1985] I.L.R. 1893 (*sub nom. Re
    Johnsen*) (Ont. H.C.).

The court declined to determine entitlement to the proceeds of life insurance policies by way
of application where the insured was a missing person abducted at gunpoint. The issues should
be determined on *viva voce* evidence.

Re Martin (1985), 47 C.P.C. 229 (Ont. H.C.).

The court granted a request by an executor to be removed from that office because of a potential conflict of interest if the accounting firm of which he was a member acted as auditor to a corporation related to the estate.

Re Skinner, [1970] 3 O.R. 35, 12 D.L.R. (3d) 227 (H.C.).

The court declined to answer a hypothetical question.

Re Bessette, [1942] O.W.N. 278, [1942] 3 D.L.R. 207 (H.C.).

The Supreme Court may, by way of interpretation of a will, determine a class of beneficiary, but may not determine the identity of the individual beneficiary.

Applications re Interpretation of Documents, Statutes and Regulations — rule 14.05(3)(d)

Seguin v. Pharmaphil Division, R.P. Scherer Canada Inc. (1995), 6 W.D.C.P. (2d) 119 (Ont. Gen. Div.).

Rule 14.05(3)(d) applies only to written contracts, not oral contracts.

Toronto (City) v. Canadian National Railway (1993), 22 C.P.C. (3d) 336 (Ont. Gen. Div.).

The court permitted a case to proceed by way of application where it appeared that the dispute turned on the construction of documents and the application of legal principles.

Canada Post Corp. v. C.U.P.W. (1989), 70 O.R. (2d) 394, 38 Admin. L.R. 305, 62 D.L.R. (4th) 724 (H.C.).

An application for a declaration that s. 21 of the *Workers' Compensation Act*, R.S.O. 1980, c. 539, did not apply to employees of Canada Post was quashed; the proceedings should have been brought by an application for judicial review.

Cineplex Odeon Corp. v. Famous Players Ltd. (1989), 69 O.R. (2d) 701, 38 C.P.C. (2d) 138, 7 R.P.R. (2d) 304 (H.C.).

An application for the interpretation of a contract which affected a land redevelopment in the proposal stages only, which could still be modified by government authorities, was permitted to proceed, as the question had practical consequences.

Re Myers and Wellesley Hospital (1986), 57 O.R. (2d) 54, 14 C.P.C. (2d) 62 (H.C.).

Where a party sought hospital records pursuant to a regulation under the *Public Hospitals Act*, the matter was properly commenced by way of application.

Reitzel v. Rej-Cap Manufacturing Ltd. (1985), 53 O.R. (2d) 116, 7 C.P.C. (2d) 77, 38 R.P.R. 254 (H.C.).

The court determined rights by way of application regarding an alleged agreement of purchase and sale notwithstanding a dispute between the parties about the existence of the contract. All facts necessary to dispose of the application had been agreed to and declining jurisdiction would have caused additional expense and delay.

Berman v. Karleton Co. (1982), 37 O.R. (2d) 176, 28 C.P.C. 168, 24 R.P.R. 8 (H.C.).

A claim for a declaration of entitlement to interest involving the purchase and sale of condominium units was permitted to proceed by way of application.

Gallant v. Veltrusy Enterprises Ltd. (1982), 32 O.R. (2d) 716, 22 C.P.C. 267, 123 D.L.R. (3d) 391 (C.A.).

The County Court had no jurisdiction to determine the rights of parties under a tenancy agreement by way of application.

Collins v. Collins (1981), 32 O.R. (2d) 358, 21 C.P.C. 148, 122 D.L.R. (3d) 141 (H.C.).

A decree *nisi* is not an "instrument."

Re Halmos (1979), 12 C.P.C. 16 (Ont. H.C.).
The court had no jurisdiction to determine the validity of a zoning by-law where inferences of fact were likely to be disputed.

Re 296616 Ont. Ltd. and Richmond Hill (1977), 14 O.R. (2d) 787 (C.A.).
The court refused to decide whether a proposed use of property would be a legal non-conforming use under a zoning by-law on the grounds that it ought not to consider a hypothetical question.

Re Doctors Hosp. and Min. of Health (1976), 12 O.R. (2d) 164, 1 C.P.C. 232, 68 D.L.R. (3d) 220 (Div. Ct.).
An application for judicial review seeking a declaration that an order in council is invalid is a proper proceeding; a full-fledged action for the declaration is not necessary.

Re Fulton and Eastern Holdings Ltd., [1973] 2 O.R. 438 (H.C.).
The court refused to determine whether forfeiture had occurred under an agreement of purchase and sale where material facts were in dispute.

Anglo Can. Fire & Gen. Ins. Co. v. Robert E. Cook Ltd., [1973] 2 O.R. 385 (H.C.).
If the interpretation or construction of the document will not end litigation and finally determine the rights of the parties, then this procedure should not be used.

Re Sekretov and Toronto, [1972] 3 O.R. 534, 28 D.L.R. (3d) 661, affirmed [1973] 2 O.R. 161, 33 D.L.R. (3d) 257 (C.A.).
An originating application to quash a municipal by-law or resolution may only be brought pursuant to the *Municipal Act*, R.S.O. 1970, c. 284, s. 286; otherwise a full-fledged action is required.

Re Mosport Park Ltd. and Twp. of Clarke, [1970] 3 O.R. 94 (H.C.).
The court refused to construe a by-law where there was a dispute of fact.

Re Clark and Supertest Petroleum Corp., [1958] O.R. 474, 14 D.L.R. (2d) 454 (H.C.).
A question regarding the right of a mortgagor to redeem may be disposed of by originating notice of motion.

Applications for Declaration of Interest in Land — rule 14.05(3)(e)

Re T.T.C. and Reuben R. Dennis Ltd., [1966] 2 O.R. 336 (C.A.).
The court may determine the effect of an unregistered sublease.

Re Edwards, [1957] O.W.N. 562 (H.C.).
The court refused to deal with a question of ownership of land summarily and required the applicant to proceed under the *Quieting Titles Act*.

Applications to Approve Transactions, etc. — rule 14.05(3)(f)

McKay Estate v. Love (1991), 6 O.R. (3d) 511, 44 E.T.R. 181 (Gen. Div.), affirmed 6 O.R. (3d) 511 at 519, 44 E.T.R. 190, 52 O.A.C. 159, additional reasons November 29, 1991, Doc. CA 841/91 (C.A.).
An application for approval of an estate sale was allowed under rule 14.05(3)(f) where the decision to sell had already been made, and the executor was acting in good faith.

Applications Including Ancillary Relief — rule 14.05(3)(g)

Re Oil, Chemical & Atomic Wkrs. Int. Union, Local 9-14 and Polymer Corp. Ltd., [1966] 1 O.R. 774, 55 D.L.R. (2d) 198 (H.C.).
Declaratory relief is available on originating motion only where specifically allowed by statute or under the Rules. Declaratory relief was denied in this case because it was not ancillary to other relief available on originating motion.

Re Principal Invts. Ltd. and Gibson, [1963] 2 O.R. 507, 40 D.L.R. (2d) 264 (C.A.).

Although the court is reluctant to make declarations on matters which will arise in the future, it may do so where the question is of significant practical importance.

Applications Where No Dispute of Facts — rule 14.05(3)(h)

Moonias v. Ontario (1994), 31 C.P.C. (3d) 149, [1995] 3 C.N.L.R. 108 (Ont. Gen. Div.).

An application for an injunction requiring the Minister to issue a commercial fishing licence without quota restrictions was ordered to proceed by way of trial as there were material facts in dispute.

Mayrand v. 768565 Ontario Ltd. (1990), 75 O.R. (2d) 167, 13 R.P.R. (2d) 1, 72 D.L.R. (4th) 706, 41 O.A.C. 141 (C.A.).

An injunction obtained by residential tenants, restraining their landlord from carrying out repairs, was set aside where each apartment had different problems and material matters were in dispute.

Danson v. Ontario (A.G.) (1987), 60 O.R. (2d) 676, 19 C.P.C. (2d) 249, 41 C.R.R. 48, 41 D.L.R. (4th) 129, 22 O.A.C. 38 (C.A.), affirmed [1990] 2 S.C.R. 1086, 74 O.R. (2d) 763n, 43 C.P.C. (2d) 165, 50 C.R.R. 59, 73 D.L.R. (4th) 686, 112 N.R. 362, 41 O.A.C. 250.

While the Supreme Court of Ontario has inherent jurisdiction to consider the constitutional validity of legislation by way of application, the application must present a factual underpinning for adjudication and a concrete issue to support the constitutional challenge. Courts cannot make a decision in a vacuum, based on the hypothetical.

Acumen Investments Ltd. v. Williams (1985), 53 O.R. (2d) 247, 6 C.P.C. (2d) 21 (*sub nom.* *Acumen Investments Ltd. v. Williams; Dominion Paving Ltd. v. Williams* (H.C.).

The court refused to interpret a municipal by-law where there were material facts in dispute.

Re London Life Ins. Co. and Ont. Human Rights Comm. (1985), 50 O.R. (2d) 748, 8 C.C.E.L. 37, 11 C.C.L.I. 104, 85 C.L.L.C. 17,012, 6 C.H.R.R. D/2891, 18 D.L.R. (4th) 557 (H.C.).

Where a declaration was sought involving interpretation of the *Human Rights Code* and no facts were in dispute, it was held that the proceeding was a proper one by application by reason of rule 14.05(3)(d) and (h).

Re Hotel Dieu Hosp. and St. Catharines (1984), 46 O.R. (2d) 657 (H.C.).

An application under the predecessor of rule 14.05(3)(d) was held to be inappropriate where facts were in dispute.

Re Burlington and Clairton (1979), 24 O.R. (2d) 586, 99 D.L.R. (3d) 170 (C.A.).

Discussion of inappropriateness of originating applications where material facts are in dispute.

Re Bitoff and Fran Restaurants Ltd. (1980), 28 O.R. (2d) 637 (H.C.).

The court refused to entertain an application to determine the enforceability of a covenant alleged to be in restraint of trade.

Re Dennis Commercial Properties Ltd. and Westmount Life Ins. Co., [1969] 2 O.R. 850, 7 D.L.R. (3d) 214, affirmed with a variation [1970] 1 O.R. 698n, 8 D.L.R. (3d) 688n (C.A.).

An assignment of a lease registered on title was expunged from the registry on an application brought by originating motion.

Re Dambrosi, [1957] O.W.N. 364 (H.C.).

The court refused to give a declaration affecting status where the material before it failed to establish that the facts were not in dispute.

TITLE OF PROCEEDING

14.06(1) Every originating process shall contain a title of the proceeding setting out the names of all the parties and the capacity in which they are made parties, if other than their personal capacity.

(2) In an action other than a divorce action, the title of the proceeding shall name the party commencing the action as the plaintiff and the opposite party as the defendant.

(3) In an application, the title of the proceeding shall name the party commencing the application as the applicant and the opposite party, if any, as the respondent and the notice of application shall state the statutory provision or rule, if any, under which the application is made.

Exception

(4) Subrules (1), (2) and (3) do not apply to proceedings under Rules 74 and 75. [am. O. Reg. 484/94, s. 6]

Title of Proceedings — Use of Pseudonyms

J. Doe v. TBH (February 16, 1996), Doc. 95-CQ-62656 (Ont. Gen. Div.).

The court permitted the plaintiff in this sexual assault case to use a pseudonym. It also permitted the defendant, which was a charitable institution who had employed the alleged perpetrator, to use a pseudonym until trial with the trial judge to determine whether the pseudonym should be used during trial. The court file was ordered to be sealed. An order was granted enjoining the disclosure of the names of the parties by anyone who learned them.

Symons v. United Church of Canada (1993), 16 O.R. (3d) 379, 68 O.A.C. 141 (Div. Ct.).

The court granted leave to appeal an order which had dismissed a motion for an order to ban publication of the applicant's name, and to amend the title of proceedings accordingly. The plaintiff alleged that she had been the victim of sexual abuse and the decision conflicted with other cases which had found that requiring publication in such circumstances might deter complainants from coming forward to make allegations of sexual abuse or sexual impropriety. There was good reason to doubt the correctness of the order since it had not addressed the established policy objective of encouraging victims to come forward.

MDS Health Group Ltd. v. Canada (Attorney General) (1993), 15 O.R. (3d) 630, 20 C.P.C. (3d) 137 (Gen. Div.).

The court refused the plaintiffs' motion to use pseudonyms and to seal a court file. Curtailment of public accessibility can only be justified where there is a need to protect social values of superordinate importance. No such values were present.

M. (S.) v. C. (J.R.) (1993), 13 O.R. (3d) 148 (Gen. Div.).

The court refused to waive compliance with rule 14.06 in this sexual assault case. The court must balance the interests of the litigants against the general public's interest in an open court process.

A.(J.) v. Can. Life Assurance Co. (1989), 66 O.R. (2d) 736, 33 C.P.C. (2d) 44 (H.C.), leave to appeal to Ont. Div. Ct. refused 70 O.R. (2d) 27, 35 C.P.C. (2d) 6.

Plaintiffs suffering from AIDS were permitted to use pseudonyms in the title of proceedings.

Re Powell, [1958] O.W.N. 84 (H.C.).

A party was allowed to conduct litigation under an adopted name which he had used for a considerable period of time.

Title of Proceeding — Miscellaneous

Silic v. Ottawa Transportation Comm., [1963] 2 O.R. 477, 40 D.L.R. (2d) 139 (H.C.).

Where the name of a party is omitted from the title of an originating process but appears in the body of the document and it is clear that such person was intended to be a party, it is an irregularity that the court may correct.

Overholt v. Williams, [1956] O.W.N. 891 (Master).

A plaintiff suing in a representative capacity must so indicate in the title.

Ward v. Southorn, [1955] O.W.N. 972 (C.A.).

Failure to indicate in the title that the plaintiff sues in a representative capacity is an irregularity and may be cured by amendment.

Re J.F. Cunningham and Son Ltd., [1955] O.W.N. 668, 35 C.B.R. 131 (Master).

Discussion of proper title in an originating application for a winding-up order.

Aitken v. Gardiner, [1953] O.W.N. 75, 555 (Master).

Discussion of title where there are multiple third and fourth parties.

McCurdy v. Aikens, [1945] O.W.N. 256 (Master).

Where a defendant is sued in an incorrect name, he should file his pleadings in his correct name and state that he was sued in an incorrect name.

HOW ORIGINATING PROCESS ISSUED

14.07(1) An originating process is issued by the registrar's act of dating, signing and sealing it with the seal of the court and assigning to it a court file number.

(2) A copy of the originating process shall be filed in the court file when it is issued.

Sprumont v. Turner (1984), 47 O.R. (2d) 432, 45 C.P.C. 118, 41 R.F.L. (2d) 1, 5 O.A.C. 292 (Div. Ct.).

The court dismissed a motion to set aside a default judgment on the ground that the date of issuance had been omitted from the originating process.

Hubert v. Cortez Explorations Ltd., [1956] O.W.N. 49 (Master).

The omission of the date and place of issue of an originating process is an irregularity and may be cured by amendment.

TIME FOR SERVICE IN ACTIONS

14.08(1) Where an action is commenced by a statement of claim, the statement of claim shall be served within six months after it is issued.

(2) Where an action is commenced by a notice of action, the notice of action and the statement of claim shall be served together within six months after the notice of action is issued.

Cross-Reference: See rule 3.02 and cases thereunder re extension of time for service.

STRIKING OUT OR AMENDING

14.09 An originating process that is not a pleading may be struck out or amended in the same manner as a pleading.

Cross-Reference: See rule 25.11 re striking out pleadings and Rule 26 re amendment of pleadings.

DISMISSAL OF ACTION WHERE DEFENDANT PAYS CLAIM

14.10(1) Where the plaintiff's claim is for money only, a defendant, on paying within the time prescribed for delivery of a defence or at any time before being noted in default, the amount of the plaintiff's claim and the amount claimed for costs, may on motion have the court dismiss the action.

(2) A defendant who considers the amount claimed for costs to be excessive may pay, within the time prescribed for delivery of a defence or at any time before being noted in default, the amount of the plaintiff's claim and the sum of $100 for costs, and the court on motion may dismiss the action and may fix and order payment of the plaintiff's costs or may order payment of the plaintiff's costs as assessed under Rule 58.

RULE 15   REPRESENTATION BY SOLICITOR

Highlights

Rule 15 deals with three aspects of representation by a solicitor.

Where solicitor is required. Rule 15.01 spells out when legal representation is or is not needed. A party who is under disability or is acting in a representative capacity must be represented by a solicitor. A corporate party must be represented by a solicitor, except with leave of the court. Any other party may act in person or be represented by a solicitor.

Authority to commence proceeding. By rule 15.02, a solicitor whose name appears on the originating process can be required to disclose whether he or she commenced or authorized the commencement of the proceeding (note that the solicitor is no longer required to disclose the client's address, but may be required to advise if a client who is a plaintiff resides in Ontario: rule 56.02). However, rule 15.02 goes further than the former Rules and incorporates the principle developed in the case law that a solicitor can be required to disclose whether his or her client authorized the commencement of the proceeding.

Solicitor's lien. Rule 15.03(4) and (5) provide a procedure for a speedy determination of whether a party's former solicitor is entitled to a lien on a party's file and the terms, if any, by which it may be discharged.

Change in representation. Rules 15.03 to 15.06 provide the procedure for changing representation, whether instituted by the client or by the solicitor.

A motion by a solicitor to be removed from the record must be served on the client, but need not be served on the opposing parties: rule 15.04(1). If the order is obtained, however, it must be served on the opposing parties as well as the client and filed with proof of service before it is effective: rule 15.05(b).

Related case law. Cases relating to motions to remove the opposing party's counsel on the grounds of possible conflict of interest, a matter not dealt with by the Rules, are collected under rule 15.04. Special note should be taken of the decision of the Supreme Court of Canada in *MacDonald Estate v. Martin*, [1990] 3 S.C.R. 1235, 48 C.P.C. (2d) 113, [1991] 1 W.W.R. 705, 77 D.L.R. (4th) 249, 70 Man. R. (2d) 241, 121 N.R. 1, in which the court comprehensively reviewed the whole question of the removal of solicitors where a solicitor who formerly worked on one side of the case moves to the law firm representing the opposing party. (For a detailed discussion of the case, see the Annual Survey of Recent Developments in Civil Procedure (SURVEY) in the 1991-92 edition of Watson and McGowan, *Ontario Civil Practice*.)

Former Rules: Rules 13, 390-394.

WHERE SOLICITOR IS REQUIRED

15.01(1) A party to a proceeding who is under disability or acts in a representative capacity shall be represented by a solicitor.

(2) A party to a proceeding that is a corporation shall be represented by a solicitor, except with leave of the court.

(3) Any other party to a proceeding may act in person or be represented by a solicitor.

Representation by Solicitor — Generally

Logan v. Logan (1993), 15 O.R. (3d) 411 (Gen. Div.).

A litigant may retain counsel for specific aspects of a case without requiring counsel to become solicitor of record. In such cases there is no general right to effect service on the litigant by serving counsel.

Re Milligan (1991), 1 C.P.C. (3d) 12 (Ont. Gen. Div.).

The inherent right of a trial judge to control his or her own court process does not carry with it the right to choose which counsel are to appear before him or her. A trial judge must take counsel as they come.

755568 Ontario Ltd. v. Linchris Homes Ltd. (1989), 70 O.R. (2d) 35 (Master).

The court permitted separate solicitors to act on a defence and on the same defendant's counterclaim where there was good reason to permit two solicitors of record to represent the one party.

Guelph (City) v. Maiocco (1988), 26 C.P.C. (2d) 34 (Ont. Master).

A party who happens to be a solicitor but is represented by solicitors of record cannot conduct the examinations for discovery personally. He must take the role of client as long as he has solicitors of record.

Ryan v. Hoover (1984), 45 O.R. (2d) 216, 40 C.P.C. 261 (Master).

After an action had been commenced by one firm of solicitors on behalf of all plaintiffs, one of the plaintiffs was permitted to change solicitors and deliver her own pleading with the court making an order as to the further method of proceeding.

Paupst v. Henry (1983), 43 O.R. (2d) 748, 3 C.C.L.I. 1, 38 C.P.C. 5, 2 D.L.R. (4th) 682 (H.C.).

Solicitors retained by an insurer to defend an action against an insured owe an independent duty to the insured to ensure that the insured is not subjected to proceedings without being properly served. The court permitted a statement of defence to be withdrawn on the eve of trial where the insured defendant had not been served with the originating process.

Battaglia v. Main (1975), 2 C.P.C. 267 (Ont. Co. Ct.).

The naming of two separate solicitors for two separate plaintiffs in an originating process is improper.

Re Canron Ltd. and Can. Wkrs. Union (1976), 12 O.R. (2d) 765, 70 D.L.R. (3d) 198 (H.C.).

As in the case of a corporation, the court may insist that a union be represented by a solicitor.

Northern Wood Preservers Ltd. v. Hall Corp. (Shipping) 1969 Ltd. (1973), 2 O.R. (2d) 335, 42 D.L.R. (3d) 679 (C.A.).

The Court of Appeal approved a requirement of the trial judge that two individual defendants and a corporate defendant having similar interests be represented by the same counsel rather than by separate counsel belonging to the same firm.

Representation by Solicitor — Natural Persons — rule 15.01(3)

92417 Can. Ltd. v. Bomac Batten Ltd. (1984), 45 O.R. (2d) 593, 41 C.P.C. 233 (Master).

A natural person may act in person or through a solicitor but not otherwise.

Bank of N.S. v. Schussler (1980), 28 O.R. (2d) 161, 111 D.L.R. (3d) 509 (H.C.).

A party representing himself may retain counsel without making him solicitor of record.

Re Letros, [1972] 2 O.R. 589, 26 D.L.R. (3d) 257 (C.A.).

A party may not be represented by a spouse who is not a solicitor.

Representation by Solicitor — Corporate Parties

Alles v. Maurice (1992), 9 C.P.C. (3d) 49, 5 B.L.R. (2d) 154 (Ont. Gen. Div.).

Discussion of appointment of counsel to represent corporate parties in oppression proceedings.

419212 Ontario Ltd. v. Astrochrome Crankshaft Toronto Ltd. (1991), 3 O.R. (3d) 116, 48 C.P.C. (2d) 268 (Master).

A motion under rule 15.04 is not the appropriate forum for considering the granting of leave under rule 15.01(2) to a corporation for it to act in person, which requires a separate application by the corporation.

92417 Can. Ltd. v. Bank of Montreal (1984), 45 C.P.C. 149 (Ont. Master).

The court permitted an officer to represent the corporate plaintiff where it could not obtain funds to retain solicitors and would otherwise be unable to seek the remedies to which it might be entitled.

Bural v. Thomas Custom Brokers Ltd. (1978), 20 O.R. (2d) 600, 7 C.P.C. 90 (H.C.).

A corporate defendant is not subject to having its defence struck out merely because it has no solicitor on the record.

DECLARATION OF AUTHORITY TO COMMENCE PROCEEDING

Demand for Declaration by Solicitor

15.02(1) A solicitor who is named in an originating process as the solicitor for the plaintiff or applicant shall, forthwith on receipt of a demand in writing from any person who has been served with the originating process, declare in writing whether he or she commenced or authorized the commencement of the proceeding or whether his or her client authorized the commencement of the proceeding, and where the solicitor fails to comply with the demand,

    (a) the court may order the solicitor to comply with the demand;

    (b) the proceeding may be stayed; and

    (c) the solicitor may be ordered to pay the costs of the proceeding.

Proceeding Commenced without Solicitor's Authority

(2) Where the solicitor declares that he or she did not commence or authorize the commencement of the proceeding, the court on motion without notice may stay or dismiss the proceeding.

Proceeding Commenced without Client's Authority

(3) Where a solicitor has commenced a proceeding without the authority of his or her client, the court on motion may stay or dismiss the proceeding and order the solicitor to pay the costs of the proceeding.

Where Proceeding Stayed

(4) Where a proceeding is stayed under this rule, no further step may be taken without leave of the court.

Cross-Reference: See rule 75.09 regarding steps which constitute a solicitor of record in contentious estate proceedings.

Authority to Act — Generally

Tenan Investments Ltd. v. Regan (1993), 21 C.P.C. (3d) 111, 67 O.A.C. 241 (Div. Ct.).

Where a solicitor's name was used on a notice of appeal without his authority, the appeal was dismissed as an abuse of process.

Battiston & Associates v. Roccari (1988), 27 C.P.C. (2d) 217 (Ont. Master).

An agent has authority to retain a solicitor on his principal's behalf and account.

MacKenzie v. Carroll (1974), 6 O.R. (2d) 706 (H.C.).

A solicitor's authority terminates on the death of his client.

Authority to Act — Corporations

Société Générale (Canada) v. 743823 Ontario Ltd. (1990), 41 C.P.C. (2d) 286 (Ont. Master).

Where a receiver had been appointed over a corporation proposed to be added as a party to an action, the directors and officers were held to have authority to conduct litigation on the corporation's behalf since their authority to do so was unimpaired by the terms of appointment of the receiver and there was no evidence of interference with the receiver's duties.

Melgold Construction Management Ltd. v. Banton Investments Ltd. (1988), 32 C.P.C. (2d) 153, 32 C.L.R. 216 (Ont. Master).

A corporate plaintiff which commences an action in the ordinary course of business need not pass a resolution authorizing the litigation.

Matsushita Elec. of Can. Ltd. v. Wacky Webster (London) Ltd. (1983), 42 O.R. (2d) 795, 37 C.P.C. 223 (H.C.).

A master does not have jurisdiction to consider the sufficiency of the plaintiff's solicitor's authority to commence the action. In this case the solicitor advised that the action had been commenced with the authority of the plaintiff but failed to produce a copy of a resolution of the plaintiff's board authorizing the action.

Sternig v. Pallett (1982), 29 C.P.C. 13 (Ont. Master).

An action against solicitors for negligence falls outside of a corporation's normal business and will be stayed unless commenced with the authority of the directors or shareholders.

Bank of Montreal v. Vola (1980), 31 O.R. (2d) 60, 18 C.P.C. 315, 13 B.L.R. 39 (H.C.).

Where authority to commence certain actions was given by the account manager of one of its branches, the bank was not required to show that express authority was given by the board of directors to commence actions on guarantees in order to maintain the actions.

Bomanak Delicatessen Ltd. v. Minakakis (1974), 4 O.R. (2d) 9 (H.C.).

An action was dismissed where it had been commenced in the name of a corporation without a meeting of the directors or shareholders.

Brismil Mines Ltd. v. Globe Exploration & Mining Co., [1970] 3 O.R. 622 (Master).

The master stayed an action which had been commenced on behalf of a corporation without a resolution of the board of directors giving special authority to do so.

Berg v. Hilco Const. Ltd., [1965] 1 O.R. 38 (Master).

A shareholder of a defendant corporation may conduct the defence where the other shareholders refuse to allow the corporation to do so.

Costs Where Proceeding Commenced Without Client's Authority

Unical Properties v. 784688 Ontario Ltd. (1990), 75 O.R. (2d) 284, 45 C.P.C. (2d) 288, 73 D.L.R. (4th) 761 (Gen. Div.).

Where an action was incorrectly commenced in the name of a partnership, costs were awarded against the partner who gave the instructions to do so, but the solicitors of record were to pay if the partner failed to do so.

Marley-King Line Const. Ltd. v. Marley, [1962] O.W.N. 253 (Master).

The court may order the solicitor for the plaintiff to bear the costs personally, but refused to do so in this case where the solicitor had not been negligent and had acted *bona fide* in the belief that his retainer was sufficient.

CHANGE IN REPRESENTATION BY PARTY

Notice of Change of Solicitor

15.03(1) A party who has a solicitor of record may change the solicitor of record by serving on the solicitor and every other party and filing, with proof of service, a notice of change of solicitor (Form 15A) giving the name, address and telephone number of the new solicitor.

Notice of Appointment of Solicitor

(2) A party acting in person may appoint a solicitor of record by serving on every other party and filing, with proof of service, a notice of appointment of solicitor (Form 15B) giving the name, address and telephone number of the solicitor of record.

Notice of Intention to Act in Person

(3) Subject to subrule 15.01(1) or (2), a party who has a solicitor of record may elect to act in person by serving on the solicitor and every other party and filing, with proof of service, a notice of intention to act in person (Form 15C) that sets out the party's address for service and telephone number.

Claim for Solicitor's Lien

(4) A party may move, on notice to the party's former solicitor of record, for an order determining whether and to what extent the solicitor has a right to a solicitor's lien.

(5) In the order, the court may impose such terms as are just in connection with the lien and its discharge. [am. O. Reg. 377/95, s. 3]

Change of Representation — rule 15.03(1), (2) and (3)

419212 Ontario Ltd. v. Astrochrome Crankshaft Toronto Ltd. (1991), 3 O.R. (3d) 116, 48 C.P.C. (2d) 268 (Master).

A corporation may use the mechanics of rule 15.03 to remove its solicitor as its solicitor of record by serving and filing a notice under rule 15.03(3) amended so as to make it subject to rule 15.01(2). A separate motion for leave under rule 15.01(2) is also required.

94272 Can. Ltd. v. 566501 Ont. Inc. (1988), 66 O.R. (2d) 58, 30 C.P.C. (2d) 71 (Master).

Where a client has served a notice of change of solicitors, a master has no inherent jurisdiction to make an order requiring the previous solicitor to deliver a file to the client.

Lutes v. Lutes (1985), 3 C.P.C. (2d) 7 (Ont. H.C.).

Delivery of a notice of change of solicitors has retroactive effect regarding previous steps taken by the new solicitor.

Solicitor's Lien — rule 15.03(4) and (5)

MOTION BY SOLICITOR FOR REMOVAL AS SOLICITOR OF RECORD

Client to be Served

15.04(1) A solicitor may move, on notice to his or her client, for an order removing him or her as solicitor of record.

(2) Service of a notice of motion for the removal of a solicitor from the record and service of the order shall be made on the client personally or by an alternative to personal service under rule 16.03 or by mailing a copy to the client at the client's last known address.

Party under Disability

(3) Where the party for whom the solicitor is acting is under disability, the notice of motion and the order shall also be served on the litigation guardian and,

(a) where the party is a minor, on the Children's Lawyer; and

(b) in any other case, on the Public Guardian and Trustee.

Contents of Order

(4) The order removing a solicitor from the record shall include,

(a) the client's last known address; and

(b) if the client is a corporation, the text of subrules (6) and (7).

Proof of Service of Order to be Filed

(5) Proof of service of the order shall be filed forthwith after it is served.

Corporations

(6) A client that is a corporation shall, within 10 days after being served with the order removing the solicitor from the record,

(a) appoint a new solicitor of record by serving a notice under subrule 15.03(2); or

(b) obtain and serve an order under subrule 15.01(2) granting it leave to be represented by a person other than a solicitor.

(7) If the corporation fails to comply with subrule (6), the court may dismiss its proceeding or strike out its defence. [am. O. Regs. 739/94, s. 1; 69/ 95, ss. 18, 19, 20]

Removal of Solicitor of Record — Grounds — Generally

Ramsbottom v. Morning (1991), 48 C.P.C. (2d) 177 (Ont. Gen. Div.).

Although otherwise warranted, the court refused to remove the defendant's solicitors where the moving party delayed more than two years in bringing its motion. It would be unfair to require the defendant to give up the solicitors of its choice after that delay.

Ely v. Rosen, [1963] 1 O.R. 47 (Master).

The application must be supported by material indicating the reasons why the solicitor should be removed from the record.

Johnson v. Toronto, [1963] 1 O.R. 627 (Master).

The refusal of the client to make a reasonable payment on account is a sufficient ground for the solicitor to be removed from the record.

Sherman v. Manley (1978), 19 O.R. (2d) 531, 6 C.P.C. 136 (C.A.).

A new trial was ordered where the trial judge refused a request at the opening of the trial by counsel for the defendant to be removed from the record because he had neither the confidence nor the instructions of his client. The antagonism between the solicitor and his client may have had a substantial impact on the outcome of the trial; the Court of Appeal was not satisfied that the defendant received a fair trial.

Removal of Solicitor of Record — Grounds — Solicitor Previously Acting for Opposing Party

Ford Motor Co. of Canada v. Osler, Hoskin & Harcourt (1996), 131 D.L.R. (4th) 419 (Ont. Gen. Div. [Commercial List]).

The court held that a law firm which had acted for Ford in anti-dumping litigation was disqualified from acting for dissenting shareholders of Ford in a subsequent valuation proceeding notwithstanding the use of a "Chinese wall".

Watson v. Trace Estate (1994), 29 C.P.C. (3d) 180 (Ont. Gen. Div.).

Where an associate of the law firm acting for the third party insurer had recently joined counsel for the plaintiff, counsel for the plaintiff was permitted to continue to act as the recommendations of the C.B.A. Task Force on Conflict of Interest were observed.

Chippewas of Kettle & Stony Point v. Canada (A.G.) (1993), 17 C.P.C. (3d) 5 (Ont. Gen. Div.), affirmed, [1994] 2 C.N.L.R. 33 (Ont. Div. Ct.).

The court removed the defendant's solicitors from the record where a former solicitor for the plaintiff joined the defendant's solicitors and timely screening measures were not taken.

Freiman v. Biletzki (January 28, 1993), Doc. 91-CU-42412 (Ont. Master).

Where a firm of solicitors had issued two statements of claim arising from a motor vehicle accident, one on behalf of a passenger against her driver and others, and one on behalf of the passenger and her driver against others, the court ordered the solicitors be removed as solicitors for the driver.

Gouveia v. Fejko (1992), 18 C.P.C. (3d) 12 at 14 (Ont. Master), affirmed 18 C.P.C. (3d) 12 (Ont. Gen. Div.).

Where a law clerk employed by the plaintiff's solicitors had taken a position with the defendant's solicitors' firm, a procedure was established to ensure that no confidential information was passed. That procedure was breached, and accordingly the court ordered that the defendant's solicitors be removed from the record.

Chief Industries Inc. v. Equisource Capital Corp. (1992), 11 C.P.C. (3d) 67 (Ont. Gen. Div.).

Where a solicitor acts against a former client there is a heavy onus to show that no relevant information has been imparted by the former client. The former client must raise the matter at the earliest opportunity.

781332 Ontario Inc. v. Mortgage Insurance Co. of Canada (1991), 5 O.R. (3d) 248, 3 C.P.C. (3d) 33 (Gen. Div.).

Where the solicitor for the plaintiff had previously acted on a related matter for one of the defendants, the plaintiff's right to choose counsel was held to be less important than the interest in preserving the integrity and appearance of the system and the plaintiff's solicitor was removed.

Van Haastrecht v. Dunbar (1991), 1 C.P.C. (3d) 57 (Ont. Gen. Div.).

Where the solicitors for the plaintiffs previously acted for one of the defendants and received confidential information, there was an appearance of impropriety. The solicitors for the plaintiffs were removed from the record.

Quebec v. Ontario (Securities Commission) (1991), 3 W.D.C.P. (2d) 2 (Ont. Div. Ct.).

The court refused to disqualify the firm of solicitors acting for the respondent where the firm had merged with a Quebec firm which had had a watching brief in a related Quebec proceeding. The Quebec firm's retainer had been very limited and there had been no access to relevant confidential information.

Calgas Investments Ltd. v. 784688 Ontario Ltd. (1991), 4 O.R. (3d) 459, 1 C.P.C. (3d) 64, 81 D.L.R. (4th) 518, additional reasons 1 C.P.C. (3d) 64n (Gen. Div.), leave to appeal to Ont. Div. Ct. refused 4 O.R. (3d) 459n.

There is a rebuttable inference to be drawn that confidences are shared among solicitors in a firm. Where a solicitor had acted for the first party and later joined a firm acting for the second party, and where the inference was not rebutted, the court ordered the firm removed from the record.

MacDonald Estate v. Martin, [1990] 3 S.C.R. 1235, 48 C.P.C. (2d) 113, [1991] 1 W.W.R. 705, 77 D.L.R. (4th) 249, 70 Man. R. (2d) 241, 121 N.R. 1.

The court removed the plaintiff's solicitors where a junior lawyer who had formerly been employed by the defendant's solicitors and was involved in the particular matter in dispute became employed by the plaintiff's solicitors. Discussion of tests and issues.

Williams v. Williams (1990), 44 C.P.C. (2d) 277 (Ont. H.C.).

The court ordered that the solicitors for the petitioner in a divorce proceeding be removed from the record where there was an appearance of professional impropriety arising from the fact that a predecessor firm had received confidential information from the respondent.

Messinger v. Bramalea Ltd. (1989), 35 C.P.C. (2d) 260 (Ont. H.C.).

The court removed solicitors acting against a former client, for whom they had drafted a will, due to an appearance of impropriety even though the litigation was unrelated.

Gavras v. Darrell Kent Real Estate Ltd. (1989), 37 C.P.C. (2d) 306 (Ont. Master), affirmed 43 C.P.C. (2d) 14 (Ont. H.C.).

The court ordered that the plaintiff's solicitors cease to act where the plaintiff's son, who had previously given advice to one of the defendants, joined the firm of solicitors representing the plaintiff.

Dzamba v. Hurst (1988), 63 O.R. (2d) 790, 25 C.P.C. (2d) 103 (Master).

The court removed the solicitors for the defendant where the solicitors had previously acted for a corporation jointly owned by the plaintiff and defendant.

Muurmans Valkenburg B.V. v. Lemmon (1987), 23 C.P.C. (2d) 269 (Ont. Master).

The court restrained the plaintiff's solicitors from continuing to act where the action involved financing documents prepared by the solicitors and executed by the defendants after discussions with the solicitors. The solicitors had not been retained by the defendants and had told the defendants to obtain independent counsel but gave advice regarding the financing intended to be relied upon by the defendants.

Crystal Heights Co-operative Inc. v. Barban Builders Inc. (1987), 19 C.P.C. (2d) 212 (Ont. Dist. Ct.).

The court held that a delay of almost two years in moving to remove a solicitor for conflict of interest in the litigation was fatal to the motion due to the prejudice and delay the removal would cause.

Royal Bank v. Appleton (1987), 17 C.P.C. (2d) 209 (Ont. H.C.)

Counsel was restrained from continuing to act for a party after joining a firm which had acted for an opposing party in the past and had thereby acquired confidential information. The appearance of unfairness outweighed any prejudice from the removal.

Negro v. Walker (1986), 7 C.P.C. (2d) 215 (Ont. Dist. Ct.).

The court refused to restrain the firm of solicitors acting for the defendants from continuing to act where a sole practitioner who had previously advised the plaintiff joined the firm on the eve of trial. The solicitor having carriage of the defendant's case had not discussed the case with his new partner, undertook not to do so in the future and undertook not to call her as a witness.

Brown v. Hodsoll (1986), 7 C.P.C. (2d) 267 (Ont. H.C.).

The court refused to restrain the firm of solicitors acting for the plaintiff from continuing to act where the solicitor who had previously had carriage of the defendants' case joined the firm. The solicitor undertook not to discuss the matter with his new colleagues and steps were taken to isolate the solicitor from any involvement with the plaintiff's case.

Flynn Development Co. v. Central Trust Co. (1985), 51 O.R. (2d) 57 (H.C.).

A law firm was restrained from acting where it had represented both parties in a transaction that was an integral part of the present litigation.

Szebelledy v. Constitution Ins. Co. of Can. ; Kozma v. Szebelledy (1985), 3 C.P.C. (2d) 170, 11 C.C.L.I. 140 (Ont. Dist. Ct.).

Where an insurer appointed the same counsel to defend both an action against its insured resulting from a motor vehicle accident and an action by the insured against the insurer under the unidentified motorist coverage, the court intervened and required it to obtain separate counsel.

Lukic v. Urquhart (1984), 47 O.R. (2d) 462, 45 C.P.C. 19, 11 D.L.R. (4th) 638 (H.C.), reversed in part on other grounds (1985), 50 O.R. (2d) 47, 15 D.L.R. (4th) 639 (C.A.).

On a motion to remove an opposing party's counsel the court must balance a party's right to be represented by his or her counsel of choice against the avoidance not only of professional impropriety but also of the appearance of professional impropriety. The court may not inquire whether the solicitor in fact received confidential information during his previous employment by the former client.

Diamond v. Kaufman (1984), 45 C.P.C. 23 (Ont. H.C.).

Where the plaintiff sought specific performance of an agreement to issue shares in the corporate defendant and, if successful, would require the corporate defendant to sue the individual defendants, the court ordered the corporate defendant and individual defendants to be represented by separate counsel.

Bank of Montreal v. MacKenzie (1984), 45 C.P.C. 29 (Ont. H.C.), leave to appeal to Ont. Div. Ct. refused 46 C.P.C. 1.

The court refused the defendant's motion to remove the plaintiff's solicitors on the grounds the solicitors also acted against the defendant in a separate action by another plaintiff who had a fiduciary relationship with the defendant.

Christo v. Bevan (1982), 36 O.R. (2d) 797, 27 C.P.C. 209, 28 R.F.L. (2d) 197 (H.C.).

Where the solicitor for one party has previously acted for an opposing party, the court may disqualify the solicitor if there is a probability of mischief or prejudice if the solicitor were permitted to act.

Falls v. Falls (1979), 12 C.P.C. 270, 12 R.F.L. (2d) 389 (Ont. Co. Ct.).

Where the wife's solicitors had previously acted for the husband in certain matters, an application to restrain them from acting for her in *Family Law Reform Act* proceedings was successful.

Steed & Evans Ltd. v. MacTavish (1976), 12 O.R. (2d) 236, 68 D.L.R. (3d) 420 (H.C.).

A party is not permitted to be represented by a solicitor who has previously represented an opposing party if there is a possibility that the solicitor may use information confidentially obtained from that opposing party.

Removal of Solicitor of Record — On Grounds that a Lawyer May Not Be Both Counsel and Witness

Woodglen & Co. v. Owens (1995), 38 C.P.C. (3d) 354 (Ont. Gen. Div.).

The defendants brought a motion to remove the plaintiffs' solicitors of record on the grounds that members of that firm might be called as witnesses at trial. The motion was dismissed as being premature, as the conflict was potential rather than actual given the stage of the proceedings.

Stevens v. Salt (1995), 22 O.R. (3d) 675 (Gen. Div.).

The court ordered that neither the solicitors who conducted the disputed real estate transaction nor those associated with them could appear as counsel.

Essa (Township) v. Guergis (1993), 15 O.R. (3d) 573, 22 C.P.C. (3d) 63 (*sub nom. Heck v. Royal Bank*) 52 C.P.R. (3d) 372 (Div. Ct.).

Where junior counsel for the plaintiff had sworn an affidavit to be used on the motion but did not intend to argue the motion, the plaintiff was not required to retain new counsel. Nor should any premature order be made by a court preventing counsel from acting at trial where a member or associate of his or her firm may be a trial witness. Rather, the court should follow a flexible approach and consider each case on its own merits.

Kitzerman v. Kitzerman (1993), 4 W.D.C.P. (2d) 43 (Ont. Master).

The court removed the plaintiff's solicitor of record where the defendant intended to call a member of the plaintiff's firm of solicitors as a witness at trial.

Newmarch Mechanical Constructors Ltd. v. Hyundai Auto Canada Inc. (1992), 13 C.P.C. (3d) 349 (Ont. Master).

Where G, a partner with the plaintiff's solicitors, was likely to be a witness at trial, the court refused to remove the solicitors from the record, but ordered that G was not to act as counsel at discovery and that the defendant could move at the opening of trial to disqualify G from acting as counsel at trial.

Crosner v. Canadian Electronic Office Equipment Inc. (1992), 7 C.P.C. (3d) 318 (Ont. Gen. Div.).

A solicitor acting for his mother, who did not qualify for legal aid because her son was a lawyer, was ordered not to act as counsel at trial where he might be required as a witness. He was permitted to act as counsel until trial.

777829 Ont. Ltd. v. 616070 Ont. Inc. (1989), 16 W.D.C.P. 227 (Ont. Master).

The court ordered that a firm cease to act for the defendants where lawyers from the firm would be witnesses at trial.

Planned Ins. Portfolios Co. v. Crown Life Ins. Co. (1989), 68 O.R. (2d) 271, 36 C.P.C. (2d) 218, 58 D.L.R. (4th) 106 (H.C.).

The court refused to remove counsel for a party where the counsel's partner would be called as a witness at trial.

Shaughnessy Brothers Investments Ltd. v. Lakehead Trailer Park (1985) Ltd. (1987), 23 C.P.C. (2d) 194 (Ont. H.C.).

Where members of a law firm and a secretary employed by the firm were defendants in a claim for fraudulent conspiracy and were represented by a solicitor who became associated with the firm after the alleged cause of action arose, the court ordered that the solicitor be removed as the solicitor for the secretary.

Removal of Solicitor of Record — Miscellaneous

Duffy v. Great Central Publishing Co. (1995), 7 W.D.C.P. (2d) 42 (Ont. Gen. Div.).

The court dismissed the defendant's motion to remove the plaintiff's solicitors on the ground they had obtained confidential information from the defendant in an earlier law suit in which they acted for another plaintiff, which information was subject to the 'implied undertaking''. The subject information could be obtained in the present suit regardless of the identity of the plaintiff's solicitors.

Chapman v. 3M Canada Inc. (1995), 25 O.R. (3d) 658 (Gen. Div.).

The court dismissed the plaintiff's motion to remove the solicitors for numerous defendants on the basis of potential conflict among the defendants. Although the plaintiff had status to raise the potential conflict, the matter was hypothetical and contrary to the facts alleged by the defendants.

ABN Amro Bank Canada v. Krupp MaK Maschinenbau GmbH (1994), 20 O.R. (3d) 36, 34 C.P.C. (3d) 94, 27 C.B.R. (3d) 228 (Gen. Div.).

A motion to remove a law firm as solicitor of record for a party was dismissed where the removal would result in confusion, delay and expense. Furthermore, there was no compelling reason for the removal as no confidential information was involved, and the moving party had delayed in bringing the motion.

Coulombe v. Beard (1993), 16 O.R. (3d) 627, 22 C.P.C. (3d) 101 (Gen. Div.).

The plaintiffs' motion to have the defendants' solicitors removed from the record was dismissed, although they had inadvertently been faxed a letter which had set out the plaintiffs' proposed trial tactics and the opinion of an expert witness who had not delivered a report. Although the information was privileged, there was no risk that the information would be used to the prejudice of the plaintiffs.

MacDonald v. Klein (1993), 17 C.P.C. (3d) 1 (Ont. Gen. Div.).

The court refused to remove the plaintiff's solicitor from the record for entering into a solicitor and client relationship with witnesses who were being cross-examined under rule 39.02.

Everingham v. Ontario (1992), 8 O.R. (3d) 121, 5 C.P.C. (3d) 118, 88 D.L.R. (4th) 755, 54 O.A.C. 224 (Div. Ct.).

The court upheld an order removing the solicitor for the respondent who had spoken with one of the applicants, a mental patient, before a scheduled cross-examination, notwithstanding that the meeting was coincidental and the subject matter of the examination not discussed.

Kennedy v. Guardian Insurance of Canada (1992), 1 C.P.C. (3d) 304 (Ont. Gen. Div.).

While the courts retain the ultimate right to determine who should be granted audience, matters such as an alleged breach of professional conduct are better handled by the Law Society.

Kuiack v. Babcock Estate (1991), 5 O.R. (3d) 650 (Gen. Div.).

The court refused to remove the plaintiff's solicitor who had also been consulted by a defendant. The defendant concerned gave no confidential information and did not object to the plaintiff's solicitor acting.

Appleton v. Hawes (1989), 17 W.D.C.P. 278 (Ont. H.C.).

Where solicitors for a party received privileged information from an investigator retained by an opposing party, the court ordered the solicitors removed from the record.

Kewell v. Paul, [1968] 2 O.R. 73 (Master).

Where a solicitor defends an action on behalf of an infant without the appointment of a litigation guardian and the Official Guardian is subsequently appointed, no order is required to remove the solicitor from the record.

Bural v. Thomas Custom Brokers Ltd. (1978), 20 O.R. (2d) 600, 7 C.P.C. 90 (H.C.).

A corporate defendant's defence will not be struck out when its solicitor is removed from the record.

DUTY OF SOLICITOR OF RECORD

15.05 A solicitor of record shall act as and remains the solicitor of record for his or her client until,

(a) the client delivers a notice under rule 15.03; or

(b) an order removing the solicitor from the record has been entered, served on the client and every other party and, where required by subrule 15.04(3), in accordance with that subrule, and filed with proof of service.

Duca Community Credit Union Ltd. v. Tay (1995), 26 O.R. (3d) 172 (Gen. Div.).

The solicitor of record must attend in court every time the proceeding is before the court notwithstanding the client's instruction to reduce costs by not attending a hearing.

R. Sherwin Enterprises Ltd. v. Municipal Contracting Services Ltd. (1994), 20 O.R. (3d) 692, 33 C.P.C. (3d) 244 (Gen. Div.).

The court removed the solicitors of record for one set of defendants where those solicitors had previously acted for the insurer of one of the other defendants regarding the same dispute.

Weldo Plastics Ltd. v. Communication Press Ltd. (1987), 19 C.P.C. (2d) 36 (Ont. Dist. Ct.).

Counsel has a duty to the court to attend at trial despite instructions from his client to the contrary, unless he is removed from the record or has withdrawn the defence.

WHERE A SOLICITOR OF RECORD HAS CEASED TO PRACTISE

15.06 Where the solicitor of record for a party has ceased to practise law, and the party for whom the solicitor acted has not served a notice under rule 15.03, any other party may serve a document on the party by mailing a copy to the party at the party's last known address, or may move for directions.

SERVICE

RULE 16   SERVICE OF DOCUMENTS

Highlights

Rule 16 provides a general code as to how all documents are to be served under the Rules or pursuant to a court order. The basic scheme (rule 16.01) is that every originating process (see the definition in rule 1.03) is to be served personally or by an alternative to personal service (except that with respect to a divorce petition only some of the alternatives to personal service may be used: rule 69.04(1)). No other document need be served personally, or by an alternative to personal service, unless so required by the Rules or a court order.

Personal service. Rule 16.02(1) contains a comprehensive listing of how personal service is to be made on a wide range of persons. A person effecting personal service does not have to produce the original or have it in his or her possession: rule 16.02(2).

Alternatives to personal service. There are four of these: acceptance of service by a solicitor (rule 16.03(2) and (3)), service by mail (rule 16.03(4)), service by leaving the document at the person's place of residence (rule 16.03(5)) and service by mail on a corporation where it cannot be found at its registered address (rule 16.03(6)). It is to be noted that there are situations under the Rules requiring personal service, where the alternatives to personal service *may not* be used, *e.g.* service of a divorce petition (rule 16.01(1), but see rule 69.04(1)), service of a notice of examination in some circumstances (rule 34.04) or a summons to a witness (rules 34.04(4) and 53.04(4)).

Other matters. The court has jurisdiction to order substituted service where for any reason it is impractical to effect prompt personal service or ''where necessary in the interest of justice'' the court may dispense with service (rule 16.04(1)). The court may grant relief where a party who has been technically served did not in fact receive the document in a timely manner (rule 16.07) and may also validate irregular service or attempted service on a person who evaded service: rule 16.08. Where service is effected by a sheriff, he or she may prove the service by a certificate of service, rather than an affidavit of service: rule 16.09(2).

The service of documents not required to be served personally has been modernized to permit service by telecopier. If the party to be served has a solicitor, service must be on the solicitor (rule 16.01(4)) either by mail, by courier, by leaving it at his or her office, by depositing it at a document exchange or by fax (*i.e.* by telephone transmission of a facsimile of the document): rule 16.05. If the person to be served is unrepresented, he or she may be served by mail or by personal service or an alternative to personal service: rule 16.01(4).

Proof of service is governed by rule 16.09 which, *inter alia*, dispenses with the requirement that an affidavit of service has to be a separate document. Rule 16.09(5) permits the use of an ink stamp or a prepared sticker incorporating an affidavit of service to be added to the backsheet. Alternatively, a printed form of backsheet might include one of the more frequently used affidavits of service.

Where it is intended in the Rules that the provisions of Rule 16 as to service are *not* to be engaged, the rule does not use the term ''serve'' but some other term, *e.g.*

"give notice ... by mail (rule 60.13(2)) or "mail a notice of listing for hearing" (rule 61.09(5)), or "give a copy of the notice to his or her client" (rule 48.14(2)).

No document may be served on Sunday without leave of the court: *Courts of Justice Act*, s. 124.

Former Rules: Rules 15-23, 200-206.

GENERAL RULES FOR MANNER OF SERVICE

Originating Process

16.01(1) An originating process shall be served personally as provided in rule 16.02 or, except in the case of a divorce petition, by an alternative to personal service as provided in rule 16.03.

(2) An originating process need not be served on a party who has delivered a defence, notice of intention to defend or notice of appearance without being served.

All Other Documents

(3) No other document need be served personally, or by an alternative to personal service, unless these rules or an order require personal service or an alternative to personal service.

(4) Any document that is not required to be served personally or by an alternative to personal service,

(a) shall be served on a party who has a solicitor of record by serving the solicitor, and service may be made in a manner provided in rule 16.05;

(b) may be served on a party acting in person or on a person who is not a party,

(i) by mailing a copy of the document to the last address for service provided by the party or person or, if no such address has been provided, to the party's or person's last known address, or

(ii) by personal service or by an alternative to personal service.

McLean v. Bradley (March 19, 1996), Doc. Sudbury C-1571/95 (Ont. Gen. Div.).

Where the defendant was served by an irregular method but delivered a notice of intent to defend, the court held it was not necessary to serve the defendant properly.

NRS London Realty Ltd. v. Glenn (1989), 67 O.R. (2d) 704 (Dist. Ct.).

In the absence of an order, service of documents by courier is not sufficient.

Fromovitz v. Fromovitz, [1962] O.R. 120, 31 D.L.R. (2d) 221 (H.C.).

Where the originating process was not served on the defendant, the entire proceeding was set aside as a nullity.

Conacher v. Conacher, [1956] O.W.N. 347 (Master).

If the copy of an originating process served does not indicate that the original has been signed and sealed, service will be set aside.

PERSONAL SERVICE

16.02(1) Where a document is to be served personally, the service shall be made,

Individual

(a) on an individual, other than a person under disability, by leaving a copy of the document with the individual;

Municipality

(b) on a municipal corporation, by leaving a copy of the document with the chairman, mayor, warden or reeve of the municipality, with the clerk or deputy clerk of the municipality or with a solicitor for the municipality;

Corporation

(c) on any other corporation, by leaving a copy of the document with an officer, director or agent of the corporation, or with a person at any place of business of the corporation who appears to be in control or management of the place of business;

Board or Commission

(d) on a board or commission, by leaving a copy of the document with a member or officer of the board or commission;

Person outside Ontario Carrying on Business in Ontario

(e) on a person outside Ontario who carries on business in Ontario, by leaving a copy of the document with anyone carrying on business in Ontario for the person;

Crown in Right of Canada

(f) on Her Majesty the Queen in right of Canada, in accordance with subsection 23(3) of the *Crown Liability Act* (Canada);

Crown in Right of Ontario

(g) on Her Majesty the Queen in right of Ontario, in accordance with section 10 of the *Proceedings Against the Crown Act*;

Attorney General

(h) on the Attorney General of Ontario, by leaving a copy of the document with a solicitor in the Crown Law Office (Civil Law) of the Ministry of the Attorney General;

Absentee

(i) on an absentee, by leaving a copy of the document with the absentee's committee, if one has been appointed or, if not, with the Public Guardian and Trustee;

Minor

(j) on a minor, by leaving a copy of the document with the litigation guardian if one has been appointed or, if not, with the minor and, where the minor resides with a parent or other person having the care or lawful custody of the minor, by leaving another copy of the document with the parent or other person, but, where the proceeding is in respect of the minor's interest in an estate or trust, the minor shall be served by leaving with the Children's Lawyer a copy of the document bearing the name and address of the minor;

Mentally Incapable Person
(k) on a mentally incapable person,
    (i) if there is a guardian or an attorney acting under a validated power of attorney for personal care with authority to act in the proceeding, by leaving a copy of the document with the guardian or attorney,
    (ii) if there is no guardian or attorney acting under a validated power of attorney for personal care with authority to act in the proceeding but there is an attorney under a power of attorney with authority to act in the proceeding, by leaving a copy of the document with the attorney and leaving an additional copy with the person,
    (iii) if there is neither a guardian nor an attorney with authority to act in the proceeding, by leaving a copy of the document bearing the person's name and address with the Public Guardian and Trustee and leaving an additional copy with the person;
(l) [Revoked O. Reg. 69/95, s. 6]

Partnership
(m) on a partnership, by leaving a copy of the document with any one or more of the partners or with a person at the principal place of business of the partnership who appears to be in control or management of the place of business; and

Sole Proprietorship
(n) on a sole proprietorship, by leaving a copy of the document with the sole proprietor or with a person at the principal place of business of the sole proprietorship who appears to be in control or management of the place of business.

(2) A person effecting personal service of a document need not produce the original document or have it in his or her possession. [am. O. Regs. 465/93, s. 3; 69/95, ss. 6, 19, 20]

Personal Service on Individuals — rule 16.02(1)(a)

Can.-Dom. Leasing Corp. Ltd. v. Corpex Ltd., [1963] 2 O.R. 497 (Master).

Service is effected if the document is brought to the notice of the recipient and the recipient has some knowledge of its contents.

Personal Service on Corporations — rule 16.02(1)(c)

Santa Marina Shipping Co. S.A. v. Lunham & Moore Ltd. (1978), 18 O.R. (2d) 315, 5 C.P.C. 146, 82 D.L.R. (3d) 295 (H.C.).

Where the defendant corporation does not carry on any part of its business in Ontario, service on an officer, director, or agent who is in Ontario for reasons unrelated to the corporation's business is invalid.

Personal Service on Persons Outside Ontario Carrying on Business in Ontario — rule 16.02(1)(e)

Interamerican Transport Systems Inc. v. Grand Trunk Western Railroad (1985), 51 O.R. (2d) 568, 10 O.A.C. 185 (Div. Ct.).

A railway company was held to carry on business in Ontario where it had a sales representative resident in Ontario soliciting business from Ontario customers.

Can. Life Assur. Co. v. C.I.B.C. (1974), 3 O.R. (2d) 70, 44 D.L.R. (3d) 486 (C.A.).

Detailed discussion of authorities.

Wee-Gee Uranium Mines Ltd. v. New York Times Co., [1969] 1 O.R. 741 (H.C.).

A newspaper which stations a reporter in Ontario for the sole purpose of gathering news does not carry on business in Ontario. "Carrying on business" is given a narrow and restrictive interpretation.

Sarco Can. Ltd. v. Pyrotherm Equipment Ltd., [1969] 1 O.R. 426, 40 Fox Pat. C. 182 (Master).

A corporate officer attending a trial in Ontario is not carrying on the business of the company in Ontario; nor is an Ontario company which distributes the foreign company's products.

Droeske v. Champlain Coach Lines Ltd., [1939] O.R. 560, 50 C.R.T.C. 248, [1939] 4 D.L.R. 210 (C.A.).

"Any person" in this provision includes any corporation. A domestic corporation selling tickets and transportation for a foreign corporation may be properly served as an agent of the foreign corporation carrying on business in Ontario.

Higgins v. Merland Oil Co., [1933] O.W.N. 679 (H.C.).

The test applied is whether the business done has continued for a substantial period of time, is done at a fixed place, and is not merely the transmission by an agent to the principal outside the jurisdiction, but rather is the actual transacting within Ontario of some of the business of the company.

Appel v. Anchor Ins. and Invt. Corp. Ltd. (1921), 21 O.W.N. 25 (H.C.).

Service can only be predicated upon an actual transaction of business within the jurisdiction, not upon some isolated act.

Personal Service on Crown — rule 16.02(1)(f), (g)

Mai v. Mississauga (City) (1990), 72 O.R. (2d) 97, 47 C.P.C. (2d) 1, 67 D.L.R. (4th) 138 (H.C.).

Since a pre-action notice of claim under the *Proceedings Against the Crown Act* is not an originating process, personal service of the notice is not required and the proper method of service is by mailing a copy of the document to the person's last known address under rule 16.01(4).

Bohatchuk v. Ont. (1983), 32 C.P.C. 220 (Ont. Dist. Ct.).

The Queen in right of Ontario may be served by serving a Crown Attorney.

Personal Service — Miscellaneous

Anglo Oriental Ltd. v. Montreal Shipping Inc. (1986), 13 C.P.C. (2d) 116 (Ont. H.C.).

Service of originating process on a ship was permitted by the court to be made by personal service on the ship's managing operator.

Maritime Life Assur. Co. v. Karapatakis (1979), 24 O.R. (2d) 311, 7 R.P.R. 229, 9 R.F.L. (2d) 265 (Master).

Discussion of interrelation of s. 43(2) of the *Family Law Reform Act* and the rules dealing with service of process.

ALTERNATIVES TO PERSONAL SERVICE

Where Available
16.03(1) **Where these rules or an order of the court permit service by an alternative to personal service, service shall be made in accordance with this rule.**

Acceptance of Service by Solicitor
(2) **Service on a party who has a solicitor may be made by leaving a copy of the document with the solicitor or an employee in the solicitor's office, but service under this subrule is effective only if the solicitor endorses on the document or a copy of it an acceptance of service and the date of the acceptance.**

(3) **By accepting service the solicitor shall be deemed to represent to the court that the solicitor has the authority of his or her client to accept service.**

Service by Mail to Last Known Address
(4) **Service of a document may be made by sending a copy of the document together with an acknowledgment of receipt card (Form 16A) by mail to the last known address of the person to be served, but service by mail under this subrule is effective,**
(a) **only if the acknowledgment of receipt card or a post office receipt bearing a signature that purports to be the signature of the person to be served is received by the sender; and**
(b) **on the date on which the sender first receives either receipt, signed as provided by clause (a).**

Service at Place of Residence
(5) **Where an attempt is made to effect personal service at a person's place of residence and for any reason personal service cannot be effected, the document may be served by,**
(a) **leaving a copy, in a sealed envelope addressed to the person, at the place of residence with anyone who appears to be an adult member of the same household; and**
(b) **on the same day or the following day mailing another copy of the document to the person at the place of residence,**
and service in this manner is effective on the fifth day after the document is mailed.

Service on a Corporation
(6) **Where the head office, registered office or principal place of business of a corporation or, in the case of an extra-provincial corporation, the attorney for service in Ontario cannot be found at the last address recorded with the Ministry of Consumer and Commercial Relations, service may be made on the corporation by mailing a copy of the document to the corporation or to the attorney for service in Ontario, as the case may be, at that address.**

Acceptance of Service by Solicitor — rule 16.03(2)

Royal Trust Corp. of Canada v. Dunn (1991), 6 O.R. (3d) 468, 6 C.P.C. (3d) 351, 86 D.L.R. (4th) 490 (Gen. Div.).

A party relying on rule 16.03(2) must assume the obligation of confirming that the solicitor who accepts service has the authority to do so. "Deemed" in rule 16.03(3) means "deemed until the contrary is proved". A default judgment based on acceptance of service by a solicitor without authority to do so was set aside.

T.D. Bank v. Palyi (1973), 3 O.R. (2d) 302 (Master).

Acceptance of service by the secretary of a solicitor was held to be sufficient where it appeared that she was acting within the scope of her authority.

SUBSTITUTED SERVICE OR DISPENSING WITH SERVICE

Where Order May be Made

16.04(1) Where it appears to the court that it is impractical for any reason to effect prompt service of an originating process or any other document required to be served personally or by an alternative to personal service under these rules, the court may make an order for substituted service or, where necessary in the interest of justice, may dispense with service.

Effective Date of Service

(2) In an order for substituted service, the court shall specify when service in accordance with the order is effective.

(3) Where an order is made dispensing with service of a document, the document shall be deemed to have been served on the date of the order for the purpose of the computation of time under these rules.

Substituted Service — Generally

Mehta v. Wellman (1988), 27 C.P.C. (2d) 180 (Ont. Dist. Ct.).

Where a defendant is too ill to instruct counsel, the court should not set aside substituted service but rather should extend the time to file the statement of defence based on medical evidence before the court. Substituted service will usually be granted on the solicitor who acted for the defendant in the transaction which is the subject-matter of the suit.

Medd v. Farm Number One Ltd. (1987), 62 O.R. (2d) 170 (Dist. Ct.).

An order for substitutional service does not preclude personal service of a statement of claim. If there has been both substitutional and personal service, the time limited for the delivery of a statement of defence runs from the earlier of the effective dates of service.

Ruby & Edwardh v. Jaffe (1986), 56 O.R. (2d) 177, 10 C.P.C. (2d) 133 (H.C.).

Service pursuant to an order for substituted service providing that service is deemed to occur on a particular date is not effective if all steps required to effect service are not actually completed by the deemed date of service.

Lower St. Lawrence Ocean Agencies Ltd. v. Samatour Shipping Co. (1984), 47 C.P.C. 199 (Fed. T.D.).

In this maritime law case the court permitted service on a non-resident defendant by serving Montreal solicitors acting for the defendant's insurer regarding another matter.

Misener v. Hotel Dieu Hosp. (1983), 42 O.R. (2d) 694, 36 C.P.C. 292 (H.C.).

A summons to witness may be ordered served substitutionally.

Babineau v. Babineau (1983), 32 C.P.C. 229 (Ont. Master).

In general, an order for substitutional service should be made only if it is probable that the party being served will receive actual notice; however, if denial of substitutional service would deprive the plaintiff of the right to relief, the requirement may be relaxed and an order made if it is *possible* there will be actual notice.

Re French and L.S.U.C. (No. 4) (1976), 12 O.R. (2d) 361 (Div. Ct.).

Deemed service under a statute may be conclusive.

Eyre v. Eyre, [1971] 2 O.R. 744 (Master).

Substituted service of an originating process will not be set aside where it appears the defendant has had notice of it; notice may be inferred where counsel appears on behalf of the defendant.

Wiley, Lowe & Co. v. Gould, [1958] O.W.N. 316 (H.C.).

An order for substituted service on a non-resident may be made if he is within the jurisdiction on the date of issue of the originating process or the date of service or if he left the jurisdiction, knowing of the originating process, to avoid service.

McLaren v. Oster, [1956] O.W.N. 666 (Master).

A non-party upon whom substituted service has been ordered has no standing to challenge the order if the party sought to be served has in fact received notice of the document served.

Rabichaud v. Rabichaud and Ramsay, [1948] O.W.N. 727 (C.A.).

Substituted service by mailing to an address out of Ontario is permissible.

Substituted Service — Service on Defendant's Insurer

Kalsar v. Irvine (1981), 24 C.P.C. 281, 126 D.L.R. (3d) 190, affirmed (1982), 133 D.L.R. (3d) 512 (Ont. Div. Ct.).

Substituted service on the defendant's insurer was permitted where the plaintiff had taken all reasonable steps to locate the defendant.

Meius v. Pippy (1980), 20 C.P.C. 215 (Ont. H.C.).

Where the plaintiff was unable to locate the defendant after taking every reasonable step, substitutional service upon the insurer was permitted.

Box v. Ergen (1978), 20 O.R. (2d) 635 at 639, 88 D.L.R. (3d) 408 at 412 (H.C.).

The court stated in *obiter dicta* that an insurance company is not the agent for service of a defendant insured.

Starosta v. Simpson (1974), 6 O.R. (2d) 384 (H.C.).

Service on an insurer as an agent of an unnamed insured was set aside where the insurer had had no contact with the insured.

Saraceni v. Rechenberg, [1971] 2 O.R. 735 (Co. Ct.).

Substituted service of an originating process on the insurer of the defendant was ordered.

Dispensing With Service

Joe v. Joe (1984), 46 O.R. (2d) 764, 39 R.F.L. (2d) 444, 10 D.L.R. (4th) 472 (C.A.), leave to appeal to Supreme Court of Canada refused 46 O.R. (2d) 764n, 10 D.L.R. (4th) 472n, 56 N.R. 396, 4 O.A.C. 318n.

Former Rule 792, which provided for dispensing with service in a divorce petition where the respondent could not be found and the only claim was for dissolution of marriage, was held not to violate s. 2(e) of the *Canadian Bill of Rights.*

Nanasi v. Nanasi (1977), 17 O.R. (2d) 591, 1 Fam. L. Rev. 80 (U.F.C.).

Where the court was satisfied that no method of service could reasonably be expected to bring notice of the proceedings to the respondent, it dispensed with service.

SERVICE ON SOLICITOR OF RECORD

16.05(1) Service of a document on the solicitor of record of a party may be made,

(a) by mailing a copy to the solicitor's office;

(b) by leaving a copy with a solicitor or employee in the solicitor's office;

(c) by depositing a copy at a document exchange of which the solicitor is a member or subscriber, but service under this clause is effective only if the document or a copy of it and the copy deposited are date stamped by the document exchange in the presence of the person depositing the copy;

(d) by telephone transmission to the solicitor's office of a facsimile of the document in accordance with subrules (3), (3.1), and (3.2) but, where service is made under this clause between 5 p.m. and midnight, it shall be deemed to have been made on the following day; or

(e) by sending a copy to the solicitor's office by courier.

(2) Service of a document by depositing a copy at a document exchange under clause (1)(c) is effective on the day following the day on which it was deposited and date stamped, unless that following day is a holiday, in which case service is effective on the next day that is not a holiday.

(2.1) Service of a document by sending a copy by courier under clause (1)(e) is effective on the second day following the day the courier was given the document, unless that second day is a holiday, in which case service is effective on the next day that is not a holiday.

(3) A document that is served by telephone transmission shall include a cover page indicating,

(a) the sender's name, address and telephone number;

(b) the name of the solicitor to be served;

(c) the date and time of transmission;

(d) the total number of pages transmitted, including the cover page;

(e) the telephone number from which the document is transmitted; and

(f) the name and telephone number of a person to contact in the event of transmission problems.

Telephone Transmission of Certain Documents

(3.1) A document of sixteen pages or more inclusive of the cover page and the backsheet may be served by telephone transmission only between 5 p.m. and 8 a.m. the following day, unless the party to be served gives prior consent.

(3.2) A motion record, application record, trial record, appeal book or book of authorities may not be served by telephone transmission at any time unless the party to be served gives prior consent. [am. O. Regs. 535/92, s. 5; 351/94, s. 1]

Logan v. Logan (1993), 15 O.R. (3d) 411 (Gen. Div.).

A litigant may retain counsel for specific aspects of a case without requiring counsel to become solicitor of record. In such cases there is no general right to effect service on the litigant by serving counsel.

SERVICE BY MAIL

Manner of Service
16.06(1) Where a document is to be served by mail under these rules, a copy of the document shall be served by regular lettermail or by registered mail.

Effective Date
(2) Service of a document by mail, except under subrule 16.03(4), is effective on the fifth day after the document is mailed but the document may be filed with proof of service before service becomes effective. [am. O. Reg. 535/92, s. 6]

Re Milton and O.M.B. (1978), 20 O.R. (2d) 257, 87 D.L.R. (3d) 413, 90 O.M.B.R. 76 (H.C.).

Service by mail was held ineffective where the sender knew the letter had not been received by the addressee. Discussion of service by mail.

WHERE DOCUMENT DOES NOT REACH PERSON SERVED

16.07 Even though a person has been served with a document in accordance with these rules, the person may show on a motion to set aside the consequences of default, for an extension of time or in support of a request for an adjournment, that the document,
(a) did not come to the person's notice; or
(b) came to the person's notice only at some time later than when it was served or is deemed to have been served.

Andrew Paving & Engineering Ltd. v. Folino (1995), 37 C.P.C. (3d) 99 (Ont. Gen. Div.).

Substituted service by mail was held to be effective notwithstanding the mail was returned unclaimed.

Don Bodkin Leasing Ltd. v. Rayzak (1993), 4 W.D.C.P. (2d) 135 (Ont. Gen. Div.). reversed on reconsideration (February 16, 1994), Doc. 92-CQ-23655 (Ont. Gen. Div.).

The onus of proving service of a statement of claim is on the plaintiff.

Allfur Trading Ltd. v. Polizos (1991), 7 C.P.C. (3d) 39 (Ont. Master).

Where the plaintiff's affidavit of service of the statement of claim is *prima facie* proper, the defendant has the onus of rebutting the evidence of service. The court did not accept a bald denial of service.

VALIDATING SERVICE

16.08 Where a document has been served in a manner other than one authorized by these rules or an order, the court may make an order validating the service where the court is satisfied that,
(a) the document came to the notice of the person to be served; or

(b) the document was served in such a manner that it would have come to the notice of the person to be served, except for the person's own attempts to evade service.

Smith v. Toronto General Hospital (Trustees of) (1994), 26 C.P.C. (3d) 99 (Ont. Gen. Div.).
The court validated service of the statement of claim 21 months after it had been issued where the defendant was not prejudiced.

Parente v. Van Holland (1988), 24 C.P.C. (2d) 233 (Ont. Dist. Ct.).
The court validated service of a document by telecopier.

De Pasquale v. Rodrigo (1985), 53 O.R. (2d) 123, 7 C.P.C. (2d) 86, 31 M.P.L.R. 99 (Dist. Ct.).
The court validated service on one respondent made by affixing the documents to his door and service on another respondent made by serving his wife and mailing a copy to him. The documents came to the attention of the respondents so served.

King v. Kokot (1980), 31 O.R. (2d) 461, 18 C.P.C. 269, 119 D.L.R. (3d) 154 (H.C.).
Although the rules for service out of Ontario had not been formally complied with, service was not set aside where there was no evidence of prejudice to the defendant.

Re Consiglio, [1971] 3 O.R. 798 (Master).
Where a document is left with a non-party and it subsequently comes to the knowledge or possession of the party to be served, the court may hold that personal service has been effected.

PROOF OF SERVICE

Affidavit of Service
16.09(1) Service of a document may be proved by an affidavit of the person who served it (Form 16B).

Sheriff's Certificate
(2) Personal service or service under subrule 16.03(5) (service at place of residence) of a document by a sheriff or sheriff's officer may be proved by a certificate of service (Form 16C).

Solicitor's Admission or Acceptance
(3) A solicitor's written admission or acceptance of service is sufficient proof of service and need not be verified by affidavit.

Document Exchange
(4) Service of a document under clause 16.05(1)(c) (document exchange) may be proved by the date stamp on the document or a copy of it.

Proof of Service on Document
(5) The affidavit or certificate of service may be printed on the back-sheet or on a stamp or sticker affixed to the backsheet of the document served.

RULE 17   SERVICE OUTSIDE ONTARIO

Highlights

Service outside Ontario may be made without leave in cases falling within the list enumerated in rule 17.02. In addition, the court is given a broad discretion to grant leave to serve the originating process outside Ontario in any case not coming within the enumerated list: rule 17.03.

A defendant served outside Ontario may challenge the service on three grounds (rule 17.06): that service is not authorized by the Rules; that an order granting leave to serve outside Ontario should be set aside; or that Ontario is not a convenient forum for the hearing of the proceeding. (Note that the court's general power to stay proceedings under s. 106 of the *Courts of Justice Act* is sometimes exercised based on convenience of forum considerations also.) It would seem that under this rule there is now no scope for a general or residual discretion to set aside service (otherwise authorized by the Rules) beyond that relating to the issue of convenient forum. In *Singh v. Howden Petroleum Ltd.* (1979), 24 O.R. (2d) 769, 11 C.P.C. 97, 100 D.L.R. (3d) 121 (C.A.), such a discretion was formerly said to exist.

A party who seeks to challenge service out of the jurisdiction should do so before delivering a defence, a notice of intent to defend or a notice of appearance, and by so doing the moving party does not submit to the jurisdiction of the court: rule 17.06(1) and (4). Following the approach now taken in most other provinces, and in the United Kingdom, the Rules make no provision for the entry of a "conditional appearance" by which the issue of jurisdiction over the person could be postponed until trial. This issue, when it arises, is one that should be determined at the outset, and if this involves fact-finding necessitating the reception of oral evidence, the master or judge can grant leave to adduce such evidence on the hearing of the motion, under rule 39.03(4). In an unusual case, leave to dispute the jurisdiction over the defendant at trial might still be granted under the closing words of rule 17.06(2) ("such other order as is just").

In *Morguard Investments Ltd. v. De Savoye*, [1990] 3 S.C.R. 1077, 46 C.P.C. (2d) 1, the Supreme Court of Canada unabashedly changed the principles with regard to the enforcement of sister province *in personam* judgments, rejecting the well-established principle that where the defendant is served outside the jurisdiction of the court, a sister province will only enforce the judgment of the original forum where the defendant either consented to or attorned to the jurisdiction of that court. The court held this approach to be inconsistent with the federal structure of our Constitution. Instead, in determining whether or not such judgment was to be enforced, consideration has to be given to the contact between the jurisdiction and the defendant or the subject-matter of the action. "There must be a real and substantial connection between the damages suffered" and the adjudicating province. The court also raised, but expressed no opinion on, the question of whether or not there may be constitutional limits on the power of the provinces to pass rules providing for service out of the jurisdiction. Noting that rules for service *ex juris* in all the provinces are broad, the court stated "that if the courts of one province are to be expected to give effect to judgments given in another province, there must be some limits to the exercise of jurisdiction against persons outside the province". Subsequently in *Hunt v. T & N plc*, [1993] 4 S.C.R. 289, the Supreme Court made it explicit that the *Morguard* principles are "Constitutional imperatives" applying to provincial legislatures and the courts.

Rule 17.05 provides for the manner of service outside of Ontario and was amended in 1990 to implement Canada's accession to the *Hague Convention on the Service Abroad of Judicial and Extrajudicial Documents in Civil or Commercial Matters*. For a detailed analysis of these provisions, see the Annual Survey of Recent Developments in Civil Procedure in the 1990 edition of this work and Holmested and Watson, *Ontario Civil Procedure*, 17 § 5.

Former Rules: Rules 25-31, 38.

DEFINITION

17.01 In rules 17.02 to 17.06, "originating process" includes a counterclaim against only parties to the main action, and a crossclaim.

SERVICE OUTSIDE ONTARIO WITHOUT LEAVE

17.02 A party to a proceeding may, without a court order, be served outside Ontario with an originating process or notice of a reference where the proceeding against the party consists of a claim or claims,

Property in Ontario
(a) in respect of real or personal property in Ontario;

Administration of Estates
(b) in respect of the administration of the estate of a deceased person,
    (i) in respect of real property in Ontario, or
    (ii) in respect of personal property, where the deceased person, at the time of death, was resident in Ontario;

Interpretation of an Instrument
(c) for the interpretation, rectification, enforcement or setting aside of a deed, will, contract or other instrument in respect of,
    (i) real or personal property in Ontario, or
    (ii) the personal property of a deceased person who, at the time of death, was resident in Ontario;

Trustee Where Assets Include Property in Ontario
(d) against a trustee in respect of the execution of a trust contained in a written instrument where the assets of the trust include real or personal property in Ontario;

Mortgage on Property in Ontario
(e) for foreclosure, sale, payment, possession or redemption in respect of a mortgage, charge or lien on real or personal property in Ontario;

Contracts
(f) in respect of a contract where,
    (i) the contract was made in Ontario,
    (ii) the contract provides that it is to be governed by or interpreted in accordance with the law of Ontario,

(iii) the parties to the contract have agreed that the courts of Ontario are to have jurisdiction over legal proceedings in respect of the contract, or

(iv) a breach of the contract has been committed in Ontario, even though the breach was preceded or accompanied by a breach outside Ontario that rendered impossible the performance of the part of the contract that ought to have been performed in Ontario;

Tort Committed in Ontario
(g) in respect of a tort committed in Ontario;

Damage Sustained in Ontario
(h) in respect of damage sustained in Ontario arising from a tort or breach of contract, wherever committed;

Injunctions
(i) for an injunction ordering a party to do, or refrain from doing, anything in Ontario or affecting real or personal property in Ontario;

Support
(j) for support;

Custody or Access
(k) for custody of or access to a minor;

Invalidity of Marriage
(l) to declare the invalidity of a marriage;

Judgment of Court Outside Ontario
(m) on a judgment of a court outside Ontario;

Authorized by Statute
(n) authorized by statute to be made against a person outside Ontario by a proceeding commenced in Ontario;

Necessary or Proper Party
(o) against a person outside Ontario who is a necessary or proper party to a proceeding properly brought against another person served in Ontario;

Person Resident or Carrying on Business in Ontario
(p) against a person ordinarily resident or carrying on business in Ontario;

Counterclaim, Crossclaim or Third Party Claim
(q) properly the subject matter of a counterclaim, crossclaim or third or subsequent party claim under these rules; or

Taxes
(r) made by or on behalf of the Crown or a municipal corporation to recover money owing for taxes or other debts due to the Crown or the municipality.

Service Outside Ontario — Validity of Rules

MacDonald v. Lasnier (1994), 21 O.R. (3d) 177 (Gen. Div.).

Any assumption of jurisdiction now has to be considered in light of *Morguard Investments Ltd., infra*, and for a provincial court to assume jurisdiction there must be a real and substantial connection between the action and the province. Even though an Ontario plaintiff had endured pain and suffering in Ontario due to the alleged failure of the Quebec doctor to diagnose a spinal fracture, and hence the action came within rule 17.02(h) re damage sustained in Ontario, the real and substantial connection was with Quebec and not Ontario and therefore the Ontario Court (General Division) did not have jurisdiction.

Morguard Investments Ltd. v. De Savoye, [1990] 3 S.C.R. 1077, 46 C.P.C. (2d) 1, 52 B.C.L.R. (2d) 160, 15 R.P.R. (2d) 1, [1991] 2 W.W.R. 217, 76 D.L.R. (4th) 256, 122 N.R. 81.

There may be constitutional limits on the powers of the provinces to pass rules providing for service out of the jurisdiction. The constitutional limit might be one requiring a substantial connection between the defendant and the forum province of the kind which makes it reasonable to infer that the litigant has voluntarily submitted himself or herself to the risk of litigation in the courts of that forum province.

Service Outside Ontario — Generally

Upper Lakes Shipping Ltd. v. Foster Yeoman Ltd. (1992), 12 C.P.C. (3d) 31, additional reasons (1993), 12 C.P.C. (3d) 40 (Ont. Master), affirmed (1993), 14 O.R. (3d) 548, 17 C.P.C. (3d) 150 (Gen. Div.).

A claim for breach of fiduciary duty is not a claim in tort and does not fall within rule 17.02(g) or (h). Leave for service outside Ontario may be available under rule 17.03.

Henry Grethel Apparel Inc. v. H.A. Imports of Can. Ltd. (1990), 42 C.P.C. (2d) 260 (Ont. Master).

The words "originating process" in rule 17.02 should be read to include a counterclaim against a person who is not already a party to the main action and accordingly service of this type of counterclaim outside Ontario is proper where the claims asserted otherwise fall within this rule.

Tridon Ltd. v. Otto Bihlier KG (1978), 21 O.R. (2d) 569, 8 C.P.C. 19, 90 D.L.R. (3d) 733 (H.C.).

Service out of Ontario without leave is proper only where *all* claims asserted against the foreign defendant fall within this rule.

Service Outside Ontario — Re Property in Ontario — rule 17.02(a)

McMahon v. Waskochil, [1945] O.W.N. 887 (Master).

An action for a declaration that foreign defendants hold land in Ontario as trustees falls within this provision.

Service Outside Ontario — Re Contracts — rule 17.02(f)

Drilco Industrial Can. Inc. v. Gregory (1988), 31 C.P.C. (2d) 112 (Ont. Master), affirmed 14 W.D.C.P. 113 (Ont. H.C.).

Service out of Ontario was proper where the assignment agreement under which the plaintiff was assignee/purchaser was governed by the law of Ontario, although the original contract which was the subject-matter of the assignment stated that the contract was to be interpreted according to the law of a foreign jurisdiction.

Hayter & Scandrett Ltd. v. Deutsche Ost-Afrika-Linie G.M.B.H. (1983), 39 C.P.C. 38 (Ont. Master), affirmed (1985), 50 C.P.C. 194, 8 O.A.C. 150 (H.C.).

The fact that the plaintiff resided in Ontario was insufficient to permit service out of province where the claim had no physical connection whatever with Ontario and all the acts out of which the alleged damage arose occurred elsewhere.

De Havilland Aircraft of Can. Ltd. v. Metroflight Inc. (1978), 29 C.P.C. 225 (Ont. H.C.).

Service of a foreign defendant was permitted under this provision although the plaintiff denied the existence of the contract and sought a declaration to that effect.

Re Viscount Supply Co., [1963] 1 O.R. 640, 4 C.B.R. (N.S.) 256, 40 D.L.R. (2d) 501 (H.C.).

Where acceptance of an offer is communicated by telephone, the contract is made in the jurisdiction in which the offeror is located. The law which governs the contract is that of the jurisdiction having the closest and most real connection with the transaction.

Laurie v. Baird, [1946] O.W.N. 600 (H.C.).

The words "which ought to have been performed within Ontario" have been interpreted to mean "which must be" or "which is bound to be" performed in Ontario, and refer to a contract which, by specific term, can be validly performed only within Ontario.

Service Outside Ontario — Re Torts — rule 17.02(g)

Anderson v. Thomas, [1935] O.W.N. 228, [1935] 3 D.L.R. 286 (H.C.).

An action for a tort committed in Ontario may be properly brought under this rule even though all the parties to the action are domiciled elsewhere.

Service Outside Ontario — Re Damage Sustained in Ontario — rule 17.02(h)

MacDonald v. Lasnier (1994), 21 O.R. (3d) 177 (Gen. Div.).

Even though an Ontario plaintiff endured pain and suffering in Ontario due to the alleged failure of a Quebec doctor to diagnose a spinal fracture, the real and substantial connection was with Quebec and not Ontario and therefore the action should be tried in Quebec.

Jaffe v. Dearing (1988), 65 O.R. (2d) 113, 26 C.P.C. (2d) 5 (H.C.).

In an action against a Florida bank for wrongfully paying on a letter of credit used to secure an appearance bond in Florida, where the plaintiff was resident in Ontario and the security for the bond came from Ontario to the knowledge of the defendant, the damage was sustained in Ontario and service outside Ontario was permitted.

Elguindy v. Core Laboratories Canada Ltd. (1987), 60 O.R. (2d) 151, 21 C.P.C. (2d) 281, 17 C.C.E.L. 13, 25 O.A.C. 243 (Div. Ct.).

Where the plaintiff's contract of employment in Ontario is induced to be breached by a telephone call by the defendants in Alberta, he has sustained damage in Ontario from a tort committed in Ontario.

Power v. Probert (1987), 19 C.P.C. (2d) 142 (Ont. Dist. Ct.).

Service outside Ontario was permitted in this action arising out of a motor vehicle accident in Alberta where the plaintiff received some treatment in Ontario and became an Ontario resident after the accident, and Ontario law was preferable for the claim.

Bowers v. MWG Apparel Corp. (1985), 6 C.P.C. (2d) 35 (Ont. Dist. Ct.).

The court set aside service outside Ontario in this wrongful dismissal action where all events relating to the employment and dismissal occurred in Manitoba and the plaintiff moved to Ontario only after his dismissal. Inclusion of a claim for mental distress possibly sustained in Ontario did not bring the case within rule 17.02(h).

Hayter & Scandrett Ltd. v. Deutsche Ost-Afrika-Linie G.M.B.H. (1985), 50 C.P.C. 194, 8 O.A.C. 150 (H.C.).

The court set aside service outside Ontario where the sole connection pleaded between the plaintiff and Ontario was that the plaintiff was incorporated and carried on business in Ontario. It was not shown that the defendant sustained damages in Ontario.

Wardell v. Tower Co. (1961) Ltd. (1984), 49 O.R. (2d) 655 (H.C.).

Where a plaintiff sued a company in Ontario for damages for wrongful dismissal in respect of a contract of employment that was signed, to be performed and breached in the Northwest Territories, service was set aside. In contract cases the damage sustained in Ontario has to be a matter of substance, not just form.

Ralph v. Halley (1982), 30 C.P.C. 73 (Ont. Master).

Service out of Ontario was set aside in an action against Newfoundland solicitors for failing to deliver a promissory note to aid in prosecuting Newfoundland actions. The damages occurred in Newfoundland since that is where the plaintiff failed to prevail in the actions, and any breach of contract occurred in Newfoundland.

Poirier v. Williston (1980), 29 O.R. (2d) 303, 113 D.L.R. (3d) 252, affirmed 31 O.R. (2d) 320, 118 D.L.R. (3d) 576 (C.A.).

Where a resident of Ontario is injured outside Ontario and returns to Ontario with pain, suffering, disability and loss of ability to earn an income, he has sustained damage in Ontario.

Can. Bronze Co. v. Shrum (1980), 17 C.P.C. 241 (Ont. Master).

A claim that the foreign assignees from the defendant of certain patents held them in trust, not constituting an allegation of conversion, is not a claim for a tort committed or damages sustained in Ontario.

Vile v. Von Wendt (1979), 26 O.R. (2d) 513, 14 C.P.C. 121, 103 D.L.R. (3d) 356 (Div. Ct.).

Where a plaintiff is hospitalized, incurs medical expenses, experiences pain and suffering, etc. in Ontario, damage has been sustained in Ontario. *Mar. v. Block* (1976), 13 O.R. (2d) 422, 1 C.P.C. 206 (H.C.), overruled.

Skyrotors Ltd. v. Carriére Technical Indust. Ltd.; Dighem Ltd. v. Société Nat. Indust. Aérospatiale (1979), 26 O.R. (2d) 207, 15 C.P.C. 105, 102 D.L.R. (3d) 323 (H.C.).

Damages in respect of loss of profits are sustained at the place where the financial records of the business are kept.

Can. Gen. Elec. Co. v. C.M. Windows & Stained Glass Ltd. (1977), 16 O.R. (2d) 188, 3 C.P.C. 298 (Master).

A large company with an Ontario presence can sue in Ontario on a debt although payment was to be made elsewhere.

Lummus Co. v. Int. Alloys, Inc. (1977), 17 O.R. (2d) 322, 5 C.P.C. 169, 80 D.L.R. (3d) 278, affirmed 17 O.R. (2d) 322n, 80 D.L.R. (3d) 278n (H.C.).

The purchaser of a defective product from a foreign supplier sustains damage in Ontario.

Service Outside Ontario — Re Custody and Access — rule 17.02(k)

Charmasson v. Charmasson (1981), 34 O.R. (2d) 498, 25 C.P.C. 45, 25 R.F.L. (2d) 41, 131 D.L.R. (3d) 74 (C.A.).

A custody order by the foreign court where the child was ordinarily resident had become void by the time the mother brought the child to Ontario. The Ontario court assumed jurisdiction after a consideration of the best interests of the child.

Service Outside Ontario — Re Judgment of Court Outside Ontario — rule 17.02(m)

Lawson v. Lawson, [1964] 2 O.R. 321 (H.C.).

Service out of Ontario is permissible in respect of an action on a foreign judgment for alimony.

Service Outside Ontario — Re Claims Authorized by Statute — rule 17.02(n)

De Havilland Aircraft of Can. Ltd. v. Metroflight Inc. (1978), 6 C.P.C. 38 (Ont. Master).

Where the sole claim was for a declaration pursuant to the *Judicature Act* that there was no legally binding contract between the parties, service out of the province was not set aside.

Service Outside Ontario — On Necessary or Proper Parties — rule 17.02(o)

Fidelity Management & Research Co. v. Gulf Canada Resources Ltd. (1995), 25 O.R. (3d) 548 (Gen. Div. [Commercial List]).

Where three directors of the federally incorporated respondent company with its head office in Alberta resided in Ontario, the court held that the other respondents were properly served *ex juris* under rule 17.02(o).

Eades v. Hamilton (1985), 52 O.R. (2d) 307, 13 C.C.L.I. 65 (Dist. Ct.).

A proceeding is not one "properly brought against another person served in Ontario" where, under the applicable conflict of laws rules, the claim made against the person served in Ontario is not one maintainable in Ontario.

Gouzenko v. Martin (1981), 34 O.R. (2d) 394, 22 C.P.C. 215 (Master).

Service out of Ontario was permitted in a libel action.

Skyrotors Ltd. v. Carriére Technical Indust. Ltd.; Dighem Ltd. v. Société Nat. Indust. Aérospatiale (1979), 26 O.R. (2d) 207, 15 C.P.C. 105, 102 D.L.R. (3d) 323 (H.C.).

A foreign manufacturer of an aircraft part alleged to be a cause of an accident is a necessary or proper party to an action against an Ontario repairer.

Vile v. Von Wendt (1979), 26 O.R. (2d) 513, 14 C.P.C. 121, 103 D.L.R. (3d) 356 (Div. Ct.).

Where there was doubt as to which of six defendants was liable, and five had been duly served, service of the sixth out of Ontario as a necessary and proper party was permitted.

Jannock Corp. v. R.T. Tamblyn & Partners (1975), 8 O.R. (2d) 622, 58 D.L.R. (3d) 678 (C.A.), leave to appeal to Supreme Court of Canada refused 8 O.R. (2d) 622n.

Where a purchaser of equipment brings an action against the designer of the equipment and the designer alleges that the non-resident company which installed the equipment is at fault, such non-resident company is a necessary and proper party notwithstanding a clause in a contract between the plaintiff and that company stating that the British Columbia courts are to have jurisdiction.

Fasig-Tipton Co. Inc. v. Willmot & Burns, [1969] 2 O.R. 1 (Master).

One foreign party may not be served under this provision merely because another foreign party has attorned to the jurisdiction and accepted service.

Service Outside Ontario — On Persons Resident or Carrying on Business in Ontario — rule 17.02(p)

Cross-Reference: See cases under rule 16.02(1)(e) re Carrying on Business in Ontario.

Applied Processes Inc. v. Crane Co. (1993), 15 O.R. (3d) 166 (Gen. Div.).

A marketing strategy including periodic visits to Ontario and advertising in Ontario was held to constitute carrying on business in Ontario.

Finnerty v. Watson, [1969] 1 O.R. 634 (H.C.).

Domicile or residence is to be determined as of the date the action is commenced rather than as of the date the cause of action arose.

SERVICE OUTSIDE ONTARIO WITH LEAVE

17.03(1) In any case to which rule 17.02 does not apply, the court may grant leave to serve an originating process or notice of a reference outside Ontario.

(2) A motion for leave to serve a party outside Ontario may be made without notice, and shall be supported by an affidavit or other evidence showing in which place or country the person is or probably may be found, and the grounds on which the motion is made.

Jannock Corp. v. R.T. Tamblyn & Partners (1975), 8 O.R. (2d) 622, 58 D.L.R. (3d) 678 (C.A.), leave to appeal to Supreme Court of Canada refused 8 O.R. (2d) 622n.

The court is more inclined to permit service on residents of other provinces than on residents of other countries.

ESB Can. Ltd. v. Duval Corp. of Can. (No. 1), [1973] 3 O.R. 781 (H.C.).

In disposing of the application: (1) the general balance of convenience to all parties is important; and (2) the substance of the issues involved in the suit must be examined. The court is less reluctant to allow service in other provinces than in foreign jurisdictions.

ESB Can. Ltd. v. Duval Corp. of Can. (No. 2), [1973] 3 O.R. 791 (H.C.).

Where an order authorizes service in one city and the defendant is served in another city, the order may be amended *nunc pro tunc*.

Cottrell v. Hanen, [1963] 1 O.R. 164 (Master).

The affidavit supporting the motion for leave must depose as to the truth of the allegations contained in the statement of claim.

ADDITIONAL REQUIREMENTS FOR SERVICE OUTSIDE ONTARIO

17.04(1) An originating process served outside Ontario without leave shall disclose the facts and specifically refer to the provision of rule 17.02 relied on in support of such service.

(2) Where an originating process is served outside Ontario with leave of the court, the originating process shall be served together with the order granting leave and any affidavit or other evidence used to obtain the order.

Davidson Partners Ltd. v. Kirsh (1990), 72 O.R. (2d) 450 (Master).

Service out of Ontario ought not to be set aside if it is in fact authorized by one of the clauses of rule 17.02, even if such clause is not referred to in the originating process.

Citadel Life Assurance Co. v. Sun Life Assurance Co. of Can. (1988), 65 O.R. (2d) 790, 22 C.P.R. (3d) 301 (Master).

Where in support of service outside Ontario the plaintiff alleged that he had "sustained damages in Ontario", the court refused to order particulars of the nature and amount of damages suffered in Ontario, since these were not issues for the purpose of pleading.

Schaffhauser Kantonalbank v. Chmiel (1988), 65 O.R. (2d) 475, 29 C.P.C. (2d) 92 (H.C.), leave to appeal refused 29 C.P.C. (2d) xlv.

Rule 17.04 does not require the statement of claim to specifically relate the facts to the various grounds for service outside the jurisdiction. The claim need only contain the facts relied on and refer to the provisions of rule 17.02 in support.

Ontario (A.G.) v. J.H. Bachmann Can. Inc. (1987), 15 C.P.C. (2d) 96 (Ont. Master).

The court set aside service outside Ontario where the statement of claim referred to specific provisions of rule 17.02 to support service outside Ontario but did not disclose facts in support of such service.

MANNER OF SERVICE OUTSIDE ONTARIO

Definitions

17.05(1) In this rule,

"contracting state" means a contracting state under the Convention;

"Convention" means the Convention on the Service Abroad of Judicial and Extrajudicial Documents in Civil or Commercial Matters signed at The Hague on November 15, 1965.

General Manner of Service

(2) An originating process or other document to be served outside Ontario in a jurisdiction that is not a contracting state may be served in the manner provided by these rules for service in Ontario, or in the manner provided by the law of the jurisdiction where service is made, if service made in that manner could reasonably be expected to come to the notice of the person to be served.

Manner of Service in Convention States

(3) An originating process or other document to be served outside Ontario in a contracting state shall be served,

(a) through the central authority in the contracting state; or

(b) in a manner that is permitted by Article 10 of the Convention and that would be permitted by these rules if the document were being served in Ontario.

Proof of Service

(4) Service may be proved,

(a) in the manner provided by these rules for proof of service in Ontario;

(b) in the manner provided by the law of the jurisdiction where service is made; or

(c) in accordance with the Convention, if service is made in a contracting state (Forms 17A to 17C). [am. O. Reg. 535/92, s. 7]

Authors' Comment

This rule was amended to give effect to the provisions of the *Hague Convention on the Service Abroad of Judicial and Extrajudicial Documents in Civil or Commercial Matters* which came into force in Canada as a result of the Government of Canada acceding to the Convention. The Convention provides uniform procedures for party states to effect service of legal documents in civil and commercial matters. However, it in effect provides for two regimes depending upon whether the country where the documents are to be served is a "non-objecting state" or an "objecting state".

Article 10 of the Convention states that "Provided the State of destination does not object, *the present convention shall not interfere with*" (a) service by mail directly to persons abroad, (b) the service of documents directly through "judicial officers, officials or *other competent persons* of the State of destination". This provision is extremely important and especially relevant with regard to commonly encountered countries (*e.g.*, the United States and the United Kingdom) where the mailing of documents to the person to be served and/or the use of local agents is acceptable. Hence, with regard to these countries such methods of service may continue to be used, despite the fact that the United States and the United Kingdom are parties to the agreement. (But as to service by mail of an *originating process*, see below and rule 17.05(3).)

If the country in which the document is to be served is a state that objects to private service, then service must be made through the Central Authority in the state (and under the Convention each country is required to appoint a Central Authority). With regard to such countries, private service is not permitted by the Convention, even though formerly it would have been recognized and been acceptable in Ontario.

The scheme of rule 17.05 is now as follows. If service is to be made in a jurisdiction that is not a contracting state, the former regime continues, *i.e.* the person may be served in a manner provided by the rules for service in Ontario, or in the manner provided by the law of the jurisdiction where service is made if service made in that manner could reasonably be expected to come to the notice of the person to be served: rule 17.05(2). However, it must be kept in mind that some states consider the service of process to be an official act which can only be performed by local authorities, and the use of private process servers or service by mail may be viewed as a violation of sovereignty and even a criminal act. A recent note (March 6, 1992) from the Swiss authorities to the Department of External Affairs made this point and indicated that such a failure to comply with Swiss law, by using service by mail, would likely render any resulting Canadian judgment unenforceable in Switzerland.

Where service is to be made in a contracting state the document is to be served either (a) through the central authority in the contracting state, or (b) in a manner permitted by the convention and that would be permitted by the Rules if the document was being served in Ontario: rule 17.05(3). In effect this means that if a contracting state is a non-objecting state, private means of service may be used. However, for an originating process, service by mail is unavailable (except in the very limited circumstances provided in rule 16.03(4)).

The Department of External Affairs advises that as of June 1, 1995, the parties to the Convention were:

Antigua and Barbuda	Italy
Barbados	Japan
Botswana	Luxembourg
Canada	Malawi
China	Netherlands
Cyprus	Norway
Czechoslovakia	Pakistan
Denmark	Portugal
Egypt	Seychelles
Federal Republic of Germany	Spain
Finland	Sweden
France	Turkey
Greece	United Kingdom
Israel	United States

Whether any other countries have become parties to the Convention may be ascertained by contacting the Treaty Registrar, Economic Law and Treaty Division of the

Department of External Affairs (613) 995-3130. For a full discussion of the operation of rule 17.05, and for the text of the convention, see Holmested and Watson, *Ontario Civil Procedure*, 17 § 5.]

Cases

Rabichaud v. Rabichaud and Ramsay, [1948] O.W.N. 727 (C.A.).

Substituted service by mailing to an address out of Ontario is permissible.

MOTION TO SET ASIDE SERVICE OUTSIDE ONTARIO

17.06(1) A party who has been served with an originating process outside Ontario may move, before delivering a defence, notice of intent to defend or notice of appearance,

 (a) for an order setting aside the service and any order that authorized the service; or

 (b) for an order staying the proceeding.

(2) The court may make an order under subrule (1) or such other order as is just where it is satisfied that,

 (a) service outside Ontario is not authorized by these rules;

 (b) an order granting leave to serve outside Ontario should be set aside; or

 (c) Ontario is not a convenient forum for the hearing of the proceeding.

(3) Where on a motion under subrule (1) the court concludes that service outside Ontario is not authorized by these rules, but the case is one in which it would have been appropriate to grant leave to serve outside Ontario under rule 17.03, the court may make an order validating the service.

(4) The making of a motion under subrule (1) is not in itself a submission to the jurisdiction of the court over the moving party.

Setting Aside Service Outside Ontario — Generally

Applied Processes Inc. v. Crane Co. (1993), 15 O.R. (3d) 166 (Gen. Div.).

The plaintiff has a *prima facie* right to have its case tried in Ontario, if it demonstrates that its action falls within rule 17.02.

Interimco Projects Engineering Corp. v. Can. Co-op. Implements Ltd. (1984), 47 C.P.C. 142 (Ont. Master).

If the plaintiff demonstrates that the action falls within the rule permitting service outside Ontario it has a *prima facie* right to have it tried in Ontario. This right can only be displaced by the defendant convincing the court that the balance of convenience requires that, in the exercise of a judicial discretion, the plaintiff should be deprived of it.

Ferranti-Packard Ltd. v. Cushman Rentals Ltd. (1980), 30 O.R. (2d) 194, 19 C.P.C. 132, 115 D.L.R. (3d) 691, affirmed 31 O.R. (2d) 799, 123 D.L.R. (3d) 766 (C.A.).

The court declined to set aside service on the ground of sovereign immunity where the defendant foreign highway authority was found not to be the alter ego or organ of a foreign state.

Tridon Ltd. v. Otto Bihlier KG (1978), 21 O.R. (2d) 569, 8 C.P.C. 19, 90 D.L.R. (3d) 733 (H.C.).

Service out of Ontario was set aside where some of the claims made did not fall within the provisions of the rule permitting service out of Ontario without leave.

Cutting Ltd. v. Lancaster Business Forms Ltd. (1977), 18 O.R. (2d) 526, 5 C.P.C. 34 (H.C.).
Service out of Ontario may not be set aside on the ground that the action is frivolous.

Setting Aside Service Outside Ontario — Onus

Frymer v. Brettschneider (1994), 19 O.R. (3d) 60, 28 C.P.C. (3d) 84, 115 D.L.R. (4th) 744, 72 O.A.C. 360 (C.A.).
Where the defendant is being served *ex juris* the burden of demonstrating that Ontario is the appropriate forum is on the plaintiff.

Vile v. Von Wendt (1979), 26 O.R. (2d) 513, 14 C.P.C. 121, 103 D.L.R. (3d) 356 (Div. Ct.).
Where the defendant himself was not resident in Quebec and there was no hardship to witnesses, the fact that the accident occurred in Quebec was insufficient to make that province the more convenient forum. The onus is on the defendant to show that Ontario is not a convenient forum.

Can. Westinghouse Co. v. Davey, [1964] 2 O.R. 282, 45 D.L.R. (2d) 321 (C.A.).
It is not sufficient that the plaintiff allege facts which would make service out of Ontario without leave proper; he must demonstrate a good arguable case that it is proper. It is not necessary, however, that it be so established beyond a reasonable doubt.

Setting Aside Service Outside Ontario — Convenience of Forum — Proper Law of Contract

Ronald A. Chisholm Ltd. v. Agro & Diverses Souscriptions Internationales - ADSI - S.A. (1991), 4 O.R. (3d) 539, 2 C.P.C. (3d) 120, 6 C.C.L.I. (2d) 132 (Gen. Div.).
The court permitted an insurance action in Ontario notwithstanding a provision in the certificate of insurance suggesting French courts had jurisdiction. The assignee of a certificate of insurance is not bound by a procedural provision with respect to the place of jurisdiction.

National Utility Service (Can.) Ltd. v. Abbott Laboratories Ltd. (1986), 56 O.R. (2d) 407, 11 C.P.C. (2d) 310 (H.C.).
The court refused to set aside service outside Ontario where the main issue was almost entirely a question of fact, although it could conceivably be affected by foreign law.

Anthes Equipment Ltd. v. Wilhelm Layher GmbH (1986), 53 O.R. (2d) 435, 6 C.P.C. (2d) 252 (H.C.).
The court set aside service on a West German defendant where the proper law of the contract sued upon was West German and the contract gave exclusive jurisdiction to a West German court.

Jones v. Ont. White Star Products Ltd. (1979), 15 C.P.C. 144 (Ont. H.C.).
Where Quebec law was the proper law of the contract and the balance of convenience was otherwise equal, Quebec was the convenient forum for a wrongful dismissal action.

Cutting Ltd. v. Lancaster Business Forms Ltd. (1977), 18 O.R. (2d) 526, 5 C.P.C. 34 (H.C.).
Service out of Ontario was set aside where Quebec law was the proper law.

Stanwell Oil & Gas Ltd. v. Blair Holdings Corp., [1954] O.W.N. 853 (Master).
The proper law of a contract is generally the law of the place where it is to be performed.

Setting Aside Service Outside Ontario — Convenience of Forum — Ontario Law Offering Legitimate Juridical Advantage

Shewan v. Canada (A.G.) (1994), 27 C.P.C. (3d) 244 (Ont. Master).
The availability of legal aid in Ontario was considered to be a juridical advantage.

Thwaites v. Simcoe Erie Group (1993), 17 C.P.C. (3d) 93 (Ont. Gen. Div.).

Notwithstanding that the defendant had satisfied the onus of establishing Manitoba as a more convenient forum than Ontario, the court refused to stay proceedings where a stay would have resulted in the loss of the substantive and legitimate juridical advantage of the plaintiff to require that the issues of fact be determined by a jury.

Amchem Products Inc. v. British Columbia (Workers' Compensation Board), [1993] 1 S.C.R. 897, 14 C.P.C. (3d) 1, 77 B.C.L.R. (2d) 62, [1993] 3 W.W.R. 441, 23 B.C.A.C. 1, 102 D.L.R. (4th) 96, 150 N.R. 321, 39 W.A.C. 1.

The test for *forum non conveniens* is that there must be some other forum more convenient and appropriate for the pursuit of the action and for securing the ends of justice. There is no reason why the loss of juridical advantage in principle should be treated as a separate and distinct condition rather than being weighed with the other factors which are considered in identifying the appropriate forum. The burden of proof on a motion to stay should not depend upon whether the defendant was served within the jurisdiction or outside the jurisdiction. Whether the burden of proof should be on the plaintiff in *ex juris* cases depends on the rule that permits service out of the jurisdiction. If it requires that service out of the jurisdiction be justified by the plaintiff, whether on a motion for an order or in defending service *ex juris* where no order is required, then the rule must govern. In any event the burden of proof should not play a significant role in this matter as it only applies in cases in which the judge cannot come to a determinative decision on the basis of the materials presented by the parties.

B. (J.) v. d. (E.) (1993), 16 C.P.C. (3d) 242 (Ont. Gen. Div.).

The court held that Ontario was a convenient forum for the plaintiff to assert a claim against family members for sexually abusing her as a child in the Netherlands since, *inter alia*, the plaintiff had a legitimate juridical advantage suing in Ontario where the defendants could be compelled to answer incriminating questions on discovery.

Kim v. Yun (1991), 4 O.R. (3d) 455, 6 C.C.L.I. (2d) 263, 35 M.V.R. (2d) 82, additional reasons 3 W.D.C.P. (2d) 59 (Gen. Div.).

Where the parties to a personal injury action arising out of a motor vehicle accident were all residents of Quebec, but the underlying accident had taken place in Ontario, the plaintiffs were permitted to proceed with an action in Ontario. The plaintiffs would be deprived of legitimate juridical advantage if Quebec law were applied.

Westminer Canada Holdings Ltd. v. Coughlan (1990), 75 O.R. (2d) 405, 73 D.L.R. (4th) 584, 41 O.A.C. 377 (Div. Ct.).

The plaintiff's burden of proving that granting a stay would deprive it of a juridical advantage can be discharged by demonstrating a danger that it *might* be so deprived. Moreover, the juridical disadvantage created by the limitation period having expired in Nova Scotia, but not in Ontario, was not removed by the fact that the defendants undertook not to raise the limitation defence in Nova Scotia, since a bare promise not to rely on the passage of time was unenforceable.

Tremblay Estate v. Demers (1988), 66 O.R. (2d) 323, 30 C.P.C. (2d) 257 (H.C.).

Where the party applying for a stay established that Quebec had the most real and substantial connection with a law suit, and the responding party failed to introduce evidence showing the loss of a personal or juridical advantage enjoyed in the domestic jurisdiction, the Ontario proceeding was stayed.

Jaffe v. Dearing (1988), 65 O.R. (2d) 113, 26 C.P.C. (2d) 5 (H.C.).

The plaintiff was permitted to prosecute his action in Ontario rather than Florida, the natural forum, where charges were pending against the plaintiff in Florida and would deter him from bringing an action there.

General Dynamics Corp. v. Veliotis (1985), 53 O.R. (2d) 371, 7 C.P.C. (2d) 169 (H.C.).

The right to claim privilege under the *Evidence Acts* and *Charter* regarding criminating statements without the right to remain silent, as opposed to the absolute right to remain silent available under U.S. law, represents a legitimate juridical advantage in being permitted to proceed in Ontario.

Pindling v. Nat. Broadcasting Corp. (1984), 49 O.R. (2d) 58, 47 C.P.C. 18, 31 C.C.L.T. 251, 14 D.L.R. (4th) 391 (H.C.).

It is permissible to choose to bring an action in Ontario to gain a legitimate juridical advantage. In this case the U.S. defendant failed to appear in a defamation action brought in the Bahamas, the natural forum. U.S. law, unlike Ontario law, would require the plaintiff to prove "actual malice". In the circumstances it was permissible to bring the action in Ontario.

Vancouver Island Helicopters Ltd. v. Borg-Warner Corp. (1980), 30 O.R. (2d) 283, 18 C.P.C. 41, 116 D.L.R. (3d) 716 (H.C.).

Service out of Ontario was permitted where a previous action concerning the same incident had failed in British Columbia due to the expiry of a limitation period, and Ontario was the convenient forum since the advantage of the forum to the plaintiff was greater than the disadvantage to the defendant.

Johnson v. Johnson (1979), 27 O.R. (2d) 698, 11 C.P.C. 224, 11 R.F.L. (2d) 231 (Master).

Where both forums do not afford the applicant similar rights, the principle of *forum conveniens* is not applicable. Therefore, service of process claiming support will not be set aside where this would compel the wife to countersue in the husband's pending divorce action in New York State, where similar relief is unavailable.

Setting Aside Service Outside Ontario — Convenience of Forum — Examples

Fidelity Management & Research Co. v. Gulf Canada Resources Ltd. (1995), 25 O.R. (3d) 548 (Gen. Div. [Commercial List]).

Where three of the directors of the federally incorporated respondent company with its head office in Alberta resided in Ontario, the court held that there was a sufficient connection to Ontario, and that the foreign respondents, who had been served *ex juris*, had failed to satisfy the court that Alberta was the more appropriate forum.

Provident Life & Accident Insurance Co. v. Walton (1994), 35 C.P.C. (3d) 147, [1995] I.L.R. 1-3145 (Ont. Gen. Div.).

Where (1) the location of witnesses was evenly divided between Ontario and British Columbia, (2) the contract was entered into in Ontario, and (3) Ontario law governed the contract, the court dismissed the motion to stay the plaintiff's action in Ontario on the ground that Ontario was not a convenient forum.

Dino v. Albertson's Inc. (1994), 28 C.P.C. (3d) 15 (Ont. Master).

The court refused to set aside service of the statement of claim in Florida where the plaintiff was an Ontario resident who had been injured in a slip and fall in Florida. The costs of transporting evidence to Florida would be harsh and unjust to the plaintiff, and the plaintiff's daughter had a claim under the *Family Law Act*, while no similar right of action existed in the State of Florida.

de Vlas v. Bruce (1994), 18 O.R. (3d) 493, 25 C.P.C. (3d) 140, 3 M.V.R. (3d) 115 (Gen. Div.).

The court permitted a plaintiff to sue in Ontario regarding a motor vehicle accident in Alberta where the balance of convenience favoured Ontario and the plaintiff had personal and juridical advantages in suing in Ontario.

Frymer v. Brettschneider (1994), 19 O.R. (3d) 60, 28 C.P.C. (3d) 84, 115 D.L.R. (4th) 744, 72 O.A.C. 360 (C.A.).

The court set aside service outside Ontario where the subject of the action related to events in Florida. Detailed review of jurisprudence regarding *forum non conveniens*.

Bailey & Co. v. Laser Medical Technology Inc. (1993), 15 O.R. (3d) 212 (Gen. Div.).

The court set aside service outside Ontario because California had the most natural, real and substantial connection with the subject dispute.

Giles v. Arnold Palmer Motors Inc. (1991), 5 O.R. (3d) 536 (Gen. Div.).

Where there is any doubt about the balance of convenience, the plaintiff should be allowed to choose the place for trial.

Furlong v. Station Mont Tremblant Lodge Inc. (1991), 4 O.R. (3d) 693, 5 C.P.C. (3d) 127, 83 D.L.R. (4th) 750 (Gen. Div.).

An Ontario resident injured in a skiing accident in Quebec brought an action in Ontario after the expiry of the applicable limitation period in Quebec. The action was dismissed as Quebec was the forum with the most real and substantial connection with the law suit.

Ronald A. Chisholm Ltd. v. Agro & Diverses Souscriptions Internationales - ADSI - S.A. (1991), 4 O.R. (3d) 539, 2 C.P.C. (3d) 120, 6 C.C.L.I. (2d) 132 (Gen. Div.).

A motion for a stay was dismissed in this action arising out of the international sale of goods. The certificate of insurance which was the subject of the action was silent with respect to jurisdiction, and the defendant was not able to establish that there was another forum more convenient than Ontario.

First Lady Coiffures Ltd. v. Laboratoire Rene Guinot (1988), 11 W.D.C.P. 45 (Ont. Master).

The court refused to set aside service on the basis that France was the most convenient forum where Ontario was more convenient for two of the three parties and there was no evidence on the relative number of witnesses. The fact that French law applied was not conclusive.

Hein v. Linwell Wood Products Ltd. (1986), 58 O.R. (2d) 799 (H.C.).

The determinative factor in establishing the forum of convenience in this case was evidence that if service were set aside there would be separate actions in two provinces, instead of only one trial in one province. Preventing a multiplicity of proceedings was a more important consideration than the applicability of the other province's law.

Bonaventure Systems Inc. v. Royal Bank (1986), 57 O.R. (2d) 270, 16 C.P.C. (2d) 32, 32 D.L.R. (4th) 721, 18 O.A.C. 112 (Div. Ct.).

The court stayed an Ontario action where justice could be done in Quebec with substantially less inconvenience and expense. The prospect of a trial in the French language in Quebec was not grounds to permit the action to proceed in Ontario.

Ang v. Trach (1986), 57 O.R. (2d) 300, 13 C.P.C. (2d) 89, 22 C.C.L.I. 67, 47 M.V.R. 120, 33 D.L.R. (4th) 90 (H.C.).

The court held that Ontario courts had jurisdiction to entertain this action arising out of an automobile accident in Quebec, that Ontario law applied, and that *Family Law Reform Act* claims could be advanced.

Mainguy v. Mainguy (1984), 42 C.P.C. 84 (Ont. Master).

After having obtained an interim support order in Belgium, the plaintiff wife moved to Ontario and commenced this action for a division of property and support. The master held that Belgium was the convenient forum. The husband, all property, and the history of the spouses together were in Belgium, Belgian law was the proper law, and the wife's right to continue her action in Belgium was still existent.

Hayter & Scandrett Ltd. v. Deutsche Ost-Afrika-Linie G.M.B.H. (1983), 39 C.P.C. 38 (Ont. Master), affirmed (1985), 50 C.P.C. 194, 8 O.A.C. 150 (H.C.).

Where the contracts involved called for interpretation by the laws of other countries, few witnesses were from Ontario, and Ontario had the least connection with the facts, Ontario was not the convenient forum even if there were difficulties in proceeding elsewhere.

Ralph v. Halley (1982), 30 C.P.C. 73 (Ont. Master).

In an action against Newfoundland solicitors for failing to deliver a promissory note to aid in prosecuting Newfoundland actions, the substance of the matter was based largely in Newfoundland and that was the convenient forum.

Greg Lund Products Ltd. v. Husband Transport Ltd. (1981), 34 O.R. (2d) 777 (Co. Ct.).

Where a defendant resident in Ontario instituted third party proceedings against a United States corporation, the court held that Ontario was the most convenient forum to dispose of the proceeding. It would be very difficult for the defendant to conduct an action for indemnity in the United States.

Re Wismer and Javelin Int. Ltd. (1981), 34 O.R. (2d) 785, 25 C.P.C. 1, 132 D.L.R. (3d) 156, leave to appeal to Ontario Div. Ct. refused 34 O.R. (2d) 785n, 793 (H.C.).

Service of a corporation resident in Quebec was ruled proper in this action where the section of the *Canada Business Corporations Act* upon which the plaintiff's claim was based has been declared unconstitutional in Quebec.

Skyrotors Ltd. v. Carriére Technical Indust. Ltd.; Dighem Ltd. v. Société Nat. Indust. Aérospatiale (1979), 26 O.R. (2d) 207, 15 C.P.C. 105, 102 D.L.R. (3d) 323 (H.C.).

Ontario is a convenient forum where it was reasonably foreseeable that the foreign manufacturer's aircraft part would be used and if carelessly made cause damage in Ontario, and much of the evidence involving other parties concerns events in Ontario.

Roger Grandmaitre Ltd. v. Can. Int. Paper Co. (1977), 15 O.R. (2d) 137, 2 C.P.C. 326 (H.C.), affirmed 4 C.P.C. 299 (C.A.).

Where there were other pending law suits in another province, all arising out of the same occurrence and involving common questions of fact and law, the balance of convenience was in favour of that province.

Submission to Jurisdiction of the Court — rule 17.06(4)

Gourmet Resources International Inc. (Trustee of) v. Paramount Capital Corp. (1991), 5 C.P.C. (3d) 140 (Ont. Gen. Div.).

A defendant's appearance to dispute jurisdiction will not be treated as an attornment to the jurisdiction of a court; however, also contesting the merits of the case does constitute voluntary submission to the jurisdiction of the court.

RULE 18   TIME FOR DELIVERY OF STATEMENT OF DEFENCE

Highlights

The filing of an "appearance" as a mandatory step in an action is no longer required (though a notice of appearance is required in an application: rule 38.07). Instead, the obligation placed on the defendant who is served with a statement of claim is to deliver a statement of defence within the appropriate time, *i.e.* 20, 40, or 60 days, depending upon where he or she is served: rule 18.01. However, provision is made for what is, in effect, an optional appearance. A defendant who has been served with a statement of claim and intends to defend the action may deliver a "notice of intent to defend" within the time prescribed for delivery of a statement of defence. By so doing the defendant becomes entitled to an additional ten days in which to file his or her statement of defence: rule 18.02. By rule 19.01(5), a defendant may deliver a statement of defence at any time prior to being noted in default.

Former Rules: Rules 28, 35-42, 44.

TIME FOR DELIVERY OF STATEMENT OF DEFENCE

18.01   Except as provided in rule 18.02 or subrule 19.01(5) (late delivery of defence) or 27.04(2) (counterclaim against plaintiff and non-party), a statement of defence (Form 18A) shall be delivered,

(a) within twenty days after service of the statement of claim, where the defendant is served in Ontario;

(b) within forty days after service of the statement of claim, where the defendant is served elsewhere in Canada or in the United States of America; or

(c) within sixty days after service of the statement of claim, where the defendant is served anywhere else.

Mehta v. Wellman (1988), 27 C.P.C. (2d) 180 (Ont. Dist. Ct.).

Where a defendant is too ill to instruct counsel the court may extend the time for delivery of a defence if proper medical evidence is before the court.

Caisse Populaire Laurier d'Ottawa Ltée v. Guertin; Caisse Populaire Laurier d'Ottawa Ltée v. Simard (1983), 43 O.R. (2d) 91, 36 C.P.C. 101, (*sub nom. Caisse Populaire Laurier d'Ottawa Ltée v. Guertin (No. 2)*) 150 D.L.R. (3d) 541, varied (1984), 46 O.R. (2d) 422, 10 D.L.R. (4th) 319 (Div. Ct.).

The *Canadian Charter of Rights and Freedoms* is not violated by requiring delivery of statements of defence by, and discovery of, parties who are also defendants in criminal proceedings.

Paupst v. Henry (1983), 43 O.R. (2d) 748, 3 C.C.L.I. 1, 38 C.P.C. 5, 2 D.L.R. (4th) 682 (H.C.).

Where an action had been defended by an insurer on behalf of an insured defendant who had never been served with the originating process and who could not be found, the court permitted the statement of defence to be withdrawn on the eve of the trial notwithstanding prejudice to the plaintiff.

McCordic v. Twp. of Bosanquet (1974), 5 O.R. (2d) 53 (H.C.).

An action was stayed to permit the defendant to obtain a survey before pleading.

Otto v. Massel (1973), 2 O.R. (2d) 706 (H.C.).

Where an originating process is issued but not served the defendant has a right to expedite the proceedings and may take his first step *gratis*.

NOTICE OF INTENT TO DEFEND

18.02(1) A defendant who is served with a statement of claim and intends to defend the action may deliver a notice of intent to defend (Form 18B) within the time prescribed for delivery of a statement of defence.

(2) A defendant who delivers a notice of intent to defend within the prescribed time is entitled to ten days, in addition to the time prescribed by rule 18.01, within which to deliver a statement of defence.

(3) Subrules (1) and (2) apply, with necessary modifications, to

(a) a defendant to a counterclaim who is not already a party to the main action and who has been served with a statement of defence and counterclaim; and

(b) a third party who has been served with a third party claim.

A.S. May & Co. v. Robert Reford Co., [1969] 2 O.R. 611, 6 D.L.R. (3d) 288 (H.C.).

A foreign defendant who entered an unconditional appearance was held to have attorned to the jurisdiction of the court.

DISPOSITION WITHOUT TRIAL

RULE 19   DEFAULT PROCEEDINGS

Highlights

The plaintiff may take default proceedings upon the defendant's failure to deliver a statement of defence or where the defence has been struck out. When this occurs the plaintiff may require the registrar to note the defendant in default: rule 19.01. A defendant noted in default is deemed to admit the truth of all allegations of fact made in the statement of claim, shall not take any other step in the action (other than a motion to set aside the noting of default) except with leave or consent, and is not entitled, with minor exceptions, to any further notice of the proceedings: rule 19.02.

Having noted the defendant in default, the plaintiff may proceed to obtain judgment by one of two routes. If the plaintiff's claim is for a debt or liquidated demand, for the recovery of land or chattels or for the foreclosure, sale or redemption of a mortgage, judgment may be obtained by the registrar signing judgment (with prejudgment interest and costs) upon the filing of a requisition: rule 19.04.

Where the plaintiff's claim is not one for which judgment may be signed (or where the claim is one for which the plaintiff could sign judgment but for any reason has not done so), the plaintiff may move for judgment: rule 19.05(1). If the claim is for unliquidated damages, a divorce or a declaration of the invalidity of a marriage, the motion must be supported by affidavit evidence: rule 19.05(2). The judge hearing the motion may grant judgment or order that the action proceed to trial and that oral evidence be presented (rule 19.05(3)) in which case it may be set down for trial immediately: rule 48.02(2).

Rule 19.08 permits the court to set aside or vary a default judgment on such terms as are just. (Note that the service of any notice of motion by the defendant will entitle the plaintiff to move for summary judgment: rule 20.01(1).)

Former Rules: Rules 48-57, 61-62, 526, 668(2).

NOTING DEFAULT

Where no Defence Delivered

19.01(1)   Where a defendant fails to deliver a statement of defence within the prescribed time, the plaintiff may, on filing proof of service of the statement of claim, require the registrar to note the defendant in default.

Where Defence Struck Out

(2)   Where the statement of defence of a defendant has been struck out,

(a)   without leave to deliver another; or

(b)   with leave to deliver another, and the defendant has failed to deliver another within the time allowed,

the plaintiff may, on filing a copy of the order striking out the statement of defence, require the registrar to note the defendant in default.

Noting of Default by Co-defendant

(3)   Where a plaintiff has failed to require the registrar to note a defendant in default, the court on motion of any other defendant who has delivered

a statement of defence, on notice to the plaintiff, may order the registrar to note the other defendant in default.

Party under Disability

(4) A defendant under disability may not be noted in default without leave of a judge obtained on motion under rule 7.07.

Late Delivery of Defence

(5) A defendant may deliver a statement of defence at any time before being noted in default under this rule.

D. & M. Building Supplies Ltd. v. Stravalis Holdings Ltd. (1976), 13 O.R. (2d) 443, 24 C.B.R. (N.S.) 53, 2 C.P.C. 343, 71 D.L.R. (3d) 328 (H.C.).

Default proceedings under the Rules are not applicable to mechanics' lien proceedings.

CONSEQUENCES OF NOTING DEFAULT

19.02(1) A defendant who has been noted in default,

(a) is deemed to admit the truth of all allegations of fact made in the statement of claim; and

(b) shall not deliver a statement of defence or take any other step in the action, other than a motion to set aside the noting of default or any judgment obtained by reason of the default, except with leave of the court or the consent of the plaintiff.

(2) Despite any other rule, where a defendant has been noted in default, any step in the action that requires the consent of a defendant may be taken without the consent of the defendant in default.

(3) Despite any other rule, a defendant who has been noted in default is not entitled to notice of any step in the action and need not be served with any document in the action, except where the court orders otherwise or where a party requires the personal attendance of the defendant, and except as provided in,

(a) subrule 26.04(3) (amended pleading);

(b) subrule 27.04(3) (counterclaim);

(c) subrule 28.04(2) (crossclaim);

(d) subrule 29.11(2) (fourth or subsequent party claim);

(e) subrule 54.08(1) (motion for confirmation of report on reference);

(f) subrule 54.09(1) (report on reference);

(g) subrule 54.09(3) (motion to oppose confirmation of report on reference);

(h) subrule 55.02(2) (notice of hearing for directions on reference);

(i) clause 64.03(8)(a) (notice of taking of account in foreclosure action);

(j) subrule 64.03(24) (notice of reference in action converted from foreclosure to sale);

(k) subrule 64.04(7) (notice of taking of account in sale action);

(l) subrule 64.06(8) (notice of reference in mortgage action);

(m) subrule 64.06(17) (report on reference in mortgage action);

(n) subrule 64.06(21) (notice of change of account);
(o) subrule 69.10(3) (counterpetition);
(p) subrules 69.16(1) (notice of Children's Lawyer's intention to inves-tigate and report) and (5) (Children's Lawyer's report). [am. O. Reg. 69/95, s. 19]

SETTING ASIDE THE NOTING OF DEFAULT

19.03(1) The noting of default may be set aside by the court on such terms as are just.

(2) Where a defendant delivers a statement of defence with the consent of the plaintiff under clause 19.02(1)(b), the noting of default against the defendant shall be deemed to have been set aside.

Metropolitan Toronto Condominium Corp. No. 706 v. Bardmore Developments Ltd. (1991), 3 O.R. (3d) 278, 49 O.A.C. 1 (C.A.).

The test for setting aside a noting in default should not be the same as that for setting aside a default judgment. In either case the court has a broad discretion which should take into account the behaviour of the plaintiff and defendant, the length of the defendant's delay, the reasons for the delay, and the complexity and value of the claim involved. Only in extreme situations should the trial judge's discretion be exercised to require an affidavit as to the merits of the defence on a motion to set aside a noting in default.

Axton v. Kent (1991), 2 O.R. (3d) 797, 49 O.A.C. 32 (Div. Ct.).

Where there has been no undue delay and there has been an intention to defend throughout, a noting of default should be set aside without the necessity of establishing a defence on the merits.

Hart v. Kowall (1990), 75 O.R. (2d) 306, 74 D.L.R. (4th) 126 (Gen. Div.).

Noting of default should be set aside without an affidavit of merits provided there was no undue delay and there was a *bona fide* intention to defend.

Rastas v. Pinetree Mercury Sales Ltd. (1989), 39 C.P.C. (2d) 287 (Ont. H.C.).

Where defendants noted in default have a *bona fide* intention to defend the action and have not unduly delayed, it is not necessary to establish a defence on the merits to set aside the noting of default.

SM Graphics International Ltd. v. Constriuzione Macchine Serigrafiche (1988), 65 O.R. (2d) 265, 28 C.P.C. (2d) 253 (Master).

There is no difference in the tests to be applied on a motion to set aside a noting in default under rule 19.03 and on a motion to set aside a default judgment under rule 19.09(1). Accordingly, where the noting in default was otherwise regular, the defendant was required to show by affidavit evidence that it had a good defence on the merits.

McKay-Weakley v. Mattuci (1987), 62 O.R. (2d) 93, 23 C.P.C. (2d) 56 (H.C.).

On appeal the court removed a term imposed when the noting of default was set aside which prevented the defendant from raising a particular defence.

Lopet v. Technor Sales Ltd. (1982), 29 C.P.C. 43 (Ont. H.C.).

Only in extreme cases is it obligatory to show a good defence on the merits before setting aside the noting of pleadings closed. *Wieder v. Williams, infra*, followed.

Wieder v. Williams (1977), 13 O.R. (2d) 528 (Master).

A motion to set aside noting of pleadings closed was granted without requiring the defendant to make out a valid defence since the application was made promptly and the failure to defend was due to inadvertance and error.

BY SIGNING DEFAULT JUDGMENT

Where Available

19.04(1) Where a defendant has been noted in default, the plaintiff may require the registrar to sign judgment against the defendant in respect of a claim for,

(a) a debt or liquidated demand in money, including interest if claimed in the statement of claim (Form 19A);

(b) the recovery of possession of land (Form 19B);

(c) the recovery of possession of personal property (Form 19C); or

(d) foreclosure, sale or redemption of a mortgage (Forms 64B to 64D, 64G to 64K and 64M).

Requisition for Default Judgment

(2) Before the signing of default judgment, the plaintiff shall file with the registrar a requisition for default judgment (Form 19D),

(a) stating that the claim comes within the class of cases for which default judgment may properly be signed;

(b) stating whether there has been any partial payment of the claim and setting out the date and amount of any partial payment;

(c) where the plaintiff has claimed prejudgment interest in the statement of claim, setting out how the interest is calculated;

(d) where the plaintiff has claimed postjudgment interest in the statement of claim at a rate other than as provided in section 129 of the *Courts of Justice Act*, setting out the rate; and

(e) stating whether the plaintiff wishes costs to be fixed by the registrar or assessed.

Registrar May Decline to Sign Default Judgment

(3) The registrar may decline to sign default judgment, and the plaintiff may make a motion to the court for default judgment, where the registrar is uncertain,

(a) whether the claim comes within the class of cases for which default judgment may properly be signed; or

(b) of the amount or rate that is properly recoverable for prejudgment or postjudgment interest.

Where Claim Partially Satisfied

(4) Where the claim has been partially satisfied, the default judgment shall be confined to the remainder of the claim.

Postjudgment Interest

(5) Where the registrar signs default judgment and the plaintiff has claimed postjudgment interest in the statement of claim at a rate other than

as provided in section 129 of the *Courts of Justice Act*, the default judgment shall provide for postjudgment interest at the rate claimed.

Costs

(6) On signing a default judgment, the registrar shall fix the costs under Tariff A to which the plaintiff is entitled against the defendant in default and shall include the costs in the judgment unless,

(a) the judgment directs a reference; or

(b) the plaintiff states in the requisition that he or she wishes to have the costs assessed,

in which case the judgment shall include costs to be determined on the reference or on assessment.

Liquidated Claims — General Principle

J. Cooke (Concrete Blocks) Ltd. v. Campbell, [1947] O.W.N. 713 (H.C.).
A claim is liquidated where the amount can be ascertained by calculation or fixed by any scale of charges or other positive data.

Liquidated Claims — Commercial Leases

High Point Mgmt. Services Ltd. v. Royal Bengal Restaurant Ltd. (1978), 19 O.R. (2d) 133, 6 C.P.C. 263 (Master).
A claim under a lease for payment of a fixed percentage of realty taxes, insurance, electricity expenses etc. is a liquidated claim.

Viking Shopping Centres Ltd. v. Foodex Systems Ltd. (1975), 11 O.R. (2d) 503 (H.C.).
A claim for rents calculated by reference to the gross sales of the tenant was held to be a liquidated demand.

Liquidated Claims — Construction Contracts

Fotopoulos v. Doukon Catering Ltd. (1979), 14 C.P.C. 259 (Ont. H.C.).
A claim on a ''cost plus'' construction contract was a liquidated demand in money.

George Wimpey Can. Ltd. v. Geist Const. Ltd. (1974), 8 O.R. (2d) 115, leave to appeal to Divisional Court dismissed 8 O.R. (2d) at 115n (H.C.).
A claim for money owing under a construction contract which set out the method of calculating the amount was held to be for a debt or liquidated demand in money.

Liquidated Claims — Deficiency Balances

Christie Corp. v. Lawrence, (January 6, 1995), Doc. 94-CQ-47505 (Ont. Gen. Div.).
A claim for a deficiency in the resale of a condominium property was held to be a liquidated demand in money.

Ont. Dev. Corp. v. Donachey (1980), 30 O.R. (2d) 378, 18 C.P.C. 169 (H.C.).
A claim for a deficiency balance was held to be a liquidated demand.

Hahn v. Wozniak (1978), 12 C.P.C. 130, leave to appeal to Ont. Div. Ct. dismissed 12 C.P.C. at 130n (H.C.).
A claim for the shortfall of principal and interest (including insurance premiums paid) on a mortgage after exercise of a power of sale was a liquidated amount, although amounts claimed for legal fees and real estate commissions related to the sale were not.

Terry-Jay Invts. Ltd. v. Cohen, [1971] 1 O.R. 46 (Master).

A claim for a deficiency owing under a chattel mortgage following the seizure and sale of the chattels is not a liquidated demand in money.

Liquidated Claims — Foreign Currency

Gross v. Marvel Office Furniture Mfg. Ltd. (1979), 22 O.R. (2d) 331, 9 C.P.C. 103, 93 D.L.R. (3d) 342 (H.C.).

A claim in United States funds is liquidated.

S. Miller (Manchester) Ltd. v. M.C. Cowan & Co., [1960] O.W.N. 362 (Master).

A debt payable in a foreign currency is liquidated.

Liquidated Claims — Work Done and Materials Supplied

Yagnik Advertising and Marketing Inc. v. Law and Business Publications Inc. (1980), 29 O.R. (2d) 60 (Master).

A claim for services rendered for "cost" plus a fixed hourly rate may be liquidated if the "cost" is amounts paid to others. Internal or indirect costs would not be liquidated.

Cantalia Sod Co. v. Patrick Harrison & Co., [1968] 1 O.R. 169 (H.C.).

A claim for work done and material supplied was held not to be "liquidated".

Consol. Frybrook Industs. Ltd. v. Jamaica Hotel Enterprises Ltd., [1960] O.R. 306 (H.C.).

A claim for work and service performed may be a claim for a liquidated demand in money.

Anderson v. Smith & Sule Ltd., [1954] O.W.N. 388 (Master).

A claim for work done is a liquidated amount if it involves a fixed scale of charges which was the subject of a bargain between the parties.

Liquidated Claims — Miscellaneous

Bank of Montreal v. Rich (1985), 4 C.P.C. (2d) 285 (Ont. Dist. Ct.).

A claim for damages for conversion is not a liquidated demand.

Diversified Bldg. Corp. Ltd. v. Mar-Ed Const. Ltd. (1982), 39 O.R. (2d) 449, 30 C.P.C. 167, 140 D.L.R. (3d) 292 (H.C.).

A claim by a purchaser to recover a deposit because of the failure of a condition was not a claim for a liquidated sum.

Roynat Inc. v. Ivey (1982), 28 C.P.C. 293, leave to appeal to Ont. Div. Ct. granted 31 C.P.C. 54 (H.C.).

A claim on a guarantee of a fixed amount is for a liquidated sum.

Gulf Can. Ltd. v. El-Cap Elliot Lake Contr. & Paving Ltd. (1980), 20 C.P.C. 145 (Ont. Co. Ct.).

A claim on a guarantee for payment was a liquidated amount where it did not include a claim for cost of collection of the account.

Neon Products Ltd. v. Children Holdings Ltd. (1979), 27 O.R. (2d) 126, 14 C.P.C. 232 (H.C.).

A claim for accelerated damages for the lease of neon signs was one for liquidated damages.

Rasins v. Place Park (Windsor) Ltd. (1977), 4 C.P.C. 63 (Ont. Master).

A claim for payments calculated as a percentage of "reasonable estimated cost" is not a liquidated sum since one must go outside the agreement to ascertain the cost.

Hammond v. Parsons (1978), 19 O.R. (2d) 162 (Master).

Where the calculation of the amount of a claim involves the calculation of United States income tax, it cannot be said that the claim is liquidated.

T.D. Bank v. Domar Systems (Can.) (1978), 6 C.P.C. 191 (Ont. Master).

A claim on a bank overdraft is a liquidated demand.

Charles Pierce Realty Co. v. Empire Hotel Co. of Timmins Ltd. (1979), 26 O.R. (2d) 511, 14 C.P.C. 262 (H.C.).

The court refused to refer to a document outside the plaintiff's claim advanced to show it was a liquidated sum.

Kennedy v. 315812 Ont. Ltd. (1976), 2 C.P.C. 281 (H.C.).

The balance due on closing in a real estate transaction will ordinarily be a liquidated balance.

Fletcher v. Wagg (1975), 11 O.R. (2d) 411 (H.C.).

An action on a written promise to pay containing two mutually exclusive modes of payment was held not to be a claim for a debt or liquidated demand in money.

Waite, Reid & Co. v. Bader, [1967] 2 O.R. 84 (H.C.).

A claim by a broker for the balance of an account is a debt or liquidated demand.

Recovery of Possession of Land — rule 19.04(1)(b)

Breglia Invts. Ltd. v. Rock, [1972] 1 O.R. 728, 24 D.L.R. (3d) 145 (Co. Ct.).

The provisions of the *Landlord and Tenant Act*, R.S.O. 1970, c. 236, regarding termination of residential tenancies supersede the Rules; a default judgment was set aside.

Recovery of Chattels — rule 19.04(1)(c)

Nat. Trust Co. v. Scoon, [1962] O.W.N. 10 (Master).

Judgment was refused where the chattels were not sufficiently identified.

Mortgage Actions — rule 19.04(1)(d)

Morris v. Century City Devs. Ltd.; Ricketts v. Century City Devs. Ltd., [1973] 1 O.R. 646 (Master).

Where a request to redeem is filed the judgment should direct a reference.

Atlantic Accept. (Toronto) Ltd. v. Ball Point Properties Ltd., [1968] 2 O.R. 712 (Master).

The plaintiff may not sign judgment with a reference unless all defendants are in default.

Requisition for Default Judgment — rule 19.04(2)

United Van Lines (Can.) Ltd. v. Petrov (1975), 13 O.R. (2d) 479, 1 C.P.C. 307 (Co. Ct.).

Where a solicitor frivolously certified that the claim was within the predecessor of this provision he could be held personally liable for costs.

Motion where registrar refuses to sign default judgment — rule 19.04(3)

Tomazio v. Rutale (1995), 26 O.R. (3d) 191 (Gen. Div.).

A master hearing a motion for default judgment pursuant to rule 19.04(3)(a) after the registrar has refused to sign judgment cannot give judgment for unliquidated damages. A judge could do so under rule 19.05(1).

BY MOTION FOR JUDGMENT

19.05(1) Where a defendant has been noted in default, the plaintiff may move before a judge for judgment against the defendant on the statement of claim in respect of any claim for which default judgment has not been signed.

(2) A motion for judgment under subrule (1) shall be supported by evidence given by affidavit if the claim is for unliquidated damages, a divorce or a declaration of the invalidity of a marriage.

(3) On a motion for judgment under subrule (1), the judge may grant judgment, dismiss the action or order that the action proceed to trial and that oral evidence be presented.

(4) Where an action proceeds to trial, a motion for judgment on the statement of claim against a defendant noted in default may be made at the trial.

Andersen v. Great-West Life Assurance Co., 24 C.P.C. (2d) 113, 30 C.C.L.I. 85, [1988] I.L.R. 1-2317 (Ont. H.C.).

Declaratory relief may be granted on motion where there is sufficient supporting evidence. *Witkin v. Del Vecchio* (1974), 6 O.R. (2d) 712 (H.C.) distinguished.

Legault v. Legault (1987), 19 C.P.C. (2d) 267 (Ont. Dist. Ct.).

On a motion for judgment, a respondent who was not only in default but also in contempt of a court order was not permitted to appear and be heard on the motion until the contempt of court was purged.

McMillan v. McMillan (1986), 54 O.R. (2d) 629 (Dist. Ct.).

A motion for judgment may be brought where the relief claimed involves child custody together with child support and spousal support.

Family Trust Corp. v. Harrison (1986), 7 C.P.C. (2d) 1 (Ont. Dist. Ct.).

A claim by an employee against an employee to reimburse the employer for an amount paid in settlement of a claim arising from the employee's misconduct is a claim for indemnity, not a claim for damages. The employer is not generally obliged to proceed to trial if the employee defaults in defending the action.

Baker v. Baker (1984), 42 C.P.C. 162 (Ont. H.C.).

A motion for judgment can be brought in a custody action. In this case judgment was granted, as the statement of claim addressed all the concerns enumerated in s. 24 of the *Children's Law Reform Act* and there was nothing to suggest that the Official Guardian should investigate and report to the court.

Anderson v. Busse, [1964] 2 O.R. 454 (Master).

Where the defendant is in default but the third party insurer is not, the plaintiff should proceed to trial.

FACTS MUST ENTITLE PLAINTIFF TO JUDGMENT

19.06 A plaintiff is not entitled to judgment on a motion for judgment or at trial merely because the facts alleged in the statement of claim are deemed to be admitted, unless the facts entitle the plaintiff to judgment.

EFFECT OF DEFAULT JUDGMENT

19.07 A judgment obtained against a defendant who has been noted in default does not prevent the plaintiff from proceeding against the same defendant for any other relief.

Cross-Reference: See *Courts of Justice Act*, s. 139.

Johnson v. Kowlessar (1981), 25 C.P.C. 179 (Ont. Master).

This provision relates merely to practice and procedure and cannot override the express provision of a statute, in this case the *Mortgages Act*, which governs the parties' substantive rights.

Capital Carbon and Ribbon Co. v. West End Bakery, [1948] O.W.N. 815, [1949] 1 D.L.R. 509 (C.A.).

Signing of default judgment against one of several joint debtors does not preclude the plaintiff from recovering against the other.

SETTING ASIDE DEFAULT JUDGMENT

19.08(1) A judgment against a defendant who has been noted in default that is signed by the registrar or granted by the court on motion under rule 19.04 may be set aside or varied by the court on such terms as are just.

(2) A judgment against a defendant who has been noted in default that is obtained on a motion for judgment on the statement of claim under rule 19.05 or that is obtained after trial may be set aside or varied by a judge on such terms as are just.

(3) On setting aside a judgment under subrule (1) or (2) the court or judge may also set aside the noting of default under rule 19.03.

Setting Aside Default Judgment — General Principles

Hunt v. Brantford (City) (1994), 34 C.P.C. (3d) 379 (Ont. Gen. Div.).

In considering whether the defendant has established a valid defence on the merits for purposes of setting aside a default judgment, the court should apply a test similar to that under Rule 20.

Bank of Montreal v. Chu (1994), 17 O.R. (3d) 691, 24 C.B.R. (3d) 136 (Gen. Div.).

Where a default judgment was granted on motion, it may be set aside only if the defendant shows a genuine issue for trial.

Don Bodkin Leasing Ltd. v. Rayzak (1993), 4 W.D.C.P. (2d) 135 (Ont. Gen. Div.), reversed on reconsideration (February 16, 1994), Doc. 92-CQ-23655 (Ont. Gen. Div.).

Where the defendant has not yet been served with the statement of claim, a default judgment obtained by the plaintiff must be set aside without conditions. The onus of proving service is on the plaintiff.

Lenskis v. Roncaioli (1992), 11 C.P.C. (3d) 99 (Ont. Gen. Div.), affirmed (February 7, 1996) (Ont. C.A.).

To set aside a default judgment the moving party must (1) move as soon as possible after becoming aware of the judgment; (2) explain the default; and (3) show an arguable case on the merits.

St. Clair Roofing & Tinsmithing Inc. v. Davidson (1992), 8 O.R. (3d) 578, 7 C.P.C. (3d) 240, 50 C.L.R. 275 (Master).

On a motion to set aside a default judgment the requirement to show a meritorious defence is the same under both the Rules of Civil Procedure and the *Construction Lien Act.* However the test to set aside noting in default is more restrictive under the Act than under the Rules.

Allfur Trading Ltd. v. Polizos (1991), 7 C.P.C. (3d) 39 (Ont. Master).

Orders setting aside default judgments are not granted simply for the asking. The court refused to do so where there had been an unexplained delay in bringing the motion and poor evidence of any defence on the merits.

Chitel v. Rothbart (1988), 29 C.P.C. (2d) 136 (Ont. C.A.), leave to appeal to Supreme Court of Canada refused (1989), 98 N.R. 132, 34 O.A.C. 399n.

The rules governing the setting aside of default judgments are not to be applied rigidly. Where a motion to set aside was promptly brought and a good defence on the merits was established, the Court of Appeal held that failure to satisfactorily explain the delay was not fatal and set aside a large default judgment, but on terms.

Dealers Supply (Agriculture) Ltd. v. Tweed Farm & Garden Supplies Ltd. (1987), 22 C.P.C. (2d) 257 (Ont. Dist. Ct.).

On a motion to set aside a default judgment, there is a broad obligation to look at all the circumstances of the case and to be satisfied that no injustice is done to the plaintiff if the judgment is set aside.

Beber v. Davis (1987), 22 C.P.C. (2d) 25 (Ont. Master).

A plaintiff seeking to obtain a default judgment on requisition must comply strictly with the Rules of Civil Procedure. If a default judgment contains an error of great substance going to the very root of the judgment the defendant is entitled to have the judgment set aside.

Martins v. Martins (1987), 60 O.R. (2d) 215, 17 C.P.C. (2d) 256 (H.C.).

A judgment obtained in a divorce proceeding can be the subject of a motion brought pursuant to rule 19.09(2).

Stabile v. Milani (1986), 9 C.P.C. (2d) 209 (Ont. Master).

On setting aside default judgments, the court has a discretion to impose terms, including allowing writs of seizure and sale to stand. Judgment was set aside where the defaulting party's affidavit raised triable issues.

C.I.B.C. v. 486163 Ont. Ltd. (1985), 2 C.P.C. (2d) 101 (Ont. Master).

A party moving to set aside a default judgment under rule [19.08(1)] must (1) show the motion has been made as soon as possible; (2) explain the default; and (3) show a defence to the action on the merits. The court may vary a default judgment to correct a typographical error without setting aside the judgment.

Grant v. Graydex Ottawa Inc. (1983), 39 C.P.C. 206 (Ont. H.C.).

In obtaining judgment where the defendant is not entitled to notice and is not represented, the plaintiff must comply strictly with the Rules, and where this was not done the judgment was set aside.

McGuigan v. McGuigan, [1955] O.W.N. 388, [1955] 4 D.L.R. 686 (H.C.).

The court has inherent jurisdiction to set aside a judgment obtained on default.

Madison Const. Ltd. v. Shields Const. Co., [1956] O.W.N. 835 (Master).

A judgment signed in a case not within the class of cases for which judgment may properly be signed will be set aside *ex debito justitiae.*

Dorner v. Grossman, [1958] O.W.N. 149 (Master).

A judgment signed in respect of a defendant against whom no proper claim has been made is a nullity.

Cafissi v. Vana, [1973] 1 O.R. 654 (Master).

A default judgment obtained by the plaintiff after being served with a notice of motion attacking the originating process was set aside *ex debito justitiae*.

Industrial Accept. Corp. Ltd. v. Golisky, [1967] 1 O.R. 278 (Master).

Where one motion to set aside a default judgment is unsuccessful, a second motion based on grounds which could have been raised in the first motion is barred. *Nemo debet bis vexari*.

Setting Aside Default Judgment — Supporting Material

National Trust Co. v. Medd (1988), 10 W.D.C.P. 275 (Ont. Dist. Ct.).

The court set aside a default judgment without evidence of the merits of the defence where the solicitor for the defendant had written the solicitor for the plaintiff advising that the statement of defence would be forthcoming and requesting default not be noted but the letter was delayed in the mail.

Allen v. 398827 Ont. Ltd. (1985), 5 C.P.C. (2d) 294 (Ont. H.C.).

The court refused to set aside a default judgment where the affidavit supporting the motion did not indicate the source of information for the belief in the merits of the defence. Further it appeared that the failure to defend the action was deliberate, not inadvertent.

Mantia v. Honour Oak Investments Ltd. (1985), 50 O.R. (2d) 788, 3 C.P.C. (2d) 28 (H.C.).

The High Court set aside a master's order setting aside a default judgment where there was no evidence before the master regarding the merits of the defence.

A.H. Al-Sagar & Bros. Engineering Project Co. v. Al-Jabouri (1984), 47 C.P.C. 33 (Ont. H.C.).

A motion to set aside a default judgment should generally be supported by an affidavit of merits, however, the court has a discretion to dispense with it.

O'Brien v. Parody (1979), 14 C.P.C. 160 (Ont. Co. Ct.).

Discussion of the onus of proof and material required on an application to set aside a default judgment.

Whitehall Dev. Corp. Ltd. v. Walker (1977), 17 O.R. (2d) 241, 4 C.P.C. 97 (C.A.).

In order to set aside a default judgment on the basis of new evidence, it must be shown that the evidence could not have been ascertained by reasonable diligence and would have resulted in a different decision.

Dayus v. Markowitz, [1972] 3 O.R. 57 (H.C.).

Where a judgment has been obtained unopposed through some slip or error on the part of the defendant, the motion to set aside the judgment should be accompanied by an affidavit setting out those facts and by a draft statement of defence.

Banks v. Upper Lakes Shipping Ltd., [1962] O.W.N. 128 (Master).

Although an affidavit of merits is almost always required before a default judgment will be set aside, the court has power to dispense with it in exceptional cases.

Danylock v. Drouillard, [1953] O.W.N. 629 (H.C.).

It is not permissible to file affidavits of non-party witnesses in support of a motion to set aside a default judgment.

Setting Aside Default Judgment — Solicitors' Errors

Morrison Financial Services Ltd. v. Spinelli (1994), 35 C.P.C. (3d) 133 (Ont. Master).

The court set aside a judgment obtained on an unopposed motion as against one of the defendants on whose behalf a joint statement of defence had been submitted but who was not aware of the motion. This defendant had an arguable case on the merits.

Halton Community Credit Union Ltd. v. ICL Computers Ltd. (1985), 1 C.P.C. (2d) 24, 8 O.A.C. 369 (C.A.).

The court set aside a judgment obtained as a result of inaction by the defendant's solicitor. A client should not be placed irrevocably in jeopardy by reason of the neglect or inattention of its solicitor if relief can be given on terms that protect the innocent adversary as to costs thrown away and as to the security of the legal position it had gained.

Howey v. Great-West Life Assur. Co. (1984), 48 C.P.C. 181 (Ont. H.C.).

The court refused to set aside a default judgment obtained where the defendant's solicitor had failed to deliver a defence despite repeated requests by the solicitors for the plaintiff.

Morris v. Century City Devs. Ltd.; Ricketts v. Century City Devs. Ltd., [1973] 1 O.R. 646 (Master).

Judgments for foreclosure were set aside where they had been obtained because of the inadvertence of the defendant's solicitor, where the application was brought promptly and where the defendant had raised a triable issue.

Shedler v. Jackson, [1954] O.W.N. 245 (Master).

The court is always ready and willing to relieve against the mistakes and omissions of a solicitor in order to prevent a miscarriage of justice to the client.

Setting Aside Default Judgment — By Non-Party

Tegelaar v. Peschmann (1985), 50 C.P.C. 23 (Ont. Master).

A default judgment for foreclosure was set aside on motion of a mortgagee who registered a mortgage the day before judgment was obtained.

Can. Trust Co. v. Kakar Properties Ltd. (1983), 32 C.P.C. 280, 26 R.P.R. 202 (Ont. Master).

A non-party has no status to move to set aside a default judgment unless the non-party acts in protection of an equitable interest.

Coulson v. Secure Holdings Ltd. (1976), 1 C.P.C. 168 (Ont. C.A.).

An *in rem* judgment, obtained without an adjudication on the merits, was set aside upon the application of interested persons who had had no notice of the proceedings, and an order was made adding them as defendants.

Doucette v. Doucette (1974), 4 O.R. (2d) 278, 47 D.L.R. (3d) 658 (H.C.).

Judgment was set aside on the application of a non-party where he should have been given notice of the action.

Anglo Petroleum Co. v. Stark, [1961] O.W.N. 93 (Master).

A stranger to the action has no standing to move to set aside a default judgment.

Setting Aside Default Judgment — To Assert Counterclaim.

Marleigh Aluminum Products Ltd. v. Scott, [1960] O.W.N. 346 (Master).

The court refused to set aside a default judgment where the proposed defence was only a counterclaim; however, it did stay execution until disposition of the counterclaim.

Plymouth Import Co. v. Kernerman, [1947] O.W.N. 301, affirmed at 305 (H.C.).

A default judgment was stayed to permit the defendant to prosecute a counterclaim on condition that the defendant pay the plaintiff's costs and post security for the judgment.

Setting Aside Default Judgment — Terms re Execution

333113 Ont. Ltd. v. Grantham (1987), 23 C.P.C. (2d) 168 (Ont. Master).

The court set aside a default judgment where the defendants showed an intention to defend and raised a triable issue, but allowed the writs of execution to stand but not be acted upon, because the signing of judgment had been regular and there had been a long though explained delay in moving to set it aside.

Bank of Montreal v. Heaps (1982), 31 C.P.C. 246 (Ont. Master).

On a motion to set aside an execution filed following a default judgment, one factor to be taken into account is whether there are some grounds for believing that there is a risk of the defendant's assets being dissipated or concealed.

T.D. Bank v. Beninato (1981), 28 C.P.C. 147 (Ont. H.C.).

Where the originating process is irregular, a default judgment ought to be set aside without a condition that the writ of execution remain on file with the sheriff.

Hegedus v. Luciani (1981), 23 C.P.C. 282 (Ont. H.C.).

Where default judgment has been signed in the face of a motion to extend the time to defend the action, the court set aside the judgment but allowed an execution under it to stand. The plaintiff was within his rights to sign judgment. If a judgment is a nullity or an irregularity an execution will be set aside with the judgment, but otherwise the court has a discretion to let the execution stand.

C.I.B.C. v. Sheahen (1978), 22 O.R. (2d) 686, 13 C.P.C. 269, 94 D.L.R. (3d) 576 (Div. Ct.).

A writ of execution can be allowed to remain in force, with proceeding thereunder stayed, as a term of an order setting aside a judgment.

Briar Invts. Ltd. v. Mintz, [1971] 2 O.R. 747 (Master).

A term of setting aside a judgment may be that an execution already issued remain in force but further proceedings thereon be stayed.

Setting Aside Default Judgment — Examples

Esprit de Corp. (1980) Ltd. v. Papadimitriou (1995), 23 O.R. (3d) 733 (Gen. Div.) (a notice of appeal has been filed).

Where the plaintiff had obtained default judgment against the corporate defendant, the court held that the plaintiff could not later move to set aside the default judgment in order to pursue its action against the individual defendants.

441612 Ontario Ltd. v. Albert (1995), 36 C.P.C. (3d) 198 (Ont. Gen. Div.).

The court set aside a default judgment where the defendant had an arguable case on the merits but had not moved promptly to set aside the default judgment nor provided a plausible explanation of the delay. The defendant was entitled to a full hearing and a determination on the merits.

Toronto Dominion Bank v. 718699 Ontario Inc. (1993), 62 O.A.C. 158 (Div. Ct.).

The court refused to set aside a default judgment where the failure to defend was intentional within the meaning of the cases, and there was no valid defence on the merits.

Bombier v. A.M. Boyd Projects Ltd. (1993), 13 O.R. (3d) 370 (Gen. Div.).

Failure to serve an amended statement of claim on a defendant noted in default was not sufficient grounds to set aside a default judgment. The defendant failed to show prejudice.

Jerez v. Kong (1993), 18 C.P.C. (3d) 389 (Ont. Gen. Div.).

Where the defendant had a defence on the merits and the long delay in bringing the motion to set aside the default judgment was the fault of her lawyer, the court set aside the default judgment provided the defendant paid the amount claimed into court.

McKay v. Sky-North Ltd., (January 3 and 29, 1992), Doc. 214A/88 (Ont. Gen. Div.).

The court refused to set aside a default judgment where a long delay in bringing the motion was not satisfactorily explained and where an affidavit of merits had been sworn not by the party but rather by the party's insurer's claims supervisor.

Bot v. Bot (1991), 4 O.R. (3d) 536, 4 C.P.C. (3d) 209 (Gen. Div.).

A motion to set aside a portion of a default judgment in a matrimonial proceeding was dismissed, as the motion was tantamount to an appeal, and was not brought within 31 days of the date of judgment as required by the *Divorce Act.*

Ivan's Films Inc. v. Kostelac (1988), 29 C.P.C. (2d) 20 (Ont. Master), leave to appeal to Ont. H.C. refused 30 C.P.C. (2d) lv.

Faced with contradictory evidence regarding service of the statement of claim, the court held that the plaintiff had not met the onus on it to prove service and set aside default judgment.

Oko v. Kwinch (1987), 60 O.R. (2d) 220, 22 C.P.C. (2d) 305 (Dist. Ct.).

A defendant was entitled to move under the previous Rules of Practice to set aside a default judgment where the judgment had been obtained prior to the implementation of the Rules of Civil Procedure and the new Rules contained no provision for setting aside the judgment.

Dinepi v. Confederation Trust Co. (1987), 19 C.P.C. (2d) 275, 25 O.A.C. 143 (Div. Ct.).

The appeal court ruled that the master below had been too rigid in refusing to set aside a default judgment where the delay was of two or three days only and was explained and a defence raising triable issues was disclosed.

Martins v. Martins (1987), 60 O.R. (2d) 215, 17 C.P.C. (2d) 256 (H.C.).

Rule 19.09 is available to set aside default judgments for divorce, in whole or in part. The court varied a divorce judgment to order the trial of an issue regarding spousal support.

Sigroum Office Management v. Milanis (1986), 10 C.P.C. (2d) 48 (Ont. Dist. Ct.).

The court set aside a default judgment where, *inter alia*, the defendant had served but not filed a statement of defence and the plaintiff failed to include in the trial record an order for trial together with another action as required by rule 48.03(1)(g).

Central Trust Co. v. Vivacom Corp. (1985), 50 C.P.C. 51, 8 O.A.C. 258 (Div. Ct.).

The court dismissed a motion to set aside a default judgment brought some sixteen months after judgment was signed. The lack of particulars contained in the originating process was a mere irregularity.

Sprumont v. Turner (1984), 47 O.R. (2d) 432, 45 C.P.C. 118, 41 R.F.L. (2d) 1, 5 O.A.C. 292 (Div. Ct.).

The court refused to set aside a default judgment for arrears of maintenance payments under a decree *nisi*, where the defendant did not challenge the correctness of the amount of the judgment but wished to have the terms of support varied pursuant to s. 11 of the *Divorce Act.*

Grant v. Graydex Ottawa Inc. (1983), 39 C.P.C. 206 (Ont. H.C.).

Where the defendant had ignored the proceedings leading up to the striking out of the statement of defence and default judgment, the judgment was set aside and leave to file a new statement of defence was given on stringent terms as to the payment of solicitor and client costs of the proceedings and the posting of security for costs.

STM Invts. Ltd. v. Crown Trust Co. (1983), 37 C.P.C. 65 (Ont. Master).

The court set aside a default judgment where the defendant explained the default and raised a triable issue by way of defence.

Johnson v. Kowlessar (1981), 25 C.P.C. 179 (Ont. Master).

In an action on the covenant the master refused the plaintiff mortgagee's motion to set aside a default judgment against the owner of the equity of redemption because, by virtue of the *Mortgages Act*, he was precluded from proceeding against the other defendant, the original mortgagor.

Royal Bank of Can. v. Mack (1981), 22 C.P.C. 21 (Ont. H.C.).

A wife's motion to set aside a default judgment against her husband and to have her added as a party defendant was refused where her only defence to the action concerned the interest calculation and there was unexplained delay.

Victoria and Grey Trust Co. v. Kaby River Lodge Ltd. (1981), 23 C.P.C. 255 (Ont. H.C.).

A default judgment for possession of mortgaged premises will not be set aside where no defence on the merits is shown and no undertaking to pay the amount owing under the mortgage is given.

Nelligan v. Lindsay, [1945] O.W.N. 295 (H.C.).

A full discussion of factors considered on a motion to set aside a judgment: a motion to set aside was denied where, *inter alia*, witnesses were no longer available; a motion to set aside a second judgment was granted upon quite onerous terms in view of the long delay on the part of the defendants and the doubtful chances of success.

APPLICATION TO COUNTERCLAIMS, CROSSCLAIMS AND THIRD PARTY CLAIMS

19.09 Rules 19.01 to 19.08 apply, with necessary modifications, to counterclaims, crossclaims and third party claims, subject to rules 28.07 (default of defence to crossclaim) and 29.07 (default of defence to third party claim).

RULE 20 SUMMARY JUDGMENT

Highlights

This Rule represented a dramatic departure from the previous practice under which a motion for summary judgment was only available to a plaintiff, and only when the claims were properly "specially endorsed". Now the procedure is available in any case to either a plaintiff or a defendant. The motion may be brought with respect to all or part of the claim.

Evidence on motion. On a motion for summary judgment, the moving party must support the motion by affidavit material or other evidence: rule 20.01. In response to a motion for summary judgment, the responding party may not rest on the allegations or denials in his or her pleadings, but must set out in affidavits or by other evidence specific facts showing that there is a genuine issue for trial.

Each party is entitled to cross-examine on any affidavit delivered by the opposing party but must deliver his or her own affidavits before doing so: rule 39.02. Affidavits for use on the motion may be made on information and belief but, where appropriate, the court on the hearing may draw adverse inferences from a party's failure to deliver affidavits of persons having personal knowledge of contested facts: rule 20.02.

Disposition of motion. The court may grant judgment where it is satisfied that there is no genuine issue for trial with respect to a claim or defence: rule 20.04(2). Since the court now has before it sworn evidence adduced by both parties, it is better able to determine whether there is a genuine factual issue for trial. The jurisprudence which has developed since Rule 20 came into force has recognized "the Court now has the duty to take a hard look at the merits of an action at this preliminary stage" (per Boland J. in *Vaughan v. Warner Communications* (1986), 56 O.R. (2d) 242, 10 C.P.C. (2d) 205, 10 C.P.R. (3d) 492 (H.C.)) and that the greater evidentiary base provided by the rule "means that proceedings under Rule 20 should require less diffidence and more assurance on the part of the motions judge than was the case under the former Rules" (per Sutherland J. in *Greenbaum v. 619908 Ont. Ltd.* (1986), 11 C.P.C. (2d) 26 (Ont. H.C.)) and see *Pizza Pizza Ltd. v. Gillespie* (1990), 75 O.R. (2d) 225, 45 C.P.C. (2d) 168, 33 C.P.R. (3d) 515 (Gen. Div.). However, in *Irving Ungerman Ltd. v. Galanis* (1991), 4 O.R. (3d) 545, 83 D.L.R. (4th) 734, the Court of Appeal held that summary judgment may only be granted where there is no genuine issue for trial. (These developments are in line with the practice under the United States Rules on which Rule 20 is modelled: see W.A. Bogart, "Summary Judgment: A Comparative and Critical Analysis" (1981), 19 Osgoode Hall L.J. 552.)

If the court is satisfied that the only issue is a question of law, it may decide the question and grant judgment accordingly (rule 20.04(4)), but where the motion is made to a master, it shall be adjourned to be heard by a judge. Where the only issue is quantum, a trial of that issue may be ordered or the court may grant judgment with a reference: rule 20.04(3). Similarly where the only issue is an accounting, judgment may be given with a reference.

If the court refuses summary judgment it may make orders to expedite the proceeding — it may specify what facts are not in dispute, define the issues to be tried and order a speedy trial: rule 20.05(1). It may also impose terms — payment into court of all or part of the claim, the giving of security for costs and placing limits on the scope of discovery: rule 20.05(3).

If the defendant requests an adjournment of the motion the court has a discretion under rule 37.13 to require a payment into court as a term of the adjournment: *Staiman Steel Ltd. v. Struxcon Ltd.* (1989), 38 C.P.C. (2d) 136 (Ont. H.C.).

While the procedure is available to any party in any action it is designed for use only where a party can show that there is no issue requiring a trial. A strong case is not sufficient. The moving party's case must be unanswerable. To discourage over-zealous use of the procedure, which can be time-consuming and expensive, cost sanctions are imposed when the motion brings no success and was unreasonable: rule 20.06(1).

Practice directions. For summary judgment appeals, see the practice direction regarding New Scheduling Procedure for Civil Appeals reproduced at Rule 61.

Former Rules: Rules 58-60, 63-64.

WHERE AVAILABLE

To Plaintiff

20.01(1) A plaintiff may, after the defendant has delivered a statement of defence or served a notice of motion, move with supporting affidavit material or other evidence for summary judgment on all or part of the claim in the statement of claim.

(2) The plaintiff may move, without notice, for leave to serve a notice of motion for summary judgment together with the statement of claim, and leave may be given where special urgency is shown, subject to such directions as are just.

To Defendant

(3) A defendant may, after delivering a statement of defence, move with supporting affidavit material or other evidence for summary judgment dismissing all or part of the claim in the statement of claim.

Iona Corp. v. Aurora (Town) (1991), 3 O.R. (3d) 579 (Gen. Div.).

Unless the motion for summary judgment is an abuse of process the court will not strike out the motion before the moving party has had an opportunity under the Rules to present its full position.

645952 Ont. Inc. v. Guardian Insurance Co. of Can. (1989), 69 O.R. (2d) 341 (H.C.).

The rule on summary judgments must be followed regardless of the state of the examinations for discovery or the exchange of documents; an incomplete examination is not a genuine issue for trial.

Heon v. Heon (1988), 67 O.R. (2d) 312, 31 C.P.C. (2d) 1, 17 R.F.L. (3d) 417, 56 D.L.R. (4th) 175, 34 O.A.C. 70 (C.A.).

Summary judgment may be granted in a divorce action. *Acchione v. Acchione* (1987), 22 C.P.C. (2d) 252, 9 R.F.L. (3d) 215 (Ont. H.C.), overruled.

Darling v. Darling (1987), 21 C.P.C. (2d) 80 (Ont. H.C.).

Motions for summary judgment are available in divorce actions, even where there is a counter-petition for corollary relief. Rule [69.19] does not exclude summary judgment motions.

AFFIDAVITS

20.02 An affidavit for use on a motion for summary judgment may be made on information and belief as provided in subrule 39.01(4), but on the hearing of the motion an adverse inference may be drawn, if appropriate,

from the failure of a party to provide the evidence of persons having personal knowledge of contested facts.

FACTUMS REQUIRED

20.03 On a motion for summary judgment, each party shall serve on every other party to the motion a factum consisting of a concise statement, without argument, of the facts and law relied on by the party, and file it, with proof of service, in the court office where the motion is to be heard, not later than 2 p.m. on the day before the hearing.

DISPOSITION OF MOTION

General
20.04(1) In response to affidavit material or other evidence supporting a motion for summary judgment, a responding party may not rest on the mere allegations or denials of the party's pleadings, but must set out, in affidavit material or other evidence, specific facts showing that there is a genuine issue for trial.

(2) Where the court is satisfied that there is no genuine issue for trial with respect to a claim or defence, the court shall grant summary judgment accordingly.

Only Genuine Issue Is Amount
(3) Where the court is satisfied that the only genuine issue is the amount to which the moving party is entitled, the court may order a trial of that issue or grant judgment with a reference to determine the amount.

Only Genuine Issue Is Question of Law
(4) Where the court is satisfied that the only genuine issue is a question of law, the court may determine the question and grant judgment accordingly, but where the motion is made to a master, it shall be adjourned to be heard by a judge.

Only Claim Is For An Accounting
(5) Where the plaintiff is the moving party and claims an accounting and the defendant fails to satisfy the court that there is a preliminary issue to be tried, the court may grant judgment on the claim with a reference to take the accounts.

Cross-Reference: See also cases under rule 20.08.

Granting Summary Judgment — General Principles

Bullen v. Proctor & Redfern Ltd. (February 5, 1996), Doc. 95-CU-85988 (Ont. Gen. Div.).

Summary judgment will often be appropriate in wrongful dismissal cases where there is no allegation of cause and the underlying facts are not in serious dispute.

Royal Bank v. Feldman (1995), 23 O.R. (3d) 798 (Gen. Div.).

Not every issue with respect to credibility constitutes a genuine issue for trial. Where, as here, the defendant's evidence is disingenuous, the court may grant summary judgment.

1061590 Ontario Ltd. v. Ontario Jockey Club (1995), 21 O.R. (3d) 547, 77 O.A.C. 196 (C.A.).

On a motion for summary judgment the court is required to take a hard look at the evidence in determining whether there is or is not a genuine issue for trial. The onus of establishing that there is no triable issue is on the moving party, however, a respondent on motion for summary judgment must "lead trump or risk losing" (rule 20.04(1)). Generally, if there is an issue of credibility which is material, a trial will be required.

Royal Bank v. Cadillac Fairview/JMB Properties (1995), 21 O.R. (3d) 783, 79 O.A.C. 303 (C.A.).

Where both plaintiff and defendant bring cross-motions for summary judgment, the court is not obliged to give judgment for either party. If the court concludes that there is a genuine issue requiring trial then both motions should be dismissed.

Rogers Cable T.V. Ltd. v. 373041 Ontario Ltd. (1994), 22 O.R. (3d) 25 (Gen. Div.).

Merely raising an issue of credibility on a motion for summary judgment will not be an answer to the motion. The issue of credibility must be genuine. Where a defendant swore that it did not owe a debt, notwithstanding overwhelming evidence to the contrary presented by the plaintiff, and in the absence of any additional evidence by the defendant to support its denial, there was no genuine issue for trial.

Filion v. 689543 Ontario Ltd. (1994), 68 O.A.C. 389 (Div. Ct.).

A motion for summary judgment should be refused unless it is clear that a trial is unnecessary. If there is an issue of credibility, it will be virtually impossible for the moving party to satisfy the requirements of Rule 20.

ITN Corp. v. ACC Long Distance Ltd. (1992), 9 O.R. (3d) 447, 42 C.P.R. (3d) 97 (Gen. Div.).

The moving party has the ultimate burden of proof but the responding party has an evidentiary burden and is encouraged to adduce primary evidence to avoid the court drawing an adverse inference under rule 20.02.

Irving Ungerman Ltd. v. Galanis (1991), 4 O.R. (3d) 545, 1 C.P.C. (3d) 248, 20 R.P.R. (2d) 49 (note), 83 D.L.R. (4th) 734, 50 O.A.C. 176 (C.A.).

If there is a genuine issue of credibility, a trial is required and summary judgment should not be granted. The resolution of the credibility issue is enhanced by the trial judge's observation of the witnesses.

Ron Miller Realty Ltd. v. Honeywell, Wotherspoon (1991), 4 O.R. (3d) 492, 1 C.P.C. (3d) 134, 46 C.L.R. 239 (Gen. Div.).

On a motion for summary judgment the court may review the merits of the action, and, on a common-sense basis, draw inferences from the evidence.

Pizza Pizza Ltd. v. Gillespie (1990), 75 O.R. (2d) 225, 45 C.P.C. (2d) 168, 33 C.P.R. (3d) 515 (Gen. Div.).

Rule 20 contemplates a radically new attitude to motions for judgment to screen out claims that ought not to proceed to trial because they cannot survive the "good hard look". Such decisions as *Mensah v. Robinson, infra*, emasculate the developing concept of the Rule and ought not to be followed.

Horton v. Joyce (1990), 45 C.P.C. (2d) 69 (Ont. H.C.).

A motion for summary judgment is not designed to require the review of all of the evidence which will be presented at trial. Such a motion is not a satisfactory substitute for a trial. Where facts are in dispute the court should be very loath to determine issues in a summary fashion.

National Trust Co. v. Maxwell (1989), 34 C.P.C. (2d) 211, 3 R.P.R. (2d) 263 (Ont. H.C.).

On a motion for summary judgment the court has to take a hard look at the merits of an action, and an apparent factual conflict in the evidence does not end the inquiry under Rule 20.

Dzamba v. Hurst (1989), 34 C.P.C. (2d) 165 (Ont. Master).

A master has jurisdiction to hear a motion for summary judgment which involves evidence obtained on examinations and cross-examinations, provided the basis of the motion is the absence of a genuine issue for trial.

Mensah v. Robinson (1989), 15 W.D.C.P. 228 (Ont. H.C.).

The court should not attempt to weigh competing affidavit material on a motion for summary judgment. Judgment should be granted only where there is no reason for doubt as to what the judgment of the court should be if the matter proceeds to trial.

Greymac Trust Co. v. Reid (1988), 31 C.P.C. (2d) 211 (Ont. Div. Ct.).

To resist a motion for summary judgment, a defendant must adduce coherent evidence with an organized set of facts showing a real issue to be tried on admissible evidence.

Riviera Farms Ltd. v. Paegus Financial Corp. (1988), 29 C.P.C. (2d) 217 (Ont. H.C.), leave to appeal to Ont. Div. Ct. granted 32 C.P.C. (2d) 164.

1. On a motion for summary judgment, the court should not decide between competing inferences from the facts.
2. Where a motion for summary judgment is adjourned from a master to a judge, the judge is not bound by the master's decision that there are no triable issues of fact.

Haick v. Smith (1988), 27 C.P.C. (2d) 193 (Ont. Master).

The master need only adjourn an issue of law to a judge where it is "genuine", meaning "arguable", with conflicting authority or no authority on the point. Otherwise, the master has jurisdiction to grant summary judgment.

St. Pierre v. Bernardo (1988), 26 C.P.C. (2d) 97, 30 C.C.L.I. 303 (Ont. H.C.).

Summary judgment may be granted notwithstanding the delivery of a jury notice. The court determined liability but not damages where the evidence on damages was incomplete.

209991 Ont. Ltd. v. C.I.B.C. (1988), 24 C.P.C. (2d) 248, 39 B.L.R. 44, 8 P.P.S.A.C. 135 (Ont. H.C.).

A lawyer or a judge schooled in the tradition that almost any substantial issue was to be determined at trial requires a material change in attitude to give appropriate effect to this rule.

Unilease Inc. v. Lee-Mar Developments Ltd. (1987), 23 C.P.C. (2d) 46 (Ont. Master).

A master has jurisdiction to construe the terms of a contract on a motion for summary judgment.

Ont. New Home Warranty Program v. Montgomery (1987), 20 C.P.C. (2d) 295, 23 O.A.C. 369 (Div. Ct.).

On a motion for summary judgment, a responding party cannot merely assert that the facts contained in a pleading are true, as this does not create a triable issue.

Mears v. Bobolia (1986), 13 C.P.C. (2d) 164 (Ont. H.C.).

Since the purpose of the rule is to reject, promptly and inexpensively, claims and defences that are bound to fail at trial, summary judgment was granted on liability in a rear-end motor vehicle collision case where there was no genuine issue for trial with regard to the issue of liability.

Greenbaum v. 619908 Ont. Ltd. (1986), 11 C.P.C. (2d) 26 (Ont. H.C.).

The court should approach motions for summary judgment with less diffidence and more assurance than under the former Rules since Rule 20 provides a better evidentiary basis for decisions.

Vaughan v. Warner Communications Inc. (1986), 56 O.R. (2d) 242, 10 C.P.C. (2d) 205, 10 C.P.R. (3d) 492 (H.C.).

A court has a duty to take a hard look at the merits of an action on a motion for summary judgment. Where there is no genuine issue for trial, the action should be dismissed.

Drysdale v. Progressive Restaurants Inc. (1985), 5 C.P.C. (2d) 214 (Ont. Dist. Ct.).

A motion for summary judgment must be supported by affidavit or other evidence.

Hattori Overseas (Hong Kong) Ltd. v. Phillip Cox Agency Inc. (1985), 2 C.P.C. (2d) 257 (Ont. Div. Ct.).

Summary judgment ought not to be granted where the defendant raises a triable issue as to the application of equitable set-off. An unliquidated claim may be set off against a liquidated claim provided they are so closely linked as to have an equity in favour of the person in the position of debtor.

426873 Ont. Ltd. v. Windermere on the Thames Ltd. (1984), 45 C.P.C. 215 (Ont. Div. Ct.).

Lack of reasons for granting summary judgment is not necessarily fatal on appeal; it is for each appellate court to determine whether it requires the reasons of the lower court to deal effectively with the appeal.

Arnoldson Y Serpa v. Confederation Life Assn., 3 O.R. (2d) 721, 46 D.L.R. (3d) 641, [1974] I.L.R. 1-606 (C.A.).

Judgment should not be granted unless the case is so clear that there is no doubt as to what the results of a trial would be. The court should not decide matters of law or fact which are in serious controversy. [*But see rule 20.04(4) re questions of law — Authors.*]

Davis v. Sawkiw (1983), 38 O.R. (2d) 466 (H.C.).

In order to succeed in a motion for summary judgment the plaintiff must make out a case so clear that there is no reason to doubt what the result at trial would be.

Bank of N.S. v. 438955 Ont. Ltd. (1983), 41 O.R. (2d) 496, 35 C.P.C. 207 (Div. Ct.).

A master must give written reasons when granting summary judgment. [*See also the cases collected under s. 134 of the Courts of Justice Act — Authors.*]

Bank of N.S. v. Nash (1983), 42 O.R. (2d) 530, 35 C.P.C. 196, reversed on other grounds (1984), 46 O.R. (2d) 283 (Div. Ct.).

A master need not give written reasons when granting summary judgment [*See also the cases collected under s. 134 of the Courts of Justice Act — Authors*].

Victoria & Grey Trust Co. v. Peddigrew (1982), 37 O.R. (2d) 440 (Div. Ct.).

Summary judgment should be granted with great caution and scrupulous discretion. The mere raising of an alleged defence does not prevent the court from examining the law and facts to determine whether the defendant is within arguable distance of grounds of defence known to law.

Royal Trust Corp. of Can. v. Zadkovich (1980), 17 C.P.C. 97 (Ont. H.C.).

Defences to the main action raised by a third party do not preclude a plaintiff from obtaining summary judgment based upon the defendant's admissions which make those defences unavailable.

Royal Bank v. Barringer; Royal Bank v. Santopolo (1983), 38 C.P.C. 196 (Ont. Master).

A successful motion to set aside a default judgment does not preclude a later motion for summary judgment. The existence of a triable issue is not *res judicata.*

Bank of Montreal v. Crosson (1979), 23 O.R. (2d) 625, 11 C.P.C. 30, 96 D.L.R. (3d) 765 (H.C.).

Where several defendants raise the same defence and a motion for judgment against one is dismissed, a subsequent motion for judgment against the others will be dismissed as an abuse of process.

Granting Summary Judgment — Affidavits and Cross-Examination

Ferring Inc. v. Richmond Pharmaceuticals Inc. (1996), 7 W.D.C.P. (2d) 168 (Ont. Div. Ct.).

On a motion for summary judgment the court permitted cross-examination on an issue raised in the pleadings which the moving party was not relying on for purposes of the motion. The "semblance of relevance" test will be most broadly applied on motions for summary judgment.

Deslauriers v. Bowen (1994), 36 C.P.C. (3d) 64 (Ont. Gen. Div.).

It is not proper to introduce an expert's report on a motion for summary judgment where that expert evidence is offered by way of an expert report attached to an affidavit from a non-expert.

Dutton v. Hospitality Equity Corp. (1994), 26 C.P.C. (3d) 209 (Ont. Gen. Div.).

The court dismissed the defendant's motion for summary judgment where expert evidence was offered by way of an expert report attached to an affidavit from a non-expert. It would not be proper to dismiss the plaintiff's action in the absence of any opportunity to cross-examine the expert.

Peirson v. Bent (1993), 13 O.R. (3d) 429 (Gen. Div.).

A party may use the transcript of his or her examination for discovery in support of a motion for summary judgment. It is permissible to file an affidavit with excerpts from the transcript in which case cross-examination is not generally appropriate.

Koressis v. Tridel Enterprises Inc. (1991), 52 O.A.C. 312 (Div. Ct.).

An appeal from an order granting summary judgment was dismissed where an adverse inference was drawn from the defendant's failure to introduce evidence from the individual with personal knowledge of the contested facts.

Royal Trust Corp. of Canada v. Adamson (1992), 14 C.P.C. (3d) 352 (Ont. Master).

The court refused the defendant's request to adjourn a motion for summary judgment where the defendant had had over one month to prepare for the motion and had not filed material or attempted a timely cross-examination on the plaintiff's affidavit and where the plaintiff had put the defendant on notice that any adjournment would be opposed.

Prousky v. American Home Assurance Co. (1992), 10 O.R. (3d) 455 (Gen. Div.).

On a cross-examination with respect to the plaintiffs' pending motion for judgment, the defendants were entitled to inquire into facts which would not only support the defence to the motion, but also support the defence to the main action.

NRS London Realty Ltd. v. Glenn (1989), 67 O.R. (2d) 704 (Dist. Ct.).

The court refused to admit a supplementary affidavit filed by the responding party defendant subsequent to the plaintiff's submissions, and granted judgment for the plaintiff.

Royal Bank v. Elwood (1988), 26 C.P.C. (2d) 84 (Ont. H.C.).

The court drew an adverse inference where an affidavit opposing a motion for summary judgment was made by the solicitor for a party rather than the party.

Ont. New Home Warranty Program v. Montgomery (1987), 20 C.P.C. (2d) 295, 23 O.A.C. 369 (Div. Ct.).

No adverse inference is to be drawn where an affidavit based on information or belief merely deposes to facts which are not contested.

Greymac Trust Co. v. Reid (1987), 19 C.P.C. (2d) 134 (Ont. Master), affirmed (1988), 31 C.P.C. (2d) 211 (Ont. Div. Ct.).

In responding to a motion for summary judgment, a defendant must present coherent affidavit evidence with an organized set of facts showing that there is a real issue to be tried on evidence which will probably be admitted.

Fasken v. Time/System Int. APS (1986), 12 C.P.C. (2d) 1 (Ont. H.C.).

Where a party fails to file an affidavit in response to a motion for summary judgment, the court is entitled to infer that the responding party was unable to attest to the facts required to make out its claim.

Bank of Montreal v. Anco Investments Ltd. (1986), 9 C.P.C. (2d) 97 (Ont. Dist. Ct.).

On a motion for summary judgment, affidavits which fail to specify the source of information and belief may be inadmissible.

Rogan v. Magnus Aerospace Corp. (1985), 50 C.P.C. 217, 7 C.P.R. (3d) 405 (Ont. H.C.).

This motion could have been decided against the responding plaintiff simply on the ground that it failed to file affidavit material or other evidence as required by the Rules. However, the motion was heard as if there were an affidavit stating that all the facts set out in the statement of claim were true and since the two paragraphs attacked disclosed no genuine issue for trial, the plantiff's claim as set out in those paragraphs was dismissed.

Saginur v. Sbrocchi (1979), 12 C.P.C. 21 (Ont. Master).

After awarding summary judgment, but before issuance of the formal judgment, the master did not permit the filing of a supplementary affidavit where all the facts surrounding the new defence existed at the time of the first affidavit and there was some doubt whether the supplementary affidavit was credible.

Hernandez v. Power Corp. of Can. Ltd. (1979), 23 O.R. (2d) 793, 13 C.P.C. 314 (H.C.).

Discussion of affidavits of merit on information and belief by employees of corporate parties under the former practice.

C.I.B.C. v. Copeland (1974), 5 O.R. (2d) 382 (Div. Ct.).

Summary judgment following cross-examination should only be granted where the defence has been completely destroyed.

Bank of Montreal v. Willow Rd. Towers Ltd. (1974), 5 O.R. (2d) 370 (Master).

It was held under the former practice that one co-defendant could not cross-examine another co-defendant on an affidavit of merits since the only purpose of such cross-examination was to show the absence of a triable issue.

Jones v. Raper, [1973] 1 O.R. 53 (C.A.).

Where an affidavit was ambiguous and on one interpretation raised a triable issue, leave was given to file a new affidavit.

Bongard v. Parry Sound, [1968] 2 O.R. 137 (H.C.).

The court refused to act on an affidavit based on information and belief.

Shapiro v. Luke, [1964] 1 O.R. 333 (Master).

Judgment will not be granted merely because cross-examination indicates that a party may well fail at trial; it is necessary that the party's case be displaced by such cross-examination.

Stone v. Kassner Invt. Corp. Ltd., [1964] 1 O.R. 329, affirmed [1964] 1 O.R. 332n (H.C.).

Where the defendant did not support its defences with sufficient particulars, summary judgment was granted to the plaintiff.

R.G. Dalton Co. v. Keith, [1948] O.W.N. 597 (Master).

It is permissible for the court to have regard to the credibility of the defendant's evidence on a motion for summary judgment.

Granting Summary Judgment — Where Counterclaim Asserted (See also rules 20.08 and 27.09.).

Kilderkin Investments Ltd. v. Mastin (1991), 47 C.P.C. (2d) 233 (Ont. Gen. Div.).

Where the conduct of the plaintiff by counterclaim was in some respects akin to fraud and the counterclaim was weak, the court refused to stay execution on the judgment in the main action notwithstanding that the insolvency of the plaintiff would make proceeding on the counterclaim pointless.

Agway Metals Inc. v. Dufferin Roofing Ltd. (1991), 46 C.P.C. (2d) 133 (Ont. Gen. Div.), varied (1994), 30 C.P.C. (3d) 295 (Ont. C.A.).

The court granted summary judgment to the plaintiff where the defendant's defence of either legal or equitable set-off was not sufficiently closely bound to the main action.

Haick v. Smith (1988), 27 C.P.C. (2d) 193 (Ont. Master).

The master granted summary judgment on a promissory note despite a defence and counterclaim of equitable set-off, since this is unavailable in bill of exchange claims. Judgment was stayed pending disposition of the counterclaim, without condition.

Davis v. Spectrix Microsystems Inc. (1987), 63 O.R. (2d) 151, 23 C.P.C. (2d) 120 (Master), affirmed (1988), 32 C.P.C. (2d) 312 (Div. Ct.).

The court granted summary judgment and did not stay execution pending determination of the counterclaim. The defendant's claim to equitable set-off was rejected.

Greymac Trust Co. v. Reid (1987), 19 C.P.C. (2d) 134 (Ont. Master), affirmed (1988), 31 C.P.C. (2d) 211 (Ont. Div. Ct.).

The court granted summary judgment to the plaintiff where the defendant failed to present coherent evidence with an organized set of facts to show that its counterclaim was meritorious, and granted a stay of execution only if the judgment amount was paid into court.

Neiman v. Edward (1987), 17 C.P.C. (2d) 133 (Ont. Dist. Ct.).

No defence by way of set-off or counterclaim for unliquidated damages can preclude summary judgment for liquidated damages; however, the court stayed enforcement of the judgment pending resolution of the counterclaim.

Krest Masonry Contractors Ltd. v. William Sorokolit Realty Ltd. (1982), 11 C.P.C. (2d) 304 (Ont. Div. Ct.).

The court granted summary judgment to the plaintiff but stayed execution regarding five per cent of the claim pending determination of the counterclaim.

Iraco Ltd. v. Staiman Steel Ltd. (1986), 54 O.R. (2d) 488, 8 C.P.C. (2d) 293, 27 D.L.R. (4th) 69 (H.C.).

Summary judgment was granted in an action brought by a holder not in due course of a cheque notwithstanding a counterclaim for damages and a claim for equitable set-off by the defendant.

C.I.B.C. v. Olympic Hotels Ltd. (1985), 4 C.P.C. (2d) 7 (Ont. Master).

In this action on a debenture, the master found that a triable issue in the nature of a counterclaim had been raised as to whether or not the defendant was given a reasonable time for payment after demand and granted summary judgment but stayed execution until the counterclaim was disposed of.

Bank Leumi Le-Israel (Can.) v. Rubin (1985), 47 C.P.C. 247 (Ont. Master).

Where the defendant substantiates a counterclaim the court has a discretion to grant or decline immediate judgment but where the defendant substantiates a defence of set-off judgment cannot be granted.

Bank of N.S. v. Nash (1984), 46 O.R. (2d) 383 (Div. Ct.).

Summary judgment against the defendant guarantors was stayed pending disposition of a counterclaim against the plaintiff bank arising out of the bank's conduct in realizing on its security.

Polar Hardware Mfg. Co. v. Zafir (1983), 42 O.R. (2d) 161, 34 C.P.C. 276 (Div. Ct.).

Where the defendant had no defence to the main action but had a counterclaim for a smaller sum, the court granted judgment to the plaintiff and stayed execution on condition that the defendant pay the full amount into court. The plaintiff was permitted to apply to have a portion of the funds paid out of court.

Smov Industrie Céramiche S.P.A. v. Sole Ceramic Importing Ltd. (1983), 32 C.P.C. 194, 141 D.L.R. (3d) 672 (Ont. H.C.).

Where the defendant did not dispute the plaintiff's claim but rather asserted a counterclaim for a smaller sum, the court granted judgment in the main action and required the defendant to pay the full claim into court. The surplus over the amount in dispute in the counterclaim was paid out to the plaintiff.

372005 Ont. Ltd. v. Right Season Insulation Ltd. (1982), 39 O.R. (2d) 199, 29 C.P.C. 314 (Master).

Where there has been no unreasonable delay in asserting a counterclaim and it raises a triable issue, there should be a stay of execution upon the plaintiff's claim.

Amer. Agronomics Corp. v. Int. Citrus of Can. Inc. (1982), 30 C.P.C. 197, 141 D.L.R. (3d) 115 (Ont. Div. Ct.).

Where there was a counterclaim with a small likelihood of success, summary judgment was granted and a stay of execution was made on the condition that the defendant pay into court the amount of the judgment.

Erie Meat Products Ltd. v. Export Packers Co. (1980), 39 O.R. (2d) 97 (C.A.).

Where on a motion for summary judgment it appears that the defendant has a counterclaim, the court may grant judgment in the main action or direct both the main action and the counterclaim to proceed to trial. If it grants judgment it may stay execution and permit the defendant to proceed with the counterclaim.

Granting Summary Judgment — Partial Judgment

Schamber v. McLaughlin (1995), 22 O.R. (3d) 572, 29 C.C.L.I. (2d) 87 (Gen. Div.).

A plaintiff in a motor vehicle case seeking partial summary judgment for damages must first succeed on a motion under s. 266 of the *Insurance Act* establishing the right to sue.

Johnson v. Bates (1994), 20 O.R. (3d) 751, 34 C.P.C. (3d) 228, 8 M.V.R. (3d) 262 (Gen. Div.).

The court granted partial summary judgment for $5,000 in this personal injury case where it was clear the plaintiff would recover a substantial amount at trial.

Maxwell v. G.E.C. Canada Ltd. (1991), 6 O.R. (3d) 253 (Gen. Div.).

A motion brought in a wrongful dismissal action for partial summary judgment based on minimum notice entitlement was dismissed, as there was a genuine issue for trial with respect to appropriate notice.

Krieger v. Krieger Estate (1990), 45 C.P.C. (2d) 92 (Ont. Master).

In an action concerning the value of shares the court granted partial judgment based on the admitted minimum value of the shares.

Re Skye Resources Ltd. and Camskye Holdings Ltd.; Roytor & Co. v. Skye Resources Ltd. (1986), 6 C.P.C. (2d) 296 (Ont. H.C.), affirmed 7 W.D.C.P. 20 (Ont. C.A.).

The phrase "part of the claim" in rule 20.01(1) is not confined to situations where there is more than one separate and distinct claim. Judgment may be granted for part of a single claim.

Rondinone v. 469046 Ont. Ltd. (1984), 48 O.R. (2d) 446 (Master).

A motion for judgment for foreclosure was dismissed as the plaintiff mortgagees were not acting *bona fide* in exercising their power of sale. Motions for judgment on the covenant and for possession were allowed but execution was stayed until trial.

372005 Ont. Ltd. v. Right Season Insulation Ltd. (1982), 39 O.R. (2d) 199, 29 C.P.C. 314 (Master).

Summary judgment will not be granted to the extent of a claim for set-off which raises a triable issue.

M. Schmitt Painting Ltd. v. Marvo Const. Co. (1977), 16 O.R. (2d) 653, 4 C.P.C. 317 (H.C.).

Judgment for part of a claim should not be given on a motion unless it is perfectly clear that such part is severable and liability for the balance of the claim will not be affected.

Electronic Games Ltd. v. Vig Northern Can. Estates Ltd. (1977), 14 O.R. (2d) 110 (C.A.).

Summary judgment was granted for a claim for the recovery of chattels where the defence alleged fundamental breach of the lease of the chattels and did not assert a right to continued possession; other issues to proceed to trial.

Savary v. Poirier, [1949] O.W.N. 553 (H.C.).

Where any part of the plaintiff's claim is admitted to be due, the plaintiff shall have judgment for that part forthwith, without prejudice to his right to sue for the remaining amount claimed and notwithstanding the defendant's claim that the amount admitted is the full amount due.

Granting Summary Judgment — Examples

First American Bank & Trust (Receiver of) v. Garay (1994), 36 C.P.C. (3d) 319 (Ont. Gen. Div.).

The plaintiff obtained summary judgment enforcing judgments obtained in Florida where the Florida judgments were final, and there had been a real and substantial connection between Florida and the subject matter of the action.

Argcen Inc. v. Federated Foods Ltd. (1995), 41 C.P.C. (3d) 137 (Ont. Gen. Div.).

The court refused to grant summary judgment where the defendant relied on a defence of equitable set-off.

1061590 Ontario Ltd. v. Ontario Jockey Club (1995), 21 O.R. (3d) 547, 16 C.E.L.R. (N.S.) 1, 43 R.P.R. (2d) 161, 77 O.A.C. 196 (C.A.).

Based on all of the evidence viewed objectively, the plaintiff acted reasonably in terminating the contract. Therefore there was no genuine issue for trial and the plaintiff was entitled to summary judgment.

Luz v. Moore Business Communication Services (1995), 37 C.P.C. (3d) 289, 9 C.C.E.L. (2d) 169 (Ont. Gen. Div.).

The court granted summary judgment for the plaintiff in this wrongful dismissal case.

Black Gold Potato Sales Inc. v. Garibaldi (1994), 20 C.P.C. (3d) 78 (Ont. Gen. Div.).

Where there was no agreement between the parties restricting the enforceability of an Ohio judgment, summary judgment was granted on the Ohio judgment. The defendant failed to rebut the presumption that the foreign judgment was valid.

York v. Pickering Toyota Ltd. (1993), 66 O.A.C. 393 (Div. Ct.).

Where there were several crucial factual issues which were the subject of contradictory affidavit evidence, the Divisional Court set aside a summary judgment. The contradictory affidavit evidence raised issues of credibility that could only be resolved by a trial judge.

Borg Investments Ltd. v. Dino Investments Ltd. (1993), 15 O.R. (3d) 191 (Gen. Div.).

Summary judgment was granted where the defendant failed to demonstrate that there was some basis upon which the trial judge could find in its favour on a crucial issue.

Aetna Life Insurance Co. of Canada v. Ungerman (1992), 17 C.P.C. (3d) 383 (Ont. Gen. Div.).

Where the master dismissed the plaintiff's motion for summary judgment but stated in his reasons for decision that three of the four defences raised by the defendant were unavailable, the court held that issue estoppel would not apply at trial and the defendants could raise those defences at trial.

Ysselstein v. Tallon (1992), 18 C.P.C. (3d) 110 (Ont. Gen. Div.).

The court dismissed the plaintiff's action on motion by the third party where the plaintiff had issued a release to the third party for injuries caused by a motor vehicle accident and the release provided the plaintiff would not sue other persons who might claim contribution from the third party. The plaintiff had then commenced this action against physicians who had treated her for her injuries and those defendants had commenced third party proceedings for contribution.

P.C.H. Inc. v. Fedyk (1992), 11 C.P.C. (3d) 77 (Ont. Gen. Div.).

In an action on a foreign judgment the court granted summary judgment for the defendant where Ontario law did not recognize the jurisdiction of the foreign court. The plaintiff was permitted to sue on the underlying cause of action.

Masciangelo v. Spensieri (1990), 1 C.P.C. (3d) 124 (Ont. H.C.).

A moving party must demonstrate that there is no genuine issue for trial. However, the credibility of a party is a genuine issue which can only be resolved at trial.

Black v. Canadian Newspapers Co. (1991), 6 C.P.C. (3d) 324 (Ont. Gen. Div.), leave to appeal refused (1992), 6 C.P.C. (3d) 324n (Ont. Gen. Div.).

The court dismissed a motion by the defendants for summary judgment awarding nominal damages against the defendants. The Rules do not contemplate such an order and, in any event, there was a genuine issue for trial.

Ottawa Mortgage Investment Corp. v. Edwards (1991), 5 O.R. (3d) 465 (Gen. Div.).

The court refused to grant summary judgment where there was an issue of credibility not susceptible to resolution on a motion.

Victorian Homes (Ontario) Inc. v. DeFreitas (1991), 47 C.P.C. (2d) 246, 16 R.P.R. (2d) 55 (Ont. Gen. Div.).

The court granted summary judgment against purchasers who refused to close on the basis of a technical deficiency in the tender. The deficiency could have been readily remedied if they had acted in good faith. The real reason for refusing to close was lack of funds.

Canada (Attorney General) v. Kinetic Contaminants Canada Ltd. (1990), 47 C.P.C. (2d) 313 (Ont. Master).

Where the plaintiff did not set out evidence contradicting the defendant's evidence on the latter's motion for summary dismissal and did not even tender evidence that third parties might have relevant evidence, the only genuine issue was a question of law and the motion was adjourned to be heard by a judge, based upon the evidence that then existed.

Grossman v. Woolf (1990), 44 C.P.C. (2d) 288, 40 O.A.C. 154 (Div. Ct.).

The court refused to grant summary judgment in an action involving vendor take-back mortgages where the defendant had introduced uncontradicted affidavit evidence alleging that he had been induced to purchase the underlying property as a result of fraudulent or negligent misrepresentations made by the plaintiff's agent. The plaintiff was precluded from relying on a disclaimer clause in the original agreement of purchase and sale in the circumstances.

Gibson v. Wageman (1990), 45 C.P.C. (2d) 98, [1991] I.L.R. 1-2690 (Ont. H.C.).

The court refused to hear a plaintiff's motion for summary judgment in a motor vehicle case on the issue of whether the defendant owner was vicariously liable for any negligence of the defendant driver.

Ont. New Home Warranty Program v. 567292 Ont. Ltd. (1990), 71 O.R. (2d) 535, 40 C.P.C. (2d) 264, 38 C.L.R. 92 (H.C.).

Where a determination as to when a limitation period commenced depended upon a mixture of facts and law, the court refused to dismiss the action on a summary basis.

Oseco Inc. v. Jansen (1989), 71 O.R. (2d) 151, 40 C.P.C. (2d) 61 (H.C.).

Where a secured creditor had taken an assignment of a cause of action, the court refused to summarily dismiss the action as being champertous. There was a triable issue as to whether the assignment was champertous.

de Gaetani v. Carpenteri (1989), 38 C.P.C. (2d) 306 (Ont. Master).

Where a foreign judgment was final, and that judgment was not impeachable by Ontario law, there was no triable issue.

Tran v. Wong (1989), 37 C.P.C. (2d) 145 (Ont. H.C.).

The court granted summary judgment where the defendants' evidence was self-contradictory and lacking in credibility. A trial judge would have limited benefit in observing the demeanour of witnesses in this case because of the use of interpreters.

Germscheid v. Valois (1989), 68 O.R. (2d) 670, 34 C.P.C. (2d) 267 (H.C.).

Where there had been findings of negligence against several defendants in a previous action, the court granted summary judgment against those same defendants on the issue of liability in a later action arising out of the same occurrence. The defendants against whom issue estoppel was raised had a full and fair opportunity to litigate the common issue of negligence in the earlier action.

Abulnar v. Varity Corp. (1989), 36 C.P.C. (2d) 87 (Ont. H.C.).

The court stayed a motion for summary judgment on behalf of 16 of 219 plaintiffs which would not substantially shorten the trial and would deprive the defendants of the ability to properly defend the action.

Halliwushka v. Thomas C. Assaly Corp. (1988), 29 C.P.C. (2d) 251 (Ont. H.C.), affirmed (1990), 48 C.P.C. (2d) 240 (Ont. C.A.).

The court granted summary judgment (on appeal) where the dispute was determinable by interpreting the contract and no additional facts would be adduced at trial.

Motor Employees (Windsor) Credit Union Ltd. v. Co-operators General Ins. Co. (1988), 26 C.P.C. (2d) 1 (Ont. H.C.).

A master has no jurisdiction to hear a motion under Rule 20 if the only genuine issue is a question of law and therefore, where the grounds for a motion were unclear, the master adjourned the motion to a judge.

T. D. Bank v. Bishop (1988), 28 O.A.C. 102 (Div. Ct.).

The court granted summary judgment on the basis of a settlement agreement which the defendant failed to honour.

Prentice v. Barrie Community Credit Union Ltd. (1988), 26 C.P.C. (2d) 178 (Ont. Dist. Ct.).

The court dismissed the plaintiff's claims where it appeared that there was no evidence available to support her claims due to her incapacity.

Financial Trust Co. v. Caisse Populaire Ste-Anne d'Ottawa Inc. (1987), 61 O.R. (2d) 538, 21 C.P.C. (2d) 24 (H.C.).

The court on a motion for summary judgment accepted the duty expressed in *Vaughan v. Warner Communications Inc., supra,* to take a hard look at the merits of the action, and granted judgment where the defendant failed to show a genuine issue for trial.

Gardner v. Wiggins (1987), 59 O.R. (2d) 475 (H.C.).

The court refused to grant summary judgment in an action for specific performance in which the defendant raised discretionary defences which must be tried on the evidence.

Royal Bank v. Geo-Air Ltée (1985), 4 C.P.C. (2d) 137 (Ont. Master).

The court granted summary judgment based upon an agreement to indemnify the plaintiff for any loss suffered from issuing a letter of guarantee where the defendant had been unsuccessful in an earlier action to restrain the plaintiff making payment under the letter of guarantee.

Rogan v. Magnus Aerospace Corp. (1985), 50 C.P.C. 217, 7 C.P.R. (3d) 405 (Ont. H.C.).

The court dismissed portions of the plaintiff's claim with respect to which there was no genuine issue for trial.

Trentmar Holdings Ltd. v. St. Paul Fire & Marine Ins. Co., 46 O.R. (2d) 222, 6 C.C.L.I. 176, [1984] I.L.R. 6894 (H.C.).

A motion made by the defendant seeking judgment for the plaintiff was granted.

Pan Amer. World Airways Inc. v. Varghese (1984), 45 O.R. (2d) 645, 7 D.L.R. (4th) 499 (H.C.), affirmed (1985), 49 O.R. (2d) 608, 15 D.L.R. (4th) 768 (C.A.).

A motion for summary judgment was granted based on a foreign judgment. The foreign judgment was a final one notwithstanding that there was a right of appeal from it.

Bedford v. Shaw (1981), 33 O.R. (2d) 766, 23 C.P.C. 12 (Master).

Whether interest pursuant to the *Judicature Act* should be awarded is not a triable issue precluding speedy judgment.

Diles v. 300919 Ont. Inc. (1981), 20 C.P.C. 280 (Ont. Co. Ct.).

Summary judgment was granted where the defendant admitted default in payment of a chattel mortgage but sought relief from the operation of an acceleration clause by remedying the default.

Cordoba Devs. Inc. v. Montreal Trust Co. (1981), 20 C.P.C. 96 (Ont. H.C.).

The plaintiff's action against a purchaser from a mortgagee seeking to set aside the sale was dismissed where the pleading did not include an offer to redeem and leave to amend was refused.

Bank of Montreal v. Cockell (1981), 20 C.P.C. 1 (Ont. Master).

Summary judgment on a promissory note was granted where the defendant failed to raise serious questions of fact or law.

Instrument Systems Corp. v. Angot Group Ltd. (1977), 5 C.P.C. 177 (Ont. Div. Ct.).

Summary judgment can be granted on the clear wording of an agreement, notwithstanding an alleged partial failure of consideration.

Krigos v. Pearl (1977), 4 C.P.C. 88, affirmed 5 C.P.C. 320 (Ont. H.C.).

Where a mortgage is only one part of a larger transaction between the parties, a motion for judgment claiming foreclosure, payment, and possession should be refused if it would effectively dispose of the totality of the dispute between the parties.

Smith-Gent Advertising Ltd. v. Marshall Cavendish Ltd., [1973] 3 O.R. 490 (H.C.).

A reference may be made with respect to a counterclaim.

Claremont Invt. Corp. Ltd. v. Massey, [1956] O.W.N. 827 (Master).

Where the defendant in a mortgage action admitted that the mortgage was in arrears but disputed the amount owing, a reference was directed to determine the amount.

WHERE A TRIAL IS NECESSARY

Powers of Court

20.05(1) Where summary judgment is refused or is granted only in part, the court may make an order specifying what material facts are not in dispute and defining the issues to be tried and may order that the action proceed to trial by being,

(a) placed forthwith, or within a specified time, on a list of cases requiring speedy trial; or

(b) set down in the normal course, or within a specified time, for trial.

(2) At the trial the facts so specified shall be deemed to be established and the trial shall be conducted accordingly, unless the trial judge orders otherwise to prevent injustice.

Imposition of Terms

(3) Where an action is ordered to proceed to trial, in whole or in part, the court may give such directions or impose such terms as are just, including an order,

(a) for payment into court of all or part of the claim;

(b) for security for costs; and

(c) that the nature and scope of discovery, if any, be limited to matters not covered by the affidavits filed on the motion and any cross-examinations on them, and that the affidavits and cross-examinations may be used at trial in the same manner as an examination for discovery.

Failure to Comply with Order

(4) Where a party fails to comply with an order for payment into court or for security for costs, the court on motion of the opposite party may dismiss the action, strike out the statement of defence or make such other order as is just.

(5) Where on a motion under subrule (4) the statement of defence is struck out, the defendant shall be deemed to be noted in default.

Cross-Reference: See also cases under rule 20.04 re imposition of terms.

Belpark Construction Ltd. v. Di Poce Management Ltd. (1995), 22 O.R. (3d) 181, 37 C.P.C. (3d) 104, 77 O.A.C. 235 (Div. Ct.).

In a proper case the court may impose a term requiring the defendant to pay part or all of a claim to the plaintiff, although in this case the court required the defendant only to make a payment into court.

Great American Puzzle Factory Inc. v. Empathy Sales Inc. (1994), 29 C.P.C. (3d) 382, additional reasons 29 C.P.C. (3d) 382 at 387 (Ont. Master).

Where the defendant admitted that it owed the money claimed, subject to its counterclaim, the court ordered that the defendant pay the funds into court pending trial.

Alliance Lumber Co. v. Mimico Planing Mills Ltd., [1947] O.W.N. 481 (Master).

A defendant which disputed only part of the plaintiff's claim was required to pay the amount admitted into court, not to the plaintiff.

COSTS SANCTIONS FOR IMPROPER USE OF RULE

Where Motion Fails

20.06(1) Where, on a motion for summary judgment, the moving party obtains no relief, the court shall fix the opposite party's costs of the motion on a solicitor and client basis and order the moving party to pay them forthwith unless the court is satisfied that the making of the motion, although unsuccessful, was nevertheless reasonable.

Where a Party Has Acted in Bad Faith

(2) Where it appears to the court that a party to a motion for summary judgment has acted in bad faith or primarily for the purpose of delay, the court may fix the costs of the motion on a solicitor and client basis and order the party to pay them forthwith.

Innovative Automation Inc. v. Candea Inc. (1995), 24 O.R. (3d) 639 (Gen. Div.).

Where the plaintiff instituted a summary judgment motion and sought leave to abandon the motion, the court awarded solicitor and client costs to the defendant. It was unreasonable to launch the motion since it was apparent that there was a genuine issue for trial.

Deslauriers v. Bowen (1994), 36 C.P.C. (3d) 64 (Ont. Gen. Div.).

The defendant's motion for summary judgment was dismissed with costs on a solicitor and client scale where there was overwhelming evidence from various witnesses that raised serious issues as to liability. Furthermore a crucial piece of evidence originally in the possession of the plaintiff had disappeared some time before the statement of claim had been issued. There was no explanation for the disappearance of the evidence, and the resultant prejudice to the defendants was a significant factor in the dismissal of the motion.

Dubinsky v. Dubinsky, (September 20, 1994), Doc. Thunder Bay 3159/92, additional reasons (1994), 34 C.P.C. (3d) 366 (Ont. Gen. Div.).

The principle of rule 20.06 applies to motions for leave to appeal. The court awarded solicitor and client costs against a party who unsuccessfully sought leave to appeal from an order dismissing a motion for summary judgment.

Thomas v. Transit Insurance Co. (1993), 12 O.R. (3d) 721 (Gen. Div.).

The plaintiffs' motion for summary judgment involved the interpretation of a section of the *Insurance Act* which had never been the subject of any binding judicial interpretation. Although the plaintiffs were unsuccessful, in the circumstances, the bringing of the motion was reasonable, and accordingly the defendant was only awarded its costs on a party and party scale.

Zimmerman v. Banack (1992), 15 C.P.C. (3d) 293 (Ont. Gen. Div.).

The court awarded party and party costs, not solicitor and client costs, against defendants who abandoned their motion for summary judgment. It was reasonable to have brought the motion and it was abandoned when new adverse facts were discovered.

EFFECT OF SUMMARY JUDGMENT

20.07 A plaintiff who obtains summary judgment may proceed against the same defendant for any other relief.

Cross-Reference: See *Courts of Justice Act*, s. 139.

STAY OF EXECUTION

20.08 Where it appears that the enforcement of a summary judgment ought to be stayed pending the determination of any other issue in the action or a counterclaim, crossclaim or third party claim, the court may so order on such terms as are just.

Cross-Reference: See cases re counterclaims under rule 20.04.

Arrowmaster Inc. v. Unique Forming Ltd. (1993), 17 O.R. (3d) 407, 29 C.P.C. (3d) 65 (Gen. Div.).

Where the plaintiff moved for summary judgment on a foreign judgment which was under appeal, judgment was granted but execution was stayed.

C.I.B.C. v. Olympic Hotels Ltd. (1985), 4 C.P.C. (2d) 7 (Ont. Master).

In this action on a debenture, the court stayed execution on the summary judgment in the main action until disposition of the counterclaim based upon the allegation that the defendant was not given a reasonable time for payment after demand.

Royal Bank v. Barringer; Royal Bank v. Santopolo (1983), 38 C.P.C. 196 (Ont. Master).

The court gave judgment but stayed execution where the counterclaim advanced by the defendant was neither frivolous nor advanced in bad faith.

Young & Biggin Ltd. v. Issler (1978), 6 C.P.C. 308 (Ont. Div. Ct.).

The court gave judgment and refused to stay execution until determination of a counterclaim arising out of separate transactions.

C. & R. Mattucci Ltd. v. Rizzuto (1977), 3 C.P.C. 187, affirmed 10 C.P.C. 98n (Ont. H.C.).

This foreclosure action was stayed on terms that the mortgage debt be paid into court, part of the amount to stand as security pending disposition of a cross-action.

I.M.L. Holdings Ltd. v. United Tire & Rubber Co. (1976), 2 C.P.C. 141 (Ont. H.C.).

Where there is doubt as to the sincerity of a counterclaim, enforcement of the summary judgment ought not to be stayed.

Lazarevich Bros. & Assoc. v. Kirra Holdings Ltd. (1974), 8 O.R. (2d) 436 (Master).

The court gave judgment on a claim for foreclosure and required the defendant to assert its claim for breach of warranty by the plaintiff in a separate action.

Pomocon Ltd. v. Golias (1974), 4 O.R. (2d) 310 (Div. Ct.).

Where a separate action pending in respect of similar matters amounted to a counterclaim, summary judgment was set aside and this action stayed pending the result of the other action.

General Printers Ltd. v. Algonquin Publishing Co., [1970] 3 O.R. 287 (C.A.).

Execution was stayed pending the determination of a counterclaim notwithstanding delay on the part of the defendant since the plaintiff had also been guilty of laches.

Hazlett v. Blueberry Point Ltd., [1967] 1 O.R. 444 (H.C.).

Where the only defence raised in a mortgage action was in effect a counterclaim, judgment was granted to the plaintiff without prejudice to the defendant asserting his counterclaim in another action.

Nat. Trust Co. v. Scoon, [1962] O.W.N. 10 (Master).

The court refused to stay enforcement of the judgment in the main action where the counterclaim was for non-monetary relief.

Hurwitz v. Baz, [1955] O.W.N. 978 (C.A.).
Where the counterclaim is not shown to be without merit, enforcement of the judgment in the main action should be stayed pending disposition of the counterclaim.

Ewerth v. Siraky, [1955] O.W.N. 13 (Master).
Enforcement of a judgment for possession of real estate was stayed pending resolution of a counterclaim for relief against forfeiture.

APPLICATION TO COUNTERCLAIMS, CROSSCLAIMS AND THIRD PARTY CLAIMS

20.09　Rules 20.01 to 20.08 apply, with necessary modifications, to counterclaims, crossclaims and third party claims.

RULE 21 DETERMINATION OF AN ISSUE BEFORE TRIAL

Highlights

This Rule provides the procedure for determining various preliminary issues which may dispose of the proceeding without a trial.

Rule 21.01(1)(a) permits the determination of a question of law where it may dispose of the whole or part of the action or where the determination of the question may substantially shorten the trial or result in a substantial saving of costs. No evidence is admissible on such motion, except with leave or on consent.

Rule 21.01(1)(b) provides for the familiar motion to strike out a pleading on the ground that it discloses no reasonable cause of action or defence. Since on such a motion the only issue is the sufficiency in law of the pleading attacked, no evidence is admissible.

Rule 21.01(3) provides for motions by a defendant to have the action stayed or dismissed on the ground that the court lacks subject-matter jurisdiction, on the ground of lack of capacity, or because of another proceeding pending between the same parties involving the same subject-matter. Provision is also made for a motion to dismiss or stay on the ground that the action is frivolous, vexatious or an abuse of the process of the court: rule 21.01(3)(d).

Rule 21 motions require a factum (rule 21.03) and are to be made promptly and the failure to do so may be taken into account in awarding costs: rule 21.02.

Former Rules: Rules 124-126.

WHERE AVAILABLE

To Any Party on a Question of Law

21.01(1) A party may move before a judge,

(a) for the determination, before trial, of a question of law raised by a pleading in an action where the determination of the question may dispose of all or part of the action, substantially shorten the trial or result in a substantial saving of costs; or

(b) to strike out a pleading on the ground that it discloses no reasonable cause of action or defence,

and the judge may make an order or grant judgment accordingly.

(2) No evidence is admissible on a motion,

(a) under clause (1)(a), except with leave of a judge or on consent of the parties;

(b) under clause (1)(b).

To Defendant

(3) A defendant may move before a judge to have an action stayed or dismissed on the ground that,

Jurisdiction

(a) the court has no jurisdiction over the subject matter of the action;

Capacity

(b) the plaintiff is without legal capacity to commence or continue the action or the defendant does not have the legal capacity to be sued;

Another Proceeding Pending
(c) another proceeding is pending in Ontario or another jurisdiction between the same parties in respect of the same subject matter; or

Action Frivolous, Vexatious or Abuse of Process
(d) the action is frivolous or vexatious or is otherwise an abuse of the process of the court,
and the judge may make an order or grant judgment accordingly.

Cross-Reference: See *Courts of Justice Act*, s. 106, re stay of proceedings.

MOTION TO BE MADE PROMPTLY

21.02 A motion under rule 21.01 shall be made promptly and a failure to do so may be taken into account by the court in awarding costs.

FACTUMS REQUIRED

21.03 On a motion under rule 21.01, each party shall serve on every other party to the motion a factum consisting of a concise statement, without argument, of the facts and law relied on by the party, and file it, with proof of service, in the court office where the motion is to be heard, not later than 2 p.m. on the day before the hearing.

Authors' Note on Organization of Cases

Cases relevant to Rule 21 have been organized as follows:

Determination of Point of Law — Generally — rule 21.01(1)(a)
Determination of Point of Law — Limitation Periods — rule 21.01(1)(a)
Striking Out Where No Cause of Action — rule 21.01(1)(b) — Generally
Striking Out Where No Cause of Action — rule 21.01(1)(b) — Examples
Striking Out Where No Cause of Action — Res Judicata
Evidence on Motion — rule 21.01(2)
Jurisdiction Over Subject of Action — rule 21.01(3)(a)
Capacity to Bring Action — rule 21.01(3)(b)
Capacity to be Sued — rule 21.01(3)(b)
Capacity to be Sued — Sovereign Immunity
Another Proceeding Pending — rule 21.01(3)(c) — General Principles
Another Proceeding Pending — rule 21.01(3)(c) — Construction Lien Proceedings
Another Proceeding Pending — rule 21.01(3)(c) — Choice of Law or Venue Clauses
Another Proceeding Pending — rule 21.01(3)(c) — Examples
Frivolous, Vexatious or Abusive Actions — rule 21.01(3)(d)

Determination of Point of Law — Generally — rule 21.01(1)(a)

MacDonald v. Ontario Hydro (1994), 19 O.R. (3d) 529, 38 C.P.C. (3d) 378, 6 C.C.P.B. 305, C.E.B. & P.G.R. 8196 (headnote only) (Gen. Div.), affirmed (1995), C.E.B. & P.G.R. 8243 (headnote only), 86 O.A.C. 37 (Div. Ct.).
The "plain and obvious" test applies to both rule 21.01(1)(a) and (b).

Colonna v. Bell Canada (1993), 15 C.P.C. (3d) 65 (Ont. Gen. Div.).

Where the plaintiff delayed 18 months in bringing a motion for determination of a point of law, the court dismissed the motion.

Trilea Centres Inc. v. Cumming Cockburn Ltd. (1991), 5 O.R. (3d) 598 (Gen. Div.).

Where the court lacks sufficient evidence to answer a question of law, it should refuse to do so. The question was an important issue of public policy and the court needed the benefit of complete factual content.

Zavitz Technology Inc. v. 146732 Canada Inc. (1991), 49 C.P.C. (2d) 26 (Ont. Gen. Div.).

Rule 21 does not apply to proceedings commenced by application.

Cimetta v. Cimetta Estate (1989), 68 O.R. (2d) 251, 20 R.F.L. (3d) 102 (H.C.).

Where the court had directed the trial of an issue without pleadings, the defendant was unable to move to have a question of law determined as there were no pleadings which revealed the point of law to be determined.

Moriarity v. Slater (1989), 67 O.R. (2d) 758, 42 B.L.R. 52 (H.C.).

The court declined to grant a motion on a preliminary question of law where the relevant statutory language was unclear and the matter was one of first impression.

Air India Flight 182 Disaster Claimants v. Air India (1987), 62 O.R. (2d) 130, 44 D.L.R. (4th) 317 (H.C.).

In order to strike out a claim under this rule the court must be satisfied that it is "plain, obvious and beyond doubt" that it cannot succeed.

Barnes v. Twps. of Kaladar, Anglesea & Effingham (1985), 52 O.R. (2d) 283, 6 C.P.C. (2d) 75 (H.C.).

The plaintiff cannot move under rule 21.01(1)(a) for a determination that, assuming the allegations in the statement of claim are true, the defendant is liable. Such a ruling would be in the realm of the hypothetical and would not shorten the trial or save costs.

Carey v. R. (1982), 28 C.P.C. 261 (Ont. H.C.).

The court refused to hear a motion to strike out the statement of claim and for leave to set down a point of law where the motion was brought just before a fixed trial date and after years of litigation.

Byrne v. Goodyear Can. Inc. (1981), 33 O.R. (2d) 800, 125 D.L.R. (3d) 695 (H.C.).

The court refused to dispose of a point of law which depended on disputed facts.

Can. Plasmapheresis Centres Ltd. v. C.B.C. (1975), 8 O.R. (2d) 55 (H.C.).

An application to dispose of a point of law raised by the pleadings should not be made prior to the close of pleadings.

Ellis v. McQueen, [1967] 2 O.R. 399, 63 D.L.R. (2d) 678 (H.C.).

The court will assume that the facts alleged in the impugned pleading are true but where the pleading relies on allegations in other proceedings, such allegations will not be assumed to be true.

Burgess v. Woodstock, [1954] O.W.N. 478 (H.C.).

The court refused to determine a point of law before trial notwithstanding the consent of both parties to do so.

Beelby v. Beelby, [1953] O.W.N. 561 (Master).

Discussion of form of pleading an objection in point of law.

Determination of Point of Law — Limitation Periods — rule 21.01(1)(a)

Murphy v. Welsh, [1993] 2 S.C.R. 1069, 14 O.R. (3d) 799 (note), 18 C.P.C. (3d) 137, 18 C.C.L.T. (2d) 101, 47 M.V.R. (2d) 1, 106 D.L.R. (4th) 404, 157 N.R. 372, 65 O.A.C. 103.

The effect of s. 47 of the *Limitations Act* is not specifically excluded by the two-year limitation period contained in s. 180(1) of the *Highway Traffic Act*, and accordingly an infant injured in a motor vehicle accident may bring an action within two years of attaining majority.

Clark v. 449136 Ontario Inc. (1996), 7 W.D.C.P. (2d) 143 (Ont. Gen. Div.).

A claim by a plaintiff injured in a motor vehicle accident against a tavern owner is subject to the general six-year limitation period for torts, not the two-year limitation period for motor vehicle accidents under the *Highway Traffic Act*.

Peixeiro v. Haberman (1995), 25 O.R. (3d) 1, 127 D.L.R. (4th) 475, 85 O.A.C. 2 (C.A.).

The "discoverability rule" applies to the two-year limitation period in the *Highway Traffic Act*. The plaintiff was allowed to commence the law suit more than two years after the date of the accident where the plaintiff did not learn of the severity of the injury until later.

Bair-Muirhead v. Muirhead (1994), 20 O.R. (3d) 744 (Gen. Div.).

The two-year limitation period contained in s. 206 of the *Highway Traffic Act* is not subject to the "discoverability rule".

Kalla v. Wolkowicz (1994), 26 C.P.C. (3d) 131, 37 C.P.C. (3d) 172 (Ont. Gen. Div.).

Discussion of the discoverability rule for limitation periods.

Karais v. Guelph (City) (1992), 11 O.R. (3d) 89, 12 C.P.C. (3d) 243 (Gen. Div.).

An action against a municipal corporation commenced beyond the applicable three-month limitation period was permitted to proceed where the words and conduct of the municipality's employee and its insurance adjuster raised triable issues based either on the principle of estoppel or waiver.

Superior Propane Inc. v. Tebby Energy Systems (1992), 9 O.R. (3d) 769, 9 C.P.C. (3d) 330, 2 C.L.R. (2d) 144 (Gen. Div.).

The limitation period for asserting a claim for contribution and indemnity under s. 2 of the *Negligence Act* is six years.

Mero v. Waterloo (Regional Municipality) (1992), 7 O.R. (3d) 102, 6 C.P.C. (3d) 250, 10 C.C.L.T. (2d) 197, 37 M.V.R. (2d) 56, 8 M.P.L.R. (2d) 1, 89 D.L.R. (4th) 533, 54 O.A.C. 334 (C.A.), leave to appeal to Supreme Court of Canada refused 9 O.R. (3d) xii, 141 N.R. 399 (note), 58 O.A.C. 239 (note).

The language of the three-month limitation period contained in the *Municipal Act* is broad enough to embrace claims framed in nuisance and negligence.

Sharma v. Ouellette, 2 C.P.C. (3d) 289, [1991] I.L.R. 1-2762 (Gen. Div.).

Although the plaintiffs' direct action against their insurer had been dismissed as being statute-barred, the plaintiffs were permitted to add their insurer as a party in a related action in order to assert a claim for declaratory relief. That claim was not statute-barred, and as the direct action had not been determined on its merits, the doctrine of *res judicata* did not apply.

Carter v. W.H. Den Ouden NV (1991), 7 C.P.C. (3d) 107 (Ont. Gen. Div.).

The discoverability rule applies to latent damage cases only and not to personal injury cases where the damage incurred is immediately obvious and known to the plaintiff.

Rostland Corp. v. Toronto (City) (1991), 2 O.R. (3d) 421, additional reasons 2 O.R. (3d) 735 (Gen. Div.).

The plaintiff brought an action in negligence and nuisance against a utility in respect of leakage of salt water from a steam heating plant. The action in negligence was barred by the six-month limitation period in s. 32 of the *Public Utilities Act*, R.S.O. 1980, c. 423, but as the leakage was ongoing, the claim of nuisance was not barred.

Sjouwerman v. Valance (1990), 46 C.P.C. (2d) 113, 37 O.A.C. 294 (C.A.), leave to appeal to Supreme Court of Canada refused (1991), 46 C.P.C. (2d) 113n, *(sub nom. Sjouwerman v. Canada Post Corp.)* 46 O.A.C. 12 (note), 126 N.R. 336 (note).

The limitation period in the *Public Authorities Protection Act* does not apply to the federal Crown.

Larche v. Middleton (1989), 69 O.R. (2d) 400, 37 C.P.C. (2d) 174 (H.C.), leave to appeal to Ont. Div. Ct. refused 1 W.D.C.P. (2d) 190.

The court refused to summarily dismiss a defamation action as limitation-barred, applying the "discoverability rule" to the alleged defamation.

Keuhl v. Beachburg (Village) (1989), 33 C.P.C. (2d) 209, 15 M.V.R. (2d) 1, 43 M.P.L.R. 273 (Ont. H.C.), reversed on other grounds (1990), 1 O.R. (3d) 154, 45 C.P.C. (2d) 225, 75 D.L.R. (4th) 193, *(sub nom. Keuhl v. Renfrew (County))* 42 O.A.C. 387 (C.A.).

The three-month limitation period in s. 284 of the *Municipal Act* is not discriminatory and is constitutionally valid.

Walton v. Cote (1989), 69 O.R. (2d) 661, 36 C.P.C. (2d) 113, 20 M.V.R. (2d) 171 (H.C.).

Where a limitation period is expressed as a number of years, the period within which an action may be commenced includes but ends on the anniversary of the day of the event giving rise to the action.

Mirhadizadeh v. Ontario (1989), 69 O.R. (2d) 422, 36 C.P.C. (2d) 1, 47 C.R.R. 342, 60 D.L.R. (4th) 597, 34 O.A.C. 393 (C.A.).

The six-month limitation period contained in s. 11 of the *Public Authorities Protection Act*, R.S.O. 1980, c. 406, did not offend the equality provisions contained in s. 15 of the *Charter of Rights*.

Martin v. Listowel Memorial Hospital (1989), 34 C.P.C. (2d) 303, additional reasons 34 C.P.C. (2d) 303 at 311 (Ont. H.C.), affirmed (1992), 3 W.D.C.P. (2d) 421 (Ont. C.A.).

Section 47 of the *Limitations Act* gives absolute protection to a minor, which is not lost by the appointment of a litigation guardian. Accordingly, an infant plaintiff was permitted to add certain physicians as defendants to a proceeding more than five years after the action was commenced.

Clark v. Cdn. National Railway Co., [1988] 2 S.C.R. 680, 32 C.P.C. (2d) 97, 47 C.C.L.T. 1, 54 D.L.R. (4th) 679, 89 N.R. 81, 89 N.B.R. (2d) 116, 226 A.P.R. 116.

A limitation period in the *Railway Act*, R.S.C. 1970, c. R-2, was *ultra vires*, as a federally imposed limitation provision regarding a personal injury action was not an integral part of the federal jurisdiction.

McQueen v. Niagara-on-the-Lake (Town) (1988), 27 C.P.C. (2d) 204, 37 M.P.L.R. 305 (Ont. Dist. Ct.).

A motion to dismiss an action as statute-barred may be brought under Rule 20 or Rule 21; Rule 21 is also designed for cases where determination of a question of law does not dispose of the action but substantially shortens the trial.

Central & Eastern Trust Co. v. Rafuse, [1986] 2 S.C.R. 147, 34 B.L.R. 187, 37 C.C.L.T. 117, 42 R.P.R. 161, 31 D.L.R. (4th) 481, 75 N.S.R. (2d) 109, 186 A.P.R. 109, [1986] R.R.A. 527, varied [1988] 1 S.C.R. 1206, 44 C.C.L.T. xxxiv.

A tort action was deemed not to "arise", nor the limitation period to commence, until the damage was discovered or ought with reasonable diligence to have been discovered by the plaintiff; this "discoverability" principle is a rule of general application, and a statutory limitation period of six years "after the cause of action arose" did not bar the plaintiff's claim.

Papamonolopoulos v. Bd. of Education for Toronto (City) (1986), 56 O.R. (2d) 1, 10 C.P.C. (2d) 176, 38 C.C.L.T. 82, 30 D.L.R. (4th) 269, 16 O.A.C. 249 (C.A.), leave to appeal to Supreme Court of Canada refused (1987), 58 O.R. (2d) 528n, 35 D.L.R. (4th) 767n, 76 N.R. 240n, 21 O.A.C. 319n.

Section 47 of the *Limitations Act*, providing that a limitation period in respect of minors' claims does not commence to run until the age of majority is reached, is a law of general application which supersedes a specific limitation in another statute in the absence of clear overriding wording in the other statute; since there was no clear overriding provision in the *Public Authorities Protection Act* the one-year limitation period in that Act did not start to run against the infant plaintiff until he reached the age of majority.

Victoria County Bd. of Educ. v. Bradstock, Reicher & Partners Ltd. (1984), 46 O.R. (2d) 674, 44 C.P.C. 314, 8 C.L.R. 182, 4 O.A.C. 72 (Div. Ct.).

An action should not be dismissed on the basis of a limitation period where there is a factual issue as to when the cause of action accrued, and the Act containing the limitation period permits the court to extend the limiation period.

Cascone v. Rodney (1981), 34 O.R. (2d) 618, 131 D.L.R. (3d) 593 (H.C.).

The application of a limitation period which does not depend on any disputed facts is a point of law appropriately raised by motion prior to trial.

Woloszczuk v. Onyszczak (1976), 14 O.R. (2d) 732, 1 C.P.C. 129, 74 D.L.R. (3d) 554 (H.C.).

The issue of whether an action is statute-barred is appropriately raised by setting down a point of law for hearing after delivery of a statement of defence.

Striking Out Where No Cause of Action — rule 21.01(1)(b) — Generally

Hanson v. Bank of Nova Scotia (1994), 19 O.R. (3d) 142, 74 O.A.C. 145 (C.A.).

The court set aside an order which had struck out a statement of claim against a law firm. The threshold for sustaining a pleading under rule 21.01(1)(b) was not a high one, and the fact that the cause of action was novel was not a bar to its proceeding to trial. Furthermore, the categories of relationships giving rise to fiduciary duties are not closed, nor are the categories of negligence in which a duty of care is owed.

Prete v. Ontario (1993), 16 O.R. (3d) 161, 18 C.C.L.T. (2d) 54, 86 C.C.C. (3d) 442, 18 C.R.R. (2d) 291, 110 D.L.R. (4th) 94, 68 O.A.C. 1 (C.A.), leave to appeal to Supreme Court of Canada refused (1994), 17 O.R. (3d) xvii (note), 20 C.C.L.T. (2d) 319 (note), 87 C.C.C. (3d) vi (note), 20 C.R.R. (2d) 192 (note), 110 D.L.R. (4th) vii (note), 175 N.R. 322 (note), 72 O.A.C. 160 (note).

On a motion under Rule 21 or Rule 25, the facts alleged in the statement of claim should be taken as true for the purpose of determining whether the claim discloses a reasonable cause of action. The court should not look beyond the pleadings and determine if the action has any chance of success. To do otherwise is to effectively conduct a summary judgment proceeding under Rule 20 without having the sworn evidence of the parties as a basis for determining whether there is a genuine issue for trial.

Morse Typewriter Co. v. Cairns (1992), 7 C.P.C. (3d) 136 (Ont. Gen. Div.).

Determinations made by a U.S. court on a motion to determine jurisdiction were held not to form the basis for issue estoppel or abuse of process. In general, determinations made in interlocutory proceedings are not designed or intended to adjudicate finally on issues of fact or law.

R.D. Belanger & Associates Ltd. v. Stadium Corp. of Ontario Ltd. (1991), 5 O.R. (3d) 778, 57 O.A.C. 81 (C.A.).

The test to be applied is whether it is plain and obvious or beyond reasonable doubt that the statement of claim discloses no reasonable cause of action.

Doe v. Metropolitan Toronto (Municipality) (Commissioners of Police) (1990), 74 O.R. (2d) 225, 50 C.P.C. (2d) 92, 5 C.C.L.T. (2d) 77, 72 D.L.R. (4th) 580, 40 O.A.C. 161 (Div. Ct.)

On a motion to dismiss for failure to disclose a cause of action (1) the material facts pleaded are taken as proved unless they are based on assumptive or speculative conclusions which are incapable of proof; (2) novelty of the cause of action is no concern; (3) the statement of claim is read generously to accommodate drafting deficiencies; and (4) if the claim has some chance of success the action is allowed to proceed.

Hunt v. T & N plc, [1990] 2 S.C.R. 959, 43 C.P.C. (2d) 105, 49 B.C.L.R. (2d) 273, 4 C.C.L.T. (2d) 1, (*sub nom. Hunt v. Carey Canada Inc.*) [1990] 6 W.W.R. 385, 74 D.L.R. (4th) 321, 117 N.R. 321.

Before a statement of claim is struck out it must be plain and obvious that it discloses no cause of action. The test is rooted in the need for courts to ensure that their process is not abused.

Montgomery v. Scholl-Plough Can. Inc. (1989), 70 O.R. (2d) 385, 40 C.P.C. (2d) 128 (H.C.), leave to appeal to Ont. Div. Ct. granted (1989), 70 O.R. (2d) 385n.

Rule 21.01(1)(b) permits the court to strike out less than the entire pleading, although this should be done only when the portion being struck is a distinct purported cause of action.

Chatelaine Homes Ltd. v. Miller (1982), 39 O.R. (2d) 611, 26 R.P.R. 68, 140 D.L.R. (3d) 319 (C.A.).

The court should not strike out a claim unless it is persuaded that the claim could not succeed if the facts alleged in the statement of claim were proved.

Schrenk v. Schrenk (1981), 32 O.R. (2d) 122, affirmed 36 O.R. (2d) 480 (C.A.).

Where on a motion to dismiss an action as disclosing no cause of action there are no issues of fact and the claim asserted is novel, it is proper to determine the question of law on preliminary motion rather than leaving it to the trial judge.

Turner v. C.P. Ltd. (1980), 27 O.R. (2d) 549, 107 D.L.R. (3d) 142 (H.C.).

The court has inherent jurisdiction to entertain a motion to dismiss an action for disclosing no cause of action at any stage of the proceedings and regardless of the state of the pleadings.

Montreal Trust Co. v. Cunningham (1977), 18 O.R. (2d) 223, 5 C.P.C. 25, 82 D.L.R. (3d) 160 (H.C.).

A third party can attack an adverse pleading.

The Dominion Bank v. Jacobs, [1951] O.W.N. 421, [1951] 3 D.L.R. 233 (H.C.).

A cause of action against one of several defendants may be properly dismissed where it is clear that no cause of action exists, and the action may proceed against the others.

R. ex rel. Tolfree v. Clark, [1943] O.R. 501, [1943] O.W.N. 403, [1943] 3 D.L.R. 684 (C.A.).

The court has an inherent jurisdiction to stay proceedings which disclose no reasonable cause of action.

Striking Out Where No Cause of Action — rule 21.01(1)(b) — Examples

Graye v. Filliter (1995), 25 O.R. (3d) 57 (Gen. Div.).

The court refused to strike out what it considered novel causes of action because of poor draftsmanship.

Dooley v. C.N. Weber Ltd. (1994), 19 O.R. (3d) 779, 7 C.C.E.L. (2d) 92, 118 D.L.R. (4th) 750 (Gen. Div.).

As absolute privilege attaches to pleadings, statements made in court, the evidence of witnesses and submissions, they may not form the basis for a cause of action such as abuse of process.

Dalex Co. v. Schwartz Levitsky Feldman (1994), 19 O.R. (3d) 463, 23 C.C.L.I. (2d) 294 (Gen. Div.).

Allegations that insurance benefits should be taken into account in determining the defendant's liability were struck out but allegations that the plaintiff's tax treatment of a loss should be taken into account in determining liability were not struck out.

Foxcroft v. Pilot Insurance Co. (1992), 8 O.R. (3d) 600 (Div. Ct.).

Claims for punitive and exemplary damages for mental distress in a breach of contract action should not be struck out merely because succeeding in such a claim is rare.

McTaggart v. Ontario (1991), 6 O.R. (3d) 456, 86 D.L.R. (4th) 556 (Gen. Div.).

An action for, *inter alia*, malicious prosecution and false imprisonment was permitted to proceed as it was not plain and obvious that the action could not succeed.

RoyNat Inc. v. Singer, Kwinter (1991), 2 C.P.C. (3d) 56 (Ont. Gen. Div.).

An action against a firm of solicitors for negligence in pursuing an earlier action was not struck out, as it was not "plain and obvious" that there was no reasonable cause of action.

Key Property Management (1986) Inc. v. Middlesex Condominium Corp. No. 134 (1991), 50 C.P.C. (2d) 255 (Ont. Gen. Div.).

A counterclaim alleging conspiracy was struck out on the grounds that it did not provide details with respect to the overt acts, times, dates or documents or any indication of the damages suffered.

Guarantee Co. of North America v. Manufacturers Life Ins. Co., 28 C.P.C. (2d) 289, [1988] I.L.R. 1-2315 (Ont. H.C.).

Where an insurer brought an action for a declaration that it was not liable to the defendants under a bond, the defendants' motion to strike out the statement of claim as disclosing no reasonable cause of action was dismissed. The plaintiff had a legitimate interest in seeing that the claim in issue was adjudicated in a timely fashion.

H. (D.L.) v. F. (G.A.) (1987), 28 C.P.C. (2d) 78, 43 C.C.L.T. 110 (Ont. H.C.).

Where a novel claim of negligence was put forward in a statement of claim, the action was not struck out for an absence of a reasonable cause of action, as it was not established that the claim was clearly unsustainable.

Bouchard v. J.L. Le Saux Ltée (1986), 58 O.R. (2d) 124, 11 C.P.C. (2d) 170 (C.A.).

The court refused to summarily dismiss an action in respect of an automobile accident in Quebec where some facts essential to the determination of the issues had not been established.

Dale Perusse Ltd. v. Kason, 6 C.P.C. (2d) 129, [1985] I.L.R. 1-1985 (H.C.), affirmed [1985] I.L.R. 1-1985n (Div. Ct.).

The court permitted a claim for punitive and exemplary damages in an action against an insurer for breach of its duty of good faith and fair dealing.

Manicom v. Oxford (1985), 52 O.R. (2d) 137, 4 C.P.C. (2d) 113, 34 C.C.L.T. 148, 30 M.P.L.R. 100, 20 C.R.R. 44, 11 O.A.C. 38 (Div. Ct.).

In this action for an injunction restraining the development of a landfill site and a declaration that the Cabinet approval of it was void by reason of s. 7 of the *Charter*, the claim against the Attorney General was dismissed as not disclosing a reasonable cause of action and the claim against the county, while disclosing a reasonable cause of action, was stayed by reason of being premature.

Latulippe v. Bank of Montreal (1985), 4 C.P.C. (2d) 102, 8 C.C.E.L. 32 (Ont. H.C.).

A derivative claim under s. 60 of the *Family Law Reform Act* cannot be maintained in a breach of contract case, such as a wrongful dismissal action.

Gibson v. Dudding (1985), 1 C.P.C. (2d) 298 (Ont. Dist. Ct.).

A child both conceived and born after an accident in which his parent was injured is not entitled to assert a claim under s. 60 of the *Family Law Reform Act*.

Seede v. Camco Inc. (1985), 50 O.R. (2d) 218, 50 C.P.C. 78 (H.C.), affirmed (1986), 55 O.R. (2d) 352 (C.A.), leave to appeal to Supreme Court of Canada refused 55 O.R. (2d) 352n, 71 N.R. 82n, 17 O.A.C. 399n.

The court struck out a claim under s. 60 of the *Family Law Reform Act* for the loss of guidance, care and companionship of an unborn child aborted as a consequence of a motor vehicle accident.

Bolton v. Avco Financial Services Can. Ltd. (1985), 48 C.P.C. 20, 7 C.C.E.L. 196 (Ont. H.C.).

The court struck out a derivative claim under s. 60 of the *Family Law Reform Act* in this wrongful dismissal action.

Ficht v. Kitchen (1984), 47 O.R. (2d) 495, 46 C.P.C. 125 (H.C.).

The spouse who married a person injured in an accident after the accident is not entitled to advance a claim for damages under Part V of the *Family Law Reform Act.*

City Nat. Leasing Ltd. v. Gen. Motors of Can. Ltd. (1984), 47 O.R. (2d) 653, 45 C.P.C. 174, 28 B.L.R. 41, 12 D.L.R. (4th) 273 (H.C.).

In an action advancing claims in contract and under the *Combines Investigation Act*, R.S.C. 1970, c. C-23, the court struck out those paragraphs relating to the latter as disclosing no cause of action. Although a trial would still be required, the resulting elimination of evidence and discovery would have a major impact on the case.

St. Joseph's Health Centre v. Sauro (1984), 45 O.R. (2d) 221, 41 C.P.C. 240 (Co. Ct.).

An action by a creditor for chronic care services against a deceased's relatives was dismissed on the basis that no right of action existed under s. 17 of the *Family Law Reform Act.*

Basse v. Toronto Star Newspapers Ltd. (1983), 37 C.P.C. 213 (Ont. H.C.).

In this libel action, an allegation of republication in aggravation of damages was struck out, where there was no suggestion that the republication was the natural and probable consequence of the original publication.

Wiedel v. Wiedel (1983), 33 C.P.C. 48 (Ont. H.C.).

The court declined to strike out a plea, alternative to a family law claim, for judgment in accordance with an agreement prior to completion of pleadings and examinations for discovery.

Cornell v. Pfizer C. & G. Inc. (1981), 23 C.P.C. 286, 81 C.L.L.C. 14,103 (Ont. H.C.).

The court declined to strike out a claim for punitive damages for breach of contract in this wrongful dismissal action. The existence of a concurrent remedy under the *Employment Standards Act* did not bar a claim for "equal pay for equal work".

Jessome v. Ont. Housing Corp. (1981), 31 O.R. (2d) 305, 18 C.P.C. 265 (Div. Ct.).

An action was not struck out where the plaintiff had failed to give notice pursuant to the *Proceedings Against the Crown Act* and where the claim was against an agent of the Crown.

Smith v. Burn (1980), 17 C.P.C. 166 (Ont. H.C.).

The court declined to strike out a statement of claim in an action brought pursuant to Part V of the *Family Law Reform Act* where the plaintiff and the defendants were foreign residents.

Paquette v. Cruji (1979), 26 O.R. (2d) 294, 12 C.P.C. 177, 103 D.L.R. (3d) 141 (H.C.).

Discussion of sufficiency of allegations in a defamation case where the plaintiff was unable to specify persons to whom the defamatory statements were made.

Striking Out Where No Cause of Action — Res Judicata (See also cases below under "Frivolous, Vexatious or Abusive Actions — rule 21.01(3)(d)".)

Municipality of Metropolitan Toronto v. Sheehan (21/2/96, Doc. 92-CU-63276) (Ont. Gen. Div.).

A decision by the Ontario Insurance Commission regarding whether the driver of a vehicle had the owner's consent does not give rise to issue estoppel or *res judicata* in a civil case involving a different party.

Bear Island Foundation v. Ontario (1995), 38 C.P.C. (3d) 215, [1996] 1 C.N.L.R. 16 (Ont. Gen. Div.).

The court found that earlier litigation between the parties had been determinative of the issues involved in an appeal, and therefore the matter was *res judicata*. Furthermore, *res judicata* applied not only to the matters originally litigated, but also to arguments which could have been pursued in that litigation.

ATL Industries Inc. v. Han Eol Ind. Co. (1995), 36 C.P.C. (3d) 288 (Ont. Gen. Div. [Commercial List]).

A corporation was held to be bound by the result of a foreign proceeding in which it was not an actual party. The corporation had knowledge of the proceeding, a clear interest in it, and the ability to intervene and be heard. *Res judicata*, issue estoppel or abuse of process applied.

Newmarch Mechanical Constructors Ltd. v. Hyundai Auto Canada Inc. (1994), 18 O.R. (3d) 766, 26 C.P.C. (3d) 289 (Gen. Div.).

An interlocutory order which finally determined an issue in the absence of an appeal, material change in circumstance or new evidence which had been suppressed or unavailable, gave rise to *res judicata* estoppel.

Aetna Life Insurance Co. of Canada v. Ungerman (1992), 17 C.P.C. (3d) 383 (Ont. Gen. Div.).

Where the master dismissed the plaintiff's motion for summary judgment but stated in his reasons for decision that three of the four defences raised by the defendant were unavailable, the court held that issue estoppel would not apply at trial and the defendants could raise those defences at trial.

Reddy v. Oshawa Flying Club (1992), 11 C.P.C. (3d) 154 (Ont. Gen. Div.).

Family members were not permitted to bring an action for derivative claims under the *Family Law Act* regarding an injured relative where the action by that relative was dismissed on the basis of *res judicata*.

Trilea Centres Inc. v. Cumming Cockburn Ltd. (1991), 5 O.R. (3d) 598 (Gen. Div.).

For issue estoppel to apply, the subject order must finally determine an issue. The subject interlocutory injunction being not final but interlocutory in nature, the court was prepared to review the issue afresh.

Greymac Properties Inc. v. Feldman (1990), 1 O.R. (3d) 686, 46 C.P.C. (2d) 125 (Gen. Div.).

Res judicata applies to all issues which were or could and should have been raised in the earlier action. An independent cause of action, which could have been but was not raised as a defence of set-off, is not barred.

Tannis Trading Inc. v. Thorne, Ernst & Whinney (1989), 69 O.R. (2d) 120, 35 C.P.C. (2d) 165, 60 D.L.R. (4th) 566 (H.C.).

Res judicata and issue estoppel did not bar an action by a creditor against a trustee in bankruptcy where the claims were not within the court's jurisdiction in a prior banking proceeding.

Four Embarcadero Center Venture v. Mr. Greenjeans Corp. (1988), 64 O.R. (2d) 746, 26 C.P.C. (2d) 248 (H.C.), appeal quashed 65 O.R. (2d) 160, 27 C.P.C. (2d) 16 (C.A.).

Where a plaintiff brought an action to enforce default judgments obtained in California, the defendant unsuccessfully moved to dismiss the action on the grounds that the judgments were under appeal and were therefore neither final nor *res judicata*. The defendant's rights could be safeguarded by staying execution of the Ontario judgment until the California appeal was determined.

Thornton v. Tittley (1985), 51 O.R. (2d) 315, 4 C.P.C. (2d) 13 (H.C.), affirmed (1987), 61 O.R. (2d) 543, 21 C.P.C. (2d) 126 (C.A.).

Where the plaintiff tenant had unsuccessfully moved for relief from forfeiture in earlier proceedings the court dismissed this action which advanced claims which merged in the earlier judgment.

Batchelor v. Morden (1985), 50 C.P.C. 39 (Ont. Dist. Ct.).

The court refused to dismiss an action by a tenant against a landlord claiming a rent rebate and damages for invasion of privacy where the tenant had brought an earlier action for breach of a covenant of quiet enjoyment in which the claims might have been included.

Re Bagaric and Juric (1984), 44 O.R. (2d) 638, 40 C.P.C. 211, 5 D.L.R. (4th) 78, 2 O.A.C. 35 (C.A.).

Under the *Child Welfare Act*, R.S.O. 1970, c. 64, a child may sue by next friend for a declaration of parentage despite the fact that similar proceedings were dismissed against the putative father. The child's claim is not barred by *res judicata*, because of the new statutory right created.

Khirkhanan v. Khirkhanan (1983), 44 O.R. (2d) 476, 40 C.P.C. 100 (H.C.).

Where the merits of the first action had not been adjudicated on, *res judicata* did not apply to bar a second action seeking similar relief.

Smith v. Eastern Airlines Inc. (1983), 39 C.P.C. 88, 2 C.C.E.L. 221, 84 C.L.L.C. 14,018 (Ont. Co. Ct.).

An action for wrongful dismissal was dismissed since there was no basis on which it could proceed because the plaintiff had been reinstated by an adjudicator under the *Canada Labour Code*.

Staff Builders Int. Inc. v. Cohen; Cohen v. Staff Builders Int. Inc. (1983), 38 C.P.C. 82 (Ont. H.C.).

The court struck out a counterclaim which raised the same issues as were raised in a previous action in which the present plaintiffs by counterclaim had consented to judgment against them.

Dom. Trust Co. v. Kay (1983), 33 C.P.C. 130, 143 D.L.R. (3d) 633 (Ont. H.C.).

This action founded on the tort of deceit was dismissed, the matter being *res judicata* by reason of the dismissal of an earlier action framed in contract based upon the same facts.

Fortino v. Rudolph (1983), 32 C.P.C. 315 (Ont. Div. Ct.).

Where an insurer recovers judgment in a subrogated action brought in the insured's name, a subsequent claim by the insured for personal injury will be dismissed on the basis of *res judicata*.

Hennig v. Northern Heights (Sault) Ltd. (1980), 30 O.R. (2d) 346, 17 C.P.C. 173 (C.A.), leave to appeal to Supreme Court of Canada refused 30 O.R. (2d) 346n.

Although a counterclaim in a prior action was not pursued at trial, the statement of claim in a later action claiming similar relief was struck out on the basis of the doctrine of *res judicata*.

Cavers v. Laycock, [1963] 2 O.R. 639, 40 D.L.R. (2d) 687 (H.C.).

A gratuitous passenger and his driver are in sufficient privity that an action by the driver against another driver precludes under the doctrine of *res judicata* a later action by the passenger against such other driver.

Evidence on Motion — rule 21.01(2)

Montreal Trust Co. of Canada v. Toronto-Dominion Bank (1992), 40 C.P.C. (3d) 389 (Ont. Gen. Div.).

A party is entitled to rely on documents referred to in the statement of claim on motions under both rule 21.01(1)(a) and 21.01(1)(b). By virtue of rule 25.06(7), a statement of claim is deemed to include documents incorporated in it by reference and which form an integral part of the plaintiff's claim.

Air Canada v. McDonnell Douglas Corp. (1990), 72 O.R. (2d) 372, 38 O.A.C. 77 (Div. Ct.), affirmed (1992), 58 O.A.C. 1 (C.A.).

Rule 21.01(2)(b) precludes the moving party from tendering any evidence on a motion to strike out a pleading.

Trendsetter Developments Ltd. v. Ottawa Financial Corp. (1989), 33 C.P.C. (2d) 16, 32 O.A.C. 327 (C.A.).

No evidence is admissible on a motion to strike out a pleading under rule 21.01(1)(b).

Eades v. Hamilton (1985), 52 O.R. (2d) 307, 13 C.C.L.I. 65 (Dist. Ct.).

The court admitted the defendant's affidavit evidence where the plaintiff did not object and it was helpful to the court.

Blakely v. 513953 Ont. Ltd. (1985), 49 O.R. (2d) 651, 49 C.P.C. 120, 31 M.V.R. 10 (H.C.).

On a motion to determine a question of law before trial, leave to admit evidence under rule 21.01(2)(a) was refused where the evidence was not relevant to the issues on the motion.

Gaudet v. Levy (1984), 47 O.R. (2d) 577, 46 C.P.C. 62, 11 D.L.R. (4th) 721 (H.C.).

The court can only rely on facts acknowledged in the pleadings or otherwise agreed to by the parties when determining a point of law regarding the applicability of a limitation period. In this case the court could not therefore be influenced by evidence from the cross-examination of the plaintiff's former solicitor regarding when the limitation period began to run.

Pala v. Oort (1982), 36 O.R. (2d) 180, 26 C.P.C. 215, 134 D.L.R. (3d) 712 (H.C.).

On a motion to dismiss an action as not being a properly constituted class action, transcripts of examinations conducted to show the plaintiff's allegations to be false were inadmissible, since the allegations of fact in the statement of claim had to be assumed to be true for the purposes of the motion.

Toronto v. Schein (1980), 19 C.P.C. 195 (Ont. H.C.).

It is not open to an applicant to make proof of a by-law or any other fact, however simple or uncontroversial.

Jurisdiction Over Subject of Action — rule 21.01(3)(a)

Ontario (Attorney General) v. Bowie (1993), 16 O.R. (3d) 476, 1 C.C.E.L. (2d) 190 (Div. Ct.).

The court dismissed an action brought by an employer against its employee for property damage arising out of a motor vehicle collision, as the court's jurisdiction was ousted by the terms of a collective agreement.

Kierrosmaki v. Mutual of Omaha Ins. Co. (1988), 26 C.P.C. (2d) 146, 31 C.C.L.I. 28 (Ont. H.C.).

Where it was not clear whether the plaintiff's claim was based on a collective agreement or an insurance policy, a motion to dismiss on the basis of lack of jurisdiction was dismissed.

Oliveira v. Greenspoon Bros. Ltd. (1979), 25 O.R. (2d) 669, 101 D.L.R. (3d) 765 (H.C.).

The court stayed an action by an employee against an employer regarding an accident during the course of employment where it appeared the matter was within the exclusive jurisdiction of the Workmen's Compensation Board.

Planned Sales Ltd. v. Einson-Freeman Int. (Americas) Ltd., [1955] O.W.N. 443 (H.C.).

The court stayed an action for breach of contract where the contract provided for arbitration in the United States.

Capacity to Bring Action — rule 21.01(3)(b)

Hal Commodities Cycles Management v. Kirsh (1993), 17 C.P.C. (3d) 320 (Ont. Gen. Div.).

Where the plaintiff was an Arizona corporation which had been dissolved and was incapable of revival under Arizona law, the court struck out the action.

International Display & Lighting Group Ltd. v. R.A.E. Industrial Electronics Ltd. (1993), 15 C.P.C. (3d) 165 (Ont. Gen. Div.).

It is not necessary to revive a dissolved Ontario corporation to prosecute an action on behalf of the corporation; however, it is necessary to do so to enforce any judgment obtained.

Canadian Council of Churches v. Canada, [1992] 1 S.C.R. 236, 5 C.P.C. (3d) 20, 2 Admin. L.R. (2d) 229, 16 Imm. L.R. (2d) 161, 8 C.R.R. (2d) 145, 88 D.L.R. (4th) 193, 49 F.T.R. 160 (note), 132 N.R. 241.

In deciding whether to grant public interest standing the court will consider (1) whether there is a serious issue raised as to the subject legislation; (2) whether the plaintiff is directly affected or has a genuine interest in the validity of the legislation; and (3) whether there is another reasonable and effective way to bring the issue to court.

Caisse Populaire Vanier Ltée v. Bales (1991), 2 O.R. (3d) 456, 3 C.B.R. (3d) 264 (Gen. Div.).

The assignment of a cause of action in tort does not amount to champerty or maintenance where the assignee has a pre-existing commercial interest.

Corp. of the Canadian Civil Liberties Assn. v. Canada (Attorney General) (1990), 74 O.R. (2d) 609, 45 C.P.C. (2d) 308, 45 Admin. L.R. 94, 72 D.L.R. (4th) 742 (H.C.).

A non-profit corporation was granted standing to challenge the constitutional validity of various provisions of the *Canadian Security Intelligence Service Act* on the grounds of public interest. The applicant had shown that it had a genuine interest in the validity of the legislation, that there was a serious issue, and that there was no other reasonable or effective manner in which the issue could be brought before the court.

Société Générale (Can.) v. 743823 Ont. Ltd. (1989), 41 C.P.C. (2d) 286 (Ont. Master).

The appointment of a receiver under a debenture was held not to affect the ability of the directors of the subject company to cause the company to continue litigation. The receiver was appointed for a limited purpose.

McNamara v. Pagecorp Inc. (1989), 38 C.P.C. (2d) 117, 76 C.B.R. (N.S.) 97 (Ont. C.A.).

An undischarged bankrupt may not sue to enforce property claims even where the property is sold by the trustee to the bankrupt before discharge.

Energy Probe v. Canada (A.G.) (1989), 68 O.R. (2d) 449, 35 C.P.C. (2d) 201, 37 Admin. L.R.
     1, 3 C.E.L.R. (N.S.) 262, 40 C.R.R. 303, 58 D.L.R. (4th) 513, 33 O.A.C. 39 (C.A.), leave
     to appeal to Supreme Court of Canada refused 102 N.R. 399, 37 O.A.C. 160n.

A public interest corporation and another plaintiff had standing to bring an action challenging
the constitutionality of the *Nuclear Liability Act*, notwithstanding that there was no evidence
that a nuclear incident had in fact occurred, nor that the plaintiff would be specifically affected;
there was a serious issue as to validity and the plaintiffs had a genuine interest, as citizens, in
the invalidity of the legislation and there was no other reasonably effective manner in which
the issue might be brought before the court.

Continental Bank of Can. v. Arthur Anderson & Co. (1987), 59 O.R. (2d) 774, 39 D.L.R. (4th)
     261 (H.C.).

On its winding-up, a bank is able to assign its causes of action, which may include pending
actions in contract and tort, to another bank; causes of action in both tort and contract may be
assigned if the assignee has a legitimate property or commercial interest in the enforcement of
the claim.

Campbell v. Ontario (A.G.) (1987), 60 O.R. (2d) 617, 35 C.C.C. (3d) 480, 42 D.L.R. (4th) 383
     (C.A.), leave to appeal to Supreme Court of Canada refused 60 O.R. (2d) 618n, 35 C.C.C.
     (3d) 480n, 42 D.L.R. (4th) 383n, 83 N.R. 24, 23 O.A.C. 317n.

The owner of a business adjoining an abortion clinic did not have standing to challenge the
Attorney General's decision to stay prosecution against three doctors.

Ross v. Moore (1982), 36 O.R. (2d) 464 (Co. Ct.).

A plaintiff whose property had been damaged by fire was held to have standing to sue notwithstanding that he had subsequently transferred the property to his wife.

Falvo Enterprises Ltd. v. Price Waterhouse Ltd. (1981), 34 O.R. (2d) 336, 40 C.B.R. (N.S.)
     305, 28 C.P.C. 134 (H.C.).

An action against the trustee in bankruptcy for the return of a deposit from an uncompleted real
estate transaction with the bankrupt was allowed to proceed although leave had not been obtained
under the *Bankruptcy Act*.

Black & White Sales Consultants Ltd. v. CBS Records Can. Ltd. (1980), 31 O.R. (2d) 46, 36
     C.B.R. (N.S.) 125, 20 C.P.C. 148, 118 D.L.R. (3d) 726 (H.C.).

An action commenced by an undischarged bankrupt while the receiving order was under appeal
was dismissed, the plaintiff having no status to bring the action.

Dehler v. Ottawa Civic Hospital (1979), 25 O.R. (2d) 749, 14 C.P.C. 4, 3 L. Med. Q. 141, 101
     D.L.R. (3d) 686, affirmed 29 O.R. (2d) 677, 117 D.L.R. (3d) 512 (C.A.).

Discussion of the standing of unborn children.

Seafarers Int. Union of Can. v. Lawrence (1979), 24 O.R. (2d) 257, 13 C.P.C. 281, 97 D.L.R.
     (3d) 324 (C.A.), leave to appeal to Supreme Court of Canada refused, 24 O.R. (2d) 257n,
     97 D.L.R. (3d) 324n.

A trade union has no status to bring an action in Ontario and therefore representatives of the
union may not bring a derivative action on behalf of the union.

Rosenberg v. Grand River Conservation Authority (1975), 12 O.R. (2d) 496, 1 C.P.C. 1, 69
     D.L.R. (3d) 384 (C.A.).

Two dissenting members of a conservation authority were refused standing to attack a decision
of that body.

Re Doctors Hospital and Min. of Health (1976), 12 O.R. (2d) 164, 1 C.P.C. 232, 68 D.L.R. (3d)
     220 (Div. Ct.).

A group of doctors who would be affected by the closing of a hospital was determined to have
status to be heard.

Green v. R., [1973] 2 O.R. 396, 34 D.L.R. (3d) 20 (H.C.).

An action for failure to maintain a provincial park was dismissed because the plaintiff, having suffered no particular damage, lacked status to maintain the action.

Denison Mines Ltd. v. A.G. Can., [1973] 1 O.R. 797, 32 D.L.R. (3d) 419 (H.C.).

The plaintiff was held to lack status to bring an action attacking the constitutionality of legislation since it did not plead it had been specifically affected or exceptionally prejudiced by such legislation.

Int. Alliance of Theatrical Stage Employees, Local 58 v. C.B.C., [1972] 1 O.R. 161, 22 D.L.R. (3d) 413 (H.C.).

An originating process naming a trade union as plaintiff was held to be a nullity incapable of amendment.

John Northway & Son Ltd. v. Dunwoody, [1962] O.W.N. 112 (H.C.).

A defendant may not object on the basis that a corporate plaintiff failed to comply with its internal management requirements to commence the action.

Dodd v. Cook, [1955] O.W.N. 411 (H.C.).

Mention of advisability of joining certain members of an unincorporated association in their personal capacities.

Capacity to be Sued — rule 21.01(3)(b)

Lukings v. I.M.A.W., Region 8 (1989), 36 C.P.C. (2d) 276, 33 O.A.C. 352 (Div. Ct.).

A union cannot be made a party to a tort action for damages in Ontario by reason of the provisions of s. 3(2) of the *Rights of Labour Act*.

McKinney v. Liberal Party of Can. (1987), 61 O.R. (2d) 680, 21 C.P.C. (2d) 118, 35 C.R.R. 353, 43 D.L.R. (4th) 706 (H.C.).

Political parties, as unincorporated private associations, do not have the legal capacity to be sued and their actions are not regulated by the *Charter of Rights*.

McGhie v. C.A.L.F.A. (1986), 58 O.R. (2d) 333 (H.C.).

An application challenging the merger of a union with another union was precluded by the *Rights of Labour Act*. The general provision in that Act effectively barred the naming of a trade union as a party to a court action, and that bar still applied under the Rules of Civil Procedure.

Beck v. Beck (1986), 56 O.R. (2d) 205, 11 C.P.C. (2d) 171, 30 D.L.R. (4th) 591 (H.C.).

The court struck out a plaintiff's personal *Family Law Reform Act* action against himself, but allowed his claim on behalf of other *Family Law Reform Act* statutory beneficiaries to proceed.

Tel-Ad Advisors Ont. Ltd. v. Tele-Direct (Publications) Inc. (1986), 8 C.P.C. (2d) 217, 11 C.P.R. (3d) 397 (Ont. H.C.).

The court dismissed an action against one defendant on the ground that it was an unincorporated association and was not capable of being sued. There were sufficient undisputed facts for the court to determine that the defendant was not a partnership.

Weaver v. Pemstar Holdings Ltd. (1986), 8 C.P.C. (2d) 137 (Ont. H.C.), affirmed Ont. C.A. Doc. CA 192/86, April 6, 1988.

The court dismissed an action against a corporation which had been dissolved by a resolution of its shareholders pursuant to the *Business Corporations Act* where the time set by statute for bringing an action after dissolution had expired.

King v. Gull Bay Indian Band (1983), 38 C.P.C. 1 (Ont. Dist. Ct.).

An "Indian Band" is a suable entity.

Khan v. Fredson Travel Inc. (1982), 35 O.R. (2d) 93, 27 C.P.C. 178 (Master).

Where the evidence before the master on a motion to add a defendant showed that the proposed defendant was not a suable entity, the motion was dismissed.

Galway Realty Ltd. v. Int. Union of Elevator Constructors (1973), 5 O.R. (2d) 29, 49 D.L.R. (3d) 343 (C.A.).

The court refused to strike out a statement of claim against a trade union where it was alleged that the head office of the union was in a jurisdiction where it was a suable entity.

Westlake v. R., [1972] 2 O.R. 605, 26 D.L.R. (3d) 273, affirmed [1973] S.C.R. vii, 33 D.L.R. (3d) 256n.

The Ontario Securities Commission is not an entity capable of being sued for damages.

Nipissing Hotel Ltd. v. Hotel & Restaurant Employees & Bartenders Int. Union, [1963] 2 O.R. 169, 38 D.L.R. (2d) 675 (H.C.).

Discussion of actions against a trade union.

Smith Transport Ltd. v. Baird, [1957] O.W.N. 405 (Master).

Representatives of a trade union may be sued if the union is possessed of a trust fund to which the plaintiff could resort to satisfy his claim. The representatives named should be those who control the fund.

Capacity to be Sued — Sovereign Immunity

Laverty v. Laverty (1994), 32 C.P.C. (3d) 91 (Ont. Gen. Div.).

The spouse of a customs attaché serving with the United States Embassy in Ottawa enjoyed statutory immunity from the jurisdiction of the court as a result of the *Vienna Convention*, and the *Foreign Missions and International Organization Act*. By virtue of the paramountcy doctrine, the *Foreign Missions and International Organization Act* overrode the provisions of the *Family Law Act* and the *Children's Law Reform Act*.

Shewan v. Canada (A.G.) (1994), 27 C.P.C. (3d) 244 (Ont. Master).

The Government of the Yukon was held to be entitled to sovereign immunity.

Walker (Litigation Guardian of) v. Bank of New York Inc. (1994), 16 O.R. (3d) 504, 111 D.L.R. (4th) 186, 69 O.A.C. 153 (C.A.), leave to appeal to Supreme Court of Canada refused (1994), 19 O.R. (3d) xvi (note), 115 D.L.R. (4th) viii (note), 178 N.R. 79 (note), 77 O.A.C. 320 (note).

In an action against the U.S. government and several of its employees for conspiracy, etc., and against a private bank and several of its employees for deceit, etc., it was held that the *State Immunity Act* provided immunity to all of the defendants, including the bank and its employees, as they came within the term "organ of the foreign state" which was a very broad term and indicated the intention of Parliament to protect individuals and institutions who act at the request of a foreign state in situations where the state would enjoy sovereign immunity.

Godin v. New Brunswick Electric Power Commission (1993), 16 C.P.C. (3d) 388 (Ont. Gen. Div.).

An action brought by an Ontario resident against a Crown corporation was stayed on the grounds of sovereign immunity. The New Brunswick *Proceedings Against the Crown Act* precluded the bringing of the action in Ontario.

Jaffe v. Miller (1993), 13 O.R. (3d) 745, 103 D.L.R. (4th) 315, 64 O.A.C. 20 (C.A.), leave to appeal to Supreme Court of Canada refused (1994), 107 D.L.R. (4th) vii (note), 166 N.R. 239 (note), 69 O.A.C. 25.

Where the statement of claim made a bald assertion of conspiracy on the part of functionaries of a foreign state, without identifying the conspirators or particularizing the acts in furtherance of the conspiracy, the plaintiff was unable to establish that the defendants fell within the exceptions provided by the common law or the *State Immunity Act*. Accordingly, the dismissal of the claim was upheld on appeal.

Tritt v. United States of America (1989), 68 O.R. (2d) 284, 33 C.P.C. (2d) 154 (H.C.).

An action against the United States of America and its functionaries for seizing property in Ontario prior to the *State Immunity Act*, S.C. 1980-81-82-83, c. 95, was dismissed on the basis of sovereign immunity.

Khan v. Fredson Travel Inc. (1982), 36 O.R. (2d) 17, 27 C.P.C. 161, 133 D.L.R. (3d) 632 (H.C.).

An action against a foreign state arising out of its operation of an airport was dismissed on the basis of sovereign immunity.

Corriveau v. Cuba (1979), 26 O.R. (2d) 674, 15 C.P.C. 177, 103 D.L.R. (3d) 520 (H.C.).

Where the law was unclear and the facts might prove important, the court refused to dismiss a landlord's action against a foreign state upon the ground of sovereign immunity.

Smith v. Can. Javelin Ltd. (1976), 12 O.R. (2d) 244, 68 D.L.R. (3d) 428 (H.C.).

An agency of a foreign sovereign is immune from being made a party to most proceedings.

Another Proceeding Pending — rule 21.01(3)(c) — General Principles (See also *Courts of Justice Act*, ss. 106 and 138.)

Hydro-Electric Commission of Kitchener-Wilmot v. A.F. White Ltd. (1992), 8 O.R. (3d) 602 (Gen. Div.).

Among the factors to be considered on a motion to perpetually stay one of two actions are (1) which action was begun first; (2) who has the chief burden of proof; (3) which is the more comprehensive in its scope; and (4) the balance of convenience.

Arab Monetary Fund v. Hashim (1992), 16 C.P.C. (3d) 352 (Ont. Gen. Div.).

Where related proceedings are under way in several jurisdictions, the court may stay the proceeding before it if required by "good management" of the multiple proceedings. Ontario proceedings were stayed for one year to await developments in related proceedings in the U.K.

Gen. Dynamics Corp. v. Veliotis (1985), 53 O.R. (2d) 371, 7 C.P.C. (2d) 169 (H.C.).

In order to stay an Ontario action the moving party must show something oppressive or vexatious or abusive in the continuance of the action. The generalized balance of convenience test stated in *MacShannon v. Rockware Glass Ltd.*, [1978] A.C. 795 (H.L.) is not the law of Ontario.

Greymac Trust Co. v. BNA Realty Inc. (1985), 50 C.P.C. 45 (Ont. H.C.).

The court has the power to restrain a person within its jurisdiction from prosecuting suits in a foreign court but such power should be exercised with extreme care. The court refused to restrain prosecution of a Quebec action.

B.L. Armstrong Co. v. Cove-Craft Indust. Inc. (1980), 27 O.R. (2d) 490, 15 C.P.C. 261, 107 D.L.R. (3d) 224 (Dist. Ct.).

The defendant must prove that (1) the continuance of the action would be unjust because it would be oppressive, vexatious or an abuse of process and (2) the stay would not cause an injustice to the plaintiff. The court refused to stay an action for the price of goods notwithstanding that the defendant had previously commenced a foreign action for damages for breach of the same contract.

Victoria Property & Invt. Co. (Can.) Ltd. v. Vitznau Mgmt. Ltd. (1978), 22 O.R. (2d) 193, 8 C.P.C. 38, 93 D.L.R. (3d) 611 (H.C.).

In determining which of two actions should be stayed, the court will consider: which action was begun first; which party has the chief burden of proof; and which action is more comprehensive.

Richardson Securities of Can. v. Cohen-Bassous (1977), 18 O.R. (2d) 439, 6 C.P.C. 226, 26 Chitty's L.J. 179, 82 D.L.R. (3d) 715 (H.C.).

An action need not be stayed merely because an action in respect of the same claim was commenced in another jurisdiction. The defendant must satisfy the court that the staying of the action would not cause injustice to the plaintiff.

Re Tuz and Tuz (1975), 11 O.R. (2d) 617, 25 R.F.L. 87, 67 D.L.R. (3d) 41 (C.A.).

Where there is a reasonable probability of conflict of jurisdiction, the inferior court has a discretion as to whether or not to proceed with the matter before it.

Huebner v. Direct Digital Industs. Ltd. (1975), 11 O.R. (2d) 372 (H.C.).

In deciding which of two actions should be perpetually stayed the court should consider: which action was commenced first; which party has the chief burden of proof; and which action has the broader scope.

Empire-Universal Films Ltd. v. Rank, [1947] O.R. 775 (H.C.).

A stay will be granted where the defendant satisfies the court that the continuance of the action would work an injustice because it would be oppressive or vexatious to him, or would be an abuse of the process of the court in some other way and that the stay would not work an injustice to the plaintiff. A mere balance of convenience is not a sufficient ground for depriving a plaintiff of the advantages of prosecuting his action if it is otherwise properly brought.

Another Proceeding Pending — rule 21.01(3)(c) — Construction Lien Proceedings

Markus Bldrs. Supply (Can.) Ltd. v. Allied Drywall Ltd. (1980), 30 O.R. (2d) 144, 116 D.L.R. (3d) 190 (H.C.).

Where a mechanics' lien action included a claim for personal judgment and a second action was commenced for the same debt, the court stayed the second action.

Meca Mechanical Industs. Ltd. v. Vaughanfield Const. Ltd. (1978), 20 O.R. (2d) 142, 10 C.P.C. 187, 87 D.L.R. (3d) 271 (Div. Ct.).

A plaintiff was permitted to institute both a mechanics' lien action and a personal action for the same debt where there was no clear prejudice to the defendant.

Pioneer Weather Systems Ltd. v. 349207 Ont. Ltd. (1978), 5 C.P.C. 202 (Ont. H.C.).

A personal action for the same monetary relief can be commenced concurrently with the filing of a claim for a mechanics' lien.

Standard Indust. Ltd. v. E.F. Wood Specialties Inc. (1977), 16 O.R. (2d) 398, 4 C.P.C. 226, 78 D.L.R. (3d) 280 (H.C.).

Where there is no prejudice to the defendant, an ordinary action concerning the same subject matter may be brought contemporaneously with a mechanics' lien action.

Rockwall Concrete Forming Ltd. v. Robintide Invts. Ltd. (1977), 15 O.R. (2d) 422, 3 C.P.C. 224 (H.C.).

A personal action for a debt was stayed where the full claim had already been paid into court in a pending mechanics' lien action.

Another Proceeding Pending — rule 21.01(3)(c) — Choice of Law or Venue Clauses

Gulf Can. Ltd. v. Turbo Resources Ltd. (1980), 18 C.P.C. 146 (Ont. H.C.).

An Ontario action was stayed where the parties had contracted to have their disputes resolved in Alberta and an Alberta action had been commenced.

Pasen v. Dom. Herb Distributors Inc., [1968] 1 O.R. 688, 67 D.L.R. (2d) 405 (H.C.), affirmed [1968] 2 O.R. 516, 69 D.L.R. (2d) 651 (C.A.).

Where an action for breach of contract had been commenced in another province and where it appeared the contract would be construed according to the laws of that province, a subsequent Ontario action was stayed.

Poly-Seal Corp. v. John Dale Ltd., [1958] O.W.N. 432 (H.C.).

Where a contract specifies that disputes be resolved by foreign courts, an Ontario court should not interfere unless it is shown that the foreign courts cannot give the relief sought.

Empire-Universal Films Ltd. v. Rank, [1947] O.R. 775 (H.C.).

It is not a sufficient ground to stay an action that the agreement on which the action is based has a term which provides that the agreement is to be construed according to the laws of another jurisdiction to which each party has submitted.

Another Proceeding Pending — rule 21.01(3)(c) — Examples

Geac Computer Corp. v. Park (January 29, 1996), Doc. 95-CU-87475 (Ont. Gen. Div.).

The court refused to stay an action notwithstanding related proceedings were pending in Texas.

Sportmart Inc. v. Toronto Hospital Foundation (1995), 62 C.P.R. (3d) 129 (Ont. Gen. Div.).

The court stayed this action where the subject dispute could be determined in a Federal Court of Canada proceeding which had been previously instituted and which was more comprehensive in scope.

Molson Cos. v. Royal Insurance Co. of Canada (1993), 20 C.P.C. (3d) 323, 20 C.C.L.I. (2d) 93, [1994] I.L.R. 1-3010 (Ont. Gen. Div.).

An Ontario action was stayed where the plaintiffs had commenced an earlier action in Italy, and the action in Ontario would not mature until the outcome of the Italian action was known.

May v. Greenwood (1992), 11 O.R. (3d) 42, 96 D.L.R. (4th) 581, 57 O.A.C. 314 (Div. Ct.).

An Ontario action was stayed pending disposition of a Manitoba action. If the *Family Law Act* claims were not dealt with in Manitoba the plaintiff could then proceed in Ontario.

Buchar (Litigation Guardian of) v. Weber (1990), 46 C.P.C. (2d) 60, 71 D.L.R. (4th) 544 (Ont. H.C.).

An Ontario court has no jurisdiction to hear a case where the subject tort occurred in another jurisdiction and all parties except an insurer were residents of that jurisdiction.

Middle East Banking Co. S.A.L. v. Al-Haddad (1989), 70 O.R. (2d) 97 (H.C.).

Where a plaintiff bank commenced an action in Ontario because of political instability in Lebanon but the defendant commenced an action in Lebanon, the court held that while Lebanon was the natural forum, the Ontario court should assume jurisdiction because the defendant was unable to show that justice could be done between the parties in a Lebanese court at substantially less inconvenience or expense.

Galtaco Redlaw Castings Corp. v. Brunswick Industrial Supply Co. (1989), 69 O.R. (2d) 478, 36 C.P.C. (2d) 225 (H.C.).

The court refused to stay an Ontario action which was more comprehensive than a related and concurrent Ohio action where the defendant could not establish that justice could be done in Ohio at substantially less inconvenience and expense.

Shell Canada Ltd. v. St. Lawrence Seaway Authority (1987), 58 O.R. (2d) 437, 36 D.L.R. (4th) 304 (H.C.), leave to appeal to Ont. Div. Ct. refused 58 O.R. (2d) 437n, 36 D.L.R. (4th) 304n.

An action commenced in the Supreme Court of Ontario against the St. Lawrence Seaway Authority was stayed, as the same plaintiffs had brought a similar action in the Federal Court of Canada. The Federal Court of Canada had concurrent jurisdiction in all the actions, and exclusive jurisdiction with regard to claims asserted against the federal Crown.

Polar Hardware Mfg. Co.v. Zafir (1984), 43 C.P.C. 156 (Ont. H.C.).

Having found that Ontario was the natural forum, a stay was refused, notwithstanding a pending action in Illinois on the same contract, in view of substantial advantages to the plaintiff in having the Ontario litigation proceed.

Hudson's Bay Co. v. PCL Const. Ltd. (1984), 45 O.R. (2d) 443, 42 C.P.C. 245, 6 D.L.R. (4th) 763 (H.C.).

The plaintiff commenced this action for damages for defective construction work. Later the defendant sued in Alberta for the contract price, and applied to stay this action. In dismissing the motion, the court rejected a balance of convenience test. The defendant must show that continuance of the action would work an injustice because it would be oppressive, vexatious or an abuse of the process of the court, and that a stay would not cause an injustice to the plaintiff.

Rosenberg v. Greymac Trust Co. (1983), 43 O.R. (2d) 463, 37 C.P.C. 105, 2 D.L.R. (4th) 58 (H.C.).

This action for recovery of a debt was stayed pending disposition of an earlier action by the defendant against the plaintiff for breach of fiduciary duty, with leave to assert the claim as a counterclaim.

Can. Systems Group (EST) Ltd. v. Allendale Mut. Ins. Co. (1983), 41 O.R. (2d) 135, 33 C.P.C. 210, 145 D.L.R. (3d) 266 (Div. Ct.).

An action under a business interruption policy was stayed at the application of defendants in a large number of other actions because of the overlapping factual issues and in order to control the stream of litigation arising out of the same facts.

Fortune King Inc. v. Burger King Can. Inc.; Burger King Can. Inc. v. Bhatt (1983), 33 C.P.C. 208 (Ont. Master).

Two actions were stayed with leave to advance a counterclaim where an earlier more comprehensive action was pending and the chief burden of proof was on the plaintiffs in that earlier action.

Rosenthal v. Fairwin Const. Co. (1983), 32 C.P.C. 110 (Ont. H.C.).

Where F commenced an action against R and R subsequently commenced an action against F and M arising out of the same facts, the court ordered the second action stayed against F with leave for R to assert a counterclaim in the first action.

Cherry v. Ivey (1982), 37 O.R. (2d) 361 (H.C.).

Where a defendant moves for a general stay of proceedings and a temporary stay of proceedings pending provision of security for costs and the latter is granted without argument on the former, he may not bring a second motion for a general stay after the required security is posted.

Exton v. Alliance Bldg. Corp. (1979), 27 O.R. (2d) 503 (H.C.).

Where two corporations were principal debtor and guarantor of the same debt, the corporations amalgamated and the creditor commenced separate actions in respect of the principal debt and the guarantee, the court stayed the second action with leave to amend the first action to include both claims.

Re Canavia Transit Inc. and Toronto (1979), 27 O.R. (2d) 191 (H.C.).

Where one person brought a motion to quash a by-law pursuant to the *Municipal Act* and a second person brought an application for judicial review to the Divisional Court, the court stayed the motion to quash with leave for that applicant to apply to the Divisional Court for judicial review also.

Imperial Oil v. Schmidt Mouldings Ltd. (1981), 23 C.P.C. 33, 55 C.P.R. (2d) 10 (Ont. H.C.).

The court declined to stay this industrial design action notwithstanding that there was a pending Federal Court action between the same parties arising out of the same facts, because the issues raised were different and the Federal Court did not have exclusive jurisdiction.

E. & S. Carpentry Contractors Ltd. v. Fedak; Nikpal v. Fedak (1980), 18 C.P.C. 307 (Ont. H.C.).

Where the plaintiff commenced a second action for relief parallel to that sought in an earlier action, the second action was dismissed as an abuse of process.

Int. Chemalloy Corp. v. Hugo (1979), 24 O.R. (2d) 818 (H.C.).

An action for negligence of a solicitor was stayed pending the outcome of an action against the same defendant in his capacity as a director of the plaintiff corporation.

General Capital Growth Ltd. v. Burlington (1979), 24 O.R. (2d) 666, 11 C.P.C. 35, 18 L.C.R. 204, leave to appeal to Ont. Div. Ct. refused 24 O.R. (2d) 666n.

An action for trespass against an expropriating authority was stayed pending a decision of the Land Compensation Board.

Canadian Marine Underwriters Ltd. v. China Union Lines Ltd., 17 O.R. (2d) 375, 5 C.P.C. 121, [1977] I.L.R. 1-910 (H.C.).

The court stayed the action where another action regarding the same matter was pending in New York State.

Stauffer v. Kinsley (1977), 17 O.R. (2d) 246 (Co. Ct.).

The second of two actions was allowed to proceed where the originating process in the first commenced action had never been served.

Flambro Realty Ltd. v. Peter Pan Drive-In Ltd. (1974), 4 O.R. (2d) 454 (H.C.).

Where a Supreme Court action was commenced prior to a County Court action, the latter action was stayed notwithstanding that the originating process in the latter action had been served first.

Harron v. Crown Trust Co., [1955] O.W.N. 48, [1955] 1 D.L.R. 840 (H.C.).

An action against an estate was stayed pending determination of the validity of a will to enable the persons found to be beneficiaries to be added as parties.

Frivolous, Vexatious or Abusive Actions — rule 21.01(3)(d) (See also the cases under rule 25.11.)

Reddy v. Oshawa Flying Club (1992), 11 C.P.C. (3d) 154 (Ont. Gen. Div.).

The doctrine of abuse of process is somewhat similar to the doctrine of *res judicata* in that it also seeks to prevent a multiplicity of proceedings or the re-litigation of an issue determined in an earlier proceeding or which might have been raised in earlier proceedings.

Donmor Industries Ltd. v. Kremlin Canada Inc. (1991), 6 O.R. (3d) 501, additional reasons (1992), 6 O.R. (3d) 506 (Gen. Div.).

A statement of claim was struck out as an abuse of process where the action was an attempt to re-litigate issues raised in an earlier action.

Temilini v. Ontario Provincial Police Commissioner (1990), 73 O.R. (2d) 664, 38 O.A.C. 270 (C.A.), leave to appeal to Supreme Court of Canada refused (1991), 1 O.R. (3d) xii, 131 N.R. 153 (note), 46 O.A.C. 238 (note).

The court refused to strike out an action under rule 21.01(3)(d) where the plaintiff had pleaded all the essentials to establish his case; the fact that the plaintiff was woefully short of evidence is not the test under the rule, which should be exercised only in the clearest cases.

Germscheid v. Valois (1989), 68 O.R. (2d) 670, 34 C.P.C. (2d) 267 (H.C.).

Defendants who had been held liable for personal injuries in an earlier action were not permitted to relitigate the issue of their liability when subsequently sued by a different plaintiff for injuries suffered in the same incident raising the same issue. To permit them to relitigate the issue would be an abuse of process. The plaintiff was granted summary judgment on the issue of liability, but because he was a "wait and see" plaintiff and should have been a party to the first action he was ordered to pay all of the defendants' costs on a solicitor and client basis.

Altobelli v. Pilot Insurance Co. (1989), 34 C.P.C. (2d) 193, 132 N.R. 196 at 198 (Ont. C.A.), affirmed [1991] 3 S.C.R. 132, 132 N.R. 196.

A plaintiff who had been unsuccessful on an issue in a prior action arising out of a motor vehicle accident was not precluded from proceeding with two other actions related to the same accident. There were different defendants involved in the later actions, and even if issue estoppel applied, there were contractual considerations which might affect the outcome.

Conroy Electronics Inc. v. Webster (1989), 33 C.P.C. (2d) 279 (Ont. H.C.).

A civil action ought not to be used to relitigate an issue tried and determined by a criminal court where there has been full opportunity to defend the issue. The defendant was permitted to use the plaintiff's criminal conviction (based on a guilty plea) as *prima facie* proof, and where on a motion for summary judgment the plaintiff had no fresh evidence, summary judgment was granted for the defendant where to permit the action to proceed to trial would be an abuse of process.

Verlysdonk v. Premier Petrenas Construction Co., 60 O.R. (2d) 65, 25 C.C.L.I. 205, 45 R.P.R. 212, 39 D.L.R. (4th) 715, [1987] I.L.R. 1-2199, 24 O.A.C. 34 (Div. Ct.).

The three requirements of issue estoppel are (1) that the same question has been decided before; (2) that the decision which is said to create the estoppel is final; and (3) that the parties to the decision or their privies were the same persons as the parties to the proceeding in which the estoppel is raised. Absent abuse of process, all three requirements must be met. On the facts of this case, a new party was held not to be in privity with the party to the earlier action.

Skuse v. Hamilton-Wentworth (Regional Mun.) (1987), 22 C.P.C. (2d) 215 (Ont. H.C.).

The court permitted the plaintiff to maintain an action against a municipality for non-repair of a highway notwithstanding that the plaintiff's separate action against an insurer under unidentified motorist coverage arising out of the same accident had previously been settled. Issue estoppel did not apply and there was no abuse of process.

Sussman v. Eales (1985), 1 C.P.C. (2d) 14, 33 C.C.L.T. 156 (Ont. H.C.).

The court struck out a defamation action by a dentist against defendants who had submitted a complaint to the Royal College of Dental Surgeons. The complaint was part of a quasi-judicial process of the college and the complainant enjoyed absolute privilege.

Demeter v. British Pacific Life Ins. Co.; Demeter v. Occidental Life Ins. Co. of California; Demeter v. Dominion Life Assur. Co., 48 O.R. (2d) 266, 8 C.C.L.I. 286, 13 D.L.R. (4th) 318, [1985] I.L.R. 1-1862, 7 O.A.C. 143 (C.A.).

Actions on life insurance policies by a convicted murderer were dismissed as an abuse of process because the plaintiff was seeking to relitigate an issue already tried.

French v. Rank City Wall Can. Ltd. (1984), 6 O.A.C. 145 (C.A.).

Where the plaintiff sought a declaration that rent increases granted by the Residential Tenancies Commission were void, the court acknowledged the commission's exclusive jurisdiction in the matter and struck out the plaintiff's action as an abuse of process.

Earl Putnam Organization Ltd. v. Macdonald (1978), 21 O.R. (2d) 815, 2 C.P.C. 208, 91 D.L.R. (3d) 714 (C.A.).

The court has inherent jurisdiction to dismiss or stay an action as an abuse of process.

Foy v. Foy (1978), 20 O.R. (2d) 747, 9 C.P.C. 141, 3 R.F.L. (2d) 286, 88 D.L.R. (3d) 761 (C.A.).

An action for assault based on facts which had been dealt with in criminal and divorce proceedings and which was brought to harass the defendant was dismissed as an abuse of process.

Cleveland v. Yukish; Hudson v. Yukish, [1965] 2 O.R. 497, 51 D.L.R. (2d) 208 (Co. Ct.).

An action commenced by an insurer in the name of its insured to assert its subrogated rights was dismissed as an abuse of process where the insured had previously commenced an action in respect of the deductible portion of his insurance. In such circumstances the insured should include the claim of the insurer in his action.

Brown v. Coldstream Copper Mines Ltd., [1954] O.W.N. 830 (H.C.).

The court should stay or dismiss an action for being frivolous or vexatious only in the clearest cases.

RULE 22   SPECIAL CASE

Highlights

Under the former practice there were two distinct procedures covering the subject now dealt with in Rule 22. Former Rule 128 enabled the parties to state a special case for the opinion of a trial court. Section 34 of the *Judicature Act* permitted a judge at first instance in any proceeding, where he or she considered a previous decision to be wrong, to refer the case before him or her to the Court of Appeal.

Rule 22 continues the former procedure whereby the parties may state a special case for the opinion of the court, but the power of a judge at first instance to himself or herself refer the case to the Court of Appeal no longer exists. However, by rule 22.03, the parties, instead of having the special case determined by the Ontario Court (General Division), may make a motion to a judge of the Court of Appeal for leave to have the special case determined in the first instance by that court.

Related case law. Although not specifically dealt with by the Rules, cases regarding *stare decisis* and related matters are collected under rule 22.03.

Former provisions: Judicature Act, s. 34 and Rule 128.

WHERE AVAILABLE

22.01(1) Where the parties to a proceeding concur in stating a question of law in the form of a special case for the opinion of the court, any party may move before a judge to have the special case determined.

(2) Where the judge is satisfied that the determination of the question may dispose of all or part of the proceeding, substantially shorten the hearing or result in a substantial saving of costs, the judge may hear and determine the special case.

Prefontaine Estate v. Frizzle, 71 O.R. (2d) 285, 40 C.P.C. (2d) 161, 45 C.C.L.I. 234, 23 M.V.R. (2d) 136, 65 D.L.R. (4th) 275, [1990] I.L.R. 1-2572, 38 O.A.C. 22 (C.A.).

The Court of Appeal determined on a special case whether an Ontario court had jurisdiction, and what law was applicable, in Ontario actions arising out of Quebec automobile accidents.

King v. Liquor Control Bd. of Ont. (1981), 33 O.R. (2d) 816, 21 C.P.C. 194, 125 D.L.R. (3d) 661 (H.C.).

The court declined to grant leave to set down a constitutional issue for hearing because of the importance of a factual underpinning in constitutional matters.

FACTUMS REQUIRED

22.02 On a motion under rule 22.01, each party shall serve on every other party to the motion a factum consisting of a concise statement, without argument, of the facts and law relied on by the party, and file it, with proof of service, in the court office where the motion is to be heard, not later than 2 p.m. on the day before the hearing.

REMOVAL INTO COURT OF APPEAL

22.03(1) A motion under rule 22.01 may be made to a judge of the Court of Appeal for leave to have a special case determined in the first instance by

that court and the judge may grant leave where subrule 22.01(2) is satisfied and where the special case raises an issue in respect of which,

(a) there are conflicting decisions of judges in Ontario and there is no decision of an appellate court in Ontario;

(b) there is a conflict between decisions of an appellate court in Ontario and an appellate court of another province, or between decisions of appellate courts of two or more other provinces; or

(c) one of the parties seeks to establish that a decision of an appellate court in Ontario should not be followed.

(2) A judge who grants leave under subrule (1) may give directions in respect of the time and form in which the case is to be listed for hearing and the exchange and filing of factums, and subject to any such directions, Rule 61 (appeals to an appellate court) applies with necessary modifications.

Leave for Determination of Special Case by Court of Appeal

Seed v. Delhey (1989), 67 O.R. (2d) 317, 33 C.P.C. (2d) 1 (C.A.).

The court declined leave where none of the requirements of rule 22.03(1)(a), (b) or (c) were met.

Stare Decisis and Related Matters

Rustecki v. Da Silva (1992), 10 O.R. (3d) 637, 11 C.P.C. (3d) 52 (Gen. Div.).

Refusal to grant leave to appeal does not imply that the appellate court approves the lower court's decision. The lower court decision carries the same authority as any unappealed judgment.

Kalinin v. Metro. Toronto, [1970] 3 O.R. 536, 13 D.L.R. (3d) 432, reversed in part on other grounds [1972] S.C.R. 564, 23 D.L.R. (3d) 89.

The Court of Appeal is not bound by its own decision.

Masse v. Dietrich, [1971] 3 O.R. 359, 20 D.L.R. (3d) 399 (Co. Ct.).

If an issue could be brought before either the High Court or the County Court and in both instances an appeal would lie to the Court of Appeal, then for purposes of that issue the High Court and County Court are of coordinate jurisdiction.

Bedard v. Isaac, [1972] 2 O.R. 391, 25 D.L.R. (3d) 551, reversed on other grounds 23 C.R.N.S. 197, 11 R.F.L. 333, 38 D.L.R. (3d) 481 (*sub nom. A.G. Can. v. Lavell*)(S.C.C.).

Decisions of the Federal Court of Appeal are of the same persuasive weight as decisions of the Courts of Appeal of other provinces.

R. v. Guertin, [1971] 2 O.R. 505, 3 C.C.C. (2d) 135 (Dist. Ct.).

An Ontario District Court judge is not bound by the decision of the Court of Appeal of another province.

Bonser v. London & Midland Gen. Ins. Co., [1973] S.C.R. 10, 29 D.L.R. (3d) 468, [1972] I.L.R. 1-477.

American precedents are particularly persuasive in insurance law matters.

FORM OF SPECIAL CASE

22.04 A special case (Form 22A) shall,

(a) set out concisely the material facts, as agreed on by the parties, that are necessary to enable the court to determine the question stated;

(b) refer to and include a copy of any documents that are necessary to determine the question;

(c) set out the relief sought, as agreed on by the parties, on the determination of the question of law; and

(d) be signed by the solicitors for the parties.

Patterson v. Scherloski, [1971] 3 O.R. 753, 21 D.L.R. (3d) 641 (H.C.).

An agreed statement of facts may be amended on consent or with leave. Conditions of granting leave should normally include that the applicant bear the costs and that the other party be at liberty to withdraw its agreement.

Murphy v. Lindzon, [1969] 2 O.R. 704, 6 D.L.R. (3d) 492 (C.A.).

Where the statement of facts did not contain all of the facts relevant to the issues between the parties the court refused to answer the questions.

HEARING OF SPECIAL CASE

22.05(1) On the hearing of a special case the court may draw any reasonable inference from the facts agreed on by the parties and documents referred to in the special case.

(2) On the determination of the question of law the court may make an order or grant judgment accordingly.

RULE 23   DISCONTINUANCE AND WITHDRAWAL

Highlights

Rule 23 regulates the discontinuance of an action by a plaintiff and the withdrawal of all or part of the statement of defence by a defendant. After the close of pleadings, consent or leave to discontinue is required: rule 23.01(1). Where an action is discontinued against a defendant who has counterclaimed, the defendant must serve a notice of election to proceed with the counterclaim within 30 days or else the counterclaim is deemed to be discontinued without costs: rule 23.02. Where an action is being discontinued against a defendant who has crossclaimed or made a third party claim, these claims are deemed to be dismissed with costs unless the court orders otherwise within 30 days: rule 23.03.

A discontinuing plaintiff is liable for the defendant's costs, including the costs of any crossclaim or third party claim deemed to be dismissed under rule 23.03, unless the court orders otherwise: rule 23.05.

The discontinuance of an action is not a defence to a subsequent action (unless a consent filed by the parties provides otherwise), but where leave to discontinue is required, the court granting leave may order that the discontinuance is a defence to any subsequent action: rule 23.04.

Former Rules: Rules 320-321, 325.

DISCONTINUANCE BY PLAINTIFF

23.01(1) A plaintiff may discontinue all or part of an action against any defendant,

(a) before the close of pleadings, by serving on all parties who have been served with the statement of claim a notice of discontinuance (Form 23A) and filing the notice with proof of service;

(b) after the close of pleadings, with leave of the court; or

(c) at any time, by filing the consent in writing of all parties.

(2) Where a party to an action is under disability, the action may be discontinued by or against that party only with leave of a judge, on notice to,

(a) the Children's Lawyer, unless,

(i) the Public Guardian and Trustee is litigation guardian of the party, or

(ii) a judge orders otherwise; and

(b) where the party under disability is a defendant, the litigation guardian. [am. O. Reg. 69/95, ss. 18, 19, 20]

Unilateral Discontinuance - rule 23.01(1)(a)

Pavonia, S.A. v. Bison Petroleum & Minerals Ltd. (1982), 25 C.P.C. 194, 132 D.L.R. (3d) 309 (Ont. Div. Ct.).

Service by mail of a notice of discontinuance, after service of originating process but before any documents have been filed by the defendant, is sufficient service.

Leave to Discontinue - rule 23.01(1)(b)

Provincial Crane Inc. v. AMCA International Ltd. (1990), 44 C.P.C. (2d) 46 (Ont. H.C.).

The court has a discretion to depart from the general rule that a defendant is entitled to costs where the plaintiff discontinues. That discretion was applied where the plaintiff had brought an action *bona fide* by reason of the defendant's conduct, but the subject matter of the action had subsequently become moot.

Commerce Capital Trust Co. v. Berk (1983), 36 C.P.C. 138 (Ont. Master).

In this action for damages for negligence and conspiracy to defraud, the allegations against a defendant solicitor were not so unfounded or improbable as to justify an award of more than party and party costs as a term of granting leave to discontinue.

Taur Mgmt. Co. v. Nir (1983), 35 C.P.C. 179 (Ont. Master).

Where a respondent to an application shows an intention to oppose the application by cross-examination on the supporting affidavit, the applicant cannot countermand the motion, but rather must obtain leave to discontinue it.

Nat. Bank of N. Amer. v. Ross (1982), 25 C.P.C. 132 (Ont. H.C.).

The court granted leave to discontinue in this case where little had been done by the plaintiff that would in substance alter the plaintiff's position from one in which it could discontinue without leave, and the defendant had taken up residence elsewhere.

Bagaric v. Juric (1981), 24 C.P.C. 38 (Ont. Master).

A plaintiff was permitted to discontinue against one defendant where an appointment to discover the other defendant had been taken out.

Silverman v. May (1979), 14 C.P.C. 43 (Ont. Master).

Leave to discontinue was refused to the plaintiff corporation where the defendant might be prejudiced in his discovery of the individual plaintiffs by his inability to obtain production of the relevant documents held by the plaintiff corporation.

Greening Holdings Ltd. v. Schnell (1976), 2 C.P.C. 350 (Ont. Co. Ct.).

Discontinuance of a foreclosure action by the plaintiff was refused when the defendant had delivered a request to redeem prior to service of originating process upon him.

Woolrich v. Woolrich, [1961] O.W.N. 323 (Master).

Where the conduct of the defendant rendered the action untenable the court granted an application to discontinue without costs.

Heakes v. George Hardy Ltd., [1955] O.W.N. 242 (Master).

The court refused leave to discontinue an action where an order had been made requiring that security for costs be furnished within a specified time, the period had not expired, and the security had not been furnished.

Effect of Discontinuance (See also cases under rules 23.02, 23.03 and 23.04.)

C.I.B.C. v. Toppan, [1966] 2 O.R. 752 (Master).

The discontinuance of an action in whole also discontinues any pending motions brought by the plaintiff.

Campbell v. The Sterling Trusts Corp., [1948] O.W.N. 557 (Master).

A notice of discontinuance served after the filing of a motion to dismiss for want of prosecution has no effect.

Setting Aside Notice of Discontinuance

Angelopoulos v. Angelopoulos (1986), 55 O.R. (2d) 101, 9 C.P.C. (2d) 285, additional reasons at 55 O.R. (2d) 101 at 110, 9 C.P.C. (2d) 285 at 296 (H.C.).

A notice of discontinuance was set aside as an abuse of process where its clear purpose was to evade the effect of an interim order.

Davis v. Campbell (1986), 54 O.R. (2d) 443, 9 C.P.C. (2d) 48, 20 C.C.L.I. 1 (H.C.).

The court set aside a notice of discontinuance which had inadvertently discontinued the action against both defendants rather than only the defendant which had reached a settlement with the plaintiff.

Cusack v. Garden City Press Ltd. (1978), 22 O.R. (2d) 126 (Master).

The court set aside a notice of discontinuance which had been filed without the instructions of the client, may not have been served, and had been ignored by all parties.

Magee v. Can. Coach Lines Ltd., [1946] O.W.N. 73 (Master).

The court does not have authority to set aside a notice of discontinuance against one defendant even though the rights of the remaining defendants for contribution over, under the *Negligence Act*, may thereby be prejudiced.

EFFECT OF DISCONTINUANCE ON COUNTERCLAIM

23.02 Where an action is discontinued against a defendant who has counterclaimed, the defendant may deliver within thirty days after the discontinuance a notice of election to proceed with the counterclaim (Form 23B), and if the defendant fails to do so, the counterclaim shall be deemed to be discontinued without costs.

Lajlo v. Noiles, [1973] 3 O.R. 666 (H.C.).

A counterclaim may not be made after the main action is discontinued.

EFFECT OF DISCONTINUANCE ON CROSSCLAIM OR THIRD PARTY CLAIM

23.03(1) Where an action is discontinued against a defendant who has crossclaimed or made a third party claim, the crossclaim or third party claim shall be deemed to be dismissed with costs thirty days after the discontinuance unless the court orders otherwise during the thirty day period.

Effect of deemed dismissal on subsequent action
(2) The deemed dismissal is not a defence to a subsequent action unless the court orders otherwise during the thirty-day period. [am. O. Reg. 770/ 92, s. 6]

EFFECT OF DISCONTINUANCE ON SUBSEQUENT ACTION

23.04(1) The discontinuance of all or part of an action is not a defence to a subsequent action, unless the order giving leave to discontinue or a consent filed by the parties provides otherwise.

(2) Where a plaintiff has discontinued and is liable for costs of an action, and another action involving the same subject matter is subsequently brought

between the same parties or their representatives or successors in interest before payment of the costs of the discontinued action, the court may order a stay of the subsequent action until the costs of the discontinued action have been paid.

I.M. - J.M. v. D.A.M. (1984), 43 R.F.L. (2d) 205 (Ont. H.C.).

Where a wife's earlier action for divorce had been discontinued, the court held that *res judicata* did not bar her subsequent action for divorce, as the former judgment had not dealt with or disposed of the claim on its merits.

Murray Duff Enterprises Ltd. v. Van Durme (1981), 23 C.P.C. 151 (Ont. Div. Ct.).

It is not an abuse of process to discontinue one action and then commence a second action seeking the same relief in order to overcome a deficiency in the first action.

Blum v. Blum, [1965] 1 O.R. 236, 47 D.L.R. (2d) 388 (C.A.).

Where the plaintiff in an annulment action sought to discontinue the action at trial, leave to do so was given on the condition that any further action would be barred.

COSTS OF DISCONTINUANCE

23.05 Where a plaintiff discontinues an action against a defendant,
(a) the defendant is entitled to the costs of the action; and
(b) where the defendant has made a crossclaim or third party claim that is deemed to be dismissed under rule 23.03, the defendant is entitled to recover from the plaintiff,
      (i) the costs payable under rule 23.03, and
      (ii) the defendant's own costs of the crossclaim or third party claim,
unless the court orders otherwise.

Korn Hotels Ltd. v. Leibel-Engel Const. Co. (1981), 20 C.P.C. 224 (Ont. Master).

Where a defendant was never served and the action was subsequently discontinued, he was not permitted to tax his costs.

Pawlowski Inc. v. Matos; Pawlowski Inc. v. Paiva; Pawlowski Inc. v. D'Assilva (1978), 6 C.P.C. 113 (Ont. H.C.).

A plaintiff who discontinued his action was not permitted to set off the costs awarded to him on an interlocutory matter against the costs to which the defendant was otherwise entitled.

WITHDRAWAL BY DEFENDANT

23.06(1) A defendant may withdraw all or part of the statement of defence with respect to any plaintiff at any time by delivering to all parties a notice of withdrawal of defence (Form 23C), but,
(a) where the defendant has crossclaimed or made a third party claim, leave to withdraw must be obtained from the court; and
(b) where the defendant seeks to withdraw an admission in the statement of defence, rule 51.05 (withdrawal of admission) applies.
(2) Where a defendant withdraws the whole of the statement of defence, the defendant shall be deemed to be noted in default.

Bazinas v. Clune, [1968] 2 O.R. 752 (Master).

Leave of the court is required before withdrawing an admission of liability.

APPLICATION TO COUNTERCLAIMS, CROSSCLAIMS AND THIRD PARTY CLAIMS

23.07 Rules 23.01 to 23.06 apply, with necessary modifications, to counterclaims, crossclaims and third party claims.

RULE 24   DISMISSAL OF ACTION FOR DELAY

Highlights

A defendant who is not in default may move to have an action dismissed for delay where the plaintiff has failed to take any of the steps listed in rule 24.01. (Where the plaintiff is under disability, notice must be given to the litigation guardian and the Official Guardian, unless a judge orders otherwise: rule 24.02). A counterclaiming defendant must deliver a notice of election to proceed within 30 days or the counterclaim shall be deemed to be discontinued without costs: rule 24.03. A crossclaim or third party claim shall be deemed to be dismissed with costs (and the defendant may recover those costs and his or her own costs from the plaintiff) unless the court orders otherwise: rule 24.04. The dismissal of an action for delay is not a defence to a subsequent action, unless the order dismissing the action provides otherwise: rule 24.05(1).

Note also rule 48.14 (status notice), which gives the court power, of its own motion, to dismiss for delay actions which have not been listed for trial within two years after the filing of the statement of defence.

Recent amendments.   Rule 24.01(d) is new and affects cases subject to the Rule 76 Simplified Procedure.

Former Rules: Rules 322-325.

WHERE AVAILABLE

24.01(1) A defendant who is not in default under these rules or an order of the court may move to have an action dismissed for delay where the plaintiff has failed,

(a) to serve the statement of claim on all the defendants within the prescribed time;

(b) to have noted in default any defendant who has failed to deliver a statement of defence, within thirty days after the default;

(c) to set the action down for trial within six months after the close of pleadings; or

(d) to deliver a notice of readiness for pre-trial conference under subrule 76.08(1); or

(e) to move for leave to restore to a trial list an action that has been struck off the trial list, within thirty days after the action was struck off. [am. O. Reg. 533/95, s. 4(1) (amendment revoked by s. 4(2) March 11, 2000)]

Dismissal for Delay — General Principles

Susin v. Harper, Haney & White (1992), 9 C.P.C. (3d) 135 (Ont. C.A.).

The defendant's failure to deliver an affidavit of documents is an inexcusable default which disentitles the defendant to an order dismissing for delay. The court imposed a timetable for the conduct of the litigation.

Wright v. Rank City Wall Can. Ltd. (1989), 36 C.P.C. (2d) 266 (Ont. H.C.), reversing in part (1989), 36 C.P.C. (2d) 266 at 267 (Ont. Master), leave to appeal refused 36 C.P.C. (2d) xli.

Although an order restoring an action to the trial list is a complete bar to a subsequent motion to dismiss for delay under rule 24.01(e), the court retains its inherent jurisdiction to dismiss for delay, and s. [106] of the *Courts of Justice Act* can still be resorted to.

Ship v. Longworth (1988), 65 O.R. (2d) 124, 27 C.P.C. (2d) 175, 29 O.A.C. 330 (Div. Ct.).

A defendants' motion to dismiss for delay was denied where they had not served an affidavit of documents and were thus "in default" under the Rules.

Greslik v. Ont. Legal Aid Plan (1988), 65 O.R. (2d) 110, 28 C.P.C. (2d) 294, 30 O.A.C. 53 (Div. Ct.).

A master has discretion to dismiss a motion to dismiss for delay where a defendant, although not technically in default, has been dilatory in complying with undertakings.

Albrecht v. Meridian Building Group Ltd. (1988), 27 C.P.C. (2d) 213, 29 O.A.C. 399 (Div. Ct.).

Actual prejudice to the defendant must be shown on a motion to dismiss an action for delay, and prejudice should not be presumed merely from the delay itself, though seven years in this case.

Brosseau v. C.A.S. of Sudbury Inc. (1986), 7 C.P.C. (2d) 312 (Ont. H.C.).

A minor having a *bona fide* cause of action is a privileged suitor. The minor and the Official Guardian acting on his behalf should not be visited with the sins of previous next friends or litigation guardians. The court refused to dismiss an action for delay although fourteen years had passed after commencement of the action.

Clairmonte v. C.I.B.C., [1970] 3 O.R. 97, 12 D.L.R. (3d) 425 (C.A.).

The defendant must show prejudice resulting from delay; the expiry of a limitation period is not itself prejudicial to the defendant.

Kowalczyk v. Scarborough Gen. Hosp. (1985), 48 C.P.C. 185 (Ont. H.C.).

Where the defendant has a *prima facie* right to bring a motion to dismiss for delay but the court considers the motion precipitous in the circumstances, the court should not dismiss the motion but rather should extend the time for the plaintiff to take the appropriate steps failing which the action would be dismissed.

Farrar v. McMullen, [1971] 1 O.R. 709 (C.A.).

The failure of the defendant to attempt to expedite the proceeding is not fatal to his application; the key is prejudice to the defendant attributable to inexcusable delay by the plaintiff.

Shoniker v. Security Record Systems Ltd., [1968] 2 O.R. 209 (Master).

An action will not be dismissed where the plaintiff fulfils his obligations before the application is made, though after the expiry of the stated time period.

Dismissal for Delay — Expiry of Limitation Period

Loblaw Cos. v. Lido Industrial Products Ltd. (1993), 19 C.P.C. (3d) 183 (Ont. Gen. Div.).

The court refused to dismiss an action for delay where there was no prejudice to the defendant. The presumption of prejudice due to expiry of the limitation period must be sustained by concrete evidence of prejudice.

Taggart v. Applied Insulation Co. (1977), 18 O.R. (2d) 664, 4 C.P.C. 148 (C.A.).

An action should not be dismissed for want of prosecution prior to the expiration of the limitation period unless the plaintiff is guilty of contumelious default or the action is frivolous or vexatious.

Hacquoil Const. Ltd. v. Uptown Motor Hotels Ltd. (1976), 2 C.P.C. 73 (Ont. H.C.).

Where a limitation period has expired, an order under this provision will not be made unless the plaintiff's delay has been intentional or contumelious or such as to give rise to a substantial risk that a fair trial will not be possible.

Worrall v. Powell, [1969] 2 O.R. 634 (C.A.).

The expiration of a limitation period raises a presumption of prejudice to the defendant.

Lepofsky v. Continental Can. Co. (1973), 1 O.R. (2d) 569 (H.C.).

Undue delay in the prosecution of an action following the expiry of a limitation period will create a presumption of prejudice to the defendant. But where the motion to dismiss was brought only two months after the expiry of the limitation period, the delay was not undue, and there being no evidence of actual prejudice, the application was dismissed.

Dismissal for Delay — Solicitor's Negligence

Vandewall v. Faria (1993), 15 C.P.C. (3d) 367, 62 O.A.C. 266 (Div. Ct.).

Where a defendant had not served an affidavit of documents but had in fact made full disclosure of documents, the court waived compliance under rule 2.01(1) and dismissed an action for delay. The subject accident had occurred more than ten years earlier and the plaintiff's counsel had been negligent.

Valleyfield Const. Ltd. v. Argo Const. Ltd. (1978), 13 C.P.C. 225 (Ont. H.C.).

Where the delay was due to the plaintiff solicitor's gross neglect, the court refused to dismiss the action in the circumstances of this case.

Gouzenko v. Sinnott News Co., [1972] 2 O.R. 296 (H.C.).

A plaintiff is responsible for delay resulting from the negligence of his solicitors.

Casson v. Gravell, [1965] 2 O.R. 218, affirmed [1965] 2 O.R. 220n (H.C.).

A lengthy delay cannot be excused solely by the faults of the former solicitor of the plaintiff.

Dismissal for Delay — Examples

Fortier v. Humphrey (1995), 25 O.R. (3d) 249 (Gen. Div.).

Where the plaintiff was not made aware of the importance of an order setting down a strict timetable for each step in the action and had not been represented by counsel at the time the order was made, the defendant's motion to dismiss the action for delay was denied.

B & B Rentals & Sales Ltd. v. Bruce Brothers Ltd. (1994), 35 C.P.C. (3d) 382, 22 C.L.R. (2d) 187 (Ont. Gen. Div.).

Where the defendant was partly to blame for the delay in the proceedings and played a significant role in causing the delay, the court refused its motion to dismiss the proceedings for delay.

Barakat v. Barakat (1994), 2 R.F.L. (4th) 219, 70 O.A.C. 135 (C.A.).

The trial judge in a family law proceeding dismissed various claims as a result of substantial delays in the litigation. The Ontario Court of Appeal allowed an appeal from the dismissals, as both spouses were at fault for the delays, and the appellant provided evidence explaining why she did not think it was appropriate to proceed to trial.

Vandewall v. Faria (1993), 15 C.P.C. (3d) 367, 62 O.A.C. 266 (Div. Ct.).

The court dismissed an action for delay nine years after it had been commenced notwithstanding the defendants had not filed an affidavit of documents. The defendants had disclosed their documents and the plaintiffs had not asked for an affidavit of documents.

Belanger v. Southwestern Insulation Contractors Ltd. (1993), 16 O.R. (3d) 457 (Gen. Div.).

The court refused to dismiss an action for delay where there had been concurrence in the delay and there was no evidence of prejudice to the defendants.

Eglington (Litigation Guardian of) v. Bederman (1993), 62 O.A.C. 391 (Div. Ct.).

An order dismissing an action for delay was set aside on appeal where the temporary irresponsibility of the plaintiff was not such as to preclude her continuing with the action.

D'Amore Construction (Windsor) Ltd. v. Ontario (1992), 13 C.P.C. (3d) 378 (Ont. Gen. Div.), affirmed (1994), 20 O.R. (3d) 42 (C.A.), leave to appeal to Supreme Court of Canada refused (February 23, 1995), Doc. 24372.

The court dismissed an action for delay where inexcusable delay by the plaintiff had caused prejudice to the defendants. Efforts by the defendants to move the case along by asking for answers to undertakings could not be used to show lack of prejudice to the defendants.

Atkinson v. Davies (1992), 37 M.V.R. (2d) 15 (Ont. Gen. Div.).

The court declined to dismiss an eight-year-old law suit for delay where the defendant's allegations of prejudice due to unavailability of documents and witnesses were not substantiated.

Evenden v. Davy (1991), 54 O.A.C. 77 (Div. Ct.).

The court dismissed an appeal from an order dismissing an action for delay where the delay had been inexcusable and there was a substantial risk that a fair trial would not be possible.

Copenace v. Fort Frances Times Ltd. (1991), 2 C.P.C. (3d) 64 (Ont. Gen. Div.).

A motion to dismiss for delay was dismissed where the delay involved was not inordinate or inexcusable, the defendants were partly responsible for the delay, and the prejudice resulting from the disappearance of a witness was not the result of the delay.

Parker Estate v. Aubé (1990), 72 O.R. (2d) 56 (H.C.).

Although the proceeding had been dormant for six years, the court refused to dismiss an action brought on a Quebec judgment for delay, where there was no prejudice to the defendant.

Hrivnak v. Steel Art Co. (1989), 34 C.P.C. (2d) 34 (Ont. Master).

The court dismissed an action for delay almost three years after expiry of the limitation period and eleven years after the alleged oral agreement upon which the claim was based.

Ship v. Longworth (1988), 65 O.R. (2d) 124, 27 C.P.C. (2d) 175, 29 O.A.C. 330 (Div. Ct.).

A defendant, by failing to serve an affidavit of documents, was not in default under the old Rules but was in default under the new Rules at the time of the motion to dismiss for delay. In view of the default, the motion was denied.

Maple Leaf Racquet Court Inc. v. Beaver Engineering Ltd. (1987), 60 O.R. (2d) 626 (Master).

A party who had failed to deliver an affidavit of documents within the time limited by the Rules was in default, and therefore was not entitled to move for an order dismissing the action.

Burwood Farms Ltd. v. Pacific Western Airlines Ltd. (1987), 21 C.P.C. (2d) 186 (Ont. H.C.).

The court dismissed an action for delay where there had been seven years of inactivity on a claim commenced twelve years before, a limitation period had expired and witnesses were lost, including the defendant's representative on discovery.

McFetters v. Drau Realty Ltd. (1986), 55 O.R. (2d) 722, 10 C.P.C. (2d) 28, 15 O.A.C. 60 (Div. Ct.).

The court dismissed an action where an unexplained and undue delay in the prosecution of an action following the expiry of a limitation period, coupled with the death or disappearance of witnesses, resulted in prejudice to the defendants.

Hatt v. Ontario (1985), 8 O.A.C. 367 (Div. Ct.).

The court refused to dismiss this action despite a four-year delay where the defendant failed to show that delay resulted in prejudice and the limitation period had not expired.

Cronkwright v. Shea (1985), 48 C.P.C. 243, 7 O.A.C. 238 (H.C.).

The court overturned an order dismissing an action for delay where there was no evidence giving particulars of prejudice to the defendant.

Wagman v. Blue Mountain Resorts Ltd. (1984), 47 C.P.C. 53 (Ont. H.C.).

The court dismissed an action for delay where the plaintiff took no steps to advance his action for four years and ignored his solicitor's requests for instructions.

Creditway Ltd. v. Ezrin (1981), 3 O.R. (2d) 776 (Div. Ct.).

Where the plaintiff's delay was not inordinate or contumelious and the limitation period had not expired, the court declined to dismiss the action but awarded costs of the motion and appeal to the defendant in the cause.

Wolfgang Zum Tobel v. Leavens Bros. Ltd. (1978), 7 C.P.C. 7 (Ont. Master).

An action was dismissed where a principal witness had died, the recollections of others would be impaired, and limitation periods had long been expired.

E.J. Piggot Enterprises Ltd. v. Bell Telephone Co. of Can., [1973] 1 O.R. 640 (Master).

Where the plaintiff obtained an interim injunction and undertook to prosecute expeditiously, but failed to do so, the action was dismissed, notwithstanding that the delay had caused no prejudice to the defendant and no limitation period had expired.

Ellis v. McQueen, [1967] 2 O.R. 399, 63 D.L.R. (2d) 678 (H.C.).

Where the defendants were partly responsible for the delay, the court refused to dismiss the action notwithstanding very serious prejudice to the defendants resulting from the delay.

NOTICE WHERE PLAINTIFF UNDER DISABILITY

24.02 Where the plaintiff is under disability, notice of a motion to dismiss the action for delay shall be served on,
   (a) the litigation guardian of the plaintiff; and
   (b) on the Children's Lawyer, unless,
      (i) the Public Guardian and Trustee is litigation guardian of the plaintiff, or
      (ii) a judge orders otherwise. [am. O. Reg. 69/95, ss. 18, 19, 20]

EFFECT OF DISMISSAL ON COUNTERCLAIM

24.03 Where an action against a defendant who has counterclaimed is dismissed for delay, the defendant may within thirty days after the dismissal deliver a notice of election to proceed with the counterclaim (Form 23B), and if the defendant fails to do so, the counterclaim shall be deemed to be discontinued without costs.

EFFECT OF DISMISSAL ON CROSSCLAIM OR THIRD PARTY CLAIM

24.04(1) Unless the court orders otherwise, where an action against a defendant who has crossclaimed or made a third party claim is dismissed for delay,

(a) the crossclaim or third party claim shall be deemed to be dismissed with costs; and

(b) the defendant may recover those costs and his or her own costs of the crossclaim or third party claim from the plaintiff.

Effect of deemed dismissal on subsequent action

(2) The deemed dismissal is not a defence to a subsequent action unless the order dismissing the action provides otherwise. [am. O. Reg. 770/92, s. 8]

EFFECT ON SUBSEQUENT ACTION

24.05(1) The dismissal of an action for delay is not a defence to a subsequent action unless the order dismissing the action provides otherwise.

(2) Where a plaintiff's action has been dismissed for delay with costs, and another action involving the same subject matter is subsequently brought between the same parties or their representatives or successors in interest before payment of the costs of the dismissed action, the court may order a stay of the subsequent action until the costs of the dismissed action have been paid.

APPLICATION TO COUNTERCLAIMS, CROSSCLAIMS AND THIRD PARTY CLAIMS

24.06 Rules 24.01 to 24.05 apply, with necessary modifications, to counterclaims, crossclaims and third party claims.

PLEADINGS

RULE 25   PLEADINGS IN AN ACTION

Highlights

Rule 25 specifies what pleadings are required or permitted and regulates the form, service and time for delivery of pleadings. Rule 25.03(1) requires every pleading to be served initially on every opposite party and on every other party who has delivered a pleading or notice of intention to defend in the action, counterclaim, crossclaim, or third or subsequent party claim and, subsequently, on every other party who has delivered a pleading or notice of intention to defend. Rule 25.03(2) requires a party adding a new party to serve on the added party all pleadings previously delivered.

Rule 25.06 sets out the rules of pleading applicable to all parties and pleadings (supplemented by rule 14.01(4), permitting the pleading of facts that occur after the commencement of an action even though the facts give rise to a new claim or defence).

Rule 25.07 imposes particular requirements on a defendant. All allegations not denied in a party's defence shall be deemed to be admitted, unless the party pleads lack of knowledge in respect of the fact. More importantly, an affirmative obligation is imposed and a denial is no longer sufficient if what the party intends to rely on is a different version of the facts than that pleaded by the opposite party. The party is required to plead his or her own version of the facts. (By rule 25.08(1) this principle is extended to a reply.)

A reply is to be delivered only by a party who intends to prove a version of the facts different from that pleaded by the opponent or to rely on any matter that might, if not specifically pleaded, take the other party by surprise or raise an issue that has not been raised by a previous pleading: rule 25.08.

A demand for particulars and the power of the court to order particulars are regulated by rule 25.10. Rule 25.11 provides a general power to strike out or expunge part or all of a pleading *or any other document* if it may prejudice or delay the trial, is scandalous, frivolous or vexatious, or is an abuse of process.

Recent amendments. Rule 25.06(8) has been amended to require particulars of malice and intent to be pleaded.

Former Rules: Rules 121-122, 138-166.

PLEADINGS REQUIRED OR PERMITTED

Action Commenced by Statement of Claim or Notice of Action

25.01(1) In an action commenced by statement of claim or notice of action, pleadings shall consist of the statement of claim (Form 14A, 14B or 14D), statement of defence (Form 18A) and reply (Form 25A), if any.

Counterclaim

(2) In a counterclaim, pleadings shall consist of the counterclaim (Form 27A or 27B), defence to counterclaim (Form 27C) and reply to defence to counterclaim (Form 27D), if any.

Crossclaim
(3) In a crossclaim, pleadings shall consist of the crossclaim (Form 28A), defence to crossclaim (Form 28B) and reply to defence to crossclaim (Form 28C), if any.

Third Party Claim
(4) In a third party claim, pleadings shall consist of the third party claim (Form 29A), third party defence (Form 29B) and reply to third party defence (Form 29C), if any.

Pleading Subsequent to Reply
(5) No pleading subsequent to a reply shall be delivered without the consent in writing of the opposite party or leave of the court.

Toronto Non-Profit Housing Corp. v. Toronto Electric Commrs. (1986), 7 C.P.C. (2d) 305 (Ont. Master).

A rejoinder may be permitted where (1) the reply introduces new and important matters; or (2) the reply introduces events subsequent to the occurrence of the loss in respect of which the action was brought; and (3) the defendant could not reasonably have anticipated the matter and pleaded to it in its statement of defence.

Firestone v. Firestone (1974), 5 O.R. (2d) 659 (H.C.).

A rejoinder may be permitted where the reply introduces a new and important matter which the defendant could not reasonably have anticipated.

Regal Films Corp. (1941) Ltd. v. Glens Falls Ins. Co., [1945] O.W.N. 130 (Master).

Leave to deliver a rejoinder will be granted where a reply introduces new and important matters which the defendant could not have anticipated.

FORM OF PLEADINGS

25.02 Pleadings shall be divided into paragraphs numbered consecutively, and each allegation shall, so far as is practical, be contained in a separate paragraph.

SERVICE OF PLEADINGS

Who Is to be Served
25.03(1) Every pleading shall be served,
(a) initially on every opposite party and on every other party who has delivered a pleading or a notice of intention to defend in the main action or in a counterclaim, crossclaim or third or subsequent party claim in the main action; and
(b) subsequently on every other party forthwith after the party delivers a pleading or a notice of intention to defend in the main action or in a counterclaim, crossclaim or third or subsequent party claim in the main action.

Service on Added Parties
(2) Where a person is added as a party to an action, the party doing so shall serve on the added party all the pleadings previously delivered in the

main action and in any counterclaim, crossclaim or third or subsequent party claim in the main action, unless the court orders otherwise.

Where Personal Service Not Required
(3) Where a pleading is an originating process, personal service on parties other than an opposite party is not required.

TIME FOR DELIVERY OF PLEADINGS

Statement of Claim
25.04(1) The time for service of a statement of claim is prescribed by rule 14.08.

Statement of Defence
(2) The time for delivery of a statement of defence is prescribed by rule 18.01.

Reply
(3) A reply, if any, shall be delivered within ten days after service of the statement of defence except where the defendant counterclaims, in which case a reply and defence to counterclaim, if any, shall be delivered within twenty days after service of the statement of defence and counterclaim.

In a Counterclaim
(4) The time for delivery of pleadings in a counterclaim is prescribed by Rule 27.

In a Crossclaim
(5) The time for delivery of pleadings in a crossclaim is prescribed by Rule 28.

In a Third Party Claim
(6) The time for delivery of pleadings in a third party claim is prescribed by Rule 29.

Cross-Reference: See also cases under rules 3.02, 18.01, and Rules 27, 28 and 29.

Time for Delivery of Reply — rule 25.04(3)

Keuhl v. Beachburg (Village) (1990), 1 O.R. (3d) 154, 45 C.P.C. (2d) 225, 75 D.L.R. (4th) 193, (*sub nom. Keuhl v. Renfrew (County)*) 42 O.A.C. 387 (C.A.).
In allowing an appeal from an order determining that a claim was statute-barred, the Court of Appeal extended the time for delivery of a reply in order to allow the plaintiff to plead her answer to the defence which was not before the judge at first instance.

Boland v. Telegram Publishing Co., [1963] 1 O.R. 629 (Master).
In the absence of lengthy delay or other special circumstances, a later reply will not be struck out.

Madden v. Madden, [1947] O.R. 866 (C.A.).
A reply cannot be delivered after the time prescribed to do so has expired unless the court extends the time.

CLOSE OF PLEADINGS

25.05　Pleadings in an action are closed when,

(a)　the plaintiff has delivered a reply to every defence in the action or the time for delivery of a reply has expired; and

(b)　every defendant who is in default in delivering a defence in the action has been noted in default.

Schram v. The Alexandra Marine and General Hospital (February 17, 1994), Doc. 5319/90 (Ont. Master).

Where a third party defends the main action, the pleadings in the main action are not closed until the plaintiff delivers its reply or the time therefor has expired.

Nelma Information Inc. v. Holt (1985), 50 C.P.C. 116 (Ont. H.C.).

A third party action is a separate action from the main action. The close of pleadings is determined separately for each action.

RULES OF PLEADING — APPLICABLE TO ALL PLEADINGS

Material Facts

25.06(1)　Every pleading shall contain a concise statement of the material facts on which the party relies for the claim or defence, but not the evidence by which those facts are to be proved.

Pleading Law

(2)　A party may raise any point of law in a pleading, but conclusions of law may be pleaded only if the material facts supporting them are pleaded.

Condition Precedent

(3)　Allegations of the performance or occurrence of all conditions precedent to the assertion of a claim or defence of a party are implied in the party's pleading and need not be set out, and an opposite party who intends to contest the performance or occurrence of a condition precedent shall specify in the opposite party's pleading the condition and its non-performance or non-occurrence.

Inconsistent Pleading

(4)　A party may make inconsistent allegations in a pleading where the pleading makes it clear that they are being pleaded in the alternative.

(5)　An allegation that is inconsistent with an allegation made in a party's previous pleading or that raises a new ground of claim shall not be made in a subsequent pleading but by way of amendment to the previous pleading.

Notice

(6)　Where a notice to a person is alleged, it is sufficient to allege notice as a fact unless the form or a precise term of the notice is material.

Documents or Conversations

(7)　The effect of a document or the purport of a conversation, if material, shall be pleaded as briefly as possible, but the precise words of the

document or conversation need not be pleaded unless those words are themselves material.

Nature of Act or Condition of Mind

(8) Where fraud, misrepresentation, breach of trust, malice or intent is alleged, the pleading shall contain full particulars, but knowledge may be alleged as a fact without pleading the circumstances from which it is to be inferred.

Claim for Relief

(9) Where a pleading contains a claim for relief, the nature of the relief shall be specified and, where damages are claimed,

(a) the amount claimed for each claimant in respect of each claim shall be stated; and

(b) the amounts and particulars of special damages need only be pleaded to the extent that they are known at the date of the pleading, but notice of any further amounts and particulars shall be delivered forthwith after they become known and, in any event, not less than ten days before trial. [am. O. Reg. 61/96, s. 1]

Cross-Reference: See also cases under rules 25.07, 25.10 and 25.11.

Pleading Material Facts and Evidence — rule 25.06(1)

735619 Ont. Ltd. v. Stone (1989), 36 C.P.C. (2d) 313 (Ont. Master).

Where the other facts contained in a pleading genuinely supported a claim for punitive and exemplary damages, the means of a defendant was a material fact and therefore could properly be pleaded.

Edwards v. Ontario (Minister of Natural Resources) (1989), 33 C.P.C. (2d) 277 (Ont. H.C.).

The court struck out a paragraph alleging remedial measures taken following an accident as pleading evidence.

Copland v. Commodore Business Machines Ltd. (1985), 52 O.R. (2d) 586, 3 C.P.C. (2d) 77 (Master).

Rule 25.06(1) requires a minimum level of material fact disclosure and if this level is not reached, the remedy is a motion to strike out the pleading rather than a motion for particulars.

Bennett v. Robert Simon Const. Ltd. (1977), 17 O.R. (2d) 190, 6 C.P.C. 110 (Co. Ct.).

Allegations dealing with an earlier flooding incident, for which no relief was claimed, were struck out as not involving material facts.

Union Gas Ltd. v. Steel Co. of Can. Ltd. (1976), 1 C.P.C. 325 (Ont. H.C.).

A paragraph alleging that other customers had experienced similar difficulties with the defendant's product was struck out with leave to amend.

Almas v. Spenceley, [1972] 2 O.R. 429, 25 D.L.R. (3d) 653 (C.A.).

The specific elements of a cause of action need not be alleged provided the facts supporting such elements are pleaded.

Sutton, Mitchell & Simpson Ltd. v. Kelore Mines Ltd., [1956] O.W.N. 648 (C.A.).

A new trial was ordered where the trial judge had determined the case on an issue altogether different than that pleaded.

Bedford Const. Co. v. Gilbert, [1956] O.W.N. 293 (C.A.).

A judgment rendered on the basis of a cause of action which had not been pleaded was set aside and a new trial ordered.

Cadillac Contr. & Devs. Ltd. v. Tanenbaum, [1954] O.W.N. 221, affirmed [1954] O.W.N. 221 at 223 (H.C.).

The allegations must be relevant to the action or they will be struck out.

Grace v. Usalkas, [1959] O.W.N. 237 (Master).

While the court is lenient in allowing the pleading of evidence other than admissions, it will not permit the complete neglect of the rules of pleading.

Cavotti v. Cavotti, [1958] O.W.N. 470 (Master).

Adultery must be pleaded with particularity.

Bilton v. Hagersville Quarries Ltd., [1948] O.W.N. 600 (H.C.).

A plea in the statement of claim that the defendant had settled a previous claim for similar damages was held to be a proper pleading of fact.

Clement v. Luesby, [1944] O.W.N. 103 (Master).

It is unnecessary to allege any matter of fact which the law presumes in favour of the party pleading; however, the facts and circumstances which place the onus on the opposing party must be pleaded.

Pleading Law — rule 25.06(2)

Ralna Ltd. v. Can. Life Assur. Co. (1982), 30 C.P.C. 96, 138 D.L.R. (3d) 747 (Ont. H.C.).

Failure to reply to a plea of law did not constitute an admission, and questions relating to the matter were permitted on discovery.

Hellenius v. Lees, [1972] S.C.R. 165, 20 D.L.R. (3d) 369.

Res ipsa loquitur is a rule of evidence and states no principle of law.

H.E.P.C. Ont. v. St. Catharines, [1971] 3 O.R. 674, 21 D.L.R. (3d) 410, affirmed [1972] 1 O.R. 806, 24 D.L.R. (3d) 278 (C.A.).

Statutory provisions which may take the opposing party by surprise should be pleaded.

Hands v. Stampede Int. Resources Ltd., [1971] 3 O.R. 44 (H.C.).

Where a foreign statute is applicable, the party pleading should set out the appropriate provision in detail, state its relevance, and specify any breach which is alleged.

Ont. Stone Corp. v. R.E. Law Crushed Stone Ltd., [1964] 1 O.R. 303 (Master).

Discussion of how to plead foreign law.

Gruen Watch Co. v. A.G. Can., [1950] O.R. 429, [1950] C.T.C. 440, [1951] 4 D.L.R. 156, reversed in part on other grounds [1951] O.R. 360, [1951] C.T.C. 94, [1951] 3 D.L.R. 18 (*sub nom. Bulova Watch Co. v. A.G. Can.*)(C.A.).

A party need not plead a statute which is declaratory of the general law.

Famous Players Can. Corp. v. J.J. Turner & Sons Ltd., [1948] O.W.N. 221 (H.C.).

It is proper to plead a conclusion of law if it is supported by the material facts upon which the conclusion is based.

Madden v. Madden, [1947] O.R. 866 (C.A.).

In a divorce action a plea that the opposite party had been guilty of acts of cruelty without the material facts particularizing those acts is a conclusion of law.

Thompson v. T.T.C., [1947] O.W.N. 920 (Master).

Where a statute is pleaded, particulars of the sections relied upon must be pleaded and where a claim over is made against a co-defendant under the *Negligence Act* the specific facts of the alleged negligence must be pleaded.

Brazier v. T.T.C., [1946] O.W.N. 890 (Master).

The pleading of a statute must be accompanied by the facts on which the application of the statute depends.

Inconsistent Pleading and New Claims — rule 25.06(4), (5)

Solid Waste Reclamation Inc. v. Philip Enterprises Inc. (1991), 2 O.R. (3d) 481, 49 C.P.C. (2d) 245 (Gen. Div.).

The court struck out new claims raised in a reply.

McComb v. American Can Can. Inc. (1986), 15 C.P.C. (2d) 242 (Ont. H.C.).

It is improper to plead a new cause of action in reply; however, leave to amend the statement of claim will be granted unless the defendant shows prejudice.

Gaskin v. Retail Credit Co., [1964] 1 O.R. 530, 43 D.L.R. (3d) 120, reversed on other grounds [1965] S.C.R. 297, 49 D.L.R. (2d) 542.

An alternative allegation, which assumes a fact previously denied, is not to be interpreted as an admission of that fact.

Burford v. Cosa Corp. of Can. Ltd., [1955] O.W.N. 8 (Master).

A new claim for relief included in a reply was struck out.

Levinson v. Levinson, [1943] O.W.N. 177 (Master).

An alternative claim raised in a reply will be struck out.

Pleading Documents or Conversations — rule 25.06(7)

Montreal Trust Co. of Canada v. Toronto-Dominion Bank (June 17, 1992) Doc. 19/92, 20/92 (Ont. Gen. Div.).

A statement of claim is deemed to include documents incorporated in it by reference and which form an integral part of the plaintiff's claim.

Brad Ind. Ltd. v. Rio Tinto M. Co., [1962] O.W.N. 126 (Master).

A party relying on an oral contract must give sufficient particulars of the contract to enable the opposing party to know the case he has to meet.

Taylor v. Krever, [1957] O.W.N. 549 (H.C.).

The court refused to allow the plaintiff to attach to his pleading a sketch of a right of way.

Pleading Nature of Act or Condition of Mind — rule 25.06(8)

Ramoska-Kaluza v. Ellis, [1955] O.W.N. 969 (C.A.).

A new trial was ordered where the fraud found at trial had not been pleaded.

Coldoff v. Brigden, [1939] O.W.N. 527 (Master).

In an action for malicious prosecution no particulars of malice need be given.

Stewart v. Bundock (1924), 25 O.W.N. 657 (H.C.).

A general allegation of fraud without specific facts is not sufficient to sustain an action.

Claim for Relief — rule 25.06(9)

Kenora (Town) Police Services Board v. Savino (1995), 36 C.P.C. (3d) 46 (Ont. Gen. Div.).
The court refused to strike out the prayer for relief in a class proceeding which did not set out the amount claimed for each class member.

Fazzari v. Pellizzari (1988), 28 O.A.C. 38 (Div. Ct.).
The court permitted a claim for punitive damages in a breach of contract case to proceed to trial.

Briand v. Sutton (No. 1) (1986), 57 O.R. (2d) 629, 15 C.P.C. (2d) 32 (H.C.).
A claim for punitive damages need not be specifically pleaded.

Dale Perusse Ltd. v. Kason, 6 C.P.C. (2d) 129, [1985] I.L.R. 1-1985 (Ont. H.C.), affirmed [1985] I.L.R. 1-1985n (Ont. Div. Ct.).
The court refused to strike out a claim for exemplary and punitive damages in an action against an insurer for breach of the duty of good faith and fair dealing.

Attam Investments Inc. v. Abrade Investments Inc. (1985), 6 C.P.C. (2d) 12 (Ont. Master).
Where several types of special damages are claimed, the amount of each should be specified if known. The circumstances of each case will dictate the extent to which particulars can reasonably be pleaded.

Royal Bank v. Keung (1985), 3 C.P.C. (2d) 22 (Ont. Dist. Ct.).
A claim for punitive damages was permitted to stand in a contract action alleging a breach of confidence by a professional for the purpose of embarrassing a client.

A.G. Ont. v. Tiberius Productions Inc. (1984), 46 O.R. (2d) 152, 44 C.P.C. 14, 8 D.L.R. (4th) 479 (H.C.).
A claim for punitive damages may not be asserted in an ordinary action for breach of a commercial contract.

Can. Southern Railway Co. v. Michigan Central Railroad Co. (1984), 45 O.R. (2d) 257, 39 C.P.C. 18, 6 D.L.R. (4th) 324 (H.C.), leave to appeal to Ont. Div. Ct. refused 39 C.P.C. 18n.
The plaintiff was permitted to make a claim for set-off against dividends payable to the defendants which were being held in escrow.

Fucella v. Ricker (1982), 35 O.R. (2d) 423 (H.C.).
Special damages should be specifically pleaded and claimed; however, it is permissible to claim a round sum and undertake to provide particulars prior to trial.

Wojcichowski v. Lakeshore Lions Club (1982), 29 C.P.C. 269 (Ont. Master).
The master struck out a claim for punitive damages in this wrongful dismissal action.

Yarnell v. Yarnell (1976), 13 O.R. (2d) 669 (Master).
A petition should specify the amounts sought for maintenance, alimony and interim alimony.

Eckland v. Eckland, [1973] 3 O.R. 472 (H.C.).
A request for ''such further and other relief as may be deemed just'' may enable the court to grant relief not specifically enumerated.

Doherty v. Doherty, [1968] 2 O.R. 518 (C.A.).
In a divorce action a prayer for ''such other relief as the court may deem just'' enables the court to award maintenance for children.

Maschinenfabrik Seydelmann K.G. v. Presswood Bros. Ltd., [1965] 1 O.R. 177, 47 D.L.R. (2d) 214, reversed on other grounds [1966] 1 O.R. 316, 53 D.L.R. (2d) 224 (C.A.).

Where an action to recover the price of goods sold failed because the contract was void, and the plaintiff had failed to claim in the alternative the return of the goods and damages, the court could not provide such relief.

Stylecraft Dress Co. v. Gotlin, [1946] O.W.N. 114 (H.C.).

Failure to state the amount of damages claimed is improper and the plaintiff must amend the statement of claim accordingly.

Acme Ruler & Advertising Co. v. Kendrick, [1944] O.W.N. 33 (Master).

A prayer for relief may be for inconsistent remedies either alternately or cumulatively.

Pleading Subsequent Facts (See also rule 14.01(4).)

Hewitt v. Hewitt, [1970] 2 O.R. 167 (Master).

An amendment alleging a new cause of action was allowed to avoid discontinuance of the present action and commencement of a new one.

Cavotti v. Cavotti, [1958] O.W.N. 470 (Master).

An amendment was permitted to allege adultery which occurred after the commencement of the action.

James Hourigan Co. Ltd. v. Cox, [1937] O.W.N. 537 (C.A.).

An alleged settlement after the commencement of an action constitutes a ground of defence, but is not grounds for staying the action.

Pleading in Defamation Actions

Kenora (Town) Police Services Board v. Savino (1995), 36 C.P.C. (3d) 46 (Ont. Gen. Div.).

The court refused to strike out a defamation claim brought by way of class proceeding on behalf of the members of the Kenora police department.

Elliott v. CBC (1993), 16 O.R. (3d) 677, 108 D.L.R. (4th) 385, 52 C.P.R. (3d) 145, 24 C.P.C. (3d) 143, 22 Admin. L.R. (2d) 272, additional reasons (1994), 24 C.P.C. (3d) 143 at 169, 22 Admin. L.R. (2d) 272 at 297 (Ont. Gen. Div.), affirmed (1995), 38 C.P.C. (3d) 332, 125 D.L.R. (4th) 534, 62 C.P.R. (3d) 19, 82 O.A.C. 115, 25 O.R. (3d) 302 (C.A.).

A class action was struck out on the ground that there is no liability for defaming a group. *Accord, McCann v. Ottawa Sun* (1993), 16 O.R. (3d) 672 (Gen. Div.).

Aboutown Transportation Ltd. v. London Free Press Printing Co. (1993), 14 O.R. (3d) 19 (C.A.).

In a libel action which pleaded a cause of action sounding in legal innuendo, the plaintiff was ordered to deliver particulars of the extrinsic facts replied upon to support the legal innuendos pleaded and the identities of those who possessed knowledge of the extrinsic facts.

Turner v. Toronto Sun Publishing Corp. (1990), 50 C.P.C. (2d) 73, 5 C.C.L.T. (2d) 184 (Ont. Gen. Div.).

The defendant in a defamation action is not at liberty to plead a lesser defamatory meaning of the words complained of and to seek to justify that meaning. *Polly Peck (Holdings) plc v. Trelford*, [1986] 2 All E.R. 84 (C.A.) and *Lucas-Box v. News Group Ltd.*, [1986] 1 All E.R. 177 (C.A.), do not reflect the law of Ontario.

Carson v. William W. Creighton Centre (1990), 73 O.R. (2d) 755, 31 C.C.E.L. 31 (Dist. Ct.).

The precise rules of pleading applicable in defamation actions do not apply to wrongful dismissal actions in which slander is alleged in the statement of claim.

Promatek Industries Ltd. v. Creative Micro Designs Inc. (1989), 33 C.P.C. (2d) 272 (Ont. Master).

The court struck out portions of a pleading which did not specify the words complained of.

Reichmann v. Toronto Life Publishing Co. (1988), 27 C.P.C. (2d) 37 (Ont. H.C.).

In a libel action, the court refused to order particulars where the plaintiff pleaded specific portions of the defamatory article and then relied on the context of the entire article for the surrounding facts by using very general phrases. Pleading the author's motive was also allowed as relevant to damages.

Jaffe v. Americans for International Justice Foundation (1987), 22 C.P.C. (2d) 286 (Ont. Master).

In an action for defamation, the plaintiff was ordered to give particulars of an allegation that there had been publication to unnamed persons, where it had not been established by affidavit that the plaintiff had no further particulars of such publication.

Cohl v. Toronto Star Newspapers Ltd. (1986), 16 C.P.C. (2d) 296 (Ont. Master).

In a libel action, the defendant may not allege that the words complained of had a meaning different from that alleged by the plaintiff and were true in that meaning.

Code v. Toronto Star Newspaper Ltd. (1984), 48 C.P.C. 64 (Ont. Master).

The plaintiff in this libel case was permitted to set out portions of the newspaper article complained of and plead that the entire article would be given in evidence at trial.

Lightfoot v. Southon (1983), 33 C.P.C. 89 (Ont. H.C.).

In this defamation case, particulars were not ordered where the three and a half-page libel complained of was uncomplicated; however, a pleading of innuendo was struck out with leave to amend to set out the specific innuendo contended for. The plaintiff was also ordered to provide particulars of to whom and when certain statements were made.

Ont. Soc. for the Prevention of Cruelty to Animals v. Toronto Sun Corp. (1982), 31 C.P.C. 252 (Ont. Master).

Although a defendant in a libel action cannot prove in mitigation that others have previously published the same libel, a defendant can in some circumstances plead that the particular damages alleged by the plaintiff flowed at least in part from other causes, whether defamatory or not. Where a defendant pleads fair comment on a matter of public interest, particulars of the facts showing that the matter is of public interest will not be ordered.

Gouzenko v. Doubleday Can. Ltd. (1981), 34 O.R. (2d) 306, 19 C.C.L.T. 167, 25 C.P.C. 146, 129 D.L.R. (3d) 549, leave to appeal to Ont. C.A. refused 35 O.R. (2d) 194n, 25 C.P.C. 146n, 142 D.L.R. (3d) 192n (H.C.).

Particulars will be ordered in a defamation action where a rolled-up plea is used to defend general allegations and where the facts relied on as a basis for the comments are not specifically stated in the alleged libel.

Pennington v. Smith (1980), 16 C.P.C. 151 (Ont. Master).

In a defamation action, an allegation that indicated neither the exact words complained of nor their purport was struck out.

Vulcan Indust. Packaging Ltd. v. C.B.C. (1979), 23 O.R. (2d) 213, 13 C.P.C. 156, 94 D.L.R. (3d) 729 (Master).

In an action for defamation based on a television broadcast, the plaintiff must indicate which portions of the programme give rise to the allegations of defamation.

Church of Scientology of Toronto v. Toronto Sun Publishing Ltd. (1977), 4 C.P.C. 207 (Ont. Master).

In a libel action, paragraphs in a statement of claim dealing with the intention of the defendant were struck out as irrelevant while others were struck out as anticipating a defence.

Canadian Plasmapheresis Centres Ltd. v. C.B.C. (1975), 8 O.R. (2d) 55 (H.C.).

Noncompliance with the notice provisions of the *Libel and Slander Act*, R.S.O. 1970, c. 243, must be specifically pleaded.

Wall v. Lalonde (1974), 7 O.R. (2d) 129, 54 D.L.R. (3d) 493 (H.C.).

A plaintiff in a defamation action was ordered to give particulars of the exact words complained of and the circumstances in which they were said.

Mengarelli v. Forrest, [1972] 2 O.R. 397 (Master).

What a defendant meant by an allegedly defamatory statement is immaterial and may not be pleaded.

Unterberger v. Prospectors Airways Co., [1962] O.W.N. 212 (Master).

The court ordered the plaintiff to give the names of persons alleged to have republished a defamatory statement.

Gouzenko v. Rasky, [1959] O.W.N. 185 (Master).

The court refused to require the plaintiff in a libel action to specify which portions of the passages in question were alleged to be untrue.

White v. Barry, [1947] O.W.N. 755 (Master).

In a slander action, where the exact date of publication of the slander was not within the knowledge of the plaintiff, a motion for particulars was refused as the defendant would have no difficulty pleading, but particulars for trial were ordered.

Meredith v. Dalton, [1944] O.W.N. 676 (Master).

In a defamation action the plaintiff must furnish the best particulars he can give of the persons present when the alleged slander was uttered; however, such particulars will not be ordered where it would be unreasonable to do so.

RULES OF PLEADING — APPLICABLE TO DEFENCES

Admissions

25.07(1) In a defence, a party shall admit every allegation of fact in the opposite party's pleading that the party does not dispute.

Denials

(2) Subject to subrule (6), all allegations of fact that are not denied in a party's defence shall be deemed to be admitted unless the party pleads having no knowledge in respect of the fact.

Different Version of Facts

(3) Where a party intends to prove a version of the facts different from that pleaded by the opposite party, a denial of the version so pleaded is not sufficient, but the party shall plead the party's own version of the facts in the defence.

Affirmative Defences

(4) In a defence, a party shall plead any matter on which the party intends to rely to defeat the claim of the opposite party and which, if not specifically pleaded, might take the opposite party by surprise or raise an issue that has not been raised in the opposite party's pleading.

Effect of Denial Agreement

(5) **Where an agreement is alleged in a pleading, a denial of the agreement by the opposite party shall be construed only as a denial of the making of the agreement or of the facts from which the agreement may be implied by law, and not as a denial of the legality or sufficiency in law of the agreement.**

Damages

(6) **In an action for damages, the amount of damages shall be deemed to be in issue unless specifically admitted.**

Cross-Reference: See also cases under rules 25.06, 25.10 and 25.11.

Pleading Denials — rule 25.07(2)

Wood Gundy Inc. v. Financial Trustco Capital Ltd. (1988), 26 C.P.C. (2d) 274 (Ont. Master).

Several defendants may file a joint statement of defence even though their defences may not be identical, but where there are defences served on behalf of some but not all of such defendants, it is necessary to frame the statement of defence so as to make clear which defendants are admitting a particular allegation, and which are denying it.

Weller v. Genereux (1980), 18 C.P.C. 254 (Ont. Master).

The first paragraph of a statement of defence containing a denial of each and every allegation in the statement of claim was allowed to stand.

Toronto v. B.A. Oil Co.; Toronto Harbour Commrs. v. B.A. Oil Co., [1947] O.W.N. 614 (H.C.).

A general denial to specific allegations in the statement of claim will be struck out.

Cherry v. Petch, [1946] O.W.N. 383 (Master).

A defence to a plaintiff's statement of claim should be set up so that the plaintiff may know the case he has to meet and so that the statement of defence contains no general denials.

Sharpe v. Reingold, [1946] O.W.N. 730 (Master).

The form of the statement of claim may determine the extent and nature of the defendant's pleading and, therefore, the application of the rules of pleading denials.

Pleading Affirmative Defences — rule 25.07(4)

Trident Holdings Ltd. v. Danand Investments Ltd. (1988), 64 O.R. (2d) 65, 39 B.L.R. 296, 30 E.T.R. 67, 49 D.L.R. (4th) 1, 25 O.A.C. 378 (C.A.).

In an action for breach of contract where the defendant's main contention was that a contract did not exist, the defendant's alternative position — that the terms of the contract had entitled it to repudiate — was rejected by the court because it had not been pleaded as required.

Johns-Manville Can. Inc. v. John Carlo Ltd. (1980), 29 O.R. (2d) 592, 12 B.L.R. 80, 113 D.L.R. (3d) 686, affirmed 32 O.R. (2d) 697, 123 D.L.R. (3d) 763 (C.A.).

A defendant in an action on a labour and material bond was not permitted to rely on a defence of lack of notice as required by the bond where the defence had not been pleaded.

Perlmutter v. Jeffery (1979), 23 O.R. (2d) 428 (H.C.).

A defence based on the *Unconscionable Transactions Relief Act*, R.S.O. 1970, c. 472, or any other statute must be specifically pleaded.

Mann v. Mann (1973), 1 O.R. (2d) 416, 11 R.F.L. 392, 40 D.L.R. (3d) 504 (H.C.).
Res judicata or estoppel by record must be specifically pleaded.

Famous Players Can. Corp. v. J.J. Turner & Sons Ltd., [1948] O.W.N. 221 (H.C.).
Estoppel must be pleaded if it is to be raised at trial.

WHERE A REPLY IS NECESSARY

Different Version of Facts
**25.08(1) A party who intends to prove a version of the facts different
from that pleaded in the opposite party's defence shall deliver a reply setting
out the different version, unless it has already been pleaded in the claim.**

Affirmative Reply
**(2) A party who intends to rely in response to a defence on any matter
that might, if not specifically pleaded, take the opposite party by surprise or
raise an issue that has not been raised by a previous pleading shall deliver a
reply setting out that matter, subject to subrule 25.06(5) (inconsistent claims
or new claims).**

Reply Only Where Required
**(3) A party shall not deliver a reply except where required to do so by
subrule (1) or (2).**

Deemed Denial of Allegations Where No Reply
**(4) A party who does not deliver a reply within the prescribed time shall
be deemed to deny the allegations of fact made in the defence of the opposite
party.**

RULES OF PLEADING — APPLICABLE TO REPLIES

Admissions
**25.09(1) A party who delivers a reply shall admit every allegation of
fact in the opposite party's defence that the party does not dispute.**

Effect of Denial of Agreement
**(2) Where an agreement is alleged in a defence, a denial of the agree-
ment in the opposite party's reply, or a deemed denial under subrule 25.08(4),
shall be construed only as a denial of the making of the agreement or of the
facts from which the agreement may be implied by law, and not as a denial
of the legality or sufficiency in law of the agreement.**

PARTICULARS

**25.10 Where a party demands particulars of an allegation in the plead-
ing of an opposite party, and the opposite party fails to supply them within
seven days, the court may order particulars to be delivered within a specified
time.**

Cross-Reference: See also cases under rule 25.06.

Particulars — General Principles

Copland v. Commodore Business Machines Ltd. (1985), 52 O.R. (2d) 586, 3 C.P.C. (2d) 77 (Master).

Rule 25.06(1) requires a minimum level of material fact disclosure and if this level is not reached, the remedy is a motion to strike out the pleading rather than a motion for particulars.

Asfordby Storage and Haulage Ltd. v. Bauer (1985), 1 W.D.C.P. 505 (Ont. H.C.).

The purpose of pleadings, particularly under the new Rules of Civil Procedure, is to define the issues as precisely as possible for the benefit of both the parties and the court. The court ordered particulars of the statement of claim.

Int. Nickel Co. v. Travellers Indemnity Co., [1962] O.W.N. 109 (C.A.).

The function of particulars for the purpose of pleading is to limit the generality of pleadings and thus to define the issues which have to be tried and as to which discovery must be given.

Henrickson v. Henrickson, [1962] O.W.N. 75 (Master).

The supplying of particulars generally precludes subsequent motions to strike out portions of a pleading; however, in this case the pleading was obviously bad for other reasons and was struck out.

Boyce, McCay, Duff & Co. v. Grace Electronics Ltd., [1953] O.W.N. 672 (Master).

Particulars will not generally be ordered of a mere traverse or negative plea. *[But note rule 25.07(3) — Authors.]*

Gribben v. Downer, [1953] O.W.N. 408 (Master).

Where particulars are ordered and a plaintiff fails to provide them, the action is automatically stayed and the defendant may move to dismiss the action for want of prosecution.

V.K. Mason Const. Ltd. v. Courtot Invts. Ltd. (1974), 6 O.R. (2d) 655 (H.C.).

A motion for particulars in a mechanics' lien action is properly brought before the master rather than a judge of the High Court.

Kilvington Bros. Ltd. v. McIntosh Granite Co., [1954] O.W.N. 463, 14 Fox Pat. C. 54, 20 C.P.R. 42 (Master).

Precedents are useful but in the last analysis the discretion of the court as to whether to order particulars is dominant and it will be exercised to do justice to all parties in the light of all the circumstances.

Hammell v. B.A. Oil Co., [1945] O.W.N. 660 (Master).

Where particulars are extensive and will cause difficulty and inconvenience in understanding the plaintiff's claim, they should be embodied in a new statement of claim.

Hebb v. Mulock and Newmarket Era & Express Ltd., [1944] O.W.N. 660 (Master).

Where the allegations referred to in the demand for particulars are plain statements of fact, further particulars will not be ordered.

Stokes v. Dayton and Tripp, [1944] O.W.N. 572 (Master).

An order for further particulars will be refused where to do so would be oppressive and the effect would be virtually to prevent the party from proceeding.

Mulvenna v. C.P.R. (1914), 5 O.W.N. 779, 26 O.W.R. 675, 15 D.L.R. 616 (H.C.).

Where there is a presumption of negligence because *res ipsa loquitur*, particulars of negligence will not be ordered.

Necessity of Affidavit Supporting Need for Particulars

Hanna v. Hanna (1986), 53 O.R. (2d) 251 (Master).

The deponent of the supporting affidavit in a motion for particulars should be the moving party. Where the party's solicitor is the deponent, privilege cannot be claimed, at least as far as to facts and issues raised in the affidavit.

Curry v. Advocate Gen. Ins. Co. of Can. (1986), 9 C.P.C. (2d) 247 (Ont. Master).

An affidavit deposing to a party's inability to plead without particulars is unnecessary where the pleading is bald, and the motion may be heard in the absence of a prior written demand for particulars where the demand would not have been heeded.

Dudziak v. Boots Drug Stores (Can.) Ltd. (1983), 40 C.P.C. 140, 3 C.C.E.L. 140 (Ont. Master).

Affidavits by solicitors on motions for particulars deposing to their clients' lack of knowledge of the allegations in a pleading, although admissible, will seldom be given much weight. An affidavit by a client deposing advice from his counsel that he was unable to plead, without indicating an inability to instruct counsel, was of no value whatsoever.

Steiner v. Lindzon (1976), 14 O.R. (2d) 122, 1 C.P.C. 237 (H.C.).

An affidavit should accompany a motion for particulars unless the need for particulars is patently obvious from the pleading itself.

Stylecraft Dress Co. v. Gotlin, [1946] O.W.N. 114 (H.C.).

Particulars will not be ordered unless it is shown by affidavit that the particulars are necessary to enable the opposite party to plead and that the particulars are not within the knowledge of the party asking for them.

Knowledge of Party Seeking Particulars

Min. of Health for Ont. v. Wilston (1975), 11 O.R. (2d) 631 (Div. Ct.).

Particulars for the purpose of pleading will not be ordered if they are within the knowledge of the party demanding them.

Physicians' Services Inc. v. Cass, [1971] 2 O.R. 626 (C.A.).

Particulars for the purpose of pleading will be ordered only if: (1) they are not within the knowledge of the party demanding them; and (2) they are necessary to enable that party to plead.

Gibson v. Gibson, [1963] 2 O.R. 436 (H.C.).

Particulars will not be ordered with respect to allegations which, by their nature, must be within the knowledge of the party seeking particulars.

Madden v. Madden, [1947] O.R. 866 (C.A.).

The principle that particulars will be ordered where the opposite party needs them in order to plead is not appropriate in all cases. In an action for alimony, based on allegations of cruelty, particulars of the acts or cruelty were ordered.

Knowledge of Party from Whom Particulars Sought

Terminal Warehouses Ltd. v. J.H. Lock & Sons Ltd., [1956] O.W.N. 581 (H.C.).

The court refused to order particulars of allegations of negligence for the purpose of trial where the defendant had greater knowledge of the allegedly negligent act than the plaintiff and the plaintiff relied on the doctrine of *res ipsa loquitur*.

Foundry Services Inc. v. Foundry Services (Can.) Ltd., [1953] O.W.N. 1 (Master).

Where a plaintiff files an affidavit stating that it is not in a position to furnish further particulars and that such particulars are within the knowledge of the defendant, particulars will not be ordered before discovery.

Schnurr v. William Hogg Coal Co., [1947] O.W.N. 456 (Master).

Where the party applying for particulars has full knowledge and the opposite party has little or no actual knowledge, a motion for particulars should be refused without prejudice to any further application for purposes of trial.

Particulars for Purpose of Offer to Settle

Wilkinson v. Slater, [1966] 1 O.R. 451 (Master).

Particulars of special damages may be ordered if they are necessary for the defendant to make a payment into court. A payment into court is a pleading.

Finn v. Coleman Packing Co., [1955] O.W.N. 189 (Master).

Particulars for the purpose of payment into court were refused where the defendant did not unequivocally indicate a *bona fide* intention to make a payment in.

Particulars of Damages (See now rule 25.06(9)(b).)

Iaboni v. Hendrich, [1965] 1 O.R. 590 (H.C.).

The court refused to order particulars of a round sum claimed for special damages.

Cook v. Brock, [1942] O.W.N. 197 (Master).

Particulars will not be ordered of a claim for general damages in a fatal accident case.

Motions for Particulars — Examples

Canadian National Railway v. Metropolitan Toronto Convention Centre Corp. (1994), 29 C.P.C. (3d) 248 (Ont. Gen. Div. [Commercial List]).

The court refused to order, for the purpose of pleading, production of documents and particulars relating to the amount of capital tax which had been paid by the plaintiff.

A. (O.) v. A. (G.), (January 18, 1993), Doc. 92-CQ-30367 (Ont. Master).

In an action alleging that the defendant had sexually assaulted the plaintiff over a period of years during the plaintiff's minority the court refused to order particulars of the dates and locations of the alleged incidents.

Peterborough (City) v. Mann (1991), 4 C.P.C. (3d) 81 (Ont. Gen. Div.).

The court ordered particulars of special damages in this conspiracy claim as well as the time frame in which the conspiracy occurred.

Del Zotto v. Cdn. Newspapers Co. (1990), 46 C.P.C. (2d) 179 (Ont. Master).

The court ordered particulars of a rolled-up plea in a defamation case.

Temelini v. Commr. of Royal Cdn. Mounted Police (1985), 6 C.P.C. (2d) 30 (Ont. Dist. Ct.).

The court ordered particulars of the plaintiff's allegations of conspiracy.

Phillips v. Inco Ltd. (1983), 39 C.P.C. 67 (Ont. Master).

In a wrongful dismissal action, particulars of a claim for mental suffering were not required.

H.A. Imports of Can. Ltd. v. General Mills Inc. (1983), 42 O.R. (2d) 645, 36 C.P.C. 296, 74 C.P.R. (2d) 257 (H.C.).

In this conspiracy action, particulars were ordered of the overt acts done in furtherance of the conspiracy, the agreements, their objects and purposes, and the damages resulting.

Teller v. Toronto, [1964] 1 O.R. 202 (Master).

Where a defendant municipality pleaded that it had been prejudiced by the failure of the plaintiff to give a notice of action pursuant to the *Municipal Act*, R.S.O. 1960, c. 249, particulars of such prejudice were ordered.

Bradley v. McLennan Plumbing & Heating Ltd., [1956] O.W.N. 275 (Master).
Particulars of a plea of unavoidable accident will be ordered only where the defendant is relying on circumstances above and beyond his exercise of ordinary care and attention.

L. v. L., [1955] O.W.N. 920 (Master).
The plaintiff in a matrimonial case was required to give particulars of desertion by the defendant alleged in the statement of claim.

Hanley v. Pearson; Fortune v. Hill, [1955] O.W.N. 746 (Master).
Discussion of particulars of basis of claim for damages in fatal accident cases.

Cassina v. Harrison, [1949] O.W.N. 106 (Master).
If facts are established to make the onus section of the *Highway Traffic Act* applicable, the plaintiff need not plead particulars of negligence.

J.K. Smit and Sons of Can. Ltd. v. Fastcut Bits Ltd., [1948] O.W.N. 729, 8 Fox Pat. C. 24 (H.C.).
In a patent infringement action where the plaintiff had been granted an order allowing inspection of the defendants premises and processes, the defendant was successful in an application for particulars.

Bilton v. Hagersville Quarries Ltd., [1948] O.W.N. 600 (H.C.).
The court held that pleading a previous claim and settlement against the defendant was relevant to the course of conduct of the defendant which the court would consider in an action seeking damages and an injunction.

Ostrander v. Blakelock, [1947] O.W.N. 874 (H.C.).
In an action for the recovery of personal property, the plaintiff was ordered to furnish particulars of title as she had pleaded other facts which made it unclear how the plaintiff alleged to have title to the goods.

STRIKING OUT A PLEADING OR OTHER DOCUMENT

25.11 The court may strike out or expunge all or part of a pleading or other document, with or without leave to amend, on the ground that the pleading or other document,
    (a) may prejudice or delay the fair trial of the action;
    (b) is scandalous, frivolous or vexatious; or
    (c) is an abuse of the process of the court.

Cross-Reference: See also cases under rules 21.01(3)(d), 25.06 and 25.07.

Striking Out Pleadings or Documents — Generally

Kwacz v. Kwacz (1985), 49 C.P.C. 82 (Ont. H.C.).
The Rules do not confer on masters or local judges the power to determine questions of law on a motion to strike out a pleading or document.

Unterreiner v. Wilson (1982), 40 O.R. (2d) 197, 24 C.C.L.T. 54, 142 D.L.R. (3d) 588 (H.C.), affirmed (1983), 41 O.R. (2d) 472, 146 D.L.R. (3d) 322 (C.A.).
The allegations of fact in the statement of claim must be taken as true or at least capable of being proved.

U.S. Fidelity and Guar. Co. v. Boland, [1957] O.W.N. 237 (H.C.).
The court should not dictate to a party how he should frame his case but the opposite party is entitled to have the case against him set out in intelligible form and free from irrelevant, prejudicial allegations.

Re Paul (1980), 28 O.R. (2d) 78 (H.C.).

Where in the trial of an issue it is ordered that affidavits are to be treated as pleadings, portions of the affidavits which are irrelevant or may tend to embarrass or delay a fair trial may be struck out.

Slan v. Beyak (1974), 3 O.R. (2d) 295 (Master).

Only one attack on a pleading is generally permitted.

Samis v. T.T.C., [1955] O.W.N. 523 (Master).

A defendant claiming over against a co-defendant under the *Negligence Act* is entitled to attack the pleading of the co-defendant.

Dolgy v. Shelter, [1949] O.W.N. 545, 16 I.L.R. 155 (Master).

An untenable defence may be struck out as embarrassing.

Patterson v. Proprietary Mines Ltd., [1945] O.W.N. 237 (Master).

A motion for particulars is normally a fresh step but where the motion is both to strike out and for particulars, the applicant may secure relief upon the motion to strike out.

Striking Out Pleadings or Documents — Granting Leave to Amend

Lido Industrial Products Ltd. v. Exbar Properties Inc. (1988), 28 O.A.C. 385 (Div. Ct.).

The court will refuse leave to amend only in the clearest of cases.

Watson v. Moore, [1973] 3 O.R. 837 (Co. Ct.).

The court endeavours to achieve substantive justice rather than procedural justice and, where a defective pleading is struck out, leave to amend should be given if the pleading can be improved and no injustice is done thereby.

Steiner v. Lindzon (1976), 14 O.R. (2d) 122, 1 C.P.C. 237 (H.C.).

Where a pleading is embarrassing for want of particularity the court will prefer to give leave to amend rather than strike it out.

Striking Out Pleadings or Documents — Jurisdiction of Master

Panalpina Inc. v. Sharma (1988), 29 C.P.C. (2d) 222 (Ont. Master).

A master has jurisdiction to strike out a plea which is "untenable" or impossible of success, but if its legal validity is arguable, the matter must be left to a judge under rule 21.01(1).

Courlebourne v. Courlebourne (1980), 18 C.P.C. 10 (Ont. Master).

The master has jurisdiction to strike out a pleading in a matrimonial action for non-compliance with a support order.

Jewel Devs. Ltd. v. Wentworth Arms Hotel Ltd. (1978), 6 C.P.C. 35 (Ont. H.C.).

Where a party wishes to attack a pleading both on the grounds that it is frivolous and vexatious and that it is prejudicial or embarrassing, the proper procedure is to bring one motion before a judge.

A.G. Ont. v. Cuttell, [1954] O.W.N. 827 (H.C.).

A master should not generally strike out a defence as being untenable but should refer the matter to the trial judge.

DePalma v. Collier (P.F.) & Son Ltd., [1946] O.W.N. 316, [1946] 3 D.L.R. 453 (Master).

The master has no jurisdiction to determine questions of fact or law but may only criticize the pleading from the standpoint of its intelligibility and compliance with the rules of pleading.

Striking Out Pleadings or Documents — Allegations Regarding Criminal Charges

Edwards v. Law Society of Upper Canada (1995), 40 C.P.C. (3d) 316 (Ont. Gen. Div.).

A motion to strike out affidavits filed in support of a motion for certification of an action as a class proceeding was allowed where the affidavits: (1) contained the reasons for judgment in a quasi-criminal proceeding; and (2) included an exhibit for which privilege was claimed and evidence as to information and belief where the source was counsel who was attempting to shield himself from cross-examination.

Hutchinson v. York Sanitation Co. (1986), 56 O.R. (2d) 778, 11 C.P.C. (2d) 22 (Master).

The court refused to strike out a paragraph concerning the defendant's quasi-criminal conviction for excessive dumping of waste where this was relevant to the claim in nuisance and negligence.

Benson v. Quattrocchi (1986), 8 C.P.C. (2d) 272 (Ont. H.C.).

A party seeking to rely on a conviction under the *Highway Traffic Act* as establishing the opposing party's negligence should plead the violation, conviction and surrounding circumstances.

Taylor v. Baribeau; Baribeau v. Jakob (1985), 51 O.R. (2d) 541, 4 C.P.C. (2d) 52, 35 M.V.R. 79, 21 D.L.R. (4th) 140 (Div. Ct.) (leave to appeal denied October 15, 1985).

A pleading alleging an opposing party's conviction of a related criminal offence, but not the reasons for conviction or findings of fact, is proper.

Jalakas v. Thompson, [1959] O.W.N. 324 (Master).

In an action for assault an allegation in the statement of defence that the defendant has been acquitted on a charge of assault is irrelevant and should be struck out.

Striking Out Pleadings or Documents — Allegations Relevant to Costs

Wood Gundy Inc. v. Financial Trustco Capital Ltd. (1988), 26 C.P.C. (2d) 274 (Ont. Master).

It is improper to plead facts which are relevant only to the issue of costs.

McLaren v. Mahaffy (1986), 10 C.P.C. (2d) 243 (Ont. H.C.).

The court refused to strike out of a statement of defence a request for costs against the plaintiff's solicitor.

Delray Dev. Corp. v. Rexe (1986), 13 C.P.C. (2d) 133 (Ont. Master).

Matters with respect to costs should not be pleaded.

A.I. Macfarlane & Associates Ltd. v. Delong (1986), 55 O.R. (2d) 89, 10 C.P.C. (2d) 25 (H.C.).

Factors relevant only to the issue of costs, such as the plaintiff's object or motive in bringing the proceeding, should not be pleaded.

Royal Bank v. Fogler, Rubinoff (1985), 3 C.P.C. (2d) 248 (Ont. H.C.).

The court permitted an allegation that the plaintiff's motive in bringing the action was to coerce the defendant to apply pressure to a non-party to pay a debt to the plaintiff. While the motive of a party is generally not relevant, it was held to be so in this case regarding the court's exercise of its discretion regarding costs.

Striking Out Pleadings or Documents — Relevance of Allegations

MacKenzie v. Wood Gundy Inc. (1989), 35 C.P.C. (2d) 272 (Ont. H.C.).

In a claim against a stock broker and his brokerage house, a pleading of similar fact evidence surrounding the broker's resignation and the findings of a disciplinary tribunal about the broker was relevant and permitted to stand.

Re Erinco Homes Ltd. (1977), 3 C.P.C. 227 (Ont. Master).

Nothing can be scandalous which is relevant.

Duggan v. Duggan, [1957] O.W.N. 547 (Master).

Any fact relating to the conduct of a party seeking custody of a child is *prima facie* relevant and therefore not scandalous.

Wilson v. Wilson, [1948] O.W.N. 326 (H.C.).

Allegations which are not properly the subject-matter of the action and which are inserted for the purpose of atmosphere should be struck out.

Welch, Anderson & Co. v. Roberts, [1946] O.W.N. 5 (H.C.).

Allegations regarding the plaintiff's motives for bringing the action are irrelevant and will be struck out.

Hammell v. B.A. Oil Co., [1945] O.W.N. 742 (Master).

Where allegations are relevant to the relief to which the plaintiff may be entitled, they will not be struck out.

Toleff v. Pember, [1944] O.W.N. 604 (Master).

In a motor vehicle action the defence that the plaintiff was unlawfully on the highway was struck out as being irrelevant.

Robinson v. Robinson, [1942] O.W.N. 410 (H.C.).

Nothing can be scandalous which is relevant and the test is whether the matter alleged to be scandalous is admissible to show the truth of an allegation material to the relief sought.

Striking Out Pleadings or Documents — Wrongful Dismissal Cases

Lobrutto v. University of St. Jerome's College (1989), 44 C.P.C. (2d) 104 (Ont. H.C.).

A claim for punitive damages in a wrongful dismissal action was struck out with leave to amend where the allegations in the statement of claim did not support that claim. A claim for aggravated damages was supportable on the pleadings, and was permitted to stand.

Desloges v. Radio-Television Representatives Ltd. (1987), 62 O.R. (2d) 633, 23 C.P.C. (2d) 1, 18 C.C.E.L. 1 (H.C.).

The court struck out a claim for damages for loss of reputation in this wrongful dismissal action. The plaintiff did not fall within the exception regarding employees for whom the promotion of their reputation is part of the employment relationship.

Manolson v. Cybermedix Ltd. (1985), 5 C.P.C. (2d) 291 (Ont. Master).

The court refused to strike out an allegation that the plaintiff in this wrongful dismissal case had committed immoral acts on the defendant's premises since that might be cause for dismissal.

Makkar v. Scarborough (1985), 48 C.P.C. 141 (Ont. H.C.).

A claim for damages for mental distress in a wrongful dismissal action must be supported by an allegation of wanton or reckless breach of contract by the defendant. The statement of claim was struck out with leave to deliver a fresh statement of claim.

Wright v. 308489 Ont. Inc. (1984), 45 C.P.C. 45 (Ont. Master).

In this wrongful dismissal action, a claim for damages for loss of reputation was struck out. A claim for damages for mental distress was also struck out, with leave to amend, as the pleading failed to allege that the distress resulted from the inadequate notice or possibly the manner of dismissal, rather than from the dismissal itself, and failed to allege that such damages were in the contemplation of the parties. The master declined to strike out the claim for punitive damages.

Phillips v. Inco. Ltd. (1983), 39 C.P.C. 67 (Ont. Master).

In a wrongful dismissal action, a claim for loss of self-esteem was permissible as being akin to a claim for mental suffering, but claims for loss of reputation and punitive damages were struck out. A claim for reinstatement was also permitted.

Mack v. Dresser Industs. Can. (1982), 38 O.R. (2d) 765 (Master).

The court struck out a claim for punitive damages in a wrongful dismissal case as being frivolous and vexatious.

Damien v. Ont. Racing Comm. (1975), 11 O.R. (2d) 489 (H.C.).

In an action for wrongful dismissal a plaintiff would be entitled to lead evidence showing the employee to be well qualified, dedicated and loyal and therefore allegations of those facts in a pleading is proper.

Striking Out Pleadings or Documents — Examples

Geo. Cluthe Manufacturing Co. v. ZTW Properties Inc. (1995), 39 C.P.C. (3d) 322 (Ont. Div. Ct.), leave to appeal to the Court of Appeal refused 39 C.P.C. (3d) 322n (Ont. C.A.).

Where the plaintiff pleaded an unlawful conspiracy, the court held that the plea added nothing to the pleas of torts of slander of title, intentional interference with contractual relations and abuse of process and could delay the fair trial of the action and ordered the pleas of unlawful conspiracy to be struck.

Welch v. Welch (1994), 27 C.P.C. (3d) 190 (Ont. Gen. Div.).

Where an affidavit contained statements regarding settlement discussion between the parties, the paragraphs were struck out as privileged.

Ontario (Attorney General) v. Dieleman (1993), 14 O.R. (3d) 697 (Gen. Div.).

Where an action for interlocutory and permanent injunctions raised *Charter* issues, the court refused to strike paragraphs from voluminous affidavit material delivered in support of a motion for an interlocutory injunction. The evidence might be relevant, and in *Charter* cases the courts encouraged parties to provide complete and wide-ranging evidence.

Sun Life Trust Co. v. Dewshi (1993), 17 C.P.C. (3d) 217, 99 D.L.R. (4th) 232 (Ont. Gen. Div.).

The court struck out portions of a pleading and affidavit which referred to a settlement.

Sun Life Assurance Co. of Canada v. 401700 Ontario Ltd. (1991), 3 O.R. (3d) 684 (Gen. Div.).

Defined terms in a pleading should not be inflammatory nor create an unnecessarily repetitive or prejudicial flavour. Where fraud is alleged against a defendant, an allegation of conspiracy to injure by fraud adds nothing and will be struck out.

Peaker v. Canada Post Corp. (1989), 68 O.R. (2d) 8 (H.C.), affirmed (November 30, 1990), Doc. CA 104/89 (Ont. C.A.).

The pleadings of a resulting or constructive trust, breach of fiduciary duty and conspiracy, which were not supported by facts or not sufficiently pleaded to allow a meaningful defence, were struck out.

Pindoff Record Sales Ltd. v. CBS Music Products Inc. (1989), 44 C.P.C. (2d) 308, 27 C.P.R. (2d) 380 (Ont. H.C.).

Allegations of conspiracy were struck from a statement of claim as there was no allegation of agreement between the particular defendants to conspire, no precise statement of the object of the conspiracy, no clear and precise account of each defendant's allegedly conspiratorial acts, and no allegation of special damages occasioned by the alleged conspiracy.

Ont. Store Fixtures Inc. v. Mmmuffins Inc. (1989), 70 O.R. (2d) 42, additional reasons 70 O.R. (2d) 42 at 47 (H.C.).

In a claim alleging intentional interference with contractual relations, the plaintiff must plead all of the elements of the tort, including (1) an enforceable contract; (2) knowledge of the plaintiff's contract; (3) an intentional act by the defendant to cause a breach; (4) wrongful interference by the defendant; and (5) resulting damage. Where there is also a claim for intentionally inducing a breach of contract, as well as a claim for breach of contract, a plaintiff must plead facts which point to a specific tortious act which is independent of the breach of contract.

U.F.C.W., Local 617P v. Royal Dressed Meats Inc. (Trustee of) (1989), 37 C.P.C. (2d) 154, 76 C.B.R. (N.S.) 79 (Ont. S.C.).

The court refused to strike out paragraphs in a factum containing excerpts from Hansard. In some circumstances the court may use Hansard as an aid in interpreting a statute.

Edwards v. Shuber (1988), 30 C.P.C. (2d) 290 (Ont. Master).

The court expunged portions of an affidavit containing unsupported hearsay and irrelevant and scandalous matters.

Iwasiw v. Essex Golf & Country Club (1988), 64 O.R. (2d) 49 (H.C.).

Where the plaintiff had given a version of certain events in his own affidavit, affidavits filed by the defence which answered the plaintiff's factual allegations and which gave a conflicting version of events could not be said to be scandalous.

Apple Bee Shirts Ltd. v. Lax (1988), 27 C.P.C. (2d) 226 (Ont. H.C.).

Discussion of the elements required to be pleaded in a statement of claim for damages for conspiracy. It is insufficient to allege that the required particulars are solely within the defendant's knowledge.

Spataro v. Handler (1988), 26 C.P.C. (2d) 28 (Ont. Dist. Ct.).

The deliberations, but not the decision, of the Discipline Committee of the Royal College of Dental Surgeons are secret. The decision may be referred to in a pleading.

Hartley v. J.B. Food Industries Inc. (1986), 10 C.P.C. (2d) 57 (Ont. H.C.).

Correspondence written in pursuit of an early settlement is privileged and should not be pleaded.

Curry v. Advocate Gen. Ins. Co. of Can. (1986), 9 C.P.C. (2d) 247 (Ont. Master).

The court struck out allegations that the defendant insurer had a practice of denying valid claims, engaged in high-handed conduct, and was in a stronger position than the plaintiff. The first allegation was irrelevant and the latter two were not supported by particulars.

J.R. Klady Agencies (1971) Ltd. v. Noma Inc. (1986), 9 C.P.C. (2d) 29 (Ont. H.C.).

A plaintiff suing for wrongful termination of a sales agency agreement is not subject to the constraints applicable to pleading in wrongful dismissal actions. It was permitted to plead its good performance of the contract but was not permitted to claim damage to its reputation.

Wilson v. Lind (1985), 3 C.P.C. (2d) 113, 35 C.C.L.T. 95 (Ont. H.C.).

The court struck out an allegation in a motor vehicle action that the defendant habitually operated his vehicle while impaired.

Bonner v. Day, 49 O.R. (2d) 268, 47 C.P.C. 278, [1985] I.L.R. 1-1865 (H.C.).

It is permissible to plead that the plaintiff is not entitled to prejudgment interest because of delay in pursuing the claim. It is embarrassing to allege that the plaintiff has failed to disclose medical reports.

Gen. Security Ins. Co. of Can. v. Vasilaros (1984), 46 C.P.C. 247 (Ont. Master).

The court struck out paragraphs which raised an aura of suspicion that non-parties related to the defendant had committed arson. Such allegations should not be made indirectly.

Marshall v. Cann, 43 C.P.C. 200, 5 C.C.L.I. 287, [1984] I.L.R. 1-1778 (Ont. H.C.).

Where the plaintiff in a motor vehicle action is not a nominal plaintiff, it is improper to plead an "inter-company settlement chart" between the insurers of the parties.

Ward v. Bosveld (1983), 40 C.P.C. 24 (Ont. H.C.).

Allegations of conspiracy were struck out where they were simply an attempt to "dress up" what was properly the subject-matter of a libel claim which was statute-barred.

Eves Lumber Ltd. v. Linton (1982), 30 C.P.C. 194, 139 D.L.R. (3d) 155 (Ont. H.C.).

In an action to set aside a fraudulent conveyance, a paragraph in the statement of claim seeking a declaration that the property was a family asset and should be partitioned and sold was struck out as embarrassing since only a spouse can assert such a claim.

Phillips v. Bongard Leslie & Co. (1982), 37 O.R. (2d) 204, (*sub nom. Re Fyffe; Phillips v. Bongard Leslie & Co.*), 28 C.P.C. 120, 11 E.T.R. 184, affirmed 28 C.P.C. 120n, 11 E.T.R. 184n (H.C.).

In an action by an executor who had obtained probate, pleadings that the deceased lacked testamentary capacity and that the will was a nullity and the plaintiff lacked status to bring the action were struck out.

Guar. Trust Co. of Can. v. Public Trustee (1978), 20 O.R. (2d) 247, 87 D.L.R. (3d) 417 (H.C.).

Discussion of allegations which may be made in support of a claim for punitive damages.

Woroniuk v. Woroniuk (1977), 17 O.R. (2d) 460, 4 C.P.C. 143 (Master).

Maintenance and champerty are not defences to an action and such pleas will be struck out.

French v. Law Soc. of Upper Can. (1975), 9 O.R. (2d) 473, 61 D.L.R. (3d) 28 (C.A.).

An action by a former solicitor and members of his family against the Law Society for negligence in the conduct of disciplinary proceedings was struck out as being frivolous and vexatious.

Everdale Place v. Rimmer (1975), 8 O.R. (2d) 641 (H.C.).

Allegations of illegality on the part of the plaintiff which could have no effect on the outcome of the action were struck out as embarrassing.

Bache & Co. Can. Ltd. v. Hirschler (1974), 4 O.R. (2d) 323 (Master).

The court refused to strike out part of an affidavit as scandalous where the party attacking the document had cross-examined on that point.

Hunter v. Marshall, [1969] 2 O.R. 589 (C.A.).

In an action where the Minister of Transport was conducting a defence under the *Motor Vehicle Accident Claims Act*, S.O. 1961-62, c. 84, all references to the Minister in the pleadings were struck out.

Morgan v. Tumosa, [1963] 1 O.R. 550 (Master).

An allegation that the defendant has committed a crime, which allegation is not necessary to the cause of action, is scandalous and should be struck out.

Ensor v. Ensor, [1961] O.W.N. 87 (H.C.).

The court struck out a scandalous portion of a report of the Official Guardian.

Elder v. Kingston, [1953] O.W.N. 409 (C.A.).

An allegation that the plaintiff had been indemnified by his insurer was struck out.

Seigel v. Seigel, [1947] O.W.N. 827 (H.C.).

A form of pleading using "and/or" which makes its meaning unclear will be struck out.

Barclay v. Taylor, [1946] O.W.N. 737 (Master).
A pleading in the statement of claim which anticipated a defence was struck out.

RULE 26   AMENDMENT OF PLEADINGS

Highlights

Rule 26 regulates when and how amendments are to be made and the service of amended pleadings. (See also rule 27.07 regarding amendments asserting a counter-claim and rule 28.03 regarding amendments asserting a crossclaim. Amendments involving a change to parties are also regulated by rules 5.04 and 9.03.)

Most importantly (in furtherance of the liberal policies stated in rules 1.04 and 2.01), rule 26.01 provides that the court *shall* grant leave to amend a pleading, at any stage of the action, on such terms as are just, unless prejudice would result that could not be compensated for by costs or an adjournment.

The use of mandatory language in the Rule has been held to reduce the court's former discretion to refuse an amendment (see *Nat. Gypsum Co. v. Lanzino* (1985), 50 C.P.C. 88 (Ont. H.C.) and *Barker v. Furlotte* (1985), 12 O.A.C. 76 (Div. Ct.)), but some discretion beyond that specified in the Rule may still survive (see *Motruk v. Jeannot* (1987), 16 C.P.C. (2d) 160 (Ont. H.C.)). Typically leave is now granted unless prejudice would result that could not be compensated for by costs or an adjournment (*e.g.* where a limitation period has intervened) or where the amendment involves withdrawal of an admission in which case rule 51.05 and the related common law tests govern: *Antipas v. Coroneos* (1988), 26 C.P.C. (2d) 63, 29 C.C.L.I. 161 (Ont. H.C.).

Rule 48.04 (consequences of setting down or consent) is no bar to an amendment under rule 26.01: *Soulos v. Korkontzilas* (1990), 74 O.R. (2d) 766 (H.C.), leave to appeal refused (1990), 1 O.R. (3d) 625n (Gen. Div.); *Vladetic v. Silvestri* (1990), 42 C.P.C. (2d) 254 (Ont. H.C.).

Former Rules: Rules 129-137, 188, 788(2).

GENERAL POWER OF COURT

26.01 On motion at any stage of an action the court shall grant leave to amend a pleading on such terms as are just, unless prejudice would result that could not be compensated for by costs or an adjournment.

Cross-Reference: See also rule 26.06 re amendments at trial and rule 51.05 re withdrawing admissions.

Amendment of Pleadings — General Principles

Vladetic v. Silvestri (1990), 42 C.P.C. (2d) 254 (Ont. H.C.).

Rule 26.01, when read with rule 1.04 and rule 2.01, supersedes rule 48.04. Accordingly, the plaintiff was permitted to amend to increase the damages claimed after setting the action down for trial where the defendant failed to establish prejudice.

Soulos v. Korkontzilas (1990), 74 O.R. (2d) 766, 45 C.P.C. (2d) 59 (H.C.), leave to appeal refused 1 O.R. (3d) 625n (Gen. Div.).

Rule 26.01 supersedes rule 48.04, and therefore a plaintiff may withdraw any part of a claim before or at trial, provided no prejudice results to the defendant. Withdrawal of a claim for damages is not withdrawal of an admission and therefore leave is not required.

Antipas v. Coroneos (1988), 26 C.P.C. (2d) 63, 29 C.C.L.I. 161 (Ont. H.C.).

Rule 51.05 supersedes rule 26.01 where the effect of the proposed amendment is to withdraw an admission.

Vaiman v. Yates (1987), 60 O.R. (2d) 696, 20 C.P.C. (2d) 33, 41 D.L.R. (4th) 186 (H.C.), leave to appeal to Ont. Div. Ct. refused 63 O.R. (2d) 211, 24 C.P.C. (2d) 135, 47 D.L.R. (4th) 359.

On a motion to amend pleadings, a master has jurisdiction to determine whether the proposed amendments are tenable at law.

Motruk v. Jeannot (1987), 16 C.P.C. (2d) 160 (Ont. H.C.).

Rule 26.01 requires that leave to amend be given in most cases, however such leave is still discretionary.

A.H.A. Automotive Technologies Corp. v. 589348 Ont. Ltd. (1985), 3 C.P.C. (2d) 9 (Ont. Master).

A party opposing an amendment is not entitled to examine the party seeking the amendment under rule 39.03 to test the truth of the allegations in the proposed amendment.

Smith v. Simmons (1985), 49 C.P.C. 28 (Ont. Master).

On a motion for leave to amend, the court should not enter into the merits of the action; however, it should determine whether or not there is a *prima facie* case set forth in the proposed amendment and where there is not, the amendment should be refused.

Barker v. Furlotte (1985), 12 O.A.C. 76 (Div. Ct.).

Rule 26.01 makes it mandatory for the court to grant leave to amend, unless prejudice would result, and the burden of showing prejudice lies with the party opposing amendment.

Nat. Gypsum Co. v. Lanzino (1985), 50 C.P.C. 88 (Ont. H.C.) (leave to appeal to Ont. Div. Ct. granted April 25, 1985; the appeal was subsequently abandoned).

The court's former discretion to refuse an amendment has been reduced by the mandatory language of rule 26.01. The court permitted a fundamental amendment to the statement of defence on the eve of trial but ordered costs of the motion and appeal and all costs thrown away to be paid by the defendant on a solicitor and client basis within fifteen days after assessment, failing which the defence would be struck out.

Robertson v. Joyce, [1948] O.R. 696 (C.A.).

An amendment to the pleadings should be allowed, no matter how careless the omission or how late the application, if it can be made without causing injustice to the other party.

Firestone v. Firestone (1975), 6 O.R. (2d) 714, 20 R.F.L. 315 (H.C.).

An amendment which places a party at a disadvantage which cannot be cured by costs or which otherwise works an injustice will not be allowed.

Neogleous v. Toffolon (No. 2) (1977), 17 O.R. (2d) 453, 4 C.P.C. 192 (H.C.).

An amendment should not be refused merely because it is inconsistent with the evidence of the party on discovery.

Overholt v. Memorial Gardens Assn. Ltd., [1958] O.W.N. 421 (H.C.).

A motion for an amendment must be supported by material indicating the nature of the proposed amendment.

George W. Crothers Ltd. v. Harvey B. White Bldrs. Ltd., [1960] O.W.N. 313 (Master).

After the issuance of an originating process, the style of cause may be amended only with leave of the court.

Union Elec. Supply Co. v. Joice Sweanor Elec. Ltd. (1974), 5 O.R. (2d) 457 (C.A.).

A master trying a mechanics' lien action may allow amendments to the pleadings on matters of substance as well as form. Once a master begins the trial he becomes exclusively seized of the matter.

Muldoon v. Simcoe Public Utilities Comm., [1945] O.W.N. 863 (Master).

Failure to make an amendment within the time limited by an order is an irregularity which can be relieved against.

Amendment of Pleadings — To Assert New Cause of Action

Gangnon v. Kohn Estate (1987), 24 C.P.C. (2d) 45, 26 O.A.C. 317 (Div. Ct.).

An amendment to raise an alternate ground for relief is not treated as a withdrawal of an admission that the plaintiff had no facts to support the alternate ground which requires leave under rule 51.05.

Vaiman v. Yates (1987), 60 O.R. (2d) 696, 20 C.P.C. (2d) 33, 41 D.L.R. (4th) 186 (H.C.), leave to appeal to Ont. Div. Ct. refused 63 O.R. (2d) 211, 24 C.P.C. (2d) 135, 47 D.L.R. (4th) 359.

On a motion to amend a statement of claim, the master ought to consider whether the amendment discloses a tenable cause of action and may refuse an amendment which does not.

Re Roebuck and Syndicated Shopping Centres Inc. (1985), 52 O.R. (2d) 265, 38 R.P.R. 160 (H.C.).

Leave was granted to amend a notice of application to claim additional relief where no prejudice would result that could not be compensated by costs and an adjournment.

Jennings v. Cummings Signs of Can. Ltd. (1983), 35 C.P.C. 83 (Ont. Master).

The court refused to permit an amendment to advance a new claim where the new claim did not disclose a reasonable cause of action.

Denton v. Jones (No. 2) (1976), 14 O.R. (2d) 382, 3 C.P.C. 137, 73 D.L.R. (3d) 636 (H.C.).

An amendment to plead a new cause of action was permitted where all facts supporting the new claim had been pleaded.

McIntyre v. Arena Dev. Ltd., [1961] O.W.N. 164 (Master).

An amendment to an originating process setting up a new cause of action will be allowed if such cause asserted by separate action would be consolidated with the existing action, and refused if such cause so asserted would not be consolidated with the existing action.

Empire-Universal Films Ltd. v. Rank, [1948] O.W.N. 704 (Master).

When service out of the jurisdiction has been made, leave should not be granted to amend so as to set up a new cause of action for which service out of the jurisdiction would not have been proper.

Amendment of Pleadings — To Withdraw Admission (See cases under rule 51.05.)

Amendment of Pleadings — After Expiry of Limitation Period (See cases under rule 5.04 re adding parties after expiry of limitation period.)

Nieuwesteeg v. Digenova (1991), 7 O.R. (3d) 506, 37 M.V.R. (2d) 127 (Gen. Div.).

When "special circumstances" exist, pleadings can be amended to add a new claim after the expiration of the limitation period. The amendments related to the same factual situation as the original pleadings and the applicant was not attempting to assert a new cause of action.

Lee v. Ontario (Minister of Transportation & Communications) (1990), 72 O.R. (2d) 343 (H.C.).

Where the plaintiff brought an action for negligence after the limitation period, he was permitted leave to amend to plead in nuisance. It was unclear whether nuisance was statute-barred, and the language of rule 26.01 was operative and mandatory, compelling the court to permit the amendment.

Willis v. Ont. Hydro (1988), 29 C.P.C. (2d) 71 (Ont. Dist. Ct.).

The court refused to permit an amendment to a statement of defence to plead *novus actus* alleging negligent medical care following an accident after expiry of the limitation periods applicable to the hospital and physician, since this would cause irreparable prejudice to the plaintiff.

Bharadwaj v. Advocate Gen. Ins. Co. of Can. (1987), 20 C.P.C. (2d) 208 (Ont. Dist. Ct.).

A plaintiff was not permitted to amend a statement of claim to include a claim for no-fault benefits outside the one-year limitation period prescribed by the *Insurance Act.* The defendant would be highly prejudiced by such an amendment, as it had been deprived of all effective opportunity to investigate the plaintiff's physical condition in a timely fashion.

Cos v. West Gwillimbury (Twp.) (1986), 56 O.R. (2d) 659 (Dist. Ct.).

Where a claim for property damage was commenced within the applicable limitation period, the plaintiff was permitted to add a claim for personal injuries and related *Family Law Act* claims.

Stoicevski v. Casement (1983), 43 O.R. (2d) 436, 43 C.P.C. 178 (C.A.).

In the circumstances of this case the court refused the defendant leave to plead the negligence of non-party doctors, as the plaintiff was entitled to assume that such a plea would be made in sufficient time to allow him to add the doctors before the applicable limitation period expired.

Casey v. Halton Bd. of Educ. (1981), 33 O.R. (2d) 71, 23 C.P.C. 24, 123 D.L.R. (3d) 402 (H.C.).

An amendment to the statement of claim was permitted to advance further claims under Part V of the *Family Law Reform Act* after the expiry of two limitation periods in this case.

Beattie v. Munro (1981), 19 C.P.C. 303 (Ont. Co. Ct.).

In a subrogated action by OHIP, the court permitted an amendment to advance a claim for general damages after a limitation period had expired.

Denton v. Jones (No. 2) (1976), 14 O.R. (2d) 382, 3 C.P.C. 137, 73 D.L.R. (3d) 636 (H.C.).

Leave to amend a pleading to allege what may have amounted to a new cause of action was given notwithstanding the expiration of a limitation period where the cause of action arose out of the same facts and there was no prejudice to the defendant except that which was inevitable from what might be a successful plea.

Royal v. Metro. Toronto (1975), 9 O.R. (2d) 522 (H.C.).

An amendment to claim damages for negligence in addition to a claim for assault was permitted notwithstanding the expiry of the limitation period where both claims arose out of the same facts and the defendant was not prejudiced.

Weston v. Copplestone (1974), 5 O.R. (2d) 724 (H.C.).

An amendment alleging mechanical unfitness of a motor vehicle was permitted after the expiry of a limitation period but an amendment alleging breach of statutory duty was refused since it amounted to a new cause of action.

Thorne v. MacGregor, [1973] 3 O.R. 54, 35 D.L.R. (3d) 687 (H.C.).

Where a claim has been made for personal injuries caused by negligence, a further claim for related property damage may be made notwithstanding the expiry of a limitation period.

Dunwoodco Ltd. v. Stermac (1970), 5 O.R. (2d) 454 (Master).

An amendment to a statement of claim setting up a new cause of action was allowed, provided that for purposes of limitation periods the action on the new claim was deemed to be commenced at the date of the amendment.

Cahoon v. Franks, [1967] S.C.R. 455, 60 W.W.R. 684, 63 D.L.R. (2d) 274.

Where a plaintiff claimed for property damage suffered in an automobile accident, a further claim for personal injuries was permitted notwithstanding the expiry of the limitation period.

Pitt v. Bank of N.S., [1956] O.W.N. 872 (Master).

Where a defendant municipality had the benefit of a special limitation period and such period had expired, an application by the plaintiff to amend his statement of claim to raise a new cause of action was refused as against the defendant municipality but granted as against the defendant bank.

Gen. Bldg. Materials v. Roy, [1956] O.W.N. 221 (Master).

An amendment setting up a defence tending to show that the proceeding was a nullity was allowed notwithstanding the expiration of the limitation period.

Long v. Mines, [1948] O.W.N. 328 (Master).

An amendment extending the claim but not amounting to the addition of new causes of action was allowed after the expiry of the limitation period.

Slattery v. Ottawa Elec. Ry. Co., [1946] O.W.N. 437 (H.C.).

A motion to amend the date of the alleged accident was refused where serious prejudice would have resulted to the defendant which had destroyed its records regarding the new date.

Amendment of Pleadings — Miscellaneous

Hales Contracting Inc. v. Towland-Hewitson Construction Ltd. (1996), 7 W.D.C.P. (2d) 151 (Ont. Gen. Div.), leave to appeal granted 7 W.D.C.P. (2d) 187.

The court granted the plaintiff's motion brought on the eve of trial to add a claim for punitive and exemplary damages but ordered the plaintiff to pay certain consequential costs.

Haikola v. Arasenau (January 19, 1996), Doc. CA C15469 (Ont. C.A.).

The Court of Appeal reversed an order refusing an amendment two weeks before trial to increase the amount claimed where the defendant failed to demonstrate prejudice.

Maxwell v. MLG Ventures Ltd. (1995), 40 C.P.C. (3d) 304 (Ont. Gen. Div.).

The plaintiff in a certified class action was not permitted to amend the statement of claim where the proposed amendments fundamentally changed the nature of the action originally certified. Other amendments which did not change the nature of the action were allowed.

Burton v. Cochrane (1995), 29 C.C.L.I. (2d) 140, 85 O.A.C. 391 (Div. Ct.).

Where the plaintiff filed an affidavit in support of its motion to amend its statement of claim, the court held that the defendants were entitled to cross-examine on the affidavit for the purpose of invoking a limitation period.

Transamerica Life Insurance Co. of Canada v. Canada Life Assurance Co. (1995), 25 O.R. (3d) 106, 41 C.P.C. (3d) 75 (Gen. Div.) (motion for leave to appeal to Div. Ct. filed).

Where the defendants failed to establish that they would suffer prejudice, the court allowed the plaintiff to file a fresh statement of claim based on information it had obtained during the examination for discovery of the defendants.

Gagro v. Morrison (1995), 40 C.P.C. (3d) 331 (Ont. Gen. Div.).

The court refused to allow an amendment increasing the amount claimed where the defendant had earlier agreed to admit liability on the basis that the plaintiff's claim was reduced to the insurance policy limits.

Walker v. York Finch General Hospital (1995), 23 O.R. (3d) 248 (Gen. Div.).

The court permitted the statement of claim to be amended notwithstanding the death of the plaintiff.

Kings Gate Development Inc. v. Colangelo (1994), 17 O.R. (3d) 841, 23 C.P.C. (3d) 137, 70 O.A.C. 140 (C.A.).

Rule 26.01 requires that leave be granted unless there is shown to be non-compensable prejudice. But because the rule can be used unreasonably and cause unfairness to the opposing party, this should be dealt with by the imposition of terms as to costs to discourage late amendments. In granting the defendant leave to amend on the eve of trial the court ordered that the defendants pay the plaintiff's costs of the motion, the fresh pleadings, production and discovery on a solicitor and client scale, in any event of the cause and before the amendment was to be permitted, such costs being fixed at $10,000.

Regin Properties Ltd. v. Logics Inc. (1994), 33 C.P.C. (3d) 86 (Ont. Master).

The court refused an untenable amendment to a pleading.

Keneber Inc. v. Midland (Town) (1993), 16 O.R. (3d) 753 (Gen. Div.).

The court refused to permit an amendment to a defence where the proposed plea of failure to mitigate was untenable.

Milosevic (Litigation Guardian of) v. Etheridge (1991), 3 C.P.C. (2d) 69 (Ont. Gen. Div.).

The court refused to grant an amendment on the eve of trial putting in issue whether the defendant was the owner of the subject motor vehicle in a personal injury case. The proposed amendment would cause prejudice.

424317 Ont. Ltd. v. Silber (1989), 70 O.R. (2d) 59 (H.C.).

The court refused to grant leave to amend a statement of claim, as it would amount to a collateral attack on a judgment which was under appeal. The issue was also hypothetical at this point, and this procedure would result in a multiplicity of legal proceedings.

Lido Industrial Products Ltd. v. Exbar Properties Inc. (1988), 28 O.A.C. 385 (Div. Ct.).

Even though a defendant's pleading was totally unsupported by allegations of fact and had been struck out, leave to amend should be granted since leave should only be refused in the clearest of cases.

Bentham v. Rothbart (1988), 26 C.P.C. (2d) 109 (Ont. Master).

A defendant was not permitted to add a counterclaim alleging abuse of process where the defendant had failed to establish evidence of a definite act or threat in furtherance of a collateral or improper purpose.

Motruk v. Jeannot (1987), 16 C.P.C. (2d) 160 (Ont. H.C.).

The plaintiff was granted leave to amend the statement of claim so as to connect a claim for slander and a claim for libel. Although the claims had been severed earlier, if the new allegations were true, they would comprise a single cause of action against both defendants.

385925 Ont. Ltd. v. Amer. Life Ins. (1984), 48 O.R. (2d) 142, 45 C.P.C. 288 (Master), affirmed (1985), 51 O.R. (2d) 382, 3 C.P.C. (2d) 137 (H.C.).

A proposed amendment to allege murder must be scrutinized with particular care and be in plain, comprehensible and unambiguous language. In this case, the motion was dismissed where the allegation gave no particulars and was without any merit, and the action was about to be pre-tried.

Simpson v. Vanderheiden; Simpson v. Phoenix Assur. Co. of Can. (1985), 49 O.R. (2d) 347, 48
  C.P.C. 7 (H.C.).

The defendant was given leave to plead that the action was statute-barred.

Josefsberg v. Wilson (1984), 45 C.P.C. 260 (Ont. H.C.).

In this motor vehicle action, an amendment was permitted to advance a claim for punitive
damages against the defendant employee of the defendant driver.

Cote v. Rooney (1982), 29 C.P.C. 261, 137 D.L.R. (3d) 371 (Ont. H.C.).

An amendment was granted in this personal injury action to allege an admission of liability by
the defendants in the course of disposing of the property damage claim notwithstanding a claim
of privilege. The nature of the communication and its admissibility at trial was a matter for the
trial judge.

Bennett v. Gage Educ. Publishing Ltd. (1980), 16 C.P.C. 241 (Ont. Master).

In a libel action, a proposed amendment to the statement of defence was refused where evidence
to prove the proposed plea would be inadmissible.

WHEN AMENDMENTS MAY BE MADE

26.02 A party may amend the party's pleading,

**(a) without leave, before the close of pleadings, if the amendment does
not include or necessitate the addition, deletion or substitution of a party
to the action;**

**(b) on filing the consent of all parties and, where a person is to be added
or substituted as a party, the person's consent; or**

(c) with leave of the court.

HOW AMENDMENTS MADE

**26.03(1) An amendment to a pleading shall be made on the face of the
copy filed in the court office, except that where the amendment is so extensive
as to make the amended pleading difficult or inconvenient to read the party
shall file a fresh copy of the original pleading as amended, bearing the date
of the original pleading and the title of the pleading preceded by the word
"amended".**

**(2) An amendment to a pleading shall be underlined so as to distinguish
the amended wording from the original, and the registrar shall note on the
amended pleading the date on which, and the authority by which, the amendment was made.**

**(3) Where a pleading has been amended more than once each subse-
quent amendment shall be underlined with an additional line for each occasion.**

North York Branson Hospital v. Union Carbide Canada Ltd. (1994), 31 C.P.C. (3d) 242 (Ont.
  Gen. Div.).

The court held that service of an amended pleading prior to the amendment being filed with the
court was a curable irregularity and not a sufficient reason to strike out the pleading.

SERVICE OF AMENDED PLEADING

Service on Every Party to Action and Related Actions

**26.04(1) An amended pleading shall be served forthwith on every per-
son who is, at the time of service, a party to the main action or to a counter-**

claim, crossclaim or third party claim in the main action, unless the court orders otherwise.

(2) Proof of service of an amended pleading other than an originating process shall be filed forthwith after it is served.

Amended Originating Process

(3) Where an amended pleading is an originating process,

(a) it need not be served personally on a party who was served with the original pleading and responded to it; and

(b) it shall be served personally or by an alternative to personal service under rule 16.03 on an opposite party who has not responded to the original pleading, whether or not the party has been noted in default.

RESPONDING TO AN AMENDED PLEADING

26.05(1) A party shall respond to an amended pleading within the time remaining for responding to the original pleading, or within ten days after service of the amended pleading, whichever is the longer period, unless the court orders otherwise.

(2) A party who has responded to a pleading that is subsequently amended and does not respond to the amended pleading within the prescribed time shall be deemed to rely on the party's original pleading in answer to the amended pleading.

AMENDMENT AT TRIAL

26.06 Where a pleading is amended at the trial, and the amendment is made on the face of the record, an order need not be taken out and the pleading as amended need not be filed or served unless the court orders otherwise.

Cross-Reference: See also cases under rule 26.01.

Amendment at or after Trial — To Increase Relief Claimed

Whiten v. Pilot Insurance Co. (1996), 7 W.D.C.P. (2d) 105 (Ont. Gen. Div.).

The court permitted an amendment to increase the amount claimed to equal a $1 million punitive damage award made by the jury.

Arslanovic v. Paterson (1993), 23 C.P.C. (3d) 190 (Ont. Gen. Div.).

The court granted the plaintiff's motion following trial to increase its claim for damages to conform with a jury's assessment of damages.

Hill v. Church of Scientology of Toronto (1992), 7 O.R. (3d) 489 (Gen. Div.).

Where no prejudice exists, a trial judge has no overriding discretion based on his or her view of the reasonableness of the amounts awarded by the jury to refuse to grant leave to amend the statement of claim.

Papadakis v. Camilleri (1989), 33 C.P.C. (2d) 291 (Ont. Dist. Ct.).

The court granted an amendment increasing the amount claimed to equal the amount awarded by the jury where the defendant could not demonstrate prejudice. Vague suggestions about what the defendant might have done differently do not establish prejudice.

Loucks v. Peterson (1988), 67 O.R. (2d) 325, 31 C.P.C. (2d) 139 (Ont. Dist. Ct.).

The court refused an amendment to increase the amount claimed to conform with the jury's assessment of damages because the jury's award was perverse.

Nevers v. T.T.C. (1987), 16 C.P.C. (2d) 259 (Ont. Dist. Ct.).

The court refused to increase the amount claimed from $25,000 to $50,000, the amount of the jury award. Such an amendment would deprive the defendant of the opportunity to transfer the action to the Supreme Court, to obtain a defence medical examination and to obtain further discovery, all of which would have been available if the amendment had been sought before trial. Further, the jury award was perverse.

370866 Ont. Ltd. v. Chizy (1987), 57 O.R. (2d) 587, 34 D.L.R. (4th) 404 (H.C.).

The court permitted an amendment at the opening of trial increasing the damages claimed tenfold, even though the claim was issued over seven years previously, where the defendant could show no prejudice.

Murray-Jensen Mfg. Ltd. v. Triangle Conduit & Cable (1968) Ltd. (1984), 46 C.P.C. 285 (Ont. H.C.).

The court amended a judgment directing a reference to limit recovery to the amount claimed in the statement of claim where the amount found due on the reference was in excess of that amount and the defendants may have acted differently if the amount claimed had been greater.

Edwards v. Harris-Intertype (Can.) Ltd. (1983), 40 O.R. (2d) 558 (H.C.).

The court permitted an amendment at trial to claim loss of capital. A claim for loss of income had been pleaded earlier.

Centennial Centre of Science and Technology v. VS Services Ltd. (1982), 40 O.R. (2d) 253, 31 C.P.C. 97 (H.C.).

An amendment at trial was permitted to advance a claim for punitive damages in this contract action where the defendant had for some time been aware of the plaintiff's intention to move, and was neither surprised nor prejudiced.

Cardwell v. Devley Mfg. Ltd. (1977), 17 O.R. (2d) 183 (C.A.).

A plaintiff was permitted to increase the amount claimed to the amount awarded at trial for breach of contract where the various items of damages were thoroughly explored at trial.

Lane v. Dominion Stores Ltd. (1977), 13 O.R. (2d) 369 (H.C.).

In a County Court action where the plaintiff obtains an amendment increasing the claim to an amount in excess of that court's monetary jurisdiction, the defendant is entitled to transfer the action to the Supreme Court notwithstanding that the original claim was also in excess of County Court jurisdiction.

Lalonde v. Kahkonen, [1972] 1 O.R. 91, 22 D.L.R. (3d) 279 (C.A.).

Where the defendant had prepared his case on the basis that he would not contest the quantum of damage claimed, the court found that an amendment at trial substantially increasing the amount claimed was seriously prejudicial to the defendant.

Anderson v. Jansen and Rochdale Credit Union Ltd., [1970] 2 O.R. 641 (C.A.).

A judge sitting without a jury should permit an amendment increasing the amount claimed to the amount actually assessed only in rare circumstances, if at all.

Dojczman v. Ste. Marie, [1969] 2 O.R. 745, 6 D.L.R. (3d) 649 (C.A.).

The Court of Appeal refused to allow an amendment increasing the amount claimed for special damages to the amount awarded at trial.

Van Den Heuvel v. Marchand, [1968] 2 O.R. 185 (H.C.).

The court refused to permit an amendment increasing the amount claimed to the amount awarded by the jury where there was good reason to believe the defence would have been conducted more vigorously if more had been claimed in the pleadings.

Quigley v. Young, [1966] 1 O.R. 407, 54 D.L.R. (2d) 27 (C.A.).

Where the amount claimed in a County Court action is within the monetary jurisdiction of that court and the jury awards damages in excess of the amount claimed, the judge should not allow an amendment increasing the amount claimed to an amount greater than the court's monetary jurisdiction.

Martin v. T.T.C., [1948] O.W.N. 628, 62 C.R.T.C. 264, reversed on other grounds [1948] O.W.N. 764 (C.A.).

The court refused to allow an amendment increasing the amount claimed where there was nothing more than the finding of the jury to justify the amendment.

Hart v. Geddes, [1948] O.W.N. 466 (H.C.).

The court allowed a plaintiff by counterclaim to amend the amount of damages claimed to a greater amount awarded by the jury.

Amendment at or after Trial - Other Examples

Myers v. Metropolitan Toronto (Municipality) Police Force (1995), 37 C.P.C. (3d) 349, 125 D.L.R. (4th) 184, 84 O.A.C. 232 (Div. Ct.).

Where the trial judge allowed the plaintiff to amend its pleadings but ordered the plaintiff to pay the costs of the wasted trial day on a solicitor/client basis within 15 days, the court held that the trial judge acted reasonably in not taking into account the plaintiff's claim of impecuniosity and would, generally, only interfere with a trial judge's discretion to award costs in limited circumstances.

National Trust Co. v. Maxwell (1989), 34 C.P.C. (2d) 211, 3 R.P.R. (2d) 263 (Ont. H.C.).

On a motion for summary judgment in an action on a mortgage, the defendant/guarantor claimed that the proceedings were premature as there had been no proper notice of default under the mortgage. In the circumstances, it was held that the guarantor would not be prejudiced by an amendment to the statement of claim at the hearing alleging that the service of the notice of sale constituted notice of default and a proper demand for payment.

Robinson v. Robinson (1989), 70 O.R. (2d) 249, 22 R.F.L. (3d) 10 (H.C.).

The defendant's motion to amend the statement of defence after all evidence had been adduced at trial was dismissed. The proposed amendment would fundamentally alter the issues and would result in palpable prejudice to the plaintiff that was not compensable in costs.

Lion Oil Trading Co. v. Shell Can. Ltd. (1987), 63 O.R. (2d) 185 (H.C.).

A defendant's motion to amend pleadings after delivery of oral judgment but before judgment was entered was denied, with solicitor and client costs, where no special circumstances were established and prejudice would result.

Gayle v. Miller (1986), 8 C.P.C. (2d) 301 (Ont. Dist. Ct.), affirmed Ont. Div. Ct., Doc. 304/86, March 10, 1987.

Where the defendants in this motor vehicle action alleged the plaintiffs' driver was at fault but did not assert a claim for contribution and indemnity either by way of a third party claim or in the statement of defence and where the jury found the defendants and the plaintiffs' driver each 50 per cent at fault, the court awarded judgment against the defendants for 100 per cent of the assessed damages and refused to permit the defendants to amend their pleadings to assert a claim for contribution and indemnity notwithstanding that the plaintiffs' driver was a party to the action in the sense she was a member of the class asserting a claim under s. 60 of the *Family Law Reform Act*.

Burns v. Pocklington (1985), 5 C.P.C. (2d) 18 (Ont. C.A.).

The court refused an amendment to assert a claim for quantum meruit after six days of a jury trial where the amendment was not being sought in good faith and the prejudice to the defendant was not compensable in costs.

Sperry Inc. v. C.I.B.C. (1985), 50 O.R. (2d) 267, 55 C.B.R. (N.S.) 68, 4 P.P.S.A.C. 314, 17
    D.L.R. (4th) 236, 8 O.A.C. 79 (C.A.).

An amendment was permitted on appeal to claim the cost of maintaining a letter of credit which the plaintiff had been required by the master to maintain as security pending the disposition of the action. There was no prejudice to the defendant that could not be compensated in costs.

Allan v. New Mount Sinai Hosp. (1981), 33 O.R. (2d) 603 (C.A.).

Where in an action for medical malpractice, the plaintiff did not specifically allege battery in his statement of claim and the trial judge found liability on that basis, the Court of Appeal ordered a new trial limited to the issue of battery.

Dominion Chain Co. v. Eastern Const. Co. (1976), 12 O.R. (2d) 201, 1 C.P.C. 13, 68 D.L.R.
    (3d) 385, affirmed (*sub nom. Giffels Associates Ltd. v. Eastern Const. Co.*) [1978] 2 S.C.R.
    1346, 4 C.C.L.T. 143, 5 C.P.C. 223, 84 D.L.R. (3d) 344, 19 N.R. 298.

An amendment to claim contribution from a co-defendant under the *Negligence Act* will be allowed after trial if there is no element of surprise.

Collins v. Haliburton, Kawartha Pine Ridge Dist. Health Unit (No. 2), [1972] 3 O.R. 643, 29
    D.L.R. (3d) 151 (H.C.).

The court permitted an amendment setting up a limitation provision as a defence after judgment had been rendered but before it had been taken out.

Sullivan v. Hoffman Bros. Ltd., [1968] 2 O.R. 201, 68 D.L.R. (2d) 500 (H.C.).

Where a jury found that the defendant had been negligent on a basis not mentioned in the statement of claim, the trial judge permitted the pleading to be amended.

Eldon Industs. Inc. v. Reliable Toy Co., [1966] 1 O.R. 409, 48 C.P.R. 109, 54 D.L.R. (2d) 97,
    31 Fox Pat. C. 186 (C.A.).

Where the plaintiffs in a passing-off action sought to amend the statement of claim at trial to allege infringement of copyright but refused to accept terms that the trial be adjourned, it was held that any claim founded upon the alleged infringement was not open to them.

Hardy v. Herr, [1965] 2 O.R. 801, 52 D.L.R. (2d) 193 (C.A.).

An amendment setting up a claim under a statute was allowed during argument at trial where the defendants were neither surprised nor prejudiced.

Dobson v. Winton and Robbins Ltd., [1958] O.W.N. 57, 14 D.L.R. (2d) 110, reversed on other
    grounds [1959] S.C.R. 775, 20 D.L.R. (2d) 164.

The court refused an amendment requested at the conclusion of the trial altering the type of relief sought where the defendant might have conducted his case differently had the relief been sought earlier.

Midanic v. Gross, [1957] O.W.N. 35 (C.A.).

An amendment on appeal was refused when it would have raised a radically different defence than those dealt with at trial and would have involved a question of fact not in issue at trial.

Sutton, Mitchell & Simpson Ltd. v. Kelore Mines Ltd., [1956] O.W.N. 648 (C.A.).

The Court of Appeal refused to allow an amendment to the statement of claim to raise an issue to make it conform with the evidence and judgment at trial because the defendant had not attempted to meet the issue at trial.

Ramoska-Kaluza v. Ellis, [1955] O.W.N. 969 (C.A.).

Trial judges and appellate courts have wide powers to allow amendments, however special care should be taken where new allegations of fraud are sought. A new trial was ordered to permit the defendant to adequately defend himself.

RULE 27   COUNTERCLAIM

Highlights

Rule 27 deals comprehensively with all aspects of counterclaims.

A defendant may assert by way of counterclaim *any* right or claim against the plaintiff and may join as a defendant to the counterclaim any other person who is a necessary or proper party to the counterclaim: rule 27.01. However, rule 27.08(2) gives the court a discretion to order that the counterclaim be tried separately or proceed as a separate action.

A counterclaim has to be issued only where a person who is not already a party to the main action is made a defendant to the counterclaim. (This is consistent with the overall policy of the Rules of not treating as an originating process a pleading which makes a claim only against an existing party: see rule 1.03.) However, where a defendant to the counterclaim is a new party to the action, there are different requirements as to the time for service, the manner of service, and the time for delivery of a defence to counterclaim: rules 27.04 and 27.05.

Prima facie, a counterclaim is to be tried together with the main action unless this would unduly complicate or delay the main action, or cause undue prejudice to a party: rule 27.08.

Where a claim or counterclaim is not disputed it may be stayed, or judgment may be granted with or without a stay of execution, until the disputed claim or counterclaim is disposed of: rule 27.09.

By amendment, rule 27.01(1) now specifically provides that a claim for contribution or indemnity under the *Negligence Act* by a defendant in respect of another party's claim against the defendant may be asserted by counterclaim. Although prior to its amendment the rule appeared to be appropriately worded to permit such a counterclaim, case law interpreted the subrule as not altering the practice established under the pre-1985 Rules of asserting such a claim for contribution and indemnity in the statement of defence: *Jacome v. McDonald* (1987), 19 C.P.C. (2d) 93 (Ont. H.C.), following and applying *Crowder v. Graham*, [1961] O.W.N. 320 (C.A.).

Set-off. See the *Courts of Justice Act*, s. 111.

Former Rules: Rules 44-47, 58(5), 114-119.

WHERE AVAILABLE

Against the Plaintiff

27.01(1) A defendant may assert, by way of counterclaim in the main action, any right or claim that he or she may have against the plaintiff including a claim for contribution or indemnity under the *Negligence Act* in respect of another party's claim against the defendant. [am. O. Reg. 396/91, s. 4].

Against the Plaintiff and Another Person

(2) A defendant who counterclaims against a plaintiff may join as a defendant to the counterclaim any other person, whether a party to the main action or not, who is a necessary or proper party to the counterclaim.

Cross-Reference: See rules 27.08(2) and 5.05 regarding relief against joinder.

Availability of Counterclaim — General Principles

Jaffe v. Miller (1991), 3 O.R. (3d) 680 (Master).
A defendant may counterclaim in a capacity different from that in which he is sued.

Wharton Enterprises Ltd. v. Brompton Financial Corp. (1990), 71 O.R. (2d) 463, 40 C.P.C.
(2d) 51, 37 C.L.R. 121, 67 D.L.R. (4th) 119 (H.C.).
A defendant may not counterclaim against a non-party in a *Construction Lien Act* claim.

Wm. Beatty Lands & Timber Co. v. New Belvedere Hotel of Parry Sound, [1947] O.W.N. 633
(C.A.).
The right to counterclaim is confined to those cases where the two claims can be conveniently
tried together. Conspiracy is not generally a proper subject of a counterclaim.

Long v. Long, [1943] O.W.N. 78 (Master).
A counterclaim may be struck out if it is oppressive or if it adds a non-party as defendant by
counterclaim and is unrelated to the main action.

Johnson v. Johnson, [1942] O.W.N. 543 (H.C.).
Where trial of the claim and counterclaim together would be inconvenient the counterclaim
may be struck out.

Bosa v. Citarella (1982), 39 O.R. (2d) 700, 31 C.P.C. 153 (Div. Ct.).
A counterclaim in a libel action may not be permitted where the issues raised in the main action
are complex and different from those raised in the counterclaim.

Roque v. Brown (1977), 2 C.P.C. 239 (Ont. H.C.).
The fact that a defendant did not counterclaim in a previous action does not prevent him from
bringing a subsequent action.

Re Huffman and Breese (1974), 3 O.R. (2d) 416 (H.C.).
A surrogate court may not entertain a counterclaim.

Arback v. Goodman (1975), 6 O.R. (2d) 49 (H.C.).
A counterclaim need not be against the plaintiff in the same capacity as that in which he sues.

Lajlo v. Noiles, [1973] 3 O.R. 666 (H.C.).
A counterclaim may not be made after the main action is discontinued.

Availability of Counterclaim — After Expiry of Limitation Period

Moio v. Gravelle (1977), 13 O.R. (2d) 558 (C.A.).
The Registrar of Motor Vehicles may be added as a defendant by counterclaim notwithstanding
the expiry of the limitation period set out in the *Highway Traffic Act,* R.S.O. 1970, c. 202, s.
146.

Dottor v. McQueen and Sorokopud (1976), 10 O.R. (2d) 592 (H.C.).
Leave was given at trial to counterclaim against the plaintiff and a co-defendant notwithstanding
that the purpose of the counterclaim appeared to be merely to provide a vehicle for asserting a
claim against the co-defendant which otherwise would have been barred by the expiry of a
limitation period.

Broadhurst v. Sartisohn, [1972] 2 O.R. 567 (H.C.).
A counterclaim commenced after the expiry of the limitation period contained in the *Highway
Traffic Act,* R.S.O. 1970, c. 202, s. 146, is not statute-barred even where a defendant by
counterclaim was not a party to the main action.

Weir v. Lazarius, [1964] 1 O.R. 158, affirmed without written reasons [1964] 1 O.R. 205n (H.C.).

Where a defence was delivered before the limitation period expired, the court permitted a counterclaim to be asserted after such expiry.

Imbro v. Nagle, [1963] 2 O.R. 570 (C.A.).

The court set aside a default judgment and gave leave to counterclaim after the expiry of the limitation period, relying on s. 147(3) of the *Highway Traffic Act*, R.S.O. 1960, c. 172.

Availability of Counterclaim — Examples

Coderre v. Lambert, 14 O.R. (3d) 453, 18 C.P.C. (3d) 17, 18 C.C.L.I. (2d) 249, 46 M.V.R. (2d) 1, 103 D.L.R. (4th) 289, [1993] I.L.R. 1-2977, 64 O.A.C. 241 (C.A.).

A defendant in a personal injury action was not permitted to add a counterclaim against the insurer of the plaintiff in an attempt to obtain a binding determination of the plaintiff's entitlement to long-term disability benefits. The defendant had no claim against the insurer in contract or tort or on any other basis. The issue was a matter for the statement of defence and not a counterclaim.

R. Cholkan & Co. v. Brinker (1990), 71 O.R. (2d) 381, 40 C.P.C. (2d) 6, 1 C.C.L.T. (2d) 291 (H.C.).

The defendants were refused leave to add a counterclaim alleging abuse of process where the defendant failed to show an improper purpose in the plaintiffs' bringing of the action and any definitive act or threat in furtherance of that purpose.

Gary Oswald Blasting Inc. v. M.J. Robinson Trucking Ltée (1989), 38 C.P.C. (2d) 195 (Ont. H.C.).

A third party's counterclaim against the plaintiff in the main action was dismissed; the counterclaim did not join the defendant in the main action.

Co-Operators Insurance Assn. v. Brown, 69 O.R. (2d) 135, 37 C.P.C. (2d) 310, 39 C.C.L.I. 190, [1989] I.L.R. 1-2509 (Dist. Ct.).

A counterclaim against an insured was struck out where the plaintiff in the main action was not the insured but an insurer seeking, in its own name, to recover its subrogated loss. A counterclaim must name the plaintiff as a party defendant.

Buchan Oil Ltd. v. Petro-Canada (1986), 12 C.P.C. (2d) 181 (Ont. H.C.).

A counterclaim for declaratory relief which included an alternative claim for rectification of an agreement was struck out where the declaratory relief was superfluous and rectification ought to have been pleaded in the statement of defence.

Beckett Elevator Ltd. v. York Condo. Corp. No. 42 (1984), 45 O.R. (2d) 669, 9 D.L.R. (4th) 159 (H.C.).

No notice is required from a condominium corporation to its owners and mortgagees before the corporation may bring a counterclaim for damages.

C.I.B.C. v. Murray Kingate Invts. Inc. (1983), 38 C.P.C. 118 (Ont. Master).

Under the former Rules, where a defendant was made a third party in a contract action he was not permitted to counterclaim against his co-defendant for contribution and indemnity but was required to issue his own third party notice. [*But see now rules 28.01 and 27.10 — Authors.*]

City Wide Lumber Co. v. 349027 Ont. Ltd.; 349207 Ont. Ltd. v. City Wide Lumber Co. (1983), 39 C.P.C. 78, 3 C.L.R. 243 (Ont. H.C.).

In a mechanics' lien action, a counterclaim alleging that registration of the lien constituted slander of title was permitted.

Reynolds Extrusion Co. v. Jolub Const. Ltd. (1982), 37 O.R. (2d) 417 (H.C.).

The court struck out portions of a counterclaim claiming contribution and indemnity with respect to a separate action against the defendant in which no third party proceedings had been taken.

Cooper v. Gales (1981), 25 C.P.C. 267 (Ont. Co. Ct.).

In this *Family Law Reform Act* action commenced by the personal representatives of the deceased wife, a counterclaim against the personal representatives in their personal capacities and raising issues involving the application of principles outside of the scope of that Act was struck out with leave to amend.

Greenwood v. Magee (1977), 15 O.R. (2d) 685, 4 C.P.C. 67 (H.C.).

A counterclaim alleging that the claim was an abuse of process was struck out.

Del Zotto v. Int. Chemalloy Corp. (1977), 2 C.P.C. 198 (Ont. H.C.).

A counterclaim alleging conspiracy was struck out where it was not made against all the plaintiffs.

Toronto v. Canada Dry Ltd., [1957] O.W.N. 471 (H.C.).

Where the plaintiff claimed an injunction restraining the defendant from using its land for certain purposes, the defendant was permitted to counterclaim for a declaration that it had a right to use the lands for those purposes.

Andoniadis v. Bell and Sykes, [1946] O.W.N. 949 (C.A.).

The court allowed the defendant to counterclaim against the plaintiff and two other parties where it was alleged that the three defendants by counterclaim were parties to a fraudulent conspiracy.

Reeder v. Reeder, [1945] O.W.N. 210 (Master).

In an action for possession of chattels by a husband against his wife, a counterclaim for arrears owing under a separation agreement was held to be proper.

Williams Tool Corp. Ltd. v. Merrickville Engineering Co., [1944] O.W.N. 384 (Master).

A counterclaim for slander was struck out in an action for a debt.

STATEMENT OF DEFENCE AND COUNTERCLAIM

27.02 A counterclaim (Form 27A or 27B) shall be included in the same document as the statement of defence and the document shall be entitled a statement of defence and counterclaim.

Liebersbach v. McArthur (1975), 11 O.R. (2d) 360 (Master).

A counterclaim and statement of defence may not be set out in separate documents.

COUNTERCLAIM TO BE ISSUED WHERE DEFENDANT TO COUNTERCLAIM NOT ALREADY PARTY TO MAIN ACTION

27.03 Where a person who is not already a party to the main action is made a defendant to the counterclaim, the statement of defence and counterclaim,

> **(a) shall be issued,**
>
> > **(i) within the time prescribed by rule 18.01 for delivery of the statement of defence in the main action or at any time before the defendant is noted in default, or**

(ii) **subsequently with leave of the court; and**
(b) **shall contain a second title of proceeding showing who is the plaintiff by counterclaim and who are defendants to the counterclaim.**

TIME FOR DELIVERY OR SERVICE OF DEFENCE AND COUNTERCLAIM

Where all Parties are Parties to Main Action
27.04(1) Where a counterclaim is only against the plaintiff, or only against the plaintiff and another person who is already a party to the main action, the statement of defence and counterclaim shall be delivered within the time prescribed by rule 18.01 for the delivery of the statement of defence in the main action, or at any time before the defendant is noted in default.

Where New Party is Brought in
(2) Where a counterclaim is against the plaintiff and a defendant to the counterclaim who is not already a party to the main action, the statement of defence and counterclaim shall be served, after it has been issued, on the parties to the main action and, together with all the pleadings previously delivered in the main action, on a defendant to the counterclaim who is not already a party to the main action, and shall be filed with proof of service,
(a) **within thirty days after the statement of defence and counterclaim is issued or at any time before the defendant is noted in default; or**
(b) **subsequently with leave of the court.**
(3) A statement of defence and counterclaim need not be served personally on any person who is a party to the main action, except where a defendant to the counterclaim is also a defendant in the main action and has failed to deliver a notice of intent to defend or a statement of defence in the main action, in which case the defendant shall be served personally or by an alternative to personal service under rule 16.03 whether or not the defendant has been noted in default in the main action.

Merit Invt. Corp. v. Mogil (1985), 49 C.P.C. 149 (Ont. Master).
The court permitted the late assertion of a counterclaim against the plaintiff but refused to permit the addition of claims against proposed new defendants by counterclaim because such claims might delay the plaintiff.

Morley v. Wiggins (1985), 49 O.R. (2d) 136, 47 C.P.C. 128, 30 M.V.R. 189, 7 O.A.C. 324 (Div. Ct.).
The court permitted a third party to assert a counterclaim against the defendants notwithstanding the expiry of the relevant limitation period.

Leblanc & Royle Communications Towers Ltd. v. Internav Ltd. (1984), 45 C.P.C. 77 (Ont. Master) (appeal dismissed without written reasons on May 9, 1984).
The master refused to grant leave to amend the statement of defence to advance a counterclaim where the action was on the eve of trial and the basis of the counterclaim had been known to the defendant for four years.

Giacomelli v. O'Reilly (1979), 23 O.R. (2d) 469, 9 C.P.C. 65 (H.C.).
The court extended the time to counterclaim in a motor vehicle case where there was no actual prejudice to the plaintiff and notwithstanding that the plaintiff's insurer had closed its file four years earlier.

Hunter v. Gallant (1979), 21 O.R. (2d) 213 (Master).

The court extended the time for service of a counterclaim notwithstanding the expiry of a limitation period, but without prejudice to raising the limitation period as a defence.

A.G. Ont. v. Palmer (1977), 15 O.R. (2d) 670, 3 C.P.C. 214 (H.C.).

Late service of a counterclaim does not render s. 146(3) of the *Highway Traffic Act*, R.S.O. 1970, c. 202, inapplicable.

TIME FOR DELIVERY OF DEFENCE TO COUNTERCLAIM

27.05(1) The plaintiff and any other defendant to a counterclaim who is already a party to the main action shall deliver a defence to counterclaim (Form 27C) within twenty days after service of the statement of defence and counterclaim.

(2) Where the plaintiff delivers a reply in the main action, the defence to counterclaim shall be included in the same document as the reply and the document shall be entitled a reply and defence to counterclaim.

(3) Except as provided in subrule 18.02(3) (notice of intent to defend) or 19.01(5) (late delivery of defence), a defendant to a counterclaim who is not already a party to the main action shall deliver a defence to counterclaim,

(a) within twenty days after service of the statement of defence and counterclaim, where the defendant to the counterclaim is served in Ontario;

(b) within forty days after service of the statement of defence and counterclaim, where the defendant to the counterclaim is served elsewhere in Canada or in the United States of America; or

(c) within sixty days after service of the statement of defence and counterclaim, where the defendant to the counterclaim is served anywhere else.

TIME FOR DELIVERY OF REPLY TO DEFENCE TO COUNTERCLAIM

27.06 A reply to defence to counterclaim (Form 27D), if any, shall be delivered within ten days after service of the defence to counterclaim.

AMENDING DEFENCE TO ADD COUNTERCLAIM

27.07(1) A defendant who has delivered a statement of defence that does not contain a counterclaim and who wishes to counterclaim only against the plaintiff or only against the plaintiff and another person who is already a party to the main action may amend the statement of defence in accordance with rules 26.02 and 26.03 in order to add the counterclaim, and rule 26.05 (responding to amended pleading) applies to the amended statement of defence and counterclaim.

(2) A defendant who has delivered a statement of defence that does not contain a counterclaim and who wishes to counterclaim against the plaintiff

and another person who is not already a party to the main action may, with leave of the court, have the registrar issue an amended statement of defence and counterclaim, and rule 26.05 (responding to amended pleading) applies to the amended statement of defence and counterclaim.

TRIAL OF COUNTERCLAIM

27.08(1) A counterclaim shall be tried at the trial of the main action, unless the court orders otherwise.

(2) Where it appears that a counterclaim may unduly complicate or delay the trial of the main action, or cause undue prejudice to a party, the court may order separate trials or order that the counterclaim proceed as a separate action.

Cross-Reference: See also cases under rule 5.05.

Severance Ordered

Royal Bank v. Kilmer van Nostrand Co. (1994), 29 C.P.C. (3d) 191 (Ont. Gen. Div.).

The court severed the trial of issues relating to a counterclaim where that would improve the management of the case and would not prejudice the defendant.

Refusal to Order Severance

Renegade Capital Corp. v. Hees International Bancorp Inc. (1991), 3 O.R. (3d) 251, 50 C.P.C. (2d) 51 (Gen. Div.).

The court declined to strike out a counterclaim and direct that it proceed as a separate action where the same key personnel, events and documents were involved in both the main action and the counterclaim.

Mogil v. Mogil (1985), 6 C.P.C. (2d) 137 (Ont. H.C.).

The court permitted a counterclaim to be tried with the main action notwithstanding the existence of a separate action involving related issues. The court could guard against the possibility of inconsistent results by ordering the two actions tried together when they were ready for trial.

DISPOSITION OF COUNTERCLAIM

Where Claim in Main Action not Disputed

27.09(1) Where a defendant does not dispute the claim of the plaintiff in the main action, but asserts a counterclaim, the court may stay the main action or grant judgment, with or without a stay of execution, until the counterclaim is disposed of.

Where Counterclaim not Disputed

(2) Where the plaintiff does not dispute the counterclaim of a defendant, the court may stay the counterclaim or grant judgment, with or without a stay of execution, until the main action is disposed of.

Where Both Claim and Counterclaim Succeed

(3) Where both the plaintiff in the main action and the plaintiff by counterclaim succeed, either in whole or in part, and there is a resulting

balance in favour of one of them, the court may in a proper case give judgment for the balance and dismiss the smaller claim and may make such order for costs of the claim and counterclaim as is just.

Stay of Action Where Claim in Main Action Not Disputed — rule 27.09(1)

Von Brevern v. Great West Saddlery Co., [1962] O.W.N. 60 (Master).
The main action should not be stayed until after judgment is obtained in it.

Granting Separate Judgments or Judgments for the Balance

Norbury Sudbury Ltd. v. Noront Steel (1981) Ltd. (1984), 47 O.R. (2d) 548, 11 D.L.R. (4th) 686 (H.C.).
Where the defendant did not maintain certain premises as agreed, the plaintiff's claim in damages succeeded. However money expended by the defendant to improve and expand the premises was set off against any damages awarded.

380631 Ont. Inc. v. Solray Invts. Ltd. (1983), 34 C.P.C. 211 (Ont. H.C.).
Where both the main action and counterclaim were successful the court permitted the debts to be set off. There were no extraneous factors such as a subrogated interest of an insurer.

Bodnar v. Hazet Holdings Ltd. (1976), 11 O.R. (2d) 414 (Master).
A master gave leave to appeal from his own report being of the opinion that he ought not to have given judgment for the balance.

Lewenza v. Ruszczak, [1960] O.W.N. 40 (C.A.).
Where the subrogated claim of an insurer was involved the court gave separate judgments for the claim and counterclaim.

Banks v. Yule, [1955] O.R. 155, [1955] 2 D.L.R. 34 (H.C.).
The court set off the amount recovered in a counterclaim against the amount recovered in the main action except to the extent that the first amount was subject to a solicitor's lien for costs.

McConnell v. Alexander, [1954] O.W.N. 266 (H.C.).
The court gave judgment for the balance owing after setting off the amount recovered in a cross-action. Cross-actions should be treated in the same way as counterclaims.

APPLICATION TO COUNTERCLAIMS, CROSSCLAIMS AND THIRD PARTY CLAIMS

27.10 Rules 27.01 to 27.09 apply, with necessary modifications, to the assertion of a counterclaim by a defendant to a counterclaim, by a defendant to a crossclaim and by a third party.

Gary Oswald Blasting Inc. v. M.J. Robinson Trucking Ltée (1989), 38 C.P.C. (2d) 195 (Ont. H.C.).
A third party may not assert a counterclaim solely against the plaintiff in the main action.

Morley v. Wiggins (1985), 49 O.R. (2d) 136, 47 C.P.C. 128, 30 M.V.R. 189, 7 O.A.C. 324 (Div. Ct.).
The court permitted a third party to assert a counterclaim against the defendants notwithstanding the expiry of the relevant limitation period.

Solomon v. Mead & Co. (1983), 42 O.R. (2d) 318, 36 C.P.C. 97 (Master).

Where a party defendant in the main action was also made a third party by a co-defendant, a counterclaim by the third party against the co-defendant was permitted.

Union Carbide Can. Ltd. v. C.N.R. (1980), 17 C.P.C. 127 (Ont. C.A.).

A third party may not counterclaim against the plaintiff.

Re Solway and Potter, [1958] O.W.N. 125 (H.C.).

A person added as a defendant by counterclaim may not himself assert a counterclaim. A plaintiff made a defendant by counterclaim may assert a counterclaim only if it arose after the commencement of the main action or is a shield against the counterclaim by the defendant; in other cases it may be raised by amending the original statement of claim [*cf. rule 27.10*].

Homes Dev. Ltd. v. Forbes, [1956] O.W.N. 668 (Master).

A plaintiff, defendant by counterclaim, may assert his own counterclaim in his reply and defence to counterclaim only if his counterclaim is not an independent claim but is merely a shield against the counterclaim of the defendant [*cf. rule 27.10*].

Smart v. The Royal Trust Co., [1947] O.W.N. 902 (Master).

A defendant who is the subject of a claim by a co-defendant may be given leave to file a counterclaim against the co-defendant.

RULE 28   CROSSCLAIM

Highlights

Rule 28 deals comprehensively with crossclaims — their availability, the time for delivering the crossclaim and defence to crossclaim, the consequences of not defending and the trial of the crossclaim.

By permitting co-defendants to claim against each other by crossclaim, the rule obviates the need for third party proceedings in such circumstances. Essentially the defendant may crossclaim in respect of any claim that is related to the claims or transactions involved in the main action (rule 28.01(1)), and the circumstances in which a crossclaim can be made against a co-defendant are identical to the circumstances in which a defendant may take third party proceedings against a non-party (because rules 28.01(1) and 29.01 use parallel language).

A defendant who claims contribution from a co-defendant under the *Negligence Act*, R.S.O. 1990, c. N.1, must do so by crossclaim (rule 28.01(2)), but a defendant against whom such a crossclaim is made need not deliver a defence to the crossclaim if he or she has delivered a statement of defence in the main action and is content to rely on the same facts: rule 28.05(2).

A claim against the plaintiff for contribution and indemnity under the *Negligence Act* regarding another party's claim may be asserted by counterclaim: rule 27.01(1).

Section 113 of the *Courts of Justice Act* provides that a crossclaim is available notwithstanding a "no action clause" in an insurance policy or other contract, purporting to prevent a defendant from asserting a crossclaim until after judgment against the defendant.

Former Rules: Rules 167-173, particularly Rule 172.

WHERE AVAILABLE

28.01(1) A defendant may crossclaim against a co-defendant who,

(a) is or may be liable to the defendant for all or part of the plaintiff's claim;

(b) is or may be liable to the defendant for an independent claim for damages or other relief arising out of,

> **(i) a transaction or occurrence or series of transactions or occurrences involved in the main action, or**

> **(ii) a related transaction or occurrence or series of transactions or occurrences; or**

(c) should be bound by the determination of an issue arising between the plaintiff and the defendant.

(2) A defendant who claims contribution from a co-defendant under the *Negligence Act* shall do so by way of crossclaim.

Crossclaims — Generally

Knudsen v. Holmes (1995), 26 O.R. (3d) 786 (Gen. Div.).

Where a party's insurer was defending a claim and refused to assert a crossclaim on behalf of the insured, it was permissible for the insured's personal solicitors to do so.

Harris v. Floyd (1991), 7 O.R. (3d) 512, [1992] I.L.R. 1-2836 (Master).

Where a crossclaim by an insurer against a defendant would add nothing to the rights or remedies of the insurer, the crossclaim was denied.

Jordan v. Guardian Ins. Co. of Can. (1985), 50 O.R. (2d) 673, 1 C.P.C. (2d) 263 (Master).

A defendant who did not defend the main action and had been noted in default was permitted to assert a crossclaim against a co-defendant.

Sgro v. Verbeek (1980), 28 O.R. (2d) 712, 111 D.L.R. (3d) 479 (H.C.).

Where a defendant alleged that the negligence of one plaintiff contributed to the cause of injury to another plaintiff and pleaded the *Negligence Act* but did not make an express claim for contribution and indemnity, the court permitted the defendant to obtain contribution and indemnity but deprived him of costs.

Ellis v. Conklin & Garrett Ltd., [1969] 2 O.R. 753 (C.A.).

It is proper to seek contribution and indemnity from a co-defendant under the *Negligence Act*, R.S.O. 1960, c. 261, in the statement of defence and also take third party proceedings claiming contractual indemnity against the same defendant. [*The contractual claim must now be asserted by crossclaim and rule 28.01(2) requires that the Negligence Act claim also be by crossclaim — Authors.*]

Metallizing Co. v. Kavanagh, [1946] O.W.N. 645 (H.C.).

A claim for contribution or indemnity against a co-defendant which has no real connection with the plaintiff's claim in the main action will be struck out.

Crossclaim for Damages — rule 28.01(1)(b)

Spott v. Gunn (1986), 10 C.P.C. (2d) 172 (Ont. Master).

Where a party has already asserted a crossclaim against a defendant for indemnity, the addition of a claim for damages in the crossclaim is only another aspect of the same cause of action. Such an additional claim was held not to be barred by the expiry of a limitation period.

STATEMENT OF DEFENCE AND CROSSCLAIM

28.02 A crossclaim (Form 28A) shall be included in the same document as the statement of defence and the document shall be entitled a statement of defence and crossclaim.

AMENDING DEFENCE TO ADD CROSSCLAIM

28.03 A defendant who has delivered a statement of defence that does not contain a crossclaim and who wishes to crossclaim may amend the statement of defence in accordance with rules 26.02 and 26.03 in order to add the crossclaim, and rule 26.05 (responding to amended pleading) applies to the amended statement of defence and crossclaim.

TIME FOR DELIVERY OF STATEMENT OF DEFENCE AND CROSSCLAIM

28.04(1) A statement of defence and crossclaim shall be delivered,
(a) within the time prescribed by rule 18.01 for delivery of the statement of defence in the main action or at any time before the defendant is noted in default; or

(b) subsequently with leave, which the court shall grant unless the plaintiff would be prejudiced thereby.

(2) A statement of defence and crossclaim need not be served personally on a defendant against whom a crossclaim is made, unless the defendant has failed to deliver a notice of intent to defend or a statement of defence in the main action, in which case the defendant shall be served personally or by an alternative to personal service under rule 16.03, whether or not the defendant has been noted in default in the main action.

Four Valleys Excavating Grading Ltd. v. Forsan Construction Ltd. (1994), 36 C.P.C. (3d) 374, 21 C.L.R. (2d) 107 (Ont. Master).
The court permitted a defendant to assert a crossclaim a few months before trial but imposed terms to avoid delay and prejudice to the plaintiff.

TIME FOR DELIVERY OF DEFENCE TO CROSSCLAIM

Defence to Crossclaim
28.05(1) Subject to subrule (2), a defence to crossclaim (Form 28B) shall be delivered within twenty days after service of the statement of defence and crossclaim.

Where Defence to Crossclaim not Required
(2) Where,
(a) a crossclaim contains no claim other than a claim for contribution or indemnity under the *Negligence Act*;
(b) the defendant to the crossclaim has delivered a statement of defence in the main action; and
(c) the defendant to the crossclaim in response to the crossclaim relies on the facts pleaded in the defendant's statement of defence in the main action and not on a different version of the facts or on any matter that might, if not specifically pleaded, take the crossclaiming defendant by surprise,
the defendant to the crossclaim need not deliver a defence to the crossclaim and shall be deemed to deny the allegations of fact made in the crossclaim and to rely on the facts pleaded in the statement of defence in the main action.

CONTENTS OF DEFENCE TO CROSSCLAIM

May Defend Against Crossclaim and Against Plaintiff's Claim Against Co-defendant
28.06(1) In a defence to crossclaim, the defendant may,
(a) defend against the crossclaim; and
(b) where appropriate, defend against the plaintiff's claim against the crossclaiming defendant, in which case the defendant may raise any defence open to the crossclaiming defendant.

Separate Part for Defence Against Plaintiff
(2) Where the defendant defends against the plaintiff's claim against the crossclaiming defendant, the defence to crossclaim shall contain a sepa-

rate part entitled a defence to plaintiff's claim against crossclaiming defendant.

Consequence of Defending Against Plaintiff
(3) A defendant who defends against the plaintiff's claim against the crossclaiming defendant,
(a) has the same rights and obligations in the action, including those in respect of discovery, trial and appeal, as a defendant to that claim; and
(b) is bound by any order or determination made in the main action between the plaintiff and the crossclaiming defendant.

Time for Reply by Plaintiff
(4) The plaintiff's reply, if any, to the defence to plaintiff's claim against crossclaiming defendant shall be delivered within ten days after service of that defence.

Consequence of Not Defending Against Plaintiff
(5) A defendant who does not defend against the plaintiff's claim against the crossclaiming defendant is bound by any order or determination made in the main action between the plaintiff and the crossclaiming defendant.

EFFECT OF DEFAULT OF DEFENCE TO CROSSCLAIM

28.07 Where a defendant against whom a crossclaim is made is noted in default in respect of the crossclaim, the crossclaiming defendant may obtain judgment against the other defendant only at the trial of the main action or on motion to a judge.

TIME FOR DELIVERY OF REPLY TO DEFENCE TO CROSSCLAIM

28.08 A reply to defence to crossclaim (Form 28C), if any, shall be delivered within ten days after service of the defence to crossclaim.

TRIAL OF CROSSCLAIM

28.09 A crossclaim shall be tried at or immediately after the trial of the main action, unless the court orders otherwise.

PREJUDICE OR DELAY TO PLAINTIFF

28.10 A plaintiff is not to be prejudiced or unnecessarily delayed by reason of a crossclaim, and on motion by the plaintiff the court may make such order to impose such terms, including an order that the crossclaim proceed as a separate action, as are necessary to prevent prejudice or delay where that may be done without injustice to the parties to the crossclaim.

APPLICATION TO COUNTERCLAIMS AND THIRD PARTY CLAIMS

28.11 Rules 28.01 to 28.10 apply, with necessary modifications, to the assertion of a crossclaim between co-defendants to a counterclaim or between third parties to a third party claim.

RULE 29   THIRD PARTY CLAIM

Highlights

Rule 29 regulates the making of "third party claims", which were formerly called "third party proceedings". It makes only minor adjustments in how these proceedings are conducted, but there are significant changes in the availability of such proceedings. A claim by one defendant against a co-defendant is no longer asserted by a third party claim, but rather by a crossclaim: see Rule 28.

Availability. Under the former Rules, a third party claim was available only in respect of claims for contribution or indemnity "or other relief over". This latter phrase was restrictive and did not permit the assertion by the defendant against a third party of a claim that was independent of the outcome of the main action.

The new Rule does not use the phrase "other relief over". Indeed, rule 29.01(b) expressly authorizes the assertion by a third party claim of an "independent claim" the defendant may have against the third party, provided it arises out of the transactions or occurrences involved in the main action or a related series of transactions or occurrences. So, for example, if P (a passenger) sues D (the driver) for damages arising out of an automobile accident, D may, by a third party claim, seek to recover from X (the driver of another car) the damages that D suffered in the same accident.

The significance of this change should not be underestimated. It changes the very nature of a third party claim. No longer is it limited to situations designed to obtain "a flow through of recovery" to D from the third party because of the judgment that the plaintiff may obtain against the defendant. Instead, it is now a general joinder device by which a defendant may engraft on to the main action any "related claim" he or she may have against non-parties, subject to the severance power given to the court by rule 29.09. (Compare the analogous "same transaction or occurrence" language used in the various general joinder rules: see rule 5.02(1)(a) and (2)(a) (joinder of multiple plaintiffs and defendants), and rule 6.01(1)(b) (consolidation)).

Although Rule 29 introduced radical changes to third party practice, it has received very little in the way of interpretation by the courts. In two cases, *Dimou v. 405455 Ont. Inc.* (1988), 66 O.R. (2d) 699 (Div. Ct.) and *Cardar Investments Ltd. v. Thorne Riddell* (1989), 71 O.R. (2d) 29, 36 O.A.C. 280 (Div. Ct.), although the decisions were (it is submitted) correct, statements were made as to the operation and scope of Rule 29 which do not appear to be sound. (For a critical analysis of these two cases see the Annual Survey of Recent Developments in Civil Procedure in the 1990 edition of this work.) See now *478649 Ontario Ltd. v. Corcoran* (1994), 20 O.R. (3d) 28, 74 O.A.C. 152 (C.A.).

Since the availability of third party claims against non-parties and crossclaims against co-defendants are designed to be parallel, rule 28.01(1) and rule 29.01 use virtually identical language.

Under the former practice, challenges to the availability of third party proceedings were almost always raised by the third party, rather than by the plaintiff in the main action. This practice was difficult to support because it amounted to the third party questioning at the outset the defendant's procedural right to sue him or her, a right the third party would not enjoy if he or she were simply made a defendant to an action in which the defendant in the main action were plaintiff. In reality a third party proceeding is simply another action (defendant v. third party) engrafted on to the main action.

On the other hand, the *plaintiff* is the party whose procedural rights may be adversely affected by the addition of third party claims. For this reason, under Rule 29 only the plaintiff in the main action, and not the third party, is given the express right to challenge the propriety of a third party claim: rule 29.09. It is, however, open to the third party to move under the general relief against joinder provision (rule 5.05) in an appropriate case.

Similarly, rule 29.02(1.2) provides that a third party claim may be issued outside of the time limited by the Rules, with leave, "which the court shall grant unless the *plaintiff* would be prejudiced thereby". The effect of this provision is that the time limited by the rule for issuing a third party claim is not to act as a limitation period in favour of the third party. If the third party has a limitation defence it should be pleaded as a defence to the third party claim, but should not influence the outcome of the motion to extend time for asserting the third party claim: see *Boylan v. Red Barn System (Can.) Ltd.* (1974), 7 O.R. (2d) 380 (Div. Ct.).

The former case law held that a "no-action clause" in an insurance contract, providing that the insurer was not liable to suit until the defendant insured suffered judgment, foreclosed third party proceedings: see *e.g. Int. Formed Tubes Ltd. v. Ohio Crankshaft Co.*, [1965] 2 O.R. 240, 50 D.L.R. (2d) 214 (C.A.). Section 113 of the *Courts of Justice Act* now provides that such agreements do not prevent the making of a third party claim.

Procedure. Basically the procedure remains the same. However, the right of the third party to defend the main action is now qualified ("where appropriate", see rule 29.05(1)) because when the third party claim is the defendant's own independent claim it will usually be inappropriate for the third party to defend the main action, since he or she will have no interest in its outcome. A third party who defends the main action is now given the same rights in the main action as the defendant in that action, and his or her participation in the trial is no longer in the discretion of the trial judge: rule 29.05(2).

Former Rules: Rules 167-173.

WHERE AVAILABLE

29.01 A defendant may commence a third party claim against any person who is not a party to the action and who,

(a) is or may be liable to the defendant for all or part of the plaintiff's claim;

(b) is or may be liable to the defendant for an independent claim for damages or other relief arising out of,

(i) a transaction or occurrence or series of transactions or occurrences involved in the main action, or

(ii) a related transaction or occurrence or series of transactions or occurrences; or

(c) should be bound by the determination of an issue arising between the plaintiff and the defendant.

Availability of Third Party Claim — Generally

[*Cases under the old Rules must be read in light of the drastic changes brought about by the new Rules — Authors.*]

Sanga v. Bettridge (1994), 17 O.R. (3d) 773, 23 C.C.L.I. (2d) 127, 3 M.V.R. (3d) 29, 113 D.L.R. (4th) 161, 70 O.A.C. 130 (C.A.).

One of the primary considerations in the application of rule 29.01(c) is that all parties involved in the same factual situation should have their rights determined without a multiplicity of proceedings.

Brampton Hydro-Electric Commission v. B.C. Polygrinders Ltd. (1992), 8 O.R. (3d) 795, 6 C.P.C. (3d) 275 (Master), affirmed (1993), 12 O.R. (3d) 625, 18 C.P.C. (3d) 84, 62 O.A.C. 42 (Div. Ct.).

The court refused to permit a third party claim where the substance of the proposed third party claim could be raised by the defendant as a defence and the third party claim itself would have no significance.

Dywidag Systems International Can. Ltd. v. Zutphen Brothers Construction Ltd., [1990] 1 S.C.R. 705, 41 C.P.C. (2d) 18, 40 C.L.R. 1, 68 D.L.R. (4th) 147, 46 C.R.R. 259, 106 N.R. 11, 97 N.S.R. (2d) 181, 258 A.P.R. 181.

Provisions of the *Federal Court Act* and the *Crown Liability Act* granting exclusive jurisdiction to the Federal Court in cases where relief is claimed against the federal Crown are not unconsitutional. A corporate defendant was not allowed to assert a third party claim against the Crown in a provincial superior court.

Cardar Investments Ltd. v. Thorne Riddell (1989), 71 O.R. (2d) 29, 36 O.A.C. 280 (Div. Ct.).

Accountants, who were sued for negligence for giving bad advice with regard to tax credits, who alleged negligence on the part of the solicitors acting for the plaintiff on the purchase of the tax credits were permitted to assert a third party claim against the solicitors under the *Negligence Act* since the solicitors might be found liable to contribute to the plaintiff's damages.

Carswell v. Traders Gen. Ins. Co. (1987), 19 C.P.C. (2d) 126, 26 C.C.L.I. 214 (Ont. Dist. Ct.), affirmed 20 C.P.C. (2d) 117, 27 C.C.L.I. 267 (Ont. H.C.).

The court's primary consideration is that all parties involved in the same factual situation have their rights determined without a multiplicity of proceedings. In this case, although denying coverage in an action on the plaintiff's insurance policy, the defendant insurer was permitted to commence a third party action against the tortfeasor which caused the damage.

Doidge v. Antonaids (1983), 42 O.R. (2d) 296, 35 C.P.C. 211, 149 D.L.R. (3d) 252 (C.A.).

A third party claim need not arise out of occurrences anterior to the main action. The court considered the common issue in the main and third party actions, the possibility of conflicting results, and the policy against multiplicity of proceedings, and permitted the third party claim to be asserted.

Husain v. Hicks (1982), 32 C.P.C. 207, 141 D.L.R. (3d) 738 (Ont. H.C.).

The court required that a claim for indemnity against one of several plaintiffs be asserted by way of third party proceedings to enable that plaintiff to plead to the claim and take proceedings for contribution and indemnity.

Lewis Insulations Ltd. v. Goodram Bros. Ltd. (1978), 21 O.R. (2d) 236, 10 C.P.C. 224, 90 D.L.R. (3d) 311 (H.C.).

A third party claim against the Queen in the right of Canada was struck out as being within the exclusive jurisdiction of the Federal Court.

Weesbach v. Supt. of Ins. (1978), 20 O.R. (2d) 398, 7 C.P.C. 206 (Div. Ct.).

The Superintendant of Insurance can add an alleged owner of an unidentified vehicle as a third party.

Anchor Shoring Ltd. v. Halton Region Conservation Authority; Dufferin Materials & Const. Ltd. v. Halton Region Conservation Authority (1977), 15 O.R. (2d) 599, 3 C.P.C. 153 (H.C.).

Third party proceedings are not permitted under the *Mechanics' Lien Act*.

Zaharuk v. Youngson, [1972] 3 O.R. 443 (H.C.).

A third party claim may be struck out where the conduct of the other parties has gravely prejudiced the third party. Here the claim was struck out because a settlement between the plaintiff and defendant prior to the issuance of the third party claim effectively deprived the third party of pre-trial procedures against the plaintiff.

Averletti v. Meertens, [1968] 2 O.R. 864 (Master).

The right to a third party proceeding may be taken away by the *Workmen's Compensation Act*, R.S.O. 1960, c. 437.

Slesar v. W. Fink Builders Ltd., [1968] 2 O.R. 594 (H.C.).

A defendant by counterclaim may take third party proceedings.

Wilson v. Hamilton Street Ry. Co., [1968] 2 O.R. 78 (Master).

The Registrar of Motor Vehicles may not be added as a third party.

English v. Royal Trust Co., [1961] O.W.N. 360 (C.A.).

A claim against one of several plaintiffs should be asserted by a counterclaim, not a third party claim.

Availability of Third Party Claim — Under Negligence Act

Canada Colors & Chemicals Ltd. v. Tenneco Canada Inc. (1995), 21 O.R. (3d) 438, 37 C.P.C. (3d) 154, 121 D.L.R. (4th) 556, 77 O.A.C. 344 (Div. Ct.).

A third party claim may not be asserted against a person where neither the plaintiff nor the defendant have a cause of action against the third party. The court struck out a negligence claim against a third party who owed no duty to either the plaintiffs or defendants.

A.G. Ont. v. Kibrick (1974), 4 O.R. (2d) 313 (C.A.).

Where an originating process names a person as a defendant but the plaintiff does not and will not serve him, a co-defendant may commence third party proceedings rather than proceeding under the *Negligence Act*, R.S.O. 1970, c. 296.

Kane v. Haman, [1971] 1 O.R. 294 (H.C.).

The addition of a party defendant or third party under s. 6 of the *Negligence Act*, R.S.O. 1960, c. 261, must be done within the relevant limitation period.

Judson v. Vasilaras, [1971] 1 O.R. 290 (H.C.).

The question of whether or not the addition of a third party under s. 6 of the *Negligence Act*, R.S.O. 1960, c. 261, must be done within the relevant limitation period should not be determined at the pleading stage; leave should be granted to issue the third party claim without prejudice to the limitation period defence.

Cooper v. Sherwood Park Resorts Ltd., [1968] 1 O.R. 99 (Master).

Third party proceedings under the *Negligence Act*, R.S.O. 1960, c. 261, should be taken within the time prescribed by the Rules.

Paul Papp Ltd. v. Fitzpatrick, [1967] 1 O.R. 565 (C.A.).

Discussion of third party proceedings under the *Negligence Act*, R.S.O. 1960, c. 261.

Durocher v. Tiffin, [1960] O.W.N. 185 (H.C.).

A claim under the *Negligence Act* by a defendant against one of several plaintiffs should be asserted in the statement of defence, not by way of third party proceedings.

Availability of Third Party Claim — Against Insurer

[See now s. 113 of the Courts of Justice Act — Authors.]

Sanga v. Bettridge (1994), 17 O.R. (3d) 773, 23 C.C.L.I. (2d) 127, 3 M.V.R. (3d) 29, 113 D.L.R. (4th) 161, 70 O.A.C. 130 (C.A.).

The court permitted a third party action to proceed against an insurer, where there was no doubt that the issues between the plaintiff and the defendant were substantially the same issues that would be raised in proceedings between the plaintiff and the third party. The insurer should be bound by the determination of the issues between the plaintiff and the defendant in the circumstances.

Peters Estate v. Armstrong (1988), 31 C.P.C. (2d) 225 (Ont. Master), affirmed 31 C.P.C. (2d) 225 at 228 (Ont. H.C.).

Disputes as to insurance coverage of the defendant can best be resolved by third party proceedings against the putative insurer.

Minassian v. Toonen (1987), 61 O.R. (2d) 765, 21 C.P.C. (2d) 267, 27 C.C.L.I. 235 (H.C.).

Rights between an insurer and its insured should not be determined on a motion under s. 226(14) of the *Insurance Act*, R.S.O. 1980, c. 218; where the insurer denies coverage, it must be made a third party.

Bissola v. Kunashko (1986), 7 C.P.C. (2d) 302 (Ont. Master).

Where the plaintiffs in a motor vehicle action sued both the tortfeasor and the plaintiff's own insurer (regarding the uninsured motorist coverage) the court refused to permit the defendant insurer to make a third party claim against the tortfeasor's insurer.

Rupolo v. Tulshi (1985), 51 O.R. (2d) 288 at 289, 49 C.P.C. 12 (Master), affirmed 51 O.R. (2d) 288, 1 C.P.C. (2d) 11, 11 C.C.L.I. 87, [1985] I.L.R. 1-1926 (H.C.).

In a motor vehicle action against the tortfeasor and the plaintiff's own insurer under the uninsured motorist coverage, it is permissible for the defendant insurer to assert a third party claim against the putative insurer of the tortfeasor to determine whether it was liable to the tortfeasor. The rule clearly permits a defendant to commence a third party claim against a person who would be bound by the determination of an issue arising between the plaintiffs and the defendant, and in so doing effects a substantial change in the law.

Maggio v. Lopes, 51 O.R. (2d) 441, 1 C.P.C. (2d) 165, [1985] I.L.R. 1-1924 (Master), affirmed 52 O.R. (2d) 694, 6 C.P.C. (2d) xlvii (Div. Ct.).

A defendant in a motor vehicle case may not take third party proceedings against the plaintiff's own no-fault insurer for a declaration that the plaintiff is entitled to no-fault benefits.

Grieve v. Milton (1982), 30 C.P.C. 113 (Ont. Master).

A third party claim by a defendant against its insurer for a declaration to defend was struck out as not being for relief over and not involving a connection of fact or subject-matter.

Grenier & Sons Ltd. v. Fortier, 29 O.R. (2d) 469, 113 D.L.R. (3d) 509, [1980] I.L.R. 1-1276 (H.C.).

A defendant in a motor vehicle action was permitted to take third party proceedings against his putative insurer for a declaration of coverage.

Hunt v. Blue Ridges Building Corp., [1964] 2 O.R. 407, affirmed [1964] 2 O.R. at 410n (H.C.).

Third party proceedings should not be taken against an insurer if a jury trial is possible, however, where the parties agree not to have a jury, or the time for serving a jury notice has passed, such proceedings are permissible.

Campbell Soup Co. v. Wm. Dalley Cartage Co., [1961] O.W.N. 337 (Master).

In a non-jury action a defendant was allowed to add its insurer as a third party.

Third Party Procedure under the Insurance Act

Carreiro v. Goszyniecki (1993), 17 C.P.C. (3d) 111 (Ont. Master).

A third party under the *Insurance Act* may not institute fourth party proceedings.

Merrill v. Sommerville (1992), 11 O.R. (3d) 444, [1993] I.L.R. 1-2902 (Gen. Div.).

Rule 29.01 does not operate to bring in an insurer as a full-fledged third party where the insurer has third party status under the *Insurance Act.*.

Bortuzzo v. Barna, 54 O.R. (2d) 598, 8 C.P.C. (2d) 277, 20 C.C.L.I. 355, [1986] I.L.R. 1-2052 (H.C.).

A third party under the *Insurance Act* is not entitled to commence fourth party proceedings.

Goldman v. Romano (1974), 5 O.R. (2d) 300 (Master).

Where the statement of defence filed by an insurer on behalf of the insured was struck out for failure of the insured to attend on discovery, the insurer was added as a third party under the *Insurance Act*, R.S.O. 1970, c. 224, s. 225(14).

Milne v. Wall, [1966] 2 O.R. 862 (Master).

An insurer added as a third party under the *Insurance Act*, R.S.O. 1960, c. 190, is bound by the determination of ownership of the vehicle made in the main action.

Schultz v. McArthur, [1964] 2 O.R. 375 (Master).

Discussion of form of order adding insurer as a third party under the *Insurance Act*, R.S.O. 1960, c. 190, s. 223(9).

Availability of Third Party Claim — Examples Where Claim Allowed

Walker Estate v. York-Finch General Hospital (1995), 26 O.R. (3d) 280 (Gen. Div.).

The court refused to strike out third party claims in this tainted blood case where it was not plain and obvious they could not succeed.

478649 Ontario Ltd. v. Corcoran (1994), 20 O.R. (3d) 28, 33 C.P.C. (3d) 292, 118 D.L.R. (4th) 682, 74 O.A.C. 152 (C.A.).

The court permitted the defendant to assert a third party claim against a solicitor who acted for the plaintiff in the subject transaction.

Botelho v. Wheatle, 59 O.R. (2d) 471, 26 C.C.L.I. 57, [1987] I.L.R. 1-2179 (H.C.).

In a motor vehicle action where the defendant failed to defend, the court permitted the defendant's insurer, which had itself added as a statutory third party, to issue a fourth party claim for contribution against another driver.

T.D. Bank v. NWP Northwood Wood Prods. Ltd. (1984), 43 C.P.C. 252 (Ont. Master).

The master refused to strike out a third party claim by the defendant guarantors based upon the allegation that but for the negligence of the third parties during the receivership the guarantors would not have been called on their guarantees.

Chatham Motors Ltd. v. Fidelity & Casualty Ins. Co. of New York (1983), 42 O.R. (2d) 464, 35 C.P.C. 217, 149 D.L.R. (3d) 94 (Div. Ct.).

A third party proceeding by the defendant in an action on a fidelity policy was permitted against an employee of the plaintiff alleged to have fraudulently appropriated funds.

Harvey Credit Union Ltd. v. G.H. Ward and Partners (1981), 15 B.L.R. 307, 24 C.P.C. 209, 128 D.L.R. (3d) 656 (Ont. H.C.).

Where the plaintiff sued its auditors for breach of contract and negligence in the preparation of financial statements, third party proceedings against the plaintiff's directors were permitted.

J. Gibb Const. Ltd. v. Toronto Truck Sufferance Terminal Ltd. (1978), 6 C.P.C. 203 (Ont. H.C.).

In an action for work done and materials supplied, a third party claim was allowed against the person alleged to be responsible for the damage necessitating the work.

Pharmacie Belisle Pharmacy Ltd. v. Mineau (1977), 17 O.R. (2d) 295, 4 C.P.C. 203 (C.A.).

A third party notice against the solicitor who acted for the defendant was upheld in an action based on a real estate transaction where the solicitor had been retained prior to the defendant entering into a binding sale agreement and part of the plaintiff's claim was for damages.

Gelinas v. Hamilton, [1970] 2 O.R. 157 (H.C.).

A third party proceeding based on gross negligence was permitted notwithstanding that the main action was based only on simple negligence.

Trans Canada Credit Corp. Ltd. v. Zaluski, [1969] 2 O.R. 496, 5 D.L.R. (3d) 702 (Co. Ct.).

A party sued on a promissory note may take third party proceedings against the person whose fraud brought about the execution of the note.

Magee v. Canada Coach Lines Ltd., [1946] O.W.N. 265 (Master).

A third party proceeding against a defendant in respect of whom the plaintiff had discontinued the main action was upheld even though a limitation period had intervened as the matter was a question of law to be determined at trial.

Availability of Third Party Claim — Examples Where Claim Struck Out

*[**Caveat:** Most or all pre-1985 cases would be decided differently under the new Rules — Authors.]*

G.W. Martin Veneer Ltd. v. Coronation Insurance Co. (1988), 30 C.C.L.I. 106 (Ont. H.C.).

Following an aircraft crash, the owners brought an action against an insurer to recover indemnity for the loss of the aircraft (the insurance action) and, together with others, brought a negligence action against the vendors and suppliers of the aircraft and against four doctors relating to the health of the pilot (the negligence action). A motion in the insurance action for leave to issue a third party claim against the defendants in the negligence action was refused.

Dimou v. 405455 Ont. Inc. (1988), 66 O.R. (2d) 699, [1989] I.L.R. 1-2401, 31 O.A.C. 308 (Div. Ct.).

The court struck out a third party notice where the parties sought to be added did not fit any of the categories enunciated in rule 29.01; in addition, it was held that a party cannot be added after judgment, where the defendant has become a judgment debtor, as was attempted in this case.

Nadrofsky Corp. v. Huron Chevrolet Oldsmobile-Cadillac Inc. (1986), 56 O.R. (2d) 117, 10 C.P.C. (2d) 248 (H.C.).

The court refused to permit the continuation of a third party claim where the main action had been settled and the limitation period governing the third party had expired.

Sterling Trust Corp. v. Fireman's Fund Ins. Co. of Can. (1982), 26 C.P.C. 209 (Ont. Master).

A third party claim by a defendant insurer against the plaintiff's employees who participated in the fraud alleged in the main action was struck out as not arising out of anterior relations.

Vanderclay Dev. Co. v. Da Costa Nunes (1980), 29 O.R. (2d) 350, 28 Chitty's L.J. 69, 113 D.L.R. (3d) 467 (Div. Ct.).

A vendor of real property, who was sued on the covenant in a mortgage when his purchaser defaulted, was not permitted to make a third party claim against his solicitor in the sale transaction for negligently failing to advise of the financial instability of the purchaser.

TIME FOR THIRD PARTY CLAIM

Issuing

29.02(1) A third party claim (Form 29A) shall be issued within ten days after the defendant delivers a statement of defence, or at any time before the defendant is noted in default, whichever is earlier.

Exception, reply

(1.1) A third party claim may be issued within ten days after the plaintiff delivers a reply in the main action to the defendant's statement of defence.

Exceptions, consent and leave

(1.2) A third party claim may be issued at any time with the plaintiff's consent or with leave, which the court shall grant unless the plaintiff would be prejudiced thereby.

Service

(2) A third party claim shall be served on the third party personally or by an alternative to personal service under rule 16.03, together with all the pleadings previously delivered in the main action or in any counterclaim, crossclaim or third or subsequent party claim in the main action, within thirty days after the third party claim is issued.

(3) A third party claim shall also be served on every other party to the main action within the time for service on the third party, but personal service is not required. [am. O. Reg. 351/94, s. 2]

Cross-Reference: See also cases under rule 3.02.

[*Authors' Note:* Notwithstanding rule 29.02(1.2), as an administrative matter it is often possible to issue a third party claim late without leave or even consent of the plaintiff and co-defendants.]

[*Caveat:* Cases refusing extension of time should now be read in light of rule 29.02(1.2) — Authors.]

Extension of Time for Third Party Claim — Generally

Tate Andale Canada Ltd. v. DiClemente (1994), 36 C.P.C. (3d) 351 at 365 (Ont. Master), affirmed (1995), 36 C.P.C. (3d) 351 (Ont. Gen. Div.).

In considering whether to extend the time for a third or subsequent party claim, the court should apply a test similar to rule 21.01(1)(b), namely: (1) material facts pleaded are taken to have been proven, (2) novelty of the cause of action is not of any importance, (3) the claim is read generously to accommodate any drafting deficiencies, and (4) the claim is allowed to proceed if it has any possibility of success.

Fire v. Longtin (1990), 71 O.R. (2d) 682, 44 C.P.C. (2d) 189 (H.C.).

A cause of action for contribution and indemnity arises when a party is sued. Accordingly, for the purpose of a third party claim for contribution and indemnity, any statute of limitation applicable to the third party runs from the date the defendant is sued.

Pringle v. Snyder's Potatoes (Preston) Ltd. (1988), 30 C.P.C. (2d) 285 (Ont. Dist. Ct.).

The defendant need not explain the delay in issuing the third party claim. The only factor the court may consider is prejudice to the plaintiff.

Bell Can. v. Olympia & York Developments Ltd. (1988), 30 C.P.C. (2d) 155, 29 C.L.R. xxiv (Ont. C.A.).

A delay in moving to add a third or fourth party is not in itself fatal to the granting of an order. However, the court refused to extend the time to issue a fourth party claim where the resultant delay of an imminent and complex trial would be prejudicial to the plaintiff.

Waterloo County Bd. of Educ. v. Mark, Musselman, McIntyre, Coombe (1982), 38 O.R. (2d) 61, 37 C.P.C. 101 (H.C.).

Factors to be considered in exercising the court's discretion to extend the time to commence third party proceedings include: time of awareness of the facts giving rise to third party claim; the expiry of the limitation period; the reason given for the delay; the length of the delay; any prejudice suffered by the third party.

Baydon Corp. v. du Pont Glore Forgan Can. Ltd. (1974), 4 O.R. (2d) 636 (Master).

Where a defendant is prompted to commence third party proceedings as a result of an amendment to the statement of claim after the close of pleadings, he should apply to the court for an extension of the time for service.

Extension of Time for Third Party Claim — Where Limitation Period Has Expired

Devincenzo v. Lemieux (1988), 30 C.P.C. (2d) 173, 40 M.P.L.R. 110 (Ont. H.C.), leave to appeal to Ont. H.C. refused (1988), 30 C.P.C. (2d) lv.

Where a defendant had issued a third party claim for contribution and indemnity against a municipality, the court dismissed the municipality's motion for summary judgment which claimed that the defendant had failed to serve a notice of action within seven days of the plaintiff's injuries, as required by the *Municipal Act*. The relevant section of that Act applied only to claims for damages or injury arising from non-repair, and not to situations where liability on the part of the municipality did not arise until judgment was awarded against the defendant.

Gay v. Calzonetti (1988), 65 O.R. (2d) 154, 27 C.P.C. (2d) 93, 6 M.V.R. (2d) 191 (H.C.).

The court permitted the addition of a third party claim after the expiry of the limitation period for adding defendants where the main action had been commenced in time and the *Highway Traffic Act* so permitted.

Ejsymont v. T.D. Bank (1984), 47 O.R. (2d) 596, 46 C.P.C. 11 (Master).

The court extended the time to commence a third party action *nunc pro tunc* notwithstanding the expiry of limitation periods contained in the *Limitations Act* and the *Professional Engineers Act* where s. 9 of the *Negligence Act*, R.S.O. 1980, c. 315, permitted the defendant to commence a later action for contribution and indemnity if the plaintiff obtained judgment.

Pek v. Levasseur (1982), 38 O.R. (2d) 108, 28 C.P.C. 179, leave to appeal refused 38 O.R. (2d) 108 at 109n (H.C.).

The court extended the time for commencement of a third party claim against a municipality notwithstanding expiry of a limitation period where it appeared that defence would fail by operation of s. 9 of the *Negligence Act*, R.S.O. 1980, c. 315.

Berardinelli v. Ont. Housing Corp. (1981), 27 C.P.C. 248 (Ont. Master).

A third party claim was set aside where the limitation period and the time prescribed in the Rules had expired and the balance of prejudice favoured the third party.

Brock Univ. v. Stewart Hinan Corp. Ltd. (1980), 27 O.R. (2d) 329, 15 C.P.C. 202, 108 D.L.R. (3d) 137 (Div. Ct.).

In view of the slowness with which the action was proceeding, and notwithstanding the expiry of a limitation period, a delay of four months before third party proceedings were taken was not untoward.

Boylan v. Red Barn System (Can.) Ltd. (1974), 7 O.R. (2d) 380 (Div. Ct.).

An application to extend the time for commencement of third party proceedings was granted notwithstanding the expiry of a limitation period, the court being of the opinion that the merits of that defence should not be resolved on an interlocutory motion of the type before it.

Black v. Horseman (1974), 4 O.R. (2d) 188 (Div. Ct.).

An application to strike out a third party proceeding which had been brought 28 days late was refused notwithstanding that one of the several claims thereby asserted was statute-barred.

Ont. Northland Transport Comm. v. New (1974), 4 O.R. (2d) 56 (Master).

An extension of time to commence a third party proceeding was denied where there had been a five-month delay and a limitation period had expired.

Buim v. Sherritt, [1972] 2 O.R. 268 (Master).

A third party claim served sixteen days late was regularized notwithstanding the expiry of a limitation period where there had been no actual prejudice to the third party.

Extension of Time for Third Party Claim — Examples

Siket v. Milczek (1993), 23 C.P.C. (3d) 204, additional reasons (July 21, 1994), Doc. Kitchener 2140/92 (Ont. Gen. Div.).

Where the examinations for discovery had been completed, a pre-trial was imminent, and the trial was set to begin in one month, the court refused to grant leave to issue a third party proceeding.

Fenix Developments G.P. Inc. v. Willemse (1994), 23 C.P.C. (3d) 376 (Ont. Gen. Div. [Commercial List]).

Leave to commence third party proceedings was granted *nunc pro tunc* where the defendant had delayed and perhaps acted in bad faith but the plaintiff had not suffered any prejudice which could not be compensated by the award of solicitor and client costs.

Hinton v. Engineering Products of Can. Ltd. (1986), 16 C.P.C. (2d) 283 (Ont. Dist. Ct.).

The court refused to extend the time to issue a third party claim where the claim would have delayed the plaintiff inordinately.

Gotaverken Energy Systems Ltd. v. Cdn. Great Lakes Casualty & Surety Co. (1985), 5 C.P.C. (2d) 41 (Ont. Master).

The court refused to permit the defendant to make a late third party claim where a fixed date had been given for a six-week trial of the main action. The plaintiff would be prejudiced by the delay of the trial.

Emco Ltd. v. Union Ins. Soc. of Canton Ltd. (1984), 45 C.P.C. 216 (Ont. Master).

The court declined to strike out the defendant fidelity insurer's third party claim against an employee of the plaintiff, even though issued eight years late and while the main action was on the trial list, since such a claim had only recently been held to be proper, extra expense and delay would be avoided, it was appropriate that the third party be bound by findings of fact based to some degree on his own evidence, and any injury to the third party could be dealt with by appropriate directions by the judge dealing with the trial list.

Pugliese v. Nat. Capital Comm.; Dunn v. Ottawa-Carleton (1981), 32 O.R. (2d) 264, 21 C.P.C. 157 (Div. Ct.).

The court extended the time for commencing third party proceedings notwithstanding unexplained delay, where no actual prejudice not compensable in costs was shown.

103 Avenue Road Ltd. v. Guardian Gas Installation & Services Ltd. (1980), 16 C.P.C. 31 (Ont. H.C.).

A motion to extend the time to commence third party proceedings was made without notice to the proposed third party. *[But see now rule 37.07(1) — Authors.]*

Jet Disposal Ltd. v. St. Paul Fire and Marine Ins. Co., 13 O.R. (2d) 603, 1 C.P.C. 184, [1976] I.L.R. 1-763 (H.C.).

The court set aside third party process, served many months late, where the defendant had long before known all the facts and the third party had been prejudiced by the completion of an examination for discovery.

Magee v. Canada Coach Lines Ltd., [1946] O.W.N. 265 (Master).

Time for service of a statement of defence was extended in order that a third party action could be regularized.

THIRD PARTY DEFENCE

29.03 Except as provided in subrule 18.02(3) (notice of intent to defend) or 19.01(5) (late filing of defence), a third party may defend against the third party claim by delivering a third party defence (Form 29B),

(a) within twenty days after service of the third party claim, where the third party is served in Ontario;

(b) within forty days after service of the third party claim, where the defendant is served elsewhere in Canada or in the United States of America; or

(c) within sixty days after service of the third party claim, where the third party is served anywhere else.

York Condominium Corp. No. 335 v. Cadillac Fairview Corp. (1983), 42 O.R. (2d) 219 (Master).

A third party is entitled to apply for particulars of the statement of claim in the main action.

REPLY TO THIRD PARTY DEFENCE

29.04 A reply to third party defence (Form 29C), if any, shall be delivered within ten days after service of the third party defence.

DEFENCE OF MAIN ACTION BY THIRD PARTY

Third Party May Defend Main Action

29.05(1) Where appropriate, the third party may defend against the plaintiff's claim against the defendant by delivering a statement of defence in the main action, in which the third party may raise any defence open to the defendant.

Consequence of Defending Main Action

(2) A third party who delivers a statement of defence in the main action,
(a) has the same rights and obligations in the main action, including those in respect of discovery, trial and appeal, as a defendant in the main action; and
(b) is bound by any order or determination made in the main action between the plaintiff and the defendant who made the third party claim.

Time for Statement of Defence

(3) The statement of defence of the third party shall be delivered within the time prescribed by rule 29.03 for the delivery of the third party defence.

Time for Reply

(4) The plaintiff's reply, if any, to the statement of defence of the third party shall be delivered within ten days after service of that statement of defence.

Consequence of Not Defending Main Action

(5) A third party who does not deliver a statement of defence in the main action is bound by any order or determination made in the main action between the plaintiff and the defendant who made the third party claim.

Gatt v. Rumack (1994), 21 O.R. (3d) 655 (Gen. Div.).

The court struck out a statement of defence to the main action filed by the third party where the third party was the defendant's insurer and the statement of defence took a position contrary to that of the defendant.

Bank of Montreal v. Pilot Insurance Co. (1992), 15 C.P.C. (3d) 92, 16 C.C.L.I. (2d) 208, [1993] I.L.R. 1-2919 (Ont. Gen. Div.).

A third party who defended the main action only on the basis of quantum of damages was held to be bound by the determination as to liability.

Evans v. Holroyd (1988), 31 C.P.C. (2d) 48 (Ont. H.C.).

The rights acquired by a third party under rule 29.05(2) include the right to move for security for costs.

Corrigan v. Employers' Ins. of Wausau A Mutual Co., 48 O.R. (2d) 354, 8 C.C.L.I. 1, 29 M.V.R. 98, 13 D.L.R. (4th) 305, [1984] I.L.R. 1-1832 (H.C.).

Where an injured plaintiff sued his own insurer on an underinsured motorist endorsement, and the insurer took third party proceedings against the tortfeasor to recover any damages the insurer might be ordered to pay, the third party was held not to have status to have the main action dismissed as premature, but was entitled to a stay of the third party proceedings.

Venton v. Chan, [1973] 3 O.R. 739 (Master).

A third party joined after the expiry of the limitation period was permitted to raise the negligence of the driver of an unidentified motor vehicle as a defence.

Hi-Grade Welding Co. v. Lytle Engineering Specialties Ltd., [1965] 1 O.R. 697 (Master).

A third party may deny allegations made by the plaintiff notwithstanding that the defendant admits them.

EFFECT OF THIRD PARTY DEFENCE

29.06 Where a third party has delivered a third party defence,
(a) the third party shall be served with all subsequent documents in the main action;
(b) judgment in the main action on consent or after the noting of the defendant in default may be obtained only on notice to the third party; and
(c) where the defendant making the third party claim has also made a crossclaim against a co-defendant, the co-defendant and the third party have the same rights to discovery from each other as if they were parties to the same action.

EFFECT OF DEFAULT OF THIRD PARTY

29.07 Where a third party has been noted in default, the defendant may obtain judgment against the third party only at the trial of the main action or on motion to a judge.

Kondo v. Hellberg and Middleton, [1949] O.W.N. 349 (C.A.).

Where a third party has defaulted, the judge may dismiss the third party claim on the merits if the defendant fails to show a *prima facie* case.

TRIAL OF THIRD PARTY CLAIM

29.08(1) After the close of pleadings in the third party claim it shall be listed for trial as an action as provided in Rule 48 without undue delay and placed on the trial list immediately after the main action.
(2) The third party claim shall be tried at or immediately after the trial of the main action, unless the court orders otherwise.

Trial of Third Party Claim — Generally

Merrett v. Lyons, [1958] O.W.N. 410 (C.A.).

An agreement between the plaintiff and the defendant as to the quantum of damages is not proof of such damages for purposes of a third party claim.

Toronto v. B.A. Oil Co., [1947] O.R. 256, [1947] 3 D.L.R. 129 (C.A.).

Discussion of trial procedure where a third party under the *Negligence Act* is involved.

Trial of Third Party Claim — Where Main Action Settled

Slater Steel Industs. Ltd. v. I.C.E. Combustion Systems Inc. (1984), 46 O.R. (2d) 45, 43 C.P.C. 259, 8 D.L.R. (4th) 254 (H.C.).

Settlement of the plaintiff's claims in the main action, in which the defendants made claims for contribution from each other, does not foreclose the prosecution of a third party claim for contribution. [*Under the new Rules the claim for contribution would be by crossclaim, not by third party claim. See rule 28.01 — Authors.*]

Morello v. Henderson, [1959] O.W.N. 121 (H.C.).

Where the main action was settled, the defendant was permitted to continue the third party action notwithstanding that the third party had been deprived of his opportunity to defend the main action.

PREJUDICE OR DELAY TO PLAINTIFF

29.09 A plaintiff is not to be prejudiced or unnecessarily delayed by reason of a third party claim, and on motion by the plaintiff the court may make such order or impose such terms, including an order that the third party claim proceed as a separate action, as are necessary to prevent prejudice or delay where that may be done without injustice to the defendant or the third party.

Symons Gen. Ins. Co. v. Can. Union Ins. Co. (1985), 50 C.P.C. 75 (Ont. Master).

A plaintiff seeking an order that a third party claim be asserted in a separate action must give notice to the third parties as well as the defendant. The motion should not be brought until it is possible to determine which third parties will defend the third party claim and which, if any, wish to defend the main action.

Victoria Trust and Savings Co. v. Puckrin, [1945] O.W.N. 321 (Master).

In a foreclosure action, a third party notice was struck out as the case was complicated and it was not possible to dispose of the third party notice without prejudicing or delaying the plaintiff.

THIRD PARTY DIRECTIONS

29.10 Any party affected by a third party claim may move for directions in respect of any matter of procedure not otherwise provided for in these rules.

Union Carbide Can. Ltd. v. C.N.R. (1980), 17 C.P.C. 127 (Ont. C.A.).

This provision authorizes directions only regarding procedural matters in the third party proceeding not specifically covered elsewhere. A third party may not counterclaim against the plaintiff.

FOURTH AND SUBSEQUENT PARTY CLAIMS

29.11(1) A third party may, by commencing a fourth party claim, assert against any person not already a party to the third party claim any claim that is properly the subject matter of a third party claim, and rules 29.01 to 29.10 apply, with necessary modifications, to the fourth party claim.

(2) A fourth party claim need not be served personally on a fourth party who is a party to the main action, unless the fourth party is a defendant in that action and has failed to deliver a notice of intent to defend or a statement of defence in the main action, in which case the fourth party shall be served personally or by an alternative to personal service under rule 16.03, whether or not the fourth party has been noted in default in the main action.

(2.1) Despite subrule 29.02(2), when a fourth party claim is served on a person who is already a party to the main action or to any counterclaim,

crossclaim or third party claim in the main action, the pleadings previously delivered in the main action or in any counterclaim, crossclaim or third party claim in the main action need not be served.

(3) A fourth or subsequent party may assert any claim that is properly the subject matter of a third party claim in like manner as a third party claim. [am. O. Reg. 770/92, s. 9]

Carreiro v. Goszyniecki (1993), 17 C.P.C. (3d) 111 (Ont. Master).
A third party under the *Insurance Act* may not institute fourth party proceedings.

Fine v. T.D. Bank, [1964] 2 O.R. 1 (Master).
A third party who is also a defendant may counterclaim against the co-defendant who took the third party proceedings, rather than taking third party proceedings against such co-defendant, thus avoiding multiplicity of proceedings. [*And see now rule 27.10 — Authors.*]

APPLICATION TO FOURTH AND SUBSEQUENT PARTY CLAIMS

29.12 The provisions of these rules that apply to third party claims apply, with necessary modifications, to fourth and subsequent party claims.

APPLICATION TO COUNTERCLAIMS AND CROSSCLAIMS

29.13 Rules 29.01 to 29.12 apply, with necessary modifications, to the assertion of a third party claim by a defendant to a counterclaim or by a defendant to a crossclaim.

DISCOVERY

Introductory Note on the Organization of the Rules Relating to Discovery (Rules 30-33) and Examinations Out of Court (Rules 34-35)

The Rules relating to discovery fall essentially into two groups. The first group, Rules 30-33, regulate the various forms of discovery, *i.e.* Discovery of Documents (Rule 30), Deemed Undertaking (Rule 30.1), Examination for Discovery (Rule 31), Inspection of Property (Rule 32), and Medical Examination of Parties (Rule 33). See the definition of "discovery" in rule 1.03. The second group, Rules 34-35, regulate the conduct of examinations for discovery. While Rule 31 provides for the nature and scope of examinations for discovery, the procedure to be followed on the conduct of the examination is regulated by Rule 34 (if it is an oral examination) and by Rule 35 (if it is to be conducted by written questions). However, Rule 34 (Procedure on Oral Examination) is not limited to examinations for discovery; it extends to the conduct of all out-of-court examinations.

Several other Rules are also relevant to disclosure or the narrowing of issues before a trial: the pre-trial conference (Rule 50), the request to admit procedure for obtaining admissions as to facts and documents (Rule 51), the disclosure of expert testimony before trial (rule 53.03) and the provision of financial statements in divorce and family law proceedings: rules 69.14 and 70.04.

RULE 30   DISCOVERY OF DOCUMENTS

Highlights

Scope of discovery. Disclosure must be made of every document relating to any matter in issue in an action that is or has been in the possession, control or power of a party, whether or not privilege is claimed in respect of the document: rule 30.02. Documents are very broadly defined (rule 30.01(1)) so as to include, *inter alia*, photographs, videotape and computer-stored information. Insurance policies under which an insurer may be liable to pay a judgment in the action or to indemnify a party to the action are discoverable: rule 30.02(3). By a court order a party can be required to disclose all relevant documents in the possession, control or power of a party's subsidiary or affiliated corporation or of a corporation controlled, directly or indirectly, by the party: rule 30.02(4).

Affidavit of documents. By rule 30.03(1), every party is required to serve an affidavit of documents within ten days after the close of pleadings and, unless the parties agree otherwise, the service of an affidavit of documents is a pre-condition to a party's right to examine for discovery: rule 31.04(1). The affidavit is to list and describe, in separate schedules, documents to be produced, documents no longer in the party's possession and documents in respect of which a claim for privilege is made: rule 30.03(2). Where a claim for privilege is made, the grounds for the claim are to be stated, and the nature and date of the document and other particulars sufficient to identify it are to be given: Forms 30A and 30B. The affidavit is to state that the party has never had possession, control or power over any relevant unlisted documents. Moreover, to ensure that the client understands the broad scope of discovery, the solicitor is to endorse on the affidavit a certificate that he or she has explained to the deponent the necessity of making full disclosure of all relevant documents: rule 30.03(4).

Continuing disclosure. A specific obligation is imposed to correct any omissions from the original affidavit and to disclose subsequently acquired non-privileged documents by means of a supplementary affidavit of documents: rule 30.07.

Production and inspection. All non-privileged documents which have been disclosed may be inspected: rule 30.04. The court may postpone production of documents which may become relevant only after the determination of an issue in the action; however, to obtain such an order, a party must show that serious prejudice would result from earlier production of the document: rule 30.04(8). Production of documents may be obtained from non-parties, but only where it is shown that the document is relevant and that it would be inequitable to require the party to proceed to trial without having discovered the document: rule 30.10. (This test is similar, but not identical, to the test imposed as a pre-condition to obtaining an order for leave to examine a non-party for discovery: rule 31.10.) Where the affidavit is incomplete or privilege has been improperly claimed, the court may order cross-examination on the affidavit or a further and better affidavit of documents, or it may inspect any document for the purposes of determining relevance or privilege: rule 30.06.

Sanctions. Provision is made for dealing with the situation where a party seeks to make use at trial of a document which has not been disclosed or produced. If the document is favourable to the party's case it may not be used, except with leave, and if it is not favourable the court may make such order as is just: rule 30.08(1). (In the United States case of *Rozier v. Ford Motor Co.* (1978), 573 F. 2d 1332 (C.A. 5th Circuit), the plaintiff was granted a new trial where the defendant had failed to disclose a document relevant to the plaintiff's case that it was obliged to disclose on discovery.)

Where a party has claimed privilege for a document, the party may not use the document at trial, except to impeach a witness or with leave of the trial judge, unless he or she abandoned the privilege in writing no later than ten days after the action was set down for trial: rule 30.09. (As to the "leave" provision in both rule 30.08(1) and rule 30.09, rule 53.08 regulates how the court should approach the issue.)

Recent amendments. New Rule 30.1 (Deemed Undertaking) regulates the general use of information obtained through the discovery process.

Former Rules: Rules 347-352.

INTERPRETATION

30.01(1) In rules 30.02 to 30.11,

(a) 'document' includes a sound recording, videotape, film, photograph, chart, graph, map, plan, survey, book of account and information recorded or stored by means of any device; and

(b) a document shall be deemed to be in a party's power if that party is entitled to obtain the original document or a copy of it and the party seeking it is not so entitled.

(2) In subrule 30.02(4),

(a) a corporation is a subsidiary of another corporation where it is controlled directly or indirectly by the other corporation; and

(b) a corporation is affiliated with another corporation where,

(i) one corporation is the subsidiary of the other,

(ii) both corporations are subsidiaries of the same corporation, or

(iii) both corporations are controlled directly or indirectly by the same person or persons.

Reichmann v. Toronto Life Publishing Co. (1988), 66 O.R. (2d) 65, 30 C.P.C. (2d) 280 (H.C.). "Document" includes a computer disc used to store information.

SCOPE OF DOCUMENTARY DISCOVERY

Disclosure
30.02(1) Every document relating to any matter in issue in an action that is or has been in the possession, control or power of a party to the action shall be disclosed as provided in rules 30.03 to 30.10, whether or not privilege is claimed in respect of the document.

Production for Inspection
(2) Every document relating to any matter in issue in an action that is in the possession, control or power of a party to the action shall be produced for inspection if requested, as provided in rules 30.03 to 30.10, unless privilege is claimed in respect of the document.

Insurance Policy
(3) A party shall disclose and, if requested, produce for inspection any insurance policy under which an insurer may be liable,
(a) to satisfy all or part of a judgment in the action; or
(b) to indemnify or reimburse a party for money paid in satisfaction of all or part of the judgment,
but no information concerning the insurance policy is admissible in evidence unless it is relevant to an issue in the action.

Subsidiary and Affiliated Corporations and Corporations Controlled by Party
(4) The court may order a party to disclose all relevant documents in the possession, control or power of the party's subsidiary or affiliated corporation or of a corporation controlled directly or indirectly by the party and to produce for inspection all such documents that are not privileged.

Authors' Note on Organization of Cases

Cases relevant to this provision have been organized as follows:

Production of Documents — Generally
Production of Documents — Medical Reports and Records
Production of Documents — Insurance Policies — rule 30.02(3)
Production of Documents — Privilege for Documents Prepared in Anticipation of Litigation
Production of Documents — Solicitor and Client Privilege
Production of Documents — Crown Privilege
Production of Documents — Privilege Regarding Settlement Negotiations
Production of Documents — Miscellaneous Privileges
Waiver of Privilege
Production of Documents — Statements Made by Opposing Party
Production of Documents — Examples

Production of Documents — Generally

Automated Tabulation Inc. v. Canadian Market Images Ltd. (1995), 24 O.R. (3d) 292 (Gen. Div.).

The court has a discretion to order that access to confidential documents be restricted to the solicitors for an opposing party and not to the opposing party itself.

Manufacturers Life Insurance Co. v. Dofasco Inc. (1989), 38 C.P.C. (2d) 47, additional reasons 38 C.P.C. (2d) 47 at 53 (Ont. H.C.).

A party was permitted to produce documents with certain portions edited out, where the expunged portions of the document were not relevant to the matters in issue.

Glowinsky v. Stephens & Rankin Inc. (1989), 38 C.P.C. (2d) 102 (Ont. Master).

Relevancy is the only test by which to judge whether a document should be produced. Documents will not be ordered produced solely on the basis that they might be useful for attacking credibility.

Reichmann v. Toronto Life Publishing Co. (1988), 66 O.R. (2d) 65, 30 C.P.C. (2d) 280 (H.C.).

A computer disc containing relevant information must be produced. It is not sufficient to produce a printout of the information.

Collins v. Beach, 24 C.P.C. (2d) 228, [1988] 1 C.T.C. 261 (Ont. H.C.).

Tax returns need only be produced to the extent that they are relevant to the matters in issue. Where only the plaintiff's income from employment was relevant, he was permitted to block out other matters disclosed on the tax returns.

Greenfield Const. Co. v. Thunder Bay (1980), 27 O.R. (2d) 257, 19 C.P.C. 282, 107 D.L.R. (3d) 508 (H.C.).

A privileged document continues to be privileged after its author is added as a defendant.

Perini Ltd. v. Parking Authority of Toronto (1975), 6 O.R. (2d) 363, 52 D.L.R. (3d) 683 (C.A.).

A document is not privileged merely because it relates exclusively to the opposite party's case.

Continental Can Co. of Can. Ltd. v. Bank of Montreal (1974), 3 O.R. (2d) 167 (Master).

A party must disclose the existence of a document in his possession with which he has no legal right to deal, but the court may refuse to order production of it.

Re Goodman & Carr and M.N.R., [1968] 2 O.R. 814, 70 D.L.R. (3d) 670, [1968] C.T.C. 484, 68 D.T.C. 5288, 5310 (H.C.).

No privilege applies to a document where fraud is alleged and a *prima facie* case is made out.

Small v. Nemez, [1963] 1 O.R. 91 (H.C.).

Documents which are once privileged are always privileged.

Toronto Gen. Trusts v. Little, [1962] O.W.N. 141 (H.C.).

Documents which are in the possession of a party in a capacity other than that in which he is engaged in the litigation are privileged.

Ivey v. Can. Trust Co., [1962] O.W.N. 62 (H.C.).

Documents which are merely loaned to a party need not be produced.

Croft v. Munnings, [1957] O.R. 211 (H.C.).

The Crown may refuse to produce certain documents if to do so would be contrary to the public interest.

Production of Documents — Medical Reports and Records (See also rules 33.04(2), 33.06(2).)

Davidson v. Grant, (April 5, 1995), Doc. 92-CU-62938 (Ont. Gen. Div.).

Where the plaintiff in this personal injury case pleaded all encompassing claims the court ordered production of clinical notes and records and OHIP records.

Micheli v. Sheppard (1994), 30 C.P.C. (3d) 297 (Ont. Gen. Div.).

Although the statement of claim in a personal injury action was broadly pleaded, the court refused to order production of clinical notes and records in relation to all matters concerning the plaintiff. The issues in the case had been narrowed to an eye injury, and therefore the request was beyond the limits of relevance.

P. (L.M.) v. F. (D.) (1994), 34 C.P.C. (3d) 172, 22 C.C.L.T. (2d) 312 (Ont. Gen. Div.).

The court ordered production of clinical notes and records relating to the plaintiff's psychotherapy treatments in this sexual abuse case but imposed confidentiality terms.

Pollard v. Esses (1994), 35 C.P.C. (3d) 398 (Ont. Gen. Div.).

Where a defendant requested and obtained an undertaking from the plaintiff to obtain clinical notes and records from non-parties, the court ordered the defendant to pay the associated costs.

Bazzi v. Allstate Insurance Co. of Canada (1994), 28 C.P.C. (3d) 166, 4 M.V.R. (3d) 310 (Ont. Gen. Div.).

Section 164 of the *Insurance Act* did not change the previous general policy which requires the defence to pay for the production of clinical notes not in the possession of the plaintiff.

W. (Y.) v. W. (L.) (1994), 28 C.P.C. (3d) 60 (Ont. Div. Ct.).

The court refused to order the production of medical records where relevance was tenuous at best. The fact that the records might have some relevance to credibility did not itself justify the ordering of production.

W. (T.) v. W. (K.R.J.) (1994), 26 C.P.C. (3d) 45, 111 D.L.R. (4th) 703 (Ont. Gen. Div.).

If a doctor has prepared a report and the report is not contradicted by the patient and is not itself ambiguous or equivocal, there will be no reason to produce the doctor's clinical notes and records.

Lonergan v. Morrissette (1993), 23 C.P.C. (3d) 186, 109 D.L.R. (4th) 758 (Ont. Gen. Div.).

Where the plaintiff placed his entire medical and emotional health in issue, the court held that the hospital records and medical reports were relevant and ordered their production.

Wilton v. Brown (1993), 22 C.P.C. (3d) 249 (Ont. Gen. Div.).

Where the plaintiff's health is placed in issue in a broad sense in the statement of claim, the clinical notes and records of the plaintiff's family physician should be produced for inspection by the defendant.

Kaptsis v. Macias (1990), 74 O.R. (2d) 189, 44 C.P.C. (2d) 285 (H.C.).

The clinical notes and records of the plaintiff's treating physician need not be disclosed where the "findings" of the physician were contained in a report which had been disclosed.

Maksimov v. Berger (1989), 68 O.R. (2d) 438 (H.C.).

The court ordered production of the entire Workers' Compensation Board file in the plaintiff's possession where the issues in the action were the same as those dealt with in the Board's file, *i.e.*, the plaintiff's back injury and his ability to work.

Clark v. Stewart (1988), 30 C.P.C. (2d) 134 (Ont. Master).

In an action for wrongful dismissal the court granted a motion by the defendant for production of all medical records and clinical notes and records relating to the plaintiff where such history was relevant to the issues in the action.

Catanzaro v. Doxtator (1988), 65 O.R. (2d) 199, 28 C.P.C. (2d) 42 (H.C.).

Where allegations in the statement of claim had brought the plaintiff's prior health into issue, the pre-accident notes of the treating physician were ordered produced.

Schultz v. Galvin (1988), 65 O.R. (2d) 13, 27 C.P.C. (2d) 253 (H.C.).

A plaintiff must make "reasonable" and not "best" efforts to obtain clinical notes, meaning a letter and follow-up call. Details of the efforts must be provided to the defendant if the notes are not obtained. The plaintiff's costs in obtaining clinical notes and records requested on discovery are payable by the defendant, even if later the notes and records are not produced by reason of irrelevance.

Djurasevic v. McAuley (1988), 10 W.D.C.P. 243 (Ont. H.C.).

The court ordered production of clinical notes and records where the plaintiff claimed she would be unable to work for the rest of her life and put the limits of her physical and mental capacities in issue.

Ontario (A.G.) v. C.E.C. Edwards Construction (1987), 60 O.R. (2d) 618, 23 C.P.C. (2d) 61 (H.C.).

The court declined to order production of clinical notes but required the plaintiff to request medical reports providing the material information contained in the notes.

Furlano v. Calarco (1987), 60 O.R. (2d) 451, 20 C.P.C. (2d) 279 (H.C.).

The test for requiring a party to produce a physician's clinical notes and records in a personal injury case is relevance. Where the plaintiff alleged broad physical and psychiatric injuries, and there was evidence of both problems in her prior medical history, the defendants obtained an order for production of the plaintiff's physician's clinical notes from two years prior to the accident to date.

Triumbari v. Bloch (1987), 20 C.P.C. (2d) 277 (Ont. H.C.).

There is no need to demonstrate a conflict between medical reports and discovery evidence before a party can be compelled to obtain a physician's clinical notes and records. If the documents so obtained are relevant, the party is obliged to prepare a supplementary affidavit of documents and produce the documents.

Couto v. T.T.C. (1987), 59 O.R. (2d) 406, 16 C.P.C. (2d) 241 (H.C.).

The court ordered production of treating physicians' clinical notes and records in this personal injury case.

Trovato v. Smith (1987), 15 C.P.C. (2d) 121 (Ont. Dist. Ct.).

The court ordered the plaintiff to seek his physician's clinical records and notes although they were not within the plaintiff's "power" within the meaning of rule 30.03(1). There is no merit, logic or support in the Rules for requiring the defendant to establish a conflict in the medical reports or discovery evidence before making such an order. If a doctor does not voluntarily produce the documents, the defence will be met with its more limited rights under rule 30.10.

Gallo v. Gillham (1987), 58 O.R. (2d) 115, 15 C.P.C. (2d) 125 (Master), affirmed 67 O.R. (2d) 734, 23 C.P.C. (2d) 109 (H.C.).

A physician's clinical notes and records of post-injury treatment are not producible where a medical report has been delivered and there is no conflict between the plaintiff's evidence and the report. *Cook v. Ip* (1985), 52 O.R. (2d) 289, 5 C.P.C. (2d) 81, 22 D.L.R. (4th) 1, 11 O.A.C. 171 (*sub nom. Cook v. Washuta*) (C.A.) did not overrule *Tilly v. Crangle* (1981), 31 O.R. (2d) 641, 120 D.L.R. (3d) 563 (C.A.).

Whitby v. Mount Sinai Hospital (1986), 57 O.R. (2d) 219, 13 C.P.C. (2d) 274 (Master), affirmed (1987), 67 O.R. (2d) 479, 24 C.P.C. (2d) 319 (H.C.).

Clinical notes and records of treating physicians are relevant productions regardless of whether a medical report is delivered and a party is obliged to make best efforts to obtain them and disclose them in his affidavit of documents.

Orr v. Warren (1986), 59 O.R. (2d) 286, 18 C.P.C. (2d) 190 (H.C.).

The court ordered the plaintiff to produce her medical records for the period prior to the accident where the defendant pleaded that a pre-existing condition caused her loss of income.

Heywood v. Nash (1986), 18 C.P.C. (2d) 154, additional reasons 18 C.P.C. (2d) 154 at 156 (Ont. H.C.).

The plaintiff was directed to request production of office and clinical notes from physicians who had treated the plaintiff both before and after a motor vehicle collision. The production of certain hospital records was not ordered as the records were not relevant to the issues between the parties.

Hathway v. Bond (1986), 11 C.P.C. (2d) 277 (Ont. Master).

A party who received medical treatment is responsible for obtaining the medical records despite any impecuniosity.

Fedorczenko v. Jamieson (1986), 56 O.R. (2d) 252, 14 C.P.C. (2d) 299 (H.C.).

The plaintiff in a personal injury action was required to use best efforts to obtain the clinical notes and records of treating physicians, a summary of hospital services received, and copies of employment records.

Griffis v. T.T.C. (1985), 15 C.P.C. (2d) 119 (Ont. H.C.).

The court ordered a plaintiff to request from her physicians and dentist and produce clinical notes and records prepared both before and after an accident regarding the physical problems in issue. If the request was refused, resort could be had directly to the professionals under rule 30.10.

Primavera v. Aetna Casualty Co. of Can. (1985), 6 C.P.C. (2d) 216 (Ont. Master).

The court refused to order production of the plaintiff's physician's clinical notes where there was no conflict between the plaintiff's evidence and any medical reports and the physician's reports were not inadequate or insufficient.

Leerentveld v. McCulloch (1985), 4 C.P.C. (2d) 26 (Ont. Master).

The plaintiff was ordered to ask his physician for his office notes and to produce them if made available or if not made available to so inform the defendant's counsel. Questions concerning medical records and x-rays must be answered unless the physicians in question were consulted solely for the purposes of litigation. Although the plaintiff had attempted to obtain the Workers' Compensation Board hospital records, the plaintiff was ordered to provide the defendant with an authorization for the release of the records.

Gibbs v. Gibbs (1985), 48 C.P.C. 163 (Ont. Master).

In this custody case the court ordered production of medical records relating to the wife's previous mental illness subject to a further *in camera* hearing if the attending physician was of the opinion it might harm the patient.

Gorin v. Ho; Gorin v. Stewart & Cass (1983), 38 C.P.C. 72 (Ont. Master).

In a personal injury action, the plaintiff has an obligation to obtain and produce medical and hospital records regarding his treatment.

Atkins v. Iwanicki (1979), 22 O.R. (2d) 182, 10 C.P.C. 269 (Master).

Where the Workmen's Compensation Board brought a subrogated action in the plaintiff's name, it was ordered to produce medical records in its possession pertaining to the plaintiff's treatment at its facilities.

Meaney v. Busby (1977), 15 O.R. (2d) 71, 2 C.P.C. 340 (H.C.).

Medical reports prepared for previous litigation are producible.

Halteh v. McCoy (1975), 6 O.R. (2d) 512 (H.C.).

A medical report obtained by a passenger under his driver's no-fault insurance policy is not privileged in an action by the passenger against the driver of another vehicle.

Boulianne v. Flynn, [1970] 3 O.R. 84 (H.C.).

A medical report prepared for one action was held not to be privileged in subsequent litigation arising out of a different accident.

Blackstone v. Mutual Life Ins. Co., [1944] O.R. 328 (C.A.).

Medical reports made in the normal course of events and before litigation was contemplated were held not to be privileged.

Production of Documents — Insurance Policies — rule 30.02(3)

DGW Electronics Corp. v. Crystal Craft Industries Inc. (1986), 15 C.P.C. (2d) 205 (Ont. H.C.).

A plaintiff prosecuting a fire case on its behalf and on a subrogated basis for its insurer was required to produce a copy of the insurance policy.

K Mart Can. Ltd./K Mart Can. Ltée v. Millmink Devs. Ltd., 56 O.R. (2d) 422, 11 C.P.C. (2d) 243, 24 C.C.L.I. 139, 31 D.L.R. (4th) 135, [1986] I.L.R. 1-2114 (H.C.).

Rules 30.02(3) and 31.06(4), requiring disclosure of insurance policies, do not constitute an unreasonable search or seizure and are not discriminatory under s. 15 of the *Charter of Rights*.

Saini v. Manolakos (1985), 1 C.P.C. (2d) 102 (Ont. Dist. Ct.).

There is no conflict between rule 30.02(3) or 31.06(4) and s. 227(2) of the *Insurance Act*, which requires production of particulars of any relevant motor vehicle liability policy when judgment is obtained against the insured.

Sabatino v. Gunning, 50 O.R. (2d) 171, 48 C.P.C. 265, [1985] I.L.R. 1-1891, 10 O.A.C. 347 (C.A.).

The purpose of rule 30.02(3) is to assist the parties in making informed and sensible decisions in circumstances where recourse to insurance moneys may play a major role in how the litigation is conducted and through what stages it should be pursued. The court ordered production of an insurance policy after trial while an appeal was pending.

Brito v. Biduke, 46 C.P.C. 3, 8 C.C.L.I. 64, [1984] I.L.R. 1-1837 (H.C.).

An insurer added as a "third party" under the *Insurance Act* may be required to produce all documents relating to insurance coverage.

Production of Documents — Privilege for Documents Prepared in Anticipation of Litigation

Tubbessing v. Bell Canada (1995), 22 O.R. (3d) 714, 9 C.C.E.L. (2d) 312 (Master).

In this wrongful dismissal case, the court ordered production of documents relating to the investigation of sexual harassment complaints by the plaintiff. There was no reasonable prospect of litigation at the time and the documents were not privileged.

Bohman v. Canada (Deputy Attorney General) (1994), 35 C.P.C. (3d) 251 (Ont. Gen. Div.).

Documents prepared by a client for counsel after learning of an investigation under the *Income Tax Act* were held to be privileged.

Tremblay v. Daum (1994), 29 C.P.C. (3d) 219, 4 M.V.R. (3d) 256 (Ont. Gen. Div.).

Where a defendant against whom the case had been dismissed gave surveillance documentation to a remaining defendant, the court held the documentation was not privileged. There was no joint privilege because the documentation was created solely by the first defendant.

Emond v. Reid (1993), 47 M.V.R. (2d) 284 (Ont. Gen. Div.).

The court applied the "substantial purpose" test rather than the "dominant purpose" test.

Hall v. Co-operators General Insurance Co., 14 C.P.C. (3d) 355, 5 C.L.R. (2d) 318, [1992] I.L.R. 1-2869 (Ont. Gen. Div.).

Courts of first instance should apply the "dominant purpose" test regarding documents prepared in anticipation of litigation as they are bound by *Ottawa-Carleton (Regional Municipality) v. Consumers' Gas Co., infra.*

Calvaruso v. Nantais (1992), 7 C.P.C. (3d) 254 (Ont. Gen. Div.).

The court refused to order production of an instructing letter from counsel to an expert witness. The letter was privileged and there was no compelling reason to require production.

Keuhl v. McConnell (1991), 3 C.P.C. (3d) 22, 32 M.V.R. (2d) 280 (Ont. Gen. Div.).

In Ontario the "substantial purpose" test, not the "dominant purpose" test, should be applied concerning the litigation privilege. *Waugh v. British Railways Bd.*, [1980] A.C. 521, [1979] 2 All E.R. 1169, not followed.

Ferber v. Gore Mutual Insurance Co. (1991), 2 W.D.C.P. (2d) 565 (Ont. Master).

In this fire insurance case, where the defendant's adjuster obtained a memorandum from a police force summarizing evidence of witnesses, the court held the document was privileged on the basis of the Divisional Court decision in *Ottawa-Carleton (Regional Municipality) v. Consumers' Gas Co., infra.* Such privilege applies not only to a collection of documents, but also to a single document.

Carlucci v. Laurentian Casualty Co. of Canada (1991), 50 C.P.C. (2d) 62 (Ont. Master).

The court refused to order the production of insurance adjuster's reports made when there was a reasonable prospect but no certainty of litigation. There must be more than a mere suspicion of litigation for privilege to apply.

Ottawa-Carleton (Regional Municipality) v. Consumers' Gas Co. (1990), 74 O.R. (2d) 637, 45 C.P.C. (2d) 293, 74 D.L.R. (4th) 742, 41 O.A.C. 65 (Div. Ct.).

Where photocopies of public documents have been obtained for the dominant purpose of use in litigation, then the photocopies, but not the original documents, are privileged.

Werner v. Warner Auto-Marine Inc. (1990), 73 O.R. (2d) 59, 44 C.P.C. (2d) 175 (H.C.).

The "substantial purpose" and not the "dominant purpose" test for privilege applies in Ontario until the Court of Appeal expressly rules otherwise.

Varga v. Huyer, 37 C.P.C. (2d) 197, [1989] I.L.R. 1-2494 (Ont. Master).

The court ordered production of a statement given by a defendant to his own insurer following a motor vehicle accident, since the accident's occurrence alone did not give rise to a definite prospect of litigation.

Lattanzio v. Jones (1989), 33 C.P.C. (2d) 160 (Ont. Dist. Ct.).

The court ordered the defendant to produce the statement of a witness taken shortly after the fire which was the subject-matter of the action. There was no evidence that the litigation was threatened or indicated at that time.

C. Itoh & Co. v. "New Jersey Maru" (The) (1988), 28 C.P.C. (2d) 7 (Ont. Master).

Although an insurance adjuster's report had been prepared prior to counsel being retained, the report was still privileged, as its dominant purpose was use in reasonably anticipated litigation.

Young's Graves Inc. (Receiver of) v. Hartford Fire Ins. Co. (1988), 27 C.P.C. (2d) 242 (Master), affirmed 27 C.P.C. (2d) 242n (H.C.).

Adjuster's reports prepared for the dominant purpose of placing before counsel for his advice, and in reasonable anticipation of litigation, were privileged. It is not essential to have selected counsel in order to claim privilege.

600254 Ont. Ltd. v. Zurich Ins. Co. (1988), 27 C.P.C. (2d) 221 (Ont. H.C.).

The court refused to order production of reports prepared in anticipation of litigation for the defendant fire insurer which suspected arson.

Proctor & Redfern Ltd. v. Lakehead Region Conservation Authority (1987), 21 C.P.C. (2d) 163 (Ont. H.C.).

The court ordered production of an expert's report obtained during negotiations prior to litigation for the dual purpose of aiding settlement discussions and assisting the defendant to assess its position in expected litigation. The court used the sole purpose test in rejecting a claim of privilege.

Yri-York Ltd. v. Commercial Union Assurance Co. of Can. (1987), 17 C.P.C. (2d) 181 (Ont. H.C.).

Statements from witnesses which were obtained prior to a law suit but in reasonable and *bona fide* anticipation of litigation, as shown by affidavit evidence, were held to be privileged.

Couto v. T.T.C. (1986), 14 C.P.C. (2d) 115 (Ont. Master), reversed in part on other grounds (1987), 59 O.R. (2d) 406, 16 C.P.C. (2d) 241 (H.C.).

The court ordered a plaintiff in a personal injury action to produce a daily diary record of her physical and emotional condition notwithstanding that it was kept on instructions of her counsel. No specific claim for privilege was made in the affidavit of documents or elsewhere.

Benson v. Quattrocchi (1986), 8 C.P.C. (2d) 272 (Ont. H.C.).

A report of a motor vehicle accident given by an insured to the insurer was held to be privileged.

Dunham v. Grant (1985), 7 C.P.C. (2d) 25 (Ont. H.C.).

The court ordered production of adjuster's reports which contained information the defendant would be required to disclose on discovery notwithstanding the lower court's finding that the reports were prepared for the dominant purpose of litigation.

Heritage Clothing (Can.) Ltd. v. Sun Alliance Ins. Co. (1985), 4 C.P.C. (2d) 154 (Ont. H.C.) (leave to appeal to Ont. Div. Ct. denied September 30, 1985).

The proper test of litigation privilege is the "dominant purpose" test.

Walters v. T.T.C. (1985), 50 O.R. (2d) 635, 4 C.P.C. (2d) 66 (H.C.).

An accident report made by the defendant's employee was ordered produced where at the time the report was prepared the employee did not have any knowledge that there might be a law suit.

Rangwala v. Rizzo, 4 C.P.C. (2d) 1, [1986] I.L.R. 1-2028 (Ont. Master) (appeal to Ont. H.C. dismissed October 30, 1985).

In this motor vehicle action, the master refused to order the defendant to produce a report made by the defendant to her insurer in compliance with her policy and the *Insurance Act.*

Falconbridge Ltd. v. Hawker Siddeley Diesels & Electrics Ltd. (1985), 50 O.R. (2d) 794, 3 C.P.C. (2d) 133 (H.C.).

The "dominant purpose" test regarding privilege attaching to documents prepared in anticipation of litigation should be applied notwithstanding the decision of the Ontario Court of Appeal in *Blackstone v. Mutual Life*, [1944] O.R. 328 adopting the "substantial purpose" test.

Armak Chemicals Ltd. v. C.N.R. (1984), 48 O.R. (2d) 381, 47 C.P.C. 219 (H.C.).

The court ordered the defendant to produce witness statements where the dominant purpose of obtaining the statements was to fulfill a statutory obligation to submit a report. *Waugh v. British Railways Bd.*, [1980] A.C. 521, [1979] 2 All E.R. 1169 (H.L.), applied.

R. v. Westmoreland, 48 O.R. (2d) 377, 15 C.C.C. (3d) 340, 14 D.L.R. (4th) 112, [1984] I.L.R. 1-1829 (H.C.).

Where prior to obtaining statements an insurance company had probable cause to believe litigation was contemplated, the statements were privileged, even though no solicitor was consulted until long after the statements were taken.

McIntyre v. C.P. Ltd. (1984), 43 C.P.C. 59 (Ont. H.C.), application for leave to appeal to Ont. Div. Ct. dismissed 43 C.P.C. 59 at 65.

The court refused to reverse the District Court Judge's ruling that photographs taken the day after a level-crossing accident be produced, where there was a statutory duty to submit a report to the Railway Commission.

Rush v. Phoenix Assur. Co. of Can., 40 C.P.C. 185, [1984] I.L.R. 1-1737 (Ont. Master).

A document may be prepared in contemplation of litigation and for the purpose of being laid before a solicitor even though there is no specific solicitor retained or in mind.

Keirouz v. Co-operators Ins. Assn., 39 C.P.C. 164, [1983] I.L.R. 1-1712 (Ont. H.C.).

In this fire case, litigation was anticipated on the date the defendant concluded that the fire was caused by arson involving the plaintiffs and documents prepared after that date were privileged, rather than the subsequent date of formal denial of the plaintiff's claim.

Schonberger v. T.T.C. (1981), 43 C.P.C. 215 (Ont. H.C.).

An employee's accident report was privileged, having been prepared with reasonable anticipation of litigation, notwithstanding the facts of this particular accident, since the defendant employer was a self-insured public carrier.

Sgambelluri v. Can. Indemnity Co. (1983), 37 C.P.C. 174 (Ont. H.C.).

In order to avoid production of documents allegedly prepared in contemplation of litigation the party seeking to establish the privilege must show that the paramount or dominant purpose of the making of the documents was use in litigation.

Wright v. Clarke (1983), 32 C.P.C. 309 (Ont. H.C.).

A diary of complaints prepared on instructions of counsel by a plaintiff in a personal injury case was held to be privileged from production.

Conn Chem Ltd. v. Canbar Products Ltd. (1982), 36 O.R. (2d) 717 (H.C.).

The court refused to require production of reports prepared regarding an industrial accident which appeared to have been prepared in contemplation of litigation.

Delta-Benco-Cascade Ltd. v. Lakes Cablevision Inc. (1982), 35 O.R. (2d) 715, 26 C.P.C. 145 (Master).

An engineering report ordered partly for the purpose of correcting defects and partly for use in contemplation of likely litigation was privileged.

Ilich v. Hartford Fire Ins. Co. (1981), 17 C.P.C. 163, affirmed 20 C.P.C. 8 (Ont. H.C.).

A document is privileged if it was prepared substantially for the purpose of, or in connection with litigation, then pending or anticipated. Some definite prospect of litigation, not merely a vague anticipation, is required. Certain reports prepared after a fire but before arson charges were laid were ordered to be produced.

Vernon v. Bd. of Educ. for North York (1975), 9 O.R. (2d) 613 (H.C.).

A document prepared in anticipation of litigation was held to be privileged notwithstanding that it was not prepared solely for that purpose.

Can. Gen. Elec. Co. v. Liverpool & London & Globe Ins. Co. (1977), 4 C.P.C. 45, affirmed 4 C.P.C. 51 (Ont. H.C.).

Where an insurer instructs an independent adjuster to investigate whether coverage under a policy exists for a claim, the report prepared is not privileged as being in contemplation of litigation.

Carleton Condominium Corp. v. Shenkman Corp. Ltd. (1977), 3 C.P.C. 211 (Ont. H.C.).

An expert's report prepared during related litigation is privileged.

Crits v. Sylvester, [1955] O.W.N. 243 (H.C.).

An expert report on the cause of an explosion was held to have been made in part for the purpose of litigation and was therefore privileged. A report required to be made to a governmental authority was held to be privileged to the extent it was based on the expert report.

Production of Documents — Solicitor and Client Privilege (See also cases under rule 31.06.)

Ontario (Attorney General) v. Ballard Estate (1994), 20 O.R. (3d) 350, 33 C.P.C. (3d) 373, 6 E.T.R. (2d) 34, 119 D.L.R. (4th) 750 (Gen. Div. [Commercial List]).

Communications between an executor or trustee and a solicitor for the estate are not privileged as against beneficiaries under the will or trust, including a beneficiary who has only a contingent interest.

R. v. McCarthy Tétrault (1992), 12 C.P.C. (3d) 42, 9 C.E.L.R. (N.S.) 12, 95 D.L.R. (4th) 94 (Ont. Prov. Div.).

An application for solicitor and client privilege under s. 160(8) of the *Provincial Offences Act* was sustained where the evidence established that the purpose of the meeting giving rise to the notes in issue was to obtain legal advice.

Pomer v. Zeppieri (1992), 8 O.R. (3d) 215 (Gen. Div.).

In an action brought by a solicitor against his former partners for a winding-up of the firm, the files assumed by the defendants subsequent to the dissolution of the firm were not the subject of solicitor and client privilege and were therefore ordered produced.

Hirji v. Scavetta (1991), 50 C.P.C. (2d) 186 (Ont. Gen. Div.).

The defendant was not required to answer questions directed to his relationship with his solicitor as solicitor and client privilege applied where the questions were directed not to facts but rather the advice given.

Goodman Estate v. Geffen, [1991] 2 S.C.R. 353, 80 Alta. L.R. (2d) 293, 42 E.T.R. 97, [1991] 5 W.W.R. 389, 81 D.L.R. (4th) 211, 127 N.R. 241, 14 W.A.C. 81.

The exception to the solicitor and client privilege permitting a solicitor to give evidence in litigation concerning a will which he or she has prepared extends to litigation involving the validity of a trust instrument after the death of the settlor.

Madge v. Thunder Bay (City) (1990), 72 O.R. (2d) 41, 44 C.P.C. (2d) 186 (H.C.).

Communications between a lawyer and client relating to the delivery of minutes of a meeting to a lawyer were privileged. The delivery of the minutes was a confidential communication, and not an act or transaction.

Dixon v. Canada (Deputy Attorney General) (1989), 91 D.T.C. 5584 (Ont. H.C.).

Discussion of solicitor and client privilege in the context of the search and seizure of documents from a law firm under the *Income Tax Act.*

York Condominium Corp. No. 227 v. York (1988), 30 C.P.C. (2d) 177 (Ont. Master).

A solicitor's file remains privileged unless privilege is lost through the intervention of an illegal act by the client. Where the client only admitted to engaging in an illegal act before retaining the solicitor, and the solicitor-client relationship was not used to further the illegal act, the solicitor-client privilege remained.

Microtel Ltd. v. Electronics Distributors Inc. (1988), 30 C.P.C. (2d) 41 (Ont. Master), affirmed 32 C.P.C. (2d) 85 (Ont. H.C.).

Although solicitor and client communications lose their privilege when they are in furtherance of a fraud, the court refused to order production where the statement of claim did not allege such a fraud, and there was nothing in the discovery or the documents in issue to show a *prima facie* case of fraud.

Mutual Life Assurance Co. of Can. v. Canada (Deputy A.G.) (1988), 28 C.P.C. (2d) 101, 88 D.T.C. 6511 (Ont. H.C.).

Communications between lawyers of a company and the employees of a wholly owned subsidiary of that same company were held to be privileged, where there was a very close relationship between the management of the two companies. Where a lawyer is an employee of the client, communications are privileged if they concern the employee's function as a lawyer, and are not privileged if the lawyer is performing a business or other function.

Bodnar v. Home Ins. Co. (1987), 25 C.P.C. (2d) 152 (Ont. Master).

An agreement between the counsel for two parties is not privileged.

Western Assurance Co. v. Can. Life Assurance Co. (1987), 63 O.R. (2d) 276, 23 C.P.C. (2d) 207 (Master).

Where two persons jointly retain a solicitor, neither has a solicitor-client privilege as against the other.

Ontario (A.G.) v. C.E.C. Edwards Construction (1987), 60 O.R. (2d) 618, 23 C.P.C. (2d) 61 (H.C.).

The court ordered production of extensive notes made by the plaintiff in this personal injury case notwithstanding that they were kept on instructions of counsel. The notes were used to refresh the plaintiff's memory. The plaintiff did not contemplate that the notes would be kept confidential.

Toronto Bd. of Education Staff Credit Union Ltd. v. Skinner (1984), 46 C.P.C. 292 (Ont. H.C.).

The party asserting solicitor and client privilege has an onus to identify the nature of the documents and state the reasons for the privilege. The privilege is limited to communications and does not extend to transactions which happen to involve the solicitor.

R. v. Church of Scientology (No. 3) (1984), 47 O.R. (2d) 90 (*sub nom. R. v. Church of Scientology (No. 2)*) 44 C.P.C. 87, 13 C.C.C. (3d) 353, 10 D.L.R. (4th) 711 (H.C.).

Discussion of availability of solicitor and client privilege.

Hamilton v. Toronto, Hamilton & Buffalo Ry.(1983), 34 C.P.C. 268 (Ont. Master).

The court ordered production of notes taken by a solicitor at a meeting between the parties which was at issue in the action.

Re Ont. Securities Comm. and Greymac Credit Corp.; Re Ontario Securities Comm. and Prousky (1983), 41 O.R. (2d) 328, 21 B.L.R. 37, 33 C.P.C. 270, 146 D.L.R. (3d) 73 (Div. Ct.).

The solicitor and client privilege applies only to communications, not transactions. Oral evidence and records concerning whether a solicitor holds or has paid or received moneys on behalf of a client, not involving communications with the client, are not privileged. Further, a solicitor cannot withhold the name of a client involved in such transactions.

Milic v. Bagby (1982), 39 O.R. (2d) 492, 30 C.P.C. 66 (Master).

Where the plaintiff and defendants had been partners, documents from the solicitor for the partnership dealing with the plaintiff's expulsion were ordered to be produced since all the parties were members of the partnership at the time of the solicitor's retainer.

Warren v. Ins. Exchange Ltd. (1982), 37 O.R. (2d) 717, 28 C.P.C. 275 (Master).

Where an important issue in the case was the knowledge that a party possessed at the time of closing the purchase of a business, documents received and generated by solicitors bearing upon the party's knowledge at the time of closing were ordered to be produced.

Silverman v. Morresi (1982), 28 C.P.C. 239 (Ont. Master).

A solicitor's file was ordered to be produced regardless of solicitor and client privilege, where there was a *prima facie* case of fraud.

Re Alcan-Colony Contracting Ltd. and M.N.R., [1971] 2 O.R. 365, 18 D.L.R. (3d) 32, 71 D.T.C. 5082 (H.C.).

The legal professional privilege extends to communications between a solicitor and an agent of the client and to information gathered by the solicitor on the instruction of the client for the purpose of giving advice.

Production of Documents — Crown Privilege

Energy Probe v. Canada (Attorney General) (1992), 10 C.P.C. (3d) 58 (Ont. Gen. Div.).

The court refused to order production of "Cabinet documents" relating to nuclear energy on the basis of Crown privilege.

Carey v. Ontario, [1986] 2 S.C.R. 637, 58 O.R. (2d) 352n, 14 C.P.C. (2d) 10, 22 Admin. L.R. 236, 30 C.C.C. (3d) 498, 35 D.L.R. (4th) 161, 72 N.R. 81, 20 O.A.C. 81.

There is no absolute privilege attaching to Cabinet documents. The court ordered that the documents be inspected by the trial judge to balance the competing interests of the proper administration of justice and government confidentiality.

South-West Oxford (Twp.) v. Ontario (A.G.) (1986), 54 O.R. (2d) 207 (Div. Ct.).

Documents prepared for use in an appeal to Cabinet were held to be subject to Crown privilege.

Production of Documents — Privilege Regarding Settlement Negotiations (See also cases under rule 31.06.)

Jones v. Appleton (1994), 32 C.P.C. (3d) 367 (Ont. Gen. Div.).

Where a plaintiff had commenced two law suits arising out of two automobile accidents, the court ordered that particulars of the settlement of the first action be disclosed to the defendant in the second action.

M.J. Development Inc. v. Downtown King West Development Corp. (1992), 12 C.P.C. (3d) 84 (Ont. Gen. Div.).

The court refused to order production of documents related to an offer of settlement made during an earlier phase of a litigious dispute. The documents were protected by privilege.

Gagne v. Smooth Rock Falls Hospital (1991), 6 C.P.C. (3d) 46, 39 C.C.E.L. 274 (Ont. Gen. Div.).

Where a letter marked "Private and Confidential" was written by the plaintiff's solicitor with a genuine intention of resolving a dispute prior to the institution of civil proceedings, the letter was inadmissible at trial on the ground of privilege.

Mueller Canada Inc. v. State Contractors Inc. (1990), 71 O.R. (2d) 397, 41 C.P.C. (2d) 291 (H.C.).

Where documents referable to settlement negotiations or the settlement document itself have relevance apart from establishing one party's liability for the conduct which is the subject of the negotiations or showing the weakness of one party's claim in respect of those matters, the documents are not privileged.

Eccles v. McCannell (1984), 44 C.P.C. 43 (Ont. Div. Ct.).

Admissions made by counsel in correspondence containing settlement negotiations are privileged and inadmissible at trial.

Abrams v. Grant (1978), 5 C.P.C. 308 (Ont. H.C.).

It is the intention of the writer and contents of a letter that govern whether it is privileged, rather than the words "without prejudice".

I. Waxman & Sons Ltd. v. Texaco Can. Ltd., [1968] 2 O.R. 452, 69 D.L.R. (2d) 543 (C.A.).

Communications written without prejudice and with a view to settlement of issues between A and C are privileged in subsequent litigation between A and B regarding the same or a closely related matter.

Production of Documents — Miscellaneous Privileges

Consolidated NBS Inc. v. Price Waterhouse (1994), 24 C.P.C. (3d) 185, 3 C.C.L.S. 186, 111 D.L.R. (4th) 656, 69 O.A.C. 236 (Div. Ct.).

The transcript of a statement given by a party to the police was held to be privileged.

Moore v. Reddy (1990), 44 C.P.C. (2d) 61 (Ont. Master).

The court refused to order production of statements made by a defendant to the Canadian Aviation Safety Board. The *Canadian Aviation Safety Board Act* provided that such statements were privileged, and were only to be disclosed if there were a supervening public interest. Those circumstances were not present.

Roussy v. Sinkins (1989), 17 W.D.C.P. 206 (Ont. H.C.).

The court recognized a legal privilege for documents relating to the peer review process in respect of hospital privileges but not for those specific documents related to the surgery which was the subject matter of the law suit.

Reichmann v. Toronto Life Publishing Co. (1988), 28 C.P.C. (2d) 11 (Ont. H.C.), leave to appeal to Ont. Div. Ct. refused 29 C.P.C. (2d) 66.

Although the "newspaper rule" protects journalists' sources of information, that rule does not protect the information itself. The defendant in a libel action was therefore ordered to produce certain documents after deletion of any reference to the confidential sources. Discussion of production of other documents in this libel action.

Benoit v. Higgins (1987), 16 C.P.C. (2d) 15 (Ont. Master).

The court held that the "public interest privilege" does not necessarily apply to the report of an investigation into the discharge of a gun by a police officer and that the documents should be submitted to the court for inspection.

Pryslak v. Anderson (1987), 57 O.R. (2d) 788, 15 C.P.C. (2d) 79 (H.C.).

The court should be wary about using Professor Wigmore's general principle of privileged communications as the basis for creating new situations of privilege notwithstanding its approval by the Supreme Court of Canada in *Slavutych v. Baker*, [1976] 1 S.C.R. 254, 38 C.R.N.S. 306, [1975] 4 W.W.R. 620, 75 C.L.L.C. 14,263, 55 D.L.R. (3d) 224.

Biomedical Information Corp. v. Pearce (1985), 49 O.R. (2d) 92, 47 C.P.C. 113, 28 B.L.R. 20, 4 C.P.R. (3d) 54 (Master).

There is no general privilege accorded to solicitor-accountant communications. In this case a letter from the defendants' solicitor to the defendants' auditor regarding pending claims was ordered produced but a legal opinion letter which had been referred to in preparing the letter to the auditor remained privileged.

McInnis v. Univ. Students' Council of Univ. of Western Ontario (1984), 47 O.R. (2d) 663, 46 C.P.C. 93, 31 C.C.L.T. 95, 12 D.L.R. (4th) 457, varied 48 O.R. (2d) 542, 14 D.L.R. (4th) 126 (H.C.), leave to appeal to Ont. Div. Ct. refused 48 O.R. (2d) 542 at 544, 14 D.L.R. (4th) 126 at 127.

Applying the "newspaper rule" in ordering the production of a reporter's notes in this libel action, the court directed that the sources of any information contained in the notes should be first deleted.

R. v. Church of Scientology (No. 2) (1984), 47 O.R. (2d) 86 *(sub nom. R. v. Church of Scientology) (No. 1))*, 44 C.P.C. 76, 13 C.C.C. (3d) 97, 10 D.L.R. (4th) 312, additional reasons 47 O.R. (2d) 765, 13 D.L.R. (4th) 639 (H.C.).

There is no privilege for religious communications, although the court will press counsel not to pursue questions that would compel a cleric to breach a confidence.

Cook v. Dufferin-Peel Roman Catholic Separate School Bd. (1983), 34 C.P.C. 178 (Ont. Master).

The court ordered production of witness statements obtained from pupils in the defendant's school system notwithstanding that the documents were purported to be included in the students' "pupil records" and therefore privileged. The statements were not properly part of the "pupil records".

Hatfield v. Globe & Mail Div. of Can. Newspapers Co. (1983), 41 O.R. (2d) 218, 34 C.P.C. 162, 25 C.C.L.T. 172 (Master).

In libel actions, the "newspaper rule", which permits newspapers to refuse to reveal the source of their information forming the basis of the alleged libel prior to trial, does not prevent production of public records used in preparing the alleged libel.

Waiver of Privilege

Woodglen & Co. v. Owens (1995), 24 O.R. (3d) 261, 38 C.P.C. (3d) 361 (Gen. Div.).

Certain privileged documents were ordered produced as the plaintiffs had put in issue the nature of the legal advice they had received, and therefore were deemed to have waived solicitor and client privilege.

Agrico Canada Ltd. v. Northgate Insurance Brokers Inc. (1994), 35 C.P.C. (3d) 370 (Ont. Gen. Div.).

Where a document which was clearly prepared in contemplation of litigation was inadvertently or accidentally disclosed, the court held that the defendant could deliver a fresh affidavit of documents and assert privilege over the document.

Air Canada v. McDonnell Douglas Corp. (1994), 19 O.R. (3d) 537, 27 C.P.C. (3d) 359 (Master), affirmed 34 C.P.C. (3d) 181 (Ont. Gen. Div.).

Disclosure of an accident investigation report to a non-party was held to waive any privilege attaching to the report.

Cineplex Odeon Corp. v. Canada (Attorney General) (1994), 26 C.P.C. (3d) 109, [1994] 2 C.T.C. 293, 114 D.L.R. (4th) 141, 94 D.T.C. 6407 (Ont. Gen. Div.).

Solicitor and client privilege may be lost by giving a privileged document to the client's auditor. In this case the same accounting firm acted both in providing tax advice, in conjunction with a solicitor, and in conducting an audit. The documents were privileged in the tax accountant's hands by extension of solicitor and client privilege through the principles of agency. The tax accountant gave the documents to the audit accountant without the client's authority. Disclosure was therefore inadvertent and the privilege was not waived.

Binkle v. Lockhart (1994), 24 C.P.C. (3d) 11 (Ont. Gen. Div.).

Where a surveillance video tape was shown to a defence expert and referred to in his report, the court held that privilege had been waived and ordered production of the video tape.

Tilley v. Hails (1993), 12 O.R. (3d) 306, 18 C.P.C. (3d) 381 (Gen. Div.).

Where privileged communications are disclosed either inadvertently or through improper conduct by a party, that party's solicitors are not entitled to make use of the documents in the litigation.

Reklitis v. Whitehall Estates Ltd. (1993), 17 C.P.C. (3d) 193 (Ont. Gen. Div.).

Allegations by a client that his solicitor had breached his duty to the client amounted to waiver of privilege regarding solicitor and client communications.

Zidenburg v. Greenberg (1993), 15 O.R. (3d) 68 (Master).

Solicitor and client privilege is waived when the party attempting to assert that privilege puts legal advice, or lack of it, in issue.

Scrafton v. Johnson Controls Ltd. (1992), 15 C.P.C. (3d) 63 (Ont. Master).

Where a privileged document had been produced in error, the court refused to order discovery questions about the document to be answered.

Lloyds Bank Canada v. Canada Life Assurance Co. (1991), 47 C.P.C. (2d) 157 (Ont. Gen. Div.).

Where a bank pleaded reliance on certain comfort letters, it was held to have waived privilege. Waiver is not automatic where a party's state of mind is in issue. Privilege is not waived where it is the person who seeks the privileged information who raises the question of reliance.

Hartz Can. Inc. v. Colgate-Palmolive Co. (1988), 27 C.P.C. (2d) 152 (Ont. H.C.).

Disclosure of part of privileged communications is not an implied waiver of the whole unless required by fairness or completeness.

Crysdale v. Carter-Baron Drilling Services Partnership (1987), 61 O.R. (2d) 663, 22 C.P.C. (2d) 232 (Master), reversed on other grounds (1988), 62 O.R. (2d) 693, 30 C.P.C. (2d) 191 (H.C.), leave to appeal to Ont. Div. Ct. refused 62 O.R. (2d) 693 at 696, 30 C.P.C. (2d) 191 at 192.

Solicitor and client privilege attaching to correspondence was waived where a party made reference to the correspondence in an affidavit.

Western Assurance Co. v. Can. Life Ins. Co. (1987), 63 O.R. (2d) 276, 23 C.P.C. (2d) 207 (Master).

Reliance on and production of privileged documents in a California law suit was held to be a voluntary waiver of privilege for purposes of an Ontario action.

Cameron v. Campbell (1987), 21 C.P.C. (2d) 53 (Ont. H.C.).

Leave was granted to appeal to the Divisional Court on the question of waiver of the privilege attaching to surveillance materials by production of a medical report based upon those materials.

Hicks Estate v. Hicks (1987), 15 C.P.C. (2d) 146, 25 E.T.R. 271 (Ont. Dist. Ct.).

The administrator of the estate of a deceased client is entitled to waive solicitor and client privilege.

Bronstetter v. Davies (1986), 11 C.P.C. (2d) 289 (Ont. H.C.).

Production of an expert's report does not act as a waiver of the privilege attaching to the expert's notes and records.

Sunwell Engineering Co. v. Mogilevsky (1986), 8 C.P.C. (2d) 14, 8 C.I.P.R. 144, 12 C.P.R. (3d) 560 (Ont. H.C.), leave to appeal to Ont. Div. Ct. refused 8 C.P.C. (2d) 14n, 8 C.I.P.R. 144n, 12 C.P.R. (3d) 560n.

The seizure of privileged documents during execution of an *ex parte* Anton Piller order does not amount to an involuntary waiver of privilege.

Columbos v. Carroll (1985), 23 C.P.C. (2d) 177 (Ont. H.C.).

Privilege attaching to an expert's report is lost if the report is provided to counsel for another party.

Production of Documents — Statements Made by Opposing Party

Uvanile v. Wawanesa Mutual Ins. Co., 44 C.P.C. 110, [1984] I.L.R. 1-1806 (Ont. H.C.).

A mere issue of credibility is insufficient to give rise to a real likelihood of the tailoring of facts and in such circumstances the court will not interfere with the full discovery process. In this case, the defendant's undertaking to produce a statement from the plaintiff was ordered fulfilled prior to that plaintiff's discovery.

Husain v. Hicks (1981), 33 O.R. (2d) 737, 24 C.P.C. 108 (Master).

The court refused the plaintiffs' motion seeking delay in production of a statement from the defendant until after discovery.

Rotondi v. Tadic (1979), 24 O.R. (2d) 317, 11 C.P.C. 17 (Master).

A party was required to produce a memorandum prepared by his insurer of a statement made by an opposing party.

Mancao v. Casino (1977), 17 O.R. (2d) 458, 4 C.P.C. 161 (H.C.).

A document reducing an oral statement of a party to writing must be produced to that party, however comments in the document not reflecting the statements of the party may be excised.

Production of Documents — Examples

Ianson v. Rukavina (1995), 22 O.R. (3d) 301, 37 C.P.C. (3d) 282 (Gen. Div.).

In this assault case against police officers, the court ordered production of complaints involving use of force by the officers.

French Estate v. French (1994), 28 C.P.C. (3d) 157 (Ont. Gen. Div.).

Where the central issue in an action was whether an advance made to the defendant was a loan or a gift, the court ordered that the plaintiff produce bank records for various accounts. The records would disclose the financial status of the plaintiff at the time of the making of the original advances, and in view of the pleadings and the evidence on discovery, the production of the records was relevant to the matters in issue.

P. (L.M.) v. F. (D.) (1994), 27 C.P.C. (3d) 38 (Ont. Gen. Div.).

Where the plaintiff alleged that the Children's Aid Society was negligent and had in its possession confidential documents relating to non-party children suggesting evidence of sexual abuse, the court ordered that the documents be produced on terms.

Consolidated NBS Inc. v. Price Waterhouse (1994), 24 C.P.C. (3d) 185, 3 C.C.L.S. 186, 111 D.L.R. (4th) 656, 69 O.A.C. 236 (Div. Ct.).

The court ordered production of documents (a) which were given to a party by a Crown Attorney as part of "Crown disclosure" in a related criminal case, and (b) which were given to a party by the Ontario Securities Commission.

Hedley v. Air Canada (1994), 23 C.P.C. (3d) 352 (Ont. Gen. Div.).

Discussion of production of documents disclosed to a party during Crown disclosure in a related criminal proceeding.

Gemini Group Automated Distribution Systems Inc. v. PWA Corp. (1993), 16 O.R. (3d) 239, 20 C.P.C. (3d) 385, 68 O.A.C. 205 (C.A.).

Documents produced in a Competition Tribunal proceeding were ordered to be listed in an affidavit of documents, whether or not privilege was claimed.

Kenyeres (Litigation Guardian of) v. Cullimore (1991), 49 C.P.C. (2d) 228, 44 O.A.C. 318 (C.A.).

In this medical malpractice case the court ordered production of the relevant portions of the transcript of the defendant's disciplinary proceedings before the Ontario College of Physicians and Surgeons.

Sharpe Estate v. Northwestern General Hospital (1990), 74 D.L.R. (4th) 43 (Ont. Master), affirmed (1991), 2 O.R. (3d) 40, 46 C.P.C. (2d) 267, 76 D.L.R. (4th) 535 (Gen. Div.).

The Red Cross was ordered to produce blood donor records in a case involving the contraction of AIDS. Restrictions were imposed as to the use of the information.

Comaplex Resources International Ltd. v. Schaffhauser Kantonalbank (1990), 42 C.P.C. (2d) 230 (Ont. Master).

Where the defendant Swiss bank had objected to production of documents on the ground that foreign law prohibited production, the court ordered production without consideration of the foreign law prohibitions. The court held that the consideration of any foreign prohibitions or restrictions with respect to disclosure should be postponed because the foreign law issues could be dealt with on any subsequent motion to consider the imposition of sanctions for non-compliance with the discovery order.

Reichmann v. Toronto Life Publishing Co. (1990), 71 O.R. (2d) 719, 41 C.P.C. (2d) 73, 66 D.L.R. (4th) 162, additional reasons, 44 C.P.C. (2d) 206 (H.C.).

The court ordered the production of the corporate plaintiff's financial statements in this libel action where, although it did not claim any special damages, the only damage which it could suffer was to its pocket.

Del Zotto v. Cdn. Newspapers Co. (1988), 65 O.R. (2d) 594, 28 C.P.C. (2d) 165, 45 C.C.L.T. 225 (Master).

Where the plaintiff in a libel action claimed exemplary damages, the plaintiff was entitled to compel production of the material upon which the article in issue was based, and to ask questions arising out of such production. This material was relevant in light of the claim for exemplary damages, as the plaintiff would have to establish that the defendants acted in knowing disregard of the plaintiff's rights.

Morgan Guaranty Trust Co. of New York v. Outerbridge (1987), 23 C.P.C. (2d) 127 (Ont. Master), affirmed (1988), 23 C.P.C. (2d) 127n (Ont. H.C.).

The court ordered production of documents relating to computer entries but not general documents about how the computer system operated. The latter documents were only relevant to a theory of the defendant which was unsupported by evidence and not pleaded.

Ontario (A.G.) v. C.E.C. Edwards Construction (1987), 60 O.R. (2d) 618, 23 C.P.C. (2d) 61 (H.C.).

The diary kept by a plaintiff in a personal injury action was ordered produced, as it was prepared for the express purpose of use at trial. It was also appropriate to require the plaintiff to request production of the treating physician's clinical notes.

Baker v. Torrance (1987), 20 C.P.C. (2d) 270 (Ont. Master).

In an action for false imprisonment, the court held that the public interest in the administration of justice outweighed the public interest in keeping certain police records confidential, and therefore the documents were ordered to be produced.

Orr v. Warren (1986), 59 O.R. (2d) 286, 18 C.P.C. (2d) 190 (H.C.).

Where the plaintiff's medical condition both before and after the subject accident was relevant to the issues in the action, the plaintiff was directed to request production of the family physician's clinical notes and records from both before and after the accident. In the event the plaintiff was unable to obtain the records, the court directed that an order would issue with respect to the family physician under rule 30.10. The defendant was also entitled to a before and after comparison of the plaintiff's work records, attendance and job evaluation, as a claim for future loss of income was involved.

Mercaldo v. Poole (1986), 13 C.P.C. (2d) 129 (Ont. H.C.).

In an action against a solicitor for professional negligence, the defendant was ordered to produce a memorandum to file recording statements made by the client after discovery of a defect in a separation agreement, subject to editing by the master. A letter to the Law Society was held to be privileged.

White v. Johnston (1986), 10 C.P.C. (2d) 63 (Ont. Dist. Ct.).

Transcripts from a real estate board's ethics committee proceedings were held to be relevant productions where the facts giving rise to the hearing were the same as those giving rise to the action. The transcripts had not been created for the dominant purpose of use in the subsequent litigation.

Duras v. Welland Gen. Hospital (1985), 51 O.R. (2d) 284, 4 C.P.C. (2d) 238 (H.C.).

The court ordered production of documents from a defendant where the documents were not relevant to any issue between the plaintiff and that defendant, but were relevant to issues between the plaintiff and other defendants.

Basse v. Toronto Star Newspapers Ltd. (1985), 1 C.P.C. (2d) 105 (Ont. Master).

The court ordered production of various internal police documents.

Donovan v. State Farm Fire & Casualty Co., 40 C.P.C. 208, [1984] I.L.R. 1-1745 (Ont. H.C.).

Disclosure of the plaintiff's financial affairs was refused in an action on a fire loss policy where the defendant insurer had not alleged a scheme by the insured to defraud, although it had pleaded that the fire had been intentionally set.

Rush v. Phoenix Assur. Co. of Can., 40 C.P.C. 185, [1984] I.L.R. 1-1737 (Ont. Master).

An underwriting file relating to the time when a policy was applied for and issued was irrelevant and not producible where the defendant admitted that the policy was in force.

Hill v. Hill (1983), 35 C.P.C. 320, 34 R.F.L. (2d) 449 (Ont. H.C.).

The respondent spouse in a divorce proceeding was required to produce financial statements of a private corporation of which he was a shareholder.

Wickes v. Redken Laboratories Can. (1983), 35 C.P.C. 53 (Ont. Master).

The court declined to order the plaintiff to produce documents in the possession of a corporation controlled by the plaintiff and one other person. Such an order could be made if notice were given to the other person involved in the corporation.

Kampus v. Bridgeford (1981), 24 C.P.C. 122, 126 D.L.R. (3d) 175, quashed on jurisdictional grounds 25 C.P.C. 169 (Ont. C.A.).

OHIP was ordered to produce the claim cards submitted by physicians and hospitals to verify that the services performed were related to an accident in respect of which a subrogated claim was asserted.

Wilson v. College of Physicians and Surgeons of Ont. (1981), 24 C.P.C. 52 (Ont. Div. Ct.).

In a proceeding under the *Health Disciplines Act*, production of materials concerning the deliberations of the complaints committee of the College of Physicians and Surgeons was refused.

Osborne v. Osborne (1981), 22 C.P.C. 297 (Ont. Master).

In this family law case, production of all corporate books and documents of a company in which the husband had an interest was refused as amounting to a discovery of a non-party. [*But see now rule 30.02(4) — Authors.*]

Campbell v. Paton (1979), 26 O.R. (2d) 4, 10 C.P.C. 229, 104 D.L.R. (3d) 428, application for leave to appeal dismissed 12 C.P.C. 133 (H.C.).

In an action against a police officer, documents prepared by the Citizens' Complaint Bureau of the police force were required to be produced.

O'Connor v. Mitzvah Holdings Ltd. (1979), 11 C.P.C. 310 (Ont. H.C.).

In an action on a promissory note, certain internal corporate documents of the guarantor were ordered produced, as they were prepared neither with a definite prospect of litigation nor to obtain the advice of solicitors.

Parr v. Butkovich (1978), 20 O.R. (2d) 491, 6 C.P.C. 237 (H.C.).

The court required that a party give his permission for the release of educational records which would otherwise be privileged by statute.

Walsh v. Metro. Toronto & Region Conservation Authority (1977), 4 C.P.C. 273 (Ont. Master).

Where a party is required by statute to file certain documents in the course of its activities, such documents are relevant and producible.

Janhevich v. Thomas (1977), 15 O.R. (2d) 765, 3 C.P.C. 303, 76 D.L.R. (3d) 656 (H.C.).

Such portions of a party's income tax returns as are relevant to matters in issue must be produced.

Re Canron Ltd. and Can. Workers Union (1976), 12 O.R. (2d) 765, 70 D.L.R. (3d) 198 (H.C.).

Where one party hires a reporter to transcribe public proceedings, the other party may have production of the transcript upon paying a proper share of the costs.

Gentle v. Gentle (1974), 3 O.R. (2d) 544, 15 R.F.L. 373, 46 D.L.R. (3d) 164 (H.C.).

The privilege under s. 10 of the *Evidence Act*, R.S.O. 1970, c. 151, regarding information which tends to prove adultery extends to the production of documents.

AFFIDAVIT OF DOCUMENTS

Party to Serve Affidavit

30.03(1) A party to an action shall, within ten days after the close of pleadings, serve on every other party an affidavit of documents (Form 30A or 30B) disclosing to the full extent of the party's knowledge, information and belief all documents relating to any matter in issue in the action that are or have been in the party's possession, control or power.

Contents

(2) The affidavit shall list and describe, in separate schedules, all documents relating to any matter in issue in the action,

(a) that are in the party's possession, control or power and that the party does not object to producing;

(b) that are or were in the party's possession, control or power and for which the party claims privilege, and the grounds for the claim; and

(c) that were formerly in the party's possession, control or power, but are no longer in the party's possession, control or power, whether or not privilege is claimed for them, together with a statement of when and

how the party lost possession or control of or power over them and their present location.

(3) The affidavit shall also contain a statement that the party has never had in the party's possession, control or power any document relating to any matter in issue in the action other than those listed in the affidavit.

Solicitor's Certificate

(4) Where the party is represented by a solicitor, the solicitor shall certify on the affidavit that he or she has explained to the deponent the necessity of making full disclosure of all documents relating to any matter in issue in the action.

Affidavit not to be Filed

(5) An affidavit of documents shall not be filed unless it is relevant to an issue on a pending motion or at trial.

Form of Affidavit

Solid Waste Reclamation Inc. v. Philip Enterprises Inc. (1991), 2 O.R. (3d) 481, 49 C.P.C. (2d) 245 (Gen. Div.).

The affidavit of documents should allocate an identifying number to each document. The number should appear on the face of each document to facilitate identification and retrieval.

Waxman v. Waxman (1991), 49 C.P.C. (2d) 113 (Ont. Div. Ct.).

Where a party has omitted to claim privilege in an affidavit of documents, the party can correct such inadvertence by serving a supplementary affidavit.

Waxman v. Waxman (1990), 42 C.P.C. (2d) 296 (Ont. Master).

Documents for which privilege is claimed should be described, with the description including the function, role, and status of the sender and receiver and their relationship to the party to the action; however, the deponent is not required to disclose names and identities of potential witnesses and experts prior to a ruling on the validity of the claim for privilege.

Temoin v. Stanley (1986), 12 C.P.C. (2d) 69 (Ont. Dist. Ct.), reversed in part on other grounds (1987), 7 W.D.C.P. 71 (Ont. H.C.).

Where a party claims privilege for a document, the author of the document must be identified in the party's affidavit of documents.

Brampton Engineering Inc. v. Alros Products Ltd. (1986), 8 C.P.C. (2d) 48 (Ont. Master).

Documents for which privilege is claimed should be described sufficiently to identify them but no details need be given which would enable the opposite party to discover indirectly the contents. The court required separate descriptions for each category of document with identification of the persons creating the documents and information about the dates of the documents.

Grossman v. Toronto Gen. Hosp. (1983), 41 O.R. (2d) 457, 35 C.P.C. 11, 146 D.L.R. (3d) 280 (H.C.).

An affidavit of documents must describe documents for which privilege is claimed and give information supporting the claim for privilege.

Miscellaneous

Atwater v. Gupta (1986), 12 C.P.C. (2d) 293 (Ont. Master).

There is no jurisdiction to order the deletion of documents from an affidavit of documents on the grounds of relevance.

C.I.B.C. v. Molony (1986), 8 C.P.C. (2d) 53 (Ont. H.C.).

The court refused to order production of documents referred to in the defendant's affidavit of documents where a supplementary affidavit was delivered pursuant to rule 30.07 indicating the documents were not in the defendant's possession, control or power.

Kap v. Sands (1980), 30 O.R. (2d) 125, (*sub nom. Zoltac v. Ross*) 22 C.P.C. 32 at 36, affirmed 22 C.P.C. 32 at 61 (H.C.).

Medical and hospital records regarding the plaintiffs or deceased persons for whose deaths the actions were brought are within the plaintiffs' power and should be listed in the affidavit of documents. It should not be necessary to move for an order requiring the hospitals and doctors to produce the documents.

INSPECTION OF DOCUMENTS

Request to Inspect

30.04(1) A party who serves on another party a request to inspect documents (Form 30C) is entitled to inspect any document that is not privileged and that is referred to in the other party's affidavit of documents as being in the party's possession, control or power.

(2) A request to inspect documents may also be used to obtain the inspection of any document in another party's possession, control or power that is referred to in the originating process, pleadings or an affidavit served by the other party.

(3) A party on whom a request to inspect documents is served shall forthwith inform the party making the request of a date within five days after the service of the request to inspect documents and of a time between 9:30 a.m. and 4:30 p.m. when the documents may be inspected at the office of the solicitor of the party served, or at some other convenient place, and shall at the time and place named make the documents available for inspection.

Documents to be Taken to Examination and Trial

(4) Unless the parties agree otherwise, all documents listed in a party's affidavit of documents that are not privileged and all documents previously produced for inspection by the party shall, without notice, summons or order, be taken to and produced at,

(a) the examination for discovery of the party or of a person on behalf or in place of or in addition to the party; and

(b) the trial of the action.

Court may Order Production

(5) The court may at any time order production for inspection of documents that are not privileged and that are in the possession, control or power of a party.

Court may Inspect to Determine Claim of Privilege

(6) Where privilege is claimed for a document, the court may inspect the document to determine the validity of the claim.

Copying of Documents

(7) **Where a document is produced for inspection, the party inspecting the document is entitled to make a copy of it at the party's own expense, if it can be reproduced, unless the person having possession or control of or power over the document agrees to make a copy, in which case the person shall be reimbursed for the cost of making the copy.**

Divided Disclosure or Production

(8) **Where a document may become relevant only after the determination of an issue in the action and disclosure or production for inspection of the document before the issue is determined would seriously prejudice a party, the court on the party's motion may grant leave to withhold disclosure or production until after the issue has been determined.**

Production of Documents Referred to in Pleadings, Affidavit, etc. — rule 30.04(2)

293818 Ont. Ltd. v. Forest Glen Shopping Centre Ltd. (1981), 22 C.P.C. 291 (Ont. Div. Ct.).
Where the plaintiff never had the document referred to in its pleading, its action was not dismissed because it could not produce it.

Trotter v. Cattan (1977), 17 O.R. (2d) 455, 5 C.P.C. 114 (H.C.).
Production was ordered of only those parts of a medical report referred to in an affidavit in support of a motion for a second medical examination.

Durall Const. Ltd. v. H.J. O'Connell Ltd., [1973] 3 O.R. 59 (Master).
A party must produce a document referred to in a pleading irrespective of any privilege attaching to the document.

Kennedy v. Diversified Mining Interest (Can.) Ltd., [1948] O.W.N. 798 (H.C.).
Where a solicitor refers in an affidavit to a written solicitor-client communication, there is a presumption that the privilege attaching to the document has been waived.

Order to Produce Documents — rule 30.04(5)

Hong Kong (Official Receiver) v. Wing (1986), 57 O.R. (2d) 216, 12 C.P.C. (2d) 217 (H.C.).
The court will only order production and inspection of documents prior to the close of pleadings where the documents are essential to pleading.

Durish v. Bent (1985), 4 C.P.C. (2d) 37 (Ont. Master).
The court declined to order production before pleading of certain documents in the possession of the plaintiffs, where the evidence did not show that the defendant needed the information to frame his defence.

McKenzie v. Bentz (1984), 44 C.P.C. 213 (Ont. H.C.).
After commencing this malpractice action but before pleading, the plaintiffs obtained an order for the production of the defendant hospital's records, to enable them to plead properly.

Morgan v. Fekete (1979), 25 O.R. (2d) 237, affirmed 25 O.R. (2d) 237n (H.C.).
The order may be made before delivery of pleadings.

Gravlev v. Venturetek Int. Ltd. (1979), 15 C.P.C. 18 (Ont. H.C.).
A party may not be required to endeavour to obtain documents from third parties where it would be unreasonable to require him so to do.

Trip v. Iezzi and Iezzi Ltd. (1978), 23 O.R. (2d) 587, 8 C.P.C. 312 (H.C.).

A party will not be compelled to produce samples of his handwriting.

Loudon v. Consolidated-Moulton Trimmings Ltd., [1956] O.W.N. 552, 24 C.P.R. 77, 15 Fox Pat. C. 167 (Master).

The court is very cautious in ordering production of documents in patent cases.

Inspection of Documents by Court — rule 30.04(6)

Falconbridge Ltd. v. Hawker Siddeley Diesels & Electrics Ltd. (1985), 50 C.P.C. 307, affirmed 50 O.R. (2d) 794, 3 C.P.C. (2d) 133 (H.C.).

Whenever possible, disputes regarding privileged documents should be determined from the affidavit of documents and other supporting material. Inspection of the documents by the court should be discouraged because it minimizes the benefit of argument by counsel.

Cost of Copies — rule 30.04(7)

Toronto Bd. of Educ. Staff Credit Union Ltd. v. Skinner (1985), 2 C.P.C. (2d) 247 (Ont. H.C.).

The court ordered a party receiving copies of voluminous documents to pay about 43.5 cents per page in copying charges.

Divided Production — rule 30.04(8) (See also cases under rule 31.06.)

McKinlay Transport Ltd. v. Motor Transport Industrial Relations Bureau of Ontario (Inc.) (1995), 37 C.P.C. (3d) 147 (Ont. Div. Ct.).

The court has an inherent jurisdiction to sever issues for trial. The court ordered the trial to proceed on liability issues with a second trial to occur, if necessary, regarding damage issues.

Mitchell v. Reed Estate (1995), 36 C.P.C. (3d) 195 (Ont. Gen. Div.).

The court refused to sever issues for trial where one party objected and severance might cause problems.

Blott, Fejer, Felkai, Rovet v. McCafferty (1989), 69 O.R. (2d) 235, 35 C.P.C. (2d) 182 (Master).

The rules on divided production and divided discovery do not apply where the responding party already has the documents or information and the only prejudice is needless expense.

Risi Stone Ltd. v. Burloak Concrete Products Ltd. (1987), 24 C.P.C. (2d) 34, 17 C.I.P.R. 166, 19 C.P.R. (3d) 90 (Ont. H.C.).

The court ordered divided production and discovery in this action for infringement of copyright and passing off. Production and discovery on the issues of damages and profits would prejudice the defendants.

L.C.D.H. Audio Visual Ltd. v. I.S.T.S. Verbatim Ltd. (1986), 54 O.R. (2d) 425, 8 C.P.C. (2d) 141 (H.C.).

The court applied the following principles in deciding whether to divide discovery: (1) the decision is a discretionary one; (2) the modern philosophy is that all issues should be resolved in one trial; (3) discovery should be divided only in the clearest cases; (4) discovery should not be divided if the issues are not clearly severable: (5) if the issues are severable and serious prejudice would result to the moving party the court must then consider whether to exercise its discretion to divide discovery; and (6) the discretion must be exercised judicially.

Diamond v. Kaufman (1985), 1 C.P.C. (2d) 1 (Ont. Master).

The court ordered divided production and discovery where the defendants operated a computer software business and the plaintiff sought an accounting of the business's receipts and disbursements. The accounting would become necessary only if the plaintiff succeeded on the issue of liability. Disclosure of the information could result in serious prejudice to the defendants.

Can. Valve Ltd. v. Sweet (1985), 49 C.P.C. 178 (Ont. Master).

The court ordered divided discovery where the issues of liability and damages were distinct, there was some question as to the strength of the plaintiff's case and production of documents regarding damages would result in economic disadvantage to the defendants.

Re Machan and Machan (1980), 26 O.R. (2d) 473, 12 R.F.L. (2d) 247 (H.C.).

The court refused to stay delivery of a statement of property pending determination of the applicability of a separation agreement.

Blake v. Great Northern Financial Corp. (1978), 18 O.R. (2d) 744 (H.C.).

In an action for an accounting the court refused to postpone production of voluminous documentation until the question of entitlement to an accounting was determined.

Respirex of Can. Ltd. v. Flynn (1974), 5 O.R. (2d) 380 (Master).

Discovery relating to damages was postponed until it was established that there was a binding contract between the parties on which to base liability.

DISCLOSURE OR PRODUCTION NOT ADMISSION OF RELEVANCE

30.05 The disclosure or production of a document for inspection shall not be taken as an admission of its relevance or admissibility.

WHERE AFFIDAVIT INCOMPLETE OR PRIVILEGE IMPROPERLY CLAIMED

30.06 Where the court is satisfied by any evidence that a relevant document in a party's possession, control or power may have been omitted from the party's affidavit of documents, or that a claim of privilege may have been improperly made, the court may,

(a) order cross-examination on the affidavit of documents;

(b) order service of a further and better affidavit of documents;

(c) order the disclosure or production for inspection of the document, or a part of the document, if it is not privileged; and

(d) inspect the document for the purpose of determining its relevance or the validity of a claim of privilege.

Heritage Clothing (Can.) Ltd. v. Sun Alliance Ins. Co. (1985), 4 C.P.C. (2d) 154 (Ont. H.C.) (leave to appeal to Ont. Div. Ct. denied September 30, 1985).

There is no time limit for production of a document for which privilege has been claimed.

Nelma Information Inc. v. Holt (1985), 50 C.P.C. 116 (Ont. H.C.).

The court ordered cross-examination on an affidavit of documents where many documents had been withheld and cross-examination appeared to be the most expeditious way of resolving the issues.

Bow Helicopters v. Textron Can. Ltd. (1981), 23 C.P.C. 212 (Ont. Master).

A motion for a further and better affidavit on production can be brought before examination for discovery. Further, an affidavit can be filed setting out the facts relied upon; however, that a document "ought to exist" is not a sufficient basis to order its production.

DOCUMENTS OR ERRORS SUBSEQUENTLY DISCOVERED

30.07 Where a party, after serving an affidavit of documents,

(a) comes into possession or control of or obtains power over a document that relates to a matter in issue in the action and that is not privileged; or

(b) discovers that the affidavit is inaccurate or incomplete,

the party shall forthwith serve a supplementary affidavit specifying the extent to which the affidavit of documents requires modification and disclosing any additional documents.

Agrico Canada Ltd. v. Northgate Insurance Brokers Inc. (1994), 35 C.P.C. (3d) 370 (Ont. Gen. Div.).

Where a document which was clearly prepared in contemplation of litigation was inadvertently or accidentally disclosed, the court held that the defendant could deliver a fresh affidavit of documents and assert privilege over the document.

Waxman v. Waxman (1991), 49 C.P.C. (2d) 113 (Ont. Div. Ct.).

Where a party has omitted to claim privilege in an affidavit of documents, the party can correct such inadvertence by serving a supplementary affidavit.

EFFECT OF FAILURE TO DISCLOSE OR PRODUCE FOR INSPECTION

Failure to Disclose or Produce Document

30.08(1) Where a party fails to disclose a document in an affidavit of documents or a supplementary affidavit, or fails to produce a document for inspection in compliance with these rules or an order of the court,

(a) if the document is favourable to the party's case, the party may not use the document at the trial, except with leave of the trial judge; or

(b) if the document is not favourable to the party's case, the court may make such order as is just.

Failure to Serve Affidavit or Produce Document

(2) Where a party fails to serve an affidavit of documents or produce a document for inspection in compliance with these rules or fails to comply with an order of the court under rules 30.02 to 30.11, the court may,

(a) revoke or suspend the party's right, if any, to initiate or continue an examination for discovery;

(b) dismiss the action, if the party is a plaintiff, or strike out the statement of defence, if the party is a defendant; and

(c) make such other order as is just.

[Note: See rule 53.08 regarding leave to admit an undisclosed document at trial — Authors.]

Gary Oswald Blasting Inc. v. M.J. Robinson Trucking Ltée (1989), 38 C.P.C. (2d) 195 (Ont. H.C.).

Where pleadings were not completed in a fourth party proceeding, the third party's motion to dismiss the main action based on the plaintiff's failure to deliver an affidavit of documents was premature.

PRIVILEGED DOCUMENT NOT TO BE USED WITHOUT LEAVE

30.09 Where a party has claimed privilege in respect of a document and does not abandon the claim by giving notice in writing and providing a copy of the document or producing it for inspection not later than ten days after the action is set down for trial, the party may not use the document at the trial, except to impeach the testimony of a witness or with leave of the trial judge.

[Note: See rule 53.08 regarding leave to admit such a document at trial — Authors.]

Giroux v. Lafrance (1993), 19 C.P.C. (3d) 12 (Ont. Gen. Div.).

Where this rule was not complied with, the court permitted surveillance evidence to be used to impeach credibility but not as substantive evidence.

Machado v. Berlet (1986), 57 O.R. (2d) 207, 15 C.P.C. (2d) 207, 32 D.L.R. (4th) 634 (H.C.).

The court permitted a defendant to use surveillance photographs to impeach the plaintiff's credibility notwithstanding that the film had not been disclosed previously. The plaintiff was permitted to explain the contents of the film since it had not been properly put to him in cross-examination.

Jones v. Heidel (1985), 6 C.P.C. (2d) 318 (Ont. H.C.).

A motion for a mistrial was dismissed where counsel for the defendant used previously undisclosed surveillance photographs when cross-examining the plaintiff. It was permissible to use the photographs to impeach the plaintiff's testimony.

PRODUCTION FROM NON-PARTIES WITH LEAVE

Order for Inspection

30.10(1) The court may, on motion by a party, order production for inspection of a document that is in the possession, control or power of a person not a party and is not privileged where the court is satisfied that,

(a) the document is relevant to a material issue in the action; and

(b) it would be unfair to require the moving party to proceed to trial without having discovery of the document.

Notice of Motion

(2) A motion for an order under subrule (1) shall be made on notice,

(a) to every other party; and

(b) to the person not a party, served personally or by an alternative to personal service under rule 16.03.

Court may Inspect Document

(3) Where privilege is claimed for a document referred to in subrule (1), or where the court is uncertain of the relevance of or necessity for discovery of the document, the court may inspect the document to determine the issue.

Preparation of Certified Copy

(4) The court may give directions respecting the preparation of a certified copy of a document referred to in subrule (1) and the certified copy may be used for all purposes in place of the original.

Production from Non-Parties — Generally

Ontario (Attorney General) v. Ballard Estate (1995), 26 O.R. (3d) 39, 129 D.L.R. (4th) 52, 86 O.A.C. 43 (C.A.).

To obtain documents from a non-party, it is not necessary to show the documents sought are vital or crucial for trial preparation. The court should consider various factors including the importance of the documents; whether pre-trial production is necessary to avoid unfairness; whether discovery from the parties is adequate and, if not, whether responsibility for the inadequacy rests with a party; whether the non-party resists production; the availability of the documents or information from other sources; and the relationship between the non-party and the parties.

550551 Ontario Ltd. v. Framingham (1991), 2 O.R. (3d) 284, 46 O.A.C. 156 (Gen. Div.).

Rule 30.10 does not apply to applications.

Peters v. Gen. Motors of Can. Ltd. (1986), 14 C.P.C. (2d) 147 (Ont. Dist. Ct.).

A motion for production from an affiliated company should proceed under rule 30.02(4) rather than rule 30.10.

Re Royal Bank of Can. and Ont. Securities Comm. (1976), 14 O.R. (2d) 783, 2 C.P.C. 132 (H.C.).

The non-party may appear and make objections to the production of documents.

Jameson v. Margetson (1975), 11 O.R. (2d) 175 (Co. Ct.).

An order was refused where production of the documents by the non-party would involve considerable time and expense.

Herrington v. Voss, [1968] 1 O.R. 250 (Master).

It is not necessary to specify the particular documents believed to be in the possession of the non-party.

Halpin v. Gillam, [1967] 2 O.R. 269 (Master).

The material in support of the motion should attempt to identify the particular types of document sought. Only documents containing important relevant material need be produced.

Weber v. Czerevko, [1962] O.W.N. 245 (H.C.).

The court refused to permit a "fishing expedition".

Production from Non-Parties — Banking Records

I.T.L. Indust. Ltd. v. Winterbottom (1980), 27 O.R. (2d) 496, 15 C.P.C. 255, 106 D.L.R. (3d) 577 (C.A.).

Production of bank documents not within the scope of s. 34 of the *Evidence Act* may, in a proper case, be ordered in an action in which the bank is not a party.

Astral Films Ltd. v. Sherman (1978), 19 O.R. (2d) 206, 5 C.P.C. 317, 3 B.L.R. 150, leave to appeal refused 19 O.R. (2d) 208n, 5 C.P.C. 317n (H.C.).

The plaintiff was permitted to inspect banking records where such records were of considerable significance and relevance to its claim. Discussion of guidelines for such applications.

Production from Non-Parties — Employment Records

Pryslak v. Anderson (1987), 57 O.R. (2d) 788, 15 C.P.C. (2d) 79 (H.C.).

The court ordered production of documents regarding the plaintiff's applications for employment to several police forces.

Wright v. Clark (1984), 48 O.R. (2d) 528, 46 C.P.C. 105 (Master).

The court refused to order production of any part of the plaintiff's employment record file where the plaintiff had undertaken to produce documents regarding the rates of pay, amounts paid and attendance record of the plaintiff.

Kap v. Sands; Keanie v. Sands (1980), 30 O.R. (2d) 125, *(sub nom. Zoltac v. Ross)* 22 C.P.C. 32 at 36, affirmed 22 C.P.C. 32 at 61 (H.C.).

The court refused to order production of employment records regarding deceased persons for whose deaths the actions were brought where it was not shown that the documents were relevant and it would be oppressive to order such production.

Woods v. Harris (1979), 25 O.R. (2d) 14, 12 C.P.C. 119 (H.C.).

The court refused to order the employer of a plaintiff making a loss of earnings claim in a motor vehicle case to produce all employment records of the plaintiff. The court must strike a balance between disclosure of relevant documents and preventing harassment of non-parties.

Production from Non-Parties — Hospital Records and Medical Reports

P. (L.M.) v. F. (D.) (1994), 34 C.P.C. (3d) 172, 22 C.C.L.T. (2d) 312 (Ont. Gen. Div.).

The court ordered the plaintiff's physician in this sexual abuse case to produce his clinical notes and records. The need to properly assess the plaintiff's damages outweighed the need to preserve confidentiality.

Mather v. Turnbull (1991), 47 C.P.C. (2d) 180 (Ont. Gen. Div.).

The court ordered production of a physician's clinical notes and psychologist's raw test data.

G. (D.M.) v. G. (S.D.) (1990), 72 O.R. (2d) 774, 44 C.P.C. (2d) 52 (Master).

Where production of psychiatric records would have had an adverse effect on a party, the court exercised its discretion to refuse production, notwithstanding the relevance of the documents.

Noonan v. Commercial Union Assurance Co. of Can. (1989), 42 C.P.C. (2d) 1 (Ont. H.C.).

As a general rule, in a personal injury case it is unfair to require the defendant to go to trial without clinical notes. Accordingly, physicians' clinical notes and records relating to post-accident treatment were to be produced. Documents relating to the plaintiff's unsuccessful application for a disability pension from the Canada Pension Plan and documents relating to insurance benefits paid to the plaintiff by another insurance company were also ordered produced. Medical records relating to pre-accident treatment were not ordered produced.

Noonan v. Commercial Union Assurance Co. of Can. (1989), 36 C.P.C. (2d) 232 (Ont. Dist. Ct.).

A psychologist was ordered to produce clinical notes and records despite objections that these documents might be misinterpreted by anyone but a psychologist. The psychologist could address that problem at trial if this occurred.

Karkanas v. Thomas (1986), 19 C.P.C. (2d) 303 (Ont. Dist. Ct.).

The court refused to order production of clinical notes of the plaintiff's family doctor for the period predating the accident where there was no *prima facie* case of an issue regarding her pre-existing condition.

Couto v. T.T.C. (1987), 59 O.R. (2d) 406, 16 C.P.C. (2d) 241 (H.C.).

In personal injury cases in which the nature and extent of the plaintiff's injuries are in issue, it is usually unfair to require the defendant to go to trial without production of the treating physician's clinical notes. A responding party opposing production of such records under rule 30.10 has the burden of establishing that production of the documents is unnecessary. *Tilly v. Crangle, infra*, is no longer the law.

Tamssot v. Belgrano (1987), 59 O.R. (2d) 57, 16 C.P.C. (2d) 189 (Master).

The court ordered production of OHIP records, but only for a time period having relevance to the issues in the action.

Trovato v. Smith (1987), 15 C.P.C. (2d) 121 (Ont. Dist. Ct.).

The court ordered the plaintiff to seek his physician's clinical records and notes although they were not within the plaintiff's "power" within the meaning of rule 30.03(1). There is no merit, logic or support in the Rules for requiring the defendant to establish a conflict in the medical reports or discovery evidence before making such an order. If a doctor does not voluntarily produce the documents, the defence will be met with its more limited rights under rule 30.10.

Jonathan v. Gore Mutual Ins. Co. (1985), 6 C.P.C. (2d) 300 (Ont. Dist. Ct.).

A hospital may insist that a patient sign the hospital's own form of authorization for release of records rather than a form prepared by the patient's solicitor.

Cook v. Ip (1985), 52 O.R. (2d) 289, 5 C.P.C. (2d) 81, 22 D.L.R. (4th) 1, 11 O.A.C. 171 (*sub nom. Cook v. Washuta*) (C.A.), leave to appeal to S.C.C. refused (1986), 68 N.R. 400n (*sub nom. OHIP v. Cook*), 18 O.A.C. 80n.

Where the plaintiff's medical condition was in issue, the court ordered production of O.H.I.P. cards relating to the plaintiff's treatment (overruling *Zdravkovic v. Paszano* (1984), 45 O.R. (2d) 550, 7 D.L.R. (4th) 328, 2 O.A.C. 293 (Div. Ct.)).

Horvath v. Home Ins. Co. (1985), 50 C.P.C. 105 (Ont. Dist. Ct.).

The court refused to order the Workers' Compensation Board to produce documents pertaining to the plaintiff relating to an industrial occurrence where the board filed a certificate pursuant to s. 30 of the *Evidence Act* objecting on the ground of privilege and that it would not be in the best interest of the public for production to be compelled.

Re Krasovskis (1985), 48 C.P.C. 159, 7 O.A.C. 316 (Div. Ct.).

Where a party obtains hospital records on the condition he will not disseminate the records further, he should request permission from the hospital to produce the records to the opposing party and advise the opposing party of the hospital's response. If the hospital refuses permission, the opposing party may move for an order that the hospital produce the records directly.

Soer v. Zorko; Zorko v. Soer (1983), 36 C.P.C. 126 (Ont. H.C.).

Clinical records will not be ordered produced by reason only of a difference of medical opinion, as opposed to a disputed question of fact.

Millward v. Reid (1981), 22 C.P.C. 101 (Ont. Div. Ct.).

Where there was reference in the medical reports to a pre-existing condition concerning the injury suffered, it was ordered that all documents relating to that condition be produced.

Tilly v. Crangle (1981), 31 O.R. (2d) 641, 120 D.L.R. (3d) 563 (C.A.).

Where the evidence of the plaintiff on examination for discovery conflicted with the contents of a medical report, the court ordered production of excerpts of the physician's clinical records dealing with the particular discrepancy. A broader order for production was refused.

Kap v. Sands; Keanie v. Sands (1980), 30 O.R. (2d) 125, (*sub nom. Zoltac v. Ross*) 22 C.P.C. 32 at 36, affirmed 22 C.P.C. 32 at 61 (H.C.).

Discussion of the proper procedure to follow to obtain production of hospital records and bank records.

Cruickshank v. Noble (1980), 29 O.R. (2d) 604 (H.C.).

(1) Where a plaintiff is requested by a defendant to obtain production of hospital records and fails to request such documents from the hospital, he should bear the costs of a motion to compel production from the hospital. If the hospital arbitrarily or unreasonably refuses to comply with the plaintiff's request, it should bear the costs of the motion. The defendant should bring the motion only if the documents are not voluntarily produced.

(2) A non-party from whom production is sought must be served personally.

Re Mitchell and St. Michael's Hosp. (1980), 29 O.R. (2d) 185, 19 C.P.C. 113, 112 D.L.R. (3d) 360 (H.C.).

The court refused to order the release of hospital records. *Strazdins v. Orthopaedic & Arthritic Hosp. (Toronto)* (1978), 22 O.R. (2d) 47, 7 C.P.C. 243, 7 C.C.L.T. 117, 2 L. Med. Q. 309 (H.C.), *infra*, not followed.

Dwyer v. Chu, 29 O.R. (2d) 156, 16 C.P.C. 188, [1980] I.L.R. 1-1226 (H.C.).

The plaintiff's no-fault insurer was ordered to produce a copy of a medical report obtained with respect to a disability benefits claim.

Sugrue v. Brown (1979), 14 C.P.C. 114 (Ont. Master).

Where a hospital refused to release records pertaining to a party's admission to hospital after written requests by his solicitor and his consent, an order was made requiring production of all the documents in the hospital's possession and costs were awarded against the hospital.

Re Sunnybrook Hosp. and Can. Gen. Accident Assur. Co. (1979), 13 C.P.C. 102 (Ont. H.C.).

A hospital was ordered to produce certain medical records to its insurer where the plaintiff patients had withheld their consent.

Atkins v. Iwanicki (1978), 22 O.R. (2d) 182 (Master).

The Workmen's Compensation Board was required to produce medical records relevant to the treatment of the plaintiff where the Board had commenced a subrogated action in the name of the plaintiff.

Strazdins v. Orthopaedic & Arthritic Hospital (Toronto) (1978), 22 O.R. (2d) 47, 7 C.P.C. 243, 7 C.C.L.T. 117, 2 L. Med. Q. 309 (H.C.).

Hospital records of a deceased person were ordered to be produced on an originating application by the personal representative of the deceased.

Bowen v. Montag (1978), 21 O.R. (2d) 801, 91 D.L.R. (3d) 719, 2 L. Med. Q. 233 (H.C.).

The court ordered production of psychiatric records where the information would promote settlement and notwithstanding that mental health was not put in issue by the pleadings.

Vanmechelen v. Vanmechelen, [1973] 3 O.R. 422, 13 R.F.L. 88 (H.C.).

The court ordered psychiatric hospitals to produce records for use regarding a custody issue with the proviso that they could not be used with respect to other issues.

Coderque v. Mutual of Omaha Ins. Co., [1970] 1 O.R. 473, [1969] I.L.R. 1-297 (H.C.).

Production of medical reports was ordered.

Kokan v. Dales, [1970] 1 O.R. 456 (H.C.).

Production of hospital records may be ordered notwithstanding that such documents may not be admissible at trial.

Petursson v. Petursson, [1966] 2 O.R. 626 (H.C.).

The court refused to order a mental hospital to produce records of the history and condition of the plaintiff because the records were highly confidential, contained hearsay and were partly irrelevant to the issues in the action.

Production from Non-Parties — Insurance Files

Belmont (Village) v. Joe Snyders Construction Ltd. (1989), 44 C.P.C. (2d) 292, 36 O.A.C. 235 (Div. Ct.).

The court refused to order production of an insurance policy from a non-party, where that policy was not relevant to a material issue in the action.

Wright v. Clark (1984), 48 O.R. (2d) 528, 46 C.P.C. 105 (Master).

The court refused to order production of the entire file of the plaintiff's no-fault insurer but did order production of documents relating to the plaintiff's disability claim.

Anger v. Dykstra, 45 O.R. (2d) 701, 43 C.P.C. 268, [1984] I.L.R. 1-1758 (H.C.).

In this personal injury action, only that portion of the file of the liability insurer of the plaintiff relating to no fault benefits was ordered produced.

Zdravkovic v. Paszana (1983), 34 C.P.C. 283 at 287 (Ont. H.C.).

The court ordered production of witness statements, adjuster's and examiner's notes, etc. from the plaintiff's insurer's files.

Production from Non-Parties — Miscellaneous

Polycellular Tires Ltd. v. Alles (1992), 12 C.P.C. (3d) 104 (Ont. Gen. Div.).

The court ordered that non-party solicitors produce their files for examination in relation to a claim for solicitor-client privilege.

Roberts (Litigation Guardian of) v. Davidson (1991), 3 C.P.C. (3d) 64 (Ont. Div. Ct.).

In a personal injury case, the court ordered production of the transcripts of the examinations for discovery in a wrongful dismissal case in which the plaintiff was involved.

Hockenhull v. Laskin (1987), 59 O.R. (2d) 157, 16 C.P.C. (2d) 200 (H.C.).

The court ordered a television station to provide a copy of certain news film at the expense of the moving party, including a component of overhead cost.

Peters v. Fireman's Fund Co. of Can., 45 O.R. (2d) 149, 4 C.C.L.I. 104, 6 D.L.R. (4th) 135, [1984] I.L.R. 1-1744 (H.C.).

Where two actions were commenced, one against the tortfeasor, and one under the underinsured motorist endorsement, and the defendant insurer sought production of the tortfeasor's insurance policy from the tortfeasor's insurer for use in the first action, the court held under the former Rules that the policy need not be produced.

Lockwood v. Ranger (1983), 42 O.R. (2d) 308, 35 C.P.C. 92 (H.C.).

The court ordered OHIP to produce claim cards regarding services rendered to the plaintiff.

Glover v. Glover (1980), 18 C.P.C. 107 (Ont. C.A.).

Bell Canada was not required to produce its records of calls to and from the residence of a third party to assist in enforcing a custody judgment.

Dand v. Mills (1978), 7 C.P.C. 86 (Ont. Master).

In an action by beneficiaries against trustees, the master refused to order production of accountant's documents concerning creation and administration of the trust.

Pocock v. Pocock, [1950] O.R. 734, affirmed [1952] O.R. 155 (C.A.).

The court may require the production of a provincial corporate tax return.

DOCUMENT DEPOSITED FOR SAFE KEEPING

30.11 The court may order that a relevant document be deposited for safe keeping with the registrar and thereafter the document shall not be inspected by any person except with leave of the court.

Automated Tabulation Inc. v. Canadian Market Images Ltd. (1995), 24 O.R. (3d) 292 (Gen. Div.).

The court has a discretion to order that access to confidential documents be restricted to the solicitors for an opposing party and not to the opposing party itself.

E.R. Squibb & Sons Inc. v. Apotex Inc. (1993), 15 C.P.C. (3d) 169, 47 C.P.R. (3d) 214 (Ont. Master).

In this case involving patent infringement the court made a protective order concerning the use and confidentiality of information disclosed in the law suit.

Inline Fiberglass Ltd. v. Omniglass Ltd. (1992), 12 C.P.C. (3d) 240, 45 C.P.R. (3d) 405 (Ont. Gen. Div.).

The court refused to order that an affidavit and transcripts from a resulting cross-examination be deposited for safe-keeping. The contents of the affidavit and the transcripts could not reasonably be said to be confidential.

Johnson v. National Life Assurance Co. of Canada (1992), 7 C.P.C. (3d) 20 (Ont. Gen. Div.), leave to appeal refused 7 C.P.C. (3d) 20n.

The court made a confidentiality order regarding documents produced in the course of the law suit.

Amer.-Can. Dev. Corp. Ltd. v. Tele Time Saver Inc. (1976), 1 C.P.C. 230, 29 C.P.R. (2d) 272 (Ont. H.C.).

The evidence in this trade secrets case was ordered sealed until trial, with access only to court and counsel. Not all trade secrets cases need be heard *in camera*.

RULE 30.1　DEEMED UNDERTAKING

Highlights

In *Goodman v. Rossi* (1995), 24 O.R. (3d) 359, the case establishing the common law "implied undertaking" as part of the law of Ontario, the Court of Appeal suggested that the law on the implied undertaking should be embodied in the Rules. In formulating the Rule, the Civil Rules Committee did not limit itself to merely codifying what had been decided in the case law to date; rather it took the opportunity to contour and refine the implied undertaking principle. Since the principle now takes its force from this Rule, it seemed appropriate to rename it a "deemed undertaking".

Application. Rule 30.1(1) stipulates what it is that attracts the deemed undertaking. It limits the operation of the principle to evidence or information obtained from *discovery procedures* and does not extend it to those procedures which are "evidence taking" in nature, *e.g.*, affidavits, cross-examination on affidavits, examination of witnesses on a pending motion. However, recognizing that the protection provided by the principle would be too narrow if it was limited literally to "evidence" obtained from discovery, the Rule extends not only to evidence but also to "information obtained" from such evidence. Consequently the implied undertaking will be breached not only by misuse of evidence, but also by misuse of the information contained in or obtained from that evidence.

If evidence revealed on discovery is known to the recipient via another source the implied undertaking does not apply: Rule 30.1(2). (This qualification was suggested by Moldaver J. in his judgment in the Divisional Court in *Goodman v. Rossi* (1994), 21 O.R. (3d) 112.)

Deemed undertaking. The undertaking deemed by the Rule is that all parties and their counsel will not use the evidence or information for any purposes other than those of the proceeding in which it was obtained (Rule 30.1(3)), but then exceptions are spelled out (Rule 30.1(4)-(7)) and the court is given a general discretionary power to relieve against the undertaking (Rule 30.1(8)).

The undertaking prevents the recipient of the information from revealing it to third parties (perhaps most particularly, but not limited to, the media) or making use of the information in a proceeding other than the one in which it was obtained.

Exception — Consent to use. The first exception is that the information may be used for another purpose if the person disclosing the information consents to such use: Rule 30.1(4). Although the rule does not specifically require that the consent be written, in general it will be unwise to make use of the information without consent in writing since it may be very difficult for the user to prove consent in the absence of a writing.

Exception — Filing or use in court. Subrule (5) places limits on the deemed undertaking principle so that it does not encroach on the principle of the "open court". Once evidence is filed with the court or given, or referred to, at a hearing the undertaking ceases to apply and the evidence or information may be used for any purpose. In *Harman v. Secretary of State for Home Department*, [1983] 1 A.C. 280, the House of Lords refused to recognize an exception for documents and evidence disclosed in open court. However, this decision was criticized and overruled by Order 24, Rule 14A of the U.K. Rules of the Supreme Court which was added in 1987. The Ontario provision, Rule 30.1(5), uses simpler and broader language than this comparable English provision.

Exception — Impeachment. Subrule (6) confirms an exception that was suggested in *Goodman* — evidence from one proceeding, even though generally subject to the undertaking, may be used in another proceeding for the purposes of impeaching the testimony of a witness. Though this exception is narrow in the sense that it permits the use of information only in the context of a court proceeding, it is to be noted that it is not limited to the use of the information against the person who made the initial disclosure. While the typical situation will be one in which the person to be impeached is a witness or party in action #2 who made disclosures in action #1 (through production of documents or on examination for discovery), the rule is not so limited. It would seem to permit information disclosed in action #1 by X to be used in action #2 to impeach Y.

A central question under this subrule is one of mechanics. How does counsel (lawyer A) who is going to do the impeachment in action #2 actually obtain the information? If the information is already known to the counsel (*e.g.*, because he or she, or another lawyer in the firm was counsel in action #1) there is no problem. But what if the information is in the possession of (an unrelated) lawyer B who acted in action #1? Are there circumstances under which lawyer B can reveal the information to lawyer A without lawyer B being in breach of the undertaking? Unless the exception is to be limited to permitting only lawyers who already have the information to use it for impeachment (which would make little or no sense in policy terms), the answer would seem to be yes. It can be argued that lawyer B may reveal the information to lawyer A on receipt of an undertaking from lawyer A that he or she will use the information only for the purpose of the impeachment.

Exception — Subsequent action. Rule 31.11(8) (subsequent action) provides that in limited circumstances if there is a subsequent action between the same parties involving the same subject matter the evidence given on an examination for discovery taken in the former action may be read into or used in evidence at the trial of the subsequent action as if it had been taken in the subsequent action. Rule 30.1(7) provides that the deemed undertaking does not prohibit the use of the evidence or information in accordance with rule 31.11(8).

Discretionary power to relieve against the undertaking. The court is given the power by subrule (8) to order that the deemed undertaking does not apply. It may do so where it is "satisfied that the interests of justice outweigh any prejudice that would result to a party who disclosed evidence" and it may impose such terms and give such directions as are just.

In *Goodman*, Morden A.C.J.O. stated that it is "a necessary and appropriate part of the implied undertaking rule that the court have the power to grant relief from its application". He quoted from *Crest Homes plc v. Marks*, [1987] 2 All E.R. 1074, where Lord Oliver had stated that the authorities on the question "illustrate no general principle beyond this, that the court will not release or modify the implied undertaking given on discovery, save in special circumstances and where the release or modification *will not occasion an injustice to the person giving discovery*" (emphasis added). In *Goodman*, Morden A.C.J.O. said that, for the purpose of the present case, he was prepared to consider the applicable test as being more liberal than that stated in *Crest Homes* — as one tolerating some injustice to the discovered party if it is outweighed by a greater injustice to the discovering party if he or she could not make use of the discovered documents. Subrule (8) confirms the balancing approach suggested by Morden A.C.J.O.

Consequential amendment to rule 51.06. Rule 51.06(1) permits a party to move for an order based on an admission made, *inter alia*, in the examination for discovery of a party or a person examined for discovery on behalf of a party in the same *or another* proceeding. Where the admission sought to be relied on is from an examination for discovery in another proceeding this would normally attract the deemed undertaking. For this reason, rule 51.06 has been amended by the addition of subrule (3) providing that if ''Rule 30.1 applies to the admission, its use in another proceeding is subject to Rule 30.1 (deemed undertaking)''.

Application

30.1(1) This Rule applies to,

(a) evidence obtained under,

    (i) Rule 30 (documentary discovery),

    (ii) Rule 31 (examination for discovery),

    (iii) Rule 32 (inspection of property),

    (iv) Rule 33 (medical examination),

    (v) Rule 35 (examination for discovery by written questions),

    (vi) Rule 60.18 (examination in aid of execution); and

(b) information obtained from evidence referred to in clause (a).

(2) This rule does not apply to evidence or information obtained otherwise than under the rules referred to in subrule (1).

Deemed Undertaking

(3) All parties and their counsel are deemed to undertake not to use evidence or information to which this Rule applies for any purposes other than those of the proceeding in which the evidence was obtained.

Exceptions

(4) Subrule (3) does not prohibit a use to which the person who disclosed the evidence consents.

(5) Subrule (3) does not prohibit the use, for any purpose, or,

(a) evidence that is filed with the court;

(b) evidence that is given or referred to during a hearing;

(c) information obtained from evidence referred to in clause (a) or (b).

(6) Subrule (3) does not prohibit the use of evidence obtained in one proceeding, or information obtained from such evidence, to impeach the testimony of a witness in another proceeding.

(7) Subrule (3) does not prohibit the use of evidence or information in accordance with subrule 31.11(8) (subsequent action).

Order that Undertaking does not Apply

(8) If satisfied that the interests of justice outweigh any prejudice that would result to a party who disclosed evidence, the court may order that subrule (3) does not apply to the evidence or to information obtained from it, and may impose such terms and give such directions as are just. [en. O. Reg. 61/96, s. 2]

[*Cases decided before April 1, 1996 when Rule 30.1 came into force should be read with great care — Authors.*]

Deemed Undertaking — Generally

Goodman v. Rossi (1995), 24 O.R. (3d) 359, 37 C.P.C. (3d) 181, 12 C.C.E.L. (2d) 105, 125 D.L.R. (4th) 613, 83 O.A.C. 38 (C.A.).

The ''implied undertaking'' is part of the law of Ontario. Discussion of circumstances where relief from the undertaking will be granted.

Rivait v. Gaudry (1994), 18 O.R. (3d) 548 (Div. Ct.) (on reserve with Court of Appeal).

Where an insurance company in an under-insured motorist coverage action had received medical information about the plaintiff, it was not precluded from making use of that information in relation to the first party benefits it was providing to the plaintiff for a disability arising out of the accident. The information was not, strictly speaking, used for a collateral purpose, and the report did not come to the insurer in a discovery process in which it was the discoverer. Furthermore, the report would have to have been produced under S.E.F. 44 requirements in any event. As a result, the court did not have to concern itself as to whether there was a rule of implied undertaking.

Carbone v. De La Rocha (1993), 13 O.R. (3d) 355 (Gen. Div.).

An implied undertaking not to use documents for collateral purposes is imposed upon a party receiving documents. Breach of the undertaking constitutes contempt of court.

Johnson v. National Life Assurance Co. of Canada (1992), 7 C.P.C. (3d) 20 (Ont. Gen. Div.), leave to appeal refused 7 C.P.C. (3d) 20n.

It is far from certain that implied undertakings are the law of Ontario. The court made an express confidentiality order.

Reichmann v. Toronto Life Publishing Co. (1990), 44 C.P.C. (2d) 206 (Ont. H.C.).

The court imposed conditions relating to the production of financial statements by the corporate plaintiff in order to safeguard their confidentiality.

National Gypsum Co. v. Dorrell (1989), 68 O.R. (2d) 689, 34 C.P.C. (2d) 1, 25 C.P.R. (3d) 15 (H.C.).

Documents which have been produced in a proceeding are always subject to an implied undertaking that they will not be used for a collateral purpose. The court therefore refused to make a non-disclosure order where there were no special circumstances.

LAC Minerals Ltd. v. New Cinch Uranium Ltd. (1985), 50 O.R. (2d) 260, 48 C.P.C. 199, 17 D.L.R. (4th) 745 (Ont. H.C.) (leave to appeal to Ont. Div. Ct. granted 2 C.P.C. (2d) 76).

The court held that documents produced in the course of litigation are subject to an implied undertaking that they will not be used for any purpose other than the conduct of the litigation in which the documents were produced, except with leave of the court or the consent of the party making production.

Anderson v. Anderson (1979), 26 O.R. (2d) 769, 14 C.P.C. 87, 12 R.F.L. (2d) 353, 105 D.L.R. (3d) 341 (H.C.).

The court has inherent jurisdiction to require parties to enter into undertakings regarding the use of documents produced for discovery. A party was required not to disclose certain documents.

Deemed Undertaking — Exceptions by Court Order

Gleadow v. Nomura Canada Inc. (1996), 7 W.D.C.P. (2d) 163 (Ont. Gen. Div.).

The court relieved the plaintiff from the "implied undertaking" so as to permit documents produced in this wrongful dismissal case to be used in related proceedings under the *Employment Standards Act*. However costs were awarded against the plaintiff because the documents had been disclosed before permission was obtained to do so.

Csak v. Mokos (1995), 7 W.D.C.P. (2d) 62 (Ont. Master).

Based on the implied undertaking, the court refused to permit the use of a pre-trial brief from one action on a motion in a second action.

Steer v. Merklinger (1995), 25 O.R. (3d) 812 (Gen. Div.).

Where the defendant's financial statements had been previously filed with the court in another proceeding, the court held that the defendant's financial statements were not subject to the implied undertaking rule and the plaintiff was free to refer to them in her affidavit.

Steer v. Merklinger (1995), 25 O.R. (3d) 812 (Gen. Div.).

While discovery evidence from another proceeding was subject to the implied undertaking rule, relief from the undertaking was granted where the prejudice to the plaintiff in not granting such relief outweighed the prejudice to the defendant.

Consolidated NBS Inc. v. Price Waterhouse (1992), 10 C.P.C. (3d) 155, 94 D.L.R. (4th) 176
(Ont. Gen. Div.), reversed in part on other grounds (1994), 69 O.A.C. 236 (Div. Ct.).

An implied undertaking not to disclose documents or information may apply to documents disclosed by the Crown in criminal prosecutions; however, such documents were ordered produced in this case since the party with the documents was not seeking to use them but rather was being asked to produce them.

Roberts (Litigation Guardian of) v. Davidson (1991), 2 W.D.C.P. (2d) 566 (Ont. Div. Ct.).

In a personal injury case, the court ordered production of the transcripts of the examinations for discovery in a wrongful dismissal case in which the plaintiff was involved.

755568 Ontario Ltd. v. Linchris Homes Ltd. (1990), 1 O.R. (3d) 649, 46 C.P.C. (2d) 157 (Gen.
Div.).

The court refused leave to provide transcripts of examinations for discovery to the police where possible violation of the *Criminal Code* was alleged.

Deemed Undertaking — Enforcement

Orfus Realty v. D.G. Jewellery of Canada Ltd. (1995), 24 O.R. (3d) 379, 41 C.P.C. (3d) 148,
83 O.A.C. 35 (C.A.).

The "implied undertaking" is the law of Ontario. Use of a document for any purpose, not necessarily a pejorative purpose, other than the litigation in which the document was produced may attract a contempt sanction.

Walker v. York Finch Hospital (1992), 15 C.P.C. (3d) 23, additional reasons (1993), 15 C.P.C.
(3d) 23 at 29 (Ont. Gen. Div.).

An order was issued restraining the telecast of a videotape of the examination of a witness under Rule 36. Such use breached an implied undertaking not to use the examination for any purpose other than for the purpose for which it was produced and would have made any subsequent order excluding witnesses under rule 52.06(1) meaningless.

RULE 31   EXAMINATION FOR DISCOVERY

Highlights

Form of the examination. An examination for discovery may be oral or by written questions and answers, but not both except with leave: rule 31.02. The procedure on examination by written questions is regulated by Rule 35, and in practice such examinations are rare.

Who may be examined. There is a right to examine any party adverse in interest (rule 31.03(1)) and, with leave, non-parties (other than expert witnesses) may be examined where there is reason to believe that they have information relevant to a material issue in the action: rule 31.10. (Note that there are specific prerequisites to the obtaining of such leave and provisions with regard to the costs of the examination). Specific provision is made as to who is to be examined in respect of various parties (*e.g.*, corporations, partnerships, persons under disability, assignees, etc.): rule 31.03.

When examination may be initiated. Unless the parties agree otherwise, no party may serve a notice of examination until he or she has served an affidavit of documents: rule 31.04.

Scope of examination. By rule 31.06, the scope of examination for discovery is redefined and broadened. Evidence is now discoverable; cross-examination, except with respect to credibility only, is permitted; and cross-examination on an affidavit of documents is permitted: rule 31.06(1). The names and addresses of witnesses, *i.e.*, persons having knowledge of transactions or occurrences in issue, are discoverable unless the court orders otherwise: rule 31.06(2).

The findings, opinions and conclusions of experts retained by a party are expressly made discoverable, but this information, and the identity of the expert, need not be disclosed if the information was obtained in preparation for contemplated or pending litigation and if the party undertakes not to call the expert as a witness at trial: rule 31.06(3). (Query whether at the discovery stage an expert's written report itself, if prepared in anticipation of litigation, still remains technically privileged so that its production can be insisted upon only on the eve of trial, under rule 53.03 or, perhaps, not later than ten days after setting down under rule 30.09 if the report itself is to be put in evidence. But *cf.* rules 33.04, 33.06 and 50.05.)

The existence and contents of any relevant insurance policy are also discoverable (rule 31.06(4)) and see also rule 30.02(3) (documentary discovery of insurance policies). In 1990, rule 31.06(4) was amended, reversing earlier case law, to specifically provide that a party may obtain disclosure of the amount of money available under the policy, and any conditions affecting its availability.

A party who subsequently discovers that an answer given on an examination was incorrect or incomplete when made, or is no longer correct and complete, is under a duty to forthwith provide the information in writing to every other party; the opposing party can require such information to be verified by affidavit or to be subject to further examination: rule 31.09(1) and (2). Failure to comply with these provisions may lead to the exclusion of the evidence at trial (see rule 53.08) or the making of such order as is just: rule 31.09(3).

Conduct of examination. This matter is principally dealt with in Rule 34. Rule 31.07 provides that a person who refuses to answer a proper question or refuses to answer on the grounds of privilege does so with some risk; unless the information is provided in writing not less than ten days after the action is set down for trial, it may not be introduced into evidence except with leave (as to the granting of such leave see rule 53.08). Where counsel, rather than the person examined, answers any question the answer is deemed to be that of the person examined, unless before the end of the examination the person repudiates or qualifies the answer: rule 31.08. However, only in the absence of an objection may counsel answer a question for a witness, even if the witness's answer is wrong; where the answer is wrong, the witness's counsel may re-examine to try to correct the answer or may correct the answer after completion of the examination pursuant to rule 31.09: *Kay v. Posluns* (1989), 71 O.R. (2d) 238 (H.C.).

Use of examination at trial. A party may read into evidence any part of the examination for discovery of an adverse party, if otherwise admissible, whether the party has already given evidence or not: rule 31.11(1). Also, the evidence given on an examination may be used for the purpose of impeaching the deponent in the same manner as any previous inconsistent statement: rule 31.11(2). Where only part of the examination is used in evidence, the trial judge may direct the introduction of any other part that qualifies the part used.

The examination of a non-party "witness" may not be read into evidence as an admission, but may be used to impeach the non-party should he or she testify: rule 31.11(1) and (2) and rule 31.10(5).

Where any person examined for discovery is unavailable at trial, leave may be granted to any party to use the examination for discovery as the evidence of the absent person: rule 31.11(6).

Recent amendments. New Rule 30.1 (Deemed Undertaking) regulates the general use of information obtained through the discovery process.

Former Rules: Rules 326, 329, 331, 333-335, 351.

DEFINITION

31.01 In rules 31.02 to 31.11, "document" has the same meaning as in clause 30.01(1)(a).

FORM OF EXAMINATION

31.02(1) Subject to subrule (2), an examination for discovery may take the form of an oral examination or, at the option of the examining party, an examination by written questions and answers, but the examining party is not entitled to subject a person to both forms of examination except with leave of the court.

(2) Where more than one party is entitled to examine a person, the examination for discovery shall take the form of an oral examination, unless all the parties entitled to examine the person agree otherwise.

Ferrovecchio v. Barbieri (1979), 10 C.P.C. 1 (Ont. Div. Ct.).

In the absence of any agreement that undertakings be answered by letter, the witness may be required to re-attend.

S.E. Lyons and Son Ltd. v. Nawoc Holdings Ltd. (1978), 20 O.R. (2d) 234, 7 C.P.C. 10, affirmed 23 O.R. (2d) 727n (H.C.).

Undertakings must be answered by the witness re-attending and giving oral evidence, unless otherwise agreed.

WHO MAY EXAMINE AND BE EXAMINED

Generally

31.03(1) A party to an action may examine for discovery any other party adverse in interest, once, and may examine that party more than once only with leave of the court, but a party may examine more than one person as permitted by subrules (3) to (8).

On Behalf of Corporation

(2) Where a corporation may be examined for discovery, the examining party may examine any officer, director or employee on behalf of the corporation, but the court on motion of the corporation before the examination may order the examining party to examine another officer, director or employee.

(3) Where an officer, director or employee of a corporation has been examined, no other officer, director or employee of the corporation may be examined without leave of the court.

On Behalf of Partnership or Sole Proprietorship

(4) Where an action is brought by or against a partnership or a sole proprietorship using the firm name, each person who was, or is alleged to have been, a partner or the sole proprietor, as the case may be, at a material time, may be examined on behalf of the partnership or sole proprietorship.

In Place of Person under Disability

(5) Where an action is brought by or against a party under disability,

(a) the litigation guardian may be examined in place of the person under disability; or

(b) at the option of the examining party, the person under disability may be examined if he or she is competent to give evidence,

but where the litigation guardian is the Children's Lawyer or the Public Guardian and Trustee, the litigation guardian may be examined only with leave of the court.

Assignee

(6) Where an action is brought by or against an assignee, the assignor may be examined in addition to the assignee.

Trustee in Bankruptcy

(7) Where an action is brought by or against a trustee of the estate of a bankrupt, the bankrupt may be examined in addition to the trustee.

Nominal Party

(8) Where an action is brought or defended for the immediate benefit of a person who is not a party, the person may be examined in addition to the party bringing or defending the action.

Limiting Multiple Examinations

(9) Where a party is entitled to examine for discovery,

(a) more than one person under this rule; or

(b) multiple parties who are in the same interest,
but the court is satisfied that multiple examinations would be oppressive, vexatious or unnecessary, the court may impose such limits on the right of discovery as are just. [am. O. Reg. 69/95, ss. 18, 19, 20]

Authors' Note on Organization of Cases

Cases relevant to this provision have been organized as follows:

Who May Be Examined — Generally — rule 31.03(1)
Examination of Representative of Corporation — Generally — rule 31.03(2)
Substitution of Representative Selected by Opposing Party — rule 31.03(2)
Who May Be Examined — Partners — rule 31.03(4)
Examination of Person Under Disability — rule 31.03(5)
Examination of Bankrupt — rule 31.03(7)
Examination of Person Represented by Nominal Party — rule 31.03(8)
Limiting Multiple Examinations — rule 31.03(9)
Examination of Representative of the Crown
Availability of Second Examination

Who May Be Examined — Generally — rule 31.03(1)

Tusa v. Walsh (1994), 23 C.P.C. (3d) 178 (Ont. Gen. Div.).

Where two actions were ordered to be tried together, the court permitted the defendants in the first action to participate in the discovery of the defendants in the second action.

Domingo v. Location Gogo Inc. (1986), 55 O.R. (2d) 123, 11 C.P.C. (2d) 282 (Master).

A third party defending the main action was not permitted to examine defendants who were not involved in the third party claim, since they were not necessarily adverse in interest.

Air Canada v. Meridien Credit Corp. Can. (1985), 6 C.P.C. (2d) 195 (Ont. Dist. Ct.).

A plaintiff was permitted to examine a third party who had not defended the main action.

Caisse Populaire Laurier d'Ottawa Ltée v. Guertin; Caisse Populaire Laurier d'Ottawa Ltée v. Simard (1983), 43 O.R. (2d) 91, 36 C.P.C. 101, 9 C.R.R. 9, (*sub nom. Caisse Populaire Laurier d'Ottawa Ltée v. Guertin (No. 2)*) 150 D.L.R. (3d) 541, varied 46 O.R. (2d) 422, 10 D.L.R. (4th) 319 (Ont. Div. Ct.).

The *Canadian Charter of Rights and Freedoms* is not violated by requiring delivery of statements of defence by, and discovery of, parties who are also defendants in criminal proceedings.

Brylowski v. Brylowski (1980), 17 C.P.C. 9 (Ont. Master).

Although no issue remained between the plaintiffs and a defendant except as to costs, the defendant was examinable by the plaintiff where a co-defendant alleged a conspiracy between the plaintiff and the defendant, and the defendant sought to be indemnified by the co-defendant for any costs awarded against him.

T.D. Bank v. Williams (1978), 13 C.P.C. 197 (Ont. Dist. Ct.).

In the circumstances of this action on a promissory note, the plaintiff was not adverse in interest to a defendant against whom judgment had been signed.

Re Lounsbury Realty Ltd. and Shekter (1978), 23 O.R. (2d) 309 (Co. Ct.).

Discovery is not available in an application under Part IV of the *Landlord and Tenant Act*, R.S.O. 1970, c. 236.

Glanc v. Min. of Revenue (Ont.) (1978), 20 O.R. (3d) 699, 7 C.P.C. 190 (H.C.).

Parties to an appeal that by statute is deemed to be an action are examinable for discovery.

Crone v. Wright (1976), 1 C.P.C. 105 (Ont. H.C.).
In an action against executors all the executors are examinable.

Wren v. Supt. of Insurance (1976), 12 O.R. (2d) 190, 1 C.P.C. 145 (H.C.).
The Superintendent of Insurance is protected by Crown privilege and is not discoverable.

Northern Heights (Sault) Ltd. v. Majic, [1968] 1 O.R. 616 (Master).
A defendant who is in default is deemed to admit the allegations of the plaintiff and is therefore adverse in interest to his co-defendants.

Ogilvie v. Gray, [1967] 2 O.R. 272 (H.C.).
A party in default may be examined.

Koczka v. Carruthers, [1967] 2 O.R. 176, leave to appeal refused [1967] 2 O.R. 178n (H.C.).
A third party added under the *Insurance Act*, R.S.O. 1960, c. 190, may be examined by the plaintiff.

Standard Int. Corp. v. Morgan, [1967] 1 O.R. 328 (Master).
In an action by minority shareholders against majority shareholders in which the company is a party defendant, the company and the majority shareholders are adverse in interest.

Higgins v. Higgins, [1957] O.W.N. 114, affirmed [1957] O.W.N. at 116 (H.C.).
A plaintiff attacking the validity of a will was held not to be adverse in interest to several defendants whose pecuniary interests under the challenged will were also in the preceding unchallenged will.

Examination of Representative of Corporation — Generally — rule 31.03(2)

452994 Ontario Ltd. v. Continental Insurance Co. of Canada (1993), 4 W.D.C.P. (2d) 187
     (Ont. Gen. Div.).
Where the plaintiff corporation was in receivership, the court ordered that an officer of the corporation be examined for discovery on behalf of the corporation notwithstanding that the officer was adverse in interest to the receiver.

Atherton v. Boycott (1989), 36 C.P.C.(2d) 250 at 252, affirmed 36 C.P.C. (2d) 250 (Ont. H.C.).
For the purposes of determining whether an individual is an employee within the meaning of rule 31.03(2), it is not necessary to strictly adhere to the common law principles establishing an employer-employee relationship.

R. v. Amway of Can. Ltd., [1989] 1 S.C.R. 21, 33 C.P.C. (2d) 163 (*sub nom. Canada v. Amway of Can. Ltd.*), 68 C.R. (3d) 97, 37 C.R.R. 235, [1989] 1 C.T.C. 255, 56 D.L.R. (4th) 309, 23 F.T.R. 160n, 91 N.R. 18, 2 T.C.T. 4074, [1989] 1 T.S.T. 2058.
A rule compelling an officer of a corporation to submit to an examination for discovery in a civil action against the corporation for forfeiture under the *Customs Act* does not violate the *Charter of Rights*.

Butler v. Dimitrieff (1988), 66 O.R. (2d) 707 (Master).
Where all officers and directors of the defendant corporation had resigned, the court ordered one of the resigned officers to attend on the examination for discovery on behalf of the corporation. This individual was knowledgeable about the matters in issue, and there was reason to doubt whether his resignation was *bona fide*.

Joseph Silaschi General Contracting (Kitchener) Ltd. v. Kitchener (1986), 8 C.P.C. (2d) 199, 19 C.L.R. 94 (Ont. H.C.).
The court refused to order the examination of an architect who had been involved on behalf of the defendant in a construction project where it appeared he was an independent contractor, not an employee.

Abitibi-Price Inc. v. Sereda (1984), 43 C.P.C. 217 (Ont. H.C.).

Where the representative produced on behalf of a corporate party gave vague and indefinite evidence, which required voluminous undertakings, a second representative was ordered produced.

Townley v. Maritime Life Assur. Co. (1982), 39 O.R. (2d) 257, 31 C.P.C. 62, 139 D.L.R. (3d) 646 (H.C.).

A third party is not obliged to accept the officer or servant selected by the plaintiff to be examined for discovery on behalf of a corporate defendant in the main action as the person to be examined in the third party proceedings.

Hamilton Harbour Commrs. v. J.P. Porter Co. (1978), 19 O.R. (2d) 66, 5 C.P.C. 297, 4 C.R. (3d) 157, 84 D.L.R. (3d) 125, leave to appeal to Div. Ct. refused 20 O.R. (2d) 632, 5 C.P.C. at 300, 88 D.L.R. (3d) 604 (H.C.).

A former corporate official was held to be examinable on behalf of the corporation where the court had not been satisfied that his resignation was not to defeat the right of the opposing party to examine him.

Royal Bank of Can. v. Paul Pogue Companies Ltd. (1972), 11 O.R. (2d) 171 (C.A.).

Statements of the person examined on behalf of a corporation bind the corporation.

Stepps Invts. Ltd. v. Security Capital Corp. Ltd. (1973), 2 O.R. (2d) 648 (H.C.).

Where the officer, director or employee resigns in good faith before the examination takes place the examining party loses its right to examine him.

Scott Transport Ltd. v. Bondy, [1973] 2 O.R. 159 (H.C.).

The officer examined must be an officer of the corporation as of the date of the examination.

Substitution of Representative Selected by Opposing Party — rule 31.03(2)

Clarkson Mews Properties Inc. v. Angel Creek Estates Ltd. (1989), 37 C.P.C. (2d) 104 (Ont. Master).

Lack of knowledge of the issues on the part of a corporate representative selected for discovery by the examining party is not a sufficient reason to order the substitution of another representative.

Cineplex Odeon Corp. v. Toronto Star Publishing Ltd. (1986), 11 C.P.C. (2d) 291 (Ont. Master).

A party's *prima facie* right to name the representative of a corporate party to be examined should not be denied merely because the court is persuaded that another person would give a better examination. The court cannot substitute its opinion for that of counsel conducting his client's case.

Kowk v. Kitchener-Waterloo Record Ltd. (1985), 2 C.P.C. (2d) 250 (Ont. Dist. Ct.).

In this wrongful dismissal action the court substituted a more senior and knowledgeable representative of the defendant for the representative selected by the plaintiff where the latter had given the plaintiff a letter of recommendation without the defendant's authority.

Andani v. Reg. Mun. of Peel (1984), 47 C.P.C. 66 (Ont. H.C.).

The court refused to substitute a senior police officer to be examined in place of the police chief who was a party defendant. The chief may have been sued personally as well as vicariously under the *Police Act*.

Roe v. Dominion Stores Ltd. (1984), 41 C.P.C. 213 (Ont. Master).

Substitution of the witness to be examined was ordered where the plaintiff had chosen to examine the president of the defendant corporation who had no first-hand knowledge of the proposed area of questioning and it would be oppressive to the defendant.

G.C.C. Ltd. v. Thunder Bay (1980), 16 C.P.C. 15 (Ont. Master), reversed on other grounds (1981), 32 O.R. (2d) 111, 20 C.P.C. 276 (H.C.).

There is a heavy onus on a litigant seeking a change of officer to be examined on the grounds of ill health.

Gibson v. Bagnall (1978), 22 O.R. (2d) 234, 93 D.L.R. (3d) 382 (H.C.).

The chief of a division of the medical staff of a hospital is examinable on behalf of the hospital. The issues on a motion to substitute one deponent for another are: (1) does he possess sufficient knowledge to be a proper person to be discovered and (2) would he be an embarrassment to the corporate party.

Sheriff v. Burrows (1977), 16 O.R. (2d) 183, 6 C.P.C. 274 (H.C.).

Where a police chief was joined as a party to an action against an officer of the force, because of the provisions of the *Police Act*, a senior administrative officer who knew as much about the subject-matter of litigation was permitted to be produced in lieu of the chief.

Protter Mgmt. Ltd. v. Ont. Housing Corp. (1975), 8 O.R. (2d) 445 (H.C.).

Where a corporation seeks to substitute a different person to be examined, it need not show the person originally chosen is not a responsible person or is not knowledgeable. In this case the first chosen person was the subject of criminal charges related to his employment and the court permitted the substitution.

Dyson v. R.H. Dyson Co., [1962] O.W.N. 25, affirmed [1962] O.W.N. 74 (H.C.).

In order to substitute the examinee the corporation must show that the person selected by the opposing party is not responsible and does not have knowledge of the matters involved in the action.

Walton v. Bank of N.S., [1960] O.W.N. 541 (H.C.).

Where the officer chosen by the defendant to be examined on behalf of the corporate plaintiff was also a third party to the action, therefore having an interest adverse to the plaintiff, the court required the defendant to examine a different representative of the plaintiff.

Who May Be Examined — Partners — rule 31.03(4)

Gemini Group Automated Distribution Systems Inc. v. PWA Corp. (1993), 16 O.R. (3d) 239, 20 C.P.C. (3d) 385, 68 O.A.C. 205 (C.A.).

A limited partner who does not engage in the management of the business was not intended to be included as one of the partners who could be examined for discovery on behalf of the partnership.

Green v. Constellation Ins. Co. (1987), 16 C.P.C. (2d) 267 (Ont. H.C.).

The court set aside a notice of examination regarding one partner and ordered the substitution of a second partner where an examination of the first-named partner would have been oppressive.

Examination of Person Under Disability — rule 31.03(5)

Emberton v. Wittick (1985), 6 C.P.C. (2d) 89 (Ont. Master).

A defendant who had suffered a stroke which impaired his ability to testify about matters prior to the stroke was required to submit to examination for discovery. The onus of establishing unsoundness of mind sufficient to foreclose the examination had not been met.

Nyilas v. Janos (1985), 50 C.P.C. 91 (Ont. Master).

A party under disability may be examined for discovery if competent to give evidence subject to the discretion of the court to impose limits where the examination would be oppressive, vexatious or unnecessary. The court permitted the examination of two plaintiffs, aged sixteen and eleven years, notwithstanding evidence that the examination might cause serious psychological damage.

Bennett v. Hartemink (1983), 42 C.P.C. 33 (Ont. H.C.).

The right to examine a minor for discovery is not absolute. The court should interview the child before exercising its discretion in that regard.

McGowan v. Haslehurst (1977), 17 O.R. (2d) 440, 5 C.P.C. 280 (H.C.).

An appointment for discovery should be struck out on the grounds of unsoundness of mind of a party only in the clearest case. The preferable course is to allow the trial judge to rule on the admissibility of the examination and the credibility of the witness.

Nemeth v. Harvey (1975), 7 O.R. (2d) 719 (Master).

A child of tender years may be examined only if, quite apart from truthfulness, it is clear he is of such intelligence that reliance can be placed upon his answers; that the child is of average intelligence for his age is not conclusive.

Marek v. Cieslak (1974), 4 O.R. (2d) 348, 48 D.L.R. (3d) 39 (H.C.).

The Public Trustee acting as the litigation guardian of a mentally incompetent person not so found was required to be examined in place of that person.

Goddard v. Hill, [1973] 3 O.R. 130 (H.C.).

Where the litigation guardian of an infant is a party in his own right, both may be examined.

Barnes v. Kirk, [1968] 2 O.R. 213 (C.A.).

The onus of establishing incompetence rests on the party alleging it.

Brown v. Silverwood Dairies Ltd., [1947] O.W.N. 310 (Master).

1. The proper manner of raising questions as to the competency or capacity of a party to be examined is by a motion to set aside the appointment, or, if there is no time, then upon the motion to commit for non-attendance.

2. Where the official examiner found the infant-plaintiff was incompetent to be sworn and the infant-plaintiff's parents subsequently explained to the infant the nature and consequences of an oath, the master found the infant competent and ordered him to re-attend for discovery.

Examination of Bankrupt — rule 31.03(7)

Knox Instruments Inc. v. Witzel, [1969] 2 O.R. 670, 13 C.B.R. (N.S.) 37 (H.C.).

An officer of a bankrupt company may be examined.

Examination of Person Represented by Nominal Party — rule 31.03(8)

Waterloo North Condominium Corp. No. 64 v. Domlife Realty Ltd. (1989), 70 O.R. (2d) 210 (H.C.).

In an action brought by a condominium corporation regarding construction defects, it was not appropriate to require the individual unit owners to attend for discovery, where they had not made specific claims with respect to their units. The evidence of the individual unit owners could be obtained through the discovery of the condominium corporation.

286018 Ont. Ltd. v. Fidinam (Can.) Ltd. (1988), 27 C.P.C. (2d) 159 (Ont. Master).

The court ordered the examination for discovery of persons who ultimately owned the nominal corporate plaintiffs as to their personal knowledge of the facts in issue.

Metro. Toronto Condo. Corp. No. 539 v. Priene Ltd. (1984), 48 O.R. (2d) 313, 46 C.P.C. 238 (Master).

In an action brought by a condominium corporation regarding construction defects, the owners of certain units containing defects, who would obtain immediate benefits if the action were successful, were ordered to be examined.

Alpha Leasing Ltd. v. Hodgson Machine & Equipment Ltd. (1984), 45 O.R. (2d) 200, 41 C.P.C. 137 (Master).

The court refused to permit an insurer in a subrogated action to substitute its own representative for discovery in place of the named plaintiff where all reasonable efforts to secure the plaintiff's attendance had not been exhausted.

Min. of Consumer & Commercial Relations v. Co-Operators Ins. Assn. (1983), 37 C.P.C. 269 (Ont. H.C.).

An action against an insurer to recover moneys paid out of the Motor Vehicle Accident Claims Fund is not brought for the immediate benefit of the motorist to whom the moneys were paid.

Consumers Glass Co. v. Farrell Lines Inc. (1982), 39 O.R. (2d) 696, 30 C.P.C. 293 (H.C.).

Where the claim of the plaintiff was entirely paid and fully subrogated to the insurance company, the party for whose benefit the action is brought is the insurer and a representative of the plaintiff's insurer was ordered to attend for discovery.

Ont. Securities Comm. v. Trustee of Re-Mor Invts. Mgmt. Corp. (1982), 26 C.P.C. 202 (Ont. H.C.).

In an action to determine who were the holders of certain mortgages, discovery was ordered of non-parties named in the statement of claim for whose immediate benefit the action was being prosecuted.

Regalcrest Builders Inc. v. Somjan Invts. Ltd. (1978), 6 C.P.C. 177, reversed 7 C.P.C. 168n (Ont. H.C.).

The fact that a non-party might materially benefit if an action was successful, through an arrangement with the plaintiffs, did not make that person examinable.

Brown and Resnick v. Stead and Austey, [1972] 3 O.R. 668 (Co. Ct.).

An officer of an insurance company was examined in respect of a counterclaim made in the name of an insured.

Limiting Multiple Examinations — rule 31.03(9)

Eversonic Inc. v. MacGirr (1986), 53 O.R. (2d) 179, 7 C.P.C. (2d) 163 (Master).

Parties are "in the same interest" only if they must stand or fall together. It is not sufficient that they are not adverse in interest and are represented by the same solicitors.

Examination of Representative of the Crown

Ontario (Attorney General) v. Ballard Estate (1995), 38 C.P.C. (3d) 81 (Ont. Gen. Div. [Commercial List]).

By virtue of the *Proceedings Against the Crown Act*, where the Crown is the plaintiff in a civil action it has the prerogative to select the representative of the Crown who will attend an examination for discovery. Accordingly, the defendant's motion to compel the production of a particular representative of the Crown for discovery was dismissed.

Can. Permanent Trust Co. v. McGregor (1982), 29 C.P.C. 27 (Ont. Master).

In the absence of a statutory enactment derogating from the Crown prerogative, the Crown cannot be compelled to submit to discovery.

Harrison Rock & Tunnel Co. v. R. (1980), 31 O.R. (2d) 573 (Master).

In an action against the Queen in right of Ontario, the Deputy Minister of Justice and Deputy Attorney General has the exclusive right to select a representative for examination for discovery.

Availability of Second Examination

Muslija v. Pilot Insurance Co. (1991), 3 O.R. (3d) 378, 50 C.P.C. (2d) 179 (Gen. Div.).

A second examination was refused in relation to a file which the plaintiff requested and was fully aware was going to be delivered to the examination where the plaintiff had clearly and unequivocally terminated the examination before the file arrived.

Chorney v. Colwill (1986), 19 C.P.C. (2d) 195 (Ont. H.C.).

The court permitted further discovery of the plaintiff where after her first examination the defendants had learned facts of great significance to the issues at trial which were known to the plaintiff before that first examination and which made her answers possibly incomplete.

April Invts. Ltd. v. Menat Const. Ltd. (1975), 11 O.R. (2d) 364 (H.C.).

A second examination was ordered with respect to facts becoming known as a result of an order for inspection of property.

Angelov v. Hampel, [1965] 2 O.R. 178 (H.C.).

A second examination was ordered where the condition of the plaintiff had deteriorated after the first examination so that the defendant could be prepared to fully meet the complaints of the plaintiff.

Boland v. Globe & Mail, [1961] O.W.N. 347 (H.C.).

Discussion of propriety of a second examination where a new trial had been ordered.

Hill-Clark-Frances Ltd. v. Schneider, [1947] O.W.N. 520 (Master).

The Rules contemplate only one examination for discovery. A party or witness subject to examination for discovery is not to be harassed by more examinations than are necessary.

Bank of Toronto v. Megaffin, [1946] O.W.N. 771 (Master).

Where a party has not obtained the discovery to which he is entitled because the opposite party has not informed himself he is entitled to another examination.

WHEN EXAMINATION MAY BE INITIATED

Examination of Plaintiff

31.04(1) A party who seeks to examine a plaintiff for discovery may serve a notice of examination under rule 34.04 or written questions under rule 35.01 only after delivering a statement of defence and, unless the parties agree otherwise, serving an affidavit of documents.

Examination of Defendant

(2) A party who seeks to examine a defendant for discovery may serve a notice of examination under rule 34.04 or written questions under rule 35.01 only after,

(a) the defendant has delivered a statement of defence and, unless the parties agree otherwise, the examining party has served an affidavit of documents; or

(b) the defendant has been noted in default.

Completion of Examination

(3) The party who first serves on another party a notice of examination under rule 34.04 or written questions under rule 35.01 may examine first

and may complete the examination before being examined by another party, unless the court orders otherwise.

Cross-Reference: See also cases under rule 34.04.

Costa v. Melo (1992), 13 C.P.C. (3d) 159 (Ont. Gen. Div.).
An affidavit of documents served before the close of pleadings is premature and cannot support a notice of examination.

Seaway Trust Co. v. Markle (1991), 47 C.P.C. (2d) 258 (Ont. Gen. Div.).
Proposed amendments to the statement of claim to add a new claim arising out of the same underlying facts did not justify delaying the examination for discovery of the defendant in the action.

Kay v. Posluns (1989), 35 C.P.C. (2d) 226 (Ont. H.C.).
Generally examinations for discovery are conducted in sequence with one being completed before the next is commenced. The court may vary the usual sequence if there are special circumstances.

Reichmann v. Toronto Life Publishing Co. (1989), 42 C.P.C. (2d) 170 (Ont. Master).
In an extraordinary case where discoveries would last many weeks the court ordered that the sequence of discovery not be governed by rule 31.04(3) but rather set alternate examination periods for the various parties.

Clark v. Stewart (1988), 30 C.P.C. (2d) 134 (Ont. Master).
An examining party should be able to substantially complete an examination for discovery of the opposite party before being obliged to be examined himself.

Risi Stone Ltd. v. Burloak Concrete Products Ltd. (1987), 45 C.P.C. (2d) 106 at 107 (Ont. H.C.).
The party who first initiates the discovery process, even by informal letter requesting examination dates, should ordinarily have the right to examine first.

Morgan Guaranty Trust Co. of New York v. Outerbridge (1986), 8 C.P.C. (2d) 257 (Ont. Master).
The court ordered the examination for discovery of the defendant to proceed notwithstanding a pending motion attacking the sufficiency of the plaintiff's affidavit of documents.

Crysdale v. Carter-Baron Drilling Services Partnership (1985), 37 C.P.C. (2d) 222 (Ont. H.C.).
Delivery of an affidavit of documents before the close of pleadings cannot support a valid notice of examination.

Von Braun v. Borovilos (1983), 40 C.P.C. 112 (Ont. Master).
The plaintiffs were unsuccessful in resisting examinations for discovery on the basis that the very bringing of the action was alleged to be an offence in concurrent criminal proceedings and they might be said to be continuing a criminal offence.

Tricontinental Invts. Co. v. Guarantee Co. of North America (1982), 39 O.R. (2d) 614, 30 C.P.C. 235, 141 D.L.R. (3d) 741 (H.C.).
A party unsuccessfully sought to postpone his discovery until after the disposition of the criminal proceedings against him.

Bow Helicopters v. Textron Can. Ltd. (1981), 24 C.P.C. 233 (Ont. H.C.).
The plaintiff was permitted to examine a second defendant, although the examination of the first defendant had not been completed.

Scott Transport Ltd. v. Bondy (1973), 1 O.R. (2d) 447 (Master).
Completion of the examination for discovery includes questions arising out of answers to undertakings.

Linklater v. Denny, [1965] 1 O.R. 298 (Master).

The party who serves the notice of appointment first is entitled to examine first provided the appointment is returnable at a reasonable time.

ORAL EXAMINATION BY MORE THAN ONE PARTY

31.05 Unless the court orders or the parties agree otherwise, where more than one party is entitled to examine a party or person for discovery without leave, there shall be only one oral examination, which may be initiated by any party adverse to the party,

　(a) who is to be examined; or

　(b) on behalf or in place of whom, or in addition to whom, a person is to be examined.

Gorin v. Ho (1983), 38 C.P.C. 72 (Ont. Master).

In general, on an examination for discovery by multiple parties, any examining party may move to compel a refused question to be answered irrespective of which counsel asked the question.

Dmitrovic v. Lazaris (1980), 28 O.R. (2d) 269, 110 D.L.R. (3d) 254 (H.C.).

Where two actions involving the same plaintiff but separate motor vehicle accidents are ordered to be tried together, the defendants are entitled to separate examinations for discovery.

SCOPE OF EXAMINATION

General

31.06(1) A person examined for discovery shall answer, to the best of his or her knowledge, information and belief, any proper question relating to any matter in issue in the action or to any matter made discoverable by subrules (2) to (4) and no question may be objected to on the ground that,

　(a) the information sought is evidence;

　(b) the question constitutes cross-examination, unless the question is directed solely to the credibility of the witness; or

　(c) the question constitutes cross-examination on the affidavit of documents of the party being examined.

Identity of Persons Having Knowledge

(2) A party may on an examination for discovery obtain disclosure of the names and addresses of persons who might reasonably be expected to have knowledge of transactions or occurrences in issue in the action, unless the court orders otherwise.

Expert Opinions

(3) A party may on an examination for discovery obtain disclosure of the findings, opinions and conclusions of an expert engaged by or on behalf of the party being examined that relate to a matter in issue in the action and of the expert's name and address, but the party being examined need not disclose the information or the name and address of the expert where,

　(a) the findings, opinions and conclusions of the expert relating to any matter in issue in the action were made or formed in preparation for contemplated or pending litigation and for no other purpose; and

(b) the party being examined undertakes not to call the expert as a witness at the trial.

Insurance Policies

(4) A party may on an examination for discovery obtain disclosure of,

(a) the existence and contents of any insurance policy under which an insurer may be liable to satisfy all or part of a judgment in the action or to indemnify or reimburse a party for money paid in satisfaction of all or part of the judgment ; and

(b) the amount of money available under the policy, and any conditions affecting its availability.

(5) No information concerning the insurance policy is admissible in evidence unless it is relevant to an issue in the action.

Divided Discovery

(6) Where information may become relevant only after the determination of an issue in the action and the disclosure of the information before the issue is determined would seriously prejudice a party, the court on the party's motion may grant leave to withhold the information until after the issue has been determined.

Authors' Note on Organization of Cases

Cases relevant to this provision have been organized as follows:

Scope of Examination — Generally
Scope of Examination — Seeking Information from Non-Parties
Scope of Examination — Solicitor and Client Privilege
Scope of Examination — Privilege re Settlement Negotiations
Scope of Examination — Questions re Adultery
Scope of Examination — Miscellaneous Privileges
Scope of Examination — Examinee's Opinion
Scope of Examination — Pleas in Related Criminal Proceedings
Scope of Examination — Preventing Tailoring of Evidence
Scope of Examination — Surveillance Information
Scope of Examination — Names of Witnesses — rule 31.06(2)
Scope of Examination — Expert Opinions — rule 31.06(3)
Scope of Examination — Insurance Matters — rule 31.06(4)
Scope of Examination — Examples
Scope of Examination — Divided Discovery — rule 31.06(6)

Scope of Examination — Generally

Air Canada v. McDonnell Douglas Corp. (1995), 22 O.R. (3d) 140 (Master), affirmed 22 O.R. (3d) 382, additional reasons 23 O.R. (3d) 156 (Gen. Div.).

Questions on an examination for discovery should be answered unless the court is satisfied that they have no semblance of relevancy. Information may be elicited on discovery even though the precise question and answer might not be admissible at trial. Questions on discovery are proper if they may lead to a line of inquiry which would uncover admissible evidence.

Kay v. Posluns (1989), 71 O.R. (2d) 238 (H.C.), additional reasons (February 1, 1991), Doc. No. Toronto 26686/88 (Gen. Div.).

1. Wide latitude is allowed on examinations for discovery. Questions are permitted so long as they have a "semblance of relevancy".

2. Rule 31.06(1)(b) merely removes cross-examination as a ground for objection. It does not authorize or encourage it. In Ontario, cross-examination in the true sense does not occur on examinations for discovery.

Pindling v. National Broadcasting Co. (1989), 15 W.D.C.P. 165 (Ont. H.C.).

In a defamation action, a defendant who pleads justification is entitled to discovery regarding specifically pleaded allegations only.

Torami v. Horton (1988), 67 O.R. (2d) 346, 31 O.A.C. 296 (Div. Ct.).

Questions may be asked about the habit of a person or routine practice of an organization. In this case questions were permitted regarding the general state of maintenance of a fleet of motor vehicles where one vehicle was involved in an accident.

Algoma Central Railway v. Herb Fraser & Associates Ltd. (1988), 66 O.R. (2d) 330, 31 O.A.C. 287 (Div. Ct.).

Questions may be asked on discovery regarding remedial measures taken subsequent to the accident which is the subject of the law suit, although the answers will not necessarily be admissible at trial. Admissibility and weight are matters for the trial judge. [*See McMahon v. Harvey (Township) (1992), 2 C.P.C. (3d) 154 (Ont. Gen. Div.), where evidence of remedial measures was not admitted at trial —Authors.*]

Charles v. Royal Bank (1987), 60 O.R. (2d) 537, 19 C.P.C. (2d) 310 (Master).

Questions eliciting incriminating answers may be asked on examination for discovery without violating the examinee's common law, statutory or constitutional privilege against self-incrimination, equality rights, or right to life, liberty and security of the person.

Leerentveld v. McCulloch (1985), 4 C.P.C. (2d) 26 (Ont. Master).

Parties are now required to give not only the evidence which they have acquired but its source as well insofar as witnesses are concerned and this includes a summary of a witness' statement. However a party need not disclose what might be called "expert research" by the party or his solicitor. A party is not required to state what inferences he has drawn from information.

Loewen, Ondaatje, McCutcheon & Co. v. Snelling (1985), 2 C.P.C. (2d) 93 (Ont. H.C.).

A party purporting to rely on facts contained in past examinations for discovery and in documents produced in the litigation is obliged to identify the facts and documents with some reasonable degree of specificity. A general statement is not sufficient.

Willroy Mines Ltd. v. New Cinch Uranium Ltd. (1983), 34 C.P.C. 13, affirmed 34 C.P.C. 13n (Ont. H.C.).

An examining party is entitled to question the representative of a corporate party regarding knowledge obtained both in his capacity as a corporate officer and in his personal capacity.

Ont. Bean Producers' Marketing Bd. v. W.G. Thompson & Sons Ltd. (1981), 32 O.R. (2d) 69, 19 C.P.C. 221, 120 D.L.R. (3d) 531, affirmed 35 O.R. (2d) 711, 27 C.P.C. 1, 134 D.L.R. (3d) 108 (Div. Ct.).

Questions as to a party's position in law are not proper.

Tridici v. M.E.P.C. Can. Properties Ltd. (1978), 22 O.R. (2d) 319, 8 C.P.C. 212 (H.C.).

An expert was permitted to assist counsel to conduct an examination where technical matters were in issue.

Mouammar v. Bruner (1978), 19 O.R. (2d) 59 (H.C.).

A party may be required to listen to a tape recording and answer questions relating thereto.

Trip v. Iezzi & Iezzi Ltd. (1978), 23 O.R. (2d) 587, 8 C.P.C. 312 (H.C.).

A party was not required to provide specimens of his signature for the purpose of comparison by a handwriting expert.

Rule-Bilt Ltd. v. Shenkman Corp. Ltd. (1977), 18 O.R. (2d) 276, 4 C.P.C. 256 (Master).

A witness may properly be asked which of many documents produced are relied on in support of a particular allegation.

Leliever v. Lindson (1977), 3 C.P.C. 245 (Ont. H.C.).

A party must indicate those parts of voluminous and complex productions upon which he intends to rely.

April Invts. Ltd. v. Menat Const. Ltd. (1975), 11 O.R. (2d) 364 (H.C.).

Facts found as a result of an order for inspection of property are discoverable.

Ohl v. Cannito, [1972] 2 O.R. 763, 26 D.L.R. (3d) 556 (H.C.).

A party may be required to answer questions disclosing facts contained in privileged documents.

Rubinoff v. Newton, [1967] 1 O.R. 402 (H.C.).

"On what facts do you rely in support of that allegation?" is a proper question.

Phillips v. Horne, [1960] O.W.N. 565, affirmed [1961] O.W.N. 53n (H.C.).

Questions requiring narrative answers are proper.

Brennan v. J. Posluns & Co., [1959] O.R. 22, 30 C.P.R. 106, 18 Fox Pat. C. 116 (H.C.).

Questions regarding facts which may support relevant arguments of law must be answered.

Madge v. Odeon Theatres (Ontario) Ltd., [1953] O.W.N. 103 (Master).

A plaintiff may be examined regarding defences raised against a co-plaintiff if he has a real interest in such defences.

Scope of Examination — Seeking Information from Non-Parties

Air Canada v. McDonnell Douglas Corp. (1995), 22 O.R. (3d) 140 (Master), affirmed 22 O.R. (3d) 382, additional reasons 23 O.R. (3d) 156 (Gen. Div.).

The person being examined for discovery on behalf of a corporation must make reasonable inquiries of fellow servants of the corporation, including individuals who are no longer employees, unless the circumstances make it unreasonable.

Pollard v. Esses (1994), 35 C.P.C. (3d) 398 (Ont. Gen. Div.).

Where a defendant requested and obtained an undertaking from the plaintiff to obtain clinical notes and records from non-parties, the court ordered the defendant to pay the associated costs.

Tax Time Services Ltd. v. National Trust Co. (1991), 3 O.R. (3d) 44 (Gen. Div.).

If the party being examined has no control over or greater access to a witness than the examining party, it need only disclose the evidence known to it.

Trovato v. Smith (1987), 15 C.P.C. (2d) 121 (Ont. Dist. Ct.).

The court ordered the plaintiff to seek his physician's clinical records and notes although they were not within the plaintiff's "power" within the meaning of rule 30.03(1). There is no merit, logic or support in the Rules for requiring the defendant to establish a conflict in the medical reports or discovery evidence before making such an order. If a doctor does not voluntarily produce the documents, the defence will be met with its more limited rights under rule 30.10.

Fedorczenko v. Jamieson (1986), 56 O.R. (2d) 252, 14 C.P.C. (2d) 299 (H.C.).

A party should make reasonable efforts to obtain documents from a non-party rather than requiring the opposing party to move under rule 30.10.

Edwards v. Valtchev (1984), 45 C.P.C. 310 (Ont. Co. Ct.).

A representative of the defendant hospital was ordered to re-attend to undertake to make certain inquiries of an intern and a resident.

Scheuermann v. Zablanczy (1984), 44 C.P.C. 97 (Ont. H.C.).

The representative of the corporate defendant was ordered to inform himself from the non-party parent corporation.

Poteck v. Pickard (1982), 31 C.P.C. 213 (Ont. Master).

The plaintiff was ordered to use her best efforts to obtain documents from a bank, to provide an authorization for the release of income tax returns, and to inquire of a daughter as to when certain discussions took place.

Wells v. Wells (1982), 29 C.P.C. 186 (Ont. Master).

The obligation to make inquiries with third parties does not require the witness to institute a lawsuit to enforce his rights to the information.

Ambler v. Ambler (1980), 15 C.P.C. 117 (Ont. Master).

In *Family Law Reform Act* matters, a spouse who is a partner or a substantial shareholder may be required to inquire whether the partner or company will consent to the supply of information concerning the worth of the spouse's investment.

Gravlev v. Venturetek Int. Ltd. (1979), 15 C.P.C. 18 (Ont. H.C.).

A party must inform himself and obtain documents from third parties unless it would be unreasonable to require him so to do.

Napoli v. Parise (1978), 21 O.R. (2d) 584, 91 D.L.R. (3d) 294 (H.C.).

A party is under no obligation to inform herself as to the knowledge of her spouse.

Vanderhoek v. Philco-Ford of Can. Ltd. (1978), 8 C.P.C. 31 (Ont. Master).

An officer was required to seek information from former employees of the defendant, who were now employees of wholly-owned subsidiaries, concerning their discussions with the plaintiff.

Concept 80 Ltd. v. W-A Const. Co. (1975), 1 C.P.C. 96 (Ont. S.C.).

An examined party cannot be compelled to inform himself from an independent contractor.

Scope of Examination — Solicitor and Client Privilege (See also cases under rule 30.02.)

London Trust & Savings Corp. v. Corbett (1994), 24 C.P.C. (3d) 226 (Ont. Gen. Div.).

Discussions between a solicitor and client were held not to be privileged because they took place in the presence of a third person not involved in the solicitor and client relationship.

Chertsey Developments Inc. v. Red Carpet Inns Ltd. (1990), 74 O.R. (2d) 665, 45 C.P.C. (2d) 84 (Master).

Solicitor and client privilege was not waived where the party resisting disclosure had not put in issue the legal advice which had been obtained. The "heart of the matter" exception did not apply.

Madge v. Thunder Bay (City) (1990), 72 O.R. (2d) 41, 44 C.P.C. (2d) 186 (H.C.).

Where the court had previously ruled that the defendant's communications with her solicitor were privileged, the defendant was not compelled to reveal the dates on which those communications had taken place.

Kupferstein v. Gottlieb, Hoffman & Kumer (1989), 40 C.P.C. (2d) 111 (Ont. Master).

The court refused to order a defendant law firm to disclose to the plaintiff the names or other information concerning clients in connection with the plaintiff's purchase of a law practice.

Hartz Can. Inc. v. Colgate-Palmolive Co. (1988), 27 C.P.C. (2d) 152 (Ont. H.C.).

It is inadvisable to limit solicitor-client privilege in Ontario to Ontario solicitors; in this case, communications between an American counsel and an Ontario client were privileged in the Ontario action.

Re Chilcott and Clarkson Co. (1984), 48 O.R. (2d) 545, (*sub nom. Re Dilawri; Clarkson Co. v. Chilcott*) 53 C.B.R. (N.S.) 251, 13 C.R.R. 41, 13 D.L.R. (4th) 481, 6 O.A.C. 291 (C.A.).

A trustee in bankruptcy may not waive solicitor-client privilege with respect to legal advice given to the bankrupt respecting his former property.

Re Ont. Securities Comm. and Greymac Credit Corp. (1983), 41 O.R. (2d) 328, 21 B.L.R. 37, 33 C.P.C. 270, 146 D.L.R. (3d) 73 (Div. Ct.).

1. The president of a company who is also a solicitor cannot assert solicitor-client privilege in respect of information acquired by him in the performance of his duties that can be, and usually are, performed by an employee or agent of the company who is not a solicitor.

2. The powers of a receiver can be validly exercised only for the purposes for which he was appointed. Where a receiver was appointed to take control and possession of the assets of certain trust companies and conduct their business, he does not have the right to waive solicitor-client privilege so that the companies' solicitors may be free to disclose confidential information to an investigative commission.

3. Where a receiver is appointed to preserve the undertaking and assets of a corporation, he can waive the solicitor-client privilege to obtain information concerning the assets and affairs of the company from a solicitor or former solicitor of the company.

Levenson v. Levenson (1982), 28 C.P.C. 263 (Ont. H.C.).

A witness was ordered to answer questions concerning his dealings with the respondent solicitor where the communications were not for the purpose of giving or receiving professional advice and there was *prima facie* evidence of fraud.

Tatone v. Tatone (1980), 16 C.P.C. 285 (Ont. Master).

Where a solicitor acted for two companies through the same man in a mortgage transaction, such that he received instructions from both companies in the presence of the other, neither could claim privilege against the other.

Nowak v. Sanyshyn (1979), 23 O.R. (2d) 797, 9 C.P.C. 303 (H.C.).

Where the communication between a solicitor and client is a fact which will be proved at trial, the communication is not privileged. A party alleging insufficient legal advice was required to divulge the advice received.

Newman v. Nemes (1979), 8 C.P.C. 229 (Ont. H.C.).

A party waives any privilege over the question of whether she gave certain instructions to her solicitor by denying that she gave the instructions and thereby putting the question in issue.

Meaney v. Busby (1977), 15 O.R. (2d) 71, 2 C.P.C. 340 (H.C.).

Communications received for the purpose of contemplated litigation cease to be privileged when the litigation is concluded.

Re Ott, [1972] 2 O.R. 5, 7 R.F.L. 196, 24 D.L.R. (3d) 517 (Surr. Ct.).

The court admitted evidence of the substance of solicitor and client communications where the client was dead and the interests of justice required it.

Re Alcan-Colony Contr. Ltd. and M.N.R., [1971] 2 O.R. 365, 18 D.L.R. (3d) 32, 71 D.T.C. 5082 (H.C.).

The legal professional privilege extends to communications between a solicitor and an agent of the client and to information gathered by the solicitor on the instructions of the client for the purpose of giving advice.

Martini v. Preston Sand & Gravel Co., [1961] O.W.N. 256 (Master).

The court refused to require a party to disclose the advice given by his solicitor regarding the purchase of lands in question.

Smith v. Smith, [1958] O.W.N. 135 (Master).

A client who voluntarily testifies, disclosing the substance of confidential communications made by him to his solicitor, thereby waives the privilege and both the solicitor and client may be fully examined in relation thereto.

Scope of Examination — Privilege re Settlement Negotiations (See also cases under rule 30.02.)

Mueller Can. Inc. v. State Contractors Inc. (1989), 71 O.R. (2d) 397, 41 C.P.C. (2d) 291 (H.C.).

The court granted the plaintiff's motion to compel the defendants to disclose information about a settlement among the defendants pertaining to the same claims and events underlying the plaintiff's action.

William Allan Real Estate Co. v. Robichaud (1987), 28 C.P.C. (2d) 47 (Ont. H.C.).

A mere claim that a discussion took place in privileged circumstances is not sufficient to render that claim valid.

William Allan Real Estate Co. v. Robichaud (1987), 17 C.P.C. (2d) 138, 37 B.L.R. 286 (Ont. H.C.), leave to appeal to Ont. Div. Ct. granted 28 C.P.C. (2d) 47.

Communications to buy peace or effect a compromise are privileged, and there need not be any express or implied agreement or clear unilateral statement that they are without prejudice.

Papineau v. Papineau (1986), 8 C.P.C. (2d) 249 (Ont. H.C.).

A party to a separation agreement who had put in issue her capacity to enter into a valid agreement was required to answer questions about "without prejudice" correspondence leading to the separation agreement.

Hillesheim v. Hillesheim (1974), 6 O.R. (2d) 647, 19 R.F.L. 42 (Master).

Discussions between spouses regarding a property settlement and provisions for support and education of children were held to be privileged notwithstanding that the words "without prejudice" were not used.

Kirschbaum v. "Our Voices" Publishing Co., [1972] 1 O.R. 737 (H.C.).

A party in a defamation action was required to answer questions relating to "without prejudice" letters where the letters may not have related only to settlement and may have been admissible at trial.

Scope of Examination — Questions re Adultery

Burt v. Burt (1979), 27 O.R. (2d) 163, 13 C.P.C. 341, 11 R.F.L. (2d) 143, 105 D.L.R. (3d) 702 (H.C.).

In a divorce action, the privilege afforded by s. 10 of the *Evidence Act*, R.S.O. 1970, c. 151, is not avoided by relying upon adultery as an act of cruelty.

Rosenberg v. Rosenberg (1974), 3 O.R. (2d) 174 (Master).

Information which tends to prove adultery and is privileged by s. 10 of the *Evidence Act*, R.S.O. 1970, c. 151, remains so notwithstanding that it may tend to prove something else at the same time.

Hunter v. Hunter, [1973] 1 O.R. 162, 11 R.F.L. 94 (H.C.).

Where a counterpetition for divorce raises the issue of adultery, the privilege relating to questions tending to show adultery applies equally in proceedings regarding the related petition for divorce.

Rayner v. Rayner, [1972] 2 O.R. 588, 7 R.F.L. 103, 26 D.L.R. (3d) 169 (C.A.).

An allegation in a pleading that a spouse had raised a reasonable apprehension that he was committing adultery is not sufficient to classify the action as "instituted in consequence of adultery".

McCarthy v. Morrison-Lamothe Bakery Ltd., [1956] O.W.N. 690, 5 D.L.R. (2d) 645 (H.C.).

The plaintiff in a fatal accident case was required to answer a question regarding adultery where it was relevant to the issue of damages.

Bradburn v. Bradburn, [1953] O.R. 882 (C.A.).

In a divorce action a party need not answer questions tending to show guilt of adultery notwithstanding that such questions may be relevant to the issue of custody.

Scope of Examination — Miscellaneous Privileges

Air Canada v. McDonnell Douglas Corp. (1995), 22 O.R. (3d) 140 (Master), affirmed 22 O.R.
   (3d) 382, additional reasons 23 O.R. (3d) 156 (Gen. Div.).

In an action arising out of an air crash, questions which related to an accident report prepared by the Department of Transport were proper. The report, while prepared in the general belief that the underlying communications were confidential, was not subject to the doctrine of qualified privilege.

Rocking Chair Plaza (Bramalea) Ltd. v. Brampton (City) (1988), 29 C.P.C. (2d) 82 (Ont. H.C.).

The court refused to permit discovery of *in camera* discussions of a municipal council as long as its decisions and recommendations were preceded by open discussion.

de Araujo v. de Araujo (1986), 11 C.P.C. (2d) 272 (Ont. Master).

Statements made by a husband during marriage counselling were communications to assist reconciliation and inadmissible in a divorce action, by s. 21(2) of the *Divorce Act*. A draft marriage contract unilaterally presented to the wife in the absence of settlement negotiations did not reflect a mutual desire to settle and was not privileged.

Royal Bank v. Wilford (1985), 2 C.P.C. (2d) 281 (Ont. Master).

A party was ordered to answer questions he refused to answer on the ground the answers might tend to incriminate him. Under s. 13 of the *Charter of Rights* protection is automatic and the witness need no longer claim protection as was necessary under the *Evidence Acts*. There is no protection against the use of the evidence by the police in the course of their investigation except that the evidence cannot be used against the defendant in any criminal proceeding other than for perjury or for the giving of contradictory evidence.

Crown Trust Co. v. Rosenberg (1983), 38 C.P.C. 109 (Ont. H.C.).

There is no privilege regarding confidential information received by a journalist or regarding the identity of the source of such information, however the court should respect the journalist's desire to protect such information and sources as much as possible. In this case the court ordered disclosure of the information but not the sources.

Torok v. Torok (1983), 44 O.R. (2d) 118, 38 C.P.C. 52 (Master).

No privilege attaches to communications between a physician and patient unless the physician is acting as a marriage counsellor or is a practising psychiatrist.

Scope of Examination — Examinee's Opinion

Air Canada v. McDonnell Douglas Corp. (1995), 22 O.R. (3d) 140 (Master), affirmed 22 O.R.
   (3d) 382, additional reasons 23 O.R. (3d) 156 (Gen. Div.).

It is proper to ask questions on an examination for discovery which might call for a conclusion on subjects within the witness's everyday expertise, or to which expertise he has ready access.

Motaharian v. Reid (1989), 39 C.P.C. (2d) 141 (Ont. H.C.).

Hypothetical questions are proper where relevant to some issue in the case, where the witness has the expertise to provide an opinion, and where the questions are not overly broad or vague. The witness, however, need not defend other persons' actions or answer for their failures.

Armak Chemicals Ltd. v. C.N.R. (1982), 37 O.R. (2d) 713, 29 C.P.C. 7 (H.C.).

A witness may be asked mixed questions of fact and opinion within his common experience.

Wade v. Sisters of Saint Joseph of the Diocese of London (1976), 2 C.P.C. 37 (Ont. H.C.).

On an examination for discovery, a party is not entitled to obtain an expert opinion from the opposite party with respect to the professional conduct of another party to the action.

Hilder v. East Gen. Hosp., [1971] 3 O.R. 777 (Master).

Defendants in a medical malpractice action were required to answer questions which elicited opinions regarding matters directly in issue in the litigation.

Weisberg v. Kerbel, [1961] O.W.N. 209 (H.C.).

A question requiring an answer based on the opinions of the examinee is improper.

Scope of Examination — Pleas in Related Criminal Proceedings

Francis v. LaFramboise (1980), 20 C.P.C. 123, affirmed 20 C.P.C. 123 at 126 (Ont. H.C.).

Questions as to whether the defendant was charged and pleaded guilty to an offence under the *Highway Traffic Act* arising out of the accident were refused where they did not relate to any allegation in the pleadings and were very general in their wording.

Rotondi v. Tadic (1979), 24 O.R. (2d) 317, 11 C.P.C. 17 (Master).

A party in a motor vehicle case was required to state whether he had pleaded guilty to traffic charges arising out of the accident.

Scope of Examination — Preventing Tailoring of Evidence

Blomme v. Eastview Racquet & Fitness Club (1995), 26 O.R. (3d) 496 (Gen. Div.).

The court ordered co-defendants not to attend each other's discovery where credibility would be the main issue at trial and the second defendant could tailor his evidence if he were aware of the first defendant's evidence.

Cardona v. Ospreay (1995), 22 O.R. (3d) 662 (Master).

The court ordered that two defendants in an assault case be excluded from each other's examinations for discovery to prevent the tailoring of evidence.

Costa v. Melo (1992), 13 C.P.C. (3d) 159 (Ont. Gen. Div.).

The court ordered that both parties be examined for discovery on the same day and that information garnered on the first examination not be disclosed to a witness being examined second.

Ceci (Litigation Guardian) v. Bonk (1992), 7 O.R. (3d) 381, 6 C.P.C. (3d) 304, 89 D.L.R. (4th) 444, 56 O.A.C. 346 (C.A.).

An order postponing the obligation to disclose particulars of surveillance reports should only be made if the evidence shows a real likelihood that the plaintiff would tailor evidence if disclosure were made. The defendant may, however, conduct the examination for discovery of the plaintiff first by serving the first appointment.

Cowan v. Wilk (1988), 17 W.D.C.P. 196 (Ont. Dist. Ct.).

The plaintiff was ordered to complete her examination for discovery before the defendant's disclosure of surveillance information. The plaintiff need not be forewarned about the possibility of being caught up in any prevarications.

Paulin v. Prince (1987), 21 C.P.C. (2d) 152 (Ont. Dist. Ct.), affirmed 23 C.P.C. (2d) 319 (Ont. H.C.), affirmed (1988), 31 C.P.C. (2d) 281 (Ont. Div. Ct.).

The court ordered the defendants to provide surveillance information prior to the plaintiffs' examination for discovery, ruling that possible prejudice resulting from the disclosure, unlike real prejudice based on a demonstrated foundation, was insufficient to permit its withholding.

Gumieniak v. Tobin (1987), 16 C.P.C. (2d) 126 (Ont. Dist. Ct.).

The court refused to order surveillance information to be withheld from the plaintiff until after her examination for discovery, where the court was not satisfied that there was a real likelihood of tailoring evidence.

Bradbury v. Traise (1986), 12 C.P.C. (2d) 261 (Ont. Dist. Ct.).

The party being examined first is obliged to provide all relevant information on examination for discovery, unless there is a real likelihood that the opposing party will tailor his evidence accordingly.

Weisz v. Gist (1986), 12 C.P.C. (2d) 190, additional reasons at 12 C.P.C. (2d) xlvi (Ont. Dist. Ct.).

The defendant was ordered to disclose information obtained from surveillance only after the discovery of the plaintiff was completed, in order to prevent the plaintiff from tailoring his discovery evidence.

Calogero v. Tersigni (1985), 49 O.R. (2d) 508, 48 C.P.C. 1 (H.C.).

The court permitted a defendant to withhold information resulting from surveillance of the plaintiff until after the plaintiff's examination for discovery. There was no valid reason why the plaintiff needed the information prior to his examination. The philosophy of complete disclosure for the purpose of trial would be served by disclosure after the plaintiff's discovery.

Parro v. Mullock (1982), 35 O.R. (2d) 168, 25 C.P.C. 273, 132 D.L.R. (3d) 65 (H.C.).

There must be a real likelihood of a tailoring of evidence before the court will order that a party not be advised before being examined for discovery of evidence given by another party on a previous examination for discovery.

Scope of Examination — Surveillance Information

Murray v. Woodstock General Hospital Trust (1988), 66 O.R. (2d) 129, 30 C.P.C. (2d) 268, 31 O.A.C. 153 (Div. Ct.).

The defendant in a personal injury action was obliged to provide details of surveillance, including (1) dates, times and precise locations, (2) particulars of the activities and observations made, and (3) the names and addresses of the persons who conducted the surveillance. The documentation itself remained privileged.

Maggio v. Lopes (1988), 29 C.P.C. (2d) 284 (Ont. Master).

The court refused to order a defendant to provide full particulars of surveillance already conducted and to be conducted of the plaintiff. Some of the information was privileged.

Patterson v. Wilkinson (1988), 28 C.P.C. (2d) 250 (Ont. H.C.).

The defendant was required to disclose to the plaintiff that surveillance-related documents existed, and the dates thereof and the names and addresses of possible witnesses in relation to them. The court refused to order disclosure of any further details.

Weiss v. Machado (1988), 65 O.R. (2d) 201, 28 C.P.C. (2d) 1 (H.C.).

The defendant in a personal injury action was required to disclose whether surveillance had been undertaken and, if undertaken, to disclose the time, place and method of surveillance, plus provide a brief synopsis of the relevant observations.

Sacrey v. Berdan (1986), 10 C.P.C. (2d) 15 (Ont. Dist. Ct.).

The defendant was required to provide information with respect to surveillance including the times and precise locations of observations of the plaintiff and everything the investigator observed on each occasion. Photographs or moving pictures taken during the course of surveillance should be set out in the affidavit of documents.

Nolan v. Grant (1986), 54 O.R. (2d) 702, 8 C.P.C. (2d) 253 (H.C.).

A party who has taken surveillance film is obliged to disclose when, where and by whom the film was taken, the activities filmed and any other material information relating to the filming but need not provide a running account of everything on the film.

Niederle v. Frederick Transport Ltd. (1985), 50 C.P.C. 135 (Ont. H.C.).

The court ordered a defendant at the outset of trial to disclose information regarding surveillance films taken of the plaintiff.

Scope of Examination — Names of Witnesses — rule 31.06(2)

Hogan v. Great Central Publishing Ltd. (1994), 16 O.R. (3d) 808, 111 D.L.R. (4th) 526 (Gen. Div.).

In a libel action brought against a magazine, the defendant was ordered to disclose the names and addresses of the writers, editors, and publisher of the article in question. The information was relevant, the magazine had actively strived to maintain anonymity, and the plaintiff had been unsuccessful in attempting to obtain this information.

Lukas v. Lawson (1993), 13 O.R. (3d) 447, 19 C.P.C. (3d) 238 (Master).

In general a solicitor cannot withhold the name of a client on whose behalf he receives, pays, or holds money if the identity of that client becomes relevant in a legal proceeding. A solicitor was obliged to divulge the name and address of a client who might reasonably be expected to have known of the mortgage transaction in question.

Tax Time Services Ltd. v. National Trust Co. (1991), 3 O.R. (3d) 44 (Gen. Div.).

Where oral summaries of the substance of the evidence of potential witnesses have been obtained through extensive cross-examination, the examining party is not also entitled to written summaries.

Dionisopoulos v. Provias (1990), 71 O.R. (2d) 547, 45 C.P.C. (2d) 116 (H.C.).

A party being examined for discovery need not provide a list of persons to be called as witnesses at trial but must provide the names and addresses of persons who might have knowledge of the matters in issue and, if requested, a summary of their evidence.

Wyse v. Ontario Hydro (1987), 21 C.P.C. (2d) 275 (Ont. Master).

On examination for discovery, the names and addresses of witnesses are to be disclosed if asked, but a summary of each witness' knowledge need not be disclosed.

Blackmore v. Slot All Ltd. (1985), 18 C.P.C. (2d) 181 (Ont. H.C.), leave to appeal refused 21 C.P.C. (2d) xlvii.

The name and address of a witness must be disclosed, as well as a summary of the evidence that the witness is expected to give.

Dudulski v. Kingston Gen. Hospital (1987), 59 O.R. (2d) 520, 16 C.P.C. (2d) 122 (Master).

The court declined to order the plaintiff to disclose the name of a nurse employed by the defendant who alerted the plaintiff to the possibility that there had been negligent treatment. The plaintiff had provided the defendant with all information on which the claim was based and the nurse would not be called by the plaintiff as a witness at trial.

Temoin v. Stanley (1986), 12 C.P.C. (2d) 69 (Ont. Dist. Ct.), reversed in part on other grounds (1987), 7 W.D.C.P. 71 (Ont. H.C.).

A party is obliged to divulge the names and addresses of those individuals who might reasonably be expected to have knowledge of the transactions or occurrences in issue regardless of whether the party plans to call those individuals as witnesses at trial.

Breivik, Scorgie, Wasylko v. Great Atlantic & Pacific Co. of Can. (1987), 58 O.R. (2d) 794, 17 C.P.C. (2d) 81 (H.C.).

The court ordered a party to provide the names and addresses of all witnesses to be called at trial and a short statement of the substance of their evidence.

Papaefthimiou v. Oberman (1986), 9 C.P.C. (2d) 138 (Ont. Dist. Ct.).

The duty to advise of names and addresses of witnesses extends to issues of damages, and not of liability only.

Nolan v. Grant (1986), 54 O.R. (2d) 702, 8 C.P.C. (2d) 253 (H.C.).

The court refused to require the defendant to provide the names and addresses of everyone interviewed during an investigation by the defendant where the defendant did not intend to rely upon the interviews at trial.

Williams v. David Brown Gear Industries Inc. (1986), 14 C.P.C. (2d) 227 (Ont. H.C.).

A party need not identify witnesses to be called at trial and state the substance of the testimony to be elicited from each.

Scope of Examination — Expert Opinions — rule 31.06(3)

Ontario (Attorney General) v. Ballard Estate (March 19, 1996), Doc. 94-CQ-54358, B217/94 (Ont. Gen. Div. [Commercial List]).

In general "finding" means the information and data obtained by the expert, contained in documents or obtained through interviews, on the basis of which conclusions are drawn and an opinion formed.

DeRidder v. DeVries (1995), 6 W.D.C.P. (2d) 377 (Ont. Gen. Div.).

The court refused to order the defendant to disclose facts obtained and observations made by the defendant's expert where the defendant undertook not to call the expert as a witness.

Award Developments (Ontario) Ltd. v. Novoco Enterprises Ltd. (1992), 10 O.R. (3d) 186 (Gen. Div.).

The words "findings, opinions and conclusions" in rule 31.06(3) are broad enough to include the field notes, raw data and records made and used by the expert in preparing its report.

Allen v. Oulahen (1992), 10 O.R. (3d) 613 (Master).

The word "findings" in rule 31.06(3) includes all the factual information that an expert relies upon in arriving at its opinions and conclusions, including research, documents, calculations and factual data.

Sandhu (Litigation Guardian of) v. Ontario (1990), 49 C.P.C. (2d) 298 (Ont. Gen. Div.).

The court ordered a defendant in this products liability case to answer questions relating to expert opinion which were not hypothetical and included mixed fact and opinion.

Kaptsis v. Macias (1990), 74 O.R. (2d) 189, 44 C.P.C. (2d) 285 (H.C.).

A party was not obliged to produce experts' clinical notes and records where the experts' reports contained their findings.

Cheaney v. Peel Memorial Hospital (1990), 73 O.R. (2d) 794, 44 C.P.C. (2d) 158 (Master).

Rule 31.06(3) is not restricted to final findings, opinions and conclusions of experts nor to written reports; it requires disclosure of any finding, opinion or conclusion of an expert that is expressed in a sufficiently coherent manner that it can be used by counsel.

Cacic v. O'Connor (1990), 71 O.R. (2d) 751, 42 C.P.C. (2d) 266 (H.C.).

The court ordered production of raw data and test scores used in formulating opinions set out in the report of a neuropsychologist; the raw test data were part of the "findings" of that expert.

Kelly v. Kelly (1990), 42 C.P.C. (2d) 181 (Ont. U.F.C.).

Preliminary drafts of a report prepared by an expert witness for the purpose of litigation are not "findings, opinions and conclusions of the expert" within the meaning of rule 31.06(3) and are privileged.

Beck v. La Haie (1989), 38 C.P.C. (2d) 67 (Ont. Master).

The court reviewed the law relating to the scope of rule 31.06(3) and concluded that raw test data resulting from psychological testing in a personal injury action were discoverable as part of the "findings" of an expert.

Athabaska Airways Ltd. v. De Havilland Aircraft of Can. Ltd. (1988), 34 C.P.C. (2d) 298 (Ont. H.C.).

The plaintiff was entitled to further examination for discovery on certain technical calculations which had been appended to the defendant's expert report. An employee of the defendant had made the calculations, and they could not be insulated from examination by inclusion in the expert's report.

Metropolitan Toronto Condominium Corp. No. 555 v. Cadillac Fairview Corp. (1988), 29 C.P.C. (2d) 110 (Ont. Master).

The notes and records on which an expert's report is based are privileged, and the privilege is not waived by production of the expert's report.

Grant v. St. Clair Region Conservation Authority (1985), 52 O.R. (2d) 729, 5 C.P.C. (2d) 281, 23 D.L.R. (4th) 137, 34 L.C.R. 70, 11 O.A.C. 232 (Div. Ct.).

The court ordered production of an appraisal report obtained by an expropriating authority to meet a statutory obligation. The report was not obtained solely for litigation and therefore was not privileged under rule 31.06(3).

Leerentveld v. McCulloch (1985), 4 C.P.C. (2d) 26 (Ont. Master).

Only the findings, opinions and conclusions of an expert, and not his report, need be disclosed at the discovery stage. There is no conflict between this provision and rule 53.03.

Flavelle v. T.T.C. (1985), 49 C.P.C. 209 (Ont. Dist. Ct.).

Where the plaintiff's psychiatrist was not going to be called at trial to give evidence, production of his report was refused since the plaintiff had brought himself within rule 31.06(3). Ordering production under rule 33.04(2)(b) would be to emasculate rule 31.06(3).

Singh v. Hooper (1983), 34 C.P.C. 218 (Ont. Master).

If a physician is consulted for advice or treatment of the plaintiff's injuries, his name, date of consultation, findings, diagnosis and prognosis must be disclosed. If he is consulted *solely* for opinions and evidence for use in the action, then his name, date of consultation, date of repors and identity of persons to whom the report was sent need be disclosed. [*But see now rule 31.06(3) — Authors.*]

Malofy v. Andrew Merrilees Ltd. (1982), 37 O.R. (2d) 711, 28 C.P.C. 284 (Div. Ct.).

The plaintiff was ordered to provide the findings, diagnosis and prognosis with respect to each medical examination relating to his injuries.

Chiarello v. Provenzano (1982), 36 O.R. (2d) 321, 28 C.P.C. 232 (Master).

The plaintiff was ordered to disclose the names of the doctors who treated him, their specialties, the complaints made, the diagnosis and prognosis, and the results of the examinations, although not with respect to doctors who the plaintiff saw purely for the purposes of preparing the action and not for obtaining treatment. [*But see now rule 31.06(3) — Authors.*]

Scope of Examination — Insurance Matters — rule 31.06(4)

Seaway Trust Co. v. Markle, 11 C.P.C. (3d) 62, [1992] I.L.R. 1-2885 (Ont. Gen. Div.).

The examining party is entitled to full disclosure of the terms of any agreement, understanding, notice or position taken, written or oral, which may affect the availability of insurance proceeds. The witness was obliged to answer, *inter alia*, whether the insurer had denied liability and, if so, on what basis.

D'Amore Construction (Windsor) Ltd. v. Ontario (No. 1), 57 O.R. (2d) 62, 12 C.P.C. (2d) 174, 21 C.L.R. 109, [1986] I.L.R. 1-2111 (H.C.).

A party is required to disclose the existence and actual terms of an insurance policy, but is not required to advise as to the amount of funds available under the policy at any given time.

K Mart Can. Ltd./K Mart Can. Ltée v. Millmink Devs Ltd., 56 O.R. (2d) 422, 24 C.C.L.I. 139, 11 C.P.C. (2d) 243, 31 D.L.R. (4th) 135, [1986] I.L.R. 1-2114 (H.C.).

Rules 30.02(3) and 31.06(4) are not contrary to the provisions of the *Canadian Charter of Rights and Freedoms.*

Guarantee Co. of North America v. Morris, Burk, Lubursky, David & Kale (1985), 50 C.P.C. 122 (Ont. Master), affirmed 50 C.P.C. 122 at 125 (Ont. H.C.).

The court refused to order a defendant to disclose whether the action was being defended pursuant to a non-waiver agreement or to disclose other information regarding dealings between the defendant and its putative insurer.

Scope of Examination — Examples

Air Canada v. McDonnell Douglas Corp. (1995), 23 O.R. (3d) 156 (Gen. Div.).

Where the plaintiff was ordered to produce two representatives for examination for discovery as experts in their respective fields, the court held that examining counsel could not ask questions of the one which he forgot to ask of the other.

Heyduk v. Love (1993), 18 C.P.C. (3d) 387 (Ont. Master).

The court ordered a witness attending for discovery to answer the question "Before coming in here today, did you review any statements that you may have made to assist you in refreshing your memory?". The question had sufficient relevance to permit it to be answered.

Scrafton v. Johnson Controls Ltd. (1992), 15 C.P.C. (3d) 63 (Ont. Master).

Where a privileged document had been produced in error, the court refused to order discovery questions about the document to be answered.

Soulos v. Korkontzilas (1990), 1 O.R. (3d) 625 (Gen. Div.), leave to appeal refused 1 O.R. (3d) 625n (Gen. Div.).

Since disgorgement of property acquired in breach of fiduciary duty is a discretionary remedy, the plaintiff was obliged to answer questions relating to damages even though the alternative claim for damages had been abandoned by the plaintiff.

Four Embarcadero Center Venture v. Kalen (1988), 65 O.R. (2d) 551, 27 C.P.C. (2d) 260 (H.C.).

The merits of a foreign judgment are irrelevant to an action for its enforcement in Ontario. Only issues relating to the foreign procedure are discoverable.

Curzon v. Waterloo County Bd. of Education (1987), 10 W.D.C.P. 144 (Ont. H.C.).

The defendant in this slip and fall case was not required to answer questions as to whether the sidewalk was repaired, replaced or cleaned after the accident where such information would require review of thousands of documents.

Lapierre v. Scarborough Centenary Hospital Assn. (1986), 8 C.P.C. (2d) 262 (Ont. H.C.).

The court refused to require the witness to answer a hypothetical and vague question but permitted the examining party to submit a written clarified question on the same subject.

Devaux v. Extendicare Ltd. (1985), 50 C.P.C. 69 (Ont. Master).

The defendant was required to answer questions about its assets and income where the plaintiff asserted a claim for punitive or exemplary damages. The means of the defendant is relevant in assessing the quantum of damages.

Guttman v. Wilson (1985), 49 O.R. (2d) 279, 47 C.P.C. 121 (Ont. H.C.).

The court required a husband claiming damages under s. 60 of the *Family Law Reform Act* to answer questions regarding his wife's pre-accident physical and emotional condition.

Daunheimer v. Queensway Auto Body Ltd. (1984), 43 C.P.C. 52 (Ont. H.C.).

A party was ordered to re-attend and listen to and identify voices on a tape recording.

Mahaney v. State Farm Fire & Casualty Co. (1983), 44 O.R. (2d) 163, 38 C.P.C. 119 (H.C.).

The court ordered the plaintiff to disclose information regarding a polygraph test taken by the plaintiff.

Gorin v. Ho (1983), 38 C.P.C. 72 (Ont. Master).

In a medical malpractice case the plaintiff must inform himself and answer questions regarding the standard of care which the defendant ought to have met.

Meilleur v. U.N.I.-Crete Canada Ltd. (1982), 30 C.P.C. 80 (Ont. H.C.).

In an action for personal injuries caused by the defendant's product, questions concerning the chemical composition of the product were proper, regardless of whether the information was obtained through an expert report. The witness had to inform himself concerning what information may have been given to the plaintiff's employer concerning safety. Questions concerning precautions taken after the accident and other prior accidents were allowed as going to the defendant's knowledge of the dangerous nature. Questions concerning subsequent accidents were refused.

Ameis v. Lebovic (1982), 30 C.P.C. 50 (Ont. Master).

Where the defendant purchaser pleaded his willingness to close in an action for breach of a real estate transaction, questions dealing with his attempts to sell his own house were permitted, although they went to his motive.

Trans Border Plastics Ltd. v. Leavens Air Charter Ltd. (1982), 36 O.R. (2d) 731, 29 C.P.C. 213, affirmed 38 O.R. (2d) 307 (H.C.).

In this products liability action, an airplane manufacturer was ordered to produce records relating to defects in aircraft of the same model built prior to the aircraft in question, and to answer questions arising from the documents.

Boushy v. Sarnia Gazette Publishing Co. (1980), 30 O.R. (2d) 667, 117 D.L.R. (3d) 171 (H.C.).

In a libel action where malice was in issue, the court required the defendant to answer questions as to whether at the time of publication he honestly believed that statements in certain newspaper articles were true.

Agnew v. O'Callaghan (1980), 18 C.P.C. 258 (Ont. H.C.).

In a libel action, where the defence of fair comment was pleaded, questions as to the belief of the defendant were ordered to be answered.

Drabinsky v. Maclean-Hunter Ltd. (1980), 28 O.R. (2d) 23, 16 C.P.C. 280, 108 D.L.R. (3d) 391 (H.C.).

Where the defences of privilege and fair comment were pleaded in a libel action, a reporter was not required to disclose his sources or produce his notes.

Re Kras and Sardo (1979), 26 O.R. (2d) 785, 12 R.F.L. (2d) 188 (U.F.C.).

The putative father in a paternity action was required to disclose the names of the other persons with whom he alleged the applicant had sexual relations.

Burt v. Burt (1979), 27 O.R. (2d) 163, 13 C.P.C. 341, 11 R.F.L. (2d) 143, 105 D.L.R. (3d) 702 (H.C.).

In a divorce action, a party is examinable as to the financial affairs of wholly-owned corporations.

Peterborough County v. Craig (1978), 14 C.P.C. 45 (Ont. Master).

Where the plaintiff's action for negligent design was based entirely on certain calculations, the defendant was entitled to obtain all the underlying information, assumptions and judgments for those calculations on discovery.

Young-Warren Food Brokerage Ltd v. Uniline Corp. (1978), 19 O.R. (2d) 332, 6 C.P.C. 45 (Master).

A corporate officer being examined on behalf of the defendant corporation was required to answer questions relating to events prior to the incorporation of the defendant, during which time he had been an employee of the parent corporation.

Kelly v. Lumley (1977), 3 C.P.C. 231 (Ont. H.C.).

In this motor vehicle action, a party was ordered to answer questions as to intoxication although there was no such specific allegation.

Gnys v. Stansfield (1975), 11 O.R. (2d) 642 (Master).

Where the defence of justification is pleaded in a defamation action, discovery is restricted to facts specifically pleaded.

Howpet Realty v. Simpsons Ltd., [1973] 3 O.R. 64 (H.C.).

An architect was required to answer the question whether certain premises were ''in good and substantial repair'' notwithstanding that it was the fundamental issue in the suit; the factual nature of the question and the expertise of the witness made the question proper.

Spatafora v. Wiebe, [1973] 1 O.R. 93 (H.C.).

Questions regarding the observations of investigators watching a party and conclusions based thereon were held to be proper.

Re Silverhill Realty Holding Ltd. and Min. of Highways for Ont., [1968] 1 O.R. 357 (C.A.).

Discussion of examinations for discovery in expropriation proceedings.

Steinberg v. Regent Const. Co., [1966] 2 O.R. 864 (H.C.).

A defendant may not question a plaintiff about the injuries to a co-plaintiff if such injuries are not relevant to the issues between the defendant and the first-mentioned plaintiff.

Re Akiba Invts. Ltd., [1963] 1 O.R. 513, affirmed without written reasons [1963] 1 O.R. 517n (C.A.).

Questions regarding the conduct of the controlling shareholder of a corporation, from which the intention of the corporation may be inferred, are proper.

Miller v. Coleman, [1959] O.W.N. 298 (Master).

In a personal injury case, questions regarding the plaintiff's previous health or injuries are proper, but questions regarding previous accidents are not.

Mills v. Toronto, [1955] O.W.N. 671 (Master).

The plaintiff was required to state what steps the defendant should have taken to avoid the accident in question.

Scope of Examination — Divided Discovery — rule 31.06(6) (See also cases under rule 30.04.)

Kinbauri Gold Corp. v. Iamgold International African Mining Gold Corp. (1995), 6 W.D.C.P. (2d) 332 (Ont. Gen. Div.).

The court divided discovery of liability and damage issues where failure to do so could have caused serious prejudice to the defendant.

McKinlay Transport Ltd. v. Motor Transport Industrial Relations Bureau of Ontario (Inc.) (1995), 37 C.P.C. (3d) 147 (Ont. Gen. Div.).

Where a single trial on all issues would result in a tremendous cost being imposed on a group of litigants at least some of whom might not be found liable, the court allowed the defendants' motion to sever the issue of damages from the issue of liability.

Allianz Life Insurance Co. of North America v. C.S.T. Foundation-Fondation C.S.T. (1995), 6 W.D.C.P. (2d) 331 (Ont. Gen. Div.).

The court refused to divide discovery of liability and damage issues where there was no prejudice to the defendant and there was no clear efficiency in splitting the proceeding.

Johnson v. Johnson (1986), 8 C.P.C. (2d) 243, 50 R.F.L. (2d) 167 (Ont. Master).

The court divided discovery in a divorce action to defer disclosure of financial information.

MacEachern v. McDougall (1981), 32 O.R. (2d) 193 (H.C.).

The court refused to divide discovery with respect to a subject which in one sense would relate to a consequential issue, but would also enable the plaintiff to endeavour to establish his right at trial.

Caddy Market Services Ltd. v. Naylor (1979), 10 C.P.C. 99 (Ont. H.C.).

The court permitted the separation of issues concerning liability from those concerning damages where the allegation was breach of an employment contract and there was a real possibility of irreparable harm.

Stermac v. Mandelbaum (1978), 8 C.P.C. 187 (Ont. Div. Ct.).

An order to withhold information was refused where the questions objected to related to basic threshold issues, as well as consequential issues, and could not be separated.

Maynard's Industrial Auctioneers & Appraisers Ltd. v. Commercial Indust. Auctioneers Ltd. (1977), 17 O.R. (2d) 745, leave to appeal to Div. Ct. refused 17 O.R. (2d) at 750n (H.C.).

Factors favouring an order for consequential discovery include serious doubt that the plaintiff will succeed on the primary issue, harm to the defendant resulting from disclosure of matters relating to the secondary issue, and undue oppression of the defendant. The modern trend is to avoid consequential discovery.

Alsop v. Alsop (1976), 13 O.R. (2d) 435, 26 R.F.L. 112 (C.A.).

Discovery should be divided only in the clearest of cases since the effect is to deprive the litigants of their normal procedural rights.

Minshall v. Minshall (1974), 4 O.R. (2d) 319, 15 R.F.L. 129 (H.C.).

In considering whether information regarding quantum should be withheld the court should consider the relative strength of the plaintiff's case and the bulk and detailed nature of the matters involved in the quantum issue.

Bean v. Bean, [1972] 2 O.R. 23 (Master).

Discovery on the question of quantum of maintenance and alimony in a divorce proceeding was postponed until the question of entitlement was determined.

Peters v. Peters, [1971] 2 O.R. 246, 5 R.F.L. 177 (H.C.).

The court refused to allow the withholding of information regarding quantum pending the resolution of an entitlement question where discovery on all issues may have assisted in determining the credibility of the parties.

EFFECT OF REFUSAL

31.07(1) Where a party, or a person examined for discovery on behalf or in place of a party, has refused to answer a proper question or to answer a question on the ground of privilege, and has failed to furnish the information in writing not later than ten days after the action is set down for trial, the party may not introduce at the trial the information refused on discovery, except with leave of the trial judge.

(2) The sanction provided by subrule (1) is in addition to the sanctions provided by rule 34.15 (sanctions for default in examination).

[*Note: See rule 53.08 regarding leave to admit such evidence at trial — Authors.*]

Snelgrove v. Steinberg Inc. (1995), 85 O.A.C. 365 (C.A.).

The court held that where a question on discovery was a proper question and an answer was not forthcoming, in order to invoke rule 31.07 no request for an undertaking was necessary, nor was it necessary to bring a motion to compel an answer.

EFFECT OF COUNSEL ANSWERING

31.08 Questions on an oral examination for discovery shall be answered by the person being examined but, where there is no objection, the question may be answered by his or her counsel and the answer shall be deemed to be the answer of the person being examined unless, before the conclusion of the examination, the person repudiates, contradicts or qualifies the answer.

Kay v. Posluns (1989), 71 O.R. (2d) 238 (H.C.), additional reasons (February 1, 1991), Doc. No. Toronto 26686/88 (Gen. Div.).

Counsel for a witness being examined for discovery may not answer a question for the witness, unless there is no objection, even if the witness's answer is wrong. The witness's counsel may re-examine to try to correct the answer or may correct the answer after completion of the examination pursuant to rule 31.09.

Eastcott v. Ruddy (1986), 9 C.P.C. (2d) 147 (Ont. H.C.).

An examining party is entitled to insist that a deponent inform herself from her solicitor and give the answer as part of her own sworn testimony, rather than simply adopt counsel's answers.

INFORMATION SUBSEQUENTLY OBTAINED

Duty to Correct Answers

31.09(1) Where a party has been examined for discovery or a person has been examined for discovery on behalf or in place of, or in addition to the party, and the party subsequently discovers that the answer to a question on the examination,

(a) was incorrect or incomplete when made; or

(b) is no longer correct and complete,
the party shall forthwith provide the information in writing to every other party.

Consequences of Correcting Answers
(2) Where a party provides information in writing under subrule (1),
(a) the writing may be treated at a hearing as if it formed part of the original examination of the person examined; and
(b) any adverse party may require that the information be verified by affidavit of the party or be the subject of further examination for discovery.

Sanction for Failing to Correct Answers
(3) Where a party has failed to comply with subrule (1) or a requirement under clause (2)(b), and the information subsequently discovered is,
(a) favourable to the party's case, the party may not introduce the information at the trial, except with leave of the trial judge; or
(b) not favourable to the party's case, the court may make such order as is just.

[*Note: See rule 53.08 regarding leave to admit undisclosed evidence at trial — Authors.*]

Snelgrove v. Steinberg Inc. (1995), 85 O.A.C. 365 (C.A.).
The court ordered a new trial where the defendant had not given the plaintiff proper discovery. The breaches were flagrant and continuing and resulted in substantial prejudice to the plaintiff.

Christie Corp. v. Alvarez (1994), 34 C.P.C. (3d) 92 (Ont. Gen. Div.).
The court refused to order a party to re-attend and answer questions arising out of written answers to undertakings where it would serve no useful purpose to do so.

Quabbin Hill Investments Inc. v. Rowntree (1993), 19 C.P.C. (3d) 113 (Ont. Gen. Div.).
Rule 31.09 does not require correction of incorrect inferences drawn by the examining party.

Machado v. Pratt & Whitney Canada Inc. (1993), 17 C.P.C. (3d) 340 (Ont. Master), leave to appeal refused 16 O.R. (3d) 250, 23 C.P.C. (3d) 115 (Gen. Div.).
The propriety of purported corrections of discovery answers is a matter for the trial judge and should not be determined by way of interlocutory motion to strike out the corrections.

Baron v. Nguyen (1991), 3 C.P.C. (3d) 67 (Ont. Gen. Div.).
Where medical reports produced after discovery indicated that the plaintiff's condition had worsened, the court permitted the defendants to have further discovery pursuant to rule 31.09(2)(b).

Cheaney v. Peel Memorial Hospital (1990), 73 O.R. (2d) 794, 44 C.P.C. (2d) 158 (Master).
A motion to compel production of expert reports which was dismissed because no reports existed yet is not *res judicata* so as to obviate the requirement for continuing disclosure under rule 31.09.

Burke v. Gauthier (1987), 24 C.P.C. (2d) 281 (Ont. H.C.).
In the absence of a prior written correction, a party was not permitted to introduce evidence at trial which was very different from the evidence given by the same party at discovery.

Mann v. Wadhera (1987), 19 C.P.C. (2d) 20 (Ont. H.C.).

The court ordered the defendant to answer questions regarding information about the plaintiff's credibility where such information had not been disclosed on discovery in response to a question as to facts being relied on with respect to either liability or damages. The plaintiff's credibility is usually relevant to liability or damages.

Gorin v. Ho (1983), 38 C.P.C. 72 (Ont. Master).

An injured plaintiff has a duty to undertake to provide medical opinions received following the examination for discovery.

Ont. Bean Producers' Marketing Bd. v. W.G. Thompson & Sons Ltd.; W.G. Thompson & Sons Ltd. v. Ont. Bean Producers' Marketing Bd. (1982), 35 O.R. (2d) 711, 134 D.L.R. (3d) 108, 27 C.P.C. 1 (Div. Ct.).

A single request for after-acquired information in respect of matters as to which questions have been put is proper.

Bowen v. Klassen (1980), 30 O.R. (2d) 15, 17 C.P.C. 80, 115 D.L.R. (3d) 167 (H.C.).

Where a party refuses an examination to undertake to furnish information subsequently obtained, the court will order his re-attendance to give such an undertaking.

Ohl v. Cannito, [1972] 2 O.R. 763, 26 D.L.R. (3d) 556 (H.C.).

A party was required to give an undertaking to disclose facts coming to his attention in the future.

DISCOVERY OF NON-PARTIES WITH LEAVE

General

31.10(1) The court may grant leave, on such terms respecting costs and other matters as are just, to examine for discovery any person who there is reason to believe has information relevant to a material issue in the action, other than an expert engaged by or on behalf of a party in preparation for contemplated or pending litigation.

Test for Granting Leave

(2) An order under subrule (1) shall not be made unless the court is satisfied that,

(a) the moving party has been unable to obtain the information from other persons whom the moving party is entitled to examine for discovery, or from the person the party seeks to examine;

(b) it would be unfair to require the moving party to proceed to trial without having the opportunity of examining the person; and

(c) the examination will not,

(i) unduly delay the commencement of the trial of the action,

(ii) entail unreasonable expense for other parties, or

(iii) result in unfairness to the person the moving party seeks to examine.

Costs Consequences For Examining Party

(3) A party who examines a person orally under this rule shall serve every party who attended or was represented on the examination with the transcript free of charge, unless the court orders otherwise.

(4) The examining party is not entitled to recover the costs of the examination from another party unless the court expressly orders otherwise.

Limitation on Use at Trial
(5) The evidence of a person examined under this rule may not be read into evidence at trial under subrule 31.11(1).

Discovery of Non-Parties — Generally

Famous Players Development Corp. v. Central Capital Corp. (1991), 6 O.R. (3d) 765, 3 C.P.C. (3d) 286, 53 O.A.C. 185 (Div. Ct.).

In order to satisfy the test under rule 31.10(2)(a), there must be a refusal, actual or constructive, by the opposing party to obtain the information from the non-party.

Lloyds Bank Canada v. Canada Life Assurance Co. (1991), 47 C.P.C. (2d) 157 (Ont. Gen. Div.).

Where the non-party declined to meet with the solicitors for the moving parties, but did provide information through the solicitors for the responding party, the court refused to order a discovery. The test in rule 31.10(2)(a) had not been met.

Famous Players Development Corp. v. Central Capital Corp. (1990), 1 O.R. (3d) 672, 46 C.P.C. (2d) 90 (Gen. Div.), affirmed (1991), 6 O.R. (3d) 765, 3 C.P.C. (3d) 286, 53 O.A.C. 185 (Div. Ct.).

The court refused to order the examination of a non-party where the non-party had cooperated in providing answers to questions asked on the discovery of one of the parties. Before obtaining such an order the moving party must establish that it was unable to obtain the information through discovery of the other parties. *Dalewood Investments Ltd. v. Canada Trust Co., infra*, was incorrectly decided.

Duguay v. Devoe (1988), 63 O.R. (2d) 499 (H.C.).

A physician who has *treated* the plaintiff may be ordered to be examined under rule 31.10. *Snively v. Schacher, infra*, disapproved.

Rothwell v. Raes (1986), 13 O.A.C. 60 (Div. Ct.).

The requirements of rule 31.10(2) are cumulative and all of them must be satisfied: the rule-makers established a number of preconditions so that the remedy could not easily be subjected to abuse: the onus is on the applicant to show that the requirements of the rule have been satisfied; to satisfy the second requirement it may be necessary to ask the person to be examined to supplement her initial response.

D'Amore Construction (Windsor) Ltd. v. Ontario (No. 2) (1986), 12 C.P.C. (2d) 178 (Ont. H.C.).

If a plaintiff has undertaken to make inquiries of a non-party, it must be given an opportunity to complete those inquiries before the defendant will be permitted to bring a motion to examine the non-party.

Snively v. Schacher (1986), 10 C.P.C. (2d) 38 (Ont. H.C.).

Discovery of a non-party was refused where the person to be examined was an expert retained by the plaintiff.

Dalewood Investments Ltd. v. Canada Trust Co. (1986), 9 C.P.C. (2d) 129 (Ont. H.C.), leave to appeal to Ont. Div. Ct. refused 9 C.P.C. (2d) 129 at 131.

The court ordered discovery of a non-party who was a former employer of one of the parties notwithstanding that party's willingness to make inquiries to the non-party.

Carleton Condo. Corp. No. 25 v. Shenkman Corp. (1986), 9 C.P.C. (2d) 233 (Ont. Master).

To obtain an order to examine a non-party for discovery the moving party must show that it is unable to obtain the information possessed by the non-party *both* from the non-party *and* from persons it is entitled to examine.

Discovery of Non-Parties — Examples

Ontario (Attorney General) v. Ballard Estate (1995), 7 W.D.C.P. (2d) 47 (Ont. Gen. Div. [Commercial List]).

The court permitted the examination for discovery of a witness who appeared to have important evidence.

Famous Players Development Corp. v. Central Capital Corp. (1990), 1 O.R. (3d) 672, 46 C.P.C. (2d) 90 (Gen. Div.), affirmed (1991), 6 O.R. (3d) 765, 3 C.P.C. (3d) 286, 53 O.A.C. 185 (Gen. Div.).

The court refused to order discovery of a non-party who had co-operated by giving written answers to questions asked of the defendants. The level of difficulty, delay or expense so created amounted to inability to obtain relevant information from the non-party.

Microtel Ltd. v. Endless Electronics Distributors Inc. (1988), 32 C.P.C. (2d) 85 (Ont. H.C.).

The court refused to permit discovery of a non-party where the plaintiff admitted to not having first attempted to obtain the information from the non-party voluntarily.

College of Physicians & Surgeons of Ont. v. Morris (1988), 28 O.A.C. 59 (Div. Ct.).

The court ordered the examination for discovery of a non-party witness at the request of the defendant where the plaintiff who planned to call the witness at trial did not know a very material fact and refused to undertake to ask the witness.

Fraser v. E.S. Gallagher Sales Ltd. (1987), 22 C.P.C. (2d) 238 (Ont. Master).

The plaintiff was not entitled to examine a former employee of the defendant where the plaintiff could have obtained the information on the original discovery of the defendant.

Nelson v. MacDonald (1987), 19 C.P.C. (2d) 115 (Ont. Dist. Ct.).

The court ordered discovery of an insurance adjuster where the only issue at trial would be the effect of releases obtained by the adjuster from the plaintiffs, the adjuster would testify at trial, and the information was not obtained from the discovery of the defendants.

Weiszman v. 491 Lawrence Avenue West Ltd. (1985), 5 C.P.C. (2d) 160 (Ont. H.C.).

Where witnesses gave statements to one party but refused to provide information not included in the statements to another party, the court granted leave to examine the witnesses for discovery.

Meneses v. Geary (1985), 49 C.P.C. 185 (Ont. Master).

The court ordered a representative of the defendant's insurer to be examined for discovery where it was alleged that the representative had made an admission of liability. In the absence of the defendant attempting to countermand or withdraw the admission, it would be unfair to require the plaintiff to proceed to trial without the admission.

USE OF EXAMINATION FOR DISCOVERY AT TRIAL

Reading in Examination of Party

31.11(1) At the trial of an action, a party may read into evidence as part of the party's own case against an adverse party any part of the evidence given on the examination for discovery of,

    (a) the adverse party; or

(b) a person examined for discovery on behalf or in place of, or in addition to the adverse party, unless the trial judge orders otherwise,

if the evidence is otherwise admissible, whether the party or person has already given evidence or not.

Impeachment

(2) The evidence given on an examination for discovery may be used for the purpose of impeaching the testimony of the deponent as a witness in the same manner as any previous inconsistent statement by that witness.

[*Note: The Evidence Act, R.S.O. 1990, c. E.23, ss. 20 and 21, requires that a prior inconsistent statement be put to the witness before its introduction into evidence. While the defendant can read in evidence from the plaintiff's examination for discovery as an admission, he or she cannot do so for impeachment purposes without complying with the Evidence Act: rule 31.11(2). See Int. Corona Resources Ltd. v. LAC Minerals Ltd., noted below under "Use of Examination for Discovery at Trial — Impeachment — rule 31.11(2)" — Authors.*]

Qualifying Answers

(3) Where only part of the evidence given on an examination for discovery is read into or used in evidence, at the request of an adverse party the trial judge may direct the introduction of any other part of the evidence that qualifies or explains the part first introduced.

Rebuttal

(4) A party who reads into evidence as part of the party's own case evidence given on an examination for discovery of an adverse party, or a person examined for discovery on behalf or in place of or in addition to an adverse party, may rebut that evidence by introducing any other admissible evidence.

Party under Disability

(5) The evidence given on the examination for discovery of a party under disability may be read into or used in evidence at the trial only with leave of the trial judge.

Unavailability of Deponent

(6) Where a person examined for discovery,

(a) has died;

(b) is unable to testify because of infirmity or illness;

(c) for any other sufficient reason cannot be compelled to attend at the trial; or

(d) refuses to take an oath or make an affirmation or to answer any proper question,

any party may, with leave of the trial judge, read into evidence all or part of the evidence given on the examination for discovery as the evidence of the person examined. to the extent that it would be admissible if the person were testifying in court.

(7) In deciding whether to grant leave under subrule (6), the trial judge shall consider,

  (a) the extent to which the person was cross-examined on the examination for discovery;

  (b) the importance of the evidence in the proceeding;

  (c) the general principle that evidence should be presented orally in court; and

  (d) any other relevant factor.

Subsequent Action

(8) Where an action has been discontinued or dismissed and another action involving the same subject matter is subsequently brought between the same parties or their representatives or successors in interest, the evidence given on an examination for discovery taken in the former action may be read into or used in evidence at the trial of the subsequent action as if it had been taken in the subsequent action.

[*Note: Accuracy of transcript. The Evidence Act, R.S.O. 1990, c. E.23, s. 48(1) provides that where an examination has been certified under the hand of the person taking it, it shall, without proof of the signature, be received and read into evidence saving all just exceptions. Section 48(2) further provides that such an examination received or read into evidence "shall be presumed to represent accurately the evidence of the party or witness, unless there is good reason to doubt the accuracy" — Authors.*]

Use of Examination for Discovery — Generally

Wallace Sign-Crafters West Ltd. v. 466126 Ontario Ltd. (1994), 28 C.P.C. (3d) 75, 72 O.A.C. 213 (Div. Ct.).

Where a witness' memory may have been impaired because of physical infirmity, the trial judge properly exercised his discretion in allowing the witness to resort to the transcript of his examination for discovery in an attempt to refresh his memory.

Seaway Trust Co. v. Markle (1991), 47 C.P.C. (2d) 258 (Ont. Gen. Div.).

The court refused to seal the transcript of the defendant's examination for discovery until after disposition of criminal proceedings against him.

Smith v. Smith (1986), 12 C.P.C. (2d) 125 (Ont. Dist. Ct.).

A transcript of an examination for discovery may be used in a criminal proceeding for the purpose of cross-examining the accused.

Int. Corona Resources Ltd. v. LAC Minerals Ltd. (1986), 8 C.P.C. (2d) 39 (Ont. H.C.).

Where an admission from an examination for discovery is read in at trial, opposing counsel can refer the judge to other evidence enlarging upon or explaining the admission only in argument.

Hamilton Harbour Commrs. v. J.P. Porter Co. (1978), 19 O.R. (2d) 66, 5 C.P.C. 297, 4 C.R. (3d) 157, 84 D.L.R. (3d) 125, leave to appeal to Div. Ct. refused 20 O.R. (2d) 632, 5 C.P.C. at 300, 88 D.L.R. (3d) 604 (H.C.).

The court gave the examined person protection under both the Canada and Ontario *Evidence Acts* and ordered copies of the discovery to be sealed and used only in the civil proceedings. The court ordered that evidence on discovery not be used directly or indirectly in related criminal proceedings except with permission of the court.

New Augarita Porcupine Mines Ltd. v. Gray, [1953] O.W.N. 24 (H.C.).

Discussion of the use of an examination for discovery in a reference to the master.

Use of Examination for Discovery — For Purposes Collateral to the Present Litigation (See also the cases collected, above, under rule 30.02 "Production of documents — Use of documents outside litigation".)

Use of Examination for Discovery at Trial — Reading in Examination of Party — rule 31.11(1)

Esson v. A.M.S. Forest Products Ltd. (1993), 18 C.P.C. (3d) 320 (Ont. Gen. Div.).

Where defence counsel had named potential defence witnesses and provided a summary of their evidence at discovery, that evidence could not be read in as evidence at trial by plaintiff's counsel. The evidence in question came from independent third parties, and as a result was inadmissible hearsay.

Claiborne Industries Ltd. v. National Bank of Can. (1989), 69 O.R. (2d) 65, 59 D.L.R. (4th) 533, 34 O.A.C. 241 (C.A.).

A corporation is bound by its representative's hearsay answers on examination for discovery, and these are admissible at trial, unless it expressly protects itself by disclaimer.

C.I.B.C. v. Int. Harvester Credit Corp. of Can. (1985), 50 O.R. (2d) 318, 49 C.P.C. 181 (H.C.).

The court permitted the defendant to read in the examination for discovery of the plaintiff at trial when the witness gave unsatisfactory or unresponsive answers at trial.

Reti v. Fox (1976), 2 C.P.C. 62 (Ont. C.A.).

A trial judge is entitled to accept part of the evidence read in from the discovery and reject the rest where it conflicts with the oral evidence.

Tecchi v. Cirillo, [1968] 1 O.R. 536 (C.A.).

A new trial was ordered where, *inter alia*, the presiding judge had read the transcript of the examinations for discovery before it had been properly introduced at trial. [*And see now rule 34.18(4) — Authors.*]

Kirkby v. Booth, [1964] 1 O.R. 286, 42 D.L.R. (2d) 32 (H.C.).

A plaintiff was permitted to withdraw excerpts of the examination for discovery of the defendant which had been read in previously and which had the effect of making the contentions of the defendant part of the plaintiff's case.

Clark v. McCrohan, [1948] O.W.N. 172, [1948] 2 D.L.R. 283 (C.A.).

Where one party reads in the examination for discovery of the opposite party it also can be used by his opponent against him. Witnesses may be called to contradict the damaging portions of the examination.

Use of Examination for Discovery at Trial — Impeachment — rule 31.11(2)

Int. Corona Resources Ltd. v. LAC Minerals Ltd. (1986), 8 C.P.C. (2d) 39 (Ont. H.C.).

Counsel can read in portions of a witness' examination for discovery to impeach the witness' testimony only if ss. 20 and 21 of the *Evidence Act* have been complied with.

Young v. Young, [1970] 3 O.R. 272, 2 R.F.L. 239, 12 D.L.R. (3d) 708 (C.A.).

Where the evidence of a party at trial varied in an important respect from his statements on discovery and the opposing party in reliance on the latter had not had a witness available to rebut such testimony, a new trial was ordered.

Use of Examination for Discovery at Trial — Unavailability of Deponent — rule 31.11(6)

Moase Enterprises Ltd. v. Clean Energy Products Inc. (1991), 2 C.P.C. (3d) 143 (Ont. Gen. Div.).

The court refused to admit at trial evidence given on an examination for discovery where the deponent was temporarily unable to testify due to infirmity or illness. The ability to cross-examine a witness at trial is an important one, and the evidence suggested the witness might be available later.

Calandra v. B. A. Cleaners Ltd. (1990), 73 O.R. (2d) 449, 11 R.P.R. (2d) 63 (Dist. Ct.).

The court permitted portions of the transcript of an examination for discovery to be read into evidence at trial where the deponent died before trial.

Howe v. Clareco Can. Ltd. (1984), 48 O.R. (2d) 155, 45 C.P.C. 303 (H.C.).

Where the plaintiff died after being examined for discovery, this action was stayed so that the trial would be deferred until after the new Rules came into force in order to permit a motion for leave under this provision to read into evidence the plaintiff's testimony.

Use of Examination for Discovery — In Subsequent Action — rule 31.11(8)

Insco Sarnia Ltd. v. Polysar Ltd. (1990), 45 C.P.C. (2d) 53 (Ont. Gen. Div.).

The court refused to accept in evidence the transcript of trial evidence given by a since deceased witness in a related criminal proceeding.

New Augarita Porcupine Mines Ltd. v. Gray, [1953] O.W.N. 24 (H.C.).

An examination for discovery is admissible in any other suit on *viva voce* proof by a witness that the examination was correctly reported.

RULE 32   INSPECTION OF PROPERTY

Highlights

This Rule, while more detailed than its predecessor, involves no change in practice, but note that the Rule refers to a "proceeding" which would appear to make it applicable to applications (see rule 1.03).

Orders for the interim preservation of property, which are a form of interim relief rather than a discovery device, are provided for in Rule 45.

Recent amendments. Rule 30.1 (Deemed Undertaking) regulates the use of evidence obtained under Rule 32.

Former Rules: Rule 372.

ORDER FOR INSPECTION

32.01(1) The court may make an order for the inspection of real or personal property where it appears to be necessary for the proper determination of an issue in a proceeding.

(2) For the purpose of the inspection, the court may,

(a) authorize entry on or into and the taking of temporary possession of any property in the possession of a party or of a person not a party;

(b) permit the measuring, surveying or photographing of the property in question, or of any particular object or operation on the property; and

(c) permit the taking of samples, the making of observations or the conducting of tests or experiments.

(3) The order shall specify the time, place and manner of the inspection and may impose such other terms, including the payment of compensation, as are just.

(4) No order for inspection shall be made without notice to the person in possession of the property unless,

(a) service of notice, or the delay necessary to serve notice, might entail serious consequences to the moving party; or

(b) the court dispenses with service of notice for any other sufficient reason.

Order for Inspection of Property — Generally

Farhi v. Wright (1987), 26 C.P.C. (2d) 88 (Ont. H.C.).

Rule 32 should be construed liberally to permit inspections.

Bell Can. v. Olympia & York Devs. Ltd. (1985), 50 C.P.C. 248, 12 C.L.R. 284 (Ont. Master).

An order may be made for the inspection of a process as well as the inspection of property. In this case the court permitted inspection of stressed tendons reinforcing concrete slabs while the tendons were being removed.

Morgan v. Fekete (1979), 25 O.R. (2d) 237 (Master).

The order may not be made until the close of pleadings.

Motordrift Aktiebolag v. Consolidated Dynamics Ltd. (1975), 11 O.R. (2d) 703 (Master).

An order may be made before discovery if it is clear that the examination for discovery would not furnish the information sought to be found by the inspection.

Coulter and Almarona Invts. Ltd. v. Estate of Carldon Aviation (1962) Ltd. (1974), 5 O.R. (2d) 378 (Master).

An order for inspection should not be made until the close of pleadings.

Langan v. Wong Aviation Ltd., [1957] O.W.N. 222 (Master).

A second inspection of property will be ordered much more readily than a second medical examination.

United Sterl-a-fone Corp. Ltd. v. Bell Telephone Co. of Can., [1953] O.W.N. 354, 18 C.P.R. 112 (Master).

The court refused to order inspection for the purpose of pleading.

Order for Inspection of Property — Terms — rule 32.01(3)

Bank of N.S. v. Wu (1986), 15 C.P.C. (2d) 283 (Ont. Dist. Ct.).

The court authorized the solicitor for the defendant to inspect the plaintiff bank's premises including the vault area on condition that the solicitor retain the information gathered in his possession and not adduce any sketches or measurements in evidence. A two-hour limit was imposed on the inspection.

Goldsman v. Sniderman, [1946] O.W.N. 417, affirmed [1946] O.W.N. at 419 (H.C.).

The court ordered that photographs and sketches resulting from the inspection be produced to the opposite party.

Wilson v. Wabash Railroad Co. and Orr, [1946] O.W.N. 733 (Master).

The plaintiff was allowed to inspect the defendant's locomotive but because of the delay by the plaintiff in applying for inspection the defendant was not required to restore and re-equip it as it was at the time of the accident or to produce it at a location more convenient to the plaintiff.

Inspection of Property — Examples

Davison v. Inco Ltd. (1992), 8 O.R. (3d) 464, 9 C.P.C. (3d) 155 (Gen. Div.).

The court permitted the defendant to inspect and conduct tests concerning the plaintiff's farming operation in this action for nuisance.

Callis v. Stop 48 Ltd. (1990), 50 C.P.C. (2d) 304 (Ont. Gen. Div.).

The court ordered inspection of a go-cart involved in an accident notwithstanding that it had been used for more than two years following the accident.

PPG Industries Can. Ltd. v. Tioxide of Can. Inc. (1986), 12 C.P.C. (2d) 158 (Ont. Master).

A plaintiff was ordered to provide the defendant with samples of its product for testing in a product liability action.

Re Macdonald and Briant (1982), 25 C.P.C. 252, leave to appeal to Ont. C.A. refused 25 C.P.C. 252n.

An order was made for preservation and inspection of a document annexed to an affidavit where there was an issue whether part of the document was forged.

Lagerquist v. Labatt's Ltd. (1978), 19 O.R. (2d) 586, 6 C.P.C. 82, 87 D.L.R. (3d) 149 (H.C.).

Where it was alleged that there was negligence in the defendant's manufacturing process, the plaintiff was permitted to have his representatives attend on the defendant's premises to make a visual examination and photograph the manufacturing process.

Allen v. Carling Breweries Ltd., [1972] 2 O.R. 294 (Master).

A plaintiff was permitted to film the manufacture, bottling, etc. of the product of the defendant where negligence had been alleged as to those processes.

Malcolm Condensing Co. v. The Employers' Liability Ins. Corp. Ltd., [1949] O.W.N. 167 (H.C.).

The defendant insurance company was denied inspection of the plaintiff's plant until after the examinations for discovery at which time evidence might be produced to support a motion for further inspection and information could be obtained which would permit the court to establish limits to the inspection where the defendant sought evidence to support a defence it did not know it would actually be able to establish.

Walker v. The McKinnon Industries Ltd., [1948] O.W.N. 537, 8 C.P.R. 129 (H.C.).

A plaintiff alleging damage from vibrations from the defendant's operations and from the settling of various gases and other emissions from the defendant's plant over his house and greenhouses was permitted an inspection of the plant and its operations. Although the plaintiff did not allege negligence on the defendant's part, the defendant's pleadings made the conduct of its plant and the nature of its machinery an issue in the action.

J.K. Smit and Sons of Can. Ltd. v. Fastcut Bits Ltd., [1948] O.W.N. 478, 729, 8 Fox Pat. C. 214 (H.C.).

In an action for an injunction to restrain the defendant from infringing a patent, the plaintiffs were permitted to inspect the defendant's machinery and processes before delivering the statement of claim after it was established that the plaintiffs had *bona fide* reason to believe the defendant's machine was an infringement of the patent of which they were licensees and that they were not merely fishing.

Proulx v. C. Caplan Ltd., [1946] O.W.N. 725, [1946] 4 D.L.R. 219 (H.C.).

An order for disinterment was made where the plaintiff's doctors made a post-mortem examination without notice to the defendants who may have been severely prejudiced without the opportunity to conduct their own examinations.

RULE 33   MEDICAL EXAMINATION OF PARTIES

Highlights

This Rule supplements s. 105 of the *Courts of Justice Act*, empowering the court to order physical or mental examinations by physicians, dentists and, pursuant to a 1989 amendment, psychologists. Taken together they brought about major changes in respect of who may be examined and the exchange of medical information regarding persons examined.

Who may be examined. The court's power to order a medical examination is no longer limited to plaintiffs or to personal injury cases: it now extends to any party whose physical or mental condition is in question in a proceeding (*Courts of Justice Act*, s. 105(2)). However, where the question of a party's physical or mental condition is not raised by the party but by another party (*e.g.*, the plaintiff in an accident case alleges that the defendant had defective eyesight, or in a divorce action the petitioner alleges that the respondent is mentally unfit to have custody) the court must be satisfied that the allegation is relevant to a material issue and there is good reason to believe there is substance to the allegation: s. 105(3).

Exchange of medical information. The Rule requires the sequential exchange of medical information relating to the person examined. Unless otherwise ordered, prior to the examination the party to be examined must provide to the examining party a copy of any report made by a health practitioner who treated or examined the party in respect of the condition in question and any hospital records or other medical document relating to the condition. However, this obligation does not extend to a report or other medical document made in preparation for contemplated or pending litigation and for no other purpose, where the party undertakes not to call the health practitioner or evidence as to the medical document at trial: rule 33.04(2).

After the examination, on receiving the examining health practitioner's report, the examining party is to serve a copy on every other party (rule 33.06(2)) even if it is "adverse".

By rule 33.08, the provisions of Rule 33 apply to any medical examination conducted on consent, except to the extent that they are waived by the consent.

Recent amendments. Rule 30.1 (Deemed Undertaking) regulates the use of evidence obtained under Rule 33.

Former provision: Judicature Act, s. 77.

MOTION FOR MEDICAL EXAMINATION

33.01 A motion by an adverse party for an order under section 105 of the *Courts of Justice Act* for the physical or mental examination of a party whose physical or mental condition is in question in a proceeding shall be made on notice to every other party.

Where Examination Will be Ordered

Robinson v. Kilby (1996), 7 W.D.C.P. (2d) 129 (Ont. Div. Ct.).

An order requiring a party, who has not placed his psychological make-up in issue, to submit to a psychological examination is a particularly intrusive step and should not be routinely ordered. Evidence in the form of an affidavit sworn by a psychologist or psychiatrist should show that such an examination is likely to produce relevant information.

Maniram v. Jagmohan (1988), 31 C.P.C. (2d) 293 at 294 (Ont. Master), affirmed 31 C.P.C. (2d) 293 (Ont. H.C.).

In ordinary circumstances, every separately represented defendant is entitled to a separate defence medical examination.

Handfield v. Lacroix (1988), 26 C.P.C. (2d) 44 (Ont. H.C.).

The mental capacity of a party to instruct counsel is not a material issue in the proceedings and the court cannot order a medical examination in that regard.

Kontosoros v. Dodoro (1987), 15 C.P.C. (2d) 247 (Ont. Master); affirmed 23 C.P.C. (2d) 111 (Ont. H.C.).

Where one set of defendants obtained an order for a medical examination the court refused the plaintiff's request for a term restricting the ability of the other defendants to obtain a separate defence medical examination. The plaintiff was ordered to pay $100 regarding his failure to attend on previously agreed physicial examinations.

Botiuk v. Toronto Free Press Publications Ltd. (1986), 56 O.R. (2d) 184, 11 C.P.C. (2d) 211 (Master).

Where a defendant moved for an order permitting him to give evidence before trial on the ground that he might not be able to testify as a result of a medical condition, the plaintiff obtained an order requiring that the defendant undergo a medical examination to assist in the defence of the motion.

Dalton v. Rassweiler (1985), 49 C.P.C. 53 (Ont. Master).

The master declined to order a defendant motorist to submit to an eye examination where there was no material filed indicating that the defendant might have eyesight problems and his evidence on discovery negatived any such suggestion.

Italiano v. Tobias (1984), 45 O.R. (2d) 380 (Co. Ct.).

Where a third party in a personal injury action seeks a psychiatric examination of the plaintiff, the third party must provide evidence justifying such an examination.

Cairns v. Schofield (1983), 40 C.P.C. 5 (Ont. Master).

Each defendant in a medical malpractice action was permitted a separate medical examination where there were separate allegations against them. Evidence might be obtained to determine which defendant's negligence led to the injury.

Proctor v. Proctor (1980), 16 C.P.C. 220 (Ont. C.A.).

The court ordered that discovery should be expanded to permit a right of psychiatric and medical examination in a non-personal injury case.

Shibley v. Western Assur. Co. (1980), 13 C.P.C. 137 (Ont. Co. Ct.).

In an action to recover disability benefits provided under a motor vehicle insurance policy, an order was made even though the quantum of recovery was set by statute.

Kathpalia v. Acker; Kathpalia v. Ferrari; Kathpalia v. Commercial Union Assur. Group (1978), 5 C.P.C. 311 (Ont. Master).

Defendants in related but separate motor vehicle actions are entitled to separate medical examinations.

ORDER FOR EXAMINATION

Contents of Order

33.02(1) An order under section 105 of the *Courts of Justice Act* may specify the time, place and purpose of the examination and shall name the health practitioner or practitioners by whom it is to be conducted.

Further Examinations

(2) The court may order a second examination or further examinations on such terms respecting costs and other matters as are just.

Place of Examination — rule 33.02(1)

Manning (Litigation Guardian of) v. Ryerson (1992), 11 C.P.C. (3d) 55 (Ont. Gen. Div.).

The choice of the physician to conduct a defence medical examination in a personal injury case should be that of the defendant unless the attendance required for the examination is unreasonably inconvenient. A plaintiff residing in the London area was required to attend in Toronto for examination.

Bauer v. Fielding (1980), 20 C.P.C. 164 (Ont. H.C.).

Where the accident occurred at Windsor, the action was commenced there, and all the relevant evidence available was there, the plaintiff was ordered to attend at Windsor for a medical examination although she resided in North Bay at the time of the order.

Brocklehurst v. Assuncao (1977), 3 C.P.C. 178 (Ont. Master).

The medical examination is to be conducted by doctors licensed to practise in Ontario, at a location determined by convenience and justice.

Lamarr v. Marsman (1976), 8 O.R. (2d) 583 (H.C.).

The court has a discretion with regard to the place of examination; it need not take place in the county where the party sought to be examined resides.

Purpose of Examination — rule 33.02(1) (See cases under rule 33.03.)

Selection of Health Practitioner — rule 33.02(1)

Fox v. Reynolds (1996), 7 W.D.C.P. (2d) 192 (Ont. Gen. Div.).

Cogent and comprehensive evidence is required to contest the defendant's choice of the physician proposed to conduct a defence medical examination.

Ontario (A.G.) v. CEC Edwards Construction (1986), 57 O.R. (2d) 782, 17 C.P.C. (2d) 268 (H.C.).

A party may be required to be examined by a psychologist, even a foreign one, but the psychologist must deliver a report pursuant to rule 33.06.

Malezian v. Knapp (1978), 17 O.R. (2d) 524 (Master).

The medical practitioner named should not be one who has previously treated the plaintiff as his own patient.

Order for Further Examination — rule 33.02(2)

Tracey v. Patterson (1985), 6 C.P.C. (2d) 86 (Ont. Dist. Ct.).

The court ordered a further defence medical examination where the plaintiff asserted a claim for damages for personality changes after the action had been set down for trial.

Mepham v. Carrier (1980), 32 O.R. (2d) 640 (C.A.).

The court permitted a second medical examination where the physician who conducted the first examination died.

Hanna v. Marr (1977), 16 O.R. (2d) 238, 77 D.L.R. (3d) 707 (H.C.).

A motion for a second examination by a psychiatrist was dismissed as not relevant as the plaintiff had not made a claim for damages other than for physical injuries.

Fine v. Weiszhaus (1977), 3 C.P.C. 50 (Ont. H.C.).

A further medical examination was ordered where the first had been without consultation with the applicants and the report had been withheld.

Halkias v. Tuharsky, [1962] O.W.N. 260 (H.C.).

A second examination was ordered where new symptoms were disclosed on discovery.

Lesser v. Radiak, [1956] O.W.N. 479 (Master).

The court will not order a subsequent examination merely for the purpose of corroborating the results of a previous examination but will do so for the purpose of obtaining the opinion of a specialist regarding a particular condition in question.

Atkinson v. Carry, [1955] O.W.N. 952 (Master).

A second examination was ordered where it was likely that the condition of the plaintiff had altered significantly in the six-month period following the first examination.

Hines v. Bird's Transfer Ltd., [1946] O.W.N. 343 (Master).

Where there was a physical examination prior to the filing of the statement of claim but the doctor could not make a prognosis on the basis of that examination, a second examination was ordered.

Davidson v. Chapman's Ltd., [1945] O.W.N. 309 (H.C.).

A second medical examination was ordered and a specialist appointed notwithstanding that the defendant should have sought an examination by a specialist in the first instance.

Goldberg v. Gardner, [1944] O.W.N. 678 (Master).

The court may order a second physical examination where the plaintiff amends the statement of claim to set up a new ground of damages.

Keller v. Darling & Co., [1944] O.W.N. 152 (Master).

An order for a second examination is justified where the physician making the first examination is unable to attend and give evidence at trial.

Gilmour v. Kerry, [1943] O.W.N. 545 (Master).

The discretion to order a second physical examination should not be applied in such a manner as to cause unnecessary inconvenience or embarrassment to the parties. But where a second examination by a specialist may be necessary to determine the condition and rights of the parties, the order is proper.

DISPUTE AS TO SCOPE OF EXAMINATION

33.03 The court may on motion determine any dispute relating to the scope of an examination.

Scope of Examination — Psychological, etc. Examinations

[Note: Pre-1990 cases should be read with care in light of the broadening of s. 105 of the Courts of Justice Act — Authors.]

Tarmohamed v. Scarborough (City) (1989), 68 O.R. (2d) 116, 31 C.P.C. (2d) 230 (H.C.).

The court may not order an examination by a medical professional other than a licensed physician unless such examination is requested by a licensed physician.

Ontario (A.G.) v. CEC Edwards Construction (1986), 57 O.R. (2d) 782, 17 C.P.C. (2d) 268 (H.C.).

The court ordered the plaintiff to submit to a psychological examination by a U.S. psychologist where it would be of assistance to a physician's examination of the plaintiff. The court ordered that the psychologist's notes and test results be provided to the plaintiff.

Vreken v. Fitchett (1984), 45 O.R. (2d) 515, 43 C.P.C. 205, 7 D.L.R. (4th) 187 (H.C.).

The court ordered the plaintiff to submit to a vocational assessment as a diagnostic aid to a defence medical examination.

Burke v. Metro. Toronto (1979), 12 C.P.C. 114 (Ont. Master).

An order for a vocational assessment of the plaintiff was refused where it was not clear that it was intended as a diagnostic aid to the physical examination, and it would involve great inconvenience to the plaintiff.

Thomas v. Stevenson (1975), 10 O.R. (2d) 648 (Div. Ct.).

A psychological examination by a person other than a legally qualified medical practitioner was ordered where it was necessary for the formulation of the conclusions of a neurological examination.

Fernandes v. Melo (1975), 6 O.R. (2d) 185 (H.C.).

An examination by a speech therapist may be ordered where an examination by a medical doctor indicates it is necessary.

Gotch v. Chittenden, [1972] 2 O.R. 272, application for leave to appeal refused [1972] 2 O.R. 588 (C.A.).

A psychological examination was ordered where it appeared it would be of assistance to a physician conducting a neurological examination.

Rysyk v. Booth Fisheries Can. Co., [1971] 1 O.R. 123, 14 D.L.R. (3d) 539 (C.A.).

Where a plaintiff alleged brain damage and a neurotic depressive reaction, a psychiatric examination was ordered. See also *Barwick v. Targon*, [1969] 1 O.R. 1 (H.C.).

PROVISION OF INFORMATION TO PARTY OBTAINING ORDER

Interpretation

33.04(1) Subrule 30.01(1) (meaning of "document", "power") applies to subrule (2).

Party to be Examined must Provide Information

(2) The party to be examined shall, unless the court orders otherwise, provide to the party obtaining the order, at least seven days before the examination, a copy of,

(a) any report made by a health practitioner who has treated or examined the party to be examined in respect of the mental or physical condition in question, other than a practitioner whose report was made in preparation for contemplated or pending litigation and for no other purpose, and whom the party to be examined undertakes not to call as a witness at the hearing; and

(b) any hospital record or other medical document relating to the mental or physical condition in question that is in the possession, control or power of the party other than a document made in preparation for contemplated or pending litigation and for no other purpose, and in respect of which the party to be examined undertakes not to call evidence at the hearing.

Zilberg v. Kinsella (1985), 6 C.P.C. (2d) 124 (Ont. Dist. Ct.).

The court refused to order production of the plaintiff's physicians' clinical notes and records under rule 33.04(2)(b). The notes were not in the plaintiff's "possession, control or power". There was no conflict between the plaintiff's evidence and the medical reports to justify production of the clinical records.

WHO MAY ATTEND ON EXAMINATION

33.05 No person other than the person being examined, the examining health practitioner and such assistants as the practitioner requires for the purpose of the examination shall be present at the examination, unless the court orders otherwise.

Barnes (Litigation Guardian of) v. London (City) Board of Education (1994), 34 C.P.C. (3d) 51, 75 O.A.C. 69 (Div. Ct.).

The parents of a plaintiff child under disability were ordered to attend a medical examination and provide information.

Bellamy v. Johnson (1989), 44 C.P.C. (2d) 77 (Ont. Master).

The court authorized plaintiffs to tape record a defence medical examination where the physician who was to conduct the examination was demonstrated to have a "defence orientation".

Simon v. Paslawski (1989), 70 O.R. (2d) 161 (H.C.).

The court refused to permit the plaintiff to tape record a defence medical examination where there was evidence the recording would interfere with the examination.

Jones v. Arnsby (1988), 22 C.P.C. (2d) 48 (Ont. Master), affirmed 29 C.P.C. (2d) 139 at 140 (Ont. H.C.), leave to appeal to Ont. Div. Ct. granted 29 C.P.C. (2d) 139 (appeal was subsequently abandoned).

The party being examined was permitted to tape record the examination.

Taub v. Noble, [1965] 1 O.R. 600, 49 D.L.R.(2d) 106 (H.C.).

The adversary system is sometimes well served by the presence of counsel.

Abbs v. Smith, [1943] O.W.N. 101, [1943] 1 D.L.R. 647 (C.A.).

The court has discretion over the conduct of a medical examination and may order that the solicitor of the party examined attend.

MEDICAL REPORTS

Preparation of Report

33.06(1) After conducting an examination, the examining health practitioner shall prepare a written report setting out his or her observations, the results of any tests made and his or her conclusions, diagnosis and prognosis and shall forthwith provide the report to the party who obtained the order.

Service of Report

(2) The party who obtained the order shall forthwith serve the report on every other party.

Primavera v. Aetna Casualty Co. of Can. (1985), 52 O.R. (2d) 181, 3 C.P.C. (2d) 198 (Master), affirmed 53 O.R. (2d) 495, 13 C.P.C. (2d) xlviii (H.C.).

A report of a defence medical examination conducted under the former Rules of Practice was not required to be produced to the plaintiff.

Davis v. Beatty (1985), 50 C.P.C. 1 (Ont. H.C.).

A report of a medical examination conducted prior to the Rules of Civil Procedure coming into force must be produced.

Stubbs v. Vanier (1985), 50 C.P.C. 7 (Ont. H.C.) (leave to appeal refused May 29, 1985).

It would be unfair to require production of a report of a medical examination conducted prior to the Rules of Civil Procedure coming into force.

PENALTY FOR FAILURE TO COMPLY

33.07 A party who fails to comply with section 105 of the *Courts of Justice Act* or an order made under that section or with rule 33.04 is liable, if a plaintiff or applicant, to have the proceeding dismissed or, if a defendant or respondent, to have the statement of defence or affidavit in response to the application struck out.

EXAMINATION BY CONSENT

33.08 Rules 33.01 to 33.07 apply to a physical or mental examination conducted on the consent in writing of the parties, except to the extent that they are waived by the consent.

Crabtree v. Mackay (1987), 61 O.R. (2d) 669, 25 C.P.C. (2d) 45 (Master).

A plaintiff who consents to a defence medical examination is not entitled to costs. On a motion brought to determine the issue, costs were awarded to the defendant in any event of the cause.

EXAMINATIONS OUT OF COURT

RULE 34　PROCEDURE ON ORAL EXAMINATIONS

Highlights

This is a rule of general application regulating the conduct of all out-of-court oral examinations (these are listed in rule 34.01). The Rule introduced a number of innovations.

Setting up the examination. Examinations may be conducted before either an official examiner or any person agreed upon by the parties: rule 34.02. A person who resides in Ontario is to be examined in his or her county unless otherwise ordered or agreed (rule 34.03) on not less than two days' notice: rule 34.05.

Rule 34.04 regulates who is to be given notice and in what form. Generally a notice of examination may be used, but persons other than parties, or persons to be cross-examined on an affidavit, are to be served personally with a summons to witness together with attendance money: rule 34.04. Rule 34.07 regulates the examination of persons residing outside of Ontario and the issuing of commissions and letters of request. Rule 34.09 spells out who has the responsibility for providing an interpreter.

Rule 34.06 makes specific provision for the holding of examinations on consent, and if the person to be examined and all parties agree, they may make different arrangements than provided in the Rule with regard to the time and place of the examination and the notice to be given.

Conduct of the examination. A party being examined for discovery must bring to the examination all non-privileged documents listed in his or her affidavit of documents or produced by him or her, unless otherwise agreed: rule 34.10(2). On other kinds of examinations, the production of documents must be specifically requested in the notice of examination or summons to witness: rule 34.10(3) and see also rule 30.10(2). Who has the right to re-examine, and the scope thereof, on the various types of examinations is defined: rule 34.11. Where a question is objected to, a brief statement of the reason for the objection is to be recorded (rule 34.12(1)) and it is specifically provided that only the court, and not the official examiner, may rule on the propriety of questions: rule 34.13. A question objected to may be answered with the objector's consent and a ruling obtained from the court before the evidence is used at a hearing: rule 34.12(2). Where an examination is being conducted improperly, it may be adjourned for the purposes of moving for directions as to the continuation or termination of the examination or for an order limiting its scope: rule 34.14.

Transcripts. A transcript of an examination need only be filed if and when it is referred to at a trial, or the day before the hearing of a motion or application: rule 34.18(2) and (4). Since on a motion or application it may be a waste of time and money to file a complete transcript when only a portion is relevant to the matter at hand, by a 1990 amendment, rule 34.18 was changed to permit a party on a motion or application to file a copy of only a portion of the transcript with the other party's consent.

It is specifically provided that the transcript is not to be given to or read by the trial judge until a party refers to it, and that the trial judge may read only those parts referred to by a party: rule 34.18(4). On consent of the parties or by order of the court, an examination may be recorded by videotape or other similar means and the recording may be filed for the use of the court along with the transcript: rule 34.19.

Former Rules: Rules 232, 282, 332, 336-345.

USE OF THE NON-RESIDENT EXAMINATION CHART

The chart deals with the examination of non-residents and indicates how the place of examination is determined, the appropriate form of summoning document and how attendance money is determined.

The chart considers separately the examination of (a) parties, (b) representatives of parties, and (c) other persons who reside outside Ontario. The appropriate column of the chart is determined by which of those three categories the witness falls within. The appropriate row of the chart depends upon whether the examination will occur in or out of Ontario.

For a discussion of the subject see *Elfe Juvenile Products Inc. v. Bern* (1993), 19 C.P.C. (3d) 355 (Ont. Gen. Div.).

NON-RESIDENT EXAMINATION CHART

		Non-resident Party	Non-resident Representative of a Party	Non-resident Person
Place of Examination		Discretionary: rule 34.07(1)(a)	Discretionary: rule 34.07(1)(a)	Discretionary: rule 34.07(1)(a)
In Ontario	Form of summoning document	Notice of examination: rule 34.04(1)	Notice of examination: rule 34.04(1)	Summons under *Interprovincial Summonses Act:* rules 34.04(7) and 53.05
In Ontario	Attendance money	Discretionary: rule 34.07(1)(e)	Discretionary: rule 34.07(1)(e)	Set by *Interprovincial Summonses Act:* rule 34.04(7)
Outside Ontario	Form of summoning document	Letters of request and commission: rule 34.07(2)	Letters of request and commission: rule 34.07(2)	Letters of request and commission: rule 34.07(2)
Outside Ontario	Attendance money	Discretionary: rule 34.07(1)(e)	Discretionary: rule 34.07(1)(e)	Discretionary: rule 34.07(4) and 34.07(1)(e)

APPLICATION OF THE RULE

34.01 Rules 34.02 to 34.19 apply to,

(a) an oral examination for discovery under Rule 31;

(b) the taking of evidence before trial under rule 36.01, subject to rule 36.02;

(c) a cross-examination on an affidavit for use on a motion or application under rule 39.02;

(d) the examination out of court of a witness before the hearing of a pending motion or application under rule 39.03; and

(e) an examination in aid of execution under rule 60.18.

BEFORE WHOM TO BE HELD

34.02 An oral examination to be held in Ontario shall be held,

(a) in the office of, but not necessarily before, an official examiner; or

(b) before any person agreed on by the parties,

at a time and place fixed by the official examiner or person agreed on.

Who May be Present on Examination

K.(G.) v. K.(D.) (1994), 36 C.P.C. (3d) 41 (Ont. Master).

The defendant in this sex abuse case was permitted to be present on the plaintiff's examination for discovery.

Comark Inc. v. King Value Centre Ltd. (1994), 35 C.P.C. (3d) 11 (Ont. Master).

Where the president of the plaintiff corporation could properly inform himself of the issues in the action, the court dismissed the plaintiff's motion to have its director of real estate present at the president's examination for discovery in order to assist.

Lamb v. Percival (1992), 7 O.R. (3d) 775 (Gen. Div.).

The court permitted co-defendants to attend one another's examinations for discovery where there was no particular reason to believe they would tailor their evidence.

Abulnar v. Varity Corp. (1989), 36 C.P.C. (2d) 87 (Ont. H.C.).

A party's foreign counsel has no inherent right to be in attendance on an examination for discovery, and therefore may only attend with leave of the court.

ICC International Computer Consulting & Leasing Ltd. v. ICC Internationale Computer & Consulting GmbH (1988), 66 O.R. (2d) 187, 31 C.P.C. (2d) 178 (H.C.).

A party, including the representative of a corporate party, has an inherent right to attend the examination for discovery of an opposite party unless cause is shown for the court to exercise its discretion to order exclusion.

Piper v. Piper (1988), 65 O.R. (2d) 196, 27 C.P.C. (2d) 170 (Master).

The court refused to permit a husband to be present during his wife's examination for discovery in their divorce action where his presence created the real possibility of intimidation.

Baywood Paper Products Ltd. v. Paymaster Cheque-writers (Can.) Ltd. (1986), 57 O.R. (2d) 229, 13 C.P.C. (2d) 204 (Dist. Ct.).

A party, including a corporate party, has an inherent right to be present at the examination for discovery of an opposite party unless cause is shown to support its exclusion.

Int. Chemalloy Corp. v. Friedman (1983), 33 C.P.C. 264 (Ont. Master).

On examination for discovery in this case, a chartered accountant familiar with the voluminous productions was permitted to be in attendance to assist counsel.

Tridici v. M.E.P.C. Can. Properties Ltd. (1978), 22 O.R. (2d) 319, 8 C.P.C. 212 (H.C.).

Where issues of technical difficulty were involved, an expert was permitted to attend the discovery to assist counsel.

Miles v. Miles, [1960] O.W.N. 57 (H.C.).
On the examination of a defendant the court permitted a co-defendant to be present to assist with documents.

Black v. Whatmough, [1955] O.W.N. 666 (Master).
An agent of the plaintiffs having intimate knowledge of the case was allowed to be present on the examination for discovery of the defendant to assist counsel.

Hofstetter v. Jones, [1950] O.W.N. 837 (H.C.).
The special examiner's discretion to exclude persons from his office during an examination will not be interfered with unless it can be shown that he exercised his discretion improperly or on a wrong principle.

Necessity of Official Examiner

Kenlinton Plaza v. 466740 Ontario Ltd. (1992), 8 O.R. (3d) 26, 9 C.P.C. (3d) 152 (Gen. Div.).
Oral examinations must take place at the office of an official examiner, unless the parties agree otherwise.

PLACE OF EXAMINATION

34.03 Where the person to be examined resides in Ontario, the examination shall take place in the county in which the person resides, unless the court orders or the person to be examined and all the parties agree otherwise.

Davis v. Howse (1982), 27 C.P.C. 319 (Ont. H.C.).
Although the plaintiff maintained an apartment in one county for business needs, he was ordered to re-attend for discovery in the county where his family resided and where he was frequently present.

HOW ATTENDANCE REQUIRED

Party
34.04(1) Where the person to be examined is a party to the proceeding, a notice of examination (Form 34A) shall be served,
(a) on the party's solicitor of record; or
(b) where the party acts in person, on the party, personally or by an alternative to personal service.

[*Authors' Comment:* Despite rule 34.04(1)(a), a notice of examination in aid of execution may not be served on the solicitor of record. See rule 60.18(7).]

Person Examined on Behalf or in Place of Party
(2) Where a person is to be examined for discovery or in aid of execution on behalf or in place of a party, a notice of examination shall be served,
(a) on the party's solicitor of record; or
(b) on the person to be examined, personally and not by an alternative to personal service.

Deponent of Affidavit
(3) Where a person is to be cross-examined on an affidavit, a notice of examination shall be served,

(a) on the solicitor for the party who filed the affidavit; or

(b) where the party who filed the affidavit acts in person, on the person to be cross-examined, personally and not by an alternative to personal service.

Others

(4) Where the person to be examined,

(a) is neither a party nor a person referred to in subrule (2) or (3); and

(b) resides in Ontario,

the person shall be served with a summons to witness (Form 34B), personally and not by an alternative to personal service.

Attendance Money

(5) When a summons to witness is served on a witness, attendance money calculated in accordance with Tariff A shall be paid or tendered to the witness at the same time.

Summons May be Issued in Blank

(6) On the request of a party or a solicitor and on payment of the prescribed fee, a registrar shall sign, seal and issue a blank summons to witness and the party or solicitor may complete the summons and insert the names of any number of witnesses.

Person outside Ontario

(7) Rule 53.05 (summons to a witness outside Ontario) applies to the securing of the attendance for examination of a person outside Ontario and the attendance money paid or tendered to the person shall be calculated in accordance with the *Interprovincial Summonses Act.*

Person in Custody

(8) Rule 53.06 (compelling attendance of witness in custody) applies to the securing of the attendance for examination of a person in custody. [am. O. Reg. 739/94, s. 2]

Sequence of Examinations (See also rule 31.04.)

Scarlett v. Clarke (1987), 25 C.P.C. (2d) 171 (Ont. Master).

Unlike examinations for discovery, on cross-examinations on affidavits there is no general rule that a party is entitled to complete his or her examination before another examination can proceed.

Herlick v. Smookler (1984), 41 C.P.C. 146 (Ont. Master).

Where the plaintiffs' solicitor was the prime mover in attempting to get discoveries commenced, and the defendants' solicitor attempted to take unfair advantage by serving an appointment first which was not returnable within a reasonable time, the appointment was struck and the plaintiffs were permitted to examine first.

Bye v. Hulin (1984), 40 C.P.C. 358 (Ont. Master).

Where there are numerous counsel and parties whose schedules are to be accommodated, the use of an appointment to obtain a scheduling advantage is not to be encouraged. The preferable order in which discoveries should proceed is the same as the order of pleadings, so the plaintiff is examined first, then the defendants, and lastly the third party. [*But see now rule 31.04(3) — Authors.*]

Scott Transport Ltd. v. Bondy (1974), 1 O.R. (2d) 447 (Master).
The party which serves a notice of appointment first is entitled to complete its examination before any examination by the opposing party.

S. Reichmann & Sons Ltd. & Co. v. The Ambassador (No. 2), [1967] 1 O.R. 538 (H.C.).
The master has jurisdiction to strike out an appointment.

Avery v. Avery, [1954] O.W.N. 364 (H.C.).
Discussion of sequence of examinations.

Attendance Money — rule 34.04(5)

Agristor Credit Corp. Can. v. Rader (1989), 68 O.R. (2d) 281, 34 C.P.C. (2d) 30 (H.C.).
The court may not reduce the attendance money required for a non-party by rule 34.04(7), but does have a discretion regarding attendance money for a party.

Simpsons-Sears Ltd. v. Kitaresku, [1972] 3 O.R. 440 (Co. Ct.).
"Conduct money" includes travelling and living expenses and a fee for daily attendance. [*And see now Tariff A, item 21 — Authors.*]

AGREEMENT TO EXAMINATION BEFORE PERSON OTHER THAN OFFICIAL EXAMINER

34.04.1(1) A person who is served with a notice of examination or summons to witness for an examination before a person who is not an official examiner shall be deemed to have agreed on the person before whom the examination is to be held unless he or she serves notice of refusal of agreement within two days after service of the notice or summons.

(2) An agreement or deemed agreement on a person before whom the examination is to be held may not be withdrawn except by consent of the parties or leave of the court. [en. O. Reg. 535/92, s. 8]

NOTICE OF TIME AND PLACE

Person to be Examined
34.05(1) Where the person to be examined resides in Ontario, he or she shall be given not less than two days notice of the time and place of the examination, unless the court orders otherwise.

Every Other Party
(2) Every party to the proceeding other than the examining party shall be given not less than two days notice of the time and place of the examination.

Firestone v. Firestone (1975), 6 O.R. (2d) 714, 20 R.F.L. 315 (H.C.).
An examination may take place on a holiday only with the consent of the parties or by order of the court.

EXAMINATIONS ON CONSENT

34.06 A person to be examined and all the parties may consent to the time and place of the examination and,

(a) to the minimum notice period and the form of notice; or

(b) to dispense with notice.

WHERE PERSON TO BE EXAMINED RESIDES OUTSIDE ONTARIO

Contents of Order for Examination

34.07(1) Where the person to be examined resides outside Ontario, the court may determine,

(a) whether the examination is to take place in or outside Ontario;

(b) the time and place of the examination;

(c) the minimum notice period;

(d) the person before whom the examination is to be conducted;

(e) the amount of attendance money to be paid to the person to be examined; and

(f) any other matter respecting the holding of the examination.

Commission and Letter of Request

(2) Where the person is to be examined outside Ontario, the order under subrule (1) shall be in (Form 34E) and shall, if the moving party requests it, provide for the issuing of,

(a) a commission (Form 34C) authorizing the taking of evidence before a named commissioner; and

(b) a letter of request (Form 34D) directed to the judicial authorities of the jurisdiction in which the person is to be found, requesting the issuing of such process as is necessary to compel the person to attend and be examined before the commissioner.

(3) The commission and letter of request shall be prepared and issued by the registrar.

Attendance Money

(4) Where the person to be examined resides outside Ontario and is not a party or a person to be examined on behalf or in place of a party, the examining party shall pay or tender to the person to be examined the amount of attendance money fixed by the order under subrule (1).

Duties of Commissioner

(5) A commissioner shall, to the extent that it is possible to do so, conduct the examination in the form of oral questions and answers in accordance with these rules, the law of evidence of Ontario and the terms of the commission, unless some other form of examination is required by the order or the law of the place where the examination is conducted.

(6) As soon as the transcript of the examination is prepared, the commissioner shall,

(a) return the commission, together with the original transcript and exhibits, to the registrar who issued it;

(b) keep a copy of the transcript and, where practicable, the exhibits; and

(c) notify the parties who appeared at the examination that the transcript is complete and has been returned to the registrar who issued the commission.

Examining Party to Serve Transcript

(7) The registrar shall send the transcript to the solicitor for the examining party and the solicitor shall forthwith serve every other party with the transcript free of charge.

Examination of Non-Resident

Praendex Inc. v. Gump (1992), 8 C.P.C. (3d) 332 (Ont. Master).

The court ordered that a non-resident witness, who was an officer of the plaintiff, be produced for examination in Ontario under rule 39.03. Issuance of a commission and letter of request was not necesssary since the witness was an officer of the plaintiff.

Royal Bank v. 55 Dennison Road East Properties Ltd. (1991), 46 C.P.C. (2d) 120 (Ont Gen. Div.).

Where the evidence of a non-resident non-party witness is sought for the purpose of a motion, it is not proper to use a notice of examination. Rather, the proper procedure is to issue a certificate under the *Interprovincial Subpoenas Act*, R.S.O. 1980, c. 220.

Ontario (Securities Commission) v. Bennett (1990), 72 O.R. (2d) 77, 66 D.L.R. (4th) 756, 13 O.S.C.B. 506 (H.C.), affirmed (1991), 1 O.R. (3d) 576, 77 D.L.R. (4th) 576 (C.A.).

In the absence of statutory authority the court has no power to appoint a commissioner to take evidence outside the province. Rules 34.01 and 34.07 are inapplicable to proceedings before an administrative tribunal since they are limited to "proceedings in court".

Agristor Credit Corp. Can. v. Rader (1989), 68 O.R. (2d) 281, 34 C.P.C. (2d) 30 (H.C.).

The master properly exercised his discretion when he ordered the third party to produce its representative, a resident of the United States, for examination for discovery in Toronto. The costs were to be shared equally by the third party and the defendants.

Kaighin Capital Inc. v. Cdn. National Sportsmen's Shows (1987), 58 O.R. (2d) 790, 17 C.P.C. (2d) 59 (H.C.).

The examining party must pay attendance money to a non-resident being cross-examined on an affidavit. "A person to be examined on behalf of or in place of a party" refers to a representative being examined for discovery or in aid of execution or perhaps for the purpose of taking evidence before trial under Rule 36. It does not generally include the deponent of an affidavit.

Re Quinn (1986), 12 C.P.C. (2d) 315, 61 C.B.R. (N.S.) 284 (Ont. S.C.).

The Registrar in Bankruptcy has jurisdiction under rule 34.07 to determine where a non-resident creditor is to be cross-examined on an affidavit of verification.

Beauclaire v. Pizzaro (1986), 9 C.P.C. (2d) 164 (Ont. Master).

The court ordered a resident party to pay the travelling expenses of a non-resident party to attend in Ontario for examination for discovery.

Kohli v. Anand (1986), 54 O.R. (2d) 506, 18 C.P.C. (2d) 101 (Master).

Where non-resident plaintiffs were shown to be impecunious and unable to meet the expense of travelling to Toronto for examinations for discovery, their discovery was ordered to take place before a commissioner in their place of residence.

Husky Oil Marketing Ltd. v. Chalet Oil Ltd. (1982), 31 C.P.C. 156 (Ont. H.C.).

The court ordered the examining party to pay a portion of the witness's transportation costs to attend in Ontario.

Aviation Traders (Engineering) Ltd. v. Price Waterhouse Ltd. (1982), 26 C.P.C. 157 (Ont. Master).

A non-resident witness was ordered to be examined in Ontario without the necessity of attendance money.

Yaeger v. Lavooy (1980), 16 C.P.C. 224 (Ont. Co. Ct.).

The defendant, who was in England, was ordered to attend in Toronto for discovery upon payment of part of his travelling expenses by the plaintiff.

G.C.C. Ltd. v. Thunder Bay (1980), 16 C.P.C. 15 (Ont. Master), reversed on other grounds (1981), 32 O.R. (2d) 111, 20 C.P.C. 276 (Ont. H.C.).

Consideration of factors in determining place of the examination where the witness resides out of Ontario.

Bigue v. Stromberg Time of Can. Ltd. (1976), 10 O.R. (2d) 456 (H.C.).

An officer being examined on behalf of a corporation was allowed conduct money based on travel from the Toronto head office rather than from his Connecticut residence.

Crooks v. Janzen Plumbing & Heating Ltd., [1968] 1 O.R. 455 (H.C.).

The court should not specify the penalty for failure to attend in an order directing discovery.

Groner v. Lake Ontario Portland Cement Co., [1958] O.W.N. 469 (Master).

A non-resident plaintiff was required to be examined in Ontario because of the preponderant balance of convenience but the defendant was required either to post security for two-thirds of the travelling expenses or to pay one-third outright.

Sharpe v. Price, [1945] O.W.N. 710 (Master).

The master discussed the factors to be taken into account when determining where a person who resides out of Ontario should be examined.

Dow v. Brady, [1944] O.W.N. 633 (Ont. Master).

Where a non-resident was injured in Ontario and then returned to Calgary, the examination for discovery was held in Calgary.

Residence of Witness

Pershadsingh v. Pershadsingh (1984), 45 C.P.C. 86 (Ont. Master).

A party holding landed immigrant status in Canada, having spent some considerable time in Ontario, and only out of Ontario to wind up his business affairs before moving finally to Ontario, was held to reside in Ontario for the purpose of the predecessor of this provision. Failure to object to examination in Ontario until the third defaulted appointment amounts to a waiver of this issue.

PERSON TO BE EXAMINED TO BE SWORN

34.08(1) Before being examined, the person to be examined shall take an oath or make an affirmation and, where the examination is conducted in Ontario, the oath or affirmation shall be administered by an official examiner or by a person authorized to administer oaths in Ontario.

(2) Where the examination is conducted outside Ontario, the oath or affirmation may be administered by the person before whom the examination

is conducted, a person authorized to administer oaths in Ontario or a person authorized to take affidavits or administer oaths or affirmations in the jurisdiction where the examination is conducted.

INTERPRETER

34.09(1) Where the person to be examined does not understand the language or languages in which the examination is to be conducted or is deaf or mute, a competent and independent interpreter shall, before the person is examined, take an oath or make an affirmation to interpret accurately the administration of the oath or affirmation and the questions to and answers of the person being examined.

(2) Where an interpreter is required by subrule (1) for the examination of,

(a) a party or a person on behalf or in place of a party, the party shall provide the interpreter;

(b) any other person, the examining party shall provide the interpreter, unless the interpretation is from English to French or from French to English and an interpreter is provided by the Ministry of the Attorney General.

Pink v. Kloss (1983), 34 C.P.C. 264 (Ont. Master).

The party being examined must supply any necessary interpreter and may, if awarded costs, recover an allowance for the fees of the interpreter.

Buccella v. Moran, [1959] O.W.N. 351 (Master).

Where there was a possibility that the interpreter would not be strictly neutral, an interpreter provided by the special examiner was used.

PRODUCTION OF DOCUMENTS ON EXAMINATION

Interpretation

34.10(1) Subrule 30.01(1) (meaning of "document", "power") applies to subrules (2), (3) and (4).

Person to be Examined Must Bring Required Documents and Things

(2) The person to be examined shall bring to the examination and produce for inspection,

(a) on an examination for discovery, all documents in his or her possession, control or power that are not privileged and that subrule 30.04(4) requires the person to bring; and

(b) on any examination, including an examination for discovery, all documents and things in his or her possession, control or power that are not privileged and that the notice of examination or summons to witness requires the person to bring.

Notice or Summons May Require Documents and Things

(3) Unless the court orders otherwise, the notice of examination or summons to witness may require the person to be examined to bring to the examination and produce for inspection,

(a) all documents and things relating to any matter in issue in the proceeding that are in his or her possession, control or power and are not privileged; or

(b) such documents or things described in clause (a) as are specified in the notice or summons.

Duty to Produce Other Documents

(4) Where a person admits, on an examination, that he or she has possession or control of or power over any other document that relates to a matter in issue in the proceeding and is not privileged, the person shall produce it for inspection by the examining party forthwith, if the person has the document at the examination, and if not, within two days thereafter, unless the court orders otherwise.

Glowinsky v. Stephens & Rankin Inc. (1989), 38 C.P.C. (2d) 102 (Ont. Master).

An undertaking to produce documents with respect to one aspect of a claim will be enforced even if the underlying claim is subsequently abandoned, unless all parties reach an agreement to the contrary.

Royal Bank of Can. v. Ont. Securities Comm. (1976), 14 O.R. (2d) 783, 2 C.P.C. 132 (H.C.).

Where a witness objects to producing documents he should appear and make such objections under oath and not on a preliminary motion.

Rule-Bilt Ltd. v. Shenkman Corp. (1977), 18 O.R. (2d) 276, 4 C.P.C. 256 (Master).

Where there are voluminous productions, it is proper to ask the witness which productions are relied upon in support of an allegation in the pleadings.

RE-EXAMINATION

On Examination for Discovery

34.11(1) A person being examined for discovery may be re-examined by his or her own counsel and by any party adverse in interest to the examining party.

On Cross-Examination on Affidavit or Examination in Aid of Execution

(2) A person being cross-examined on an affidavit or examined in aid of execution may be re-examined by his or her own counsel.

Timing and Form

(3) The re-examination shall take place immediately after the examination or cross-examination and shall not take the form of a cross-examination.

On Examination for Motion or Application

(4) Re-examination of a witness examined,

(a) before the hearing of a motion or application, is governed by subrule 39.03(2); and

(b) at the hearing of a motion or application, is governed by subrule 39.03(4).

On Examination Before Trial

(5) Re-examination of a witness examined before trial under Rule 36 is governed by subrule 36.02(2).

OBJECTIONS AND RULINGS

34.12(1) Where a question is objected to, the objector shall state briefly the reason for the objection, and the question and the brief statement shall be recorded.

(2) A question that is objected to may be answered with the objector's consent, and where the question is answered, a ruling shall be obtained from the court before the evidence is used at a hearing.

(3) A ruling on the propriety of a question that is objected to and not answered may be obtained on motion to the court.

Kay v. Posluns (1989), 71 O.R. (2d) 238, additional reasons (February 1, 1991), Doc. No. Toronto 26686/88 (H.C.).

If objection is taken to a question, an argument should not ensue on the record. It should be dealt with in accordance with rule 34.12.

Del Zotto v. Canadian Newspapers Co. (1988), 65 O.R. (2d) 594, 28 C.P.C. (2d) 165, 45 C.C.L.T. 225 (Master).

Where a disagreement arose as to the scope of discovery, the parties set out their positions on the record and a motion was brought for directions as to the scope of discovery before any questions were asked; while observing that this was a procedure that should be followed only in rare cases, because of the danger of making rulings in the abstract, the court gave directions in this case.

RULINGS BY OFFICIAL EXAMINER

34.13 An official examiner may make rulings in respect of the conduct of an examination, other than a ruling on the propriety of a question, but an examiner's ruling is subject to review on a motion to set aside or vary the ruling.

Hofstetter v. Jones, [1950] O.W.N. 837 (H.C.).

The special examiner's discretion to exclude persons from his office during an examination will not be interfered with unless it can be shown that he exercised his discretion improperly or on a wrong principle.

IMPROPER CONDUCT OF EXAMINATION

Adjournment to Seek Directions

34.14(1) An examination may be adjourned by the person being examined or by a party present or represented at the examination, for the purpose of moving for directions with respect to the continuation of the examination or for an order terminating the examination or limiting its scope, where,

(a) the right to examine is being abused by an excess of improper questions or interfered with by an excess of improper interruptions or objections;

(b) the examination is being conducted in bad faith, or in an unreasonable manner so as to annoy, embarrass or oppress the person being examined;

(c) many of the answers to the questions are evasive, unresponsive or unduly lengthy; or

(d) there has been a neglect or improper refusal to produce a relevant document on the examination.

Sanctions for Improper Conduct or Adjournment

(2) Where the court finds that,

(a) a person's improper conduct necessitated a motion under subrule (1); or

(b) a person improperly adjourned an examination under subrule (1), the court may order the person to pay personally and forthwith the costs of the motion, any costs thrown away and the costs of any continuation of the examination and the court may fix the costs and make such other order as is just.

Kay v. Posluns (1989), 71 O.R. (2d) 238, additional reasons (February 1, 1991), Doc. No. Toronto 26686/88 (H.C.).

(1) Counsel for a witness being examined for discovery may not answer the question for the witness, unless there is no objection, even if the witness's answer is wrong; the witness's counsel may re-examine to try to correct the answer or may correct the answer after completion of the examination pursuant to rule 31.09. (2) Interruptions by counsel may be necessary so that he or she may find the relevant document involved in the question or so he or she can understand the question and in principle this is quite proper.

413528 Ont. Ltd. v. 951 Wilson Avenue Inc. (1989), 71 O.R. (2d) 40, 42 C.P.C. (2d) 78 (Master).

Counsel for a witness being cross-examined on an affidavit may not discuss with the witness during any recess or adjournment the evidence which has already been given or to be given. When the examination is completed subject to undertakings counsel may communicate with the witness.

Hall v. Youngson (1989), 39 C.P.C. (2d) 149 (Ont. Master).

The court ordered a fresh examination where on the first examination counsel for the party being examined had wrongfully interfered with the examination by an excess of improper interruptions, objections and argument.

Peel Condominium Corp. No. 199 v. Ont. New Home Warranties Plan (1988), 30 C.P.C. (2d) 118, 32 O.A.C. 1 (Div. Ct.).

On a cross-examination, a witness should not be harassed by repetitive questions on the same subject when he has already given his answer and should not be asked to state his opinion on a point of law, although the questioner is entitled to know the position of the opposite party on the issues of the proceeding.

Eversonic Inc. v. MacGirr (1987), 19 C.P.C. (2d) 209 (Ont. H.C.).

There is no rule of general application as to when an answer becomes unduly lengthy, and considerable latitude must be given to the witness.

McLeod v. Cdn. Newspapers Co. (1987), 58 O.R. (2d) 721, 15 C.P.C. (2d) 151 (Master).

During the examination the solicitor for the witness being examined should not engage in private communications with the witness as to whether a question should be answered, how it should be answered, or the manner in which the witness is giving her testimony.

Kingsberg Developments Ltd. v. MacLean (1985), 3 C.P.C. (2d) 241 (Ont. Master).

Rule 34.14 is not intended to permit a motion for a general ruling regarding a legitimate disagreement between counsel as to the scope of examination. Rather the examination should proceed and a motion should be brought regarding the specific questions in dispute.

Sonntag v. Sonntag (1979), 24 O.R. (2d) 473, 11 C.P.C. 13 (H.C.).

A solicitor was ordered to pay the costs of an aborted examination where his conduct had unduly interfered with the examination.

Burndy Can. Ltd. v. Brown (1978), 5 C.P.C. 266 (Ont. H.C.).

The court may order a cross-examination to be conditional upon examining counsel undertaking to maintain the confidentiality of information obtained thereby, and may restrict a party's right to attend.

SANCTIONS FOR DEFAULT OR MISCONDUCT BY PERSON TO BE EXAMINED

34.15(1) Where a person fails to attend at the time and place fixed for an examination in the notice of examination or summons to witness or at the time and place agreed on by the parties, or refuses to take an oath or make an affirmation, to answer any proper question, to produce a document or thing that he or she is required to produce or to comply with an order under rule 34.14, the court may,

(a) where an objection to a question is held to be improper, order or permit the person being examined to reattend at his or her own expense and answer the question, in which case the person shall also answer any proper questions arising from the answer;

(b) where the person is a party or, on an examination for discovery, a person examined on behalf or in place of a party, dismiss the party's proceeding or strike out the party's defence;

(c) strike out all or part of the person's evidence, including any affidavit made by the person; and

(d) make such other order as is just.

(2) Where a person does not comply with an order under rule 34.14 or subrule (1), a judge may make a contempt order against the person.

Ordering Re-Attendance — rule 34.15(1)(a)

Royal Bank v. 55 Dennison Road East Properties Ltd. (1991), 46 C.P.C. (2d) 120 (Ont. Gen. Div.).

Where the defendant's affiant failed to attend for cross-examination on his affidavit, the court refused to strike out the statement of defence, but ordered the witness to attend to be cross-examined and to pay costs.

Union Industries Inc. v. Beckett Packaging Ltd. (1988), 10 W.D.C.P. 377 (Ont. Master).

The court declined to enforce an undertaking given on the basis of a mutual mistake of fact.

S.E. Lyons & Son Ltd. v. Nawoc Holdings Ltd. (1978), 20 O.R. (2d) 234, 7 C.P.C. 10, affirmed 23 O.R. (2d) 727n (H.C.).

A party can insist that an undertaking be fulfilled by re-attendance rather than correspondence.

Toronto v. Zec (1982), 35 C.P.C. 229 (Ont. Master).

The master has no jurisdiction to order a witness examined in respect of a pending motion to re-attend to answer questions refused on the examination as he has no power to enforce the order.

Tan v. Solomon (1982), 24 C.P.C. 275 (Ont. Master).

Where the plaintiff, a pedestrian in a motor vehicle case, had made an allegation of negligence but refused to supply particulars of the negligence when asked on discovery, an order was made for re-attendance.

Borins v. Honest Ed's Ltd. (1980), 29 O.R. (2d) 79, 17 C.P.C. 207, 112 D.L.R. (3d) 190 (H.C.).

Failure to seek an order striking out the corporate defendant's pleading in the alternative to re-attendance does not affect the master's jurisdiction to order an officer to re-attend.

Dismissing Action or Striking Out Defence for Non-Attendance — rule 34.15(1)(b)

Landry v. Pollock (1995), 7 W.D.C.P. (2d) 17 (Ont. C.A.).

The Court of Appeal set aside an order dismissing an action for failure to fulfill undertakings.

Chiaravalle v. Lloyds Non-Marine Underwriters (1994), 34 C.P.C. (3d) 183 (Ont. Gen. Div.).

Where the defendant had failed to comply with an order to answer undertakings, the court ordered the defendant to do so within 16 days, failing which the statement of defence would be struck out.

James Sturino Realty Ltd. v. Andrew Michaels Group Ltd. (1988), 64 O.R. (2d) 410, 28 O.A.C. 354 (Div. Ct.).

Where the defendants repeatedly failed to fulfill undertakings, their defence was struck out and the plaintiff obtained default judgment. A motion by the defendants to set aside the default judgment was dismissed.

Anlagen und Treuhand Contor GMBH v. Int. Chemalloy Corp. (1982), 27 C.P.C. 195 (Ont. C.A.).

An action was not dismissed for failure to attend for examination for discovery where the failure to attend arose through the inadvertence of counsel and the action was not completely without merit.

Van Kooten v. Doy (1980), 31 O.R. (2d) 247, 20 C.P.C. 32 (H.C.).

Where the action was being defended pursuant to the *Motor Vehicle Accident Claims Act*, the defence was not struck out where the Minister was unable to produce a defaulting defendant for discovery.

Chisholm v. Chisholm (1974), 2 O.R. (2d) 535 (Div. Ct.).

The court set aside an order dismissing an alimony action due to the plaintiff's failure to attend an examination for discovery where the plaintiff appeared to have a valid medical excuse.

Breslin v. Whalen, [1970] 3 O.R. 562 (Master).

A third party action was dismissed because the defendant failed to attend for examination and notwithstanding that the defence and third party proceedings were being conducted under the *Motor Vehicles Accident Claims Act*, S.O. 1961-62, c. 84.

Crooks v. Janzen Plumbing & Heating Ltd., [1968] 1 O.R. 455 (H.C.).

A defence may not be struck out for failure to attend where the action is being defended under the *Motor Vehicle Accident Claims Act*, S.O. 1961-62, c. 84.

Other Sanctions — rule 34.15 (1)(d)

Snelgrove v. Steinberg Inc. (1995), 85 O.A.C. 365 (C.A.).

Where the plaintiff was severely prejudiced by the defendant's inaccurate, incomplete and late disclosure and non-disclosure of relevant information, the court ordered a new trial.

Process Industrial Co. v. G.R.W. Industries (1985) Ltd. (1992), 6 C.P.C. (3d) 264 (Ont. Gen. Div.).

Where a defendant refused to answer proper discovery questions in the face of an order to do so, which also provided judgment would go for the plaintiff on default, the court granted judgment for the plaintiff.

EXAMINATION TO BE RECORDED

34.16 Every examination shall be recorded in its entirety in question and answer form in a manner that permits the preparation of a typewritten transcript of the examination, unless the court orders or the parties agree otherwise.

TYPEWRITTEN TRANSCRIPT

34.17(1) Where a party so requests, the official examiner or person who recorded an examination shall have a typewritten transcript of the examination prepared and completed within four weeks after receipt of the request.

(2) The transcript shall be certified as correct by the person who recorded the examination, but need not be read to or signed by the person examined.

(3) As soon as the transcript is prepared, the official examiner or person who recorded the examination shall send one copy to each party who has ordered and paid for a transcript and, if a party so requests and pays for it, shall provide an additional copy for the use of the court.

FILING OF TRANSCRIPT

Party to Have Transcript Available

34.18(1) It is the responsibility of a party who intends to refer to evidence given on an examination to have a copy of the transcript of the examination available for filing with the court.

Filing for Use on Motion or Application

(2) Where a party intends to refer to a transcript on the hearing of a motion or application, a copy of the transcript for the use of the court shall be filed in the court office where the motion or application is to be heard, not later than 2 p.m. on the day before the hearing.

(3) The party may file a copy of a portion of the transcript if the other parties consent.

Filing for Use at Trial

(4) A copy of a transcript for the use of the court at trial shall not be filed until a party refers to it at trial, and the trial judge may read only the portions to which a party refers.

VIDEOTAPING OR OTHER RECORDING OF EXAMINATION

34.19(1) On consent of the parties or by order of the court, an examination may be recorded by videotape or other similar means and the tape or other recording may be filed for the use of the court along with the transcript.

(2) Rule 34.18 applies, with necessary modifications, to a tape or other recording made under subrule (1).

Kay v. Posluns (1989), 71 O.R. (2d) 238, additional reasons (February 1, 1991), Doc. No. Toronto 26686/88 (H.C.).

An order for videotaping of an examination for discovery should be granted only in rare cases and was refused where the plaintiff complained that the defendant's counsel was conducting himself improperly through making unnecessary objections.

Attica Invt. Inc. v. Gagnon (1984), 47 C.P.C. 316 (Ont. Master).

The court ordered an examination *de bene esse* to be recorded on videotape.

RULE 35   PROCEDURE ON EXAMINATION FOR DISCOVERY BY WRITTEN QUESTIONS

Highlights

This Rule is entirely new — under the former practice examination for discovery could be conducted only by means of an oral examination. Rule 31.02(1) provides that a party may not be examined by both written questions and an oral examination, except with leave of court. This provision was included to avoid the United States practice of "two waves of discovery" — first examining a party by written questions and then following up with a second, oral examination. Note also that where more than one party is entitled to examine a person it must be by oral examination, unless all the parties entitled to examine agree otherwise: rule 31.02(2).

As a discovery mechanism, an examination by written questions is usually considered to be less effective than an oral examination, because the answers are often drafted by opposing counsel rather than being the immediate responses of the party personally, and because it is less easy to quickly follow up on a newly discovered line of questions (but note rule 35.04(1)). However, an examination by written questions may be useful, for example, where the witness is not readily accessible, the questions sought to be asked are straightforward, and an opportunity to assess the quality of the witness is not important.

Former provisions: None.

QUESTIONS

35.01 An examination for discovery by written questions and answers shall be conducted by serving a list of the questions to be answered (Form 35A) on the person to be examined and every other party.

ANSWERS

35.02(1) Written questions shall be answered by the affidavit (Form 35B) of the person being examined, served on the examining party within fifteen days after service of the list of questions.

(2) The examining party shall serve the answers on every other party forthwith.

OBJECTIONS

35.03 An objection to answering a written question shall be made in the affidavit of the person being examined, with a brief statement of the reason for the objection.

FAILURE TO ANSWER

Further List of Questions
35.04(1) Where the examining party is not satisfied with an answer or where an answer suggests a new line of questioning, the examining party

may, within ten days after receiving the answer, serve a further list of written questions which shall be answered within fifteen days after service.

Court Order for Further Answers

(2) Where the person being examined refuses or fails to answer a proper question or where the answer to a question is insufficient, the court may order the person to answer or give a further answer to the question or to answer any other question either by affidavit or on oral examination.

Court Order for Oral Examination

(3) Where the court is satisfied, on reading all the answers to the written questions, that some or all of them are evasive, unresponsive or otherwise unsatisfactory, the court may order the person examined to submit to oral examination on such terms respecting costs and other matters as are just.

Additional Sanctions

(4) Where a person refuses or fails to answer a proper question on a written examination or to produce a document that he or she is required to produce, the court may, in addition to imposing the sanctions provided in subrules (2) and (3),

    (a) if the person is a party or a person examined on behalf or in place of a party, dismiss the party's action or strike out the party's defence;

    (b) strike out all or part of the person's evidence; and

    (c) make such other order as is just.

Love v. Mixing Equipment Co. (1986), 10 C.P.C. (2d) 237 (Ont. Master).

A party is entitled to ask further questions only if they are related to the initial list of questions.

IMPROPER CONDUCT OF EXAMINATION

35.05 On motion by the person being examined, or by any party, the court may terminate the written examination or limit its scope where,

    (a) the right to examine is being abused by an excess of improper questions; or

    (b) the examination is being conducted in bad faith, or in an unreasonable manner so as to annoy, embarrass or oppress the person being examined.

FILING QUESTIONS AND ANSWERS

35.06 Rule 34.18 applies, with necessary modifications, to the filing of written questions and answers for the use of the court.

RULE 36   TAKING EVIDENCE BEFORE TRIAL

Highlights

This Rule authorizes the taking of evidence before trial, both in and outside Ontario, for use at the trial. This is not a discovery device, but the actual taking of evidence in lieu of calling the witness at trial. The Rule replaced the former procedure of taking evidence *de bene esse* or on commission, and involved a number of important changes.

A person may be examined for the purposes of having his or her testimony available to be tendered as evidence at the trial, either by leave of the court or on consent of the parties: rule 36.01(1). The grounds upon which the court may make such an order are considerably broadened (rule 36.01(2)) and are no longer limited to situations where it can be established that, at the time of trial, the witness will likely be out of the jurisdiction or incapable of testifying, *e.g.* the convenience of the witness or the saving of costs may be sufficient grounds for an order.

Where the person to be examined is an expert, before moving for leave, the moving party must provide to every other party a copy of the expert's report, unless the court otherwise orders: rule 36.01(3).

The procedure for the examination is regulated by Rule 34, except that the witness is to be examined, cross-examined and re-examined as at trial: rule 36.02. The examination may be videotaped (rule 34.19) and since it is likely that the examination will be used at trial in lieu of calling the witness, this is highly desirable: see *Wright v. Whiteside* (1983), 40 O.R. (2d) 732, 34 C.P.C. 91 at 95 (H.C.).

Where the court makes an order for the examination of a witness out of Ontario, if the moving party so requests, the order shall provide for a letter of request enabling the assistance of the foreign court to be sought to compel the attendance of the witness: rule 36.03. This is a beneficial change in the law which formerly required that it must first be established that the witness will not voluntarily attend the examination (which could be difficult to prove without first making a trip to the foreign country).

The principles governing the use of such examinations at trial have been changed. Formerly, before the examination could be used, leave of court had to be obtained and this required establishing that the witness was presently unavailable or incapable of attending the trial. Now, by rule 36.04, the transcript or videotape of the examination of a witness who is not a "party" as defined by rule 36.04(1) may be used, unless the court orders otherwise, and the witness shall not be called to give evidence at trial except with leave. Use of the transcript or videotape of the examination of a witness who is a "party" requires leave of the court or consent of the parties: rule 36.04(4).

Related case law. Although not specifically dealt with by the Rules, cases regarding incoming letters rogatory are collected under rule 36.03.

Former Rules: Rules 270, 276-289.

WHERE AVAILABLE

By Consent or by Order

36.01(1) A party who intends to introduce the evidence of a person at trial may, with leave of the court or the consent of the parties, examine the

person on oath or affirmation before trial for the purpose of having the person's testimony available to be tendered as evidence at the trial.

Discretion of Court

(2) In exercising its discretion to order an examination under subrule (1), the court shall take into account,

(a) the convenience of the person whom the party seeks to examine;

(b) the possibility that the person will be unavailable to testify at the trial by reason of death, infirmity or sickness;

(c) the possibility that the person will be beyond the jurisdiction of the court at the time of the trial;

(d) the expense of bringing the person to the trial;

(e) whether the witness ought to give evidence in person at the trial; and

(f) any other relevant consideration.

Expert Witness

(3) Before moving for leave to examine an expert witness under subrule (1), the moving party shall serve on every other party the report of the expert witness referred to in subrule 53.03(1) (calling expert witness at trial) unless the court orders otherwise.

Walker v. York Finch Hospital (1992), 15 C.P.C. (3d) 23, additional reasons (1993), 15 C.P.C. (3d) 23 at 29 (Ont. Gen. Div.).

An order was issued restraining the telecast of a videotape of the examination of a witness under Rule 36. Such use breached an implied undertaking not to use the examination for any purpose other than for the purpose for which it was produced and would have made any subsequent order excluding witnesses under rule 52.06(1) meaningless.

Proietti v. Raisauda (1992), 7 C.P.C. (3d) 11 (Ont. Gen. Div.).

The court refused to issue a commission to obtain the evidence of a defendant who did not reside in Canada and might not attend at trial.

White v. Weston (1986), 14 C.P.C. (2d) 121 (Ont. H.C.).

The court granted a defence motion to take the evidence of the 77-year-old defendant before trial on the undertaking of the defendant's counsel to call his client at trial unless the client was unable to appear by reason of death, infirmity or sickness.

Botiuk v. Toronto Free Press Publications Ltd. (1986), 56 O.R. (2d) 184, 11 C.P.C. (2d) 211 (Master).

Where a defendant moved for an order permitting him to give evidence before trial on the ground that he might not be able to testify as a result of a medical condition, the plaintiff obtained an order requiring that the defendant undergo a medical examination to assist in the defence of the motion.

Simpson v. Vanderheiden; Simpson v. Phoenix Assur. Co. of Can. (1985), 49 O.R. (2d) 347, 48 C.P.C. 7 (H.C.).

The court ordered that the evidence of two eyewitnesses be taken by commission in Alberta as the witnesses appeared unwilling to travel to Ontario for trial. Their testimony was to be recorded on videotape or film.

Singer v. Singer (1983), 38 C.P.C. 63 (Ont. Master).

The court ordered evidence to be taken on commission notwithstanding that the evidence was likely to be controversial.

Wright v. Whiteside (1983), 40 O.R. (2d) 732, 34 C.P.C. 91 (H.C.).

The fact that a witness is 70 years of age or more is *prima facie* grounds for ordering the taking of evidence before trial. The court ordered the examination to be videotaped.

Union Carbide Can. Ltd. v. Vanderkop (1974), 6 O.R. (2d) 448 (H.C.).

A commission was issued to take the evidence out of Ontario where the persons sought to be examined were reluctant to enter the jurisdiction because of possible criminal proceedings and could not be compelled to attend the trial.

Copps v. Time Int. of Can. Ltd., [1964] 1 O.R. 229 (Master).

The order may be made notwithstanding that the opposing party may be prejudiced by being unable to cross-examine in open court.

Niewiadomski v. Langdon, [1956] O.W.N. 762, 6 D.L.R. (2d) 361 (H.C.).

The fact that the evidence of the witness is highly controversial is not grounds to refuse a motion to take evidence before trial.

Dodd v. Charlton Transport Ltd., [1956] O.W.N. 230 (H.C.).

A commission was granted for the examination of an eyewitness to an accident.

Guiry v. Wheeler, [1954] O.W.N. 381 (Master).

An examination out of Ontario may be refused if it would prevent necessary cross-examination of the witness.

Mamarbachi v. Cockshutt Plow Co., [1953] O.W.N. 44 (Master).

Useful discussion of circumstances in which examinations out of Ontario will be permitted.

Maynard v. Maynard, [1947] O.W.N. 493 (Master).

A motion for a commission was dismissed where the evidence sought was only corroborative of the applicant's own evidence.

PROCEDURE

36.02(1) Subject to subrule (2), Rule 34 applies to the examination of a witness under rule 36.01, unless the court orders otherwise.

(2) A witness examined under rule 36.01 may be examined, cross-examined and re-examined in the same manner as a witness at trial.

EXAMINATIONS OUTSIDE ONTARIO

36.03 Where an order is made under rule 36.01 for the examination of a witness outside Ontario, the order shall, if the moving party requests it, provide for the issuing of a commission and letter of request under subrules 34.07(2) and (3) for the taking of the evidence of the witness and, on consent of the parties, any other witness in the same jurisdiction, and the order shall be in (Form 34E).

Commissions — Generally

Electric Reduction Co. v. Crane, [1959] O.W.N. 241 (H.C.).

An appeal from the ruling of a commissioner should be to the trial judge.

Letters Rogatory — Outgoing

Nacevich v. Nacevich, [1962] O.W.N. 105 (H.C.).

A letter of request was issued to obtain the evidence of a witness residing in Yugoslavia.

Quality Steels (London) Ltd. v. Atlas Steels Ltd., [1950] O.W.N. 221 (H.C.).

On appeal by the defendants, the court affirmed the order of the master permitting the plaintiff the issuance of a commission to take evidence in Switzerland. Letters rogatory in aid were denied because there was nothing to indicate that the foreign witnesses would be uncooperative. [*But note now rule 36.03 — Authors.*]

Letters Rogatory — Incoming (See rules 34.01 and 34.07.)

[*Older cases should be considered in light of the amendment to the Evidence Act, s. 60(1), made by the Courts of Justice Act, 1984, s. 176(2) — Authors.*]

W.R. Grace Co. v. Brookfield Development Corporation (1995), 41 C.P.C. (3d) 130 (Ont. Gen. Div.).

The court enforced letters rogatory from a Minnesota court seeking to inspect documents.

World Youth Day Inc. v. Perry (1995), 41 C.P.C. (3d) 133 (Ont. Gen. Div.).

The court refused to enforce letters rogatory from a Colorado court seeking an examination for discovery purposes of representatives of a company which was to be added as a party to the Colorado law suit. An order enforcing ordinary discovery of a party to a foreign action will not ordinarily be granted.

Hooft v. Heineken NV (1994), 33 C.P.C. (3d) 233 (Ont. Gen. Div.).

The court enforced a letter of request from a Dutch court.

Somerset Pharmaceuticals Inc. v. Interpharm Inc. (1994), 25 C.P.C. (3d) 12, 52 C.P.R. (3d) 317, 109 D.L.R. (4th) 593 (Ont. Gen. Div.).

The *Charter* was held not to apply to an order enforcing letters rogatory. The court enforced letters rogatory from a Florida court.

Gourmet Resources International Inc. (Trustee of) v. Paramount Capital Corp. (1991), 3 O.R. (3d) 286 (Gen. Div.).

The court enforced letters rogatory and required the respondent to answer disputed questions on a judgment debtor examination regarding a New York judgment notwithstanding that the respondent was also being sued in Ontario to enforce the New York judgment.

France (Republic) v. De Havilland Aircraft of Canada Ltd. (1991), 3 O.R. (3d) 705, 1 C.P.C. (3d) 76, 65 C.C.C. (3d) 449, 49 O.A.C. 283 (C.A.).

The court gave effect to letters rogatory issued by a French court regarding a criminal matter.

Coats Co. v. Bruno Wessel Ltd. (1990), 46 C.P.C. (2d) 316 (Ont. Gen. Div.).

The court refused to grant an order enforcing letters rogatory where the applicant failed to show the evidence requested was relevant to the foreign proceeding.

United States v. Pressey (1988), 65 O.R. (2d) 141, 26 C.P.C. (2d) 122, 51 D.L.R. (4th) 152, 27 O.A.C. 304 (C.A.).

Where a party is being examined under oath with respect to criminal proceedings in the United States pursuant to letters rogatory, the forum of the examination remains Canadian, and accordingly evidentiary matters are governed by Canadian law.

Scholnick v. Bank of N.S. (1987), 59 O.R. (2d) 538 (H.C.).

The court refused to enforce letters of request from a United States court seeking the production of a wide class of documents which were only vaguely identified. There is no power in the court to limit a specific request as to production of documents from a foreign court and the request for such a great mass of documents, not specified or identified except in a general way, could not stand.

Southam Inc. v. Theriault (1987), 61 O.R. (2d) 758, 23 C.P.C. (2d) 133 (H.C.).

The court gave effect to letters of request seeking an examination of the chief of Canada's defence staff notwithstanding a claim of Crown prerogative.

Four Embarcadero Center Venture v. Mr. Greenjeans Corp. (1987), 59 O.R. (2d) 229, 16 C.P.C. (2d) 205 (H.C.), affirmed (1988), 65 O.R. (2d) 256 (C.A.).

The court gave effect to letters of request from a California court for the examination of witnesses in aid of execution notwithstanding that an appeal was pending from the California judgment. California law did not provide for a stay of execution pending appeal. The court varied the schedule of examinations sought in the letters of request.

Friction Division Products Inc. v. E.I. DuPont de Nemours & Co. (No. 2) (1986), 56 O.R. (2d) 722, 12 C.P.C. (2d) 221, 10 C.I.P.R. 97, 12 C.P.R. (3d) 2, 32 D.L.R. (4th) 105 (H.C.).

Where earlier evidentiary shortcomings had been corrected, an application to give effect to letters of request issued by a Delaware court was allowed, even though an earlier application had been dismissed.

Mulroney v. Coates; Southam Inc. v. Mulroney (1986), 54 O.R. (2d) 353, 8 C.P.C. (2d) 109, 27 D.L.R. (4th) 118 (H.C.).

Pursuant to s. 60(1) of the Ontario *Evidence Act,* effect may now be given to requests by foreign courts for examination for discovery of non-parties.

Friction Division Products Inc. v. E.I. Du Pont de Nemours & Co. (1985), 51 O.R. (2d) 244, 6 C.P.R. (3d) 66 (H.C.).

The court refused to enforce U.S. letters of request on the grounds that (1) a Canadian court will not order a Canadian resident to submit to the process of a foreign court unless it is necessary; (2) it was not clearly established that the evidence was required for trial as opposed to discovery; (3) the order sought was more burdensome to a witness than would be the case if the action had been brought in Ontario; (4) in its scope the order sought was oppressive and an improper burden on the respondents. [*But see the amendment to s. 60(1) of the Ontario Evidence Act and rule 31.10 — Authors.*]

Dist. Ct. of St. Gallen v. Nagel (1985), 50 C.P.C. 109 (Ont. Dist. Ct.).

The court adjourned an application to permit the gathering of evidence to establish that the foreign court was a court of competent jurisdiction in the proceeding before it and that the foreign court had the authority to direct the taking of evidence in a foreign jurisdiction (*i.e.* Ontario).

Re A.G. Becker Inc. (1984), 45 C.P.C. 163 (Ont. H.C.).

The court refused to enforce letters rogatory issued by the United States Securities and Exchange Commission.

I.A.M. v. Qantas Airways Ltd. (1983), 42 O.R. (2d) 387, 35 C.P.C. 97, 149 D.L.R. (3d) 38 (H.C.).

The court enforced letters rogatory issued by a California court to obtain evidence in respect of a motion for summary judgment.

Pan American World Airways Inc. v. TAS Int. Travel Service Inc. (1982), 37 O.R. (2d) 59, 27 C.P.C. 98, 135 D.L.R. (3d) 81 (H.C.).

An order for the examination of witnesses pursuant to a commission issued by a New York court was granted notwithstanding the absence of formal letters rogatory.

U.S. Dist. Ct., Middle Dist. of Florida v. Royal Amer. Shows Inc.; U.S.A. v. Royal Amer. Shows Inc., [1982] 1 S.C.R. 414, 19 Alta. L.R. (2d) 97, 25 C.P.C. 287, 27 C.R. (3d) 1, [1982] 3 W.W.R. 481, 36 A.R. 361, 66 C.C.C. (2d) 125, 134 D.L.R. (3d) 32, 41 N.R. 181.

The court ordered production of documents sought in letters rogatory for use at trial notwithstanding that the request did not include examination of any party or witness.

R. v. Zingre, [1981] 2 S.C.R. 392, 23 C.P.C. 259, 61 C.C.C. (2d) 465, 127 D.L.R. (3d) 223, 10 Man. R. (2d) 62, 38 N.R. 272.

The Supreme Court of Canada gave effect to letters rogatory notwithstanding that the evidence sought related to a pre-trial proceeding.

Medical Ancillary Services v. Sperry Rand Corp. (1979), 23 O.R. (2d) 406 (H.C.).

Discussion of examination of a corporation pursuant to letters rogatory.

Re Galamar Industs. and Microsystems Int. Ltd. (1975), 11 O.R. (2d) 405, 23 C.P.R. (2d) 19, 66 D.L.R. (3d) 221 (Co. Ct.).

An order giving effect to letters rogatory should only be granted if the examination sought is shown by the party seeking the order to be intended for use at trial and not for purposes of discovery. *[But see now the Evidence Act, s. 60(1) as amended by the Courts of Justice Act, 1984, s. 176(2) — Authors.]*

Re Raychem Corp. v. Canusa Coating Systems Inc., [1971] 1 O.R. 192, 64 C.P.R., 1984, 247, 14 D.L.R. (3d) 684 (C.A.).

Letters rogatory requesting examinations of persons in the nature of discovery will not be enforced; such orders will be made only if the examinations are for the purpose of trial. *[See note to Re Galamar, supra.]*

Re McCarthy and Menin and U.S. Securities and Exchange Comm., [1963] 2 O.R. 154, 38 D.L.R. (2d) 660 (C.A.).

Discussion of requests by foreign tribunals for the assistance of Ontario courts in obtaining evidence from witnesses in Ontario.

Re Barcelona T.L. & P. Co., [1960] O.W.N. 415 (H.C.).

Discussion of Spanish letters of request.

Re Geneva and Comtesse, [1959] O.R. 668, (*sub nom. Re Comtesse and Zelig*) 23 D.L.R. (2d) 506 (H.C.).

Discussion of material required in support of an application to act on letters rogatory.

Re Radio Corp. of Amer. v. Rauland Corp., [1956] O.R. 630, 26 C.P.R. 29, 5 D.L.R. (2d) 424, 16 Fox Pat. C. 46 (H.C.).

The court gave effect to letters rogatory requesting the oral examination of a non-party but refused to order production of documents on the scale requested.

Re Paramount Film Distributing Corp. and Ram, [1954] O.W.N. 753 (H.C.).

Discussion of form of letters rogatory and the applicability of the Ontario *Evidence Act* and the *Canada Evidence Act*.

USE AT TRIAL

36.04(1) In subrules (2) to (7), where an action,
(a) is brought by or against a corporation, "party" includes an officer, director or employee of the corporation;
(b) is brought by or against a partnership or a sole proprietorship using the firm name, "party" includes each person who was, or is alleged to have been, a partner or the sole proprietor, as the case may be;

(c) is brought by or against a party under disability, "party" includes the litigation guardian;

(d) is brought by or against an assignee, "party" includes the assignor;

(e) is brought by or against a trustee of the estate of a bankrupt, "party" includes the bankrupt;

(f) is brought or defended for the immediate benefit of a person who is not a party, "party" includes the person for whose immediate benefit the action is brought or defended.

(2) At trial any party may use the transcript and videotape or other recording of an examination under rule 36.01 or 36.03 of a witness who is not a party as the evidence of the witness, unless the court orders otherwise on the ground that the witness ought to give evidence at trial or for any other sufficient reason.

(3) A witness who is not a party and whose evidence has been taken under rule 36.01 or 36.03 shall not be called to give evidence at the trial, except with leave of the trial judge.

(4) With leave of the trial judge or the consent of the parties, a party may use at trial the transcript and a videotape or other recording of an examination under rule 36.01 of a witness who is a party as the evidence of the witness.

(5) In exercising its discretion under subrule (4), the court shall take into account,

(a) whether the party is unavailable to testify by reason of death, infirmity or sickness;

(b) whether the party ought to give evidence in person at the trial; and

(c) any other relevant consideration.

(6) Use of evidence taken under rule 36.01 or 36.03 is subject to any ruling by the trial judge respecting its admissibility.

(7) The transcript and a videotape or other recording may be filed with the court at trial and need not be read or played at trial unless a party or the trial judge requires it. [am. O. Reg. 69/95, s. 18]

Sykes v. Sykes, [1950] O.W.N. 235 (H.C.).
The court will refuse to permit use of evidence at trial if there are valid objections.

MOTIONS AND APPLICATIONS

RULE 37   MOTIONS — JURISDICTION AND PROCEDURE

Highlights

This Rule applies to "motions" (formerly called interlocutory motions): the jurisdiction and procedure on "applications" (formerly called originating motions) is regulated by Rule 38. Rule 37 should be read in conjunction with Rule 39 (Evidence on Motions and Applications).

Scope of the Rule. The Rule not only defines the subject-matter jurisdiction of judges and masters over motions (rule 37.02), it also mandates the place of hearing of motions, *i.e.* in which county they are to be brought (rule 37.03) and to whom motions should be made assuming that the subject-matter and place of hearing requirements have been met (rule 37.04).

In the context of such detailed regulation, recall that s. 110 of the *Courts of Justice Act* provides that where a step in a proceeding is taken before the wrong court, judge or officer it may be transferred or adjourned to the proper court, judge or officer.

In addition, the Rule sets out the basic procedure for the making and hearing of motions: rules 37.05-37.12.1.

Appeals from interlocutory orders are now classified as appeals, not as a form of motion as under the former Rules, and are governed by their own rule: see rule 62.01.

Jurisdiction. A judge has jurisdiction to hear any motion in a proceeding: rule 37.02(1).

Masters may (with a few specified exceptions, the most important being where jurisdiction is expressly conferred on a judge) also hear any motion in a proceeding: rule 37.02(2).

These jurisdictional grants find their basis in the *Courts of Justice Act* — see particularly ss. 16, 87(2) and 66(2)(h).) The resulting scheme of motion jurisdiction is as follows: if a statute or rule provides for a motion to be made to "the court" (as opposed to "a judge") the motion is within the jurisdiction of a master unless it comes within the exceptions set forth in rule 37.02(2). As the definition in rule 1.03 indicates, the term "the court" is a neutral term covering judges and masters.

Similarly, if a rule provides for the making of an order but does not specify the forum (*e.g.* rule 34.13), or if a motion not expressly provided for is brought to enforce an obligation in the Rules, a master may grant the order unless one of the rule 37.02(2) exceptions applies.

On the other hand, if a statute or rule requires a motion to be to "a judge", the jurisdiction of the master is ousted (rule 37.02(2)(a)) and it must be made to a judge. Where a motion is made in connection with a reference, the motion shall be heard by the referee: rule 54.05(1).

Rule 37.04 requires that a motion be made to the "court" if it is within a master's jurisdiction and otherwise it is to be made to a judge.

Place of hearing. The general rule is that a motion made on notice is to be made and heard in the county where the solicitor's office of any responding party is located: rule 37.03(2)(a). Consequently, except on consent or where the other limited exceptions to the general rule apply, motions must be brought in the responding party's solicitor's bailiwick. Motions may not automatically be brought at Toronto, notwithstanding that the master there may have subject-matter jurisdiction. Where a motion is made in the wrong location, the court may grant leave to hear the motion, but deprive a successful moving party of costs (*Rogan v. Magnus Aerospace Ltd.* (1985), 50 C.P.C. 217, 7 C.P.R. (3d) 405 (Ont. H.C.)) or where leave is not granted the order made may be set aside on appeal so as not to encourage motions in the wrong location: *Bright v. Clanahan* (1987), 24 C.P.C. (2d) 268 (Ont. H.C.).

Hearing date. Where there is a practice direction in effect at the place of hearing, it governs the scheduling of the hearing; otherwise a motion may be set down for hearing on any day on which a judge or master is scheduled to hear motions, and if counsel estimates that the hearing of the motion will be more than two hours, a hearing date shall be obtained from the registrar before the notice of motion is served (rule 37.05(1) and (2)). But an urgent motion may be set down for hearing on any day on which motions are scheduled to be heard: rule 37.05(3).

Other features of Rule 37. A notice of motion is required to be detailed and informative: rule 37.06.

Motion records are required, unless ordered otherwise, on all motions made on notice: rule 37.10(1). Only the record, and not the court file unless requested by the judge or master or requisitioned by a party, shall be placed before the judge or master.

Generally no factum is required on a motion (contrast the situation re applications: rule 38.09), but a number of rules do require factums on the hearing of specific motions: *e.g.* motions for summary judgment (rule 20.03), determination of an issue before trial (rule 21.03), special case (rule 22.02), discharge of a certificate of pending litigation (rule 42.02(2)) and motions for leave to appeal (rules 61.03(2) and 62.02(6)). However, on any motion a party is entitled to deliver a factum: rule 37.10(6).

The Rule defines the circumstances in which motions may be heard in the absence of the public, and the category of motions which may be so heard is quite limited: rule 37.11.

Provision is made for the hearing of motions by means of a conference telephone call: rule 37.12.

Motions may be heard without oral argument under rule 37.12.1. This applies not only to consent and unopposed motions and motions without notice (rule 37.12.1(1)), but also to opposed motions (rule 37.12.1(4)) if the parties choose not to make oral submissions.

On the hearing of any motion the court may order a speedy trial: rule 37.13(1)(a).

A party who is abusing the process through vexatious motions may be prohibited from bringing further motions except with leave: rule 37.16. Rule 57.03(1) encourages the court to order costs payable forthwith on motions more often (it is to do so where it is "satisfied that the motion ought not to have been made or opposed"): rule 57.03(1).

In complicated proceedings all motions may be assigned to be heard by a particular judge: rule 37.15.

A motion is defined to include "a motion in a proceeding or an intended proceeding" (rule 1.03) and hence leave to commence a proceeding, where leave is required, is obtained on motion (rule 14.01(3)) and in an urgent case (*e.g.* an interlocutory injunction) a motion may be made before the commencement of a proceeding: rule 37.17. Rule 9.02(1) also provides for a pre-proceeding motion to appoint a litigation administrator.

Commercial list. Motions concerning matters on the Commercial List are dealt with in the Commercial List practice direction. Changes are required in the form of the notice of motion and the method of obtaining a hearing date. See the practice directions reproduced following the Highlights of Rule 38.

Summary of procedure. For a summary of the procedure on a motion, see Procedural Charts (CHARTS).

Practice directions. Practice directions regarding motions and applications in Motions Court (Weekly Court), family law motions in the Toronto Region, motions before the master, motions before the master in Commercial List matters, motions adjourned *sine die* in the Toronto master's office, and motions and applications, civil pre-trial conferences and costs in interlocutory proceedings in the Central East Region and motions in the North East Region are set out following these Highlights. For local procedures regarding motions in the Central South Region see chapters 5 and 8 of the *Administrative Procedures Manual for the Central South Region* published by direction of Regional Senior Justice Fedak.

Former Rules: Rules 207-223, 235-239.

Practice Directions

The following practice directions are reproduced below:

Motions and Applications in Motions Court (Weekly Court), Toronto Region

Family Law Motions, Toronto Region

Motions before the Master, Toronto Region

Notice to Users of the Commercial List — Motion before a Master

Motions Adjourned Sine Die — Master's Office — Toronto

Notice to the Profession, Improved Service to the Profession for Master's Court, Office of the Master

Motions and Applications, Civil Pre-trial Conferences and Costs in Interlocutory Proceedings, Central East Region

Motions in the Ontario Court (General Division), North East Region

---

PRACTICE DIRECTION
Toronto Region

MOTIONS AND APPLICATIONS IN MOTIONS COURT (WEEKLY COURT)
SETTING DOWN FOR HEARING

1. All motions and applications are to be set down for hearing at the Motions Court office, 145 Queen Street West, Toronto, with the exception of motions for leave to appeal to the Divisional Court, which are to be set down for hearing at the Divisional Court office, Osgoode Hall.

HEARING DATES FOR MOTIONS AND APPLICATIONS

2. With respect to motions and applications of average or moderate complexity which will require no more than two hours to be argued, counsel for the moving party or applicant is at liberty to chose any date for the return of the motion or application. However, before determining the return date counsel for the moving party or applicant must consult with opposing counsel,

if known, to select a return date convenient to all counsel and which will provide sufficient time for counsel to file all necessary materials and conduct any cross-examinations or other examinations and to agree upon a timetable for doing so. As well, counsel are to jointly estimate the time required to argue the motion or application. Before agreeing upon a hearing date counsel may wish to communicate with the Motions Court office to determine the status of the list of motions and applications set down for the contemplated return date.

3. With respect to more complex motions and applications which will require more than two hours, but less than a full day, to be argued, counsel for the moving party or applicant must obtain a hearing date from the Motions Court office before a notice of motion or notice of application is served. Before requesting a hearing date, counsel for the moving party or applicant must follow the procedure contained in paragraph 2.

4. With respect to more complex motions and applications which will require more than one day to be argued, counsel for the moving party or applicant must obtain a hearing date from the supervising Motions Court judge, currently Mr. Justice Borins. After complying with the procedure contained in paragraph 2, counsel for the moving party or applicant should communicate with the supervising judge by telephone transmission of a letter to (416) 327-5417 setting out a description of the motion or application and several dates which are convenient to counsel. Counsel will be advised in writing of the hearing date or dates assigned by the supervising judge.

5. The intent of the procedure required by paragraphs 2, 3 and 4 is to ensure that the hearing date is a *real* hearing date when the motion or application will be argued, if not settled, and will avoid the usual request for an adjournment by the responding party for time to file materials, conduct cross-examinations and examinations, and so on. Where counsel for the responding party is unknown, as is often the case on an application, or the responding party is unrepresented by counsel, in respect to paragraph 2 counsel may select a convenient hearing date and in respect to paragraphs 3 and 4 counsel must obtain a hearing date from the Motions Court office or the supervising Motions Court judge, respectively.

6. Counsel should communicate with the Motions Court office by telephoning (416) 327-5467 or by telephone transmission of a document to that office at (416) 327-5527.

7. With respect to urgent motions or applications regardless of complexity or estimated hearing time, except for *ex parte* motions for interim or interlocutory injunctive relief and any other *ex parte* motions, if counsel experience difficulties in obtaining a hearing date counsel should contact the supervising Motions Court judge. All requests with respect to the hearing of *ex parte* motions should be directed to Mr. William J. Sheehan, Manager, Trial Scheduling.

CONFIRMATION OF HEARING DATES

8. Unless counsel for the moving party or applicant confirms that the motion or application is to proceed as scheduled by 2:00 p.m. on the day prior to the scheduled hearing date, the documents pertaining to that proceeding will not be forwarded to a judge and the motion or application will not be heard on the date scheduled.

9. Counsel for the moving party or applicant may confirm the hearing date by delivery of Form A, or a similar document, to the Motions Court office or by telephone transmission of Form A to that office at (416) 327-5527. In the event that a motion or application is settled after the transmission of Form A counsel must notify the Motions Court office by telephone at (416) 327-5467 of the settlement. As this is a voice mail telephone number it is available for use at any time.

10. Before delivering or transmitting Form A counsel for the moving party or applicant is required to discuss the following matters with opposing counsel:

(a)   whether the motion or application is to proceed as scheduled;

(b)   if so, whether it is to proceed by way of argument on all or some issues, consent order, or adjournment;

(c)   if the motion or application is to proceed by way of argument on some issues, what those issues are;

(d)   whether the time estimate given when the motion or application was originally set down remains accurate, and if not, the revised time estimated to argue the motion or application.

Counsel for the moving party or applicant is to advise the Motions Court judge if he or she has been unable to obtain the co-operation of opposing counsel in respect to the above information.

ADHERENCE TO TIME ESTIMATES

11. In arguing a motion or application counsel will not be permitted to exceed the time which they have estimated for its hearing.

UNOPPOSED MOTIONS AND APPLICATIONS

12. In regard to unopposed motions and applications and in regard to those in which an order or judgment is to be granted on consent, counsel should prepare a draft order or judgment for the assistance of the presiding judge.

CONSENT ADJOURNMENTS

13. Where the parties consent to an adjournment of a motion or application, the adjournment can be arranged by telephoning the Motions Court office at (416) 327-5467 by 2:00 p.m. on the day prior to the scheduled hearing date and attendance of counsel in Motions Court will not be required unless the adjournment is to be on terms.

MATERIALS FOR USE ON MOTIONS AND APPLICATIONS

14. The Rules of Civil Procedure will apply in relation to all other matters concerning the hearing of motions and applications. In particular, the attention of counsel is directed to rule 37.10 and rule 38.09 which concern materials for use on motions and applications, respectively.

15. In respect of most motions, the filing of a factum is optional: subrule 37.10(7). However, the preparation and filing of a factum is mandatory in respect to certain motions including motions for summary judgment (subrule 20.03), for the determination of a question of law or striking out a pleading on the ground that it discloses no reasonable cause of action or defence (subrule 21.03), in the form of a special case (subrule 22.02), by way of appeal from the order of a master (subrule 62.01(7)(8)) and for leave to appeal to the Divisional Court from an interlocutory order of a judge (subrule 62.02(6)). As well, the preparation and filing of a factum is required in respect to all applications: subrules 38.09(1)(a) and (2)(a). Although the filing of a factum is optional in regard to most motions, many counsel have adopted the practice of preparing a factum for all motions, which is of great assistance to Motions Court judges. Counsel are, therefore, encouraged to prepare factums for all contested motions and, in particular, motions for interlocutory injunctive relief and the appointment of an interim receiver.

June 15, 1993

[Sgd.] THE HONOURABLE F.W. CALLAGHAN
CHIEF JUSTICE OF THE ONTARIO COURT

(Form A)

Court File #

ONTARIO COURT
(GENERAL DIVISION)

BETWEEN:

(*name*)

(Moving Party *or* Applicant)

– and –

(*name*)

(Respondent)

I, _____ , COUNSEL FOR THE _____ (MOVING PARTY *or* APPLICANT), CONFIRM THAT I HAVE DISCUSSED WITH OPPOSING COUNSEL THE MATTERS REFERRED TO BELOW, AND THAT:

(A)   THE _____ (MOTION *OR* APPLICATION)
       (*strike out inapplicable word(s)*)

          IS   IS NOT

       PROCEEDING ON _____ , 199__ (*indicate date*) AS
       SCHEDULED.

(B)   THE MOTION OR APPLICATION IS PROCEEDING BY WAY OF:
       (*mark appropriate box or boxes* [x])

        ARGUMENT ON ALL ISSUES   [   ]

        ARGUMENT ON THE ISSUES DESCRIBED IN PARA-   [   ]
        GRAPH (C) BELOW

        CONSENT ORDER   [   ]

        ADJOURNMENT ON CONSENT   [   ]

        ADJOURNMENT ON TERMS   [   ]

        ADJOURNMENT TO BE REQUESTED BY MOVING PARTY   [   ]
        or RESPONDENT
        (*strike out inapplicable words*)
        WHICH IS TO BE OPPOSED   [   ]

(C)   (*to be completed only if the motion or application is* not *proceeding by way of argument on all issues, consent order or adjournment*)
       THE ARGUMENT WILL PROCEED ON THE FOLLOWING ISSUES:

       _____
       _____
       _____
       _____

       (*briefly describe the issues on which the argument is to proceed*)

(D)   THE TIME ESTIMATE OF _____ (*indicate original time estimate*) GIVEN WHEN THE MOTION OR APPLICATION WAS ORIGINALLY SET DOWN (*strike on inapplicable word(s)*)

        DOES   DOES NOT

                REMAIN ACCURATE.

(E)   (*to be completed only if the original time estimate* does not *remain accurate*)
      THE REVISED TIME ESTIMATE IS _____
      (*indicate revised time estimate*).

_____   _____
(*Date and Time*)   (*Signature*)

TO: THE DEPUTY LOCAL REGISTRAR
      ONTARIO COURT OF JUSTICE
      (GENERAL DIVISION)
      MOTIONS COURT OFFICE
      ROOM 123
      145 QUEEN STREET WEST
      TORONTO, ONTARIO
      M5H 2N9

      FAX #327-5527

NOTE: NOTWITHSTANDING THAT A MOTION OR APPLICATION IS SET
       DOWN FOR HEARING ON A PARTICULAR DATE, UNLESS COUN-
       SEL FOR THE MOVING PARTY OR APPLICANT CONFIRMS THAT
       THE MOTION OR APPLICATION IS TO PROCEED AS SCHEDULED
       BY 2:00 p.m. ON THE DAY PRIOR TO THE SCHEDULED HEARING
       DATE, THE DOCUMENTS PERTAINING TO THAT PROCEEDING
       WILL NOT BE FORWARDED TO A JUDGE AND THE MOTION OR
       APPLICATION WILL NOT BE HEARD ON THE DATE SCHEDULED.

       IF AN ADJOURNMENT IS TO BE REQUESTED COUNSEL MUST
       AGREE ON THE RETURN DATE AND CONFIRM WITH THE MO-
       TIONS COURT THE AVAILABILITY OF THE DATE.

PRACTICE DIRECTION
Toronto Region

FAMILY LAW MOTIONS

Setting down for Hearing

1. All motions, case managed matters and applications (except Divisional Court leave applications) are to be set down for hearing at the Family Law Office, 145 Queen Street West,
   Toronto, Room 311.

2. Except for otherwise scheduled matters, all motions will be heard at 10:00 a.m.

Confirmation of Hearing Date

3. While it is the primary duty of counsel for the moving party to confirm that the motion is
   to proceed as scheduled **by 2:00 p.m.** two days prior to the scheduled hearing date, either
   party may confirm. If neither party confirms that the motion is to proceed, the documents
   pertaining to the motion will not be forwarded to a judge and the motion will not be heard
   on the date scheduled.

4. Counsel may confirm the hearing date by delivery or facsimile transmission of Form A to
   the Family Law Office at (416) 327-6137. (**This number is for purposes of transmitting
   Form A only, and is not to be used for filings of Court documents.**) Counsel must

provide opposing counsel with a copy of Form A immediately upon transmittal to the Family Law Office. In the event that a motion is settled after the transmission of Form A counsel **MUST** notify the Family Law Office.

5. Before delivering or transmitting Form A counsel for the moving party is **REQUIRED** to discuss the following matters with opposing counsel:

    (a) whether the motion and, if applicable, cross motion, are to proceed as scheduled;

    (b) if so, whether the motion and cross motion are to proceed by way of argument on all or some issues, consent order, or adjournment;

    (c) if the motion and cross motion are to proceed by way of argument on some issues, what those issues are;

    (d) time estimate for the motion and cross motion combined.

Counsel for the moving party is to advise the Family Law Motions Court judge if he or she has been unable to obtain the co-operation of opposing counsel in respect to the above information and so indicate on Form A.

Adherence to Time Estimates

6. **IN ARGUING A MOTION COUNSEL WILL NOT BE PERMITTED TO EXCEED THE TIME WHICH THEY HAVE ESTIMATED FOR ITS HEARING.**

7. If argument is expected to take 30 minutes or more, an appointment must be scheduled with the Family Law Office so that it will not interfere with the normal operation of the Motions Court. Where the issues are complex or there is substantial material to be filed, the judge assigned to the motion may require that factums be filed. (This is in addition to the requirement of factums in motions for summary judgment as required by the Rules of Practice).

Consent Adjournments

8. Where the parties consent to an adjournment of a motion, the adjournment can be arranged by delivery of Form A or a similar document to the Family Law Office or by facsimile transmission of that document to that office at (416) 327-6137 by 2:00 p.m., two days prior to the scheduled hearing date and attendance of counsel in Family Law Motions Court will not be required unless the other party seeks an order. If a motion is settled after that time, a notice must be sent to the Family Law Office by facsimile transmission no later than the close of business the day prior to the motion, stating that the Judge should not read the materials and that the matter will be spoken to.

Duty of Counsel where no Continuing Record

9. Unless a continuing record is used, a Statement of Prior Legal Proceedings must be filed and it is the responsibility of each counsel to ensure, no later than 2:00 p.m. two days prior to the hearing date, that all material necessary for use on the motion is properly organized in the file to be placed before the Judge. It is also counsel's duty to see that material irrelevant to the motion is not placed before the judge.

Consent Motions

10. Consent motions should be made returnable ''the week of . . .'' and filed in the Family Law Office. The Court will require a notice of motion, supporting affidavit, the consent or minutes of settlement and two copies of a draft order. This material need not be in record form. Counsel's attendance is not necessary. Once reviewed by the presiding Motions Court Judge, the documents will be returned to the Family Law Office.

Motions Without Notice

11. The half-hour period between 9:00 and 9:30 a.m. each day a Trial Court Judge is sitting is reserved for motions without notice *only if* there is extreme **urgency**. Proceedings must

have been commenced beforehand, the motion material must be in Record form and counsel must attend at the Family Law Office to prepare an application form for the motion.

12. This Practice Direction comes into force on May 16, 1994.

DATED: April 5, 1994

THE HONOURABLE
A.G. CAMPBELL
REGIONAL SENIOR JUSTICE
TORONTO REGION

THE HONOURABLE
R. ROY McMURTRY
CHIEF JUSTICE OF THE
ONTARIO COURT

Form A   **Court File No.**

ONTARIO COURT (GENERAL DIVISION)

BETWEEN: Moving Party

— and —

Responding Party

I, _____, COUNSEL FOR THE MOVING/RESPOND-ING PARTY, CONFIRM THAT I HAVE:

[ ] DISCUSSED WITH _____, OPPOSING COUNSEL, THE MATTERS REFERRED TO BELOW AND CONFIRM, OR

[ ] I HAVE BEEN UNABLE TO CONFIRM WITH OPPOSING COUNSEL BECAUSE
_____
_____

(A) THE MOTION IS PROCEEDING ON _____
AS SCHEDULED.

(B) THE MOTION IS PROCEEDING BY WAY OF:

— ARGUMENT ON ALL ISSUES   [ ]

— ARGUMENT ON THE ISSUES DESCRIBED IN
PARAGRAPH (C) BELOW.   [ ]

— CONSENT ORDER   [ ]

— ADJOURNMENT ON CONSENT FROM _____TO
_____ [ ]

— OPPOSED ADJOURNMENT TO BE REQUESTED BY _____[ ]

(C) THE ARGUMENT WILL PROCEED ON THE FOLLOWING ISSUES:

(D) THE FOLLOWING MOTION RECORDS SHOULD BE READ BY THE JUDGE:

(E) TIME ESTIMATE:_____ + _____ = _____
          (moving party)   *(responding party)*   *(total)*

(F) JUSTICE _____is ASSIGNED TO THIS MATTER.

_____   _____
(Date and Time)   *(Counsel's Name — please print)*

TO: FAMILY LAW OFFICE

_____
(*Counsel's Signature*)

FACSIMILE 327-6137
(*confirmations only — no filings will be accepted*)

_____
(*Phone Number*)

_____
(*Facsimile Number*)
(*no transmittal page required*)

PRACTICE DIRECTION
Toronto Region

MOTIONS BEFORE THE MASTER

A: APPLICATION OF THESE DIRECTIONS

1. Unless specifically otherwise stated, (see heading C, "Construction Liens", below) or the context requires otherwise, these directions pertain exclusively to civil motions within the jurisdiction of the Master whether brought in actions or applications, and apply as well to motions brought in actions and applications that were

   (1)   formerly in the District Court of Ontario, OR

   (2)   formerly in the Supreme Court of Ontario.

2. These directions do not apply to motions brought in actions which are the subject of case management.

B: CIVIL MOTIONS

GENERAL PROVISIONS

3. (a)   When setting down a motion brought on notice, it will be necessary to accurately estimate the length of time required to hear the motion and to supply a signed certification to that effect.

   (b)   Only lawyers, law students under articles or litigants-in-person may speak to motions on a list. Other persons, with leave of the court, may speak to motions brought without notice.

   (c)   All Masters' orders are entered on the first floor (east end) at 145 Queen Street West, Toronto, Ontario M5H 2N9.

MOTIONS WITHOUT NOTICE (EX PARTE)

4. EX PARTE motions will be heard every week-day morning at 145 Queen Street West between 10:00 a.m. and 11:30 a.m. according to the availability of a Master. Courtroom location will be posted.

5. When no EX PARTE Master is available an urgent EX PARTE motion may be dealt with by the Master presiding in the non-appointment court.

CONSENT ORDERS

6. All material in support of a consent order (including two copies of the draft order) is to be filed in the motions office on the first floor (west end) at 145 Queen Street West for disposition. Signed orders may be picked up at the same location.

MOTIONS BROUGHT ON NOTICE
FILING MATERIAL

7. All material to be used on a motion brought on notice will be filed at the motions office at 145 Queen Street West.

8. No motion material shall be filed earlier than one month before the return date of the motion.

9. In the case of a motion for which an appointment has been granted, the material must be filed at least two weeks in advance of the return date of the motion. In default of so filing, the motion will be transferred to the non-appointment list (see below).

MOTIONS BY APPOINTMENT

10. Upon request made at the motions office, and subject to the availability of time, appointments will be granted for motions brought on notice where the motion is estimated to require less than 2 hours' hearing time.

NON-APPOINTMENT LIST

11. Where no appointment has been requested, the motion will be assigned to the non-appointment list when the notice of motion is filed. Motions on this list will only be heard when all motions for which appointments have been granted, all urgent EX PARTE motions have been disposed of and time permits.

ADJOURNMENTS

12. Masters' motions (other than Long Motions) may be adjourned by phone or fax addressed to the motions office to be received no later than 4:00 p.m. the day before the return of the motion. Otherwise, a lawyer or a student must attend on the return of the motion to speak to it.

Telephone: 416-327-5479
Fax: 416-327-5484

LONG MOTIONS BY SPECIAL APPOINTMENT

13. Long motions are those civil motions that are likely to require more than two hours of hearing time.

14. Special appointments will be granted to hear long motions. Such appointments can be arranged by conference telephone call among all counsel (or parties) and Master Clark, or by personal attendance before Master Clark. Dates for telephone conferences and personal attendances must be arranged through Master Clark's secretary. Call Mrs. Mary Gay at 327-5493.

15. Special instructions as to the filing of material will be given when the appointment is granted.

16. Adjournments are to be arranged directly through Master Clark.

C: CONSTRUCTION LIEN MOTIONS

MOTIONS WITHOUT NOTICE

17. EX PARTE Motions are heard from 9:30 a.m. to 10:00 a.m. every week-day subject to the availability of the Master. Courtroom location will be posted.

CONSENT ORDERS

18. Consent orders in respect of which no motion has been brought, will be dealt with as EX PARTE motions.

19. Motions brought on notice will be heard on Monday of each week, by appointment arranged through Maria Kolliopoulos in the construction lien office in Room 225, 145 Queen Street West, telephone 327-5481, regardless of the length of motion, but subject to the availability of the Master. Courtroom location will be posted.

FILING MATERIAL

20. All material to be used on construction lien motions brought on notice is to be filed in Room 225 at 145 Queen Street West, Toronto, Ontario and not in the motions court office.

ADJOURNMENTS

21. Construction lien motions may be adjourned by telephone or fax addressed to the construction lien office provided the notice of adjournment is received at the construction lien office by 4:00 p.m., the day before the return of the motion. Otherwise a lawyer or student must attend on the return of the motion to speak to it.

Telephone: 416-327-5481
Fax: 416-327-5484

June 15, 1993   [Sgd.] THE HONOURABLE F.W. CALLAGHAN
                                     CHIEF JUSTICE OF THE ONTARIO COURT

PRACTICE DIRECTION

NOTICE TO USERS OF COMMERCIAL LIST

MOTION BEFORE A MASTER

You may find that it is more efficient to bring a motion before Master B. Clark in matters within his jurisdiction provided you are not involved in an action under the Toronto Case Management Rules. The matter should have already been admitted to the Commercial List (if it cannot qualify under the specified categories pursuant to the Practice Direction then in effect, counsel may attend before the presiding judge in chambers at 9:30 a.m. through Courtroom 46). Any motions brought before Master Clark should be arranged directly with his office; however filing of materials should go through the Commercial List Office in the ordinary course. Please prominently mark the material as being for Master Clark. Counsel are reminded that the Commercial List expects counsel to use common sense, courtesy and cooperation to resolve matters amongst themselves.

Examples of motions that may be dealt with by Master Clark:

(a)   R. 15.04   Motion by Solicitor for Removal as Solicitor of Record

                           Note: This motion should be brought well in advance of any pending motion in the Commercial List (and the Commercial List Office should be separately advised) as it may affect the hearing of the pending motion.

(b)   R. 25.10   Particulars of Pleadings
      R. 25.11   Striking Out A Pleading Or Other Document

(c)	R. 42	Certificate of Pending Litigation
(d)	R. 34.15	Sanctions For Default Or Misconduct By Person to Be Examined
(e)	R. 19.08 R. 19.09	Setting Aside The Noting of Default Setting Aside Default Judgment
(f)	R. 20	Summary Judgment
(g)	R. 30.10 R. 31.10	Production From Non-Parties With Leave Discovery of Non-Parties With Leave
(h)	R. 56	Security For Costs
(i)	R. 26	Amendment of Pleadings
(j)	R. 5.04	Misjoinder, Non-Joinder and Parties Incorrectly Named
(k)	R. 32.01	Order For Inspection Of Property
(l)	R. 34.12(3) R. 35.04(2)	Objections and Rulings — Oral Examinations Further Answers — Written Questions
(m)	R. 43	Interpleader

The use of this facility will be monitored to ensure (i) that it serves a useful purpose and (ii) that is continues to be compatible with the informal regime of individual judge case management in the Commercial List.

Osgoode Hall, Toronto　　　　　　　James M. Farley
February 3, 1992

Judge In Charge of
The Commercial List

NOTICE
Master's Office — Toronto

RE MOTIONS ADJOURNED SINE DIE

Recently motion records have disappeared at an increasing rate and this represents great inconvenience and expense both to the profession and to the staff of the Motions Office.

Those records that seem to be mislaid the most are those that have been *adjourned sine die.*

Therefore as of December 1, 1992 records in all Masters motions that have been *adjourned sine die* will be segregated and stored separately.

In order to bring back on a motion that has been *adjourned sine die* simply file the notice of return of motion at the Motions Office in the usual manner on the first floor at 145 Queen St. West.

Any further material for use on a motion that has been *adjourned sine die* will likewise be filed at the Motions Office in the usual manner.

These arrangements apply to all records filed in the Masters Court regardless of where the action was commenced.

Master B. T. Clark, Q.C.
MANAGING MASTER

NOTICE TO THE PROFESSION
Office of the Master

AN IMPROVED SERVICE TO THE PROFESSION FOR MASTERS COURT

Your attention is drawn to the voice message provided to the Profession to help decide the best day to have motions dealt with in Court. The Masters Court is changing the telephone message on (416) 327 5479 effective March 25/94. This message is available 24 hours a day, 7 days a week.

The message deals with "Court Loading", which is defined as the number of practice motions set down for a given day.

The objective of the Court is to spread the work load. The Profession can benefit by setting their motion down on low number days.

The message you will hear will give the day, the date, and the number of motions already set down for that date, for example — Monday, March 28th — 60 motions.

The message will provide you with 15 days of Court loading. The message will be updated every working Friday, and will always give you loading information for 15 days from the date of the message.

In addition to Court loading information, the message will tell you what days the 'Without Notice' Court will be sitting, but, be aware that any date given in advance is subject to last minute change.

The Masters Court is doing its best to serve the Profession as efficiently as possible within the limited personnel resources at its disposal.

The Profession can help themselves and the Masters Court by helping to spread the workload. Please take a few moments to listen to the message, and make your choice, but do try and set your motion down on a low number day. A bad day would be a day with the number in the seventies.

Sincerely,

Derek G. Dunmore
for Managing Master Clark

March 25, 1994

PRACTICE DIRECTION
Central East Region

MOTIONS AND APPLICATIONS, CIVIL PRE-TRIAL CONFERENCES AND COSTS IN INTERLOCUTORY PROCEEDINGS

This compendious Practice Direction applies to all motions and applications, civil pre-trial conferences and awards of costs in interlocutory proceedings occurring in Central East Region.

The decision to deal with costs in interlocutory proceedings in the Practice Direction has been taken as a result of consultations with the Regional Bench and Bar Committee. The practice described in paragraphs 34 through 38 will be followed in awarding such costs, subject always to the discretion of the presiding justice.

Several provisions of the Practice Direction make reference to contacting court officials by telephone or facsimile transmission. For example, in paragraph 6, reference is made to adjournment of motions and applications by letter, telephone call and facsimile transmission to the local trial coordinators. Paragraph 15 refers to the scheduling by the Regional Trial Coordinator of motions and applications involving specialized subject matter. Paragraph 21 refers to the manner in which Pre-Trial Conferences are to be arranged. For ease of reference, relevant telephone and facsimile numbers are set out in Appendix C.

June 15,1993   [Sgd.] THE HONOURABLE F.W. CALLAGHAN
                                    CHIEF JUSTICE OF THE ONTARIO COURT

MOTIONS AND APPLICATIONS

1. Except in cases of urgency or complexity, *ex parte* and consent matters will not be heard in motions court and will be dealt with only on the basis of materials filed. Where a matter is of some urgency, but not sufficient urgency to warrant being placed on the motion list, counsel should draw this to the attention of the counter staff so it will be given priority.

2. Records must be filed for *ex parte* and consent matters.

3. All motions and applications on notice shall be set down for hearing through the local coordinator in the centre where the matter is to be heard.

4. All motion and application records and materials shall be filed by the deadlines prescribed by rule 37.10. When the filing deadlines have not been complied with, the materials shall be filed only with leave of the justice presiding in motions court.

5. All affidavits of service should be filed separately from the served material (ie. not attached with a staple) so they do not obscure the motion material.

6. Matters may be adjourned by telephone, letter or fax requests to the local trial coordinator on consent of all parties at any time before 4:00 p.m. on the day before the hearing date. Thereafter someone will have to attend to complete a consent order form.

7. On motion days parties may have matters disposed of in their absence by filing minutes of settlement or a memorandum advising of a consent adjournment on terms or otherwise. The proposed endorsement shall be written on the back of the record or on a Form A and left with the motion court registrar. Where the parties know that a matter is to be disposed of on this basis the endorsement or Form A shall be completed before 10:00 a.m.

8. Motion lists shall show matters in the order in which they were filed. Matters adjourned from a previous date shall be placed on the list as if filed on that previous date.

9. The court registrar shall open court on motion days at 9:30 a.m. to enable parties to dispose of any consent matter by completing an endorsement or a Form A. At 10:00 a.m. the presiding justice shall begin proceedings and deal with the list in the following manner:

   i)   All parties on each matter will be asked to estimate the time required to argue their matter. At this time parties may also make representations if they wish their matter heard out of order. If no one is present to speak to a matter at 10:00 a.m. and there is no time estimate on the counsel slip, the matter shall be placed at the end of the list.

   ii) All parties with matters which are not on the list shall be given an opportunity to request leave to have the matter placed on the list.

   iii) The presiding justice shall then advise all parties of the order in which matters will be heard, which matters, if any are to be adjourned and whether counsel may leave the courtroom and return later in the day. Permitting counsel to return later in the day will depend on whether there appear to be sufficient matters preceding their particular motion or application.

iv) Then all short matters (e.g. those estimated to take approximately 15 minutes or less) shall be heard. These will include short matters of all kinds (e.g. urgent *ex parte* matters, matters which are unopposed, contested matters, contested adjournments, etc.). The remaining matters shall be dealt with in the order they appear on the list, subject to special considerations such as urgency, length and complexity.

v) If the list is not completed before the noon break the afternoon session shall begin with another review of the list so that parties who will not be reached can request adjournments or be excused until later in the afternoon.

vi) Where no one appears on a matter and no adjournment or consent order has been properly arranged by the time court adjourns for the day, the matter will be endorsed ''no one appeared'' and will not be placed on a hearing list again unless a new notice of return of motion or application is delivered.

10. All endorsements and Form A's completed by parties (other than adjournments without terms) shall be reviewed and signed by the presiding justice. If any proposed disposition is not approved, the applicant's counsel will be advised by telephone.

11. In Barrie, Newmarket and Whitby no motion shall be heard on a regular motion day if it is estimated to take longer than 90 minutes. At other centres the maximum length is two hours. In matters longer than these, the applicant shall apply to the local trial coordinator for a special appointment which may be scheduled anywhere in the Region designated by the local trial coordinator in consultation with the Regional Trial Coordinator. Counsel are reminded that very few matters will require special appointments if proper materials are filed and a request made in advance that they be reviewed. If on a motion day the parties estimate that the argument will take longer than the maximum stated above, the matter will be removed from the motion list.

12. Because it will not be known which matters will proceed, justices shall not be expected to read any material in advance of the hearing unless there is a note on the file that a specific counsel so requested. Such requests should be made by telephone, letter or fax by 2:00 p.m. on the day before the hearing. Parties should not make such a request until shortly before the hearing date when they will be in a position to know what issues are outstanding.

13. All counsel should begin their submissions by stating which order they seek and then either advise the presiding justice what materials should be read before argument proceeds or, alternatively, advise the justice during argument where the information is located in the material. In a complicated matter, counsel should file a chronology without argument or begin their oral submissions by providing the chronology.

14. Counsel must comply with rules 69.15(1) and 70.08 in family law matters and failure to do so may result in cost sanctions.

SCHEDULING OF SPECIALIZED MATTERS AND HEARINGS BY TELEPHONE

15. Motions and applications which involve specialized subject matter may be scheduled by counsel for a special hearing on a fixed date by applying to the Regional Senior Justice or her designate by motion on notice to all parties, which motion must be scheduled through the Regional trial coordinator.

16. Counsel should also consider an application for a special hearing under rule 37.15 where it is anticipated that there may be a series of motions in a matter or it requires case management.

17. All motions seeking an order certifying a proceeding as a class proceeding shall be brought only by way of an application for a special hearing.

18. Requests for a telephone hearing of a motion or application under rules 37.12 and 38.12 may be made to the local trial coordinator.

CIVIL PRE-TRIAL CONFERENCES

19. All cases must be pre-tried before they will be placed on the ready list or assigned a week for trial.

20. Pre-trial conferences ("pre-trials") before a justice will be arranged on application by letter or fax by a counsel or a party acting in person. If all parties agree, they may arrange a private pre-trial before any person who is approved in advance by the Regional Senior Justice.

21. Pre-trials may be arranged in only three situations:

i)   when an application is sent by letter or fax to the local trial coordinator stating that the trial record has been filed;

ii)   when an application is sent by letter or fax to the local trial coordinator stating that the case has not reached the stage where a trial record can be filed but the request is being made with the consent of all parties;

iii)   when an application by way of motion with notice to all parties is sent to the Regional Senior Justice before the trial record is filed and without the consent of all parties and special reason is shown.

Where a pre-trial is held in situation (ii) or (iii) the matter will not normally be placed on the trial list until a further pre-trial is held.

22. After making written application, the applicant shall arrange the pre-trial by obtaining a date from the local trial coordinator, and confirming with all parties that it is agreeable. The applicant shall then so advise the local trial coordinator who shall fix the date and note whether or not it is on consent. Parties may raise the basis of disagreement as a matter of costs. Once the date is fixed, the applicant shall forthwith notify all parties in writing.

23. On an experimental basis and subject to further change, pre-trials at Whitby, Newmarket, Barrie and Bracebridge shall be allotted 45 minutes. Pre-trials at Cobourg, Lindsay and Peterborough shall be scheduled for 15, 30, 45, or 60 minutes on the basis of the estimate provided by the applicant and subject to the discretion of the local trial coordinator. If the applicant believes that a longer appointment is required, this may be arranged at the discretion of the local trial coordinator.

24. Pre-trial memoranda and, where required by the rules, financial statements and net family property statements, shall be filed by 15 days before the pre-trial date. Where no party has filed the required materials by that deadline, the pre-trial shall be automatically cancelled by the local trial coordinator and another pre-trial scheduled in its place.

25. All local trial coordinators shall keep a list of cases which qualify under paragraph 21 and in which all parties have advised that they are ready for a pre-trial to be scheduled on short notice. Cases will be placed on this list only when all parties have filed the pre-trial materials required by the rules. When pre-trials are cancelled they shall be replaced with cases from this list.

26. Counsel should limit the length of materials filed so that the materials of all parties can be read in a total of 15 to 30 minutes. Counsel should indicate which of the materials should be read and which are filed only as reference material. Passages of special importance may be highlighted.

27. When a party wishes to cancel a pre-trial, he or she should contact all other parties to ascertain their position and then telephone the local trial coordinator to make the request

and advise of the position of the other parties. Where all parties consent to the cancellation, the local trial coordinator shall decide whether the reason is sufficient. Sufficient reasons include but are not limited to, the death of a related person, illness of counsel and being called for trial in another matter. In order that court time not be wasted, adjournments shall be more difficult to obtain when there are no cases which can be scheduled as replacements.

28. Where any party objects to the proposed cancellation, the pre-trial shall not be cancelled and inappropriate objections can be raised at the pre-trial as a matter of costs.

29. It is recognized that sometimes it will be impracticable for counsel with carriage of a case to attend the pre-trial or to have an informed substitute attend. However, if a pre-trial is unproductive for this reason, then costs may be awarded under rule 57.07 against counsel personally if counsel does not satisfy the pre-trial judge that reasonable efforts were made to make alternate arrangements.

30. Where a pre-trial proceeds, any party who has not filed a memorandum or, where required by rules 70.04 or 69.14, a financial statement or net family property statement, no later than 15 days before the pre-trial date shall, as a general rule and subject to the discretion of the pre-trial judge, be ordered to pay each other party costs fixed at a minimum of $250 and payable forthwith. The costs shall be awarded against the counsel or the party depending on the reason for the default. Counsel are hereby given notice that they should come to the pre-trial prepared to make representations as contemplated by rule 57.07.

31. At the conclusion of a pre-trial, materials filed shall be returned to the parties and the pre-trial Justice shall complete Form B and read it to the parties.

32. Counsel shall ensure that their clients are available to the courthouse or can be contacted promptly by telephone in order to give instructions. In family law cases the parties must be present in the court house at the time of the pre-trial.

33. Requests for a pre-trial conference by telephone under rule 50.08 may be made to the local trial coordinator.

COSTS

34. Where costs are awarded on motions, applications and pre-trials they shall normally be fixed and made payable forthwith.

35. Costs on motions and applications, including *ex parte* matters shall normally be awarded on the basis of the grid in Appendix A.

36. Counsel should have available at the hearing of a motion, application or pre-trial information of the kind outlined in Appendix B so that costs can be fixed at the hearing.

37. Costs shall not be awarded on *ex parte* matters dealt with on filed materials unless the applicant files a signed memorandum containing the required information mentioned in Appendix B.

38. Parties are reminded of rules 49.02, 57.03, 69.15(5) and 70.08 concerning motions which ought not to have been made or opposed, any offers made and, in family law matters, any failure to make an offer with respect to a motion for interim relief.

FORM A

PROPOSED ENDORSEMENT

Short Title of Proceeding: Court File #

Date:

Endorsement:

(If more space required continue on back)

Requested by:

Counsel for	Counsel for	Counsel for
tel: _____	tel: _____	tel: _____

_____ Approved

_____ Not approved   By Justice _____

_____ Checkmark indicates court staff has advised counsel for applicant that proposed endorsement was not approved.

FORM B

REPORT ON PRE-TRIAL

Short title of proceeding: Court File #

Date:

ORDERS made under rule 50.02(1)(b):

Deadline

(   ) undertakings of _____ to be answered by
(   ) undertakings of _____ to be answered by
(   ) affidavit of documents of _____ to be delivered by
(   ) affidavit of documents of _____ to be delivered by
Other orders:

Motion at trial will be brought: Time Estimate

– by _____ for _____

– by _____ for _____

Estimated length of trial:

To be put on list for sittings commencing:

Presiding justice _____

APPENDIX A

GUIDELINES AS TO WHAT PARTIES CAN EXPECT AS COSTS ON A MOTION

PARTY & PARTY SCALE	SOLICITOR & CLIENT SCALE	
Hourly Rates for Preparation (including preparing materials, cross-examination, records, factum, correspondence, research, etc.)		
Law Clerks & Articling Students	$35	$45
Lawyers: 1-5 Years	$70	$100
6-10 Years	$100	$140
11-15 Years	$120	$160
over 15 Years	$140	$175-275
Counsel Fee - Simple Motion		
.25 Hours	Up to $150	Up to $300
1.0 Hours	Up to $300	Up to $800
2.0 Hours (Half Day)	Up to $750	Up to $1000
Counsel Fee - Difficult Motion		
1.0 Hours	Up to $600	Up to $1000
2.0 Hours (Half Day)	Up to $900	Up to $1800
1 Day	Up to $1500	Up to $2500

CAUTION: NOTWITHSTANDING THE ABOVE, COSTS ARE IN THE DISCRETION OF THE COURT (COURTS OF JUSTICE ACT, s. 131)

NOTES:

1.   An award of costs shall normally include sums for preparation, counsel fee and assessable disbursements.

2.   A junior fee is not usually allowed on a motion taking less than one day.

3.   Goods and Services Tax (G.S.T.) of 7% shall be added to any awards of costs on either scale.

4.   The amount of the counsel fee may be increased to reflect not only the time spent on argument but also non-productive waiting time at court.

APPENDIX B

INFORMATION TO SUPPORT CLAIMS FOR COSTS

Ex parte matters on which no counsel appears

Where costs are claimed on *ex parte* motions filed to be determined without the attendance of counsel, a letter or memorandum must be filed with the material in the following form:

1. It must be signed by a solicitor.

2. Where costs are claimed on a party and party scale it must state:
   a. the number of hours spent by category of timekeeper
   b. the years of experience of any lawyer involved
   c. the assessable disbursements claimed.

3. Any other material relied on should be attached (eg. copies of orders, offers, etc.)

Example

Memorandum re Claim for Costs

preparation time:

lawyer time (5 years' experience)	1 hour	@ $70 =	$ 70.00
clerk time	2 hours	@ $35 =	70.00
assessable disbursements: issue statement of claim			125.00
transcript			90.00
			$ 355.00

(Signature of lawyer)

All other motions

1. Counsel should be prepared to file with the court, or advise the court at the hearing of, the same information as required in paragraphs 2 and 3 above.

2. Where costs are claimed on a solicitor and client scale the hourly rates for that scale on Appendix A shall be used and counsel should also be prepared to advise the court of any disbursements claimed in addition to assessable disbursements.

(In addition, to preparation time and disbursements the presiding justice may fax a counsel fee for attendance and argument based on the guidelines in Appendix A).

APPENDIX C

TELEPHONE AND FAX NUMBERS

	Telephone:	Fax:
Regional Senior Justice	(905) 853-4827	853-4826
Regional Trial Coordinator	(905) 853-4822	853-4826
Local Trial Coordinator		
Barrie	(705) 739-6151	739-6578
Bracebridge	(705) 645-9522	745-7901
Cobourg }	(905) 372-8241	372-9952
Lindsay }		
Peterborough }		
Newmarket	(905) 853-4823	853-8591
Whitby	(905) 668-9131	668-0004

PRACTICE DIRECTION
North East Region

MOTIONS IN THE ONTARIO COURT (GENERAL DIVISION)

1. All consent and routine matters not requiring notice are to be dealt with by a judge in chambers, unless otherwise requested by counsel.

2. All uncontested motions for adjournment are to be made on the consent order form attached as Schedule "A" to this Practice Direction and are to be delivered to the Registrar's office at any time prior to the day the motion is made returnable or to the clerk in court prior to the commencement of the hearing of motions on the return date. The record will be endorsed accordingly without attendance by counsel.

3. The Registrar in each Judicial District in the Region shall determine whether requests for adjournments of motions will be accepted by telephone. If such requests are determined to be acceptable, the Registrar shall notify counsel in that Judicial District, in writing, of the procedure to be followed.

4. In the event a motion is adjourned for a third time, the third adjournment will be without date, to be brought back on by any party on four days' notice to all other parties, unless otherwise ordered by a Judge.

5. A Notice of Motion will not be placed on a motions list unless it is accompanied by a Motion Record.

6. In addition to the documents required by the Rules of Civil Procedure, a Motion Record shall contain a certificate on the prescribed form, attached as Schedule "B" to this Practice Direction, signed by a lawyer estimating the time required by all parties to argue the motion. The Registrar shall refuse to accept any Motion Record which does not contain the lawyer's certificate.

7. Counsel are advised that the presiding Motions Judge will hold them strictly to the estimated time set out in the certificates.

8. The Registrar shall prepare the motions list under the following three guidelines:

    (a) "Express" (10 minutes or less)
    (b) "Short" (30 minutes or less)
    (c) "Long" (more than 30 minutes).

9. The Motions Judge will hear the Express motions first, then the Short motions, and then the Long motions in the order that the Notices of Motion have been properly filed with the Registrar, or in such other order as the Motions Judge shall determine.

10. In the event any Short motions or Long motions are not reached by the end of the day, such motions will automatically be adjourned to the trial co-ordinator who shall set fixed dates for the hearing of those motions. In the alternative, counsel who file a Long motion may apply directly to the trial co-ordinator for an appointment to hear the motion.

11. Factums are not required for an Express motion or for a Short motion unless the Motions Judge makes an order to the contrary.

12. Notwithstanding the provisions of paragraph 11, counsel are urged to file factums on Short motions.

13. Factums will be required for Long motions, save and except when the motion is for interim relief under the *Divorce Act*, the *Family Law Act* or the *Children's Law Reform Act*, or when the Motions Judge otherwise orders.

14. In the event the applicant in a Long motion has not filed his/her factum by 2:00 p.m. on the day before the motion, the Registrar shall automatically strike the motion off the list,

unless in the Notice of Motion the moving party asks for an order dispensing with the delivery of a factum.

15. This practice direction comes into force on April 1, 1994.

Dated March 24, 1994

The Honourable S.D. Loukidelis	The Honourable R.R. McMurtry
Regional Senior Justice	Chief Justice
North East Region	Ontario Court of Justice (General Division)

SCHEDULE "A"

ACTION # _____

BETWEEN:

_____

Applicant

— and —

_____

Respondent

ON CONSENT ORDER TO GO

_____   _____
Counsel for Applicant   Counsel for Respondent

_____   _____
Date   Judge

SCHEDULE "B"

ACTION # _____

BETWEEN:

_____

Applicant

— and —

_____

Respondent

CERTIFICATE

I hereby certify that the attached motion will require

_____ Hours
_____ Minutes

for argument.

_____   _____
Date   Name of Lawyer

NOTICE OF MOTION

37.01 A motion shall be made by a notice of motion (Form 37A) unless the nature of the motion or the circumstances make a notice of motion unnecessary.

JURISDICTION TO HEAR A MOTION

Jurisdiction of Judge

37.02(1) A judge has jurisdiction to hear any motion in a proceeding.

Jurisdiction of a Master

(2) A master has jurisdiction to hear any motion in a proceeding, and has all the jurisdiction of a judge in respect of a motion, except a motion,

(a) where the power to grant the relief sought is conferred expressly on a judge by a statute or rule;

(b) to set aside, vary or amend an order of a judge;

(c) to abridge or extend a time prescribed by an order that a master could not have made;

(d) for judgment on consent in favour of or against a party under disability;

(e) relating to the liberty of the subject;

(f) under section 4 or 5 of the *Judicial Review Procedure Act*; or

(g) in an appeal.

Jurisdiction of Judge — Generally

Toronto-Dominion Bank v. Berthin (1992), 11 C.P.C. (3d) 58 (Ont. Gen. Div.).

Where, in a case subject to the Toronto Civil Case Management Project, a judge other than the case management judge or a designated substitute case management judge made an order dealing with the case, the order was set aside on the basis of lack of jurisdiction. Once a case is assigned to case management in Toronto, a case management judge must deal with all matters before trial.

Re Sherwood Park Restaurant Inc. and Markham; Wendy v. Markham (1984), 43 C.P.C. 317, 10 C.R.R. 190 (Ont. H.C.).

Where a matter is otherwise properly before a judge in motions court, his jurisdiction is not ousted by the fact that an issue under the *Charter of Rights* is raised.

Jurisdiction of Master

Green v. F.W. Woolworth Co. (1992), 16 C.P.C. (3d) 34 (Ont. Master).

A master has jurisdiction to hear a motion which seeks to compel a solicitor to deliver files to his or her former client.

Georbay Developments Inc. v. Smahel (1990), 72 O.R. (2d) 200 (H.C.).

A master is without jurisdiction to discharge a certificate of pending litigation granted by a judge by reason of rule [37.02(2)(b)].

Lasch v. Lasch (1988), 64 O.R. (2d) 464, 13 R.F.L. (3d) 434 (H.C.).

The master has no jurisdiction to grant injunctive relief and hence an order made by a master pursuant to s. 12 of the *Family Law Act* merely requires a spouse to account for his or her assets at the trial.

Lido Industrial Products Ltd. v. Exbar Properties Inc. (1988), 28 O.A.C. 385 (Div. Ct.).

Although a master has jurisdiction to strike out pleadings on the ground that they are scandalous, frivolous or vexatious under rule 25.11, he or she does not have jurisdiction to do so on the ground that they disclose no reasonable cause of action or defence under rule 21.01(1)(b), since such jurisdiction is expressly conferred upon a judge.

Sharp Electronics of Can. Ltd. v. Dean (1988), 66 O.R. (2d) 748, 32 C.P.C. (2d) 181 (Master).

A master does not have jurisdiction to set aside an order of a registrar dismissing the action for failure to comply with an order of a judge made at a status hearing.

Holden Corp. v. Gingerfield Properties Ltd. (1988), 65 O.R. (2d) 454, 30 C.P.C. (2d) 302 (H.C.).

A master has no jurisdiction to hear a "recycled" motion which collaterally results in the master reviewing, varying, changing or reversing or affirming the order of a judge of the High Court.

Dickson v. Dickson (Rankin) (1988), 28 C.P.C. (2d) 45 (Ont. Master).

The jurisdiction of a master with respect to interlocutory proceedings is not displaced until the trial of an action commences.

Schrittwieser v. Morris (1987), 60 O.R. (2d) 704 (Master), reversed on other grounds 62 O.R. (2d) 177, 47 R.P.R. 185 (H.C.).

A master had jurisdiction to hear a motion for the discharge of a motion pursuant to s. 11 of the *Mortgages Act*, R.S.O. 1980, c. 296.

Young v. Gnosis Medical Systems (Can.) Ltd. (1987), 59 O.R. (2d) 61, 16 C.P.C. (2d) 135 (Master).

A master has jurisdiction to grant leave to sell land under power of sale without notice pursuant to s. 38 of the *Mortgages Act*, R.S.O. 1980, c. 296.

Inversen v. Smith (1987), 58 O.R. (2d) 733, 16 C.P.C. (2d) 215 (*sub nom. Iversen v. Smith*), 22 O.A.C. 232 (Div. Ct.).

A motion to disqualify solicitors from acting for a party may be heard by a master.

Young v. 503708 Ont. Ltd. (1986), 56 O.R. (2d) 411, 12 C.P.C. (2d) 245 (H.C.).

A master has jurisdiction to hear a motion for an order discharging a certificate of pending litigation.

Ruby & Edwardh v. Jaffe (1986), 56 O.R. (2d) 177, 10 C.P.C. (2d) 133 (H.C.).

A master has jurisdiction to hear a motion to set aside the report of an assessment officer.

Angelopoulos v. Angelopoulos (1986), 55 O.R. (2d) 101, 9 C.P.C. (2d) 285, additional reasons 55 O.R. (2d) 101 at 110, 9 C.P.C. (2d) 285 at 296 (H.C.).

A master has jurisdiction to make restraining orders and orders to preserve property under the *Family Law Act.*

Pantry v. Pantry (1986), 53 O.R. (2d) 667, 50 R.F.L. (2d) 240, 25 D.L.R. (4th) 636, 13 O.A.C. 48 (C.A.).

The master has jurisdiction to make an order for interim relief under the *Divorce Act* notwithstanding that a final order for custody and support has been made under the *Family Law Reform Act* prior to the commencement of the divorce proceedings.

Cineplex Odeon Corp. v. Toronto Star Publishing Ltd. (1986), 9 C.P.C. (2d) 7 (Ont. Master).

A master has jurisdiction to extend a time period prescribed by the order of a judge provided the order is one which could originally have been made by a master.

Cooke v. Cooke (1985), 53 O.R. (2d) 43, 6 C.P.C. (2d) 304, 23 D.L.R. (4th) 401 (H.C.).

A master has jurisdiction to stay an action on the basis of convenience of forum but does not have jurisdiction to stay an action based on a determination that the Supreme Court of Ontario does not have any jurisdiction over the case. The latter issue must be determined by a judge.

Re Zurich Ins. Co. and Torbay Dining Ltd. (1985), 49 C.P.C. 26 (Ont. Master).

Where an insurer paid money into court pursuant to s. 118 of the *Insurance Act*, R.S.O. 1980, c. 218, a "motion" for payment out of the moneys was held to be beyond the jurisdiction of a master, and was transferred to a judge. The proceeding under the *Insurance Act* was spent. There was no current proceeding in which a motion could be brought for payment out. Even if such a proceeding were still current, a final determination would be made on the hearing of an application, and not on a motion.

Dumas v. Dumas (1985), 49 C.P.C. 140 (Ont. Master).

The master does not have jurisdiction to hear a motion for an order removing the opposing party's solicitor from the record.

Long v. Long (1979), 27 O.R. (2d) 61, 14 C.P.C. 220 (Master).

A master has jurisdiction to release the automatic stay of proceedings under s. 20 of the *Family Law Reform Act* when a divorce action is commenced.

Re Robins and Partners and Randell (1978), 20 O.R. (2d) 496, (*sub nom. Re Randell and Solicitors*) 7 C.P.C. 168n (C.A.).

The master has no jurisdiction to deal with an application to tax a solicitor and client bill after payment.

Re Solicitors (1978), 7 C.P.C. 17, affirmed (*sub nom. Re Peel Terminal Warehouses Ltd. and Wootten, Rinaldo & Rosenfield*) 21 O.R. (2d) 857, 10 C.P.C. 160 (C.A.).

A master cannot refer a solicitor's bill of costs for taxation.

Epp v. Epp (1977), 17 O.R. (2d) 575, 4 C.P.C. 164 (Master).

An application to vary an interim alimony order may be heard by a master other than the one who made the original order.

O'Connor v. Mitzvah (1977), 15 O.R. (2d) 812, 3 C.P.C. 204 (Master).

A master cannot stay proceedings unless permitted by the Rules.

Papp v. Papp, [1970] 1 O.R. 331, 8 D.L.R. (3d) 389 (C.A.).

Rules approved by the court which delegate authority to the master to decide matters of interim custody are constitutional.

Wardak v. Fluxgold, [1968] 2 O.R. 849 (H.C.).

The master has jurisdiction until the case is called in court to be heard and in the absence of other jurisdictional problems he should dispose of motions on their merits and not refer them to the trial judge.

Krendel v. Frontwell Invts. Ltd., [1966] 1 O.R. 455 (Master).

While the master has jurisdiction to hear a motion on the eve of trial, he may choose to refer it to the senior judge presiding at the sittings.

Shiffman v. T.T.C., [1953] O.W.N. 367 (Master).

Where a motion within the jurisdiction of the master and a countermotion not within the jurisdiction of the master are brought before a master, the countermotion may be adjourned to be heard by a judge and the motion may be adjourned to be heard by the master after disposition of the countermotion.

A.G. Eng. v. Royal Bank, [1948] O.W.N. 782 (H.C.).

The master has no jurisdiction to determine questions of law or fact in an action but may stay the action until a party is added as a defendant.

Kerner v. Angus & Co., [1946] O.W.N. 624 (Master).

The master has no jurisdiction to hear a motion to add a party defendant if the action has come on for trial and been adjourned.

PLACE OF HEARING

Motion Made Without Notice

37.03(1) A motion properly made without notice may be made in the county where,

(a) the proceeding was commenced;

(b) any party resides; or

(c) the solicitor's office of the solicitor of record for any party is located.

Motion Made on Notice — Generally

(2) Unless the parties agree otherwise, and subject to subrules (3) and (4), a motion made on notice shall be made,

(a) in the county where the solicitor's office of any responding party is located or where a responding party who acts in person resides; or

(b) where there is no responding party residing in Ontario, in the county where the proceeding was commenced or where the solicitor's office of the solicitor of record for any party is located.

(3) Where a party has served a notice of motion naming a place of hearing in accordance with subrule (2), any other party may make a motion at the same place and time to the same judge or, if the motion is within a master's jurisdiction, to the same master.

Leave to Hear Motion on Notice at Another Place

(4) On the ground of urgency or hardship or for another sufficient reason, the court may grant leave for the hearing of a motion on notice at a place elsewhere than provided in subrule (2), and the motion for leave may be made in any county.

(5) Where leave is refused on a motion under subrule (4), the court shall fix the costs of any responding party who appeared at the hearing of the motion on a solicitor and client basis, together with travelling expenses, and order the moving party or his or her solicitor to pay those costs and expenses forthwith, unless the court is satisfied that the making of the motion for leave, although unsuccessful, was nevertheless reasonable. [am. O. Reg. 535/92, s. 9]

Milkovich v. Milkovich (1990), 25 R.F.L. (3d) 444 (Ont. Dist. Ct.).

Where the respondent in a divorce proceeding retained Toronto counsel after being served with a motion returnable in Thunder Bay, the court held that the motion had been properly made at Thunder Bay since the respondent resided there and had no solicitor of record when the motion was served.

SAF Drive Systems Inc. v. O'Bireck (1990), 45 C.P.C. (2d) 134 (Ont. Gen. Div.).

The court permitted a motion for leave to appeal to be heard where the solicitors for the moving party, rather than the responding party, practised because the original motion had been heard in that place and if leave were given the appeal would be heard in that region.

Boyle v. Coady (1990), 71 O.R. (2d) 595, 45 C.P.C. (2d) 129 (H.C.).

Where the solicitors for the responding party have offices in two counties, the moving party may bring the motion in either county. *Kasiurak v. Amery, infra,* overruled. [*But see now rules 37.03(2) and 1.03 "solicitor's office" — Authors.*]

Ridley v. Ridley (1989), 37 C.P.C. (2d) 167 (Ont. H.C.).

Financial hardship is a ground for ordering the hearing of a motion in a place where neither party resides.

Kasiurak v. Amery (1989), 69 O.R. (2d) 474 (Master).

A motion must be brought in the place where the responding party's solicitors who are actually dealing with the matter are located, despite the existence of other firm offices.

National Trust Co. v. Maxwell (1989), 34 C.P.C. (2d) 211, 3 R.P.R. (2d) 263 (Ont. H.C.).

Where a motion was made returnable in Hamilton and on the initial return of the motion the responding parties were unrepresented but retained a Toronto solicitor prior to the ultimate hearing of the motion, the order made by the local judge in Hamilton without indicating why the motion ought not to be heard in Toronto was set aside.

Murray v. Murray (1988), 30 C.P.C. (2d) 78 (Ont. H.C.), affirmed 36 C.P.C. (2d) 53 (Ont. H.C.).

Where the respondent had only retained counsel after service of a notice of motion and supporting material, and that counsel did not practise in the county where the motion was originally returnable, the motion was adjourned to be heard in the county where the respondent's solicitor practised.

Motor Employees (Windsor) Credit Union Ltd. v. Co-operators General Ins. Co. (1988), 26 C.P.C. (2d) 1 (Ont. H.C.).

A motion brought before a master in Toronto was adjourned to a local judge in Windsor where the preponderance of convenience favoured hearing the motion in Windsor.

Bright v. Clanahan (1987), 24 C.P.C. (2d) 268 (Ont. H.C.).

An order resulting from a motion brought in the wrong venue was set aside. Where a court concludes that a motion has been brought in the wrong venue and leave is not granted to bring it elsewhere, the court should not hear the substance of the motion because to do so would encourage motions being brought in the wrong venue.

Greymac Trust Co. v. Burnett (1987), 59 O.R. (2d) 50, 16 C.P.C. (2d) 75 (H.C.).

The court held that a motion was properly heard in Toronto because several of the responding parties were represented by Toronto solicitors notwithstanding that the responding party who was the "target" of the motion was represented by a Windsor solicitor.

Bonczuk v. Bonczuk (1986), 12 C.P.C. (2d) 299 (Ont. H.C.).

A motion to commit for contempt should be brought in the location where the alleged contempt has been committed.

Bank of Montreal v. Beck (1986), 10 C.P.C. (2d) 45 (Ont. Dist. Ct.).

Where the solicitors for the responding party maintain offices in several counties, the moving party may bring the motion in any of those counties.

G.C. Rentals & Enterprises Ltd. v. Giamnarino (1986), 9 C.P.C. (2d) 10 (Ont. H.C.).

The court held that a plaintiff bringing a motion for examination of a witness outside Ontario was not required to bring the motion in the place where the defendant's solicitors practised.

Rogan v. Magnus Aerospace Corp. (1985), 50 C.P.C. 217, 7 C.P.R. (3d) 405 (Ont. H.C.).

Where a moving party chose an incorrect place of hearing the court proceeded to hear the motion to avoid waste of time. The moving party was successful on the motion but was deprived of costs because of its failure to comply with rule 37.03(2).

Mutual Life Assur. Co. of Can. v. Windsor Westchester at the Lake Ltd. (1985), 47 C.P.C. 12 (Ont. Master).

The court gave leave that a motion be brought in Toronto rather than Windsor because the responding party's counsel had consented to two other motions being heard in Toronto and was therefore not prejudiced.

Secord v. Bank of Montreal (1984), 47 O.R. (2d) 538, 44 C.P.C. 296 (Master).

The master has no jurisdiction to make an order as to the place of hearing of all further motions based on an alleged agreement between counsel as to venue.

MOTIONS — TO WHOM TO BE MADE

37.04 A motion shall be made to the court if it is within a master's jurisdiction and otherwise shall be made to a judge.

HEARING DATE FOR MOTIONS

Where no practice direction
37.05(1) At any place where no practice direction concerning the scheduling of motions is in effect, a motion may be set down for hearing on any day on which a judge or master is scheduled to hear motions.

Exception, lengthy hearing
(2) If counsel estimates that the hearing of the motion will be more than two hours long, a hearing date shall be obtained from the registrar before the notice of motion is served.

Urgent motion
(3) An urgent motion may be set down for hearing on any day on which a judge or master is scheduled to hear motions, even if counsel estimates that the hearing is likely to be more than two hours long. [re-en. O. Reg. 770/92, s. 10]

CONTENT OF NOTICE

37.06 Every notice of motion (Form 37A) shall,
(a) state the precise relief sought;
(b) state the grounds to be argued, including a reference to any statutory provision or rule to be relied on; and
(c) list the documentary evidence to be used at the hearing of the motion.

Symons Gen. Ins. Co. v. Can. Union Ins. Co. (1985), 50 C.P.C. 75 (Ont. Master).

The failure to comply with rule 37.06 is sufficient grounds to adjourn or dismiss a motion, without prejudice to a further motion, if the responding party is prejudiced by the non-observance of the rule.

Malthouse v. R. (1977), 3 C.P.C. 351 (Ont. H.C.).

A party moving against an irregularity should itself be free of any irregularity in its motion. A late application for leave to appeal an order validating originating process was dismissed in this case.

Conacher v. Conacher, [1956] O.W.N. 347 (Master).

Where a notice of motion failed to specify the nature of an alleged irregularity in an order the court refused to hear an attack on the order.

SERVICE OF NOTICE

Required as General Rule

37.07(1) The notice of motion shall be served on any person or party who will be affected by the order sought, unless these rules provide otherwise.

Where Not Required

(2) Where the nature of the motion or the circumstances render service of the notice of motion impracticable or unnecessary, the court may make an order without notice.

(3) Where the delay necessary to effect service might entail serious consequences, the court may make an interim order without notice.

(4) Unless the court orders or these rules provide otherwise, an order made without notice to a person or party affected by the order shall be served on the person or party, together with a copy of the notice of motion and all affidavits and other documents used at the hearing of the motion.

Where Notice Ought to Have Been Served

(5) Where it appears to the court that the notice of motion ought to have been served on a person who has not been served, the court may,

(a) dismiss the motion or dismiss it only against the person who was not served;

(b) adjourn the motion and direct that the notice of motion be served on the person; or

(c) direct that any order made on the motion be served on the person.

Minimum Notice Period

(6) Where a motion is made on notice, the notice of motion shall be served at least three days before the date on which the motion is to be heard. [am. O. Reg. 219/91, s. 3]

> *Cross-Reference:* See rule 39.01(6) re duty of disclosure on motion made without notice.

M. (S.) v. C. (J.R.) (1993), 13 O.R. (3d) 148 (Gen. Div.).

Evidence showing notice is impracticable or unnecessary must be provided before a court will make an order without notice.

Canada (Attorney General) v. Cardinal Insurance Co. (1991), 7 C.P.C. (3d) 167 (Ont. Gen. Div.).

On a motion by a liquidator to approve a settlement of a law suit commenced by the company in liquidation, the parties to the law suit proposed to be settled are entitled to notice.

Launch! Research & Dev. Inc. v. Essex Dist. Co. (1977), 4 C.P.C. 261 (Ont. H.C.).

A plaintiff should only apply for an injunction without notice where it is genuinely impossible to give any notice to the defendant of the order sought without defeating the purposes of the order.

FILING OF NOTICE OF MOTION

37.08(1) Where a motion is made on notice, the notice of motion shall be filed with proof of service at least two days before the hearing date in the court office where the motion is to be heard.

(2) Where service of the notice of motion is not required, it shall be filed at or before the hearing.

ABANDONED MOTIONS

37.09(1) A party who makes a motion may abandon it by delivering a notice of abandonment.

(2) A party who serves a notice of motion and does not file it or appear at the hearing shall be deemed to have abandoned the motion unless the court orders otherwise.

(3) Where a motion is abandoned or is deemed to have been abandoned, a responding party on whom the notice of motion was served is entitled to the costs of the motion forthwith, unless the court orders otherwise.

Yang v. Mao (1995), 23 O.R. (3d) 466, 39 C.P.C. (3d) 10 (Gen. Div.).

Where the plaintiff abandoned its motion for an injunction without explanation, the court awarded costs on a solicitor and client scale.

Zimmerman v. Banack (1992), 15 C.P.C. (3d) 293 (Ont. Gen. Div.).

The court awarded party and party costs, not solicitor and client costs, against defendants who abandoned their motion for summary judgment. It was reasonable to have brought the motion and it was abandoned when new adverse facts were discovered.

MATERIAL FOR USE ON MOTIONS

Where Motion Record Required

37.10(1) Where a motion is made on notice, the moving party shall, unless the court orders otherwise before or at the hearing of the motion, serve a motion record on every other party to the motion and file it, with proof of service, in the court office where the motion is to be heard, at least two days before the hearing, and the court file shall not be placed before the judge or master hearing the motion unless he or she requests it or a party requisitions it.

Contents of Motion Record

(2) The motion record shall contain, in consecutively numbered pages arranged in the following order,

(a) a table of contents describing each document, including each exhibit, by its nature and date and, in the case of an exhibit, by exhibit number or letter;

(b) a copy of the notice of motion;

(c) a copy of all affidavits and other material served by any party for use on the motion;

(d) a list of all relevant transcripts of evidence in chronological order, but not necessarily the transcripts themselves; and

(e) a copy of any other material in the court file that is necessary for the hearing of the motion.

Responding Party's Motion Record

(3) Where a motion record is served a responding party who is of the opinion that it is incomplete may serve on every other party, and file, with proof of service, in the court office where the motion is to be heard, not later than 2 p.m. on the day before the hearing, a responding party's motion record containing, in consecutively numbered pages arranged in the following order,

(a) a table of contents describing each document, including each exhibit, by its nature and date and, in the case of an exhibit, by exhibit number or letter; and

(b) a copy of any material to be used by the responding party on the motion and not included in the motion record.

Material may be Filed as Part of Record

(4) A notice of motion and any other material served by a party for use on a motion may be filed, together with proof of service, as part of the party's motion record and need not be filed separately.

Transcript of Evidence

(5) A party who intends to refer to a transcript of evidence at the hearing of a motion shall file a copy of the transcript as provided by rule 34.18.

Factum

(6) A party may serve on every other party and file, with proof of service, in the court office where the motion is to be heard, not later than 2 p.m. on the day before the hearing, a factum consisting of a concise statement, without argument, of the facts and law relied on by the party.

HEARING IN ABSENCE OF PUBLIC

37.11(1) A motion may be heard in the absence of the public where,

(a) the motion is to be heard and determined without oral argument;

(b) because of urgency, it is impractical to have the motion heard in public;

(c) the motion is to be heard by conference telephone under rule 37.12;

(d) the motion is made in the course of a pre-trial conference; or

(e) the motion is before a single judge of an appellate court.

(2) The hearing of all other motions shall be open to the public, except as provided in section 135 of the *Courts of Justice Act*, in which case the presiding judge or officer shall endorse on the notice of motion leave for a hearing in the absence of the public. [am. O. Reg. 465/93, s. 4]

HEARING BY CONFERENCE TELEPHONE

37.12 By appointment obtained from the judge or officer before whom the motion is to be heard, the motion may be heard in whole or in part by means of a conference telephone call. [am. O. Reg. 535/92, s. 10]

HEARING WITHOUT ORAL ARGUMENT

Consent motions, unopposed motions and motions without notice

37.12.1(1) Where a motion is on consent, unopposed or without notice under subrule 37.07(2), the motion may be heard in writing without the attendance of the parties, unless the court orders otherwise.

(2) Where the motion is on consent, the consent and a draft order shall be filed with the notice of motion.

(3) Where the motion is unopposed, a notice from the responding party stating that the party does not oppose the motion and a draft order shall be filed with the notice of motion.

Opposed Motions in Writing

(4) Where the issues of fact and law are not complex, the moving party may propose in the notice of motion that the motion be heard in writing without the attendance of the parties, in which case,

(a) the motion shall be made on at least fourteen days notice;

(b) the moving party shall serve with the notice of motion and immediately file, with proof of service in the court office where the motion is to be heard, a motion record, a draft order and a factum entitled factum for a motion in writing, setting out the moving party's argument;

(c) the motion may be heard in writing without the attendance of the parties, unless the court orders otherwise.

(5) Within ten days after being served with the moving party's material, the responding party shall serve and file, with proof of service, in the court office where the motion is to be heard,

(a) a consent to the motion;

(b) a notice that the responding party does not oppose the motion;

(c) a motion record, a notice that the responding party agrees to have the motion heard and determined in writing under this rule and a factum entitled factum for a motion in writing, setting out the party's argument; or

(d) a notice that the responding party intends to make oral argument, along with any material intended to be relied upon by the party.

(6) Where the responding party delivers a notice under subrule (5) that the party intends to make oral argument, the moving party may either attend the hearing and make oral argument or not attend and rely on the party's motion record and factum. [en. O. Reg. 465/93, s. 4; am. O. Reg. 766/93, s. 1]

DISPOSITION OF MOTION

37.13(1) On the hearing of a motion, the presiding judge or officer may grant the relief sought or dismiss or adjourn the motion, in whole or in part and with or without terms, and may,

(a) where the proceeding is an action, order that it be placed forthwith, or within a specified time, on a list of cases requiring speedy trial; or

(b) where the proceeding is an application, order that it be heard at such time and place as are just.

(2) A judge who hears a motion may,

(a) in a proper case, order that the motion be converted into a motion for judgment; or

(b) order the trial of an issue, with such directions as are just, and adjourn the motion to be disposed of by the trial judge.

(3) Where on a motion a judge directs the trial of an issue, subrules 38.10(2) and (3) (issue treated as action) apply with necessary modifications.

Exception, motions in estate matters

(4) Clause (2)(b) and subrule (3) do not apply to motions under Rules 74 and 75. [am. O. Reg. 484/94, s. 7]

Effect of Disposition of Motion — Res Judicata

Newmarch Mechanical Constructors Ltd. v. Hyundai Auto Canada Inc. (1994), 18 O.R. (3d) 766, 26 C.P.C. (3d) 289 (Gen. Div.).

An interlocutory order which finally determined an issue in the absence of an appeal, material change in circumstances, or new evidence which had been suppressed or unavailable, gave rise to *res judicata* estoppel.

Ward v. Dana G. Colson Management Ltd. (1994), 24 C.P.C. (3d) 211 (Ont. Gen. Div.), affirmed (December 2, 1994), Doc. CA C18299 (Ont. C.A.).

Where an issue is raised and determined in the context of an interlocutory motion, as a general rule issue estoppel applies and neither party will be permitted to re-litigate the issue in the same or a subsequent proceeding.

Famous Players Development Corp. v. Central Capital Corp. (1990), 1 O.R. (3d) 672, 46 C.P.C. (2d) 90 (Gen. Div.), affirmed (1991), 6 O.R. (3d) 765, 3 C.P.C. (3d) 286, 53 O.A.C. 185 (Div. Ct.).

Estoppel by *res judicata* does not apply to interlocutory orders which are not final such as an order dismissing a motion to examine a non-party for discovery under rule 31.10.

William Allan Real Estate Co. v. Robichaud (1990), 72 O.R. (2d) 595, 9 R.P.R. (2d) 48, 68 D.L.R. (4th) 37, additional reasons 72 O.R. (2d) 595 at 615, 68 D.L.R. (4th) 37 at 57 (H.C.).

Where documents had been held at the interlocutory stage, on the facts then before the court, to have been made as part of without prejudice settlement discussions, this decision was held not to be *res judicata* at trial on the question of whether or not the documents were privileged on that ground.

Royal Bank v. Barringer; Royal Bank v. Santopolo (1983), 44 O.R. (2d) 506, 38 C.P.C. 196 (Master).

A decision on a motion to set aside a default judgment that a triable issue exists does not bar a motion for summary judgment. Since the first decision was an interlocutory one, *res judicata* does not apply.

Goulding v. Ternoey (1982), 35 O.R. (2d) 29, 25 R.F.L. (2d) 113, 132 D.L.R. (3d) 44 (C.A.).

The dismissal of a motion "without prejudice" merely prevents the respondent from raising the defence of *res judicata* on a subsequent motion. It does not affect time limitations or any other application of the law.

Pickard v. Reynolds Int. Pen Co. [1946] O.W.N. 907 (Master).

A dismissal of a motion without a judicial determination of its merits does not preclude a second motion on fresh material.

Terms of Adjournment

Staiman Steel Ltd. v. Struxcon Ltd. (1989), 38 C.P.C. (2d) 136 (Ont. H.C.).

On the adjournment of a motion for summary judgment the court imposed a term that the defendant pay $100,000 into court.

Ordering Trial of an Issue — rule 37.13(2)(b) (See also cases under rule 38.10.)

Shepley v. Libby McNeil & Libby of Can. Ltd. (1979), 23 O.R. (2d) 354, 9 C.P.C. 201 (Div. Ct.).

The court has no jurisdiction to order the trial of an issue where a jury notice is outstanding.

Ball v. New York Central Railroad Co., [1954] O.W.N. 41, 71 C.R.T.C. 132 (H.C.).

The trial of an issue should be directed only to decide a matter collateral to and necessary for a decision on the motion in which the issue is directed.

McCaw v. Eames, [1948] O.W.N. 774 (H.C.).

Discussion of the jurisdiction of a local judge to direct a trial of an issue. [*But see now rules 38.02, 38.10(1) — Authors.*]

Shields v. The London and Western Trusts Co., [1924] S.C.R. 25, [1924] 1 D.L.R. 163.

The ordering of the trial of an issue is in the discretion of the judge of first instance.

Conduct of Hearing of Motion

Re Ferguson and Imax Systems Corp. (1984), 47 O.R. (2d) 225, 44 C.P.C. 17, 52 C.B.R. (N.S.) 255, 11 D.L.R. (4th) 249, 4 O.A.C. 188 (Div. Ct.).

The court may impose a time limit for oral argument in a proper case.

SETTING ASIDE, VARYING OR AMENDING ORDERS

Motion to Set Aside or Vary

37.14(1) A person who,

(a) is affected by an order obtained on motion without notice;

(b) fails to appear on a motion through accident, mistake or insufficient notice; or

(c) is affected by an order of a registrar,

may move to set aside or vary the order, by a notice of motion that is served forthwith after the order comes to the person's attention and names the first available hearing date that is at least three days after service of the notice of motion.

(2) On a motion under subrule (1), the court may set aside or vary the order on such terms as are just.

Order Made by Registrar

(3) A motion under subrule (1) or any other rule to set aside, vary or amend an order of a registrar may be made to a judge or master, at a place in accordance with rule 37.03 (place of hearing of motions).

Order Made by Judge

(4) A motion under subrule (1) or any other rule to set aside, vary or amend an order of a judge may be made,

(a) to the judge who made it, at any place; or

(b) to any other judge, at a place determined in accordance with rule 37.03 (place of hearing of motions).

Order Made by Master

(5) A motion under subrule (1) or any other rule to set aside, vary or amend an order of a master may be made,

(a) to the master who made it, at any place; or

(b) to any other master or to a judge, at a place determined in accordance with rule 37.03 (place of hearing of motions).

Order Made in Court of Appeal or Divisional Court

(6) A motion under subrule (1) or any other rule to set aside, vary or amend an order made by a judge or panel of the Court of Appeal or Divisional Court may be made,

(a) where the order was made by a judge, to the judge who made it or any other judge of the court; or

(b) where the order was made by a panel of the court, to the panel that made it or any other panel of the court.

Cross-Reference: See also cases under rule 38.11 and rule 39.01(6).

Ewert v. Chapnick (1995), 37 C.P.C. (3d) 76 (Ont. Gen. Div.).

Where counsel's non-attendance on a motion was by her own volition, the court refused to set aside the order.

Murphy v. Dodd (1989), 70 O.R. (2d) 681, 63 D.L.R. (4th) 515 (H.C.).

The court set aside an order prohibiting an abortion where the respondent had not attended on the original application. The application had been brought on short notice and the respondent had not fully appreciated the significance of the proceedings.

Warger v. Nudel (1989), 39 C.P.C. (2d) 290 (Ont. Master), affirmed (1990), 49 C.P.C. (2d) 126 (Ont. Div. Ct.).

Analysis of a master's jurisdiction to review and set aside previous orders made by a master. In the circumstances the court declined to exercise its jurisdiction to set aside the previous order.

Bayside Realty Inc. v. P.D.L. Developments (Overseas) Ltd. (1989), 38 C.P.C. (2d) 155 (Ont. Master).

The court set aside an order dismissing the action where the plaintiff claimed not to have notice of the motion for the order, no limitation period had expired, and the plaintiff's case was *prima facie* meritorious.

Tong v. Ing (1988), 67 O.R. (2d) 20 (Master).

The court refused to set aside an order made where the solicitor for the responding party was unable to argue the motion on the hearing date due to conflicting engagements but did not arrange for someone to attend and seek an adjournment.

Waites v. Alltemp Products Co. (1987), 19 C.P.C. (2d) 185 (Ont. Dist. Ct.).

The issue on a motion to set aside an order is not only whether the order should have been granted initially, but also if, having been made, it should be set aside.

Axelrod v. City of Toronto (No. 2) (1985), 52 O.R. (2d) 440, 5 C.P.C. (2d) 221 (*sub nom. Axelrod v. City of Toronto*) (H.C.).

The court varied its own order and eliminated a fine it had imposed for contempt.

Merker v. Leader Terrazzo Tile Mosaic Ltd. (1983), 43 O.R. (2d) 632, 37 C.P.C. 1, 2 D.L.R. (4th) 117 (H.C.).

An *ex parte* order, obtained by the plaintiff on misleading affidavit material, was set aside although the cross-examination disclosed information sufficient to support the order made. The court awarded costs on a solicitor and client scale, payable by the plaintiff's solicitors personally.

Merker v. Leader Terrazzo Tile Mosaic Ltd. (1983), 32 C.P.C. 223, reversed on other grounds 43 O.R. (2d) 632, 37 C.P.C. 1, 2 D.L.R. (4th) 117 (H.C.).

A party moving to set aside an *ex parte* order is entitled to cross-examine on an affidavit filed in support of the *ex parte* motion.

Bosch v. Bosch (1982), 2 F.L.R.A.C. 109 (Ont. Master).

The court set aside an order where counsel for the responding party inadvertently left the hearing date out of her diary and was not in attendance when the order was made.

Strazisar v. Can. Universal Ins. Co. (1981), 21 C.P.C. 51 (Ont. Co. Ct.).

The respondent should be permitted to file further material or a motion to set aside an order made without notice if: (1) it was not obtainable by reasonable diligence at the time of the original hearing, (2) if admitted it would have an important influence on the result; and (3) it is apparently credible.

Re Sneath (1979), 13 C.P.C. 111 (Ont. Master).

An application to set aside a certificate of taxation of a solicitor and client bill must be brought before a taxing officer, or perhaps a motion court judge.

Palmateer v. Bach, 9 O.R. (2d) 693, [1975] I.L.R. 1-667 (H.C.).

An insurer of a defendant has status by virtue of the *Insurance Act*, R.S.O. 1970, c. 224, s. 225, to bring an application to set aside an order extending the time for service of an originating process.

McCart v. A.B.C. Auto Wrecking Supply Co., [1966] 1 O.R. 546 (Master).

While a *praecipe* order is an order made without notice, there is no limitation on the time allowed in which to attack such an order as having been made without proper authority.

MOTIONS IN A COMPLICATED PROCEEDING OR SERIES OF PROCEEDINGS

37.15(1) Where a proceeding involves complicated issues or where there are two or more proceedings that involve similar issues, the Chief Justice or Associate Chief Justice of the Ontario Court, a regional senior judge of the General Division or a judge designated by any of them may direct that all motions in the proceeding or proceedings be heard by a particular judge, and rule 37.03 (place of hearing of motions) does not apply to those motions.

(2) A judge who hears motions pursuant to a direction under subrule (1) shall not preside at the trial of the actions or the hearing of the applications.

Chippewas of Sarnia Band v. Canada (Attorney General) (1996), 7 W.D.C.P. (2d) 172 (Ont. Gen. Div.).

It is for the Chief Justice or the Regional Senior Judge of the region where the case will be tried to decide whether a judge should be designated pursuant to rule 37.15(1) to hear motions in a class action. If a judge is so designated, rule 37.03 regarding venue for motions does not apply.

Control and Metering Ltd. v. Karpowicz (1994), 17 O.R. (3d) 431, 23 C.P.C. (3d) 275 (Gen. Div.).

While a judge case-managing an action may well take into account views of the facts and legal issues formed in prior motions, that is what the Case Management Rules mandate and the judge may not be disqualified on the basis of an apprehension of bias.

Morgan v. Morgan (1992), 6 C.P.C. (3d) 261 (Ont. Gen. Div.).

A judge was designated to hear all motions in this proceeding where there had been ten motions over a four-month period and the motions appeared to depend on and require a review of the previous motions.

PROHIBITING MOTIONS WITHOUT LEAVE

37.16 On motion by any party, a judge or master may by order prohibit another party from making further motions in the proceeding without leave, where the judge or master on the hearing of the motion is satisfied that the other party is attempting to delay or add to the costs of the proceeding or otherwise abuse the process of the court by a multiplicity of frivolous or vexatious motions.

MOTION BEFORE COMMENCEMENT OF PROCEEDING

37.17 In an urgent case, a motion may be made before the commencement of a proceeding on the moving party's undertaking to commence the proceeding forthwith.

Aroland First Nation v. Ontario (1996), 7 W.D.C.P. (2d) 138 (Ont. Gen. Div.).

The court has jurisdiction to add a party to an intended action where a motion has been brought under rule 37.17.

Warkentin v. Sault Ste. Marie Bd. of Educ. (1985), 49 C.P.C. 31 (Ont. Dist. Ct.).

The court entertained a motion for an interim injunction in a situation of urgency where the plaintiffs had not yet commenced a proceeding but where they undertook, through their counsel, to commence the proceeding forthwith.

RULE 38   APPLICATIONS — JURISDICTION AND PROCEDURE

Highlights

This Rule regulates the jurisdiction and procedure on "applications" (formerly called originating motions). It should be read in conjunction with Rule 14 (Originating Process) which states when proceedings may be taken by application, and Rule 39 (Evidence on Motions and Applications). Rule 38 applies to all applications in the Ontario Court (General Division), though parts of the Rule are inapplicable to applications for judicial review in the Divisional Court: rules 38.01(2) and 68.02(1).

Jurisdiction. Under the Rules the masters have no jurisdiction to hear applications, however, statutes confer some jurisdiction on them: see the *Mortgages Act*, R.S.O. 1990, c. M.40, s. 39.

Notice of application. The notice of application must be detailed and informative (rule 38.04) and it must be issued by the court to commence the proceeding: rule 38.05.

The notice of application must be served ten days before the hearing date, or twenty days before the hearing date when it is served out of Ontario: rule 38.06(3).

Hearing date. Where there is a practice direction in effect at the place of hearing, it governs the scheduling of the hearing; otherwise, an application may be set down for hearing on any day on which a judge is scheduled to hear applications, and if counsel estimates that the hearing of the application will be more than two hours, a hearing date shall be obtained from the registrar before the notice of application is served (rule 38.03(2) and (3)). But an urgent application may be set down for hearing on any day on which applications are scheduled to be heard: rule 38.03(3.1).

Except with respect to certain family law proceedings (see rule 70.05) and applications under the *Landlord and Tenant Act* (rule 38.03(1.1)) there is no requirement that applications be heard in a particular county.

Appearance. A respondent served with a notice of application must forthwith deliver a "notice of appearance" (rule 38.07(1)) and a respondent who fails to do so is generally not entitled to receive further notice or documents, to file material, to examine or cross-examine witnesses or to be heard at the hearing of the application, except with leave (rule 38.07(2)) and need not be served with the application record and factum: rule 38.09(1).

Counter-applications. These are specifically provided for in rule 38.03(4).

Miscellaneous. The applicant and the respondent must each deliver an application record and factum for use on the hearing, unless dispensed with by a judge: rule 38.09.

Specific provision is made for abandoning applications (rule 38.08), for setting aside judgment given without notice (rule 38.11) and for the court's powers on the hearing of the application, including the power to direct the trial of an issue in which event the proceeding in effect becomes an action (rule 38.10).

Commercial list. Applications concerning matters on the Commercial List are dealt with in the Commercial List practice direction reproduced below, following the Highlights. See also the practice direction under Rule 37 regarding masters motions in Commercial List matters.

Summary of procedure. For a summary of the procedure on an application, see Procedural Charts (CHARTS).

Practice directions. For applications in Toronto's Motion Court (Weekly Court) or for applications in the Central East Region, see the practice directions reproduced following the Highlights of Rule 37. For local procedures regarding applications in the Central South Region see chapter 5 of the *Administrative Procedures Manual for the Central South Region* published by direction of Regional Senior Justice Fedak.

Former Rules: Rules 10, 35, 48, 127, 209-217, 235, 238-239, 608, 613.

PRACTICE DIRECTION
Toronto Region

THE COMMERCIAL LIST

The Commercial List was established in 1991 for the hearing of certain actions, applications and motions in the Ontario Court (General Division) in the Toronto Region involving issues of commercial law. The special procedures adopted for the hearing of matters on the Commercial List which expedite the hearing and determination of these matters have met with considerable approval and they have expedited the hearing and determination of these matters.

These procedures continue to be developmental. This revision of the Practice Direction contains numerous modifications from the June 15, 1993 version (reported at (1993), 13 O.R. (3d) 453). All counsel appearing in matters on the Commercial List are expected to know and follow the current Practice Direction. Since the Commercial List is well established, many of the provisions of the governing practice direction can be shortened and simplified. It is expected that the Practice Direction covers most areas of general inquiry which have been made to the Commercial List Office. Reference should also be made to *Ashmore v. Corp. of Lloyd's*, [1992] 2 All E.R. 486 (H.L.).

The Commercial List remains, in the first instance, voluntary, except for bankruptcy matters. Applicants and plaintiffs may continue to set matters that qualify for the Commercial List down for hearing either on the Commercial List or elsewhere. There is, however, provision for any party to have a matter transferred to, or removed from, the Commercial List.

A continuous re-evaluation process by the Court and the Users' Committee determines whether (i) other matters should be added to those matters which may be listed on the Commercial List or (ii) its procedures should be further modified or continued. Co-operation, communication and common sense will continue to be the watchwords of the Commercial List. This Practice Direction is to govern the conduct of matters on the Commercial List after December 31, 1995, subject to further amendments as required.

Osgoode Hall   THE HONOURABLE R. ROY MCMURTRY
August 8, 1995   CHIEF JUSTICE OF THE ONTARIO COURT

Matters Eligible for the Commercial List

1. Matters which may be listed on the Commercial List are applications, motions and actions which in essence involve the following:
   (a) *Bankruptcy and Insolvency Act*;
   (b) *Bank Act*, relating to realizations and priority disputes;
   (c) *Business Corporations Act (Ontario)* and *Canada Business Corporations Act*:
   (d) *Companies' Creditors Arrangements Act*;
   (e) *Limited Partnerships Act*;
   (f) *Pension Benefits Act*;
   (g) *Personal Property Security Act*;
   (h) receivership applications and all interlocutory motions to appoint, or give directions to, receivers and receiver/managers;

(i) *Securities Act*;
(j) *Winding-Up Act*; and
(k) such other commercial matters as a judge presiding over the Commercial List may direct to be listed on the Commercial List (See *771225 Ontario Inc. v. Bramco Holdings Co. Ltd.*, [1993] O.J. No. 1772).

In considering whether to make a direction under sub-paragraph 1(k), the judge may take into account the current and expected caseload of matters listed on the Commercial List.

Judges, Court Officials and Courtrooms

2. The Commercial List will be administered through the facilities of the Commercial List Office, Room 118, 145 Queen Street West, Toronto.
3. Matters listed on the Commercial List, including bankruptcy matters, will usually be heard in courtrooms at 145 Queen Street West, Toronto. The Commercial List will also use the facilities of the ADR Centre at 77 Grenville Street, Toronto and counsel will be advised of these cases the day before the hearing. Counsel appearing at the ADR Centre will not be gowned, while counsel appearing elsewhere will be gowned.
4. If counsel are aware that a judge sitting on the Commercial List should not hear a particular matter, the Commercial List Office should be advised.

Originating Process

5. Actions and applications intended to be listed, in whole or in part, on the Commercial List will be issued in the appropriate office of the Ontario Court (General Division), as provided in the Rules of Civil Procedure.
6. For all applications, an initial return date, obtained from the Commercial List Office or selected by counsel in conformity with the provisions of paragraphs 14 and 15, as the case may be, must be used.

Place of Hearing

7. For the time being, only Toronto Region matters can be listed on the Commercial List (unless, for special reasons, authorization is given by the supervising judge) and matters listed on the Commercial List will only be heard in Toronto. With respect to motions concerning matters from outside the Toronto Region, including transfers, either a consent must be obtained or a general leave for a particular matter may be granted concerning rule 37.03.

Applications for Transfer

8. Matters may be transferred to or removed from the Commercial List on a motion to a judge sitting to hear matters on the Commercial List. Such motions will be dealt with as a regular motion or, if urgent, as a Chambers Matter as provided in paragraph 24.
9. A matter may be provisionally transferred to the Commercial List by a judge who is hearing the matter or a proceeding in the matter but who is not sitting to hear matters on the Commercial List, with the consent of all parties appearing. Such provisional transfer will be for the purpose of bringing an application for transfer in accordance with paragraph 8 by one of the parties or as the judge may direct. A new Commercial List file number will be assigned to transferred matters and that file number will be used exclusively thereafter, except that the original file number shall be used to indicate on the Request Form that the matter has been previously dealt with.
10. A matter may be transferred to the Commercial List by the Commercial List Office staff if the transfer is on consent of all parties, a Request Form and Case Timetable are fully completed and the matter is a Toronto matter which clearly falls within the categories of sub-paragraphs 1(a)-(j).

Court Documents

11 The name of the court in the title of proceedings of matters listed on the Commercial List will be: "Ontario Court (General Division) — Commercial List". All Notices of Application and Notices of Motion involving the Commercial List will state that the application or motion will be made to "a judge presiding over the Commercial List at 145 Queen Street West, Toronto".

12. All parts of the front and back of a Request Form must be completed for all cases and for each proceeding (including 9:30 a.m. matters, matters added to the Commercial List and all other attendances) and the form must be signed by all counsel or an explanation for not doing so must be given. If all counsel cannot sign the same form, they may sign individual copies. Completed Request Forms may be faxed to the Commercial List Office at (416) 327-6228. Copies of the current Request Form are available from the Commercial List Office.

13. A Case Timetable should be completed to accompany the Request Form. If this cannot be done before the matter is first spoken to (it being recognized that the schedule may depend on the setting of a hearing date), a Case Timetable should be agreed among counsel as soon as possible thereafter and a copy sent to the Commercial List Office. In the event that counsel cannot agree on a schedule, counsel should attend before the supervising judge in chambers (see paragraph 24). It is expected that matters will be completed sufficiently in advance of the deadline dates to allow for consideration of the matter by counsel and subsequent slippage in the matter. If a step is not completed in accordance with the Case Timetable, counsel are expected to get the matter back on schedule as soon as possible. (See *Mernick (Re)* (1992), 14 C.B.R. (3d) 263). Copies of the current Case Timetable form are available from the Commercial List Office.

Dates for Applications, Motions and Trials

14. The Commercial List Office will maintain the Commercial List. The office staff and the supervising judge in chambers may assign initial hearing dates for matters requiring 2 days or less for hearing ("short matters").

15. For applications and motions which are expected to take 3 days or more ("long" matters), the application or motion will initially be made returnable in the assignment court held on the first Monday of a month (or the first Tuesday, if Monday is a holiday) beginning at 9:30 a.m. The date for hearing will thereafter be assigned by the supervising judge. Notices of Application and Notices of Motion for such matters will state that the application or motion is to be heard on the initial return date "and thereafter as the judge may direct". Dates for the hearing of petitions in bankruptcy will also be set at this assignment court.

16. For trials and trials of issues, a motion to set a hearing date will be made, unless the matter is otherwise scheduled by the supervising judge in chambers on consent or on the appearance of all parties. The motion should be made to the supervising judge or designate either as a chambers motion under paragraph 24 or by special appointment. A trial date will not be set unless the applicable steps noted in the Tariff/Hearing Requirements Memorandum have been completed and a pre-trial has been held. Provision for these steps should be made in the Case Timetable.

17. A Trial/Hearing Requirements Memorandum should be obtained from the Commercial List Office at an early stage and the applicable steps completed. If the applicable steps have not been materially completed by the time of the pre-trial, they must be completed before a trial date will be set. The witness milestones shall have been completed before the pre-trial; this determination is essential to permit the correct calculation of the time required for the trial, as other trials will be scheduled to follow immediately thereafter.

18. For a scheduling motion to a judge to be heard at an assignment court, counsel should try to provide a list of 3 mutually convenient and disparate dates from which the judge may select. Counsel are expected to check with the Commercial List Office for available dates immediately prior to the motion.

19. Except where special circumstances otherwise require, in selecting a return date for a matter, counsel are expected to allow reasonable time for all preliminary steps (such as cross-examinations and the filing of additional affidavits) to take place before the return date, in order that the matter can be dealt with effectively by the Court. Counsel are encouraged and expected to consult among themselves in this regard, so that matters can be dealt with on their return and without further adjournment.

20. Counsel may specify the return date for a matter as "on a date to be established by the Commercial List Office". A list of these matters will be maintained by the Commercial List Office. Matters set down on this basis which are not heard within 3 months will be struck from the list, unless otherwise ordered on a chambers motion to the supervising judge. If counsel are not able to resolve scheduling issues among themselves, a chambers motion may be made for a date and draft timetables shall be provided to the judge by each party.

21. A list of matters scheduled to be heard the following day will be posted on the bulletin board at 145 Queen Street West by 4:00 p.m. Information about matters listed for the following day may also be obtained by calling 327-5045 after 4:00 p.m.

Estimates of Required Time

22. A realistic estimate of the time required for hearing the matter must be stated in the Request Form. If such an estimate cannot be given on the initial return of a matter, the Request Form must be appropriately amended when the matter is subsequently re-scheduled. If all parties do not sign the Request Form, the initial return of the matter shall be for a 10 minute scheduling hearing. Counsel are expected to allocate the estimated hearing time appropriately among themselves, failing which the Court will assume that counsel have agreed to an equal division of time. If the time estimates in the Request Form become obsolete, then it is to be revised by notice to the Commercial List Office, giving the reason for the change.

23. The Court will attempt to fix not only the date, but also the time, of the hearing, in appropriate situations. This will require the co-operation of all counsel to correctly estimate the time required for their matters, to complete them within the time previously scheduled and to minimize wasted time for all concerned.

Chambers Matters

24. The supervising judge will be available in chambers (Room 422) adjoining courtroom 46 at 145 Queen Street West at 9:30 a.m. on each day to deal with *ex parte*, urgent, scheduling and consent matters which will take no more than 10 minutes. Counsel must book these chambers matters through the Commercial List Office and these bookings will be made so as to allow the Chambers Judge to finish the chambers matters by 10:00 a.m. If additional judges are required for the 9:30 a.m. matters, the Commercial List Office will attempt to arrange for them. In appropriate cases, counsel should file the materials for the appointment on the previous day, so that the judge is aware of the nature of the matter to be considered.

25. *Ex parte* matters on the Commercial List will be rare. Counsel will be required to justify the reason for not notifying the respondents. In most cases, notice will be required, particularly if the matter is part of an ongoing dispute and there are solicitors known to be representing the respondents, even if in respect of other matters.

26. Motions to have matters listed on the Commercial List under paragraph 1(k) should be accompanied by the consent of the other counsel involved or a completed Request Form so that the judge may endorse a fiat either granting or refusing the motion.

27. Following the completion of a Chambers matter, counsel are expected to return the Court materials to the Commercial List Office (after checking with the registrar attending on the Chambers judge) and to ensure that the fees involved for such attendance have been paid.

Adjournments and Settlement

28. Counsel will be expected to be ready to proceed with matters for which hearing times have been agreed to or otherwise set; adjournments of previously scheduled matters will be granted only in special circumstances and for a material reason. Counsel are expected conscientiously to have sought to resolve most adjournments and waiting periods among themselves before a hearing, in a way which minimizes inconvenience and difficulty for the parties. Parties are expected to have retained counsel promptly and requests for adjournments because counsel have not been retained promptly or because new counsel have been retained just prior to the hearing will be dealt with accordingly. Applications for adjournments should be spoken to at the 9:30 a.m. sittings as soon as possible to allow re-allocations of the scheduled time. It is expected that the first counsel to speak to a proposed adjournment will be in a position to outline the position of other counsel appearing.

29. If a matter is adjourned to permit the continuation of effective settlement discussions and the matter is not settled within a reasonable time, a report should be made to the judge through the Commercial List Office on the status of those discussions. This report should be made within 30 days and may be made in court, in chambers or by letter, as appropriate.

30. Where appropriate, matters may be scheduled to be heard on a "standby" basis for a particular date. In these cases, counsel should be prepared to proceed on short notice or they must keep the Bankruptcy Office advised of times when they become unavailable.

31. If an adjournment of a previously scheduled matter is to be sought or appears likely to be required, the Commercial List Office must be alerted as soon as possible to accommodate rescheduling of another matter or alerting counsel on standby matters.

32. Counsel on Commercial List matters are expected conscientiously and continuously to canvass the matter of settlement and to advise promptly of all settlements, or matters which are reasonably likely to settle, so that other matters may be rescheduled.

Judge to Hear Whole Matter

33. It is expected that a judge who determines a substantive proceeding in a matter will continue to hear all subsequent substantive proceedings in that matter. Arrangements for these subsequent proceedings may be made directly with the Commercial List Office. For matters of sufficient complexity or duration, in the event that the original judge is not sitting on the Commercial List at the time or has not been then designated to a future Commercial List team, the judge should be contacted in writing about the nature of the matter to be heard and a list of times which are convenient to all counsel, so that the judge can conveniently schedule the matter or can refer it back to the Commercial List Office for re-assignment.

Case Management

34. It is expected that most matters of substance and of an ongoing nature on the Commercial List will be subject to a form of case management by a Commercial List judge. In particular, this concept will apply to the following matters:

    (a) those actions which are subject to formal case management as a result of the Toronto Region Civil Case Management Pilot Project commencing December 2, 1991 (arrangements have been made with the Pilot Project judges for Commercial List judges to case manage such cases; notice should be given to the Pilot Project of such transfers; such matters will be treated as complex track matters);

    (b) other actions listed on or transferred to the Commercial List;

    (c) applications, where the trial of an issue is directed;

    (d) any other matters where a party moves for case management and a Commercial List judge so directs.

Note, however, that paragraph 33 already provides for significant informal case management for each case on the Commercial List. Where an order is made under sub-paragraph (a), (b) or (c) of this paragraph, a case management judge will be appointed as part of the order.

35. Where a Commercial List matter is subject to case management, a Scheduling Conference (if not already held at the time of transfer or otherwise) will be held with the case management judge not later than 1 month after the close of pleadings or the date of the order referred to in paragraph 34. The purpose of the Scheduling Conference is to determine a plan to process the case in a timely and reasonable fashion and to deal with any matters of a procedural nature which should be addressed at an early stage of the proceedings. The prospects for settlement should also be addressed. The results of a Scheduling Conference will be recorded in a Case Timetable.

36. Counsel will be expected to have conferred among themselves, prior to the Scheduling Conference, for the purpose of preparing a plan to process the case, including a time schedule, for review with the case management judge.

37. Unless otherwise ordered, a Case Conference will be held with the case management judge not later than 1 month after the completion of discoveries. The plaintiff or applicant will have the onus of arranging the Case Conference. The purpose of the Case Conference is to monitor the progress of the matter, to canvass settlement or other disposition of all or as many of the issues as possible, and to provide whatever directions as may be necessary or appropriate with respect to the disposition of the matter.

38. A Case Conference may be held at any other time during the proceeding where the parties consent or where a party moves for the scheduling of a Case Conference and the case management judge so directs.

Alternative Dispute Resolution and Pre-Trials

39. Resort to the techniques of "alternative dispute resolution" (ADR), where appropriate, is recognized and encouraged as an effective aid in the disposition of issues and matters on the Commercial List.

40. It will be the duty of the case management judge and the obligation of counsel to explore methods to resolve the contested issues between the parties, including the resort to ADR, at the Case Conferences and on whatever other occasions it may be fitting to do so.

41. At any time, particularly on consent of the parties, the case management judge may refer any issue for ADR, as appears appropriate.

42. A matter selected for ADR may be referred to the Pilot Project of the ADR Centre or to a person selected from among those supernumerary or retired judges designated from time to time by the Chief Justice of the Ontario Court and such other individuals as are designated from time to time by the Chief Justice. Those individuals (or organizations on their behalf) wishing to be designated should apply in writing to the Users' Committee, Attention: Mr. Justice Blair, for that purpose. A list of the supernumerary or retired judges and other individuals who are designated from time to time will be available from the Commercial List Office.

43. When a matter, or any issue within a matter, has been referred to ADR, counsel will report to the case management judge at regular intervals as to the progress of the ADR proceedings. The timing of such reports will be agreed upon between counsel and the case management judge.

44. The Court may schedule intensive pre-trials for both entire cases and significant matters within cases. These pre-trials should be booked through the Commercial List Office and with enough time for the matters in issue and the possibility of settlement to be canvassed thoroughly. The pre-trial will also deal with arrangements for managing the trial or hearing. A trial date under paragraph 16 will not be set before the pre-trial procedures have been concluded.

Materials for use of the Court

45. It is expected that materials filed for the use of the Court will be filed with the Commercial List Office at least within the time prescribed by the Rules. Early filing is recommended

and all materials must be filed by 2:00 p.m. of the day before the hearing. If commercial couriers are used for filing, they must be advised of the need to comply with this schedule.

46. The Commercial List Office should be advised of what specific materials from those files are required for the hearing of any particular proceeding. This is particularly important where the matter is on-going or the materials in the court files are voluminous. It is suggested that counsel co-ordinate on a common marking scheme for the records, transcripts, factums, authorities and other materials intended for use by the Court and that a representative attend at the Commercial List Office the day before a hearing to ensure that the correct materials are available.

47. In appropriate cases, to supplement any required formal Record, counsel are requested to consider preparing an informal Compendium of the key materials to be referred to in argument (fair extracts of documents, transcripts, previous orders, authorities, etc.) to assist in focusing the case for the Court. (See *Saskatchewan Egg Producers' Marketing Board v. Ontario*, [1993] O.J. No. 434.) It will be helpful to draw the attention of the Court to pertinent information about each document (*e.g.* the date, the deponent of an affidavit, the parties to a contract, the significance of a particular passage or provision, etc.) by appropriate commentary in the index of the Compendium or on the first page of the document or both. Relevant portions of the Compendium should be highlighted or marked. Counsel are urged to consult among themselves in the preparation of a joint Compendium, if possible. The Compendium should contain only essential materials. The use of a loose-leaf format is particularly helpful to the Court both for conducting hearings and for writing decisions.

48. The Court invites the use of diagrams, corporate organization charts, list of persons involved, point-form chronologies and other synopses of complex or technical evidence.

49. The prior preparation of draft orders for consideration by the Court at the end of a hearing will greatly expedite the issuance of orders.

50. For trials, the Court encourages the use of sworn witness statements to replace examination in chief, in whole or in part. All such witness statements must be exchanged with all other parties and counsel well in advance of the hearing And, unless a prior order is made, the witness should be available for cross-examination at the trial. (Also see rule 53.02.)

Reasons for Decision

51. If a decision is hand-written or dictated and not transcribed by the Court, counsel for the plaintiff or moving party will assist the Court in preparing a typed draft of the decision and providing to the court the typed draft for editing by the judge, along with an electronic version of the draft on diskette and a copy of the hand-written decision or dictation tape, noting any passages which were difficult to read.

Costs

52. The Court will seek to award and fix costs at the end of the hearing of a matter. Counsel should be prepared to deal with costs (including both liability and amount) at the conclusion of the hearing of the matter or, if absolutely necessary, by written submissions immediately thereafter.

Users' Committee

53. A Commercial List Users' Committee has been established, consisting of practitioners familiar with the operation of the Commercial List and appointed by the Chief Justice of the Ontario Court. The names of the members of the Users' Committee may be obtained from the Commercial List Office. Persons who wish to join the Users' Committee should advise Mr. Justice Farley. The Users' Committee will meet regularly with representatives of the judges hearing matters from the Commercial List to consider

improvements to the organization and operation of the Commercial List and to make recommendations to the Chief Justice in that regard. The Users' Committee welcomes suggestions, compliments and complaints from other practitioners who have had cases on the Commercial List. Communications to the Users' Committee may be sent by fax to Charles F. Scott at (416) 865-7380.

Enquiries

54.   If you wish to make comments about the Commercial List directly to the Court, contact Mr. Justice Farley in writing or by telephone (327-5731). He or his designate may also be contacted about the scheduling of trials and long matters. In such cases, it is expected that counsel will give details of the matter, the urgency, if any, expected length and mutually convenient dates. A Request Form and Case Timetable may be used for this purpose.

Commercial List Forms

55.   Current versions of the Request Form and Case Timetable forms may be obtained from the Commercial List Office. These forms will be revised concurrently with the issuance of this Practice Direction.

Effective Date

56.   This practice direction is effective from January 1, 1996 and replaces the previous Practice Direction Concerning the Commercial List, dated June 15, 1993.

Commercial List — Procedural Matters

Maple Valley Acres Ltd. v. Canadian Imperial Bank of Commerce (1992), 13 C.P.C. (3d) 358 (Ont. Gen. Div.).

The court refused to transfer an action to the Commercial List where it had been commenced in Brampton and the plaintiff opposed the transfer.

APPLICATION OF THE RULE

38.01(1) Rules 38.02 to 38.11 apply to all proceedings commenced by a notice of application under rule 14.05, subject to subrule (2).

(2) Rules 38.02 and rule 38.09 do not apply to applications to the Divisional Court.

Cross-Reference: Note the limitations in rule 14.05 as to what matters may be dealt with by application.

Delage v. Papineau Roman Catholic Separate School Trustees, [1954] O.W.N. 206 (H.C.).

An application is "made" when it comes on in whole or in part before the court.

APPLICATIONS — TO WHOM TO BE MADE

38.02 An application shall be made to a judge.

PLACE AND DATE OF HEARING

Place

38.03(1) The applicant shall name in the notice of application as the place of hearing a place in which the court normally sits.

Applications under the Landlord and Tenant Act

(1.1) An application under the *Landlord and Tenant Act* shall be made in the county in which the premises are located and shall be heard and determined in that county.

Hearing date where no practice direction

(2) At any place where no practice direction concerning the scheduling of applications is in effect, an application may be set down for hearing on any day on which a judge is scheduled to hear applications.

Exception, lengthy hearing

(3) If counsel estimates that the hearing of the application will be more than two hours long, a hearing date shall be obtained from the registrar before the notice of application is served.

Urgent application

(3.1) An urgent application may be set down for hearing on any day on which a judge is scheduled to hear applications, even if counsel estimates that the hearing is likely to be more than two hours long.

Counter-Application

(4) Where a notice of application has been served, and the respondent wishes to make an application against the applicant, or against the applicant and another person, the respondent may make the application at the same place and time to the same judge. [am. O. Regs. 175/92, s. 2; 770/92, s. 11]

CONTENT OF NOTICE

38.04 Every notice of application (Form 14E, 68A, 73A, 74.44 or 75.5) shall state,
(a) the precise relief sought;
(b) the grounds to be argued, including a reference to any statutory provision or rule to be relied on; and
(c) the documentary evidence to be used at the hearing of the application. [am. O. Reg. 484/94, s. 8]

ISSUING OF NOTICE

38.05 A notice of application shall be issued as provided by rule 14.07 before it is served.

SERVICE OF NOTICE

Generally

38.06(1) The notice of application shall be served on all parties and, where there is uncertainty whether anyone else should be served, the applicant may make a motion without notice to a judge for an order for directions.

Where Notice Ought to Have Been Served

(2) Where it appears to the judge hearing the application that the notice of application ought to have been served on a person who has not been served, the judge may,

(a) dismiss the application or dismiss it only against the person who was not served;

(b) adjourn the application and direct that the notice of application be served on the person; or

(c) direct that any judgment made on the application be served on the person.

Minimum Notice Period

(3) The notice of application shall be served at least ten days before the date of the hearing of the application, except where the notice is served outside Ontario, in which case it shall be served at least twenty days before the hearing date.

Filing Proof of Service

(4) The notice of application shall be filed with proof of service at least three days before the hearing date in the court office where the application is to be heard.

NOTICE OF APPEARANCE

38.07(1) A respondent who has been served with a notice of application shall forthwith deliver a notice of appearance (Form 38A).

(2) A respondent who has not delivered a notice of appearance is not entitled to,

(a) receive notice of any step in the application;

(b) receive any further document in the application, unless,

(i) the court orders otherwise, or

(ii) the document is an amended notice of application that changes the relief sought;

(c) file material, examine a witness or cross-examine on an affidavit on the application; or

(d) be heard at the hearing of the application, except with leave of the presiding judge.

(3) Despite subrule (2), a party who is served with a notice of application outside Ontario may make a motion under subrule 17.06(1) before delivering a notice of appearance and is entitled to be served with material responding to the motion.

Exception, applications to pass accounts
(4) Subrules (1) and (2) do not apply to a notice of application to pass accounts under Rule 74. [am. O. Regs. 351/94, s. 3; 484/94, s. 9]

ABANDONED APPLICATIONS

38.08(1) The applicant may abandon an application by delivering a notice of abandonment.

(2) An applicant who fails to appear at the hearing shall be deemed to have abandoned the application unless the court orders otherwise.

(3) Where an application is abandoned or is deemed to have been abandoned, a respondent on whom the notice of application was served is entitled to the costs of the application, unless the court orders otherwise.

(4) Where a party to an application is under disability, the application may be abandoned by or against that party only with leave of a judge, on notice to,
(a) the Children's Lawyer, unless,
(i) the Public Guardian and Trustee is litigation guardian of the party, or
(ii) a judge orders otherwise; and
(b) where the party under disability is a respondent, the litigation guardian. [am. O. Reg. 69/95, ss. 18, 19, 20]

MATERIAL FOR USE ON APPLICATION

Application Record and Factum
38.09(1) The applicant shall,
(a) serve an application record, together with a factum consisting of a concise statement, without argument, of the facts and law relied on by the applicant, at least three days before the hearing, on every respondent who has served a notice of appearance; and
(b) file the application record and factum, with proof of service, not later than 2 p.m. on the day before the hearing, in the court office where the application is to be heard.

(2) The applicant's application record shall contain, in consecutively numbered pages arranged in the following order,
(a) a table of contents describing each document, including each exhibit, by its nature and date and, in the case of an exhibit, by exhibit number or letter;
(b) a copy of the notice of application;
(c) a copy of all affidavits and other material served by any party for use on the application;
(d) a list of all relevant transcripts of evidence in chronological order, but not necessarily the transcripts themselves; and
(e) a copy of any other material in the court file that is necessary for the hearing of the application.

Respondent's Application Record and Factum

(3) The respondent shall serve on every other party a factum consisting of a concise statement, without argument, of the facts and law relied on by the respondent and may, where the respondent is of the opinion that the application record is incomplete, serve on every other party a respondent's application record containing, in consecutively numbered pages arranged in the following order,

(a) a table of contents describing each document, including each exhibit, by its nature and date and in the case of an exhibit, by exhibit number or letter; and

(b) a copy of any material to be used by the respondent on the application and not included in the application record,

and the respondent's factum and application record shall be filed, with proof of service, in the court office where the application is to be heard, not later than 2 p.m. on the day before the hearing.

Dispensing with Record and Factum

(4) A judge, before or at the hearing of the application, may dispense with compliance with this rule in whole or in part.

Material May be Filed as Part of Record

(5) Any material served by a party for use on an application may be filed, together with proof of service, as part of the party's application record and need not be filed separately if the record is filed within the time prescribed for filing the notice or other material.

Transcript of Evidence

(6) A party who intends to refer to a transcript of evidence at the hearing of an application shall file a copy of the transcript as provided by rule 34.18.

Exceptions, applications in estate matters

(7) Subrules (1) to (6) do not apply to applications under Rule 74.

(8) Subrules (1) to (6) apply to applications under Rule 75, but neither the applicant nor the respondent is required to serve a factum. [am. O. Reg. 484/94, s. 10]

DISPOSITION OF APPLICATION

38.10(1) On the hearing of an application the presiding judge may,

(a) grant the relief sought or dismiss or adjourn the application, in whole or in part and with or without terms; or

(b) order that the whole application or any issue proceed to trial and give such directions as are just.

(2) Where a trial of the whole application is directed, the proceeding shall thereafter be treated as an action, subject to the directions in the order directing the trial.

(3) Where a trial of an issue in the application is directed, the order directing the trial may provide that the proceeding be treated as an action

in respect of the issue to be tried, subject to any directions in the order, and shall provide that the application be adjourned to be disposed of by the trial judge.

Exception, applications in estate matters
   (4) Clause (1)(b) and subrules (2) and (3) do not apply to applications under Rules 74 and 75. [am. O. Reg. 484/94, s. 11]

Ordering the Trial of an Issue (See also cases under rule 37.13.)

Olivier v. Olivier, (January 5, 1995), Doc. St. Catharines 33,482/94 (Ont. Gen. Div.).
A motions court judge has jurisdiction to order an application be converted to an action.

E. J. Hannafin Enterprises Ltd. v. Esso Petroleum Canada (1994), 17 O.R. (3d) 258, 24 C.P.C. (3d) 195 (Gen. Div.).
The court refused to convert an application to an action notwithstanding that several trials of issues could be necessary. Fragmentation of trial may be permissible if the end result is to enable the parties to process their dispute more expeditiously and efficiently.

West v. Edson Packaging Machinery Ltd. (1993), 16 O.R. (3d) 24 (Gen. Div.).
The court ordered that an application for an oppression remedy be converted to a trial where the dispute could not be fairly and satisfactorily resolved without a trial.

BPCO Inc. v. Imperial Oil Ltd. (1993), 17 C.P.C. (3d) 130 (Ont. Gen. Div.).
The court refused to convert an application into an action notwithstanding the respondent's submission that oral evidence should be admitted in evidence to support a rectification argument.

Renegade Capital Corp. v. Hees International Bancorp Inc. (1990), 73 O.R. (2d) 311 (H.C.).
The court stayed an application for an order under the *Securities Act* and required the matter to proceed as an action where there were complex and disputed questions of fact, issues of credibility and a requirement for oral evidence.

Energy Probe v. Canada (A.G.) (1989), 68 O.R. (2d) 449, 35 C.P.C. (2d) 201, 37 Admin. L.R. 1, 3 C.E.L.R. (N.S.) 262, 40 C.R.R. 303, 58 D.L.R. (4th) 513, 33 O.A.C. 39 (C.A.), leave to appeal to Supreme Court of Canada refused 102 N.R. 399, 37 O.A.C. 160 (note).
A *Charter* challenge commenced by application was converted to an action by the appellate court, on consent; a trial court would be in a better position to deal with certain differences as to factual matters and to balance the evidence of justification under s. 1 of the *Charter* if this became necessary.

Assn française des conseils scolaires de l'Ontario v. Ontario (1988), 66 O.R. (2d) 599, 55 D.L.R. (4th) 394 (C.A.).
Trial of constitutional issues was ordered where the issues were complex and additional evidence was required to resolve the issues.

Re Island of Bob-Lo Co. and Township of Malden, [1969] 2 O.R. 535 (C.A.).
Where affidavit evidence was insufficient in setting out several relevant factors, the trial of an issue was directed.

Re Dougmor Realty Holdings Ltd., [1968] 1 O.R. 61, 11 C.B.R. (N.S.) 153, 65 D.L.R. (2d) 419 (C.A.).
Where the plaintiff confines his case to grounds narrower than those encompassed in the order directing the trial of an issue and the defendant accordingly does not cross-examine or call evidence on other points, the judge should base his decision on the points argued.

Re Hunter Infants, [1955] O.W.N. 477 (H.C.).

If the trial of an issue is treated as an action, discovery is available to the parties. [*See now rule 38.10(2) — Authors.*]

SETTING ASIDE JUDGMENT ON APPLICATION MADE WITHOUT NOTICE

38.11(1) A person who is affected by a judgment on an application made without notice or who fails to appear at the hearing of an application through accident, mistake or insufficient notice may move to set aside or vary the judgment, by a notice of motion that is served forthwith after the judgment comes to the person's attention and names the first available hearing date that is at least three days after service of the notice of motion.

(2) A motion under subrule (1) may be made,

(a) at any place, to the judge who granted the judgment;

(b) at a place determined in accordance with rule 37.03 (place of hearing of motions), to any other judge;

(c) to the Divisional Court, in the case of a judgment of that court.

(3) On a motion under subrule (1), the judgment may be set aside or varied on such terms as are just.

Cross-Reference: See also cases under rule 37.14.

Re Geneva and Comtesse, [1959] O.R. 668, (*sub nom. Re Comtesse and Zelig*) 23 D.L.R. (2d) 506 (H.C.).

The court has an inherent jurisdiction to review *ex parte* orders.

HEARING BY CONFERENCE TELEPHONE

38.12 By appointment obtained from the judge or officer before whom the application is to be heard, the application may be heard in whole or in part by means of a conference telephone call. [en. O. Reg. 535/92, s. 11]

RULE 39   EVIDENCE ON MOTIONS AND APPLICATIONS

Highlights

This Rule is concerned with how evidence may be given on motions and applications, *i.e.* by affidavit (rule 39.01), by cross-examination on affidavits (rule 39.02), by the examination of a witness before the hearing of a pending motion or application, or with leave, orally at the hearing (rule 39.03) or by the use of an examination for discovery on the hearing of a motion (rule 39.04).

Contents of affidavit. The general rule as to the contents of affidavits is stated in rule 4.06(2): they are to be confined to the personal knowledge of the deponent or "to other evidence that the deponent could give if testifying as a witness in court, except where these rules provide otherwise".

Information and belief is permitted in affidavits to be used on a motion: rule 39.01(4). Affidavits for use on an application may contain information and belief to a limited extent, *i.e.* with respect to matters that are not contentious: rule 39.01(5). In either case the source of the information and the fact of belief must be specified. What was formerly a common law requirement, that on a motion or application made without notice full and fair disclosure of all material facts must be made, is codified: rule 39.01(6).

Cross-examination on affidavits. Cross-examination on affidavits is regulated with a view to streamlining the process and to avoiding abuse, and the right to cross-examine on affidavits is subject to several specific restrictions.

A party may not cross-examine until he or she has served every affidavit on which he or she intends to rely and completed all examinations under rule 39.03 (rule 39.02(1)) and this precondition is enforced by rule 39.02(2): a party who has cross-examined on an opponent's affidavit may not subsequently deliver an affidavit or conduct an examination under rule 39.03, except with leave or consent.

The right to cross-examine must be exercised with reasonable diligence and where a party fails to do so the court may refuse an adjournment of the hearing for the purposes of cross-examination: rule 39.02(3).

Two further conditions are imposed that do not apply to applications, a motion for summary judgment or a contempt order, but which apply to all other motions. A cross-examining party, if he or she orders a transcript, is obliged to purchase and provide a free copy to every adverse party. The cross-examining party is also liable to pay the costs of the adverse party in respect of the examination regardless of the outcome of the proceeding, unless the court orders otherwise: rule 39.02(4).

A deponent who is cross-examined must make inquiries and inform himself of relevant information readily available to him (*Mutual Life Assurance Co. of Can. v. Buffer Investments Inc.* (1985), 52 O.R. (2d) 335, 5 C.P.C. (2d) 5 (H.C.)) and may be questioned about matters not connected with the merits of the pending application or motion for the purpose of showing bias (*Di Giacomo v. D & G Mangan Investments Inc.* (1986), 8 C.P.C. (2d) 175 (Ont. Master)) or to attack his credibility: *Seaway Trust Co. v. Markle* (1988), 25 C.P.C. (2d) 64 (Ont. Master).

Evidence by examination for discovery. In 1996, rule 39.04, dealing with this subject, was amended to resolve the issue (as to which there was conflict in the case law) of whether a party may use its own examination for discovery on a motion. It may not be so used unless the parties consent to its use.

Recent amendments. Rule 39.04 has been amended to clarify restrictions on the use of a party's own examination for discovery.

Former Rules: Rules 228-231, 237, 292, 297, 628, 775lb.

EVIDENCE BY AFFIDAVIT

Generally

39.01(1) Evidence on a motion or application may be given by affidavit unless a statute or these rules provide otherwise.

Service and Filing

(2) Where a motion or application is made on notice, the affidavits on which the motion or application is founded shall be served with the notice of motion or notice of application and shall be filed with proof of service in the court office where the motion or application is to be heard not later than 2 p.m. on the day before the hearing.

(3) All affidavits to be used at the hearing in opposition to a motion or application or in reply shall be served and filed with proof of service in the court office where the motion or application is to be heard not later than 2 p.m. on the day before the hearing.

Contents — Motions

(4) An affidavit for use on a motion may contain statements of the deponent's information and belief, if the source of the information and the fact of the belief are specified in the affidavit.

Contents — Applications

(5) An affidavit for use on an application may contain statements of the deponent's information and belief with respect to facts that are not contentious, if the source of the information and the fact of the belief are specified in the affidavit.

Full and Fair Disclosure on Motion or Application Without Notice

(6) Where a motion or application is made without notice, the moving party or applicant shall make full and fair disclosure of all material facts, and failure to do so is in itself sufficient ground for setting aside any order obtained on the motion or application.

Affidavit Evidence — Generally

Saccon (Litigation Guardian of) v. Sisson (1992), 9 C.P.C. (3d) 383 (Ont. Gen. Div.).

It is improper for a commissioner for taking affidavits to simply sign the *jurat* in an affidavit. The commissioner must administer an oath or affirmation. Although the affidavit was not properly sworn in this case, the defendant had conducted a cross-examination and the evidence from the cross-examination was proper and admissible.

Warren Industrial Feldspar Co. v. Union Carbide Canada Ltd. (1986), 54 O.R. (2d) 213, 8 C.P.C. (2d) 1 (H.C.).

Documents cannot simply be filed with the court in a motion record, but must be proved by affidavit or oral evidence.

Hrivnak v. Steel Art Co. (1989), 34 C.P.C. (2d) 34 (Ont. Master).

The court is not bound to accept uncontradicted affidavit evidence where that evidence is not persuasive or consistent with other evidence and the inferences which could be fairly drawn from the absence of other evidence.

Unilease Inc. v. Lee-Mar Developments Ltd. (1987), 23 C.P.C. (2d) 46 (Ont. Master).

The court held that paragraphs in an affidavit filed on a motion, which depended for their probative value on documents which were not sworn to as exhibits and therefore inadmissible, should be disregarded.

Vinski v. Lack (1987), 61 O.R. (2d) 379, 21 C.P.C. (2d) 208 (Master).

The court refused to admit into evidence on a motion made without notice an affidavit taken before a commissioner whose signature was an illegible scrawl and who was not otherwise identified.

Chitel v. Rothbart; Rothbart v. Chitel (1984), 42 C.P.C. 217 (Ont. Master), affirmed (1985), 2 C.P.C. (2d) xlix (Ont. Div. Ct.), leave to appeal to Ont. C.A. refused 15 C.P.C. (2d) xlviii.

The master refused to accept a further affidavit tendered by the applicant following an adjournment after argument on the motion had started and certain weaknesses had started to appear in the applicant's case. No satisfactory explanation had been given as to why the affidavit could not have been delivered at the outset.

Clay-Jen Holdings Ltd. v. Inner Core Corp. (1983), 37 C.P.C. 246 (Ont. Master).

A solicitor who has made an affidavit for use on a motion should not conduct a cross-examination of another deponent of an affidavit to be used on the motion.

Imperial Oil Ltd. v. Grabarchuk (1974), 3 O.R. (2d) 783 (C.A.).

In arguing a motion, counsel may not rely on his own affidavit.

Baydon Corp. Ltd. v. du Pont Glore Forgan Can. Ltd. (1974), 4 O.R. (2d) 290 (H.C.).

The deponent of the affidavit must not be the solicitor who argues the matter before the court.

Zajac v. Zwarycz, [1963] 2 O.R. 209, 39 D.L.R. (2d) 6, affirmed [1965] 1 O.R. 575, 49 D.L.R. (2d) 52 (C.A.).

Proof may be required that the foreign equivalent of an affidavit is in the form required by the law of the foreign jurisdiction.

Service of Affidavit — rule 39.01(2)

Westbury Canada Life v. Newall (1992), 6 C.P.C. (3d) 281 (Ont. Master).

The court refused to permit the responding party to a motion for summary judgment to deliver an affidavit on the day of the hearing where that party had neglected to do so for two months.

NRS London Realty Ltd. v. Glenn (1989), 67 O.R. (2d) 704 (Dist. Ct.).

The court rejected a supplementary affidavit and factum delivered after the opposite party had made its submissions.

Ontario Jockey Club v. Toronto (City) (1986), 53 O.R. (2d) 151, 23 D.L.R. (4th) 693 (H.C.), affirmed 61 O.R. (2d) 131, 41 D.L.R. (4th) 767 (Div. Ct.).

The failure to serve an affidavit together with the notice of motion was excused where there was no prejudice to the responding party who appeared and cross-examined on the affidavit without objection.

Re King Nursing Home Ltd. and Grossman (1983), 43 O.R. (2d) 355, 38 C.P.C. 179, 1 D.L.R. (4th) 766 (Div. Ct.).

Failure to serve the affidavit with the notice of motion is an irregularity which may be ignored; however, in this case the court ordered examinations by the applicant under various subpoenas not to proceed until the affidavit was served.

Muir v. Hamilton, [1946] O.W.N. 862 (Master).

The court has a discretion to excuse a default in serving the affidavit with the notice of motion where the circumstances justify it.

Affidavit Based on Information and Belief — rule 39.01(4), (5)

Manraj v. Bour (1995), 6 W.D.C.P. (2d) 441 (Ont. Gen. Div.).

A solicitor who was the source of information as to an important issue contained in an affidavit sworn on information and belief was not permitted to make submissions to the court.

Csak v. Mokos (1995), 7 W.D.C.P. (2d) 62 (Ont. Master).

The court struck out an affidavit where, *inter alia*, it did not properly distinguish between personal knowledge and facts based on information and belief.

Peirson v. Bent (1993), 13 O.R. (3d) 429 (Gen. Div.).

The only significance to a law clerk's affidavit exhibiting medical reports was that expert evidence had been received. It did not prove the contents of the medical reports.

Cameron v. Taylor (1992), 10 O.R. (3d) 277 (Gen. Div.).

Paragraphs in an affidavit to be used on an application, which failed to state the source of the deponent's information and belief as to contentious matters, were struck out.

Li Santi v. Li Santi (1990), 24 R.F.L. (3d) 174 (Ont. Fam. Ct.).

The court struck out an exhibit to an affidavit which contained unsworn hearsay statements and which did not disclose the source of the information or the belief of its truth.

791715 Ontario Inc. v. Robinson (1989), 72 O.R. (2d) 337, 49 C.P.C. (2d) 158 (Master), affirmed (1990), 72 O.R. (2d) 337n, 49 C.P.C. (2d) 158n (H.C.).

Where no source of information was given with regard to an assertion in an affidavit the assertion was held to be inadmissible.

Edwards v. Shuber (1988), 30 C.P.C. (2d) 290 (Ont. Master).

The court expunged portions of an affidavit containing unsupported hearsay and irrelevant and scandalous matters.

Evans v. Holroyd (1988), 31 C.P.C. (2d) 48 (Ont. H.C.).

Where an affidavit does not state the source of the information and the fact of the belief, the court may not waive the irregularity if an objection is made.

Abco Box & Carton Co. v. Dafoe & Dafoe Inc. (1987), 20 C.P.C. (2d) 128, 65 C.B.R. (N.S.) 292 (Ont. Dist. Ct.).

The failure to identify the source of information and the fact of belief in an affidavit was not fatal where the information was found in the exhibits to the affidavit.

539618 Ontario Inc. v. Olympic Foods (Thunder Bay) Ltd. (1987), 22 C.P.C. (2d) 195, 65 C.B.R. (N.S.) 143 (Ont. S.C.), affirmed 65 C.B.R. (N.S.) 285 (Ont. S.C.).

Hearsay evidence in an affidavit, disguised as personal knowledge, was ignored by the court when exposed by cross-examination.

Re Becker (1986), 57 O.R. (2d) 495, 25 E.T.R. 174 (*sub nom. Stadelmier v. Hoffman*) (Surr. Ct.).

On this application a matter determined to be "contentious" could not be disposed of on the basis of affidavits on information and belief.

Re A.G. Can. and Continental Trust Co. (1985), 52 O.R. (2d) 157, 21 D.L.R. (4th) 591 (H.C.).

Where an affidavit filed in a winding-up proceeding recited facts obtained from a firm of chartered accountants and the deponent did not attest to his belief in the facts, the affidavits were nevertheless held to be admissible. The accountants' reports were admissible as findings of public officers, and, in any event, the respondents had chosen not to cross-examine on the affidavit.

Copenhagen Handelsbank A/S v. Peter Makos Furs Ltd. (1984), 46 C.P.C. 21, 28 B.L.R. 26 (Ont. H.C.).

The court disregarded paragraphs in an affidavit based on information and belief which did not disclose the source of the information.

Erie Mfg. Co. (Can.) Ltd. v. Rogers (1982), 24 C.P.C. 132 (Ont. H.C.).

If contested, an affidavit which offends this rule ought not to be received unless something is shown to justify its admission.

Ontario (A.G.) v. Canadian Union of Public Employees (1981), 31 O.R. (2d) 618, 20 C.P.C. 208, 119 D.L.R. (3d) 428 (H.C.).

Parts of an affidavit which did not disclose the source of the information were held inadmissible.

Bee Chemical Co. v. Plastic Paint & Finish Specialties Ltd. (1980), 15 C.P.C. 288, 47 C.P.R. (2d) 172, leave to appeal to Supreme Court of Canada refused 47 C.P.R. (2d) 286n, 33 N.R. 83n.

Affidavits based upon information and belief are not admissible in contempt proceedings.

Armstrong v. Gardner (1978), 20 O.R. (2d) 648 (H.C.).

An application by minority shareholders for leave to commence a representative action may be supported by an affidavit on information and belief.

City Buick Pontiac Cadillac Ltd. v. Allan (1977), 6 C.P.C. 182 (Ont. H.C.).

An affidavit based on information and belief must state who advised the affiant and the reason the advisor knows what he states.

Lawrence Square Ltd. v. Pape (1978), 6 C.P.C. 51 (Ont. H.C.).

Where objection was taken to an affidavit on an interlocutory motion which did not state the grounds for the beliefs set out, the irregularity was not waived and the offending paragraphs were disregarded.

Wiley, Lowe & Co. v. Gould, [1958] O.W.N. 316 (H.C.).

The court may refuse to receive affidavits based on information and belief and may invoke the best evidence rule.

Statements by Counsel

Real Securities of Can. Ltd. v. Beland (1987), 16 C.P.C. (2d) 230 (Ont. Dist. Ct.).

Prejudicial allegations of fact made from the counsel table will be disregarded by the court except in considering costs against their maker.

Zuker v. Schaefer (1982), 30 C.P.C. 279 (Ont. H.C.).

A judge or a master hearing a motion can base his decision on matters that do not appear to be in controversy which are stated to him by counsel.

Non-Disclosure of Facts on Motion Made Without Notice — rule 39.01(6)

830356 Ontario Inc. v. 156170 Canada Ltd. (1995), 6 W.D.C.P. (2d) 159 (Ont. Gen. Div.).

The court vacated a certificate of pending litigation obtained *ex parte* where the plaintiff failed to make full and fair disclosure of all material facts.

Bank of Nova Scotia v. Rawifilm Inc. (1994), 18 O.R. (3d) 743 (Master).

Where an *ex parte* motion was brought to obtain a certificate of pending litigation on the basis of an alleged fraudulent conveyance, the plaintiff was under an obligation to make full disclosure of all material facts it knew that could reasonably relate to the transferor's intent. A failure to make such full disclosure resulted in the certificate of pending litigation being set aside.

BBM Bureau of Measurement v. Cybernauts Ltd. (1992), 8 C.P.C. (3d) 293, 42 C.P.R. (3d) 180 (Ont. Gen. Div.).

The court set aside an *ex parte* "Mareva" injunction and "Anton Piller" order where on the *ex parte* motion there had been a combination of failure to disclose material matters, misrepresentation as to the contents of documents, misstated sources of information and withholding of material documentation.

358426 Ontario Ltd. v. Liappas (1991), 1 C.P.C. (3d) 95 (Ont. Master).

Where a party obtained certificates of pending litigation *ex parte* without disclosing all relevant information, the certificates were discharged.

Lynian Ltd. v. Dubois (1990), 45 C.P.C. (2d) 231 (Ont. Gen. Div.).

The court set aside an "Anton Piller" order for failure to make full disclosure.

Pazner v. Ontario (1990), 74 O.R. (2d) 130 (H.C.).

An order extending the time for service of a statement of claim was not set aside where some facts had not been disclosed on the original motion but the undisclosed facts were not material.

607722 Ont. Ltd. v. Knott Hotels Co. of Can. (1989), 15 W.D.C.P. 219 (Ont. Master).

Where a certificate of pending litigation is vacated because of non-disclosure on the *ex parte* motion pursuant to which the certificate was issued, a subsequent motion, on proper material, to issue a new certificate will be dismissed as *res judicata*.

Passarelli v. Di Cienzo (1989), 67 O.R. (2d) 603, 34 C.P.C. (2d) 54 (H.C.).

The court discharged a certificate of pending litigation where there had been serious non-disclosures on the *ex parte* motion to obtain the certificate.

Russell v. Burke (1989), 33 C.P.C. (2d) 52 (Ont. Master).

Where, by mistake, incorrect facts were contained in an affidavit supporting an *ex parte* motion but the other portions of the affidavit were sufficient to obtain the order, the court declined to set aside the order.

Corsi v. di Cecco (1988), 25 C.P.C. (2d) 1 (Ont. Master), reversed on other grounds 32 C.P.C. (2d) 310 (Ont. H.C.).

Where the moving party takes a position in good faith that a fact is untrue, he cannot be criticized for failing to disclose the fact on a motion made without notice even if the court finds that the fact is true.

Waites v. Alltemp Products Co. (1987), 19 C.P.C. (2d) 185 (Ont. Dist. Ct.).

The court refused to set aside an order for lack of full and frank disclosure where, although the original *ex parte* material was incomplete, it was not misleading and no material facts were deliberately withheld.

MRA Technologies Ltd. v. Nanotec Research Ltd. (1985), 3 C.P.C. (2d) 73 (Ont. Master).

An order obtained without notice to require the sheriff to seize certain documents was set aside where the supporting affidavit did not disclose certain contractual terms alleged by the defendant.

Hess v. Mandzuk (1984), 44 C.P.C. 179, 34 R.P.R. 90 (Ont. H.C.).

A certificate of pending litigation was vacated where on the original *ex parte* motion for the certificate the moving party failed to disclose information which if disclosed would have given the court serious concerns.

Merker v. Leader Terazzo Tile Mosaic Ltd. (1983), 43 O.R. (2d) 632, 37 C.P.C. 1, 2 D.L.R. (4th) 117 (H.C.).

An *ex parte* order, obtained by the plaintiff on misleading affidavit material, was set aside although the cross-examination disclosed information sufficient to support the order made. The court awarded costs on a solicitor and client scale, payable by the plaintiff's solicitors personally.

J & P Goldfluss Ltd. v. 306569 Ont. Ltd. (1977), 4 C.P.C. 296 (Ont. H.C.).

Where there has been serious non-disclosure in the affidavit material upon which a certificate of pending litigation was obtained, the certificate will be vacated.

Launch! Research & Dev. Inc. v. Essex Dist. Co. (1977), 4 C.P.C. 261 (Ont. H.C.).

Failure to disclose a material fact on a motion for an injunction without notice is fatal to its continuance.

Atlantic Sugar Refineries Co. v. R.T. Tamblyn and Partners Ltd. (1974), 3 O.R. (2d) 195, 45 D.L.R. (3d) 28, reversed on other grounds, 8 O.R. (2d) 622 (C.A.), leave to appeal to S.C.C. refused 8 O.R. (2d) 622n.

Failure to disclose a material fact is not a conclusive reason to rescind an order.

EVIDENCE BY CROSS-EXAMINATION ON AFFIDAVIT

On a Motion or Application

39.02(1) A party to a motion or application who has served every affidavit on which the party intends to rely and has completed all examinations under rule 39.03 may cross-examine the deponent of any affidavit served by a party who is adverse in interest on the motion or application.

(2) A party who has cross-examined on an affidavit delivered by an adverse party shall not subsequently deliver an affidavit for use at the hearing or conduct an examination under rule 39.03 without leave or consent, and the court shall grant leave, on such terms as are just, where it is satisfied that the party ought to be permitted to respond to any matter raised on the cross-examination with evidence in the form of an affidavit or a transcript of an examination conducted under rule 39.03.

To be Exercised with Reasonable Diligence

(3) The right to cross-examine shall be exercised with reasonable diligence, and the court may refuse an adjournment of a motion or application for the purpose of cross-examination where the party seeking the adjournment has failed to act with reasonable diligence.

Additional Provisions Applicable to Motions

(4) On a motion other than a motion for summary judgment or a contempt order, a party who cross-examines on an affidavit,

(a) shall, where the party orders a transcript of the examination, purchase and serve a copy on every adverse party on the motion, free of charge; and

(b) is liable for the party and party costs of every adverse party on the motion in respect of the cross-examination, regardless of the outcome of the proceeding, unless the court orders otherwise.

Cross-Reference: See Rule 34 as to the procedure on such an examination.

Availability of Cross-Examination

Norton v. Norton (1990), 27 R.F.L. (3d) 179 (Ont. Master).

Rules 39.02 and 39.03 do not confer a right to examine on an Official Guardian's Report but rather s. 112 of the *Courts of Justice Act* applies. Rule 39.03 does apply where the Official Guardian has not been appointed.

Ridley v. Ridley (1989), 37 C.P.C. (2d) 167 (Ont. H.C.).

Cross-examination is not an absolute right and the court refused to adjourn a motion where the responding party did not file material or take steps to cross-examine during the three weeks after receiving the notice of motion.

A.H. Al-Sagar & Bros. Engineering Project Co. v. Al-Jabouri (1984), 47 C.P.C. 33 (Ont. H.C.).

Cross-examination on an affidavit is not an absolute right and the court may refuse an adjournment to permit cross-examination.

Toronto Bd. of Education Staff Credit Union Ltd. v. Skinner (1984), 47 O.R. (2d) 70, 45 C.P.C. 55 (H.C.).

Where a motion has been brought to vacate a certificate of pending litigation, the moving party is entitled to cross-examine the deponent of an affidavit made in support of the *ex parte* motion for the certificate.

Re Ferguson and Imax Systems Corp. (1984), 47 O.R. (2d) 225, 44 C.P.C. 17, 52 C.B.R. (N.S.) 255, 11 D.L.R. (4th) 249, 4 O.A.C. 188 (Div. Ct.).

The Divisional Court held that in the circumstances of this case the responding party to a motion should not have been denied the opportunity to cross-examine on an affidavit delivered the day before the motion.

Bardeau v. Bardeau (1983), 38 C.P.C. 140 (Ont. Master).

The master held that where an applicant informally withdrew a motion, the respondent could not cross-examine on an affidavit filed in support of the motion.

Butler Mfg. (Can.) Ltd. v. M.N.R. (1983), 42 O.R. (2d) 784, 37 C.P.C. 251, 83 D.T.C. 5361 (Master).

The master granted an application by a taxpayer for an order compelling the deponent of an affidavit, filed on an *ex parte* motion by the Minister of National Revenue for an order permitting search and seizure, to attend for cross-examination.

Wise v. Benda (1982), 30 C.P.C. 148 (Ont. Master).

An appointment for cross-examination on an affidavit in order to obtain evidence to set aside the caution was set aside since the proceeding for which the affidavit had been filed had been disposed of.

Thomson v. Atlas Transport Equipment Ltd. (1981), 24 C.P.C. 278 (Ont. H.C.).

Where an affidavit of the client was an exhibit to an affidavit of the solicitor in support of a motion, cross-examination of the client was permitted.

Re Canadian Wkrs. Union and Frankel Steel Ltd. (1976), 12 O.R. (2d) 560, 76 C.L.L.C. 14,010 (H.C.).

An affidavit may not be withdrawn in order to avoid cross-examination on it.

Re Botiuk and Hurowitz (1975), 9 O.R. (2d) 299, 60 D.L.R. (3d) 227 (Div. Ct.).

Where the court, without sufficient justification, refused a party the opportunity to cross-examine the resulting order was set aside.

Sherman v. Manley (1974), 6 O.R. (2d) 518 (Master).

A party has no right to cross-examine on an affidavit filed for use upon a motion in which he has no real interest.

Re Kaplan (1973), 4 O.R. (2d) 58 (Co. Ct.).

There is no right to cross-examine on an affidavit verifying the accounts of the committee of a mental incompetent.

Bank of N.S. v. Metropolitan Trust Co., [1966] 2 O.R. 1 (Master).

There is no inherent right to cross-examine on an affidavit.

Stauffer v. Sampson, [1962] O.W.N. 115 (H.C.).

Where the court had already disposed of a motion, leave to cross-examine on an affidavit and re-argue the motion was refused.

Volckmar v. Krupp, [1958] O.W.N. 303 (H.C.).

On a motion to rescind or vary an *ex parte* order, the applicant may cross-examine on an affidavit filed in support of the *ex parte* application.

Re Miles; Miles v. Miles, [1958] O.W.N. 293 (Master).

The court has inherent power to refuse or restrict cross-examination. It may do so if there is a more appropriate time to explore the subject-matter of the cross-examination.

Holmested v. Township of North York, [1955] O.W.N. 837 (Master).

Where an affidavit is served the deponent is subject to cross-examination notwithstanding that the affidavit is never filed.

Conduct of Examination

Peel Condominium Corp. No. 199 v. Ontario New Home Warranties Plan (1988), 30 C.P.C. (2d) 118, 32 O.A.C. 1 (Div. Ct.).

A witness being cross-examined on an affidavit should make inquiries as to the relevant information readily available to him or her.

Stein v. Stein (1984), 49 C.P.C. 99 (Ont. Master).

Where a witness was ordered to re-attend and answer a question asked on a cross-examination on an affidavit and proper questions flowing therefrom the court ordered that the examining party disclose to the witness prior to the re-attendance certain documents relevant to the cross-examination. Fairness to the witness outweighed the risk of evidence-tailoring.

Bank of Montreal v. Carrick (1973), 1 O.R. (2d) 574, affirmed 1 O.R. (2d) 574n (H.C.).

A deponent of an affidavit may be required to inform himself in order to answer questions on cross-examination.

Scope of Cross-Examination

Moyle v. Palmerston Police Services Board (1995), 25 O.R. (3d) 127 (Div. Ct.).

A witness who has sworn an affidavit regarding a pending application may be cross-examined on any issue of fact relevant to the application and may be asked questions to elicit information discrediting the witness in respect of the truth of the facts in the affidavit. However questions designed to impeach the character of the witness will rarely if ever be proper since determining the credibility of the witness, as part of the process of resolving the material facts in dispute, is beyond the proper role of the judge hearing the application.

Land v. Kaufman (1991), 1 C.P.C. (3d) 234 (Ont. Gen. Div.).

A solicitor who pleads that he or she misunderstood the client's instructions cannot hide behind solicitor/client privilege when the opposite party seeks to explore whether there is any merit to that claim.

Westminer Can. Holdings Ltd. v. Coughlan (1989), 33 C.P.C. (2d) 27 (Ont. Master), affirmed 37 C.P.C. (2d) 314 (Ont. H.C.).

On a cross-examination regarding a motion to stay an action because Ontario was not the convenient forum, the court refused to require the witness to produce documents and answer questions which would have been tantamount to an examination for discovery. Detailed examination of the merits of the case would be oppressive and an abuse of process.

Crysdale v. Carter-Baron Drilling Services Partnership (1987), 61 O.R. (2d) 663, 22 C.P.C. (2d) 232 (Master), reversed on other grounds 62 O.R. (2d) 693, 30 C.P.C. (2d) 191 (H.C.), leave to appeal to Divisional Court refused 62 O.R. (2d) 693 at 696, 30 C.P.C. (2d) 191 at 192.

A party who referred to privileged communications in an affidavit was compelled to answer questions relating to the details of the communications.

Seaway Trust Co. v. Markle (1988), 25 C.P.C. (2d) 64 (Ont. Master).

A question on a cross-examination on an affidavit is proper if (1) it is relevant to any matter in issue on the motion on which the affidavit is to be used, (2) it is fair, and (3) it is directed in a *bona fide* way to an issue on the motion or to the credibility of the witness.

Di Giacomo v. D & G Mangan Investments Inc. (1986), 8 C.P.C. (2d) 175 (Ont. Master).

A deponent may be questioned about matters not connected with the merits of the pending application for the purpose of showing bias.

Mutual Life Assurance Co. of Can. v. Buffer Investments Inc. (1985), 52 O.R. (2d) 335, 5 C.P.C. (2d) 5 (H.C.).

The deponent must make inquiries and inform himself of relevant information readily available to him.

Rodrigues v. Madill (1985), 3 C.P.C. (2d) 1 (Ont. Master).

Reference in an affidavit to instructions by a client to his solicitor was held not to constitute waiver of solicitor and client privilege.

Toronto Board of Education Staff Credit Union Ltd. v. Skinner (1984), 46 C.P.C. 292 (Ont. H.C.).

A deponent may be cross-examined on any matters that are relevant to the pending motion, but need not answer questions that go to the general issues in the action.

C.I.B.C. v. Molony (1983), 32 C.P.C. 213 (Ont. H.C.).

An affiant may be cross-examined on any matter relevant to the issue in respect of which the affidavit was filed, not on any issue raised in the action. Where the motion is for an interlocutory injunction, however, virtually all matter raised in the action will be relevant to the motion as well.

Occhipinti v. Occhipinti (1981), 21 C.P.C. 239 (Ont. Master).

On a cross-examination on an affidavit, questions directed solely to the credibility of the person being examined need not be answered.

Cobbold v. Time Can. Ltd. (1976), 13 O.R. (2d) 567, 1 C.P.C. 228, 71 D.L.R. (3d) 629 (H.C.).

Cross-examination as to the credibility of an undertaking as to damages in an affidavit in support of an application for an interlocutory injunction is permitted.

James v. Maloney, [1973] 1 O.R. 656 (H.C.).

Upon the cross-examination on an affidavit any document which is referred to in the affidavit and forms one of the bases for the motion or application may be required to be produced notwithstanding any privilege. [*And see rule 34.10 — Authors.*]

Wojick v. Wojick and Donger, [1971] 2 O.R. 687 (H.C.).

A party may cross-examine on an issue raised in an affidavit notwithstanding that such issue is irrelevant to the merits of the case.

Re Lubotta and Lubotta, [1959] O.W.N. 322 (Master).

Cross-examination need not be confined to the four corners of the affidavit but may cover any matters relevant to the issue in respect of which the affidavit is filed.

Re Routley's Ltd. and Boland, [1956] O.W.N. 708 (Master).

The cross-examiner has a broad scope to ask questions to lay a foundation for further questions going to credibility or relevant to the issue in respect of which the affidavit has been filed.

Superior Discount Ltd. v. N. Perlmutter and Co., [1951] O.W.N. 897 (Master).

Cross-examination on an affidavit is proper where the questions are: (1) relevant to the issue in respect of which the affidavit is filed, (2) fair, and (3) based on a *bona fide* intention of directing the question to the issue in the proceeding or to the credibility of the witness.

Leave to File Affidavit or Examine a Witness — rule 39.02(2)

Grant Brown National Leasing Inc. v. Nuclar-Greco (1994), 25 C.P.C. (3d) 228 (Ont. Gen. Div.).

Where cross-examination of the defendant led to the plaintiff's obtaining the transcript of the defendant's evidence in a criminal proceeding, the filing of the transcript did not offend the rule in *Browne v. Dunn* (1893), 6 R. 67 (H.L.) or rule 39.02(2).

K.A. Sharpe & Partners Inc. v. Sterling Drug Ltd. (1993), 27 C.P.C. (3d) 173 (Ont. Master).

The court granted leave to file an affidavit after cross-examinations had been conducted where the affidavit contained relevant evidence and there was no prejudice to the opposing party which could not be dealt with by terms or costs.

Fremont Reinsurance Co. v. Symons General Insurance Co., 72 O.R. (2d) 129, 43 C.C.L.I. 161, 66 D.L.R. (4th) 760, [1990] I.L.R. 1-2597 (H.C.).

The court refused leave to file a further affidavit where the affidavit related to matters that had been put in issue prior to cross-examination and not dealt with in cross-examination.

Davis v. Spectrix Microsystems Inc. (1987), 63 O.R. (2d) 151, 23 C.P.C. (2d) 120 (Master), affirmed 32 C.P.C. (2d) 312 (Div. Ct.).

Leave to file an affidavit should only be granted if the cross-examination raises some matter not raised earlier in the litigation.

Swatch S.A. v. Cdn. Tire Corp. (1987), 21 C.P.C. (2d) 48 (Ont. Master), affirmed 10 W.D.C.P. 199 (Ont. H.C.).

Discussion of factors to be considered on an application for leave to conduct an examination under rule 39.03 after cross-examining on an affidavit.

Diligence in Conducting Cross-Examination — rule 39.02(3)

Zuker v. Schaefer (1982), 30 C.P.C. 279 (Ont. H.C.).

Where the matter was adjourned once to permit cross-examination and no steps were taken to obtain such cross-examination before the return of the motion, the master did not err in refusing a further adjournment.

Boow v. Edgar (1982), 39 O.R. (2d) 409, 30 C.P.C. 162, 139 D.L.R. (3d) 533 (H.C.).

The refusal of a local judge to grant an adjournment to permit cross-examination on an affidavit was upheld on appeal.

Cross-Examination on Affidavit — Miscellaneous

MacDonald v. Klein (1993), 17 C.P.C. (3d) 1 (Ont. Gen. Div.).

The solicitor for a party may create an actual or potential conflict of interest by acting as the solicitor for a witness being cross-examined.

Ostrower v. Genereux (1985), 5 C.P.C. (2d) 35 (Ont. H.C.).

Where an affidavit denied that the deponent had knowledge of certain transactions involving the deponent's husband, the court held that the deponent had waived the husband and wife privilege provided by s. 11 of the *Evidence Act*, R.S.O. 1980, c. 145.

Re Camco Inc.; C.G.E. Co. v. GSW Inc. (1982), 33 C.P.C. 97 at 98, 19 B.L.R. 302, reversed in part 33 C.P.C. 97, 22 B.L.R. 1 (Ont. H.C.).

In this case the deponent of an affidavit filed in support of an application for a winding-up order successfully relied upon the privilege afforded to documents filed under the *Foreign Investment Review Act*, but was obliged to produce correspondence passing between the applicant and its parent.

Armak Chemicals Ltd. v. C.N.R. Co. (1983), 32 C.P.C. 258, 143 D.L.R. (3d) 85 (Ont. H.C.).

On cross-examination on an affidavit in support of a motion to dismiss a fourth party proceeding commenced out of time on the grounds the fourth party was prejudiced by its having no recollection of the events giving rise to the action, the court refused to order production of statements made by employees of the fourth party. The documents were privileged and while the examining party was entitled to inquire about their existence, it was not entitled to production.

Re MacDonald and Briant (1982), 35 O.R. (2d) 161, 24 C.P.C. 257 (Master).

An affiant was not required to answer questions where to do so would contravene the laws of the Bahamas; however, the affidavit was struck out.

Burndy Canada Ltd. v. Brown (1978), 5 C.P.C. 266 (Ont. H.C.).

Counsel may be required by order to undertake to hold confidential evidence disclosed upon the cross-examination of the opposite party and also to limit his or her party's presence at such a cross-examination where this is appropriate.

Young v. Neumann (1978), 19 O.R. (2d) 666, 6 C.P.C. 17 (H.C.).

A deponent was ordered to answer similar questions on separate cross-examinations in separate proceedings where the questions were relevant to each proceeding.

Christoff v. Gray, [1961] O.W.N. 115 (Master).

The applicant was allowed to rely on evidence given on the cross-examination on his own affidavit.

Costs of Cross-Examination

Van Bork v. Van Bork (1994), 3 R.F.L. (4th) 59, additional reasons 34 C.P.C. (3d) 342, 5 R.F.L. (4th) 174 (Ont. C.A.).

Where the court had not adjudicated on the costs of cross-examination but the order had been issued and entered, the court re-opened the issue and awarded cross-examination costs to the party who had been successful on the motion.

Trimel Corp. v. Gervais (1992), 17 C.P.C. (3d) 175 (Ont. Gen. Div.).

Rule 39.02(4)(b) will apply in all instances unless the court clearly orders otherwise. The words "the costs of the entire motion are to be in the cause" did not constitute such an order.

Woodslee Credit Union Ltd. v. Taylor (1988), 66 O.R. (2d) 248, 33 C.P.C. (2d) 299 (H.C.).

Where a defendant cross-examined on an affidavit delivered by the plaintiff on the plaintiff's motion for particulars, and the plaintiff subsequently abandoned the motion, the defendant was still obliged to pay the costs of the cross-examination where the plaintiff's original motion had been reasonable.

EVIDENCE BY EXAMINATION OF A WITNESS

Before the Hearing

39.03(1) Subject to subrule 39.02(2), a person may be examined as a witness before the hearing of a pending motion or application for the purpose of having a transcript of his or her evidence available for use at the hearing.

(2) A witness examined under subrule (1) may be cross-examined by the examining party and any other party and may then be re-examined by the examining party on matters raised by other parties, and the re-examination may take the form of cross-examination.

To be Exercised with Reasonable Diligence

(3) The right to examine shall be exercised with reasonable diligence, and the court may refuse an adjournment of a motion or application for the purpose of an examination where the party seeking the adjournment has failed to act with reasonable diligence.

At the Hearing

(4) With leave of the presiding judge or officer, a person may be examined at the hearing of a motion or application in the same manner as at a trial.

Summons to Witness

(5) The attendance of a person to be examined under subrule (4) may be compelled in the same manner as provided in Rule 53 for a witness at a trial.

Cross-Reference: See Rule 34 as to the procedure on such an examination.

Examination of a Witness — Generally

Elfe Juvenile Products Inc. v. Bern (1994), 35 C.P.C. (3d) 117, 76 O.A.C. 54 (Div. Ct.).

Where a non-party is examined on a motion or application, the scope of allowable questions is more limited than on an examination for discovery. Questions must relate to the issues in the motion or application and have a semblance of relevancy.

Donway West Properties Inc. v. Nitsopoulos (1993), 22 C.P.C. (3d) 290 (Ont. Master).

An opposing party and an opposing party's solicitor may be examined under rule 39.03 unless it would be an abuse of process to do so.

Praendex Inc. v. Gump (1992), 8 C.P.C. (3d) 332 (Ont. Master).

The court ordered that a non-resident witness, who was an officer of the plaintiff, be produced for examination in Ontario under rule 39.03. Issuance of a commission and letter of request was not necessary since the witness was an officer of the plaintiff.

Iona Corp. v. Aurora (Town) (1991), 3 O.R. (3d) 579 (Gen. Div.).

Where the persons summonsed have some relevant personal knowledge, the summonses will not be struck out even though there may be other potential witnesses who have better knowledge. It may be an abuse of process if such other witnesses are subsequently summonsed.

Royal Bank v. 55 Dennison Road East Properties Ltd. (1991), 46 C.P.C. (2d) 120 (Ont. Gen. Div.).

A non-party who resides outside Ontario can be compelled to attend for examination under the *Interprovincial Subpoenas Act*, R.S.O. 1980, c. 220, as contemplated by rule 34.04(7).

Agnew v. Assn. of Architects (Ont.) (1987), 64 O.R. (2d) 8, 30 Admin. L.R. 285, 26 O.A.C. 354 (Div. Ct.).

Members of tribunals are no more compellable to testify about their decision-making process than are judges; anyone attempting to subpoena a member must establish that the purpose of the subpoena and the actual questions to be asked would not involve any aspect of the decision process; in this case the applicant had sought to ask questions directed to the decision process.

Horvat v. Feldman (1986), 15 C.P.C. (2d) 220 (Ont. H.C.).

If the scope of the examination goes beyond what is relevant for the motion, the person being examined or a party present or represented at the examination may adjourn it pursuant to rule 34.14(1).

Horvat v. Feldman (1985), 5 C.P.C. (2d) 267 (Ont. Master), affirmed (1986), 15 C.P.C. (2d) 220 (Ont. H.C.).

A party attacking a summons to witness has the onus to show the summons is an abuse of process or the witness has no relevant information.

Faulkner v. Faulkner (1985), 47 R.F.L. (2d) 26 (Ont. Master).

Discussion of when leave should be given for evidence to be given orally on an interim custody motion.

Sherwood Park Restaurant Inc. v. Crawford (1984), 47 O.R. (2d) 501, 45 C.P.C. 226 (H.C.).

A party was not precluded from examining a witness under the predecessor of this provision simply because the plaintiffs failed to request the sought-after information from the defendant at the time of his cross-examination.

Crutcher v. Crutcher (1982), 30 C.P.C. 308 (Ont. Master).

A summons to examine a witness prior to the completion of the cross-examination of the other party on his affidavit was set aside.

Fort Norman Explorations Inc. v. McLaughlin (1982), 36 O.R. (2d) 787, 28 C.P.C. 218 (H.C.).

There is no general rule requiring examination of the parties before resorting to this provision.

Beck v. Bradstock (1976), 14 O.R. (2d) 333, 2 C.P.C. 90 (H.C.).

An examination pursuant to this rule will not be permitted for the purpose of aiding a motion which is itself an abuse of process.

Hamilton Harbour Commrs. v. J.P. Porter Co. (1976), 13 O.R. (2d) 199, 1 C.P.C. 191, 70 D.L.R. (3d) 535 (H.C.).

A party being examined on a pending motion need only answer questions relevant to the subject-matter of the motion.

Re Can. Metal Co. and Heap (1975), 7 O.R. (2d) 185, 54 D.L.R. (3d) 641 (C.A.).

1. A party has a *prima facie* right to make relevant examinations and need not examine the opposing parties before examining non-parties; however, the court will not permit examinations which amount to abuse of process.

2. In considering whether an examination should be permitted the court will consider whether the evidence sought to be obtained from the proposed examination is relevant to the issue raised by the motion and whether, having regard to the range and number of examinations proposed, the examination would be vexatious to the opposing party or an unwarranted imposition upon the proposed witnesses.

Bergen v. Bergen, [1972] 3 O.R. 822, 10 R.F.L. 374 (Master).

Where a party serves a summons to witness on non-parties, an opposing party may move to set aside such summons without instructions from the witnesses. The party serving the summons has the onus to show that the proposed examinations are reasonable.

Examination of a Witness — Examples

Transamerica Life Insurance Co. of Canada v. Canada Life Assurance Co. (1995), 7 W.D.C.P. (2d) 48 (Ont. Gen. Div.).

The court permitted an examination under rule 39.03 regarding a motion for summary judgment subject to certain restrictions.

Ellis-Don Ltd. v. Ontario (Labour Relations Board), 16 O.R. (3d) 698, 24 Admin. L.R. (2d) 122, 94 C.L.L.C. 14,012, 110 D.L.R. (4th) 731, 68 O.A.C. 216, [1994] O.L.R.B. Rep. 113 (Div. Ct.), leave to appeal to Supreme Court of Canada refused 24 Admin. L.R. (2d) 122n, 118 D.L.R. (4th) vi (note), [1995] O.L.R.B. Rep. 92 (note).

The court refused to permit members of the Ontario Labour Relations Board to be examined as witnesses on a pending motion for an application for judicial review, by virtue of s. 111 of the *Labour Relations Act.*

Ontario (Attorney General) v. Dieleman (1993), 16 O.R. (3d) 39, 21 C.P.C. (3d) 49, 19 C.R.R. (2d) 345, 110 D.L.R. 94th) 343 (Gen. Div.), leave to appeal refused 16 O.R. (3d) 39 at 46, 110 D.L.R. (4th) 349 (Gen. Div.).

The court granted an order requiring the Attorney General of Ontario to attend for examination on a pending motion, where the Attorney General was seeking an interim order restraining the defendants from protest activities. The evidence sought to be elicited could reasonably be expected to be relevant, and Ministers of the Crown do not enjoy any special protection or exemption from testifying under rule 39.03.

Benlolo v. Silverman (1993), 17 C.P.C. (3d) 304 (Ont. Master).

The court set aside as an abuse of process a summons issued by the plaintiff to the physician proposed to conduct a defence medical examination.

Litton Systems of Canada Ltd. v. Olympia Engineering Ltd. (1993), 17 C.P.C. (3d) 289 (Ont. Gen. Div.).

The court permitted the examination of a party's solicitor notwithstanding the claim of solicitor and client privilege where the circumstances showed waiver of privilege.

Randeno v. Standevan (1987), 61 O.R. (2d) 726 (H.C.).

A plaintiff was permitted to adduce *viva voce* evidence on a motion, to identify certain proposed defendants whose identities were uncertain.

Ledger Commerce Ltd. v. Ultrasecure Tempest Research Corp. (1987), 17 C.P.C. (2d) 87 (Ont. H.C.).

The court refused to set aside a summons to witness where the proposed witness was knowledgeable and the moving party failed to show an abuse of process.

Reiger v. Chief of Police (1987), 58 O.R. (2d) 203 (*sub nom. Reiger v. Burrows*), 14 C.P.C. (2d) 318 (Master).

A defendant seeking security for costs pursuant to s. 14 of the *Public Authorities Protection Act*, R.S.O. 1980, c. 406, may examine the plaintiff under rule 39.03(1).

Hong Kong (Official Receiver) v. Wing (1986), 13 C.P.C. (2d) 113 (Ont. Master).

A party seeking to prevent the examination of a witness for a pending motion has the onus to show that the examination is an abuse. Where the expense involved in examining a witness in Panama was small relative to the amount in issue, the examination was ordered.

Trigon Management Inc. v. Greyhound Leasing & Financial Co. of Can. Ltd. (1986), 53 O.R. (2d) 489, 7 C.P.C. (2d) 221 (Master).

The court permitted examination of an officer of the defendant regarding a motion for summary judgment.

Canadu Copier Corp. v. Sharp Electronics of Can. Ltd. (1985), 4 C.P.C. (2d) 235, 20 C.R.R. 26 (Ont. Master).

Notices of examination served on persons allegedly in contempt of court were set aside as being contrary to s. 11(c) of the *Charter of Rights.*

J.G. Drapeau Ltd. v. Livingston Estates Ltd. (1985), 51 O.R. (2d) 96, 2 C.P.C. (2d) 229, 11 O.A.C. 312 (C.A.).

Ordinarily it would be an abuse of process to examine an employee of the plaintiff to obtain evidence for a motion under rule 56.01(d) however it was permitted in this case because the plaintiff filed an affidavit containing information obtained from the proposed witness.

Kendal v. Greymac Mtge. Corp. (1985), 49 C.P.C. 272 (Ont. Master).

The court set aside a summons to witness regarding a pending motion for particulars of a pleading. No affidavit had been delivered regarding the motion for particulars and therefore that motion would be determined based solely on the contents of the pleading. The examination sought would be a premature discovery and a fishing expedition.

Re Seaway Trust Co. and Ont. (1983), 35 C.P.C. 124, 143 D.L.R. (3d) 623 (Ont. Div. Ct.).

The court declined to quash subpoenas to a Minister, Deputy Minister, and several other government officials to obtain evidence to support an application attacking certain legislation as being unconstitutional.

Welch v. Reeh (1982), 29 C.P.C. 228 (Ont. Master).

An examination conducted as a cross-examination and without notice to the opposite parties was set aside and the transcript expunged. [*As to cross-examination, see now rule 39.03(2) — Authors.*]

Idean Contractors Ltd. v. St. Davids Invts. Ltd. (1981), 24 C.P.C. 302 (Ont. Master).

An order compelling the attendance of a non-resident witness for examination in support of a motion for an injunction was refused.

Morgan v. Morgan (1980), 19 C.P.C. 259 (Ont. Div. Ct.).

Where reasonable, this provision may be used in aid of a motion for the production of documents from a non-party.

Beck v. Bradstock (1976), 14 O.R. (2d) 333, 2 C.P.C. 90 (H.C.).

In a motion to add a defendant, leave will not be given to examine the person sought to be added.

Re Dominion Stores Ltd. and United Trust Co., [1972] 3 O.R. 662 (H.C.).

A solicitor for a party may be so examined with questions of privilege being determined on the examination. The court has jurisdiction to prevent a vexatious or unreasonable examination.

EVIDENCE BY EXAMINATION FOR DISCOVERY

Adverse Party's Examination

39.04(1) On the hearing of a motion, a party may use in evidence an adverse party's examination for discovery or the examination for discovery of any person examined on behalf or in place of, or in addition to, the adverse

party, and rule 31.11 (use of discovery at trial) applies with necessary modifications.

Party's Examination
(2) On the hearing of a motion, a party may not use in evidence the party's own examination for discovery or the examination for discovery of any person examined on behalf or in place of, or in addition to, the party unless the other parties consent. [re-en. O. Reg. 534/96, s. 1]

PRESERVATION OF RIGHTS IN PENDING LITIGATION

RULE 40   INTERLOCUTORY INJUNCTION OR MANDATORY ORDER

Highlights

The Rule supplements two sections of the *Courts of Justice Act, i.e.* s. 101 (which authorizes the granting of interlocutory injunctions and mandatory orders) and s. 102 (which regulates the granting of labour injunctions). Both of these statutory provisions essentially reproduce similar provisions in the former *Judicature Act.*

Rule 40.02 regulates the granting and the extension of injunctions and mandatory orders made on a motion without notice. The rule does not apply to labour injunctions (rule 40.02(4)) because s. 102 of the Act more specifically regulates the granting and the extension of such injunctions in labour disputes.

Rule 40.03 generally requires the moving party to give an undertaking regarding damages as a condition of obtaining an interlocutory injunction.

There is a three-part test for granting an interlocutory injunction: (1) Is there a serious question to be tried? (2) Will the applicant suffer irreparable harm if the injunction is not granted? (3) Which party will suffer the greater harm from granting or refusing the remedy pending a decision on the merits? Part (1) is to be determined on the basis of common sense and an extremely limited merits review. However, a detailed merits review will be appropriate (a) where the result of the motion will, in effect, amount to a final determination and (b) where the only issue is a simple question of law, or (possibly) where the factual record is largely settled: *RJR-Mac-Donald Inc. v. Canada (Attorney General)*, [1994] 1 S.C.R. 311.

Former provisions: Judicature Act, ss. 19(1), 20.

HOW OBTAINED

40.01 An interlocutory injunction or mandatory order under section 101 or 102 of the *Courts of Justice Act* may be obtained on motion to a judge by a party to a pending or intended proceeding.

Authors' Note on Organization of Cases

Cases relevant to this provision have been organized as follows:

General Principles Regarding Granting of Interlocutory Injunctions
"Mareva" Injunctions — Interim Injunctions Restraining Disposition of Property
Imposition of Conditions or Requirement of Security
Examples Where Interlocutory Injunctions Granted
Examples Where Interlocutory Injunctions Refused
Miscellaneous Cases

General Principles Regarding Granting of Interlocutory Injunctions

Yule Inc. v. Atlantic Pizza Delight Franchise (1968) Ltd. (1977), 17 O.R. (2d) 505, 35 C.P.R. (2d) 273, 80 D.L.R. (3d) 725 (Div. Ct.).

Following *American Cyanamid Co. v. Ethicon Ltd.*, [1975] A.C. 396, [1975] 1 All E.R. 504, [1975] 2 W.L.R. 316 (H.L.), on a motion for an interlocutory injunction the moving party need not establish a strong *prima facie* case. He must establish that there is a substantial issue to be tried; and then the granting of relief will depend on other matters, including the threatened harm to the moving party which might not be adequately compensated by damages, the balance of convenience and the effect of the injunction on both parties.

RJR-MacDonald Inc. v. Canada (Attorney General), [1994] 1 S.C.R. 311, 54 C.P.R. (3d) 114, 111 D.L.R. (4th) 385, 164 N.R. 1, 60 Q.A.C. 241.

There is a three-part test for granting an interlocutory injunction: (1) Is there a serious question to be tried? (2) Will the applicant suffer irreparable harm if the injunction is not granted? (3) Which party will suffer the greater harm from granting or refusing the remedy pending a decision on the merits? Part (1) is to be determined on the basis of common sense and an extremely limited merits review. However, a detailed merits review will be appropriate (a) where the result of the motion will, in effect, amount to a final determination and (b) where the only issue is a simple question of law, or (possibly) where the factual record is largely settled.

Barwell Food Sales Inc. v. Snyder & Fils Inc. (1988), 24 C.P.R. (3d) 102 (Ont. H.C.).

Although *res judicata* does not apply, an Ontario court will give great weight to the outcome of an injunction application in another jurisdiction involving the same party and issues as are in dispute in Ontario.

CDC Life Sciences Inc. v. Institut Merieux S.A. (1988), 39 B.L.R. 275 (Ont. H.C.).

An interlocutory injunction is an extraordinary remedy which must remain flexible, and the test set forth in *American Cyanamid, supra*, may not always be suitable.

Aspen Cleaners & Launderers Ltd. v. Toronto (City) (1988), 32 C.P.C. (2d) 87 (Ont. H.C.).

The moving party may have to meet a higher than usual standard to obtain relief against a public authority.

Ticketnet Corp. v. Air Canada (1987), 21 C.P.C. (2d) 38 (Ont. H.C.).

The standard for granting an interlocutory mandatory injunction is higher than for an interlocutory prohibitory injunction and requires a "high degree of assurance that at trial it will appear" to have been "rightly granted".

C-Cure Chemical Co. v. Olympia & York Devs. Ltd. (1983), 33 C.P.C. 192, 71 C.P.R. (2d) 153 (Ont. Div. Ct.), leave to appeal to Ont. C.A. refused 33 C.P.C. 192n.

Where there is no real conflict on the facts or it is possible to make a reasonable determination of what facts are likely to be proven at trial, the "strong *prima facie* case" test can be applied. Where that is not so, *Amer. Cyanamid v. Ethicon Ltd., supra*, may be used.

Rapp v. McClelland & Stewart Ltd. (1981), 34 O.R. (2d) 452, 19 C.C.L.T. 68, 128 D.L.R. (3d) 650 (H.C.).

An injunction restraining publication of allegedly defamatory material should only issue where the words complained of are so manifestly defamatory that any jury verdict to the contrary would be considered perverse.

Athabasca Holdings Ltd. v. ENA Datasystems Inc. (1980), 30 O.R. (2d) 527, 116 D.L.R. (3d) 318 (H.C.).

If a statutory remedy provides an adequate alternative, that remedy should be pursued before the injunction is sought.

London (City) v. Talbot Square Ltd. (1978), 22 O.R. (2d) 21 (Div. Ct.).

Interlocutory injunctions are granted with a view to preserving the status quo, ensuring that the subject-matter of the litigation is not destroyed or irreversibly altered before trial, and protecting the right of the plaintiff as set up in the action from being defeated by some act of the defendant before trial.

Bernard v. Valentini (1978), 18 O.R. (2d) 656, 3 B.L.R. 139, 83 D.L.R. (3d) 440 (H.C.).

The moving party need not establish a strong *prima facie* case; it is sufficient to satisfy the court that the case is not frivolous and that there are substantial issues to be tried.

Empire Stevedores (1973) Ltd. v. Sparringa (1978), 19 O.R. (2d) 610, 4 B.L.R. 103, leave to appeal refused 19 O.R. (2d) 610n (H.C.).

An interim injunction restraining the defendant from competing with the plaintiff, his former employer, was refused where the balance of convenience favoured the defendant and there was very grave doubt that the plaintiff would succeed at trial.

Wald v. Pape (1978), 22 O.R. (2d) 163, 92 D.L.R. (3d) 378 (H.C.).

On a motion for an interim injunction the court ought not to resolve factual issues but should dispose of the matter using the balance of convenience test. *Yule Inc., supra*, followed.

Steel Art Co. v. Hrivnak (1979), 27 O.R. (2d) 136, 14 C.P.C. 252, 48 C.P.R. (2d) 262, 105 D.L.R. (3d) 716 (H.C.).

An injunction was refused where an employer sought to prevent an ex-employee from establishing a competing business on the grounds that the balance of convenience was in the employee's favour. *Yule Inc., supra*, followed.

Thirty-Six Toronto St. Ltd. v. 517988 Ont. Ltd. (1984), 46 C.P.C. 73 (Ont. H.C.).

The court refused to grant an injunction which would have determined the real issue between the parties and left no substantial issue to be tried. The interlocutory remedy is not meant to preclude the *lis* by deciding the issue for all time.

A.G. Ont. v. Hale (1983), 38 C.P.C. 292, 13 C.E.L.R. 19 (Ont. H.C.).

Where the Attorney General seeks an injunction to enforce the law, the court should still consider the impact of the order on the parties and the public. Such an injunction was refused where it would put the defendants out of business and inconvenience the public, while withholding it would not cause harm to the public or environment.

Heathview Devs. Ltd. v. Credit Foncier (1982), 37 O.R. (2d) 262 (H.C.).

In determining a motion for an interlocutory injunction, the court should first consider whether there is a serious issue to be tried and, if so, it should then consider the compensatory nature of damages and finally the balance of convenience.

Bank of Montreal v. James Main Holdings Ltd. (1982), 28 C.P.C. 157 (Ont. Div. Ct.).

Where an applicant seeks an interlocutory injunction restraining the breach of a negative covenant, if it cannot show inadequacy of damages as a remedy and a favourable balance of convenience, then it must satisfy the court that there has been or is about to be a clear breach of that covenant.

Carlton Realty Co. v. Maple Leaf Mills Ltd. (1978), 22 O.R. (2d) 198, 4 B.L.R. 300, 93 D.L.R. (3d) 106 (H.C.).

The exercise of discretion on a motion for an interlocutory injunction should not be bound by any ironclad rule set up by semantics of phrases.

A.G. Ont. v. Grabarchuk (1975), 11 O.R. (2d) 607, 67 D.L.R. (3d) 31 (Div. Ct.).

The court may grant an interim injunction to prevent the continued violation of a statute notwithstanding that the statute provides penalties for the violation. The usual criteria for granting interim injunctions do not apply in such a case.

Geometrics and Geometrics Services (Can.) Ltd. v. Smith (1975), 11 O.R. (2d) 112, 25 C.P.R. (2d) 202, 65 D.L.R. (3d) 62 (H.C.).

Where the granting of an interlocutory injunction may deprive the defendant of his livelihood and the refusal to do so may result in the plaintiff having difficulty in proving damages, the balance of convenience militates against granting the injunction.

Teledyne Industs. Inc. v. Lido Indust. Products Ltd. (1978), 19 O.R. (2d) 740, 41 C.P.R. (2d) 60, 86 D.L.R. (3d) 446 (C.A.).

Generally an interlocutory injunction will not be granted in patent cases when the validity or infringement of the patent is disputed, the patent is of recent origin, its validity has not been established by a court decision, and the defendant gives an undertaking to the court to keep an account.

Can. Metal Co. v. C.B.C. (1975), 7 O.R. (2d) 261, 55 D.L.R. (3d) 42 (Div. Ct.).

Discussion of an extreme reluctance to grant an injunction restraining the publication of alleged libels.

Benincasa v. Ballentine (1978), 7 C.P.C. 81 (Ont. H.C.).

An injunction will not be granted where an application for similar relief is pending before an administrative tribunal.

Maker v. Davanne Holdings Ltd., [1954] O.R. 935, [1955] 1 D.L.R. 728 (H.C.).

The party opposing the making of an interlocutory injunction has the burden of proof to establish that damages would be an adequate remedy.

"Mareva" Injunctions — Interim Injunctions Restraining Disposition of Property

R. v. Consolidated Fastfrate Transport Inc. (1995), 24 O.R. (3d) 564, 40 C.P.C. (3d) 160, 99 C.C.C. (3d) 143, 61 C.P.R. (3d) 339, 125 D.L.R. (4th) 1, 83 O.A.C. 1 (C.A.).

Although a civil court has jurisdiction to grant a Mareva injunction to preserve the assets of a party facing a criminal prosecution and a possible fine, the Crown must, *inter alia*, show that the accused is deliberately disposing of assets for the improper purpose of making them unavailable to pay a fine in the event of a conviction.

Pan-Abode Distributors (Eastern) Ltd. v. Lindal Cedar Homes Inc. (1993), 27 C.P.C. (3d) 177 (Ont. Gen. Div.).

Funds paid into court pursuant to a Mareva injunction were allowed to be released if alternative security were provided.

Manufacturers Life Insurance Co. v. Suggett (1992), 13 C.P.C. (3d) 171 (Ont. Gen. Div.).

The court ordered the net sale proceeds of the sale of the defendants' home paid into court where there was substantial and unanswered evidence of fraud, notwithstanding a lack of evidence that the defendants were going to leave Ontario.

Yonge Street Shopping Centre General Partner Ltd. v. Nimo's Lighting World Inc. (1992), 9 C.P.C. (3d) 350 (Ont. Gen. Div.).

The right to freeze exigible assets by means of a Mareva injunction exists only if there is a genuine risk of disappearance of the assets either inside or outside the jurisdiction.

Israel Discount Bank of Canada v. Genova (1992), 13 C.P.C. (3d) 104 (Ont. Gen. Div.).

The court refused to continue an *ex parte* "Mareva" injunction where there was a lack of evidence concerning removal of assets from the jurisdiction.

Kuehne & Nagel International Ltd. v. Redirack Ltd. (1991), 47 C.L.R. 241 (Ont. Gen. Div.).

An element of fraud or improper purpose is not necessary to obtain a "Mareva" injunction. The court ordered a defendant which was liquidating most of its assets for business reasons to pay $690,000 into court.

Di Menza v. Richardson Greenshields of Canada Ltd. (1989), 74 O.R. (2d) 172, 43 C.P.C. (2d) 87 (Div. Ct.).

The mere possibility of the removal of any assets rendering any judgment nugatory is not a sufficient ground for granting a "Mareva" injunction since it has the same effect as execution before judgment.

NEC Corp. v. Steintron Int. Electronics Ltd. (1985), 52 O.R. (2d) 201, 5 C.P.C. (2d) 187 (H.C.).

The court granted an interim injunction restraining the defendant, which had lost but was appealing a related British Columbia action, from disposing of its Ontario assets.

Aetna Financial Services Ltd. v. Feigelman, [1985] 1 S.C.R. 2, 29 B.L.R. 5, 55 C.B.R. (N.S.) 1, [1985] 2 W.W.R. 97, 4 C.P.R. (3d) 145, 15 D.L.R. (4th) 161, 32 Man. R. (2d) 241, 56 N.R. 241.

The Supreme Court of Canada recognized the right of superior provincial courts to issue "Mareva" injunctions. English jurisprudence does not take into account the nature of Canada's federal system. Rightful removal of assets in the ordinary course of business by a resident defendant from one province to another province does not by itself entitle the plaintiff to a "Mareva" injunction.

Chitel v. Rothbart (1982), 39 O.R. (2d) 513, 30 C.P.C. 205, 141 D.L.R. (3d) 268, 69 C.P.R. (2d) 62 (C.A.).

Discussion of the principles and guidelines to be followed in granting "Mareva" injunctions. There must be a strong *prima facie* case on the merits and a real risk that the defendant is about to remove his assets from the jurisdiction to avoid the possibility of a judgment. A Mareva injunction was dissolved where the plaintiff had failed to make full disclosure on the interim motion made without notice, so that an incomplete and misleading picture of the relationship between the parties had resulted. [*As to full disclosure on motions made without notice, see rule 39.01(6) — Authors.*]

Aksoy v. Sadak (1984), 45 C.P.C. 50 (Ont. H.C.).

The court declined to grant a Mareva injunction where there was no demonstrated risk that the responding parties would leave the jurisdiction and the moving party had failed to make out a strong *prima facie* case on the merits.

Quinn v. Marsta Cession Services Ltd. (1982), 37 O.R. (2d) 373, 16 B.L.R. 131, 37 C.P.C. 78 (H.C.).

As a general proposition, granting a Mareva injunction should not be made in circumstances where it would prevent the payment of a debt.

Caisse Populaire Laurier D'Ottawa v. Guertin; Caisse Populaire Laurier D'Ottawa v. Simard (1983), 42 O.R. (2d) 35, 36 C.P.C. 63 (H.C.).

A Mareva injunction was dissolved where the material before the court did not indicate that there was a real risk that the defendant was about to remove his assets from the jurisdiction or that he was otherwise dissipating or disposing of his assets in a manner distinct from his usual or ordinary course of business. *Chitel v. Rothbart, supra*, followed.

Bank of Montreal v. James Main Holdings Ltd. (1982), 26 C.P.C. 266, 23 R.P.R. 180 (Ont. H.C.).

A Mareva injunction to prevent the defendant from dealing with her property was refused where there was no unusual circumstance relating to the risk of removal or disposition of assets.

Can. Pac. Airlines Ltd. v. Hind (1981), 32 O.R. (2d) 591, 14 B.L.R. 233, 22 C.P.C. 179, 122 D.L.R. (3d) 498 (H.C.).

Where the defendant's dishonesty was shown, and there was a great risk that he would dispose of any assets available to him, a Mareva injunction was permitted.

Liberty Nat. Bank and Trust Co. v. Atkin (1981), 31 O.R. (2d) 715, 20 C.P.C. 55, 121 D.L.R. (3d) 160 (H.C.).

A Mareva injunction should issue, subject to certain safeguards, where there is a danger of the defendant absconding or assets being removed from the jurisdiction or disposed of so that if the plaintiff obtains judgment he may not be able to satisfy it.

Mills v. Petrovic (1980), 30 O.R. (2d) 238, 12 B.L.R. 224, 18 C.P.C. 38, 118 D.L.R. (3d) 367 (H.C.).

Where there was substantial evidence that the defendant had defrauded or stolen from the plaintiff, an interlocutory injunction issued restraining the defendant from disposing of his property.

Robert Reiser & Co. v. Nadore Food Processing Equipment Ltd. (1977), 17 O.R. (2d) 717, 25 C.B.R. (N.S.) 162, 81 D.L.R. (3d) 278 (H.C.).

In an action to set aside a conveyance of personal property, an interim injunction prohibiting dealing with the property may be granted if the applicant is a creditor of the defendant and shows strong indication that the conveyance may have been fraudulent.

Imposition of Conditions or Requirement of Security

Cemasco Management Ltd. v. Analysis Film Releasing Corp. (1979), 24 O.R. (2d) 389, 46 C.P.R. (2d) 189, 98 D.L.R. (3d) 573 (H.C.).

As a term of dismissing a motion for an interlocutory injunction the defendant was required to undertake to keep records which would facilitate proof of damages.

Int. Chemalloy Corp. v. Kawecki Berylco Industs. Inc. (1977), 3 C.P.C. 53 (Ont. H.C.).

An interlocutory injunction was continued and pledged shares ordered released, on condition that money be paid into court to stand as security.

C. & G. Customs Builders Co. v. Applewood Air Conditioning Ltd. (1975), 10 O.R. (2d) 399, 63 D.L.R. (3d) 395 (H.C.).

The court's power to grant an injunction or order of *mandamus* includes the ability to order the removal of a notice of conditional sale registered against land and to impose conditions on the person seeking the order.

80 Wellesley St. East Ltd. v. Fundy Bay Builders Ltd., [1972] 2 O.R. 280, 25 D.L.R. (3d) 386 (C.A.).

An interim mandatory order was made removing a document from title on the condition the applicant first supply certain security.

Examples Where Interlocutory Injunctions Granted

Eveready Canada v. Duracell Canada Inc. (1995), 64 C.P.R. (3d) 348 (Ont. Gen. Div.).

The court made an interim order restraining the defendant from televising an advertisement using a pink bunny representing the plaintiff's trademark where the potential damage to the plaintiff from continuing to air the advertisement outweighed the potential damage to the defendant if the advertisement ceased.

Ontario (Attorney General) v. Dieleman (1994), 20 O.R. (3d) 229, 117 D.L.R. (4th) 449, additional reasons (1995), 22 O.R. (3d) 785, 123 D.L.R. (4th) 757, further additional reasons (1995), 22 O.R. (3d) 785 at 794, 123 D.L.R. (4th) 766 (Gen. Div.).

The Attorney General has a broad standing to sue on behalf of the public interest in respect of a flouting of the law contrary to the public interest, and based on an inclusive right to seek to enjoin conduct constituting a public nuisance. In the result, the Attorney General's application to enjoin certain anti-abortion activity was granted.

Lakewood by the Park Ltd. v. Ontario Home Warranty Programme (1991), 5 O.R. (3d) 527, 49 C.L.R. 241 (Gen. Div.).

The court granted a mandatory injunction to prevent return of a letter of credit.

Rennie v. Canada Trustco Mortgage Co. (1991), 1 C.P.C. (3d) 272, 19 R.P.R. (2d) 271 (Ont. Gen. Div.).

The court granted an injunction restraining a mortgagee from selling under power of sale proceedings where the mortgagor had not received notice of the power of sale proceedings, had acted in good faith, and had the intention and economic capacity to redeem the property.

Peat Marwick Thorne v. Canadian Broadcasting Corp. (1991), 5 O.R. (3d) 747, 4 C.P.C. (3d) 233, 39 C.P.R. (3d) 58, 84 D.L.R. (4th) 656 (Gen. Div.).

The court issued an interim injunction restraining the CBC from broadcasting a documentary containing confidential information in breach of an alleged agreement not to use such without consent. The court conducted the hearing *in camera* and sealed the court file.

Ontario (Attorney General) v. Bear Island Foundation (1989), 70 O.R. (2d) 758, [1990] 4 C.N.L.R. 25, 63 D.L.R. (4th) 756 (H.C.).

The Attorney General was granted an injunction, without having to show irreparable harm, where an Indian band obstructed road construction on land in which the court found that it had no aboriginal or ownership claim. The fact that other procedures existed (*i.e.* arrest) to prevent the obstruction is not relevant since one purpose of the injunction is to have the breaching party face the sanctions of being in contempt of court.

Assad v. Cambridge Right to Life (1989), 69 O.R. (2d) 598 (H.C.).

An injunction was granted to stop picketing outside offices where abortions were performed.

Baron Philippe de Rothschild S.A. v. Casa de Habana Inc. (1987), 17 C.I.P.R. (2d) 185, 19 C.P.R. (3d) 114 (Ont. H.C.).

An interlocutory injunction was issued preventing the defendant's use of the name "Rothschild", without proof of injury or damage, since it constituted a breach of the *Trademarks Act* and an unlawful appropriation of personality.

Engineered Sound Systems Ltd. v. Datel Communications Ltd. (1987), 22 C.P.C. (2d) 240 (Ont. Dist. Ct.), reversed in part 22 C.P.C. (2d) 240n, 19 C.P.R. (3d) 105 (Ont. H.C.).

Where there was some evidence of misuse of confidential information, an injunction was granted against the plaintiff's ex-employee. The injunction did not extend to the defendant's new employer, where the balance of convenience was in its favour, and the plaintiff was sufficiently protected without the necessity of such an order.

Profast (London) Ltd. v. Wright (1986), 14 C.P.C. (2d) 284, 14 C.P.R. (3d) 118 (Ont. H.C.), leave to appeal refused 14 C.P.C. (2d) 484n.

The court restrained former employees of the plaintiff from soliciting the plaintiff's customers.

Tsambalieros v. McKean (1986), 11 C.P.C. (2d) 1, 12 C.P.R. (3d) 62 (Ont. H.C.).

The court granted an injunction to enforce a restrictive covenant voluntarily executed by the defendant even though the plaintiff was unable to show damage to date on a balance of convenience test.

Wallace Welding Supplies Ltd. v. Wallace (1986), 8 C.P.C. (2d) 157, 32 B.L.R. 99, 11 C.C.E.L. 108, 9 C.P.R. (3d) 514 (Ont. H.C.).

The court granted an injunction restraining the plaintiff's former employees from certain competitive activities breaching common law and contractual obligations owing by the former employees to the plaintiff.

Hunt v. Fanshawe College of Applied Arts & Technology (1985), 52 O.R. (2d) 759, 6 C.P.C. (2d) 159, 10 C.C.E.L. 138 (H.C.).

The court enjoined the defendant college from disseminating information critical of the plaintiff's professional and personal reputation.

Creditel of Can. Ltd. v. Boothe (1985), 7 C.P.C. (2d) 20, 6 C.P.R. (3d) 507 (Ont. H.C.).

The court restrained the defendants from using confidential client lists obtained from the plaintiff which was the former employer of two of the defendants.

H & S. Bookspan Invts. Ltd. v. Axelrod (1984), 47 O.R. (2d) 604, 45 C.P.C. 318 (H.C.).

Although the law leans against the granting of remedies that tend to restrict a mortgagee from exercising its rights under the mortgage, in this action there was a triable issue as to whether the mortgage was in good standing and the court granted an injunction to prevent the operation of the notice of power of sale.

G.T. Precision Welding (Ont.) Ltd. v. Nelligan (1984), 45 C.P.C. 194, 3 C.P.R. (3d) 511 (Ont. H.C.).

An injunction was made restraining the defendants, former senior managerial employees of the plaintiff, from soliciting the plaintiff's customers for a period of one year or until trial, whichever came first.

Metro. Toronto v. N.B. Theatrical Agencies Inc. (1984), 44 O.R. (2d) 574, 40 C.P.C. 191, 24 M.P.L.R. 241, 4 D.L.R. (4th) 678 (H.C.).

An injunction was granted to prevent violations of municipal by-laws pending a decision challenging the constitutional validity of the by-laws.

ATV Music Publishing of Can. Ltd. v. Rogers Radio Broadcasting Ltd. (1982), 35 O.R. (2d) 417, 134 D.L.R. (3d) 487 (H.C.).

The court restrained the defendant from playing the words to the song "Constitution" to the tune of Lennon and McCartney's song "Revolution" where there could be irreparable harm to the plaintiff if the defendant were permitted to do so.

Hoskin v. Price Waterhouse Ltd. (1982), 35 O.R. (2d) 350 (H.C.).

The court enjoined the bank from proceeding with power of sale proceedings under two mortgages given by a guarantor of corporate debts as collateral security. It appeared the receiver appointed by the bank may have been negligent in disposing of the corporate assets and necessitating recourse to the mortgages.

Rosen v. Pullen (1981), 16 B.L.R. 28, 126 D.L.R. (3d) 62 (Ont. H.C.).

The court declined to dissolve an interlocutory injunction restraining payment by a bank pursuant to a letter of credit where the applicant made out a good *prima facie* case of fraud.

C.D.N. Research & Dev. Ltd. v. Bank of N.S. (1980), 18 C.P.C. 62 (Ont. H.C.).

An interlocutory injunction was granted to prevent a bank from making payment pursuant to a demand on an irrevocable letter of credit.

A.G. Ont. v. Yeotes; A.G. Ont. v. Harry (1980), 28 O.R. (2d) 577, 16 C.P.C. 60, 12 R.P.R. 166, 111 D.L.R. (3d) 488, reversed on other grounds 31 O.R. (2d) 589, 14 M.P.L.R. 156, 18 R.P.R. 161, 120 D.L.R. (3d) 128, leave to appeal to S.C.C. dismissed 37 N.R. 356.

The Attorney General obtained an interlocutory injunction to prevent the partition of lands without *Planning Act* compliance.

Turf Care Products v. Crawford's Mowers & Marine (1979), 23 O.R. (2d) 292, 1 P.P.S.A.C. 25, 95 O.L.R. (3d) 378 (Div. Ct.).

The court granted an interlocutory interim injunction restraining the defendants from selling collateral to a challenged security agreement.

Sheddon v. Ont. Major Junior Hockey League (1978), 19 O.R. (2d) 1, 36 C.P.R. (2d) 81, 83 D.L.R. (3d) 734 (H.C.).

An interim injunction was granted enjoining the respondents from preventing the applicant from playing hockey with a team in the respondent league.

Creditel of Can. Ltd. v. Faultless (1977), 18 O.R. (2d) 95, 2 B.L.R. 239, 36 C.P.R. (2d) 88, 81 D.L.R. (3d) 567 (H.C.).

An interlocutory injunction was made restraining the defendants from divulging certain confidential business information and from enticing customers away from the plaintiff.

Hardee Farms Int. Ltd. v. Cam & Crank Grinding Ltd., [1973] 2 O.R. 170, 10 C.P.R. (2d) 42, 33 D.L.R. (3d) 266 (H.C.).

An interim injunction may be granted to prohibit the breach of a negative covenant.

Canadian Tire Corp. Ltd. v. Desmond, [1972] 2 O.R. 60, 24 D.L.R. (3d) 642 (H.C.).

An interim injunction was granted restraining the defendant, a disgruntled customer of the plaintiff, from picketing the premises of the plaintiff carrying a defamatory sign.

McMillin v. Yandell, [1972] 1 O.R. 146, 22 D.L.R. (3d) 398 (H.C.).

An interlocutory injunction was granted on the motion of a minority of members of a trade union local to restrain merger of their local with another union.

Mahas v. C.I.B.C., [1963] 2 O.R. 447, 40 D.L.R. (2d) 25 (H.C.).

The court granted an interlocutory injunction restraining a landlord from demolishing certain premises but refused to compel the landlord to repair the premises.

R. v. Trudel, [1947] O.W.N. 175, [1947] 2 D.L.R. 238 (H.C.).

The court has power to grant a mandatory injunction against trespassers restraining them from remaining in illegal possession of premises.

Examples Where Interlocutory Injunctions Refused

967305 Ontario Ltd. v. North American Trust Co. (1996), 7 W.D.C.P. (2d) 158 (Ont. Gen. Div.).

The court refused to grant an injunction restraining steps being taken under a notice of sale under mortgage.

Cellular Rental Systems Inc. v. Bell Mobility Cellular Inc. (1995), 23 O.R. (3d) 766, 21 B.L.R. (2d) 91, 61 C.P.R. (3d) 204, 123 D.L.R. (4th) 742, 82 O.A.C. (3d) 86 (Div. Ct.).

Where a permanent injunction was not requested in the statement of claim or the notice of motion, the court held that it did not have the jurisdiction to grant an interlocutory injunction restraining the defendants from breaching the *Competition Act*. In any event, the court lacked the jurisdiction under the *Competition Act* to restrain a breach of the Act.

Duarte v. LensCrafters International Inc. (1994), 31 C.P.C. (3d) 321, 57 C.P.R. (3d) 418 (Ont. Gen. Div.).

Where the plaintiff moved to restrain the defendant from terminating the lease of his eye examination clinic, the court held that the plaintiff would not suffer irreparable harm as a result of the termination and dismissed the motion.

Hardware Agencies Ltd. v. Medeco Security Locks Canada (1995), 39 C.P.C. (3d) 297, additional reasons 39 C.P.C. (3d) 297 at 311 (Ont. Gen. Div.).

Where the plaintiff failed to establish that there was a serious issue to be tried that it should not be bound by a 30-day termination clause in the distributor agreements, the court dismissed the plaintiff's motion for an interlocutory injunction.

Burlington (City) v. Video Matic 24 Hr Movie Rentals Inc. (1994), 34 C.P.C. (3d) 54, 21
    M.P.L.R. (2d) 217 (Ont. Gen. Div.).

The court refused to grant an injunction restraining the alleged breach of a municipal by-law.

Lackner Centre Developments Inc. v. Toronto Dominion Bank (1993), 17 C.P.C. (3d) 60, 32
    R.P.R. (2d) 204 (Ont. Gen. Div.).

The court refused to restrain a bank from shutting down branches in violation of leases where
damages would be an adequate remedy.

Toronto Blue Jays Baseball Club v. John Doe (1992), 9 O.R. (3d) 622 (Gen. Div.).

The court refused to grant an *ex parte* order against persons unknown permitting the plaintiff
to seize baseball tickets from scalpers. The plaintiff did not establish any present unlawful
intention and had not established any irreparable harm.

Adno v. Physiotherapy Assn. (Ontario) (1991), 6 O.R. (3d) 209 (Gen. Div.).

A motion for an injunction was dismissed where the defendant had taken remedial steps in
respect of the matter complained of in the statement of claim, and the plaintiff had failed to
meet the normal tests to be met on such a motion.

Drewlo Homes Inc. v. Ontario New Homes Warranty Programme (1991), 4 O.R. (3d) 629, 49
    C.L.R. 185 (Gen. Div.).

A motion for an injunction prohibiting the defendant from distributing a Home Buyer's Guide
was dismissed, as the withdrawal of the Guide would harm the public.

Gerrard v. Century 21 Armour Real Estate Inc. (1991), 4 O.R. (3d) 191, 35 C.C.E.L. 128, 35
    C.P.R. (3d) 448 (Gen. Div.), leave to appeal to Ont. Div. Ct. refused 4 O.R. (3d) 191n, 35
    C.P.R. (3d) 448n.

A motion for an interlocutory injunction relating to breach of a restrictive covenant was denied
where the applicant failed to make out a strong *prima facie* case and the evidence as to irreparable
harm was speculative.

Dylex Ltd. v. Factory Carpet Corp. (1989), 44 C.P.C. (2d) 96 (Ont. H.C.).

A motion for an interlocutory injunction was dismissed where the plaintiff failed to show a
strong *prima facie* case, and the plaintiff's failure to move expeditiously for an interlocutory
injunction forced the conclusion that it was not suffering irreparable harm.

Ontario (A.G.) v. Temagami Wilderness Society (1989), 38 C.P.C. (2d) 296 (Ont. H.C.).

The court refused to enjoin a proposed blockade of a logging road where there was no existing
illegal act or injury by the respondent. The respondent had the freedom to express its opposition
to the road within the law.

Doherty v. Irish Dance Teachers' Assn. of Can. (1987), 24 C.P.C. (2d) 50, 18 C.C.E.L. 206
    (Ont. H.C.).

The court refused to order the defendant to reinstate the plaintiff as a member. Discussion of
circumstances where the court will intervene in the expulsion of a member of an association.

Mercury Marine Ltd. v. Dillon (1986), 56 O.R. (2d) 266, 11 C.P.C. (2d) 235, 12 C.P.R. (3d)
    158, 30 D.L.R. (4th) 627 (H.C.).

The court refused an interim injunction restraining a former employee from working for the
plaintiff's competitor and dealing with the plaintiff's customers where a strong *prima facie* case
was not established.

Bramalea Ltd. v. Can. Safeway Ltd. (1985), 4 C.P.C. (2d) 144, 37 R.P.R. 191 (Ont. H.C.).

The court declined to grant an interlocutory injunction requiring a large food store to continue
to operate its business at the plaintiff's shopping centre, where there was serious doubt whether
the plaintiff would succeed at trial and it was not clear that the plaintiff would suffer irreparable
harm if the order were not made. Additionally, the court would have difficulty in the supervision
of such a mandatory order.

Greenlaw v. Ont. Major Junior Hockey League (1984), 48 O.R. (2d) 371, 2 C.P.R. (3d) 556
(H.C.).

A motion by a hockey player for an interlocutory injunction to preclude a draft to a North Bay
hockey club was dismissed. Although there was a serious issue to be tried, the balance of
convenience favoured the defendant league.

First City Financial Corp. Ltd. v. Genstar Corp. (1981), 33 O.R. (2d) 631, 15 B.L.R. 60, 125
D.L.R. (3d) 303 (H.C.).

The court will refuse to grant an injunction where the applicant has an alternative and effective
remedy available to it. In this case the court refused to issue an injunction regarding a takeover
bid where it appeared that the Ontario Securities Commission could deal with the matter.

Re Mactan Holdings Ltd. and 431736 Ont. Ltd. (1980), 31 O.R. (2d) 37, 118 D.L.R. (3d) 91
(H.C.).

The court refused to grant an interim injunction restraining the sale of land where the applicant
had obtained a certificate of pending litigation regarding the property in question.

Cantol Ltd. v. Brodi Chemicals Ltd. (1978), 23 O.R. (2d) 36, 5 B.L.R. 177, 42 C.P.R. (2d) 111,
94 D.L.R. (3d) 265 (H.C.).

The court refused to grant an interlocutory injunction restraining a former employee of the
plaintiff from breaching a non-solicitation agreement.

Capitol Records — EMI of Can. Ltd. v. Gosewich (1977), 17 O.R. (2d) 501, 36 C.P.R. (2d) 36,
80 D.L.R. (3d) 737 (H.C.).

An interim injunction prohibiting a former employee of the moving party, who had covenanted
not to disclose confidential business information or to solicit business from its clientele, from
being employed by a competitor was refused.

Brown v. Gananoque (1977), 17 O.R. (2d) 228, 4 M.P.L.R. 127 (H.C.).

An interim injunction prohibiting a municipality from extending sewer works was refused.

Gretzky v. Ont. Minor Hockey Assn. (1975), 10 O.R. (2d) 759, 24 C.P.R. (2d) 275, 64 D.L.R.
(3d) 467 (H.C.).

An interim injunction to enforce contractual rights was refused because the contract was
voidable at the option of the moving parties and because the moving parties had not exhausted
appeal procedures available under the contract.

Greenback Invts. (Hamilton) Ltd. v. O'Connell, [1972] 3 O.R. 656, 29 D.L.R. (3d) 164 (H.C.).

The court refused to grant an interim injunction restraining the defendant police from raiding
the plaintiff's premises, since if the plaintiff were successful at trial it could be adequately
compensated in damages.

George v. Vaughan, [1971] 3 O.R. 701, 21 D.L.R. (3d) 513 (H.C.).

An interim injunction to restrain a municipality from participating in the operation of a sanitary
landfill and gravel pit was refused.

Arnold v. Bronstein, [1971] 1 O.R. 467, 15 D.L.R. (3d) 649 (H.C.).

An interim injunction restraining a mortgagee from exercising his power of sale was refused
where the mortgagee was acting in good faith and without fraud.

Cummings v. Hydro-Electric Power Comm. of Ont., [1966] 1 O.R. 605, 54 D.L.R. (2d) 583
(H.C.).

An interlocutory injunction to restrain a defendant employer from applying to the Lieutenant
Governor in Council for changes in its pension plan was denied.

Miscellaneous Cases

Amchem Products Inc. v. British Columbia (Workers' Compensation Board), [1993] 1 S.C.R. 897, 14 C.P.C. (3d) 1, 77 B.C.L.R. (2d) 62, [1993] 3 W.W.R. 441, 102 D.L.R. (4th) 96, 150 N.R. 321, 23 B.C.A.C. 1, 39 W.A.C. 1.

Discussion of the circumstances in which the court will issue an ''anti-suit'' injunction restraining the defendant from prosecuting an action in a foreign jurisdiction.

Cahill v. Metro. Toronto (1985), 6 C.P.C. (2d) 189 (Ont. H.C.).

A class action cannot be maintained to enjoin a public nuisance.

Greymac Trust Co. v. BNA Realty Inc. (1985), 50 C.P.C. 45 (Ont. H.C.).

The court has the power to restrain a person within its jurisdiction from prosecuting suits in a foreign court but such power should be exercised with extreme care. The court refused to restrain prosecution of a Quebec action.

Bourganis v. larentzos (1978), 19 O.R. (2d) 327, 6 C.P.C. 301, 85 D.L.R. (3d) 446 (H.C.).

An interlocutory injunction was dissolved where the plaintiff had taken no steps in the year following the granting of the injunction to bring the action to trial and had refused to co-operate with the defendant in his efforts to proceed with the matter.

Can. Metal Co. v. C.B.C. (No. 2) (1976), 11 O.R. (2d) 167, 29 C.C.C. (2d) 325, 65 D.L.R. (3d) 231 (C.A.).

The Supreme Court of Ontario can entertain a proceeding for an injunction against the C.B.C., since it is not a federal Board, etc., over which the Federal Court has exclusive jurisdiction.

Adrian Messenger Services v. The Jockey Club Ltd. (No. 2), [1972] 2 O.R. 619, 26 D.L.R. (3d) 287 (C.A.).

An interim injunction obtained by a plaintiff who is then unsuccessful at trial will be extended pending appeal only in rare cases.

Pasen v. Dominion Herb Distributors Inc., [1968] 2 O.R. 516, 69 D.L.R. (2d) 651 (C.A.).

An interim injunction is a discretionary order with which the Court of Appeal will not interfere if there was material before the court of first instance which could justify its decision.

WHERE MOTION MADE WITHOUT NOTICE

Maximum Duration

40.02(1) An interlocutory injunction or mandatory order may be granted on motion without notice for a period not exceeding ten days.

Extension

(2) Where an interlocutory injunction or mandatory order is granted on a motion without notice, a motion to extend the injunction or mandatory order may be made only on notice to every party affected by the order, unless the judge is satisfied that because a party has been evading service or because there are other exceptional circumstances, the injunction or mandatory order ought to be extended without notice to the party.

(3) An extension may be granted on a motion without notice for a further period not exceeding ten days.

Labour Injunctions Excepted

(4) Subrules (1) to (3) do not apply to a motion for an injunction in a labour dispute under section 102 of the *Courts of Justice Act*.

Cross-Reference: See cases under rule 37.14.

M. (S.) v. C. (J.R.) (1993), 13 O.R. (3d) 148 (Gen. Div.).

Rule 40.02(1) is of no assistance where the moving party is seeking preservation of long-term rights and not rights pending resolution of the litigation.

Launch! Research & Dev. Inc. v. Essex Dist. Co. (1977), 4 C.P.C. 261 (Ont. H.C.).

A plaintiff should only apply for an injunction without notice where it is genuinely impossible to give any notice to the defendant of the order sought without defeating the purposes of the order.

The Chesapeake and Ohio Ry. Co. v. Ball, [1953] O.R. 843, appeal quashed [1953] O.R. 877
   (C.A.).

An interlocutory injunction will rarely be granted without hearing both sides; however, in cases of emergency the order may be made *ex parte.*

UNDERTAKING

40.03 On a motion for an interlocutory injunction or mandatory order, the moving party shall, unless the court orders otherwise, undertake to abide by any order concerning damages that the court may make if it ultimately appears that the granting of the order has caused damage to the responding party for which the moving party ought to compensate the responding party.

Vetech Laboratories Ltd. v. 621870 Ontario Ltd. (1991), 2 C.P.C. (3d) 135 (Ont. Gen. Div.).

The omission of an undertaking as to damages in an injunction proceeding was an irregularity curable under rule 59.06. The court refused to dissolve the injunction obtained by the defendant where irreparable harm would result to the defendant.

Metropolitan Toronto (Municipality) v. N.B. Theatrical Agencies Inc. (1991), 2 O.R. (3d) 260,
   4 M.P.L.R. (2d) 93, 76 D.L.R. (4th) 522 (Gen. Div.).

Where a municipality had obtained an interlocutory injunction against a hotel which had deliberately and persistently flouted a municipal by-law, but the municipality had failed to uphold it in a final judgment, the court dismissed the hotel's motion for leave to enforce the undertaking given to obtain the injunction. The hotel's conduct had disentitled it to the exercise of the court's discretion in its favour.

John F. Renshaw (Can.) Inc. v. Captiva Investments Ltd. (1989), 70 O.R. (2d) 458 (H.C.).

A defendant may not counterclaim for damages pursuant to an undertaking given by the plaintiff regarding an injunction. The proper method of enforcing the undertaking is to apply to the trial judge for leave to prove damages.

Maybank Foods Inc. Pension Plan v. Gainers Inc. (1988), 63 O.R. (2d) 687, *(sub nom. Micallef
   v. Gainers Inc.)* 25 C.P.C. (2d) 248 (H.C.).

An injunction was granted restraining the vendor of a business from transferring pension funds out of one plan into another, without any undertaking as to damages.

Nelson Burns & Co. v. Gratham Industries Ltd. (1987), 23 C.P.C. (2d) 279, 18 C.I.P.R. 153,
   19 C.P.R. (3d) 71, 25 O.A.C. 89 (C.A.), leave to appeal to S.C.C. refused (1988), 19 C.P.R.
   (3d) vi, 88 N.R. 318, 30 O.A.C. 77n.

An unsuccessful plaintiff will ordinarily be obliged to pay damages in accordance with his undertaking without quibble. The plaintiffs' success on a claim unrelated to the interlocutory injunction did not prevent enforcement of the undertaking.

A.G. Ont. v. Harry (1982), 35 O.R. (2d) 248, 25 C.P.C. 67, 132 D.L.R. (3d) 73 (H.C.).

The court to whom an undertaking as to damages has been given by an unsuccessful plaintiff retains a discretion to refuse to enforce it where there are special circumstances or the defendant's conduct has been inequitable.

Sherk v. Horwitz, [1973] 3 O.R. 979, 12 C.P.R. (2d) 190, 39 D.L.R. (3d) 17 (H.C.).

The undertaking should be enforced by proving the damages before the trial judge.

Merchants Gas Co. v. Hall, [1956] O.W.N. 820 (H.C.).

Where a permanent injunction is refused, damages in respect of an interlocutory injunction should be confined to the immediate natural consequences of the injunction which were within the knowledge of the party obtaining the injunction.

RULE 41   APPOINTMENT OF RECEIVER

Highlights

This Rule is supplementary to the general power in s. 101 of the *Courts of Justice Act* by which a judge may appoint a receiver, or receiver-manager, by an interlocutory order.

It would appear that only a court-appointed receiver may apply for directions under rule 41.05, but a privately appointed receiver may apply for directions if he comes within the provisions of the *Canada Business Corporations Act*, R.S.C. 1985, c. C-44, s. 100.

A creditor may not obtain an order appointing a receiver, which is in effect execution before judgment, unless there is strong evidence that the creditor's right to recovery is in serious jeopardy: *Ryder Truck Rental Can. Ltd. v. 568907 Ont. Ltd. (Trustee of)* (1987), 16 C.P.C. (2d) 130 (Ont. H.C.).

Former provisions: Judicature Act, s. 19(1).

DEFINITION

41.01 In rules 41.02 to 41.06, "receiver" means a receiver or receiver and manager.

HOW OBTAINED

41.02 The appointment of a receiver under section 101 of the *Courts of Justice Act* may be obtained on motion to a judge in a pending or intended proceeding.

Appointment of Receiver — Generally

Confederation Trust Co. v. Dentbram Developments Ltd. (1992), 9 C.P.C. (3d) 399 (Ont. Gen. Div.).

When receivers proposed by each party possess similar qualities, generally the receiver proposed by the creditor, who has carriage of the proceedings, should be appointed.

Third Generation Realty Ltd. v. Twigg Holdings Ltd. (1991), 6 C.P.C. (3d) 366 (Ont. Gen. Div.).

The test regarding the appointment of a receiver is whether the appointment is just and convenient having regard to the nature of the property and the rights of the parties in relation thereto. A receiver should not be appointed to relieve a mortgagee in possession of its responsibilities as such, however, the fact that the plaintiff is a mortgagee in possession is not an objection *per se.*

Fisher Investments Ltd. v. Nusbaum (1988), 31 C.P.C. (2d) 158, 71 C.B.R. (N.S.) 185 (Ont. H.C.).

Appointment of an interim receiver-manager is extraordinary relief which prejudges the conduct of a litigant and should be granted sparingly.

539618 Ont. Inc. v. Olympic Foods (Thunder Bay) Ltd. (1987), 22 C.P.C. (2d) 195, 65 C.B.R. (N.S.) 143 (Ont. S.C.), application to vary refused 65 C.B.R. (N.S.) 285 (Ont. S.C.).

An *ex parte* order appointing an interim receiver was set aside where cross-examination disclosed that the affidavit material used to obtain the order contained hearsay on important points, failed to disclose relevant facts, and was deliberately crafted so as to hide the real source of the deponent's information.

Ryder Truck Rental Can. Ltd. v. 568907 Ont. Ltd. (Trustee of) (1987), 16 C.P.C. (2d) 130 (Ont. H.C.).

The court will not appoint a receiver, which is in effect execution before judgment, unless there is strong evidence that the creditor's right to recovery is in serious jeopardy.

Canadian Commercial Bank v. Gemcraft Ltd. (1985), 3 C.P.C. (2d) 13 (Ont. H.C.).

The court appointed a receiver and manager at the motion of a secured party whose security was in jeopardy. The defendant's financial condition had deteriorated and several events of default had occurred under the security agreement.

Bank of Montreal v. Appcon Ltd. (1981), 33 O.R. (2d) 97, 37 C.B.R. (N.S.) 281, 123 D.L.R. (3d) 394 (S.C.).

On a motion to appoint a receiver, it is proper to consider security held by the moving party entitling it to appoint a receiver privately. In this case the court appointed a receiver with a term restraining the disposition of the defendant's assets other than in the ordinary course of business in order to preserve for the moving party the benefits of its security.

Cantamar Holdings Ltd. v. Tru-View Aluminum Products (1979), 23 O.R. (2d) 572, 6 B.L.R. 209 (H.C.).

The court may appoint a receiver notwithstanding that the moving party holds security registered under the *Personal Property Security Act.*

Bee Chemical Co. v. Plastic Paint & Finish Specialties Ltd. (1979), 13 C.P.C. 131 (Ont. Master).

Pending an appeal to the Court of Appeal, the High Court appointed a receiver where the appellant was clearly ignoring the injunction granted as part of the judgment.

Re Federal Trust Co. and Frisina (1976), 20 O.R. (2d) 32, 28 C.B.R. (N.S.) 201, 86 D.L.R. (3d) 591 (H.C.).

The court will not appoint a person as receiver-manager in circumstances which would raise in the mind of a reasonable and intelligent person a real apprehension that he lacks impartiality and disinterestedness.

Goldex Mines Ltd. v. Revill (1974), 7 O.R. (2d) 216 (C.A.).

The injunctive and directory powers of the court were broad enough to protect minority shareholders and the court refused to appoint an interim receiver.

Sanden v. Price, [1973] 1 O.R. 55, 18 C.B.R. (N.S.) 71 (H.C.).

A master lacks jurisdiction to appoint a receiver. [*And see now Courts of Justice Act, s. 101(1), and rules 40.01, 37.02(2)(a) — Authors.*]

Re Wardlaw & Whittaker, [1970] 1 O.R. 86 (C.A.).

A receiver may be appointed in an application to wind up a partnership.

Chapman v. Rose-Snider Fur Co. (1922), 51 O.L.R. 603, 69 D.L.R. 639 (H.C.).

In making an *ex parte* order appointing a receiver the court must be satisfied that delay would or might entail serious mischief. Any *ex parte* order appointing a receiver should contain an undertaking as to damages.

Appointment of Receiver — By Way of Execution

[*See rule 60.02(1)(d) re appointment of a receiver to enforce an order for the payment of money. Also note that under rule 60.08 a notice of garnishment now reaches future debts — Authors.*]

Carter (Receiver of) v. Carter (1988), 29 C.P.C. (2d) 150, 69 C.B.R. (N.S.) 137 (Ont. H.C.).

The court recognized and confirmed a British Columbia Supreme Court order appointing a receiver in aid of execution, although the order was under appeal.

Lavigne v. Robern (1986), 56 O.R. (2d) 385, 12 C.P.C. (2d) 87, 30 D.L.R. (4th) 756 (H.C.).

A receiver in aid of execution was appointed to collect pension benefits paid pursuant to the *Public Service Superannuation Act* where a debtor had made himself "judgment proof".

Cdn. Film Development Corp. v. Perlmutter (1986), 53 O.R. (2d) 283, 6 C.P.C. (2d) 262 (H.C.), leave to appeal refused 8 C.P.C. (2d) 237.

The court appointed a receiver where the judgment debtor structured his affairs to prevent the plaintiff from recovering on its judgment while maintaining an extravagant lifestyle.

Simon v. Simon (1984), 45 O.R. (2d) 534, 42 C.P.C. 133, 50 C.B.R. (N.S.) 161, 38 R.F.L. (2d) 198, C.E.B. & P.G.R. 8166, 7 D.L.R. (4th) 128, 2 O.A.C. 299 (Div. Ct.).

The court appointed a receiver by way of equitable execution of future pension benefits, where it was practically very difficult, if not impossible, to enforce the judgment otherwise.

Martin v. Martin (1981), 33 O.R. (2d) 164, 22 C.P.C. 209, 24 R.F.L. (2d) 211, 123 D.L.R. (3d) 718 (H.C.).

Where the husband, a Crown employee, had disposed of his exigible assets and then arbitrarily reduced his maintenance payments, the court appointed the sheriff as receiver-manager of such amounts of the husband's future salary as necessary to make the payments. *Noriega v. Noriega, infra,* distinguished.

Noriega v. Noriega (1979), 23 O.R. (2d) 520, 30 C.B.R. (N.S.) 169, 13 C.P.C. 263 (H.C.).

A receiver cannot be appointed to collect the future earnings of a judgment debtor.

Gorman v. Young (1976), 2 C.P.C. 245 (Ont. Dist. Ct.).

Where a judgment debtor is a federal Crown employee, not subject to garnishment, a receiver may be appointed to collect his wages, pay him a sum to maintain himself, and distribute the balance to creditors.

Dowell v. Aikenhead, [1961] O.W.N. 174 (H.C.).

The court refused to appoint a receiver by way of equitable execution in respect of moneys payable only on a contingency.

Conduct of Receivership

Ernst & Young Inc. v. Ontario (1995), 25 O.R. (3d) 623 (Gen. Div.).

The court refused to dismiss under Rule 21 an action for a receiver's fees where the appointment of the receiver had been made by a judge on the judge's own initiative but the appointment was later set aside by the Court of Appeal.

Bank of America Canada v. Willann Investments Ltd. (1993), 17 C.P.C. (3d) 296, 20 C.B.R. (3d) 223 (Ont. Gen. Div.).

The court may approve a receiver's activities retroactively.

Demysh v. Demysh, [1993] W.D.F.L. 393 (Ont. Gen. Div.).

The court reduced a receiver's fees by 15 per cent due to inefficiency. The court apportioned the fees between the plaintiff and defendant.

Canada (Attorney General) v. Cardinal Insurance Co. (1991), 7 C.P.C. (3d) 167 (Ont. Gen. Div.).

Discussion of the procedure on a motion by a liquidator to approve the settlement of an action.

Société Générale (Canada) v. 743823 Ontario Ltd. (1990), 41 C.P.C. (2d) 286 (Ont. Master).

Where a receiver had been appointed over a corporation proposed to be added as a party to an action, the directors and officers were held to have authority to conduct litigation on the corporation's behalf since their authority to do so was unimpaired by the terms of appointment of the receiver and there was no evidence of interference with the receiver's duties.

Olympic Foods (Thunder Bay) Ltd. v. 539618 Ont. Inc. (1989), 40 C.P.C. (2d) 280 (Ont. H.C.).
Discussion of assessment of receiver's fees.

Crown Trust Co. v. Rosenberg (No. 3) (1987), 60 O.R. (2d) 87, 22 C.P.C. (2d) 131, 67 C.B.R.
(N.S.) 320, 39 D.L.R. (4th) 526 (H.C.).

On a motion to approve the sale of certain properties, the court should not proceed against the
recommendations of its receiver-manager except in special circumstances and where the necessity and propriety of doing so are plain.

NEC Corp. v. Steintron Int. Electronics Ltd. (1986), 14 C.P.C. (2d) 305 (Ont. H.C.).

A receiver is an officer of the court with a fiduciary duty to act to the best advantage of all
interested parties, not just the creditor at whose motion it was appointed. The court refused to
authorize a receiver to commence on action in its own name.

Victoria Ins. Co. of Can. v. Young's-Graves Bloodstock Inc. (1985), 49 O.R. (2d) 47, 47 C.P.C.
119 (H.C.).

The court refused leave to commence County Court proceedings against a receiver appointed
by the Supreme Court. The receiver was under Supreme Court supervision and any proceedings
against it should be in the Supreme Court.

Del Zotto v. Int. Chemalloy Corp. (1976), 14 O.R. (2d) 72, 22 C.B.R. (N.S.) 268, 2 C.P.C. 198
(H.C.).

Where there is a court-appointed receiver over the defendant's assets, leave should be obtained
prior to the defendant delivering a counterclaim.

Re Allan, [1939] O.W.N. 7 (H.C.).

A receiver by way of equitable execution has no right to take any proceedings without first
obtaining the leave of the court.

FORM OF ORDER

41.03 An order appointing a receiver shall,

**(a) name the person appointed or refer that issue in accordance with
Rule 54;**

**(b) specify the amount and terms of the security, if any, to be furnished
by the receiver for the proper performance of the receiver's duties, or
refer that issue in accordance with Rule 54;**

**(c) state whether the receiver is also appointed as manager and, if nec-
essary, define the scope of the receiver's managerial powers; and**

(d) contain such directions and impose such terms as are just.

REFERENCE OF CONDUCT OF RECEIVERSHIP

**41.04 An order appointing a receiver may refer the conduct of all or
part of the receivership in accordance with Rule 54.**

DIRECTIONS

**41.05 A receiver may obtain directions at any time on motion to a judge,
unless there has been a reference of the conduct of the receivership, in which
case the motion shall be made to the referee.**

DISCHARGE

41.06 A receiver may be discharged only by the order of a judge.

RULE 42   CERTIFICATE OF PENDING LITIGATION

Highlights

This Rule is supplementary to s. 103 of the *Courts of Justice Act*, which provides for the issuing, registering and discharging of a certificate of pending litigation (formerly called a certificate of *lis pendens*) and imposes liability for damages on a party who registers a certificate without a reasonable claim.

Obtaining a certificate. It is a precondition to a motion for a certificate that the moving party has made a claim for a certificate in the proceeding: rule 42.01(2) (as to when a pleading may commence a proceeding without itself being an originating process, see rule 14.01(2)). A court order must be obtained before the registrar may issue a certificate but the order may be obtained on a motion without notice. A master has jurisdiction to grant this order: see rule 37.02(2).

Registering a certificate. Under the former practice, the certificate of *lis pendens* procedure only operated with regard to land under the *Registry Act.* When land was under the *Land Titles Act*, a caution had to be registered and such a caution could be obtained only upon application to the land registrar, even if a certificate had been issued by the court. Now, by s. 103(2), a certificate of pending litigation issued by the court may be registered whether the land is under the *Land Titles Act* or the *Registry Act.*

Discharging a certificate. (Formerly the term "vacating" was used.) The grounds upon which a certificate may be discharged are more specifically stated than before (s. 103(6)) but there appears to be no major change. The master is given power to discharge a certificate since by s. 103(6) and rule 42.02 this power is given to the "court" and hence the master has jurisdiction: see rule 37.02(2).

A factum is required on a motion to discharge a certificate: rule 42.02(2).

Unlike the former legislation, s. 103 does not deal with the question of appealing discharge orders, but they are appealable under the general appeal provisions of the *Courts of Justice Act*, s. 17 or s. 19, and the registration of a discharge order can be stayed under Rule 63.

Former provisions: Judicature Act, ss. 38-39 and Rules 11a and 32.

ISSUING OF CERTIFICATE

Court Order Required

42.01(1) A certificate of pending litigation (Form 42A) under section 103 of the *Courts of Justice Act* may be issued by a registrar only under an order of the court.

Claim for Certificate to be in Originating Process

(2) A party who seeks a certificate of pending litigation shall include a claim for it in the originating process or pleading that commences the proceeding, together with a description of the land in question sufficient for registration.

Motion Without Notice

(3) A motion for an order under subrule (1) may be made without notice.

Order to be Served Forthwith

(4) A party who obtains an order under subrule (1) shall forthwith serve it, together with a copy of the notice of motion and all affidavits and other documents used at the hearing of the motion, on all parties against whom an interest in land is claimed in the proceeding. [am. O. Reg. 219/91, s. 4]

DISCHARGE OF CERTIFICATE

42.02(1) An order discharging a certificate of pending litigation under subsection 103(6) of the *Courts of Justice Act* may be obtained on motion to the court.

Factum

(2) Each party to a motion under subrule (1) shall, unless the motion is made on consent, serve on every other party a factum consisting of a concise statement, without argument, of the facts and law relied on by the party, and file it, with proof of service, in the court office where the motion is to be heard, not later than 2 p.m. on the day before the hearing.

Cross-Reference: For cases regarding certificates of pending litigation see s. 103 of the *Courts of Justice Act.*

RULE 43   INTERPLEADER

Highlights

The Rule provides for two kinds of interpleader proceedings: by an ordinary stake-holder (rule 43.02) or by a sheriff (rule 43.05).

Where the proceeding is by an ordinary stake-holder, interpleader is by motion if there is an existing proceeding (rule 43.03(2)) or by application where there is no existing court proceeding (rule 43.03(1)).

Prior to the 1989 amendment a similar situation prevailed with regard to sheriff's interpleader, *i.e.*, a motion was to be used if there was an existing proceeding or an application where there was no existing court proceeding. However, this has now been modified by an amendment. The rules relating to sheriff's interpleader where the sheriff has executions from different courts (rule 43.05(6) and (7)) were amended to make the rules as simple as possible. The approach is that if a sheriff has an execution from the General Division, the interpleader is done by a motion in that court. If the sheriff has no execution from the new court, but only executions from other courts (which will include the former High Court and District Court) the sheriff must seek an interpleader order by way of application to the General Division. While this imposes upon a sheriff the minor inconvenience of having to make an application rather than a motion in some cases, it has avoided the need to spell out in the rule a detailed list of which executions from the former courts may be dealt with on motion, and which must be dealt with by application.

Former Rules: Rules 632-655.

DEFINITION

43.01   In rules 43.02 to 43.04, ''property'' means personal property and includes a debt.

WHERE AVAILABLE

43.02   Where two or more persons make adverse claims in respect of property against a person who,
  (a)   claims no beneficial interest in the property, other than a lien for costs, fees or expenses; and
  (b)   is willing to deposit the property with the court or dispose of it as the court directs,
that person may seek an interpleader order (Form 43A).

Smeltzer v. Bank of Nova Scotia (1992), 13 C.P.C. (3d) 46 (Ont. Master).

To qualify for an interpleader order, the moving party must be a mere stakeholder and not involved, directly or indirectly, in the litigation.

Cam-Nest Developments Ltd. v. Penta Stolp Corp. (1992), 10 C.P.C. (3d) 71 (Ont. Gen. Div.).

The court granted an interpleader order pursuant to s. 53(2) of the *Conveyancing and Law of Property Act* where the assignor of a debt raised an issue about payment of the debt to the assignee.

Minden, Gross, Grafstein & Greenstein v. Stoller (1979), 10 C.P.C. 35 (Ont. Master).

An interpleader order was made where the applicants had no claim to any portion of the particular sum in dispute, although they did have a different claim against one of the parties to the dispute.

Clarkson Co. v. Hamilton, [1972] 3 O.R. 762 (H.C.).
A motion was denied where the pleadings indicated a real claim against the applicant.

Skelhorn v. T.D. Bank, [1966] 2 O.R. 594 (H.C.).
A bank sued by a depositor and another person for funds held by it was found to be a mere stakeholder and entitled to an interpleader order.

Hoffman Bros. Ltd. v. Carl E. Miller Const. Ltd., [1963] 2 O.R. 435 (H.C.).
The court granted an application for interpleader notwithstanding that the applicant claimed a small portion of the funds in question.

White v. Can. Bank of Commerce, [1960] O.W.N. 265 (C.A.).
The court refused a motion for interpleader where one of two owners of a joint account sued a bank for dishonouring a cheque and the other owner, while not a party, also claimed the funds.

A.G. Eng. v. Can. Bank of Commerce, [1948] O.W.N. 785 (H.C.).
The stakeholder must show real foundation for the expectation of multiple claims; mere anticipation of conflicting claims is insufficient.

Murdoch v. Guaranty Trust Co. of Can., [1948] O.W.N. 169 (H.C.).
Where the stakeholder claimed a lien upon the property it held, an interpleader order was denied.

HOW OBTAINED

By Application Where no Proceeding Commenced
43.03(1) Where no proceeding has been commenced in respect of the property in question, a person seeking an interpleader order shall make an application to a judge naming all the claimants as respondents and shall, in the notice of application, require them to attend the hearing to substantiate their claims.

By Motion Where Proceeding has been Commenced
(2) Where a proceeding has been commenced in respect of the property, a person seeking an interpleader order shall make a motion in the proceeding to the court on notice to all the claimants and shall, in the notice of motion, require them to attend the hearing to substantiate their claims.

Affidavit in Support
(3) The application or motion shall be supported by an affidavit identifying the property and containing the names and addresses of all claimants to the property of whom the deponent has knowledge and stating that the applicant or moving party,

(a) claims no beneficial interest in the property, other than a lien for costs, fees or expenses;

(b) does not collude with any of the claimants; and

(c) is willing to deposit the property with the court or dispose of it as the court directs.

Evans v. Jacobs, [1962] O.W.N. 209 (H.C.).
The court may not bar a claimant's rights for failure to attend unless the notice of motion called on him to appear and maintain or relinquish his claim.

Re U.S. Fidelity & Guaranty Co. and Mastrangelo, [1954] O.W.N. 46 (Master).
A claimant must file an affidavit to substantiate its claim.

DISPOSITION OF APPLICATION OR MOTION

43.04(1) On the hearing of an application or motion for an interpleader order, the court may,

(a) order that the applicant or moving party deposit the property with an officer of the court, sell it as the court directs or, in the case of money, pay it into court to await the outcome of a specified proceeding;

(b) declare that, on compliance with an order under clause (a), the liability of the applicant or moving party in respect of the property or its proceeds is extinguished; and

(c) order that the costs of the applicant or moving party be paid out of the property or its proceeds.

(2) In an order under subrule (1), the court may,

(a) order a claimant to be made a party to a proceeding already commenced in substitution for or in addition to the moving party;

(b) order the trial of an issue between the claimants, define the issue to be tried and direct which claimant is to be plaintiff and which defendant;

(c) where the question is one of law and the facts are not in dispute, decide the question without directing the trial of an issue;

(d) on the request of a claimant, determine the rights of the claimants in a summary manner, if, having regard to the value of the property and the nature of the issues in dispute, it seems desirable to do so;

(e) where a claimant fails to attend the hearing, or attends and fails to comply with an order made in the course of the proceeding, make an order declaring that the claimant and all persons claiming under the claimant are forever barred from prosecuting a claim against the applicant or moving party and all persons claiming under the applicant or moving party, without affecting the rights of the claimants as between themselves;

(f) stay any further step in a proceeding in respect of the property; and

(g) make such other order as is just.

(3) Where a motion for an interpleader order is made to a master and raises a genuine issue of fact or of law, the motion shall be adjourned to be heard by a judge.

Danbrie Agri-Products Manufacturing Ltd. v. Martens Pipe Products Inc. (1987), 16 C.P.C. (2d) 175 (Ont. Dist. Ct.).
On a sheriff's interpleader motion the court held that where the goods seized are not in the actual or apparent possession of the judgment debtor the onus is upon the execution creditor to establish his right to seize them.

Hudson's Bay Co. v. ICC Euroleasing Co. (1986), 13 C.P.C. (2d) 304 (Ont. H.C.), leave to appeal to Ont. Div. Ct. refused 13 C.P.C. (2d) 304n.
The court refused to summarily dispose of an interpleader application and ordered the trial of an issue where facts were in dispute, the amount in issue was substantial, and material filed in the application was hearsay evidence.

Young v. LeMon (1985), 3 C.P.C. (2d) 163 (Ont. Dist. Ct.).

On a sheriff's interpleader motion the court held that the claim of an execution creditor to real property registered in the name of the execution debtor was subordinate to the interest of the beneficiary under a trust agreement which was not registered at the time the execution was filed.

Di Domizio Const. Ltd. v. Sambura Holdings Ltd.; Di Domizio Const. Ltd. v. Amboseli Holdings Ltd. (1979), 12 C.P.C. 56 (Ont. Master).

Where the value of the subject-matter in dispute exceeded $90,000 and concerned a claim by Revenue Canada, the master refused to dispose of the merits of the claims in a summary manner and granted an interpleader application.

Bank of Montreal v. Inco Ltd.; Conveyor Belt Maintenance Service Ltd. v. Inco Ltd.; Laurentian Electric Ltd. v. Blezard Piping & Welded Products Ltd. (1979), 10 C.P.C. 205 (Ont. H.C.).

Where the defendant had been co-operative with various claimants, it was not ordered to pay interest on the moneys held by it prior to its obtaining an interpleader order.

Re Bishop and Traders Finance Corp. Ltd., [1966] 2 O.R. 343 (C.A.).

The court required unsuccessful claimants to pay the costs of the applicant.

Ex parte Perini Ltd., [1959] O.W.N. 307 (H.C.).

The master refused to summarily determine the rights of the claimants where $3000 was involved.

SHERIFF'S INTERPLEADER

Definition

43.05(1) In this rule,
"property" means real or personal property and includes a debt;
"writ of execution" and "execution" include an order of attachment under the *Absconding Debtors Act*.

Sheriff May Move in Respect of Property Seized

(2) A sheriff may make a motion for an interpleader order (Form 43B) in respect of property or the proceeds of property taken or intended to be taken by the sheriff in the execution of any enforcement process where,

(a) the sheriff has received a claim in respect of the property; and

(b) an execution creditor has given the sheriff notice under rule 60.13 disputing the claim or the execution creditor at whose direction the sheriff took or intended to take the property has not given the notice required by subrule 60.13(2) within the time prescribed by that subrule.

Procedure

(3) The sheriff shall make only one motion in respect of the property.

(4) The motion may be made in any proceeding in which a writ of execution was issued against the debtor, subject to subrules (6) and (7), and shall name as responding parties every claimant and all execution creditors, even though their executions were not issued in the same proceeding.

Sale of Property that is Security for Debt

(5) Where personal property has been seized in execution by a sheriff, and a claimant claims to be entitled to the property as security for a debt,

the court may order a sale of the property and direct that the proceeds of sale or an amount sufficient to answer the claim be paid into court pending determination of the claim.

Executions from Different Courts

(6) A sheriff who has an execution issued by the Ontario Court (General Division) shall make the interpleader motion in that court, even if he or she also has an execution issued by another court, and despite rule 37.03 (place of hearing of motions), the motion shall be heard in the sheriff's county.

(7) A sheriff who has no execution issued by the Ontario Court (General Division) but has an execution issued by another court shall make an application for an interpleader order to a judge of the Ontario Court (General Division), although subrule (2) provides for a motion, and rules 43.01 to 43.04 and subrules (1) to (5) apply with necessary modifications.

RULE 44 INTERIM RECOVERY OF PERSONAL PROPERTY

Highlights

This Rule, and s. 104 of the *Courts of Justice Act*, replace the *Replevin Act* and the order of replevin with a more streamlined but not dissimilar procedure of an "interim order for the recovery of possession of personal property".

The order is available only in an action claiming recovery of possession of personal property: s. 104(1). The order may not be obtained on requisition (as could a replevin order) and a motion to the court is required (s. 104(1) and rule 44.01(1)), but in appropriate circumstances the motion may be made without notice: rule 44.01(2).

On the motion the plaintiff must establish that he or she is the owner of the property or entitled to possession of it and that the property was unlawfully taken or detained by the defendant: rule 44.01(1). The court will not embark on a full trial on the question of title and the plaintiff need only show substantial grounds for its claim in order to obtain interim possession: *R.N. Holdings Ltd. (Receiver of) v. Wong* (1990), 45 C.P.C. (2d) 101 (Ont. Master).

Where the motion is on notice to the defendant the court may (a) direct the sheriff, upon the plaintiff giving security, to take the property from the defendant and give it to the plaintiff; (b) direct that the defendant, on giving security, retain the property, or (c) make such other order as is just. However, when the motion is without notice to the defendant upon the plaintiff giving security, the goods are to be held by the sheriff for ten days before being given to the plaintiff. This permits the defendant to move against the order made without notice, under rule 44.05.

The sheriff is required to serve the order on the defendant when the property is recovered or as soon thereafter as is possible: rule 44.07(2).

Provision is made for situations where the defendant prevents the recovery of the property by the sheriff. Gone is the obscure poetry of the former Rules that the goods "have been eloigned by the defendant out of the bailiwick of the sheriff" and hence the sheriff could take other goods "in withernam". However, basically the procedure is the same: in such circumstances the court may order the sheriff to seize other personal property of the defendant to the same value and give it to the plaintiff to hold until the defendant surrenders the original property: rule 44.08.

By s. 104(2) a person who obtains possession of personal property by obtaining or setting aside an interim order is liable for any loss suffered by the person ultimately found to be entitled to possession, and rule 44.04(1) assists in the satisfaction of any such liability by making the term of any security given, that the party providing the security will pay any damages and costs that the opposite party has sustained by reason of the interim order.

Former provisions: Replevin Act and Rules 359-369.

MOTION FOR INTERIM ORDER

44.01(1) An interim order under section 104 of the *Courts of Justice Act* for recovery of possession of personal property may be obtained on motion by the plaintiff, supported by an affidavit setting out,

(a) a description of the property sufficient to make it readily identifiable;

(b) the value of the property;

(c) that the plaintiff is the owner or lawfully entitled to possession of the property;

(d) that the property was unlawfully taken from the possession of the plaintiff or is unlawfully detained by the defendant; and

(e) the facts and circumstances giving rise to the unlawful taking or detention.

(2) The notice of motion shall be served on the defendant unless the court is satisfied that there is reason to believe that the defendant may improperly attempt to prevent recovery of possession of the property or that, for any other sufficient reason, the order should be made without notice.

Clark Door of Canada Ltd. v. Inline Fiberglass Ltd. (1996), 7 W.D.C.P. (2d) 100 (Ont. Gen. Div.).

To obtain an order for interim possession the plaintiff must establish (1) substantial grounds for its claim that its property is being unlawfully detained by the defendant and (2) the balance of convenience favours the plaintiff.

Peco Tool & Die Ltd. v. 939991 Ontario Ltd. (1993), 19 C.P.C. (3d) 123 (Ont. Gen. Div.).

The plaintiff must show substantial grounds for its claim to ownership of the property in question. The mere possibility that the plaintiff may succeed at trial is insufficient.

Businex Business Centres (Canada) Inc. v. TR Services Ltd. (1992), 17 C.P.C. (3d) 313 (Ont. Gen. Div.).

To obtain interim possession the plaintiff need only show that at the time of the commencement of the action he or she was the owner or was entitled to the possession of the chattel in question and that it was being wrongfully detained, though the court should also consider the equities of the situation.

Toronto Blue Jays Baseball Club v. John Doe (1992), 9 O.R. (3d) 622 (Gen. Div.).

The court refused to grant an *ex parte* order against persons unknown permitting the plaintiff to seize baseball tickets from scalpers. The plaintiff did not establish any present unlawful intention and had not established any irreparable harm.

R.N. Holdings Ltd. (Receiver of) v. Wong (1990), 45 C.P.C. (2d) 101 (Ont. Master).

To succeed on a motion for interim possession, the plaintiff need only show substantial grounds for its claim. The court will not embark on a full trial on the question of title.

Triathlon Leasing Inc. v. Gemma Plastics Corp. (1989), 17 W.D.C.P. 132 (Ont. Master).

Where the moving party establishes it has title to the subject property or is lawfully entitled to possession of it, the court has a discretion to decide who should have possession. Where the test is not met the motion should be dismissed.

Abel/Noser Corp. v. C.P.M.S. Computerized Portfolio Management Services Inc. (1987), 58 O.R. (2d) 633, 15 C.P.C. (2d) 135 (H.C.).

The court refused to give the plaintiff interim possession of the personal property which was the subject of the action where the plaintiff could not identify the property and the equities favoured the defendant.

Haessler-DeWay Ltd. v. Color Tech. Inc. (1985), 49 C.P.C. 156, 4 C.I.P.R. 77, 5 C.P.R. (3d) 191 (Ont. Dist. Ct.).

The court refused to grant an interim order for the possession of certain property in favour of an unpaid vendor who failed to establish it had retained title to the property.

Edwards v. Phillips (1983), 36 C.P.C. 239 (Ont. Master).

A replevin order will be granted only if the plaintiff shows substantial grounds for the claim.

Robert Cooper Productions Inc. v. J.S. Kastner Associates Ltd. (1982), 24 C.P.C. 269 (Ont. Master).

A replevin order was refused where the main issue in the case was the ownership of the chattels, and that issue fell to be determined by arbitration pursuant to an agreement of the parties.

Aggio v. Rosenburg (1981), 24 C.P.C. 7 (Ont. Master).

An order was made requiring a litigant's former solicitors to deliver correspondence belonging to the litigant to her new solicitors.

Susin v. 297509 Ont. Ltd. (1978), 6 C.P.C. 206 (Ont. Master).

A replevin order was not granted where the defendants did not claim title to or a right to possession of the goods but sought to retain them only as security.

Ryder Truck Rental Ltd. v. Walker, [1960] O.W.N. 70, affirmed [1960] O.W.N. 114 (H.C.).

If the plaintiff shows facts affording substantial grounds for his claim, the order should be granted. The court will not undertake a full trial on the question of title.

ORDER TO CONTAIN DESCRIPTION AND VALUE OF PROPERTY

44.02 An interim order for recovery of possession of personal property shall contain a description of the property sufficient to make it readily identifiable and shall state the value of the property.

DISPOSITION OF MOTION

Where Made on Notice

44.03(1) On a motion for an interim order for recovery of possession of personal property made on notice to the defendant, the court may,

(a) order the plaintiff to pay into court as security twice the value of the property as stated in the order, or such other amount as the court directs, or to give the appropriate sheriff security in such form and amount as the court approves, and direct the sheriff to take the property from the defendant and give it to the plaintiff;

(b) order the defendant to pay into court as security twice the value of the property as stated in the order, or such other amount as the court directs, or to give the plaintiff security in such form and amount as the court approves, and direct that the property remain in the possession of the defendant; or

(c) make such other order as is just.

Where Made Without Notice

(2) On a motion for an interim order for the recovery of possession of personal property made without notice to the defendant, the court may,

(a) order the plaintiff to pay into court as security twice the value of the property as stated in the order, or such other amount as the court directs, or to give the appropriate sheriff security in such form and amount as the court approves, and direct the sheriff to take and detain the property

for a period of ten days after service of the interim order on the defendant before giving it to the plaintiff; or

(b) make such other order as is just.

Gray Metal Industs. Inc. v. 55319 Ont. Ltd. (1984), 41 C.P.C. 314 (Ont. Master).

Where the taking of equipment could cause substantial damages to the defendants, interim recovery was ordered on the basis that security be posted to cover the value of such equipment and the possible damages. An order that the defendant be permitted to retain the equipment upon posting security for the plaintiff's claim could not be made, even though the defendants could make better use of the equipment than the plaintiff. [*See now rule 44.03(1)(b) — Authors.*]

Susin v. 297509 Ont. Ltd. (1978), 6 C.P.C. 206 (Ont. Master).

The plaintiff was permitted to post a surety bond as security in lieu of paying cash into court, set in the amount claimed plus the estimated costs of the action.

CONDITION AND FORM OF SECURITY

44.04(1) Where an interim order for the recovery of possession of personal property requires either party to give security, the condition of the security shall be that the party providing the security will return the property to the opposite party without delay when ordered to do so, and pay any damages and costs the opposite party has sustained by reason of the interim order.

(2) Where the security is by bond, the bond shall be in (Form 44A) and shall remain in force until the security is released under rule 44.06.

(3) Where the bond is to be given by a person other than a guarantee company to which the *Guarantee Companies Securities Act* applies, the person giving the bond shall first be approved by the court.

Authors' Note

The following is a list of corporations currently approved as guarantee companies under the *Guarantee Companies Securities Act* (approved by Order in Council 292/96, February 21, 1996).

SCHEDULE "A"

Aetna Casualty & Surety Company of Canada

Allstate Insurance Company of Canada

Alta Surety Company

AXA Insurance (Canada)

Boreal Insurance Inc.

Boreal Property & Casualty Insurance Company

Canadian General Insurance Company

The Canadian Surety Company

Chubb Insurance Company of Canada

CIGNA Insurance Company of Canada

The Citadel General Assurance Company

Coachman Insurance Company

Commerce and Industry Insurance Company of Canada

Commercial Union Assurance Company of Canada

The Continental Insurance Company

Continental Insurance Limited

Co-Operators General Insurance Company

CUMIS General Insurance Company

The Dominion of Canada General Insurance Company

Economical Mutual Insurance Company

Elite Insurance Company

Federal Insurance Company

Federated Insurance Company of Canada

Federation Insurance Company of Canada

Fireman's Fund Insurance Company

The General Accident Assurance
Company of Canada

Gerling Global General Insurance
Company

Gore Mutual Insurance Company

The Guarantee Company of North
America

Guardian Insurance Company of Canada

The Halifax Insurance Company

The Hartford Fire Insurance Company

London Guarantee Insurance Company

Lumbermens Mutual Casualty Company

Markel Insurance Company of Canada

The Mortgage Insurance Company of
Canada

New Rotterdam Insurance Company

Northern Indemnity, Inc.

Pilot Insurance Company

Reliance Insurance Company

Royal Insurance Company of Canada

St. Paul Fire and Marine Insurance
Company

Scottish & York Insurance Co. Limited

Seaboard Surety Company of Canada

Simcoe & Erie General Insurance
Company

The Sovereign General Insurance
Company

State Farm Fire and Casualty Company

The Wawanesa Mutual Insurance
Company

Western Surety Company

Zurich Indemnity Company of Canada

Zurich Insurance Company

SETTING ASIDE ORDER

44.05 The court on motion may set aside or vary an interim order for the recovery of possession of personal property or stay enforcement of the order.

Thompson v. Thompson and Woodbine Cartage & Movers, [1947] O.W.N. 393 (Master).

Goods were returned to the defendants upon condition that they post security for twice the value of the goods. Common sense dictates that goods be used by a party rather than stored pending disposition of the case.

RELEASE OF SECURITY

44.06 Any security furnished pursuant to an order made under rule 44.03 may be released on the filing of the written consent of the parties or by order of the court.

DUTY OF SHERIFF

44.07(1) Before proceeding to enforce an interim order for the recovery of possession of personal property, the sheriff shall ascertain that any security required by the order has been given.

(2) The sheriff shall serve the order on the defendant when the property or any part of it is recovered or as soon thereafter as is possible.

(3) Where the sheriff is unable to comply with the order, or it is dangerous to do so, the sheriff may move for directions from the court.

(4) The sheriff shall, without delay after attempting to enforce the order and in any event within ten days after service of the order, report to the

plaintiff on what property has been recovered and, where the sheriff has failed to recover possession of all or part of the property, on what property has not been recovered and the reason for his or her failure to recover it.

WHERE DEFENDANT PREVENTS RECOVERY

44.08 Where the sheriff reports that the defendant has prevented the recovery of all or part of the property, the court may make an order,

(a) directing the sheriff to take any other personal property of the defendant, to the value of the property that the sheriff was prevented from recovering, and give it to the plaintiff; and

(b) directing the plaintiff to hold the substituted property until the defendant surrenders to the plaintiff the property that the sheriff was prevented from recovering.

RULE 45   INTERIM PRESERVATION OF PROPERTY

Highlights

This Rule governs interim preservation of property and is one of several Rules providing procedures for preserving rights in pending litigation.

The power of the court (rule 45.01(1)) to make an order for the custody or preservation of property extends not only to any property in question in a proceeding, but also to any property that is relevant to an issue in the proceeding, *i.e.* a material article of real evidence (compare rule 30.11 (safekeeping of documents)). In an appropriate case a court could, for example, order evidence to be preserved under rule 45.01(1), photographed under rule 32.01, and then sold under rule 45.01(2).

Provision is made for ordering the payment of a specific fund in question into court: rule 45.02.

While rule 45.03 respecting the recovery of personal property held as security is not new, subrule (2) is, and it seeks to protect non-parties with secured interests that rest on possession as opposed to registration. When an order is made under rule 45.03 and the plaintiff recovers the personal property, the money paid into court is to await the outcome of the proceeding.

Former Rules: Rules 369-371.

INTERIM ORDER FOR PRESERVATION OR SALE

45.01(1) The court may make an interim order for the custody or preservation of any property in question in a proceeding or relevant to an issue in a proceeding, and for that purpose may authorize entry on or into any property in the possession of a party or of a person not a party.

(2) Where the property is of a perishable nature or likely to deteriorate or for any other reason ought to be sold, the court may order its sale in such manner and on such terms as are just.

Interim Order for Preservation or Sale — Generally

Werner v. Warner Auto-Marine Inc. (1995), 35 C.P.C. (3d) 215, additional reasons (May 10, 1995), Doc. 8769/88, 26070/88Q, 330778/88 (Ont. Gen. Div.).

Where, contrary to a preservation order, the plaintiff carried out destructive tests on real evidence, the court dismissed the plaintiff's claim.

Auto Enterprise Ltd. v. Oakville Motors Sales & Leasing Inc., (March 14, 1995), Doc. 95-CQ-61234 (Ont. Gen. Div.).

The court refused to grant a preservation order regarding certain vehicles where the vehicles did not appear to be at risk and were likely to depreciate in value.

Cornish v. Gnyp (1993), 17 C.P.C. (3d) 68 (Ont. Gen. Div.).

The court may order property sold where it is just and equitable to do so notwithstanding that the property is not perishable or likely to deteriorate.

Marchand v. Public General Hospital Society of Chatham (1993), 20 C.P.C. (3d) 68 (Ont. Gen. Div.).

In a medical malpractice case the court ordered the defendants to produce for examination samples of the plaintiff's tissue taken during a caesarean section.

Colebourne v. Colebourne (1981), 2 F.L.R.A.C. 104 (Ont. H.C.).

In this family law action the court made an interim preservation order regarding a house in Florida which was a matrimonial asset.

Musson v. Head (1924), 27 O.W.N. 157 (H.C.).

A plaintiff seeking specific performance of an alleged contract to exchange his farm and livestock for another property was permitted to sell his livestock and other perishable goods pending trial but the burden was on the plaintiff to show that the price received for the goods represented their true value.

"Anton Piller" Orders — Ex Parte Orders for Seizure, Inspection, etc. of Documents and Property

Israel Discount Bank of Canada v. Genova (1992), 13 C.P.C. (3d) 104 (Ont. Gen. Div.).

The court refused to continue an *ex parte* "Anton Piller" order where, *inter alia*, the plaintiff lacked a strong *prima facie* case. Such a remedy is a most exceptional one and an extremely high standard is expected from the plaintiff.

Lynian Ltd. v. Dubois (1990), 45 C.P.C. (2d) 231 (Ont. Gen. Div.).

The moving party must have a very high standard of disclosure and ought to err on the side of excessive disclosure. The court set aside an "Anton Piller" order for non-disclosure.

Bardeau Ltd. v. Crown Food Service Equipment (1982), 38 O.R. (2d) 411, 26 C.P.C. 297 at 306, 67 C.P.R. (3d) 198 (H.C.).

An "Anton Piller" order permitting the plaintiff to inspect, copy and photograph the defendant's documents and property may be made *ex parte* if the plaintiff shows an extremely strong *prima facie* case and there is a serious concern that the evidence will be destroyed if the order is not made. Specific safeguards should be imposed regarding enforcement of the order. In this case such an order was made but subsequently discharged because of non-disclosure of a material fact.

Nintendo of Amer. Inc. v. Coinex Video Games Inc., [1983] 2 F.C. 189, 34 C.P.C. 108, 69 C.P.R. (2d) 122, 46 N.R. 311 (C.A.).

An "Anton Piller" order may be granted where (1) the plaintiff has an extremely strong *prima facie* case; (2) the damage, potential or actual, is very serious for the plaintiff; (3) there is clear evidence the defendants possess incriminating documents or property; and (4) there is a real possibility the defendant may destroy such material before a motion on notice can be made. Terms regarding enforcement should be imposed to protect the defendant.

SPECIFIC FUND

45.02 Where the right of a party to a specific fund is in question, the court may order the fund to be paid into court or otherwise secured on such terms as are just.

Tom Jones Corp. v. Mishemukwa Developments Ltd. (1996), 7 W.D.C.P. (2d) 183 (Ont. Gen. Div.).

The court ordered the defendants to pay into court the contents of a disputed trust account.

Maybank Foods Inc. Pension Plan v. Gainers Inc. (1988), 63 O.R. (2d) 687, (*sub nom. Micallef v. Gainers Inc.*) 25 C.P.C. (2d) 248 (H.C.).

The court ordered $3,000,000 of disputed pension funds paid into court.

Rotin v. Lechcier-Kimel (1985), 3 C.P.C. (2d) 15 (Ont. H.C.).

The phrase "specific fund" refers to a reasonably indentifiable fund earmarked for the pending litigation.

RECOVERY OF PERSONAL PROPERTY HELD AS SECURITY

45.03(1) Where in a proceeding a party from whom the recovery of personal property is claimed does not dispute the title of the party making the claim, but claims the right to retain the property as security for a debt, the court may order the party claiming recovery of the property to pay into court or otherwise give security for the debt and such further sum, if any, for interest and costs as the court directs.

(2) The affidavit in support of a motion under subrule (1) shall disclose the name of every person asserting a claim to possession of the property of whom the party claiming recovery has knowledge and every such person shall be served with notice of the motion.

(3) On compliance with an order under subrule (1), the property shall be given to the party claiming recovery and the money in court or the security shall await the outcome of the proceeding.

838388 Ontario Ltd. v. Wellington Inc. (1990), 45 C.P.C. (2d) 222 (Ont. H.C.).

The court held that a "refundable" deposit in a real estate transaction was not a specific fund.

Ness Bros. Ltd. v. Barrie Airways Ltd., [1963] 2 O.R. 109 (H.C.).

The quantum of the security for costs should be the full amount likely to be taxed in the action.

Otaco Ltd. v. Salem Engineering (Can.) Ltd., [1944] O.W.N. 449 (Master).

The party seeking delivery of property was required to pay only the amount claimed by the party under the lien and not any storage charges claimed.

PRE-TRIAL PROCEDURES

RULE 46   PLACE OF TRIAL

Highlights

This Rule governs the choice of the place of trial and motions to change the place of trial. The only proceedings in which the Rules designate the place of trial are divorce actions and family law proceedings: rule 46.01(3). The Rule recognizes that occasionally statutes may require trial at a particular place (rule 46.01(2)), but the former provision (in the *Judicature Act*, s. 58) requiring actions against a municipality for the non-repair of a highway to be tried in the county where the municipality is located was not carried over into the *Courts of Justice Act*.

The grounds upon which a change in the place of trial may be ordered are stated more specifically than under the former Rule. Rule 46.03(2)(a) may represent some change from the former practice, since it frames the convenience test in terms of "the balance of convenience substantially favours the holding of the trial at another place", rather than in terms of a preponderance of convenience or an overwhelming preponderance of convenience as did the former case law. (Balance of convenience would seem to be broad enough to cover the often encountered situation where, in multiple actions ordered to be tried together, different places of trial have been named.) Rule 46.03(2)(b) permits a change on the basis of the unavailability of a fair trial at the place named by the plaintiff.

The *Courts of Justice Act*, s. 114, sets out the effect of agreements as to the place of trial, although in somewhat different terms than the former statutory provision.

Practice directions. For local procedures regarding change of venue in the Central South Region see chapter 4 of the *Administrative Procedures Manual for the Central South Region* published by direction of Regional Senior Justice Fedak.

Former provisions: Judicature Act, s. 61 and Rules 245, 775f.

TO BE NAMED IN STATEMENT OF CLAIM

46.01(1) The plaintiff shall name in the statement of claim as the place of trial a place in which the court normally sits in the county in which the plaintiff proposes that the action be tried.

(2) Where a statute requires an action to be tried in a particular county, the plaintiff shall name as the place of trial a place in which the court normally sits in that county.

(3) In a divorce action, the place of trial shall be named in accordance with rule 69.17, and in a family law proceeding, it shall be named in accordance with rule 70.05.

Bye v. Hulin (1983), 39 C.P.C. 279 (Ont. Master).

The personal convenience of the plaintiff's medical experts was a valid reason for the choice of venue where there was no mandatory venue or overwhelming preponderance of convenience for another venue.

Freeman v. Gabriel (1981), 33 O.R. (2d) 846 (H.C.).

It is *prima facie* improper to name a place of trial which has no connection with the parties or the cause of action.

Lido Drywall Ltd. v. Campeau Corp. (1976), 1 C.P.C. 301, leave to appeal granted 1 C.P.C. 305 (Ont. H.C.).

A venue may be selected to obtain a speedy trial, though there be no real connection between the venue selected and the subject of the litigation.

WHERE TRIAL TO BE HELD

46.02 The trial shall be held at the place named in the statement of claim unless the court makes an order under rule 46.03 changing the place of trial.

ORDER CHANGING PLACE OF TRIAL

46.03(1) Where a plaintiff has named as the place of trial a place other than that required by statute, the court on motion by any party shall order that the trial be held at the place required.

(2) In any other case, the court on motion by any party may order that the trial be held at a place other than that named in the statement of claim where the court is satisfied that,

(a) the balance of convenience substantially favours the holding of the trial at another place; or

(b) it is likely that a fair trial cannot be had at the place named in the statement of claim.

Changing Place of Trial — Balance of Convenience — General Principles

Chippewas of Sarnia Band v. Canada (Attorney General) (1996), 7 W.D.C.P. (2d) 172 (Ont. Gen. Div.).

Litigation that directly affects a community should be heard in the court that serves the community. The court changed the place of trial of this land claim case from Toronto to Sarnia, where the land was situated, notwithstanding the plaintiff's desire to have the trial elsewhere to avoid a confrontational atmosphere.

Laurin v. Favot (1996), 7 W.D.C.P. (2d) 171 (Ont. Gen. Div.).

Although the plaintiff, as *dominus litis*, has the right to choose the place of trial, it may be changed if a substantial preponderance of convenience favours trial in another location. Factors include location of witnesses, the need to take a view, the delay or expedition of the trial, the relative costs, whether the case has a connection with the place proposed, and the judicial caseload in the place proposed. It is *prima facie* improper to name a place of trial which has no connection with either the parties or the cause of action. It is not fair to cases properly tried in a particular venue to be delayed by cases with no connection to that venue.

Continental Breweries v. 707517 Ontario Ltd. (1990), 46 C.P.C. (2d) 151 (Ont. Master).

A substantial difference in the balance of convenience is necessary to change the place of trial. In considering the balance of convenience the court can consider the convenience of the witnesses, the speeding up of the trial and the effect of venue on costs including travelling time for counsel.

Latkiewicz v. Murray (1985), 53 O.R. (2d) 306, 5 C.P.C. (2d) 260 (H.C.).

A slight possibility of a view being required at trial should not affect the balance of convenience.

Marshall v. Kirby (1977), 5 C.P.C. 23 (Ont. H.C.).

The public interest in having public officials and doctors near their place of duty and the fees if any to be paid to witnesses are relevant considerations.

J.G. Fitzgerald & Sons Ltd. v. Kapuskasing District High School, [1968] 1 O.R. 136 (Master).

The fact that a cause of action arose in a particular county is not determinative.

Treutlein v. Mockle, [1961] O.W.N. 237 (H.C.).

The failure of a party resisting change of the place of trial to file material indicating the convenience of his witnesses justifies an adverse inference as to their convenience.

Winter-Seal of Can. Ltd. v. Winter-Seal Windows (London) Ltd., [1957] O.W.N. 33 (H.C.).

Delay in reaching trial is a factor when considering a change of place of trial but it will rarely be decisive.

C.P.R. v. Cementation Co. (Can.) Ltd., [1956] O.W.N. 447 (Master).

The possibility of a view by the jury is only infrequently a significant factor in determining the appropriate place of trial.

Hoan v. Hoan, [1955] O.W.N. 514 (H.C.).

Where communication and transportation facilities between two proximate places of trial are good (*e.g.* as between Toronto and Hamilton) it is difficult to conceive of a case where a sufficient preponderance of convenience could be shown to warrant a change of place of trial.

Reeve v. Andrulis, [1953] O.W.N. 823 (H.C.).

A party who obtains an order to change the venue on the basis that he intends to call certain witnesses may be penalized in costs if the witnesses are not called.

Leskiw v. Chenery, [1949] O.W.N. 714 (H.C.).

Where two actions in which different places of trial have been named are to be tried together, the preponderance of convenience, however slight, and the scope of each action should be considered in determining the place of trial.

Kemp v. Filiatreault, [1949] O.W.N. 525 (H.C.).

The difficulty of bringing physicians to a distant place of trial is a proper consideration.

Stewart v. Doan, [1944] O.W.N. 426 (H.C.).

Where the trial court judge might wish to view the site which is the subject of litigation, a change of venue may be ordered.

Axelrod v. Beth Jacob, [1942] O.W.N. 191 (Master).

To enable the court to decide whether the witnesses to be called are material and necessary, the name of each witness and the evidence such witness can give must usually be shown.

Changing Place of Trial — Balance of Convenience — Examples

Pizza Pizza Ltd. v. Boyack (1995), 38 C.P.C. (3d) 306 (Ont. Gen. Div.).

On a motion to change the venue of a trial, the court discounted the significance of where the cause of action arose, and found that the balance of convenience did not substantially favour a change of venue.

Conway v. Ontario (1993), 14 O.R. (3d) 543 (Gen. Div.).

An action brought by a psychiatric patient relating to an incident which had occurred while he was a patient at a facility in Barrie was ordered to be tried in Brockville, although the majority of defendants resided in Barrie. To force the plaintiff to proceed in Barrie would result in his having to move back to the very institution which was the source of the original claim. In the circumstances, the balance of convenience favoured the holding of trial at Brockville where the patient was now located.

Kuyntjes v. Kuyntjes (1984), 45 C.P.C. 32 (Ont. Master).

In this family law proceeding, the master ordered the place of trial to be changed to the site of the matrimonial home, around which the historical and current issues revolved, rather than the city where the wife and child had recently moved.

Green v. Dixon Road Car Wash Ltd. (1981), 33 O.R. (2d) 353, 22 C.P.C. 263, 124 D.L.R. (3d) 503 (H.C.).

An action based on non-repair of a sidewalk was ordered to take place in the county where the sidewalk was situate.

Bank of Montreal v. Perry (1981), 31 O.R. (2d) 700 (H.C.).

The place of trial in an action by a bank on a promissory note made at a branch in the county in which the defendant resides should be that county. The bank is a resident of such location where it operates a branch. The cause of action arises at the branch where the loan transaction is made.

Luxenberg v. Nekechuk (1975), 14 O.R. (2d) 672 (H.C.).

A third party action against a municipality should be tried in the county in which the municipality is situate.

Diening v. Ashley Motors Toronto (1977), 4 C.P.C. 23 (Ont. Master).

Where a large majority of the witnesses necessary for trial were in Toronto, the place of trial was changed from Ottawa to Toronto.

Changing Place of Trial — Trial of Several Actions Together

Ryan v. Air Terminal Transport Ltd., [1961] O.W.N. 169 (H.C.).

Where several actions arose out of the same circumstances, some being jury cases brought in Ottawa and some being non-jury cases brought in Toronto, the court ordered that all actions be put on the Toronto jury list.

Chinn v. Walters, [1959] O.W.N. 195 (Co. Ct.).

The master refused to transfer the second commenced of two County Court actions to the county in which the first action was commenced where the balance of convenience favoured the second county.

Pace v. Pietrobon, [1958] O.W.N. 317 (Master).

Where it appears that two actions should be tried together and different places of trial have been named in each action, it is not necessary that as great a preponderance of convenience should be shown as on a motion concerning a single action.

Hutchins Transport Co. v. Sharpe, [1955] O.W.N. 63 (Master).

Where three actions arose out of the same accident and two different places of trial had been chosen, the court transferred one action to facilitate trial together.

Rintoul v. Dominion Stores Ltd., [1955] O.W.N. 114 (H.C.).

The court changed the place of trial of an action to facilitate trial together with another action.

Changing Place of Trial — To Obtain Fair Trial

Oliver v. Gothard (1992), 10 O.R. (3d) 309, 11 C.P.C. (3d) 342 (Gen. Div.).

In light of the connections of the parties and the subject matter of the proceedings previously held in Kitchener, the court held that it was conducive to the appearance of fairness that the trial be held in another location.

Ridley v. Ridley (1989), 37 C.P.C. (2d) 167 (Ont. H.C.).

Financial hardship is a ground for ordering a change of trial venue since "fair trial" is to be read broadly.

Thompson v. Beaulieu (1987), 63 O.R. (2d) 171 (Fam. Ct.).

Child support proceedings brought against a respondent in the court of which the respondent's father was senior judge were not transferred outside the judicial district, but were ordered to be heard by a judge who did not ordinarily preside therein.

Commodore v. Fortier (1985), 3 C.P.C. (2d) 225, 35 M.V.R. 18 (Ont. Master).

The court dismissed a motion to change the place of trial on account of a newspaper report adverse to the defendants, where the newspaper had published a retraction.

Grant v. Todorovic, [1970] 3 O.R. 292 (Master).

The place of trial was changed where the plaintiff was a prominent public official and the defendants had been the subject of adverse newspaper publicity.

Empson v. Cooney, [1953] O.W.N. 925 (C.A.).

A trial judge has a discretion to change the place of trial from the county in which the parties reside and the cause of action arose, regardless of the balance of convenience, if the interests of justice so require.

Changing Place of Trial — Time for Motion

Acli Int. Commodity Services Inc. v. Samuel Varco Ltd. (1977), 17 O.R. (2d) 518, 4 C.P.C. 195 (H.C.).

An application to change the place of trial should not be made until the issues involved have been defined through the exchange of pleadings.

Drage v. T.D. Bank, [1972] 1 O.R. 583 (H.C.).

The taking of a fresh step after having knowledge of an irregularity with respect to the place of trial does not foreclose a motion to change the venue.

Godbout v. Truaisch, [1955] O.W.N. 929 (H.C.).

The motion may be brought before the close of pleadings if the issues in the action are clear.

Dixon v. Wrightman, [1949] O.W.N. 697 (H.C.).

Where a case had been adjourned until a witness could be served with a subpoena and a trial date set, it was held to be much too late for an application for change of venue.

Leadbetter v. Township of Darlington, [1949] O.W.N. 365 (H.C.).

An objection to venue where a statute stipulates the place of trial is not waived by filing a statement of defence.

Wall v. Caswell, [1947] O.W.N. 845 (H.C.).

A motion to change the place of trial may be brought after service of the notice of trial.

RULE 47   JURY NOTICE

Highlights

This Rule has to be read together with s. 108(1)-(3) of the *Courts of Justice Act*, which regulate the availability of jury trial.

Availability of jury trial. Section 108(2) lists the types of claims with respect to which a jury may not determine issues of fact or assess damages and provides that jury trial is unavailable for any relief claimed against a municipality (*cf. Judicature Act*, s. 58). In cases other than those listed, or where another statute prohibits trial by jury (*e.g. Proceedings Against the Crown Act*, R.S.O. 1990, c. P.27, s. 11), a party may require issues of fact to be tried or damages assessed, or both, by a jury (s. 108(1)) by delivering a jury notice at any time before the close of pleadings: rule 47.01.

Pursuant to a 1989 amendment, s. 108 has been amended to make a correction with respect to the right to jury trial. Under the former *Judicature Act* (s. 60(4)) the right to have issues of fact tried or damages assessed by a jury did not apply "to causes, matters, or issues over the subject of which the Court of Chancery had exclusive jurisdiction", but it was provided by the former Rules of Practice (Rule 257) that where equitable issues were raised by the pleadings, they were to be tried (and damages incidental thereto assessed) by the judge without the intervention of a jury, unless the trial judge otherwise directed. Hence, this gave the court discretion to permit equitable issues to be tried by jury. The former *Courts of Justice Act* provision (s. 121(2) of the 1984 Act) had inadvertently changed the law by requiring a trial without a jury whenever equitable relief (*e.g.*, an injunction) was claimed even though other relief of a non-equitable nature was also claimed (*e.g.*, damages for defamation): see *Reichmann v. Toronto Life Publishing Co.* (1989), 69 O.R. (2d) 242 (H.C.), leave to appeal refused 17 W.D.C.P. 5, and (1991), 1 O.R. (3d) 160 (Gen. Div.), leave to appeal to Ont. Div. Ct. refused 2 W.D.C.P. (2d) 62. The section (now 108(2)) was amended with the intention of restoring the law to the situation that a jury is only prohibited in respect of the claim for one of the enumerated kinds of relief (*e.g.*, equitable relief), so that a jury may still determine the issues of fact with respect to other claims in the action.

Unlike the former *Judicature Act*, the present Act does not make jury trial mandatory in actions for defamation, malicious arrest, malicious prosecution and false imprisonment, but jury trial is available in such cases if a jury notice is served.

Striking out a jury notice. Where the delivery of a jury notice is irregular (*i.e.* because a statute requires trial without a jury, or the notice was delivered out of time), it may be struck out on motion to the court, *i.e.* to a master or a judge: rule 47.02(1). A jury notice may also be struck out, on motion to a judge, where a jury trial, though not prohibited, is inappropriate (rule 47.02(2)). Such a motion may be premature if it is brought prior to examinations for discovery: *Pipher v. Shelburne Dist. Hospital* (1985), 5 C.P.C. (2d) 110, 12 C.C.E.L. 182 (Ont. H.C.); *Sussman v. Eales* (1987), 61 O.R. (2d) 316, 24 C.P.C. (2d) 99 (H.C.).

Former provisions: Judicature Act, ss. 57-60 and Rule 400.

ACTIONS TO BE TRIED WITH A JURY

47.01 A party to an action may require that the issues of fact be tried or the damages be assessed, or both, by a jury, by delivering a jury notice

(Form 47A) at any time before the close of pleadings, unless section 108 of the *Courts of Justice Act* or another statute requires that the action be tried without a jury.

Taylor v. Santos (Doc. SC 2308/90, Milton) (Ont. Gen. Div.).

Where the only party who has served a jury notice is let out of the law suit before trial, the trial will proceed without a jury.

Schram v. The Alexandra Marine and General Hospital (February 17, 1994), Doc. 5319/90 (Ont. Master).

Where a third party defends the main action, the pleadings in the main action are not closed until the plaintiff delivers its reply or the time therefor has expired.

Intertechnique Hair Salons Inc. v. Marathon Realty Co. (1983), 44 O.R. (2d) 382, 40 C.P.C. 1 (H.C.).

Where there are multiple defendants the time for delivery of a jury notice is based on the close of pleadings against all defendants.

STRIKING OUT JURY NOTICE

Where Jury Notice not in Accordance with Statute or Rules

47.02(1) A motion may be made to the court to strike out a jury notice on the ground that,

(a) a statute requires a trial without a jury; or

(b) the jury notice was not delivered in accordance with rule 47.01.

Where Jury Trial Inappropriate

(2) A motion to strike out a jury notice on the ground that the action ought to be tried without a jury shall be made to a judge.

Discretion of Trial Judge

(3) Where an order striking out a jury notice is refused, the refusal does not affect the discretion of the trial judge, in a proper case, to try the action without a jury.

Cross-Reference: See s. 108 of the *Courts of Justice Act.*

Authors' Note on Organization of Cases

Cases relevant to this provision have been organized as follows:

Striking Out Jury Notice — Non-Compliance with Statute — rule 47.02(1)
Striking Out Jury Notice — Where Jury Trial Inappropriate — rule 47.02(2)
Striking Out Jury Notice — Professional Malpractice Cases
Extension of Trial to Deliver Jury Notice
Discretion of Trial Judge — Generally — rule 47.02(3)
Discretion of Trial Judge — Mention of Insurance — rule 47.02(3)

Striking Out Jury Notice — Non-Compliance With Statute — rule 47.02(1)

MacLennan v. National Life Assurance Co. of Canada, 28 C.P.C. (3d) 35, 5 C.C.P.B. 136, [1994] I.L.R. 1-3085 (Ont. Gen. Div.).

In an action in which the plaintiff claimed a declaration of total disability, and payment of disability benefits, the defendant's jury notice was struck. The plaintiff's true claim was for a declaration, and the claim for damages was only incidental to that declaratory relief.

Constitution Insurance Co. of Canada v. Coombe (1992), 11 O.R. (3d) 783, 14 C.P.C. (3d) 322, 98 D.L.R. (4th) 573, [1993] I.L.R. 1-2897 (Gen. Div.).

The court struck out a jury notice where the relief sought by the plaintiff was in the nature of a declaratory order delineating the rights of the parties, notwithstanding the plaintiff did not specifically ask for a declaration but did claim damages.

Gracey v. Thomson Newspapers Corp. (1991), 4 O.R. (3d) 180, 1 C.P.C. (3d) 21, 82 D.L.R. (4th) 244 (Gen. Div.).

Although the delivery of a jury notice as against one defendant was barred by s. 26 of the *Crown Liability Act*, the remaining defendants were permitted to serve a jury notice as s. 26 does not prohibit a jury for a separate claim in the same action.

Guldborg v. Lautenbach (1990), 73 O.R. (2d) 610, 70 D.L.R. (4th) 747 (H.C.).

The court struck out a jury notice served by a co-defendant in this action against a municipality.

Sutherland v. Clarke (1989), 70 O.R. (2d) 453 (H.C.).

The prohibition against jury trials contained in the *Proceedings Against the Crown Act* does not apply to Crown agents and accordingly the jury notice was permitted to stand.

Jenkins v. Burlington Hydro-Electric Comm. (1989), 71 O.R. (2d) 137, 43 C.P.C. (2d) 250 (H.C.).

A jury notice was permitted to stand in an action against the defendant notwithstanding that it was an entity owned by a municipality.

Woodslee Credit Union Ltd. v. Taylor (1988), 66 O.R. (2d) 248, 33 C.P.C. (2d) 299 (H.C.).

Although a party had claimed a declaration and injunctive relief with respect to certain mortgaged property, that party's jury notice was permitted to stand as the claim was essentially one for breach of contract. In any event, the claim for the injunction was only for an interim order, and accordingly it would not go to the jury.

Gillespie v. Van Der Biezen (1987), 24 C.P.C. (2d) 315 (Ont. H.C.).

The court struck out a jury notice in an action involving trust issues.

447927 Ont. Inc. v. Pizza Pizza Ltd. (1987), 16 C.P.C. (2d) 277 (Ont. H.C.).

The court struck out a jury notice where the case involved equitable issues of mixed fact and law as to whether fiduciary obligations existed and were breached.

Brown v. Chief of Police of Thunder Bay (City) (1986), 11 C.P.C. (2d) 159 (Ont. Dist. Ct.).

A jury notice should not be struck out merely because a claim for declaratory relief is made, where that relief is only a precursor to a claim for damages. An action against the chief of police was held not to be relief against a municipality under this section.

Bank of Montreal v. Ewing (1982), 27 C.P.C. 118 (Ont. Master).

The jury notice was struck out in this action to set aside a fraudulent conveyance.

Dorland v. Apollo Leasing (1981), 36 O.R. (2d) 16, 25 C.P.C. 196 (C.A.), leave to appeal to Supreme Court of Canada refused (1982), 36 O.R. (2d) 16, 25 C.P.C. 196, 42 N.R. 354.

A jury notice in a main action was not struck out merely because a defendant instituted third party proceedings against a municipality alleging non-repair of a highway where the non-repair claim was required by statute to be heard without a jury.

Damien v. O'Mulvenny (1981), 34 O.R. (2d) 448, 19 C.C.L.T. 48, 128 D.L.R. (3d) 258 (H.C.).

An action for breach of a duty of confidentiality is a matter in which the Courts of Chancery had exclusive jurisdiction and may not be tried with a jury.

Perrier v. Sorgat (1979), 25 O.R. (2d) 645, 13 C.P.C. 171, 101 D.L.R. (3d) 318 (Co. Ct.).

An action against a commissioner and officer of the Ontario Provincial Police for damages for assault, false imprisonment and malicious prosecution is not a procedure against the Crown and may be tried by jury.

Roberts v. Barbosa (1976), 12 O.R. (2d) 260, 1 C.P.C. 81 (H.C.).

A jury notice was struck out because third party proceedings had been taken against the Crown.

Toronto Star v. C.B.C. (1976), 11 O.R. (2d) 289 (Master).

A defamation action against the Crown may not be tried with a jury.

Colquhoun v. Kitchen (1975), 4 O.R. (2d) 376 (H.C.).

An action for an injunction to restrain a common law nuisance may be tried with a jury. [*But see now the Courts of Justice Act, s. 108(2)1 — Authors.*]

Carolan v. Olivetti Can. Ltd. (1974), 8 O.R. (2d) 252 (H.C.).

An action for wrongful dismissal may be tried with a jury.

Striking Out Jury Notice — Where Jury Trial Inappropriate — rule 47.02(2)

Oliver v. Gothard (1992), 10 O.R. (3d) 309, 11 C.P.C. (3d) 342 (Gen. Div.).

Where two actions were to be tried together, and only one was the subject of a jury notice, the court ordered that the actions be tried without a jury because mixed questions of law and fact were involved.

Wheater v. Walters (1992), 7 C.P.C. (3d) 197 (Ont. Gen. Div.).

The court struck out a jury notice where the plaintiff had been involved in four separate motor vehicle accidents, each giving rise to an action with all actions to be tried together. The case was too complex for a jury.

Jeschkeit v. State Farm Insurance Co. (1990), 44 C.P.C. (2d) 140 (Ont. H.C.).

A jury notice was not struck out simply because the action was a claim under the unidentified motorist coverage of a standard automobile policy of insurance.

Strojny v. Chan (1988), 26 C.P.C. (2d) 38 (Ont. H.C.).

The fact that a judge is better able than a jury to comprehend, recollect, analyze, and weigh evidence is insufficient reason to strike out a jury notice. There is a *prima facie* right to have common law actions tried by jury.

Irfan v. Loftus (1987), 22 C.P.C. (2d) 277 (Ont. Dist. Ct.).

Where the plaintiff had been involved in two separate collisions which resulted in overlapping injuries, a jury notice was struck out. It would be unreasonable to expect that a jury could properly assess and differentiate between the injuries in the two collisions.

Sussman v. Eales (1987), 61 O.R. (2d) 316, 24 C.P.C. (2d) 99 (H.C.).

A motion to strike out a jury notice prior to discoveries in this libel action was dismissed as premature.

Pipher v. Shelburne Dist. Hospital (1985), 5 C.P.C. (2d) 110, 12 C.C.E.L. 182 (Ont. H.C.).

The court declined to strike out a jury notice prior to discoveries in this wrongful dismissal action.

MacDougall v. Midland Doherty Ltd. (1984), 48 O.R. (2d) 602, 47 C.P.C. 166, 7 C.C.E.L. 28 (H.C.).

A jury is inappropriate where difficult questions of law are required to be determined. The court struck out a jury notice in a wrongful dismissal case where the plaintiff claimed damages for mental distress.

Markovski v. Allstate Ins. Co. of Can., 42 O.R. (2d) 689, 35 C.P.C. 30, 1 C.C.L.I. 148, [1983] I.L.R. 1-1665 (Div. Ct.).

The court refused to strike out a jury notice served in an action against an insurer pursuant to the uninsured motorist provisions of a standard automobile policy.

Fulton v. Fort Erie (1982), 40 O.R. (2d) 235, 31 C.P.C. 47, 142 D.L.R. (3d) 487 (H.C.).

The court struck out the jury notice in this wrongful dismissal action in which a claim for damages for mental distress was being advanced and difficult questions of fact and law were raised.

Whealy v. Torbar Ltd. (1982), 40 O.R. (2d) 378 (H.C.).

The court dismissed a jury at trial in a case involving complicated evidence regarding neurological injuries.

Frederick v. Abstainers' Ins. Co., 35 O.R. (2d) 592, 133 D.L.R. (3d) 146, [1982] I.L.R. 1-1494 (H.C.).

A jury notice was struck out in an action against an insurer under the uninsured motorist coverage of a standard automobile poicy.

Rahmaty v. Kentner; Rahmaty v. Jaquith (1982), 31 C.P.C. 300 (Ont. H.C.).

The jury notices were struck out where two actions arising out of separate motor vehicle accidents were to be tried together and complicated medical and actuarial evidence would be led.

Demeter v. Occidental Life Ins. Co. of California (1979), 23 O.R. (2d) 31, 9 C.P.C. 332, 94 D.L.R. (3d) 465, affirmed 26 O.R. (2d) 391, 12 C.P.C. 125 (Div. Ct.).

Substantial publicity concerning previous criminal proceedings and the prospect of a long and complicated trial did not warrant striking out a jury notice in this case.

Brodie v. Heath (1975), 13 O.R. (2d) 365, 7 C.P.C. 94 (Dist. Ct.).

A jury notice will not be struck out merely because a claim against one defendant is based in gross negligence and a claim against another defendant is based in negligence.

Otonabee Motors Ltd. v. B.A. Oil Co., [1968] 1 O.R. 573 (C.A.).

Where it is not clearly shown that the issues are too complicated to be tried with a jury, the decision should be left to the trial judge.

Arrow Transit Lines Ltd. v. Tank Truck Transport Ltd., [1968] 1 O.R. 154, 65 D.L.R. (2d) 683 (H.C.).

A jury notice was struck out where the evidence was likely to be technical.

Cole v. Trans-Canada Air Lines, [1966] 2 O.R. 188, 56 D.L.R. (2d) 234 (H.C.).

The court refused to strike out a jury notice before trial in a fatal accident case merely because there would be actuarial and other evidence pertaining to the future value of money, the appropriate discounts for the cash value of the verdict, etc.

Kovacs v. Skelton, [1966] 1 O.R. 6 (H.C.).

A jury notice was struck out where the case involved seven serious injuries and one fatality, liability was in dispute, and a good deal of medical evidence would be required.

Ryan v. Whitton, [1964] 1 O.R. 111 (C.A.).

Where it appears possible, but not certain, that a complicated legal issue may arise at trial, the question of striking out the jury notice should be left for the determination of the trial judge after it is clear whether such an issue has indeed arisen.

Such v. Dominion Stores Ltd., [1961] O.R. 190, 26 D.L.R. (2d) 696 (C.A.).

In an action of a character which may usually be tried by a jury, the jury notice should not be struck out in the absence of special circumstances.

Martin v. Reutch, [1943] O.R. 683 (C.A.).

An order striking out a jury notice before trial can be appealed but should not be interfered with unless it can be demonstrated that an injustice will result or the order is clearly wrong.

Gordon v. Imperial Tobacco Sales Co. Ltd., [1937] O.R. 576, 69 C.C.C. 156, [1937] 3 D.L.R. 550 (C.A.).

Where only part of an action is to be tried with a jury, separate trials need not be ordered. The trial judge may deal with the issues at his discretion.

Striking Out Jury Notice — Professional Malpractice Cases

Campbell v. Singal (1989), 35 C.P.C. (2d) 283 (Ont. H.C.).

The court dismissed a motion to strike out the jury notice in this medical malpractice action. There is no practice which absolutely precludes juries in such cases and juries should be struck only where they could not reasonably be expected to follow the evidence or properly apply the judge's charge.

Meringolo v. Oshawa Gen. Hospital (1986), 10 C.P.C. (2d) 272 (Ont. H.C.).

In a medical malpractice action where expert testimony would be given on complex scientific matters, the jury notice was struck out.

Anderson v. Wilgress (1985), 6 C.P.C. (2d) 172 (Ont. H.C.).

The court refused to strike out a jury notice in this medical malpractice case where the medical reports indicated the issues would not be as complex as the pleadings indicated and the effect of striking the notice would be to delay the trial for two years. The motion could be renewed before the pre-trial judge.

Granger v. Craan (1985), 7 C.P.C. (2d) 39 (Ont. H.C.).

The court struck out the jury notice in this action against a dermatologist for negligence in prescribing a drug.

Zeller v. Toronto Gen. Hosp. (1984), 45 C.P.C. 221 (Ont. H.C.).

The court declined to strike out the jury notice in this medical malpractice case.

Soldwisch v. Toronto Western Hosp. (1983), 43 O.R. (2d) 449, 38 C.P.C. 309, 1 D.L.R. (4th) 446 (Div. Ct.).

There is no longer a practice requiring that a jury be struck out in medical malpractice cases. A motions court judge has a discretion separate and distinct from that of the trial judge, but if there is doubt about whether the action ought to be tried without a jury the motion to strike must fail.

Coop v. Greater Niagara Gen. Hosp. (1983), 34 C.P.C. 6 (Ont. H.C.).

The court declined to strike out a jury notice in a medical malpractice case where it was not shown the issue would be too complex for a jury.

Goodman v. Siskind, Taggart and Cromarty (1980), 31 O.R. (2d) 308, 20 C.P.C. 177, 119 D.L.R. (3d) 438 (H.C.).

An application to strike out a jury notice in a solicitor malpractice action was dismissed.

McArthur v. McMaster Univ. Medical Centre (1979), 26 O.R. (2d) 285, 3 L. Med. Q. 149 (H.C.).

There has been a substantial change in the judicial approach to whether juries should be allowed in medical malpractice cases, in favour of allowing juries.

Law v. Woolford (1976), 2 C.P.C. 197 (Ont. H.C.).

In a medical malpractice action, a jury notice requiring that only damages be assessed by a jury was not struck out.

Faffray v. Sisters of St. Joseph of Sault Ste. Marie, [1966] 2 O.R. 304 (H.C.).
An action against a nurse for negligence in her professional duties should be tried without a jury.

Extension of Time to Deliver Jury Notice

Nardo v. Fluet (1993), 13 O.R. (3d) 220 (Gen. Div.).
Leave to amend pleadings has the effect of re-opening pleadings for all purposes, including the delivery of a jury notice, unless some limitation in purpose is indicated.

Vataner v. Rossi (1991), 2 C.P.C. (3d) 156 (Ont. Master).
Where a jury notice was delivered by the defendant after completion of examinations for discovery, the plaintiff's motion to strike the notice was allowed. A decision to proceed with a trial by jury only after discoveries amounted to an unconscionable and unjustified delay.

Jeschkeit v. State Farm Insurance Co. (1990), 44 C.P.C. (2d) 140 (Ont. H.C.).
A one-week extension for delivery of a jury notice was permitted where there was no unconscionable delay or likelihood of prejudice to the defendant.

Black v. Sinclair (1989), 16 W.D.C.P. 69 (Ont. H.C.).
The court validated the plaintiffs' jury notice served almost five months late in this medical malpractice case.

Goldman v. H.A. Brown Ltd. (1988), 30 C.P.C. (2d) 299 (Ont. H.C.).
Where all parties had delayed the proceedings to some extent, and the delivery of a jury notice would only result in a delay of two or three months, there was no unconscionable delay or significant prejudice.

Desjardine v. Neron (1987), 24 C.P.C. (2d) 311 (Ont. Master).
The time for delivery of a jury notice should be extended unless there has been an unconscionable delay or the opposite parties are likely to suffer prejudice. The court granted a six-month extension.

Dragicevic v. Menna (1987), 25 C.P.C. (2d) 53 (Ont. Master).
The court dismissed a motion to extend the time to file a jury notice by four years. There had been an unconscionable delay in seeking leave and there might be a delay in obtaining a jury trial.

Jackson v. Hautala (1983), 42 O.R. (2d) 153, 35 C.P.C. 108 (Div. Ct.).
A party should not be deprived of the right to a jury trial except for cogent reasons. The court extended the time for delivery of a jury notice by three months where the defendant changed his solicitor and where there was no prejudice to the plaintiff.

Graham v. Smith (1982), 38 O.R. (2d) 404, 27 C.P.C. 237 (Master), affirmed 38 O.R. (2d) 404 at 410 (H.C.).
Where an amendment is not such as to suggest for the first time that a jury trial would be appropriate, pleadings are not thereby re-opened to allow delivery of a jury notice.

Waters v. Cadillac Fairview Corp. (1981), 33 O.R. (2d) 778, 22 C.P.C. 271 (H.C.).
Where the defendant had delivered an amended statement of defence on consent after discoveries, the plaintiff was permitted to serve a jury notice as pleadings had been re-opened.

Levin v. T.T.C. (1977), 18 O.R. (2d) 231 (Master).
Where a plaintiff was given leave to bring a motion to amend his pleading after certifying his readiness for trial, and the motion was granted, pleadings were not re-opened for the purpose of serving a jury notice.

Westall v. Smith (1977), 15 O.R. (2d) 695, 4 C.P.C. 61 (H.C.).

An insurer added as a third party pursuant to the *Insurance Act* cannot require trial by jury.

Warren v. Lowery (1976), 2 C.P.C. 137 (Ont. H.C.).

An extension of time for delivering a jury notice was refused where a considerable time had passed from the date prescribed.

Pankowski v. Halifax Ins. Co., [1960] O.W.N. 383 (H.C.).

A jury notice served after the close of pleadings is not necessarily validated by the re-opening of pleadings.

Freeman v. Parker, [1956] O.W.N. 561 (H.C.).

An order amending a statement of claim and permitting consequent amendment of the statement of defence and reply re-opens pleadings and unless it is specifically otherwise provided any party may serve a jury notice.

Discretion of Trial Judge — Generally — rule 47.02(3)

Chrastina v. Patterson Estate (1995), 81 O.A.C. 52 (C.A.), leave to appeal to Supreme Court of Canada refused (February 15, 1996), Doc. 24864.

Where the plaintiff withdrew its motion to strike the jury, the court held that the trial judge could no longer discharge the jury on his own initiative.

Wilson v. Martinello (1993), 29 C.P.C. (3d) 18 (Ont. Gen. Div.).

The court struck out the jury where an early ruling required hearing evidence in two stages.

Ball v. Vincent (1993), 27 C.P.C. (3d) 148 (Ont. Gen. Div.).

The trial judge discharged the jury at the outset of trial where a number of issues made the case too complex for a jury trial.

Cosford v. Cornwall (1992), 9 O.R. (3d) 37, 7 C.P.C. (3d) 387, 93 D.L.R. (4th) 123, 56 O.A.C. 47 (C.A.).

The trial judge may not discharge the jury on his own initiative but rather, in general, may do so only on motion by one of the parties. The Court of Appeal ordered a new trial where the trial judge had done so on his own initiative.

De Boer v. Bosweld (1991), 5 O.R. (3d) 413 (Gen. Div.).

Only when the facts, the law, or both are such that a jury cannot reasonably be expected to be able to follow the evidence properly or to apply the judge's charge properly should a jury be struck. The trial judge can exercise such discretion at any point in the proceedings.

Sloane v. Toronto Stock Exchange (1991), 5 O.R. (3d) 412, 4 C.P.C. (3d) 278, 52 O.A.C. 177 (C.A.).

The right to trial by jury is an important substantive right. The Court of Appeal ordered a new trial in this wrongful dismissal case where the trial judge had dismissed the jury due to complexity of the claims for mental distress and punitive damages.

Aitken v. Forsell (1991), 50 C.P.C. (2d) 176, 30 M.V.R. (2d) 125, 81 D.L.R. (4th) 542, 50 O.A.C. 337 (C.A.).

Appellate review of a trial judge's exercise of discretion to discharge a jury is limited. The test is whether justice can be done to the litigants in the particular case and whether that is better accomplished by retention or by discharge of the jury.

Graham v. Rourke (1990), 75 O.R. (2d) 622, 74 D.L.R. (4th) 1, 40 O.A.C. 301 (C.A.), affirmed on reconsideration 75 O.R. (2d) 622 at 644 (C.A.).

Appellate review of a trial judge's exercise of the discretion to discharge a jury is limited. If the trial judge has considered the relevant factors and committed no error of law, the discretion cannot be interfered with.

Murray v. Collegiate Sports Ltd. (1989), 40 C.P.C. (2d) 1 (Ont. C.A.).

The presence of difficult and unsettled questions of law is not in itself grounds for discharging a jury.

Iona Corp. v. Rooney (1987), 62 O.R. (2d) 179, 25 C.P.C. (2d) 174 (H.C.).

The court struck out a jury notice in one of three related actions because injunctive relief was claimed. Jury notices were permitted to stand in the other two actions subject to the discretion of the trial judge. The effect of pre-trial publicity should be left to the trial judge to consider at the time of trial.

Kostopoulos v. Jesshope (1985), 50 O.R. (2d) 54, 48 C.P.C. 209, 6 O.A.C. 326 (C.A.), leave to
     appeal to S.C.C. refused 50 O.R. (2d) 800n, 61 N.R. 319.

The trial judge discharged the jury where a member of the jury was a former patient of a psychiatrist who gave evidence. There was a risk the juror may have conveyed her opinion of the witness to the other jurors.

Isaacs v. MHG Int. Ltd. (1984), 45 O.R. (2d) 693, 4 C.C.E.L. 197, 7 D.L.R. (4th) 570, 3 O.A.C.
     301 (C.A.).

Where there is a possibility that complicated legal issues may arise at trial, the trial judge should not exercise his or her discretion until evidence is heard and a determination made that such an issue has, in fact, arisen.

Nag v. McKellar, [1969] 1 O.R. 764, 4 D.L.R. (3d) 53 (C.A.).

The trial judge should not discharge the jury merely because visual evidence in the form of motion pictures is introduced.

Majcenic v. Natale, [1968] 1 O.R. 189, 66 D.L.R. (2d) 50 (C.A.).

Motions at trial to discharge a jury should be heard either in open court in the absence of the jury or in chambers in the presence of a court reporter.

Martin v. St. Lawrence Cement Co., [1968] 1 O.R. 94 (C.A.).

A new trial was ordered where the trial judge had discharged the jury before any evidence had been led in an uncomplicated occupier's liability case.

Neelands v. Haig, [1957] O.W.N. 337, 9 D.L.R. (2d) 165 (C.A.).

A new trial was ordered where the trial judge discharged the jury without sufficient reason.

Flynn v. Saunders, [1947] O.W.N. 975 (C.A.).

The power of the trial judge to dispense with a jury ends when the case is submitted to the jury.

Discretion of Trial Judge — Mention of Insurance — rule 47.02(3)

Schon v. Hodgins (1988), 11 W.D.C.P. 273 (Ont. Dist. Ct.).

In a motor vehicle case the judge has a discretion to dismiss the jury if insurance is mentioned. In this case there was a risk of injustice and the jury was dismissed.

Jackson v. Inglis (1985), 50 C.P.C. 126, 7 O.A.C. 377 (C.A.).

The Court of Appeal refused to interfere with the discretion of a trial judge who discharged a jury because of the mention of a possible claim under Schedule C of a standard automobile policy.

Morin v. Rochon, 42 O.R. (2d) 301, 1 C.C.L.I. 139, 38 C.P.C. 215, 148 D.L.R. (3d) 573, [1983]
     I.L.R. 1-1679 (H.C.).

Where the plaintiff in a motor vehicle case mentioned the insurer of one of the defendants at trial, the judge refused to discharge the jury.

Dickison v. Montgomery, [1960] O.R. 544 (C.A.).

The Court of Appeal refused to set aside the verdict of a jury notwithstanding that the trial judge had mentioned possible recourse to the unsatisfied judgment fund in response to a question regarding insurance from the foreman.

Koebel v. Rive, [1958] O.R. 448 (C.A.).

Where something occurs during trial from which the jury may reasonably infer that a defendant is insured, the jury should be discharged and counsel should elect whether to obtain another jury or proceed without one.

Poyner v. Ferguson, [1955] O.W.N. 1, [1955] 2 D.L.R. 281 (H.C.).

A jury was discharged where there had been mention of insurance premiums and, more importantly, the press had published reports of the amount of damages claimed.

Theakston v. Bowhey, [1950] O.R. 524, [1950] 3 D.L.R. 804, affirmed [1951] S.C.R. 679, [1951] 4 D.L.R. 150.

Where the mention of insurance is not such that the jury is likely to infer that the defendant is insured, the jury may be retained.

RULE 48   LISTING FOR TRIAL

Highlights

This Rule sets out the procedure by which actions are listed for trial. This involves a one-step procedure for setting down and listing cases for trial: defended cases are automatically listed for trial after 60 days from being set down for trial. The status notice procedure comes into play when an action is not listed for trial in a timely manner.

Prior to its amendment in 1991, Rule 48 required a two-step process in order to list defended actions for trial. First, the action had to be "set down for trial" by serving and filing a notice of readiness for trial and a trial record and filing the notice and trial record. Then, 60 days later, the action could be placed on a list for trial by serving a notice of listing for trial. By contrast, undefended actions were set down for trial and then automatically added to a trial list without the need to serve a notice of trial.

Setting down. In a defended action a party who is ready for trial may set the action down by serving a trial record on every other party and forthwith filing it with proof of service: rule 48.02(1). Any party who sets an action down, or consents to the action being placed on the trial list, may not initiate or continue any motion or form of discovery (with certain defined exceptions) without leave of the court: rule 48.04.

Placing on a trial list. The registrar is to automatically place a defended action on a trial list 60 days after the action has been set down for trial, or earlier if all parties consent: rule 48.06(1).

Once an action is placed on a trial list all parties are deemed to be ready for trial and a pre-trial conference or the trial will proceed unless otherwise ordered by a judge or the person presiding at the pre-trial conference: rule 48.07.

While a party who sets the action down, or who consents to the action being placed on a trial list, may not initiate or continue any motion or form of discovery, except with leave. However, no other party is every directly prohibited from initiating or conducting motions or discovery, but he or she is obligated to be ready to proceed with a pre-trial or the trial, once the action is placed on a trial list.

Provision is made for a separate speedy trial list (rule 48.09) and speedy trials may be ordered under rule 20.05(1)(a) (on a motion for summary judgment) and rule 37.13(1)(a) (on the disposition of any motion).

Commercial list. Actions on the Commercial List are subject to the Commercial List practice direction. A motion is required to obtain a trial date in such cases. See the practice direction reproduced following the Highlights of Rule 38.

Status notice. The status notice procedure provides a degree of court control over the progress of litigation. This procedure (formerly called "status hearings") was reviewed in 1991 and at that time it was resolved to retain the procedure, but to amend the rule to make it more economic in its use of the parties' time and judicial resources. The rule was amended to reshape the procedure along the lines of that provided in rule 61.13(2) for dismissal of appeals for delay.

In actions which have not been listed for trial or disposed of within two years from the filing of a statement of defence, the registrar shall mail to the parties a "status notice": rule 48.14(1). This notice (a copy of which must be given by a solicitor to his client) gives the parties 90 days in which to set the action down for trial, terminate the action or request a status hearing before a judge. If none of these steps are taken the registrar shall dismiss the action for delay: rule 48.14(3).

At a status hearing the judge may set a timetable for placing the action on the trial list or dismiss the action for delay: rule 48.14(8). Where an action is not thereafter set down for trial as ordered, or otherwise terminated, the registrar is to dismiss the action for delay: rule 48.14(4). Where a registrar has dismissed an action for delay under this rule the court nevertheless has authority under rule 37.14(1) to set aside the registrar's order: rule 48.14(11) and see *Harvey Hubbell Can. Inc. v. Thornhurst Corp.* (1987), 62 O.R. (2d) 799 (Div. Ct.).

Duty to inform registrar of settlement. Whether or not an action has been placed on a trial list, every party is now under an express obligation to promptly inform the registrar of any settlement: rule 48.12.

Practice directions. A practice direction regarding cases commenced under the *Construction Lien Act* in the East Region is reproduced below. For local procedures regarding listing for trial, assignment court, and trial lists in the Central South Region see chapter 4 of the *Administrative Procedures Manual for the Central South Region* published by direction of Regional Senior Justice Fedak.

PRACTICE DIRECTION
East Region

CONSTRUCTION LIEN ACT

Effective August 3rd, 1994 all cases commenced under the authority of the Construction Lien Act R.S.O. 1990, Chapter 30 must comply with the provisions of section 60 of the Act, or with Rule 48 when satisfying the requirements of section 37 of the Act.

A separate Construction Lien list will continue to be maintained notwithstanding the practice for setting down is changing by virtue of this Direction.

Dated July 15, 1994

Regional Senior Justice R.C. Desmarais

Chief Justice R. Roy McMurtry

WHEN AND BY WHOM ACTION MAY BE SET DOWN FOR TRIAL

48.01 After the close of pleadings, any party to an action or to a counterclaim or crossclaim in the action who is not in default under these rules or an order of the court and who is ready for trial may set the action down for trial, together with any counterclaim or crossclaim.

HOW ACTION IS SET DOWN FOR TRIAL

Defended Action
48.02(1) Where an action is defended, a party who wishes to set it down for trial may do so by serving a trial record prepared in accordance with

rule 48.03 on every party to the action or to a counterclaim or crossclaim in the action and on any third or subsequent party and forthwith filing the trial record with proof of service.

Undefended Action

(2) Where the court orders the trial of an undefended action, a party who wishes to set it down for trial may do so by filing a trial record prepared in accordance with rule 48.03.

Defended Third Party Claim

(3) Where an action is a defended third party claim, a party who wishes to set it down for trial shall, in addition to complying with subrule (1), serve the trial record in the third party claim on the plaintiff in the main action within the time for service on the parties to the third party claim and shall forthwith file proof of service.

Undefended Third Party Claim

(4) Where an action is an undefended third party claim, a party who wishes to set it down for trial shall serve the trial record in the third party claim on the plaintiff in the main action and shall forthwith file proof of service.

Trial at Another Place

(5) Where an action is to be tried at a place other than where it was commenced, the party filing the trial record shall by requisition require the court file, including the trial record, to be sent to the court office at the place of trial. [am. O. Reg. 396/91, s. 5]

TRIAL RECORD

48.03(1) The trial record shall contain, in the following order,

(a) a table of contents, describing each document by its nature and date;

(b) a copy of any jury notice;

(c) a copy of the pleadings, including those relating to any counterclaim or crossclaim;

(d) a copy of any financial statement delivered under rule 69.14 or 70.04 or waiver of financial statements filed under subrule 69.14(3);

(e) a copy of any demand or order for particulars of a pleading or financial statement and the particulars delivered in response;

(f) a copy of any notice of amounts and particulars of special damages delivered under clause 25.06(9)(b);

(g) a copy of any order respecting the trial; and

(h) a certificate signed by the solicitor setting the action down, stating,

    (i) that the record contains the documents required by clauses (a) to (g),

    (ii) that the time for delivery of pleadings has expired,

    (iii) where applicable, that a defendant who has failed to deliver a statement of defence has been noted in default, and

(iv) where applicable, that judgment has been obtained or that the action has been discontinued or dismissed against a defendant.

(2) It is the responsibility of the party who filed the trial record to place with the record, before the trial, a copy of,

(a) any notice of amounts and particulars of special damages delivered after the filing of the trial record;

(b) any order respecting the trial made after the filing of the trial record;

(c) any memorandum signed by counsel, or any order made by the court, following a pre-trial conference;

(d) any financial statement delivered under subrule 69.14(14) or 70.04(14) after the filing of the trial record;

(e) in an undefended action, any affidavit to be used in evidence; and

(f) any report of the Children's Lawyer and supporting affidavit and any dispute of, or waiver of the right to dispute, the report or affidavit. [am. O. Reg. 69/95, s. 19]

CONSEQUENCES OF SETTING DOWN OR CONSENT

48.04(1) Any party who has set an action down for trial and any party who has consented to the action being placed on a trial list shall not initiate or continue any motion or form of discovery without leave of the court.

(2) Subrule (1) does not,

(a) relieve a party from complying with undertakings given by the party on an examination for discovery;

(b) relieve a party from any obligation imposed by,

(i) rule 30.07 (disclosure of documents or errors subsequently discovered),

(ii) rule 30.09 (abandonment of claim of privilege),

(iii) rule 31.07 (disclosure of information refused on discovery),

(iv) rule 31.09 (disclosure of information subsequently obtained),

(v) rule 51.03 (duty to respond to request to admit),

(vi) rule 53.03 (service of report of expert witness), or

(vii) rule 69.14 or 70.04 (delivery of financial statement); or

(c) preclude a party from resorting to rule 51.02 (request to admit facts or documents).

Leave to Initiate or Continue Motions or Discovery — Generally

Keldie v. Pilot Insurance Co. (1995), 24 O.R. (3d) 521 (Gen. Div.).

An agreement between litigants to set a case down for trial without prejudice to discovery rights is unenforceable.

Gloucester Organization Inc. v. Canadian Newsletter Managers Inc. (1995), 21 O.R. (3d) 753, 37 C.P.C. (3d) 111 (Gen. Div.).

The liberal amendment policy reflecting in rule 26.01 requires the court to grant leave to bring a motion to amend a pleading more readily than leave for other motions.

CBL Investments Inc. v. Menkes Corp. (1994), 17 O.R. (3d) 147 (Gen. Div.).

Setting an action down for trial does not preclude a party from enforcing a previous order that the opposite party answer questions refused on discovery.

Walls v. Mulkani (1994), 21 O.R. (3d) 715, 34 C.P.C. (3d) 327 (Gen. Div.).

The court refused leave to the plaintiffs to conduct an examination for discovery after setting the action down for trial where there had been no substantial or unexpected change in circumstances.

Theodore Holdings Ltd. v. Anjay Ltd. (1993), 18 C.P.C. (3d) 160 (Ont. Gen. Div.).

Once a party has listed an action for trial, a motion for summary judgment may not be brought without leave being obtained. In determining whether to grant leave, consideration should be given to whether the facts underpinning the proposed motion were known prior to the action being listed for trial and whether the motion would dispose of all of the outstanding issues.

Hill v. Ortho Pharmaceutical (Canada) Ltd. (1992), 11 C.P.C. (3d) 236 (Ont. Gen. Div.).

Setting down an action for trial is not a mere technicality. Before leave is granted for further interlocutory proceedings, there must be a substantial or unexpected change in circumstances.

Glykis v. Pardy (1985), 5 C.P.C. (2d) 147 (Ont. Master).

Where a solicitor delivers a notice of readiness without knowledge of a change of circumstances of which the client is aware, leave may be granted to bring a motion arising out of the change of circumstances.

Financial Trust Co. v. Royal Trust Corp. of Can.; Yale & Partners Ltd. v. Royal Trust Corp. of Can. (1985), 5 C.P.C. (2d) 114 (Ont. Master).

In determining whether to grant leave to initiate a motion the court should consider: (1) the facts known to the party when the notice of readiness was served; (2) whether there has been a change of circumstances; (3) the object of the request for leave; and (4) whether the motion in respect of which leave is sought would likely be granted.

Weiss v. Walwyn Stodgell Cochran Murray Ltd. (1984), 45 C.P.C. 65 (Ont. Master).

The court will give no effect to agreements between counsel purporting to preserve the right to examination for discovery in the face of the predecessor to this provision. In this case, the master refused to give leave to continue the examinations for discovery of the defendant's directors.

Tolbend Const. Ltd. v. Freure Homes Ltd. (1984), 45 C.P.C. 42 (Ont. Div. Ct.).

Leave to amend the pleadings in order for new counsel to restructure the action was refused, as there had been no change of circumstances.

Stedelbauer v. Can. Cartage System Ltd. (1979), 28 O.R. (2d) 318, 15 C.P.C. 212 (H.C.).

Leave under the predecessor of this provision is not necessary to obtain an order for the production of hospital records where it is an attempt to shorten the trial, and is not part of the discovery process.

Valleyfield Const. Ltd. v. Argo Const. Ltd. (1978), 20 O.R. (2d) 245 (H.C.).

Leave will be given for motions to enforce undertakings.

Trotter v. Cattan (1977), 15 O.R. (2d) 800, 3 C.P.C. 159, affirmed 17 O.R. (2d) 455, 5 C.P.C. 114 (H.C.).

The predecessor of this provision did not preclude a motion in response to and only by reason of a motion by another party.

Kovary v. Heinrich (1974), 5 O.R. (2d) 365 (H.C.).

Leave for further interlocutory proceedings or discovery should be given only if there is a substantial and unexpected change in circumstances so that refusal would be manifestly unjust.

Leave to Initiate or Continue Motions or Discovery — Examples Where Leave Granted

Vladetic v. Silvestri (1990), 42 C.P.C. (2d) 254 (Ont. H.C.).

The plaintiff was permitted to increase the claim for damages after setting the action down for trial where there was no prejudice to the defendant. Rule 48.04 and rule 26.01 must be balanced.

Sigfusson Transportation Co. v. Min. of Natural Resources (1985), 1 C.P.C. (2d) 204 (Ont. H.C.).

The court gave leave to file a reply pleading estoppel notwithstanding the delivery of a certificate of readiness.

Lister v. Mount Sinai Hosp. (1984), 46 C.P.C. 132 (Ont. H.C.).

The court granted leave to move to add the plaintiff's adoptive father and new-born brother as *Family Law Reform Act* plaintiffs. Counsel for the plaintiff had no expectation of the adoption or birth when he delivered the certificate of readiness. It is the expectation of counsel, not of the client, which is the controlling consideration.

York Condominium Corp. No. 202 v. Kuhl (1980), 17 C.P.C. 124 (Ont. Master).

The plaintiffs were permitted further discovery where before all defendants had been examined they had inadvertently certified that no further motions or discovery would be initiated.

Greenspan v. Whiting (1979), 12 C.P.C. 73 (Ont. Co. Ct.).

Where liability had been admitted and no discovery of the defendant conducted, the plaintiff was permitted to have discovery into surveillance conducted after it was learned at the pre-trial that there had been surveillance.

Vallender v. Marbella Boutique Imports Ltd. (1977), 15 O.R. (2d) 664, 3 C.P.C. 238 (H.C.).

Examination for discovery of one of the defendants was permitted in this case to avoid manifest injustice.

Sriubiskis v. Hyshka (1976), 1 C.P.C. 346 (Ont. H.C.).

Leave to seek an order for a medical examination was granted where the medical report subsequently received indicated possible injuries not pleaded by the plaintiff.

Leave to Initiate or Continue Motions or Discovery — Examples Where Leave Refused

Machado v. Pratt & Whitney Canada Inc. (1993), 16 O.R. (3d) 250, 23 C.P.C. (3d) 115 (Gen. Div.).

The court refused the plaintiff leave to appeal from a decision of the master which was released after the plaintiff set the action down for trial.

Worsley Estate v. Lichong (1993), 14 O.R. (3d) 649, 20 C.P.C. (3d) 5, additional reasons (1994), 17 O.R. (3d) 615, further additional reasons (March 1, 1994), Doc. 1069, 16422 (Gen. Div.).

The plaintiffs were not entitled to examine the defendants for discovery after several actions had been set down. Although the actions had been set down inadvertently, the plaintiffs had failed to arrange or proceed with examinations for discovery until they were faced with motions to dismiss for delay.

Lando & Partners Ltd. v. Upshall (1983), 39 C.P.C. 45, 48 C.B.R. (N.S.) 313 (Ont. H.C.).

A trustee in bankruptcy who continued a bankrupt's action after a certificate of readiness had been delivered was refused discovery.

Singh v. Incardona (1983), 43 O.R. (2d) 213, 37 C.P.C. 80 (Master).

Where the parties had agreed to set the action down for trial, without prejudice to the plaintiff's right to examine the defendant for discovery in the event that liability was not admitted, leave to move to compel the defendant's attendance was declined.

3001 Invts. Ltd. v. Pegg (1982), 32 C.P.C. 74 (Ont. Master).

The court refused to grant leave to the plaintiff to amend its statement of claim to seek additional relief after the plaintiff had delivered a certificate of readiness.

PLACING UNDEFENDED ACTION ON TRIAL LIST

48.05(1) In an undefended action, on receipt of the trial record the registrar at the place of trial shall forthwith place the action on the appropriate trial list.

(2) An undefended action shall not be placed on a trial list for a sitting outside Toronto unless the trial record is received by the registrar at the place of trial at least ten days before the commencement of the sitting, except where a judge orders otherwise.

(3) [Revoked O. Reg. 396/91, s. 6]

PLACING DEFENDED ACTION ON TRIAL LIST

48.06(1) A defended action shall be placed on the appropriate trial list by the registrar sixty days after the action is set down for trial or, if the consent in writing of every party other than the party who set the action down is filed earlier, on the date of filing.

(2) A defended action shall not be placed on a trial list for a sitting outside Toronto later than ten days before the commencement of the sitting, except where a judge orders otherwise. [re-en. O. Reg. 396/91, s. 7]

CONSEQUENCES OF ACTION BEING PLACED ON TRIAL LIST

48.07 Where an action is placed on a trial list,
(a) all parties shall be deemed to be ready for trial;
(b) a pre-trial conference in the action shall proceed as scheduled unless the judge or officer presiding at the conference orders otherwise; and
(c) the trial shall proceed when the action is reached on the trial list unless a judge orders otherwise.

SEPARATE TRIAL LISTS

48.08(1) Actions to be tried with a jury shall be placed on a trial list of jury actions and actions to be tried without a jury shall be placed on a trial list of non-jury actions.

(2) Where the next scheduled sitting in a place outside Toronto is for the trial of jury actions, the trial list of non-jury actions shall be added at the end of the trial list of jury actions.

SEPARATE SPEEDY TRIAL LIST

48.09 The registrar shall keep a separate speedy trial list on which only actions for which a speedy trial has been ordered shall be listed.

ACTIONS TRAVERSED OR REMAINING ON LIST AT CONCLUSION OF SITTING

48.10 Unless a judge orders otherwise, all actions traversed to the next sitting and all actions remaining on the trial list at the conclusion of a sitting shall stand in the same order at the beginning of the next appropriate trial list.

ACTIONS STRUCK OFF TRIAL LIST

48.11 Where an action is struck off a trial list, it shall not thereafter be placed on any trial list except with leave of a judge.

DUTY TO INFORM REGISTRAR OF SETTLEMENT

48.12 Every party to an action, whether it is placed on a trial list or not, shall promptly inform the registrar of any settlement of the action and shall confirm in writing that the action has been settled.

APPLICATION OF THE RULE

48.13 Rules 48.01 to 48.12 apply to any proceeding in which the court has directed the trial of an issue, unless the court orders otherwise.

ACTION NOT ON TRIAL LIST WITHIN TWO YEARS

Status Notice
48.14(1) Where an action in which a statement of defence has been filed has not been placed on a trial list or terminated by any means within two years after the filing of a statement of defence, the registrar shall serve on the parties a status notice (Form 48C) that the action will be dismissed for delay unless it is set down for trial or terminated within ninety days after service of the notice.

(2) A solicitor who receives a status notice shall forthwith give a copy of the notice to his or her client.

Dismissal by Registrar
(3) The registrar shall dismiss the action for delay, with costs, ninety days after service of the status notice, unless

    (a) the action has been set down for trial;

    (b) the action has been terminated by any means; or

    (c) a judge presiding at a status hearing has ordered otherwise.

(4) Where an action is not set down for trial or terminated by any means within the time specified in an order made at a status hearing, the registrar shall dismiss the action for delay, with costs.

(4.0.1) The registrar shall serve an order made under subrule (3) or (4) (Form 48D) on the parties.

(4.1) A solicitor who is served with an order dismissing the action for delay shall forthwith give a copy of the order to his or her client, and shall file proof that a copy was given to the client.

Status Hearing

(5) Where a status notice has been served, any party may request that the registrar arrange a status hearing, in which case the registrar shall mail to the parties a notice of the hearing, and the hearing shall be held before a judge.

Attendance at Status Hearing

(6) The solicitors of record shall attend, and the parties may attend, the status hearing.

(7) Where a party represented by a solicitor does not attend the hearing, the party's solicitor shall file proof that a copy of the status notice and notice of the time and place of the status hearing were given to the party.

Disposition at Status Hearing

(8) At the status hearing, the plaintiff shall show cause why the action should not be dismissed for delay, and,

(a) if the presiding judge is satisfied that the action should proceed, the judge may set time periods for the completion of the remaining steps necessary to have the action placed on a trial list and may order that it be placed on a trial list within a specified time, or may adjourn the status hearing to a specified date, on such terms as are just; or

(b) if the presiding judge is not satisfied that the action should proceed, the judge may dismiss the action for delay.

Plaintiff Under Disability

(9) Where the plaintiff is under disability, the action may be dismissed for delay only if,

(a) the defendant gives notice to the Children's Lawyer or, if the Public Guardian and Trustee is litigation guardian of the plaintiff, to the Public Guardian and Trustee; or

(b) the presiding judge or a judge on motion orders otherwise.

Effect of Dismissal

(10) Rules 24.03 to 24.05 (effect of dismissal for delay) apply to an action dismissed for delay under subrule (3), (4), or (8).

(11) An order under this rule dismissing an action may be set aside under rule 37.14. [am. O. Regs. 219/91, s. 5; 396/91, s. 8; 770/92, s. 13; 212/93, s. 4; 69/95, ss. 18, 19, 20]

Mandal v. 575419 Ontario Ltd. (1994), 23 C.P.C. (3d) 172 (Ont. Gen. Div.).

Where an action was dismissed for failure to list for trial in accordance with the status hearing judge's order, the court refused to set aside the Registrar's order as the plaintiff demonstrated no interest in prosecuting the matter and the plaintiff's lawyer was negligent.

Bruzzese v. Peterkin (1994), 25 C.P.C. (3d) 246 (Ont. Gen. Div.).

The court set aside the dismissal of the action for failure to comply with a deadline set at a status hearing. The plaintiff explained the delay and there was no substantial prejudice to the defendant.

Currie v. Toronto (City) (1992), 7 O.R. (3d) 796 (Gen. Div.), affirmed (1995), 22 O.R. (3d) 127 (note) (C.A.).

The court has the jurisdiction to set aside a status hearing order dismissing an action for delay. The criteria to be applied are those set out in rule 37.14.

Knight v. Buckley (1991), 6 O.R. (3d) 339 (C.A.).

Where plaintiff's counsel had no intention to list an action for trial at any material time, the court refused to overturn an order dismissing a motion to set aside an order of dismissal.

Molevelt v. Sowinski (1991), 6 O.R. (3d) 112 (Gen. Div.).

A motion to set aside an order dismissing an action was allowed where plaintiff's counsel had been unaware of the consequences of failing to list the action, and the defendants were not prejudiced by the delay.

Sinnett v. Sullivan (1991), 49 C.P.C. (2d) 122 (Ont. Gen. Div.).

In the absence of any reason for the delay in taking any steps to proceed with the action or to list it for trial, the court refused to set aside an order dismissing the action for delay in view of the probable actual prejudice suffered by the defendant.

Brazeau v. E.B. Eddy Forest Products Ltd. (1988), 27 C.P.C. (2d) 35 (Ont. Dist. Ct.).

Where the plaintiff's solicitor fails to attend on a status hearing and the action is dismissed, the order should be set aside if any reason for failing to appear is shown, there is no prejudice to the defendant and the motion to set aside the order is brought promptly.

Harvey Hubbell Can. Inc. v. Thornhurst Corp. (1987), 62 O.R. (2d) 799, 26 O.A.C. 331 (Div. Ct.).

The court has authority under rule 37.14(1)(c) to set aside an order of the registrar made under rule 48.14(6). *Mior v. Project Lift Inc., infra*, overruled.

McCraw v. Dresser Can. Inc. (1987), 60 O.R. (2d) 154, 19 C.P.C. (2d) 26 (H.C.).

The court suspended operation of a judge's status hearing order and the registrar's consequent dismissal of an action where the order had not been complied with through inadvertence.

Mior v. Project Lift Inc. (1987), 59 O.R. (2d) 222, 16 C.P.C. (2d) 112 (H.C.).

The court refused to set aside the dismissal of an action for failure of the plaintiff to place the action on the trial list within the time specified by the judge conducting the status hearing. The dismissal by the registrar was merely an administrative act. The substance behind it was the judge's order which had not been altered by appeal.

Central Can. Travel Services v. Bank of Montreal (1986), 57 O.R. (2d) 633, 13 C.P.C. (2d) 119 (H.C.).

The court set aside the dismissal of an action at a status hearing where the plaintiff failed to attend the hearing through inadvertence and there had been no delay.

RULE 49   OFFER TO SETTLE

Highlights

This Rule represents a major innovation of the 1985 Rules and has had a significant impact on the conduct of litigation in terms of encouraging and facilitating settlements. It replaced the former "payment into court in satisfaction" procedure but is considerably broader. The Rule applies to actions and applications alike, is not restricted to monetary claims and is equally available to plaintiffs, applicants, defendants and respondents.

General principle: Cost consequences for failure to accept. A party may serve on any other party a written offer to settle any one or more or the claims in a proceeding on the terms set out in the offer: rule 49.02.

An offer may be made at any time, but provided it is made at least seven days before the commencement of the hearing (and is not withdrawn and does not expire before the commencement of the hearing) certain *prima facie* cost consequences follow if it is not accepted.

If it is the plaintiff's offer and the plaintiff obtains a judgment as favourable as or more favourable than the terms of the offer, the plaintiff is entitled to party and party costs to the date of the offer and solicitor and client costs thereafter, unless the court orders otherwise: rule 49.10(1). If it is the defendant's offer and the plaintiff obtains a judgment, but that judgment is merely as favourable as or is less favourable than the terms of the offer, the plaintiff is entitled to party and party costs to the date of the offer and the defendant is entitled to party and party costs thereafter, unless the court orders otherwise: rule 49.10(2).

The Court of Appeal has held that courts should depart from the *prima facie* costs consequences in rule 49.10 only where, after giving proper weight to the policy of the rule and the importance of a reasonable predictability and the even application of the rule, the interests of justice require departure; the good faith of the party who did not accept an offer should not be given significant weight: *Niagara Structural Steel (St. Catharines) v. W.D. Laflamme Ltd.* (1987), 58 O.R. (2d) 773, 19 C.P.C. (2d) 163, 19 O.A.C. 142 (C.A.). Where an offer provides a lump sum for damages including prejudgment interest, the court will compare the damages awarded at trial plus prejudgment interest as of the date of the offer to the lump sum in order to determine whether the judgment is as favourable as the offer: *Mathur v. Commercial Union Assurance Co. of Can.* (1988), 24 C.P.C. (2d) 225, 28 O.A.C. 55 (Div. Ct.).

Although not expressly provided by the Rules, where the plaintiff fails to accept a significant offer to settle by the defendant and the action is then dismissed, the Court of Appeal held in *S. & A. Strasser Ltd. v. Richmond Hill (Town)* (1990), 1 O.R. (3d) 243, 49 C.P.C. (2d) 234, 45 O.A.C. 394 (C.A.), that the defendant should be awarded party and party costs to the date of the offer and solicitor and clients costs thereafter. Nevertheless the trial judge retains a discretion simply to award party and party costs to the defendant in such circumstances, which has been the usual disposition both under the offer to settle rules since 1985 and the payment into court mechanism under the former Rules.

The Supreme Court of Canada in *Fletcher v. Manitoba Public Insurance Corp.* (1990), 75 O.R. (2d) 373, held that where the plaintiff sought the benefit of the costs consequences provided by rule 49.10(1) (because of the defendant's failure to accept the plaintiff's offer to settle) the burden was on the *defendant* to establish that the plaintiff was not entitled to such costs. The Civil Rules Committee considered that if

Fletcher stated a general proposition, that proposition was wrong in principle. Hence rule 49.10 was amended to deal expressly with the onus of establishing that a judgment is as favourable as or more or less favourable than the terms of the offer; it placed the burden on the party who seeks the benefit of the costs consequences provided for in the rule.

Even where the offer is not made at least seven days before the hearing, or is withdrawn or has expired, or perhaps was made before the proceeding was commenced, the court is given a discretion to take it into account in exercising its discretion as to costs: rule 49.13.

Withdrawal, expiry and acceptance. An offer to settle may be withdrawn at any time before acceptance by serving a withdrawal of the offer, and an offer may specify a time within which it may be accepted and it expires at that time if not previously accepted: rule 49.04.

An offer to settle may be accepted by serving an acceptance of offer before it is withdrawn (rule 49.07(1)) and an offer is not terminated by a counter-offer or a rejection: rule 49.07(2) (this alters the common law and reverses the decision in *Tam v. Tam* (1982), 38 O.R. (2d) 718, 29 C.P.C. 278, 29 R.F.L. (2d) 162, 138 D.L.R. (3d) 302 (C.A.), and is necessary to preserve the Rule's potential costs benefits).

A written offer to settle may be withdrawn only by a written notice of withdrawal: *York North Condominium Corp. No. 5 v. Van Horne Clipper Properties Ltd.* (1989), 70 O.R. (2d) 317, 40 C.P.C. (2d) 156, 35 O.A.C. 364 (C.A.).

A plaintiff's offer may make it a term of acceptance that the defendant pay money into court or to a trustee, and the plaintiff may accept a defendant's offer with the condition that the defendant pay money into court or to a trustee: rule 49.07(3) and (4). In this way the benefits of the former "payment into court in satisfaction" procedure is retained, but the procedure itself has disappeared and is replaced by this much broader offer to settle procedure.

Where an offer is accepted, the plaintiff may have his or her costs assessed if the offer does not provide for the disposition of costs (rule 49.07(5)) and the court may incorporate any term of the offer into a judgment: rule 49.07(6).

Where a party fails to comply with the terms of an accepted offer, the other party may move for judgment in terms of the accepted offer or continue the proceedings as if there had been no accepted offer: rule 49.09.

Special provisions apply where there is a party under disability (rule 49.08) or there are multiple defendants (rule 49.11).

Also, provision is made for offers to contribute where defendants are alleged to be jointly and severally liable: rule 49.12.

Practice directions. A practice direction regarding the Alternative Dispute Resolution Pilot Project in the Toronto Region is reproduced below following the Chart.

Former Rules: Rules 306-318a, 775i.

A chart showing the cost consequences of failure to accept offers to settle is set out below.

USE OF OFFER TO SETTLE COST CONSEQUENCES CHART

The usual cost consequences (*i.e.* unless the court orders otherwise) of failure to accept offers to settle can be seen by determining the location of the plaintiff's recovery at trial on the continuum set out below.

If the plaintiff's recovery is equal to or greater than the amount of a plaintiff's offer to settle, the plaintiff should usually receive party and party costs up to the date of service of the offer and solicitor and client costs thereafter: rule 49.10(1).

If the plaintiff's recovery is more than any defendant's offer but less than any plaintiff's offer, the plaintiff should usually receive party and party costs throughout the action.

If the plaintiff's recovery is equal to or less than a defendant's offer, the plaintiff should usually receive party and party costs only up to the date of service of the offer and the defendant should usually receive party and party costs after that date: rule 49.10(2).

If the plaintiff's action is dismissed, the defendant will usually receive party and party costs throughout the action.

The chart assumes that the offers to settle are served at least seven days before the hearing and are not withdrawn and do not expire before commencement of the hearing.

The chart is not directly applicable if non-monetary relief is involved.

OFFER TO SETTLE COST CONSEQUENCES CHART

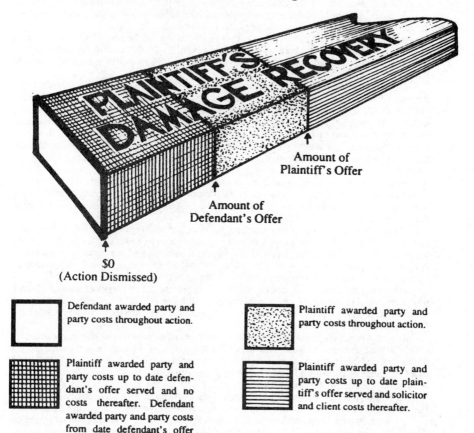

$0
(Action Dismissed)

Defendant awarded party and party costs throughout action.

Plaintiff awarded party and party costs throughout action.

Plaintiff awarded party and party costs up to date defendant's offer served and no costs thereafter. Defendant awarded party and party costs from date defendant's offer served.

Plaintiff awarded party and party costs up to date plaintiff's offer served and solicitor and client costs thereafter.

PRACTICE DIRECTION
Toronto Region

ALTERNATIVE DISPUTE RESOLUTION PILOT PROJECT

In order to provide litigants with a timely and cost-effective alternative to the conventional means of resolving civil disputes, the Ontario Court of Justice (General Division) and the Ministry of the Attorney General have initiated a two year pilot project under which court-based Alternative Dispute Resolution ("A.D.R.") services are being offered in Toronto Region. The project is being funded through the Ministry of the Attorney General's "Investment Strategy", which aims to strategically add resources to the Ontario justice system.

This pilot project has been designed and is being implemented by a steering committee comprised of members of the Court, representatives of the Bar and Ministry officials. An A.D.R. Users' Committee has been convened and meets regularly with the Court's representatives to consider improvements to the project's operation.

A facility known as the A.D.R. Centre has been established at 77 Grenville Street, Toronto, which can be contacted by telephone at (416) 314-8355 and by fax at (416) 314-8483. All filings required at the A.D.R. Centre may be made by fax in accordance with the *Rules of Civil Procedure.*

Commencing in 1994, new civil cases commenced in this Region, cases already in the Region's civil inventory and matters emanating from the Commercial List may be referred to the A.D.R. Centre. Construction lien matters may be referred by the masters. Referral may occur at any point subsequent to the filing of a statement of defence. Where all parties consent and to the extent that resources permit, cases not previously referred to the A.D.R. Centre may be referred to it. A stand-by list has been established for this purpose. It is not anticipated that in its initial stages, this project will deal with motor vehicle negligence or family law cases.

When a referral has been made, counsel are obliged to certify that all parties represented were immediately provided with a copy of the Memorandum to Parties (Form 5) which came to counsel attached to the Notice of Referral, and advised as to the availability and nature of A.D.R. processes.

Cases selected will receive a mediation session of up to three hours conducted by either dispute resolution officers or judges. In order to assist them in providing these services, the judges participating in the project and the dispute resolution officers have been trained in A.D.R. techniques. The primary technique in use at the Centre is mediation, supplemented by neutral evaluation and, when long trials are anticipated, mini-trials.

Alternatively, the parties may choose to utilize private A.D.R. services instead of those provided by the Court, in which case the parties will be responsible for fees charged by the private A.D.R. service providers. A directory of private A.D.R. service providers is available for perusal at the A.D.R. Centre.

If a case is not resolved after using the A.D.R. process, it will continue in the ordinary course to trial. Pursuant to Rule 48.07(c) of the Rules of Civil Procedure and paragraph 7.1 of this Practice Direction, those cases will proceed to trial on the filing with the A.D.R. Centre of a Certificate of Inability to Resolve (Form 4) prescribed by this Practice Direction. Cases referred to the A.D.R. Centre and not proceeded with by the parties within six months of referral will be returned to the litigation track and a Certificate of Default placed in the court file. This may be referred to at the final disposition of the litigation, in speaking to costs.

At least 10 days before attending at the A.D.R. Centre, the parties or counsel acting on their behalf are required to meet and confer about the dispute to narrow the issues and to attempt to settle. If the dispute is not settled at that pre-session conference, the parties are required to submit a joint Statement of Issues in the prescribed form (Form 2), identifying the factual and legal issues in dispute. The purpose is not to duplicate the pleadings but to briefly set out each party's best case, and to list any documents of central importance to the case. It would be a very unusual case where more than three issues or five documents are identified. This Statement of Issues, any appended material, and the Confidentiality Agreement required to be signed (Form 3) will form the basis for the A.D.R. Session. If settlement is achieved at the pre-session conference or at any time before the scheduled A.D.R. Session, the A.D.R. Centre should be advised forthwith by fax in order to enable other litigants to utilize the three-hour appointment.

Parties and their counsel or in-house counsel are expected to attend the A.D.R. Session. It is of central importance that the parties attend in person to maximize the effectiveness of the mediation. If the party representative attending the session does not have full authority to settle the dispute, arrangements must be made prior to the session for ready telephone access to the decision-maker for the entire duration of the session, including after regular office hours. The benefits of the mediation process include face to face meetings, assessments, attempts at persuasion and sharing of interests by the parties. Without the right parties in attendance, the process is compromised from the outset.

Only in the most exceptional cases should counsel attend without their clients, and then only with the consent of the other parties and the consent of the Project Director, obtained at least 10 days before the A.D.R. Session. Consent of the Project Director will be granted only in circumstances where counsel are able to give assurances of their full authority to settle the case including full autonomy to consider a wide range of non-monetary options for settlement. If the required consents are not obtained in a timely fashion and counsel attends the A.D.R. Session without a party representative, that counsel may be required to appear before the presiding Commercial List judge at the A.D.R. Centre to explain the failure to obtain the requisite consents. A Certificate of Default will be issued by the Project Director, which may be used in speaking to costs following final disposition of the action. The schedule A.D.R. Session will not proceed in the absence of the party representative.

It will be rescheduled at an early date consented to by counsel and the parties, or ordered by the presiding judge.

It is the joint responsibility of all counsel and unrepresented parties to find a mutually agreeable date for the A.D.R. Session. While it is also the joint responsibility of counsel for the parties to confirm at least seven days before the date of the scheduled session, that the A.D.R. Session is to proceed as scheduled, either party may confirm that the session is proceeding, or is being adjourned as set out below, and that the Statement of Issues has been filed. If neither party confirms that the session is to proceed, the documents pertaining to the session will not be forwarded to the judge or dispute resolution officer assigned, and the session will not proceed on the date scheduled. A Certificate of Default will be issued by the Project Director and placed in the court file. All parties and counsel with carriage of the case may be required to attend before a judge to give an explanation for the default. Counsel may indicate Confirmation of Attendance by delivery or fax of Form 6 to the A.D.R. Centre, with a simultaneous copy to opposing counsel. Counsel for either party is to advise the A.D.R. Centre if he or she has been unable to obtain the co-operation of opposing counsel in respect to the above information, and so indicate on Form 6.

Written adjournment requests received at least ten days before the scheduled session, to a fixed date within three months of the session, provided by and consented to by the parties, will be accommodated by the A.D.R. Centre. Adjournment requests in the week preceding the scheduled A.D.R. Session may be denied by the Project Director. Adjournment requests made within two working days of the session will not normally be granted. Application for late adjournments are subject to a cancellation fee and must be made in person by counsel with carriage of the case to the presiding judge of the Commercial List at the A.D.R. Centre on the closest 9:30 a.m. motion day. Appointments with the Commercial List judge must be booked with the scheduling co-ordinator of the A.D.R. Centre on notice to all counsel and unrepresented parties. If a timely adjournment is not sought as prescribed, and counsel and/ or parties do not appear at the scheduled time and date of the A.D.R. Session, a cancellation fee will be levied and a Certificate of Default will be issued and placed in the court file.

It is not anticipated that the power to award costs pursuant to s. 141 of the *Courts of Justice Act* and Rule 57 of the *Rules of Civil Procedure* will be exercised in relation to A.D.R. Sessions attended by the parties and counsel appearing on their behalf. When a Certificate of Default has been issued, it may be taken into account in speaking to costs following the final disposition of the action.

This pilot project is designed to provide enhanced, more timely and more cost-effective access to justice for both defendants and plaintiffs. Ultimately, its success will depend on the co-operation of all parties to a dispute, and their counsel.

The procedures applicable to the pilot project are set out below.

July 31, 1995

THE HONOURABLE R. ROY McMURTRY
CHIEF JUSTICE OF THE ONTARIO COURT

THE HONOURABLE A.G. CAMPBELL
REGIONAL SENIOR JUSTICE

Alternative Dispute Resolution Pilot Project Procedures

1. Definitions

1.1   In this Practice Direction,

1. "alternative dispute resolution" or "A.D.R." refers to a range of processes designed to aid parties in resolving their disputes outside of a formal judicial proceeding. These processes include but are not limited to mediation, neutral evaluation and mini-trial;
2. "A.D.R. Centre" refers to the court-based Alternative Dispute Resolution Centre established pursuant to this Practice Direction;
3. "A.D.R. Session" refers principally to a mediation presided over by either a judge of the Court or a dispute resolution officer, and attended by counsel and parties to a dispute to which this Practice Direction applies;
4. "mediation" is a process in which a judge of the Court or a dispute resolution officer facilitates communication between parties to assist them in reaching a mutually acceptable resolution of that dispute;
5. "dispute resolution officer" means a person other than a judge, providing A.D.R. services through the A.D.R. Centre;
6. "'neutral evaluation" is a process in which a judge of the Court or a dispute resolution officer evaluates the relative strengths and weaknesses of the positions advanced by the parties, and the probable outcome at trial, and advises the parties accordingly; and
7. "mini-trial" is a process in which opposing counsel present their best case to the parties and to a judge of the Court who moderates the presentations and renders a non-binding opinion as to the probable resolution of the dispute after a trial.

2. Referral to A.D.R. Centre

2.1 At any time after the delivery of a statement of defence, new civil actions commenced in Toronto Region and cases already in the Region's civil inventory, including the Commercial List, may be referred to the A.D.R. Centre upon notice to counsel for the parties, or where the parties are not represented, to the parties themselves.

2.2 The notice referred to in subparagraph 2.1 shall be in Form 1 and it shall be served on counsel along with a Form 5 Memorandum to Parties. Copies of both shall be placed in the court file for the case.

2.3 Upon receipt of a notice in Form 1, counsel for a party shall immediately give a copy of the Memorandum to Parties (Form 5) to his/her client. Counsel is expected to fully advise his/her client as to the availability and nature of A.D.R. processes and will be obliged to certify that his/her client has been so provided and advised by faxing to the A.D.R. Centre an executed copy of Page 1 of the Memorandum to Parties.

3. Choice Between Court-Based and Private A.D.R. Services

3.1 Nothing in this practice direction limits the ability of litigants to resort to private A.D.R. service providers as a means of resolving disputes of the nature described in paragraph 2, and in fact, resort to such services is encouraged. An A.D.R. Session held before a private provider will, upon completion of Form 4 or the settlement of the action and written confirmation to the A.D.R. Centre, as the case may be, completely satisfy the requirement to have an A.D.R. Session in the matter.

3.2 A directory of those indicating a willingness to provide private A.D.R. services is available for perusal at the A.D.R. Centre.

4. Procedure Where Case Referred to the A.D.R. Centre

4.1 At least 10 days before attending an A.D.R. Session, the parties or counsel acting on their behalf are required to meet and confer about the dispute to narrow the issues and attempt to settle.

4.2 If the dispute is not resolved, the parties shall submit a joint Statement of Issues (Form 2), confirming that they have met and conferred about the dispute, identifying the factual and legal issues in dispute, briefly setting out each party's best case, and listing any documents which are of central importance to the case.

4.3 It is the obligation of all parties that the Statement of Issues (Form 2) is filed with the A.D.R. Centre at least 7 days prior to the attendance together with a confirmation of attendance (Form 6). In default of filing Form 2 and Form 6 as required, the case may be struck from the A.D.R. Centre list, a cancellation fee may be levied, and a Certificate of Default issued and placed in the court file.

4.4 Parties and their counsel or in-house counsel are expected to attend the A.D.R. Session. It is of central importance that the parties attend in person to maximize the effectiveness of the mediation. If the party litigant attending the session does not have full and final authority to settle the dispute, arrangements must be made prior to the session for ready telephone access to the decision maker for the entire duration of the session, including after regular office hours. The benefits of the mediation process include face to face meetings, assessments, attempts at persuasion and sharing of interests by the parties. Without the right parties in attendance, the process is compromised from the outset.

4.5 Only in the most exceptional cases should counsel attend without their clients, and then only with the consent of other parties and the consent of the Project Director, obtained at least ten days before the A.D.R. Session. Consent of the Project Director will be granted only in circumstances where counsel are able to give assurances of their full authority to settle the case including full autonomy to consider a wide range of non-monetary options for settlement. If the required consents are not obtained in a timely fashion and counsel attends the A.D.R. Session without a party representative, that counsel will be required to appear before the presiding Commercial Court judge at the A.D.R. Centre to explain the failure to obtain the consents. The scheduled A.D.R. Session will not proceed in the absence of the party representative. It will be rescheduled at an early date consented to by counsel and the parties or ordered by the presiding judge.

4.6 Written adjournment requests received 10 days before the scheduled session, to a fixed date within 3 months of the session, consented to by the parties, will be accommodated by the A.D.R. Centre. Adjournment requests in the week preceding the scheduled A.D.R. Session may be denied by the Project Director. Adjournment requests made within two working days of the session will not normally be granted. Application for such an adjournment must be made in person by counsel with carriage of the case to the presiding judge of the Commercial List at the A.D.R. Centre on the closest 9:30 a.m. motion day. Appointments with the Commercial List judge must be booked with the scheduling co-ordinator of the A.D.R. Centre on notice to all counsel and unrepresented parties. The party requesting the late adjournment will be required to pay a cancellation fee. If an adjournment is not sought as prescribed, and counsel and/or parties do not appear at the scheduled time and date of the A.D.R. Session, a cancellation fee will be levied against each party not appearing, and a Certificate of Default will be issued and placed in the court file.

4.7 A.D.R. Sessions shall be presided over by a judge of the court or by a dispute resolution officer.

4.8 If after the pre-session conference and after forwarding to the A.D.R. Centre proof of service of the Memorandum to Parties, the parties all agree that an A.D.R. Session is unlikely to succeed, they may opt out of the A.D.R. process by executing and filing a request to opt out in Form 4 with the A.D.R. centre at least 10 days prior to the scheduled A.D.R. Session. A cancellation fee may be levied against each party for requests made in the week preceding the scheduled A.D.R. Session. Requests to opt out made within 2 working days of the session will be subject to a cancellation fee. The latter requests must be made in person by all counsel with carriage of the case, in the presence of all the parties, to the presiding judge of the Commercial List at the A.D.R. Centre on the closest 9:30 a.m. motion day. Appointments with the Commercial List judge must be booked with the scheduling co-ordinator at the A.D.R. Centre on notice to all counsel and unrepresented parties.

4.9 If it is determined in the A.D.R. Session that neutral evaluation would be an appropriate step in resolving the dispute, counsel with the assistance of the mediator will set out the one or two issues to be referred to the neutral evaluator on Form 8. The parties will be required to forward to the A.D.R. Centre at least 7 days before the scheduled date a memorandum of no more than 10 pages, double spaced, setting out the argument in support of the issue(s) to be evaluated. Highlighted excerpts from the one or two relevant cases should also be provided. The adjournment provisions found in paragraph 4.6 will apply.

4.10 Upon receipt of Form 8, the A.D.R. Centre will schedule a 45 minute session before a judge/neutral evaluator to consider the issue(s) presented. In that session counsel will present the core of the case in the presence of the parties. The neutral evaluator then gives a candid assessment of the strengths and weaknesses of the case. If settlement does not result, the case is returned to the litigation track by filing Form 4 as set out in para. 7.1(b).

5.0 Confidentiality of Proceedings/Immunity of Neutrals

5.1 Prior to participating in an A.D.R. session, the parties are required to enter into and file at the A.D.R. Centre an agreement in Form 3, indicating their agreement that

(a) statements made and documents produced in an A.D.R. Session or in the pre-session conference, and not otherwise discoverable, are not subject to disclosure through discovery or any other process and are not admissible into evidence for any purpose, including impeaching credibility,

(b) the notes, record, and recollections of the judge or dispute resolution officer conducting the A.D.R. Session are confidential and protected from disclosure for all purposes, and

(c) the judge or dispute resolution officer conducting the A.D.R. session has the immunity described in s. 82 of the *Courts of Justice Act*, with necessary changes to points of detail.

5.2 Users of private A.D.R. services may wish to enter into express agreements addressing, among other things, the matters described in paragraph 5.1, clauses (a) and (b).

6.0 Recording the Outcome of the A.D.R. Session

6.1 If an agreement to resolve the dispute is reached, it shall be reduced to writing and signed by the parties or their counsel. The parties shall provide written notice of the resolution of the case to the A.D.R. Centre within 10 days of the agreement and the agreement may be filed with the Court. The parties shall then take appropriate steps to dispose of the action.

6.2 A written settlement agreement concluded by the parties at an A.D.R. Session is deemed to be an Offer to Settle which has been accepted within the meaning of Rule 49 of the *Rules of Civil Procedure*.

6.3 If the parties do not reach any agreement to resolve the dispute as a result of the A.D.R. Session, no record of the A.D.R. Session shall be available to the trial judge other than the Certificate of Inability to Resolve through A.D.R. in Form 4, referred to in paragraph 7.1.

7.0 Proceeding to Trial Where No Resolution is Reached

7.1 A case which has been referred to the A.D.R. Centre may proceed to trial only where one of the following certificates has been filed as stated below, along with proof that the certificate has been given to all parties:

(a) if an A.D.R. Session has not yet been held, a Certificate of Inability to Resolve through A.D.R. (Form 4) has been executed on behalf of all parties and filed at the A.D.R. Centre; or

(b) if an A.D.R. Session has been held, a Certificate of Inability to Resolve through A.D.R. (Form 4) has been executed on behalf of at least one of the parties and by their counsel and filed at the A.D.R. Centre; or

(c) if an A.D.R. Session has not yet been held within six months of the date of the Notice of Referral, the Project Director has issued a Certificate of Default, placed it in the court file, and the case is then returned to the litigation track.

7.2 Notwithstanding paragraph 7.1, clause (b), where an A.D.R. Session has been held and it is possible to do so, the parties are encouraged to file a joint Certificate of Inability to Resolve through A.D.R. in Form 4.

8.0 Users' Committee

8.1 A Users' Committee has been established, consisting of practitioners and parties familiar with A.D.R. and appointed by the Chief Justice of the Ontario Court. The names of members of the Users' Committee may be obtained from the A.D.R. Centre. The Users' Committee meets regularly with representatives of the judges involved in the pilot project to consider improvements to the organization and operation of the pilot project and to make recommendations to the Chief Justice in that regard. The Users' Committee welcomes suggestions, compliments and complaints from other practitioners who have had cases referred to the A.D.R. Centre.

This Practice Direction concerning the Alternative Dispute Resolution Pilot Project becomes effective on September 5, 1995.

Osgoode Hall   The Honourable R. Roy McMurtry
August 8, 1995   Chief Justice of the Ontario Court

FORM 1
(*General Heading*)
NOTICE OF REFERRAL TO THE A.D.R. CENTRE

The parties are notified that the action described above has been referred to the Alternative Dispute Resolution ("A.D.R.") Centre of the Ontario Court of Justice (General Division), for an A.D.R. Session. The A.D.R. Session will take place at the A.D.R. Centre, 8th Floor, 77 Grenville Street, Toronto, on _____, 199__, at _____:_____.m.

Another date can be arranged by immediately faxing to the Centre a date no more than 3 months away which is agreed to by all parties.

The A.D.R. Session will be conducted under the authority of the Practice Direction from the Chief Justice relating to the Alternative Dispute Resolution Pilot Project published in the Ontario Reports. The purpose of this initiative is to provide additional court services and significantly improve access to justice.

NOTE: Paragraph 2.3 of the Practice Direction requires that upon receipt of this Notice, **counsel shall immediately give a copy of the Memorandum to Parties (Form 5) to his/her client and file the completed certification (Form 5, p. 1) with the A.D.R. Centre**

At least ten days before attending at the A.D.R. Centre, the parties or their counsel are required to meet and confer about the dispute, to narrow the issues and to attempt to settle. If no settlement results from the pre-session meeting, **at least 7 days prior** to the A.D.R. Session the parties must file with the A.D.R. Centre a joint statement in Form 2, briefly identifying the factual and legal issues in dispute, setting out their best case and listing any documents which they consider to be of central importance to the case. In order to avoid a cancellation fee, a Confirmation of Attendance (Form 6) or a Certificate of Inability to Resolve (Form 4) must also be filed at this time.

Parties to the litigation are expected to attend the A.D.R. Session in person along with their counsel or in-house counsel in order to maximize the effectiveness of the mediation. It is also important that the party litigant attend with full autonomy to consider a wide range of options for settlement. If the party litigant attending the session does not have full and final authority to settle the dispute, arrangements must be made prior to the session for ready telephone access to the decision-maker for the entire duration of the session, including after regular office hours. The benefits of the mediation process include face to face meetings, assessments, attempts at persuasion and sharing of interests by the parties. Without the right parties in attendance, the process is compromised from the outset.

Only in the most exceptional cases should counsel attend without their clients, and then only with the consent of the other parties and the consent of the Project Director, obtained **at least 10 days before** the A.D.R. Session. Consent of the Project Director will be granted only in circumstances where counsel are able to give assurances of their full authority to settle the case including full autonomy to consider a wife range of non-monetary options for settlement. If the required consents are not obtained in a timely fashion and counsel attends the A.D.R. Session without a party representative, that counsel will be required to appear before the presiding Commercial List judge at the A.D.R. Centre to explain the failure to obtain the requisite consents, a Certificate of Default will be issued and a cancellation fee may be levied. The A.D.R. Session will not proceed in the absence of the party representative. It will be rescheduled at an early date consented to by counsel and the parties, or ordered by the presiding judge.

Prior to an A.D.R. Session, the parties must file with the A.D.R. Centre a Confidentiality Agreement (Form 3), which is designed to protect the parties' interests in the event that the action proceeds to trial.

As an alternative to attending at the A.D.R. Centre, the parties may choose a private A.D.R. service provider at their own expense.

Documents to be filed at the A.D.R. Centre may be filed by fax at (416) 314-8483.

FORM 2
(General Heading)

PARTIES' JOINT STATEMENT IN ANTICIPATION OF A.D.R. SESSION

(File at the A.D.R. Centre at least 7 days prior to the A.D.R. Session along with Form 6 Confirmation of Attendance)

The parties or counsel acting on their behalf have met and have conferred about the dispute but have been unable to resolve it.

The parties state that the following legal and factual issues remain to be resolved (*Please be brief*):

1. _____
2. _____
3. _____
4. _____

In separate appendices to this form, each of the parties has stated his, her or its case at its best and has listed any key documents.

Dated:

_____   _____
Counsel for the Plaintiff   Counsel for the Defendant

(signatures of unrepresented and further parties may be attached to this form)

FORM 3
(General Heading)

CONFIDENTIALITY AGREEMENT

The parties will participate in an Alternative Dispute Resolution ("A.D.R.") Session to be conducted in accordance with the Practice Direction regarding the A.D.R. Pilot Project. Through their counsel or individually, the parties agree that:

(a) statements made and documents produced in an A.D.R. Session or in the pre-session conference and not otherwise discoverable are not subject to disclosure through discovery or any other process and are not admissible into evidence for any purpose, including impeaching credibility,

(b) the notes, records, and recollections of the judge or dispute resolution officer conducting the A.D.R. Session are confidential and protected from disclosure for all purposes, and

(c) the judge or dispute resolution officer presiding over the A.D.R. Session has the immunity described in s. 82 of the *Courts of Justice Act*, with necessary changes to points of detail.

Dated:

_____   _____
Counsel for the Plaintiff   Counsel for the Defendant

(signatures of unrepresented and further parties may be attached to this form)

FORM 4
(General Heading)

CERTIFICATE OF INABILITY TO RESOLVE THROUGH A.D.R.

(File at the A.D.R. Centre with proof that all parties and counsel served)

Through their counsel, the parties certify that they have been advised by their counsel of the availability of a range of processes known as Alterative Dispute Resolution ("A.D.R."), designed to aid parties in resolving their disputes outside of a formal judicial proceeding, and of the existence of the court-based A.D.R. Centre where the court has offered them that settlement assistance.

The parties further certify that A.D.R. techniques: (check one)

[ ] have been considered but are unlikely to succeed and wish to cancel the session scheduled for them at the A.D.R. Centre; or

[ ] have been tried and have not succeeded in resolving the dispute.

If this form is received more than 48 hours [excluding weekends and holidays] prior to the scheduled session, no cancellation fee will be charged.

The parties therefore request that this action proceed to trial and estimate that the trial will take ___ court days.

The parties further state that it is anticipated that the following legal or factual issues will remain to be determined at trial: (additional issues may be attached)

1. _____

2. _____

3. _____

4. _____

Dated:

_____   _____
Counsel for the Plaintiff   Counsel for the Defendant

(*signatures of unrepresented and further parties may be attached to this form*)

_____

FORM 5

Ontario Court (General Division) **Alternative Dispute Resolution Centre**
77 Grenville Street, 8th Floor
Toronto, Ontario, M5S 1B3

(*General Heading*)

MEMORANDUM TO PARTIES

> Counsel hereby certifies that this memo was provided to his/her client on, _____,
> 199__ at _____
>   (give party's address, not that of counsel)
>
>   _____
>   Counsel for Plaintiff/defendant (Circle one)

Your case has been scheduled for a **three-hour** A.D.R. Session on _____,
199__ at ___:___ ___.m. at the A.D.R. Centre at 77 Grenville Street, Suite 800, Toronto.

The A.D.R. Centre pilot project is designed to provide enhanced, more timely and more cost-effective access to justice for both defendants and plaintiffs. Ultimately its success will depend on the co-operation of all parties to any dispute, and their counsel.

A.D.R. means *Alternative Dispute Resolution*, and it is an alternative to trial. At the A.D.R. Centre you will be given the opportunity to participate in a mediation session conducted by a court-appointed mediator or judge (the "mediator"). Mediation is, quite simply, assisted negotiation. The purpose of the session is to provide the parties with the opportunity to reach their own mutually acceptable resolution of the issues in dispute. The mediator assists the parties by structuring the negotiation and maintaining the channels of communication. The mediator has no decision-making authority. If a settlement is reached among the parties, the official court process is terminated.

If no settlement is reached, the case continues to trial in the ordinary way. Negotiations and settlements, if any, are private among the parties. Discussions are not subject to examination at trial. Before coming to the session, you must sign a Confidentiality Agreement (Form 3) which is designed to protect your interests in the event that no settlement is achieved and the case proceeds to trial.

As part of the mediation process, other dispute resolution options are available. **Neutral evaluations** is a process in which a judge evaluates the relative strengths and weaknesses of the case, and gives the parties an opinion as to the probable outcome at trial.

As a party you are expected to attend the A.D.R. Session in person, along with your counsel or in-house counsel, in order to maximize the effectiveness of the mediation. It is also important that you come with full authority to consider a wide range of options for settlement. If you do not have full and final authority to settle the case, you must make arrangements before the session for easy telephone access to the decision-maker for the entire duration of the session, including after regular office hours. Feel free to bring with you anyone who would assist you in coming to a decision to settle your case.

The objective of the A.D.R. Centre is to facilitate access to the justice system by contributing to the productivity and effectiveness of the system. You can help in two ways:

1.   Accept responsibility to participate in the mediation session. You have the opportunity to resolve this dispute. Seek the support of your lawyer in negotiating the resolution of the dispute. Contact the other parties at an early date and test their commitment to the process. The A.D.R. Centre may be in a position to schedule your mediation session at an earlier date.

2.   If you really do not want to resolve your dispute by mediation, then discuss this with your lawyer and the other parties at an early date and have your lawyer notify the A.D.R. Centre so that your 3-hour session can be used by others.

If an adjournment is requested by any party within 2 working days of the session, you and your lawyer and the other parties with their lawyers will all have to appear before a judge to state your reasons for the late adjournment. The judge may turn down the request. **A cancellation fee, to be paid by the requesting party, applies to all late adjournment requests.**

FORM 6
(General Heading)

CONFIRMATION OF ATTENDANCE AT A.D.R. CENTRE

(Fax at least 7 days prior to A.D.R. Session)

[ ] The parties and their counsel confirm their attendance at the A.D.R. Session scheduled for _____, 199__.

[ ] Counsel for the plaintiff/defendant (circle one) advise that no confirmation of attendance can be given because of a lack of co-operation [ ] or lack of response [ ] from opposing counsel. My client and I are available [ ] not available [ ] to attend the scheduled A.D.R. Session.

[ ] The Statement of Issues is filed herewith. (If no co-operation, file your own).

[ ] The session is not proceeding because: (check one only)
- parties have opted out and Form 4 has been filed   [ ]
- adjournment on consent to _____ [ ]
- opposed adjournment to be requested by plaintiff/defendant (circle one) and 9:30 a.m. appointment before a judge
- requested for _____ [ ]

Dated:

_____
Counsel's Name (Please print)

_____
Counsel's Signature

_____
Phone Number

_____
Fax Number

To: A.D.R. Centre
Fax (416) 314-8483
CC: Opposing Counsel

No transmittal page required.

FORM 7
(General Heading)

CERTIFICATE OF DEFAULT

I, CHRISTINE E. HART, Director of the Alternative Dispute Resolution Pilot Project, hereby certify that:

1. This case was referred to the A.D.R. Centre and notice was properly given to counsel for the parties or, where the parties are not represented, to unrepresented parties.

2. Counsel for the plaintiff/defendant (circle one) failed to comply with the requirements of the pilot project Practice Direction as follows:

    [   ] failed to certify service on client of Memorandum to Parties (para 2.3)

    [   ] failed to meet about the dispute to narrow the issues and to attempt settlement prior to the A.D.R. Session (para 4.1)

    [   ] failed to co-operate in providing a joint statement of issues (para. 4.2, 4.3)

    [   ] failed to attend the A.D.R. Session with a person having authority to settle the dispute as required by paragraphs 4.4 and 4.5.

    [   ] failed to attend the A.D.R. Session without appropriate notice (para. 4.3, 4.6, 4.8)

    [   ] failed to convene the A.D.R. Session within 6 months of referral (para. 7.1(c))

3. The plaintiff/defendant attended the scheduled A.D.R. Session but after 30 minutes no one appeared for the plaintiff/defendant.

Dated:

Director, A.D.R. Pilot Project

FORM 8
(General Heading)

ISSUES FOR NEUTRAL EVALUATOR

(To be filed by the mediator at the conclusion of the mediation session)

The parties and counsel acting on their behalf have participated in a mediation session and believe that a neutral evaluation by a judge on the one or two outstanding issues will assist them in concluding a settlement of the dispute. To assist the court they have indicated their availability for a 45-minute session on the following dates:

1. _____
2. _____
3. _____

The parties state with the assistance of the mediator that the following issues are to be submitted to the neutral evaluator for an opinion, (*Please be brief*)

1. _____
2. _____

The session will not proceed unless supporting argument is filed at least 7 days before the scheduled date as set out in paragraphs 4.9 and 4.10 of the Practice Direction.

Dated:

_____   _____
Counsel for the Plaintiff   Counsel for the Defendant

(*signatures of unrepresented and further parties may be attached to this form*)

DEFINITIONS

49.01 In rules 49.02 to 49.14,
"defendant" includes a respondent;
"plaintiff" includes an applicant.

WHERE AVAILABLE

49.02(1) A party to a proceeding may serve on any other party an offer to settle any one or more of the claims in the proceeding on the terms specified in the offer to settle (Form 49A).

(2) Subrule (1) and rules 49.03 to 49.14 do not apply to motions, but nothing in this subrule prevents a party from making a proposal for settlement of a motion or the court from taking the proposal into account in making an order in respect of costs.

To Whom and by Whom Offer May be Made

Tan (Litigation Guardian of) v. Diamanti (1995), 41 C.P.C. (3d) 291 (Ont. Gen. Div.).
For a party to a crossclaim to obtain Rule 49 costs consequences an offer to settle must be made identified with the crossclaim.

McKinnon Fuels Ltd. v. Funston (1992), 10 O.R. (3d) 567 (Gen. Div.).
The provisions of Rule 49 pertaining to offers to settle are applicable in actions for the recovery of moneys owing under a mortgage.

J. Friedman Receivers & Trustees Ltd. v. George Wimpey Can. Ltd. (1984), 44 C.P.C. 66 (Ont. Master).
A third party cannot pay moneys into court.

Hoffman v. Longworth, 17 O.R. (2d) 47, 4 C.P.C. 134, [1978] I.L.R. 1-929 (C.A.).
An insurer made a third party pursuant to the *Insurance Act* may pay money into court.

McKinnon v. Thompson, [1962] O.W.N. 134 (H.C.).

A payment into court may be made notwithstanding that the plaintiff is under disability. [*And see now rule 49.08 — Authors.*]

Terms of Offer (See rule 49.02(1) and Form 49A.)

Skinner v. Royal Victoria Hospital, (May 10, 1993), Doc. 15953/86, additional reasons (1995), 35 C.P.C. (3d) 290 (Ont. Gen. Div.).

It is doubtful that a proposal to agree to quantum of damages and litigate only liability issues is an "offer to settle" within the meaning of Rule 49.

Smith v. Canada (1993), 13 O.R. (3d) 215 (Gen. Div.), leave to appeal to Div. Ct. refused (1994), 17 O.R. (3d) 468, 23 Imm. L.R. (2d) 235.

The court may take a settlement proposal into account regarding costs of a motion.

Lamprakos v. Pickering (1987), 63 O.R. (2d) 649 (H.C.).

An offer to settle term regarding party and party costs as assessed or agreed was interpreted as including costs to the date of acceptance of the offer.

Di Nardo v. Palermo (1983), 42 O.R. (2d) 524, 36 C.P.C. 258 (H.C.).

The defendant had paid a sum into court without specifying an allocation thereof as between claims or causes of action. The statement of defence set out such an allocation. The court dismissed the plaintiff's motion for payment out of one of the specified sums, without prejudice to the plaintiff's right to apply to strike out the notice of payment into court.

Ross v. Martin, [1966] 2 O.R. 306 (H.C.).

The failure to state the proportion of a payment into court allocated to each of several claims is an irregularity which does not prevent an award of costs to the payor.

Britnell v. Macfie Explorations Ltd., [1954] O.W.N. 889 (H.C.).

The notice need not specify the amounts attributable to property damage, personal injury or other constituent elements of the claim.

Bickerton v. Caughell, [1946] O.W.N. 841 (Master).

Where the defendant paid money into court but did not specify which cause it was in respect of the notice of payment in was struck out.

Form of Offer and Acceptance

Johnson & Johnson Inc. v. Bristol-Myers Squibb Canada Inc. (January 23, 1996), Doc. Toronto 94-CQ-58779 (Ont. Gen. Div.).

A proposal to settle a motion need not be in writing to form the basis for a solicitor and client costs award.

Veilleux v. Ranger (1995), 25 O.R. (3d) 759 (Gen. Div.).

An oral offer is incapable of being served pursuant to rule 49.02.

John Logan Chevrolet Oldsmobile Inc. v. Baldwin (1994), 28 C.P.C. (3d) 393 (Ont. Gen. Div.).

An oral offer to settle does not attract the costs consequences of Rule 49.

Andani v. Peel (Regional Municipality) (1993), 66 O.A.C. 137 (C.A.), leave to appeal to Supreme Court of Canada refused (1994), 71 O.A.C. 78 (note), 179 N.R. 320 (note).

Although the plaintiffs' written offer of settlement contained a provision which gave the plaintiffs the option of placing all or part of the settlement funds in a structured settlement, the offer was still properly viewed as a settlement offer within Rule 49.

Pollard v. Pollard (1992), 4 W.D.C.P. (2d) 58 (Ont. Gen. Div.).

An oral settlement offer may not form the foundation for an award of solicitor and client costs on an interim family law motion. A written offer is necessary.

Bruce v. DPCE Computer Services Inc. (1992), 10 O.R. (3d) 630, 42 C.C.E.L. 233 (Gen. Div.).

No slavish conformity with the forms prescribed in the Rules is necessary to accept offers to settle.

Lindsay Paper Box Co. v. Schubert International Manufacturing Inc. (1992), 8 O.R. (3d) 437 (Gen. Div.).

An offer to settle does not have to be in the form prescribed by Rule 49 in order to be effective.

Leffen v. Zellers Inc. (1986), 9 C.P.C. (2d) 149 (Ont. H.C.).

An offer of settlement may be made in correspondence between counsel. The prescribed forms are guides only.

Owen Commercial Equip. Ltd. v. Gen. Motors of Can. Ltd. (1985), 49 O.R. (2d) 647, 49 C.P.C. 58 (Master).

Where funds had been paid into court in satisfaction prior to the Rules of Civil Procedure coming into force, the court permitted the defendants to substitute an offer to settle in the same amount and, if the plaintiff did not accept the offer within 20 days, the funds were to be paid out of court to the defendants.

Roach v. Roach (1985), 49 O.R. (2d) 684, 50 C.P.C. 302 (Dist. Ct.).

The court enforced a settlement based on an offer and acceptance contained in letters. It may well be that the use of the prescribed forms is permissive and that any written or proven verbal offer and acceptance are effective. [*See Acadia Hotels Ltd. v. Smith, 43 B.C.L.R. 202, 34 C.P.C. 50, [1983] 6 W.W.R. 462, 149 D.L.R. (3d) 15 (B.C. C.A.) regarding a verbal revocation of an offer — Authors.*]

TIME FOR MAKING OFFER

49.03 An offer to settle may be made at any time, but where the offer to settle is made less than seven days before the hearing commences, the costs consequences referred to in rule 49.10 do not apply.

Veilleux v. Ranger (1995), 25 O.R. (3d) 759 (Gen. Div.).
A late written offer was not perfected by an earlier oral offer.

Bodenhamer v. Bodenhamer (1991), 2 O.R. (3d) 767 (Gen. Div.).

An offer of settlement made prior to commencement of a proceeding does not constitute an offer within the meaning of Rule 49. As the common law governs, if such an offer is rejected, it cannot be accepted at a later date.

WITHDRAWAL OR EXPIRY OF OFFER

Withdrawal
49.04(1) An offer to settle may be withdrawn at any time before it is accepted by serving written notice of withdrawal of the offer on the party to whom the offer was made.

(2) The notice of withdrawal of the offer may be in (Form 49B).

Offer Expiring after Limited Time
(3) Where an offer to settle specifies a time within which it may be accepted and it is not accepted or withdrawn within that time, it shall be deemed to have been withdrawn when the time expires.

Offer Expires when Court Disposes of Claim

(4) An offer may not be accepted after the court disposes of the claim in respect of which the offer is made.

Withdrawal of Offer

Diefenbacher v. Young (1995), 22 O.R. (3d) 641, 123 D.L.R. (4th) 641, 80 O.A.C. 216 (C.A.).
Where a plaintiff serves two offers to settle during the course of a law suit and the second offer is lower than the first and is silent about the first offer, the second offer withdraws the first offer by implication. The situation is similar where a defendant makes two offers, the second of which is higher than the first and is silent about the first offer.

Mortimer v. Cameron (1994), 17 O.R. (3d) 1, 19 M.P.L.R. (2d) 286, 111 D.L.R. (4th) 428, 68 O.A.C. 332, additional reasons (June 24, 1994), Doc. CA C12036 (C.A.), leave to appeal to Supreme Court of Canada refused (1994), 19 O.R. (3d) xvi (note), 23 M.P.L.R. (2d) 314 (note), 114 D.L.R. (4th) vii (note), 178 N.R. 146 (note), 76 O.A.C. 400 (note).
The court held that the plaintiff's making of a second offer, lower than the first offer, did not constitute a withdrawal of the first offer.

Payne v. Scottish & York Insurance Co. (1992), 10 C.P.C. (3d) 222 (Ont. Gen. Div.).
Where the plaintiff accepted an outstanding offer to settle eight months after it was made and three months after the expiry of the applicable limitation period, the court granted judgment in accordance with the terms of the accepted offer. The mere expiration of a limitation period is not sufficient to signify a revocation of an offer.

Smith v. Robinson (1992), 7 O.R. (3d) 550, 4 C.P.C. (3d) 262, 87 D.L.R. (4th) 360 (Gen. Div.).
A written offer made pursuant to Rule 49 can only be withdrawn in writing, not by oral discussions.

Cyanamid of Canada Ltd. v. Bigelow Liptak of Canada Ltd./Bigelow Liptak du Canada Ltée (1991), 43 C.P.C. (2d) 1 (Ont. H.C.).
A second offer to settle, stipulating that the original offer is included in and superseded by the second offer, does not amount to a withdrawal of the first offer.

York North Condominium Corp. No. 5 v. Van Horne Clipper Properties Ltd. (1989), 70 O.R. (2d) 317, 40 C.P.C. (2d) 156, 35 O.A.C. 364 (C.A.).
A written offer to settle may only be withdrawn in writing. *Siluszyk v. Massey-Ferguson Industries Ltd.*, *infra*, overruled.

D & R Equipment Repairs Ltd. v. Mardave Construction Ltd. (1989), 69 O.R. (2d) 48, 35 C.P.C. (2d) 266 (H.C.).
An offer to settle remains open for acceptance until there is a clear and unequivocal oral withdrawal or written withdrawal thereof.

Fraser Inc. v. Aitken (1989), 33 C.P.C. (2d) 46 (Ont. H.C.).
The sudden withdrawal of an offer to settle after commencement of the hearing does not affect the cost consequences of the offer.

Mlodzinska v. Malicki (1987), 63 O.R. (2d) 180, 25 C.P.C. (2d) 26, 27 O.A.C. 199 (Div. Ct.).
Where during the course of trial the defendants' counsel gave the plaintiffs' counsel a notice of withdrawal of an offer a split second before plaintiffs' counsel delivered a notice of acceptance of offer, the court held that the offer had been validly withdrawn. An ambiguous oral statement and gesture by the defendants' counsel was ignored.

Coté v. Scott (1986), 16 C.P.C. (2d) 292 (Ont. H.C.).
A verbal withdrawal of an offer is effective. A statement by counsel for the offeror to counsel for the offeree that the trial would proceed unless an amount, which was greater than the amount in the prior written offer, was paid was held to constitute withdrawal of the prior written offer.

Lefebvre v. Lefebvre (1986), 10 C.P.C. (2d) 97 (Ont. Dist. Ct.).

Where a party advises that he or she is about to serve a written acceptance of an offer to settle, an attempt to withdraw the offer verbally before service of the written acceptance is not effective.

Siluszyk v. Massey-Ferguson Industries Ltd. (1986), 53 O.R. (2d) 509, 7 C.P.C. (2d) 247 (H.C.).

An offer may be withdrawn by an oral statement.

Expiry of Offer

Denison v. M. Loeb Ltd. (1993), 16 O.R. (3d) 130, 24 C.P.C. (3d) 191 (Gen. Div.).

An offer to settle which was open "until the trial of this action" was not revived where a mistrial was declared three days after commencement of trial.

Atikian v. Flitcroft (1989), 34 C.P.C. (2d) 231 (Ont. Dist. Ct.).

Where an offer to settle expired one minute prior to the commencement of trial, the court refused to make a costs order based on the offer.

Gillevet v. Crawford & Co. Ins. Adjusters (1988), 66 O.R. (2d) 665, 31 C.P.C. (2d) 170, 35 C.C.L.I. 49 (Dist. Ct.).

An offer to settle is not revoked by the expiry of the relevant statutory limitation period but it does expire if not accepted within a reasonable time. [*The events in this case predated the Rules of Civil Procedure. The issue regarding expiry of the offer if not accepted within a reasonable time would likely be decided differently under the new Rules — Authors.*]

EFFECT OF OFFER

49.05 An offer to settle shall be deemed to be an offer of compromise made without prejudice.

Messere v. Dacosta (1986), 11 C.P.C. (2d) 266, 43 M.V.R. 159, 23 C.C.L.I. 98, additional reasons February 13, 1987 (Ont. Dist. Ct.).

In a motor vehicle accident claim, settlement discussions with the insurer were held not to be a waiver of the insurer's right to rely on a limitation period, nor did they constitute an admission of liability or undertaking to waive the limitation defence. The insurer was granted summary judgment based on the limitation period.

DISCLOSURE OF OFFER TO COURT

49.06(1) No statement of the fact that an offer to settle has been made shall be contained in any pleading.

(2) Where an offer to settle is not accepted, no communication respecting the offer shall be made to the court at the hearing of the proceeding until all questions of liability and the relief to be granted, other than costs, have been determined.

(3) An offer to settle shall not be filed until all questions of liability and the relief to be granted in the proceeding, other than costs, have been determined.

Ariganello v. Dun & Bradstreet Canada Ltd. (1993), 15 C.P.C. (3d) 121, 46 C.C.E.L. 278 (Ont. Master).

The court permitted the defendant to plead offers to settle made to the plaintiff in this wrongful dismissal case where the plaintiff claimed punitive damages and the defendant did not allege cause.

Lakefront Growers Ltd. v. Inco Ltd. (1989), 34 C.P.C. (2d) 95 (Ont. H.C.).

The plaintiff was permitted to plead previous settlements, without figures, where such settlements might be relevant to injunctive relief claimed by the plaintiff.

Peel Condominium Corp. No. 199 v. Ont. New Home Warranties Plan (1988), 30 C.P.C. (2d) 118, 32 O.A.C. 1 (Div. Ct.).

Settlement negotiations conducted without prejudice may be taken into account by the court where a question of laches is raised as a defence.

Bonneville v. Hyundai Auto Canada Inc. (1988), 24 C.P.C. (2d) 235 (Ont. H.C.).

The court struck out a paragraph of the statement of claim in this wrongful dismissal case pleading that the defendant made an offer of severance pay when the plaintiff was dismissed.

C.I.B.C. v. Val-Dal Construction Ltd. (1987), 63 O.R. (2d) 283, 28 C.P.C. (2d) 87 (Master).

A settlement proposal made prior to the commencement of the action is not governed by rule 49.06, but disclosure of the proposal may be restricted by the common law.

Burke v. Kongskilde Ltd. (1987), 16 C.P.C. (2d) 108 (Ont. Assess. O.), affirmed 21 C.P.C. (2d) 36 (Ont. H.C.).

An offer to settle an assessment of costs may be disclosed to the court after it assesses the bill of costs but before it disposes of the costs of the assessment.

Hartley v. J.B. Food Industries Inc. (1986), 10 C.P.C. (2d) 57 (Ont. H.C.).

Correspondence written in pursuit of an early settlement is privileged and should not be pleaded.

Williamson v. Grant Brown National Leasing Inc. (1986), 54 O.R. (2d) 776, 9 C.P.C. (2d) 169, 11 C.C.E.L. 279 (H.C.).

An oral offer to settle made prior to the commencement of litigation may be pleaded where there has been no formal offer and the oral offer was not made on a without prejudice basis.

Leffen v. Zellers Inc. (1986), 9 C.P.C. (2d) 149 (Ont. H.C.).

An offer to settle is not admissible in evidence except when the court has determined all matters other than costs and may not be disclosed for any other purpose.

Taulbee v. Bowen (1986), 54 O.R. (2d) 763, 9 C.P.C. (2d) 90 (H.C.).

A reference to an offer to settle in material in support of a motion for security for costs was struck out.

Kuyntjes v. Kuyntjes (1984), 45 C.P.C. 32 (Ont. Master).

In this family law proceeding, material filed in support of a motion for a change of venue disclosed details of three offers to settle. The offending paragraphs were ordered struck out, and the offers to settle, which had been filed with the material, were ordered sealed, to be opened only by the court on notice to both counsel. Offers of settlement of several issues must be accepted in the terms offered initially, and remain privileged, even if a counter-offer is at least partially similar.

ACCEPTANCE OF OFFER

Generally

49.07(1) An offer to settle may be accepted by serving an acceptance of offer (Form 49C) on the party who made the offer, at any time before it is withdrawn or the court disposes of the claim in respect of which it is made.

(2) Where a party to whom an offer to settle is made rejects the offer or responds with a counter-offer that is not accepted, the party may thereafter

accept the original offer to settle, unless it has been withdrawn or the court has disposed of the claim in respect of which it was made.

Payment into Court or to Trustee as Term of Offer
(3) An offer by a plaintiff to settle a claim in return for the payment of money by a defendant may include a term that the defendant pay the money into court or to a trustee and the defendant may accept the offer only by paying the money in accordance with the offer and notifying the plaintiff of the payment.

Payment into Court or to Trustee as a Condition of Acceptance
(4) Where a defendant offers to pay money to the plaintiff in settlement of a claim, the plaintiff may accept the offer with the condition that the defendant pay the money into court or to a trustee and, where the offer is so accepted and the defendant fails to pay the money in accordance with the acceptance, the plaintiff may proceed as provided in rule 49.09 for failure to comply with the terms of an accepted offer.

Costs
(5) Where an accepted offer to settle does not provide for the disposition of costs, the plaintiff is entitled,
    (a) where the offer was made by the defendant, to the plaintiff's costs assessed to the date the plaintiff was served with the offer; or
    (b) where the offer was made by the plaintiff, to the plaintiff's costs assessed to the date that the notice of acceptance was served.

Incorporating into Judgment
(6) Where an offer is accepted, the court may incorporate any of its terms into a judgment.

Payment out of Court
(7) Where money is paid into court under subrule (3) or (4), it may be paid out on consent or by order.

Acceptance of Offer — Generally

McNeil, Mantha Inc. v. Menzies (1992), 12 C.P.C. (3d) 217 (Ont. Gen. Div.).
Where the defendant's written offer to settle was accepted, subject to an oral agreement to change the date on which payment was to be made, the acceptance was binding on the defendant.

McDougall v. McDougall (1992), 7 O.R. (3d) 732, 6 C.P.C. (3d) 308 (Gen. Div.).
A settlement proposal in the form of a letter which complies with the essential requirements of rule 49.02 should be treated as an offer to settle under the Rules, not as a common law offer. Accordingly it does not expire if there is a counter-offer, but rather remains open for acceptance. As a matter of policy, Rule 49 should apply unless a litigant expressly opts out of that regime.

Chruszczyk v. Gerrie (Litigation Guardian of) (1991), 6 C.P.C. (3d) 337 (Ont. Gen. Div.).
The intention of the offeror when the offer was made determines whether some offerees can accept the offer and settle their claims while other offerees proceed with the litigation. In the case the offer was construed as being a single offer, not a separate offer to each plaintiff.

Meadowfield Ventures Inc. v. Kennedy (1990), 75 O.R. (2d) 760, 45 C.P.C. (2d) 113, 42 O.A.C. 319 (C.A.).

Rule 49.07(2) does not apply to an offer made pending appeal. Such an offer is terminated by a counter-offer or a rejection.

Szebelledy v. Constitution Ins. Co. of Can. (1986), 19 C.P.C. (2d) 197 (Ont. Dist. Ct.).

The assessment of damages and the apportionment of liability by the jury constitute an effective disposition of the plaintiff's claim. An offer to settle may not be accepted after the jury makes such findings even though the offer has not been formally withdrawn.

459853 Ont. Ltd. v. Ameristar Properties Inc. (1986), 12 C.P.C. (2d) 213 (Ont. Dist. Ct.).

If a party adds a time-limit to the condition permitted by rule 49.07(4), a counter-offer is created.

Re Desanto and Cretzman (1986), 53 O.R. (2d) 732, 8 C.P.C. (2d) 191 (Dist. Ct.).

Acceptance of some but not all of the terms of an offer to settle is ineffective. The Rules require an unqualified and unconditional acceptance of the terms of the offer.

Roach v. Roach (1985), 49 O.R. (2d) 684, 50 C.P.C. 302 (Dist. Ct.).

An offer made and rejected prior to rule 49.07(2) coming into force on January 1, 1985 remains open for acceptance unless it is formally revoked.

Lederer v. Dunlop (1985), 49 O.R. (2d) 72, 47 C.P.C. 242 (H.C.).

Acceptance of a payment into court made by one of two defendants was held not to be satisfaction of the plaintiff's claim against the second defendant where the claims against the two defendants were expressly made in the alternative.

Dukaj v. Murphy (1979), 27 O.R. (2d) 198, 14 C.P.C. 244, 106 D.L.R. (3d) 575 (H.C.).

Where the plaintiff accepts the money paid into court, the interest earned thereon belongs to the defendant.

Saikeley v. Royal Ins. Co. of Can. (1979), 24 O.R. (2d) 601, 27 Chitty's L.J. 134, 98 D.L.R. (3d) 575 (H.C.).

A plaintiff who accepts a payment into court is not entitled to prejudgment interest.

Glengair Invts. Ltd. v. North Ennisclare Realty Ltd. (1975), 10 O.R. (2d) 595 (H.C.).

Where a payment into court and surrender of counterclaim are accepted by a plaintiff, he is entitled to the costs of the counterclaim as well as of the main action.

Bussman v. Bickford (1974), 4 O.R. (2d) 301, leave to appeal to Div. Ct. refused 4 O.R. (2d) 310n.

A notice of acceptance was set aside where important material facts came to the attention of the defendant after the payment in and, before acceptance thereof, he moved for payment out. [*In respect of changed circumstances, consideration will now have to be given whether the failure to comply with the continuing discovery provisions — rules 30.07, 31.09 — may vitiate an offer to settle or an acceptance where a material non-disclosure occurs — Authors.*]

Acceptance of Offer — Whether Client Bound by Solicitor

Davis v. Kalkhoust (1986), 12 C.P.C. (2d) 241 (Ont. H.C.).

If a solicitor having ostensible authority to act settles a claim, the settlement will be enforced against the client where no limitation of the solicitor's ostensible authority has been communicated to the opposing party.

Mantha v. Mantha (1984), 47 C.P.C. 176 (Ont. Dist. Ct.).

A solicitor may bind his client in a settlement unless the client has limited his authority and the opposing side has knowledge of the limitation. However where the intervention of the court is required to make an order, it has a discretion to inquire into the circumstances and grant or withhold its intervention.

Campbell v. James (1984), 41 C.P.C. 51 (Ont. Co. Ct.).

Where there was a limitation on the retainer of a solicitor, a settlement reached with an adjuster was not enforced even though the solicitor had apparent authority.

Thornton v. Thornton (1983), 35 C.P.C. 317, 33 R.F.L. (2d) 266 (Ont. C.A.).

The court refused to grant a motion for judgment based on a solicitor's agreement to minutes of settlement where the minutes were not signed, the solicitor's authority was disputed, and the client repudiated the alleged settlement. The court directed trial of the issues.

Fabian v. Bud Mervyn Const. Ltd. (1981), 35 O.R. (2d) 132, 23 C.P.C. 140, 127 D.L.R. (3d) 119 (Div. Ct.).

A settlement concluded by a solicitor acting within his apparent authority is binding upon his client where the retainer is not disputed.

Acceptance of Offer — Costs Consequences

Smith v. Klosler (1984), 46 C.P.C. 254 (Ont. H.C.).

Where one of several plaintiffs accepted a payment into court, she was held to be entitled to tax her costs immediately rather than waiting for the final determination of the entire law suit.

Hasenflue v. Keleher, [1972] 3 O.R. 719 (T.O.).

Where only one of several plaintiffs accepts a payment into court, that plaintiff may not tax his costs until the conclusion of the action.

"Mary Carter" Agreements

Schmieder v. Singh (February 20, 1996), Doc. 67472/91Q, 91-CQ-4785 (Ont. Gen. Div.).

Several parties entered into a "Mary Carter" agreement designed to maximize the liability of certain parties and reduce the exposure of another party. The court did not require the amounts involved to be disclosed.

Pettey v. Avis Car Inc. (1993), 13 O.R. (3d) 725, 18 C.P.C. (3d) 50, 103 D.L.R. (4th) 298 (Gen. Div.).

A "Mary Carter" agreement was not an abuse of process where the court had been fully informed of the terms of the agreement and was able to control the process of the trial. Procedural fairness requires disclosure of a "Mary Carter" type agreement, excepting the dollar amounts. The disclosure of the dollar amount is in the discretion of the court.

J & M Chartrand Realty Ltd. v. Martin (1981), 22 C.P.C. 186 (Ont. H.C.).

The court declined to determine the validity of a "Mary Carter" agreement but held that where such an agreement is entered into it must be revealed to counsel for all parties and to the court before the trial of the action, and in the absence of such disclosure a successful non-contracting defendant was awarded costs against the contracting co-defendant as well as the plaintiff. (A "Mary Carter" agreement is one made between the plaintiff and one of two co-defendants under which the contracting defendant advances settlement moneys to the plaintiff and remains in the trial, but the plaintiff agrees to repay those funds from any recovery against the other defendant. The effect of such an agreement is to make the plaintiff and the contracting defendant "partners" in attacking the other defendant.)

Bodnar v. Home Insurance Co. (1987), 25 C.P.C. (2d) 152 (Ont. Master).

Any secret agreement between two or more parties which may affect the outcome of the litigation, whether or not it was a true "Mary Carter" agreement, should be revealed to other counsel and to the court. Such disclosure may be ordered at the pre-trial stage and is not protected from disclosure by privilege.

PARTIES UNDER DISABILITY

49.08 A party under disability may make, withdraw and accept an offer to settle, but no acceptance of an offer made by the party and no acceptance by the party of an offer made by another party is binding on the party until the settlement has been approved as provided in rule 7.08.

FAILURE TO COMPLY WITH ACCEPTED OFFER

49.09 Where a party to an accepted offer to settle fails to comply with the terms of the offer, the other party may,

(a) make a motion to a judge for judgment in the terms of the accepted offer, and the judge may grant judgment accordingly; or

(b) continue the proceeding as if there had been no accepted offer to settle.

Cross-Reference: See also cases under rule 49.07.

Enforcement of Settlement

McIntosh v. Smith (1995), 6 W.D.C.P. (2d) 440 (Ont. Gen. Div.).

The court refused to enforce a settlement where the defendant accepted a three-year-old offer by the plaintiff, which, while never withdrawn, was premised on prompt acceptance. It would be unfair to enforce the settlement and deprive the plaintiff of prejudgment interest.

Ellis-Don Construction Ltd. v. Halifax Insurance Co., 41 C.P.C. (3d) 341, [1995] I.L.R. 1-3230 (Ont. Gen. Div.).

The court enforced a settlement where the plaintiff served a single offer to settle three separate actions and the defendant accepted the offer after the trial of the first action. Under the express terms of the offer it was open for acceptance until the commencement of all three trials.

Cellular Rental Systems Inc. v. Bell Mobility Cellular Inc. (1995), 6 W.D.C.P. (2d) 169 (Ont. Gen. Div.), affirmed (December 6, 1995), Doc. CA C21473 (Ont. C.A.).

Where parties agreed on a settlement "subject to finalizing mutually acceptable settlement documentation" but failed to reach agreement on the form of the documents, the court made an order enforcing the settlement. Settlement implies a promise to furnish a release but no party is bound to execute a complex or unusual form of release.

Coulombe (Litigation Guardian of) v. Excelsior Life Insurance Co., 26 C.P.C. (3d) 104, [1994] I.L.R. 1-3082 (Ont. Gen. Div.).

The court refused to add a term to a settlement that payments to the plaintiff be tax-free. While both parties expected the settlement funds would be used to create a structured settlement providing for a series of tax-free payments, the offer did not include such language and it would have the effect of creating a guarantee from the defendant to make up any shortfall resulting from changes in the income tax treatment of the payments.

Belanger v. Southwestern Insulation Contractors Ltd. (1993), 16 O.R. (3d) 457 (Gen. Div.).

Where a solicitor accepted an offer to settle with both the actual and apparent authority of her clients, the court granted the defendant judgment in accordance with the terms of the settlement. It was reasonable to infer that the solicitor had acted on the instruction of her clients and there were no special circumstances present.

Trembath v. Trembath (1993), 4 W.D.C.P. (2d) 117 (Ont. Gen. Div.).

The court dismissed a motion to enforce a settlement where it found there was no intention to create a binding settlement agreement.

Canadian Imperial Bank of Commerce v. Weinman (1992), 6 C.P.C. (3d) 189 (Ont. Gen. Div.).
The court declined to enforce an accepted offer to settle where the offer was unreasonable on its face and had been accepted by mistake.

Smith v. Robinson (1992), 7 O.R. (3d) 550, 4 C.P.C. (3d) 262, 87 D.L.R. (4th) 360 (Gen. Div.).
The court refused to grant judgment based on an accepted offer to settle where the offer had been forgotten for several years and the offeror's solicitor had no authority to leave the offer open for acceptance.

Fretz v. Roman Catholic Episcopal Corp. of Hamilton (1991), 4 C.P.C. (3d) 204 (Ont. Gen. Div.).
The court enforced minutes of settlement notwithstanding the contention that the plaintiff's solicitor did not have authority to execute the minutes. The court ought not to inquire into a solicitor's authority where the parties are of full age and capacity and neither the retainer nor terms agreed upon by the solicitors are disputed.

Marlin-Watson Home Corp. v. Taylor (1991), 3 C.P.C. (3d) 82 (Ont. Gen. Div.).
The court enforced a settlement negotiated by a legal assistant in the office of the solicitor for the plaintiff.

Barrett v. Berman (1991), 2 C.P.C. (3d) 78 (Ont. Gen. Div.), affirmed (July 23, 1992), Doc. CA 530/91 (Ont. C.A.).
The court granted judgment where the defendants had received independent legal advice and agreed to minutes of settlement. Minutes of settlement should not be enforced by a motion for summary judgment, but rather by a motion under Rule 49.

Draper v. Sisson (1991), 50 C.P.C. (2d) 171 (Ont. Gen. Div.).
Where plaintiff's counsel accepted an offer to settle based on a misunderstanding of the terms of the settlement, the court refused to enforce the settlement. The defendants had not changed their position in reliance on the acceptance, and it would be inequitable for the defendants to be permitted to take advantage of the mistake.

Thomson v. Elliott (1989), 35 C.P.C. (2d) 34 (Ont. Dist. Ct.).
The court enforced a settlement where the offer to settle was accepted in writing with the addition of the words "I await your advice as to ... costs"; these words did not negate enforceability.

Cambrian Ford Sales (1975) Ltd. v. Horner (1989), 69 O.R. (2d) 431, 37 C.P.C. (2d) 225, 35 O.A.C. 259 (Div. Ct.).
The court refused to re-open a settlement in a personal injury action where injuries proved more serious than first supposed; a misapprehension of the facts is no ground for doing so.

Shortill v. Karmark Construction Ltd. (1989), 67 O.R. (2d) 481, 32 C.P.C. (2d) 209 (H.C.).
The court held that acceptance of an offer by one of two parties to whom it was made was ineffective. In the circumstances of this case the offer constituted a single offer, not separate proposals to the two parties.

Lunardi v. Lunardi (1988), 31 C.P.C. (2d) 27 (Ont. H.C.).
The court enforced an oral agreement to settle a civil non-family law case. There was no reason for the court to exercise its discretion to refuse enforcement. The settlement was fair.

Dixon v. Sperry Inc. (1988), 10 W.D.C.P. 278 (Ont. H.C.).
Where after one or two months' delay by the defendant in implementing a settlement the plaintiff served a motion to enforce the settlement and within a few days the defendant paid, the court declined to award the plaintiff interest, but did award costs of the launching but not of the hearing of the motion.

Re Lem Estate (1987), 16 C.P.C. (2d) 139 (Ont. Surr. Ct.).

The court refused to enforce a purported settlement where the offeror had made a unilateral mistake and the offeree was aware of the mistake when she accepted the offer.

Sylman v. Sylman (1986), 10 C.P.C. (2d) 231 (Ont. H.C.).

The court enforced a settlement where the parties had entered into the settlement with the assistance of duly authorized counsel.

Harvey v. Harvey (1986), 55 O.R. (2d) 60, 10 C.P.C. (2d) 160 (H.C.).

The court dismissed a motion to enforce an alleged settlement of property issues in a divorce action. The petition claimed a decree of divorce and no other relief and the decree had been granted on an undefended basis. Any agreement regarding division of property could not be enforced in this proceeding.

Campbell v. Campbell (1985), 52 O.R. (2d) 206, 6 C.P.C. (2d) 79, 47 R.F.L. (2d) 392 (H.C.).

The court granted judgment on the basis of a letter signed by the parties containing terms to be incorporated into a formal separation agreement notwithstanding the defendant's signature was not witnessed as required by s. 54 of the *Family Law Reform Act*.

Rodic v. Rodic (1985), 6 C.P.C. (2d) 201, 48 R.F.L. (2d) 299 (Ont. Dist. Ct.).

The court granted judgment enforcing an accepted offer to settle notwithstanding the allegation that the solicitor who served the offer to settle lacked authority to do so. Where lack of authority is not made known to the offeree before acceptance of the offer, the court should not go behind the document. A motion under rule 49.09 should be granted upon proof of compliance with rules 49.02 and 49.07 unless it involves a party under disability.

Lutes v. Lutes (1985), 3 C.P.C. (2d) 7 (Ont. H.C.).

An agreement not to defend a divorce action is against public policy and will not be enforced.

U.S. Billiards Inc. v. Carr (1984), 44 O.R. (2d) 591, 41 C.P.C. 221 (*sub nom. U.S. Billiards Inc. v. Howie Carr Amusements Ltd.*) 2 O.A.C. 364 (Div. Ct.).

The court can give effect to a settlement of an action, between parties who are *sui juris*, without the delivery of a statement of claim or other proceedings in the action where the claim is simply for a money judgment.

Cameron Packaging Ltd. v. Ruddy (1983), 41 C.P.C. 154, affirmed (1984), 41 C.P.C. 154n (Ont. C.A.).

Where settlements were reached and were subsequently repudiated, without prejudice correspondence and discussions leading up to the settlements were admissible in evidence on a motion for judgment.

COSTS CONSEQUENCES OF FAILURE TO ACCEPT

Plaintiff's Offer

49.10(1) Where an offer to settle,

(a) is made by a plaintiff at least seven days before the commencement of the hearing;

(b) is not withdrawn and does not expire before the commencement of the hearing; and

(c) is not accepted by the defendant,

and the plaintiff obtains a judgment as favourable as or more favourable than the terms of the offer to settle, the plaintiff is entitled to party and party costs to the date the offer to settle was served and solicitor and client costs from that date, unless the court orders otherwise.

Defendant's Offer

(2) Where an offer to settle,

(a) is made by a defendant at least seven days before the commencement of the hearing;

(b) is not withdrawn and does not expire before the commencement of the hearing; and

(c) is not accepted by the plaintiff,

and the plaintiff obtains a judgment as favourable as or less favourable than the terms of the offer to settle, the plaintiff is entitled to party and party costs to the date the offer was served and the defendant is entitled to party and party costs from that date, unless the court orders otherwise.

Burden of Proof

(3) The burden of proving that the judgment is as favourable as the terms of the offer to settle, or more or less favourable, as the case may be, is on the party who claims the benefit of subrule (1) or (2). [en. O. Reg. 219/91, s. 6]

Failure to Accept Offer — General Principles

Niagara Structural Steel (St. Catharines) Ltd. v. W.D. Laflamme Ltd. (1987), 58 O.R. (2d) 773, 19 C.P.C. (2d) 163, 19 O.A.C. 142 (C.A.).

The court should depart from the *prima facie* costs consequences in rule 49.10 only where, after giving proper weight to the policy of the rule and the importance of reasonable predictability and the even application of the rule, the interests of justice require a departure. The good faith of the party who did not accept the offer should not be given significant weight. The provisions of rule 49.10 do not apply to appeals.

Data General (Canada) Ltd. v. Molnar Systems Group Inc. (1991), 6 O.R. (3d) 409, 85 D.L.R. (4th) 392 (C.A.).

An offer to settle need not contain an element of compromise and a plaintiff's offer to settle for 100 per cent of a liquidated claim may result in an award of solicitor and client costs. However, the absence of an element of compromise is a fact that the court may consider in exercising its discretion to "order otherwise".

S & A Strasser Ltd. v. Richmond Hill (Town of) (1990), 1 O.R. (3d) 243, 49 C.P.C. (2d) 234, 45 O.A.C. 394 (C.A.).

Where the plaintiff did not accept the defendant's offer to settle and the plaintiff's action was dismissed at trial, the court awarded the defendant party and party costs up to the date of the offer and solicitor and client costs thereafter. The award was based on rule 57.01, not Rule 49.

Berdette v. Berdette (1988), 66 O.R. (2d) 410 at 428, 16 R.F.L. (3d) 360 (H.C.), affirmed (1991), 3 O.R. (3d) 513, 41 E.T.R. 126, 33 R.F.L. (3d) 113, 81 D.L.R. (4th) 194, 47 O.A.C. 345 (C.A.).

The general rule as to costs applies to matrimonial litigation in order to discourage protracted cases and to ensure that the spouses attempt to reach a reasonable settlement. *Andrews v. Andrews* (1980), 32 O.R. (2d) 29 (C.A.) not followed.

Failure to Accept Offer — Generally

Hunger Project v. Council on Mind Abuse (C.O.M.A.) Inc. (1995), 22 O.R. (3d) 29, 34 C.P.C. (3d) 1, 121 D.L.R. (4th) 734 (Gen. Div.).

An offer to settle on terms the court could not award may nonetheless attract costs consequences. Where the plaintiff offered to settle a defamation claim in exchange for a retraction and apology, the defendant failed to accept the offer, and the plaintiff obtained judgment for $25,000 at trial, the court awarded solicitor and client costs to the plaintiff from the date of the offer.

Daniels v. Crosfield (Canada) Inc. (1994), 19 O.R. (3d) 430, 28 C.P.C. (3d) 1 (Gen. Div.).

1. Where the plaintiff served an offer for $43,000 plus interest and solicitor and client costs and obtained judgment for about $45,000 plus interest, the court declined to award solicitor and client costs. By including solicitor and client costs as a term of the offer, the plaintiff made it very difficult to obtain solicitor and client costs provided by rule 49.10(1).

2. The costs consequences of offers to settle apply not only to judgments granted after trial but also on motions for summary judgment.

Douglas Hamilton Design Inc. v. Mark (1994), 20 C.P.C. (3d) 224, 66 O.A.C. 44 (C.A.).

The Court of Appeal refused to award solicitor and client costs of an appeal where the successful respondent had delivered an offer to settle. Rule 49 has no application to offers to settle appeals, and the limited compromise offered by the respondent did not justify a departure from the usual order as to costs.

Mortimer v. Cameron (1994), 17 O.R. (3d) 1, 19 M.P.L.R. (2d) 286, 111 D.L.R. (4th) 428, 68 O.A.C. 332, additional reasons (June 24, 1994), Doc. CA C12036 (C.A.), leave to appeal to Supreme Court of Canada refused (1994), 19 O.R. (3d) xvi (note), 23 M.P.L.R. (2d) 314 (note), 114 D.L.R. (4th) vii (note), 178 N.R. 146 (note), 76 O.A.C. 400 (note).

In the absence of wrongdoing, the mere failure to make a reasonable offer to settle did not warrant an award of solicitor and client costs.

Yepremian v. Weisz (1993), 16 O.R. (3d) 121, 20 C.P.C. (3d) 357 (Gen. Div.).

The costs consequences of rule 49.10 were not applicable to an offer which was by its terms continuously variable. Rule 49.10 was intended to provide that a fixed, certain and understandable offer be outstanding in order for there to be costs consequences.

Smith v. Canada (1993), 13 O.R. (3d) 215 (Gen. Div.), leave to appeal to Div. Ct. refused (1994), 17 O.R. (3d) 468, 23 Imm. L.R. (2d) 235.

The court may take a settlement proposal into account regarding costs of a motion.

Huh v. 512208 Ontario Ltd. (1992), 7 O.R. (3d) 125 (Gen. Div.), leave to appeal granted 8 O.R. (3d) 435 (Gen. Div.).

Parties can make offers to settle which do not trigger the costs consequences provided by the Rules. Parties must make it clear that they are making written offers outside the Rules. However, such offers are subject to common law principles of offer and acceptance.

Canadian Newspapers Co. v. Kansa General Insurance Co. (1991), 1 C.P.C. (3d) 16 (Ont. Gen. Div.).

The inherent difficulty of a case is not a material consideration in the exercise of the discretion conferred by rule 49.10.

Re Olenchuk Estate (1991), 4 C.P.C. (3d) 6, 43 E.T.R. 146 (Ont. Gen. Div.).

The usual costs consequences of offers to settle are not determinative in estate litigation.

588147 Ontario Inc. v. 500105 Ontario Ltd. (1990), 44 C.P.C. (2d) 43 (Ont. Dist. Ct.).

The court refused to award solicitor and client costs to the defendant where the defendant's offer to settle was not accepted and the action was dismissed. It is not the intention of the rule that defendants receive solicitor and client costs in such circumstances.
bn
Hagyard v. Keele Plumbing & Heating Ltd. (1989), 15 W.D.C.P. 375 (Ont. Dist. Ct.).

Where the plaintiff serves two offers to settle and recovers judgment for more than each offer, the second offer is deemed to nullify the first offer unless otherwise specified, and the plaintiff should receive party and party costs to the date of service of the second offer and solicitor and client costs thereafter.

Jacuzzi Can. Ltd. v. A. Mantella & Sons Ltd. (1988), 31 C.P.C. (2d) 195 (Ont. H.C.).

The intent of the rule is to induce settlements and avoid trials. Tinkering with the *prima facie* operation of rule 49.10 will destroy the predictability necessary for the rule to accomplish its purpose.

Bray Associates Inc. v. Electrical Contacts Ltd. (1988), 30 C.P.C. (2d) 265 (Ont. H.C.).

The court should not depart from the general rule, even where the defendant had been acting in good faith and was not unreasonable in declining the plaintiff's offer to settle; otherwise reasonable predictability respecting the incidents of costs would disappear.

Balogh v. Citicom Inc. (1988), 26 C.P.C. (2d) 226, 29 O.A.C. 259 (Div. Ct.).

While the court has a discretion to decline to award solicitor and client costs under rule 49.10, that discretion should only be resorted to where good reason is shown.

Berry v. Berry (1985), 1 C.P.C. (2d) 257, 45 R.F.L. (2d) 41 (Ont. Dist. Ct.).

In family law cases, unless the case falls within rule 49.10, the court should apply *Andrews v. Andrews* (1980), 32 O.R. (2d) 29 (C.A.), in exercising its discretion as to costs.

Foulis v. Robinson (1978), 21 O.R. (2d) 769, 8 C.P.C. 198, 92 D.L.R. (3d) 134 (C.A.).

The defendants are entitled to put the plaintiff to the proof. There is no obligation to settle.

Boyuk v. Blake, [1961] O.W.N. 283 (H.C.).

Discussion of costs following acceptance of payment in by one of several plaintiffs represented by the same solicitor.

Presley v. Township of Beckwith, [1933] O.W.N. 485 (C.A.).

Where the plaintiff recovers the amount paid into court, he is only entitled to costs incurred prior to the payment in, even where only one of two defendants made the payment in.

Failure to Accept Offer — "Commencement of the Hearing"

Bontje v. Campbell, Roy & Brown Insurance Brokers Inc. (1994), 21 O.R. (3d) 545 (Gen. Div.).

A civil non-jury trial commences when the action is called for trial, not when evidence is adduced. *Jonas v. Barma, infra*, not followed.

Jonas v. Barma (1987), 22 C.P.C. (2d) 274 (Ont. Dist. Ct.).

In a civil case, a hearing does not commence when a jury is chosen, but rather after the first evidence is called.

Kirkpatrick v. Crawford (1987), 22 C.P.C. (2d) 86 (Ont. Dist. Ct.).

The "commencement of the hearing" takes place when evidence is first adduced, not when the jury is selected.

Ont. Store Fixtures Inc. v. Uni-versa Store Equipment Ltd. (1986), 13 C.P.C. (2d) 189 (Ont. Dist. Ct.).

An offer to settle expressly expiring "at the commencement of the trial" does not expire "before the commencement of the trial" and therefore may attract automatic costs consequences under rule 49.10.

Hausman v. O'Grady (1986), 14 C.P.C. (2d) 188 (Ont. H.C.).

The automatic costs consequences provided by the rule were held not to apply where the offer was withdrawn in the courtroom just before the case was called to trial.

Failure to Accept Offer — Perverse Jury Awards

Loffredi v. Simonetti (1988), 29 C.P.C. (2d) 10 (Ont. Dist. Ct.).

The court considered a perverse jury verdict in exercising discretion with respect to the effect on costs of an offer to settle under rule 49.10(2).

Kirkpatrick v. Crawford (1987), 22 C.P.C. (2d) 86 (Ont. Dist. Ct.).

Whether a jury award is perverse is a question for the appellate court and is not a proper factor in the awarding of costs by the trial judge.

Rajcic v. Argue (1987), 25 C.P.C. (2d) 49 (Ont. H.C.).

Where the plaintiff declined the defendant's offer of $40,000 and was awarded $4,000 by the jury the judge declined to award costs in favour of the defendant. The evidence justified a higher award than that made by the jury and the plaintiff was in a pitiful plight.

Green v. Bateman (1986), 15 C.P.C. (2d) 203 (Ont. Dist. Ct.).

The fact that the trial judge views the jury's award of damages as perversely low is not valid grounds to depart from the automatic costs consequences provided by rule 49.10(2)(c).

Baboi v. Gregory (1986), 56 O.R. (2d) 175, 9 C.P.C. (2d) 230 (Dist. Ct.).

The plaintiff recovered less than an advance payment and an earlier offer to settle. Although the jury assessment appeared perverse, there was no ground on which to deny party and party costs to the defendant from the date of the offer to settle.

Venn v. McAllister (1986), 8 C.P.C. (2d) 268 (Ont. Dist. Ct.).

The court awarded party and party costs to the plaintiff notwithstanding the plaintiff recovered less than the defendant's offer to settle where the jury's award to the plaintiff was unreasonably low.

McCann v. B & M Renovating (1983), 34 C.P.C. 188 (Ont. H.C.).

Where a jury's award of damages was less than the amount paid into court, but the judge viewed the award as unduly low, he declined to award costs to the defendant.

Segreti v. Toronto (1981), 20 C.P.C. 110 (Ont. H.C.).

Where the court was of the view that the jury had been improperly influenced by counsel for the defendant expressing his personal opinions in his address, costs were awarded to the plaintiff although the damages awarded were less than the payment in.

Failure to Accept Offer — Effect of Prejudgment Interest

Emery v. Royal Oak Mines Inc. (1995), 26 O.R. (3d) 216, 15 C.C.E.L. (2d) 49 (Gen. Div.).

In comparing an offer to settle, which is inclusive of prejudgment interest, to the result at trial, the court should compare the damage award at trial plus interest to the date of the offer to the amount of the offer.

Merrill Lynch Canada Inc. v. Cassina (1992), 15 C.P.C. (3d) 264 (Ont. Gen. Div.).

In determining whether or not a judgment is as favourable or more favourable than an offer to settle, which was stated to be inclusive of costs and interest, the proper test is to compare the amount offered to the amount recovered plus interest and costs up to the date of the offer.

Energy Management Consultants v. Venpower Ltd. (1992), 3 W.D.C.P. (2d) 196 (Ont. Gen. Div.).

In determining whether a judgment at trial is as favourable as an offer to settle, the court should compare the offer to the damages awarded at trial with prejudgment interest on such damages to the date of the offer, not the date of the trial.

Mathur v. Commercial Union Assurance Co. of Can. (1988), 24 C.P.C. (2d) 225, 28 O.A.C. 55 (Div. Ct.).

Where an offer provides a lump sum for damages including prejudgment interest, the court will compare the damages awarded at trial plus prejudgment interest as of the date of the offer to the lump sum in order to determine whether the judgment is as favourable as the offer. In this case the plaintiff offered to accept $9000 for damages and interest. The damages at trial plus interest to the date of the offer was less than $9000 although the damages plus interest to the date of trial was more than $9000. The plaintiff was awarded party and party costs throughout.

Von Cramm v. Riverside Hospital of Ottawa (1988), 66 O.R. (2d) 705 (H.C.).

Where the plaintiff made an offer to settle for $200,000 plus prejudgment interest and after a week of trial the parties settled for $210,000 including interest, the plaintiff was awarded party and party costs.

Orsini v. Sherri (1987), 16 C.P.C. (2d) 194 (Ont. Dist. Ct.).

Where the plaintiff's offer sought $25,000 for damages and was silent regarding interest and the plaintiff recovered at trial about $18,000 damages and about $9,000 in interest, the court awarded costs to the plaintiff on a party and party basis to the date of the offer and on a solicitor and client basis thereafter.

Barsalona v. Green (1986), 8 C.P.C. (2d) 234 (Ont. Dist. Ct.).

Where the plaintiff's offer to settle contained a fixed sum for prejudgment interest and the total amount of the offer was more than the damages awarded at trial plus interest to the date of service, but less than the said damages plus interest to the date of trial, the court awarded costs to the plaintiff on a party and party basis rather than on a solicitor and client basis in the peculiar circumstances of the case.

Baker v. Gascon (1981), 26 C.P.C. 43 (Ont. Co. Ct.).

Prejudgment interest to the date of judgment was added to the recovery in determining whether the plaintiff's recovery exceeded the payment into court. Discussion of reasons for ordering costs to plaintiff even if total judgment did not exceed payment in.

Morozuk v. Boon (1979), 28 O.R. (2d) 130, 108 D.L.R. (3d) 607 (Co. Ct.).

Where the plaintiff's recovery, exclusive of interest, is less than the payment into court, he should be deprived of costs. Prejudgment interest is not included in the determination of whether the recovery exceeds the payment in.

Rushton v. Lake Ontario Steel Co. (1980), 29 O.R. (2d) 68, 16 C.P.C. 191, 112 D.L.R. (3d) 144 (H.C.).

In determining whether the amount of judgment exceeds the payment into court for the purposes of costs, the amount of prejudgment interest due is to be included in the judgment.

Failure to Accept Offer — Effect of Terms re Costs

Gagro v. Morrison (1995), 6 W.D.C.P. (2d) 460 (Ont. Gen. Div.).

The court refused to award costs in favour of a defendant which had served an offer to settle providing that the plaintiffs pay costs if they accepted the offer after one month, notwithstanding the amount offered was more than that awarded at trial. The costs term created instability which was inconsistent with Rule 49.

Noyes v. Attfield (1994), 19 O.R. (3d) 319, 29 C.P.C. (3d) 184 (Gen. Div.).

Where the defendant's offer to settle included a fixed sum for costs, the defendant was unable to establish the judgment at trial was more favourable and costs were awarded to the plaintiff. The court refused to enter into a *ad hoc* assessment of costs as at the date of the offer.

Friesen v. Invacare Canada (1986), 8 C.P.C. (2d) 290 (Ont. Dist. Ct.).

Where the plaintiff did not accept the defendant's offer to settle for $3,500 and obtained judgment for only $2,060 at trial, the court awarded party and party costs to the plaintiff up to the date of the offer and party and party costs to the defendant thereafter. The court rejected the plaintiff's submission that since the defendant's offer was silent as to costs and the plaintiff's costs incurred up to that point exceeded $1,500, the plaintiff should be awarded costs throughout.

Failure to Accept Offer — Examples

Cugliari v. White (1995), 24 O.R. (3d) 57 (Gen. Div.).

Where a jury award was greater than the defendant's offer but the trial judge ruled certain disability benefits were to be deducted from the award, reducing it to less than the defendant's offer, the defendant was awarded party and party costs from the date of the offer.

Daniels v. Crosfield (Canada) Inc. (1994), 19 O.R. (3d) 430, 28 C.P.C. (3d) 1 (Gen. Div.).

Although the plaintiff obtained monetary judgment which exceeded the amount of his offer to settle, that offer to settle had required the defendant to pay solicitor and client costs from the date of the offer to the date of its acceptance. As a result, the judgment which the plaintiff obtained did not produce a judgment as favourable as the terms of his offer to settle, and therefore rule 49.10(1) did not apply.

Balkos v. Cook (1994), 29 C.P.C. (3d) 375 (Ont. Gen. Div.).

The court held that the plaintiff's offer to accept $1 million was more favourable than the award of $900,000 at trial with a right to "structure" any portion thereof. Accordingly, the plaintiff was awarded party and party costs to the date of the offer and solicitor and client costs thereafter.

Ecuimates v. Rix (1993), 27 C.P.C. (3d) 301 (Ont. Gen. Div.).

Where the plaintiff failed to accept the defendant's offer and the action was dismissed, the defendant was awarded party and party costs to the date of the offer and solicitor and client costs thereafter.

Calabogie Peaks (1983) Inc. v. Bannock (1992), 4 W.D.C.P. (2d) 5 (Ont. Gen. Div.).

Where the plaintiff's action was dismissed and the defendant had made an offer to settle which had not been accepted, the court distinguished *S. & A. Strasser Ltd. v. Richmond Hill* (1990), 1 O.R. (3d) 243 (C.A.) and awarded costs to the defendant on a party and party basis, not on a solicitor and client basis.

Scarcello v. Whalley (1992), 10 C.P.C. (3d) 19 (Ont. Gen. Div.).

Where an offer to settle was served on September 13 and the trial commenced on September 20, the offer was made "at least seven days" before the commencement of the hearing within the meaning of rules 3.01 and 49.10.

Ligate v. Abick (1992), 8 O.R. (3d) 49, 2 C.P.C. (3d) 216 (Gen. Div.).

A successful plaintiff had made an offer to settle on a structured basis, but in the absence of evidence comparing the offer to settle and the damage award granted at trial, the plaintiff was awarded party and party costs. Upon submission of further evidence as to the value of the offer to settle, the court awarded the plaintiff solicitor and client costs from the date of the offer.

Soulos v. Korkontzilas (1991), 4 O.R. (3d) 51 at 71, 2 C.P.C. (3d) 70 (Gen. Div.).

Where the defendant had delivered an offer to settle, and the action was dismissed, the defendant was awarded costs from the date of the offer to settle. Although the plaintiff had succeeded in establishing a breach of duty on the part of the defendant, it had suffered no loss as a result.

Berdette v. Berdette (1991), 3 O.R. (3d) 513, 41 E.T.R. 126, 33 R.F.L. (3d) 113, 81 D.L.R. (4th) 194, 47 O.A.C. 345 (C.A.), leave to appeal to Supreme Court of Canada refused 85 D.L.R. (4th) viii (note), 137 N.R. 388 (note), 55 O.A.C. 397 (note).

Where one spouse tries to settle, is reasonable and makes favourable offers to settle but the other spouse wants to litigate a novel point and is unsuccessful, the latter should pay for the litigation.

Bruce v. Waterloo Swim Club (1990), 75 O.R. (2d) 173 (H.C.).

The spirit of this provision is to reward the party making a genuine effort to settle and to punish the party who does not. Although the plaintiff recovered less than his offers to settle, he had attempted to negotiate while the defendant made no offer at all. The plaintiff was awarded party and party costs to the date of the second offer and solicitor and client costs thereafter.

Ray Plastics Ltd. v. Dustbane Products Ltd. (1990), 47 C.P.C. (2d) 280, 33 C.P.R. (3d) 219 at 237 (Ont. H.C.).

The plaintiffs' offer did not come within rule 49.10(1), where although the judgment was more favourable than the offer's monetary terms, the term concerning injunctive relief was wider than that awarded at trial. The plaintiff had not suggested that the terms of the injunction could be negotiated.

Moorcroft v. Doraty & Kebe (1990), 72 O.R. (2d) 320, 67 D.L.R. (4th) 479 (H.C.).

The plaintiffs were ordered to pay the defendant's party and party costs from the date of the defendant's offer to settle. Despite the plaintiff's allegations of criminal wrongdoing, solicitor and client costs were not awarded; the plaintiffs had appeared on their own behalf and the award of party and party costs was a sufficient deterrent for the future.

Imperial Brass Ltd. v. Jacob Electric Systems Ltd. (1989), 72 O.R. (2d) 17 (H.C.).

As the plaintiff had recovered more than its offer to settle, it was entitled to solicitor and client costs as against the unsuccessful defendant. However, those costs were limited to four days of a five-day trial, because one day was allocated to the plaintiff's case against the defendant who had been wholly successful.

Albrecht v. Opemoco Inc. (1989), 70 O.R. (2d) 221, 62 D.L.R. (4th) 541 (H.C.).

Where a plaintiff delivered an offer to settle for 90 per cent of the claim, plus interest and costs, and recovered the full claim at trial, solicitor and client costs were awarded from the date of the offer.

Cavoulakos v. 616550 Ont. Ltd. (1989), 68 O.R. (2d) 788, 5 R.P.R. (2d) 40 (H.C.).

A party made an offer more than seven days before a hearing, and in the result obtained an order identical to the offer. The offeror received party and party costs to the date of the offer, and solicitor and client costs thereafter.

Heon v. Heon (1988), 70 O.R. (2d) 781, 23 R.F.L. (3d) 408 (H.C.).

Where both husband and wife made offers to settle less favourable than the final judgment in this action for equalization of net family property and child support and spousal support, no costs were awarded.

Pinder v. Aregers (1988), 30 O.A.C. 137 (Div. Ct.).

In a proceeding involving a claim to title to real property by prescription where the plaintiffs failed in their claim for a possessory title, but were successful in obtaining a declaration that they had a prescriptive right to an easement, the court held that non-monetary offers made by the parties were not a sufficient foundation for invoking Rule 49 and awarding solicitor and client costs.

Jacuzzi Can. Ltd. v. A. Mantella & Sons Ltd. (1988), 31 C.P.C. (2d) 195 (Ont. H.C.).

Where the plaintiff offered to settle for $100,000 before trial, withdrew the offer during trial, made a second offer for $175,000, and recovered $116,000, the trial judge awarded costs to the plaintiff on a party and party basis to the date of the first offer and on a soliitor and client basis thereafter.

Bray Associates Inc. v. Electrical Contacts Ltd. (1988), 30 C.P.C. (2d) 265 (Ont. H.C.).

The court awarded solicitor and client costs against the defendant notwithstanding it was acting in good faith and was not unreasonable in declining the plaintiff's offer. In order to maintain predictability the provisions of rule 49.10 should be applied unless the interests of justice require a departure.

Pitter v. Williamson (1988), 11 W.D.C.P. 329 (Ont. Dist. Ct.).

Where the defendant served an offer for (a) damages of $13,006.28 to the injured plaintiff; (b) $100 for all *Family Law Act* plaintiffs; (c) prejudgment interest; and (d) costs to be agreed or assessed and the plaintiffs purported to accept (a) and continue the action regarding (b), (c) and (d), the court held that there had been a binding settlement of claim (a). The offer did not state that the amounts were not severable.

Roberts v. Dresser Industries Can. Ltd. (1988), 11 W.D.C.P. 265 (Ont. Dist. Ct.).

A defendant was awarded costs on the basis of an offer which exceeded the plaintiff's recovery by only $78.12. A line must be drawn somewhere and it has been drawn by the rule.

Century 21 Kelleher Real Estate Ltd. v. Zahlan (1988), 11 W.D.C.P. 337 (Ont. Dist. Ct.).

The court applied *Niagara Structural Steel (St. Catharines) Ltd. v. W.D. Laflamme Ltd., supra,* and awarded solicitor and client costs to the plaintiff.

Moore v. Moore (1987), 21 C.P.C. (2d) 191 (Ont. H.C.).

Where a divorce case did not fall strictly within rule 49.10, the court applied the rule in *Andrews v. Andrews* (1980), 32 O.R. (2d) 29 (C.A.), to award costs.

Royal Homes Ltd. v. Delvasto (1986), 12 C.P.C. (2d) 150 (Ont. Dist. Ct.).

A plaintiff which had obtained a result at trial only slightly better than its offer to settle was awarded solicitor and client costs from the date of completion of discoveries, although its offer was delivered before those discoveries.

Buckle v. Mother Parker's Foods Ltd. (1986), 8 C.P.C. (2d) 265, 11 C.C.E.L. 299, 15 O.A.C. 116 (Div. Ct.).

The Divisional Court refused to award solicitor and client costs to the successful plaintiff respondent who had obtained judgment at trial for $13,663 and after the defendant commenced an appeal had served an offer to settle for $12,000. The offer represented a relatively small reduction from the recovery at trial and was served less than one month prior to the hearing of the appeal.

Sauer v. Grozelle (1986), 8 C.P.C. (2d) 183 (Ont. Dist. Ct.).

The court ordered that costs incurred by the plaintiff after serving an offer to settle for $44,000 be paid on a solicitor and client basis where judgment had been obtained for $45,000. The defendant had offered about $18,000.

Monarch Kitchen Cabinets Ltd. v. LaPosta (1985), 49 C.P.C. 239 (Ont. Dist. Ct.).

Where the plaintiff recovered more at trial than its offer to settle, it was awarded party and party costs to the date of the offer and solicitor and client costs thereafter.

Halpern v. Locurto; Norman Hall & Associates Ltd. v. Prosser (1984), 45 C.P.C. 285 (Ont. H.C.).

Where the payment in in satisfaction of all claims was more than the liability of the corporate defendant, which did not participate in the payment in, but less than that of the other defendants due to an award of punitive damages against them, the corporate defendant was not entitled to its costs following the payment in.

Hare v. Maple Leaf Mills Ltd. (1984), 45 C.P.C. 223 (Ont. Co. Ct.) (under appeal to Ont. C.A.).

Where at trial the plaintiff failed to recover more than the defendant's offer, made just prior to the long weekend following which the trial commenced, the plaintiff was awarded his costs up to the time of the offer plus one day's counsel fee at trial.

Wagar v. Wagar (1982), 27 C.P.C. 32, 27 R.F.L. (2d) 459 (Ont. H.C.).

Where the judgment was substantially the same as the husband's offer to settle, but to award no costs would have a serious effect upon the maintenance of the wife, costs were awarded on a party and party basis.

Cameron v. Cameron (1978), 19 O.R. (2d) 18, 2 R.F.L. (2d) 184, 3 R.F.L. (2d) 277, 83 D.L.R. (3d) 765 (H.C.).

Where a petitioner for divorce refused an offer of settlement which was more generous than the ultimate award by the court, the court deprived the petitioner of costs from the date of the offer; had the petitioner been in a better financial position the court would have awarded such costs to the respondent.

Fahel v. Portener (1976), 11 O.R. (2d) 635 (T.O.) [reversed without written reasons 12 O.R. (2d) 264].

Where the payment in was made the day before trial and the plaintiff was awarded costs up to that time, the plaintiff is not entitled to a counsel fee for the first day of trial.

MULTIPLE DEFENDANTS

49.11   Where there are two or more defendants, the plaintiff may offer to settle with any defendant and any defendant may offer to settle with the plaintiff, but where the defendants are alleged to be jointly or jointly and severally liable to the plaintiff in respect of a claim and rights of contribution or indemnity may exist between the defendants, the costs consequences prescribed by rule 49.10 do not apply to an offer to settle unless,

(a) in the case of an offer made by the plaintiff, the offer is made to all the defendants, and is an offer to settle the claim against all the defendants; or

(b) in the case of an offer made to the plaintiff,

(i) the offer is an offer to settle the plaintiff's claim against all the defendants and to pay the costs of any defendant who does not join in making the offer; or

(ii) the offer is made by all the defendants and is an offer to settle the claim against all the defendants, and, by the terms of the offer, they are made jointly and severally liable to the plaintiff for the whole amount of the offer.

OFFER TO CONTRIBUTE

49.12(1)   Where two or more defendants are alleged to be jointly or jointly and severally liable to the plaintiff in respect of a claim, any defendant may make to any other defendant an offer to contribute (Form 49D) toward a settlement of the claim.

(2)   The court may take an offer to contribute into account in determining whether another defendant should be ordered,

(a) to pay the costs of the defendant who made the offer; or

(b) to indemnify the defendant who made the offer for any costs that the defendant is liable to pay to the plaintiff,

or to do both.

(3)   Rules 49.04, 49.05, 49.06 and 49.13 apply to an offer to contribute as if it were an offer to settle.

Fatal v. Burton (1995), 24 O.R. (3d) 234, 40 C.P.C. (3d) 347 (Gen. Div.).

Where a defendant made an offer to a co-defendant to divide liability 75 per cent-25 per cent and the co-defendant was found 100 per cent liable at trial, the court awarded the first defendant party and party costs of the crossclaim to the date of the offer and solicitor and client costs thereafter.

Denzler v. Aull (1994), 19 O.R. (3d) 507, 29 C.P.C. (3d) 99 (Gen. Div.).

The court may order one defendant to pay another defendant's solicitor and client costs based on an offer to contribute notwithstanding the omission of rule 49.10 from rule 49.12(3).

Ryan v. Richards (1992), 11 C.P.C. (3d) 152 (Ont. Gen. Div.).

The court considered an offer to contribute in determining whether a defendant should be ordered to pay the costs of a co-defendant.

AKW Insurance Brokers (1985) Ltd. (Trustees of) v. Guarantee Co. of North America (1992), 12 C.P.C. (3d) 115, 16 C.C.L.I. (2d) 294 at 308 (Ont. Gen. Div.).

The court refused to award solicitor and client costs to a successful defendant which had delivered an offer to contribute in light of the factors set out in rule 57.01(1).

Leroux v. James (1989), 38 C.P.C. (2d) 132 (Ont. H.C.).

Where two defendants offered to contribute $275,000 and the remaining defendant offered to consent to a dismissal of the actions without costs, and the plaintiff was awarded only $63,000 by the jury, the court held that the two offers triggered rule 49.10 and awarded costs against the plaintiff.

Stewart v. Lanark Mutual Ins. Co. (1988), 30 C.P.C. (2d) 311 (Ont. Dist. Ct.).

Where a defendant proposed by a letter to a co-defendant that liability to the plaintiff be equally divided, and the proposal was rejected by the co-defendant but the trial judge found a 50 per cent division of liability, the co-defendant was ordered to pay the costs of the defendant incurred regarding the liability issue after the proposal.

DISCRETION OF COURT

49.13 Despite rules 49.03, 49.10 and 49.11, the court, in exercising its discretion with respect to costs, may take into account any offer to settle made in writing, the date the offer was made and the terms of the offer.

McCullough v. Bursey (1995), 25 O.R. (3d) 655 (Gen. Div.).

Where the plaintiff agreed to dismiss his action against defendant B but defendant C, who had crossclaimed against defendant B, refused to agree, defendant C was ordered to pay the costs of defendant B on a solicitor and client scale.

Mortimer v. Cameron (1994), 17 O.R. (3d) 1, 19 M.P.L.R. (2d) 286, 111 D.L.R. (4th) 428, 68 O.A.C. 332, additional reasons (June 24, 1994), Doc. CA C12036 (C.A.) leave to appeal to Supreme Court of Canada refused (1994), 19 O.R. (3d) xvi (note), 23 M.P.L.R. (2d) 314 (note), 114 D.L.R. (4th) vii (note), 178 N.R. 146 (note), 76 O.A.C. 400 (note).

Where the conditions of rule 49.10 are not met, rule 49.13 does not confer wide discretion to award solicitor and client costs.

Bell Canada v. Olympia & York Developments Ltd. (1994), 17 O.R. (3d) 135, 26 C.P.C. (3d) 368, 111 D.L.R. (4th) 589, 70 O.A.C. 101 (C.A.).

The successful party is entitled to a reasonable expectation that it will be awarded costs in the absence of special circumstances. It was held to be an error in principle to deprive a successful party of costs on the basis of failure to make an offer of settlement.

Douglas Hamilton Design Inc. v. Mark (1993), 20 C.P.C. (3d) 224, 66 O.A.C. 44 (C.A.).

Although Rule 49 does not apply to offers to settle appeals, the existence of the offer is a factor in the exercise of the appellate court's discretion in awarding costs.

Terham Management Consultants Ltd. v. OEB International Ltd. (1993), 17 C.P.C. (3d) 270 (Ont. Gen. Div.).

The court ordered costs against a successful plaintiff which had refused second settlement offers for amounts approximately equal to or greater than the award at trial.

Merrill Lynch Canada Inc. v. Cassina (1993), 15 C.P.C. (3d) 264 (Ont. Gen. Div.).

The court awarded solicitor and client costs to a defendant who had verbally offered to settle by dismissal of the action and counterclaim where the result at trial was more favourable to the defendant.

Hamilton v. Canadian National Railway Co. (1991), 50 C.P.C. (2d) 271, 80 D.L.R. (4th) 470 at 474 (Ont. C.A.).

Although rule 49.10 does not apply to appeals, the court exercised its discretion and awarded a respondent costs of an appeal on a party and party basis where it had delivered an offer to settle on terms more favourable than the outcome of the appeal.

Ultramar Canada Inc. v. Montreal Pipe Line Ltd. (1990), 75 O.R. (2d) 498, 46 C.P.C. (2d) 184 (Gen. Div.).

The mere fact that the defendant made an unrealistic offer and therefore the plaintiff had no choice but to have the matter tried does not justify an award of solicitor and client costs.

Al-Qahtani-Shaw-Leonard Ltd. v. Crossworld Freight Ltd. (1987), 60 O.R. (2d) 565 at 581, 23 C.P.C. (2d) 77, 40 D.L.R. (4th) 656 at 673 (H.C.), varied on other grounds (1988), 66 O.R. (2d) 256, 34 C.C.L.I. xix, 54 D.L.R. (4th) 192 (C.A.).

Where the plaintiff had delivered offers during the course of trial, the court refused to exercise its jurisdiction with respect to solicitor and client costs in favour of the plaintiff.

Adamson v. Watts & Henderson (Atlantic) Ltd. (1987), 21 C.P.C. (2d) 215 (Ont. H.C.).

The court refused to award solicitor and client costs to a plaintiff who had recovered slightly less than his offer to settle, and rule 49.10 did not apply.

Marchand v. Simcoe County Bd. of Education (1986), 12 C.P.C. (2d) 140 (Ont. H.C.).

The defendants were not awarded costs under rule 49.13 where their offer to settle did not meet the requirements of rule 49.11 and was merely a conditional offer to settle part of the plaintiff's claim.

Arthur J. Fish Ltd. v. Moore (1985), 53 O.R. (2d) 65, 8 C.P.C. (2d) 77, 17 C.L.R. 137, 23 D.L.R. (4th) 424, 13 O.A.C. 117 (*sub nom. Arthur J. Fish Ltd. v. Superstructure Door of Can. (Trustee of)*) (Div. Ct.).

Unsuccessful efforts to arrive at settlement do not affect the issue of costs unless a party has made an offer which is open for acceptance by another party, or has paid money into court.

Datamex Ltd. v. Eberline Int. Corp., a division of Thermo Electron Corp. (1986), 7 C.P.C. (2d) 159 (Ont. H.C.).

Where the defendants made an offer to settle which was withdrawn after eleven days and the plaintiff was awarded a smaller amount at trial, the court exercised its discretion under this rule and awarded no costs to any party.

Sharp v. Sharp (1981), 32 O.R. (2d) 794, 123 D.L.R. (3d) 383 (H.C.).

Where, in a family law action, the offer to settle of the wife was too high and the offer of the husband was too low but the husband was in a better financial position to bear costs, costs were awarded to the wife.

Bregman v. Bregman (1978), 21 O.R. (2d) 724, 1 F.L.R.A.C. 79, 7 R.F.L. (2d) 201, 91 D.L.R. (3d) 470, affirmed 25 O.R. (2d) 254, 104 D.L.R. (3d) 703 (C.A.).

Where a petitioner had offered to accept more than the ultimate award and the respondent had offered to pay less than the ultimate award, and the petitioner had not been reasonable in the settlement negotiations, the petitioner was deprived of costs.

APPLICATION TO COUNTERCLAIMS, CROSSCLAIMS AND THIRD PARTY CLAIMS

    49.14 Rules 49.01 to 49.13 apply, with necessary modifications, to counterclaims, crossclaims and third party claims.

RULE 50   PRE-TRIAL CONFERENCE

Highlights

The Rule expressly authorizes a pre-trial conference to be conducted, not only by a judge, but also by an "officer", *e.g.* a commissioner (often a retired judge), appointed under former s. 24 of the *Courts of Justice Act.* (Section 24 is repealed but existing commissioners continue in office.) An officer who conducts a pre-trial conference cannot make certain orders that a judge may make, *i.e.* orders as to the conduct of a proceeding (rule 50.02(1)) or as to the costs of the pre-trial conference (rule 50.06). Although a judge conducting a pre-trial conference has greater jurisdiction, contentious rulings should not be made at pre-trial conferences unless there has been clear notice and a full opportunity to respond: *Essa (Township) v. Guergis* (1993), 15 O.R. (3d) 573 (Div. Ct.).

The encouragement of settlement is expressly recognized as a function of the pre-trial conference (rule 50.01(a)) and the advisability of appointing a court expert (see rule 52.03) is added to the list of matters for consideration at the conference: rule 50.01(g).

An express prohibition is imposed with regard to the subsequent communication of any statement made at a pre-trial conference, except as disclosed in the pre-trial memorandum or order, to any judge or officer presiding at the hearing of the proceeding or any motion or reference in the proceeding: rule 50.03.

The general principle that a judge who conducts a pre-trial conference may not preside at the trial is retained (rule 50.04). Prior to 1986 there was a specific qualification in respect of divorce actions to the effect that when a pre-trial conference resolved all the issues in a divorce action, with the consent of the parties the judge who conducted the pre-trial could preside at the trial. This provision was deleted by amendment in 1986 because under the new *Divorce Act* there is no longer a requirement that there be a trial, and after a successful pre-trial conference the petitioner can bring a motion for judgment under rule 69.19. As redrafted, rule 50.04 (since it merely prevents a judge who conducts a pre-trial conference from presiding at the *trial* of the action or the hearing of an *application*) does not prevent the judge who conducts a pre-trial conference from hearing a subsequent *motion* for judgment in a divorce action.

Practice directions. For pre-trial conferences in the Central East Region, see the practice direction reproduced following the Highlights of Rule 37. For local procedures regarding pre-trial dates and pre-trial conference memoranda in the Central South Region see chapter 4 of the *Administrative Procedures Manual for the Central South Region* published by direction of Regional Senior Justice Fedak.

Former Rules: Rule 244.

WHERE AVAILABLE

50.01 In an action or application, a judge may, at the request of a party or on his or her own initiative, direct the solicitors for the parties, either with or without the parties, and any party not represented by a solicitor, to appear before a judge or officer for a pre-trial conference to consider,

(a) the possibility of settlement of any or all of the issues in the proceeding;

(b) the simplification of the issues;

(c) the possibility of obtaining admissions that may facilitate the hearing;

(d) the question of liability;

(e) the amount of damages, where damages are claimed;

(f) the estimated duration of the hearing;

(g) the advisability of having the court appoint an expert;

(h) the advisability of fixing a date for the hearing;

(i) the advisability of directing a reference; and

(j) any other matter that may assist in the just, most expeditious and least expensive disposition of the proceeding.

Bowser (Litigation Guardian of) v. Bowser, (February 16, 1995), Docs. 24581/87 B, 24577/87 (Ont. Gen. Div.).

Where an authoritative representative of a party failed to attend a pre-trial conference pursuant to a court order, the court ordered a representative to attend at a later date and threatened to award solicitor and client costs.

Campbell v. Stainton (1985), 50 O.R. (2d) 283 (H.C.).

The pre-trial judge may, of her own motion, make an order changing the place of trial.

Pears v. Shelby (1983), 42 O.R. (2d) 539, 36 C.P.C. 108 (H.C.).

A local judge has no jurisdiction to direct or conduct a pre-trial conference.

Murch v. Murch (1981), 24 R.F.L. (2d) 1 (Ont. H.C.).

Where a solicitor for a party fails to attend a pre-trial conference directed by the court, the court has inherent jurisdiction to strike out the party's pleading.

Can. Permanent Trust Co. v. Wortsman (1978), 21 O.R. (2d) 846 (H.C.).

A reference may be directed at the time of a pre-trial conference.

MEMORANDUM OR ORDER

50.02(1) At the conclusion of the conference,

(a) counsel may sign a memorandum setting out the results of the conference; and

(b) where the conference is conducted by a judge, the judge may make such order as he or she considers necessary or advisable with respect to the conduct of the proceeding,

and the memorandum or order binds the parties unless the judge or officer presiding at the hearing of the proceeding orders otherwise to prevent injustice.

(2) A copy of a memorandum or order under subrule (1) shall be placed with the trial or application record.

Essa (Township) v. Guergis (1993), 15 O.R. (3d) 573, 22 C.P.C. (3d) 63 (*sub nom. Heck v. Royal Bank*) 52 C.P.R. (3d) 372 (Div. Ct.).

Generally, pre-trial judges should not make significant contentious rulings at pre-trial conferences in the absence of clear notice and opportunity to meet and respond to the order sought.

Kakeway v. Ontario (1993), 4 W.D.C.P. (2d) 98 (Ont. Gen. Div.).

The court refused to make an order based on settlement comments of the responding party in his pre-trial conference memorandum. Effectiveness of the pre-trial conference system depends on frank discussion and that would be undermined if pre-trial comments were used in such a manner. The court did make an earlier pre-trial conference order for an examination *de bene esse* but that was a procedural matter which did not prejudice any rights in issue at trial.

NO DISCLOSURE TO THE COURT

50.03 No communication shall be made to the judge or officer presiding at the hearing of the proceeding or a motion or reference in the proceeding with respect to any statement made at a pre-trial conference, except as disclosed in the memorandum or order under rule 50.02.

Bell Canada v. Olympia & York Developments Ltd. (1994), 17 O.R. (3d) 135, 26 C.P.C. (3d) 368, 111 D.L.R. (4th) 589, 70 O.A.C. 101 (C.A.).

Evidence of what occurred at a pre-trial conference should not be used by the trial court even if the parties consent to admission of the evidence. Litigants must be assured that at a pre-trial they can speak freely, negotiate openly, and consider recommendations from the pre-trial judge, without concern that their positions in the litigation will be affected.

PRE-TRIAL JUDGE CANNOT PRESIDE AT HEARING

50.04 A judge who conducts a pre-trial conference shall not preside at the trial of the action or the hearing of the application.

DOCUMENTS TO BE MADE AVAILABLE

50.05 All documents intended to be used at the hearing that may be of assistance in achieving the purposes of a pre-trial conference, such as medical reports and reports of experts, shall be made available to the pre-trial conference judge or officer.

Kungl v. Fallis (1988), 26 C.P.C. (2d) 102 (Ont. H.C.).

Rule 50.05 applies only to documents and evidence in existence at the time of the pre-trial. The date of a pre-trial does not establish a cut-off date for the introduction of expert evidence at trial.

COSTS OF PRE-TRIAL CONFERENCE

50.06 A judge who conducts a pre-trial conference may make an order for costs of the pre-trial conference but in the absence of such an order or where the conference is conducted by an officer, the costs shall be assessed as part of the costs of the proceeding.

CONFERENCE BEFORE TRIAL JUDGE

50.07 Subrule 50.04(1) does not prevent a judge before whom a proceeding has been called for hearing from holding a conference either before

or during the hearing to consider any matter that may assist in the just, most expeditious and least expensive disposition of the proceeding without disqualifying himself or herself from presiding at the hearing.

Majcenic v. Natale, [1968] 1 O.R. 189, 66 D.L.R. (2d) 50 (C.A.).

A court reporter should be present at all conferences among the trial judge and counsel so that a record is available for purposes of appeal.

PRE-TRIAL CONFERENCE BY CONFERENCE TELEPHONE

50.08 Where all counsel and parties not represented by counsel participating in the pre-trial conference and the judge or other officer of the court conducting it consent, the pre-trial conference may be conducted by means of a conference telephone call.

RULE 51   ADMISSIONS

Highlights

This Rule deals with three distinct aspects of admissions. First, it provides a "request to admit" procedure. Second, it regulates the withdrawal of admissions. Third, it provides a summary procedure for obtaining judgments based upon admissions.

Request to admit. Rules 51.01 to 51.04 provide a procedure that permits a party, at any time, to serve a request to admit on another party, requesting that the truth of a fact or the authenticity of a document be admitted. The procedure is available in both actions and applications. Its purpose is to limit the issues at a hearing by obtaining admissions as to facts and documents which otherwise would have to be proved and it is a useful adjunct to the discovery process.

The party on whom the request is served must respond within twenty days, otherwise he or she shall be deemed to have made the requested admission: rule 51.03(1) and (2). The response to the request must be specific: unless the response either specifically denies the truth of the fact or the authenticity of the document, or refuses to admit and sets forth the reason for the refusal, the party served with the request shall be deemed to have made the requested admission: rule 51.03(3). The court will refuse to entertain interlocutory motions as to the propriety of requests to admit and such issues should be left to the discretion of the trial judge: *RSC Management Ltd. v. Cadillac Fairview Corp.* (1985), 51 O.R. (2d) 107, 2 C.P.C. (2d) 53 (Master). Similarly, a response to a request to admit should be based on the truth of the fact or authenticity of the document, and not on whether the fact or document is admissible in evidence, and objections regarding admissibility or relevance should be made at trial: *Canpotex v. Graham* (1985), 5 C.P.C. (2d) 233 (Ont. H.C.).

Costs consequences may attach to a party's denial or refusal to admit: if the fact or document is subsequently proved at the hearing, the court may take the denial or refusal into account in exercising its discretion as to costs (rule 51.04 and see also rules 57.01(1)(g) and 58.06(1)(g)).

It is to be noted that a request to admit is much broader than the notice to admit procedure provided in s. 55 of the *Evidence Act*, R.S.O. 1990, c. E.23. The latter extends only to documents (and not to facts) and merely establishes the correctness or genuineness of the copies: due execution, and authenticity generally, must still be proved (see J. Sopinka and S.N. Lederman, *The Law of Evidence in Civil Cases* (1974), pp. 285-6). By contrast, a request to admit under Rule 51 can lead to an admission of the authenticity of either the original or a copy of the document.

Withdrawal of admissions. Rule 51.05 permits an admission made pursuant to Rule 51, or in a pleading, to be withdrawn on consent or with leave of the court. Rule 51.05 is not overridden by rule 26.01 (the general power of amendment). The traditional requirement that a proposed amendment which amounts to a withdrawal of admission must be supported by material showing: (1) the proposed amendment raises a triable issue; (2) the admission was made inadvertently or the solicitor was wrongly instructed; and (3) the withdrawal of the admission will not cause injustice to the other parties (it being understood that there is no injustice if the other parties can be compensated by costs) enunciated in *Philmor Developments (Richmond Hill) Ltd. v. Steinberg* (1986), 9 C.P.C. (2d) 20 (Ont. Master), affirmed 9 C.P.C. (2d) 43 (Ont. H.C.), may have been relaxed by the decision in *Antipas v. Coroneos* (1988),

26 C.P.C. (2d) 63, 29 C.C.L.I. 161 (Ont. H.C.), which suggested that any reasonable explanation may satisfy point (2).

Judgment based on admission. By rule 51.06, a party may move for such judgment or other order as he or she may be entitled to based on admissions. The procedure applies not only to admissions made in pleadings or on an examination, but also to admissions made in an affidavit or in response to a request to admit. Moreover, an admission made in an affidavit or on examination in one proceeding may form the basis of a judgment in another proceeding.

Former Rules: Rules 63, 132.

INTERPRETATION

51.01 In rules 51.02 to 51.06, ''authenticity'' includes the fact that,
(a) a document that is said to be an original was printed, written, signed or executed as it purports to have been;
(b) a document that is said to be a copy is a true copy of the original; and
(c) where the document is a copy of a letter, telegram or telecommunication, the original was sent as it purports to have been sent and received by the person to whom it is addressed.

REQUEST TO ADMIT FACT OR DOCUMENT

51.02(1) A party may at any time, by serving a request to admit (Form 51A), request any other party to admit, for the purposes of the proceeding only, the truth of a fact or the authenticity of a document.

(2) A copy of any document mentioned in the request to admit shall, where practicable, be served with the request, unless a copy is already in the possession of the other party.

Csak v. Csak (1993), 15 C.P.C. (3d) 124, 44 R.F.L. (3d) 255 (Ont. Gen. Div.).

Where a party served an unresponsive response to a request to admit, the court ordered the party to serve an amended response.

Lake v. Commercial Union Assurance Co. (1989), 17 W.D.C.P. 47 (Ont. Master).

Where in a response to request to admit the reason given for refusing to admit a fact is irrelevant or patently inappropriate, the court may strike out the response under rule 25.11 as being an abuse of process and vexatious.

Canpotex Ltd. v. Graham (1985), 5 C.P.C. (2d) 233 (Ont. H.C.).

A response to a request to admit should be based on the truth of the fact or authenticity of the document and not on whether the fact or document is admissible in evidence. Objections regarding admissibility or relevance should be made at trial.

RSC Management Ltd. v. Cadillac Fairview Corp. (1985), 51 O.R. (2d) 107, 2 C.P.C. (2d) 53 (Master).

The master ought not make rulings on the propriety of requests to admit, rather the issue should be left to the discretion of the trial judge. If an improper request is made the trial judge may require the party serving the request to pay costs in compensation for requiring the opposite party to review and respond to it.

EFFECT OF REQUEST TO ADMIT

Response Required Within Twenty Days

51.03(1) A party on whom a request to admit is served shall respond to it within twenty days after it is served by serving on the requesting party a response to request to admit (Form 51B).

Deemed Admission Where No Response

(2) Where the party on whom the request is served fails to serve a response as required by subrule (1), the party shall be deemed, for the purposes of the proceeding only, to admit the truth of the facts or the authenticity of the documents mentioned in the request to admit.

Deemed Admission Unless Response Contains Denial or Reason for Refusal to Admit

(3) A party shall also be deemed, for the purposes of the proceeding only, to admit the truth of the facts or the authenticity of the documents mentioned in the request, unless the party's response,

(a) specifically denies the truth of a fact or the authenticity of a document mentioned in the request; or

(b) refuses to admit the truth of a fact or the authenticity of a document and sets out the reason for the refusal.

Wunsche v. Wunsche (1994), 18 O.R. (3d) 161, 114 D.L.R. (4th) 314, 70 O.A.C. 380 (C.A.).

A valuation report had been the subject of a request to admit before trial. The appellant was specifically requested to admit the truth of the fact that the valuator had placed a particular valuation on a business interest. The appellant's faillure to respond to that request to admit did not mean the appellant was deemed to have accepted the valuation, but rather simply constituted an admission that the valuator had concluded the shares in issue had a particular value. The valuation report should not have been permitted into evidence in the circumstances.

COSTS ON REFUSAL TO ADMIT

51.04 Where a party denies or refuses to admit the truth of a fact or the authenticity of a document after receiving a request to admit, and the fact or document is subsequently proved at the hearing, the court may take the denial or refusal into account in exercising its discretion respecting costs.

Cross-Reference: See also rule 57.01(1)(g).

WITHDRAWAL OF ADMISSION

51.05 An admission made in response to a request to admit, a deemed admission under rule 51.03 or an admission in a pleading may be withdrawn on consent or with leave of the court.

Withdrawal of Admissions — In Pleadings (Cases under former Rule should be applied with care.)

Szelazek Investments Ltd. v. Orzech (February 2, 1996), Doc. CA C21539 (Ont. C.A.).

The appropriate test to determine whether to permit an amendment withdrawing an admission is that set out in *Antipas v. Coroneos, infra.*

Zellers Inc. v. Group Resources Inc. (1994), 21 O.R. (3d) 522 (Gen. Div.).

The court granted leave to withdraw an ambiguous admission which had been made inadvertently.

Antipas v. Coroneos (1988), 26 C.P.C. (2d) 63, 29 C.C.L.I. 161 (Ont. H.C.).

If an amendment withdrawing an admission raises a triable issue and does not cause prejudice, it will be permitted if the party withdrawing the admission provides a reasonable explanation for the change in position. A new claim exceeding the limits of an insurance policy explained the withdrawal of an admission of liability. In considering whether there is a triable issue, the court will examine the evidence at the time of the motion. It is not necessary to show new evidence found after the admission was made.

Philmor Developments (Richmond Hill) Ltd. v. Steinberg (1986), 9 C.P.C. (2d) 20 (Ont. Master), affirmed 9 C.P.C. (2d) 43 (Ont. H.C.).

Rule 26.01 does not override rule 51.05. A proposed amendment which amounts to a withdrawal of an admission must be supported by material showing: (1) the proposed amendment raises a triable issue; (2) the admission was made inadvertently or the solicitor was wrongfully instructed; and (3) the withdrawal of the admission will not cause injustice to the other parties (it being understood that there is no injustice if the other parties can be compensated by costs).

Machinefabriek D. Barth & ZN. B.V. v. Roberts Welding & Fabricating Ltd. (1985), 7 C.P.C. (2d) 123 (Ont. Master).

The court refused to permit an amendment to a pleading withdrawing an admission where a key witness for opposing party had become uncooperative. Such prejudice could not be compensated in costs.

Baydon Corp. Ltd. v. du Pont Glore Forgan Can. Ltd. (1974), 4 O.R. (2d) 290 (H.C.).

An amendment withdrawing an admission may be made where it is shown: (1) that the fact admitted is not true; (2) that the admission was inadvertent or the solicitor wrongly instructed; and (3) that any prejudice to the other parties caused by the withdrawal can be compensated in costs.

Paletta v. Paletta (1984), 46 C.P.C. 147 (Ont. H.C.).

The court refused to permit the defendant to withdraw an admission of the existence of a partnership where the draftsman of one of two agreements related to the partnership died and the file regarding the second agreement could not be found.

Sampson & McNaughton Ltd. v. Nicholson (1984), 46 O.R. (2d) 339, 43 C.P.C. 134 (H.C.).

The plaintiff/defendant by counterclaim was refused leave to withdraw an allegation of a written agreement and allege an oral one instead.

Skellett v. Kline (1983), 42 C.P.C. 1 (Ont. H.C.).

An admission of liability in this motor vehicle action, made before the insurer realized that the claim was in excess of the policy limits, was not allowed to be withdrawn, where the material in support of the motion was silent as to the involvement of an alleged unknown motorist.

Gould v. Ariss Haulage Ltd. (1979), 27 O.R. (2d) 291, 15 C.P.C. 150, 106 D.L.R. (3d) 369 (H.C.).

On an application for leave to withdraw an admission of fact, the court modified the test outlined in *Baydon Corp. Ltd. v. duPont Glore Forgan Can. Ltd., supra,* by replacing the first element with the requirement that the court be satisfied that what is proposed to replace the admission raises a triable issue.

Jones v. Union Gas Co. of Can. Ltd. (1978), 20 O.R. (2d) 229 (Master).

A defendant was permitted to withdraw an admission where there was serious controversy as to whether the admission was true, and where a co-defendant had always contested the issue.

Tsigas v. Amourgis (1977), 3 C.P.C. 100 (Ont. Master).

A party seeking to withdraw an admission must satisfy the court, *inter alia*, that the admission is probably untrue.

Rowan v. Landriault (1975), 2 C.P.C. 25 (Ont. Co. Ct.).

Although the plaintiff was permitted to increase the damages claimed, the defendant was not permitted to withdraw an admission of liability where he had not shown such admission was incorrect and inadvertently made.

Visipak Ltd. v. Deerfield Laminations Ltd., [1973] 1 O.R. 97 (H.C.).

A defendant was refused leave to withdraw an admission of liability where the resulting prejudice to the plaintiff could not be compensated in costs and the defendant failed to show that the admission was false.

Brohman v. Aroutsidis, [1969] 2 O.R. 791 (Master).

An amendment to withdraw an admission was refused where there was no satisfactory evidence that the admission was untrue and where the opposing party would have been prejudiced by such an amendment.

Anderson v. Woods, [1955] O.W.N. 585 (H.C.).

A defendant was permitted to withdraw an admission of liability made on his behalf but without his knowledge where the plaintiff could be adequately compensated in costs.

Can. Permanent Mtge. Corp. v. Toronto, [1951] O.R. 726, [1951] 4 D.L.R. 587 (C.A.).

A motion to amend a pleading by withdrawing an admission must be supported by evidence that the fact admitted was untrue.

Withdrawal of Admissions — From Requests to Admit

National Utility Service (Canada) Ltd. v. Kenroc Tools Inc. (1995), 34 C.P.C. (3d) 362 (Ont. Gen. Div.).

Where the defendant's solicitor inadvertently failed to give a timely response to a request to admit, the court granted leave to withdraw a deemed admission under rule 51.03(2).

ORDER BASED ON ADMISSION OF FACT OR DOCUMENT

Motion

51.06(1) Where an admission of the truth of a fact or the authenticity of a document is made,

(a) in an affidavit filed by a party,

(b) in the examination for discovery of a party or a person examined for discovery on behalf of a party; or

(c) by a party on any other examination under oath or affirmation in or out of court,

any party may make a motion to a judge in the same or another proceeding for such order as the party may be entitled to on the admission without waiting for the determination of any other question between the parties, and the judge may make such order as is just.

(2) Where an admission of the truth of a fact or the authenticity of a document is made by a party in a pleading or is made or deemed to be made by a party in response to a request to admit, any party may make a motion in the same proceeding to a judge for such order as the party may be entitled to on the admission without waiting for the determination of any question between the parties, and the judge may make such order as is just.

Exception: Deemed Undertaking
(3) If Rule 30.1 applies to the admission, its use in another proceeding is subject to Rule 30.1 (deemed undertaking). [am. O. Reg. 61/96, s. 3]

Dzamba v. Hurst (1989), 34 C.P.C. (2d) 165 (Ont. Master).

Rule 51.06 does not oust the jurisdiction of a master to hear a motion for summary judgment based in part on admissions made on an examination.

C.I.B.C. v. Wadsworth (1985), 3 C.P.C. (2d) 83 (Ont. Dist. Ct.).

The court granted judgment based on admissions from the defendant's examination for discovery notwithstanding allegations in the statement of defence that the plaintiff had not mitigated its damages. The defendant cannot require a trial by pleading unsubstantiated allegations.

Boni v. Banack, [1971] 2 O.R. 783 (C.A.).

Statements by the husband of a defendant, answering questions on discovery on behalf of his wife by consent of the parties, were not admissions binding on the wife.

TRIALS

RULE 52   TRIAL PROCEDURE

Highlights

This Rule regulates some aspects of the conduct of trials, however much of the procedure at trial is determined by the common law, not by the Rules.

Court-appointed experts. A judge is empowered, on motion by a party or on his or her own initiative to appoint an independent expert to inquire into and report on any question of fact or opinion relevant to an issue in the action: rule 52.03(1). The Rule makes it clear that the role of the expert is that of a witness (as opposed to one who sits with or advises the judge) and specific provision is made for the parties to receive the expert's written report and to cross-examine on it: rule 52.03(7)-(10).

Exclusion of witnesses. The general power of the court to exclude witnesses until called to give evidence is subject to the specific proviso that a party or a witness whose presence is essential to instruct counsel may not be excluded, but may be required to testify before other witnesses: rule 52.06(2). It is also specifically provided that no communication is to be made to an excluded witness of testimony given in his or her absence, except with leave, until after he or she has testified: rule 52.06(3).

Order of presentation in jury trials. With leave of the trial judge, a defendant may make an opening address immediately after the plaintiff's opening: rule 52.07(1)2. The circumstances in which a defendant may address the jury last are specifically defined: a defendant loses the right to go last only if he or she calls evidence-in-chief — putting a document into evidence during the cross-examination of a plaintiff's witness will not lead to the loss of the right: rule 52.07(1)5.

Reply evidence. Evidence in rebuttal is permitted where the defence has raised some new matter or defence which the plaintiff had no opportunity to deal with, and could not have reasonably anticipated; rebuttal evidence will not be permitted regarding the matters which merely confirm or reinforce earlier evidence in the plaintiff's case which could have been brought before the defence was made; moreover, where the new evidence is with respect to a collateral matter, no rebuttal evidence will be permitted: *Krause v. R.*, [1986] 2 S.C.R. 466, 14 C.P.C. (2d) 156, 7 B.C.L.R. (2d) 273, 54 C.R. (3d) 294, [1987] 1 W.W.R. 97, 29 C.C.C. (3d) 385, 33 D.L.R. (4th) 267, 71 N.R. 61.

Related case law. Although not specifically dealt with by the Rules, cases regarding non-suit are collected under rule 52.10. See the cases collected under rules 30.04(8) and 31.06(6) regarding dividing issues for trial.

Practice directions. See below.

Former Rules: Rules 252-253, 255-256, 262-263, 265-267, 509-511.

NOTICE TO THE PROFESSION

CIVIL BACKLOG INITIATIVE — 1996

The public is entitled to an affordable and timely resolution of civil disputes. In six of the eight regions of the province a high percentage of civil cases remain on the trial list for more than a year before these cases are tried.

The Civil Justice Review, which is a collaborative effort of the judiciary, the bar, the Ministry of the Attorney General and the public, made the following recommendation in regard to civil backlog:

> "We recommend that two dedicated teams, a trial team and a pre-trial settlement team, be created for the purpose of pre-trying and trying the backlogged cases in the court centres around the province where this is needed most. We recommend that the trial team be drawn from existing judicial resources."

I have accepted this recommendation of the Civil Justice Review and have created a civil backlog trial team consisting of eight justices of the court. Each of the eight regions has contributed one justice to this initiative. The team of justices will sit for four weeks in each of the backlogged regions (five weeks in Toronto). The scheduling of the civil backlog trial team is as follows:

	The weeks of:
Toronto Region	March 25, April 1, 8, 15, 22
East Region	May 6, 13, 20 and 27
North East Region	June 3, 10, 17, 24
Central East	August 26, September 2, 9, 16
Central West Region	September 23, 30, October 7, 15
South West Region	November 4, 11, 18, 25

The mandate of the civil backlog trial team is to try the oldest civil cases first. It is expected that counsel and the litigants will be fully prepared to proceed on the date assigned for trial. Any request for an adjournment of the proceedings will be scrutinized very carefully and cases will only be adjourned in exceptional circumstances. In an effort to ensure consistency of the adjournment policy, a designated justice in each area will be assigned to hear any adjournment requests during the civil backlog initiative period.

The initiative will significantly reduce the backlog of civil cases and assist members of the public in obtaining a timely resolution of their civil disputes. It is crucial that counsel assist the Court in this important undertaking by providing accurate information to trial co-ordinators regarding the readiness of cases for trial and the estimated trial time required.

Each Regional Senior Justice in the six affected regions will be releasing a scheduling announcement to the bar on the specifics of how the visiting justices will be assigned to the civil backlog in the regions. These scheduling announcements will be released in early 1996.

Osgoode Hall, Toronto
December 15, 1995

R. Roy McMurtry
Chief Justice, Ontario Court of Justice

FAILURE TO ATTEND AT TRIAL

52.01(1) Where an action is called for trial and all the parties fail to attend, the trial judge may strike the action off the trial list.

(2) Where an action is called for trial and a party fails to attend, the trial judge may,

(a) proceed with the trial in the absence of the party;

(b) where the plaintiff attends and the defendant fails to attend, dismiss the counterclaim, if any, and allow the plaintiff to prove the claim;

(c) where the defendant attends and the plaintiff fails to attend, dismiss the action and allow the defendant to prove the counterclaim, if any; or

(d) make such other order as is just.

(3) A judge may set aside or vary, on such terms as are just, a judgment obtained against a party who failed to attend at the trial.

Setting Aside Judgment — rule 52.01(3)

Guerriero v. Paul (1990), 73 O.R. (2d) 25, 42 C.P.C. (2d) 318 (H.C.).

Where the defendant had relied on his counsel's assurance that a trial adjournment would be granted, but the trial had proceeded and judgment had been granted against the defendant, the judgment was set aside.

Sigroum Office Management v. Milanis (1986), 10 C.P.C. (2d) 48 (Ont. Dist. Ct.).

Default judgment was set aside where the defendants had served a statement of defence, but had not filed a copy with the local registrar. Furthermore one of the affidavits which had been employed at trial was not sworn and the trial record was incomplete.

Garbe v. Winton (1980), 19 C.P.C. 64 (Ont. H.C.).

The court may set aside a judgment obtained at trial after default was noted.

Burbank v. O'Flaherty (1975), 13 O.R. (2d) 769, 2 C.P.C. 3 (Co. Ct.).

The predecessor of this provision was held to be inapplicable where a defendant had not delivered pleadings; however, a judgment obtained in circumstances where a defendant is in default of defence may be set aside through the exercise of the court's inherent jurisdiction.

Nelligan v. Lindsay, [1945] O.W.N. 295 (H.C.).

A full discussion of factors considered on a motion to set aside a judgment. A motion to set aside was denied where, *inter alia*, witnesses were no longer available, a motion to set aside a second judgment was granted upon quite onerous terms in view of the long delay on the part of the defendants, and the chances of success were doubtful.

ADJOURNMENT OF TRIAL

52.02 A judge may postpone or adjourn a trial to such time and place, and on such terms, as are just.

Atlas Construction Inc. v. Brownstones Ltd. (1996), 7 W.D.C.P. (2d) 184 (Ont. Gen. Div.).

Generally a trial should be adjourned where there is an outstanding appeal of an interlocutory order which may affect the course of the trial. Discussion of circumstances where consenting to the commencement of trial may waive rights relating to interlocutory motions and orders.

Cousineau v. St. Joseph's Health Centre (1990), 49 C.P.C. (2d) 306 (Ont. H.C.).

The court should be reluctant to second-guess counsel as to the necessity of an adjournment where there is a reason for an adjournment.

Findlay v. Diver (1989), 43 C.P.C. (2d) 316 (Ont. H.C.).

Where the parties agreed to split the trial and that the jury would decide the question of liability and the judge alone would then assess damages, and the jury found the defendants not liable, the judge granted the plaintiff's request not to proceed with the assessment of damages pending an appeal of the jury's verdict on liability.

Khan v. Pfeugel (1984), 44 C.P.C. 154 (Ont. H.C.).

Where a case was called for a jury trial and the trial judge made a ruling on an evidentiary point, the trial was held to have commenced notwithstanding the jury had not been empanelled and no evidence had actually been heard. The judge ought not to have adjourned the case to permit an appeal from the ruling.

Monarch Life Assur. Co. v. Lionstar Invts. Ltd. (1979), 10 C.P.C. 240 (Ont. Div. Ct.).

Where exceptional circumstances did not exist, a motion for adjournment was refused even though new counsel had been retained only the day prior to the hearing.

Pellegrini v. Haggar (1974), 4 O.R. (2d) 52 (C.A.).

Orders made at assignment court do not fetter the discretion of the trial judge.

Hannah v. Shannon, [1968] 1 O.R. 69 (C.A.).

A punitive order as to costs against a party not present made on the judge's own motion is a denial of natural justice and cannot stand.

MacDonald v. Stace, [1958] O.W.N. 1 (C.A.).

Where it appeared that the defendants were endeavouring to delay the trial without any sufficient reason, the trial judge refused an adjournment and proceeded to try the case notwithstanding the withdrawal of the defendants.

COURT APPOINTED EXPERTS

Appointment by Judge

52.03(1) On motion by a party or on his or her own initiative, a judge may, at any time, appoint one or more independent experts to inquire into and report on any question of fact or opinion relevant to an issue in the action.

(2) The expert shall be named by the judge and, where possible, shall be an expert agreed on by the parties.

Contents of Order Appointing Expert

(3) The order shall contain the instructions to be given to the expert and the judge may make such further orders as he or she considers necessary to enable the expert to carry out the instructions, including, on motion by a party, an order for,

(a) inspection of property under Rule 32; or

(b) the physical or mental examination of a party under section 105 of the *Courts of Justice Act*.

Remuneration of Expert

(4) The remuneration of an expert shall be fixed by the judge who appoints the expert, and shall include a fee for the expert's report and an appropriate sum for each day that attendance at the trial is required.

(5) The responsibility of the parties for payment of the remuneration of an expert shall be determined in the first instance by the judge.

(6) Where a motion by a party for the appointment of an expert is opposed, the judge may, as a condition of making the appointment, require the party seeking the appointment to give such security for the remuneration of the expert as is just.

Report

(7) The expert shall prepare a report and send it to the registrar and the registrar shall send a copy of the report to every party.

(8) The report shall be filed as evidence at the trial of the action unless the trial judge orders otherwise.

(9) The judge may direct the expert to make a further or supplementary report, and subrules (7) and (8) apply to that report.

Cross-examination of Expert
(10) Any party may cross-examine the expert at the trial.

Liability of Parties for Remuneration of Expert
(11) The liability of the parties for payment of the remuneration of the expert shall be determined by the trial judge at the end of the trial, and a party who has paid the expert in accordance with a determination under subrule (5), if not the party determined to be liable for payment under this subrule, shall be indemnified by the party determined to be liable.

Ericsson Communications Inc. v. Novatel Communications Ltd. (February 19, 1996), Doc. Ottawa 68656/92 (Ont. Gen. Div.).

The court appointed an accounting firm to act as an independent expert and review documentation relating to damage issues.

Featherstone v. Grunsven, [1972] 1 O.R. 490 (C.A.).

The parties have a right to examine all documents resulting from the appointment of the expert.

Phillips v. Ford Motor Co. of Can. Ltd., [1971] 2 O.R. 637, 18 D.L.R. (3d) 641 (C.A.).

Discussion of limitations of the use of court experts.

Blowes v. Hamilton, [1970] 1 O.R. 310, 8 D.L.R. (3d) 320 (H.C.).

The court appointed a doctor as an expert who was permitted to ask questions directly of the witness.

MacDonald Electric Ltd. v. Cochrane, [1955] O.W.N. 255 (H.C.).

The court appointed an expert to investigate the functioning of electronic equipment.

Richard v. Gray Coach Lines Ltd., [1950] O.W.N. 136 (H.C.).

In a personal injury action having complicated medical evidence, the court, with the consent of both parties, appointed a doctor to help assess damages and fixed the doctor's remuneration.

EXHIBITS

Marking and Numbering
52.04(1) Exhibits shall be marked and numbered consecutively, and the registrar attending the trial shall make a list of the exhibits, giving a description of each exhibit, and stating by whom it was put in evidence and, where the person who produced it is not a party or a party's solicitor, the name of that person.

Return of Exhibits
(2) At any time following the trial judgment, on requisition by the solicitor or party who put an exhibit in evidence or the person who produced it and on the filing of the consent of all parties represented at the trial, the registrar may return the exhibit to the person making the requisition.

(3) Subject to subrule (2), the exhibits shall remain in the possession of the registrar or the registrar of the court to which an appeal is taken,
 (a) until the time for an appeal has expired; or

(b) where an appeal has been taken, until it has been disposed of.

(4) On the expiration of the time for appeal or on the disposition of the appeal, the registrar on his or her own initiative, shall return the exhibits to the respective solicitors or parties who put the exhibits in evidence at the trial.

Gaulin v. Gaulin (1978), 8 C.P.C. 302 (Ont. Div. Ct.).
A party was permitted the return of the exhibits which he had filed.

VIEW BY JUDGE OR JURY

52.05 The judge or judge and jury by whom an action is being tried or the court before whom an appeal is being heard may, in the presence of the parties or their counsel, inspect any property concerning which any question arises in the action, or the place where the cause of action arose.

Kubarsepp v. Jeppesen, [1953] O.W.N. 805 (H.C.).
Where members of a jury take an unauthorized view, a new trial may be ordered.

Chambers v. Murphy, [1953] O.W.N. 399, [1953] 2 D.L.R. 705 (C.A.).
It is improper for a trial judge to use his observations on a view in assessing the credibility of witnesses.

Paul v. Fadden, [1953] O.W.N. 306 (C.A.).
A view is for the purpose of enabling the trial judge properly to evaluate the evidence adduced at trial.

EXCLUSION OF WITNESSES

Order for Exclusion
52.06(1) The trial judge may, at the request of any party, order that a witness be excluded from the courtroom until called to give evidence, subject to subrule (2).

Order not to Apply to Party or Witness Instructing Counsel
(2) An order under subrule (1) may not be made in respect of a party to the action or a witness whose presence is essential to instruct counsel for the party calling the witness, but the trial judge may require any such party or witness to give evidence before any other witnesses are called to give evidence on behalf of that party.

No Communication with Excluded Witnesses
(3) Where an order is made excluding a witness from the courtroom, there shall be no communication to the witness of any evidence given during his or her absence from the courtroom, except with leave of the trial judge, until after the witness has been called and has given evidence.

Exclusion of Persons Interfering with Trial
(4) Nothing in this rule prevents the trial judge from excluding from the courtroom any person who is interfering with the proper conduct of the trial.

Taylor Estate v. McCully (1994), 20 O.R. (3d) 373, 32 C.P.C. (3d) 247 (Gen. Div.).

Where an order had been made excluding witnesses from trial, the court refused to subsequently exempt the defence experts from the order. The plaintiff had been obliged to produce evidence subject to the order, and granting an exemption midway through the proceeding would result in prejudice to the plaintiff which could not be cured by an award of costs.

Drosos v. Chong (1992), 8 C.P.C. (3d) 312 (Ont. Gen. Div.).

The court awarded costs of a mistrial against the plaintiff's counsel who had discussed trial testimony with an expert witness notwithstanding an exclusion order. The order did not contain an exception for expert witnesses.

C.C.A.S., Hamilton-Wentworth v. S. (M.) (1985), 10 C.P.C. (2d) 60 (Ont. U.F.C.).

The exclusion of witnesses is a discretionary matter for the trial judge. Generally where credibility is in issue witnesses should be excluded if a party so requests.

Crawford v. Ferris, [1953] O.W.N. 713 (H.C.).

Communication among witnesses in the face of an order for exclusion of witnesses seriously undermines the weight of the affected evidence.

ORDER OF PRESENTATION IN JURY TRIALS

52.07(1) On the trial of an action with a jury, the order of presentation shall be regulated as follows, unless the trial judge directs otherwise:

1. The plaintiff may make an opening address and, subject to paragraph 2, shall then adduce evidence.

2. A defendant may, with leave of the trial judge, make an opening address immediately after the opening address of the plaintiff, and before the plaintiff adduces any evidence.

3. When the plaintiff's evidence is concluded, the defendant may make an opening address, unless he or she has already done so, and shall then adduce evidence.

4. When the defendant's evidence is concluded, the plaintiff may adduce any proper reply evidence and the defendant shall then make a closing address, followed by the closing address of the plaintiff.

5. Where a defendant adduces no evidence after the conclusion of the plaintiff's evidence, the plaintiff shall make a closing address, followed by the closing address of the defendant.

(2) Where the burden of proof in respect of all matters in issue in the action lies on the defendant, the trial judge may reverse the order of presentation.

(3) Where there are two or more defendants separately represented, the order of presentation shall be as directed by the trial judge.

(4) Where a party is represented by counsel, the right to address the jury shall be exercised by counsel.

Address to Jury

Gellie v. Naylor (1986), 55 O.R. (2d) 400, 9 C.P.C. (2d) 123, 28 D.L.R. (4th) 762, 15 O.A.C. 129 (C.A.).

A new trial was ordered where the trial judge had deprived the plaintiff of the right to address the jury last.

Contents of Address to Jury (These cases must now be read in light of s. 118.)

Allan v. Bushnell T.V. Co., [1969] 2 O.R. 6, 4 D.L.R. (3d) 212 (C.A.).
Counsel should not express their views as to quantum of damages to be awarded.

Gray v. Alanco Devs. Ltd., [1967] 1 O.R. 597, 61 D.L.R. (2d) 652 (C.A.).
In a jury trial neither the judge nor counsel should express views as to the quantum of general damages. The jury should not be informed of the amount claimed in the statement of claim. Witnesses are not permitted to express views on the monetary value to be allowed for pain and suffering, etc.

Ross v. Lamport, [1955] O.R. 542, [1955] 4 D.L.R. 826, reversed in part [1956] S.C.R. 366, 2 D.L.R. (2d) 255.
A new trial was ordered where, *inter alia*, an address to the jury had been inflammatory.

Stewart v. Speer, [1953] O.R. 502 (C.A.).
Discussion of manner in which the amount claimed by the plaintiff may be disclosed to the jury.

Reply Evidence — rule 52.07(1)4

Krause v. R., [1986] 2 S.C.R. 466, 14 C.P.C. (2d) 156, 7 B.C.L.R. (2d) 273, 54 C.R. (3d) 294, [1987] 1 W.W.R. 97, 29 C.C.C. (3d) 385, 33 D.L.R. (4th) 267, 71 N.R. 61.
During a cross-examination in a civil trial, if new evidence emerges concerning the merits of the case, the other party may be allowed to call evidence in rebuttal. However, where the new evidence is with respect to a collateral matter, no rebuttal evidence will be allowed.

Allcock Laight & Westwood Ltd. v. Patten, Bernard and Dynamic Displays Ltd., [1967] 1 O.R. 18 (C.A.).
The plaintiff may not introduce evidence in reply, the main purpose of which is to confirm his case in chief; a new trial was ordered where the plaintiff did so.

Judge's Charge to Jury (These cases must now be read in light of s. 118. See also the cases under s. 134.)

Howes v. Crosby (1984), 45 O.R. (2d) 449, 29 C.C.L.T. 60, 6 D.L.R. (4th) 698, 2 O.A.C. 375 (C.A.).
In an action for damages for personal injury or wrongful death, a trial judge may not charge the jury respecting the possible range of damages. This is particularly so where a solicitor has expressly asked the judge not to direct the jury on this matter. However, a judge may instruct a jury as to the upper limit on non-pecuniary damages that may be awarded in "catastrophe" cases.

DISAGREEMENT OF THE JURY

52.08(1) Where the jury,
(a) disagrees;
(b) makes no finding on which judgment can be granted; or
(c) answers some but not all of the questions directed to it or gives conflicting answers, so that judgment cannot be granted on its findings, the trial judge may direct that the action be retried with another jury at the same or any subsequent sitting, but where there is no evidence on which a judgment for the plaintiff could be based or where for any other reason the plaintiff is not entitled to judgment, the judge shall dismiss the action.

(2) Where the answers given by a jury are sufficient to entitle a party to judgment on some but not all of the claims in the action, the judge may grant judgment on the claims in respect of which the answers are sufficient, and subrule (1) applies to the remaining claims.

Gauthier v. Gauvin, [1968] 2 O.R. 809, 70 D.L.R. (2d) 665 (C.A.).

A new trial was ordered by the Court of Appeal where the jury failed to make a clear finding of fact on the critical issue, namely which party went through a red light.

Allen v. Brazeau, [1967] 2 O.R. 665, 65 D.L.R. (2d) 37 (C.A.).

Where the jury fails to make a finding on a crucial question of fact, it may be sent back to do so.

Terkuc v. Herd, [1958] O.R. 37 (C.A.).

Discussion of circumstances under which a jury should be sent back to clarify indefinite or inconclusive answers.

RECORDING JURY VERDICT

52.09 The verdict of a jury shall be endorsed on the trial record.

Playford v. Freiberg (1993), 15 C.P.C. (3d) 195 (Ont. Gen. Div.).

The court should not accept evidence from a juror with respect to what happened in the jury room. The court refused to strike out the jury verdict and order a new trial or to reconvene and recharge the jury.

Loffredi v. Simonetti (1988), 29 C.P.C. (2d) 10 (Ont. Dist. Ct.).

When faced with a perverse jury verdict, the trial judge must enter judgment in accordance with the verdict.

Baboi v. Gregory (1986), 56 O.R. (2d) 175, 9 C.P.C. (2d) 230 (Dist. Ct.).

A trial judge does not have the authority to declare a jury verdict to be perverse.

Segreti v. Toronto (1981), 20 C.P.C. 110 (Ont. H.C.).

Although the verdict of the jury concerning damages was perverse, the trial judge refused to substitute his assessment of damages.

FAILURE TO PROVE A FACT OR DOCUMENT

52.10 Where, through accident, mistake or other cause, a party fails to prove some fact or document material to the party's case,

    (a) the judge may proceed with the trial subject to proof of the fact or document afterwards at such time and on such terms as the judge directs; or

    (b) where the case is being tried by a jury, the judge may direct the jury to find a verdict as if the fact or document had been proved, and the verdict shall take effect on proof of the fact or document afterwards as directed, and, if it is not so proved, judgment shall be granted to the opposite party, unless the judge directs otherwise.

Failure to Prove Facts — Generally

Kerbel v. Carson, Dunlop & Associates Ltd. (1994), 27 C.P.C. (3d) 114, 15 C.L.R. (2d) 1 (Ont. Gen. Div.).

Where proof of professional certification would bar a claim against the defendant engineer, the court granted leave to file such proof within one week.

J.R.I. Food Corp. v. Yonadam (1993), 16 C.P.C. (3d) 345 (Ont. Gen. Div.).

Where as a result of a mistake, the plaintiff had failed to prove documents relevant to its case, the court granted leave to adduce further evidence. In the circumstances, costs of the motion were payable by the plaintiff on a solicitor and client basis in any event of the cause.

Hengab Invts. Ltd. v. Vicente (1981), 24 C.P.C. 192 (Ont. Co. Ct.).

Review of relevant considerations in permitting a plaintiff to prove material facts to its case after the action had been dismissed on a non-suit but prior to the formal judgment being taken out, where the failure to prove such facts was through inadvertence or mistake.

Ont. Motor Sales Ltd. v. Steeves, [1959] O.W.N. 205 (C.A.).

Where the plaintiff omits to prove a non-controversial but necessary fact he should be permitted to re-open his case and correct the omission.

Motion for Non-Suit

Eagleson v. Dowbiggan (January 10, 1996), Doc. 93-CQ-45766, additional reasons (February, 1996), Doc. 93-CQ-45766 (Ont. Gen. Div.).

On a motion for non-suit in a defamation case, the defendants are not put to the usual election as to whether or not they will call evidence. The judge may either decide the motion or reserve her decision until the conclusion of the defendants' case. Here the judge decided the motion and dismissed the case.

Bank of Montreal v. Horan (1986), 54 O.R. (2d) 757 (H.C.).

A motion for a non-suit should not be entertained until the defendants have elected whether or not to call evidence.

Brazeau Transport Inc. v. Canfor Ltd. (1982), 38 O.R. (2d) 414, 27 C.P.C. 51 (Co. Ct.).

On a motion for non-suit, evidence of the applicant's co-defendant should be considered in determining the sufficiency of evidence against the applicant.

Hall v. Pemberton (1974), 5 O.R. (2d) 438, 50 D.L.R. (3d) 518 (C.A.).

The test is whether the evidence supporting the plaintiff's case is sufficient in law to result in judgment for the plaintiff, assuming all such evidence is true and drawing all reasonable and favourable inferences therefrom.

Nadler v. Chornij, [1973] 2 O.R. 1, 32 D.L.R. (3d) 651 (C.A.).

The trial judge ought not to make findings of fact when disposing of a motion for non-suit.

Johnstone v. Ottawa Electric Ry. Co., [1950] O.R. 16, 65 C.R.T.C. 104, [1950] 1 D.L.R. 530 (C.A.).

Where the plaintiff has shown that one or all defendants have been negligent but has not shown *which* defendant was negligent, no non-suit should be granted, but the trial should continue so the court can determine on all the evidence which, if any, defendant was negligent.

RULE 53   EVIDENCE AT TRIAL

Highlights

This Rule regulates various aspects of evidence at trial. It is, of course, merely supplementary to the *Evidence Act* and the common law of evidence. Nevertheless, it contains a number of minor clarifications or changes in the law and several changes that are major.

Evidence by the examination of witnesses. The basic rule that witnesses are to be examined orally in court by direct, cross- and re-examination is codified, as is the trial judge's right to exercise reasonable control over the interrogation of witnesses, to protect a witness from harassment or embarrassment and to direct a witness to be recalled for further examination: rule 53.01(1)-(3).

It is specifically provided that where a witness appears unwilling or unable to give responsive answers, the trial judge may permit examination by leading questions: rule 53.01(4).

Where there are language problems, an interpreter is to be provided by the party calling the witness, unless in the case of French-English or English-French translations an interpreter is provided by the Attorney General: rule 53.01(5) and (6).

Evidence by affidavit. Affidavit evidence may be used only with leave of the court obtained at or before trial. (Note, however, that where an action is undefended the plaintiff may make *a motion* for judgment supported by affidavit evidence: see rule 19.05.)

Expert witnesses. As a precondition to calling an expert, at least ten days before the trial, a copy of the expert's report setting out the expert's qualifications and the substance of his or her proposed testimony must be served on every other party. Unless this is done the expert may not testify, except with leave: rule 53.03. Where the expert is a health practitioner, s. 52 of the *Evidence Act*, which is reproduced below following rule 53.03, must be complied with.

The evidence of an expert should not be excluded simply on the ground that a report was not timely delivered, unless the court is satisfied that the prejudice to justice involved in receiving the evidence exceeds the prejudice involved in excluding it (see rule 53.08). Appropriate terms may be imposed. For example, in *Hunter v. Ellenberger* (1988), 25 C.P.C. (2d) 14 (Ont. H.C.), the expert evidence was received with time allowed to opposing counsel to call responding evidence and with a costs penalty.

Compelling attendance at trial. The former subpoena is re-named a "summons to witness" (rule 53.04(1)) and it is to be noted that the summons is to be served personally and not by the alternatives to personal service provided in rule 16.03. A form of summons is provided to compel the attendance of witnesses outside Ontario under the *Interprovincial Summonses Act*, R.S.O. 1990, c. I.12: rule 53.05.

The procedure for securing the attendance of an adverse party by a notice to his or her solicitor extends to an officer, director or sole proprietor of an adverse party, and to partners in a partnership that is an adverse party, and ten days' notice is required: rule 53.07(1). Such persons, and an adverse party, may be cross-examined by the person calling them, as of right: rule 53.07(3).

Evidence admissible only with leave. Several rules provide that, with regard to certain types of evidence, unless various preconditions are met, the evidence is not admissible, except with leave. Rule 53.08 gives the court direction as to the granting of such leave by providing that leave shall be granted on such terms as are just and with an adjournment if necessary, unless to do so would cause prejudice to the opposite party or would cause undue delay in the conduct of the trial.

Calculation of future pecuniary damages. Rule 53.09 provides for a 2.5 per cent discount rate for future pecuniary damages and sets out a formula for a gross-up to offset income tax liability.

Prejudgment interest. Rule 53.10 sets the prejudgment interest rate for non-pecuniary loss in personal injury cases at five per cent per year.

Former Rules: Rules 232, 254, 267a, 268, 272-275.

EVIDENCE BY WITNESSES

Oral Evidence as General Rule

53.01(1) Unless these rules provide otherwise, witnesses at the trial of an action shall be examined orally in court and the examination may consist of direct examination, cross-examination and re-examination.

Trial Judge to Exercise Control

(2) The trial judge shall exercise reasonable control over the mode of interrogation of a witness so as to protect the witness from undue harassment or embarrassment and may disallow a question put to a witness that is vexatious or irrelevant to any matter that may properly be inquired into at the trial.

(3) The trial judge may at any time direct that a witness be recalled for further examination.

Leading Questions on Direct Examination

(4) Where a witness appears unwilling or unable to give responsive answers, the trial judge may permit the party calling the witness to examine him or her by means of leading questions.

Interpreter

(5) Where a witness does not understand the language or languages in which the examination is to be conducted or is deaf or mute, a competent and independent interpreter shall, before the witness is called, take an oath or make an affirmation to interpret accurately the administration of the oath or affirmation to the witness, the questions put to the witness and his or her answers.

(6) Where an interpreter is required under subrule (5), the party calling the witness shall provide the interpreter, unless the interpretation is to be from English to French or from French to English and an interpreter is provided by the Ministry of the Attorney General.

Evidence by Witnesses — Generally

Carpenter v. Carpenter (1993), 19 C.P.C. (3d) 18 (Ont. Gen. Div.).

The court re-opened the trial where important new evidence came to light after the conclusion of trial but before reasons for judgment had been given.

Rodger v. Strop (1992), 14 C.P.C. (3d) 289, 42 M.V.R. (2d) 174 (Ont. Gen. Div.).

The admissibility of photographs, including videotape, depends upon (1) their accuracy in truly representing the facts; (2) their fairness and absence of any intention to mislead; and (3) their verification by a person capable to do so. In this jury case the court admitted surveillance videos of the plaintiff and photos of the plaintiff's motor vehicle taken after the accident.

Kennedy v. Guardian Insurance of Canada (1992), 1 C.P.C. (3d) 304 (Ont. Gen. Div.).

It is for a solicitor to determine whether he or she will give evidence on behalf of his or her client at trial, but where a solicitor decides to give such evidence, the solicitor must relinquish the role of advocate.

Telenga v. Raymond European Car Services Ltd. (1991), 3 C.P.C. (3d) 79 (Ont. Gen. Div.).

There is a duty to use reasonable care to prevent the spoliation of evidence. However, distinguishing U.S. jurisprudence, the court refused to grant summary judgment or preclude expert evidence where spoliation had occurred.

Paquette v. Chubb (1988), 65 O.R. (2d) 321, 31 C.P.C. (2d) 87, 52 D.L.R. (4th) 1, 29 O.A.C. 243 (C.A.), leave to appeal to Supreme Court of Canada refused (1989), 66 O.R. (2d) xi, 35 C.P.C. (2d) xlviii, 55 D.L.R. (4th) vii, 100 N.R. 239, 34 O.A.C. 400n.

Lengthy discussion of what constitutes corroborative evidence in civil cases.

Planned Insurance Portfolios Co. v. Crown Life Insurance Co. (1989), 68 O.R. (2d) 271, 36 C.P.C. (2d) 218, 58 D.L.R. (4th) 106 (H.C.).

A lawyer was permitted to give evidence in a matter in which a partner was acting as counsel. There was no conflict of interest, and it was not a jury trial.

Moysa v. Alberta (Labour Relations Bd.), [1989] 1 S.C.R. 1572, 34 C.P.C. (2d) 97, 67 Alta. L.R. (2d) 193, [1989] 4 W.W.R. 596, 97 A.R. 368, 89 C.L.L.C. 14,028, 60 D.L.R. (4th) 1, 96 N.R. 70.

Section 2(b) of the *Canadian Charter of Rights and Freedoms* does not provide reporters with immunity from testimonial compulsion.

Grineage v. Coopman (1988), 27 C.P.C. (2d) 187 (Ont. H.C.).

While the *Charter* protection against self-crimination is not limited to criminal proceedings, but extends to provincial statutes providing for penalties, cross-examination on previous testimony at a provincial offences trial was permitted in a related civil action where it went mainly to credibility.

Erco Industries Ltd. v. Allendale Mutual Ins. Co. (1988), 62 O.R. (2d) 766, 29 C.C.L.I. 4, 25 O.A.C. 130 (C.A.).

A plaintiff was not permitted to enter new evidence in reply which would contradict the defendant's expert witness, where the plaintiff had chosen not to cross-examine the defence expert on the point in issue.

Omnia Pelts Inc. v. C.P. Airlines Ltd. (1986), 57 O.R. (2d) 568, 15 C.P.C. (2d) 99 (H.C.).

The trial judge should permit a witness to be cross-examined by both senior and junior counsel provided: (1) the complexity of the case makes division of the cross-examination desirable; (2) the areas to be covered by each counsel are defined at the outset of the cross-examination; and (3) there is no overlap.

Deep v. Wood (1983), 33 C.P.C. 256, 143 D.L.R. (3d) 246 (Ont. C.A.).

In a civil action, cross-examination at trial concerning prior findings of professional misconduct involving dishonesty may be used to diminish the credibility of a witness.

Wingold v. W.B. Sullivan Const. Ltd. (1980), 20 C.P.C. 76 (Ont. H.C.).

Discussion of the circumstances in which counsel may cross-examine a witness called by a co-defendant.

Richards v. Richards, [1946] O.W.N. 129 (H.C.).

Discussion of the proof of service of documents and the desirability of the process-server testifying in court.

Murray v. Haylow, 60 O.L.R. 629, [1927] 3 D.L.R. 1036 (C.A.).

Nothing can justify the treating of the religious belief of a witness with contempt and questions which do so will be disallowed.

Examination of Witnesses — Intervention by Judge

J.M.W. Recycling Inc. v. A.G. Can. (1982), 35 O.R. (2d) 355, 133 D.L.R. (3d) 363 (C.A.).

The Court of Appeal ordered a new trial where the trial judge had intervened too frequently in the examination of witnesses.

Majcenic v. Natale, [1968] 1 O.R. 189, 66 D.L.R. (2d) 50 (C.A.).

Where questions by the trial judge amount to an unwarranted interference with counsel's conduct of the trial, a new trial may be ordered.

EVIDENCE BY AFFIDAVIT

With Leave of Court

53.02(1) Before or at the trial of an action, the court may make an order allowing the evidence of a witness or proof of a particular fact or document to be given by affidavit, unless an adverse party reasonably requires the attendance of the deponent at trial for cross-examination.

(2) Where an order is made under subrule (1) before the trial, it may be set aside or varied by the trial judge where it appears necessary to do so in the interest of justice.

Affidavit Evidence With Leave of the Court — rule 53.02(1)

Leclerc v. St-Louis (1984), 47 O.R. (2d) 584, 45 C.P.C. 137, 11 D.L.R. (4th) 765, (*sub nom. Vien v. Vien*) 5 O.A.C. 307 (Div. Ct.).

An affidavit made by a wife, who later died, claiming against her deceased husband's estate, was ruled admissible in evidence at the trial.

Lumbreras-Ximeuez v. Allstate Ins. Co. of Can., 11 O.R. (2d) 639, [1975] I.L.R. 1-710 (H.C.).

Affidavit evidence should not be allowed where such evidence is strongly contested and depends upon the credibility of the witness.

Konapecki v. Konapecki, [1944] O.W.N. 685 (H.C.).

The court discussed the advantage of bringing a motion under the predecessor of this provision before trial rather than at trial.

Parker v. Parker, [1948] O.W.N. 834 (H.C.).

Notice must be given to the opposing party of an intention to seek an order permitting the use of affidavit evidence at trial.

EXPERT WITNESSES

53.03(1) A party who intends to call an expert witness at trial shall, not less than ten days before the commencement of the trial, serve on every other

party to the action a report, signed by the expert, setting out his or her name, address and qualifications and the substance of his or her proposed testimony.

(2) No expert witness may testify, except with leave of the trial judge, unless subrule (1) has been complied with.

[Note: See rule 53.08 regarding leave to admit expert evidence on short or no notice — Authors.]

Evidence Act Provision

Section 52 of the *Evidence Act*, R.S.O. 1990, c. E.23, must be complied with regarding medical evidence and is as follows. (The amending Act [1989, c. 68] transitional provision is similar to that contained in S.O. 1989, c. 67, and causes the same difficulties. See the Authors' Comment following *Courts of Justice Act* s. 116.)

Definition
52.—(1) In this section,
''practitioner'' means,
(a) a person licensed to practise under the *Health Disciplines Act*,
(b) a drugless practitioner registered under the *Drugless Practitioners Act*,
(c) a denture therapist under the *Denture Therapists Act*,
(d) a chiropodist registered under the *Chiropody Act*,
(e) a registered psychologist under the *Psychologists Registration Act*, or
(f) a person licensed or registered to practise in another part of Canada under an Act that is similar to an Act referred to in clause (a), (b), (c), (d) or (e).

Medical reports
(2) A report obtained by or prepared for a party to an action and signed by a practitioner and any other report of the practitioner that relates to the action are, with leave of the court and after at least ten days notice has been given to all other parties, admissible in evidence in the action.

Entitlement
(3) Unless otherwise ordered by the court, a party to an action is entitled, at the time that notice is given under subsection (2), to a copy of the report together with any other report of the practitioner that relates to the action.

Report required
(4) Except by leave of the judge presiding at the trial, a practitioner who signs a report with respect to a party shall not give evidence at the trial unless the report is given to all other parties in accordance with subsection (2).

If practitioner called unnecessarily
(5) If a practitioner is required to give evidence in person in an action and the court is of the opinion that the evidence could have been produced as effectively by way of a report, the court may order the party that required the

attendance of the practitioner to pay as costs therefor such sum as the court considers appropriate.

Experts' Reports — Generally

Toronto Helicopters Ltd. v. Intercity Ford Ltd. (January 18, 1995), Doc. Thunder Bay 7676A-90 (Ont. Gen. Div.).

Evidence of an experiment is not necessarily expert evidence in respect of which a report is a necessary prerequisite. The court conducted a *voir dire* to determine whether certain other evidence was lay opinion evidence which did not require a report or expert opinion evidence which does ordinarily require a report.

Tulshi v. Ioannou (1994), 27 C.P.C. (3d) 153 (Ont. Gen. Div.).

A report from a deceased expert was permitted to be filed at trial.

Hock (Next Friend of) v. Hospital for Sick Children (1993), 19 C.P.C. (3d) 349 (Ont. Gen. Div.).

The court refused to order that one party's expert reports be provided to the opposite party before the opposite party obtained its own reports.

Gibson v. Toth (1990), 44 C.P.C. (2d) 137 (Ont. Div. Ct.).

A new trial was ordered where the trial judge had refused to permit the introduction of a specialist's evidence because of the plaintiff's failure to serve a report pursuant to s. 52(3) of the *Evidence Act*. The plaintiff had been unable to serve a report because the specialist had refused to provide one.

Ricketts v. Woods (1989), 69 O.R. (2d) 128 (C.A.).

The court would not interfere with a jury's findings despite the admission at trial of an undisclosed expert's opinion.

Hunter v. Ellenberger (1988), 25 C.P.C. (2d) 14 (Ont. H.C.).

Evidence should not be excluded on technical grounds, such as lack of timely delivery of an expert report, unless the court is satisfied that the prejudice to justice involved in receiving the evidence exceeds the prejudice to justice involved in excluding it. In this case the expert evidence was received with time allowed to opposing counsel to call responding evidence and with a costs penalty.

Bronstetter v. Davies (1986), 11 C.P.C. (2d) 289 (Ont. H.C.).

Production of an expert's report does not act as a waiver of the privilege attaching to the expert's notes and records.

Gorgichuk v. American Home Assurance Co., 5 C.P.C. (2d) 166, 14 C.C.L.I. 32, [1985] I.L.R. 1-1984 (Ont. H.C.).

The court excused the late delivery of an expert's report where the trial list unexpectedly collapsed and as much notice as possible was given. The court also excused the failure to give full disclosure of the expert's qualifications.

Scope of Experts' Testimony

Fraser River Pile & Dredge Ltd. v. Empire Tug Boats Ltd. (1995), 92 F.T.R. 26 (Fed. T.D.).

The court refused to admit expert evidence which appeared to be advocacy dressed up as expert opinion.

Piché v. Lecours Lumber Co. (1993), 13 O.R. (3d) 193, 19 C.P.C. (3d) 200 (Gen. Div.).

Privilege over an expert's file is not lost by calling the expert as a witness but may be considered waived regarding facts or assumptions provided to the expert by counsel if such facts or assumptions form the basis for the expert's opinion and are not otherwise in evidence.

Cousineau v. St. Joseph's Health Centre (1990), 49 C.P.C. (2d) 306 (Ont. H.C.).

An expert witness consulted but not retained by one party may be called at trial by the opposite party but may not, due to litigation privilege, disclose confidential information received from the first party's counsel.

Walters v. Walters (1990), 45 C.P.C. (2d) 215 (Ont. Gen. Div.).

An expert who was retained for a period of time by the defendant and was subsequently retained by the plaintiff was not permitted to give evidence.

Bell Can. v. Olympia & York Developments Ltd. (1989), 68 O.R. (2d) 103, 36 C.P.C. (2d) 193, 33 C.L.R. 258 (H.C.).

An expert called as a witness at trial may not be compelled to disclose privileged information provided by the solicitor for the party who retained him.

Henderson v. Probert (1988), 28 C.P.C. (2d) 64 (Ont. H.C.), affirmed (1989), 41 C.P.C. (2d) 298 (Div. Ct.), leave to appeal to Ont. C.A. refused 41 C.P.C. (2d) 298n.

A non-medically trained "rehabilitation consultant" was not permitted to testify as an expert as to the pain experienced by an injured plaintiff; the witness lacked the relevant expertise and, moreover, his opinion was based upon interviews he conducted with persons who had not been called as witnesses at the trial and this raised a serious impediment to the admission of the opinion as it was based on hearsay.

Stribbell v. Bhalla (1988), 32 C.P.C. (2d) 269 (Ont. H.C.).

Where the plaintiff filed a medical report obtained by the defendant and the defendant cross-examined the physician, the defendant was not permitted to ask questions about matters which were wholly outside the scope of the report. Cross-examination cannot indirectly elicit opinions which should have been set forth earlier pursuant to rule 53.03(1).

C.C.A.S., Hamilton-Wentworth v. S. (J.C.) (1986), 9 C.P.C. (2d) 265 (Ont. U.F.C.).

The court refused to hear opinion evidence from a witness with superficial formal training and limited experience. Discussion of expert witness qualifications.

McEachrane v. C.A.S., Essex (County) (1986), 10 C.P.C. (2d) 265 (Ont. H.C.).

The court refused to permit an expert to testify where his report listed topics of testimony but did not provide the substance of his proposed testimony.

Transmetro Properties Ltd. v. Lockyer Bros. Ltd. (1985), 4 C.P.C. (2d) 273 (Ont. H.C.).

The court granted an adjournment where the plaintiff's expert's report contained only conclusions. The defendant was entitled to the documents, calculations and data upon which the expert's opinions and conclusions were based.

Thorogood v. Bowden (1978), 21 O.R. (2d) 385, 89 D.L.R. (3d) 604 (C.A.).

The testimony of an expert is not to be narrowly confined and limited to the precise contents of his report; he may expand and amplify but may not open a new field.

Quantrill v. Alcan-Colony Contracting Co. (1978), 18 O.R. (2d) 333 (C.A.).

The defendant's medical expert was allowed to comment on the findings and opinions of the plaintiff's medical experts notwithstanding that he had not outlined that testimony in his own medical report.

de Genova v. de Genova, [1971] 3 O.R. 304, 5 R.F.L. 22, 20 D.L.R. (3d) 264 (H.C.).

Discussion of instances where a report would be unnecessary.

Iler v. Beaudet, [1971] 3 O.R. 644 (Co. Ct.).

Where an expert's report failed to substantially disclose certain evidence offered in the expert's testimony, the trial judge refused to admit the evidence and granted an adjournment so that a proper report could be prepared.

Medical Expert — Use of Report at Trial

Etienne v. McKellar General Hospital (1995), 38 C.P.C. (3d) 342 (Ont. Gen. Div.).

The court refused to grant leave to the plaintiff to introduce two medical reports into evidence where the authors were not available for cross-examination at trial. The proposed evidence was hearsay, and the test of necessity could not be met in the circumstances of the case.

Scime v. Guardian Ins. Co. of Can. (1988), 30 C.P.C. (2d) 149 (Ont. Dist. Ct.).

A defence medical report was admitted at trial notwithstanding the examining physician had died before trial.

Stribbell v. Bhalla (1988), 32 C.P.C. (2d) 272 (Ont. H.C.).

The plaintiff was permitted to file a report prepared by a physician conducting a defence medical examination. The defendant was obliged to arrange attendance of the physician for cross-examination by the defendant.

Black v. Royal Bank (1988), 33 C.P.C. (2d) 93 (Ont. Dist. Ct.).

A detailed record made by a physician and contained in hospital records was held to be a medical report subject to s. 52 of the *Evidence Act* and not admissible as a business record under s. 35 of the *Evidence Act.*

Briand v. Sutton (1986), 57 O.R. (2d) 629, 15 C.P.C. (2d) 32 (H.C.).

A party filing a medical report at trial pursuant to the provisions of the *Evidence Act* will ordinarily be required to produce the physician for cross-examination if desired by the opposing party.

Harris v. Windsor Air Line Limousine Services Ltd. (1985), 6 C.P.C. (2d) 156 (Ont. H.C.).

Where the plaintiff wishes to file a medical report and the defendant wishes to cross-examine the physician who made it, the physicians should be called as part of the plaintiff 's case.

Rousam v. Cambridge (1982), 30 C.P.C. 203 (Ont. C.A.).

Dentists' reports cannot be admitted into evidence pursuant to s. 52 of the *Evidence Act.*

Carew v. Loblaws Ltd. (1977), 18 O.R. (2d) 660, 83 D.L.R. (3d) 603 (H.C.).

Where a physician made two medical reports three years apart and the first was introduced in evidence, it was held that the second report must also be introduced.

Ferraro v. Lee (1974), 2 O.R. (2d) 417, 43 D.L.R. (3d) 161 (C.A.).

A party must usually elect between calling a medical practitioner to give *viva voce* evidence and entering the medical report in evidence.

Gazdig v. Desjardins (1974), 1 O.R. (2d) 457, 40 D.L.R. (3d) 649 (C.A.).

Where a medical expert is examined *viva voce*, a medical report containing very damaging information which had not been touched upon during such testimony ought not be admitted.

Foster v. Hoerle; Parker v. Registrar of Motor Vehicles, [1973] 2 O.R. 601, 34 D.L.R. (3d) 648 (H.C.).

The giving of notice waives any privilege which may have attached to the report.

Snyder v. Siutters, [1970] 3 O.R. 789, 14 D.L.R. (3d) 173 (H.C.).

It is permissible to enter a medical report in evidence and also have the practitioner give oral evidence.

Re Brady Infants, [1970] 2 O.R. 262, 3 R.F.L. 15, 10 D.L.R. (3d) 432 (Co. Ct.).

Discussion of admissibility of conclusions in psychiatric report which were based solely on hearsay.

Kapulica v. Dumancic, [1968] 2 O.R. 438 (C.A.).

Evidence admitted by way of report is restricted to evidence which would be admissible if the medical practitioner testified *viva voce*. The opposite party has an absolute right to cross-examine the medical practitioner.

Leave of Trial Judge — rule 53.03(2)

Pavao v. Pinarreta (1995), 40 C.P.C. (3d) 84 (Ont. Div. Ct.).

The Divisional Court ordered a new trial where the trial judge had refused to let the defendant introduce expert evidence at trial. Although no report had been filed under rule 53.03(1), on the facts of the case there would have been no prejudice from allowing the testimony.

Paramount Tavern (Toronto) Ltd. v. Global Real Estate Co. (1993), 29 C.P.C. (3d) 217 (Ont. Div. Ct.).

A motions court judge who granted an adjournment on the eve of a trial had no jurisdiction to rule that expert evidence could not be called at trial.

C. (M.) v. M. (F.) (1990), 46 C.P.C. (2d) 254, 74 D.L.R. (4th) 129 (Ont. Gen. Div.).

Leave to call the evidence of an expert was refused where no report had been served. Although the court has a discretion to permit expert evidence in those circumstances, the late preparation of a report would have caused an unreasonable delay, and the trier of fact was able to form its own opinion with respect to the matter in issue. In any event, the expert's evidence was directed to the issue of exemplary damages, and as the facts of the case did not merit such an award, the expert's opinion was not required.

Sevidal v. Chopra (1987), 64 O.R. (2d) 169, 41 C.C.L.T. 179, 45 R.P.R. 79, 2 C.E.L.R. (N.S.) 173 (H.C.).

A second report by an expert, which had not been timely served, was admitted pursuant to rule 53.08 where the defendants could be adequately compensated by an appropriate award of costs.

COMPELLING ATTENDANCE AT TRIAL

By Summons to Witness

53.04(1) A party who requires the attendance of a person in Ontario as a witness at a trial may serve the person with a summons to witness (Form 53A) requiring him or her to attend the trial at the time and place stated in the summons, and the summons may also require the person to produce at the trial the documents or other things in his or her possession, control or power relating to the matters in question in the action that are specified in the summons.

Summons may be Issued in Blank

(2) On the request of a party or a solicitor and on payment of the prescribed fee, a registrar shall sign, seal and issue a blank summons to witness and the party or solicitor may complete the summons and insert the names of any number of witnesses.

Where Document may be Proved by Certified Copy

(3) No summons to witness for the production of an original record or document that may be proved by a certified copy shall be served without leave of the court.

Summons to be Served Personally

(4) A summons to witness shall be served on the witness personally and not by an alternative to personal service and, at the same time, attendance money calculated in accordance with Tariff A shall be paid or tendered to the witness.

(5) Service of a summons to witness and the payment or tender of attendance money may be proved by affidavit.

Summons in Effect until Attendance No Longer Required

(6) A summons to witness continues to have effect until the attendance of the witness is no longer required.

Sanctions for Failure to Obey Summons

(7) Where a witness whose evidence is material to an action is served with a summons to witness and the proper attendance money is paid or tendered to him or her, and the witness fails to attend at the trial or to remain in attendance in accordance with the requirements of the summons, the presiding judge may by a warrant for arrest (Form 53B) cause the witness to be apprehended anywhere within Ontario and forthwith brought before the court.

(8) On being apprehended, the witness may be detained in custody until his or her presence is no longer required, or released on such terms as are just, and the witness may be ordered to pay the costs arising out of the failure to attend or remain in attendance.

Desmarais v. Morrissette (1993), 79 C.C.C. (3d) 444, 69 O.A.C. 76 (C.A.).

A *subpoena duces tecum* should not be quashed before trial on the basis of privilege, but rather the documents should be brought to trial and the claim for privilege determined by the trial judge.

Bettes v. Boeing Canada/DeHavilland Division, 10 O.R. (3d) 768, 12 C.P.C. (3d) 226, 8 Admin. L.R. (2d) 232, [1992] O.L.R.B. Rep. 1136 (Gen. Div.), affirmed [1993] O.L.R.B. Rep. 275 (Div. Ct.).

An applicant for judicial review issued a summons to witness to a tribunal member to secure evidence for use on a judicial review application. The court quashed the summons to witness, as there was no reasonable and relevant evidentiary basis for the issuance of the summons and the applicant had failed to establish a *prima facie* case for examining the witness.

Everingham v. Ontario (1991), 3 C.P.C. (3d) 93 (Ont. Gen. Div.).

The court refused to set aside a summons to witness, but imposed a confidentiality term where the records sought were relevant.

Smerchanski v. Lewis (1980), 30 O.R. (2d) 370, 18 C.P.C. 29, 117 D.L.R. (3d) 716 (C.A.).

An order quashing a subpoena to a stranger to the action was a final order and an appeal was permitted in the midst of the trial.

Pollock v. Lin (1978), 19 O.R. (2d) 748 (Master).

The omission of the name of the witness renders the summons a nullity. [*Now compare rule 2.01 — Authors.*]

Stewart v. Waterloo Mutual Ins. Co., 3 C.P.C. 236, [1977] I.L.R. 1-878 (Ont. H.C.).

In the absence of improper purpose, a summons will not be set aside, although a person named has no knowledge of the matters in issue.

Rideout v. Rideout, [1956] O.W.N. 644 (H.C.).

The court dismissed contempt proceedings arising out of failure to obey a subpoena issued under C.S.C. 1859, c. 79, s. 4, requiring attendance before the Superior Court of Montreal where the default had not been wilful and the nature of the Quebec proceedings was unclear.

Mobilex Ltd. v. Hamilton, [1950] O.W.N. 721 (H.C.).

Where there is no possibility that a trial will take place during current sittings of the court, a subpoena will be set aside as an abuse of process. The time when a witness is to attend must be stated in the subpoena and until notice of trial is given such time cannot be determined.

INTERPROVINCIAL SUBPOENA

53.05 A summons to a witness outside Ontario to compel his or her attendance under the *Interprovincial Summonses Act* shall be in (Form 53C).

COMPELLING ATTENDANCE OF WITNESS IN CUSTODY

53.06 The court may make an order (Form 53D) for attendance of a witness in custody whose evidence is material to an action, directing the officer having custody of a prisoner to produce him or her, on payment of the fee prescribed under the *Administration of Justice Act*, for an examination authorized by these rules or as a witness at a hearing.

McGuire v. McGuire, [1953] O.R. 328, 16 C.R. 177, 105 C.C.C. 335, [1953] 2 D.L.R. 394 (C.A.).

The court only has jurisdiction over witnesses in custody in Ontario.

CALLING ADVERSE PARTY AS WITNESS

Securing Attendance

53.07(1) A party may secure the attendance of a person who is,
(a) an adverse party;
(b) an officer, director or sole proprietor of an adverse party; or
(c) a partner in a partnership that is an adverse party,
as a witness at a trial by,
(d) serving the person with a summons to witness; or
(e) serving on the adverse party or the solicitor for the adverse party, at least ten days before the commencement of the trial, a notice of intention to call the person as a witness,
and at the same time paying or tendering attendance money calculated in accordance with Tariff A.

When Adverse Party may be Called

(2) Where a person referred to in subrule (1) is in attendance at the trial, a party may call the person as a witness without previous notice or the payment of the attendance money, unless,
(a) the person has already testified; or
(b) the adverse party or the adverse party's counsel undertakes to call the person as a witness.

Cross-examination

(3) A party calling a witness referred to in subrule (1) may cross-examine him or her.

Failure to Testify

(4) Where a person required to testify under this rule,

(a) refuses or neglects to attend at the trial or to remain in attendance at the trial;

(b) refuses to be sworn; or

(c) refuses to answer any proper question put to him or her or to produce any document or other thing that he or she is required to produce,

the court may grant judgment in favour of the party calling the witness, adjourn the trial or make such other order as is just.

Whiten v. Pilot Insurance Co. (1995), 7 W.D.C.P. (2d) 105 (Ont. Gen. Div.).

Where an adverse party is called as a witness under rule 53.07, the party calling the witness is entitled to cross-examine, but counsel for the witness is not entitled to cross-examine but rather may ask only non-leading questions.

Caron v. Chodan Estate (1989), 17 W.D.C.P. 226 (Ont. H.C.).

Where the plaintiff called one of several co-defendants pursuant to rule 53.07, counsel for the other defendants, who were not adverse in interest to the party called, were permitted to cross-examine, but not to lead the witness so as to put words in his mouth, nor to ask leading questions for the purpose of eliciting testimony concerning new matters constituting an element of the case of those defendants.

Caron v. Chodan Estate (1989), 16 W.D.C.P. 238 (Ont. H.C.).

Where a person's attendance at trial is secured by a party under rule 53.07(1), that party may call the person as a witness notwithstanding an undertaking by the person's counsel to call him as a witness. Rule 53.07(2)(b) cannot be invoked to defeat the exercise of the right given in rule 53.07(1). *Crutchfield v. Crutchfield, infra,* not followed. [*This decision would seem to be incorrect. See Crutchfield, infra — Authors.*]

Crutchfield v. Crutchfield (1987), 10 R.F.L. (3d) 247 (Ont. H.C.).

Rule 53.07(1) does not confer any right to call a party, it merely provides a method to ensure that the adverse party is in attendance at trial. It is subrule (2) that regulates when an adverse party may be called and it applies whether the party is at trial voluntarily or by virtue of subrule (1), and the adverse party may not be called if his counsel undertakes to call him as a witness.

Haviv v. Estée Lauder Cosmetics Ltd. (1986), 9 C.P.C. (2d) 285 (Ont. Master), affirmed 9 C.P.C. (2d) 185 at 186 (Ont. H.C.).

This rule applies to persons irrespective of their residence. The power to set aside a notice of intention must be exercised sparingly and with great caution.

EVIDENCE ADMISSIBLE ONLY WITH LEAVE

53.08(1) Where evidence is admissible only with leave of the trial judge under,

(a) subrule 30.08(1) (failure to disclose document);

(b) rule 30.09 (failure to abandon claim of privilege);

(c) rule 31.07 (refusal to disclose information on discovery);

(d) subrule 31.09(3) (failure to correct answers on discovery);

(e) subrule 53.03(2) (failure to serve expert's report); or

(f) subrule 76.04(2) (failure to disclose witness),

leave shall be granted on such terms as are just and with an adjournment if necessary, unless to do so will cause prejudice to the opposite party or will cause undue delay in the conduct of the trial. [am. O. Reg. 533/95, s. 5(1) (amendment revoked by s. 5(2) March 11, 2000)]

Cross-Reference: See cases under the particular rules mentioned in rule 53.08.

CALCULATION OF AWARDS FOR FUTURE PECUNIARY DAMAGES

Discount Rate

53.09(1) The discount rate to be used in determining the amount of an award in respect of future pecuniary damages, to the extent that it reflects the difference between estimated investment and price inflation rates, is 2.5 per cent per year.

Gross Up

(2) In calculating the amount to be included in the award to offset any liability for income tax on income from investment of the award, the court shall,

(a) assume that the entire award will be invested in fixed income securities; and

(b) determine the rate to be assumed for future inflation in accordance with the following formula:

$$g = \left(\frac{1+i}{1+d} \right) - 1$$

where

"g" is the rate to be assumed for future inflation;

"i" is the average yield on Government of Canada marketable bonds for durations of over ten years, as published in the edition of the Bank of Canada's Weekly Financial Statistics appearing on or not more than six days before the date that the trial commenced, rounded to the nearest half of one per cent; and "d" is the discount rate specified in subrule (1). [am. O. Reg. 465/93, s. 5]

International Corona Resources Ltd. v. LAC Minerals Ltd. (1986), 53 O.R. (2d) 737, 32 B.L.R. 15, 39 R.P.R. 113, 9 C.P.R. (3d) 7, 25 D.L.R. (4th) 504 (H.C.), affirmed (1987), 62 O.R. (2d) 1, 28 E.T.R. 245, 46 R.P.R. 109, 18 C.P.R. (3d) 263, 44 D.L.R. (4th) 592, 23 O.A.C. 263 (C.A.), affirmed (1989), 69 O.R. (2d) 287, 26 C.P.R. (3d) 97, 61 D.L.R. (4th) 14, 101 N.R. 239 (S.C.C.).

Because of the risks and variables associated with a gold mine a higher discount rate was applied.

McDermid v. Ontario (1985), 53 O.R. (2d) 495, 5 C.P.C. (2d) 299 (H.C.).

The court has a discretion to depart from the prescribed discount rate if justified by the evidence and circumstances.

Dziver v. Smith (1983), 41 O.R. (2d) 385, 146 D.L.R. (3d) 314 (C.A.).

The court held the predecessor of rule 53.09 did not prevent the parties from showing that there are other factors which, in the particular circumstances, ought to be taken into consideration. If no evidence is adduced by either side as to additional factors, the court should apply the prescribed discount rate.

PREJUDGMENT INTEREST RATE FOR NON-PECUNIARY DAMAGES

53.10 The prejudgment interest rate on damages for non-pecuniary loss in an action for personal injury is 5 per cent per year.

Skinner v. Royal Victoria Hospital (1995), 6 W.D.C.P. (2d) 59 (Ont. Gen. Div.).

Rule 53.10 does not apply to causes of action arising on or before October 23, 1989.

Tait v. Roden (1994), 20 O.R. (3d) 20 (Gen. Div.).

Prejudgment interest on damages for libel should be calculated under s. 128(1) of the *Courts of Justice Act*. Damages for libel are not analogous to "damages for non-pecuniary loss" under rule 53.10.

REFERENCES

RULE 54   DIRECTING A REFERENCE

Highlights

Rule 54 deals with the directing of a reference — when and to whom a reference may be directed (rules 54.02 and 54.03), motions on a reference (rule 54.05), and the resulting report and its confirmation (rules 54.06-54.09). The actual procedure to be followed on a reference is regulated by Rule 55.

When a reference may be directed. This is now governed by the Rules (pursuant to the *Courts of Justice Act*, s. 66(2)(q)), rather than by statute as was formerly the case. Moreover, the circumstances in which a reference may be directed were narrowed. The power of a judge to direct a reference of the whole proceeding or an issue therein, in specified circumstances, remains essentially unchanged: rule 54.02(1) and *cf.* the *Judicature Act*, s. 71. However, the former virtually unlimited general power in a judge to direct a reference of a particular question or issue (*cf.* the *Judicature Act*, s. 70) has been replaced by a more limited power, restricted to specified circumstances: rule 54.02(2). So now, for example, the issue of the assessment of damages can normally only be referred if all parties consent under rule 54.02(1)(a).

In addition to the reference powers conferred by Rule 54, additional reference powers are also located elsewhere in the Rules: see, e.g., rules 69.21 and 70.07 (references to family law commissioners), rule 65.02 (proceedings for administration), rules 64.02 and 19.04(1) (default judgments)), and rule 20.04(3) and (5) (summary judgments)).

To whom references may be directed. The person to whom a reference is to be directed is stated (rule 54.03, and see also rule 64.02 re mortgage actions). References may be directed to the referring judge, a registrar, or other officer (including a master), to a person agreed upon by the parties or, in certain circumstances, to a family law commissioner: rule 54.03(1).

Motions. A referee is specifically directed to hear all motions made in connection with the reference, but with his or her consent or in his or her absence, a motion may be heard by a judge or master: rule 54.05(1). An order made by a referee on a motion may be set aside or varied by a motion made to a judge: rule 54.05(2).

Confirmation of reports. The procedures for the confirmation of reports made on a reference depend upon whether or not the initial order directing the reference itself requires the referee to "report back" (and in this regard note rule 54.04(2)).

Where a report back is required, the report may be confirmed only on a motion, which normally must be made to the judge who directed the reference: see rule 54.08. A judge should confirm a report unless there has been an error in principle, an absence or excess of jurisdiction, or some patent misapprehension of the evidence, and the report should not be disturbed unless it appears unsatisfactory on all the evidence: *Jordan v. McKenzie* (1987), 26 C.P.C. (2d) 193 (Ont. H.C.), affirmed (1990), 39 C.P.C. (2d) 217 (Ont. C.A.).

When the order directing the reference does not require a report back, the report is confirmed on the expiration of fifteen days after the report is filed, unless a notice of motion to oppose confirmation is served within that time: rule 54.09(1).

If a party desires immediate confirmation of a report that does not have to be reported back, he or she may seek confirmation on motion to a judge: rule 54.09(4).

It is to be noted that, unlike the situation under the former practice (see the *Judicature Act*, s. 74, and former Rules 512-513) it is not possible to appeal from the report on a reference as such. The report is of no effect until it is confirmed: rule 54.07. A party who wishes to challenge a report should do so by a motion to oppose confirmation (when no report back is required) or on the hearing of the motion to confirm the report (where a report back is required). Once an order has been made confirming a report or refusing to confirm a report an appeal may be taken from such an order.

Rule 69.21 (reference to a family law commissioner) provides its own procedure for confirming the report and requires a motion to confirm in every case.

Former provisions: *Judicature Act*, ss. 70-74 and Rules 402, 512-513.

APPLICATION OF RULES 54 AND 55

54.01　Rules 54 and 55 apply to references directed,
(a)　under rule 54.02 or any other rule; and
(b)　under a statute, subject to the provisions of the statute.

WHERE REFERENCE MAY BE DIRECTED

Reference of Whole Proceeding or Issue
54.02(1)　Subject to any right to have an issue tried by a jury, a judge may at any time in a proceeding direct a reference of the whole proceeding or a reference to determine an issue where,
(a)　all affected parties consent;
(b)　a prolonged examination of documents or an investigation is required that, in the opinion of the judge, cannot conveniently be made at trial; or
(c)　a substantial issue in dispute requires the taking of accounts.

Reference of Issue
(2)　Subject to any right to have an issue tried by a jury, a judge may at any time in a proceeding direct a reference to determine an issue relating to,
(a)　the taking of accounts;
(b)　the conduct of a sale;
(c)　the appointment by the court of a guardian or receiver, or the appointment by a person of an attorney under a power of attorney;
(d)　the conduct of a guardianship or receivership or the exercise of the authority of an attorney acting under a power of attorney; or
(e)　the enforcement of an order. [am. O. Reg. 69/95, s. 7]

Elcano Acceptance Ltd. v. Richmond, Richmond, Stambler & Mills (1986), 55 O.R. (2d) 56, 9 C.P.C. (2d) 260, 16 O.A.C. 69 (C.A.).

The court has an inherent jurisdiction to split a trial in the interests of justice and order a reference or a separate trial of issues, but the power is narrowly circumscribed and should be exercised only in the clearest cases.

Can. Permanent Trust Co. v. Wortsman (1978), 21 O.R. (2d) 846 (H.C.).

A reference may be directed at the time of a pre-trial conference. [*See now rule 50.01(i) — Authors.*]

Tukara v. Krizmanic (1976), 2 C.P.C. 301 (Ont. Div. Ct.).

Where litigants would be forced to lead evidence before the referee, most of which has already been led before the trial judge, a reference should not be directed.

V.K. Mason v. Courtot Invts. (1975), 9 O.R. (2d) 325 (H.C.).

A mechanics' lien action brought in the Judicial District of York must be heard by a judge of the Supreme Court except on consent or if the other requirements are met.

Western Caissons Ltd. v. T.T.C., [1966] 2 O.R. 528 (H.C.).

Special circumstances, such as the possibility of bias, must be shown before a reference will be revoked.

Imperial Trusts Co. v. Jackson (1917), 12 O.W.N. 126 (Master).

The policy of the court is to try cases if possible and to avoid references.

TO WHOM REFERENCE MAY BE DIRECTED

Judge or officer
54.03(1) A reference may be directed to the referring judge, to a registrar or other officer of the court, to a family law commissioner (in the case of a reference directed under rule 69.21 or 70.07) or to a person agreed on by the parties.

Person Agreed on by Parties
(2) Where a reference is directed to a person agreed on by the parties, the person is, for the purposes of the reference, an officer of the court directing the reference.
(3) The judge directing a reference to a person agreed on by the parties may,
(a) determine his or her remuneration and the liability of the parties for its payment;
(b) refer that issue to the person to whom the reference is directed; or
(c) reserve that issue until the report on the reference is confirmed.

ORDER DIRECTING A REFERENCE

54.04(1) An order directing a reference shall specify the nature and subject matter of the reference and who is to conduct it and may,
(a) direct in general terms that all necessary inquiries be made, accounts taken and costs assessed;
(b) contain directions for the conduct of the reference; and
(c) designate which party is to have carriage of the reference.
(2) An order of a master or registrar directing a reference shall not require a report back, and the report or an interim report on the reference shall be confirmed under rule 54.09 (confirmation by passage of time).
(3) A referee has, subject to the order directing the reference, all the powers these rules give to a referee.

Mason v. Intercity Properties Ltd. (1988), 66 O.R. (2d) 8 (H.C.).

Where a judgment ordered shares to be purchased at their fair value on a particular date and directed a reference to determine value, and the reference did not take place for five years after the date of the order, in which time the properties owned by the companies had increased in value by in excess of 300 per cent, it was held that the change in value should not be taken into account; while the judge ordering the evaluation date may not have contemplated a delay of five years, he must have contemplated some delay and intended the valuation to be as of the date fixed; although the result may have been inequitable, the judgment was final and not subject to review.

Olympia & York Devs. Ltd. v. Chicquen (1978), 6 C.P.C. 221 (Ont. H.C.).

Contentions as to priorities cannot be raised on a reference, unless the judge in granting judgment specifically refers them for consideration and report.

Goyer v. Shurtleff, [1947] O.W.N. 656 (H.C.).

Discussion of contents of an order of reference.

MOTIONS ON A REFERENCE

54.05(1) A referee shall hear and dispose of any motion made in connection with the reference, but in the absence of or with the consent of the referee, a motion may be heard and disposed of by a judge or master.

(2) Rule 37.03 (place of hearing of motions) does not apply to a motion made in connection with a reference and heard by the referee.

(3) Where a referee has made an order on a motion in the reference, a person who is affected by the order may make a motion to a judge to set aside or vary the order by a notice of motion served within seven days after the order is made and naming the first available hearing date that is at least three days after service of the notice of motion. [am. O. Reg. 219/91, s. 7]

REPORT ON REFERENCE

54.06 A referee shall make a report that contains his or her findings and conclusions.

Vukovic v. Zeljko (1982), 31 C.P.C. 158, affirmed 31 C.P.C. 158n (Ont. H.C.).

A master is *functus officio* after his report has been signed.

Rosen v. Anglin, [1955] O.W.N. 643 (C.A.).

A County Court Judge to whom a Supreme Court matter has been referred must give his decision in the form of a report and not in the form of a judgment.

REPORT MUST BE CONFIRMED

54.07(1) A report has no effect until it has been confirmed.

(2) A report shall be entered immediately after it has been confirmed and rule 59.05 (entry of order) applies, with necessary modifications. [am. O. Reg. 396/91, s. 9]

Baker v. Dumaresq, [1934] S.C.R. 665, [1935] 1 D.L.R. 148.

A report of a master, once confirmed, is a final judgment from which appeals may be taken in the usual way, including to the Supreme Court of Canada.

CONFIRMATION ON MOTION WHERE REPORT BACK REQUIRED

54.08(1) Where the order directing a reference requires the referee to report back, the report or an interim report on the reference may be confirmed only on a motion to the judge who directed the reference, subject to subrule **69.21(3)** (reference to family law commissioner), on notice to every party who appeared on the reference, and the judge may require the referee to give reasons for his or her findings and conclusions and may confirm the report in whole or in part or make such other order as is just.

(2) Where the judge who directed the reference is unable for any reason to hear a motion for confirmation, the motion may be made to another judge.

Kaymic Developments (Ontario) Ltd. v. Ontario Housing Corp. (1990), 73 O.R. (2d) 670, 43 C.P.C. (2d) 81 (H.C.).

The standard of review of a report set out in *Jordan v. McKenzie* (1987), 26 C.P.C. (2d) 193 (Ont. H.C.), affirmed (1990), 39 C.P.C. (2d) 217 (Ont. C.A.), also applies where the master is required to report back under rule 54.08.

CONFIRMATION BY PASSAGE OF TIME WHERE REPORT BACK NOT REQUIRED

Fifteen-Day Period to Oppose Confirmation

54.09(1) Where the order directing a reference does not require the referee to report back, the report or an interim report on the reference is confirmed,

(a) immediately on the filing of the consent of every party who appeared on the reference; or

(b) on the expiration of fifteen days after a copy, with proof of service on every party who appeared on the reference, has been filed in the office in which the proceeding was commenced, unless a notice of motion to oppose confirmation of a report is served within that time.

To Whom Motion to Oppose Confirmation Made

(2) A motion to oppose confirmation of a report shall be made to a judge other than the one who conducted the reference.

Notice of Motion to Oppose Confirmation

(3) A notice of motion to oppose confirmation of a report shall,

(a) set out the grounds for opposing confirmation;

(b) be served within fifteen days after a copy of the report, with proof of service on every party who appeared on the reference, has been filed in the office in which the proceeding was commenced; and

(c) name the first available hearing date that is at least three days after service of the notice of motion.

Motion for Immediate Confirmation

(4) A party who seeks confirmation before the expiration of the fifteen day period prescribed in subrule (1) may make a motion to a judge for confirmation.

Disposition of Motion

(5) A judge hearing a motion under subrule (2) or (4) may require the referee to give reasons for his or her findings and conclusions and may confirm the report in whole or in part or make such other order as is just. [am. O. Reg. 396/91, s. 10]

Solmon Rothbart Goodman v. Davidovits (1996), 7 W.D.C.P. (2d) 174 (Ont. Gen. Div.).

Generally affidavit evidence is not admissible on a motion to oppose confirmation of a report. One exception would be if there was an issue whether the referee exceeded his jurisdiction or failed to accept it.

Komorowski v. Van Weel (1993), 12 O.R. (3d) 444, 9 C.L.R. (2d) 39 (Gen. Div.).

On a motion to oppose confirmation of a master's report on a reference, the decision should stand unless some palpable or overriding error of fact is demonstrated or it is clearly wrong.

Thompson v. Hermon (1988), 65 O.R. (2d) 538, 30 C.L.R. 184 (H.C.).

On a motion to oppose confirmation of a report under rule 54.09, the court should not interfere if the master's findings were within the scope of the referring order and were supported by the evidence.

Jordan v. McKenzie (1987), 26 C.P.C. (2d) 193 (Ont. H.C.), affirmed (1990), 39 C.P.C.(2d) 217 (Ont. C.A.).

On a motion to oppose confirmation of a report the judge ought not to interfere with the result unless there has been an error in principle, an absence or excess of jurisdiction, or some patent misapprehension of the evidence. Further the award should not be disturbed unless it appears unsatisfactory on all of the evidence.

C. Battison (Battiston) & Sons Inc. v. Mauti (1985), 50 O.R. (2d) 599, 11 C.L.R. 173 (H.C.), reversed on other grounds (1986), 58 O.R. (2d) 82, 25 C.L.R. 298, 34 M.P.L.R. 242, 34 D.L.R. (4th) 700 (Div. Ct.).

A motion to oppose confirmation may be brought in a reference under the *Mechanics' Lien Act,* R.S.O. 1980, c. 216, notwithstanding the Act was not amended by the *Courts of Justice Act, 1984* to so state.

REFEREE UNABLE TO CONTINUE OR COMPLETE REFERENCE

54.10 Where a referee is unable for any reason to continue or complete a reference, any party to the reference may make a motion to a judge for directions for continuation or completion of the reference.

RULE 55   PROCEDURE ON A REFERENCE

Highlights

Rule 55 sets out the procedure to be followed on references. Additional provisions applicable to mortgage references are to be found in rule 64.06. The directing of references, the confirmation of the referee's report, and who may hear motions on a reference are dealt with in Rule 54.

While Rule 55 involves numerous changes in terminology, the procedure to be followed on a reference largely follows the former practice and the Rule involves no major changes.

Former Rules: Rules 403-462.

GENERAL PROVISIONS FOR CONDUCT OF REFERENCE

Simple Procedure to be Adopted

55.01(1) A referee shall, subject to any directions contained in the order directing the reference, devise and adopt the simplest, least expensive and most expeditious manner of conducting the reference and may,

(a) give such directions as are necessary; and

(b) dispense with any procedure ordinarily taken that the referee considers to be unnecessary, or adopt a procedure different from that ordinarily taken.

Special Circumstances to be Reported

(2) A referee shall report on any special circumstances relating to the reference and shall generally inquire into, decide and report on all matters relating to the reference as fully as if they had been specifically referred.

General Procedure

(3) Subject to subrule (1), a reference shall be conducted as far as possible in accordance with rules 55.01 to 55.07.

PROCEDURE ON A REFERENCE GENERALLY

Hearing for Directions

55.02(1) The party having carriage of the reference shall forthwith have the order directing the reference signed and entered and, within ten days after entry, request an appointment with the referee for a hearing to consider directions for the reference and, in default, any other party having an interest in the reference may assume carriage of it.

(2) A notice of hearing for directions (Form 55A) and a copy of the order directing the reference shall be served on every other party to the proceeding at least five days before the hearing unless the referee directs or these rules provide otherwise.

The Trusts and Guarantee Co. v. Trustee of the Property of The National Debenture Corp. Ltd., [1946] O.W.N. 385 (C.A.).

Failure to give notice of the reference to all parties makes the proceeding a nullity. [*But cf. now rule 2.01 — Authors.*]

Directions
(3) At the hearing for directions, the referee shall give such directions for the conduct of the reference as are just, including,

(a) the time and place at which the reference is to proceed;
(b) any special directions concerning the parties who are to attend; and
(c) any special directions concerning what evidence is to be received and how documents are to be proved.

Re Solloway Mills, [1935] O.R. 275, [1935] O.W.N. 183, [1935] 2 D.L.R. 459 (Master).
Discussion of procedure on a reference and power to direct delivery of particulars as opposed to delivery of pleadings.

(4) The directions may be varied or supplemented during the course of the reference.

Spearin v. Rohn, [1944] O.W.N. 459 (H.C.).
The powers of the master are discretionary and will be interfered with on appeal only if the master has proceeded on an incorrect principle.

Adding Parties
(5) Where it appears to the referee that any person ought to be added as a party to the proceeding, the referee may make an order adding the person as a defendant or respondent and direct that the order, together with the order directing the reference and a notice to party added on reference (form 55B), be served on the person, and on being served the person becomes a party to the proceeding.

(6) A person served with a notice under subrule (5) may make a motion to a judge to set aside or vary the order directing the reference or the order adding the person as a party, by a notice of motion served within ten days after service of the notice under subrule (5), or where the person is served outside Ontario, within such further time as the referee directs, and naming the first available hearing date that is at least three days after service of the notice of motion.

Failure to Appear on Reference
(7) A party who is served with notice of a reference under subrule (2) or (5) and does not appear in response to the notice is not entitled to notice of any step in the reference and need not be served with any document in the reference, unless the referee orders otherwise.

Representation of Parties with Similar Interests
(8) Where it appears to the referee that two or more parties have substantially similar interests and can be adequately represented as a class, the referee may require them to be represented by the same solicitor and, where they cannot agree on a solicitor to represent them, the referee may designate a solicitor on such terms as are just.

(9) A party referred to in subrule (8) who insists on being represented by a different solicitor shall not recover the costs of the separate represen-

tation and, unless the referee orders otherwise, shall pay all costs incurred by the other parties as a result of the separate representation.

Amendment of Pleadings

(10) The referee may grant leave to make any necessary amendments to the pleadings that are not inconsistent with the order of reference.

Western Caissons Ltd. v. T.T.C., [1966] 2 O.R. 528 (H.C.).
There is no power to allow amendments which alter the issues referred.

Procedure Book

(11) The referee shall keep a procedure book in which he or she shall note all steps taken and all directions given in respect of the reference, and the directions need not be embodied in a formal order or report to bind the parties.

Transferring Carriage of Reference

(12) Where the party having carriage of the reference does not proceed with reasonable diligence, the referee may, on the motion of any other interested party, transfer carriage of the reference to another party.

Evidence of Witnesses

(13) Witnesses on a reference shall be examined orally unless the referee directs otherwise, and evidence taken orally shall be recorded.

(14) The attendance of a person to be examined on a reference may be compelled in the same manner as provided in Rule 53 for a witness at a trial.

Fisk v. Fisk, [1957] O.W.N. 521, 11 D.L.R. (2d) 50 (C.A.).
Evidence of witnesses should be recorded so that a transcript is available on appeal.

Expert Witnesses

(14.1) Rule 53.03 (expert witness) and rule 53.08 (evidence admissible only with leave) apply, with necessary modifications, to the calling of an expert witness on a reference. [en. O. Reg. 535/92, s. 12]

Expert Appointed by Referee

(14.2) A referee may appoint an independent expert and rule 52.03 (court appointed expert) applies, with necessary modifications. [en. O. Reg. 535/92, s. 12]

Examination of Party and Production of Documents

(15) The referee may require any party to be examined and to produce such documents as the referee thinks fit and may give directions for their inspection by any other party.

Filing of Documents

(16) While a reference is pending, all documents relating to it shall be filed with the referee and, on completion of the reference, the documents shall be returned to the office in which the proceeding was commenced.

Gostick v. C.B.C., [1966] 1 O.R. 583, affirmed [1966] 1 O.R. 789n (H.C.).
It is not necessary to file the certificate of a party and party taxation.

Execution or Delivery of Instrument

(17) Where a person refuses or neglects to execute or deliver an instrument that becomes necessary under an order directing the reference, the referee may give directions for its execution or delivery.

Rulings

(18) Where the referee has made a ruling on the admissibility of evidence or any other matter relating to the conduct of the reference, the referee shall, on the request of any party, set out the ruling and the reasons for it in the report or, in the discretion of the referee, in an interim report on the reference.

Preparation of Report

(19) When the hearing of the reference is completed, the referee shall fix a date to settle the report and the party having carriage of the reference shall serve notice of the date on all parties who appeared on the reference unless the referee dispenses with notice.

(20) The party having carriage of the reference shall prepare a draft report and present it to the referee on the day fixed for settling the report.

(21) When the referee has settled and signed the report, the party having carriage of the reference shall forthwith serve it on all parties who appeared on the reference and file a copy with proof of service.

(22) In a proceeding for the administration of the estate of a deceased person, the report shall, as far as possible, be in (Form 55C).

PROCEDURE TO ASCERTAIN INTERESTED PERSONS AND VERIFY CLAIMS

Publication of Advertisements

55.03(1) The referee may direct the publication of advertisements for creditors or beneficiaries of an estate or trust, other unascertained persons, or their successors.

Filing of Claims

(2) The advertisement shall specify a date by which and a place where interested persons may file their claims and shall notify them that, unless their claims are so filed, they may be excluded from the benefit of the order, but the referee may nevertheless accept a claim at a later time.

Examination of Claims

(3) Before the day specified by the referee for the consideration of claims filed in response to the advertisement, the executor, administrator or trustee, or such other person as the referee directs, shall examine the claims and prepare an affidavit verifying a list of the claims filed in response to the advertisement and stating which claims he or she believes should be disallowed and the reasons for that belief.

Adjudication of Contested Claims

(4) **If a claim is contested, the referee shall order that a notice of contested claim (Form 55D), fixing a date for adjudication of the claim, be served on the claimant.**

PROCEDURE ON TAKING OF ACCOUNTS

Powers of Referee

55.04(1) On the taking of accounts, the referee may,

(a) take the accounts with rests or otherwise;

(b) take account of money received or that might have been received but for wilful neglect or default;

(c) make allowance for occupation rent and determine the amount;

(d) take into account necessary repairs, lasting improvements, costs and other expenses properly incurred; and

(e) make all just allowances.

Preparation of Accounts

(2) Where an account is to be taken, the party required to account, unless the referee directs otherwise, shall prepare the account in debit and credit form, verified by affidavit.

(3) The items on each side of the account shall be numbered consecutively, and the account shall be referred to in the affidavit as an exhibit and shall not be attached to the affidavit.

Books of Accounts as Proof

(4) The referee may direct that the books in which the accounts have been kept be taken as proof, in the absence of evidence to the contrary, of the matters contained in them.

Production of Vouchers

(5) Before hearing a reference, the referee may fix a date for the purpose of taking the accounts and may direct the production and inspection of vouchers and, where appropriate, cross-examination on his or her affidavit of the party required to account or of the person who filed the affidavit on the party's behalf or in the party's place, with a view to ascertaining what is admitted and what is contested between the parties.

Questioning Accounts

(6) A party who questions an account shall give particulars of the objection, with specific reference by number to the item in question, to the party required to account, and the referee may require the party to give further particulars of the objection.

DIRECTION FOR PAYMENT OF MONEY

Payment into Financial Institution

55.05(1) Where under an order directing a reference the referee directs money to be paid at a specified time and place, the referee shall direct it to

be paid into a financial institution to the credit of the party entitled or to the joint credit of the party entitled and the Accountant of the Ontario Court or local registrar.

Payment Out
(2) Where money is directed to be paid out of court to the credit of the party entitled, the party may name the financial institution into which the party wishes it to be paid.

(3) Where money has been paid to the joint credit of the party and the Accountant or registrar, the Accountant or registrar shall sign the cheque or direction for payment out on the production of the consent of the party paying in, verified by affidavit, or of the party's solicitor, or, in the absence of the consent, on the order of the referee.

Money Belonging to Minor
(4) Where it appears that money in court belongs to a minor, the referee shall require evidence of the age of the minor and shall, in the report, state the minor's birth date and full address.

Money to be Paid to Creditors
(5) Where an order of reference or a report directs the payment of money out of court to creditors, the person having carriage of the reference shall deposit with the Accountant or registrar a copy of the order or report and shall serve a notice to creditor (Form 55E) on each creditor stating that payment of the creditor's claim, as allowed, may be obtained from the Accountant or registrar.

REFERENCE FOR CONDUCT OF SALE

Method of Sale
55.06(1) Where a sale is ordered, the referee may cause the property to be sold by public auction, private contract or tender, or partly by one method and partly by another.

Advertisement
(2) Where property is directed to be sold by auction or tender, the party having carriage of the sale shall prepare a draft advertisement according to the instructions of the referee showing,
(a) the short title of the proceeding;
(b) that the sale is by order of the court;
(c) the time and place of the sale;
(d) a short description of the property to be sold;
(e) whether the property is to be sold in one lot or several and, if in several, in how many, and in what lots;
(f) the terms of payment;
(g) that the sale is subject to a reserve bid, if that is the case; and
(h) any conditions of sale different from those set out in (Form 55F).

Conditions of Sale

(3) **The conditions of sale by auction or tender shall be those set out in (Form 55F), subject to such modifications as the referee directs.**

Hearing for Directions

(4) **At a hearing for directions under subrule 55.02(3), the referee shall,**

(a) **settle the form of the advertisement;**

(b) **fix the time and place of sale;**

(c) **name an auctioneer, where one is to be employed;**

(d) **give directions for publication of the advertisement;**

(e) **give directions for obtaining appraisals;**

(f) **fix a reserve bid, if any; and**

(g) **make all other arrangements necessary for the sale.**

Norwich Union Life Ins. Soc. v. Oke, [1933] O.W.N. 673 (Master).
Discussion of the procedure for fixing the time of sale.

Who May Bid

(5) **All parties may bid except the party having carriage of the sale and any trustee or agent for the party or other person in a fiduciary relationship to the party.**

(6) **Where the party having carriage of the sale wishes to bid, the referee may transfer carriage of the sale to another party or to any other person.**

Who Conducts Sale

(7) **Where no auctioneer is employed, the referee or a person designated by the referee shall conduct the sale.**

Purchaser to Sign Agreement

(8) **The purchaser shall enter into an agreement of purchase and sale at the time of sale.**

Deposit

(9) **The deposit required by the conditions of sale shall be paid to the party having carriage of the sale or the party's solicitor at the time of sale and the party or solicitor shall forthwith pay the money into court in the name of the purchaser.**

Interim Report

(10) **Where a sale is made through an auctioneer, the auctioneer shall make an affidavit concerning the result of the sale, and where no auctioneer is employed, the referee shall enter the result in the procedure book and, in either case, the referee may make an interim report on the sale (Form 55G).**

Objection to Sale

(11) **A party may object to a sale by making a motion to the referee to set it aside, and notice of the motion shall be served on all parties to the reference and on the purchaser, who shall be deemed to be a party for the purpose of the motion.**

Completion of Sale

(12) The purchaser may pay the purchase money or the balance of it into court without order and, after the confirmation of the report on the sale, on notice to the party having carriage of the sale, the purchaser may obtain a vesting order.

Sparling v. 10 Nelson Street Ltd. (1980), 30 O.R. (2d) 609, 18 R.P.R. 1, 118 D.L.R. (3d) 182 (H.C.).

Discussion of circumstances prior to confirmation of the interim report in which the court will interfere with the sale.

Scott v. Rauf (1975), 10 O.R. (2d) 468, 21 C.B.R. (N.S.) 123, 63 D.L.R. (3d) 580 (C.A.).

The purchaser may not obtain a vesting order until after confirmation of the report of the sale.

(13) Where possession is wrongfully withheld from the purchaser, either the purchaser or the party having carriage of the sale may move for a writ of possession.

(14) The purchase money may be paid out of court in accordance with the report,

(a) on consent of the purchaser or the purchaser's solicitor; or

(b) on proof to the Accountant or registrar that the purchaser has received a transfer or vesting order of the property for which the money in question was paid into court.

(15) No transfer shall be approved until the referee is satisfied that the purchase money has been paid into court and, where a mortgage is taken for part of the purchase money, that the mortgage has been registered and deposited with the Accountant or registrar.

REFERENCE TO APPOINT COMMITTEE, GUARDIAN OR RECEIVER

55.07(1) Where, by an order directing a reference, a referee is directed to appoint a committee, guardian or receiver, the referee shall not report on the appointment until he or she has settled and approved any security required by the order and until the security has been filed with the Accountant or registrar.

(2) Where, by an order directing a reference or a report, the person so appointed is required to pass accounts or to pay money into court and has not done so, the referee may, on the passing of accounts, disallow any compensation and may charge the person with interest. [am. O. Reg. 69/95, s. 18]

Toronto Packing Co. v. Abrams (1921), 21 O.W.N. 29 (H.C.).

Security must be provided unless otherwise ordered.

COSTS

RULE 56   SECURITY FOR COSTS

Highlights

This Rule sets out the procedure for a defendant or respondent to obtain an order for security for costs. In 1989, the availability of security for costs was expanded to include a party to a garnishment, interpleader or other issue who is an active claimant (rule 56.01(2)) and to appeals (rule 61.06).

Availability. The situations in which security may be ordered are set out in rule 56.01(1). The most important grounds are the plaintiff or applicant being a non-resident or a "shell" corporation (rule 56.01(1)(a) and (d), respectively).

Constitutional validity of Rule. Case law across Canada has generally held that security for costs rules are not contrary to the equality provisions of s. 15(1) of the *Charter*. See, *e.g., Gerald Shapiro Holdings Inc. v. Nathan Tessis & Associates Inc.* (1986), 13 C.P.C. (2d) 288, additional reasons 6 W.D.C.P. 320 (Ont. Master), and see generally Holmested and Watson, *Ontario Civil Procedure*, 56 § 6.

General approach of the court to motions for security. On a motion for security for costs, the initial onus is on the defendant or respondent to show that the plaintiff or applicant falls within one of the enumerated categories. If this onus is met, the court has discretion to grant or refuse an order for security, and if the court makes an order, it has a discretion as to the quantum and means of payment of the order: *Hallum v. Canadian Memorial Chiropractic College* (1989), 70 O.R. (2d) 119 (H.C.). The plaintiff or applicant may avoid the order for security by showing either (a) that the order is unnecessary because it has sufficient assets or (b) that it should be permitted to proceed to trial despite its inability to pay costs should it fail: *John Wink Ltd. v. Sico Inc* (1987), 57 O.R. (2d) 705, 15 C.P.C. (2d) 187 (H.C.), leave to appeal to Ont. Div. Ct. granted 22 C.P.C. (2d) 311; *Warren Industrial Feldspar Co. Ltd. v. Union Carbide Canada Ltd.* (1986), 54 O.R. (2d) 213, 8 C.P.C. (2d) 1 (H.C.); *Smith Bus Lines Ltd. v. Bank of Montreal* (1987), 61 O.R. (2d) 688 at 690, 20 C.P.C. (2d) 38 (H.C.), leave to appeal to Ont. Div. Ct. refused 61 O.R. (2d) 688, 25 C.P.C. (2d) 255 (H.C.). Thus, in the exercise of its discretion, the court may consider the plaintiff's or applicant's financial ability to proceed with the action should it be ordered to provide security for costs; *i.e.,* the court may consider the plaintiff's or applicant's impecuniosity and may decline to order security for costs or to order nominal security if because of impecuniosity, the requirement of security for costs might work an injustice by denying a worthy claimant the opportunity of having its claim adjudicated: *Smallwood v. Sparling* (1983), 42 O.R. (2d) 53, 34 C.P.C. 24, affirmed 42 O.R. (2d) 53, 34 C.P.C. 24 at 29 (H.C.); *John Wink Ltd. v. Sico Inc., supra.* Where the plaintiff or applicant establishes its impecuniosity, then to show that its claim ought to be allowed to proceed despite an inability to be responsible for costs, the plaintiff or applicant must also show that its claim is not devoid of merits; it need not show that its claim is likely to succeed but rather that the claim is not almost certain to fail: *John Wink Ltd. v. Sico Inc., supra*; *Hallum v. Canadian Memorial Chiropractic College, supra*; *Rackley v. Rice* (1992), 8 O.R. (3d) 105 (Div. Ct.). In its consideration of whether to make an order for security for costs, the court may consider the merits of the case: *Hawaiian Airlines Inc. v. Chartermasters Inc.* (1985), 50 O.R. (2d) 575, 50 C.P.C. 224 (Master); *Horvat v. Feldman* (1985), 5 C.P.C. (2d) 267, affirmed

(1986), 15 C.P.C. (2d) 220 (Ont. H.C.); *Heck v. Royal Bank* (1986), 56 O.R. (2d) 168, 11 C.P.C. (2d) 109 (H.C.). Under the former Rules, it was doubtful whether this was so: *Re Agar*, [1957] O.W.N. 208 (Master).

Impecuniosity. If a plaintiff establishes that it is impecunious to the point where it cannot deposit security for costs, and the law suit will be "stopped in its tracks" by an order for security, the plaintiff should be allowed to proceed unless the claim is plainly devoid of merit: *John Wink Ltd. v. Sico Inc., supra.* However, "impecuniosity" is something quite different from having "insufficient assets in Ontario to pay the costs of the defendant" and in order to establish impecuniosity, a corporate plaintiff must establish that moneys are not available to it from its shareholders or other sources to deposit as security: *Smith Bus Lines v. Bank of Montreal* (1987), 61 O.R. (2d) 688 at 690, 20 C.P.C. (2d) 38 (H.C.), leave to appeal to Ont. Div. Ct. refused 61 O.R. (2d) 688, 25 C.P.C. (2d) 255; *Continental Breweries Inc. v. 707517 Ontario Ltd.* (1990), 46 C.P.C. (2d) 151 (Ont. Master).

Miscellaneous. The procedure for a declaration as to the plaintiff's/applicant's place of residence (rule 56.02) is necessary because under the Rules there is no obligation for the residence of the plaintiff/applicant to be stated in the originating process.

The Rule recognizes that there may be multiple defendants/respondents, only one of whom moves for security for costs, and requires notice of the motion to be given to all the defendants/respondents (rule 56.03) and that a dismissal for default in giving security is only effective as against the defendant/respondent who has obtained an order: rule 56.06.

The effect of an order for security for costs is clarified: there is no general stay, only the plaintiff/applicant is prohibited from taking any step until security is given, and it is made clear that even the plaintiff/applicant may proceed to the extent of appealing the order.

Former Rules: Rules 373-382.

WHERE AVAILABLE

56.01(1) The court, on motion by the defendant or respondent in a proceeding, may make such order for security for costs as is just where it appears that,

(a) the plaintiff or applicant is ordinarily resident outside Ontario;

(b) the plaintiff or applicant has another proceeding for the same relief pending in Ontario or elsewhere;

(c) the defendant or respondent has an order against the plaintiff or applicant for costs in the same or another proceeding that remain unpaid in whole or in part;

(d) the plaintiff or applicant is a corporation or a nominal plaintiff or applicant, and there is good reason to believe that the plaintiff or applicant has insufficient assets in Ontario to pay the costs of the defendant or respondent;

(e) there is good reason to believe that the action or application is frivolous and vexatious and that the plaintiff or applicant has insufficient assets in Ontario to pay the costs of the defendant or respondent; or

(f) a statute entitles the defendant or respondent to security for costs.

(2) Subrule (1) applies with necessary modifications to a party to a garnishment, interpleader or other issue who is an active claimant and would, if a plaintiff, be liable to give security for costs.

Cross-Reference: See rule 61.06 and cases collected thereunder for security for costs of an appeal.

Authors' Note on Organization of Cases

Cases relevant to this provision have been organized as follows:

Security from Non-Residents — Corporate Residence
Security from Non-Residents — Effect of Reciprocal Enforcement of Judgments Legislation
Security from Non-Residents — Assets in Ontario
Security from Non-Residents — Multiple Plaintiffs
Security from Non-Residents — Counterclaim by Non-Resident Defendant
Security from Non-Residents — Family Law Proceedings
Security from Non-Residents — Estate Proceedings
Security from Non-Residents — Miscellaneous
Security for Costs — Generally
Security for Costs — Impecunious Plaintiffs
Security for Costs — Other Proceeding Pending — rule 56.01(1)(b)
Security for Costs — Unpaid Costs from Previous Proceeding — rule 56.01(1)(c)
Security for Costs — Nominal Plaintiff — rule 56.01(1)(d)
Security for Costs — Corporate Plaintiff — rule 56.01(1)(d)
Security for Costs — Frivolous and Vexatious Actions — rule 56.01(1)(e)
Security for Costs — Statutory Provisions — rule 56.01(1)(f)
Security for Costs — Evidence on Motion
Security for Costs — Examination of Witnesses
Security for Costs of Multiple Defendants
Security for Costs of Third Party

Security from Non-Residents — Corporate Residence

Valleyfield Const. Ltd. v. Argo Const. Ltd.; Argo Const. Ltd. v. Valleyfield Const. Ltd. (1984), 44 C.P.C. 107 (Ont. Master).

Mere evidence that a corporation's head office is outside Ontario is insufficient to establish that it resides outside Ontario.

St. Anne-Nackawic Pulp & Paper Co. v. Tywood Industs. Ltd. (1980), 15 C.P.C. 77 (Ont. H.C.).

Incorporation in another province is not a sufficient ground for an order for security for costs. The existence of reciprocal enforcement of judgments legislation is only a factor to be considered in the exercise of the court's discretion.

Pet Milk Can. Ltd. v. Olympia & York Devs. (1974), 4 O.R. (2d) 640 (Master).

Where a majority of the directors of a company resided out of the jurisdiction and the "head office" of the company in Ontario was merely a mailing address, it was held that the company was not a resident of Ontario.

McDougall & Christmas Ltd. v. Genser, [1963] 2 O.R. 737 (H.C.).

A Quebec company which had had a permanent office in Ontario for at least five years and which carried on a substantial business in the province was held not to "reside out of Ontario".

Security from Non-Residents — *Effect of Reciprocal Enforcement of Judgments Legislation*

Krushnisky v. Clitherow (1986), 9 C.P.C. (2d) 155 (Ont. Master), varied 5 W.D.C.P. 371 (Ont. H.C.), leave to appeal refused (November 24, 1986), Doc. 16934/84.

The court ordered security from a plaintiff residing in a province with reciprocal enforcement of judgment legislation where there was no evidence of assets likely to satisfy an adverse costs order.

Williams v. Turner (1986), 56 O.R. (2d) 505, 13 C.P.C. (2d) 55, additional reasons 6 W.D.C.P. 142 (Master).

On a motion for security for costs, plaintiffs subject to reciprocal enforcement legislation were not treated differently than other foreign plaintiffs where they failed to show possession of sufficient conveniently realizable assets to answer for costs.

Stewart v. Perrault (1985), 50 C.P.C. 59 (Ont. Master).

The court declined to order security for costs from a Manitoba resident with substantial assets in that province. Ontario has an arrangement for reciprocal enforcement of judgments with Manitoba.

McCormack v. Newman (1983), 35 C.P.C. 298 (Ont. Master).

The onus is on a non-resident plaintiff seeking to avoid security for costs on the basis of having assets in a jurisdiction having reciprocal enforcement of judgments legislation, to show such assets exist and would likely satisfy an order for costs.

Smallwood v. Sparling (1983), 40 O.R. (2d) 796, 34 C.P.C. 24, affirmed 42 O.R. (2d) 53, 34 C.P.C. 24 at 29 (H.C.).

Security for costs will not generally be required from a non-resident plaintiff who has sufficient assets to answer a judgment for costs in a jurisdiction with reciprocal enforcement of judgments legislation. The plaintiff has the onus to show the sufficiency of the assets.

Richmond v. Can. Nat. Exhibition Assn. (1979), 24 O.R. (2d) 781, 11 C.P.C. 184, 104 D.L.R. (3d) 317 (H.C.).

A plaintiff who resided in a jurisdiction in which reciprocal enforcement of judgments legislation applied was not required to post security for costs.

Security from Non-Residents — *Assets in Ontario*

Cortes v. Lipton Bldg. Ltd., [1963] 1 O.R. 187 (Master).

The court refused to order security for costs where the defendant in a mortgage action admitted that the non-resident plaintiff was owed a large sum under the mortgage.

Re White and White, [1960] O.W.N. 384 (Master).

Where a non-resident applicant in partition proceedings was registered as a joint tenant of the property in question, the court refused to order security for costs. [*Note Rule 56 applies to both actions and applications — Authors.*]

Security from Non-Residents — *Multiple Plaintiffs*

Wong v. Silverstein (1987), 25 C.P.C. (2d) 161 (Ont. Master).

The court may order security for costs against a non-resident *Family Law Act* plaintiff notwithstanding that the injured plaintiff resides in Ontario, but declined to do so in this case where there was no evidence that the non-resident's claims materially increased the defence costs.

Williams v. Turner (1986), 56 O.R. (2d) 505, 13 C.P.C. (2d) 55, additional reasons at 6 W.D.C.P. 142 (Master).

Where non-resident plaintiffs had presented several rather than joint claims, each plaintiff was required to post security for costs.

Willowtree Invts. Inc. v. Brown (1985), 48 C.P.C. 150 (Ont. Master).

Where multiple plaintiffs assert a joint claim, security for costs will not be required from a non-resident plaintiff if there is a plaintiff within Ontario. However if the claims are several, so that the non-resident plaintiff may fail while the resident plaintiff succeeds, security may be required from the non-resident.

Zotos v. Hanover Insurance Co. (1985), 4 C.P.C. (2d) 309 (Ont. Master).

Where a number of plaintiffs assert claims which are several and not joint, a non-resident plaintiff may be ordered to provide security despite another plaintiff's residing in Ontario.

Security from Non-Residents — Counterclaim by Non-Resident Defendant

Standard Conveyor Co. v. Heakes, [1953] O.W.N. 821 (Master).

A non-resident plaintiff by counterclaim asserting a claim in part against a stranger to the action may be required to provide security for costs.

Engebretson Grupe Co. v. Grossman, [1937] O.W.N. 393 (Master).

Where the defendants did not deny the plaintiff's claim but set up a counterclaim, the defendants were characterized as the active parties to the action and an order for security for costs was set aside.

Wilkins v. Towner, [1936] O.W.N. 137 (H.C.).

Security for costs from a non-resident plaintiff by counterclaim was denied because he had been brought into the jurisdiction to defend the main action and counterclaim was connected with the main action.

Security from Non-Residents — Family Law Proceedings

Marcocchio v. Marcocchio (1981), 32 O.R. (2d) 536 (Master).

The court refused to require security for costs from a non-resident spouse in a custody case. The welfare of the child is paramount and such an order might deter the spouse from proceeding.

Josuph v. Josuph, [1971] 2 O.R. 90 (Master).

Discussion of security for costs in divorce cases.

Re Agar, [1957] O.W.N. 208 (H.C.).

A non-resident parent was required to furnish security for costs on an appeal from a dismissal of a *habeas corpus* proceeding involving the custody of her child.

Security from Non-Residents — Estate Proceedings

Re Bisyk (1979), 23 O.R. (2d) 600, 13 C.P.C. 324 (H.C.).

The court refused to require non-resident heirs-at-law to post security for costs in an action challenging the validity of a will where there were reasonable grounds to question the capacity of the testator.

Cooper v. Nat. Trust Co., [1962] O.W.N. 119 (H.C.).

In an action regarding the administration of an estate the court is reluctant to order security for costs if it appears costs would likely be paid to all parties out of the estate.

Security from Non-Residents — Miscellaneous

Green v. Copperthorne Industries 86 Ltd. (1993), 12 O.R. (3d) 728 (Gen. Div.).
The court may order security for costs of a solicitor and client assessment of costs where the client resides outside Ontario.

Borthwick v. St. James Square Associates Inc. (1987), 61 O.R. (2d) 790 (Master).
Security for costs was denied in a real estate transaction case where the defendant held a deposit sufficient to satisfy costs and the action involved joint claims of resident and non-resident plaintiffs.

Evans v. Holroyd (1988), 31 C.P.C. (2d) 48 (Ont. H.C.).
A third party who defends the main action may obtain security for costs from the plaintiff.

Four Embarcadero Center Venture v. Mr. Greenjeans Corp. (1986), 10 C.P.C. (2d) 105 (Ont. Master).
The fact that an applicant or plaintiff holds a foreign judgment is not a proper factor to be considered in determining whether security for costs should be ordered.

Re Allan, [1939] O.W.N. 183 (Master).
An order for security for costs was denied where the non-resident plaintiff had an outstanding judgment against the defendant.

Lake Sulphite Pulp Co. v. Charles W. Cox Ltd., [1938] O.W.N. 300 (Master).
An order for security for costs was granted against the non-resident receiver of a resident plaintiff corporation.

Security for Costs — Generally

Sutherland v. Canadian Red Cross Society (1994), 25 C.P.C. (3d) 118 (Ont. Gen. Div.).
The court dismissed a motion for security for costs in a class action where, although the plaintiffs resided outside Ontario, they undertook to seek funding from the Class Proceedings Committee. If funding were granted, the Class Proceedings Fund would become responsible for defence costs.

423322 Ontario Ltd. v. Bank of Montreal (1988), 66 O.R. (2d) 123, 41 C.P.C. (2d) 249 (H.C.).
The court declined to order security for costs having regard to the delay in bringing the motion and the fact that the plaintiff's action was not frivolous or vexatious and was founded upon the actions of the defendant which the plaintiff alleged caused its insolvency.

Budline Millwork Ltd. v. Torindo Ltd. (1988), 29 C.L.R. 319 (Ont. Master).
Rule 56.01 applies to proceedings under the *Construction Lien Act.*

286018 Ont. Ltd. v. Fidinam (Can.) Ltd. (1988), 27 C.P.C. (2d) 159 (Ont. Master).
A motion for security for costs may be made at the pre-trial conference where no prejudice is shown to the plaintiff.

ICC International Computer Consulting & Leasing Ltd. v. ICC Internationale Computer & Consulting GmbH (1989), 33 C.P.C. (2d) 40 (Ont. H.C.).
No party will be required to give security for costs as a condition for defending itself. Security will not be required from a plaintiff by counterclaim where the counterclaim is closely related to the main action.

423322 Ont. Ltd. v. Bank of Montreal (1988), 66 O.R. (2d) 123 (H.C.).
Even where there was no contradictory evidence, the court was not required to accept the plaintiff's allegation that it had been prejudiced by the defendant's failure to bring a motion for security for costs promptly. However, as no explanation was given for the delay in bringing the motion, and the action was not frivolous or vexatious, the court refused to make an order for security for costs.

Maple Leaf Racquet Court Inc. v. Beaver Engineering Ltd. (1987), 60 O.R. (2d) 626 (Master).
An appeal is not a "proceeding" within the meaning of rule 56.01.

Sydlo v. Mixing Equipment Co. (No. 3) (1987), 18 C.P.C. (2d) 79, 22 O.A.C. 231 (*sub nom. Love v. Mixing Equipment Co.*) (Div. Ct.).
An order to continue based on an assignment of the cause of action by a corporation to an individual for the purpose of avoiding an order requiring the corporation to post security for costs was held to be an abuse of process. The court permitted the order to continue to stand provided the plaintiff posted security for costs.

Mangold v. 330002 Ont. Ltd. (1986), 57 O.R. (2d) 716 (H.C.).
Section 15 of the *Charter of Rights* can only be relied upon by litigants who are deprived of their rights as a result of proven impecuniosity and prove that the rule requiring security for costs would effectively deny them equal protection of the law; in this case the plaintiff had not established that she was unable to pay security, but merely that it would be a hardship, and while this was a factor to be considered on the motion, it did not justify a finding that the rule was invalid.

Gerald Shapiro Holdings Inc. v. Nathan Tessis & Associates Inc. (1986), 13 C.P.C. (2d) 288, 27 C.R.R. 161, additional reasons at 6 W.D.C.P. 320 (Ont. Master).
Rule 56.01(a) and (d), permitting an order for security for costs against a non-resident, corporate or nominal plaintiff, do not offend the mobility or equality provisions of the *Charter of Rights*.

Hawaiian Airlines Inc. v. Chartermasters Inc. (1985), 50 O.R. (2d) 575, 50 C.P.C. 224 (Master).
The court has a discretion to require security for costs by instalments, *i.e.* to fix an amount as security for proceedings up to a particular point in the action with a further motion to be made at that time to determine the amount of further security required. The court may order dollar-for-dollar security and need not apply the "two-thirds rule".

Mutual Life Ins. Co. of Can. v. Buffer Investments Inc. (1986), 56 O.R. (2d) 480 (H.C.).
A motion to set aside a final order of foreclosure is not a proceeding, and therefore cannot be subject to a motion for security for costs.

Security for Costs — Impecunious Plaintiffs

Paul v. General Magnaplate Corp. (1995), 7 W.D.C.P. (2d) 79 (Ont. Gen. Div.).
The court refused to require non-resident plaintiffs to provide security where the defendants had *de facto* security through possession of assets of the plaintiffs and, although the plaintiffs could not show impecuniosity, requiring security would have the effect of depriving the plaintiffs of a *bona fide* cause of action.

Solcan Electric Corp. v. Viewstar Canada Inc. (1994), 25 C.P.C. (3d) 181 (Ont. Gen. Div.).
The court dismissed a motion for security for costs where the plaintiff was impecunious and injustice would result if the action were not allowed to proceed.

LaCoe v. Che (1992), 17 C.P.C. (3d) 181 (Ont. Gen. Div.).
Proof of impecuniosity does not require a specific statement that the plaintiff cannot raise or borrow money where other evidence shows impecuniosity.

Continental Breweries Inc. v. 707517 Ontario Ltd. (1990), 46 C.P.C. (2d) 151 (Ont. Master).
The plaintiff was ordered to post security for costs although it had no realizable assets. The shareholders of the plaintiff could fund the action, and it would not be just for the defendant to be sued by a corporate "shell" who was at no risk if it lost, and could never satisfy a costs award.

Shadows v. Travelers Can. Corp. (1990), 40 C.P.C. (2d) 118 (Ont. H.C.).

Although the plaintiff was without assets, if failed to show that it was impecunious. Accordingly, security for costs was ordered.

Das v. Coles (1989), 71 O.R. (2d) 57, 64 D.L.R. (4th) 345 (H.C.).

In resisting an order for security for costs, plaintiffs with a meritorious case who establish impecuniosity are not required to sell or encumber assets necessary for life, and any such assets should not be considered as supporting an order for security.

Hallum v. Cdn. Memorial Chiropractic College (1989), 70 O.R. (2d) 119 (H.C.).

A non-resident alleging impecuniosity must do more than adduce some evidence. The onus rests on him to satisfy the court that he is impecunious.

Holt v. Caven (1989), 35 C.P.C. (2d) 190 (Ont. Master).

Where the plaintiffs were impecunious and their case was not "plainly devoid of merit" the court refused to order security for costs.

Kurzela v. 526442 Ont. Ltd. (1988), 66 O.R. (2d) 446, 32 C.P.C. (2d) 276, 31 O.A.C. 303 (Div. Ct.).

In order to establish inpecuniosity a corporate plaintiff must establish that its shareholders are unable to provide funds to post as security.

Conklin Lumber Co. v. C.I.B.C. (1988), 28 C.P.C. (2d) 245 (Ont. Master), affirmed 65 O.R. (2d) 373, 28 C.P.C. (2d) 245n (H.C.).

As an impecunious plaintiff could not have been required to post security for costs pursuant to the former Rules of Practice, a plaintiff was not required to post such costs where an action had been instituted in November 1982, and where there was an unexplained delay on the part of the defendant in moving for security for costs.

Trottier Foods Ltd. v. LeBlond (1987), 24 C.P.C. (2d) 272 (Ont. Master).

The court refused to excuse the responding parties from posting security for costs on the grounds of impecuniosity where they did not provide evidence establishing that the order sought would prevent them from proceeding with the action.

Smith Bus Lines v. Bank of Montreal (1987), 61 O.R. (2d) 688 at 690, 20 C.P.C. (2d) 38 (H.C.), leave to appeal to Ont. Div. Ct. refused 61 O.R. (2d) 688, 25 C.P.C. (2d) 255.

"Impecuniosity" is quite different from having "insufficient assets in Ontario to pay the costs of the defendant", and in order to establish impecuniosity, a corporate plaintiff must establish that moneys are not available to it from its shareholders or other sources to deposit as security.

John Wink Ltd. v. Sico Inc. (1987), 57 O.R. (2d) 705, 15 C.P.C. (2d) 187 (H.C.), leave to appeal to Ont. Div. Ct. granted 22 C.P.C. (2d) 311.

Where the defendant establishes good reason to believe that the plaintiff has insufficient assets to satisfy the costs of the action, the onus shifts to the plaintiff to establish either that it has sufficient assets or that it should be permitted to proceed to trial in spite of the lack of assets. Where the plaintiff admits its poverty the plaintiff may proceed to trial if it establishes it is not almost certain to fail. Unless a claim is plainly devoid of merit it should be allowed to proceed.

D.W. Buchanan Construction Ltd. v. 392720 Ont. Ltd. (1986), 11 C.P.C. (2d) 226 (Ont. Master).

Security for costs was ordered where the plaintiff alleged impecuniosity but gave inadequate and contradicting evidence in that regard.

Clark v. Tiger Brand Knitting Co. (1986), 10 C.P.C. (2d) 288 (Ont. H.C.).

A party who seeks to avoid payment of security for costs on the ground of impecuniosity should not rely on a solicitor's affidavit nor may the moving party rely on its own examination for discovery.

408466 Ont. Ltd. v. Fidelity Trust Co. (1986), 10 C.P.C. (2d) 278 at 282 (Ont. H.C.).

If the moving party is *prima facie* entitled to security for costs, the onus to establish impecuniosity is on the plaintiff. Where there was no evidence as to the financial position of the sole shareholder of the plaintiff, impecuniosity was not established.

Warren Industrial Feldspar Co. v. Union Carbide Can. Ltd. (1986), 54 O.R. (2d) 213, 8 C.P.C. (2d) 1 (H.C.).

A plaintiff seeking to avoid security for costs because it is impecunious must lead evidence to demonstrate its impecuniosity and to show why justice demands it be permitted to proceed without posting security. The court may consider the merits of the action.

City Paving Co. v. Port Colborne (1985), 3 C.P.C. (2d) 316 (Ont. Master).

An order for security for costs by instalments was made where the plaintiff was impecunious and the amount of security required was substantial.

Security for Costs — Other Proceeding Pending — rule 56.01(1)(b)

Maple Leaf Racquet Court Inc. v. Beaver Engineering Ltd. (1987), 60 O.R. (2d) 626 (Master).

A motion for security for costs was dismissed where a party had commenced a second action while an appeal from an earlier action with respect to the same wrong was pending. The outstanding appeal was not a pending proceeding within the meaning of rule 56.01(1)(b).

Security for Costs — Unpaid Costs from Previous Proceeding — rule 56.01(1)(c)

Davidson v. Kewatin (Town of) (1990), 45 C.P.C. (2d) 64 (Ont. H.C.).

The court refused to order security for costs due to improper conduct by the solicitor for the defendant.

Tricontinental Investments Co. v. Guarantee Co. of North America (1989), 70 O.R. (2d) 461, 39 C.P.C. (2d) 113, 35 O.A.C. 253 (C.A.).

Costs awarded by an order which is under appeal do not form the basis for security for costs under rule 56.01(1)(c).

Ostrander v. Bawden (1978), 8 C.P.C. 34 (Ont. Master).

Security for costs was ordered where the plaintiff had not paid the costs awarded against him in a previous action dealing with the same rights, questions and facts, although for a different cause of action.

Security for Costs — Nominal Plaintiff — rule 56.01(1)(d)

Loblaw Cos. v. Lido Industrial Products Ltd. (1993), 19 C.P.C. (3d) 183 (Ont. Gen. Div.).

The court required a bankrupt plaintiff by counterclaim to provide security for costs where the counterclaim was being prosecuted for the benefit of the bankrupt's secured creditor.

Mancini Estate (Trustee of) v. Falconi (1989), 70 O.R. (2d) 171, 38 C.P.C. (2d) 208 (H.C.).

An order for security for costs should not be made against a trustee in bankruptcy where it is acting in a representative capacity for the benefit of all creditors. Furthermore, the moving parties had not established that the plaintiff had insufficient assets in Ontario to pay the costs of the defendant, if ordered to do so.

David C. Heaslip Enterprises Ltd. v. Petrosar Ltd. (1987), 28 C.P.C. (2d) 285 (Ont. Master), affirmed 28 C.P.C. (2d) 285n (Ont. H.C.).

It would be procedurally unfair to apply the provisions of rule 56.01(1)(d) to a plaintiff where the action had been commenced and prosecuted under the former Rules of Practice.

J.G. Drapeau Ltd. v. Livingston Estates Ltd. (1985), 51 O.R. (2d) 96, 2 C.P.C. (2d) 229, 11 O.A.C. 312 (C.A.).

Ordinarily it would be an abuse of process to examine an employee of the plaintiff to obtain evidence for a motion under rule 56.01(1)(d), however it was permitted in this case because the plaintiff filed an affidavit containing information obtained from the proposed witness.

Janlaw Mgmt. Inc. v. Uxbridge Gold Enterprises Ltd. (1984), 44 C.P.C. 94 (Ont. Master).

A shelf corporation used to enter into an agreement of purchase and sale as trustee for certain beneficiaries and as a matter of convenience was held to be a nominal plaintiff.

Pugh v. Stather (1982), 31 C.P.C. 108 (Ont. Co. Ct.).

Security for costs will not be ordered in a subrogated damages action if the insurer's counsel files an affidavit undertaking on the insurer's behalf to indemnify the defendant for any costs that might be awarded to him.

Lincoln Terrace Restaurant Ltd. v. Bray (1980), 19 C.P.C. 290 (Ont. Master).

A plaintiff corporation does not become a nominal plaintiff by virtue of its dissolution after the action has commenced.

York Condominium v. Bramalea Consolidated Devs. Ltd. (1975), 10 O.R. (2d) 459 (Master).

A condominium corporation is not *per se* a nominal plaintiff.

DeGuzman v. Cruikshank Motors Ltd. (1976), 1 C.P.C. 318 (Ont. H.C.).

An undertaking by the insurer to pay any order of costs made against the plaintiff is insufficient to disentitle the defendant to an order for security for costs.

Rolmac Const. Co. v. Rio Tinto Mining Co., [1961] O.W.N. 269, affirmed [1961] O.W.N. 272 (H.C.).

A nominal plaintiff is one who lacks a beneficial interest in the result of the action.

Trustee of Altridge Ltd. v. Cook, [1960] O.W.N. 310 (H.C.).

The court refused to require a trustee in bankruptcy to furnish security for costs.

Security for Costs — Corporate Plaintiff — rule 56.01(1)(d)

Superstars Mississauga Inc. v. Ambler-Courtney Ltd. (1993), 15 O.R. (3d) 437, 17 C.P.C. (3d) 27 (Master).

A limited partner is not, in the normal course, ordered to pay the costs of an action if it fails. The defendant must look to the general partner and where the general partner is a corporation rule 56.01(2) applies.

671122 Ontario Ltd. v. Canadian Tire Corp. (1993), 15 O.R. (3d) 65, 20 C.P.C. (3d) 392, 107 D.L.R. (4th) 207, 66 O.A.C. 1 (C.A.).

The court should consider the quality, sufficiency and *bona fides* of the plaintiff's assets but should not countenance extensive and speculative inquiries as to the future availability and value of the assets.

206084 Ontario Ltd. v. Sun Alliance Insurance Co. (1992), 9 O.R. (3d) 462 (Gen. Div.).

Security for costs was granted as the property of the plaintiff corporation had been forfeited to the Crown upon its dissolution pursuant to the *Business Corporations Act*.

Buffer Investments Inc. v. Roynat Inc. (1988), 26 C.P.C. (2d) 55 (Ont. H.C.).

The court ordered corporate plaintiffs to provide security for the costs of the trial of an issue.

Novarode NV/SA v. Nova Coated Products Ltd. (1987), 19 C.P.C. (2d) 156 (Ont. Master).

A non-resident defendant-by-counterclaim and non-resident third party were awarded security for costs against an Ontario corporation which lacked assets.

Warren Industrial Feldspar Co. v. Union Carbide Can. Ltd. (1986), 54 O.R. (2d) 213, 8 C.P.C. (2d) 1 (H.C.).

In a motion under rule 56.01(1)(d) the defendant need not *prove* the plaintiff has insufficient assets to answer for costs so long as it establishes "good reason to believe" such is the case.

Brain-Hulst Ltd. v. H.E. Pierre Enterprises Ltd. (1985), 2 C.P.C. (2d) 90, 56 C.B.R. (N.S.) 146 (H.C.).

A bankrupt corporation was not required to provide security for costs where the trustee in bankruptcy had been added as a party plaintiff and, at the time of the motion, the estate had sufficient assets to satisfy an adverse order of costs.

RCVM Enterprises Ltd. v. Int. Harvester Can. Ltd. (1985), 50 O.R. (2d) 508, 50 C.P.C. 278 (Master).

The court required an impecunious corporate plaintiff to provide security for costs. The plaintiff failed to show why, despite the impecuniosity, justice demanded that it be permitted to continue the action without security for costs. The court applied the "two-thirds rule".

Security for Costs — Frivolous and Vexatious Actions — rule 56.01(1)(e)

Logan v. Logan (1993), 15 O.R. (3d) 411 (Gen. Div.).

The court refused security for costs of proceedings to vary an access order on the basis the proceedings were frivolous and vexatious. There were serious allegations and children were at risk.

MacDonald v. Lange (1986), 56 O.R. (2d) 89, 3 R.F.L. (3d) 288 (H.C.).

Security for costs were ordered against a mother seeking a declaration of paternity where her earlier claims for support had been unsuccessful.

Willowtree Invts. Inc. v. Brown (1985), 48 C.P.C. 150 (Ont. Master).

The defendant must show not only that the action is likely frivolous and vexatious but also that the plaintiff has insufficient assets in Ontario to satisfy an award of costs.

Security for Costs — Statutory Provisions — rule 56.01(1)(f)

Van Riessen v. Canada (Attorney General) (1994), 35 C.P.C. (3d) 165 (Ont. Gen. Div.).

The court ordered the plaintiffs to provide security for costs pursuant to s. 10 of the *Public Authorities Protection Act.*

Rackley v. Rice (1992), 8 O.R. (3d) 105, 89 D.L.R. (4th) 62, 56 O.A.C. 349 (Div. Ct.).

A motion for security for costs under s. 14 of the *Public Authorities Protection Act* was dismissed where an impecunious plaintiff showed that the action was not almost certain to fail.

Hunter v. Pittman (1988), 25 C.P.C. (2d) 145 (Ont. H.C.).

Section 14 of the *Public Authorities Protection Act*, R.S.O. 1980, c. 406, does not violate the equality provision in s. 15 of the *Charter of Rights* in permitting security for costs against plaintiffs without sufficient property to answer for costs.

Reiger v. Chief of Police (1987), 58 O.R. (2d) 203 (*sub nom. Reiger v. Burrows*), 14 C.P.C. (2d) 318 (Master).

A defendant seeking security for costs pursuant to s. 14 of the *Public Authorities Protection Act*, R.S.O. 1980, c. 406, may examine the plaintiff under rule 39.03(1).

Hull v. Deare (1983), 40 C.P.C. 59 (Ont. Master).

There is no right to conduct an examination under s. 20(2) of the *Libel and Slander Act*, R.S.O. 1980, c. 237, unless a notice of motion has been delivered.

Shewchun v. McMaster Univ. (1983), 33 C.P.C. 35, 143 D.L.R. (3d) 238 (Ont. Master).

A defendant seeking security for costs under the *Libel and Slander Act* need not deliver his supporting affidavit before being entitled to examine the plaintiff pursuant to that statute.

Gunn v. North York Public Library (1976), 14 O.R. (2d) 554, 2 C.P.C. 68 (H.C.).

Discussion of the security for costs provisions of the *Libel and Slander Act*, R.S.O. 1970, c. 243, and the *Public Authorities Protection Act*, R.S.O. 1970, c. 374.

Raffman v. Crawford, [1963] 2 O.R. 37 (Master).

Discussion of security for costs provisions of the *Public Authorities Protection Act*, R.S.O. 1960, c. 318.

Goudie v. Oliver, [1957] O.W.N. 575 (Master).

Special statutory provisions entitling certain defendants to security for costs do not limit the availability of such relief under the Rules.

Davidson v. Millward, [1955] O.W.N. 941 (Master).

The general purpose of security for costs provisions under the Rules and various statutes is to grant protection in certain classes of actions where the plaintiff is unable to satisfy or the defendant is unable to enforce a judgment for costs against the plaintiff. Discussion of provision in *Public Authorities Protection Act*, R.S.O. 1950, c. 303.

Security for Costs — Evidence on Motion

Heck v. Royal Bank (1986), 56 O.R. (2d) 168, 11 C.P.C. (2d) 109 (H.C.).

Where a solicitor has delivered an affidavit in response to a motion for security for costs, the solicitor may be required to answer questions with respect to the merits of the action on cross-examination.

Taulbee v. Bowen (1986), 54 O.R. (2d) 763, 9 C.P.C. (2d) 90 (H.C.).

Evidence with respect to an offer to settle is inadmissible on a motion for increased security for costs.

Security for Costs — Examination of Witnesses

Carnival Leisure Industries Ltd. v. Brigante (1993), 4 W.D.C.P. (2d) 209 (Ont. Gen. Div.).

Where the plaintiff does not allege impecuniosity, questions regarding the merits of the case are generally not permitted in cross-examining on the plaintiff's affidavit.

Mar-Flite Ltd. v. Guardall Warranty Corp. (Trustee of) (1989), 75 C.B.R. (N.S.) 203 (Ont. S.C.).

The court refused to permit a cross-examination going to the merits of the action, in order to obtain evidence for a motion for security for costs, where the plaintiff had not alleged impecuniosity.

Quinn v. Dimoff (1988), 31 C.P.C. (2d) 167 (Ont. Master).

Both plaintiff and defendant may be examined regarding the merits of the action as witnesses on a pending motion. The defendant, however, may not examine the plaintiff regarding his assets or financial position unless the plaintiff has filed an affidavit raising that issue.

Walker v. Peel & Maryborough Mutual Fire Ins. Co. (1987), 59 O.R. (2d) 400 (Dist. Ct.).

When testing affidavit evidence filed in opposition to a motion for security for costs, a defendant may cross-examine a plaintiff on its financial situation prior to a determination of whether the plaintiff is a nominal plaintiff.

Heck v. Royal Bank (1986), 56 O.R. (2d) 168, 11 C.P.C. (2d) 109 (H.C.).

The court may permit a deponent who files an affidavit on a motion for security for costs to be cross-examined as to the merits of the action.

Horvat v. Feldman (1985), 5 C.P.C. (2d) 267 (Ont. Master), affirmed (1986), 15 C.P.C. (2d) 220 (Ont. H.C.).

The court permitted the defendant to be examined regarding the merits of the action since that was a relevant consideration to the exercise of the court's discretion regarding security for costs.

Andross Const. Ltd. v. Laidlaw (1982), 25 C.P.C. 279 (Ont. Master).

A plaintiff will only be compelled to answer questions concerning his property in Ontario on his examination for discovery if answers have already been obtained which provide a reasonably sound basis for the belief that the action is frivolous and vexatious.

3001 Invts. Ltd. v. Pegg (1982), 25 C.P.C. 246 at 251 (Ont. H.C.).

A subpoena served on an officer of the plaintiff to examine him in support of a motion under the predecessor of this provision, following completion of examinations for discovery, was struck out. *Patland Invts. Ltd. v. Kates, infra,* approved.

Patland Invts. Ltd. v. Kates (1978), 16 O.R. (2d) 420, 4 C.P.C. 241 (Master).

A defendant cannot examine the plaintiff by summons in support of a motion for security for costs.

Security for Costs of Multiple Defendants

Comtois v. Edmonson, [1954] O.W.N. 733 (Master).

The court may order the plaintiff to provide security for each of several defendants.

Finnegan v. Dzus, [1953] O.W.N. 635 (Master).

Discussion of apportionment of security among multiple defendants.

Five-Star Mysteries Inc. v. Martin, [1948] O.W.N. 683 (H.C.).

Where the plaintiff provided security for costs following a motion for such security by one of several defendants, the court denied the plaintiff's motion for an order that the security provided stand as security for the costs of all the defendants because the other defendants had no notice of the motion.

Security for Costs of Third Party

Williams v. Turner (1989), 68 O.R. (2d) 433, 36 C.P.C. (2d) 47 (Master).

Although rule 56.01 permits a third party to seek security for costs from a plaintiff, no security was ordered where it was unlikely that the plaintiff would be ordered to bear the third party's costs at trial.

Evans v. Holroyd (1988), 31 C.P.C. (2d) 48 (Ont. H.C.).

A third party who delivers a statement of defence in the main action acquires the right to move for security for costs against a non-resident plaintiff in the same manner as a defendant.

Griffith v. Muir (1982), 38 O.R. (2d) 1, 28 C.P.C. 236 (Master).

Non-resident plaintiffs were ordered to give security for costs in respect of a third party who defended the main action.

Monda v. Niagara Imperial Motel Ltd., [1970] 1 O.R. 736 (Master).

The order may be made for the benefit of a third party.

McLean v. Beausaert, [1960] O.W.N. 257 (H.C.).

A non-resident plaintiff was required to post security for costs at the instance of a third party added under the *Insurance Act*.

Shaw v. Brown, [1955] O.W.N. 472 (Master).

The court refused to order a non-resident defendant to provide security for the costs of a third party added under the *Negligence Act*.

DECLARATION OF PLAINTIFF'S OR APPLICANT'S PLACE OF RESIDENCE

56.02 The solicitor for the plaintiff or applicant shall, forthwith on receipt of a demand in writing from any person who has been served with the originating process, declare in writing whether the plaintiff or applicant is ordinarily resident in Ontario, and where the solicitor fails to respond to the demand, the court may order that the action or application be stayed or dismissed.

Whelan v. Farrell (1982), 28 C.P.C. 258 (Ont. H.C.).

The court ordered a solicitor to disclose his client's address to permit surveillance of the plaintiff.

MOTION FOR SECURITY

56.03(1) In an action, a motion for security for costs may be made only after the defendant has delivered a defence and shall be made on notice to the plaintiff and every other defendant who has delivered a defence or notice of intent to defend.

(2) In an application, a motion for security for costs may be made only after the respondent has delivered a notice of appearance and shall be made on notice to the applicant and every other respondent who has delivered a notice of appearance.

423322 Ont. Ltd. v. Bank of Montreal (1988), 65 O.R. (2d) 136, 27 C.P.C. (2d) 9 (Master), affirmed 66 O.R. (2d) 123 (H.C.).

The court refused to order security for costs where delay in bringing the motion for security was unexplained and lulled the plaintiff into a false sense of security. Generally, the appropriate time for the motion is after discovery of the plaintiff.

Community Web Printing, A Div. of Houle Printing Ltd. v. Cosmos Graphics Inc. (1985), 3 C.P.C. (2d) 209 (Ont. Master).

Where a defendant by counterclaim sought security for costs after delivering a statement of defence which itself asserted a new counterclaim but before delivery of a defence to the new counterclaim, the court dismissed the motion as premature. A motion for security for costs should not be heard until the issues in the action have been defined by the pleadings.

Cohen v. Power, [1971] 2 O.R. 742 (Master).

Unexplained delay in bringing a motion for security for costs will be fatal to its success.

AMOUNT AND FORM OF SECURITY AND TIME FOR FURNISHING

56.04 The amount and form of security and the time for paying into court or otherwise giving the required security shall be determined by the court.

Mabri Construction Ltd. v. Thomas C. Assaly Corp. (1974), 6 O.R. (2d) 178 (H.C.).
Where the defendant makes a counterclaim the costs of the counterclaim should not be included in any security for costs.

Albino & Mike Contracting Ltd. v. James (1992), 17 C.P.C. (3d) 331 (Ont. Master).
The court permitted a corporate plaintiff to provide security for costs by way of undertakings from its principals to pay personally any award of costs against the plaintiff.

FORM AND EFFECT OF ORDER

56.05 A plaintiff or applicant against whom an order for security for costs (Form 56A) has been made may not, until the security has been given, take any step in the proceeding except an appeal from the order, unless the court orders otherwise.

DEFAULT OF PLAINTIFF OR APPLICANT

56.06 Where a plaintiff or applicant defaults in giving the security required by an order, the court on motion may dismiss the proceeding against the defendant or respondent who obtained the order, and the stay imposed by rule 56.05 no longer applies unless another defendant or respondent has obtained an order for security for costs.

Leonard v. Prior (1994), 118 D.L.R. (4th) 442 (Ont. Gen. Div.).
The court dismissed an action where the plaintiff had failed to provide the required security and did not have a credible proposal to rectify the default.

AMOUNT MAY BE VARIED

56.07 The amount of security required by an order for security for costs may be increased or decreased at any time.

Levy-Russell Ltd. v. Tecmotiv Inc. (1992), 10 C.P.C. (3d) 52 (Ont. Gen. Div.).
Where security for costs in the sum of $150,000 had been ordered on consent but in hindsight was inadequate, the court ordered that further security be provided in the sum of $450,000.

Novarode NV/SA v. Nova Coated Products Ltd. (1987), 19 C.P.C. (2d) 156 (Ont. Master).
The court has jurisdiction to increase the security for costs provided for in a consent order, but an increase should not be awarded lightly and should be awarded only where there is a significant gap between the order and what later appears necessary.

NOTICE OF COMPLIANCE

56.08 On giving the security required by an order, the plaintiff or applicant shall forthwith give notice of compliance to the defendant or respondent who obtained the order, and to every other party.

SECURITY FOR COSTS AS TERM OF RELIEF

56.09 Despite rules 56.01 and 56.02, any party to a proceeding may be ordered to give security for costs where, under rule 1.05 or otherwise, the court has a discretion to impose terms as a condition of granting relief and, where such an order is made, rules 56.04 to 56.08 apply, with necessary modifications.

Sydlo Inc. v. Mixing Equipment Co. (No. 3) (1987), 18 C.P.C. (2d) 79, 22 O.A.C. 231 (*sub nom. Love v. Mixing Equipment Co.*) (Ont. Div. Ct.).

When granting relief under rule 56.09, the onus of proof applicable on a motion for security for costs is not relevant.

RULE 57   COSTS OF PROCEEDINGS
BETWEEN PARTY AND PARTY

Highlights

Rule 57 deals with the awarding of costs as between parties to the litigation. The "assessment" of such costs, formerly called "taxation", is governed by Rule 58. (The Rules no longer regulate solicitor and client assessments at all, the former Rules on the subject have been transferred to the *Solicitors Act.*)

The court's general discretion to determine by whom and to what extent costs shall be paid is set forth in s. 131(1) of the *Courts of Justice Act.* But that section is expressly made subject to the Rules, and rule 57.01 lists numerous factors the court may take into account in awarding costs. Most of these factors are familiar, but particular note should be taken of the prominence given to any "offer to settle made in writing".

Rule 57.01(2) "overrules" some former case law by specifically providing that the court may order costs against a successful party in a proper case.

While referring costs for assessment remains the normal practice, the court is given express power to fix costs with or without reference to the Tariffs: rule 57.01(3).

Where costs are to be assessed the court may give directions to the assessment officer: rule 57.02.

Specific costs provisions in Rule 57. Several of these provisions are worthy of note. In order to discourage unnecessary motions, rule 57.03 provides that if the court is satisfied that a contested motion ought not to have been brought or opposed it shall order the costs to be paid forthwith. (Case law now indicates that in disposing of interlocutory motions the court will generally fix costs and order for them to be paid forthwith: *Axton v. Kent* (1991), 2 O.R. (3d) 797 (Div. Ct.).)

Specific provision is made for costs to be assessed where a settlement provides for their recovery but does not fix them: rule 57.04.

In respect of the costs of a litigation guardian, rule 57.06 permits the court to limit the liability of a successful party to pay the costs of a litigation guardian who acted for an unsuccessful defendant.

The court's power to order a solicitor to pay costs personally is largely codified in rule 57.07.

Specific costs provisions in other Rules. In addition to Rule 57, there are scattered throughout the Rules many express provisions for costs awards that may well govern the ultimate disposition of costs. The following are examples.

On a motion for summary judgment the court may fix costs on a solicitor-client basis and order that they be paid forthwith where the motion fails and was unreasonable, or where a party to the motion has acted in bad faith or primarily for the purposes of delay: rule 20.06. A party examining a non-party for discovery is not entitled to recover the costs of the examination from another party, unless the court expressly orders otherwise: rule 31.10(4). If the court finds an oral examination out of court was improperly conducted or adjourned it may order the person to pay personally and forthwith the costs of the motion, any costs thrown away and the costs of any continuation of the examination: rule 34.14(2). Where leave is refused for the hearing of a motion in other than the respondent's solicitor's county, the court shall fix the costs of the responding party on a solicitor-client basis together with travelling expenses and order the moving party or his or her solicitor to pay those costs forthwith, unless the court is satisfied that the making of the motion was reasonable: rule

37.03(5). Generally, a party who cross-examines on an affidavit on a motion is liable for the party and party costs of every adverse party on the motion in respect of the cross-examination, regardless of the outcome of the proceeding, unless the court orders otherwise: rule 39.02(4)(b).

Important *prima facie* costs sanctions are provided by rule 49.10 where an offer to settle is refused and the proceeding goes to judgment. Where a party fails to respond affirmatively to a request to admit and the fact or document in respect of which the admission was sought is subsequently proved at the hearing, the court may take the denial or refusal into account in exercising its discretion respecting costs: rule 51.04 (and see also rule 57.01(1)(g)).

Practice directions. For costs in interlocutory proceedings in the Central East Region, see the practice direction reproduced following the Highlights of Rule 37.

Former provisions: Judicature Act, s. 80, and Rule 656 *et seq.*

GENERAL PRINCIPLES

Factors in Discretion

57.01(1) In exercising its discretion under section 131 of the *Courts of Justice Act* to award costs, the court may consider, in addition to the result in the proceeding and any offer to settle made in writing,

    (a) the amount claimed and the amount recovered in the proceeding;

    (b) the apportionment of liability;

    (c) the complexity of the proceeding;

    (d) the importance of the issues;

    (e) the conduct of any party that tended to shorten or to lengthen unnecessarily the duration of the proceeding;

    (f) whether any step in the proceeding was,

        (i) improper, vexatious or unnecessary, or

        (ii) taken through negligence, mistake or excessive caution;

    (g) a party's denial of or refusal to admit anything that should have been admitted;

    (h) whether it is appropriate to award any costs or more than one set of costs where a party,

        (i) commenced separate proceedings for claims that should have been made in one proceeding, or

        (ii) in defending a proceeding separated unnecessarily from another party in the same interest or defended by a different solicitor; and

    (i) any other matter relevant to the question of costs.

Costs Against Successful Party

(2) The fact that a party is successful in a proceeding or a step in a proceeding does not prevent the court from awarding costs against the party in a proper case.

Costs may be Fixed or Assessed

(3) In awarding costs, the court may fix all or part of the costs with or without reference to the Tariffs, instead of referring them for assessment, and where the costs are not fixed, they may be assessed under Rule 58.

Authority of Court

(4) Nothing in this rule or rules 57.02 to 57.07 affects the authority of the court under section 131 of the *Courts of Justice Act*,

(a) to award or refuse costs in respect of a particular issue or part of a proceeding;

(b) to award a percentage of assessed costs or award assessed costs up to or from a particular stage of a proceeding; or

(c) to award all or part of the costs on a solicitor and client basis.

Cross-Reference: See cases collected under rule 49.10 regarding the effect of offers to settle on the disposition of costs.

Authors' Note on Organization of Cases

Cases relevant to this provision have been organized as follows:

Exercise of Discretion — Amount in Issue — rule 57.01(1)(a)
Exercise of Discretion — Divided Success — rule 57.01(1)(b)
Exercise of Discretion — Importance of Issues — rule 57.01(1)(d)
Exercise of Discretion — Conduct Affecting Duration of Proceedings — rule 57.01(1)(e) and 57.01(4)
Exercise of Discretion — Improper, etc., Steps — rule 57.01(1)(f)
Exercise of Discretion — Failure to Make Admissions — rule 57.01(1)(g)
Exercise of Discretion — Number of Sets of Costs — rule 57.01(1)(h)
Exercise of Discretion — Other Matters — rule 57.01(1)(i)
"Bullock", "Sanderson" Orders, etc.
Award of Costs to or Against a Non-Party
Award of Costs — GST
Award of Costs — Miscellaneous
Costs Against Successful Party or Withholding of Costs to Successful Party — rule 57.01(2)
Award of Costs on Solicitor and Client Basis — rule 57.01(4)(c)

Exercise of Discretion — Amount in Issue — rule 57.01(1)(a)

Doyle v. Sparrow (1979), 27 O.R. (2d) 206, 106 D.L.R. (3d) 551, leave to appeal to Supreme Court of Canada refused 27 O.R. (2d) 206n, 32 N.R. 180n, 106 D.L.R. (3d) 551n.

The Court of Appeal refused to interfere with the discretion of a trial judge who awarded costs to the plaintiff in a defamation action who had recovered judgment for only $2. The amount of damages recovered is only one factor in awarding costs.

Krouse v. Chrysler Can. Ltd., [1972] 2 O.R. 133, 25 D.L.R. (3d) 49, 5 C.P.R. (2d) 30, reversed on other grounds 1 O.R. (2d) 225, 40 D.L.R. (3d) 15, 13 C.P.R. (2d) 28 (C.A.).

A successful plaintiff in a Supreme Court action was awarded costs on the usual scale, notwithstanding that only $1000 was recovered in damages, because the proceeding involved an important question of principle with practical commercial consequences.

Mitz v. Eastern & Chartered Trust Co., [1968] 2 O.R. 109 (H.C.).

Where a third party successfully defends a claim by a defendant and the defendant is found liable to the plaintiff, the costs of the third party are based on the amount recovered by the plaintiff from the defendant rather than the amount claimed.

Exercise of Discretion — Divided Success — rule 57.01(1)(b)

Skye v. Matthews (1996), 7 W.D.C.P. (2d) 73 (Ont. C.A.).

The Court of Appeal overturned a distributive costs order. While such orders are not totally foreclosed, they do not make sense in light of the objectives of the offer to settle rules and are rarely if ever appropriate.

Laven Associates Ltd. v. Price (1993), 20 C.P.C. (3d) 86 (Ont. Gen. Div.).

Where the plaintiff had been successful, but the defendant's claim for set-off and counterclaim had resulted in an overall reduction of the plaintiff's recovery by approximately 10 per cent, the plaintiff's costs award was reduced by 10 per cent to reflect the defendant's partial success.

539618 Ontario Ltd. v. Stathopoulos (1992), 11 O.R. (3d) 364, 97 D.L.R. (4th) 1, 58 O.A.C. 308 (C.A.).

A set-off as against the plaintiff's successful claim should not obscure the fact that the plaintiff succeeded in his claim when assessing costs. The success and/or failure of the defendant's counterclaim needs also to be taken into account when assessing the costs of the counterclaim.

Oakville Storage & Forwarders Ltd. v. Canadian National Railway Co. (1991), 5 O.R. (3d) 1 (*sub nom. Armak Chemicals Ltd. v. Canadian National Railway Co.*), 4 C.P.C. (3d) 280, 84 D.L.R. (4th) 326, 52 O.A.C. 188 (C.A.), leave to appeal to Supreme Court of Canada refused (1992), 6 O.R. (3d) xiii (note), 86 D.L.R. (4th) viii (note), 137 N.R. 238 (note), 55 O.A.C. 320 (note).

It is doubtful if an award of costs on the "distributive costs" principle is ever appropriate under the present Rules of Civil Procedure.

Gregoric v. Gregoric (1991), 4 O.R. (3d) 604 (Gen. Div.).

Where success in a family law proceeding was divided, and the petitioner had not demanded financial disclosure at the time of entering into a separation agreement, no order as to costs was made.

Ultramar Canada Inc. v. Montreal Pipe Line Ltd. (1990), 75 O.R. (2d) 498, 46 C.P.C. (2d) 184 (Gen. Div.).

The plaintiff was awarded party and party costs of an application to fix the fair value of shares where the plaintiff had achieved substantial success and neither party's offer to settle was effective.

William Allan Real Estate Co. v. Robichaud (1990), 72 O.R. (2d) 595, 9 R.P.R. (2d) 48, 68 D.L.R. (4th) 37, additional reasons 72 O.R. (2d) 595 at 615, 68 D.L.R. (4th) 37 at 57 (H.C.).

The court refused to apply the "distributive costs" principle where the plaintiff had succeeded on its main factual contention, although it had been unsuccessful on the balance of the issues raised at trial.

Tricontinental Investments Co. v. Guarantee Co. of North America (1988), 29 C.P.C. (2d) 99, 34 C.C.L.I. 293 (Ont. H.C.).

The court refused to apply the "distributive costs" principle where a defendant defeated the entire claim, even though the defendant lost on three out of four defences raised.

Oakville Storage and Forwarders Ltd. v. C.N.R. (1987), 27 C.P.C. (2d) 56 (Ont. H.C.).

The court has a discretion to divide costs according to the distributive cost principle where various parties succeed on various issues. The party in whose favour judgment is given is awarded the general costs of the action. The court then awards costs to and against particular parties based on the outcome of the major issues in controversy. The court applied the distributive cost principle in a very complex action which required 95 days of trial.

Sorensen v. Sorensen (1979), 24 O.R. (2d) 659, 7 C.P.C. 306, 8 R.F.L. (2d) 185 (Div. Ct.).

A petitioner for divorce who succeeded in the claim for divorce but failed on the question of custody was awarded 75 per cent of her costs on a party and party basis as on a contested basis.

Exercise of Discretion — Importance of Issues — rule 57.01(1)(d)

Janigan v. Harris (1989), 70 O.R. (2d) 5, 62 D.L.R. (4th) 293, additional reasons 70 O.R. (2d) 5 at 27, 62 D.L.R. (4th) 293 at 314 (H.C.).

Both the appellant's and respondent's costs of an appeal from a disputed municipal election result were ordered borne by the municipality on a solicitor and client basis. The appeal was in the public interest, and both parties achieved some measure of success on the appeal.

Exercise of Discretion — Conduct Affecting Duration of Proceedings — rule 57.01(1)(e) and 57.01(4)

Gerula v. Flores (1995), 126 D.L.R. (4th) 506, 83 O.A.C. 128 (C.A.).

Where the defendant's attempt to frustrate the proceedings by deception resulted in the action being drawn out prior to trial, the court affirmed an award of solicitor and client costs against the defendant up to the date of trial.

H. v. W. (1993), 13 O.R. (3d) 437 (Gen. Div.).

Where a spouse in this family law case delayed until the eve of trial before accepting a settlement offer, the court required the spouse to pay for expert reports obtained by the other spouse.

Brinkos v. Brinkos (1989), 69 O.R. (2d) 798, 61 D.L.R. (4th) 766, additional reasons 69 O.R. (2d) 798 at 800, 61 D.L.R. (4th) 766 at 768 (C.A.).

A husband was denied the discretionary recovery of his costs where his conduct prior to and during matrimonial litigation was disgraceful.

Abbott v. Reuter-Stokes Can. Ltd. (1988), 32 C.P.C. (2d) 161 (Ont. H.C.).

Impecuniosity is no shield to a costs order based on a party's obstructionism and unreasonable conduct.

Lawlor v. Sherrard (1986), 10 C.P.C. (2d) 164 (Ont. H.C.).

The court ordered a defendant to pay certain costs on a solicitor and client scale where it had raised a silly and scandalous defence, including unfounded allegations about the competence of the plaintiff's medical advisors.

Trottier v. Minto Management Ltd. (1986), 56 O.R. (2d) 193, 30 D.L.R. (4th) 744, 16 O.A.C. 373 (Div. Ct.).

Successful appellants were only awarded costs for one day on a two-day hearing, where they had put forward many arguments which were not pursued.

Zlatkovic v. Wladyczanski (1981), 20 C.P.C. 310 (Ont. H.C.).

Where the plaintiff called unnecessary witnesses, the plaintiff's counsel fee was reduced and the fees for the unnecessary witnesses were disallowed.

Firestone v. Firestone (No. 2) (1979), 25 O.R. (2d) 314, 1 F.L.R.A.C. 534, 11 R.F.L. (2d) 175 (H.C.).

A successful petitioner for divorce was deprived of costs in respect of three days' worth of evidence on an unfounded allegation.

Williamson v. Joseph Baruch Const. Ltd. (1979), 12 C.P.C. 122 (Ont. H.C.).

An appeal from taxation, on the ground that costs should be reduced because the plaintiff wasted time pursuing a higher claim than was likely attainable, was refused where the trial judge had indicated that the damages issue was a difficult one.

Abramsen v. Abramsen (1979), 12 C.P.C. 26 (Ont. H.C.).

Where both parties engaged in tactics which unnecessarily protracted custody proceedings, no costs were awarded after trial except each party was ordered to share the costs of the Official Guardian and a psychiatrist.

Foulis v. Robinson (1979), 21 O.R. (2d) 769, 8 C.P.C. 198, 92 D.L.R. (3d) 134 (C.A.).

The trial judge should avoid second-guessing how a trial should have been conducted.

Morton Terminal Ltd. v. Seaway Forwarding Agencies Ltd. (1978), 8 C.P.C. 87 (Ont. H.C.).

Where the plaintiff was successful, but he did not succeed on two issues pleaded which were not unreasonable to allege and which did not inordinately lengthen the trial, the costs were not reduced.

Batcher v. Lendvai (1978), 19 O.R. (2d) 347 (H.C.).

Costs of a mistrial payable forthwith were ordered against a plaintiff who, having been admonished not to disclose the fact that the defendant was insured, led evidence on that point.

Kalesky v. Kalesky (1974), 5 O.R. (2d) 546, 17 R.F.L. 321, 51 D.L.R. (3d) 30 (C.A.).

The refusal of a trial judge to award costs to a respondent in a divorce proceeding, on the grounds she need not have appeared since the granting of the divorce was inevitable, was overturned where the spouse had a vital interest in the question of maintenance.

Collins v. Haliburton, Kawartha Pine Ridge Dist. Health Unit (No. 2), [1972] 3 O.R. 643, 29 D.L.R. (3d) 151 (H.C.).

Where the defendant raised a limitation provision as a defence only after judgment had been rendered in favour of the plaintiff, the action was dismissed, but without costs.

Exercise of Discretion — Improper, etc., Steps — rule 57.01(1)(f)

Bifolchi v. Sherar (Administrator) (1995), 25 O.R. (3d) 637 (Gen. Div.).

Where the plaintiff's offer to settle was unclear and the conduct of counsel unduly prolonged the trial, the court awarded costs to the successful plaintiff on a party and party scale reduced by one-half.

Smith v. Harrington (1994), 36 C.P.C. (3d) 209 (Ont. Gen. Div.).

The court ordered solicitor and client costs against the defendants where a mistrial was declared as a result of improper cross-examination on behalf of the defendants.

Merrill Lynch Canada Inc. v. Cassina (1993), 15 C.P.C. (3d) 264 (Ont. Gen. Div.).

A successful party was allowed costs in connection with preparation for trial when the case was about to proceed but was adjourned.

V. Kelner Airways Ltd. v. Standard Aero Ltd. (1991), 2 C.P.C. (3d) 140 (Ont. Gen. Div.).

A defendant was awarded costs on a party and party basis up to the date of service of its offer, and thereafter on a solicitor and client basis, where the action had been dismissed. Solicitor and client costs were awarded because counsel for the plaintiff had acted unreasonably in the course of the proceeding.

Jengle v. Keetch (1989), 68 O.R. (2d) 238, 5 R.P.R. (2d) 184 (H.C.).

Solicitor and client costs were awarded against an unsuccessful plaintiff where the matter could have been resolved easily and without any need for litigation by the plaintiff granting a licence.

Taillefer v. St. Germain (1988), 26 C.P.C. (2d) 209 (Ont. H.C.).

Where a mistrial was caused by a counsel's repeated reference to insurance and to the criminal trial of one of the parties, the court awarded all parties costs against that counsel's client.

Credit Heights Ltd. v. United States Fidelity & Guaranty Co. (1987), 59 O.R. (2d) 209 (H.C.).

Where a successful plaintiff had made an excessive claim for damages and had wasted time at trial, it was awarded only 50 per cent of the costs of the action and the defendant was awarded a counsel fee for four and one-half days of the 13-day trial. Both counsel were awarded a counsel fee for written arguments which the court found helpful.

Mattabi Mines Ltd. v. Schmachtel (1987), 59 O.R. (2d) 199 (H.C.).

An employer's solicitor responded to a wrongful dismissal demand letter with a letter requesting time for client consultation, and then commenced an action for a declaration that the employee's dismissal was justified. In permanently staying the action, the court held that the solicitor was bound to notify plaintiff's counsel that there would be no settlement discussions, contrary to the impression created by his letter, *before* commencing the action, and awarded solicitor and client costs of the stay motion to the employee.

Real Securities of Can. Ltd. v. Beland (1987), 16 C.P.C. (2d) 230 (Ont. Dist. Ct.).

Prejudicial allegations of fact made from the counsel table will be disregarded by the court except in considering costs against their maker.

Lefebvre v. Osborne (1983), 38 C.P.C. 93 (Ont. H.C.).

A successful party was deprived of costs where it had failed to give proper disclosure and production of documents.

Fiege v. Cornwall Gen. Hosp. (1980), 30 O.R. (2d) 691, 117 D.L.R. (3d) 152, 4 L. Med. Q. 124 (H.C.).

The court awarded costs on a solicitor and client basis where the defendant failed to produce a relevant unprivileged document on discovery and subsequently relied on the document at trial, thereby unnecessarily extending the trial.

Moreira v. Dasilva (1977), 5 C.P.C. 73 (Ont. H.C.).

Solicitor and his own client costs were awarded against an unsuccessful party who had attempted to mislead and deceive the court.

Re Schiller and Scarborough Gen. Hosp. (1975), 9 O.R. (2d) 648 (C.A.).

Each party was ordered to bear its own costs in an appeal which was quashed for lack of jurisdiction where, *inter alia*, the question of jurisdiction was not raised prior to the hearing.

Union Carbide Can. Ltd. v. Vanderkop (1976), 1 C.P.C. 114 (Ont. H.C.).

Where the defendant presented forged documents in an attempt to deceive the court, costs on a solicitor and own client basis were awarded against him.

Grys v. Sewell and Jaffary, [1972] 1 O.R. 864 (H.C.).

Commencement of an action in an attempt to stifle public discussion of a matter of public interest and importance is a gross abuse of the process of the court which may be penalized in costs.

Truglia v. Travelers Indemnity Co., [1966] 1 O.R. 364, 53 D.L.R. (2d) 309 (H.C.).

The court deprived a defendant insurer of costs partly because of bad faith in the actions of its adjusters.

Exercise of Discretion — Failure to Make Admissions — rule 57.01(1)(g)

Gibbs v. Grand Bend Village (1990), 72 O.R. (2d) 697, 68 D.L.R. (4th) 474 (H.C.).

The successful plaintiffs were not entitled to solicitor and client costs where the defendant's failure to admit facts and the authenticity of documents was not a deliberate frustration of the proceedings.

Tricontinental Investments Co. v. Guarantee Co. of North America (1988), 29 C.P.C. (2d) 99, 34 C.C.L.I. 293 (Ont. H.C.).

The court deprived a successful defendant of the costs of six out of nine days at trial since it refused to admit a fact which the plaintiff proved at significant expense.

Reeve v. Andrulis, [1953] O.W.N. 823 (Master).

A party who obtains an order to change the venue on the basis that he intends to call certain witnesses may be penalized in costs if the witnesses are not called.

Exercise of Discretion — Number of Sets of Costs — rule 57.01(1)(h)

Ash v. Corp. of Lloyd's (1992), 9 O.R. (3d) 755 at 761, 7 C.P.C. (3d) 372, 60 O.A.C. 241 at 261, 95 D.L.R. (4th) 766 (C.A.), leave to appeal to Supreme Court of Canada refused 10 O.R. (3d) xv (note), 94 D.L.R. (4th) vii, 59 O.A.C. 160 (note).

On an appeal where only one factum was filed by the successful parties and their counsel divided the argument, only one set of costs was awarded.

Baribeau v. Can. Permanent Trust Co., 59 O.R. (2d) 21, 20 C.P.C. (2d) 162, 27 C.C.L.I. 137, 36 D.L.R. (4th) 157, [1987] I.L.R. 1-2188 (H.C.).

Where an insurer and its insured retained separate counsel in two actions arising out of a motor vehicle accident, only one set of costs was awarded.

Boland v. Ostrander, [1949] O.W.N. 231 (H.C.).

An award of "costs to the defendants" generally entitles separately represented defendants to tax separate bills.

Exercise of Discretion — Other Matters — rule 57.01(1)(i)

Routley v. Routley (1980), 16 C.P.C. 288 (Ont. Prov. Ct.).

Where no claim for costs had been made in an application for support, the successful applicant was denied costs.

McLean v. Guillet, 22 O.R. (2d) 175, 3 E.T.R. 51, 92 D.L.R. (3d) 398, [1978] I.L.R. 1-1041 (Dist. Ct.).

Where a husband failed to change the beneficiary of a life insurance policy from his first wife to his second wife and the latter brought an unsuccessful action, her costs were ordered paid out of the insurance proceeds.

"Bullock", "Sanderson" Orders, etc.

PAYMENT OF COSTS INCURRED BY SUCCESSFUL DEFENDANT

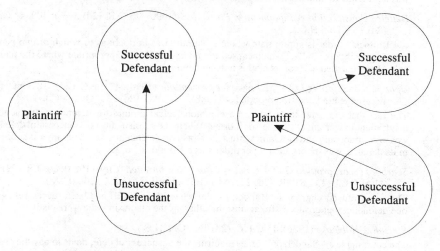

　　　　"SANDERSON" ORDER　　　　　　　"BULLOCK" ORDER
　　(Unsuccessful Defendant pays　　　(Plaintiff pays Successful Defendant and is
　　Successful Defendant directly)　　　reimbursed by Unsuccessful Defendant)

Widdis v. Hall (1995), 22 O.R. (3d) 187, 9 M.V.R. (3d) 252 at 262 (Gen. Div.).

The *prima facie* rule is that a successful defendant is entitled to look to the plaintiff for its costs. A "Sanderson" order relieving the plaintiff from that obligation and imposing it directly on an unsuccessful defendant should not be made if there is a real risk that the successful defendant will not receive those costs from the unsuccessful defendant because of the latter's impecuniosity. A "Bullock" order may issue where the plaintiff seeks judgment against two or more defendants on the ground that all of them are liable, provided the litigation arose because of the conduct of the unsuccessful defendant and so long as it was reasonable that the plaintiff should add the successful defendant.

Mortimer v. Cameron (1994), 17 O.R. (3d) 1, 19 M.P.L.R. (2d) 286, 111 D.L.R. (4th) 428, 68 O.A.C. 332, additional reasons (June 24, 1994), Doc. CA C12036 (Ont. C.A.), leave to appeal to Supreme Court of Canada refused (1994), 19 O.R. (3d) xvi (note), 23 M.P.L.R. (2d) 314 (note), 114 D.L.R. (4th) vii (note), 178 N.R. 146 (note), 76 O.A.C. 400 (note).

Where the plaintiff had sued multiple defendants, and had met with divided success, the court held that either a "Bullock" order or a "Sanderson" order was justified, as it had been reasonable and proper to join the successful defendants.

Hague v. Billings (1993), 13 O.R. (3d) 298, 15 C.C.L.T. (2d) 264, 46 M.V.R. (2d) 254, 102 D.L.R. (4th) 44, 64 O.A.C. 219 (C.A.).

The Court of Appeal refused to interfere with the exercise of a trial judge's discretion in refusing to make a "Bullock" order, where the plaintiff had met with divided success. There was no error in the exercise of the trial judge's discretion.

AKW Insurance Brokers (1985) Ltd. (Trustees of) v. Guarantee Co. of North America (1992), 12 C.P.C. (3d) 115, 16 C.C.L.I. (2d) 294 at 308 (Ont. Gen. Div.).

The court made a "Bullock" order where the plaintiff had been successful against one defendant, but unsuccessful against another. Although the amount claimed against the two defendants was not identical, both claims arose out of the same set of circumstances.

Dellelce Construction & Equipment v. Portec Inc. (1990), 73 O.R. (2d) 396 at 400, 44 C.P.C. (2d) 165 (Ont. H.C.).

A "Bullock" order is appropriate where a plaintiff was in doubt as to which of two persons was responsible for the act which caused the injury, and is not appropriate where the plaintiff could have pursued each of its claims independently.

Upper Lakes Shipping Ltd. v. St. Lawrence Cement Inc. (1990), 41 C.P.C. (2d) 318 (Ont. H.C.), re-adjudicating decision reported at (1988), 28 C.P.C. (2d) 270 (Ont. H.C.).

The fact that the defendants rely on a common factual ground for defence to the action is insufficient to warrant a "Sanderson" order. Where the claim against one successful defendant was in contract only and the claim against the other two defendants, one of whom was successful in its defence, was in tort, the proper order was a "Bullock" order.

Scarboro (Scarborough) Golf & Country Club v. Scarborough (City) (1988), 66 O.R. (2d) 257, 41 M.P.L.R. 1, 1 R.P.R. (2d) 225, 54 D.L.R. (4th) 1, 31 O.A.C. 260 (C.A.).

The court refused to grant a "Bullock" order where the plaintiff had been successful against one defendant, but unsuccessful against the other, as the claims in issue were distinct.

Watson v. Holyoake (1986), 15 C.P.C. (2d) 262 (Ont. H.C.).

The court made a "Sanderson" order requiring the unsuccessful defendants to pay the costs of a successful defendant directly, but required the plaintiff to pay the costs of a second successful defendant where the claim against it was unrelated to the claims against the other defendants.

Bardoel v. St. Clair-Wilkerson Ltd. (1984), 47 C.P.C. 173 (Ont. H.C.).

The court made a "Bullock" order where the unsuccessful defendant had rebuffed the plaintiff's suggestion after one day of trial that the other defendant be let out of the action.

Rowe v. Investors Syndicate Ltd; Anglin v. Investors Syndicate Ltd. (1984), 46 C.P.C. 209 (Ont. H.C.).

An unsuccessful defendant will be required to pay the costs of a successful defendant, if the plaintiff acted reasonably in joining the successful defendant and the conduct of the unsuccessful defendant necessitated the action. Whether a "Sanderson" order (requiring the unsuccessful defendant to pay the successful defendant's costs directly) or a "Bullock" order (requiring the unsuccessful defendant to pay the successful defendant's costs indirectly by indemnifying the plaintiff for such costs) is made depends upon the equitable issue between the plaintiff and successful defendant of who should bear the risk of the unsuccessful defendant being unable to pay.

Babcock v. Carr (1982), 34 O.R. (2d) 65, 127 D.L.R. (3d) 77 (H.C.).

The court made a "Sanderson" order, requiring unsuccessful defendants to pay the costs of the successful defendants directly, rather than a "Bullock" order.

W.H. Bosley & Co. v. Marathon Realty Co. (1982), 39 O.R. (2d) 144, 29 C.P.C. 255 (H.C.).

A "Bullock" order should not be made where independent causes of action are alleged against separate defendants, however closely interwoven the facts upon which the allegations are based.

J & M Chartrand Realty Ltd. v. Martin (1981), 22 C.P.C. 186 (Ont. H.C.).

A defendant was awarded costs against its co-defendants as well as the plaintiff where the co-defendants had an agreement with the plaintiff, which was not disclosed until after trial, limiting their exposure and permitting them to share in the judgment.

Mitt v. Henriksson, [1968] 1 O.R. 373 (H.C.).

An insurer added as a third party under the *Insurance Act*, R.S.O. 1960, c. 190, which unsuccessfully defended the plaintiffs' claim against its insured was made directly liable to the plaintiffs for costs necessitated by such defence.

Gilbert v. Barron, [1958] O.W.N. 98, 13 D.L.R. (2d) 262 (H.C.).

The court ordered an unsuccessful defendant to pay the costs of a successful defendant rather than making a "Bullock" order.

Award of Costs to or Against a Non-Party

Smith v. Canadian Tire Acceptance Ltd. (1995), 22 O.R. (2d) 433, 36 C.P.C. (3d) 175 (Gen. Div.), affirmed 26 O.R. (3d) 94, 40 C.P.C. (3d) 129 (C.A.).

The court awarded costs of an unsuccessful class action against non-parties who had purported to sell rights in the proceeds of the action to the public.

Gulf Canada Resources Ltd. v. Merlac Marine Inc. (1994), 18 O.R. (3d) 239 (Gen. Div.).

The court has authority to award costs against a non-litigant where: (a) the non-party did not believe the plaintiff had a good cause of action; (b) the non-party counselled commencement of the action; (c) the non-party financed the action; and (d) the non-party in effect conducted the action from the sidelines up to and including trial.

Quabbin Hill Investments Inc. v. Rowntree (1993), 19 C.P.C. (3d) 113 (Ont. Gen. Div.).

The court refused to award costs against a non-party who was the directing mind of the corporate plaintiff.

931473 Ontario Ltd. v. Coldwell Banker Canada Inc. (1992), 5 C.P.C. (3d) 271 (Ont. Gen. Div.).

The shareholders of the unsuccessful plaintiff corporation were not held liable for costs where the defendants failed to establish that the plaintiff corporation was a "straw man" intentionally put forth to avoid payment of costs if the proceedings were unsuccessful.

Ridgely v. Ridgely Design Inc. (1991), 3 O.R. (3d) 695 (Gen. Div.).

The court may fix the real litigant with liability for costs.

R.L. Wilson Engineering & Construction Ltd. v. Metropolitan Life Ins. Co. (1988), 32 C.P.C. (2d) 76 (Ont. H.C.).

The court declined to order costs against the principal of the unsuccessful insolvent corporate plaintiff.

Yared Realty Ltd. v. Topalovic (1981), 45 C.P.C. 189 (Ont. H.C.).

The trial judge amended his judgment to award costs against certain non-parties on whose behalf the action was brought where the successful defendant had been unable to collect the award of costs from the plaintiff who had become bankrupt.

Assaf v. Koury (1980), 16 C.P.C. 202 (Ont. H.C.).

An award of costs was made against a person not a party where he had counselled the commencement of the action, financed it, and previously engaged in a long history of litigation regarding the estate involved.

Rockwell Devs. Ltd. v. Newtonbrook Plaza Ltd., [1972] 3 O.R. 199, 27 D.L.R. (3d) 651 (C.A.).

Costs should not be awarded against a person who is not a party or a solicitor in the proceedings and who has not procured a party to take proceedings on his behalf.

Horvath v. Mackie, [1968] 2 O.R. 855 (H.C.).

Where a municipality successfully conducts a defence of an action against its police chief in circumstances where it would be obliged by statute to indemnify the police chief for any judgment against him, it is entitled to the benefit of an award of costs to the police chief.

Re Harmer, [1963] 2 O.R. 690, 40 D.L.R. (2d) 825, affirmed [1964] 1 O.R. 367, 42 D.L.R. (2d) 321, affirmed 46 D.L.R. (2d) 521 (S.C.C.).

A corporate executor whose employee had prepared a badly framed will was required to bear the costs of a motion to construe its provisions.

Award of Costs — GST

Ligate v. Abick (1991), 5 O.R. (3d) 332, 2 C.P.C. (3d) 209 (Gen. Div.), additional reasons (1992), 8 O.R. (3d) 49, 2 C.P.C. (3d) 216 (Gen. Div.).

In order to maintain the level of indemnification intended by an award of party and party costs, the court ordered that GST be paid to the extent that those costs would be subject to that tax.

MacMillan v. White (1991), 3 W.D.C.P. (2d) 25 (Ont. Gen. Div.).

The trial judge awarded GST on party and party costs. An order is necessary to recover GST on costs since the Tariffs have not yet been amended to provide for it.

Award of Costs — Miscellaneous

Hill v. Church of Scientology of Toronto (1994), 18 O.R. (3d) 385, 20 C.C.L.T. (2d) 129, 114 D.L.R. (4th) 1, 71 O.A.C. 161 (C.A.), affirmed [1995] 2 S.C.R. 1130, 24 O.R. (3d) 865 (note), 25 C.C.L.T. (2d) 89, 30 C.R.R. 189, 126 D.L.R. (4th) 129, 184 N.R. 1, 84 O.A.C. 1.

Where the major portion of a defamation trial was devoted to a plea of justification asserted by the first defendant, and the majority of damages were awarded against that first defendant alone, the second defendant was ordered to pay only 30 per cent of the plaintiff's trial costs, with the first defendant to pay the balance. However, the parties remained jointly and severally liable for all of the costs of the plaintiff, with each having a claim over against the other for any excess paid.

Pittman Estate v. Bain (1994), 19 C.C.L.T. (2d) 1, 112 D.L.R. (4th) 257, additional reasons 112 D.L.R. (4th) 482, further additional reasons 35 C.P.C. (3d) 55, 112 D.L.R. (4th) 494, further additional reasons (1994), 35 C.P.C. (3d) 67 (Ont. Gen. Div.).

A judge fixing costs determines what the legal services are worth using the Tariff as a reference point, but does not assess costs on an item by item basis as would be done by an assessment officer.

Van Bork v. Van Bork (1994), 30 C.P.C. (3d) 116, additional reasons (July 21, 1994), Doc. D120320/84 (Ont. Gen. Div.).

The court fixed the costs of a divorce action in which the wife was entitled to her party and party costs for part of the proceeding, and her solicitor and client costs thereafter. With respect to the party and party costs, the court considered what the services devoted to the proceeding were worth according to the submissions of counsel and their experience, and with some regard to what would be taxed on the party and party scale. With respect to the solicitor and client costs, the successful litigant was entitled to complete indemnification except for extra charges which were beyond the reasonable scope of the litigation and the preparation and presentation of the case.

Blair v. Consolidated Enfield Corp. (1993), 15 O.R. (3d) 783, 12 B.L.R. (2d) 303, 106 D.L.R. (4th) 193, 66 O.A.C. 121 (C.A.), affirmed (March 21, 1995), Doc. 23887 (S.C.C.).

The director of a corporation who had acted honestly and in good faith with a view to the best interests of the corporation, and who had acted reasonably in the defence of litigation, was entitled to indemnity for his legal costs pursuant to s. 136(1) of the *Business Corporations Act*.

Kenyeres (Litigation Guardian of) v. Cullimore (1992), 13 C.P.C. (3d) 385 (Ont. Gen. Div.), affirmed (March 7, 1994), Doc. CA C12531/92 (Ont. C.A.).

The court permitted counsel for a successful minor plaintiff to recover solicitor and client fees above the party and party costs recoverable from the defendant.

Ontario (Securities Commission) v. Consortium Construction Inc. (1992), 9 O.R. (3d) 385, 11 C.P.C. (3d) 352, 14 C.B.R. (3d) 6, 93 D.L.R. (4th) 321, 57 O.A.C. 241 (C.A.).

Where a receiver is appointed pursuant to the *Securities Act* the court has the jurisdiction to make an order as to costs imposing upon trust assets in receivership, although such discretion should be used sparingly.

Van Heeswyk v. Van Heewsyk (1992), 44 R.F.L. (3d) 42 (Ont. Gen. Div.).

Generally, the petitioner in an uncontested divorce based on marriage breakdown as evidenced by a one-year separation should be awarded costs representing one half of the counsel fee set out in Tariff B and one half of the disbursements incurred.

Beach v. Canada (Deputy Minister of National Revenue Customs & Excise) (1992), 10 O.R. (3d) 572 (C.A.).

The court has jurisdiction to award costs to or against the Crown in any proceedings to which the Crown is a party pursuant to the *Crown Liability and Proceedings Act.*

Re Olenchuk Estate (1991), 4 C.P.C. (3d) 6, 43 E.T.R. 146 (Ont. Gen. Div.).

In estate litigation costs are generally paid out of the estate if the litigation originates in the fault of the testator or the residual beneficiaries. Further, an unsuccessful party may be relieved of the costs of the successful party if there were reasonable grounds to question execution, testamentary capacity, undue influence or fraud.

David v. Pilot Insurance Co. (1991), 49 C.P.C. (2d) 282 (Ont. Gen. Div.).

The court awarded costs of this action jointly against the plaintiff and an intervenor under Rule 13.

Wilson v. Conley (1990), 46 C.P.C. (2d) 85, 1 B.L.R. (2d) 220 (Ont. Gen. Div.).

Pending adjournment of a motion for interim costs of an application for an oppression remedy, interim interim costs were granted pursuant to s. 248(4) of the *Business Corporations Act*, S.O. 1982, c. 4, having regard to the applicant's strong *prima facie* case and the applicant's financial difficulty arising from the allegedly oppressive conduct of the respondent.

Greymac Credit Corp. v. Outerbridge (1988), 11 W.D.C.P. 233 (Ont. H.C.).

The court may award costs against an unsuccessful receiver or liquidator in priority to other creditors.

Mayberry v. Scottish & York Ins. Co. (1987), 24 C.P.C. (2d) 54, 27 C.C.L.I. 215 (Ont. Dist. Ct.).

An insurer sued under uninsured motorist coverage who was successful in a crossclaim against the uninsured motorist was awarded costs against the uninsured motorist on a party and party basis regarding the crossclaim and on a solicitor and client basis regarding the defence of the main action.

Cdn. Newspapers Co. v. Canada (A.G.) (1986), 56 O.R. (2d) 240, 12 C.P.C. (2d) 203, 27 C.R.R. 52, 32 D.L.R. (4th) 292 at 304 (H.C.).

Costs were awarded on a party and party basis against the Attorney General of Canada where an applicant had successfully challenged the constitutional validity of certain provisions of the *Criminal Code.*

Andrews v. Andrews (1980), 32 O.R. (2d) 29, 20 C.P.C. 88, 20 R.F.L. (2d) 348, 120 D.L.R. (3d) 252 (C.A.).

Discussion of the factors relevant to the awarding of costs in a family law case.

Cobbold v. Time Can. Ltd. (1980), 28 O.R. (2d) 326, 16 C.P.C. 102, 109 D.L.R. (3d) 611 (H.C.).

The general rule that a successful defendant is entitled to his costs was applied in a class action suit.

Re MacBeth and Curran, [1948] O.R. 444, [1948] 3 D.L.R. 85 (Master).

The Crown is not in the same position as ordinary litigants with respect to costs. Costs can only be awarded against the Crown in special and limited circumstances.

Costs Against Successful Party or Withholding of Costs to Successful Party — rule 57.01(2)

Bell Canada v. Olympia & York Developments Ltd. (1994), 17 O.R. (3d) 135, 26 C.P.C. (3d) 368, 111 D.L.R. (4th) 589, 70 O.A.C. 101 (C.A.).

The successful party is entitled to a reasonable expectation that it will be awarded costs in the absence of special circumstances. It was held to be an error in principle to deprive a successful party of costs on the basis of failure to make an offer of settlement.

Ruhl v. Royal Bank (1993), 13 O.R. (3d) 58, 31 R.P.R. (2d) 71 (Gen. Div.).

Where a mortgagee obtains a final order of foreclosure it is not entitled to costs since the mortgagee has become the owner of the property and exhausted its rights against the mortgagor.

King v. Gulf Canada Ltd. (1992), 45 C.C.E.L. 238, 60 O.A.C. 139 (C.A.).

In a wrongful dismissal action, the Court of Appeal awarded the unsuccessful plaintiff solicitor and client costs both at trial and on appeal where the employer's conduct had been reprehensible and contrary to its own moral commitment in a policy letter to all employees.

B. (R.) v. Children's Aid Society of Metropolitan Toronto (1992), 10 O.R. (3d) 321, 43 R.F.L. (3d) 36, 96 D.L.R. (4th) 45, 58 O.A.C. 93 (C.A.), affirmed [1995] 1 S.C.R. 315, 21 O.R. (3d) 479 (note), 9 R.F.L. (4th) 157, 26 C.R.R. (2d) 202, 122 D.L.R. (4th) 1, 176 N.R. 161, 78 O.A.C. 1.

In a *Charter* case, the Attorney General was ordered to pay the costs of the unsuccessful litigants where the actions of the state had triggered the litigation, and the issue was of national importance.

Singh v. Singh (1992), 10 C.P.C. (3d) 42, additional reasons [1992] W.D.F.L. 1072 (Ont. Gen. Div.).

The court awarded costs against a successful party who had failed to make proper pre-trial disclosure.

Jordan v. Hall (1987), 17 C.P.C. (2d) 285 (Ont. Dist. Ct.).

The court ordered a successful defendant to pay solicitor and client costs to the plaintiffs due to improper conduct of defence counsel during the jury trial.

Fox v. Bourget (1987), 17 C.P.C. (2d) 94 (Ont. Dist. Ct.), affirmed 9 W.D.C.P. 142 (Ont. H.C.).

Where a party seeks an indulgence and is unsuccessfully opposed by a second party, the second party is entitled to costs. The price of indulgence is payment of the costs of those who have sought, unsuccessfully, to prevent its being granted.

Ledyit v. Alford (1986), 58 O.R. (2d) 223 (C.A.).

In affiliation proceedings, no costs were awarded because the case involved a novel issue as to the significance of a blood test.

Watson v. Holyoake (1986), 15 C.P.C. (2d) 262 (Ont. H.C.).

The court refused to deprive a successful plaintiff of costs where she had made unsubstantiated allegations of conspiracy.

Alan D'Orsay Const. v. A & D Pallet Truck Inc. (1984), 45 C.P.C. 126, 8 C.L.R. 296 (Ont. H.C.).

In this construction lien action the court limited the plaintiff to 80 per cent of the costs of the full trial since the plaintiff ignored the defendant's offer, which was less than the award at trial, and did not make a counter-offer, contrary to the spirit and intent of the *Construction Lien Act* and contrary to good advocacy counselling.

Contractors Machinery & Equipment Ltd. v. Guy (1980), 30 O.R. (2d) 51, 115 D.L.R. (3d) 252 (H.C.).

The court refused to require an unsuccessful third party to pay the defendant's costs of defending the main action where such defence had been unreasonable. The third party action against another third party was dismissed without costs where it had been reasonable to join the party.

Can. Acceptance Corp. Ltd. v. Biluk (1978), 10 C.P.C. 178 (Ont. Dist. Ct.).

Unless misconduct has been proved, a successful defendant should not be ordered to pay costs.

Hartford v. Langdon Coach Lines Co. (1975), 10 O.R. (2d) 617, 64 D.L.R. (3d) 213 (H.C.).

A completely successful litigant against whom no misconduct is shown may not be ordered to pay the costs of the opposing party, although it is proper for the court to refrain from awarding costs to such litigant. [*But cf. now rule 57.01(2) — Authors.*]

Can. Metal Co. v. C.B.C. (No. 2) (1975), 8 O.R. (2d) 375, 23 C.C.C. (2d) 445, 59 D.L.R. (3d) 430 (C.A.).

Where a judge refuses to commit an alleged contemnor to jail because he holds a reasonable doubt as to guilt, costs may not be denied on the basis that the contemnor had not removed all suspicion of guilt.

Sidmay Ltd. v. Wehttam Invts. Ltd., [1966] 1 O.R. 457, 54 D.L.R. (2d) 194, reversed on other grounds [1967] 1 O.R. 508, 61 D.L.R. (2d) 358, affirmed [1968] S.C.R. 828, 69 D.L.R. (2d) 336.

Where a plaintiff obtained a declaration that a mortgage was void due to the failure of the defendant mortgagee to register under the *Loan and Trust Corporations Act*, R.S.O. 1960, c. 222, the court refused to award costs as they would be an additional unjust hardship on the defendant.

Re Thompson Estate, [1944] O.R. 290, [1944] O.W.N. 260 (C.A.).

There is no principle upon which the court can order an unsuccessful litigant to pay the solicitor and client costs of the successful party. Where the executors of an estate successfully defend an action concerning a trust which is part of the estate, they cannot recover the excess costs over party and party costs from the trust fund. The excess costs must be recovered from the estate.

Inc. Synod of Diocese of Huron v. Ferguson (1924), 56 O.L.R. 161 (H.C.).

A successful plaintiff was deprived of costs where a matter which could have been disposed of by originating application was asserted by action.

Award of Costs on Solicitor and Client Basis — rule 57.01(4)(c) (See also cases re rule 57.01(1)(e) and (f) above.)

Murano v. Bank of Montreal (1995), 41 C.P.C. (3d) 143 (Ont. Gen. Div. [Commercial List]).

The court awarded solicitor and client costs against a defendant which had made unfounded allegations of dishonesty against the plaintiff in its pleadings and at trial.

Goulin v. Goulin (1995), 26 O.R. (3d) 472 (Gen. Div.).

The court awarded solicitor and client costs to a defendant where the plaintiff had made unfounded allegations of fraud and wrong-doing and had consented to the dismissal of the action after the statement of defence had been filed. The court has jurisdiction to make such an award at any stage of the proceeding.

Harnden v. Kosir (1995), 26 O.R. (3d) 588 (Gen. Div.).

Perjury may justify an award of solicitor and client costs.

Ontario (Attorney General) v. Dieleman (1995), 22 O.R. (3d) 758, 123 D.L.R. (4th) 757, additional reasons 22 O.R. (3d) 785 at 794, 123 D.L.R. (4th) 766 (Gen. Div.).

Solicitor and client costs were awarded to two defendants against whom the Attorney General had unsuccessfully sought an injunction restraining picketing at abortion clinics.

Myers v. Metropolitan Toronto (Municipality) Police Force (1995), 37 C.P.C. (3d) 349, 125 D.L.R. (4th) 184, 84 O.A.C. 232 (Div. Ct.).

Where the trial judge allowed the plaintiff to amend its pleadings but ordered the plaintiff to pay the costs of the wasted trial day on a solicitor/client basis within 15 days, the court held that the trial judge acted reasonably in not taking into account the plaintiff's claim of impecuniosity and would, generally, only interfere with a trial judge's discretion to award costs in limited circumstances.

Equity Waste Management of Canada Corp. v. Halton Hills (Town) (1995), 22 O.R. (3d) 796, 27 M.P.L.R. (2d) 123 (Gen. Div.).

A solicitor and client costs award may be for more than the docketed time multiplied by usual billing rates. Inclusion of such a premium does not require a specific agreement between the solicitor and client at the outset of the law suit.

Wallace Sign-Crafters West Ltd. v. 466126 Ontario Ltd. (1994), 28 C.P.C. (3d) 75, 72 O.A.C. 213 (Div. Ct.).

The court set aside the trial judge's award of solicitor and client costs to a successful defendant. The plaintiff's pursuit of its action could not be characterized as the type of reprehensible conduct which would give rise to an award of solicitor and client costs.

Rodriguez v. Allstate Insurance Co., [1995] I.L.R. 1-3169 (Ont. Gen. Div.).

The court awarded solicitor and client costs against an insurer who, *inter alia*, denied coverage to an insured on extremely flimsy and weak grounds and whose conduct reflected a shameful exercise of power and ineptitude.

Hibbs v. Billings (1994), 6 W.D.C.P. (2d) 36 (Ont. Gen. Div.).

The court ordered solicitor and client costs against the plaintiffs where the amount of the jury verdict was less than the aggregate of the no-fault benefits and the advance payments by the defendants.

Denzler v. Aull (1994), 19 O.R. (3d) 507, 29 C.P.C. (3d) 99 (Gen. Div.).

The court may consider an offer to contribute in determining whether solicitor and client costs should be awarded.

Dia v. Gore Mutual Insurance Co. (1993), 12 O.R. (3d) 637 (Gen. Div.).

An insurer had acted unreasonably in reducing and then discontinuing no-fault benefits with a view to compelling another no-fault insurer to assume liability for the payments. As a result, on an application to determine which of the two insurers was liable to pay no-fault benefits, the insured was awarded solicitor and clients costs as against the unsuccessful insurer.

Moyer v. Polsin (1992), 11 O.R. (3d) 216, 28 R.P.R. (2d) 103, 60 O.A.C. 281 (Div. Ct.).

Solicitor and client costs were awarded to the respondents on an unsuccessful appeal where the appellants' defence was without merit and had not been undertaken in good faith.

Gerula v. Flores (1993), 16 C.P.C. (3d) 362 (Ont. Gen. Div.).

The court awarded solicitor and client costs against the defendant surgeon who had altered medical records and lied to the plaintiff's solicitor.

Coughlin v. Mutual of Omaha Insurance Co. (1992), 10 O.R. (3d) 787, 96 D.L.R. (4th) 551 (Gen. Div.).

Where possible, a trial judge should fix costs at the conclusion of trial or as soon thereafter as is possible. In the result, costs were fixed on a solicitor and client scale where the defendant's ''hardball'' conduct had forced the plaintiff to bring an action to establish his full rights.

Dube v. Penlon Ltd. (1992), 10 O.R. (3d) 190 (Gen. Div.).

Where a blameless plaintiff was required to embark on an extremely difficult, complex and costly course of litigation, and the plaintiff had been totally disabled as a result of the matters in issue, the court awarded the plaintiff costs on a solicitor-and-client basis.

131843 Canada Inc. v. Double "R" (Toronto) Ltd. (1992), 7 C.P.C. (3d) 15, additional reasons 3 W.D.C.P. (2d) 251; 11 C.P.C. (3d) 190; (January 21, 1993) (Ont. Gen. Div.).

The court awarded solicitor and client costs against a plaintiff who had made unfounded allegations of dishonesty analogous to fraud and had rejected favourable settlement offers and whose action had been dismissed at trial.

Lawson v. Toronto Hospital Corp. (1991), 52 O.A.C. 186, additional reasons 54 O.A.C. 75 (Div. Ct.).

Solicitor and client costs were awarded where the unsuccessful applicant on an interlocutory injunction had made allegations that the respondent had acted for a wrongful purpose, in an arbitrary manner and in bad faith with complicity.

Shier v. Fiume (1991), 6 O.R. (3d) 759 (Gen. Div.).

Costs of an action were awarded on a solicitor and client scale to the successful plaintiff, where the plaintiff had fully disclosed the strength of his case to the defendant, and yet the defendant had nonetheless proceeded to trial without a reasonably arguable case.

S & A Strasser Ltd. v. Richmond Hill (Town of) (1990), 1 O.R. (2d) 243, 49 C.P.C. (2d) 234, 45 O.A.C. 394 (C.A.).

Where the plaintiff did not accept the defendants' offer to settle and the plaintiff's action was dismissed at trial, the court awarded the defendant party and party costs up to the date of the offer and solicitor and client costs thereafter. The award was based on rule 57.01, not Rule 49.

Procor Ltd. v. U.S.W.A. (1989), 71 O.R. (2d) 410, 65 D.L.R. (4th) 287, additional reasons 71 O.R. (2d) 410 at 434, 65 D.L.R. (4th) 287 at 310 (H.C.).

The court awarded solicitor and client costs in this injurious falsehood action against a defendant who had persisted in serious and unfounded allegations of customs fraud.

Maximilian v. M. Rash & Co. (1987), 62 O.R. (2d) 206 (Dist. Ct.).

The plaintiff received solicitor and client costs in an action where it was found that he had been the victim of a breach of trust.

Johnston v. Jenkins Leaside Travel Ltd. (1987), 19 C.P.C. (2d) 300 (Ont. Dist. Ct.).

A successful defendant was denied solicitor and client costs of the trial although the plaintiff was inexcusably absent for one and a half days during his evidence and admitted perjuring himself. The increased scale is to be awarded only in "rare and exceptional" cases.

Isaacs v. MHG Int. Ltd. (1984), 45 O.R. (2d) 693, 4 C.C.E.L. 197, 7 D.L.R. (4th) 570, 3 O.A.C. 301 (C.A.).

A trial judge should only exercise his discretion to order costs on a solicitor-client basis in rare cases. It is wrong for a trial judge to punish through such costs in a case where oppressive conduct is pleaded, but later abandoned.

Kierans v. Kierans (1984), 45 C.P.C. 84 (Ont. H.C.).

In this family law proceeding, the court declined to award costs on a solicitor and client basis. The recovery by the plaintiff was significantly higher than any settlement offer made by the defendant and while there had been some "foot-dragging" there was no deliberate failure to make financial disclosure.

Foulis v. Robinson (1979), 21 O.R. (2d) 769, 8 C.P.C. 198, 92 D.L.R. (3d) 134 (C.A.).

The Court of Appeal set aside an award of solicitor and client costs. Discussion of circumstances in which such costs are appropriate.

Estok v. Tamassy (1975), 10 O.R. (2d) 308 (C.A.).

An award of costs to a plaintiff on a solicitor and his own client basis was reduced to party and party costs where, *inter alia*, the defendant was not given an opportunity to speak to the question of costs.

Brown v. Roque (1973), 2 O.R. (2d) 100 (H.C.).

Costs against a party on a solicitor and client basis were denied notwithstanding that the party had deliberately given false evidence.

Vanderclay Dev. Co. v. Inducon Engineering Ltd., [1969] 1 O.R. 41, 1 D.L.R. (3d) 337 (H.C.).

Costs should be awarded on a solicitor and client basis only in exceptional cases.

Collins v. Forest Hill Invt. Ltd., [1967] 2 O.R. 351, 63 D.L.R. (2d) 492 (Co. Ct.).

A contractual provision stating that legal costs are payable as between solicitor and client is valid and binding.

DIRECTIONS TO ASSESSMENT OFFICER

57.02(1) Where costs are to be assessed, the court may give directions to the assessment officer in respect of any matter referred to in rule 57.01.

(2) The court shall record,

(a) any direction to the assessment officer;

(b) any direction that is requested by a party and refused; and

(c) any direction that is requested by a party and that the court declines to make but leaves to the discretion of the assessment officer.

COSTS OF A MOTION

Contested Motion

57.03(1) Where, on the hearing of a contested motion, the court is satisfied that the motion ought not to have been made or opposed, as the case may be, the court shall,

(a) fix the costs of the motion and order them to be paid forthwith; or

(b) order the costs of the motion to be paid forthwith after assessment.

(2) Where a party fails to pay the costs of a motion as required under subrule (1), the court may dismiss or stay the party's proceeding, strike out the party's defence or make such other order as is just.

Motion Without Notice

(3) On a motion made without notice, there shall be no costs to any party, unless the court orders otherwise.

Cross-Reference: For motions in the Central East Region, see the practice direction regarding motions and applications, civil pre-trial conferences and costs in interlocutory proceedings following the Highlights of Rule 37.

Costs of Motion — When to be Assessed and Paid

Axton v. Kent (1991), 2 O.R. (3d) 797, 49 O.A.C. 32 (Div. Ct.).

Generally the practice should be to order costs payable forthwith on interlocutory matters unless the justice of the case suggests otherwise.

Apotex Inc. v. Egis Pharmaceuticals (1991), 2 O.R. (3d) 126, 32 C.P.R. (3d) 559 at 568 (Gen. Div.), leave to appeal to Ont. Div. Ct. refused 2 O.R. (3d) 126n, 32 C.P.R. (3d) 559n.

Fixed costs payable forthwith on a solicitor and client scale were awarded where a motion for an interlocutory injunction grounded on unfounded allegations of fraud, deceit and conspiracy was dismissed. In disposing of interlocutory motions, the court will generally fix costs and order them to be paid forthwith.

592123 Ont. Ltd. v. Captiva Investments Ltd. (1987), 19 C.P.C. (2d) 279 (Ont. Assess. O.).

A party to whom costs of a motion are awarded ''in the cause'' is not entitled to recover such costs unless it is subsequently awarded costs of the application or action in which the motion is brought. It is not sufficient that the party is awarded other relief not including costs.

Staff Builders Int. Inc. v. Cohen (1983), 40 C.P.C. 169 (Ont. T.O.).

Costs of a motion awarded ''in any event of the appeal forthwith after taxation thereof'' were taxable immediately. Discussion of when costs are taxable on various interlocutory awards.

Anchor Shoring Ltd. v. Halton Conservation Authority (1979), 12 C.P.C. 220 (Ont. H.C.).

Where costs on an interlocutory motion were awarded ''in any event of the cause . . . payable forthwith after taxation'', such costs were not permitted to be taxed until the cause had been determined.

Can. Metal Co. v. C.B.C. (1976), 14 O.R. (2d) 112, 2 C.P.C. 105, affirmed 14 O.R. 112 at 114, 2 C.P.C. 108 (H.C.).

Where costs in any event of the cause are awarded on an interlocutory motion, recovery must await the final disposition of the action.

Costs of Motion — Examples

Shimcor Investments Ltd. v. Toronto (City) (1993), 12 O.R. (3d) 794 (Gen. Div.).

On the plaintiff's motion for leave to appeal the dismissal of a Mareva injunction, the defendants moved to quash the motion for leave. In the result both motions were dismissed, with costs of the motion for leave to appeal awarded on a party and party basis to the defendants, subject to a set-off of the costs awarded to the plaintiffs in relation to the unsuccessful motion to quash.

Lawson v. Toronto Hospital Corp. (1991), 54 O.A.C. 75 (Div. Ct.).

Solicitor and client costs in the amount of $89,235.81 were awarded to the respondents in respect of an unsuccessful motion for an injunction. The costs award was based on a senior counsel fee of $325.00 per hour, a junior counsel fee of $210.00 per hour, a student-at-law at $65.00 per hour, and law clerks at $85.00 per hour.

International Corona Resources Ltd. v. LAC Minerals Ltd. (1988), 66 O.R. (2d) 610 at 630, 54 D.L.R. (4th) 647 at 666 (H.C.).

Where a motion was brought to set aside a trial judgment on the ground that it was fraudulently obtained, and the moving party had itself been guilty of improper conduct, including misuse of the criminal process for tactical benefit, shredding of documents, alteration of records, and failure to comply with production orders, the court awarded costs to all responding parties to the motion on a solicitor and client basis.

Abbott v. Reuter-Stokes Can. Ltd. (1988), 32 C.P.C. (2d) 161 (Ont. H.C.).

The court ordered costs payable forthwith where the plaintiff had been obstructionist on his cross-examination, requiring an unnecessary motion for re-attendance.

Crabtree v. Mackay (1987), 61 O.R. (2d) 669, 25 C.P.C. (2d) 45 (Master).

Where the plaintiff's health was clearly in issue and there were no special circumstances why the proposed defence medical examination should not be held, the court ordered a defence medical examination with costs to the defendant in any event of the cause.

Century Customs Brokers Ltd. v. P.C.B. Freight Services Ltd. (1985), 49 C.P.C. 165 (Ont. Master).

The court fixed costs at $2000 and ordered payment forthwith where a defendant wrongfully withheld possession of goods, forced the plaintiff to bring a motion for possession and delayed in consenting to the motion.

Lavery v. Sherway Contr. (Windsor) Ltd. (1983), 43 O.R. (2d) 264, 38 C.P.C. 134 (H.C.).

Where the plaintiff failed to *praecipe* a County Court action to the Supreme Court upon the defendant disputing the monetary jurisdiction of the County Court, and the defendant was obliged to bring a motion for that purpose, the court fixed the costs of the motion and ordered them paid forthwith.

Grossman v. Toronto Gen. Hosp. (1983), 41 O.R. (2d) 457, 35 C.P.C. 11, 146 D.L.R. (3d) 280 (H.C.).

Where the defendants' conduct amounted to a deliberate refusal to comply with their obligation to produce documents, the court awarded costs of a motion on a solicitor and client basis taxable and payable forthwith.

Bank of N.S. v. Schussler (1980), 28 O.R. (2d) 161, 111 D.L.R. (3d) 509 (H.C.).

A party who had no solicitor of record may be awarded costs in respect of counsel retained for particular motions.

COSTS ON SETTLEMENT

57.04 Where a proceeding is settled on the basis that a party shall pay or recover costs and the amount of costs is not included in or determined by the settlement, the costs may be assessed under Rule 58 on the filing of a copy of the minutes of settlement in the office of the assessment officer.

COSTS WHERE ACTION BROUGHT IN WRONG COURT

Recovery within Monetary Jurisdiction of Small Claims Court
57.05(1) If a plaintiff recovers an amount within the monetary jurisdiction of the Small Claims Court, the court may order that the plaintiff shall not recover any costs.

(2) Subrule (1) does not apply to an action transferred to the General Division under section 107 of the *Courts of Justice Act.*

Default Judgment within Monetary Jurisdiction of Small Claims Court
(3) If the plaintiff obtains a default judgment that is within the monetary jurisdiction of the Small Claims Court, costs shall be assessed in accordance with that court's tariff.

Proceeding Dismissed for Want of Jurisdiction
(4) Where a proceeding is dismissed for want of jurisdiction, the court may make an order for the costs of the proceeding. [am. O. Reg. 377/95, s. 4]

Comtois v. Johnson, [1969] 1 O.R. 336 (H.C.).

It is the amount recovered as opposed to the amount claimed which is determinative.

COSTS OF LITIGATION GUARDIAN

57.06(1) **The court may order a successful party to pay the costs of the litigation guardian of a party under disability who is a defendant or respondent, but may further order that the successful party pay those costs only to the extent that the successful party is able to recover them from the party liable for the successful party's costs.**

(2) **A litigation guardian who has been ordered to pay costs is entitled to recover them from the person under disability for whom he or she has acted, unless the court orders otherwise.**

Brewitt v. Duke, [1956] O.W.N. 107 (H.C.).

The litigation guardian of an unsuccessful infant defendant is entitled to recover his costs from the plaintiff and the plaintiff may in turn recover those costs from the infant. [*But see now rule 57.06(1) — Authors.*]

Re Fennell, [1955] O.W.N. 617, [1955] 5 D.L.R. 116 (H.C.).

The excess of solicitor and client costs taxed against the litigation guardian over party and party costs contained in a settlement was ordered to be paid out of funds awarded to the infant plaintiff.

Rooney v. Jasinski, [1952] O.R. 869, [1953] 1 D.L.R. 225 (C.A.).

Where costs are incurred *bona fide* and for the benefit of the party under disability, he may be liable to indemnify the litigation guardian.

Petrie v. Speers Taxi Ltd., [1952] O.R. 731, [1953] 1 D.L.R. 349 (C.A.).

Where the Official Guardian had been litigation guardian for an unsuccessful defendant, his costs were ordered to be paid by the successful plaintiff and added to the amount of the judgment. [*But see now rule 57.06(1) — Authors.*]

LIABILITY OF SOLICITOR FOR COSTS

57.07(1) **Where a solicitor for a party has caused costs to be incurred without reasonable cause or to be wasted by undue delay, negligence or other default, the court may make an order,**

    (a) **disallowing costs between the solicitor and client or directing the solicitor to repay to the client money paid on account of costs;**

    (b) **directing the solicitor to reimburse the client for any costs that the client has been ordered to pay to any other party; and**

    (c) **requiring the solicitor personally to pay the costs of any party.**

(2) **An order under subrule (1) may be made by the court on its own initiative or on the motion of any party to the proceeding, but no such order shall be made unless the solicitor is given a reasonable opportunity to make representations to the court.**

(3) **The court may direct that notice of an order against a solicitor under subrule (1) be given to the client in the manner specified in the order.**

Liability of Solicitor — rule 57.07(1)

Young v. Young, [1993] 4 S.C.R. 3, 84 B.C.L.R. (2d) 1, 49 R.F.L. (3d) 117, [1993] 8 W.W.R. 513, 34 B.C.A.C. 161, 18 C.R.R. (2d) 41, 108 D.L.R. (4th) 193, 160 N.R. 1, 56 W.A.C. 161.

Courts must be extremely cautious in awarding costs personally against a lawyer, given the duties upon the lawyer to guard the confidentiality of instructions and to bring forward with courage even unpopular causes.

Bridlepath Progressive Real Estate Inc. v. Unique Homes Corp. (1992), 12 C.P.C. (3d) 109 (Ont. Master).

Costs were awarded against a solicitor personally, where the solicitor had caused costs to be incurred without reasonable cause, and where costs had been wasted by undue delay and negligence on the part of the solicitor. Costs were not awarded personally against the junior solicitor who had been acting upon the instructions of the client and a senior partner of his firm.

931473 Ontario Ltd. v. Coldwell Banker Canada Inc. (1992), 5 C.P.C. (3d) 271 (Ont. Gen. Div.).

An order for payment of costs by a solicitor is not available in cases of mistake, error of judgment, or mere negligence. Rather the conduct of the solicitor must be inexcusable and merit reproof.

Drosos v. Chong (1992), 8 C.P.C. (3d) 312 (Ont. Gen. Div.).

The court awarded costs of a mistrial against the plaintiff's counsel who had discussed trial testimony with an expert witness notwithstanding an exclusion order. The order did not contain an exception for expert witnesses.

Donmor Industries Ltd. v. Kremlin Canada Inc. (1992), 6 O.R. (3d) 506 (Gen. Div.).

Costs of a motion to strike a statement of claim were ordered to be paid by the plaintiff's counsel personally, where that counsel had caused the defendants to incur costs without reasonable cause.

Kennedy v. Guardian Insurance Co. of Canada (1991), 1 C.P.C. (3d) 291 (Ont. Gen. Div.), leave to appeal refused (September 24, 1991), Doc. Thunder Bay 5956-90 (Ont. Gen. Div.).

Where the conduct of a solicitor demonstrates unreasonable interference with the conduct of the cross-examination by examining counsel and constitutes obstruction, an award of costs on a solicitor and client basis will be ordered as against the solicitor personally.

Hockey v. Hockey (1989), 69 O.R. (2d) 338, 21 R.F.L. (3d) 105, 60 D.L.R. (4th) 765, 35 O.A.C. 257 (Div. Ct.).

Solicitor and client costs were awarded against a solicitor personally where his "reckless" letter exacerbated the dispute and an access order was disregarded.

640612 Ont. Inc. v. 253547 Ont. Ltd. (1987), 26 C.P.C. (2d) 93 (Ont. Master).

The court ordered a solicitor to pay the costs of a motion brought on behalf of his client where part of the relief sought was completely unfounded and the balance of the relief sought was premature.

Cini v. Micallef (1987), 60 O.R. (2d) 584, 20 C.P.C. (2d) 229 (H.C.).

Something more than mere negligence is required on the part of counsel before the court will order costs against a solicitor personally. There must be gross negligence or a failure to carry out the professional duty before such an award is justified.

Weldo Plastics Ltd. v. Communication Press Ltd. (1987), 19 C.P.C. (2d) 36 (Ont. Dist. Ct.).

The inability of counsel to control his client is not a basis for an award of costs against the solicitor.

Christie Group Ltd. v. Parfum Jean Duvalier Inc. (1987), 16 C.P.C. (2d) 219 (Ont. Master).

Before bringing a motion the moving party's solicitor must ensure that the evidence supporting the motion is sufficient to accomplish the objective of the motion. If there are no *bona fide prima facie* grounds, the solicitor is at risk personally regarding costs.

Lough v. Digital Equipment of Can. Ltd. (1986), 57 O.R. (2d) 456, 62 C.B.R. (N.S.) 216, 15 C.C.E.L. 1, 33 D.L.R. (4th) 318 (H.C.).

A motion seeking an award of costs against the plaintiff's solicitors personally for failing to advise the defendant of the plaintiff's bankruptcy was dismissed by the court where aspects of the claim were personal and did not rest in the trustee.

Kern v. Kern (1986), 54 O.R. (2d) 11, 8 C.P.C. (2d) 31, 50 R.F.L. (2d) 77 (H.C.).

The High Court reversed an order of the District Court awarding costs against a solicitor who had represented a client in a family law proceeding and had acted for the client in the sale of certain assets, the proceeds of which were removed from Canada.

Lukic v. Urquhart (1985), 50 O.R. (2d) 47 (C.A.).

An order for costs against the solicitor personally was reversed on appeal where the solicitor had not been given notice that the order was to be made against him and the solicitor had not "knowingly or willingly committed any impropriety".

Aliferis v. Parfeniuk (1985), 1 C.P.C. (2d) 41, 9 O.A.C. 215 (C.A.).

The court awarded costs against the solicitor for the plaintiff regarding interlocutory proceedings to extend the time for service of an originating process.

Dobud v. Herbertz (1985), 50 C.P.C. 283 (Ont. Dist. Ct.).

The court awarded costs against a solicitor personally where his inept handling of the case deprived the clients of the opportunity to advance certain claims.

Re Bisyk (No. 2) (1980), 32 O.R. (2d) 281 (H.C.), affirmed (1981), 32 O.R. (2d) 281n (C.A.).

The court awarded costs against a solicitor personally where the solicitor was responsible for irresponsible and unfounded allegations against the integrity and good faith of an executive.

Evans v. The Savarin Ltd. (1980), 27 O.R. (2d) 705, 109 D.L.R. (3d) 510 (H.C.).

The court awarded costs against solicitors personally where it appeared they had commenced or continued proceedings without authority and had not been frank with the court.

Sonntag v. Sonntag (1979), 24 O.R. (2d) 473, 11 C.P.C. 13 (H.C.).

A solicitor was ordered to pay the costs of an aborted examination where his conduct had unduly interfered with the examination.

United Van Lines (Can.) Ltd. v. Petrov (1975), 13 O.R. (2d) 479, 1 C.P.C. 307 (Co. Ct.).

A solicitor may be held liable for costs where he improperly makes an improper certification in a specially endorsed writ.

Re Consiglio Trusts (No. 2), [1973] 3 O.R. 329, 36 D.L.R. (3d) 661 (C.A.).

A solicitor was ordered to bear costs personally where the proceeding was ill-conceived and brought on behalf of an infant for whom no litigation guardian had been appointed.

Re Solicitor, [1971] 1 O.R. 138 (T.O.).

The assessment officer may totally disallow a fee where the solicitor has been seriously negligent or inept.

Right to be Heard — rule 57.07(2)

Fekete v. 415585 Ont. Ltd. (1988), 64 O.R. (2d) 552, 27 C.P.C. (2d) 121 (Master).

Discussion of the proper procedure to be followed in seeking or ordering costs against a solicitor personally.

Fekete v. 415585 Ont. Ltd. (1988), 64 O.R. (2d) 542, 27 C.P.C. (2d) 108, additional reasons 64 O.R. (2d) 542 at 552, 30 C.P.C. (2d) 10 (H.C.).

The court set aside a costs order against a solicitor personally where it appeared that the solicitor had not been afforded a real opportunity to oppose liability.

Dairy Queen Frozen Products (Can.) Ltd. v. Tweedledum Invts. Ltd.; Dairy Queen Frozen Products (Can.) Ltd. v. J. McCauley & Sons (1976), 2 C.P.C. 186 (Ont. C.A.).

Where notice and an opportunity to be heard were given, the court had jurisdiction to award costs against a solicitor personally.

Notice to Client — rule 57.07(3)

Bateman v. Stasyszyn (1979), 25 O.R. (2d) 247 (H.C.).

The court ordered that clients not be charged by their solicitors in respect of certain motions and required a copy of the reasons for decision to be sent to the client.

RULE 58   ASSESSMENT OF COSTS

Highlights

This Rule governs the quantification of costs, a process now called "assessment" rather than "taxation" of costs. The assessment is conducted by assessment officers who are determined, not by this Rule, but by s. 90 of the *Courts of Justice Act, i.e.* masters and such other persons as are specifically appointed as assessment officers. Also by rule 58.02(2) a referee is deemed to be an assessment officer for purposes of assessing costs of the reference.

Circumstances in which costs may be assessed. While the court has power to fix costs without assessment (rule 57.01(3)), where a rule or an order provides that a party is entitled to costs and those costs are not fixed by the court, they may be assessed: rule 58.01.

The most common authority for assessment will be a court order, but there are a number of situations where a party may, pursuant to a rule, have costs assessed without a court order, *e.g.* discontinuance of an action (rule 23.05); abandoned motion (rule 37.09(3)); abandoned application (rule 38.08(3)); where an accepted offer does not provide for costs (rule 49.07(5)); where a settlement provides that a party is entitled to costs but they are not determined by the settlement (rule 57.04); the expenses of doing an act required to be done under an order where the judgment debtor fails to do so (rule 60.11(10)); the costs of an examination in aid of execution and certain other enforcement costs (rule 60.19).

The mechanics of an assessment where there is no court order are variously dealt with in rules 57.04, 58.03(1) and 58.07.

Assessment. Costs may be assessed by an assessment officer where the proceeding was commenced or where it was heard, or in any place agreed to by the parties (rule 58.02(1)). It is not otherwise possible for a party to require the assessment to take place at Toronto as was formerly permitted.

Costs are to be assessed in accordance with the Tariffs (rule 58.05(1)). The assessment officer is given a list of factors to be taken into consideration (rule 58.06) and, in addition, he or she is to give effect to any direction given by the court under rule 57.02. Express power is given to an assessment officer to award and fix the costs of an assessment itself: rule 58.05(6).

While all investigatory work engaged in by an expert and his or her assistants leading to an expert's report is recoverable under the tariff (*Chatham Motors Ltd. v. Fidelity & Casualty Ins. Co. of New York* (1986), 53 O.R. (2d) 581, 7 C.P.C. (2d) 251 (H.C.), varied on other grounds (1988), 63 O.R. (2d) 205, 27 C.P.C. (2d) 31 (C.A.)), an assessment officer cannot allow a disbursement to an expert witness for preparation time prior to trial: *Burns Fry Ltd. v. Aetna Casualty Co. of Can.* (1987), 19 C.P.C. (2d) 119 (Ont. Assess. O.), affirmed 23 C.P.C. (2d) 167 (Ont. H.C.). However, a trial judge may award costs of an expert attending in court while the opposing experts testify (*Oakville Storage and Forwarders Ltd. v. C.N.R.* (1987), 27 C.P.C. (2d) 56 (Ont. H.C.)) or may order all of the expert's fees to be paid: *Bye v. Hulin* (1988), 32 C.P.C. (2d) 314 (Ont. H.C.).

Tariffs. Tariff A, Part I (Solicitors' Fees), includes allowances for financial statements (item 2), for notices and offers (item 11), for assignment court (item 13) and for seizure or seizure and sale under a writ of execution or notice of garnishment (item 20). A specific allowance is made for examinations in aid of execution (item 19) to dovetail with the procedure (see rule 60.19) which allows a judgment creditor to add certain costs of enforcement to his or her execution. Item 29.1, introduced in 1991, provides for the recovery of a reasonable amount for the translation into English or French of a document that has been filed, or ordered by the presiding judge or officer.

Under Tariff A, Part II (Disbursements), a reasonable amount is recoverable for experts' reports supplied to other parties that were reasonably necessary for the conduct of the proceeding (item 26) and it is no longer a precondition that the report be used at trial. A reasonable amount is also allowable for copies of documents and authorities prepared for the use of the court and supplied to other parties (item 31) and for the copies of records, appeal books and factums (item 32). A general power is given to the presiding judge or officer to make an order for the recovery of "any other disbursement reasonably necessary for the conduct of the proceeding" (item 35). GST is recoverable under item 36, introduced in 1994.

Related case law. Although the Rules do not govern assessment of costs under the *Solicitors Act* or the *Expropriation Act*, cases dealing with these matters are collected following rule 58.12.

Former Rules: Rules 667-696 and Tariffs.

Cross-Reference: For solicitor's lien issues, see rule 15.03(4) and (5) and the cases collected there.

GENERAL

58.01 Where a rule or order provides that a party is entitled to the costs of all or part of a proceeding between party and party and the costs have not been fixed by the court, they shall be assessed in accordance with rules 58.02 to 58.12.

Basman v. Beck (1989), 34 C.P.C. (2d) 201, 32 E.T.R. 292 (Ont. Surr. Ct.).
Rule 58 applies to the assessment of costs in Surrogate Court.

Ojo v. Willett Hospital (1985), 3 C.P.C. (2d) 34 (Ont. Assess. O.).
The entitlement to costs must be positively established by statute, rule, order or judgment. Where costs reserved to a particular court are not expressly dealt with, they cannot be recovered.

WHO MAY ASSESS COSTS

General Rule
58.02(1) Costs shall be assessed by an assessment officer, subject to subrule (2), in the place where the proceeding was commenced or heard or in a county agreed on by the parties.

Reference
(2) The costs of a reference may be assessed by an assessment officer or by the referee, and for the purposes of rules 58.03 to 58.12, the referee shall be deemed to be an assessment officer.

Cross-Reference: See *Courts of Justice Act*, s. 90(4), re the assessment of costs of a proceeding before a tribunal.

Vacations Inns Inc. v. Income Trust Co. (1991), 6 O.R. (3d) 573 (Assess. O.).

Costs to be assessed pursuant to [s. 43(4)] of the *Mortgages Act* are assessable in the county or district in which the property is located.

Willowrun Investment Corp. v. Greenway Homes Ltd. (1987), 21 C.P.C. (2d) 129 (Ont. H.C.).

An appeal from a confirmed reference report does not stay an assessment of the costs of the reference and, *semble*, an assessment of the reference costs may be done before confirmation.

Royal College of Dental Surgeons of Ont. v. Rival (1976), 14 O.R. (2d) 337, 2 C.P.C. 291,
    affirmed 14 O.R. (2d) 337 at 340, 2 C.P.C. 293 (H.C.).

Where costs of a discipline hearing are to be "as far as practicable, . . . the same as in the Supreme Court", the fees and expenses of the members of the committee cannot be taxed.

ASSESSMENT AT INSTANCE OF PARTY ENTITLED

By Filing Bill of Costs and Obtaining Appointment

58.03(1)   A party entitled to costs may obtain a notice of appointment for assessment of costs (Form 58A) from the appropriate assessment officer on filing a bill of costs and a copy of the order or other document giving rise to the party's entitlement to costs with the assessment officer.

(2)   The notice and the bill of costs shall be served on every party interested in the assessment at least seven days before the date fixed for the assessment.

Appleton v. Hawes (1990), 47 C.P.C. (2d) 151 (Ont. H.C.), additional reasons (January 17,
    1991), Doc. No. Toronto 14715/84 (Ont. Gen. Div.).

Where a party assigned to its solicitors an award of party and party costs but then changed solicitors, the solicitors were not entitled to proceed with the assessment of costs. Only a party or its solicitors of record may obtain an appointment to assess costs.

Mintz v. Mintz (1984), 46 C.P.C. 234 (Ont. T.O.).

Where a party delayed unreasonably in taxing her costs, the taxing officer reduced the bill by the amount of interest accrued during the period of excessive delay.

Fairview Electronics Ltd. v. De Boer Int. Ltd. (1983), 39 C.P.C. 272, 48 C.B.R. (N.S.) 102
    (Ont. T.O.).

A taxation of costs against a bankrupt was not stayed under the *Bankruptcy Act* (Can.) since it was not a proceeding for the recovery of a claim provable in bankruptcy, but merely a step to quantify that claim which had already been established.

Lee v. Armstrong (1976), 13 O.R. (2d) 527 (T.O.).

There is no general requirement that the bill of costs be served with the notice of appointment, provided the bill is delivered well in advance of the return date of the notice of appointment.

ASSESSMENT AT INSTANCE OF PARTY LIABLE

By Obtaining Appointment and Serving Notice

58.04(1)   Where a party entitled to costs fails or refuses to file or serve a bill of costs for assessment within a reasonable time, any party liable to pay the costs may obtain a notice to deliver a bill of costs for assessment (Form 58B) from the appropriate assessment officer.

(2)   The notice shall be served on every party interested in the assessment at least twenty-one days before the date fixed for the assessment.

Delivery of Bill of Costs

(3) On being served with the notice, the person required to deliver a bill of costs shall file and serve a copy of the bill on every party interested in the assessment at least seven days before the date fixed for the assessment.

Failure to Deliver Bill of Costs

(4) Where a party required to deliver a bill of costs for assessment fails to do so at the time set out in the notice and thereby prejudices another party, the assessment officer may fix the costs of the defaulting party at an appropriate sum in order to prevent further prejudice to the other party.

ASSESSMENT IN ACCORDANCE WITH TARIFFS

Generally

58.05(1) Where party and party costs are to be assessed, the assessment officer shall assess and allow,

(a) solicitors' fees and disbursements in accordance with the Tariffs; and

(b) disbursements for fees paid to the court, a court reporter, an official examiner or a sheriff under the regulations under the *Administration of Justice Act*,

and no other fees, disbursements or charges shall be assessed or allowed unless the court orders otherwise.

Students-at-Law and Law Clerks

(2) Where students-at-law or law clerks have rendered services of a nature that the Law Society of Upper Canada authorizes them to render, the fees for those services shall be assessed and allowed at one-half of the amount that would have been allowed under the Tariffs for a solicitor.

Disbursements

(3) No disbursements other than fees paid to the court shall be assessed or allowed unless it is established by affidavit or by the solicitor appearing on the assessment that the disbursement was made or that the party is liable for it.

Directions

(4) An assessment officer may direct production of books and documents and give directions for the conduct of an assessment.

Set Off of Costs

(5) Where parties are liable to pay costs to each other, the assessment officer may adjust the costs by way of set off.

Costs of Assessment

(6) The assessment officer may, in his or her discretion, award or refuse the costs of an assessment to either party, and fix those costs.

Cross-Reference: For assessment of solicitor and client costs under the *Solicitors Act*, see the cases collected following rule 58.12.

Authors' Note on Organization of Cases

Cases relevant to this provision have been organized as follows:

Assessment of Costs — Generally

Ontex Resources Ltd. v. Metalore Resources Ltd. (1996), 7 W.D.C.P. (2d) 152 (Ont. Master).
The hourly rates allowed for appeal work are independent of the rates allowed for trial work.

Eastwalsh Homes Ltd. v. Anatal Development Corp. (1995), 80 O.A.C. 141 (C.A.).
In assessing costs it is not helpful to compare the ratio of time spent in preparation and time spent in court. The appeal court requires a high standard of preparation and thoroughness and counsel may very well incur large amounts of preparation time for relatively short appeal hearings.

MacMillan v. White (1991), 3 W.D.C.P. (2d) 25 (Ont. Gen. Div.).
The trial judge awarded GST on party and party costs. An order is necessary to recover GST on costs since the Tariffs have not yet been amended to provide for it.

Paletta v. Mackesy, Smye, Turnbull, Grilli & Jones (1989), 70 O.R. (2d) 404, 38 C.P.C. (2d) 291 (H.C.).
Reducing a solicitor's account on assessment as a result of a three-and-a-half-year delay in rendering that account was not an error in principle.

Cavotti v. Cavotti (1987), 22 C.P.C. (2d) 109 (Ont. Assess. O.).
The experience of counsel is a relevant factor in determining whether excessive time has been spent on a tariff item.

Singh v. Nicholls (1984), 45 C.P.C. 205 (Ont. T.O.).

The suggested possible settlement figure or the amount offered by the defendant were not considered as factors in an assessment in determining the degree of success realized in the proceedings.

Beyak v. Min. of Natural Resources (1982), 46 C.P.C. 49 (Ont. H.C.).

The taxing officer must tax the costs on the scale imposed by the court. He or she has no discretion to impose a punitive scale of costs.

Ronald Elwyn Lister Ltd. v. Dayton Tire Can. Ltd. (1983), 32 C.P.C. 95 (Ont. H.C.).

Where a judgment after trial directs a reference regarding quantum of damages and awards costs of the trial, it is not necessary to wait for the damages to be determined before taxing such costs. Quantum of damages awarded is a relevant but not essential factor in taxing costs.

Briarfield Acres Dev. Ltd. v. Min. of Transportation and Communications (1982), 37 O.R. (2d) 433 (H.C.).

Where a party is awarded costs without any order regarding apportionment between his successful and unsuccessful claims he is entitled to recover costs incurred for both the successful and unsuccessful claims.

Graham v. Reynard (1981), 32 O.R. (2d) 541, 21 C.P.C. 245 (T.O.).

A taxing officer's discretion is not limited by views expressed only in the court's reasons for judgment.

Takes v. Chiropractic Review Ctee. of the Bd. of Directors of Chiropractic (1981), 20 C.P.C. 258 (Ont. T.O.).

The taxing officer held that he had jurisdiction to increase as well as decrease the amount claimed under the various tariff items that are expressly left to his discretion.

Kinnear v. Kinnear (1978), 18 O.R. (2d) 549, 7 C.P.C. 14, 83 D.L.R. (3d) 286 (T.O.).

Costs arising from a change of solicitors are not recoverable unless the change was reasonably necessary.

Fothergill v. Fothergill, [1973] 1 O.R. 708 (H.C.).

A legally-aided person may recover costs in excess of the total amount paid or payable for costs by him.

Bertrand v. Bowman, [1969] 2 O.R. 385 (T.O.).

An award of costs to a party "if demanded" is taxed in the same way as an ordinary award.

Commodore Invts. Ltd. v. Buddell, [1968] 1 O.R. 418 (T.O.).

There is no strict rule that an award of solicitor and client costs is equal to one and a third of the amount of party and party costs.

Formea Chemicals Ltd. v. Polymer Corp. Ltd., [1967] 2 O.R. 424, 53 C.P.R. 228 (T.O.).

Party and party costs may exceed the amount of fees paid to the solicitors of the successful party but may not exceed the total of fees and disbursements so paid.

Carlson v. McMurrich, [1967] 2 O.R. 179, affirmed without written reasons and leave to appeal to C.A. refused [1967] 2 O.R. 182n.

If an unsuccessful party affirmatively proves the successful party is not liable to pay his solicitors, no costs are taxable.

Sloan v. Sloan, [1965] 2 O.R. 828 (H.C.).

In a proceeding between spouses, party and party costs may be taxed more generously than would otherwise be usual.

Hoblitzell v. Masticote, [1960] O.W.N. 438 (H.C.).

The court allowed several successful defendants to tax only one bill of costs where they had been represented by the same counsel and had supported one another's positions.

Denberg v. Denberg and Schaffer, [1954] O.W.N. 461 (H.C.).

The costs of abortive proceedings are not taxable unless so ordered by the court or unless the successful party is not responsible for the proceedings proving abortive.

Assessment of Costs — Evidence on Assessment

Dical Investments Ltd. v. Morrison (1993), 13 C.P.C. (3d) 305 (Ont. Gen. Div.).

On a party and party assessment the usual practice is for the solicitors appearing to make unsworn statements to assist the assessment officer. Usually no formal evidence is heard.

Arthur v. Signum Communications Ltd. (1992), 16 C.P.C. (3d) 38 (Ont. Gen. Div.).

Viva voce evidence is not part of the usual procedure on a party and party assessment, and should only be introduced in an exceptional case.

Szewczyk v. Ralph (1987), 16 C.P.C. (2d) 227 (Ont. H.C.).

On the assessment of party and party costs the assessment officer need not hear *viva voce* evidence and have a transcript taken of the proceedings.

Staff Builders International Inc. v. Cohen (1985), 3 C.P.C. (2d) 158 (Ont. Assess. O.).

The practice on assessment of costs is not to take evidence under oath. It is not necessary for every solicitor who worked on the case to give evidence.

Coutts v. C.I.B.C. (1984), 42 C.P.C. 72 (Ont. H.C.).

The procedure to be followed on an assessment of costs is the same, whether awarded on a solicitor and client or a party and party basis. Only in an exceptional case is *viva voce* evidence heard. The procedure to be followed here did not involve any denial of fundamental justice contrary to s. 7 of the *Charter of Rights*.

Andrews v. Andrews (1983), 38 C.P.C. 175 (Ont. H.C.).

Affidavit evidence beyond a statement of disbursements is not admissible on a party and party taxation.

Tylman v. Tylman (1981), 38 C.P.C. 50 (Ont. H.C.).

The taxing officer should hear *viva voce* evidence on the taxation of party and party costs.

Assessment of Costs — Award on Solicitor and Client Basis

Arthur v. Signum Communications Ltd. (1992), 16 C.P.C. (3d) 38 (Ont. Gen. Div.).

On a party and party assessment on a solicitor and client scale, costs incurred prior to the commencement of the action were recoverable when they related to necessary preliminary steps. Further, it is not proper to limit the successful party to a *per diem* allowance for the fees relating to attendance at trial.

Deloitte, Haskins & Sells Ltd. v. Bell Canada (1992), 10 O.R. (3d) 761 (Gen. Div.).

An award of solicitor and client costs is intended to provide an indemnity for legal costs, to the exclusion of services that are not reasonably necessary for the proper presentation of the case. There is no "rule of thumb" for the assessment of solicitor-client costs based upon party and party costs plus one-third.

Dical Investments Ltd. v. Morrison (1993), 13 C.P.C. (3d) 305 (Ont. Gen. Div.).

A written retainer is not necessary on the assessment of party and party costs awarded on a solicitor and client basis where there is no dispute between the solicitor and client as to the retainer.

Apotex Inc. v. Egis Pharmaceuticals (1991), 4 O.R. (3d) 321, 37 C.P.R. (3d) 335 (Gen. Div.).

In fixing costs on a solicitor and client basis, the judge applied rates of up to $390 per hour for senior counsel. There is no formula or rule of thumb according to which solicitor and client costs should be calculated on the basis of "party and party costs plus one-third".

O'Connell v. Gelb (1988), 29 C.P.C. (2d) 124 (Ont. H.C.).

Solicitor and client costs awarded to the plaintiff were assessed at $116,000, notwithstanding that the plaintiff's recovery for damages and interest was only $15,000.

Kimpe v. Union Gas Ltd. (1984), 45 C.P.C. 265 (Ont. T.O.).

In this assessment of costs on a solicitor and client basis of a complicated application to a tribunal, the taxing officer made substantial reductions due to inaccuracies in dockets and lack of concern over how time was spent, but made allowance for aging and inflation over the long period of the retainer. An expert's account was substantially reduced due to unreliable docketing habits, lack of control over time spent by subordinates, and lack of expertise. A reasonable mark-up of subordinates' hourly rates was allowed. Nothing was allowed for the result or complexity.

Mintz v. Mintz (1983), 43 O.R. (2d) 789, 38 C.P.C. 125 (H.C.).

Where a party was ordered to pay his opponent's costs on a solicitor and client basis, the court ordered production of dockets, accounts and correspondence subject to inspection by the master regarding claims of privilege.

Simone v. Toronto Sun Publishing Ltd. (1979), 11 C.P.C. 340 (Ont. T.O.).

An award of costs on a solicitor and client basis at trial does not entitle the successful party to costs of interlocutory proceedings in which no order as to costs were made.

Singer v. Singer (1975), 11 O.R. (2d) 775, leave to appeal to Div. Ct. refused 11 O.R. (2d) 775n.

Where costs are awarded on a solicitor and client basis, an allowance for work done by a law student or law clerk which would otherwise have been done by a solicitor is proper. [*See now rule 58.05(2) — Authors.*]

Re Seitz (1974), 6 O.R. (2d) 460, 53 D.L.R. (3d) 223 (H.C.).

Costs payable "as between a solicitor and his client" are intended to be a complete indemnification for costs essential to and arising within the four corners of the litigation, therefore an award in respect of successful lobbying to obtain a statutory amendment favourable to the case is allowable.

Prager v. Kobayashi, [1968] 1 O.R. 694 (T.O.).

An award of costs on a solicitor and client basis means the amount charged by the solicitor to the client for services reasonably necessary for the presentation of the case rendered between the commencement of the proceedings and judgment.

Re Malton and Township of Toronto, [1965] 2 O.R. 792 (Master).

Where costs are awarded on a solicitor and client basis, disbursements for expert witnesses made after the commencement of the proceedings and fairly incurred in properly preparing and presenting the case are fully recoverable.

Assessment of Costs — Salaried Solicitor (See also s. 131 of the *Courts of Justice Act.*)

Feldman v. Law Society of Upper Can. (1989), 68 O.R. (2d) 157, 33 C.P.C. (2d) 213 (H.C.).

The Law Society was not permitted to recover a counsel fee for services rendered by a salaried solicitor. English authority permitting such recovery was reluctantly held not to be the law of Ontario.

Willowrun Investment Corp. v. Greenway Homes Ltd. (1987), 21 C.P.C. (2d) 129 (Ont. H.C.).
The court allowed an amount for a contracted research solicitor which exceeded the amount paid to that solicitor by the party's solicitors.

Demeter v. Dominion Life Assur. Co. (1983), 40 C.P.C. 248 (Ont. T.O.).
Where a corporation seeks to recover costs for a salaried solicitor, there should be an agreement with the solicitor making such costs part of his remuneration at the time the services are rendered but certainly no later than when the order or judgment of the court is delivered.

Dehler v. Whitton and Hastey, [1964] 1 O.R. 165 (T.O.).
Where a corporation employs a salaried solicitor and there is no agreement that the costs of an action are to be added to his salary, the corporation may recover disbursements only.

Assessment of Costs — Miscellaneous

Ojo v. Willett Hospital (1985), 3 C.P.C. (2d) 34 (Ont. Assess. O.).
Where costs of a motion are reserved to the court disposing of the proceeding and that court makes no specific order regarding the costs of the motion, no such costs are recoverable.

Turner v. MacDonnell (1985), 1 C.P.C. (2d) 46 (Ont. Assess. O.)
Costs may be recovered for work done by a solicitor not qualified to practise in Ontario if the solicitor has not been paid at the time of the assessment.

Franco v. Kornatz (1982), 29 C.P.C. 38 (Ont. H.C.).
The costs of an application to the Workmen's Compensation Board to determine whether a personal injury action can be brought are not taxable in the subsequent suit.

Sheppard v. Supt. of Ins. (1978), 19 O.R. (2d) 254, 6 C.P.C. 212 (T.O.).
Where a party obtains a judgment including a claim subrogated to OHIP, OHIP must pay its share of the costs notwithstanding that it is unable to actually recover under the judgment because it exceeds the maximum liability of the Superintendent of Insurance.

Kleiner v. Kleiner, [1973] 1 O.R. 160 (T.O.).
Costs of enforcing an award of interim alimony in Provincial Court (Family Division) are not recoverable as part of the party and party bill in the main action for divorce.

Effect of Revision of Tariff (See also rule 1.02.)

Shea v. Miller, [1971] 1 O.R. 199 (C.A.).
Amendments to cost provisions are "procedural" and therefore have retrospective effect. Judgments signed and entered before such amendments come into force are not affected. [*But see now rule 1.02(4) — Authors.*]

Warren v. Stuart House Int. Ltd. and Stuart, [1970] 2 O.R. 220 (T.O.).
A revised tariff of costs applies only to awards of costs made after the effective date of the amendments unless there is clear intent that such changes are to have retrospective effect.

Tariff Item 4 — Stated Case

Barkwell v. Ludyka (1988), 30 C.P.C. (2d) 143 (Ont. H.C.).
Tariff item 4 establishes only part of the counsel fee for the determination of a stated case. It does not include the costs of the other steps involved in such a motion, which are governed by item 7.

Tariff Item 7 — Motions

Singer v. Singer (No. 2) (1976), 13 O.R. (2d) 556 (T.O.).

A motion to quash an appeal was held to be taxable as a "contested motion" rather than a "motion to an appellate court".

McNally v. Grant Brown Leasing Ltd., [1969] 1 O.R. 264 (T.O.).

Costs of a motion to vary a judgment made in response to an appeal by the opposing party are limited to costs arising as a result of the motion and not as a result of the main appeal.

Tariff Item 8 — Applications

Imrie v. Institute of Chartered Accountants of Ont., [1973] 1 O.R. 326 (T.O.).

Counsel fee was allowed on an originating application at $2,500 and on cross-examination on affidavits at $400.

McFarland v. Trenton, [1957] O.W.N. 118 (H.C.).

A motion to commit for failure to obey a subpoena should be taxed as an originating motion. [*But compare rule 60.11 — Authors.*]

Tariff Item 9 — Examinations

Ronald Elwyn Lister Ltd. v. Dayton Tire Can. Ltd. (1983), 32 C.P.C. 95 (Ont. H.C.).

The fee for examinations for discovery should be based on the amount of time occupied. Where the time occupied is unknown, the fee may be based on the length of the transcript. A fee of $5 to $6 per page was allowed.

Tariff Item 12 — Preparation for Trial and Counsel Fee on Settlement

Ontex Resources Ltd. v. Metalore Resources Ltd. (1996), 7 W.D.C.P. (2d) 152 (Ont. Master).

In assessing costs incurred over a period of five years, the court used one set of hourly rates for the first three years and another set for the last two years.

Eastwalsh Homes Ltd. v. Anatal Development Corp. (1995), 80 O.A.C. 141 (Gen. Div.).

The court did not reduce the plaintiff's party and party costs on the basis the plaintiff had used a "team approach" whereby various lawyers had different responsibilities in the prosecution of the claim; however the usual factors such as duplication of effort were applied.

Walker v. CFTO Ltd. (1994), 23 C.P.C. (3d) 296, additional reasons 24 C.P.C. (3d) 280 (Ont. Master).

Where damage issues had to be re-tried, the court refused to reduce the preparation time for the second trial.

Pittman Estate v. Bain (1994), 19 C.C.L.T. (2d) 1, 112 D.L.R. (4th) 257, additional reasons 112 D.L.R. (4th) 482, further additional reasons 35 C.P.C. (3d) 55, 112 D.L.R. (4th) 494, further additional reasons (1994), 35 C.P.C. (3d) 67 (Ont. Gen Div.).

A solicitor called to the bar in 1973 was allowed an hourly rate of $175 on a party and party basis. A junior counsel and a clerk were allowed at $85 and $40 per hour respectively.

Minuteman Press of Canada Co. v. Touche Ross & Co. (1994), 27 C.P.C. (3d) 70 (Ont. Gen. Div.).

The hourly rates for senior counsel called in 1969 and 1977 were allowed at $175 and $160 respectively.

Canadian Express Ltd. v. Blair (1992), 8 O.R. (3d) 769, 10 C.P.C. (3d) 141, 91 D.L.R. (4th) 559 (Gen. Div.).

The court reduced the allowance for preparation time where it exceeded the hearing time by a multiple of 20. On a party and party assessment, no allowance is permitted for ungowned lawyers attending the hearing to advise counsel. The court allowed hourly rates of up to $150 for senior counsel and up to $120 for junior counsel.

Jaffe v. Dearing (1992), 7 C.P.C. (3d) 225, additional reasons (April 10, 1992), Doc. Toronto 5236/85, 10453/86 (Ont. Gen. Div.).

A solicitor-litigant was allowed fees for preparation and appearance at trial.

Schlau v. Boyesko (1989), 17 W.D.C.P. 231 (Ont. H.C.).

Trial preparation is not limited to that which immediately precedes trial. Good trial preparation commences when the client walks in the door.

Stewart v. Davies (1988), 25 C.P.C. (2d) 57 (Ont. Assess. O.).

The decision in *Carpenter v. Malcolm, infra*, must not be interpreted to prevent the assessment officer from disallowing excessive costs.

Crabtree v. Mackay (1987), 61 O.R. (2d) 669, 25 C.P.C. (2d) 45 (Master).

Time spent considering whether to consent to a request from the opposing party can be assessed as part of preparation for trial.

Cavotti v. Cavotti (1987), 22 C.P.C. (2d) 109 (Ont. Assess. O.).

The preparation time of a previous solicitor was not allowed where it was not clearly shown that such time was solely for preparation for trial.

Carpenter v. Malcolm (1985), 6 C.P.C. (2d) 176 (Ont. H.C.).

Counsel fee for preparation for trial should include all time legitimately expended and should not be subject to arbitrary reduction.

Regent Holidays Ltd. v. Kinsella Investments Ltd. (1985), 5 C.P.C. (2d) 197 (Ont. Assess. O.).

No allowance is recoverable for attendance at assignment court.

Bentley v. Davidson Partners Ltd. (1985), 4 C.P.C. (2d) 168 (Ont. Assess. O.).

The fee is not limited as to the time when preparation for trial is done. The assessment officer may consider factors other than the expenditure of time, such as the success achieved.

Ramsay v. Can. Corporate Mgmt. Co. (1984), 42 C.P.C. 278 (Ont. T.O.).

Some counsel fee should be allowed on the acceptance of an offer to settle prior to examinations for discovery.

Ronald Elwyn Lister Ltd. v. Dayton Tire Can. Ltd. (1983), 32 C.P.C. 95 (Ont. H.C.).

The amount awarded by way of *per diem* counsel fee at trial includes an allowance for counsel's preparation for trial on a particular day the trial is in session. An additional fee should be taxed for time spent on weekends or on other days when the trial is not in session.

Weiner v. Gemtey Co. (1982), 38 O.R. (2d) 463, 30 C.P.C. 105 (T.O.).

No allowance for preparation for trial was made where that preparation was done before the delivery of pleadings.

Endicott v. Halliday (1982), 28 C.P.C. 114 (Ont. T.O.).

A solicitor-litigant was permitted an allowance for preparation time.

Lake Ontario Steel Co. v. United Steel Wkrs. of Amer., Local 6571 (1980), 18 C.P.C. 87 (Ont. T.O.).

In determining the fee for preparation, one of the factors considered was the experience of counsel and a higher rate was allowed for senior counsel.

Lovery v. C.N.R. (1979), 23 O.R. (2d) 314, 13 C.P.C. 106 (H.C.).

Where parties settle for an amount less than an amount agreed to be the damages of the plaintiff, the amount of the settlement should be a factor in determining the counsel fee.

Haida Industs. Ltd. v. Field Aviation Co. (1978), 20 O.R. (2d) 174, 6 C.P.C. 115 (T.O.).

Where an action settles before trial, a counsel fee may be awarded for work in preparation for trial which does not fall under other Tariff items.

Rattner v. Mercantile Bank of Can. (1978), 19 O.R. (2d) 91, 6 C.P.C. 303, affirmed 19 O.R. (2d) 91n (H.C.).

All solicitor's work will be classified as preparation for trial, except those services otherwise clearly identifiable, such as preparation of pleadings, examinations, and correspondence.

Falcone v. Diceman (1974), 4 O.R. (2d) 116 (T.O.).

The gross fee for preparation for trial does not vary with the experience of counsel, however, a less experienced solicitor may take longer to prepare, therefore reducing his hourly rate.

Waters v. Smith, [1973] 3 O.R. 962 (H.C.).

The allowance for preparation for trial may be made in respect of work performed for that purpose even before the commencement of the action.

Harrington v. Na-Churs Plant Food Co. (Can.) Ltd., [1971] 2 O.R. 514 (T.O.).

Where a payment into court is accepted, the counsel fee may be substantial and need not be calculated on an hourly basis.

Hazelton v. Quality Products Ltd. and Heywood, [1971] 1 O.R. 1 (C.A.).

Preparation for trial means work done after it becomes likely there will be a trial and with a view to being ready to present the case at trial.

Thompson v. Kerr, [1959] O.W.N. 285 (H.C.).

A substantial counsel fee was awarded notwithstanding that the action had been settled and only a brief court appearance had been necessary. The fee had been earned in negotiating the settlement.

Tariff Item 14 — Counsel Fee at Trial

Canadian Express Ltd. v. Blair (1992), 8 O.R. (3d) 769, 10 C.P.C. (3d) 141, 91 D.L.R. (4th) 559 (Gen. Div.).

An assessment officer may not award more than one senior counsel fee and one junior counsel fee unless so directed by the trial judge.

Wotherspoon v. Cdn. Pacific Ltd. (1988), 33 C.P.C. (2d) 74 (Ont. Assess. O.).

Unless the trial judge orders otherwise, the assessment officer may allow only one senior counsel fee and one junior counsel fee.

Riverside Landmark Corp. v. Northumberland Gen. Ins. Co. (1985), 48 C.P.C. 178 (Ont. Assess. O.).

In a complicated action with a thirteen-day trial a counsel fee of $57,750 was allowed including $35,900 for preparation.

Deep v. Pitfield, MacKay, Ross & Co. (1985), 48 C.P.C. 138 (Ont. Assess. O.).

Counsel fee for a trial which lasted slightly less than two days was allowed at $3,600, composed of $200 for correspondence, $1,200 for preparation, $2,000 for the days at trial and $200 for assignment courts.

389079 Ont. Ltd. v. WBC Production Ltd. (1984), 43 C.P.C. 92 (Ont. T.O.).

On this assessment of a party and party bill on a solicitor and client basis, the counsel fee claimed by a senior solicitor, lacking in litigation experience, for a relatively simple matter was reduced to that of a junior litigation counsel.

Wright v. Inaugural Invts. Ltd. (1982), 24 C.P.C. 296 (Ont. Master).

On a party and party taxation, where the action was settled at trial, a counsel fee at trial was allowed, but no settlement fee. Time spent by a student assisting in the preparation for trial was not allowed. Time spent and experience were used only as guides in determining the difficulty of the preparation.

Lovery v. C.N.R. (1979), 23 O.R. (2d) 314, 13 C.P.C. 106 (H.C.).

The amount of the recovery, not the agreed amount of damages, should influence the amount allowed as counsel fee.

Ritopecki v. Dominion Stores Ltd. (1976), 13 O.R. (2d) 488 (T.O.).

An allowance for waiting time in the counsel fee is proper in extreme circumstances.

Bradshaw v. Boothe's Marine Ltd. (1973), 2 O.R. (2d) 593 (T.O.).

Discussion of counsel fee component of party and party costs.

Tariff Item 14 — Fee for Junior Counsel

Ultramar Canada Inc. v. Montreal Pipe Line Ltd. (1990), 75 O.R. (2d) 498, 46 C.P.C. (2d) 184 (Gen. Div.).

The plaintiff was entitled to costs of all three counsel whom it used during portions of a complex action involving voluminous documentation.

Takes v. Chiropractic Review Ctee. of the Bd. of Directors of Chiropractic (1981), 20 C.P.C. 258 (Ont. T.O.).

Costs arising out of a junior solicitor's time in assisting with preparation were permitted although he was not counsel at the hearing.

Re Solicitors (1978), 6 C.P.C. 49 (Ont. T.O.).

A junior counsel fee will not be allowed where the work involved a duplication of effort.

Pasut v. Larabie, [1971] 3 O.R. 849 (T.O.).

Even where a junior counsel fee is not appropriate, a brief fee for the junior may be.

Degre v. Berrea and Registrar of Motor Vehicles, [1967] 2 O.R. 493 (T.O.).

A junior counsel fee is proper in all but the most routine cases involving small amounts of money.

Cloverdale Shopping Centre Ltd. v. Township of Etobicoke, [1967] 2 O.R. 192 (T.O.).

Counsel fee allowed to a senior counsel assisted by a junior will be less than that allowed if acting alone.

Enright v. Trans-Canada Air Lines, [1966] 2 O.R. 905 (H.C.).

A sole practitioner who retains outside counsel but also attends at trial himself is treated as a junior counsel for purposes of taxation.

R. v. Public Accountants Council, [1961] O.W.N. 351 (T.O.).

A junior counsel fee was not allowed on the hearing of an originating motion but was allowed on an appeal therefrom.

Re Hatch Estate, [1957] O.W.N. 215 (H.C.).

In considering a junior counsel fee, the taxing officer should decide whether the case warranted the employment of junior counsel and, if so, set the fee in accordance with the importance of the issues involved.

Tariff Item 16 — Appeals

Cavotti v. Cavotti (1987), 22 C.P.C. (2d) 109 (Ont. Assess. O.).

Correspondence was disallowed because it was not provided for in Tariff item [16(a) or 16(b)].

Heymich v. Fred Fisher Equipment Ltd. (1975), 11 O.R. (2d) 416 (T.O.).

Where costs are awarded on a cross-appeal they are limited to the work occasioned solely by the cross-appeal and not attributable to the main appeal.

Henry Morgan & Co. v. Hamilton, [1960] O.W.N. 150 (H.C.).

Discussion of costs on motion for leave to appeal to the Supreme Court of Canada.

Tariff Item 17 — References

Sween v. Sween (1973), 1 O.R. (2d) 216 (T.O.).

Where a decree *nisi* awarded costs to a party and directed a reference as to amount of maintenance, the party was held not to be entitled to the costs of the reference.

Kyte v. Oxford Fruit Co-op., [1972] 3 O.R. 561 (T.O.).

Where a judgment in the Supreme Court orders a reference and unconditionally awards costs, such costs are payable on the usual scale notwithstanding that the amount found due on the reference is within the monetary jurisdiction of the Small Claims Court.

Tariff Item 21 — Attendance Money

Tri-Associates Ins. Agency Ltd. v. Douglas (1986), 9 C.P.C. (2d) 227 (Ont. H.C.).

The court disallowed the cost of subpoenas and attendance money for witnesses who did not testify or even appear at trial.

Freedman v. Maple Leaf Gardens Ltd. (1978), 7 C.P.C. 18 (Ont. T.O.).

Witness fees for a subpoenaed witness who is on call, but never attends, are taxable. A plaintiff can recover his costs attributable to an unsuccessful claim against one defendant from the defendant liable in costs.

Spooner v. Spooner (1977), 16 O.R. (2d) 46, 3 C.P.C. 337 (T.O.).

A party's own cost of transportation to trial is not recoverable on a party and party taxation.

Trim Trends Can. Ltd. v. Dieomatic Metal Products Ltd., [1969] 2 O.R. 593 (T.O.).

Expenses of foreign witnesses are taxed on the same inadequate basis as domestic witnesses.

Tariff Item 22 — Official Examiner, etc., Fees

Sunstrum v. Sunstrum (1975), 12 O.R. (2d) 37 (T.O.).

Actual and reasonable disbursements to a special examiner were allowed on taxation notwithstanding that the figure exceeded the amount permitted by the Tariff.

Tariff Item 24 — Pre-trial Examinations and Transcripts

See cases collected under Tariff Item 34.

Tariff Item 25 — Models, etc.

Allore v. Greer (1980), 30 O.R. (2d) 541, 18 C.P.C. 58 (H.C.).

A document prepared by an accountant concerning calculations of adjusted income was not a "model" within the meaning of the Tariff.

Waters v. Smith, [1973] 2 O.R. 490, reversed on other grounds [1973] 3 O.R. 962 (H.C.).

Partial indemnification for a survey was allowed. The taxing officer ought not to "second guess" counsel with respect to such matters as the necessity of surveys, photos etc. unless it is quite clear they were unnecessary or unreasonable.

Tariff Item 26 — Expert Reports

Blanshard v. Dean Estate (1990), 44 C.P.C. (2d) 301 (Ont. H.C.).

Included in "reports" are any activities which are reasonably necessary to the producing of a report which will be useful to the court. On an assessment, the onus is on the party whose bill is being assessed to show that the item presented falls within item 24.

Ultramar Canada Inc. v. Montreal Pipe Line Ltd. (1990), 75 O.R. (2d) 498, 46 C.P.C. (2d) 184 (Gen. Div.).

The court awarded 60 per cent of the cost of an expert's report notwithstanding that the expert was not called as a witness.

Jordan v. McKenzie (1989), 37 C.P.C (2d) 108 (Ont. Assess. O.).

Discussion of the allowable fees for a valuation expert.

Bye v. Hulin (1988), 32 C.P.C. (2d) 314 (Ont. H.C.).

All charges of expert witnesses, including charges for consultations or reading other reports and references, were allowed on appeal where the court had ordered that taxable disbursements and "all fees of expert witnesses" were to be paid.

Bratt v. Hanes (1988), 65 O.R. (2d) 612, 31 C.P.C. (2d) 198 (H.C.).

The assessment officer has no discretion to allow expert fees which fall outside Tariff items 24 and 26.

Chatham Motors Ltd. v. Fidelity & Casualty Ins. Co. of New York (1986), 53 O.R. (2d) 581, 7 C.P.C. (2d) 251 (H.C.), varied on other grounds (1988), 63 O.R. (2d) 205, 27 C.P.C. (2d) 31 (Ont. C.A.).

All investigatory work engaged in by an expert and his assistants leading to the expert's report is recoverable under the tariff.

Tariff Item 28 — Expert Witnesses

Abate v. Borges (1992), 12 C.P.C. (3d) 391 (Ont. Gen. Div.).

The court allowed a disbursement relating to the cost of retaining a second expert to resolve conflicting views between other experts. However, the time spent by that expert reviewing the other parties' report was not a recoverable disbursement.

Dellelce Construction & Equipment v. Portec Inc. (1990), 73 O.R. (2d) 396 at 440, 44 C.P.C. (2d) 165 (H.C.).

Generally a witness will not be considered an expert for the purpose of an assessment unless a report has been delivered.

Ultramar Canada Inc. v. Montreal Pipe Line Ltd. (1990), 75 O.R. (2d) 498, 46 C.P.C. (2d) 184 (Gen. Div.).

The court awarded only 60 per cent of the fees of the plaintiff's expert not called at trial where there was no timely disclosure that the expert would not testify and the defendant was greatly inconvenienced.

Stribbell v. Bhalla (1990), 73 O.R. (2d) 748, 42 C.P.C. (2d) 161 (H.C.).

The trial judge permitted the plaintiff to recover the cost of a videotape used at trial and of all experts' reports supplied to the defendants where both were reasonably necessary for the conduct of the proceedings; however, the amount of certain experts' reports was reduced.

Khan v. Mitchell (1989), 34 C.P.C. (2d) 208 (Ont. Assess. O.).

The court refused to grant leave to the plaintiffs to call their experts to give evidence concerning their accounts on an assessment of costs. An assessment officer should apply general knowledge in assessing the reasonableness of expert accounts.

Khan v. Mitchell (1988), 27 C.P.C. (2d) 52, varied on other grounds on reconsideration 34 C.P.C. (2d) 208 (Ont. Assess. O.).

The assessment officer allowed physicians' charges at rates from $100 to $150 per hour, a psychologist's charges at $120 per hour, a rehabilitation consultant's charges at $70 per hour and a financial consultant's charges at $75 per hour.

Oakville Storage & Forwarders Ltd. v. C.N.R., (1987), 27 C.P.C. (2d) 56 (Ont. H.C.).

The trial judge awarded costs regarding the attendance of an expert in court while opposing experts testified.

Chitel v. Rothbart (1987), 20 C.P.C. (2d) 291 (Ont. H.C.), leave to appeal to Ont. Div. Ct. refused 21 C.P.C. (2d) xlvii.

An assessment officer may allow a disbursement for expert evidence used on a motion for default judgment, without appearance by counsel before the judge hearing the motion, where the action involves unliquidated damages.

Burns Fry Ltd. v. Aetna Casualty Co. of Can. (1987), 19 C.P.C. (2d) 119 (Ont. Assess. O.), affirmed 23 C.P.C. (2d) 167 (Ont. H.C.).

An assessment officer cannot allow a disbursement to an expert witness for preparation time prior to trial.

Cheskin v. Schrage (1986), 10 C.P.C. (2d) 150 (Ont. H.C.).

Expert witness fees are recoverable costs, regardless of whether the expert's evidence is accepted or rejected at trial, provided the litigant was reasonable in calling the expert.

Davies v. Robertson (1984), 44 C.P.C. 150 (Ont. Master).

In assessing the reasonableness of an expert's fee, the court needs information as to his or her qualifications and experience, the time spent, and the hourly rate charged by the expert and by similar experts.

Micacchi v. Jones (1980), 18 C.P.C. 276 (Ont. T.O.).

On a party and party taxation, both a witness fee for a doctor who testified at trial and the cost of a medical report were allowed.

Smale v. Van Der Weer (1979), 13 C.P.C. 169 (Ont. Master).

"Day" means a 24-hour period.

Morton Terminal Ltd. v. Seaway Forwarding Agencies Ltd. (1978), 8 C.P.C. 87 (Ont. H.C.).

Costs for witness fees for experts were given only for those days on which testimony was given, and not for each day on which those witnesses were in attendance to hear other evidence. [*But see now item 28 — Authors.*]

Ray Kennedy Const. Ltd. v. Moore Park Homes Ltd. (1975), 10 O.R. (2d) 127 (Div. Ct.).

The court has no jurisdiction in a mechanics' lien action to award costs for the services of professional engineers.

Hickey v. Morrissette, [1961] O.W.N. 75 (H.C.).

In calculating the length of a trial the second day is deemed to begin 24 hours after the trial commenced, and so on.

Tariff Item 31 — Cost of Copying Documents

Toronto Bd. of Educ. Staff Credit Union Ltd. v. Skinner (1985), 2 C.P.C. (2d) 247 (Ont. H.C.).

The court ordered a party receiving copies of voluminous documents to pay about 43.5 cents per page in copying charges.

Tariff Item 34 — Cost of Transcripts

Canadian Express Ltd. v. Blair (1992), 8 O.R. (3d) 769, 10 C.P.C. (3d) 141, 91 D.L.R. (4th) 559 (Gen. Div.).

The assessment officer has a discretion to award the cost of expediting a transcript within the prescribed amounts.

Ultramar Canada Inc. v. Montreal Pipe Line Ltd. (1990), 75 O.R. (2d) 498, 46 C.P.C. (2d) 184 (Gen. Div.).

The court awarded the cost of daily transcripts where the transcripts were used by counsel and assisted the court.

Tariff Note 2 — Counterclaims, etc.

Cavotti v. Cavotti (1987), 22 C.P.C. (2d) 109 (Ont. Assess. O.).

A successful defendant was awarded costs of an action but not of a counterclaim where the amounts claimed in the counterclaim were also claimed in the statement of defence as a set-off.

Kalogirou v. Large (1975), 13 O.R. (2d) 532, 26 Chitty's L.J. 251 (T.O.).

A successful counterclaimant who has been awarded costs is entitled only to those costs peculiar to the counterclaim.

Limon v. London Frozen Foods Ltd., [1964] 2 O.R. 235 (H.C.).

Costs of a counterclaim are restricted to the amount by which costs were increased as a result of the counterclaim.

Simpson v. McGee and Fitzpatrick, [1964] 1 O.R. 31, 41 D.L.R. (2d) 38 (H.C.).

Discussion of taxation of party and party costs where both a claim and a counterclaim are successful.

Disbursements — Generally

Bratt v. Hanes (1988), 65 O.R. (2d) 612, 31 C.P.C. (2d) 198 (H.C.).

Absent a court direction under rule 57.02 or an order under s. [131(1)] of the *Courts of Justice Act*, a disbursement outside the Tariff is not to be allowed. The court thus denied recovery of expert's fees related to educating counsel.

Barrow v. T.T.C. (1983), 35 C.P.C. 268 (Ont. T.O.).

The onus is on the party seeking to recover a disbursement to establish that the disbursement was reasonable.

Morgenstern v. Faludi, [1962] O.W.N. 189 (T.O.).

The taxing officer on a party and party taxation may only allow expenses falling under a Tariff item. [*And see now item 35 — Authors.*]

Students-at-Law and Law Clerks — rule 58.05(2)

Equity Waste Management of Canada Corp. v. Halton Hills (Town) (1995), 22 O.R. (3d) 796, 27 M.P.L.R. (2d) 123 (Gen. Div.).

No costs were awarded regarding the attendance of a student at a hearing where the attendance was simply a learning experience for the student and did not benefit the client.

Can.-Johns Manville Co. v. Mungin, [1973] 2 O.R. 610 (T.O.).

A solicitor is entitled to an allowance for services of a law clerk acting under his supervision.

Set-Off of Costs — rule 58.05(5)

York Condominium Corp. No. 329 v. Dazol Devs. Ltd. (1979), 12 C.P.C. 182 (Ont. T.O.).

A set-off of costs in separate actions was not permitted, notwithstanding that the two parties were the same.

Costs of Assessment — rule 58.05(6)

Borden & Elliot v. Deer Home Investments Ltd. (1992), 14 C.P.C. (3d) 269 (Ont. Gen. Div.).

The costs of an assessment involving accounts rendered to various corporations should not be awarded against the individual representing the corporations on the assessment, where there is no inappropriate conduct on the part of that individual.

Burke v. Kongskilde Ltd. (1987), 16 C.P.C. (2d) 108 (Ont. Assess. O.), affirmed 21 C.P.C. (2d) 36 (Ont. H.C.).

An offer to settle an assessment of costs may be disclosed to the court after it assesses the bill of costs but before it disposes of the costs of the assessment.

FACTORS TO BE CONSIDERED ON ASSESSMENT

58.06(1) In assessing costs the assessment officer may consider,

(a) the amount involved in the proceeding;

(b) the complexity of the proceeding;

(c) the importance of the issues;

(d) the duration of the hearing;

(e) the conduct of any party that tended to shorten or to lengthen unnecessarily the duration of the proceeding;

(f) whether any step in the proceeding was,

> **(i) improper, vexatious or unnecessary, or**
>
> **(ii) taken through negligence, mistake or excessive caution;**

(g) a party's denial of or refusal to admit anything that should have been admitted; and

(h) any other matter relevant to the assessment of costs.

(2) In assessing costs the assessment officer is bound by the court's direction or refusal to make a direction under rule 57.02, but is not bound where the court declines to make a direction and leaves the matter to the assessment officer's discretion.

Fothergill v. Fothergill, [1973] 1 O.R. 708 (H.C.).

The taxing officer is not generally entitled to know whether a party is assisted by legal aid.

Re Godkin Estate, [1945] O.W.N. 219 (H.C.).
A creditor who insisted on separate representation was refused costs.

COSTS OF ABANDONED MOTION, APPLICATION OR APPEAL

58.07 The costs of a motion, application or appeal that is abandoned or deemed to be abandoned may be assessed on filing in the office of the assessment officer,

>   **(a) the notice of motion or application served, together with an affidavit that the notice was not filed within the prescribed time or that the moving party or applicant did not appear at the hearing; or**
>
>   **(b) the notice of abandonment served.**

Sargeant v. Sargeant (1983), 35 C.P.C. 233 (Ont. T.O.).
No formal notice countermanding a motion is required to enable the respondent to tax his costs. A letter countermanding the motion is sufficient.

Diamond v. Kaplan (1982), 24 C.P.C. 230 (Ont. T.O.).
Where two attendances were made with respect to a motion subsequently abandoned, costs of those proceedings were permitted.

COSTS OF PARTICULAR PROCEEDINGS

Passing of Accounts
58.08(1) The costs of passing the accounts of a trustee, attorney under a power of attorney, guardian or other person having similar duties relating to the management of assets shall be determined in accordance with subrules 74.18(10) to (13) (costs of passing of accounts of estate trustees).

Costs out of Fund or Estate
(2) Where costs are to be paid out of a fund or estate, the assessment officer may direct what parties are to attend on the assessment and may disallow the costs of the assessment of any party whose attendance is unnecessary because the interest of the party in the fund or estate is small, remote or sufficiently protected by other interested parties. [am. O. Reg. 69/95, s. 8]

Re Burden (1974), 3 O.R. (2d) 626 (H.C.).
Where costs ordered payable out of an estate exceeded the value of the estate, the costs of the executors were given priority.

CERTIFICATE OF ASSESSMENT

58.09 On the assessment of party and party costs, the assessment officer shall set out in a certificate of assessment of costs (Form 58C) the amount of costs assessed and allowed.

OBJECTIONS TO ASSESSMENT

58.10(1) On request, the assessment officer shall withhold the certificate for seven days or such other time as he or she directs, in order to allow a

party who is dissatisfied with the decision of the assessment officer to serve objections on every other interested party and file them with the assessment officer, specifying concisely the grounds for the objections.

(2) A party on whom objections have been served may, within seven days after service or such other time as the assessment officer directs, serve a reply to the objections on every other interested party and file it with the assessment officer.

(3) The assessment officer shall then reconsider and review the assessment in view of the objections and reply and may receive further evidence in respect of the objections, and the assessment officer shall decide on the objections and complete the certificate accordingly.

(4) The assessment officer may, and if requested shall, state in writing the reasons for his or her decision on the objections.

Bailey v. Bailey (1988), 30 O.A.C. 181 (Div. Ct.).

Where an assessment officer hastily signed a certificate following taxation without giving counsel an opportunity to request time to serve and file objections pursuant to rule [58.10], the certificate was set aside and the appellant was permitted seven days to serve and file objections; the purpose of the provision is to ensure that on an appeal the appellate court will have a full record before it and the appellant was effectively deprived of an appeal route pursuant to rule [58.11] because the opportunity to serve and file objections had been denied.

Russello v. Jannock Ltd. (1987), 61 O.R. (2d) 384 (Assess. O.).

An assessment officer has no jurisdiction to consider objections to his assessment after the certificate has been issued. Counsel must request that the certificate be withheld at the conclusion of the assessment if objections are to be made.

Re Sneath (1979), 13 C.P.C. 111 (Ont. Master).

This provision has no application to taxations under the *Solicitors Act*.

Rowland v. Sackmar, [1960] O.W.N. 522 (C.A.).

The court permitted objections to the decision of the taxing officer to be filed notwithstanding the inadvertent failure to request that the certificate be withheld.

APPEAL FROM ASSESSMENT

58.11 The time for and the procedure on an appeal under clause 6(1)(c) or 17(b) or subsection 90(4) of the *Courts of Justice Act* from a certificate of an assessment officer on an issue in respect of which an objection was served is governed by rule 62.01.

Re Knipfel (1982), 37 O.R. (2d) 92, 11 E.T.R. 93, 133 D.L.R. (3d) 662 (C.A.).

The court will not interfere with the discretion of the taxing officer where the dispute involves no principle but only a question of amount unless the amount is so grossly large as to be beyond all question improper.

Re Solicitor (1976), 3 C.P.C. 148 (Ont. C.A.).

A retaxation was ordered where the taxing officer had made no findings.

Re Solicitors (1976), 1 C.P.C. 227 (Ont. Div. Ct.).

A further appeal from a solicitor and client taxation lies from the High Court to the Court of Appeal.

Sloan v. Sloan, [1965] 2 O.R. 828 (H.C.).
It is permissible to award costs of an appeal from a taxing officer against the unsuccessful party.

Balnave v. Park Ave. Apts. Ltd., [1960] O.W.N. 84 (C.A.).
Where possible an appeal from a party and party taxation should be taken before the judge who tried the action.

Re Hatch Estate, [1957] O.W.N. 215 (H.C.).
The fact that the amount taxed is grossly excessive is in itself evidence that the taxing officer proceeded on incorrect principles.

COSTS OF A SHERIFF

Party may Require Assessment

58.12(1) A sheriff claiming fees or expenses that are not prescribed by the regulations under the *Administration of Justice Act* or that have not been assessed shall, on being required by a party, furnish the party with a bill of costs and have the costs assessed by an assessment officer.

(2) A sheriff who has been required to have his or her fees or expenses assessed shall not collect them until they have been assessed.

(3) Either the sheriff or the party requiring the assessment may obtain an appointment for the assessment and the procedure on the assessment shall be the same as in the case of an assessment between party and party.

Reduction of Fees on Motion by Debtor

(4) A person liable under a writ of execution who is dissatisfied with the amount of fees or expenses claimed by a sheriff in respect of the enforcement of the writ may make a motion, before or after payment, on notice to the sheriff and, if the amount appears to be unreasonable, even though it is in accordance with Tariff A, the court may reduce the amount or order the amount to be refunded on such terms as are just.

(5) Nothing in subrule (4) authorizes the court to reduce or order a refund of a fee that is prescribed by the regulations under the *Administration of Justice Act*.

Solicitors Act Assessment — General Matters

[*Note: The provisions formerly contained in the Rules with regard to solicitor and client assessment have not been carried over to the new Rules: some have been transferred to the Solicitors Act: Courts of Justice Act, 1984, s. 214.*]

Frei v. Robinson (March 19, 1996), Doc. 93-MU-5690, 93-MU-5691 (Ont. Gen. Div.).
Where a client disputes the retainer on a solicitor and client assessment but does not bring a timely motion to set aside the order for assessment, the assessment officer may proceed with the assessment.

McCarthy Tétrault v. Signum Communications Ltd. (1995), 36 C.P.C. (3d) 169 (Ont. Gen. Div.).
A motion to oppose confirmation of an assessment officer's report on a solicitor and client assessment was dismissed where there was no error in principle, no absence or excess of jurisdiction, and no patent misapprehension of the evidence. The assessment officer had properly refused to accept evidence which compared the accounts in issue to those rendered by counsel for the opposite party, and had properly refused to take into account the total fees paid by the client throughout the litigation, where only the last accounts rendered by the solicitors were in issue on the assessment.

Minkarious v. Abraham, Duggan (1995), 27 O.R. (3d) 26, 129 D.L.R. (4th) 311 (Gen. Div.).
Where the solicitors rendered a series of interim bills and a final bill and the client had paid most of the interim bills, the court referred all of the bills for assessment.

Green v. Copperthorne Industries 86 Ltd. (1993), 12 O.R. (3d) 728 (Gen. Div.).
The court may order security for costs of a solicitor and client assessment of costs where the client resides outside Ontario.

Mitchell v. Morris (1992), 16 C.P.C. (3d) 267 (Ont. Gen. Div.).
The court has a discretion regarding the venue for a *Solicitors Act* assessment of costs. As the client chose a Toronto solicitor, the court ordered that the assessment be in Toronto.

Stribbell v. Bhalla (1990), 73 O.R. (2d) 748, 42 C.P.C. (2d) 161 (H.C.).
Where the parents consented, the trial judge permitted counsel for a successful minor plaintiff to recover out of the judgment proceeds costs in excess of the usual party and party scale. Justice requires that deserving actions be prosecuted by competent counsel, and competent counsel are entitled to be paid a reasonable fee for the value of the work done.

Conrad v. Quinel International Ltd. (1989), 69 O.R. (2d) 223, 37 C.P.C. (2d) 302 (Div. Ct.).
Only a client may require assessment of a solicitor's account; a third party who is contractually bound to indemnify the client for the account may not.

Gardiner, Roberts v. MacLean (1988), 30 C.P.C. (2d) 85 (Ont. Assess. O.).
A solicitor has an obligation to ensure that, when the contract of retainer is entered into, the client has fee information that is as complete and accurate as a careful solicitor can provide. Therefore, where the solicitor fails to give the client that information, the solicitor's account should be reduced accordingly.

Sopha v. Total Engineering Ltd. (1979), 10 C.P.C. 121 (Ont. H.C.).
Discussion of principles applicable to solicitor and client taxation including preparation of the bill and review on appeal where the services involved are not governed by the Tariff.

Bliss, Kirsh v. Jackson (1979), 9 C.P.C. 238 (Ont. T.O.).
A solicitor's bill need not be drawn in a form related to the court Tariffs, and may set out a lump sum fee for services.

Re Solicitors (1978), 6 C.P.C. 197 (Ont. Master).
A taxing officer has no jurisdiction to deal with issues of retainer.

Re Solicitors (1977), 4 C.P.C. 308 (Ont. Master).
Where a bill is rendered after trial indicating "To: fees on account", there is no obligation on the solicitor to accept only that amount and he is entitled to further fees after the appeal.

Re Solicitors (1977), 4 C.P.C. 275 (Ont. T.O.).
Where a solicitor intends his retainer to be used to secure his services only and not to be applied to his account, he must fully and carefully explain that to the client.

Re Solicitors, [1967] 2 O.R. 691 (T.O.).
Discussion of form of solicitor and client bill of costs.

Re Solicitors, [1967] 2 O.R. 137 (H.C.).
Discussion of distinctions between "solicitor and client" costs and "solicitor and his own client" costs.

Solicitors Act Assessment — Agreement With Client

Solmon Rothbart Goodman v. Ondrey (1995), 38 C.P.C. (3d) 76 (Ont. Gen. Div.).
Where an individual agrees to assume personal liability for a corporation's legal bills, the solicitor should obtain written confirmation to be able to enforce the agreement.

Leach v. Goodwin (1993), 15 O.R. (3d) 14 (Gen. Div.).

Despite having a hostile client who was constantly demanding advice, a solicitor's fees were reduced where he failed to advise the client that his original cost estimate had become inadequate.

Erickson v. Baxter (1988), 66 O.R. (2d) 133 (H.C.).

An assessment officer's failure to inquire into an alleged agreement concerning remuneration was an error in principle.

Cohen v. Kealey & Blaney (1985), 26 C.P.C. (2d) 211, 10 O.A.C. 344 (C.A.).

Where a solicitor and client have a firm understanding as to the maximum fee to be charged depending on the success of a proceeding, the terms of that understanding are a significant consideration on assessment.

Thomson, Rogers v. Edwards (1984), 47 C.P.C. 75 (Ont. T.O.).

An estimate of fees given by a solicitor to a client is a relevant consideration on a solicitor and client taxation but the solicitor is not bound by the client's misunderstanding of the estimate.

Fox v. Blechman (1984), 47 C.P.C. 70 (Ont. T.O.).

A solicitor has a duty to make clear to his client what is involved when he estimates his fees.

Thomson, Rogers v. Croydon Furniture Systems Inc. (1982), 30 C.P.C. 298 (Ont. T.O.).

Where the work becomes more complicated and time-consuming than originally anticipated, the solicitor ought to inform the client that the fee will exceed that quoted. Where the solicitor failed to do so, the fee was reduced to an amount more in accordance with the original estimate.

Re Solicitors and Kozaroff (1981), 21 C.P.C. 3 (Ont. T.O.).

The expectations of the client as to the fee, based on the conduct of the solicitor and any discussion with the client, are a factor in assessing on a *quantum meruit* basis the solicitor's charges.

Re Paolini and Evans, Keenan (1976), 13 O.R. (2d) 767, 2 C.P.C. 113 (H.C.).

An ambiguity in an agreement respecting costs should be resolved in favour of the client. In this case "approximately $6,000" was interpreted as having an upper limit of $6,600.

Re Day, Wilson, Campbell and Brennan (1976), 13 O.R. (2d) 726, 11 L.C.R. 3 (T.O.).

Where a client is led to believe that if successful the opposing litigant will pay *all* his legal fees, his solicitor is not entitled to any additional fees.

Cuttell v. Roberts (1974), 4 O.R. (2d) 649 (C.A.).

An oral agreement between a solicitor and client in respect of remuneration was held to be unenforceable by the solicitor.

Re Solicitor, [1973] 1 O.R. 652 (C.A.).

A solicitor rendering services pursuant to an oral agreement is entitled to taxation on a *quantum meruit* basis.

Solicitors Act Assessment — Reference for Assessment

Borden & Elliot v. Barclays Bank of Canada (1993), 15 O.R. (3d) 352, 106 D.L.R. (4th) 478 (*sub nom. Lorenzetti Development Corp. v. Barclays Bank of Canada*) (Gen. Div.).

A person who has assumed the client's costs liability is entitled to a reference for assessment.

Fitzsimmons, McFarlane, Slocum & Harpur v. Tepperman (1993), 4 W.D.C.P. (2d) 114, additional reasons 4 W.D.C.P. (2d) 353 (Ont. Gen. Div.).

Where a client has paid a solicitor's bill an order will not be made referring the bill for assessment unless (1) the application is brought within 12 months of payment and (2) there are special circumstances.

Mitchell v. Morris (1992), 16 C.P.C. (3d) 267 (Ont. Gen. Div.).

The size of the solicitor's account compared to the recovery of the plaintiff, the lack of a trial to obtain a settlement for the client, and a misunderstanding between the solicitor and client were considered to be "special circumstances" within both s. 10 and s. 25 of the *Solicitors Act.* Accordingly the court extended the time to assess the account.

Re Weir & Foulds (1989), 68 O.R. (2d) 342 (H.C.), leave to appeal to Ont. Div. Ct. granted 68 O.R. (2d) 342n.

The solicitor and client accounts incurred by a public company in resisting a takeover bid were referred for assessment. The takeover had been successful, and the shareholders should be satisfied that the actions taken by the outgoing management were in the best interests of the company.

Tory, Tory, Deslauriers & Binnington v. Concert Productions Int. Inc. (1985), 7 C.P.C. (2d) 54 (Ont. H.C.).

The court dismissed an application by a third party liable to pay a solicitor's account for a reference to have the account assessed after it had been paid where no "special circumstances" were shown.

Re Landau and Official Guardian (1984), 47 O.R. (2d) 346 (Master).

Where the Official Guardian hired a solicitor to represent a child in a proceeding under the *Child Welfare Act,* and costs were to be taxed, the Official Guardian contended that there was no solicitor-client relationship between the solicitor and the Official Guardian. As this dispute existed, a *praecipe* order for taxation was set aside.

Re Peel Terminal Warehouses Ltd. and Wooten, Rinaldo and Rosenfield (1978), 21 O.R. (2d) 857, 10 C.P.C. 160 (C.A.).

Where a client wishes to dispute his bill after one month from its delivery, but before the expiry of twelve months, the master has no jurisdiction under the *Solicitors Act* to direct a reference to the taxing officer, although a judge has inherent jurisdiction.

Re Robins and Randell (1977), 17 O.R. (2d) 242, 6 C.P.C. 68, reversed on jurisdictional grounds 20 O.R. (2d) 496, *(sub nom. Re Randell and Solicitors)* 7 C.P.C. 168n (H.C.).

An application to extend the time for filing a solicitor and client taxation was held to be an originating motion and therefore an affidavit based on information and belief was not admissible.

Re Sternig (1977), 4 C.P.C. 221 (Ont. Master).

Where a solicitor delivered a general account to his client, then a particularized account later, the period for bringing a taxation under the *Solicitors Act* commenced only after delivery of the particularized bill. In any event, where there is clearly overcharging, special circumstances exist such as to allow the court to exercise its discretion to allow a taxation after the twelve-month period.

Re Reid and Goodman & Goodman (1974), 4 O.R. (2d) 447 (H.C.).

The court has jurisdiction to direct a reference to review a solicitor and client bill even where the motion is made more than one month but less than twelve months following delivery of the bill. No special circumstances need be shown.

Re Solicitors (1973), 2 O.R. (2d) 765 (Master).

Where the retainer is not in dispute, the master has jurisdiction to refer a solicitor and client bill for taxation, however he should not do so on *ex parte* application.

Re Solicitor, [1972] 2 O.R. 571 (H.C.).

A client may tax the costs of his solicitor notwithstanding that the solicitor has failed to deliver a bill of costs as ordered.

Re Solicitor, [1966] 2 O.R. 601 (Master).

A *praecipe* order for taxation of a solicitor and client bill will not normally be set aside unless the retainer is disputed before the order was taken out, however, where the clients had reasonable grounds to dispute the retainer the order was so set aside.

Re Solicitor, [1966] 2 O.R. 295 (C.A.).

The taxing officer lacks jurisdiction to set aside a *praecipe* order for taxation of a solicitor and client bill without a formal motion being brought for that purpose.

Re S., [1955] O.W.N. 918 (Master).

The certificate of the taxing officer on a taxation under the *Solicitors Act* must be confirmed in the same way as a report on a reference before execution.

Solicitors Act Assessment — Evidence on Assessment

McCarthy Tétrault v. Signum Communications Ltd. (1995), 36 C.P.C. (3d) 169 (Ont. Gen. Div.).

On a solicitor and client assessment the court refused to admit evidence of the legal costs of the opposing party.

Lash, Johnston v. Wells (1982), 28 C.P.C. 126 (Ont. T.O.).

On a solicitor and client taxation, the value of certain work was not allowed where there was no evidence of personal knowledge that the work had been performed.

Richards v. Bittenbinder (1979), 10 C.P.C. 291 (Ont. T.O.).

On a solicitor and client taxation, the solicitor was permitted to call experienced lawyers as witnesses concerning the complexities of the issues and the manner in which they were dealt with.

Re Solicitors, [1972] 2 O.R. 565 (T.O.).

The rules of evidence apply on a taxation; hearsay evidence will be rejected.

Re Solicitor, [1960] O.W.N. 392 (C.A.).

The taxing officer must hear evidence in order to determine the value of the services rendered.

Solicitors Act Assessment — Exercise of Discretion — General Principles

Desmoulin v. Blair (1994), 21 O.R. (3d) 217, 120 D.L.R. (4th) 700, 76 O.A.C. 1 (C.A.).

On a solicitor and client assessment the court should take into account the solicitor's risk of not being paid by the client. In this personal injury case liability was in doubt and the solicitor could only expect to be paid if the case were successful. The action was successful and the recovery was about $643,000. Solicitors' fees were allowed by the Court of Appeal at $150,000 although on an hourly rate basis they would only have been about $92,000.

Re Solicitors, [1972] 3 O.R. 433 (T.O.).

Discussion of the factors relevant in setting solicitor and client fee: (1) the time expended by the solicitor; (2) the legal complexity of the matters dealt with; (3) the degree of responsibility assumed by the solicitor; (4) the monetary value of the matters in issue; (5) the importance of the matters to the client; (6) the degree of skill and competence demonstrated by the solicitor; (7) the results achieved; and (8) the ability of the client to pay.

Paletta v. Mackesy, Smye, Turnbull, Grilli & Jones (1989), 70 O.R. (2d) 404, 38 C.P.C. (2d) 291 (H.C.).

Delay in rendering a bill may deprive the client of an opportunity to assess the bill effectively and is a proper ground to reduce the bill.

Re Greenglass (1988), 32 C.P.C. (2d) 55 (Ont. H.C.).

Time expended and hourly rates form the preliminary basis for many accounts; however, the mechanical application of an hourly rate will sometimes lead to error. The court allowed a fee of $5,000 where only 23 hours were spent but party and party costs of $3,750 had been recovered in this personal injury case.

Morayniss v. McArthur (1984), 46 C.P.C. 256 (Ont. H.C.).

Lack of success should result in reduction of a solicitor and client bill only if the solicitor acted improperly in some way. A solicitor who charges at a low hourly rate is entitled to charge more hours than the norm.

Campbell v. Nichols (1984), 44 C.P.C. 72 (Ont. T.O.).

The size of the claim must play a part in the assessment of costs, even where the client has caused the solicitor to do more than he would have had he known that the claim would prove to be very small.

Re Kruger and Giverty (1981), 23 C.P.C. 3 (Ont. H.C.).

If a client insists upon proceeding with litigation against his counsel's advice, the fees will not necessarily be related to the amount in issue or the amount of recovery.

Re Solicitors (1978), 6 C.P.C. 49 (Ont. T.O.).

A solicitor is entitled to be paid for travelling time, but not at the same hourly rate he is paid for doing solicitors' work.

Re Solicitors (1977), 4 C.P.C. 263 (Ont. T.O.).

A solicitor need not accept fees less than he could tax merely because a third party has agreed to pay his client's legal costs as part of a settlement.

Re Solicitors (1976), 2 C.P.C. 298 (Ont. H.C.).

In a solicitor and client taxation, lack of success may be considered in reducing the bill.

Re Solicitor (1974), 7 O.R. (2d) 496 (T.O.).

Where a settlement includes a payment for party and party costs, the calculation of solicitor and client costs should be made without reference to such payment.

Re Solicitor, [1973] 1 O.R. 107 (C.A.).

The solicitor and client bill of the successful party must bear some reasonable relation to the amount recovered in the action.

Re Solicitors, [1971] 3 O.R. 470 (T.O.).

Discussion of where an allowance for services of law students and law clerks is appropriate.

Re Solicitors, [1970] 1 O.R. 407 (T.O.).

Discussion of limited utility of County Law Association Tariffs as a guide to a taxing officer.

Re Solicitor, [1968] 1 O.R. 45 (T.O.).

The factors to be considered in establishing a reasonable fee for a solicitor's service in a criminal case are the complexity of the matter in question, the importance of the matter to the client, the time devoted by the solicitor, the skill and experience of the solicitor, and the results achieved.

Solicitors Act Assessment — Exercise of Discretion — Quality of Work

Re Solicitors and Kern (1980), 16 C.P.C. 253 (Ont. T.O.).

Where the work done was not utterly useless, an error in judgment by the solicitor did not result in the reduction of his account.

Re Solicitor (1979), 8 C.P.C. 85 (Ont. T.O.).

Where the taxing officer found the services rendered by the solicitor were of no use to the client, no fee for services was allowed.

Re Solicitor, [1960] O.W.N. 260 (T.O.).

The taxing officer refused to consider allegations of negligence against the solicitor in fixing the fee.

Solicitors Act Assessment — Costs of Assessment

Wright & McTaggart v. Soapak Industries Ltd. (Receiver of) (1990), 75 O.R. (2d) 394 (Assess. O.).

Discussion of circumstances in which costs of assessment of the account of a dissolved partnership can include counsel and witness fees for former partners.

Re Solicitor, [1969] 2 O.R. 823 (T.O.).

Costs of the taxation of a solicitor and client bill will normally be awarded to the client if the bill is excessive and to the solicitor if the bill is patently reasonable. No costs will be awarded if the bill appears excessive but is in fact reasonable.

Re Kingsmill, Jennings and Belusa (1981), 25 C.P.C. 157 (Ont. T.O.).

On a solicitor and client taxation, where the solicitor's account was reduced to the extent of time docketed twice in error, no costs were awarded.

Solicitors Act Assessment — Estate Matters

Re Cook (1975), 10 O.R. (2d) 61 (T.O.).

Discussion of costs in an estate matter of "average complexity" where value of estate exceeded $300,000.

Re Kimberley & Naylor and Prior (1974), 5 O.R. (2d) 593 (T.O.).

Discussion of solicitor and client costs in estate work when solicitor performs both legal and executor's work.

Re Freeburne, [1973] 1 O.R. 423 (H.C.).

Beneficiaries under a will may require the taxation of a bill of costs notwithstanding that it has already been approved and paid by the executors.

Solicitors Act Assessment — Miscellaneous Matters

Weir & Foulds v. Punjani (1994), 28 C.P.C. (3d) 32 (Ont. Gen. Div.).

The court refused to stay collection of a costs award where there was a pending negligence action against the solicitors. The assessment had been undertaken on consent, and in all of the circumstances, it would have been wrong to stay execution.

Woods v. Chamberland (1991), 6 O.R. (3d) 419, 5 C.P.C. (3d) 217 (Gen. Div.).

The court ordered that an assessment of costs under the *Solicitors Act* be conducted by a judge rather than an assessment officer where there was a serious allegation of negligence or misconduct by the solicitor.

Greenspan, Rosenberg v. Buxbaum (1987), 17 C.P.C. (2d) 213 (Ont. H.C.).

A retainer agreement need not be reviewed in the solicitor's county of residence. A client must pay the accounts before seeking to refer them for assessment.

Bristow, Catalano, Moldaver & Gilgan v. Paparde (1984), 46 C.P.C. 180 (Ont. T.O.).

A solicitor should advise his client if the solicitor's hourly rate increases during the currency of the retainer.

Elliott, Warne, Carter v. Scott (1982), 24 C.P.C. 300 (Ont. T.O.).

The taxing officer held that he did not have jurisdiction to award interest to a client on the sum overpaid to the solicitor.

Re Solicitors and Roy (1981), 24 C.P.C. 27 (Ont. T.O.).

Costs were not reduced although much of the solicitors' work had been done two years earlier when the hourly rates were lower.

Campeau Corp. v. Vice and Hunter (1977), 18 C.P.C. 141 (Ont. H.C.).

A motion to move a solicitor and client taxation from Ottawa to Toronto was refused.

Bagnall & Catalano v. Groff (1980), 14 C.P.C. 227 (Ont. Master).

Where the solicitors had tendered an account to the client and no steps were taken to have the bill taxed, the solicitors were permitted to deliver an amended account for a larger sum.

Re Solicitors (1980), 13 C.P.C. 228 (Ont. H.C.).

A solicitor cannot withdraw an account already delivered and substitute a new bill in a greater amount for the same services without leave.

Re Solicitors, [1973] 2 O.R. 550 (C.A.).

The taxing officer has no authority to dispense with service of notice of filing of his certificate.

Re Solicitor, [1973] 1 O.R. 652 (C.A.).

The taxing officer is empowered to award interest chargeable 30 days following the tendering of the bill.

Re Solicitor, [1972] 2 O.R. 106 (T.O.).

If a solicitor wishes to charge an hourly rate greater than that which *quantum meruit* would justify, he must follow the procedure set out in the *Solicitors Act*, R.S.O. 1970, c. 441, s. 18.

Re Solicitor, [1971] 1 O.R. 90 (T.O.).

The fee for an uncomplicated divorce case was allowed at $500.

Costs in Expropriation Proceedings

Farquhar v. R. (1983), 33 C.P.C. 79 (Ont. T.O.).

The taxing officer reduced the hourly rate charged, to reflect the rates of the years when the services were rendered, in this expropriation action.

Stanton v. Scarborough Bd. of Educ. (No. 3) (1983), 33 C.P.C. 58, 26 L.C.R. 292 (Ont. T.O.).

In expropriation cases, the cost of an appraisal report reasonably incurred must also be proportionate to its value before being taxable. Interest on the cost of an appraisal report is only taxable if legally payable under the account.

Greenslade v. Min. of the Environment (1982), 24 C.P.C. 307, 23 L.C.R. 289 (Ont. T.O.).

Interest charged by an appraiser on his outstanding accounts was allowed on the taxation in an expropriation proceeding.

Kolbuch v. Ont. Min. of Housing (1982), 24 C.P.C. 20, 23 L.C.R. 1, reversed 38 O.R. (2d) 333, 25 L.C.R. 261, 137 D.L.R. (3d) 459 (H.C.).

Discussion of taxation of expert's fees and solicitor's fees in expropriation proceedings.

Eddy v. Min. of Transportation & Communications (No. 3) (1976), 13 O.R. (2d) 424, 10 L.C.R. 92 (T.O.).

Costs incurred by the claimant in taxing the costs of an expropriation proceeding are part of the "reasonable legal, appraisal and other costs actually incurred by [him] for the purposes of determining the compensation payable" and may be taxed as well.

Martin v. Regional Municipality of Ottawa-Carleton (1978), 3 C.P.C. 294, 12 L.C.R. 201, affirmed (*sub nom. Martin v. Ottawa-Carleton (No. 2)*) 16 L.C.R. 289 (Ont. Div. Ct.).

In this expropriation proceeding, the costs of a second appraiser not called as a witness and whose report was not disclosed were allowed. The costs of taxation are part of the costs of the expropriation.

Christian & Missionary Alliance v. Metro. Toronto (1973), 3 O.R. (2d) 655, 6 L.C.R. 393 (T.O.).

Discussion of costs in expropriation proceeding.

Shiner v. Metro. Toronto (No. 2), [1973] 1 O.R. 274, 3 L.C.R. 101 (T.O.).

Discussion of taxation of party and party bill in expropriation proceedings.

Four Thousand Yonge Street v. Metro. Toronto (1973), 1 O.R. (2d) 100, 5 L.C.R. 22 (T.O.).

Discussion of costs in a difficult expropriation case.

Ansco Invts. Ltd. v. Metro. Toronto, [1973] 1 O.R. 267 (T.O.).

The Rules of the Supreme Court were held not to apply to a taxation under the *Expropriations Act*, R.S.O. 1970, c. 154, s. 33.

Peloquin v. Junction Creek Conservation Authority, [1973] 1 O.R. 258 (T.O.).

Party and a party costs in an expropriation proceeding must be reasonable, must have actually been incurred by the owner, and must have been incurred in order to determine the compensation payable for the property.

Kingston Enterprises Ltd. v. Min. of Highways, [1971] 1 O.R. 712 (T.O.).

The Ontario Municipal Board had no jurisdiction under s. 33(1) of the *Expropriations Act*, S.O. 1968-69, c. 36, to refer the assessment of costs to the taxing master.

Re Dufferin-Lawrence Devs. Ltd. and North York Bd. of Educ., [1970] 1 O.R. 729 (H.C.).

Taxation in expropriation cases is on a more liberal scale than ordinary party and party costs.

Salvadore v. Ont. Min. of Highways, [1970] 1 O.R. 116 (T.O.).

Taxations under s. 33(1) of the *Expropriations Act*, S.O. 1968-69, c. 36, are on a *quantum meruit* basis; the Tariffs do not apply.

ORDERS

RULE 59   ORDERS

Highlights

This Rule deals with the non-enforcement aspect of orders. The enforcement of orders is regulated by Rule 60.

"Orders" is a generic term, defined to include judgments: rule 1.03. Rule 59 covers their effective date (rule 59.01), the initial endorsement by the court (rule 59.02), the process of preparing, settling and signing the formal order (rules 59.03-59.04), the entry and filing of the formal order (rule 59.05) and also the amending, setting aside and varying of orders (rule 59.06) and the acknowledgment of the satisfaction of an order (rule 59.07).

Preparation, settling and signing of orders. By rule 59.04(1), the registrar at the place of hearing or where the proceeding was commenced may sign every order, unless it has been signed by the court, judge or officer who made it. To facilitate this procedure, rule 59.02 generally requires the court at the time of making the order to endorse it on the relevant court papers, *i.e.* the appeal book, record, notice of motion or notice of application.

Approval as to the form of the order is to be sought from all parties represented at the hearing (rule 59.03(1)). Hence, approval is necessary where the order is one for the recovery of a sum certain after a hearing (contrast former Rule 534).

Forms are provided for orders, judgments and orders or certificates on appeal (Forms 59A, 59B and 59C) and they employ terminology that is more modern and direct than under the former practice.

Entry and filing. By rule 59.05, in addition to the order being entered, a copy of the order must be filed in the court file at the place where the proceeding was commenced.

Amending, setting aside or varying orders. The grounds upon which an order may be amended (rule 59.06(1)) or set aside or varied on the basis of fraud, the discovery of new facts, *etc.*, (rule 59.06(2)) remain unchanged. In addition, there are numerous provisions throughout the Rules for setting aside or varying particular orders on other grounds, *e.g.* orders made on default (rules 19.08 and 52.01(3)); orders made on motion (rule 37.14), on an application (rule 38.11) or on a reference (rule 54.05(3)); orders made by the registrar in an appellate court (rule 61.16(5)); and final orders for corollary relief (rule 69.24).

Satisfaction of order. Provision is made for the filing and entering of an acknowledgment of the satisfaction of an order (rule 59.07).

Summary of procedure. For a summary of the procedure for settling, signing and entering orders, see Procedural Charts (CHARTS).

Former Rules: Rules 264, 517-539.

EFFECTIVE DATE

59.01 An order is effective from the date on which it is made, unless it provides otherwise.

ENDORSEMENT BY JUDGE OR OFFICER

59.02(1) An endorsement of every order shall be made on the appeal book, record, notice of motion or notice of application by the court, judge or officer making it, unless the circumstances make it impractical to do so.

(2) Where written reasons are delivered,

(a) in an appellate court, an endorsement is not required;

(b) in any other court, the endorsement may consist of a reference to the reasons,

and a copy of the reasons shall be filed in the court file.

PREPARATION AND FORM OF ORDER

Preparation of Draft Formal Order

59.03(1) Any party affected by an order may prepare a draft of the formal order and send it to all other parties represented at the hearing for approval of its form.

(2) [Revoked O. Reg. 739/94, s. 3]

General Form of Order

(3) An order shall be in (Form 59A (order), 59B (judgment) or 59C (order or certificate on appeal)) and shall contain,

(a) the name of the judge or officer who made it;

(b) the date on which it was made; and

(c) a recital of the particulars necessary to understand the order, including the date of the hearing, the parties who were present or represented by counsel and those who were not, and any undertaking made by a party as a condition of the order.

(4) The operative parts of an order shall be divided into paragraphs, numbered consecutively.

Order Directing Payment for Minor

(5) An order directing payment into court or to a trustee on behalf of a minor shall show the minor's birth date and full address and shall direct that a copy of the order be served on the Children's Lawyer.

Order for Costs

(6) An order for the payment of costs shall direct payment to the party entitled to receive the costs and not to the party's solicitor.

Order on which Interest Payable

(7) An order for the payment of money on which postjudgment interest is payable shall set out the rate of interest and the date from which interest is payable.

Support Order

(8) An order for the payment of support shall set out, under the signature line, the last known address of the support creditor and debtor. [am. O. Regs. 739/94, s. 3; 69/95, s. 19]

Canada (Attorney General) v. Bitove Corp. (1996), 7 W.D.C.P. (2d) 164 (Ont. Gen. Div. [Commercial List]).

The formal judgment should set out only the relief granted as that constitutes the operative effect of the court's reasoning. It should not set out the dispositions of each issue made to reach the relief granted since such dispositions are not "operative".

Broad v. Ellis, [1956] O.W.N. 180 (Master).

Where a party had approved the draft of an order, he was held to be bound by it prior to service on him of a copy of the signed order.

SIGNING ORDERS

General

59.04(1) Every order shall be submitted in accordance with subrules (5) to (9) for the signature of,

(a) in the case of an order of the Court of Appeal, the Registrar of the court; or

(b) in any other case, the registrar at the place of hearing or where the proceeding was commenced,

unless the court, judge or officer who made the order has signed it.

(2) Where an order states that it may be signed only on the filing of an affidavit or the production of a document, the registrar shall examine the affidavit or document and ascertain that it is regular and sufficient before signing the order.

(3) Where a judge ceases to hold office or becomes incapacitated after making an order but before it is signed, another judge may settle and sign it.

(4) Where a master ceases to hold office or becomes incapacitated after making an order but before it is signed, another master or a judge may settle and sign it.

Signing Where Form of Draft Order Approved

(5) Where all the parties represented at the hearing have approved the form of the order, the party who prepared the draft order shall,

(a) file the approval of all the parties represented at the hearing, together with a copy of the order; and

(b) leave the order with the registrar for signing.

(6) [Revoked O. Reg. 739/94, s. 4]

Support Order

(7) A party who leaves a support order with the registrar for signing shall also leave a copy of the order for filing in the office of the Director of the Family Support Plan.

Where Registrar Satisfied

(8) Where the registrar is satisfied that the order is in proper form, he or she shall sign the order and return it to the party who left it to be signed.

Where Registrar not Satisfied

(9) Where the registrar is not satisfied that the order is in proper form, he or she shall return the order unsigned to the party who left it to be signed and the party may,

(a) submit the order in proper form and, if required by the registrar, file the approval of the parties to the order in that form, together with a copy of the order; or

(b) obtain an appointment to have the order settled by the court, judge or officer that made it and serve notice of the appointment on all other parties who were represented at the hearing.

Appointment to Settle Where Form of Draft Order not Approved

(10) Where approval is not received within a reasonable time, a party may obtain an appointment to have the order settled by the registrar or, where the registrar considers it necessary, by the court, judge or officer that made it, and notice of the appointment shall be served on all other parties who were represented at the hearing.

Urgent Cases

(11) In a case of urgency, the order may be settled and signed by the court, judge or officer that made it without the approval of any of the parties who were represented at the hearing.

Appointment to Settle Disputed Order before Judge or Officer

(12) Where an objection is taken to the proposed form of the order in the course of its settlement before a registrar, the registrar shall settle the order in the form he or she considers proper and the objecting party may obtain an appointment with the court, judge or officer that made the order to settle the part of the order to which objection has been taken and serve notice of the appointment on all other parties who were represented at the hearing.

(13) Where the order was made by a court that consisted of more than one judge, the appointment shall be with the judge who presided at the hearing or, where he or she is unavailable, any other judge who was present at the hearing.

(14) The judge with whom an appointment is obtained under subrule (13) may refer the settling of the order to the full court that made the order.

(15) Where an appointment is not obtained under subrule (12) or (13) within seven days after the registrar settles the order, a party may require the registrar to sign the order as settled by him or her.

(16) After an order has been settled under subrule (12) by the judge or officer who made it, or under subrule (13) or (14), the registrar shall sign it unless it was signed by a judge or officer at the time it was settled. [am. O. Regs. 351/94, s. 4; 739/94, s. 4]

Chrysler Credit Canada Ltd. v. 734925 Ontario Ltd. (1991), 5 O.R. (3d) 65 (Master).

A solicitor has an ethical obligation — owed to the court and to the other solicitors — to approve an order as to which there is no legitimate objection. Ceasing to act for the client or instructions from the client not to approve the order do not relieve the solicitor of this obligation.

Wessel v. Wessel (1978), 20 O.R. (2d) 494, 5 R.F.L. (2d) 397 (C.A.).

Where a compromise is reached before a trial judge and a dispute subsequently arises as to its terms, a second judge has no jurisdiction to hear a motion to interpret the terms.

ENTRY OF ORDER

Every Order to be Entered and Filed

59.05(1) Every order shall be entered in accordance with subrules (2) to (6) immediately after it is signed and the party having the order signed shall give to the registrar the original and a sufficient number of copies for the purpose of entering and filing it.

(2) The registrar shall enter an order by,

(a) noting at the foot of the original the entry book in which a copy is to be inserted or the microfilm on which the original is to be photographed, together with the date of the insertion or photograph; and

(b) inserting a copy in an entry book or microfilming the original.

Where Order to be Entered and Filed

(3) Every order shall be entered in the office of the registrar in which the action or application was commenced and a copy of the order as entered shall be filed in the court file.

(4) Where an order in a subsequent action or application affirms, reverses, sets aside, varies or amends an earlier order, it shall be entered not only in the office described in subrule (3) but also in the office in which the earlier order was entered.

(5) An order of the Court of Appeal shall be entered not only in the office described in subrule (3) but also in the office of the Registrar of the Court of Appeal.

(6) The certificate of the Registrar of the Supreme Court of Canada in respect of an order made on an appeal to that court shall be entered by the local registrar at Toronto and by the registrar in the office where the action or application was commenced, and all subsequent steps may be taken as if the order had been made in the court from which the appeal was taken. [am. O. Reg. 61/96, s. 4]

Brunelle v. Brunelle, [1964] 1 O.R. 113 (H.C.).

A party may compel the solicitor of an opposing party to enter any signed judgment in his possession, notwithstanding any solicitor's lien.

Pearson v. Park Plaza Corp., [1961] O.W.N. 22 (Master).

A *praecipe* order must be entered.

AMENDING, SETTING ASIDE OR VARYING ORDER

Amending

59.06(1) An order that contains an error arising from an accidental slip or omission or requires amendment in any particular on which the court did not adjudicate may be amended on a motion in the proceeding.

Setting Aside or Varying

(2) A party who seeks to,

(a) have an order set aside or varied on the ground of fraud or of facts arising or discovered after it was made;

(b) suspend the operation of an order;
(c) carry an order into operation; or
(d) obtain other relief than that originally awarded,
may make a motion in the proceeding for the relief claimed.

Change of Disposition Prior to Issuance of Order

Applecrest Investments Ltd. v. Guardian Insurance Co. (1992), 13 C.P.C. (3d) 394 (Ont. Gen. Div.).

The court re-opened and continued a trial where, after trial but before entry of the judgment, important new evidence was discovered which might well affect the outcome of the case.

Fekete v. 415585 Ont. Ltd. (1988), 64 O.R. (2d) 542 at 552, 30 C.P.C. (2d) 10 (H.C.).

A court retains the jurisdiction to clarify the terms of its own order prior to the issue and entry of that order.

Smith Bus Lines Ltd. v. Bank of Montreal (1987), 61 O.R. (2d) 688, 25 C.P.C. (2d) 255 (H.C.).

Where a judge did not give counsel a full opportunity to make submissions before issuing reasons for decision, he withdrew his reasons and referred the matter to another judge for hearing *de novo*. Discussion of propriety of communicating with a judge by letter. Discussion of one judge conferring with another to clarify an endorsement.

Saginur v. Sbrocchi (1979), 12 C.P.C. 21 (Ont. Master).

Where formal judgment had not been issued, the master retained jurisdiction to change the disposition of a motion.

Canadian Acceptance Corp. Ltd. v. Biluk (1978), 10 C.P.C. 178 (Ont. Dist. Ct.).

Until formal judgment is signed and entered, the trial judge may reconsider the judgment already given.

Rombeek v. Co-operators Ins. Assn. (Guelph) (1977), 4 C.P.C. 69 (Ont. H.C.).

Amendments to a judgment which has not been issued may be allowed, notwithstanding that a notice of appeal has been served.

Holmes Foundry Ltd. v. Point Edward, [1963] 2 O.R. 404, 39 D.L.R. (2d) 621 (C.A.).

An order may be withdrawn, altered, or modified by a judge either on his own initiative or on the application of a party until such time as the order has been drawn up, passed, and entered.

Correction of Errors — rule 59.06(1)

Vetech Laboratories Ltd. v. 621870 Ontario Ltd. (1991), 2 C.P.C. (3d) 135 (Ont. Gen. Div.).

The omission of an undertaking as to damages in an injunction proceeding was an irregularity curable under rule 59.06. The court refused to dissolve the injunction obtained by the defendant where irreparable harm would result to the defendant.

Vicckies v. Vicckies (1990), 45 C.P.C. (2d) 200 (Ont. H.C.).

Rule 59.06 is sufficiently broad and general that the court may amend a judgment where there has been an inadvertent error by the court which can be easily rectified.

Monarch Construction Ltd. v. Buildevco Ltd. (1988), 26 C.P.C. (2d) 164 (Ont. C.A.).

A consent judgment is final and binding and can only be amended when it does not express the real intentions of the parties or where there is fraud; in other words, a consent judgment can only be rectified on the same grounds on which a contract can be rectified. There was no allegation of fraud and no basis upon which the court could grant rectification. The contract was unambiguous on its face and should be performed in accordance with its terms.

Re Permanent Invt. Corp. Ltd. and Township of Ops and Graham, [1967] 2 O.R. 13, 62 D.L.R. (2d) 258 (C.A.).

The registrar may, on consent, allow alterations which he believes would be sanctioned by the court if mentioned to the court, and such alterations are binding on the parties.

Amato v. Amato, [1955] O.W.N. 313 (Master).

The jurisdiction of the master to correct clerical errors is restricted to *praecipe* orders and judgments and to orders, reports or judgments made in his office. [*See now rules 37.02(2), 37.14 — Authors.*]

Amendment re Matters Not Adjudicated — rule 59.06(1)

Imperial Roadways Ltd. v. C.P. Ltd. (1982), 28 C.P.C. 151, 134 D.L.R. (3d) 149 (Ont. H.C.).

The trial judge amended his judgment to indicate that it was to bear postjudgment interest after disposition of an appeal.

Moyer v. Moyer (1980), 30 O.R. (2d) 698, 17 C.P.C. 225, 117 D.L.R. (3d) 661 (Surr. Ct.).

The court amended a consent judgment after entry to provide for the payment of postjudgment interest.

Chester v. Chester and Sutton (1977), 2 C.P.C. 121 (Ont. H.C.).

A trial judge who fails to consider whether a divorce action should be treated as contested for the purposes of costs retains jurisdiction to deal with that matter.

Leaseconcept Ltd. v. French (1976), 1 C.P.C. 160 (Ont. H.C.).

Where upon motion for the alternative remedies of committal and sequestration the court had granted the order without adjudicating on the sequence of relief, the order was amended after entry.

Robertson v. Robertson (1975), 8 O.R. (2d) 253, 20 R.F.L. 397 (H.C.).

Where the court inadvertently failed to specify that costs in a divorce proceeding should be taxed on a contested basis, the decree was corrected notwithstanding that it had been made absolute.

Rocke v. Rocke, [1956] O.W.N. 481 (C.A.).

The court amended an order to specify the scale of costs after the order had been signed and entered.

Setting Aside or Varying Orders — Fraud — rule 59.06(2)(a)

International Corona Resources Ltd. v. LAC Minerals Ltd. (1988), 66 O.R. (2d) 610, 54 D.L.R. (4th) 647, additional reasons 66 O.R. (2d) 610 at 630, 54 D.L.R. (4th) 647 at 666 (H.C.).

A motion to set aside a judgment for fraud is subject to the following principles: 1) fraud must be proved on a reasonable balance of probability; 2) the fraud must go to the foundation of the case; 3) the fraud must not have been known at the time of the trial; 4) the moving party must establish it acted with due diligence; 5) fraud by a non-party requires a higher standard than fraud by a party; 6) due diligence is measured by an objective test; 7) the moving party must not delay unreasonably in bringing the motion; 8) the moving party's conduct is relevant; and 9) the new facts must provide a reason to set aside the judgment.

Davidson Estate v. Karfilis (1987), 22 C.P.C. (2d) 188 (Ont. H.C.).

The evidence contained in an agreed statement of facts used in a disciplinary proceeding was held not to constitute evidence of fraud sufficient to warrant the setting aside of an earlier judgment.

Bldg. Materials Corp. v. Cermar Imports (Ont.) Ltd. (1978), 7 C.P.C. 30 (Ont. H.C.).
Unsubstantiated allegations of fraud form no basis for staying entry of judgment.

Pajelle Invts. Ltd. v. Guaranty Trust Co. (1977), 3 C.P.C. 221 (Ont. H.C.).
The mere possibility of fraud did not in this case outweigh the need for finality.

100 Main Street East Ltd. v. Sakas (1976), 8 O.R. (2d) 385, 58 D.L.R. (3d) 161 (C.A.).
A judgment may be set aside as obtained by fraud if it is shown the fraud *may* have affected
the result; it is not necessary to show it *did* affect the result.

Suriano v. Suriano, [1972] 1 O.R. 125, 6 R.F.L. 100, 22 D.L.R. (3d) 377 (C.A.).
A motion to impeach a judgment or order on the grounds of fraud practised upon the court is
properly made to the trial court, not to the Court of Appeal.

Re Cook and Morley and Forster, [1950] O.W.N. 739 (H.C.).
Before a judgment will be set aside on the ground of fraud by perjured evidence, the evidence
must be shown to have been material to the court's decision.

Setting Aside or Varying Orders — Fresh Evidence — rule 59.06(2)(a). (See also
cases under *Courts of Justice Act*, s. 134(4)(b).)

Saeglitz v. Saeglitz (1995), 6 W.D.C.P. (2d) 120 (Ont. U.F.C.).
The court refused to re-open a trial to admit fresh evidence where the evidence would probably
not affect the outcome and was available through reasonable diligence at trial.

Mele v. Royal Bank (1994), 29 C.P.C. (3d) 3 (Ont. Gen. Div.).
Where new counsel was retained after summary judgment was granted, but before the formal
judgment was issued and entered, the court re-opened the matter and permitted fresh evidence.

Dawi v. Armstrong (1992), 17 C.P.C. (3d) 196 (Ont. Gen. Div.), affirmed (September 27, 1993),
    Doc. CA C12417 (Ont. C.A.).
On a motion to set aside summary judgment based on fresh evidence, it must be shown that the
new evidence (1) has an important influence on the decision of whether or not there is a triable
issue; (2) is apparently credible; and (3) could not have been obtained by reasonable diligence
before summary judgment.

Saviro International v. Cadillac Gage Co. (1992), 14 C.P.C. (3d) 229 (Ont Gen. Div.), affirmed
    (1993), 14 C.P.C. (3d0 252 (Ont. C.A.), leave to appeal to Supreme Court of Canada
    refused 19 C.P.C. (3d) 21 (note), 65 O.A.C. 320 (note), 162 N.R. 400 (note).
Two years after an action had been struck, the plaintiff brought a motion to set aside the order
on the basis of new evidence. The motion was dismissed as the plaintiff had failed to act with
reasonable diligence and had provided no justification for the excessive delay.

Qit Fer et Titane Inc. v. Upper Lakes Shipping Ltd. (1991), 3 O.R. (3d) 165 (Gen. Div.).
After judgment but before its entry, the court declined to admit a response to a request to admit
under Rule 51 which would probably not have changed the result and could have been relied
on at trial. The issues had been fully developed and the response would, at best, set up a technical
defence.

Castlerigg Investments Inc. v. Lam (1991), 2 O.R. (3d) 216, 47 C.P.C. (2d) 270 (Gen. Div.).
The trial judge has an unfettered discretion to re-open a trial to hear new evidence where the
judge is not *functus*. It is not necessary to show that the evidence in issue could have been
obtained for trial with the exercise of reasonable diligence. The fundamental consideration is
to ensure that a miscarriage of justice does not occur.

Rosenberg v. Geist (1984), 48 O.R. (2d) 373, 48 C.P.C. 271 (H.C.).

A judgment or order cannot be set aside on the ground of a matter arising subsequent to its making unless it is shown that the evidence relied upon could not have been discovered by the party complaining.

394363 Ont. Ltd. v. Fuda (1984), 44 O.R. (2d) 698 (Div. Ct.).

On a motion to submit further evidence and set aside a summary judgment, the master should only admit the evidence where it was not obtainable through reasonable diligence before judgment was given.

Indust. Dev. Bank v. Bertolo, [1970] 3 O.R. 697, 14 D.L.R. (3d) 21 (C.A.).

Where a motion is brought for a new trial on the grounds of fresh evidence and the applicant alleges that the judgment was obtained by fraud, the court will not view the fresh evidence with the strictness that would otherwise apply; however since the evidence here was tenuous, the appropriate procedure was to bring an action rather than a motion attacking the previous judgment.

Scott v. Cook, [1970] 2 O.R. 769, 12 D.L.R. (3d) 113 (H.C.).

In an application to re-open a trial to adduce further evidence made after reasons for judgment have been delivered but before judgment is entered, the applicant must show that the new evidence could not reasonably have been obtained before trial and that such evidence would *probably* have changed the result; the test is less stringent than that in a similar motion before an appellate court.

Setting Aside or Varying Orders — Obtaining Other Relief — rule 59.06(2)(d)

Lesyork Holdings Ltd. v. Munden Acres Ltd. (1976), 13 O.R. (2d) 430, 1 C.P.C. 261 (C.A.).

The court may vary a judgment of specific performance and award damages.

Setting Aside or Varying Orders — Solicitor's Lack of Authority

Atkins v. Holubeshen (1984), 43 C.P.C. 166 (Ont. H.C.), affirmed (1985), 50 C.P.C. 94 (Ont. Div. Ct.), affirmed (1986), 23 C.P.C. (2d) 192 (Ont. C.A.).

A consent *ex parte* order dismissing an action pursuant to an agreement between counsel as to the time for fulfilling certain undertakings was set aside two years later when the plaintiff first learned of the order, pursuant to the predecessor of this provision and the court's inherent jurisdiction.

Thomson v. Gough (1977), 17 O.R. (2d) 420, 5 C.P.C. 43, 80 D.L.R. (3d) 598 (H.C.).

A consent order dismissing an action will not be set aside after issuance on the ground of the solicitor's lack of authority.

Johnston v. Nelson, [1965] 2 O.R. 556, 51 D.L.R. (2d) 386 (H.C.).

Where a solicitor agrees to a settlement without the authority of his client, a judgment based on such purported settlement may be set aside.

Setting Aside or Varying Orders — Miscellaneous

Hussein v. Sharif (1994), 30 C.P.C. (3d) 223, 6 R.F.L. (4th) 105 (Ont. U.F.C.).

The court refused a request to amend retroactively an order, prior to its issue and entry, where the purpose of the request was to ensure that a right of appeal still existed. It was for the appellate court to determine the commencement of the relevant appeal period.

Bakshi v. Kouretsos (1993), 21 C.P.C. (3d) 70 (Ont. Gen. Div.).

The court will not vary postjudgment interest after judgment except in unusual circumstances or in cases of error arising from accidental slip, omission or fraud.

Gray Estate v. Winkfield (1992), 4 W.D.C.P. (2d) 4 (Ont. Gen. Div.).

The trial judge varied a judgment after it had been issued and entered to provide that the plaintiff executor was liable for costs in his personal capacity.

Hanil Bank Canada v. Maria's Fashion Place (Edmonton) Ltd. (1992), 9 O.R. (3d) 799, 10 C.P.C. (3d) 295 (Master).

The court does not have jurisdiction to amend a judgment registered in Ontario under the *Reciprocal Enforcement of Judgments Act*, R.S.O. 1990, c. R.5, notwithstanding s. 4(b) of the Act.

Strelchuk v. Vella (1990), 44 C.P.C. (2d) 172 (Ont. Dist. Ct.).

The court refused to reconsider an issued and entered judgment in the absence of fraud or clerical error. The fact that costs were reserved in the judgment did not alter its finality.

A.H. Al-Sagar & Brothers Engineering Project Co. v. Al-Jabouri (1989), 46 C.P.C. (2d) 69 (Ont. H.C.).

A motion to set aside a High Court judgment on grounds of new evidence should be brought in the High Court rather than the Court of Appeal. It is not necessary to bring the motion before the trial judge.

Formglas Inc. v. Plasterform Inc. (1989), 34 C.P.C. (2d) 27, additional reasons 17 W.D.C.P. 26 (Ont. H.C.), leave to appeal to Ont. Div. Ct. granted (September 29, 1989), Doc. No. Toronto 29840/88.

The court has no jurisdiction to declare the intention of or interpret a previous order.

McCraw v. Dresser Can. Inc. (1987), 60 O.R. (2d) 154, 19 C.P.C. (2d) 26 (H.C.).

Where a plaintiff's solicitor had failed to comply with an order made on a status hearing, and the failure was due to inadvertence, the plaintiff was permitted to restore the matter to the trial list.

Sandwich West (Twp.) v. Bubu Estates Ltd. (1986), 56 O.R. (2d) 147, 12 C.P.C. (2d) 169, 30 D.L.R. (4th) 477, 17 O.A.C. 177 (C.A.).

Where a consent judgment had purported to bind non-parties who had rights independent of the defendants, the judgment was varied to delete references to non-parties.

Theofanous v. Commercial Union Assurance Co. of Can. (1986), 11 C.P.C. (2d) 70, 22 C.C.L.I. 24 (Ont. Dist. Ct.).

The court has discretion to set aside a judgment after it has been signed and entered and satisfaction acknowledged, and did so when counsel were mistaken as to the basis and effect of the settlement which resulted in the judgment.

Murray-Jensen Mfg. Ltd. v. Triangle Conduit & Cable (1968) Ltd. (1984), 46 C.P.C. 285 (Ont. H.C.).

The court amended a judgment directing a reference to limit recovery to the amount claimed in the statement of claim where the amount found due on the reference was in excess of that amount and the defendants may have acted differently if the amount claimed had been greater.

R.A.M.S. Invts. Ltd. v. Blantax Mgmt. Services Can. Ltd. (1984), 44 C.P.C. 1 (Ont. Co. Ct.).

The court varied a judgment by striking out the provisions for payment out of court of the moneys in issue, after learning of a prior "stop order".

Chitel v. Rothbart; Rothbart v. Chitel (1984), 42 C.P.C. 217 (Ont. Master), affirmed (1985), 2 C.P.C. (2d) xlix (Ont. Div. Ct.), leave to appeal to Ont. C.A. refused 15 C.P.C. (2d) xlviii.

A consent order is a contract and can only be varied by subsequent consent or on any ground which would invalidate a contract.

Yared Realty Ltd. v. Topalovic (1981), 45 C.P.C. 189 (Ont. H.C.).

The trial judge amended his judgment to award costs against certain non-parties on whose behalf the action was brought, where the successful defendant had been unable to collect the award of costs from the plaintiff who had become bankrupt.

Ont. Securities Comm. v. Turbo Resources Ltd. (1983), 33 C.P.C. 50 (Ont. H.C.).

The court refused to vary a mandatory order that was issued and entered a year before, requiring the officers and directors of the defendant to carry out a transaction, where there was no fraud, slip or error in expressing the court's intention.

Braithwaite v. Haugh (1978), 19 O.R. (2d) 288, 84 D.L.R. (3d) 590 (Co. Ct.).

Where the insurers of the plaintiff had obtained judgment for their subrogated claim for property damages and the plaintiff was then unaware of the effect such judgment would have on his action for personal injuries, the judgment was set aside.

Lesyork Holdings Ltd. v. Munden Acres Ltd. (1976), 13 O.R. (2d) 430, 1 C.P.C. 261 (C.A.).

Relief may not be granted for a cause of action which has arisen subsequent to the issuance of the judgment.

Goodman Invts. Ltd. v. Abraham (1976), 1 C.P.C. 258 (Ont. H.C.).

A mistake avoidable through reasonable diligence is not a ground for variation of an order after entry.

SATISFACTION OF ORDER

59.07 A party may acknowledge satisfaction of an order in a document signed by the party before a witness, and the document may be filed and entered in the court office where the order was entered.

Heitman Financial Services Ltd. v. Towncliff Properties Ltd. (1981), 35 O.R. (2d) 189, 24 C.P.C. 116 (H.C.).

A satisfaction piece given to some but not all defendants does not constitute a release of all defendants.

McClelland v. McClelland, [1972] 1 O.R. 236, 6 R.F.L. 91, 22 D.L.R. (3d) 624 (H.C.).

Discussion of attack on satisfaction piece.

RULE 60   ENFORCEMENT OF ORDERS

Highlights

This Rule on the enforcement of "orders" (a generic term defined to include judgments: rule 1.03) is composed of three parts. The first is a convenient catalogue of the various methods of enforcing different types of orders (rules 60.02-60.05). In the second part, various methods of enforcement (*i.e.* the writ of seizure and sale, garnishment, writ of sequestration, writ of possession, contempt order) are each dealt with in detail (rules 60.07-60.11). The third part consists of a miscellaneous group of provisions dealing with the role of the sheriff, examinations in aid of execution and the costs of enforcement (rules 60.13-60.19).

Writ of seizure and sale. A return of a *nulla bona* is no longer required as a prerequisite to a sale of land under a writ of seizure and sale (*cf.* former Rule 563) and a creditor need no longer wait twelve months before resorting to the sale of land (see former Rule 561): a sale of land may be held six months after the writ is filed with the sheriff (rule 60.07(18)), but the sale procedure may not be set in motion until four months after the writ is filed (rule 60.07(17)). These changes give effect to the recommendations of the Ontario Law Reform Commission's *Report on The Enforcement of Judgment, Debts and Related Matters* (1981), Part III, c. 2.

To aid the sheriff in determining how much money he or she has to raise, the creditor must provide to him or her as part of the direction to enforce detailed information as to the amount of the order, the amount and date of any payment, the rate of postjudgment interest where payable and the costs of enforcement: rule 60.07(13). Where an execution creditor has filed a writ of seizure and sale with the sheriff and he or she thereafter receives payment from a debtor, the creditor must give the sheriff notice of the payment forthwith: rule 60.16(1). Where an order is satisfied in full, the creditor is obligated to withdraw all writs relating to that order from the sheriff's office: rule 60.16(2).

The writ of seizure and sale must give the creditor's address (in addition to that of any solicitor filing the writ) and when the time for renewal is approaching, the sheriff is to direct the notice of expiration to the creditor rather than to the solicitor: rule 60.07(7). This is a useful change since this event will take place six years after the filing of the writ, when the solicitor-client relationship may have terminated. Changes of address by the creditor or the solicitor may be recorded under rule 60.07(12.1).

Garnishment. The most significant change in Rule 60 from the former practice has to do with two modifications to the garnishment procedure.

First, the procedure does not require an initial court application for a garnishment order: the procedure begins with the administrative act of the registrar issuing a notice of garnishment: rule 60.08(4) and (6). However, pursuant to a 1990 amendment, leave is required if six years or more has elapsed since the date of the order or if its enforcement is conditional.

Second, garnishment is "continuing" in the sense that it catches not only debts immediately due and owing, but also most future debts: rule 60.08(4)(e), (11), (12) and (13). Consequently, the relevant form (Form 60H Notice of Garnishment) has been modified to provide for a series of payments by the garnishee (*e.g.* from the debtor's wages or salary). This new garnishment procedure is also based on recommendations made in the Ontario Law Reform Commission's *Report, supra*, Part II, c. 3.

Since 1989, the Ontario Crown is subject to garnishment proceedings. Formerly the Crown was subject to garnishment proceedings only for orders for support or maintenance. Special procedures apply to garnishment proceedings against the Crown and are set out in R.R.O. 1990, Regulation 940 under the *Proceedings Against the Crown Act*.

A 1996 amendment to rule 60.08 clarifies that a notice of garnishment may name only one debtor and only one garnishee.

Sheriffs. When a writ has been fully executed or has expired, the sheriff is not required to return it to the registrar's office: rule 60.15. Specific provision is made for a motion for directions to the court, by the sheriff or any interested person, where questions arise in relation to the measures to be taken by the sheriff in the course of execution: rule 60.17.

Examination in aid of execution. This is the new name for judgment debtor examinations. The scope of such examinations is broadly stated (rule 60.18(2)), and the persons who may be examined, in addition to the judgment debtor, are broadly defined: rule 60.18(6).

Costs of enforcement. A deficiency in the former law is remedied by rule 60.19 which entitles a party enforcing an order to certain postjudgment enforcement costs.

Former Rules: Rules 2(j) and (k), 540-606.

DEFINITIONS

60.01 In rules 60.02 to 60.19,
"creditor" means a person who is entitled to enforce an order for the payment or recovery of money;
"debtor" means a person against whom an order for the payment or recovery of money may be enforced.

ENFORCEMENT OF ORDER FOR PAYMENT OR RECOVERY OF MONEY

General
60.02(1) In addition to any other method of enforcement provided by law, an order for the payment or recovery of money may be enforced by,
    (a) a writ of seizure and sale (Form 60A) under rule 60.07;
    (b) garnishment under rule 60.08;
    (c) a writ of sequestration (Form 60B) under rule 60.09; and
    (d) the appointment of a receiver.

Recovery of Costs without Order Awarding Costs
(2) Where under these rules a party is entitled to costs on the basis of a certificate of assessment of costs without an order awarding costs, and the costs are not paid within seven days after the certificate of assessment of costs is signed, the party may enforce payment of the costs by the means set out in subrule (1) on filing with the registrar an affidavit setting out the basis of entitlement to costs and attaching a copy of the certificate of assessment.

Cross-Reference: See cases under rule 41.02 regarding appointment of a receiver by way of execution.

Tintner v. Tintner, [1968] 1 O.R. 538 (Master).

An order for interim alimony may be enforced notwithstanding other remedies provided in the Rules.

ENFORCEMENT OF ORDER FOR POSSESSION OF LAND

60.03 An order for the recovery or delivery of the possession of land may be enforced by a writ of possession (Form 60C) under rule 60.10.

ENFORCEMENT OF ORDER FOR RECOVERY OF PERSONAL PROPERTY

60.04(1) An order for the recovery of possession of personal property other than money may be enforced by a writ of delivery (Form 60D), which may be obtained on filing with the registrar where the proceeding was commenced a requisition together with a copy of the order as entered.

(2) Where the property is not delivered up under a writ of delivery, the order may be enforced by a writ of sequestration (Form 60B) under rule 60.09. [am. O. Reg. 396/91, s. 11]

ENFORCEMENT OF ORDER TO DO OR ABSTAIN FROM DOING ANY ACT

60.05 An order requiring a person to do an act, other than the payment of money, or to abstain from doing an act, may be enforced against the person refusing or neglecting to obey the order by a contempt order under rule 60.11.

Cross-Reference: See cases under rule 60.11.

Re Leponiemi and Leponiemi (1982), 35 O.R. (2d) 440, 25 C.P.C. 240, 26 R.F.L. (2d) 320, 132 D.L.R. (3d) 701 (C.A.).

The Court of Appeal doubted that an order requiring the police to enforce a custody order should be made *ex parte.*

ENFORCEMENT BY OR AGAINST A PERSON NOT A PARTY

60.06(1) An order that is made for the benefit of a person who is not a party may be enforced by that person in the same manner as if the person were a party.

(2) An order that may be enforced against a person who is not a party may be enforced against that person in the same manner as if the person were a party.

WRIT OF SEIZURE AND SALE

Where Available Without Leave
60.07(1) Where an order may be enforced by a writ of seizure and sale, the creditor is entitled to the issue of one or more writs of seizure and sale

(Form 60A), on filing with the registrar where the proceeding was commenced a requisition setting out,

(a) the date and amount of any payment received since the order was made; and

(b) the amount owing and the rate of postjudgment interest,

together with a copy of the order as entered and any other evidence necessary to establish the amount awarded and the creditor's entitlement.

Where Leave is Required

(2) If six years or more have elapsed since the date of the order, or if its enforcement is subject to a condition, a writ of seizure and sale shall not be issued unless leave of the court is first obtained.

(3) An order granting leave to issue a writ of seizure and sale ceases to have effect if the writ is not issued within one year after the date of the order granting leave, but the court may grant leave again on a subsequent motion.

Order for Payment into Court

(4) Where an order is for the payment of money into court, the writ of seizure and sale shall contain a notice that all money realized by the sheriff under the writ is to be paid into court.

Order for Payment at Future Time

(5) Where an order is for payment at or after a specified future time, the writ of seizure and sale shall not be issued until after the expiration of that time.

Duration and Renewal

(6) A writ of seizure and sale remains in force for six years from the date of its issue and for a further six years from each renewal.

(7) Where a writ of seizure and sale is filed with a sheriff, the sheriff shall, not less than thirty days nor more than sixty days before expiration of the writ, mail a notice of its expiration to the creditor, at the address shown on the writ or the most recent request to renew it.

(8) A writ of seizure and sale that is filed with a sheriff may be renewed before its expiration by filing a request to renew (Form 60E) with the sheriff, and the sheriff shall endorse on the writ a memorandum stating the date of its renewal.

(9) A writ of seizure and sale that is not filed with a sheriff may be renewed before its expiration by filing with the registrar who issued it a requisition to renew the writ and the registrar shall endorse on the writ a memorandum stating the date of its renewal.

Change or Variation of Debtor's Name

(10) Where a debtor named in a writ of seizure and sale,

(a) changes his, her or its name after the writ is issued;

(b) uses an alias; or

(c) uses a variation of spelling of the name,

the creditor may on motion made without notice seek a change or variation to the writ.

(11) On a motion referred to in subrule (10), the court may order the sheriff to,

(a) amend the writ by adding the words "now or also known as", followed by the new name of the debtor, the alias or the spelling variation;

(b) amend the index of writs to show the new name, the alias or the spelling variation; and

(c) if a copy of the writ was sent to the land registrar for filing under the *Land Titles Act*, send a copy of the amended writ to the land registrar.

Writ to Bear Creditor's Address

(12) Every writ of seizure and sale shall bear the name and address of the creditor and the creditor's solicitor, if any.

Change of Address

(12.1) If the address of the creditor or the creditor's solicitor changes after the writ is issued, the creditor may have the new address noted on the writ by filing a requisition to that effect with the sheriff.

Authors' Comment. This amendment places the obligation on the creditor to keep the address on the filed writ current. In the absence of any change of address, the sheriff will mail the notice of expiration of the writ as provided in rule 60.07(7) (address shown on the writ).

Direction to Enforce

(13) A creditor who has filed a writ of seizure and sale with a sheriff may file with the sheriff a direction to enforce (Form 60F) setting out,

(a) the date of the order and the amount awarded;

(b) the rate of postjudgment interest payable;

(c) the costs of enforcement to which the creditor is entitled under rule 60.19;

(d) the date and amount of any payment received since the order was made; and

(e) the amount owing, including postjudgment interest,

and directing the sheriff to enforce the writ for the amount owing, subsequent interest and the sheriff's fees and expenses.

Property in Hands of Receiver

(14) A writ of seizure and sale shall not be enforced against property in the hands of a receiver appointed by a court.

Seizure of Personal Property

(15) Where personal property is seized under a writ of seizure and sale, the sheriff shall, on request, deliver an inventory of the property seized to the debtor or the debtor's agent or employee before or, where this is not practicable, within a reasonable time after the property is removed from the premises on which it was seized.

Sale of Personal Property

(16) Personal property seized under a writ of seizure and sale shall not be sold by the sheriff unless notice of the time and place of the sale has been,

(a) mailed to the creditor at the address shown on the writ or the creditor's solicitor and to the debtor at the debtor's last known address, at least ten days before the sale; and

(b) published in a newspaper of general circulation in the place where the property was seized.

Sale of Land

(17) A creditor may not take any step to sell land under a writ of seizure and sale until four months after the writ was filed with the sheriff or, where the writ has been withdrawn, four months after the writ was re-filed.

(18) No sale of land under a writ of seizure and sale may be held until six months after the writ was filed with the sheriff or, where the writ has been withdrawn, six months after the writ was re-filed.

(19) A sale of land shall not be held under a writ of seizure and sale unless notice of the time and place of sale has been,

(a) mailed to the creditor at the address shown on the writ or to the creditor's solicitor and to the debtor at the debtor's last known address, at least thirty days before the sale;

(b) published in *The Ontario Gazette* once at least thirty days before the sale and in a newspaper of general circulation in the place where the land is situate, once each week for two successive weeks, the last notice to be published not less than one week nor more than three weeks before the date of sale; and

(c) posted in a conspicuous place in the sheriff's office for at least thirty days before the sale.

(20) The notice shall set out,

(a) a short description of the property to be sold;

(b) the short title of the proceeding;

(c) the time and place of the intended sale; and

(d) the name of the debtor whose interest is to be sold.

(21) The sheriff may adjourn a sale to a later date where the sheriff considers it necessary in order to realize the best price that can be obtained in all the circumstances, and where the sale is adjourned, it may be conducted on the later date with such further notice, if any, as the sheriff considers advisable.

(22) Where notice of a sale of land under a writ of seizure and sale is published in *The Ontario Gazette* before the writ expires, the sale may be completed by a sale and transfer of the land after the writ expires.

Abortive Sale

(23) Where personal property or land seized under a writ of seizure and sale remains unsold for want of buyers, the sheriff shall notify the creditor of the date and place of the attempted sale and of any other relevant circumstances.

(24) On receipt of a notice under subrule (23), the creditor may instruct the sheriff in writing to sell the personal property or land in such manner as the sheriff considers will realize the best price that can be obtained. [am. O. Regs. 396/91, s. 12; 770/92, s. 14; 739/94, s. 5]

Writ of Seizure and Sale — Generally

Re Sicurella (1987), 60 O.R. (2d) 260, 19 C.P.C. (2d) 243, 65 C.B.R. (N.S.) 81, 40 D.L.R. (4th) 188 (S.C.).

A motion to vacate a writ of execution must be brought before the court out of which the execution issued. A bankruptcy court judge has no jurisdiction to vacate an execution issued in District Court.

C.I.B.C. v. Sheahen (1978), 22 O.R. (2d) 686, 94 D.L.R. (3d) 576 (Div. Ct.).

A writ of seizure and sale, like other writs, enjoys an existence independent of the judgment to which it relates. Consequently a writ of execution can be allowed to remain in force, with proceedings thereunder stayed, as a term of an order setting aside a judgment.

Seel Enterprises Ltd. v. McArthur, [1962] O.W.N. 7 (Master).

Where an action on the covenant in a mortgage was stayed after judgment upon payment of arrears, the writ of *fi. fa.* was ordered to be withdrawn.

Schipper v. Linkon Co., [1957] O.W.N. 481, 11 D.L.R. (2d) 283 (H.C.).

The court has no inherent power to delay the issuance of a writ of seizure and sale.

Writ of Seizure and Sale — Priorities

Central Guaranty Trust Co. v. Sudbury (City) (1992), 8 O.R. (3d) 565 (Gen. Div.).

A judgment creditor who files an execution against land after the sale of the land under power of sale is not entitled to share in the proceeds of sale.

Wright v. Canada (A.G.), 62 O.R. (2d) 737, 23 C.P.C. (2d) 218, 67 C.B.R. (N.S.) 93, 13 R.F.L. (3d) 343, 36 C.R.R. 361, [1988] 1 C.T.C. 107, 88 D.T.C. 6041, 46 D.L.R. (4th) 182, 26 O.A.C. 372 (Div. Ct.).

An execution filed by the federal Crown was held to take priority over a charging order under s. 146 of the *Judicature Act* based on a claim for arrears under a support judgment.

Young v. Le Mon (1985), 3 C.P.C. (2d) 163 (Ont. Dist. Ct.).

A writ of seizure and sale is subordinate to an unregistered trust agreement made prior to the issuance of the writ.

Leave to Issue Writ of Seizure and Sale — rule 60.07(2)

Scott v. Scott (1981), 19 C.P.C. 184 (Ont. H.C.).

The court refused to grant leave to issue execution for arrears of support where the applicant had not been misled and her failure for three years to act indicated a lack of need.

United Brotherhood of Carpenters and Joiners of Amer., Local 3054 v. Cassin-Remco Ltd. (1979), 11 C.P.C. 116 (Ont. H.C.).

Having issued execution against the employer, a union has status to bring a motion to issue execution against a person found to be a "successor employer" under the *Labour Relations Act*.

Shmegilsky v. Slobodzian, [1964] 1 O.R. 633 (Master).

Leave will be granted where it is shown that the judgment was obtained within the relevant limitation period, that it remains unsatisfied, and that the writ may be properly enforced against the judgment debtor personally; there is no jurisdiction to refuse leave on equitable grounds.

Duration and Renewal of Writ of Seizure and Sale — rule 60.07(6)

McLay v. Molock (1993), 21 C.P.C. (3d) 189 (Ont. Gen. Div.).

Where a writ of execution had not been renewed due to inadvertence, the court granted leave to issue an *alias* writ.

Smyth v. Toronto Dominion Bank (1989), 35 C.P.C. (2d) 256, 75 C.B.R. (N.S.) 147 (Ont. H.C.).

Neither the *Bankruptcy Act* nor the Rules require a judgment creditor to withdraw a writ of seizure and sale which is extinguished by operation of law when the debtor is discharged in bankruptcy.

Colombe v. Caughell (1985), 52 O.R. (2d) 767, 6 C.P.C. (2d) 314 (Dist. Ct.).

An *alias* writ of seizure and sale may be issued if the original writ is not renewed within the six-year period.

Weiner v. Persin, [1962] O.W.N. 117, 3 C.B.R. (N.S.) 290, affirmed 9 C.B.R. (N.S.) 320n (S.C.).

An execution issued before an assignment in bankruptcy cannot be enforced after the judgment debtor is discharged from bankruptcy. The debt must be proved in bankruptcy.

Peterboro Dist. Co-op. Services v. Raison, [1960] O.W.N. 495 (Master).

The court will rarely renew a writ out of time but may issue an *alias* writ in such circumstances.

Re Solicitor, [1959] O.W.N. 8 (Master).

Where a writ is not renewed before it expires, an *alias* writ may be issued. Discussion of supporting material.

Zacks v. Glazier, [1945] O.W.N. 205 (Master).

An *ex parte* motion for leave to issue an *alias* writ to replace an expired writ was refused where the writ had lapsed through an oversight and the defendants were available to be served.

Douglas v. Hannah (1920), 18 O.W.N. 397 (H.C.).

The writ expires at the end of the day before the anniversary date of its issuance.

Direction to Enforce — rule 60.07(13)

Leboeuf v. Downing (1991), 4 C.P.C. (3d) 174 (Ont. Gen. Div.).

On a motion for directions regarding the sale of real estate pursuant to a writ of seizure and sale, the court held that the judgment creditor need not certify to the sheriff whether or not the property is a matrimonial home.

Seizure of Personal Property — rule 60.07(15)

Re Bishop and Traders Finance Corp. Ltd., [1966] 2 O.R. 343, 56 D.L.R. (3d) 685 (C.A.).
Discussion of actual and "walking" possession.

Robinson v. Robinson, [1965] 1 O.R. 326, 7 C.B.R. (N.S.) 209, 48 D.L.R. (2d) 42 (C.A.).

A judgment debtor should challenge a seizure by a motion in the action rather than an originating motion.

Sale of Personal Property — rule 60.07(16)

Maple Leaf Lumber Co. v. Caldbick and Pierce (1917), 40 O.L.R. 512 (C.A.).

Where a sheriff is negligent in disposing of chattels at a low price, the sale is not invalid but the sheriff is liable to the judgment creditor.

Sale of Land

Zingone v. Zingone (1986), 53 O.R. (2d) 411, 7 C.P.C. (2d) 113, 38 R.P.R. 106, 25 D.L.R. (4th) 416 (H.C.).

Where an execution was satisfied after the sheriff had accepted a bid to purchase real estate owned by the judgment debtor but before the sale transaction had been completed, the sheriff was held not to be obliged to complete the transaction.

GARNISHMENT

Where Available

60.08(1) A creditor under an order for the payment or recovery of money may enforce it by garnishment of debts payable to the debtor by other persons.

Where Leave Required

(2) If six years or more have elapsed since the date of the order, or if its enforcement is subject to a condition, a notice of garnishment shall not be issued unless leave of the court is first obtained.

(3) An order granting leave to issue a notice of garnishment ceases to have effect if the notice is not issued within one year after the date of the order granting leave, but the court may grant leave again on a subsequent motion.

Obtaining Notice of Garnishment

(4) A creditor under an order for the payment or recovery of money who seeks to enforce it by garnishment shall file with the registrar where the proceeding was commenced a requisition for garnishment (Form 60G) together with a copy of the order as entered, any other evidence necessary to establish the amount awarded and the creditor's entitlement, and an affidavit stating,

(a) the date and amount of any payment received since the order was made;

(b) the amount owing, including postjudgment interest;

(c) details of how the amount owing and the postjudgment interest are calculated;

(c.1) the address of the debtor;

(d) the name and address of each person to whom a notice of garnishment is to be directed;

(e) that the creditor believes that those persons are or will become indebted to the debtor and the grounds for the belief;

(f) such particulars of the debts as are known to the creditor;

(g) where a person to whom a notice of garnishment is to be directed is not in Ontario, that the debtor is entitled to sue that person in Ontario to recover the debt, and the basis of entitlement to sue in Ontario; and

(h) where a person to whom a notice of garnishment is to be directed is not then indebted but will become indebted to the debtor, such particulars of the date on and the circumstances under which the debt will arise as are known to the creditor. [am. O. Reg. 535/92, s. 13]

(5) The affidavit required by subrule (4) may contain statements of the deponent's information and belief, if the source of the information and the fact of the belief are specified in the affidavit.

(6) On the filing of the requisition and affidavit required by subrule (4), the registrar shall issue notices of garnishment (Form 60H) naming as garnishees the persons named in the affidavit and shall send a copy of each notice of garnishment to the sheriff of the county in which the debtor resides or, if the debtor resides outside Ontario, to the sheriff of the county in which the proceeding was commenced.

(6.1) A notice of garnishment issued under subrule (6) shall name one debtor and one garnishee.

Service of Notice of Garnishment

(7) The creditor shall serve the notice of garnishment,

(a) on the debtor, together with a copy of the affidavit required by subrule (4); and

(b) on the garnishee, with a blank garnishee's statement (Form 60I) attached.

(8) The notice of garnishment shall be served by ordinary mail, or by personal service or an alternative to personal service under rule 16.03.

(9) A notice of garnishment may be served outside Ontario if the debtor would be entitled to sue the garnishee in Ontario to recover the debt.

(10) Where the garnishee is a bank, loan or trust corporation, credit union, caisse populaire or the Province of Ontario Savings Office, the garnishee shall be served at the branch at which the debt is payable.

Garnishee Liable from Time of Service

(11) The garnishee is liable to pay to the sheriff any debt of the garnishee to the debtor, up to the amount shown in the notice of garnishment or supplementary notice of garnishment, less $10 for the cost of making each payment, within ten days after service on the garnishee or ten days after the debt becomes payable, whichever is later.

(12) For the purposes of subrule (11), a debt of the garnishee to the debtor includes a debt payable at the time the notice of garnishment is served and a debt,

(a) payable within six years after the notice is served; or

(b) payable on the fulfilment of a condition within six years after the notice is served.

(13) For the purposes of subrule (11), a debt of the garnishee to the debtor does not include,

(a) if the garnishee is a bank, loan or trust corporation, credit union, caisse populaire or the Province of Ontario Savings Office, money in an account opened after the notice of garnishment is served;

(b) if the garnishee is an employer, a debt arising out of employment that commences after the notice is served; or

(c) if the garnishee is an insurer, a debt payable under an insurance policy that is entered into after the notice is served.

Payment by Garnishee to Sheriff

(14) A garnishee who admits owing a debt to the debtor shall pay it to the sheriff in the manner prescribed by the notice of garnishment, subject to section 7 of the *Wages Act.*

Garnishee Must Serve Statement to Dispute Garnishment

(15) A garnishee who wishes for any reason to dispute the garnishment or who pays to the sheriff less than the amount set out in the notice of garnishment as owing by the garnishee to the debtor shall, within ten days after service of the notice of garnishment, serve on the creditor and the debtor and file with the court a garnishee's statement (Form 60I) setting out the particulars.

Garnishment Hearing

(16) On motion by a creditor, debtor, garnishee or any other interested person, the court may,

(a) where it is alleged that the debt of the garnishee to the debtor has been assigned or encumbered, order the assignee or encumbrancer to appear and state the nature and particulars of the claim;

(b) determine the rights and liabilities of the garnishee, the debtor and any assignee or encumbrancer;

(c) vary or suspend periodic payments under a notice of garnishment; or

(d) determine any other matter in relation to a notice of garnishment, and the court may proceed in a summary manner, but where the motion is made to a master and raises a genuine issue of fact or of law, it shall be adjourned to be heard by a judge.

Enforcement against Garnishee

(17) Where the garnishee does not pay to the sheriff the amount set out in the notice of garnishment as owing by the garnishee to the debtor and does not serve and file a garnishee's statement, the creditor is entitled on motion to the court, on notice to the garnishee, to an order against the garnishee for payment of the amount that the court finds is payable to the debtor by the garnishee, or the amount set out in the notice, whichever is less.

Payment by Garnishee to Person other than Sheriff

(18) Where, after service of a notice of garnishment, the garnishee pays a debt attached by the notice to a person other than the sheriff, the garnishee remains liable to pay the debt in accordance with the notice.

Payment to Sheriff Discharges Garnishee
   (19) **Payment of a debt by a garnishee in accordance with a notice of garnishment is a valid discharge of the debt, as between the garnishee and the debtor, to the extent of the payment, including the amount deducted for the cost of making payment under subrule (11).**

Creditor to Give Notice when Order Satisfied
   (20) **When the amount owing under an order that is enforced by garnishment has been paid, the creditor shall forthwith serve a notice of termination of garnishment (Form 60J) on the garnishee and on the sheriff. [am. O. Reg. 534/95, s. 2]**

Cross-Reference: See s. 143.1 of the *Courts of Justice Act* regarding restrictions on garnishing amounts paid under the *Family Benefits Act* or the *General Welfare Assistance Act.*

Garnishment — Generally

Wayfarer Holidays Ltd. v. Hoteles Barcelo (1993), 12 O.R. (3d) 208, 18 C.P.C. (3d) 36 (Gen. Div.).
The court has an equitable discretion whether or not to make a garnishee order. The court will not order a garnishee to pay money to a judgment creditor where the payment would leave the garnishee liable to an action to recover the same debt in a foreign court to whose jurisdiction the garnishee is subject.

Hong Kong Bank of Canada v. Slesers (1992), 7 O.R. (3d) 117, 7 C.P.C. (3d) 27 (Gen. Div.).
Where the debtor was a physician receiving payments from OHIP, which were not exempt from attachment under the *Wages Act*, the court nevertheless permitted the debtor to retain 62 per cent of his fees earned.

Director of Support & Custody Enforcement v. Jones (1991), 5 O.R. (3d) 499, 3 C.P.C. (3d) 206, 37 R.F.L. (3d) 282, 85 D.L.R. (4th) 375, 52 O.A.C. 47 (Div. Ct.).
A judgment creditor may not garnishee a bank account held jointly by the judgment debtor and a non-party. *Empire Fertilizers Ltd. v. Cioci*, [1934] O.W.N. 535 (C.A.) not followed.

Director of Support & Custody Enforcement v. Galea (1990), 50 C.P.C. (2d) 85 (Ont. Prov. Div.).
Discussion of grounds to dispute garnishment.

Director of Support & Custody Enforcement v. Drosos (1988), 27 C.P.C. (2d) 23 (Ont. Fam. Ct.).
Garnishment is entirely a creature of the Rules and has no common law ancestry.

Jewell v. Ross (1987), 16 C.P.C. (2d) 46 (Ont. Dist. Ct.).
A judgment creditor is entitled to enforce an order against a garnishee obtained under rule 60.08(12) notwithstanding the subsequent bankruptcy of the judgment debtor.

Kucherepa v. Guse (1985), 6 C.P.C. (2d) 16 (Ont. Dist. Ct.).
The solicitor for the creditor may make the affidavit required by rule 60.08(2).

Royal Bank v. Wheler (1985), 5 C.P.C. (2d) 278 (Ont. Master).

Rule 60.08 contemplates that the notice of garnishment [(Form 60H)] will contain a statement of the amount owing by the garnishee to the judgment debtor but [Form 60H] itself does not require such a statement. Where the garnishee was the employer of the judgment debtor and the judgment creditor did not know the amount owing by the garnishee and the garnishee did not respond to the notice of garnishment, the court made an order that the garnishee pay the entire amount of the judgment debt.

MacKinnon v. MacKinnon (1979), 14 C.P.C. 94, 3 Fam. L. Rev. 151 (Ont. Div. Ct.).

After a decree *nisi* obtained in another jurisdiction is filed with the Supreme Court Registrar, it becomes a judgment upon which garnishment may issue.

Garnishment of Particular Funds

Cadillac Fairview Corp. v. Grandma Lee's Ontario Inc. (1995), 6 W.D.C.P. (2d) 432 (Ont. Gen. Div.).

Rent jointly payable to a landlord by a lessee who was a judgment debtor and its sublessee who was a garnishee was held not to be subject to garnishment.

Kaufman v. Royal Bank (1994), 34 C.P.C. (3d) 334 (Ont. Small Cl. Ct.).

Where a judgment debtor cashes a cheque but does not deposit it in his account, a notice of garnishment directed to the bank does not affect the funds.

Stratton v. Jantree No. 15 Ltd. Partnership (1991), 4 C.P.C. (3d) 200 (Ont. Gen. Div.).

A deposit pledged by the debtor to the bank as security is not subject to garnishment.

Jantunen v. Ross (1991), 5 O.R. (3d) 433, 6 C.P.C. (3d) 218, 39 C.C.E.L. 93, 85 D.L.R. (4th) 461 (Div. Ct.).

Where the judgment debtor is a waiter and receives gratuities by way of credit card payments, the gratuities are subject to garnishment but 80 per cent are exempt from garnishment pursuant to the *Wages Act.*

Cram v. Bellman (1991), 2 O.R. (3d) 607, 35 C.C.E.L. 268 (*sub nom. Cram v. Rideau Group Realty Ltd.*) (Gen. Div.).

The commissions payable to a real estate salesperson are wages within the meaning of the *Wages Act,* and accordingly are subject to the 80 per cent exemption contained therein.

Dimosvki v. Director of Support & Custody Enforcement (1988), 17 R.F.L. (3d) 445 (Ont. Fam. Ct.).

A joint bank account is not subject to garnishment.

Director of Support & Custody Enforcement v. Drosos (1988), 27 C.P.C. (2d) 23 (Ont. Fam. Ct.).

Conditional debts such as prepayments by defendant insurance companies are subject to attachment.

Bank of N.S. v. Robson, 63 O.R. (2d) 159, 27 C.C.L.I. 167, [1988] I.L.R. 1-2281 (Dist. Ct.).

The cash surrender value of a life insurance policy owned by a judgment debtor is not subject to garnishment.

Westcoast Commodities Inc. v. Chen (1986), 55 O.R. (2d) 264, 9 C.P.C. (2d) 197, 28 D.L.R. (4th) 635 (H.C.).

Moneys standing in a joint bank account are not properly seizable to satisfy a judgment against one of the account holders.

Redpath Industries Ltd. v. Wibsco Building Products Ltd. (1986), 7 C.P.C. (2d) 297 (Ont. Dist. Ct.).

Where the judgment debtor was a salesman working on a commission basis who had obtained a draw from his employer against potential earnings, the court held that future commissions could be attached by the judgment creditor.

Etherden v. Etherden (1985), 52 O.R. (2d) 349, 6 C.P.C. (2d) 167, 48 R.F.L. (2d) 444 (U.F.C.).

Discussion of garnishment of Workers' Compensation benefits.

Bliss, Kirsh v. Doyle (1983), 44 O.R. (2d) 129, 39 C.P.C. 97, 48 C.B.R. (N.S.) 142, 16 E.T.R. 290, 3 D.L.R. (4th) 425 (H.C.).

Moneys held in a R.R.S.P. are trust funds and not subject to garnishment proceedings.

Blais v. Blais (1983), 43 O.R. (2d) 513, 41 C.P.C. 206, 36 R.F.L. (2d) 193 (Dist. Ct.).

A pensioner was not an employee and the benefits he received were not attachable under the *Family Law Reform Act.*

Garnishment — Priorities

Canada Mortgage & Housing Corp. v. Apostolou (1995), 22 O.R. (3d) 190, 9 P.P.S.A.C. (2d) 89 (Gen. Div.).

A notice of garnishment was held to have priority over an assignment of wages which had not been perfected under the *Personal Property Security Act* at the time the notice of garnishment was served.

Take-A-Break Coffee Service v. Raymond (1987), 26 C.P.C. (2d) 184 (Ont. Prov. Ct.).

Discussion of garnishee proceedings against the federal Crown where there are multiple executions from Ontario and Quebec.

Re Desjarlais and Desjarlais (1985), 52 O.R. (2d) 796, 5 C.P.C. (2d) 217, 48 R.F.L. (2d) 412 (Master).

A garnishee who employs a judgment debtor is not entitled to deduct from the judgment debtor's salary in priority to the rights of the judgment creditor amounts owing by the judgment debtor to the garnishee.

Brampton Brick Ltd. v. Viran Const. Ltd.; Vacca v. Brampton Brick Ltd. (1981), 21 C.P.C. 212 (Ont. Co. Ct.).

Where a joint debt is sought to be attached, the court should inquire into the respective rights of the joint owners of the debt, and only so much as is found belonging to the judgment debtor may be applied against the judgment debt.

Garnishment Involving Support Orders

Canadian Pacific Forest Products Ltd. v. Bjorklund (1993), 12 O.R. (3d) 596, 15 C.P.C. (3d) 155 (Gen. Div.).

A family support creditor is entitled to attach up to 50 per cent of the debtor's wages and an ordinary judgment creditor is entitled to garnishee only 20 per cent. Where less than 20 per cent is sufficient to satisfy the family support creditor, the ordinary judgment creditor is entitled only to the balance of the 20 per cent and the debtor is entitled to keep the remaining 80 per cent.

Director of Support & Custody Enforcement v. Villneff (1988), 27 C.P.C. (2d) 1 (Ont. Fam. Ct.).

In Provincial Court (Family Division) a debtor may file a dispute of garnishment proceedings in the court closest to his residence, and may file a change of venue motion with the dispute.

Swami v. Swami (1988), 26 C.P.C. (2d) 294, 13 R.F.L. (3d) 161 (Ont. Dist. Ct.).

Where the judgment debtor's employer deposited wages into the judgment debtor's bank account after deducting an amount garnished and the judgment creditor then seized the bank account, the court made an order permitting the judgment creditor to keep 50 per cent of his wages.

Blair (Cheetham) v. Blair (1985), 51 O.R. (2d) 126, 2 C.P.C. (2d) 318 (H.C.).

Where 50 per cent of the judgment debtor's wages were subject to garnishment because of an outstanding support order, rather than only 20 per cent which would otherwise have been attached, the court ordered that 30 per cent be paid to the support order creditor and that 20 per cent be distributed among all judgment creditors including the support order creditor.

Dubreuil v. Courjaud (1985), 51 O.R. (2d) 124, 2 C.P.C. (2d) 315 (H.C.).

Where the judgment debtor's wages were subject to garnishment only because a support order was outstanding against him, the court directed the funds be paid to the support order creditor only and not distributed among other judgment creditors.

Bank of N.S. v. Cameron (1985), 1 C.P.C. (2d) 18 (Ont. Prov. Ct.).

Where a garnishee receives notices of garnishment from both the Small Claims Court and the District Court priority should be given to the notice received first.

Dainard v. Dainard (1981), 22 C.P.C. 283 (Ont. Prov. Ct.).

Discussion of the collection of a support order in the Small Claims Court.

WRIT OF SEQUESTRATION

Leave Required

60.09(1) A writ of sequestration (Form 60B), directing a sheriff to take possession of and hold the property of a person against whom an order has been made and to collect and hold any income from the property until the person complies with the order, may be issued only with leave of the court, obtained on motion.

(2) The court may grant leave to issue a writ of sequestration only where it is satisfied that other enforcement measures are or are likely to be ineffective.

(3) In granting leave to issue a writ of sequestration, the court may order that the writ be enforced against all or part of the person's real and personal property.

Variation or Discharge

(4) The court on motion may discharge or vary a writ of sequestration on such terms as are just.

WRIT OF POSSESSION

Leave Required

60.10(1) A writ of possession (Form 60C) may be issued only with leave of the court, obtained on motion without notice or at the time an order entitling a party to possession is made.

(2) The court may grant leave to issue a writ of possession only where it is satisfied that all persons in actual possession of any part of the land have

received sufficient notice of the proceeding in which the order was obtained to have enabled them to apply to the court for relief.

Duration

(3) A writ of possession remains in force for one year from the date of the order authorizing its issue, and may, before its expiry, be renewed by order for a period of one year from each renewal.

Leave to Issue Writ of Possession

Can. Trustco Mortgage Co. v. McLean; Can. Permanent Trust Co. v. Newman (1983), 33 C.P.C. 117, 27 R.P.R. 131, 143 D.L.R. (3d) 101 (H.C.).

The plaintiff is entitled to leave to issue a writ of possession upon establishing that notice has been given. There is no discretion to refuse leave on the grounds of hardship.

Community Trust Co. v. Pollock (1982), 36 C.P.C. 227 (Ont. Master).

A spouse in possession of mortgaged premises must be a party defendant in proceedings for possession, by reason of the rights conferred by s. 43 of the *Family Law Reform Act.*

Kinross Mtge. Corp. v. Balfour (1981), 33 O.R. (2d) 213, 22 C.P.C. 161, 124 D.L.R. (3d) 137 (H.C.).

Leave to issue a writ of possession was refused where judgment for possession had not been obtained against a mortgagor.

Jamort (Invts.) Ltd. v. Fitzgerald, [1968] 1 O.R. 541 (Master).

Discussion of purpose of provision and nature of material which should be put before the master.

Duration of Writ of Possession — rule 60.10(3)

Re Metro. Toronto and Bremner (No. 2) (1980), 30 O.R. (2d) 385, 18 C.P.C. 179, 16 R.P.R. 147, 117 D.L.R. (3d) 621 (C.A.).

A writ of possession issued pursuant to the *Landlord and Tenant Act* was held not to expire after one year.

CONTEMPT ORDER

Motion for Contempt Order

60.11(1) A contempt order to enforce an order requiring a person to do an act, other than the payment of money, or to abstain from doing an act, may be obtained only on motion to a judge in the proceeding in which the order to be enforced was made.

(2) The notice of motion shall be served personally on the person against whom a contempt order is sought, and not by an alternative to personal service, unless the court orders otherwise.

(3) An affidavit in support of a motion for a contempt order may contain statements of the deponent's information and belief only with respect to facts that are not contentious, and the source of the information and the fact of the belief shall be specified in the affidavit.

Warrant for Arrest

(4) A judge may issue a warrant (Form 60K) for the arrest of the person against whom a contempt order is sought where the judge is of the opinion

that the person's attendance at the hearing is necessary in the interest of justice and it appears that the person is not likely to attend voluntarily.

Content of Order

(5) In disposing of a motion under subrule (1), the judge may make such order as is just, and where a finding of contempt is made, the judge may order that the person in contempt,

    (a) be imprisoned for such period and on such terms as are just;

    (b) be imprisoned if the person fails to comply with a term of the order;

    (c) pay a fine;

    (d) do or refrain from doing an act;

    (e) pay such costs as are just; and

    (f) comply with any other order that the judge considers necessary,

and may grant leave to issue a writ of sequestration under rule 60.09 against the person's property.

Where Corporation is in Contempt

(6) Where a corporation is in contempt, the judge may also make an order under subrule (5) against any officer or director of the corporation and may grant leave to issue a writ of sequestration under rule 60.09 against his or her property.

Warrant of Committal

(7) An order under subrule (5) for imprisonment may be enforced by the issue of a warrant of committal (Form 60L).

Discharging or Setting Aside Contempt Order

(8) On motion, a judge may discharge, set aside, vary or give directions in respect of an order under subrule (5) or (6) and may grant such other relief and make such other order as is just.

Order that Act be done by Another Person

(9) Where a person fails to comply with an order requiring the doing of an act, other than the payment of money, a judge on motion may, instead of or in addition to making a contempt order, order the act to be done, at the expense of the disobedient person, by the party enforcing the order or any other person appointed by the judge.

(10) The party enforcing the order and any person appointed by the judge are entitled to the costs of the motion under subrule (9) and the expenses incurred in doing the act ordered to be done, fixed by the judge or assessed by an assessment officer in accordance with Rule 58.

Authors' Note: Warrants of committal are enforced by the police, not the sheriff. For Metropolitan Toronto, the police officer responsible for court services can be reached through the 361 University Ave. courthouse, room 105.

Contempt Orders — Generally

McClure v. Backstein (1987), 17 C.P.C. (2d) 242 (Ont. H.C.).

Rule 60.11 does not violate the *Charter of Rights and Freedoms.*

R. v. B.E.S.T. Plating Shoppe Ltd. (1987), 59 O.R. (2d) 145, 19 C.P.C. (2d) 174, 1 C.E.L.R. (N.S.) 145, 32 C.C.C. (3d) 417, 21 O.A.C. 62 (C.A.).

Contempt proceedings must be conducted in accordance with the principles of fundamental justice, including the right to be presumed innocent until proven guilty beyond a reasonable doubt and to have a reasonable time to prepare a defence and to call witnesses. An alleged contemnor is entitled to the trial of an issue, on request, where facts are in dispute.

Olteanu v. Olteanu (1985), 3 C.P.C. (2d) 215, 47 R.F.L. (2d) 96 (Ont. H.C.).

The court may punish a person in default of an order for maintenance or support by a fine but not by imprisonment.

Re Seguin and Seguin (1979), 22 O.R. (2d) 649, 8 R.F.L. (2d) 388 (U.F.C.).

The Unified Family Court has no power to punish contempt regarding an order of the High Court.

Bee Chemical Co. v. Plastic Paint & Finish Specialties Ltd. (1978), 9 C.P.C. 100 (Ont. H.C.).

This jurisdiction may be exercised by a judge of the High Court where a judgment of that court is under appeal and not stayed.

Re R. and Monette (1975), 10 O.R. (2d) 762, 28 C.C.C. (2d) 409, 64 D.L.R. (3d) 470 (H.C.).

Only superior courts have inherent jurisdiction to deal with contempt not in the face of the court. Such proceedings are quasi-criminal and must be proved beyond a reasonable doubt.

Can. Metal Co. v. C.B.C. (No. 2) (1975), 4 O.R. (2d) 585, 19 C.C.C. (2d) 218, 48 D.L.R. (3d) 641 (H.C.), affirmed 11 O.R. (2d) 167, 29 C.C.C. (2d) 325, 65 D.L.R. (3d) 231 (C.A.).

Misconduct must be proved beyond a reasonable doubt.

Contempt Orders — Procedural Matters

Ontario (Attorney General) v. Paul Magder Furs Ltd. (1992), 12 O.R. (3d) 72 (Gen. Div.).

The court refused to take the defendant's apology as purging contempt. The apology was not a sincere or genuine one.

Paul Magder Furs Ltd. v. Ontario (Attorney General) (1991), 6 O.R. (3d) 188, 3 C.P.C. (3d) 240, 85 D.L.R. (4th) 694, 52 O.A.C. 151 (C.A.), leave to appeal to Supreme Court of Canada refused 9 O.R. (3d) xii (note), 91 D.L.R. (4th) viii (note), 141 N.R. 394 (note), 57 O.A.C. 102 (note).

The court refused to hear the plaintiff's appeal until it purged its contempt.

Ontario (Attorney General) v. Paul Magder Furs Ltd. (1991), 5 O.R. (3d) 560, additional reasons (July 16, 1992), Doc. RE 2782/89 (Gen. Div.).

The court may refuse to hear a party who is in contempt of an order of the court.

R. v. B.E.S.T. Plating Shoppe Ltd. (1987), 59 O.R. (2d) 145, 19 C.P.C. (2d) 174, 1 C.E.L.R. (N.S.) 145, 32 C.C.C. (3d) 417, 21 O.A.C. 62 (C.A.).

Proceedings for a contempt order may be initiated by service of a notice of application returnable before a Supreme Court judge, who has inherent jurisdiction to punish for contempt. A trial of an issue should be ordered where there are controverted facts relating to matters essential to the court's decision.

Axelrod v. City of Toronto (No. 2) (1985), 52 O.R. (2d) 440, 5 C.P.C. (2d) 221 (*sub nom. Axelrod v. City of Toronto*) (H.C.).

The court varied its own order and eliminated a fine it had imposed for contempt.

Hitchcock v. Stevens (1974), 4 O.R. (2d) 634, 48 D.L.R. (3d) 690 (C.A.).

Where a person is ordered to be imprisoned for contempt, appeal lies to the Court of Appeal and that court may grant a stay of execution of the order.

Dare Foods (Biscuit Division) Ltd. v. Gill, [1973] 1 O.R. 637 (H.C.).
The notice of motion itself must set out particulars of the alleged contempt.

General Printers Ltd. v. Thomson, [1965] 1 O.R. 81, 46 D.L.R. (2d) 697 (H.C.).
Statements of fact in an affidavit filed in support of a motion to commit should be confined to statements within the personal knowledge of the deponent. *[But see now rule 60.11(3) — Authors.]*

Contempt Orders — Liability of Non-Parties

Can. Metal Co. v. C.B.C. (No. 2) (1975), 4 O.R. (2d) 585, 19 C.C.C. (2d) 218, 48 D.L.R. (3d) 641 (H.C.), affirmed 11 O.R. (2d) 167, 29 C.C.C. (2d) 325, 65 D.L.R. (3d) 231 (C.A.).
Non-parties having notice of the substance of an order are under an obligation to obey it and failure to do so may result in contempt proceedings.

Re Tilco Plastics Ltd. and Skurjat, [1966] 2 O.R. 547, 49 C.R. 99, [1967] 1 C.C.C. 131, 57 D.L.R. (2d) 596 (H.C.), affirmed and leave to appeal to S.C.C. refused by C.A. and S.C.C. [1967] 1 O.R. 609n, [1967] 2 C.C.C. 196n, 61 D.L.R. (2d) 664n.
A non-party can be found guilty of contempt for knowingly acting in contravention of a court order.

Contempt Orders — Examples

Leo Sakata Electronics Canada Ltd. v. McIntyre (1995), 96 C.L.L.C. 210-016 (Ont. Gen. Div.).
The court held a union official in contempt for failing to fulfill an undertaking which had been incorporated into a court order.

Werner v. Warner Auto-Marine Inc. (1995), 35 C.P.C. (3d) 215, additional reasons (May 10, 1995), Doc. 8769/88, 26070/88Q, 330778/88 (Ont. Gen. Div.).
Where, contrary to a preservation order, the plaintiff carried out destructive tests on real evidence, the court dismissed the plaintiff's claim.

Pilpel v. Pilpel (1993), 27 C.P.C. (3d) 157 (Ont. Gen. Div.).
The court ordered that a contemnor be jailed for 45 days unless he purged his contempt.

Ontario (Attorney General) v. Paul Magder Furs Ltd. (1992), 10 O.R. (3d) 46, 13 C.P.C. (3d) 364, 94 D.L.R. (4th) 748, 57 O.A.C. 145 (C.A.).
On an appeal from fines imposed for contempt of court, the court refused to stay the fines pending appeal because of the flagrant conduct of the appellant.

Director, Support & Custody Enforcement v. McLeod (1991), 4 C.P.C. (3d) 292, 36 R.F.L. (3d) 331 (Ont. Prov. Div.).
A debtor in a family law matter was the subject of an order to pay arrears or else be committed. The debtor's motion to vary the order as a result of his incurring legal fees was dismissed, as it was not a material change in circumstances.

Dominion of Canada General Insurance Co. v. Dusome (June 5, 1992), Doc. Hamilton 91-CU-41778 (Ont. Gen. Div.).
The court fined the contemnor, a non-party, $2,000 for refusing to obey an order to produce documents.

Surgeoner v. Surgeoner (1991), 6 C.P.C. (3d) 318 (Ont. Gen. Div.).
Sending a person to jail is a last resort. The court adjourned this contempt motion to allow the respondent to purge his contempt.

777829 Ontario Ltd. v. McNally (1991), 9 C.P.C. (3d) 257 (Ont. Gen. Div.).

A contemnor was ordered imprisoned for twelve months where he had breached an order not to dispose of assets.

Re Axelrod and Toronto (1984), 48 O.R. (2d) 586, 46 C.P.C. 308, 13 D.L.R. (4th) 634 (H.C.), varied on reconsideration (1985), 52 O.R. (2d) 440 (*sub nom. Re Axelrod and Toronto (No. 2),* 5 C.P.C. (2d) 221 (H.C.).

An order holding a municipality in contempt and imposing a fine for failure to comply with a *mandamus* was varied on consent on the ground that the earlier non-compliance had been prompted by deeply held convictions and since remedied.

Crown Trust Co. v. Rosenberg (1984), 45 C.P.C. 97 (Ont. H.C.).

Where a defendant had disregarded a clear and unambiguous injunction restraining dealings in certain assets except in the ordinary course of business, the court appointed a receiver, ordered the defendant to submit to an oral examination as to his assets and to discharge certain mortgages, and adjourned the matter of sanctions for the contempt until completion of the examination and discharges.

Stratford Professional Firefighters Assn., Loc. 534, I.A.F.F. v. Stratford (1981), 23 C.P.C. 250 (Ont. H.C.).

Where an arbitrator's award required the defendant to reconsider a decision, without laying down a precise formula to bind the defendant, it could not be enforced by contempt proceedings.

Bank of Montreal v. Togel (1979), 24 O.R. (2d) 359, 98 D.L.R. (3d) 380 (Co. Ct.).

The court does not have jurisdiction on interlocutory motion to require a party to execute a release even where the release was a term of a settlement of the action. A separate action is necessary.

Re I.W.A. and Patchogue Plymouth, Hawkesbury Mills (1976), 14 O.R. (2d) 118, 2 C.P.C. 98 (H.C.).

An order for sequestration or fine was not made where the party had relied on the common practice in believing a matter to be stayed pending judicial review.

Can. Metal Co. v. C.B.C. (No. 2) (1975), 4 O.R. (2d) 585, 19 C.C.C. (2d) 218, 48 D.L.R. (3d) 641 (H.C.), affirmed 11 O.R. (2d) 167, 29 C.C.C. (2d) 325, 65 D.L.R. (3d) 231 (C.A.).

Where the contemnors intended no disrespect to the court and had apologized, fines of $700 and $350 were imposed.

Re Petryczka and Petryczka, [1973] 2 O.R. 866, 10 R.F.L. 321, 35 D.L.R. (3d) 526 (H.C.).

A parent awarded interim custody who refused to obey orders allowing the other parent interim access was jailed for 24 hours.

Standard Industries Ltd. v. Rosen, [1955] O.W.N. 262, 14 Fox Pat. C. 173, 24 C.P.R. 41, [1955] 4 D.L.R. 363 (H.C.).

Where a person stupidly, but not maliciously, breached an injunction, an order for committal was refused but a cost sanction was imposed.

Re Ross and Toronto Bd. of Commissioners of Police, [1953] O.R. 947, 107 C.C.C. 147, [1954] 1 D.L.R. 706 (H.C.).

Where the contemnors complied with the order of the court only after a motion for committal had been brought, costs were awarded on a solicitor and client basis.

Harding v. Liprovitch (1929), 35 O.W.N. 361 (H.C.).

Where the defendant had made some effort to comply with an injunction to entirely discontinue the wrongful acts against which an injunction had been granted, a fine was imposed in lieu of a committal.

Browne v. Britnell & Co. (1924), 27 O.W.N. 232 (H.C.).

Where the officers and servants of the defendant company knew that a nuisance was being committed, but "took chances", a writ of sequestration was issued.

Mackell v. Ottawa Separate School Trustees (1917), 12 O.W.N. 265 (H.C.).

An officer of a corporation who had knowledge of a judgment which the corporation disobeyed was committed for contempt.

FAILURE TO COMPLY WITH INTERLOCUTORY ORDER

60.12 Where a party fails to comply with an interlocutory order, the court may, in addition to any other sanction provided by these rules,
  (a) stay the party's proceeding;
  (b) dismiss the party's proceeding or strike out the party's defence; or
  (c) make such other order as is just.

DISPUTE OF OWNERSHIP OF PROPERTY SEIZED BY SHERIFF

60.13(1) A person who makes a claim in respect of property or the proceeds of property taken or intended to be taken by a sheriff in the execution of any enforcement process against another person shall give notice to the sheriff of the claim and the address for service of the person making the claim.

(2) On receiving a claim, the sheriff shall forthwith give notice of claim (Form 60M) to every creditor of the debtor who has filed an enforcement process with the sheriff, by mail addressed to the creditor at the address shown on the enforcement process, and the creditor shall within seven days after receiving the notice give the sheriff notice in writing stating whether the creditor admits or disputes the claim.

(3) Where the sheriff,
  (a) receives a notice admitting the claim from every creditor; or
  (b) receives a notice admitting the claim from the creditor at whose
       direction the sheriff took or intended to take the property and does not
       receive a notice disputing the claim from any other creditor,
he or she shall release the property in respect of which the claim is admitted.

(4) On receiving a notice disputing a claim, or on the failure of the creditor at whose direction the sheriff took or intended to take the property to give the required notice within the time prescribed by subrule (2), the sheriff may make a motion or application under rule 43.05 for an interpleader order.

SHERIFF'S REPORT ON EXECUTION OF WRIT

60.14(1) A party or solicitor who has filed a writ with a sheriff may in writing require the sheriff to report the manner in which he or she has executed the writ and the sheriff shall do so forthwith by mailing to the party or solicitor a sheriff's report (Form 60N).

(2) Where the sheriff fails to comply with a request made under subrule (1) within a reasonable time, the party serving the request may move before a judge for an order directing the sheriff to comply with the request.

REMOVAL OR WITHDRAWAL OF WRIT FROM SHERIFF'S FILE

Executed and Expired Writs

60.15(1) When a writ has been fully executed or has expired, the sheriff shall endorse a memorandum to that effect on the writ, remove it from his or her file and retain it in a separate file of executed and expired writs.

Withdrawal of Writ

(2) A party or solicitor who has filed a writ with a sheriff may withdraw it as against one or more of the debtors named in it by giving the sheriff written instructions to that effect.

(3) When a writ is withdrawn, the sheriff shall record the date and time of the withdrawal in a memorandum on the writ, and where it is withdrawn as against all debtors named in it, shall remove the writ from his or her file and return it to the person who withdrew it.

DUTY OF PERSON FILING WRIT WITH SHERIFF

60.16(1) Where a writ of seizure and sale has been filed with a sheriff and any payment has been received by or on behalf of the creditor, the creditor shall forthwith give the sheriff notice of the payment.

(2) Where an order has been satisfied in full, the creditor shall withdraw all writs of execution relating to the order from the office of any sheriff with whom they have been filed.

(3) Where the creditor fails to withdraw a writ as required by subrule (2), the court on motion by the debtor may order that the writ be withdrawn.

Julian v. Northern and Central Gas Corp. Ltd., 31 O.R. (2d) 388 at 389, 11 C.C.L.T. 1, 16 C.P.C. 92, 118 D.L.R. (3d) 458 at 459, [1980] I.L.R. 1-1173 (C.A.).

Payments made on account of a judgment are applicable to discharge first the interest component of the award and secondly the principal.

MOTION FOR DIRECTIONS

60.17 Where a question arises in relation to the measures to be taken by a sheriff in carrying out an order, writ of execution or notice of garnishment, the sheriff or any interested person may make a motion for directions,

(a) to the judge or officer who made the original order, at any place;

(b) to a judge or officer who had jurisdiction to make the original order, in the sheriff's county, despite rule 37.03 (place of hearing of motions); or

(c) where an appeal has been taken from the original order, to a judge of the court to which the appeal has been taken, at any place.

EXAMINATION IN AID OF EXECUTION

Definitions

60.18(1) In subrules (2) to (6),
"creditor" includes a person entitled to obtain or enforce a writ of possession, delivery or sequestration;
"debtor" includes a person against whom a writ of possession, delivery or sequestration may be or has been issued.

Examination of Debtor

(2) A creditor may examine the debtor in relation to,
(a) the reason for nonpayment or nonperformance of the order;
(b) the debtor's income and property;
(c) the debts owed to and by the debtor;
(d) the disposal the debtor has made of any property either before or after the making of the order;
(e) the debtor's present, past and future means to satisfy the order;
(f) whether the debtor intends to obey the order or has any reason for not doing so; and
(g) any other matter pertinent to the enforcement of the order.

(3) An officer or director of a corporate debtor, or, in the case of a debtor that is a partnership or sole proprietorship, a partner or sole proprietor against whom the order may be enforced, may be examined on behalf of the debtor in relation to the matters set out in subrule (2).

(4) Only one examination under subrule (2) or (3) may be held in a twelve month period in respect of a debtor in the same proceeding, unless the court orders otherwise.

(5) Where it appears from an examination under subrules (2) to (4) that a debtor has concealed or made away with property to defeat or defraud creditors, a judge may make a contempt order against the debtor.

Examination of Person other than Debtor

(6) Where any difficulty arises concerning the enforcement of an order, the court may,
(a) make an order for the examination of any person who the court is satisfied may have knowledge of the matters set out in subrule (2); and
(b) make such order for the examination of any other person as is just.

Service on Debtor

(7) Despite clause 34.04(1)(a) (service on solicitor), a party who is to be examined in aid of execution shall be served with a notice of examination personally or by an alternative to personal service. [am. O. Regs. 739/94, s. 6; 377/95, s. 5]

Examination of Judgment Debtor

C.M. *Oliver & Co. v. Gilroy*, [1959] O.R. 316, 18 D.L.R. (2d) 280 (H.C.).

A judgment debtor may be required to answer incriminating questions. A master lacks jurisdiction to order a re-attendance. [*But see now rule 34.15 — Authors.*]

Examination in Aid of Execution — Generally

Fidelity Electronics of Canada Ltd. v. Flomo Canada Inc. (1993), 22 C.P.C. (3d) 294, 24 C.B.R. (3d) 253 (Ont. Gen. Div.).

The transcript of an examination in aid of execution is admissible on a motion to appoint a receiver in aid of execution.

Bock v. Fairborn (1990), 40 C.P.C. (2d) 277 (Ont. Dist. Ct.).

A motion to examine a judgment debtor's spouse was dismissed where there was no evidence that the judgment creditor had exhausted all other means available to satisfy the judgment. Furthermore, it could not be shown that the judgment debtor had made a deliberate attempt to hide assets or income.

Chitel v. Rothbart (1987), 60 O.R. (2d) 38, 17 C.P.C. (2d) 276 (Master).

The court permitted a person to be examined in aid of execution where the person was not a party to an outstanding action to set aside a conveyance notwithstanding that her evidence would cover the same subject-matter as the outstanding action.

Parks v. Sullivan (1982), 29 C.P.C. 124 (Ont. Master).

It is established practice for masters to make orders under the predecessor of this provision. This provision applies to the enforcement of an order against a garnishee. An order should only be made when the judgment creditor has exhausted all other means available.

Egan Visual Inc. v. Futuric Office Furniture Distributors Ltd. (1983), 33 C.P.C. 111 (Ont. Master).

A master has jurisdiction to make an order permitting an examination in aid of execution. [*And see now rule 37.02(2) — Authors.*]

C.I.B.C. v. Sutton (1981), 34 O.R. (2d) 482, 21 C.P.C. 303, 126 D.L.R. (3d) 330 (C.A.).

This procedure is not limited to judgments other than those for the recovery of money.

Spiegel v. Klein, [1962] O.W.N. 37 (Master).

The judgment creditor need not establish conclusively that the person sought to be examined has possession of property of the judgment debtor; reasonable grounds for so supposing are sufficient.

Saddy v. Prosser, [1955] O.W.N. 241 (Master).

An order requiring a non-party to submit to examination should not be made *ex parte*.

Examination in Aid of Execution — Transferee of Property

Chitel v. Rothbart (1988), 28 C.P.C. (2d) 5 (Ont. Div. Ct.).

A consent order requiring a non-party to attend for an examination in aid of execution was enforced, even though one of the judgment creditors had subsequently commenced an action against the non-party in California. The consent order was a contract, and there was no common mistake, misrepresentation, fraud or other ground which would invalidate such a contract.

Patrons Acceptance Ltd. v. Born (1983), 34 C.P.C. 186 (Ont. Co. Ct.).

The court will permit examination of a transferee of the judgment debtor's property in aid of execution provided the examination is sought prior to commencement of proceedings against the transferee.

Examination in Aid of Execution — Solicitors

Maynard's Auctioneers & Appraisers Ltd. v. Commercial Industrial Auctioneers Ltd. (1979), 18 C.P.C. 132 (Ont. Master).

Where there was reason to suspect that a corporate solicitor was in possession of share certificates owned directly or indirectly by the judgment debtor, an examination of the solicitor was permitted.

Ideal Electric Ltd. v. Lepofsky, [1960] O.W.N. 548 (Master).

A solicitor being examined by the judgment creditor was required to answer a question as to whether he possessed a stock certificate registered in the name of the judgment debtor.

COSTS OF ENFORCEMENT

60.19(1) A party who is entitled to enforce an order is entitled to the costs of an examination in aid of execution and the issuing, service, enforcement and renewal of a writ of execution and notice of garnishment, unless the court orders otherwise.

(2) A party entitled to costs under subrule (1) may include in or collect under a writ of execution or notice of garnishment,

(a) the amounts prescribed in the regulations under the *Administration of Justice Act* and in Tariff A for issuing, renewing and filing with the sheriff the writ of execution or notice of garnishment;

(b) disbursements paid to a sheriff, registrar, official examiner, court reporter or other public officer and to which the party is entitled under subrule (1), on filing with the sheriff or registrar a copy of a receipt for each disbursement;

(c) the minimum amount prescribed in Tariff A for conducting an examination in aid of execution, on filing with the sheriff or registrar an affidavit stating that the examination was conducted; and

(d) any other costs to which the party is entitled under subrule (1), on filing with the sheriff or registrar a certificate of assessment of the costs.

APPEALS

RULE 61   APPEALS TO AN APPELLATE COURT

Highlights

This Rule regulates the procedure on appeals to an appellate court, *i.e.* the Court of Appeal or the Divisional Court (see definition in rule 1.03), whether from another court or from an administrative tribunal. It does not regulate the procedure in respect of the Divisional Court's non-appellate jurisdiction, *i.e.* applications for judicial review (which is regulated by Rule 68). Nor does the Rule confer any rights of appeal. This is a matter of statute (see *e.g. Courts of Justice Act*, s. 6 (Court of Appeal) and s. 19 (Divisional Court) and the Appeal Route Charts (CHARTS)). Other rules regulate the procedure on appeals to other than an appellate court: rule 62.01 (appeals to a judge from an interlocutory order of a master, or from a certificate of assessment of costs, or pursuant to statutes other than the *Courts of Justice Act* where no other procedure is provided), rule 70.10 (appeals from Ontario Court (Provincial Division)), rules 71.02, 71.03 (*Child and Family Services Act* appeals).

The Rule regulates how and when appeals (including cross-appeals) are to be commenced (rules 61.04 and 61.07); certificates or agreements as to the evidence to be reproduced (rule 61.05); the perfecting of appeals (*i.e.* the preparation and delivery of appeal books, factums and a certificate of perfection: rules 61.09-61.12); the dismissal of appeals for delay (rule 61.13); the abandonment of appeals (rules 61.14-61.15); and motion practice in appellate courts (rule 61.16). It also deals with motions for leave to appeal to an appellate court where leave of the appellate court is required (rule 61.03). However motions for leave to appeal to the Divisional Court with leave of a judge are regulated by rule 62.02.

Time limits. The time for serving a notice of appeal to an appellate court under the Rules is thirty days after the date of the order appealed from: rule 61.04(1). The time for serving a notice of cross-appeal is fifteen days after the service of the notice of appeal (rule 61.07(1)) and the time for perfecting the appeal where evidence is required is thirty days after the appellant receives notice that the evidence has been transcribed: rule 61.09(1).

By rule 61.04(2) and Form 61B the title of the proceeding in an appellate court (the former "style of cause") is specifically prescribed.

Certificate or agreement as to evidence. The parties are required to attempt to limit the evidence to be reproduced for the appeal, and an agreement as to evidence may be filed (rule 61.05(4)) as an alternative to the use of certificates as to evidence.

Cross-appeals. A respondent must deliver a notice of cross-appeal not only where he seeks to set aside or vary the order appealed from, but also where he will seek, in the event that the appeal is allowed in whole or in part, other or different relief or a disposition other than that given by the order appealed from: rule 61.07(1).

Perfecting appeals. On perfecting an appeal, it is the appellant's obligation to file a certificate of perfection: rule 61.09(3)(c). In the Court of Appeal there are no longer monthly lists of cases to be heard: they are replaced by a running list of "cases to be heard" : rule 61.09(5).

Appeal books and factums. The Registrar is empowered to refuse to accept an appeal book which does not comply with the Rules or which is illegible: rule 61.10(2). The Rules have been brought into conformity with commonly used terminology so that the appellant's and the respondent's statements are now called "factums": rule

61.11. The factums must include, *inter alia*, the text of all relevant provisions of statutes, regulations and by-laws: rules 61.11(1)(f) and 61.12(3)(f).

Security for costs. A judge of the appellate court may require security for costs of the appeal (1) on the grounds mentioned in rule 56.01, or (2) if the appeal is frivolous and vexatious and the appellant does not have sufficient assets in Ontario to pay such costs, or if there is "other good reason" to order security for costs: rule 61.06. (Note that this second ground, introduced in 1989, permits ordering security against an appellant irrespective of whether the appellant was originally a plaintiff or defendant in the court below.)

Dismissal for delay. A comprehensive procedure is provided for dismissal of an appeal, either by the Registrar on his own motion or on the motion of the respondent, where the appellant has not met the time limits respecting the appeal: rule 61.13.

Motion practice. The legislation is specific as to what matters may be decided by single judges of an appellate court on motion, and provision is made for review of such decisions by a motion to a panel of the court to set aside or vary the decision: see the *Courts of Justice Act*, s. 21 (Divisional Court) and s. 7 (Court of Appeal). There is also an express right of review, on motion to a single judge, of orders or decisions of the Registrar: rule 61.16(5).

Motions for leave to appeal to the Court of Appeal. By rule 61.03.1 such motions must be made in writing and they will be disposed of without an oral hearing, unless otherwise ordered.

Practice directions. Practice directions regarding motions to the Court of Appeal in civil matters, title of proceedings in civil appeals in the Court of Appeal, unnecessary evidence in civil appeals in the Court of Appeal, factums in civil appeals in the Court of Appeal, books of authorities in the Court of Appeal and the Divisional Court, filing material and the new scheduling procedures for civil appeals are reproduced following these Highlights. See *Courts of Justice Act* s. 21 for a practice direction regarding proceedings to be heard by a single judge in the Divisional Court.

Summary of procedure. For a summary of the procedure on an appeal to an appellate court, see Procedural Charts (CHARTS).

Appeal routes. For charts depicting the appeal routes from final and interlocutory orders, see Procedural Charts (CHARTS).

Former Rules: Rules 497-503, 667.

Cross-Reference: As to the powers of a court to which an appeal is taken, see *Courts of Justice Act*, ss. 119 and 134.

Practice Directions

The following practice directions are reproduced below:

Motions to the Court of Appeal in Civil Matters
Title of Proceeding in Civil Appeals in the Court of Appeal
Unnecessary Evidence in Civil Appeals in the Court of Appeal
Factums in Civil Appeals in the Court of Appeal
Books of Authorities
Filing Motion Material in the Court of Appeal
New Procedure Respecting Motions for Leave to Appeal to the Court of Appeal in Writing
Books of Authorities — Divisional Court

PRACTICE DIRECTION

MOTIONS TO THE COURT OF APPEAL IN CIVIL MATTERS

1. All motions to a panel of the Court of Appeal (except motions which must be made to the panel hearing the appeal under rule 61.16(2)) will be heard on every Monday (or on the following Tuesday, if Monday is a holiday) in each month (except during July and August and from December 24 to the following January 6, both dates inclusive).

2. In cases of urgency, a justice of appeal in chambers may direct that a motion be heard on another day on which the court is scheduled to sit.

3. Generally speaking, on a motion for leave to appeal counsel for the moving party will be expected to make his or her submissions in approximately 15 minutes and counsel for the responding party will be expected to make his or her submissions in approximately 10 minutes.

4. The court hearing the motion may grant leave to appeal generally, or upon specific points of law or mixed law and fact, where the answers to such questions will be decisive of the appeal. In general, reasons for the granting or refusing of leave will not be given.

5. This Practice Direction continues the Practice Direction dated December 21, 1984.

May 1, 1993   [Sgd.] C.L. Dubin
[13 O.R. (3d) 65]   Chief Justice of Ontario
                                                                  For the Court

PRACTICE DIRECTION

TITLE OF PROCEEDING IN CIVIL APPEALS
IN THE COURT OF APPEAL

1. The title of a proceeding in the Court of Appeal shall be in accordance with rule 61.04(2) and Form 61B.

2. This Practice Direction continues the Practice Direction dated December 21, 1984.

May 1, 1993   [Sgd.] C.L. Dubin
[13 O.R. (3d) 66]   Chief Justice of Ontario
                                                                  For the Court

PRACTICE DIRECTION

UNNECESSARY EVIDENCE IN CIVIL
APPEALS IN THE COURT OF APPEAL

The transcription of unnecessary evidence and the reproduction of unnecessary exhibits only result in delays in the hearing of appeals and substantially increase the cost of litigation.
In order to eliminate the transcription of evidence and the reproduction of exhibits which are not required for the disposition of an appeal by the Court of Appeal, the attention of the

profession is directed to rule 61.05 respecting the service of certificates (Form 61C and Form 61D) or an agreement respecting evidence.

It is appreciated that where the counsel who acted at trial is not taking the appeal, the assistance of the counsel who took the trial may be required in completing the certificates or making the agreement.

In appeals where the facts are not in dispute, an agreed statement of facts should take the place of a transcript. The directions of a judge of the Court of Appeal in Chambers should be obtained where required under rule 61.09(4).

Unless otherwise ordered by a judge of the Court of Appeal, there shall be omitted from all transcripts of evidence for civil appeals:

(a) all proceedings on the challenge of the array or of jurors for cause;

(b) any opening address of the trial judge;

(c) the opening and closing addresses of counsel;

(d) all proceedings in the absence of the jury and all argument in the absence of the jury (excepting objections to a charge and the trial judge's ruling thereon together with any reasons for his ruling), and all argument where there is no jury;

(e) all objections to the admissibility of evidence excepting only a notation that an objection was made. (The ruling of the trial judge including any reasons for his ruling will be transcribed).

The court reporters have been instructed that after a transcript has been ordered for a civil appeal, the completion of the transcript is not to be suspended without an order of a judge of the Court of Appeal. This does not apply to appeals where a provisional legal aid certificate has been issued and a decision as to the granting of legal aid has not yet been made by the Area Committee.

This Practice Direction continues the Practice Direction dated December 21, 1984.

May 1, 1993   [Sgd.] C.L. Dubin
[13 O.R. (3d) 66]   Chief Justice of Ontario
                                             For the Court

PRACTICE DIRECTION

FACTUMS IN CIVIL APPEALS IN THE COURT OF APPEAL

1. The attention of the profession is drawn to rules 61.11 and 61.12 which deal with the appellant's and the respondent's factums. Particular regard should be had to the emphasis in these rules on the necessity for a "concise summary" of the relevant facts and a "concise" statement of the law. In the majority of appeals, because of the emphasis on oral argument, the factums should be no longer than 10 pages and other than in exceptional cases should not exceed 30 pages. If counsel is of the opinion that more than 30 pages of factum is needed in any particular case, counsel should obtain the consent of the chambers judge to the filing of such factum.

2. This Practice Direction continues the Practice Direction dated December 21, 1984.

May 1, 1993   [Sgd.] C.L. Dubin
[13 O.R. (3d) 67]   Chief Justice of Ontario
                                             For the Court

PRACTICE DIRECTION

BOOKS OF AUTHORITIES — COURT OF APPEAL

It is of great assistance to the Court of Appeal to have case books filed containing photostatic copies of the authorities to which they intend to refer on the hearing of the appeal. Such case books of authorities:

1. Should include *only* the cases to which counsel actually intend to refer in the oral argument. The particular passages in the cases to which counsel wish to refer should be clearly marked.

2. Should indicate whether they are filed by the appellant or the respondent. There should be consultation between counsel to avoid any duplication of the authorities included in their respective case books. A joint case book is, of course, acceptable.

3. Should have a tab for each case (either numerical or alphabetical), should include an index of the authorities and indicate the tab where the authority is reproduced. It is not necessary to number the pages in the case book so long as the photostats show the page numbers of each authority.

4. Should be filed, if possible, not later than the Monday of the week preceding the hearing of the appeal as they are of great assistance to the judges in preparing for the hearing.

This Practice Direction continues the Practice Direction of September, 1986.

May 1, 1993   [Sgd.] C.L. Dubin
                                                        Chief Justice of Ontario
                                                                For the Court

---

PRACTICE DIRECTION

FILING MOTION MATERIAL IN THE COURT OF APPEAL

All of the material for motions before a judge in chambers in the Court of Appeal must be filed by 12:00 noon the day prior to the hearing.

In urgent situations where this time limit cannot be complied with, leave to file may be obtained from the judge or the Registrar.

May 1, 1993   [Sgd.] C.L. Dubin
[13 O.R. (3d) 68]   Chief Justice of Ontario
                                                                For the Court

---

PRACTICE DIRECTION

NEW SCHEDULING PROCEDURES FOR CIVIL APPEALS

Following an internal review, the Court of Appeal has approved changes in its scheduling procedures for civil appeals. The purpose of these changes is to reduce the time between the date of perfection of appeals and their hearing. This Practice Direction provides particulars of these changes.

I. EXPEDITED APPEALS

The following appeals should be expedited:

(a) Family law appeals unless the issues in the appeal do not directly or indirectly affect children.
(b) Summary judgment appeals.
(c) Appeals that may delay the progress of an ongoing action.

   (d)   Appeals expedited by the Chief Justice, the Associate Chief Justice or a panel of the Court.

II. THE LIST JUDGE

1.   A judge of the Court, designated by the Chief Justice as the List Judge, shall supervise the civil list.
2.   The List Judge shall perform the duties set out in this Practice Direction.

III. SPECIAL PROVISIONS FOR SUMMARY JUDGMENT APPEALS

(a) Perfected Summary Judgment Appeals

1.   Commencing December, 1995 the Registrar will commence listing perfected unlisted appeals from summary judgments on a first-perfected basis.
2.   The Registrar will send a letter to counsel for the appellant and for the respondent informing them:
    (a)   of the date fixed for the appeal;
    (b)   that oral argument will be limited to one hour; 30 minutes for the appellant, 20 minutes for the respondent, and 10 minutes for reply;
    (c)   that motions to change the date for time for argument should be made to the List Judge through the Motions Clerk.

(b) Unperfected Appeals from Summary Judgments

1.   Once perfected, summary judgment appeals shall be expedited and listed for hearing.
2.   The argument of summary judgment appeals shall be limited to one hour: 30 minutes for the appellant, 20 minutes for the respondent, and 10 minutes for reply. Counsel may make a motion to the List Judge through the Motions Clerk for more time.

IV. PERFECTED APPEALS FROM OTHER THAN SUMMARY JUDGMENTS

1.   In all perfected unlisted civil appeals, other than summary judgment appeals, the Registrar will send a letter to counsel for the appellant and for the respondent requesting the following information:
    (a)   whether the appeal is still active;
    (b)   counsel's certified estimate of the time, in fractions of an hour or hours (*e.g.* 3/4 of an hour or 1-1/2 hours), of his or her oral argument not including, in the case of appellant's counsel, the time for reply;
    (c)   any days when counsel cannot argue the appeal.
2.   The following scheduling practices shall be implemented effective February 1, 1996:
    (a)   If both counsel respond to the letter, the appeal will be listed on a first-perfected basis, using the information provided by counsel.
    (b)   If only one counsel responds, the appeal will be listed using the information provided by that counsel.
    (c)   If neither counsel responds, the appeal will be placed on a purge list to be spoken to.
    (d)   If counsel wish to change the hearing date given by the Registrar, they must make a motion to the List Judge through the Court of Appeal Motions Clerk.
    (e)   Counsel will be expected to provide realistic time estimates for oral argument and to adhere to those estimates.
3.   All perfected family law appeals, with priority being given to those appeals which concern children, will be expedited and immediately listed for hearing.

V. UNPERFECTED APPEALS

1. Counsel shall certify in the factum his or her estimate of the time, in fractions of an hour or hours (*e.g.* 3/4 of an hour or 1-1/2 hours), of his or her oral argument not including, in the case of appellant's counsel, the time for reply. Appropriate cost sanctions will be imposed on respondents who do not file their factums within the time provided in Rule 61.12(2).

2. The Court expects counsel to provide realistic time estimates. These time estimates shall be published on the weekly court lists and shall be provided to the panel hearing the appeal. The Court expects counsel to adhere to their time estimates.

3. Appeals estimated to take longer than one day, and other appeals in which the time estimates appear inconsistent or unreasonable, shall not be listed until reviewed by the List Judge or the Associate Chief Justice.

4. Appeals shall be scheduled for hearing in two stages:
    (a) Six (6) months before an appeal is to be heard it will be listed for hearing during a given week. If within 30 days of such listing counsel agree on a day during the assigned week when they wish to argue the appeal, they shall immediately notify the Registrar in writing of the agreed upon day.
    (b) One (1) month before the week's appeals are to be argued the Registrar will fix the daily list for the week. The Registrar will attempt to accommodate counsel's agreement and the interests of non-Toronto counsel.

5. Counsel who seek to change a hearing date set by the Registrar or who seek more time for oral argument must make a motion to the List Judge through the Motions Clerk.

6. The Court expects counsel to notify the Registrar immediately of any appeal that is settled or abandoned.

VI. APPEALS WITHOUT ORAL ARGUMENT

1. The Court may decide appeals without oral argument on the consent of counsel. Counsel who wish an appeal to be decided without oral argument shall, after delivering their factums, file a written consent with the Registrar.

2. In appeals without oral argument the appellant shall be permitted to file a reply factum.

3. Where practicable, the court shall render judgment within 60 days of the filing of the consent.

VII. FILING OF MATERIAL FOR USE ON AN APPEAL

1. Transcripts of evidence may be printed on both sides of the page.

2. Documents for use on an appeal, including transcripts of evidence, may be filed in miniscript.

3. Counsel are permitted and encouraged to file diskettes containing any computer-generated material filed on the appeal, including the parties' factums, formatted in DOS/WordPerfect 6.0a, or earlier.

4. In a complex case, counsel are encouraged to file an extract book for the use of the panel hearing the appeal. The extract book should contain relevant extracts from the appeal book and transcripts of evidence and relevant case references.

VIII. APPEALS BY VIDEO CONFERENCE

Upon installation of the required equipment counsel may make arrangements through the Registrar's Office to argue an appeal by video conference.

IX. PRE-HEARING CONFERENCES

The Motions Court Judge shall conduct a pre-hearing conference in any appeal in which all counsel request such a conference. Arrangements for a pre-hearing conference shall be made through the Registrar's Office.

X. MOTIONS

1. In motions before a panel, the oral argument shall be limited to 15 minutes for the moving party, 10 minutes for the responding party, and 5 minutes for reply. Counsel who seek more time for oral argument must make a motion to the List Judge through the Motions Clerk.
2. Motions before the List Judge may be argued by telephone conference call.
3. Where appropriate, motions before the Associate Chief Justice or the Chief Justice may be argued by telephone conference call.

December 18, 1995

Sgd. C.L. Dubin
Chief Justice of Ontario
for the Court

PRACTICE DIRECTION

BOOKS OF AUTHORITIES — DIVISIONAL COURT

It is of great assistance to the Divisional Court to have case books filed by counsel containing photostatic copies of the authorities to which they intend to refer on the hearing of the matter. Such case books of authorities:

1. Should include *only* the cases to which counsel actually intend to refer in the oral argument. The particular passages in the cases to which counsel wish to refer should be clearly marked.

2. Should be prepared jointly in accordance with this direction. Where counsel are unable to agree, then such case books should indicate whether they are filed by the appellant or the respondent. There should be consultation between counsel to avoid any duplication of the authorities included in their respective case books.

3. Should have a tab for each case (either numerical or by letters), should include an index of the authorities and indicate the tab where the authority is reproduced. It is not necessary to number the pages in the case book so long as the photocopies show the page numbers of each authority.

4. Should be filed, if possible, not later than the Monday of the week preceding the hearing of the matter as they are of great assistance to the judges in preparing for the hearing.

February, 1987

W.D. Parker
Chief Justice of the High Court

APPLICATION OF THE RULE

61.01 Rules 61.02 to 61.16 apply to all appeals to an appellate court except as provided in clause 62.01(1)(b) or rule 71.03 and, with necessary modifications, to proceedings in an appellate court by way of,

(a) stated case under a statute;

(b) special case under rule 22.03, subject to any directions given under subrule 22.03(2); and

(c) reference under section 8 of the *Courts of Justice Act*.

DEFINITION

61.02 In rules 61.03 to 61.16, "Registrar" means,

(a) in the Court of Appeal, the Registrar of the Court of Appeal; or

(b) in the Divisional Court, the registrar in the regional centre of the region where the appeal is to be heard in accordance with subsection 20(1) of the *Courts of Justice Act.*

In May 1996, the authors were advised that the regional centres for the Divisional Court referred to in rule 61.02 were as follows:

1. *Northwest Region (Thunder Bay)*
    Court House
    277 Camelot Street
    Thunder Bay, Ontario
    P7A 4B3
    TELEPHONE NUMBER: (807) 343-2725

2. *Northeast Region (Sudbury)*
    Court House
    155 Elm Street West
    Sudbury, Ontario
    P3C 1T9
    TELEPHONE NUMBER: (705) 671-5958

3. *Central East Region (Newmarket)*
    Court House
    50 Eagle Street West
    Newmarket, Ontario
    L3Y 6B1
    TELEPHONE NUMBER: (905) 853-4809

4. *Central West Region (Milton)*
    Court House
    491 Steeles Avenue East
    Milton, Ontario
    L9T 1Y7
    TELEPHONE NUMBER: (905) 878-7281

5. *Central South Region (Hamilton)*
    Court House
    50 Main Street East
    Hamilton, Ontario
    L8N 1E9
    TELEPHONE NUMBER: (905) 308-7218

6. *Southwest Region (London)*
    Court House
    80 Dundas Street
    London, Ontario
    N6A 2P3
    TELEPHONE NUMBER: (519) 660-3026

7.   *East Region (Ottawa)*
     Court House
     161 Elgin Street
     Ottawa, Ontario
     K2P 2K1
     TELEPHONE NUMBER: (613) 239-1089

8.   *Toronto Region*
     Osgoode Hall
     130 Queen Street West
     Toronto, Ontario
     M5H 2N5
     TELEPHONE NUMBER: (416) 327-5100

MOTION FOR LEAVE TO APPEAL TO DIVISIONAL COURT

Notice of Motion for Leave

61.03(1) Where an appeal to the Divisional Court requires the leave of that court, the notice of motion for leave shall,

(a) state that the motion will be heard on a date to be fixed by the Registrar;

(b) be served within fifteen days after the date of the order or decision from which leave to appeal is sought, unless a statute provides otherwise; and

(c) be filed with proof of service in the office of the Registrar, within five days after service.

Motion Record, Factum and Transcripts

(2) On a motion for leave to appeal to the Divisional Court, the moving party shall serve,

(a) a motion record containing, in consecutively numbered pages arranged in the following order,

(i) a table of contents describing each document, including each exhibit, by its nature and date and, in the case of an exhibit, by exhibit number or letter,

(ii) a copy of the notice of motion,

(iii) a copy of the order or decision from which leave to appeal is sought, as signed and entered,

(iv) a copy of the reasons of the court or tribunal from which leave to appeal is sought with a further typed or printed copy if the reasons are handwritten,

(iv.1) a copy of any order or decision that was the subject of the hearing before the court or tribunal from which leave to appeal is sought,

(iv.2) a copy of any reasons for the order or decision referred to in subclause (iv.1), with a further typed or printed copy if the reasons are handwritten,

(v) a copy of all affidavits and other material used before the court or tribunal from which leave to appeal is sought,

(vi) a list of all relevant transcripts of evidence in chronological order, but not necessarily the transcripts themselves, and

(vii) a copy of any other material in the court file that is necessary for the hearing of the motion;

(b) a factum consisting of a concise statement, without argument, of the facts and law relied on by the moving party; and

(c) relevant transcripts of evidence, if they are not included in the motion record,

and shall file three copies of the motion record, factum and transcripts, if any, with proof of service, within thirty days after the filing of the notice of motion for leave to appeal.

(3) On a motion for leave to appeal to the Divisional Court, the responding party may, where he or she is of the opinion that the moving party's motion record is incomplete, serve a motion record containing, in consecutively numbered pages arranged in the following order,

(a) a table of contents describing each document, including each exhibit, by its nature and date and, in the case of an exhibit, by exhibit number or letter; and

(b) a copy of any material to be used by the responding party on the motion and not included in the motion record,

and may serve a factum consisting of a concise statement, without argument, of the facts and law relied on by the responding party, and shall file three copies of the responding party's motion record and factum, if any, with proof of service, within fifteen days after service of the moving party's motion record, factum and transcripts, if any.

Notice and Factum to State Questions on Appeal

(4) The moving party's notice of motion and factum shall, where practicable, set out the specific questions that it is proposed the Divisional Court should answer if leave to appeal is granted.

Date for Hearing

(5) The Registrar shall fix a date for the hearing of the motion which shall not, except with the responding party's consent, be earlier than fifteen days after the filing of the moving party's motion record, factum and transcripts, if any.

Time for Delivering Notice of Appeal

(6) Where leave is granted, the notice of appeal shall be delivered within seven days after the granting of leave.

Costs Appeal Joined with Appeal as of Right

(7) Where a party seeks to join an appeal under clause 133(b) of the *Courts of Justice Act* with an appeal as of right,

(a) the request for leave to appeal shall be included in the notice of appeal as part of the relief sought;

(b) leave to appeal shall be sought from the panel of the Divisional Court hearing the appeal as of right; and

(c) where leave is granted, the panel may then hear the appeal.

Costs Cross-Appeal Joined with Appeal or Cross-Appeal as of Right
(8) Where a party seeks to join a cross-appeal under clause 133(b) of the *Courts of Justice Act* with an appeal or cross-appeal as of right,

(a) the request for leave to appeal shall be included in the notice of appeal or cross-appeal as part of the relief sought;

(b) leave to appeal shall be sought from the panel of the Divisional Court hearing the appeal or cross-appeal as of right; and

(c) where leave is granted, the panel may then hear the appeal.

Application of Rules
(9) Subrules (1) to (6) do not apply where subrules (7) and (8) apply.
[am. O. Regs. 534/95, s. 3; 61/96, s. 5; 175/96, s. 1]

Nicholson v. Haldimand-Norfolk Regional Bd. of Commissioners of Police (1980), 31 O.R. (2d) 195, 117 D.L.R. (3d) 604 (C.A.), leave to appeal to Supreme Court of Canada refused [1981] 1 S.C.R. 92, 31 O.R. (2d) 195n, 117 D.L.R. (3d) 750, 37 N.R. 395.

The granting of leave to appeal from the Divisional Court to one party does not entitle the opposite party to cross-appeal without leave.

Re Can. Metal Co. and Heap (1975), 7 O.R. (2d) 185, 54 D.L.R. (3d) 641 (C.A.).

Appeal to the Court of Appeal is available with leave from both final and interlocutory orders of the Divisional Court. [*And see now the Courts of Justice Act, s. 18(1)(a) — Authors.*]

Re United Glass & Ceramic Wkrs. and Dom. Glass Co., [1973] 2 O.R. 763, 74 C.L.L.C. 14,203, 5 L.A.C. (2d) 224n (C.A.).

Leave to appeal from the Divisional Court to the Court of Appeal will be granted more readily where the judgment appealed from was an exercise of original jurisdiction rather than appellate jurisdiction.

Sault Dock Co. v. Sault Ste. Marie, [1973] 2 O.R. 479, 34 D.L.R. (3d) 327 (C.A.).

Leave to appeal from the Divisional Court to the Court of Appeal will usually be granted only if there is an arguable issue involving: (1) the interpretation of a statute or regulation of Canada or Ontario including its constitutionality; (2) the interpretation, clarification or propounding of some general rule or principle of law; (3) the interpretation of a municipal by-law where the point in issue is a question of public importance; or (4) the interpretation of an agreement where the point in issue involves a question of public importance.

MOTION FOR LEAVE TO APPEAL TO COURT OF APPEAL

Motion in Writing
61.03.1(1) Where an appeal to the Court of Appeal requires the leave of that court, the motion for leave shall be made in writing, without the attendance of parties or counsel.

Notice of Motion
(2) The notice of motion for leave to appeal shall state that the motion will be submitted to the court for consideration 36 days after service of the

moving party's motion record, factum and transcripts, if any, or on the filing of the moving party's reply factum, if any, whichever is earlier.

(3) The notice of motion,

(a) shall be served within 15 days after the date of the order or decision from which leave to appeal is sought, unless a statute provides otherwise; and

(b) shall be filed with proof of service in the office of the Registrar within five days after service.

Moving Party's Motion Record, Factum and Transcripts

(4) The moving party shall serve a motion record and transcripts of evidence, if any, in accordance with subrule 61.03(2), and a factum consisting of the following elements:

1. Part I, containing a statement identifying the moving party and the court from which it is proposed to appeal, and stating the result in that court.

2. Part II, containing a concise summary of the facts relevant to the issues on the proposed appeal, with such reference to the evidence by page and line as is necessary.

3. Part III, containing the specific questions that it is proposed the court should answer if leave to appeal is granted.

4. Part IV, containing a statement of each issue raised, immediately followed by a concise statement of the law and authorities relating to that issue.

5. Schedule A, containing a list of the authorities referred to.

6. Schedule B, containing the text of all relevant provisions of statutes, regulations and by-laws.

(5) Parts I to IV shall be arranged in paragraphs numbered consecutively throughout the factum.

(6) The moving party shall file three copies of the motion record, factum and transcripts, if any, and may file three copies of a book of authorities, if any, with proof of service, within 30 days after the filing of the notice of motion for leave to appeal.

Responding Party's Motion Record and Factum

(7) The responding party may, if of the opinion that the moving party's motion record is incomplete, serve a motion record in accordance with subrule 61.03(3).

(8) The responding party shall serve a factum consisting of the following elements:

1. Part I, containing a statement of the facts in the moving party's summary of relevant facts that the responding party accepts as correct and those facts with which the responding party disagrees and a concise summary of any additional facts relied on, with such reference to the evidence by page and line as is necessary.

2. Part II, containing the responding party's position with respect to each issue raised by the moving party, immediately followed by a concise statement of the law and authorities relating to it.

3. Part III, containing a statement of any additional issues raised by the responding party, the statement of each issue to be followed by a concise statement of the law and authorities relating to it.

4. Schedule A, containing a list of the authorities referred to.

5. Schedule B, containing the text of all relevant provisions of statutes, regulations and by-laws.

(9) Parts I to III shall be arranged in paragraphs numbered consecutively throughout the factum.

(10) The responding party shall file three copies of the factum, and of the motion record, if any, and may file three copies of a book of authorities, if any, with proof of service within 25 days after service of the moving party's motion record and other documents.

Moving Party's Reply Factum

(11) If the responding party's factum raises an issue on which the moving party has not taken a position in the moving party's factum, that party may serve a reply factum.

(12) The reply factum shall contain consecutively numbered paragraphs setting out the moving party's position on the issue, followed by a concise statement of the law and authorities relating to it.

(13) The moving party shall file three copies of the reply factum with proof of service within 10 days after service of the responding party's factum.

Determination of Motion

(14) Thirty-six days after service of the moving party's motion record and factum, and transcripts, if any, or on the filing of the moving party's reply factum, if any, whichever is earlier, the motion shall be submitted to the court for consideration, and

(a) if it appears from the written material that no oral hearing is warranted, the court shall determine the motion;

(b) otherwise, the court shall order an oral hearing to determine the motion.

Date for Oral Hearing

(15) If the court orders an oral hearing, the Registrar shall fix a date for it.

Time for Delivering Notice of Appeal

(16) Where leave is granted, the notice of appeal shall be delivered within seven days after the granting of leave.

Costs Appeal Joined with Appeal as of Right

(17) Where a party seeks to join an appeal under clause 133(b) of the *Courts of Justice Act* with an appeal as of right,

(a) the request for leave to appeal shall be included in the notice of appeal as part of the relief sought;

(b) leave to appeal shall be sought from the panel of the Court of Appeal hearing the appeal as of right;

(c) where leave is granted, the panel may then hear the appeal.

Costs Cross-Appeal Joined with Appeal or Cross-Appeal as of Right

(18) Where a party seeks to join a cross-appeal under clause 133(b) of the *Courts of Justice Act* with an appeal or cross-appeal as of right,

(a) the request for leave to appeal shall be included in the notice of appeal or cross-appeal as part of the relief sought;

(b) leave to appeal shall be sought from the panel of the Court of Appeal hearing the appeal or cross-appeal as of right;

(c) where leave is granted, the panel may then hear the appeal.

Application of Rules

(19) Subrules (1) to (16) do not apply where subrules (17) and (18) apply. [en. O. Reg. 61/96, s. 6; am. O. Reg. 175/96, s. 2]

COMMENCEMENT OF APPEALS

Time for Appeal and Service of Notice

61.04(1) An appeal to an appellate court shall be commenced by serving a notice of appeal (Form 61A) together with the certificate required by subrule 61.05(1) on every party whose interest may be affected by the appeal, other than,

(a) a defendant who was noted in default; or

(b) a respondent who has not delivered a notice of appearance, unless he or she was heard at the hearing with leave,

and on any person entitled by statute to be heard on the appeal, within thirty days after the date of the order appealed from, unless a statute or these rules provide otherwise.

Title of Proceeding

(2) The title of the proceeding in an appeal shall be in accordance with (Form 61B).

Notice of Appeal

(3) The notice of appeal (Form 61A) shall state the relief sought and the grounds of appeal.

(4) The notice of appeal, with proof of service, shall be filed in accordance with subrule 4.05(4) (leaving in or mailing to court office) in the Registrar's office within ten days after service.

Cross-Reference: See cases under rule 3.02 regarding extension of time for appeals.

Canadian Express Ltd. v. Blair (1991), 6 O.R. (3d) 212, 5 C.P.C. (3d) 161, 53 O.A.C. 397 (Div. Ct.).

A party may appeal only from an order, not from the related reasons for decision. Even where the reasoning may prejudice a party in another proceeding, there is no appeal; the prejudice should be dealt with in the other proceeding.

Can. Acceptance Corp. Ltd. v. Biluk (1978), 10 C.P.C. 178 (Ont. Dist. Ct.).

Where any substantial matter remains to be determined on the settlement of a judgment, the time for appealing runs from the date of entry of the judgment and not the date of pronouncement.

Brown v. Brown (1978), 22 O.R. (2d) 50, 7 R.F.L. (2d) 398 (C.A.).

The respondent must be served with the notice of appeal whether or not he appeared at first instance. [*But compare now rules 19.02(3) and 61.04(1) — Authors.*]

Re Permanent Invt. Corp. Ltd. and Township of Ops and Graham, [1967] 2 O.R. 13, 62 D.L.R. (2d) 258 (C.A.).

The time for appeal usually runs from the date of pronouncement of a judgment but where a substantial matter remains to be determined on the settlement of the judgment the time runs from the date of entry.

Toronto v. B.A. Oil Co.; Toronto Harbour Commrs. v. B.A. Oil Co., [1947] O.W.N. 88, reversed on other grounds [1947] O.R. 256, [1947] 3 D.L.R. 129 (C.A.).

Where the master made an order but entertained further argument on the settling of the order ten days later and the formal order was taken out two days after that, the time for serving a notice of appeal ran from the date of the final formal order.

CERTIFICATE OR AGREEMENT RESPECTING EVIDENCE

Appellant's Certificate Respecting Evidence

61.05(1) In order to minimize the number of documents and the length of the transcript required for an appeal, the appellant shall serve with the notice of appeal an appellant's certificate respecting evidence (Form 61C) setting out those portions of the evidence that, in the appellant's opinion, are not required for the appeal.

Respondent's Certificate Respecting Evidence

(2) Within fifteen days after service of the appellant's certificate, the respondent shall serve on the appellant a respondent's certificate respecting evidence (Form 61D), confirming the appellant's certificate or setting out any additions to or deletions from it.

(3) A respondent who fails to serve a respondent's certificate within the prescribed time shall be deemed to have confirmed the appellant's certificate.

Agreement Respecting Evidence

(4) Instead of complying with subrules (1) to (3), the parties may, within thirty days after service of the notice of appeal, make an agreement respecting the documents to be included in the appeal books and the transcript required for the appeal.

Ordering Transcripts

(5) The appellant shall within thirty days after filing the notice of appeal file proof that the appellant has ordered a transcript of all oral evidence that the parties have not agreed to omit, subject to any direction under subrule 61.09(4) (relief from compliance).

(6) A party who has previously ordered a transcript of oral evidence shall forthwith modify the order in writing to comply with the certificates or agreement.

(7) When the evidence has been transcribed, the court reporter shall forthwith give written notice to all parties and the Registrar.

Costs Sanctions for Unnecessary Evidence
(8) The court may impose costs sanctions where evidence is transcribed or exhibits are reproduced unnecessarily.

> *Cross-Reference:* See the practice direction regarding unnecessary evidence in civil appeals in the Court of Appeal following the Highlights of Rule 61.

Valiquette v. Vandelac (1979), 9 C.P.C. 203 (Ont. Div. Ct.).
An appeal was dismissed where the appellant decided to proceed with the appeal after having countermanded the ordering of the evidence, in circumstances indicating a "devious manoeuvre".

Can. Memorial Chiropractic College v. Metro. Toronto, [1967] 1 O.R. 244, affirmed [1968] S.C.R. 198, 66 D.L.R. (2d) 268.
A party may be penalized in costs for including in its appeal books evidence and exhibits irrelevant to the issues in appeal.

SECURITY FOR COSTS OF APPEAL

61.06(1) In an appeal where it appears that,
(a) there is good reason to believe that the appeal is frivolous and vexatious and that the appellant has insufficient assets in Ontario to pay the costs of the appeal;
(b) an order for security for costs could be made against the appellant under rule 56.01; or
(c) for other good reason, security for costs should be ordered,
a judge of the appellate court, on motion by the respondent, may make such order for security for costs of the proceeding and of the appeal as is just.

(2) If an appellant fails to comply with an order under subrule (1), a judge of the appellate court on motion may dismiss the appeal. [am. O. Reg. 465/93, s. 6]

Aegis Biomedical Technologies Ltd. v. Jackowski (March 26, 1996), Doc. CA C22356, M17783 (Ont. C.A.).
The court awarded security for costs of both the appeal and the trial. There is no principle limiting the court's discretion to order security for the trial costs.

967084 Ontario Inc. v. Ahola (1995), 24 O.R. (3d) 89 (Gen. Div.).
A costs award which is an integral part of the order under appeal cannot form the basis for security for costs under rule 61.06(1)(c).

Canadian Imperial Bank of Commerce v. 437544 Ontario Inc. (1995), 86 O.A.C. 241 (C.A.).
The court refused to order security for costs of an appeal by a trustee in bankruptcy. If the appeal were unsuccessful, the trustee would be personally liable for costs.

Schmidt v. Toronto Dominion Bank (1995), 24 O.R. (3d) 1, 37 C.P.C. (3d) 383, 82 O.A.C. 233 (C.A.).
Security for costs was ordered where there was good reason to believe the appeal was frivolous and vexatious. It was not necessary to find the appeal was in fact devoid of merit.

McKee v. Di Battista, Gambin Development Ltd. (1995), 22 O.R. (3d) 700, 80 O.A.C. 9 (C.A.).

To obtain an order for security for costs it is necessary that the appeal *appears to be* frivolous or vexatious, not that the appeal *is* frivolous or vexatious.

Societe Sepic S.A. v. AGA Stone Ltd. (1995), 21 O.R. (3d) 542, 34 C.P.C. (3d) 206, 77 O.A.C. 306 (C.A.).

The Court of Appeal does not have jurisdiction to order security for costs of a motion for leave to appeal.

Horton v. Joyce (1994), 20 O.R. (3d) 59, 36 C.P.C. (3d) 242, 73 O.A.C. 395 (C.A.).

On a motion for security for costs of an appeal under rule 61.06(1)(a), the respondent must show that the appeal is not *bona fide* in two respects: (1) that the appeal is frivolous to the point of being manifestly devoid of merit; and (2) that the appellant lacks substance to the point where it would be unjust to permit the appeal to continue without protecting the respondent with respect to costs.

Jaffe v. Miller (1994), 32 C.P.C. (3d) 242, 76 O.A.C. 15 (C.A.), affirmed (March 17, 1995) (Ont. C.A.), leave to appeal to Supreme Court of Canada refused (December 14, 1995), Doc. 24971.

The court ordered the appellants to post $150,000 security for costs of the appeal but did not require security for the costs of the trial.

Toys "R" Us (Canada) Ltd. v. Rotisseries St-Hubert Ltée/St-Hubert Bar-B-Q Ltd. (1994), 20 O.R. (3d) 814, 32 C.P.C. (3d) 88, 75 O.A.C. 242 (C.A.).

Rule 61.06(1)(b) cannot be applied to require a non-resident defendant or respondent to provide security for costs of an appeal.

Grenier v. Southam Inc. (1994), 19 O.R. (3d) 799, 74 O.A.C. 150 (C.A.).

The court dismissed a motion for security for costs where the appellant was employed and had some assets and where there was no evidence the appeal was frivolous and vexatious.

GEAC Canada Ltd. v. Craig Erickson Systems Inc. (1994), 26 C.P.C. (3d) 355, 74 O.A.C. 136 (C.A.).

The Court of Appeal refused to order security for costs on an appeal from a finding of contempt. Although the appellant had apologized to the court of first instance, the apology had not amounted to an unqualified admission of contempt or a confession that the appeal was without merit. A respondent cannot rely upon rule 61.06(1)(b) to obtain an order for security for costs of an appeal against a defendant/appellant.

Hall-Chem Inc. v. Vulcan Packaging Inc. (1994), 27 C.P.C. (3d) 104, 72 O.A.C. 303 (C.A.).

The court held that a finding of fraud at trial was a special circumstance warranting an order for security for costs. Furthermore, it appeared that an order for security for costs would not prevent the appellant from proceeding with the appeal.

Tricontinental Investments Co. v. Guarantee Co. of North America (1989), 70 O.R. (2d) 461, 39 C.P.C. (2d) 113, 35 O.A.C. 253 (C.A.).

The court will not grant security for costs of an appeal simply because the appellant has not paid the costs awarded by the order under appeal. Rules [61.06(1)(b)] and 56.01(1)(c) cannot be combined to produce such a result.

T.D. Bank v. Szilagyi Farms Ltd. (1988), 65 O.R. (2d) 433, 28 C.P.C. (2d) 231, 29 O.A.C. 357 (C.A.).

The court has no jurisdiction under rule 56.01 to order security for costs of an appeal by a defendant. Furthermore, the inherent jurisdiction of the court does not justify ordering security for costs in the absence of specific statutory authority. [*But see now rule 61.06 — Authors.*]

Fabing v. Conceicao (1986), 54 O.R. (2d) 402, 9 C.P.C. (2d) 36, 15 O.A.C. 66 (C.A.).

On a motion for security for costs pending appeal the court considered the merits of the case and awarded dollar for dollar security including the costs of trial.

Dona v. Dona (1986), 54 O.R. (2d) 256, 9 C.P.C. (2d) 161, 2 R.F.L. (3d) 107, 16 O.A.C. 356 (C.A.).

The successful applicant in an application to vary a decree *nisi* of divorce is not entitled to security for costs from the respondent regarding an appeal launched by the respondent. [*Note the rule has now been amended to apply to applications— Authors.*]

Greensteel Industs. Ltd. v. Binks Mfg. Co. of Can. Ltd. (1982), 35 O.R. (2d) 45, 131 D.L.R. (3d) 343 (C.A.).

The court refused to order security for costs on appeal because the appellant, a Manitoba corporation, had substantial assets, no previous motion for security had been brought, there was reciprocal enforcement of judgments legislation with Manitoba and there was no suggestion the appeal was frivolous.

Cheng v. Hadley (1978), 10 C.P.C. 76 (Ont. Master).

A motion for security for costs pending an appeal must be made to the appellate court. The master has no jurisdiction.

K.V.C. Electric Ltd. v. Louis Donolo Inc. [1964] 1 O.R. 565, 43 D.L.R. (2d) 198 (H.C.).

The court no longer has inherent jurisdiction to order security for costs and since the Rules do not provide for such an order on an appeal by an unsuccessful non-resident defendant, it cannot be made.

Poole v. Hirsh, [1960] O.W.N. 532 (H.C.).

A non-resident defendant appellant was required to post security for two-thirds of the estimated costs of the appeal.

Van Fleet v. Public Trustee, [1948] O.W.N. 524 (H.C.).

A non-resident defendant with no assets in the jurisdiction was ordered to provide security for the costs of an appeal from a decision against her.

CROSS-APPEALS

61.07(1)　A respondent who,
(a)　seeks to set aside or vary the order appealed from; or
(b)　will seek, if the appeal is allowed in whole or in part, other relief or a different disposition than the order appealed from,
shall, within fifteen days after service of the notice of appeal, serve a notice of cross-appeal (Form 61E) on all parties whose interests may be affected by the cross-appeal and on any person entitled by statute to be heard on the appeal, stating the relief sought and the grounds of the cross-appeal.

(2)　The notice of cross-appeal, with proof of service, shall be filed in the office of the Registrar within ten days after service.

(3)　Where a respondent has not delivered a notice of cross-appeal, no cross-appeal may be heard except with leave of the court hearing the appeal.

Lesyork Holdings Ltd. v. Munden Acres Ltd. (1976), 13 O.R. (2d) 430, 1 C.P.C. 261 (C.A.).

Time for cross-appealing will not be extended where the appeal has been abandoned.

AMENDMENT OF NOTICE OF APPEAL OR CROSS-APPEAL

Supplementary Notice to be Served and Filed

61.08(1)   The notice of appeal or cross-appeal may be amended without leave, before the appeal is perfected, by serving on each of the parties on whom the notice was served a supplementary notice of appeal or cross-appeal (Form 61F) and filing it with proof of service.

Argument Limited to Grounds Stated

(2)   No grounds other than those stated in the notice of appeal or cross-appeal or supplementary notice may be relied on at the hearing, except with leave of the court hearing the appeal.

Relief Limited

(3)   No relief other than that sought in the notice of appeal or cross-appeal or supplementary notice may be sought at the hearing, except with the leave of the court hearing the appeal.

McGillis v. Sullivan, [1947] O.W.N. 459 (C.A.).

An application for leave to re-argue an appeal on the basis of a new ground of appeal was granted.

Shoprite Stores v. Gardiner, [1935] S.C.R. 637, [1936] 2 D.L.R. 479.

Where an appellant failed to include a ground of appeal in a notice of appeal, the Supreme Court of Canada refused to entertain argument on that point.

PERFECTING APPEALS

Time for Perfecting

61.09(1)   The appellant shall perfect the appeal by complying with sub-rules (2) and (3),

(a)   where no transcript of evidence is required for the appeal, within thirty days after filing the notice of appeal; or

(b)   where a transcript of evidence is required for the appeal, within thirty days after receiving notice that the evidence has been transcribed.

Record and Exhibits

(2)   The appellant shall cause to be forwarded to the Registrar the record and the original exhibits from the court or tribunal from which the appeal is taken.

Material to be Served and Filed

(3)   The appellant shall,

(a)   serve on every other party to the appeal and any person entitled by statute or an order under rule 13.03 (intervention in appeal) to be heard on the appeal,

(i)   the appeal book referred to in rule 61.10,

(ii)   the transcript of evidence, and

(iii)   the appellant's factum referred to in rule 61.11;

(b) file with the Registrar, with proof of service,

    (i) in an appeal to the Court of Appeal, five copies, or

    (ii) in an appeal to the Divisional Court, three copies,

of the documents served under clause (a); and

(c) file with the Registrar a certificate of perfection stating that the record, exhibits, appeal book, transcript and appellant's factum have been filed, and setting out the name, address and telephone number of the solicitor for,

    (i) every party to the appeal, and

    (ii) any person entitled by statute or an order under rule 13.03 (intervention in appeal) to be heard on the appeal,

or, where a party or person acts in person, the person's name, address for service and telephone number.

Relief from Compliance

(4) Where compliance with the rules governing appeal books or transcripts of evidence would cause undue expense or delay, a judge of the appellate court may give special directions.

Notice of Listing for Hearing

(5) When an appeal is perfected, the Registrar shall place it on the list of cases to be heard at the appropriate place of hearing and shall mail a notice of listing for hearing (Form 61G) to every person listed in the certificate of perfection.

Davis v. Beatty (1988), 63 O.R. (2d) 779, 26 C.P.C. (2d) 140, 28 O.A.C. 42 (Div. Ct.).

Where an appellant broke into the court reporter's home and stole transcripts and tapes of the trial, the court refused to extend the time to perfect the appeal and dismissed the appeal.

Durall Const. Ltd. v. W.A. McDougall Ltd. (1983), 34 C.P.C. 10 (Ont. Div. Ct.).

The court ordered an appeal expedited where the subject of the appeal was a ruling made in the course of a lengthy trial regarding the participation of a non-party and where the trial would not be resumed until the appeal was heard.

APPEAL BOOK

61.10(1) The appeal book shall contain, in consecutively numbered pages arranged in the following order, a copy of,

(a) a table of contents describing each document, including each exhibit, by its nature and date and, in the case of an exhibit, by exhibit number or letter;

(b) the notice of appeal and any notice of cross-appeal or supplementary notice of appeal or cross-appeal;

(c) the order or decision appealed from as signed and entered;

(d) the reasons of the court or tribunal appealed from with a further typed or printed copy if the reasons are handwritten;

(d.1) if an earlier order or decision was the subject of the hearing before the court or tribunal appealed from, a copy of the order or decision, as signed and entered, and a copy of any reasons for it, with a further typed or printed copy if the reasons are handwritten;

(e) the pleadings or notice of application or any other document that initiated the proceeding or defines the issues in it;

(f) any affidavit evidence, including exhibits, that the parties have not agreed to omit;

(g) all documentary exhibits filed at a hearing or marked on an examination that the parties have not agreed to omit, arranged in order by date and not by exhibit number or, where there are documents having common characteristics, arranged in separate groups in order by date;

(h) the certificates or agreement respecting evidence referred to in rule 61.05;

(i) any order made in respect of the conduct of the appeal;

(j) any other document relevant to the hearing of the appeal; and

(k) a certificate (Form 61H) signed by the appellant's solicitor, or on the solicitor's behalf by someone he or she has specifically authorized, stating that the contents of the appeal book are complete and legible.

(2) The Registrar may refuse to accept an appeal book if it does not comply with these rules or is not legible. [am. O. Reg. 61/96, s. 7]

APPELLANT'S FACTUM

61.11(1) The appellant's factum shall be signed by the appellant's counsel, or on counsel's behalf by someone he or she has specifically authorized, and shall consist of,

(a) Part I, containing a statement identifying the appellant and the court or tribunal appealed from and stating the result in that court or tribunal;

(b) Part II, containing a concise summary of the facts relevant to the issues on the appeal, with such reference to the evidence by page and line as is necessary;

(c) Part III, containing a statement of each issue raised, immediately followed by a concise statement of the law and authorities relating to that issue;

(d) Part IV, containing a statement of the order that the appellate court will be asked to make, including any order for costs;

(e) a certificate stating how much time (expressed in hours or fractions of an hour) counsel estimates will be required for his or her oral argument, not including reply;

(f) Schedule A, containing a list of the authorities referred to; and

(g) Schedule B, containing the text of all relevant provisions of statutes, regulations and by-laws.

(2) Parts I to IV shall be arranged in paragraphs numbered consecutively throughout the factum. [am. O. Reg. 534/95, s. 4]

Cross-Reference: See the practice direction regarding factums in civil appeals in the Court of Appeal following the Highlights of Rule 61.

U.F.C.W., Local 617P v. Royal Dressed Meats Inc. (Trustee of) (1989), 37 C.P.C. (2d) 154, 76 C.B.R. (N.S.) 79 (Ont. S.C.).

The court refused to strike references to *Hansard* which were included as an aid to statutory construction in a factum in an appeal to a judge in bankruptcy.

Crone and Robert Crone Pictures Ltd. v. Orion Ins. Co., [1966] 1 O.R. 221, 53 D.L.R. (2d) 98, affirmed [1967] S.C.R. 157, [1967] I.L.R. 1-179, 60 D.L.R. (2d) 630.

A statement of points of law and fact intended to be argued should not include argument.

RESPONDENT'S FACTUM

Filing and Service

61.12(1) Every respondent shall prepare a respondent's factum and shall file with the Registrar,

(a) in an appeal to the Court of Appeal, five copies; or

(b) in an appeal to the Divisional Court, three copies,

with proof of service on all other parties to the appeal.

Time for Delivery

(2) A respondent's factum shall be delivered within thirty days after service of the appeal book, transcript of evidence and appellant's factum.

Contents

(3) The respondent's factum shall be signed by the respondent's counsel, or on counsel's behalf by someone he or she has specifically authorized, and shall consist of,

(a) Part I, containing a statement of the facts in the appellant's summary of relevant facts that the respondent accepts as correct and those facts with which the respondent disagrees and a concise summary of any additional facts relied on, with such reference to the evidence by page and line as is necessary;

(b) Part II, containing the position of the respondent with respect to each issue raised by the appellant, immediately followed by a concise statement of the law and the authorities relating to that issue;

(c) Part III, containing a statement of any additional issues raised by the respondent, the statement of each issue to be immediately followed by a concise statement of the law and the authorities relating to that issue;

(d) Part IV, containing a statement of the order that the appellate court will be asked to make, including any order for costs;

(e) a certificate stating how much time (expressed in hours or fractions of an hour) counsel estimates will be required for his or her oral argument;

(f) Schedule A, containing a list of the authorities referred to; and

(g) Schedule B, containing the text of all relevant provisions of statutes, regulations and by-laws that are not included in Schedule B to the appellant's factum.

(3.1) Parts I to IV shall be arranged in paragraphs numbered consecutively throughout the factum.

Cross-Appeal

(4) Where a respondent has served a notice of cross-appeal under rule 61.07,

(a) the respondent shall prepare a factum as an appellant by cross-appeal and deliver it with or incorporate it in the respondent's factum; and

(b) the appellant shall deliver a factum as a respondent to the cross-appeal within ten days after service of the respondent's factum. [am. O. Reg. 534/95, s. 5]

Cross-Reference: See the practice direction regarding factums in civil appeals in the Court of Appeal following the Highlights of Rule 61.

Netherton v. Johnson (1976), 2 C.P.C. 21 (Ont. C.A.).

Where there is inexcusable delay in the delivery of a respondent's statement, costs of a successful appeal may be awarded on a solicitor and client scale.

DISMISSAL FOR DELAY

Motion by Respondent

61.13(1) Where an appellant has not,

(a) filed proof that a transcript of evidence that the parties have not agreed to omit was ordered within the time prescribed by subrule 61.05(5); or

(b) perfected the appeal within the time prescribed by subrule 61.09(1) or by an order of the appellate court or a judge of that court,

the respondent may make a motion to the Registrar, on ten days notice to the appellant, to have the appeal dismissed for delay.

Notice by Registrar

(2) Where the appellant has not,

(a) filed a transcript of evidence within thirty days after the Registrar received notice that the evidence has been transcribed; or

(b) perfected the appeal within one year after filing the notice of appeal, the Registrar may serve notice on the appellant that the appeal will be dismissed for delay unless it is perfected within ten days after service of the notice.

(2.1) If the appeal is from a summary judgment and the appellant has not perfected it within the time prescribed by subrule 61.09(1) or by an order of the appellate court or a judge of that court, the Registrar may serve notice on the appellant that the appeal will be dismissed for delay unless it is perfected within 10 days after service of the notice.

Registrar to Dismiss where Default not Cured

(3) Where the appellant does not cure the default,

(a) in the case of a motion under subrule (1), before the hearing of the motion; or

(b) in the case of a notice under subrule (2) or (2.1), within 10 days after service of the notice;
or within such longer period as a judge of the appellate court allows, the Registrar shall make an order in (Form 61I) dismissing the appeal for delay, with costs and shall serve the order on the respondent.

Tsalamatas v. Wawanesa Mutual Ins. Co. (1983), 37 O.R. (2d) 461, 28 C.P.C. 254, 137 D.L.R. (3d) 62 (C.A.).

A single judge of the Court of Appeal does not have jurisdiction to make an order dismissing an appeal for want of prosecution. The appropriate course is to move before the Registrar.

Meridian Property Mgmt. v. Fournier, [1973] 2 O.R. 322 (H.C.).

An appeal to the Divisional Court which has been dismissed as an abandoned appeal may be restored to the list for hearing only by an order of the full Divisional Court or by a judge designated for that purpose by the court. [*See now rule 61.16(5) — Authors.*]

Cross-Appeals
(4) Where a respondent who has served a notice of cross-appeal has not delivered a factum in the cross-appeal within thirty days after service of the appeal book, transcript of evidence and appellant's factum, the appellant may make a motion to the Registrar, on five days notice to the respondent, to have the cross-appeal dismissed for delay.

(5) Where the respondent does not deliver a factum in the cross-appeal before the hearing of the motion under subrule (4) or within such longer period as a judge of the appellate court allows, the Registrar shall make an order in (Form 61I) dismissing the cross-appeal for delay, with costs.

Motions for Leave
(6) On a motion for leave to appeal, where the moving party has not served and filed the motion record and other documents in accordance with subrule 61.03(2) or subrules 61.03.1(4) to (6), the responding party may make a motion to the Registrar, on 10 days notice to the moving party, to have the motion for leave to appeal dismissed for delay.

(7) On a motion for leave to appeal, where the moving party has not served and filed the motion record and other documents within 60 days after the filing of the notice of motion for leave to appeal, the Registrar may serve notice on the moving party that the motion will be dismissed for delay unless the documents are served and filed within 10 days after service of the notice.

(8) On a motion for leave to appeal, where the moving party,
(a) in the case of a motion under subrule (6), does not serve and file the documents before the hearing of that motion, or within such longer period as a judge of the appellate court allows;
(b) in the case of a notice under subrule (7), does not serve and file the documents within ten days after service of the notice or within such longer period as a judge of the appellate court allows,
the Registrar shall make an order in (Form 61J) dismissing the motion for delay, with costs. [am. O. Regs. 351/94, s. 5; 534/95, s. 6; 61/96, s. 8]

Barry Gilmour Holdings Inc. v. Hall (March 29, 1996), Doc. CA M16992, M17714 (Ont. C.A.).
Where a motion under rule 61.13(6) is brought in writing, rule 37.12.1(4)(a) applies and 14 days' notice must be given.

Christensen v. Scarborough (City Clerk) (1991), 3 C.P.C. (3d) 16, 44 O.A.C. 310 (Div. Ct.).
An appeal was dismissed where the appellant failed to perfect his appeal within the prescribed time. Where there is a demand for certainty and finality, as in election cases, the court will adhere to a strict application of the time periods set by the Rules.

Langer v. Yorkton Securities Inc. (1986), 57 O.R. (2d) 555, 14 C.P.C. (2d) 134, 19 O.A.C. 394 (C.A.).
A party responding to a motion under rule [61.13(4)] should move before a judge to obtain an order extending the time before the Registrar hears the motion under rule [61.13(4)].

ABANDONED APPEALS

Delivery of Notice of Abandonment
61.14(1) A party may abandon an appeal or cross-appeal by delivering a notice of abandonment (Form 61K).

Deemed Abandonment
(2) A party who serves a notice of appeal or cross-appeal and does not file it within ten days after service shall be deemed to have abandoned the appeal or cross-appeal, unless the court orders otherwise.

Effect of Abandonment
(3) Where an appeal or cross-appeal is abandoned or is deemed to have been abandoned, the appeal or cross-appeal is at an end, and the respondent or appellant is entitled to the costs of the appeal or cross-appeal, unless a judge of the appellate court orders otherwise.

Re Rogers, [1956] O.W.N. 22 (C.A.).
A notice of abandonment of an appeal was allowed to be withdrawn where it had not been served on all the respondents, had not been filed, and had been repudiated promptly.

CROSS-APPEAL WHERE APPEAL DISMISSED FOR DELAY OR ABANDONED

61.15(1) Where an appeal is dismissed for delay or is abandoned, a respondent who has cross-appealed may,
(a) within fifteen days thereafter, deliver a notice of election to proceed (Form 61L); and
(b) make a motion to a judge of the appellate court for directions in respect of the cross-appeal.
(2) Where the respondent does not deliver a notice of election to proceed within fifteen days, the cross-appeal shall be deemed to be abandoned without costs unless a judge of the appellate court orders otherwise.

MOTIONS IN APPELLATE COURT

Rule 37 Applies Generally

61.16(1) Rule 37, except rules 37.02 to 37.05 (jurisdiction to hear motions, place of hearing, to whom to be made, hearing date), 37.10 (motion record) and 37.17 (motion before commencement of proceeding), applies to motions in an appellate court, with necessary modifications.

Motion to Receive Evidence

(2) A motion under clause 134(4)(b) of the *Courts of Justice Act* (motion to receive further evidence) shall be made to the panel hearing the appeal.

Motions Required to be Heard by One Judge

(2.1) A motion required by subsection 7(2) or 21(3) of the *Courts of Justice Act* to be heard and determined by one judge may be heard and determined by a panel hearing an appeal or another motion in the proceeding properly made to the panel.

Motion to be Heard by More Than One Judge

(3) Where a motion in an appellate court is to be heard by more than one judge, the notice of motion shall state that the motion will be heard on a date to be fixed by the Registrar.

Motion Record and Factum

(4) On a motion referred to in subrule (3),

(a) the moving party shall serve a motion record that contains the documents referred to in subrule 37.10(2) and a factum consisting of a concise statement, without argument, of the facts and law relied on by the moving party, and shall file three copies of the motion record and factum, with proof of service, at least three days before the hearing; and

(b) the responding party,

(i) may, where of the opinion that the motion record is incomplete, serve a motion record that contains the documents referred to in subrule 37.10(3), and

(ii) shall serve a factum consisting of a concise statement, without argument, of the facts and law relied on by the responding party,

and shall file three copies of the responding party's motion record and factum, with proof of service, at least two days before the hearing; and

(c) a party who intends to refer to a transcript of evidence at the hearing shall ensure that three copies of it are filed at least two days before the hearing.

Review of Registrar's Order

(5) A person affected by an order or decision of the Registrar may make a motion to a judge of the appellate court to set it aside or vary it by a notice of motion that is served forthwith after the order or decision comes to the person's attention and names the first available hearing date that is at least three days after service of the notice of motion.

Review of Single Judge's Order

(6) A person who moves to set aside or vary the order of a judge of an appellate court under subsection 7(5) or 21(5) of the *Courts of Justice Act* shall do so by a notice of motion that is served within four days after the order is made and states that the motion will be heard on a date to be fixed by the Registrar. [am. O. Reg. 770/92, s. 15]

> *Cross-Reference:* As to when motions in an appellate court can be heard by a single judge, see the *Courts of Justice Act*, s. 7(2) and (3) (Court of Appeal), s. 21(3) and (4) (Divisional Court) and rule 37.14(6). See also the practice directions regarding motions to the Court of Appeal in civil matters and filing motion material in the Court of Appeal following the Highlights of Rule 61.

> *Lesyork Holdings Ltd. v. Munden Acres Ltd.* (1976), 13 O.R. (2d) 430, 1 C.P.C. 261 (C.A.).
> An appeal manifestly devoid of merit may be quashed on a motion brought for that purpose.

RULE 62   APPEALS FROM INTERLOCUTORY ORDERS AND OTHER APPEALS TO A JUDGE

Highlights

General. This Rule deals with two distinct aspects of appeals from interlocutory orders. First, rule 62.01 provides the procedure to be followed on appeals which may be taken as of right to a judge from interlocutory orders of a master or a certificate of assessment of costs. Second, rule 62.02 governs the granting of leave to appeal to the Divisional Court from an interlocutory order of a judge.

Right of appeal. Whether there is a *right* of appeal from an interlocutory order made on the hearing of a motion depends upon the person hearing the motion. If a "court" motion was heard by a master there will be an automatic right of appeal to a judge; however, if the motion is heard in the first instance by a judge, then there will be an appeal only with leave.

Appeals to a judge. An interlocutory order of a master may be appealed as of right to a judge: *Courts of Justice Act*, s. 17(a). An appeal from a certificate of assessment of costs in a proceeding in the General Division is to a judge of the General Division: s. 17(b). An appeal from a certificate of assessment of costs in a proceeding in the Court of Appeal is to a judge of the Court of Appeal: ss. 6(1)(c) and 7(2). Where the certificate relates to both courts, the appeal may be heard by a judge of the Court of Appeal: s. 6(2). An appeal from a certificate of assessment of costs is only available on issues in respect of which objections have been served under rule 58.10.

The appeal to a judge is commenced by the service of a notice of appeal which must be served within seven days after the date of the order appealed from.

The place of hearing of the appeal is governed by rule 37.03 and will generally be the county where the solicitor's office of the respondent is located: rule 62.01(6).

An appeal record and factums from both appellant and respondent are required on all interlocutory appeals, unless dispensed with by a judge: see rule 62.01(7)-(9).

Motions for leave to appeal to the Divisional Court. The appeal route is to the Divisional Court, with leave, from interlocutory orders made by a judge. Leave must be obtained from a judge other than the one appealed from: rule 62.02(1).

Leave is obtained by a notice of motion which must be served within seven days after the date of the order from which leave to appeal is sought (rule 62.02(2)). In addition to the normal motion record requirements (see rule 37.10), the parties must file factums: rule 62.02(6). See rule 12.06 regarding leave to appeal to the Divisional Court in class proceedings.

Final v. interlocutory orders. An order which finally determines a proceeding brought by way of application is a final order whether or not it finally resolves the real underlying dispute between the parties: *Buck Brothers Ltd. v. Frontenac Builders Ltd.* (1994), 19 O.R. (3d) 97 (C.A.); *Automatic Systems Inc. v. E.S. Fox Ltd.* (1994), 12 B.L.R. (2d) 148 (Ont. C.A.).

Summary of procedure. For a summary of the procedure on an appeal from an interlocutory order, see Procedural Charts (CHARTS).

Appeal routes. For charts depicting the appeal routes from final and interlocutory orders, see Procedural Charts (CHARTS).

Former Rules: Rules 220, 499, 514.

PROCEDURE ON APPEAL

Application of Rule

62.01(1) Subrules (2) to (10) apply to an appeal that is made to a judge,

(a) from an interlocutory order of a master, under clause 17(a) of the *Courts of Justice Act*;

(b) from a certificate of assessment of costs, under clause 6(1)(c) or 17(b) or subsection 90(4) of that Act; or

(c) under any other statute, unless the statute or a rule provides for another procedure.

Time For Appeal

(2) An appeal shall be commenced by serving a notice of appeal (Form 62A) on all parties whose interests may be affected by the appeal, within seven days after the date of the order or certificate appealed from.

Hearing Date

(3) The notice of appeal shall name the first available hearing date that is not less than seven days after the date of service of the notice of appeal, and rule 37.05 (hearing date for motions) applies, with necessary modifications.

Notice of Appeal

(4) The notice of appeal (Form 62A) shall state the relief sought and the grounds of appeal, and no grounds other than those stated in the notice may be relied on at the hearing, except with leave of the judge hearing the appeal.

(5) The notice of appeal shall be filed in the court office where the appeal is to be heard, with proof of service, not later than three days before the hearing date.

Place of Hearing

(6) The appeal shall be heard at a place determined in accordance with rule 37.03 (place of hearing of motions).

Appeal Record

(7) The appellant shall, not later than three days before the hearing, serve on every other party and file, with proof of service, in the court office where the appeal is to be heard, an appeal record containing, in consecutively numbered pages arranged in the following order,

(a) a table of contents describing each document, including each exhibit, by its nature and date and, in the case of an exhibit, by exhibit number or letter;

(b) a copy of the notice of appeal;

(c) a copy of the order or certificate appealed from, as signed and entered, and the reasons, if any, as well as a further typed or printed copy of the reasons if they are handwritten; and

(d) such other material that was before the judge or officer appealed from as is necessary for the hearing of the appeal, and a factum consisting of a concise statement, without argument, of the facts and law relied on by the appellant.

(8) The respondent shall, not later than 2 p.m. on the day before the hearing, serve on every other party and file with proof of service, in the court office where the appeal is to be heard,

(a) any further material that was before the judge or officer appealed from and is necessary for the hearing of the appeal; and

(b) a factum consisting of a concise statement, without argument, of the facts and law relied on by the respondent.

(9) A judge may dispense with compliance with subrules (7) and (8), in whole or in part, before or at the hearing of the appeal.

Abandoned Appeals

(10) Rule 61.14 applies, with necessary modifications, to the abandonment of an appeal under this rule.

Cross-Reference: See cases collected under *Courts of Justice Act*, s. 134, for effect of lack of reasons by the court of first instance.

Interlocutory Appeals — Generally

CBL Investments Inc. v. Menkes Corp. (1994), 17 O.R. (3d) 147 (Gen. Div.).

The court had inherent jurisdiction to dismiss an interlocutory appeal for delay.

Anthes Equipment Ltd. v. Wilhelm Layher GmbH (1986), 53 O.R. (2d) 435, 6 C.P.C. (2d) 252 (H.C.).

A judge of the High Court does not lose his or her jurisdiction as a judge of the Divisional Court simply because he or she is sitting in one courtroom rather than another. Where an appeal which should be brought before a judge of the Divisional Court sitting singly is brought incorrectly before a judge in Weekly Court, or vice versa, the judge should hear the appeal in his or her other capacity so that the parties are not shuttled back and forth between courts.

Courtney v. Schneider (1982), 31 C.P.C. 105, 139 D.L.R. (3d) 537 (Ont. H.C.).

Following the commencement of trial, a party cannot proceed with a pending interlocutory appeal.

Pitts v. Hawthorne (1979), 23 O.R. (2d) 369, 13 C.P.C. 178 (Div. Ct.).

An interlocutory order in a County Court action may be appealed to a judge of the High Court and no further. [*See now Courts of Justice Act, s. 19(1)(b) — Authors.*]

Interlocutory Appeals — Standard of Review of Decision of Court of First Instance

Air Canada v. McDonnell Douglas Corp., (December 2, 1994), Potts J. (Ont. Gen. Div.).

A master's determination of whether a document is relevant and producible is a discretionary decision and an appeal will not be heard *de novo. Trigg v. MI Movers Int. Transport Services Ltd., infra,* not followed.

Carnival Leisure Industries Ltd. v. Brigante (1993), 4 W.D.C.P. (2d) 209 (Ont. Gen. Div.).

An appeal from a decision of a master regarding the relevance of questions on a cross-examination on an affidavit should be heard *de novo.*

Swan (Committee of) v. Stroud (1993), 12 O.R. (3d) 378 (Gen. Div.).

A judge hearing an appeal from an order of a master, made without written reasons, concerning the propriety of a large number of discovery questions should not, in general, conduct a hearing *de novo*.

Borden & Elliot v. Deer Home Investments Ltd. (1992), 14 C.P.C. (3d) 269 (Ont. Gen. Div.).

An appeal from an assessment of costs is an interlocutory appeal, and therefore the appellate court should not interfere with an order unless it is clearly wrong. However, where the client was denied a full, fair and complete hearing at the assessment, the matters were referred back for re-assessment by way of hearing *de novo*.

Westminer Canada Holdings Ltd. v. Coughlan (1990), 75 O.R. (2d) 405, 73 D.L.R. (4th) 584, 41 O.A.C. 377 (Div. Ct.).

A decision of the master staying a proceeding on the grounds of inconvenient forum involves an issue vital to the disposition of the law suit and accordingly it may be considered by the court *de novo*: *Marleen Investments v. McBride, infra*, does not apply.

Canada Life Assurance Co. v. Spago Ristorante Inc. (1990), 46 C.P.C. (2d) 166 (Ont. Gen. Div.).

Marleen Investments Ltd. v. McBride, infra, does not apply to appeals concerning relevance of questions on examinations for discovery and cross-examinations or to claims of privilege.

Passarelli v. Di Cienzo (1989), 67 O.R. (2d) 603, 34 C.P.C. (2d) 54 (H.C.).

A judge hearing an appeal from a master's order regarding issuing a certificate of pending litigation may substitute his discretion for the master's discretion. *Marleen Investments v. McBride, infra*, does not apply.

Trigg v. MI Movers Int. Transport Services Ltd. (1986), 13 C.P.C. (2d) 150 (Ont. H.C.).

The relevance of documents to the issues in an action is not a discretionary matter and an appeal from a master's order thereon is not governed by *Marleen Investments v. McBride, infra*.

Tru-Style Designs Inc. v. Greymac Properties Inc. (1986), 56 O.R. (2d) 462, 11 C.P.C. (2d) 117, 31 D.L.R. (4th) 253 (H.C.).

An appeal from an interlocutory order involving a question vital to the final issue of a case requires a rehearing in which the appeal judge may substitute his discretion for that exercised below.

Elmore v. Nanticoke (1985), 6 C.P.C. (2d) 211 (Ont. H.C.).

The High Court reversed a discretionary order of a District Court judge to the extent there was no evidence to support the exercise of the discretion, but did not interfere to the extent there was such evidence.

Picotte Insulation Inc. v. Mansonville Plastics (B.C.) Ltd. (1985), 48 C.P.C. 169 (Ont. H.C.).

A judge hearing an appeal from an interlocutory ruling on issues vital to the final disposition of the case may substitute his own discretion for that of the court of first instance.

Stoicevski v. Casement (1983), 43 O.R. (2d) 436, 43 C.P.C. 178 (C.A.).

There is an exception to the general rule against conducting a rehearing on an appeal from a discretionary order of a master where the order deals with issues vital to the final disposition of the case. In such circumstances the appellate court may substitute its own discretion.

Wagman v. Blue Mountain Resorts Ltd. (1984), 47 C.P.C. 53 (Ont. H.C.).

Where a master makes a discretionary order without giving reasons the appellate court must, of necessity, proceed to a rehearing of the matter *de novo*.

Marleen Investments Ltd. v. McBride (1979), 23 O.R. (2d) 125, 13 C.P.C. 221, 27 Chitty's L.J. 69 (H.C.).

An appeal from an interlocutory order of the master involving the exercise of discretion should not be heard by way of a rehearing and should only be allowed if the order is clearly wrong.

Whether Orders are Final or Interlocutory

[*The following cases are organized by subject-matter in the same sequence as the subjects are referred to in the Rules and generally correspond with the sequence in which the subjects would arise in the conduct of an action — Authors.*]

Orders Made Disposing of Applications

Buck Brothers Ltd. v. Frontenac Builders Ltd. (1994), 19 O.R. (3d) 97, 34 C.P.C. (3d) 76, 117 D.L.R. (4th) 373, 73 O.A.C. 298 (C.A.).

An order made in a proceeding by way of application that terminates that proceeding is a final order, notwithstanding that it may not have finally decided the real underlying matter in dispute between the parties. An order made on an application, that it should be left to arbitrators to decide whether the conditions for arbitration were satisfied, is final for the purposes of appeal.

Automatic Systems Inc. v. E.S. Fox Ltd. (1994), 12 B.L.R. (2d) 148, 13 C.L.R. (2d) 165 (Ont. C.A.)

Where defendants in a pending construction lien action brought an application (not a motion in the action) to stay the action on the basis of an arbitration clause, the order dismissing the application was final since that order finally disposed of the entire matter raised in that proceeding, *i.e.*, in the application.

Orders re Parties

Micaleff v. Gainers Inc. (1990), 77 D.L.R. (4th) 236, 44 O.AC. 48 (C.A.).

An order refusing intervenor status is final for purposes of appeal.

Bryson v. Kerr (1976), 13 O.R. (2d) 672, 2 C.P.C. 46 (Div. Ct.).

An order refusing a motion to add a party defendant is final for purposes of appeal.

Meadow Woode Corp. Ltd. v. Eurasia Realty Invts. Ltd. (1976), 1 C.P.C. 62 (Ont. Div. Ct.).

An order adding a party defendant is interlocutory for purposes of appeal.

Orders re Service

MacKay v. Queen Elizabeth Hospital (1989), 68 O.R. (2d) 92 (Div. Ct.).

An order setting aside service outside Ontario is final for purposes of appeal. *Mar v. Block* (1976), 13 O.R. (2d) 422, 1 C.P.C. 206 (H.C.) overruled.

Davies v. Hodson and Rose, [1956] O.W.N. 583, 6 D.L.R. (2d) 634 (C.A.).

An order extending the time for service of an originating process is interlocutory for purposes of appeal.

Orders re Default and Summary Judgment

Albert v. Spiegel (1993), 17 C.P.C. (3d) 90, 64 O.A.C. 239 (C.A.).

An order dismissing a motion for summary judgment is interlocutory and an appeal lies to the Divisional Court with leave. The Court of Appeal has no jurisdiction to grant such leave.

Laurentian Plaza Corp. v. Martin (1992), 7 O.R. (3d) 111, 6 C.P.C. (3d) 381, 89 D.L.R. (4th) 50, 54 O.A.C. 329 (C.A.).

An order setting aside a default judgment with a term requiring the defendant to provide security for the amount of the judgment is interlocutory for purposes of appeal.

Yepremian v. Fitzsimmons (1977), 3 C.P.C. 345 (Ont. Master).

An order dismissing a motion to set aside a default judgment without prejudice to a future application on other grounds is final.

Broadhead v. Rutman, [1966] 2 O.R. 834 (C.A.).

An order reinstating a default judgment is final for purposes of appeal.

Bennington Dev. Ltd. v. Cohen, [1966] 2 O.R. 837 (H.C.).

An order refusing a motion to set aside a default judgment is final for purposes of appeal.

Shoolbred v. Reliable Transport Ltd., [1959] O.W.N. 356 (C.A.).

An order setting aside a default judgment is interlocutory for purposes of appeal.

Industrial Int. Leasing Ltd. v. Macaroni Machine Ltd. (1976), 13 O.R. (2d) 555 (H.C.).

A summary judgment with a reference to determine quantum is "final" for purposes of appeal.

Orders re Stay of Proceedings

Hamel v. Intellad Marketing Ltd. (1986), 11 C.P.C. (2d) 137 (Ont. H.C.).

An order perpetually staying an Ontario action on the ground that Alberta is the *forum conveniens* is a final order.

General Capital Growth Ltd. v. Burlington (1979), 24 O.R. (2d) 669, 11 C.P.C. 35, 18 L.C.R. 204 (C.A.).

An order staying an action pending disposition of proceedings before an administrative tribunal is interlocutory for purposes of appeal.

I.M.L. Holdings Ltd. v. United Tire v. Rubber Co. (1976), 2 C.P.C. 141 (Ont. H.C.).

An order staying execution of a judgment pending disposition of a counterclaim is interlocutory.

Re Presswood and Int. Chemalloy Corp. (1975), 9 O.R. (2d) 399 (Div. Ct.).

An order removing a stay of proceedings is interlocutory for purposes of appeal.

Orders re Discontinuance

Bank of N.S. v. Schussler (1980), 28 O.R. (2d) 161, 111 D.L.R. (3d) 509 (H.C.).

An order granting leave to discontinue an action is interlocutory for purposes of appeal.

Orders Resolving Questions of Law

Ball v. Donais (1993), 13 O.R. (3d) 322, 45 M.V.R. (2d) 319, 64 O.A.C. 85 (C.A.).

An order under Rule 21 holding that the plaintiff's claim was not statute-barred was a final order since its effect was to preclude the defendant from thereafter raising the limitation period as a defence. While the order did not finally dispose of the rights of the parties to the litigation, it did finally dispose of the issue raised by that defence and thereby deprived the defendant of a substantive right which would be determinative of the entire action.

Orders re Pleadings

424317 Ont. Ltd. v. Silber (1989), 70 O.R. (2d) 59 (H.C.).

An order barring a plaintiff from amending its statement of claim to allege a breach of fiduciary duty is a final order for purposes of appeal.

Four Embarcadero Center Venture v. Mr. Greenjeans Corp. (1988), 65 O.R. (2d) 160, 27 C.P.C. (2d) 16 (C.A.).

An order refusing to strike out a statement of claim and grant summary dismissal is interlocutory.

385925 Ont. Ltd. v. American Life Ins. Co. (1985), 51 O.R. (2d) 382, 3 C.P.C. (2d) 137 (H.C.).

An order dismissing a motion to amend a statement of defence to raise a new defence is final for purposes of appeal.

Denton v. Jones (1976), 13 O.R. (2d) 419, 1 C.P.C. 65 (H.C.).

An order dismissing a motion to amend a statement of claim to allege a new cause of action is final for purposes of appeal.

Four Seasons Travel Ltd. v. Laker Airways Ltd. (1974), 6 O.R. (2d) 453 (Div. Ct.).

An order striking out a statement of defence is final for purposes of appeal.

Ainsworth v. Bickersteth, [1947] O.R. 525, [1947] 3 D.L.R. 517 (C.A.).

An order striking out a statement of claim as frivolous and vexatious is final.

Delaney Boat Lines & Services Ltd. v. Barrie (1976), 15 O.R. (2d) 675, 2 C.P.C. 103 (C.A.).

An order to strike out a counterclaim is a final order for the purposes of appeal.

Orders re Third Parties

Khalil v. United Invt. Services Ltd. (1975), 11 O.R. (2d) 707 (Div. Ct.).

An order dismissing a motion for leave to issue third and fourth party claims is final for purposes of appeal.

Genier v. Commercial Credit Corp. Ltd. (1975), 11 O.R. (2d) 493 (H.C.).

An order striking out a third party claim is final for purposes of appeal.

Binkley v. Matera, [1973] 1 O.R. 386 (C.A.).

An order refusing to extend the time for commencement of a third party claim is final for purposes of appeal.

Orders re Discovery

Belmont (Village) v. Joe Snyders Construction Ltd. (1989), 44 C.P.C. (2d) 292, 36 O.A.C. 235 (Div. Ct.).

An order that a non-party produce a document is a final order.

Kampus v. Bridgeford (1982), 25 C.P.C. 169 (Ont. C.A.).

Where the plaintiff included a claim on behalf of OHIP in his personal injury action, an order on appeal requiring OHIP to produce certain records was held to be interlocutory, although OHIP was not a party.

Frishke v. Royal Bank of Can. (1977), 17 O.R. (2d) 388, 4 C.P.C. 279, 80 D.L.R. (3d) 393 (C.A.).

Where a party is added only for the purpose of enforcing an injunction, an order requiring production and disclosure by it is a final order.

Guaranty Trust Co. v. Fleming & Talbot, [1946] O.W.N. 833, [1946] O.R. 817, [1947] 1 D.L.R. 184 (C.A.).

An order permitting the examination of a non-party is interlocutory as between plaintiff and defendant, but is final *vis-à-vis* the witness.

Orders re Trial of an Issue

Karbaliotis v. Anaheim Unit Investors (1996), 7 W.D.C.P. (2d) 149 (Ont. C.A.).
An order setting aside a certificate of assessment of solicitor and client costs and ordering the trial of an issue is interlocutory for purposes of appeal.

Tanenbaum v. Tanenbaum (1976), 14 O.R. (2d) 208, 26 R.F.L. 83 (C.A.).
An order directing the trial of an issue to resolve factual matters does not finally dispose of the rights of the parties and is therefore interlocutory for purposes of appeal.

Maynard v. Maynard, [1949] O.W.N. 547 (C.A.).
An order for the trial of an issue arising out of a motion was held to be final in the circumstances of this case.

Orders re Interim Relief

R. v. Consolidated Fastfrate Transport Inc. (1995), 40 C.P.C. (3d) 160, 24 O.R. (3d) 564, 99 C.C.C. (3d) 143, 61 C.P.R. (3d) 339, 125 D.L.R. (4th) 1, 83 O.A.C. 1 (C.A.).
A Mareva injunction obtained by the Crown for the purpose of assisting in a separate criminal law proceeding is a final order.

Ont. Medical Assn. v. Miller (1976), 14 O.R. (2d) 468, 2 C.P.C. 125 (C.A.).
The refusal to grant an interlocutory injunction restraining the release of information is interlocutory for purposes of appeal notwithstanding that the practical effect may be to end the litigation.

The Chesapeake and Ohio Ry. Co. v. Ball, [1953] O.R. 877 (C.A.).
An order dissolving an interim injunction is interlocutory for purposes of appeal.

McCart v. McCart and Adams, [1946] O.W.N. 776, [1946] O.R. 729, [1946] 4 D.L.R. 568 (C.A.).
An order appointing a receiver is interlocutory.

313473 Ont. Ltd. v. Lornal Const. Ltd. (1976), 3 C.P.C. 240 (Ont. Div. Ct.).
An order dismissing a motion to vacate a certificate of pending litigation is interlocutory.

Archer v. Archer (1975), 11 O.R. (2d) 432 (C.A.).
An order vacating a notice of pending litigation is interlocutory for purposes of appeal.

Orders re Summons to Witness

Smerchanski v. Lewis (1980), 30 O.R. (2d) 370, 18 C.P.C. 29, 117 D.L.R. (3d) 716 (C.A.).
An order quashing a subpoena to a stranger to the action was a final order and an appeal was permitted in the midst of the trial.

Orders re Set-Off of Judgments

Lewenza v. Ruszczak, [1959] O.W.N. 317, 20 D.L.R. (2d) 156 (C.A.).
An order setting off the amount owing on a counterclaim against the amount owing in the main action is final for purposes of appeal.

Orders re Costs

Somerleigh v. Brayshaw (1993), 15 C.P.C. (3d) 160 (Ont. Div. Ct.).
An order of a judge varying the report of an assessment officer regarding a solicitor and client assessment of costs is final for purposes of appeal.

Yakabuski v. Yakabuski Estate (1989), 36 C.P.C. (2d) 189, 31 O.A.C. 257 (Div. Ct.).

A provision as to costs contained in an interlocutory order is interlocutory for purposes of appeal. The fact that there was no appeal with respect to an interlocutory order, and only an appeal with respect to costs, did not convert the costs order into a final order.

Re Stabile, Maniaci, DiPoce & Angeletti and 413582 Ont. Ltd. (1981), 34 O.R. (2d) 52, 25 C.P.C. 153, 128 D.L.R. (3d) 489 (H.C.).

A master's order setting aside a *praecipe* order for taxation of a solicitor's account is final, an appeal from which lies to the Divisional Court.

Rickwood v. Aylmer, [1955] O.R. 470, [1955] 2 D.L.R. 726 (C.A.).

An order made on an appeal from a party and party taxation is interlocutory for purposes of further appeal.

Orders re Mortgage Actions

Lipson v. 365414 Ont. Ltd. (1982), 36 O.R. (2d) 729, 29 C.P.C. 18 (Div. Ct.).

An order refusing to extend the time for redemption beyond the period fixed by a judgment in a foreclosure action is interlocutory.

Lundy v. Travail Holdings Ltd. (1980), 30 O.R. (2d) 747, 20 C.P.C. 5, 14 R.P.R. 303, 117 D.L.R. (3d) 416 (Div. Ct.).

An order refusing to extend the time for redemption of a mortgage is a final order.

McGovern v. Mayhart Developers Ltd., [1972] 1 O.R. 545, 23 D.L.R. (3d) 529 (C.A.).

An order refusing to extend the time in which to file a request to redeem is final for purposes of appeal.

Orders re Family Law Proceedings

King v. King (1978), 20 O.R. (2d) 145, 9 R.F.L. (2d) 26, 86 D.L.R. (3d) 744 (H.C.).

An appeal from a preliminary judgment of a local judge regarding jurisdiction to make an order varying a decree *nisi* is to a judge of the High Court.

Whittaker v. Whittaker (1977), 5 C.P.C. 49 (Ont. C.A.).

An order refusing to vary the amount of maintenance fixed in a decree *nisi* is final.

Re McCurdy, [1954] O.W.N. 117 (C.A.).

An order awarding custody of a minor under the *Infants Act*, R.S.O. 1950, c. 180, is final for purposes of appeal.

Orders re Miscellaneous Matters

Aptowitzer v. Ontario (1995), 26 O.R. (3d) 254, 128 D.L.R. (4th) 574, 86 O.A.C. 73 (C.A.).

An order removing a party's solicitors of record is interlocutory for purposes of appeal.

Loblaws Inc. v. Ancaster (Town) Chief Building Official (1993), 4 W.D.C.P. (2d) 39 (Ont. Div. Ct.).

An order granting standing is interlocutory for purposes of appeal. An order refusing standing is final for purposes of appeal.

Hughes v. Eglinton Warden Merchants Market Inc. (1991), 2 C.P.C. (3d) 313 (Ont. Gen. Div.).

An order setting aside minutes of settlement is final for purposes of appeal.

Goldberg v. Goldberg (1989), 68 O.R. (2d) 124, 33 C.P.C. (2d) 30, additional reasons 68 O.R. (2d) 124 at 128 (H.C.).

An order dismissing a motion to enforce a purported settlement is interlocutory for purposes of appeal.

Murphy v. Welsh (1987), 62 O.R. (2d) 159n, 31 C.P.C. (2d) 209 (Div. Ct.).

An order retroactively extending the time for the commencement of an action is interlocutory for the purpose of appeal.

Goldman v. Hoffman-La Roche Ltd. (1987), 60 O.R. (2d) 161, 35 C.C.C. (3d) 488, 42 D.L.R. (4th) 436, 16 C.P.R. (3d) 289, (*sub nom. Dir. of Investigation & Research, Competition Act v. Hoffman-La Roche Ltd.*) 22 O.A.C. 85 (C.A.).

A search warrant issued pursuant to the *Competition Act* (Canada) is an investigative tool, and is not properly characterized as a final order.

Inversen v. Smith (1987), 58 O.R. (2d) 733, 16 C.P.C. (2d) 215 (*sub nom. Iversen v. Smith*), 22 O.A.C. 232 (Div. Ct.).

An order restraining solicitors from acting for a party is interlocutory.

Billes v. Parkin Partnership Architects Planners (1983), 40 O.R. (2d) 525, 31 C.P.C. 198, 143 D.L.R. (3d) 55 (C.A.).

An order dismissing a motion seeking leave to enforce an award under the *Arbitrations Act*, where the real issue is entitlement to interest on the award, is final.

Re Top Banana Ltd. and Foodcorp Ltd. (1981), 32 O.R. (2d) 289, 122 D.L.R. (3d) 319 (C.A.).

An order dismissing an application for a declaration under the *Landlord and Tenant Act* that the landlord was not entitled to interfere with the tenant's possession is final for purposes of appeal however the proper forum for the appeal is the Divisional Court pursuant to provisions of the *Judicature Act.*

Re McEnaney, [1949] O.W.N. 755 (C.A.).

An order removing proceedings from the Surrogate Court to the Supreme Court is interlocutory.

MOTION FOR LEAVE TO APPEAL

Leave to Appeal from Interlocutory Order of a Judge

62.02(1) Leave to appeal to the Divisional Court under clause 19(1)(b) of the Act shall be obtained from a judge other than the judge who made the interlocutory order.

Time for Service of Motion

(2) The notice of motion for leave shall be served within seven days after the date of the order from which leave to appeal is sought or such further time as is allowed by the judge hearing the motion.

Hearing Date

(3) The notice of motion for leave shall name the first available hearing date that is at least three days after service of the notice of motion.

Grounds on Which Leave May Be Granted

(4) Leave to appeal shall not be granted unless,

(a) there is a conflicting decision by another judge or court in Ontario or elsewhere on the matter involved in the proposed appeal and it is, in

the opinion of the judge hearing the motion, desirable that leave to appeal be granted; or

(b) there appears to the judge hearing the motion good reason to doubt the correctness of the order in question and the proposed appeal involves matters of such importance that, in his or her opinion, leave to appeal should be granted.

Motion Record

(5) On a motion for leave, the requirement of rule 37.10 respecting a motion record may be satisfied by,

(a) requisitioning that the motion record used on the motion that gave rise to the order from which leave to appeal is sought be placed before the judge hearing the motion for leave; and

(b) serving and filing a supplementary motion record containing the notice of motion for leave to appeal, a copy of the order from which leave to appeal is sought and a copy of any reasons given for the making of the order as well as a further typed or printed copy of the reasons if they are handwritten.

Factums Required

(6) On a motion for leave, each party shall serve on every other party to the motion a factum consisting of a concise statement, without argument, of the facts and law relied on by the party, and file it with proof of service in the court office where the motion is to be heard, not later than 2 p.m. on the day before the hearing.

Reasons for Granting Leave

(7) The judge granting leave shall give brief reasons in writing.

Subsequent Procedure Where Leave Granted

(8) Where leave is granted the notice of appeal required by rule 61.04, together with the appellant's certificate respecting evidence required by subrule 61.05(1), shall be delivered within seven days after the granting of leave, and thereafter Rule 61 applies to the appeal. [am. O. Regs. 212/93, s. 5; 465/93, s. 7]

Cross-Reference: See rule 12.06 regarding leave to appeal under the *Class Proceedings Act.*

Test on Motion for Leave

Comtrade Petroleum Inc. v. 490300 Ontario Ltd. (1992), 7 O.R. (3d) 542, 6 C.P.C. (3d) 271, 55 O.A.C. 316 (Div. Ct.).

In order to satisfy rule [62.02(4)(a)] it is insufficient to show that two courts have exercised their discretion to produce different results. It is necessary to demonstrate a difference in the principles chosen as a guide to the exercise of such discretion.

Greslik v. Ont. Legal Aid Plan (1988), 65 O.R. (2d) 110, 28 C.P.C. (2d) 294, 30 O.A.C. 53 (Div. Ct.).

Leave under rule [62.02(4)(b)] will be granted only for matters of public importance and matters relevant to the development of the law and the administration of justice.

Rankin v. McLeod, Young, Weir Ltd. (1986), 57 O.R. (2d) 569, 13 C.P.C. (2d) 192 (H.C.).

Leave to appeal from an interlocutory order of the High Court will only be given where the appeal involves matters of general or public importance which transcend the interests of the parties, warranting resolution by a higher level of judicial authority.

Stubbs v. Vanier (1985), 1 C.P.C. (2d) 191 (Ont. H.C.).

In seeking leave to appeal from a decision of a High Court judge, a contrary decision of a District Court judge is not a "conflicting decision" within the meaning of rule [62.02(4)]. *[But see Masse v. Dietrich, [1971] 3 O.R. 359, 20 D.L.R. (3d) 399 (Co. Ct.) — Authors.]*

Van Brugge v. Arthur Frommer Int. Ltd. (1982), 35 O.R. (2d) 333, 16 B.L.R. 143 (H.C.).

The court granted leave to appeal to determine the availability of "Mareva" injunctions in Ontario. It was an important issue on which there had been no appellate decisions.

Can. Egg Marketing Agency v. Sunnylea Foods Ltd. (1977), 3 C.P.C. 348 (Ont. H.C.).

For there to be "good reason to doubt the correctness" of the decision appealed from, a judge need not consider it to be wrong or even probably wrong.

Can. Metal Co. v. C.B.C. (1976), 2 C.P.C. 61 (Ont. H.C.).

Leave to appeal should not be granted where the judge hearing the application would himself dismiss the appeal.

Int. Formed Tubes Ltd. v. Ohio Crankshaft Co., [1965] 1 O.R. 621, 49 D.L.R. (2d) 127 (C.A.).

A conflicting decision from another jurisdiction may provide "good reason to doubt the correctness" of the decision or order in respect of which an appeal is sought.

Recourse from Disposition of Motion for Leave

Cameron v. Blair Holdings Corp., [1955] O.W.N. 61 (C.A.).

There is no appeal from an order granting leave to appeal and a motion to quash the appeal so granted on the ground that the order ought not have been made will not succeed.

The Chesapeake and Ohio Ry. Co. v. Ball, [1953] O.R. 877 (C.A.).

Where a party applies to a judge for leave to appeal and leave is refused, that decision is final and the party may not seek leave from another judge.

Motion for Leave — Miscellaneous

Silverberg v. Lichty (1993), 20 C.P.C. (3d) 373 (Ont. Div. Ct.).

The court refused to grant leave to appeal from a pre-trial order where there was no good reason to doubt the correctness of the order. Although the order may have been broader than required, it involved a procedural matter between the parties, and did not involve matters of such importance that leave should be granted.

Toms v. Agro (1992), 8 O.R. (3d) 95 (Gen. Div.), affirmed 11 O.R. (3d) 62 (Div. Ct.).

A motion for leave to appeal an interlocutory order granting the plaintiffs injunctive relief was allowed where the motions court judge did not have jurisdiction to grant the order appealed from.

Comtrade Petroleum Inc. v. 490300 Ontario Ltd. (1992), 7 O.R. (3d) 542, 6 C.P.C. (3d) 271, 55 O.A.C. 316 (Div. Ct.).

Where leave to appeal has been granted without reasons as required by rule 62.02(7), the appellate court may explore the issue of leave *de novo*.

Emberley v. Hans (1991), 48 C.P.C. (2d) 212 (Ont. Gen. Div.).

Although an extension of time should be granted with respect to a motion for leave to appeal if the justice of the case requires it, delays in family law proceedings are a particular concern. The merits of the proposed appeal were reviewed, and in the result, the justice of the case did not require an extension of time for leave to appeal.

Re Funt (1983), 41 C.P.C. 224 (Ont. Div. Ct.).

Leave is required to appeal an interlocutory order of a surrogate court judge to the Divisional Court.

Roynat Inc. v. Ivey (1982), 28 C.P.C. 293, leave to appeal to Ont. Div. Ct. granted 31 C.P.C. 54 (Ont. H.C.).

A judge hearing an appeal from a master refused to consider whether leave to appeal from his own order dismissing the appeal ought to be given.

Ferguson v. Imax Systems Corp. (1982), 38 O.R. (2d) 59, 28 C.P.C. 290, 134 D.L.R. (3d) 519, reversed on other grounds 43 O.R. (2d) 128, 150 D.L.R. (3d) 718 (C.A.).

Leave is not required to appeal an interlocutory order made in proceedings under a federal statute, where an absolute right of appeal is granted.

90207 Can. Ltd. v. Maple Leaf Village Ltd., (1981), 24 C.P.C. 152 (Ont. H.C.).

On an application for leave to appeal, affidavit material disclosing evidence which was or could have been before the judge of first instance was not admitted.

Texpack Ltd. v. Rowley, [1972] 2 O.R. 91 (C.A.).

An interlocutory injunction regarding a labour dispute may be appealed without leave. [*See Courts of Justice Act, s. 102(10) — Authors.*]

Kettle v. Jack, [1947] O.W.N. 267 (C.A.).

Leave to extend the time to move was granted where the law as laid down by the Court of Appeal was not brought to the attention of the trial judge and the appellants showed a *bona fide* intention to seek relief from the trial judgment.

RULE 63   STAY PENDING APPEAL

Highlights

Under the former Rules the procedures for obtaining a stay pending appeal varied depending upon who made the decision to be appealed and whether the order was final or interlocutory. Now, by Rule 63, common principles apply irrespective of who made the order or whether it is interlocutory or final.

Rule 63.01(1) provides the basic rule. On the delivery of a notice of appeal there is an automatic stay of any order, final or interlocutory, for the payment of money other than a support order or support enforcement order. There is also an automatic stay of certain landlord and tenant matters: rule 63.01(2). However, a judge of the court to which the appeal has been taken may lift the stay: rule 63.01(3).

This basic rule is supplemented by the power, given by rule 63.02, for a stay to be granted by court order. This power is important to permit a stay pending the delivery of a notice of appeal and to permit a stay in respect of orders for non-monetary relief. The scheme for such court-ordered stays is somewhat complicated. The court whose decision is to be appealed may order a stay in any type of case: rule 63.02(1)(a). However, such a stay expires on the happening of either one of two events: when the time for delivery of the notice of motion for leave to appeal or the time for delivery of a notice of appeal expires, or when a notice of motion for leave to appeal or notice of appeal is delivered.

The impact of this provision will vary depending upon the type of order and whether leave to appeal is required. If the order is one that can be appealed without leave and it is for the payment of money (other than support or support enforcement), then on the delivery of the notice to appeal the automatic stay under rule 63.01 will become effective. However, if the order is one that requires leave to appeal, or is for non-monetary relief, support, or support enforcement, then on the delivery of the notice of motion for leave to appeal or the notice of appeal, a stay obtained from the court below (under rule 63.02(1)(a)) will automatically expire: rule 63.02(1). If the appealing party wants to continue this stay, a motion will have to be made, under rule 63.02(1)(b), to the court to which a motion for leave to appeal has been made or an appeal has been taken. (*Note:* when leave to appeal is necessary this may involve two motions: the motion for leave to appeal — which may not come on for hearing for some time — and an immediate, urgent, motion for a stay).

While a stay prevents the judgment creditor from directing the sheriff to enforce execution, the creditor may now, notwithstanding the stay, have a writ of execution issued and file it with the sheriff or the land registry office so that it will bind the judgment debtor's land: rule 63.03(3).

Changes in Rule 63 introduced in 1989 enlarged the category of orders which were not automatically stayed pending appeal from injunctions, mandatory orders and certain family law orders to all orders for non-monetary relief, or support enforcement, other than provisions in orders under the *Landlord and Tenant Act* declaring a tenancy agreement terminated or directing that a writ of possession issue. The most dramatic effect of this revision relates to interlocutory orders. Formerly most interlocutory orders were stayed automatically but now almost all interlocutory orders will not be stayed automatically because they do not "provide for the payment of money." For example, an order discharging a certificate of pending litigation will no longer be stayed automatically and the defendant will be able to clear the title to the subject property unless a further order is made imposing a stay pending appeal.

Changes in Rule 63 introduced in 1993 provided that an appeal from an order refusing to set aside a default judgment does not stay the default judgment and introduced a special provision dealing with appeals of orders under the *Co-operative Corporations Act.*

The provisions of an order containing both monetary and non-monetary relief are treated separately to determine which provisions are stayed automatically. For example, an appeal from an order awarding damages and granting a permanent injunction would automatically stay the payment of damages but not the injunctive relief.

In deciding whether to grant a stay by order the test is the same as for an interlocutory injunction, *i.e.* the court should consider (1) Is there a serious issue to be decided? (2) Would compliance with the order under appeal cause irreparable harm? and (3) What is the balance of convenience: *RJR-MacDonald Inc. v. Canada (Attorney General)*, [1994] 1 S.C.R. 311.

Former Rules: Rules 505-508, 514.

USE OF STAY PENDING APPEAL STATUS CHART

Whether and how an order is stayed can be determined on the Stay Pending Appeal Status Chart (below) by cross-referencing the column containing the correct classification of the relief awarded by the subject order (*i.e.* whether or not the order provides for the payment of money other than support or support enforcement and other than a default judgment) with the row containing the correct classification of the appeal rights which apply to the subject order (*i.e.* whether or not leave to appeal is required). To determine if leave to appeal is required, see the Appeal Route Charts (CHARTS).

The Stay Pending Appeal Status Chart does not apply to appeals to the Supreme Court of Canada.

STAY PENDING APPEAL STATUS CHART

		RELIEF AWARDED BY ORDER	
		Monetary Relief (other than support or support enforcement or re default judgments)	Non-Monetary Relief (or support or support enforcement or re default judgments)
APPEAL RIGHTS	No leave to appeal required	**AUTOMATIC STAY** — automatic stay when notice of appeal delivered: rule 63.01(1) — court whose decision is to be appealed may grant stay: rule 63.02(1)(a) and (2) — court appealed to may lift automatic stay: rule 63.01(5) — an appeal from an order refusing to set aside a default judgment does *not* automatically stay the judgment. A stay order is necessary: rule 63.01(2)	**MUST OBTAIN STAY** — court whose decision is to be appealed may grant stay: rule 63.02(1)(a) and (2) — court appealed to may grant stay: rule 63.02(1)(b) — court appealed to may lift stay previously ordered: rule 63.02(3) — *Landlord and Tenant Act* or *Co-operative Corporations Act* orders terminating tenancy agreement or occupancy rights or granting writ of possession are *automatically* stayed when notice of appeal delivered: rule 63.01(3) and (4)
	Leave to appeal required	**MUST OBTAIN STAY PENDING LEAVE** — court whose decision is to be appealed may grant stay: rule 63.02(1)(a) and (2) — court to whom motion has been made for leave to appeal may grant stay: rule 63.02(1)(b) — court which may grant leave or court appealed to may lift stay previously ordered: rule 63.02(3) — automatic stay when leave to appeal obtained and notice of appeal delivered: rule 63.01(1) — court appealed to may lift automatic stay: rule 63.01(5)	**MUST OBTAIN STAY** — court whose decision is to be appealed may grant stay: rule 63.02(1)(a) and (2) — court to whom motion has been made for leave to appeal may grant stay: rule 63.02(1)(b) — court appealed to may grant stay: rule 63.02(1)(b) — court which may grant leave or court appealed to may lift stay previously ordered: rule 63.02(3)

AUTOMATIC STAY ON DELIVERY OF NOTICE OF APPEAL

Payment of Money

63.01(1) The delivery of a notice of appeal from an interlocutory or final order stays, until the disposition of the appeal, any provision of the order for the payment of money, except a provision that awards support or enforces a support order.

Exception, Default Judgment

(2) The delivery of a notice of appeal from an order refusing to set aside a default judgment does not stay the default judgment, but it may be stayed by order and rule 63.02 applies as if the appeal were from the default judgment.

Landlord and Tenant Orders

(3) **The delivery of a notice of appeal from an interlocutory or final order made under the *Landlord and Tenant Act* stays, until the disposition of the appeal, any provision of the order declaring a tenancy agreement terminated or directing that a writ of possession issue.**

Co-operative Housing Orders

(4) **The delivery of a notice of appeal from an interlocutory or final order made under the *Co-operative Corporations Act* stays, until the disposition of the appeal, any provision of the order declaring occupancy rights terminated or directing that a writ of possession issue.**

Lifting Stay

(5) **A judge of the court to which the appeal is taken may order, on such terms as are just, that the stay provided by subrule (1), (3) or (4) does not apply. [re-en. O. Reg. 465/93, s. 8]**

[*Caveat: Cases decided before the 1989 amendments must be read with care — Authors* .]

Automatic Stay Pending Appeal — Generally

Kiani v. Abdullah (1989), 70 O.R. (2d) 697, 7 R.P.R. (2d) 161, 36 O.A.C. 34 (C.A.).
A judgment for an equitable order remedy, such as rescission, resulting in an imperative order is not automatically stayed upon the delivery of a notice of appeal.

Houdaille Industries of Can. Ltd. v. Top Iron & Metal Co. (1986), 9 C.P.C. (2d) 26 (Ont. H.C.).
A representative of a judgment debtor was required to submit to an examination in aid of execution notwithstanding a pending appeal from an order dismissing a motion to set aside an order lifting a stay of execution of the judgment.

Kennedy v. Kennedy (1985), 45 R.F.L. (2d) 109 (C.A.).
In an appeal in a family law action where the court was satisfied that the husband was likely to part with assets he had been ordered to turn over to his wife, he was ordered to lodge certain assets with the Registrar.

Orange v. Mokund (1980), 17 C.P.C. 119 (Ont. Co. Ct.).
Execution on a judgment in the main action is not stayed pending the disposition of an appeal in the third party proceedings.

Panagopoulos v. Consumers' Gas Co. (1979), 25 O.R. (2d) 765, 102 D.L.R. (3d) 452 (C.A.).
Execution is stayed automatically notwithstanding that the appeal is regarding costs only, but the stay may be restricted to an amount estimated to cover the costs in dispute on appeal.

Re Marathon Realty Co. and Koumoudouros (1977), 5 C.P.C. 50 (Ont. Div. Ct.).
A tenant was ordered to post a bond as security for damages of the landlord by reason of the stay, pending an appeal from an order granting relief from forfeiture.

Re I.W.A. and Patchogue Plymouth, Hawkesbury Mills (1976), 14 O.R. (2d) 118, 2 C.P.C. 98 (H.C.).
Arbitration awards are not automatically stayed upon the filing of an application for judicial review.

Parkinson v. Parkinson (1974), 4 O.R. (2d) 130 (H.C.).

An appeal from an interim order for corollary relief under the *Divorce Act,* R.S.C. 1970, c. D-8, does not stay the order.

Downsview Meadows Ltd. v. Wright-Winston Ltd., [1965] 2 O.R. 566, 51 D.L.R. (2d) 396 (C.A.).

Federal legislation governs stays of execution pending appeal to the Supreme Court of Canada.

Lifting Automatic Stay

797 Don Mills Ltd. v. NN Life Insurance Co. of Canada (February 29, 1996), Doc. CA C23839, M17709, M17731 (Ont. C.A.).

The court lifted a stay of execution in order to require a tenant to pay rent to a landlord.

Savarin Ltd. v. Fasken & Calvin (1995), 42 C.P.C. (3d) 129 (Ont. C.A.).

The court lifted an automatic stay and ordered security for costs where the appeal appeared to be frivolous and vexatious.

Eurocollection Canada Ltd. v. L.M. Molds Concepts Inc. (1995), 80 O.A.C. 146 (C.A.).

The court lifted the automatic stay of execution regarding $130,000 of a $263,000 judgment.

Boulanger v. Liddle (1995), 34 C.P.C. (3d) 284 (Ont. C.A.).

The court lifted a stay of execution where the appeal bordered upon being frivolous. A condition was imposed that any funds recovered be paid into court pending the outcome of the appeal.

GEAC Canada Ltd. v. Craig Erickson Systems Inc. (1994), 26 C.P.C. (3d) 355, 74 O.A.C. 136 (C.A.).

Where the Court of Appeal refused to lift the automatic stay of appeal, it also refused to order security for the costs of the proceeding below as the request for security was intended to achieve substantially the same result as the request to lift the stay.

Hall-Chem Inc. v. Vulcan Packaging Inc. (1994), 27 C.P.C. (3d) 104, 72 O.A.C. 303 (C.A.).

The court lifted the automatic stay under rule 63.01(1) after consideration of the grounds of the appeal, the general circumstances of the case including the trial judge's reasons, and the probable delay between the trial and the appeal which could not be controlled by the parties.

Ryan v. Laidlaw Transportation Ltd. (1994), 19 O.R. (3d) 547, 31 C.P.C. (3d) 188, 6 C.C.E.L. (2d) 161, 118 D.L.R. (4th) 708, 74 O.A.C. 67 (C.A.).

An employer appealed from a judgment for damages for wrongful dismissal, and the successful plaintiff brought a motion to lift the automatic stay under rule 63.01(1). The court permitted a partial lifting of the stay, as the plaintiff was in dire financial condition and the appellant's chances of success on the appeal were not overwhelming.

Stein v. Sandwich West (Township) (1993), 16 O.R. (3d) 321 (C.A.).

The defendants in a serious personal injury action appealed a trial judgment which awarded the plaintiffs in excess of $9 million. The Court of Appeal granted an order partially lifting the automatic stay of execution where the circumstances spoke compellingly for relief against hardship. The appeal on the existing record did not appear likely to succeed, and the respondents' needs outweighed the risk of non-recovery to the appellants if the appeal was successful.

Babbitt v. Paladin Inc. (1993), 20 C.P.C. (3d) 399 (Ont. C.A.).

The defendants were ordered to provide security for a judgment, and security for costs including the costs of appeal within 10 days, or the automatic stay would be lifted. Given the defendants' past actions, there was a risk that assets might be transferred, but lifting the stay entirely would have had devastating consequences for them.

Quabbin Hill Investments Inc. v. Yorkminster Investments Properties Ltd. (1992), 8 O.R. (3d)
     278, 55 O.A.C. 199 (C.A.).

The court ordered the removal of a stay of judgment pending appeal, to the extent of allowing
an examination in aid of execution to proceed.

Arthur v. Signum Communications Ltd. (1991), 2 C.P.C. (3d) 74 (Ont. Gen. Div.).

A partial lift of a stay of judgment was granted after taking into account the perceived merit of
the appeal, the amount likely to be paid as a minimum in an appeal including damages, and any
hardship to the appellant.

Oswell v. Oswell (1991), 2 O.R. (3d) 145, 47 C.P.C. (2d) 209, 31 R.F.L. (3d) 441, 76 D.L.R.
     (4th) 444, 46 O.A.C. 316, additional reasons 2 O.R. (3d) 145 at 149, 31 R.F.L. (3d) 441
     at 445, 76 D.L.R. (4th) 444 at 448, 46 O.A.C. 316 at 319 (C.A.).

The court will exercise its discretion to lift the automatic stay more readily in family law cases
than in other cases.

Bannon Estate v. Wisotzki (1990), 1 O.R. (3d) 142, 44 C.P.C. (2d) 39, 41 O.AC. 59 (C.A.).

The court partially lifted the stay pending appeal of quantum of damages and apportionment of
fault where the delay would cause hardship to the plaintiff.

Peper v. Peper (1990), 1 O.R. (3d) 145, 45 C.P.C. (2d) 157, 29 R.F.L. (3d) 1, 73 D.L.R. (4th)
     131, 46 O.A.C. 241 (C.A.).

1. The institutional delay in processing appeals justifies reconsideration of the somewhat
inflexible approach taken in the past to the lifting of an automatic stay of a money judgment,
particularly in relation to disputes under the *Family Law Act.*
2. It is not necessary for the court to find that an appeal is frivolous before lifting the stay of
the order under appeal. The court lifted the stay in this family law case.

LeBlanc v. Digiammatteo (1989), 71 O.R. (2d) 130, 64 D.L.R. (4th) 507, 35 O.A.C. 380 (C.A.).

Where the defendants appealed from a judgment awarding the plaintiffs $513,000 plus interest
but did not dispute liability, the court lifted the stay of execution to the extent of $100,000.

Walter E. Heller Financial Corp. v. American Gen. Supply of Can. (1969) Ltd. (1986), 56 O.R.
     (2d) 257, 12 C.P.C. (2d) 129, 30 D.L.R. (4th) 600 (C.A.).

An appellant was ordered to pay into court security for a judgment pending appeal where the
appellant had disposed of its assets outside of the usual course of business and was no longer
carrying on business in Canada.

Cudmore v. Knight (1977), 16 O.R. (2d) 127, 4 C.P.C. 55 (C.A.).

Pending an appeal with respect to damages alone, a stay of execution was lifted as to that portion
of the damage assessment the appellate court would likely leave intact related to the payment
into court.

Antone v. Monk, [1958] O.W.N. 337 (C.A.).

The court refused to remove a stay of execution pending appeal where it was not demonstrated
with any degree of certainty that the appeal was frivolous. It is not sufficient to show that the
current assets of the judgment debtor may not be available by the time the appeal is disposed
of.

STAY BY ORDER

By Trial Court or Appeal Court

     **63.02(1) An interlocutory or final order may be stayed on such terms
as are just,**

        (a) by an order of the court whose decision is to be appealed;

(b) by an order of a judge of the court to which a motion for leave to appeal has been made or to which an appeal has been taken.

Expiry of Trial Court Stay
(2) A stay granted under clause (1)(a) expires if no notice of motion for leave to appeal or no notice of appeal, as the case may be, is delivered and the time for the delivery of the relevant notice has expired.

Setting Aside or Varying Stay
(3) A stay granted under subrule (1) may be set aside or varied, on such terms as are just, by a judge of the court to which a motion for leave to appeal may be or has been made or to which an appeal may be or has been taken.

Support or Custody Order
(4) A party who obtains a stay of a support or custody order shall obtain a certificate of stay under subrule 63.03(4) and file it forthwith in the office of the Director of the Family Support Plan. [re-en. O. Reg. 465/93, s. 8; am. O. Regs. 351/94, s. 6; 534/95, s. 7]

Stay by Order — Generally

RJR-MacDonald Inc. v. Canada (Attorney General), [1994] 1 S.C.R. 311, 54 C.P.R. (3d) 114, 111 D.L.R. (4th) 385, 164 N.R. 1, 60 Q.A.C. 241.

In deciding whether to grant a stay by order the test is the same as for an interlocutory injunction, *i.e.* (1) Is there a serious issue to be decided? (2) Would compliance with the order under appeal cause irreparable harm? and (3) What is the balance of convenience.

820099 Ontario Inc. v. Harold E. Ballard Ltd. (1991), 49 C.P.C. (2d) 239, 50 O.A.C. 254 (Div. Ct.).

On a motion to impose a stay pending appeal the court will apply a balance of convenience test, similar to that on an interlocutory injunction, but with greatest weight being given to the fact that the adjudication has already taken place and is regarded as *prima facie* correct. The court refused to stay most relief granted in this oppression proceeding under the *Business Corporations Act* .

Rocket v. Royal College of Dental Surgeons of Ont. (1988), 66 O.R. (2d) 73, 30 C.P.C. (2d) 34, 29 O.A.C. 260 (C.A.).

There is no jurisdiction in a single judge of the Court of Appeal to stay an order pending the Supreme Court of Canada hearing an application for leave to appeal. However, to avoid a hiatus where no stay could effectively be made, the matter was dealt with by a panel of judges of the Court of Appeal by virtue of its inherent jurisdiction to control its own process.

International Corona Resources Ltd. v. LAC Minerals Ltd. (1987), 21 C.P.C. (2d) 260, 23 O.A.C. 378 (C.A.).

The court applied a balance of convenience test in granting a stay pending the hearing of an application for leave to appeal to the Supreme Court of Canada, in the absence of any statutory provision.

International Corona Resources Ltd. v. LAC Minerals Ltd. (1986), 21 C.P.C. (2d) 252 (Ont. C.A.).

The court granted a stay of judgment pending appeal where the status quo was in the best interests of both parties and would not prejudice the respondent.

Bijowski v. Caicco (1985), 3 C.P.C. (2d) 295, 45 R.F.L. (2d) 266 (Ont. C.A.).

Rule 63.02 confers a restricted jurisdiction on the trial judge or another judge of the court to order a stay of execution pending delivery of a notice of appeal or expiry of the appeal period. Thereafter it is for the appellate court to determine whether execution should be stayed pending disposition of the appeal.

Talsky v. Talsky (No. 2) (1973), 1 O.R. (2d) 148, 14 R.F.L. 36, 39 D.L.R. (3d) 516 (C.A.).

A judge of the High Court has inherent jurisdiction to stay execution of an order of that court pending an appeal to the Supreme Court of Canada.

James McWilliams Blue Line Inc. v. Joy Oil Co., [1950] O.W.N. 712 (C.A.).

The Ontario Court of Appeal has no jurisdiction to stay execution on a judgment pending appeal of a counterclaim to the Supreme Court of Canada.

Stay by Order — Administrative Tribunals

Re Rose (1982), 38 O.R. (2d) 162, 29 C.P.C. 235, 137 D.L.R. (3d) 365 (Div. Ct.).

Where the tribunal from whom an appeal is taken has jurisdiction to stay its order, an application for such relief should in the first instance be made to that tribunal.

Re Dylex Ltd. and Amalgamated Clothing & Textile Wkrs. Union Toronto Joint Bd. (1977), 17 O.R. (2d) 448, 77 C.L.L.C. 14,105 (H.C.).

A judge of the High Court has inherent jurisdiction to stay a certification order made by the Ontario Labour Relations Board pending judicial review.

Re Metro. Toronto Police Commrs. Bd. and Metro. Toronto Police Assn. (1975), 7 O.R. (2d) 198, 54 D.L.R. (3d) 654 (C.A.).

The Court of Appeal cannot stay the execution of a decision of a tribunal pending an appeal to the Supreme Court of Canada if it has already completed its review of the decision.

Re Great Northern Capital Corp. and Toronto (1973), 1 O.R. (2d) 160 (H.C.).

In considering whether to stay the execution of an order in the nature of *mandamus* the court should consider the *bona fides* of the appeal, the substance of the grounds for appeal, and the hardship to the respective parties if a stay were granted or refused. The court refused to stay the execution of an order requiring the issuances of building permits.

Re Occhipinti and Discipline Ctee. of Ont. College of Pharmacy, [1970] 1 O.R. 741 (C.A.).

An appellate court may stay execution of all judgments over which it has appellate jurisdiction including those of statutory tribunals.

Stay by Order — Examples

Vassallo v. Mulberry Street Ltd. (1995), 83 O.A.C. 386 (C.A.).

The court stayed execution of a contempt order and expedited the appeal.

Stroh v. Millers Cove Resources Inc. (1995), 83 O.A.C. 202 (Div. Ct.).

The court ordered a stay of an appointment of a receiver where not to grant the stay would have rendered the appeal nugatory.

Stan-Canada Inc. v. Calibrated Instruments Inc. (1995), 37 C.P.C. (3d) 142, 77 O.A.C. 50 (C.A.).

The court granted a stay of execution on the condition that the appellant make certain payments to the respondent.

Ontario Home Builders' Assn. v. York Region Board of Education (1993), 103 D.L.R. (4th) 92, 64 O.A.C. 72 (C.A.).

Where the Divisional Court had declared by-laws imposing educational development charges on new homes unconstitutional, the Court of Appeal refused to grant a stay permitting the school boards to continue to levy the development charges pending appeal. A stay in such circumstances would not have the normal effect of preventing the successful party from executing on judgment pending appeal, but rather would permit the unsuccessful party to continue to act as if the decision had never been rendered.

Wijngaarden v. Tzalalis (1992), 11 O.R. (3d) 779, 60 O.A.C. 236 (C.A.).

Where a treating physician and hospital had obtained a declaration that they were at liberty to administer a transfusion to a Jehovah's Witness seriously injured in a motor vehicle accident, the Court of Appeal refused to stay the order pending appeal. The transcripts from the original hearing were not available, and therefore the court was not in a position to substitute its decision for that of the trial judge.

Loblaws Inc. v. Ancaster (Town) Chief Building Official (1992), 14 C.P.C. (3d) 333, 62 O.A.C. 108 (Div. Ct.).

The court granted a partial stay pending appeal where the appeal was *bona fide* and the appellant would otherwise suffer hardship. The judgment under appeal restrained the appellant from selling certain goods.

Hoar v. Hoar (1992), 39 R.F.L. (3d) 125, 54 O.A.C. 397 (C.A.).

On an application to stay a *Family Law Act* judgment pending appeal, the court granted a stay of the property division and spousal maintenance provisions of the judgment on terms, but refused to stay the child support provisions of the judgment.

820099 Ontario Inc. v. Harold E. Ballard Ltd. (1991), 49 C.P.C. (2d) 239, 50 O.A.C. 254 (Div. Ct.).

The court refused to grant a stay of a trial judgment pending appeal where the stay would prejudice the party which had been successful at first instance.

Spring v. L.S.U.C. (1987), 60 O.R. (2d) 699, 41 D.L.R. (4th) 374 (Div. Ct.), affirmed (1988), 63 O.R. (2d) 736 (Div. Ct.).

A party found guilty of professional misconduct by the Law Society of Upper Canada appealed his disbarment, and then applied to Divisional Court seeking an order staying the disbarment and banning publication until determination of the appeal. In the result, the stay was not granted as the only issue on appeal was the adequacy of the penalty, not the finding of liability. The issue was not of such gravity as to engage the authority of the court to stay the proceeding.

EFFECT OF STAY

Generally

63.03(1) Where an order is stayed, no steps may be taken under the order or for its enforcement, except,

(a) by order of a judge of the court to which a motion for leave to appeal has been made or an appeal has been taken; or

(b) as provided in subrules (2) and (3).

Entry of Order and Assessment of Costs

(2) A stay does not prevent the settling, signing and entering of the order or the assessment of costs.

Writ of Execution

(3) A stay does not prevent the issue of a writ of execution or the filing of the writ in a sheriff's office or land registry office, but no instruction or direction to enforce the writ shall be given to a sheriff while the stay remains in effect.

Certificate of Stay

(4) Where an order is stayed, the registrar of the court,

(a) that granted the stay; or

(b) to which an appeal has been taken,

shall issue, on requisition by a party to the appeal, a certificate of stay (Form 63A) and, when the certificate has been filed with the sheriff, the sheriff shall not commence or continue enforcement of the order until satisfied that the stay is no longer in effect.

(5) A requisition for a certificate of stay shall state whether the stay is under subrule 63.01(1) or by order under subrule 63.02(1), and if by order, shall set out particulars of the order.

McGregor v. Royal Victoria Hospital of Barrie Inc. (1991), 3 C.P.C. (3d) 309 (Ont. C.A.).
A stay does not prevent the assessment of costs. A court may in an unusual case order otherwise.

Roynat Inc. v. Graat (1986), 56 O.R. (2d) 511, 12 C.P.C. (2d) 152 (H.C.).
The filing of a certificate of stay with the sheriff prevents the enforcement of a writ of execution, but the judgment debtor's lands are still bound by the writ pending the outcome of the appeal.

Panagopoulos v. Consumers' Gas Co. (1979), 25 O.R. (2d) 765, 102 D.L.R. (3d) 452 (C.A.).
Where an appeal was with respect to costs only, the court allowed money in court to be paid out, except an amount sufficient to cover the costs of the appeal.

Nanticoke v. Walker (1979), 14 C.P.C. 215, 10 R.P.R. 49 (Ont. Co. Ct.).
Where a certificate of the Registrar of the Court of Appeal was lodged with the sheriff, the execution did not bind the lands of the judgment debtor.

Setting Aside Writ of Execution

(6) A judge of the court to which a motion for leave to appeal has been made or an appeal has been taken may set aside the issue or filing of a writ of execution where the moving party or appellant gives security satisfactory to the court.

PARTICULAR PROCEEDINGS
RULE 64   MORTGAGE ACTIONS

Highlights

General. Mortgage actions are commenced by a special form of statement of claim: Form 14B. The documents to be delivered by a defendant in order to redeem or to compel a sale have been renamed, from "notice D.O.R." to "request to redeem," and from "notice D.O.S." to "request for sale." (By a 1996 amendment these documents, which formerly had only to be filed, must now also be served on the plaintiff.)

The redemption period, in both foreclosure and sale actions, is sixty days after the taking of the mortgage account: rules 64.03(8) and 64.04(7). The minimum notice of the taking of the account is seven days.

In order to redeem in a sale action, the mortgagor need only pay the plaintiff's claim and is no longer required to redeem all the encumbrancers: rule 64.04(9).

A subsequent encumbrancer seeking a sale in a foreclosure action must post $250 as security for costs: rule 64.03(19). The mortgagor is not required to post security for costs if he requires a sale.

Where a foreclosure has been converted to a sale and it appears that the sale will not yield enough to pay out to the plaintiff, the court or referee may reconvert the action to a foreclosure: rule 64.03(23).

Execution creditors and construction lien claimants who are named as defendants in the statement of claim must be served in the ordinary way, that is, personally or by an alternative to personal service under rule 16.03. Special service rules apply only to execution creditors and construction lien claimants added on a reference: rule 64.06(5).

For changes in the procedure on references generally, see Rules 54 and 55.

DEFINITION

64.01 In rules 64.02 to 64.06, "subsequent encumbrancer" means a person who has a lien, charge or encumbrance on the mortgaged property subsequent to the mortgage in question in the action.

DEFAULT JUDGMENT WITH REFERENCE

64.02 A reference directed by a default judgment in a mortgage action shall be directed to a judge or master sitting in the county where the action was commenced or to the registrar in that county.

FORECLOSURE ACTIONS

Persons to be Joined

64.03(1) In an action for foreclosure, all persons interested in the equity of redemption shall be named as defendants in the statement of claim, subject to subrule (2).

Kung v. Zambrano (1980), 16 C.P.C. 239 (Ont. H.C.).

In the case of acquired *pendente lite*, the burden or onus is on the person acquiring the interest to apply to be added as a party defendant.

Maritime Life Assur. Co. v. Karapatakis (1979), 10 C.P.C. 301, 7 R.P.R. 229, 9 R.F.L. (2d) 265 (Ont. Master).

Discussion of proper procedure that a mortgagee must follow in dealing with a spousal interest in a foreclosure action.

Pape v. Edfield Holdings Ltd., [1968] 1 O.R. 369 (Master).

A conditional sales vendor whose goods are affixed to realty prior to an advance under a mortgage made without notice of the conditional sale is a proper defendant; but in other circumstances he would have no interest in the realty to be foreclosed.

Poloniato v. Regina Macaroni Holding Ltd., [1955] O.W.N. 627, [1955] 4 D.L.R. 845 (H.C.).

The assignee of a conditional sales contract regarding chattels affixed to realty was added as a party.

(2) The plaintiff may commence a foreclosure action without naming subsequent encumbrancers as defendants where it appears expedient to do so by reason of their number or otherwise, but the plaintiff may make a motion without notice on a reference after judgment to add as defendants all subsequent encumbrancers who were not originally made parties.

(3) On a reference, where the referee considers that subsequent encumbrancers should have been named as defendants in the statement of claim, the referee may refuse to allow the additional costs of adding them on the reference.

Statement of Claim

(4) The statement of claim in a foreclosure action shall be in (Form 14B).

Claims that May be joined

(5) In a foreclosure action a mortgagee may also claim,

(a) payment of the mortgage debt by any party personally liable for it; and

(b) possession of the mortgaged property.

Can. Permanent Trust Co. v. Welton Ltd., [1973] 2 O.R. 245, 33 D.L.R. (3d) 417 (H.C.).

Where an action is commenced for possession and for payments due under the mortgage, the plaintiff may not exercise the power of sale contained in the mortgage.

The Toronto Mtge. Co. v. Killoran, [1941] O.W.N. 37 (Master).

Where the mortgagor breached a covenant to pay taxes, the mortgagee was successful in its action for possession without seeking foreclosure.

Request to Redeem

(6) A defendant in a foreclosure action who wishes to redeem the mortgaged property shall serve on the plaintiff and file with proof of service a request to redeem (Form 64A) within the time prescribed by rule 18.01 for

delivery of a statement of defence, or at any time before being noted in default, whether the defendant delivers a statement of defence or not.

(7) A request to redeem filed by a defendant who is a subsequent encumbrancer shall contain particulars, verified by affidavit, of the claim and the amount owing.

Effect of Filing Request to Redeem
(8) A defendant who has filed a request to redeem is entitled to,
(a) seven days notice of the taking of the account of the amount due to the plaintiff; and
(b) sixty days after the taking of the account of the amount due to the plaintiff, to redeem the mortgaged property,
but a defendant who is a subsequent encumbrancer is entitled to redeem only if the claim is proved on a reference or is not disputed.

Solnicki v. Redruth Investments Ltd. (1977), 16 O.R. (2d) 121, 1 R.P.R. 125 (H.C.).
Where the defendant has filed a request to redeem the plaintiff may not discontinue the action without leave.

Christian v. Noble, [1963] 1 O.R. 115, 36 D.L.R. (2d) 211 (C.A.).
The court exercised its discretion to reduce the redemption period.

Default Judgment where no Request to Redeem
(9) Where a defendant in a foreclosure action has been noted in default and has not filed a request to redeem, the plaintiff,
(a) if the plaintiff wishes a reference concerning subsequent encumbrancers, may require the registrar to sign judgment for foreclosure with a reference (Form 64B); or
(b) if the plaintiff does not wish a reference concerning subsequent encumbrancers, may require the registrar to sign judgment for immediate foreclosure (Form 64C).

Default Judgment where Request to Redeem Filed
(10) Where a defendant in a foreclosure action has been noted in default but has filed a request to redeem, the plaintiff,
(a) if the plaintiff wishes a reference concerning subsequent encumbrancers, may require the registrar to sign judgment for foreclosure with a reference (Form 64B); or
(b) if the plaintiff does not wish a reference concerning subsequent encumbrancers, may require the registrar,
(i) to take an account of the amount due to the plaintiff,
(ii) where more than one party is entitled to redeem, to determine the priority in which each is so entitled, and
(iii) to sign judgment for foreclosure (Form 64D).
(11) Where, on the taking of the account or in determining priorities, any dispute arises between the parties, or the registrar is in doubt, the registrar may sign judgment for foreclosure with a reference (Form 64B).

Redemption by Named Defendant

(12) In a foreclosure action, a defendant named in the statement of claim,

(a) who has filed a request to redeem; and

(b) whose claim is proved on a reference or is not disputed, if he or she is a subsequent encumbrancer,

may redeem the mortgaged property on paying, within the time fixed by the judgment or report on a reference, the amount, including costs, found due to the plaintiff.

Redemption by Encumbrancer added on Reference

(13) A subsequent encumbrancer added on a reference who attends on the reference and whose claim is proved or is not disputed is entitled to redeem the mortgaged property within the time fixed by the report on the reference.

Foreclosure of Subsequent Encumbrancers

(14) Where a subsequent encumbrancer has been served with a notice of reference under subrule 64.06(4), (7) or (8) and fails to attend and prove a claim on the reference, the referee shall so report and, on confirmation of the report, the claim of that party is foreclosed and the plaintiff may obtain a final order of foreclosure (Form 64E) against that party on motion to the court without notice.

Final Order of Foreclosure

(15) Where no defendant other than a subsequent encumbrancer has filed a request to redeem, and where no subsequent encumbrancer has attended and proved a claim on the reference, the referee shall so report and, on confirmation of the report, a final order of foreclosure may be obtained against all defendants on motion to the court without notice.

Ruhl v. Royal Bank (1993), 13 O.R. (3d) 58, 31 R.P.R. (2d) 71 (Gen. Div.).

Where a mortgagee obtains a final order of foreclosure it is not entitled to costs since the mortgagee has become the owner of the property and exhausted its rights against the mortgagor.

Ont. Housing Corp. v. Ong (1987), 58 O.R. (2d) 125, 15 C.P.C. (2d) 279 (H.C.), affirmed (1988), 63 O.R. (2d) 799, 26 C.P.C. (2d) 139 (C.A.).

The court exercised its equitable jurisdiction to set aside a final order of foreclosure where service of the statement of claim had been dispensed with by order and where the default judgment for foreclosure had been signed a day early. A vesting order was made in favour of the innocent purchasers of the property. The mortgagee was required to account to the mortgagor for the proceeds of sale.

Marcovitch v. Foster (1978), 6 C.P.C. 143 (Ont. Master).

The discretion to re-open a final order of foreclosure was not exercised where the failure to make timely redemption was due to poor office procedures and lack of communication and concern.

(16) On default of payment according to the judgment or report on a reference in a foreclosure action, a final order of foreclosure may be obtained against the party in default on motion to the court without notice.

Conversion from Foreclosure to Sale

(17) A defendant in a foreclosure action who is not a subsequent encumbrancer, and who wishes a sale but does not wish to defend the action, shall serve on the plaintiff and file with proof of service a request for sale (Form 64F) within the time prescribed by rule 18.01 for delivery of a statement of defence, or at any time before being noted in default, and the plaintiff may require the registrar to sign judgment for sale (Form 64G or 64H).

(18) A subsequent encumbrancer named as a defendant in the statement of claim in a foreclosure action who wishes a sale, but does not wish to defend the action or redeem the mortgaged property, shall within the time prescribed by rule 18.01 for delivery of a statement of defence, or at any time before being noted in default,

    (a) pay into court the sum of $250 as security for the costs of the plaintiff and of any other party having carriage of the sale; and

    (b) serve on the plaintiff, and file with proof of service a request for sale (Form 64F), together with particulars, verified by affidavit, of the claim and the amount owing,

and the plaintiff may require the registrar to sign judgment for sale (Form 64I) conditional on proof of the subsequent encumbrancer's claim.

(19) A subsequent encumbrancer added on a reference in a foreclosure action who wishes a sale shall within ten days after service on the encumbrancer of notice of the reference, or where served outside Ontario, within such further time as the referee directs,

    (a) pay into court the sum of $250 as security for the costs of the plaintiff and of any other party having carriage of the sale; and

    (b) serve on the plaintiff, and file with proof of service, a request for sale (Form 64F), together with particulars, verified by affidavit, of the claim and the amount owing,

and where the subsequent encumbrancer attends and proves a claim on the reference, the referee shall make an order amending the judgment from a judgment for foreclosure to a judgment for sale.

(20) On the reference, the referee may require the subsequent encumbrancer to pay an additional sum of money into court as security for costs.

(21) The referee shall deal with the security given under subrule (18), (19) or (20) in the report on the reference.

Power to Convert from Foreclosure to Sale

(22) On the motion of any party, made to the court before judgment or to the referee after judgment, a sale may be directed instead of foreclosure and an immediate sale may be directed without previously determining the priorities of encumbrancers or giving the usual or any time to redeem.

Silver Tam Enterprises Ltd. v. Seavy (1986), 56 O.R. (2d) 793, 12 C.P.C. (2d) 267, 17 O.A.C. 225, 42 R.P.R. 265 (C.A.).

If a final order of foreclosure has been granted, a mortgagor and subsequent encumbrancers no longer have any status to request relief under rule 64.03(22).

Coronation Credit (Ont.) Ltd. v. Franklin Motel (North Bay) Ltd., [1966] 2 O.R. 300 (Co. Ct.).
Where the motion to convert is made after judgment and after expiry of the time for redemption, the applicants must show a reasonable possibility of a profitable sale.

Victoria Trust and Savings Co. v. Puckrin, [1947] O.W.N. 178 (Master).
An order was made that a mortgaged property be sold unless the amount necessary to redeem was paid into court.

Power to Reconvert to Foreclosure
(23) In a foreclosure action that has been converted into a sale action, on the motion of any party, made to the court before judgment or to the referee after judgment, the action may be converted back into a foreclosure action where it appears that the value of the property is unlikely to be sufficient to satisfy the claim of the plaintiff.

426034 Ontario Ltd. v. Pasquale Marra Enterprises Inc. (1994), 20 O.R. (3d) 65, 31 C.P.C. (3d) 92, 41 R.P.R. (2d) 1, 74 O.A.C. 344 (C.A.).
Where a sale proved abortive, the court ordered that the sale action be converted back into a foreclosure action notwithstanding that the value of the property was greater than the mortgage debt.

Where Judgment for Sale Obtained in Foreclosure Action
(24) Where a judgment for sale has been obtained in a foreclosure action, a subsequent encumbrancer is entitled to notice of the hearing for directions on the reference for sale, whether the encumbrancer has filed a request to redeem the mortgaged property or not.

Chauvin v. Lauzon, [1973] 3 O.R. 1012 (H.C.).
Execution creditors should be given notice of the proceedings and may be made parties.

(25) A plaintiff who wishes to transfer carriage of the sale to the defendant requesting the sale may do so by serving on the defendant a notice of election to transfer carriage of the sale and filing it with proof of service, and the defendant then has carriage of the sale and is entitled to the return of the deposit paid into court under subrule (18), (19) or (20).

Stansbury v. UCD Realty Dev. Ltd. (1973), 2 O.R. (2d) 107 (Master).
The defendant, not the plaintiff, is responsible for the costs of an abortive sale.

Penn Mutual Life Ins. Co. v. Brookdale Shopping Plaza Ltd., [1973] 2 O.R. 54 (Master).
The plaintiff may ordinarily make his election at any time up to the return of the appointment before the master to obtain instructions for the conduct of the sale.

Procedure on Reference where Foreclosure Action Converted to Sale
(26) Where a foreclosure action is converted to a sale action under subrule (17), (18), (19) or (22), the reference shall proceed in the same manner as in a sale action. [am. O. Reg. 534/95, s. 8]

SALE ACTIONS

Persons to be Joined

64.04(1) In an action for sale of a mortgaged property, all persons interested in the equity of redemption, other than subsequent encumbrancers, shall be named as defendants in the statement of claim.

(2) In a sale action, subsequent encumbrancers shall be added as parties on a reference after judgment.

Statement of Claim

(3) The statement of claim in a sale action shall be in (Form 14B).

Claims that may be Joined

(4) In a sale action, a mortgagee may also claim,

(a) payment of the mortgage debt by any party personally liable for it; and

(b) possession of the mortgaged property.

Request to Redeem

(5) A defendant in a sale action who wishes to redeem the mortgaged property shall serve on the plaintiff and file with proof of service a request to redeem (Form 64A) within the time prescribed by rule 18.01 for delivery of a statement of defence, or at any time before being noted in default, whether the defendant delivers a statement of defence or not.

Zuker v. Schaefer (1982), 30 C.P.C. 279 (Ont. H.C.).

Leave to amend to withdraw a claim for sale on the grounds that it was made inadvertently was refused where it was brought three and a half weeks after the defendants had filed a request to redeem. The acquisition of the right to redeem is not affected by the assertion on behalf of the plaintiff that its claim was advanced by inadvertence.

(6) In a sale action, a subsequent encumbrancer is not entitled to file a request to redeem, and where a foreclosure action is converted to a sale action, a subsequent encumbrancer is not entitled to redeem even though the encumbrancer has filed a request to redeem.

Effect of Filing Request to Redeem

(7) A defendant who has filed a request to redeem is entitled to,

(a) seven days notice of the taking of the account of the amount due to the plaintiff; and

(b) sixty days after the taking of the account of the amount due to the plaintiff, to redeem the mortgaged property.

Default Judgment

(8) Where a defendant in a sale action has been noted in default and,

(a) has not filed a request to redeem, the plaintiff may require the registrar to sign judgment for immediate sale with a reference (Form 64J); or

(b) has filed a request to redeem, the plaintiff may require the registrar to sign judgment for sale with a reference (Form 64K).

Redemption by Named Defendant

(9) In a sale action a defendant named in the statement of claim who has filed a request to redeem may redeem the mortgaged property on paying, within the time fixed by the report on the reference, the amount, including costs, found due to the plaintiff.

Final Order for Sale

(10) Where no defendant has filed a request to redeem and where no subsequent encumbrancer has attended and proved a claim on the reference, the referee shall so report and, on confirmation of the report, a final order for sale (Form 64L) may be obtained on motion to the court without notice.

(11) On default of payment according to the judgment or a report on a reference in a sale action, a final order for sale may be obtained on motion to the court without notice.

Purchase Money

(12) Where an order for sale has been obtained, the property shall be sold under the referee's direction, and the purchaser shall pay the purchase money into court unless the referee directs otherwise.

(13) The purchase money shall be applied in payment of what has been found due to the plaintiff and the other encumbrancers, if any, according to their priorities, together with subsequent interest and subsequent costs.

Order for Payment of Deficiency on Sale

(14) Where the purchase money is not sufficient to pay what has been found due to the plaintiff, the plaintiff is entitled, on motion to the court without notice, to an order for payment of the deficiency by any defendant liable for the mortgage debt. [am. O. Reg. 534/95, s. 9]

REDEMPTION ACTIONS

Persons to be Joined

64.05(1) In an action for redemption of a mortgaged property, all persons interested in the equity of redemption, other than subsequent encumbrancers, shall be named as plaintiffs or defendants in the statement of claim.

(2) In a redemption action, subsequent encumbrancers shall be added as defendants only where the plaintiff is declared foreclosed.

Claims that May Be Joined

(3) In a redemption action, a person interested in the equity of redemption may also claim possession of the mortgaged property.

Judgment

(4) In a redemption action, where the defendant has been noted in default, the plaintiff may require the registrar to sign judgment for redemption (Form 64M).

(5) Every judgment for redemption shall direct a reference, whether or not there are any subsequent encumbrancers.

Where Plaintiff Fails to Redeem
(6) On default of payment according to the report in a redemption action, the defendant is entitled, on motion to the court without notice, to a final order of foreclosure against the plaintiff or to an order dismissing the action with costs.

Ina Devs. Ltd. v. Smith, [1971] 3 O.R. 448, 20 D.L.R. (3d) 648 (H.C.).
The proper procedure to re-open a final order for foreclosure is to apply for relief in the original action, not to commence a separate action.

(7) Where the plaintiff is declared foreclosed, directions may be given, in the final order foreclosing the plaintiff or by a subsequent order, that the reference be continued for redemption or foreclosure, or for redemption or sale, against any subsequent encumbrancers, or for the adjustment of the relative rights and liabilities of the original defendants among themselves.

(8) Where the reference is continued under subrule (7),
(a) for redemption or foreclosure, the reference shall proceed in the same manner as in a foreclosure action;
(b) for redemption or sale, the reference shall proceed in the same manner as in a sale action,
and for that purpose the last encumbrancer shall be treated as the owner of the equity of redemption.

(9) Where the plaintiff is declared foreclosed, a subsequent encumbrancer who attends and proves a claim on the reference is entitled to thirty days to redeem the mortgaged property.

Where Nothing Due to Defendant
(10) Where, on a reference in a redemption action, nothing is found due to the defendant, the defendant is liable for the costs of the action and the defendant shall pay any balance due to the plaintiff forthwith after confirmation of the report on the reference.

PROCEDURE ON MORTGAGE REFERENCES GENERALLY

Rule 55 Applies
64.06(1) Rule 55 (procedure on a reference) applies to a reference in an action for foreclosure, sale or redemption, except as provided in this rule.

Plaintiff to File Material Concerning Subsequent Encumbrancers
(2) On a reference in an action for foreclosure, sale or redemption, the plaintiff shall file sufficient evidence to enable the referee to determine who appears to have a lien, charge or encumbrance on the mortgaged property subsequent to the mortgage in question.

Duties and Powers of Referee

(3) On the reference the referee shall,

(a) add subsequent encumbrancers as defendants in accordance with subrule (4);

(b) fix a time and place for determining the validity of the claims of subsequent encumbrancers;

(c) determine who has a lien, charge or encumbrance on the mortgaged property subsequent to the mortgage in question;

(d) take an account of what is due on the mortgage and what is due to subsequent encumbrancers who prove a claim;

(e) fix or assess the costs of the parties;

(f) fix a time and place for payment, where applicable;

(g) where the reference is for immediate sale, give directions for the sale and defer taking accounts until after the sale is held or proves abortive;

(h) where a sale is being conducted on the request of a subsequent encumbrancer, determine that the encumbrancer has a valid claim before giving directions for the sale;

(i) take all necessary steps for redemption by or foreclosure of the parties entitled to redeem the mortgaged property and, where applicable, for sale of the mortgaged property; and

(j) take subsequent accounts and fix or assess subsequent costs as required.

Royal Bank of Can. v. Dees (1980), 19 C.P.C. 178 (Ont. H.C.).

All costs, whether incurred before or after commencement of an action, included with the mortgage account or not, referable to a specific tariff item or not, are taxable.

Queen's Park Civil Service Credit Union Ltd. v. Tobin, [1972] 3 O.R. 926 (Master).

Where the payor appoints a nominee, an order to continue must be obtained before the nominee applies for a final order of foreclosure in the action.

Adding Subsequent Encumbrancers

(4) Subject to subrule 64.05(2) (subsequent encumbrancers in redemption action), the referee shall direct all persons who appear to have a lien, charge or encumbrance on the mortgaged property subsequent to the mortgage in question and who were not named as defendants in the statement of claim to be added as defendants and to be served with a notice of reference to subsequent encumbrancer added on reference (Form 64N).

(5) A subsequent encumbrancer added under subrule (4) may be served with documents on the reference,

(a) in the case of an execution creditor, by mail at the address shown on the writ of execution or the most recent request to renew it or, if the creditor's address is not shown, by serving the creditor's solicitor in a manner authorized by subrule 16.05(1);

(b) in the case of a person who has registered a claim for lien under the *Construction Lien Act*, by mail at the address for service shown on the claim for lien; or

(c) in any other case, personally or by an alternative to personal service under rule 16.03.

(6) A person served with a notice under subrule (4) may move within ten days after service, or where the person is served outside Ontario, within such further time as the referee directs, to set aside or vary the judgment in the action or the order adding the person as a defendant.

(7) Where it appears to the referee that a person who was named as a defendant in the statement of claim may have a lien, charge or encumbrance on the mortgaged property subsequent to the mortgage in question, although the person was not alleged to be a subsequent encumbrancer in the statement of claim, the referee shall direct that defendant to be served with a notice of reference to subsequent encumbrancer named as original party (Form 64O).

Notice of Reference to Original Defendants

(8) Subject to subrule (10), all persons who were named as defendants in the statement of claim shall be served with a notice of reference to original defendants (Form 64P), stating the names and nature of the claims of all those appearing to have a lien, charge or encumbrance on the mortgaged property.

(9) Any person named as a defendant in the statement of claim who is not a subsequent encumbrancer and who has not filed a request to redeem or a request for sale may be served with the notice of reference by mail at the persons's last known address.

(10) A subsequent encumbrancer who was named as a defendant in the statement of claim and who has not filed a request to redeem or a request for sale is not entitled to notice of a reference for foreclosure.

Adding Parties Other than Encumbrancers

(11) Where on a reference it appears that there are persons interested in the equity of redemption, other than subsequent encumbrancers, who are not already defendants to the action, the referee may order that they be added as defendants on the reference on such terms as are just, and the order shall be served on them, together with the judgment in the action and a notice to added party (Form 64Q), personally or by an alternative to personal service under rule 16.03.

(12) A defendant added under subrule (11) may move within ten days after service of the material referred to in subrule (11), or where the defendant is served outside Ontario, within such further time as the referee directs, to set aside or vary the judgment in the action or the order adding the person as a defendant.

Where more than one Party Entitled to Redeem

(13) One day shall be fixed for payment by all the parties entitled to redeem and, where more than one party is entitled to redeem, the referee shall determine the priority in which they are so entitled.

(14) Where more than one defendant entitled to redeem makes payment, any such defendant may make a motion on the reference for further directions.

Proof of Account where Mortgage Assigned
(15) In an action for foreclosure or sale by, or for redemption against, an assignee of a mortgagee, a statement of the mortgage account, verified by affidavit of the assignee, may be taken as proof of the state of the account and an affidavit is not required from the mortgagee or any intermediate assignee denying any payment to the mortgagee or intermediate assignee, unless the mortgagor or the mortgagor's assignee, or any party entitled to redeem, denies by affidavit the correctness of the statement of account.

Referee's Report
(16) The referee shall set out in the report on the reference,
(a) the names of,
   (i) all persons who were parties on the reference,
   (ii) all subsequent encumbrancers who were served with notice of the reference, and
   (iii) all subsequent encumbrancers who failed to attend on the reference and prove their claims;
(b) the amount and priority of the claims of the parties who attended and proved their claims on the reference, and the report shall show those parties as the only encumbrancers of the property; and
(c) the date on which the report was settled.

(17) The report shall be served on all parties who attended on the reference and on any defendant who filed a request to redeem or a request for sale and shall be filed with proof of service.

(18) Where any period fixed for payment expires within fifteen days after confirmation of the report, a new account shall be taken.

Mortgagee to Transfer Property where Redeemed
(19) Subject to the *Mortgages Act*, where a party pays the amount found due on the mortgage, the mortgagee shall, unless the judgment directs otherwise, transfer the mortgaged property to the party making the payment or the party's nominee, free and clear of all encumbrances incurred by the mortgagee, and the mortgagee shall deliver up all instruments in the mortgagee's possession, control or power that relate to the mortgaged property.

Registrar May Request Directions
(20) A registrar who is of the opinion that a mortgage reference directed to him or her ought to be dealt with by a judge may request directions from a judge.

Change of Account
(21) Where the state of account as ascertained by an order or report has changed before the day fixed for payment, the mortgagee may, at least

fifteen days before that day, serve notice of the change of account on the person required to pay, giving particulars of the change of account and of the sum to be paid.

Cameron v. D'Estrada, [1939] O.W.N. 399 (Master).

The court set aside a final order of foreclosure where the last notice of change of account was delivered after the original date set for redemption.

(22) Where notice of a change of account has been served and the sums mentioned in it are proper, the court may make a final order without further notice or, on the motion for a final order, may fix a new day for payment and may require notice to be served.

(23) A party served with notice of change of account who is dissatisfied may make a motion to the court to determine the amount to be paid and to fix a new day for payment.

(24) Where the state of account has changed before the day fixed for payment and notice of the change has not been served,

(a) where the amount payable for redemption is reduced, a new day shall be fixed for payment, on notice to the persons entitled to redeem; or

(b) where the amount payable for redemption has increased, the mortgagee may move for a final order after the day fixed for payment, without the fixing of a new day.

(25) Where the state of the new account has changed after the day fixed for payment, it is not necessary to fix a new day, unless the court so directs on the motion for a final order.

(26) Where it becomes necessary to fix a new day for payment after the expiration of the original period, the further time allowed shall be thirty days, unless the court orders otherwise.

(27) Despite subrule (26), the court may, on motion of any party, extend or abridge the time for redemption for such time and on such terms as are just.

Dominion Sportservice Ltd. v. Trustee of H.D. Electronics Ltd., [1965] 2 O.R. 282 (H.C.).

The master has jurisdiction to vary a date for redemption which has previously been set by a judge. [*See now rule 37.02(2)(c) — Authors.*]

RULE 65   PROCEEDINGS FOR ADMINISTRATION

Highlights

Provisions governing proceedings for the administration of the estate of a deceased person or the execution of a trust have been retained, on the advice of the Surrogate Court Subcommittee of the Rules Committee, notwithstanding that such proceedings are rare.

Former Rules: Rules 615-650.

WHERE AVAILABLE

65.01(1) A proceeding for the administration of the estate of a deceased person or for the execution of a trust may be commenced by notice of application,

(a) by a person claiming to be a creditor of the estate of the deceased person;

(b) by a person claiming to be a beneficiary under the will or on the intestacy of the deceased person or under the instrument of trust; or

(c) by an executor or administrator of the estate of the deceased person or a trustee.

(2) A judgment for administration of an estate (Form 65A) or for execution of a trust shall be granted only if the judge is satisfied that the questions between the parties cannot otherwise be properly determined.

(3) Where no accounts or insufficient accounts have been rendered, the judge may, instead of granting judgment for administration of the estate or for execution of the trust, order that the executors, administrators or trustees render to the applicant a proper statement of their accounts and may stay the application in the meantime.

Re Sievert (1921), 51 O.L.R. 305, 67 D.L.R. 199 (C.A.).

A beneficiary was denied an order for the sale of an asset, where the executors were acting *bona fide* and had good reasons to delay the sale.

Re Cronan (1916), 10 O.W.N. 300 (Master).

Discussion of circumstances where a judgment for administration will be granted to an executor.

WHERE A REFERENCE IS DIRECTED

65.02(1) A judgment for administration of an estate or for execution of a trust shall direct a reference, and the referee has power to deal with the property of the estate or trust, including power to give all necessary directions for its realization, and shall finally wind up all matters connected with the estate or trust without any further directions, except where the special circumstances of the case require interim reports or interlocutory orders.

(2) Interest on accounts taken in administration proceedings shall be computed on the debts of the deceased from the date of the judgment and on

legacies from the end of one year after the death of the deceased, unless the will directs another time for payment.

(3) All money realized from the estate or trust shall forthwith be paid into court, and no money shall be distributed or paid out except by order of a judge or, on a reference, by order of the referee. [am. O. Reg. 465/93, s. 9]

Re Kendrick, Kendrick and Cramp, [1949] O.W.N. 144, [1949] 2 D.L.R. 348 (C.A.).

Any question of the liability of an executor *de son tort* is outside the scope of a reference to the master and must be established in a proceeding to which that person is properly made a party.

Re Hill; Guaranty Trust Co. of Can. v. Hill, [1949] O.W.N. 63 (H.C.).

The report of the master is not binding on non-parties.

RULE 66   PARTITION PROCEEDINGS

Highlights

This Rule essentially reproduces the former Rules on this subject, modified so as to fit the framework and terminology of the new Rules.
Former Rules: Rules 622-623.

cm

WHERE AVAILABLE

66.01(1) A person who is entitled to compel partition of land may commence an action or application under the *Partition Act.*

(2) A proceeding for partition or sale by or on behalf of a minor shall be on notice to the Children's Lawyer. [am. O. Regs. 770/92, s. 16; 69/95, s. 19]

Ostler v. Rogers (1978), 5 R.F.L. (2d) 83 (Ont. Div. Ct.).

A trial of an issue to determine the interests of the parties was directed where complex issues of fact or of mixed fact and law were raised in the affidavits and in the cross-examinations as to the intent of the parties at the time of the transfer of the property into the names of the parties.

Cook v. Johnston, [1970] 2 O.R. 1 (H.C.).

The court will only order a sale if it is more advantageous to the parties than a partition, even if one of the parties requests a sale.

Szuba v. Szuba, [1950] O.W.N. 669, [1951] 1 D.L.R. 387 (H.C.).

The applicant for partition having a *prima facie* right to it, arriving with clean hands, and not acting for oppressive or vexatious reasons, should receive the benefit of the court's discretion ordering partition.

Kulczycki v. Kulczycki, [1949] O.W.N. 177 (C.A.).

Where there was a real dispute as to the ownership of the land, the court directed a reference to the master first to determine that matter.

FORM OF JUDGMENT

66.02 A judgment for partition or sale shall be in (Form 66A).

PROCEEDS OF SALE

66.03 All money realized in a partition proceeding from sale of land shall forthwith be paid into court, unless the parties agree otherwise, and no money shall be distributed or paid out except by order of a judge or, on a reference, by order of the referee. [am. O. Reg. 396/91, s. 13]

RULE 67   PROCEEDINGS CONCERNING THE ESTATES OF MINORS

Highlights

This Rule essentially reproduces the former provisions with only minor changes: *e.g.* the affidavit in support must give details as to all the property (and not just the personal property) to which the minor is entitled (rule 67.02(1)(a)) and the court is given express power to dispense with the filing of the consent of a minor over the age of 16 (rule 67.03(2)).

Former Rules: Rules 625-628.

HOW COMMENCED

67.01 A proceeding for approval of the sale, mortgage, lease or other disposition of property of a minor may be commenced by notice of application on notice to the Children's Lawyer. [am. O. Reg. 69/95, s. 19]

AFFIDAVIT IN SUPPORT

67.02(1) The affidavit in support of the application shall state,

(a) the nature and amount of all the property to which the minor is entitled;

(b) the nature and value of the property to be disposed of;

(c) what annual income the property yields; and

(d) the facts relied on to establish the necessity for the proposed disposition.

(2) Where an allowance is sought for maintenance of the minor, the affidavit shall state the amount required and the facts relied on to establish the need for the allowance and, where applicable, shall show the necessity for resorting to the property to provide the allowance.

(3) Where the appointment of a guardian is sought, the affidavit shall state the reasons for the appointment and the facts relied on to justify the appointment of the person proposed.

WHERE CONSENT REQUIRED

67.03(1) Approval of the sale, mortgage, lease or other disposition of property of a minor over the age of sixteen years shall not be given unless the consent of the minor has been filed, together with a solicitor's affidavit stating the solicitor's belief that the minor understood the consent when the solicitor read and explained it.

(2) A judge hearing an application referred to in subrule (1) may dispense with the necessity of filing the minor's consent and solicitor's affidavit.

(3) The judge may examine the minor with respect to his or her consent.

(4) Where the minor is outside Ontario, the judge may direct an inquiry to be made concerning the minor's consent in such manner as is just.

RULE 68   PROCEEDINGS FOR JUDICIAL REVIEW

Highlights

This Rule regulates applications for judicial review pursuant to the *Judicial Review Procedure Act*, R.S.O. 1990, c. J.1.

Application to a judge of the General Division. Urgent judicial review applications to a judge of the General Division are governed exclusively by the procedure provided in Rule 38 (see rule 68.02(2)) and Rule 68 is inapplicable to such proceedings.

Applications to Divisional Court. The procedure on applications to the Divisional Court is governed in part by Rule 38 and in part by Rule 68: see rules 38.01(2) and 68.02(1). Rule 38 applies, with the exception of rules 38.02 and 38.09 (which are irrelevant to Divisional Court applications). Rules 68.03 to 68.06 apply to Divisional Court applications: rule 68.02(1).

A special form of notice of application (Form 68A) is to be used when the application is to the Divisional Court (rule 68.01(1)), which is to state that the application is to be heard on a date to be fixed by the registrar at the place of hearing (rule 68.03). It must also include the address of the court office at the place where the application is to be heard: rule 4.02(2)(d). Following the 1989 ''court reform'' amendments to the *Courts of Justice Act*, the Divisional Court operates regionally, rather than being centralized in Toronto. Judicial review applications in the Divisional Court may be brought in any region (s. 20(2)). Although the Act does not *require* judicial review applications to be heard regionally, it is anticipated that the normal practice will be for judicial review applications to be heard at regional centres. If the application is not commenced at a regional centre, the local registrar at the office where it is commenced is to transfer a copy of the notice of application and any material filed in support to the court office in the regional centre of the region where the application is to be heard, and all further documents in the application shall be filed there: rule 68.01(2) and 4.05(3). By virtue of s. 109 of the *Courts of Justice Act*, if the constitutional validity or applicability of a statute, regulation, by-law or common law rule is in question, or a remedy is claimed under s. 24(1) of the *Charter* concerning an act or omission of the Governments of Canada or Ontario, notice of a constitutional question (rule 4.11) must be given to the Attorney General of Canada and the Attorney General of Ontario. Even in the absence of any constitutional question, the *Judicial Review Procedure Act*, s. 9(4), provides that notice of any application for judicial review shall be served upon the Attorney General for Ontario.

Summary of procedure. For a summary of the procedure on an application for judicial review in the Divisional Court, see Procedural Charts (CHARTS). Section 10 of the *Judicial Review Procedure Act* provides that where notice of an application for judicial review has been served on a tribunal, it is to forthwith file a record of its proceedings. If the tribunal is one governed by the *Statutory Powers Procedure Act*, s. 21 of that Act sets out what is to be the content of the record. Pursuant to rule 68.06 an application for judicial review may be dismissed for delay either on the motion of the respondent (to the registrar) or by the registrar on his or her own motion. This procedure is akin to that for appeals (*cf.* rule 61.13).

HOW COMMENCED

68.01(1) An application to the Divisional Court or to the Ontario Court (General Division) for judicial review under the *Judicial Review Procedure*

Act shall be commenced by notice of application, and where the application is to the Divisional Court the notice of application shall be in (Form 68A).

(2) If the application is made to the Divisional Court and is not commenced at a regional centre, the local registrar in the place where it is commenced shall forthwith transfer a copy of the notice of application and of any material filed in support of the application to the court office in the regional centre of the region where the application is to be heard, and all further documents in the application shall be filed there.

Re Union Felt Products (Ont.) Ltd. and R. (1975), 8 O.R. (2d) 438 (H.C.).

Proceedings following the laying of an information under the *Environmental Protection Act*, S.O. 1971, c. 86, are not criminal in nature and any application for prohibition in respect of them should be made to the Divisional Court.

APPLICABLE PROCEDURE

Divisional Court
68.02(1) Rule 38, except as provided in subrule 38.01(2), and rules 68.03 to 68.06 apply to applications to the Divisional Court for judicial review.

General Division
(2) Rule 38 applies to applications to the Ontario Court (General Division) for judicial review under subsection 6(2) of the *Judicial Review Procedure Act.*

HEARING DATE IN DIVISIONAL COURT

68.03 A notice of application shall state that the application is to be heard on a date to be fixed by the registrar at the place of hearing.

APPLICATION RECORDS AND FACTUMS

Applicant
68.04(1) The applicant shall deliver an application record and a factum,
(a) where the nature of the application requires a record of the proceeding before the court or tribunal whose decision is to be reviewed, within thirty days after the record is filed; or
(b) where the nature of the application does not require such a record, within thirty days after the application is commenced.
(2) The applicant's application record shall contain, in consecutively numbered pages arranged in the following order,
(a) a table of contents describing each document, including each exhibit, by its nature and date and, in the case of an exhibit, by exhibit number or letter;
(b) a copy of the notice of application;
(b.1) a copy of the reasons of the court or tribunal whose decision is to be reviewed, with a further typed or printed copy if the reasons are handwritten;

(c) a copy of all affidavits and other material served by any party for use on the application;

(d) a list of all relevant transcripts of evidence in chronological order, but not necessarily the transcripts themselves; and

(e) a copy of any other material in the court file that is necessary for the hearing of the application.

(3) The applicant's factum shall be signed by the applicant's counsel, or on counsel's behalf by someone he or she has specifically authorized, and shall consist of,

(a) Part I, containing a statement identifying the applicant and the court or tribunal whose decision is to be reviewed and stating the result in that court or tribunal;

(b) Part II, containing a concise summary of the facts relevant to the issues on the application, with specific reference to the evidence;

(c) Part III, containing a statement of each issue raised, immediately followed by a concise statement of the law and authorities relating to that issue;

(d) Part IV, containing a statement of the order that the court will be asked to make, including any order for costs;

(e) Schedule A, containing a list of the authorities referred to; and

(f) Schedule B, containing the text of all relevant provisions of statutes, regulations and by-laws,

in paragraphs numbered consecutively throughout the factum.

Respondent
(4) The respondent shall deliver an application record and a factum within thirty days after service of the applicant's application record and factum.

(5) The respondent's application record shall contain, in consecutively numbered pages arranged in the following order,

(a) a table of contents describing each document, including each exhibit, by its nature and date and, in the case of an exhibit, by exhibit number or letter; and

(b) a copy of any material to be used by the respondent on the application and not included in the application record.

(6) The respondent's factum shall be signed by the respondent's counsel, or on counsel's behalf by someone he or she has specifically authorized, and shall consist of,

(a) Part I, containing a statement of the facts in the applicant's summary of relevant facts that the respondent accepts as correct and those facts with which the respondent disagrees and a concise summary of any additional facts relied on, with specific reference to the evidence;

(b) Part II, containing the position of the respondent with respect to each issue raised by the applicant, immediately followed by a concise statement of the law and the authorities relating to that issue;

(c) **Part III, containing a statement of any additional issues raised by the respondent, the statement of each issue to be immediately followed by a concise statement of the law and the authorities relating to that issue;**

(d) **Part IV, containing a statement of the order that the court will be asked to make, including any order for costs;**

(e) **Schedule A, containing a list of the authorities referred to; and**

(f) **Schedule B, containing the text of all relevant provisions of statutes, regulations and by-laws that are not included in Schedule B to the applicant's factum,**

in paragraphs numbered consecutively throughout the factum.

Copies for Use of the Court
(7) **The parties shall file three copies of their application records and factums for the use of the court.**

Material may be Filed as Part of Record
(8) **Any material served by a party for use on an application may be filed, together with proof of service, as part of the party's application record and need not be filed separately if the record is filed within the time prescribed for filing the notice or other material.**

Transcript of Evidence
(9) **A party who intends to refer to a transcript of evidence at the hearing shall file three copies of the transcript with the application record and factum, despite subrule 34.18(2) (time for filing transcript). [am. O. Reg. 219/91, s. 8]**

CERTIFICATE OF PERFECTION

68.05(1) The applicant shall file with the application record a certificate of perfection, stating that all the material required to be filed by the applicant for the hearing of the application has been filed, and setting out the name, address and telephone number of the solicitor for,

(a) **every party to the proceeding; and**

(b) **any person entitled by statute or an order under rule 13.03 (intervention) to be heard on the application,**

or, **where a party or person acts in person, the party's name, address for service and telephone number.**

(2) **When the certificate of perfection has been filed, the registrar shall place the application on a list for hearing and give notice of listing for hearing (Form 68B) by mail to the parties and the other persons named in the certificate of perfection.**

DISMISSAL FOR DELAY

Motion by Respondent
68.06(1) Where the applicant has not,
(a) delivered an application record and factum within the time prescribed by subrule 68.04(1); or
(b) filed a certificate of perfection as required by subrule 68.05(1),
the respondent may make a motion to the registrar at the place of hearing, on ten days notice to the applicant, to have the application dismissed for delay.

Notice by Registrar
(2) Where the applicant has not delivered an application record and factum and filed a certificate of perfection within one year after the application was commenced, the registrar may serve notice on the applicant that the application will be dismissed for delay unless the applicant delivers an application record and factum and files a certificate of perfection within ten days after service of notice.

Registrar to Dismiss where Default not Cured
(3) Where the applicant does not cure the default within ten days after service of a notice under subrule (1) or (2) or such longer period as a judge of the Divisional Court allows, the registrar shall make an order in (Form 68C) dismissing the application for delay, with costs.

Review of Registrar's Dismissal
(4) A party affected by an order of the registrar under subrule (3) may make a motion under subrule 61.16(5) to set aside or vary the order.

RULE 69   DIVORCE ACTIONS

Highlights

The new *Divorce Act* (Canada) in 1986 necessitated a re-drafting of this Rule to reflect changes brought about by the Act and the former Rule was revoked in its entirety and a new Rule substituted in its place. In many respects the new Rule mirrors the former Rule, but there are numerous important changes which are summarized below.

Petition and service. There are two forms of petition (see rule 69.03(1)) since it is now possible for the spouses to jointly commence a divorce action without a respondent (see rule 69.03(5) and (6), and s. 8(1) of the Act). It is no longer necessary to name the other person involved in an act of adultery (rule 69.03(4)), but where such a person is named he or she must be served (rule 69.04(3)). By rule 69.03(7) a dollar amount must now be stated in respect of any claim for support or for division of property. Under former Rule 70 a petition had to be served personally and the alternatives to personal service were unavailable. Now by rule 69.04 a petition may, in addition to personal service, be served by mail with an acknowledgment of receipt card or by acceptance of service by a solicitor. If personal service is used the process server must ask the respondent to acknowledge service by signing the back of the petition: this marks a return to a procedure which existed under the former (pre-1985) Rules of Practice, Rule 791(3)-(4).

Financial statements. The automatic filing of financial statements in custody cases is no longer required, but the court may order a short form financial statement in custody cases: rule 69.14(7). Where a material change has taken place in a spouse's finances this must now be disclosed "forthwith", not just seven days before a pre-trial or trial as was formerly the case: rule 69.14(13). Where a claim is made for a division of property, provision is now made for each spouse to deliver seven days prior to a pre-trial conference, a motion for judgment or a trial, a "net family property statement" — a form which shows each party's view of what the net family property picture is.

Interim relief. A notice of motion for interim relief must now state the amount of support claimed for each dependant: rule 69.15(1).

Children's Lawyer's report. Pursuant to s. 112 of the *Courts of Justice Act* (see the Ministry Comment to s. 112), in actions commenced after February 2, 1987, the Children's Lawyer may elect whether or not to investigate and report to the court concerning custody of or access to a child. In previously commenced actions such investigations and reports are automatic: rule 69.16.

Place of trial. The place of trial is now left up to the petitioner to select unless there is a claim for custody or access in which case the trial must be where the child resides: rule 69.17.

Motion for judgment. Where the respondent has defaulted it is no longer necessary for the petitioner to proceed to trial and instead he or she may make a motion for judgment supported by affidavit evidence. Rule 69.19 sets out in considerable detail the procedure to be followed and the content of the affidavit on a motion for judgment under rule 19.05. It sets out much of what used to appear in practice directions. However, the petitioner is not compelled to support a motion for judgment by affidavit evidence and may instead call oral evidence on the hearing of the motion: rule 69.19(6).

Judgment. Rule 69.19(7)-(11) create a new procedure for mailing out of the judgment (formerly the decree). The new Act replaces the "Decree Absolute" with a "Certificate of Divorce" and rule 69.22 reflects this.

Variation of orders. In respect of applications to vary final orders for corollary relief, financial statements are to be automatic in respect of variations of support orders, financial statements may be ordered where variation is sought only with regard to custody and the contents of affidavits for use on variation applications are prescribed: rule 69.24. The new Act creates interprovincial variation of support orders: the Act itself supplies most of the procedures, but these provisions are supplemented by rule 69.24(8)-(13).

Support enforcement. Rule 69.27, added on March 1, 1992, by O. Reg. 73/92, makes the support order enforcement provisions of rule 70.10.1 apply to divorce actions. See the "Highlights" to Rule 70 for an analysis of the amendments.

Forms. An extensive set of new forms accompanies Rule 69.

Summary of procedure. For a summary of the procedure in a divorce action, see Procedural Charts (CHARTS).

Former Rules: Rules 775d, 775g, 775i, 7751a, 7751b, 776-809.

APPLICATION OF RULES OF CIVIL PROCEDURE

69.01 All the Rules of Civil Procedure that apply in an action apply in a divorce action, with necessary modifications, except where rules 69.03 to 69.27 provide otherwise. [am. O. Reg. 73/92, s. 2]

DEFINITIONS

**69.02 In rules 69.02 to 69.26,
"Act" means the *Divorce Act* (Canada);
"child of the marriage" has the same meaning as in section 2 of the Act.**

Boyce v. Boyce, [1973] 2 O.R. 868, 10 R.F.L. 393, 35 D.L.R. (3d) 528 (H.C.).

"Petition" includes counterpetition for purposes of the *Divorce Act*, R.S.C. 1970, c. D-8.

PETITION

General
69.03(1) The originating process for the commencement of a divorce action is a petition for divorce (Form 69A or 69B), except as provided by subrule 69.09(6) (counterpetition against person not already a party (Form 69G)).

(2) A certificate of the marriage or of the registration of the marriage shall be filed before a petition is issued, unless the petition states that it is impossible to obtain the certificate, or that the certificate will be filed before the action is set down for trial or a motion is made for judgment.

(3) The party commencing the action is called the petitioner and the opposite party is called the respondent.

Person Alleged to Have Been Involved in Adultery

(4) In a petition in which it is alleged that the respondent spouse has committed adultery, it is not necessary to set out the name of the other person alleged to have been involved.

Joint Petition for Divorce

(5) Spouses may commence a divorce action jointly without a respondent.

(6) A joint petition for divorce shall not contain a claim for any relief other than a divorce and, if applicable, an order on consent.

Claim for Relief

(7) A petition that contains a claim for support or division of property shall set out the nature and amount of relief claimed and, if support is claimed, the amount for each dependant.

Young v. Young (1983), 40 C.P.C. 106 (Ont. Master).

Where a petitioner wishes to plead adultery as a particular of alleged cruelty, the person alleged to be involved in the adultery must be named, added as a respondent, and given particulars of the date and place. [*See now rule 69.03(4) — Authors.*]

Dungey v. Dungey (1982), 31 C.P.C. 273 (Ont. H.C.).

The requirement to name persons involved in matrimonial offences does not apply to a petition for divorce on the ground of cruelty.

Bell v. Bell, [1973] 1 O.R. 51, 10 R.F.L. 369 (Master).

A non-party to a divorce proceeding who had had *de facto* custody of a child of the marriage was given extensive rights to participate in the determination of the custody issue.

T. v. T., [1970] 2 O.R. 139, 1 R.F.L. 23, 10 D.L.R. (3d) 125 (H.C.).

Where a person has been involved in a matrimonial offence with the respondent only to the extent of being a victim of his alleged rape, she need not be joined as a party unless the court so orders. [*See now rule 69.03(4) — Authors.*]

SERVICE OF PETITION

Manner of Service

69.04(1) A petition shall be served on the respondent personally or in accordance with subrules 16.03(2) to (4) (acceptance of service by solicitor, service by mail with acknowledgment of receipt card), unless the court makes an order under rule 16.04 for substituted service or dispensing with service.

(2) A person who effects personal service of a petition shall ask the respondent to complete and sign the acknowledgment of service on the back of the petition and shall sign as witness to the respondent's signature, or record the fact that the respondent declined to sign the acknowledgment of service, as the case may be.

Person Alleged to Have Been Involved in Adultery

(3) If a petition sets out the name of a person alleged to have been involved in adultery with the respondent, it shall be served on the person, unless the court orders otherwise, by any method authorized by Rule 16 for

service of an originating process, or by mailing a copy of the petition to the person at his or her last known address.

Petitioner not to Effect Personal Service

(4) A petition that is served personally shall be served by someone other than the petitioner.

Service Outside Ontario

(5) A petition may be served outside Ontario without a court order.

Substituted Service by Advertisement

(6) Where substituted service of a petition by advertisement in a newspaper is ordered by the court, the advertisement shall be in (Form 69C).

TIME FOR SERVICE OF PETITION

69.05 A petition shall be served within six months after it is issued.

PLEADINGS

69.06(1) In a divorce action, pleadings shall consist of the petition (Form 69A or 69B), answer (Form 69D) and reply (Form 69E), if any.

(2) In a counterpetition, pleadings shall consist of the counterpetition (Form 69F or 69G), answer to counterpetition (Form 69H) and reply to answer to counterpetition (Form 69I), if any.

Weindl v. Weindl (1980), 16 C.P.C. 51 (Ont. Master).

Where in a divorce action the relief sought was available under the *Divorce Act*, a claim under the *Family Law Reform Act*, which was not made in the alternative, was struck out.

Resnick v. Resnick, [1970] 1 O.R. 524 (C.A.).

Facts supporting allegations of cruelty and claims for corollary relief must be set out in a divorce petition as in other pleadings.

ANSWER

Time for Delivery of Answer

69.07(1) Except as provided in subrule (3), 19.01(5) (late delivery of defence) or 69.10(2) (counterpetition against petitioner and non-party), a respondent who wishes to oppose a claim made in the petition shall deliver an answer,

(a) within twenty days after service of the petition, where the respondent is served in Ontario;

(b) within forty days after service of the petition, where the respondent is served elsewhere in Canada or in the United States of America; or

(c) within sixty days after service of the petition, where the respondent is served anywhere else.

Notice of Intent to Defend

(2) A respondent served with a petition who intends to defend the action may deliver a notice of intent to defend (Form 69J) within the time prescribed for delivery of the answer.

(3) A respondent who delivers a notice of intent to defend within the prescribed time is entitled to ten days, in addition to the time prescribed by subrule (1), within which to deliver an answer.

Lutes v. Lutes (1985), 3 C.P.C (2d) 7 (Ont. H.C.).

An agreement not to defend a divorce action is unenforceable.

REPLY

69.08 A reply, if any, shall be delivered within ten days after service of the answer.

COUNTERPETITION

Where Available

69.09(1) A respondent who claims any relief against the petitioner, other than dismissal of the action and costs, shall do so by way of counterpetition.

(2) A respondent who counterpetitions against the petitioner may join as a respondent to the counterpetition any other person, whether a party to the main action or not, who is a necessary or proper party to the counterpetition.

Person Alleged to Have Been Involved in Adultery

(3) Subrules **69.03(4)** and **69.04(3)** (naming and service of person alleged to have been involved in adultery) apply, with necessary modifications, to a counterpetition.

Counterpetition to be in Same Document as Answer

(4) A respondent shall include the counterpetition (Form 69F or 69G) and the answer in a single document entitled an answer and counterpetition.

Claim for Relief

(5) A counterpetition that contains a claim for support or division of property shall set out the nature and amount of relief claimed and, if support is claimed, the amount for each dependant.

Counterpetition to be Issued where Respondent to Counterpetition not Already Party to Main Action

(6) Where a person who is not already a party to the main action is made a respondent to the counterpetition, the answer and counterpetition,

    (a) shall be issued,

        (i) within the time prescribed by rule 69.07 for the delivery of an answer in the main action, or at any time before the respondent is noted in default, or

        (ii) subsequently with leave of the court; and

    (b) shall contain a second title of proceeding showing who is petitioner by counterpetition and who are respondents to the counterpetition.

Service Outside Ontario

(7) A counterpetition may be served outside Ontario without a court order.

Baboi v. Baboi (1982), 31 C.P.C. 195 (Ont. Master).

A request for an order of enforcement of a separation agreement can be incorporated in a party's answer and counterpetition.

Kadin v. Kadin (1975), 11 O.R. (2d) 358, 23 R.F.L. 277 (Master).

A respondent seeking maintenance should do so in an answer and counterpetition rather than in an answer.

Gentile v. Gentile, [1970] 3 O.R. 294 (H.C.).

It is not necessary that a counterpetition claiming alimony also claim a decree of divorce.

TIME FOR DELIVERY OR SERVICE OF ANSWER AND COUNTERPETITION

Where all Parties are Parties to the Main Action

69.10(1) Where a counterpetition is only against the petitioner, or only against the petitioner and another person who is already a party to the main action, the answer and counterpetition shall be delivered within the time prescribed by rule 69.07 for the delivery of the answer in the main action, or at any time before the respondent has been noted in default.

Where New Party is Brought In

(2) Where a counterpetition is against the petitioner and a respondent to the counterpetition who is not already a party to the main action, the answer and counterpetition shall be served, after it has been issued, on the parties to the main action and, together with all the pleadings previously delivered in the main action, on the respondent to the counterpetition who is not already a party to the main action, and shall be filed with proof of service,

(a) within thirty days after the answer and counterpetition is issued or at any time before the respondent is noted in default; or

(b) subsequently with leave of the court.

(3) An answer and counterpetition need not be served personally on any person who is a party to the main action, except where a respondent to the counterpetition is also a respondent in the main action and has failed to deliver a notice of intent to defend or an answer in the main action, in which case the respondent shall be served in the manner prescribed by subrule 69.04(1), whether or not the respondent has been noted in default in the main action.

AMENDING ANSWER TO ADD COUNTERPETITION

69.11(1) A respondent who has delivered an answer that does not contain a counterpetition and who wishes to counterpetition only against the petitioner, or only against the petitioner and another person who is already a party to the main action, may amend the answer in accordance with rules 26.02 and 26.03 in order to add the counterpetition, and rule 26.05 (responding to amended pleading) applies to the amended answer and counterpetition.

(2) A respondent referred to in subrule (1) who wishes to counterpetition against the petitioner and another person who is not already a party to

the main action may, with leave of the court, have the registrar issue an amended answer and counterpetition, and rule 26.05 (responding to amended pleading) applies to the amended answer and counterpetition.

ANSWER TO COUNTERPETITION

By Petitioner and Other Party to Main Action

69.12(1)   The petitioner and any other respondent to a counterpetition who is already a party to the main action shall deliver an answer to counterpetition (Form 69H) within twenty days after service of the counterpetition.

(2)   Where the petitioner delivers a reply in the main action, the answer to counterpetition and the reply shall be included in a single document entitled a reply and answer to counterpetition.

By Respondent added by Counterpetition

(3)   Except as provided in subrule (5) or 19.01(5) (late delivery of defence), a respondent to a counterpetition who is not already a party to the main action shall deliver an answer to counterpetition (Form 69H),

(a)   within twenty days after service of the answer and counterpetition, where the respondent to the counterpetition is served in Ontario;

(b)   within forty days after service of the answer and counterpetition, where the respondent to the counterpetition is served elsewhere in Canada or in the United States of America; or

(c)   within sixty days after service of the answer and counterpetition, where the respondent to the counterpetition is served anywhere else.

(4)   Where a respondent to a counterpetition who is not already a party to the main action is served with a counterpetition and intends to defend the action, he or she may deliver a notice of intent to defend (Form 69J) within the time prescribed for delivery of the answer to counterpetition.

(5)   A respondent to a counterpetition who delivers a notice of intent to defend within the prescribed time is entitled to ten days, in addition to the time prescribed by subrle (3), within which to deliver an answer to counterpetition.

REPLY TO ANSWER TO COUNTERPETITION

69.13   A reply to answer to counterpetition (Form 69I), if any, shall be delivered within ten days after service of the answer to counterpetition.

FINANCIAL STATEMENTS

Where Required

69.14(1)   Where a petition contains a claim for support or division of property, the petitioner shall file and serve a financial statement (Form 69K) with the petition and the respondent spouse shall deliver a financial statement with the answer.

(2) Where no claim for support or division of property is made in the petition, but such a claim is made in the counterpetition, the respondent spouse shall deliver a financial statement with the answer and counterpetition and the petitioner shall deliver a financial statement with the answer to counterpetition.

Waiver of Financial Statements

(3) Subrules (1) and (2) do not apply in respect of a claim for support under the Act if both spouses have filed a waiver of financial statements (Form 69L), but the spouses may not waive the obligation to deliver financial statements in respect of a claim under the *Family Law Act.*

Registrar to Refuse Documents Unless Accompanied by Financial Statements

(4) Where a financial statement is required to be filed or delivered with a petition or counterpetition, or an answer to it, the registrar shall not accept the petition, counterpetition or answer for issuing or filing without the financial statement.

Respondent must File Even When Not Defending

(5) A respondent spouse who does not intend to defend a claim for support or division of property shall nevertheless deliver a financial statement within the time prescribed for delivery of an answer or answer to counterpetition, but the failure of the respondent spouse to do so does not prevent the petitioner from setting the action down for trial or moving for judgment.

Order to Require Delivery

(6) Where a respondent spouse fails to deliver a financial statement within the time prescribed for delivery of the answer or answer to counterpetition, the court may, on motion without notice, make an order requiring the delivery of a financial statement within a specified time.

(7) If a claim is made in the action for custody of a child, the court may order the parties to deliver financial statements (short form) (Form 69M) within a specified time.

Particulars of Financial Statement

(8) Where a financial statement lacks particularity, a spouse may demand particulars and if the other spouse fails to supply them within seven days the court may, on such terms as are just,

    (a) order particulars to be delivered within a specified time; or

    (b) strike out the financial statement and order that a new financial statement be delivered within a specified time.

Sanctions for Failure to Deliver Financial Statement or to Give Particulars

(9) Where a spouse fails to comply with an order to deliver a financial statement, a new financial statement or particulars,

    (a) the court may dismiss the spouse's action or strike out his or her answer; and

    (b) a judge may make a contempt order against the spouse.

Cross-examination on Financial Statement

(10) A spouse may cross-examine the other spouse on his or her financial statement.

(11) A cross-examination on a financial statement may be used,

(a) on a motion for interim relief; and

(b) at trial, in the same manner as an examination for discovery.

(12) A spouse who has set the action down for trial or who has consented to the action being placed on a trial list may not cross-examine before trial on the other spouse's financial statement without leave of the court, but is not relieved of the obligation imposed by subrules (13) to (15).

Duty to Correct Financial Statement and Answers on Cross-examination

(13) A spouse who has delivered a financial statement and subsequently discovers,

(a) that any information in the financial statement or answer on cross-examination on it was incorrect or incomplete when made; or

(b) that there has been a material change in any information contained in it,

shall forthwith provide information concerning the change or correction in writing to the other spouse, and subrules 31.09(2) and (3) (correcting answers and sanctions for failure to correct) apply, with necessary modifications.

(14) A spouse who has delivered a financial statement shall deliver a fresh financial statement at least seven days before the commencement of the trial of the action, but may not be cross-examined before trial on the fresh financial statement except with leave of the court.

Net Family Property Statement

(15) In an action in which a claim is made for a division of property, each spouse shall deliver a net family property statement (Form 69N) at least seven days before each of the following:

1. A pre-trial conference.

2. A motion for judgment.

3. The trial.

Heron v. Heron (1987), 19 C.P.C. (2d) 218, 9 R.F.L. (3d) 41 (Ont. H.C.), leave to appeal to Ont. Div. Ct. refused 19 C.P.C. (2d) 218n.

Rule [31.06(6)] on divided discovery applies to the filing of financial statements in divorce proceedings under rule [69.14]. Where the party seeking to withhold the information satisfies the onus under the former rule, he should file a completed financial statement with a request for its sealing until the preliminary issues are determined.

Steinhoff v. Steinhoff (1983), 35 C.P.C. 113 (Ont. Co. Ct.).

Financial statements are pleadings but are not evidence of their contents. Evidence must be led on the subject at trial.

Hoffman v. Hoffman (1983), 41 O.R. (2d) 80, 34 C.P.C. 158, 32 R.F.L. (2d) 428, 145 D.L.R. (3d) 377 (H.C.).

The court held in a divorce action that claim for maintenance based on a separation agreement was not a claim for corollary relief and that a statement of financial information need not be filed. [*But see now the language of rule 69.14(1) — Authors.*]

Anderson v. Anderson (1979), 26 O.R. (2d) 769, 14 C.P.C. 87, 12 R.F.L. (2d) 353, 105 D.L.R. (3d) 341 (H.C.).

Where there were concerns that the respondent's daughter would obtain and use the information provided by her in a matrimonial dispute to harass him in other matters, and that the dissemination of such financial information could hurt the competitive status of his business, an order was made restricting the disclosure of the documents to the parties and their solicitors and financial advisors and preventing the statements of property and cross-examinations thereon from being part of the public record.

Re Machan and Machan (1979), 26 O.R. (2d) 473, 12 R.F.L. (2d) 247 (H.C.).

The court refused to stay delivery of a statement of property pending determination of the applicability of a separation agreement.

Ambler v. Ambler (1980), 15 C.P.C. 117 (Ont. Master).

A spouse who is a partner or substantial shareholder may be required to inquire whether the partner or company will consent to the supply of information concerning the worth of the spouse's investment. [*And see now rule 30.02(4) — Authors.*]

INTERIM RELIEF

Notice of Motion
69.15(1) A notice of motion for interim relief shall set out the precise relief sought, including the amount of support claimed for each dependant.

Pre-motion Conference
(2) At the hearing of the motion the court may direct a pre-motion conference to consider the possibility of settling any or all the issues raised by the motion or the action.

(3) The costs of a pre-motion conference shall be assessed as part of the costs of the action, unless a judge or master who conducts the conference orders otherwise.

(4) A judge or officer who conducts a pre-motion conference under subrule (2) shall not preside at a motion for interim relief, the trial, a reference in the action or a motion for judgment, except that where the pre-trial conference has resolved all the issues in the action, a judge who conducted it may preside at a motion for judgment on consent of the parties.

Written Proposal for Settlement and Costs of Interim Motion
(5) In exercising his or her discretion concerning costs, the judge or officer who hears a motion for interim relief shall take into account any written proposal for settlement of the motion or the failure to make such a proposal.

Failure to Comply with Interim Order
(6) Where a party fails to comply with an order for interim relief and the court is satisfied that the party is able to comply with the order, the court may postpone the trial of the action or strike out any pleading or affidavit of the party in default.

Interim Relief Generally

Hill v. Hill (1988), 63 O.R. (2d) 618, 27 C.P.C. (2d) 319 (H.C.).
The court may award interim disbursements in an application for spousal support under the *Family Law Act*.

Page v. Page (1986), 50 R.F.L. (2d) 275 (Ont. Dist. Ct.).
Discussion of principles applicable to a motion for interim support where there was a separation agreement between the parties.

Patti v. Patti (1982), 37 O.R. (2d) 209, 29 C.P.C. 10, 27 R.F.L. (2d) 209 (Master).
On a motion for interim preservation, assets should be considered to be family assets and an order should issue, unless there is clear evidence to the contrary.

Goodfellow v. Goodfellow (1982), 38 O.R. (2d) 54, 28 C.P.C. 212 (Master).
A wife was permitted to bring an interim motion for support in a divorce action where prior proceedings for support under the *Family Law Reform Act* had been concluded.

Meleszko v. Meleszko (1981), 24 C.P.C. 272 (Ont. Master).
An interim order for exclusive possession of part of a house was made.

Holle v. Holle (1981), 24 C.P.C. 137, 25 R.F.L. (2d) 105 (Ont. H.C.).
When a party sought to vary an interim support order and file new affidavit material after cross-examinations, an adjournment was granted to permit further cross-examinations on the new material.

Spridgeon v. Spridgeon (1980), 20 C.P.C. 272 (Ont. Master).
Where the parties had entered into a separation agreement, an order for increased interim maintenance was made to provide more for the children.

Epp v. Epp (1977), 17 O.R. (2d) 575, 4 C.P.C. 164 (Master).
A master may vary an award of interim maintenance made by another master where there has been a change in circumstances. *[And see now rule 37.14(4) — Authors.]*

Sinclair v. Sinclair, [1973] 1 O.R. 334, 11 R.F.L. 91 (Master).
The master has jurisdiction to award interim relief in a divorce proceeding notwithstanding the existence of a prior Supreme Court judgment granting alimony.

Lipson v. Lipson, [1972] 3 O.R. 403, 7 R.F.L. 186 (C.A.).
The court has jurisdiction to vary an interim order for corollary relief.

I.J. v. H.H., [1971] 3 O.R. 222, 5 R.F.L. 214 (Master).
On a motion for interim alimony and maintenance the merits of the petition for divorce are not relevant provided the proceeding is not frivolous or vexatious.

Davis v. Davis, [1971] 2 O.R. 780, 4 R.F.L. 160 (H.C.).
A motion for interim alimony will be granted once a *de facto* marriage is established; the determination of the parties right *de jure* is not a relevant consideration on the application for interim alimony.

Dyment v. Dyment, [1969] 2 O.R. 748 (C.A.).
Discussion of considerations in awarding interim custody.

Miller v. Miller, [1951] O.W.N. 201 (Master).
A delay in applying for interim alimony may be excused where a party receives payments after separation but before institution of the action for alimony.

Failure to Comply With Interim Order — rule 69.15(6)

Underhill v. Underhill (1985), 49 C.P.C. 237 (Ont. H.C.).

Rule [69.15(6)] does not permit a pleading in one proceeding to be struck out where an interim order in a separate proceeding is not complied with.

Vanderschilden v. Vanderschilden (1982), 28 C.P.C. 228, 26 R.F.L. (2d) 407 (Ont. Master).

Where the husband could not make the required payments for reasons beyond his control, the order was varied rather than strike out his pleadings.

Twigg v. McCusker, [1947] O.W.N. 389 (C.A.).

An appeal was struck off the list until the appellant obeyed an order for payment of interim disbursements.

CHILDREN'S LAWYER'S REPORT

Notice of Intention to Investigate and Report

69.16(1) Where the Children's Lawyer intends to investigate and report to the court concerning custody of or access to a child, he or she shall serve notice of that intention (Form 69O) on the parties and shall file a copy of the notice with proof of service.

(2) Service of the notice on a party who has been noted in default shall be effected by mail addressed to the party at his or her last known address, unless the court orders otherwise.

Service of Documents on Children's Laywer

(3) Where the Children's Lawyer has served notice, a party who subsequently serves an answer, reply or notice of motion or any other document that relates to custody of or access to the child or relates to the child's support or education shall also serve it on the Children's Lawyer within the time prescribed for service on the parties.

Discovery by Children's Lawyer

(4) Where the Children's Lawyer has served notice, he or she has the right to discovery in respect of any matter that relates to custody of or access to the child or relates to the child's support or education.

Service of Report

(5) The Children's Lawyer shall serve his or her report on the parties interested in custody of or access to the child or in the child's support or education, within sixty days after serving notice under subrule (1), and shall then forthwith file a copy of the report and supporting affidavit, if any, with proof of service.

(6) Subrule (2) applies, with necessary modifications, to service of the report.

Dispute of Report

(7) A party on whom the report is served may dispute a statement in it or in any supporting affidavit by serving a concise statement of the nature of the dispute on every other party interested in custody of or access to the

child or in the child's support or education, and on the Children's Lawyer, and filing the statement, with proof of service, within fifteen days after service of the report.

(8) Where the Children's Lawyer has served notice under subrule (1), the action shall not be tried and no motion for judgment shall be heard until,

(a) all disputes have been filed or the time for filing disputes has expired; or

(b) every party interested in custody of or access to the child or in the child's support or education has filed a waiver (Form 69P) of the right to dispute the report.

Application of Former Rule

(9) Rule 70.16 as it read on February 2, 1987 continues to apply to divorce actions commenced on or before that date. [am. O. Reg. 69/95, s. 19]

Custody — Jurisdiction

G. (P. A.) v. G. (K. A.) (1992), 10 O.R. (3d) 641, 17 C.P.C. (3d) 205, 43 R.F.L. (3d) 84, 96 D.L.R. (4th) 731, 58 O.A.C. 217 (C.A.).

A foreign custody order will be recognized in Ontario unless the statutory exceptions under the *Children's Law Reform Act* are met.

O. v. O. (1980), 30 O.R. (2d) 588, 19 C.P.C. 276, 17 R.F.L. (2d) 336, 117 D.L.R. (3d) 159 (H.C.).

Where a child is physically present in Ontario but not ordinarily resident in Ontario, the court will assume jurisdiction over the child if it is shown that the child would otherwise be harmed.

Mudd v. Mudd (1980), 18 C.P.C. 72 (Ont. H.C.).

The Ontario courts were found to have jurisdiction to determine custody where the children had a real and substantial connection with Ontario.

Saulnier v. Saulnier (1980), 17 C.P.C. 303, 3 Fam. L. Rev. 214, reversed on other grounds 3 Fam. L. Rev. 215 (Ont. H.C.).

The jurisdiction under the *Family Law Reform Act* to award custody in the face of a custody order in a divorce proceeding in another province should be exercised only for powerful reasons related to the child's welfare.

Re Allison and Allison (1979), 23 O.R. (2d) 329 (H.C.).

One parent cannot unilaterally change the ordinary residence of a child by surreptitiously removing the child from the jurisdiction.

Nielsen v. Nielsen, [1971] 1 O.R. 541, 5 R.F.L. 313, 16 D.L.R. (3d) 33 (H.C.).

If a child is ordinarily resident in Ontario the court has jurisdiction to determine issues concerning the child's welfare, notwithstanding its physical absence from the province. Discussion of meaning of "ordinarily resident".

Custody — Miscellaneous

Glover v. Glover, 29 O.R. (2d) 392, 16 C.P.C. 77, 18 R.F.L. (2d) 116, [1980] C.T.C. 531, 113 D.L.R. (3d) 161, 80 D.T.C. 6262, affirmed (*sub nom. Glover v. M.N.R.*) 25 R.F.L. (2d) 335, [1982] C.T.C. 29, 130 D.L.R. (3d) 383n, 82 D.T.C. 6035 (S.C.C.).

The court held it was without jurisdiction to order the Minister of National Revenue to disclose the address of a party for the purpose of enforcing a custody order.

Re Reid and Reid (1975), 11 O.R. (2d) 622, 25 R.F.L. 209, 67 D.L.R. (3d) 46 (Div. Ct.).

The court may order representation for children who are the subject of custody proceedings.

Bell v. Bell, [1973] 1 O.R. 51, 10 R.F.L. 369 (Master).

A non-party to a divorce proceeding who had had *de facto* custody of a child of the marriage was given extensive rights to participate in the determination of the custody issue.

Children's Lawyer's [Official Guardian's] Report

Wallin v. Wallin, [1973] 2 O.R. 870, 13 R.F.L. 305 (H.C.).

No final decision should be made until the report of the Official Guardian is available.

Wrightsell v. Wrightsell, [1973] 1 O.R. 649, 11 R.F.L. 271 (H.C.).

Where the report of the Official Guardian is not available, the court may require additional evidence on the points which would have been dealt with in the report or, in clear cases, may proceed without the report or additional evidence.

Steward v. Steward, [1970] 1 O.R. 738 (H.C.).

A motion in a divorce proceeding to dispense with service of the Official Guardian's report may be made to the master.

Johnston v. Johnston, [1969] 2 O.R. 198 (H.C.).

Where the parties' offspring have been adopted by other persons, the Official Guardian need not be served with the pleadings.

H. v. H., [1965] 2 O.R. 175 (H.C.).

The report of the Official Guardian may contain hearsay statements if they are relevant to the issues before the court.

Williams v. Williams, [1956] O.W.N. 85 (Master).

The Official Guardian need not be served with the originating process within the time limited for service on the defendant.

NAMING PLACE OF TRIAL AND TRIAL JUDGE

Place of Trial

69.17(1) The petitioner shall name in the petition as the place of trial a place where the court normally sits in the county in which the petitioner proposes that the action be tried.

(2) A petitioner who makes a claim for custody of or access to a child who ordinarily resides in Ontario shall name in the petition as the place of trial a place where the court normally sits in the county in which the child ordinarily resides.

(3) The trial shall be held at the place named in the petition unless an order is made to change the place of trial under rule 46.03.

Kerr v. Irvine (1989), 70 O.R. (2d) 275, 22 R.F.L. (3d) 462 (Div. Ct.).

Applications to vary orders for custody are to be brought in the place where the court normally sits in the county in which the child ordinarily resides.

MARRIAGE CERTIFICATE AND CERTIFICATE RESPECTING PRIOR PENDING PROCEEDINGS

69.18 No divorce action shall be tried and no motion for judgment in a divorce action shall be heard until the registrar has received and attached to the trial or motion record,

(a) a certificate of the marriage or of the registration of the marriage, unless the petition states that it is impossible to obtain a certificate; and

(b) a certificate or report with respect to prior pending proceedings commenced by either spouse, issued under the Divorce Regulations (Canada) after the petition was filed.

MOTION FOR JUDGMENT

Requisition and Notice of Motion

69.19(1) A requisition to note the respondent in default and a notice of motion for judgment in a divorce action under subrule 19.05(1) (motion for default judgment) shall be combined in Form 69Q.

Petitioner's Affidavit

(2) The affidavit of the petitioner in support of the motion (Form 69R) shall,

(a) contain sufficient information for the court to satisfy itself that there is no possibility of the reconciliation of the spouses, or that the circumstances of the case are of such a nature that it would clearly not be appropriate to do so;

(b) confirm that all the information in the petition is correct, except as specified in the affidavit;

(c) if the certificate of marriage or of registration of marriage filed in the action is not signed and sealed by the Registrar General of Ontario, refer to the certificate by its title, date and place of issue and the name and office of the person who issued it and state that it contains the correct particulars of the marriage;

(d) if no certificate of marriage or of registration of marriage has been filed in the action, state,

(i) what efforts have been made to obtain a certificate and why it is impossible to obtain one,

(ii) the date and place of marriage, and

(iii) sufficient particulars to prove the marriage;

(e) set out particulars of the grounds for divorce;

(f) state that there has been no agreement, conspiracy, understanding or arrangement to which the petitioner is either directly or indirectly a party for the purpose of subverting the administration of justice, fabricating or suppressing evidence or deceiving the court;

(g) if the petitioner is relying on the respondent's adultery or cruelty, state that the petitioner has not condoned or connived at the act or conduct complained of, or if there has been condonation or connivance, set out the circumstances that indicate that the public interest would be better served by granting the divorce;

(h) provide particulars of the present and proposed custody and access arrangements in respect of each child of the marriage, if different from those set out in the petition;

(i) if the petitioner claims support, provide particulars of his or her and the children's needs and of the respondent's means, with reference to the financial statements filed in the action, and set out particulars of any change in circumstances since the financial statements were filed;

(j) if the petitioner does not claim a division of property, confirm that he or she does not wish to claim a division of property at this time and state that he or she is aware that a claim for a division of property may be barred after the divorce;

(k) if the petitioner wishes to include in the judgment provisions of a consent, settlement, separation agreement or previous court order, refer to the document as an exhibit and refer to the specific provisions to be included;

(l) if the petitioner claims costs, set out sufficient facts to enable the court to determine whether costs should be awarded;

(m) if the petitioner seeks to have the divorce take effect earlier than thirty-one days after it is granted, set out the special circumstances that justify the earlier effective date, state that the spouses have agreed that no appeal will be taken from the judgment and refer to the agreement as an exhibit; and

(n) provide the respondent spouse's last known address and state the means by which the address is known.

Respondent's Affidavit

(3) An affidavit made by a respondent spouse in support of the motion (Form 69S) shall,

(a) state that the respondent is the petitioner's spouse;

(b) provide the respondent's address for service of the judgment;

(c) if the petitioner is relying on the respondent's adultery and the respondent is prepared to admit the adultery, state that the respondent is aware that he or she is not obliged to give evidence that he or she has committed adultery, but that he or she is willing to give that evidence;

(d) contain the matters referred to in clauses (2)(a), (b), (f), (g), (h) and (i); and

(e) if the respondent does not claim a division of property, confirm that he or she does not wish to claim a division of property at this time and state that he or she is aware that a claim for a division of property may be barred after the divorce.

Where Counterpetitioner Moves for Judgment

(4) If the motion for judgment is made by the counterpetitioner, subrules (2) and (3) (petitioner's and respondent's affidavits) apply and refer-

ences to the petition and petitioner shall be deemed to be references to the counterpetition and counterpetitioner.

Affidavit of Person Involved in Adultery

(5) Where a person with whom a respondent spouse is alleged to have committed adultery is prepared to admit the adultery and files an affidavit in support of the motion, the affidavit shall state that the person is aware that he or she is not obliged to give evidence that the respondent spouse committed adultery with him or her, but that he or she is willing to give that evidence.

Oral Evidence at Hearing of Motion

(6) Instead of or in addition to filing an affidavit in support of the motion, the petitioner or counterpetitioner may examine witnesses at the hearing of the motion and subrule 39.03(4) (leave to examine witness at hearing) does not apply.

Draft Judgment

(7) The moving party shall file with the notice of motion four copies of the draft divorce judgment (Form 69T), a stamped envelope addressed to each of the parties and, where the Children's Lawyer has prepared a report in the action, a stamped envelope addressed to the Children's Lawyer.

(8) If a draft judgment provides for the payment of support, the moving party shall file with the notice of motion a fifth copy for filing by the registrar in the office of the Director of the Family Support Plan.

Registrar to Present Motion to Judge

(9) The registrar shall present the notice of motion and the evidence filed in support to a judge.

(10) Before presenting the motion to a judge, the registrar shall examine the notice of motion, the evidence filed in support and the draft divorce judgment and shall complete a registrar's certificate (Form 69U).

Judgment

(11) If judgment is granted on the motion in accordance with the draft filed, the registrar shall forthwith sign and enter judgment and mail a copy of it in each envelope provided under subrule (7).

(12) If judgment is to be granted on the motion, but not in accordance with the draft filed, the judge shall hear submissions on behalf of the moving party or adjourn the motion for that purpose. [am. O. Regs. 351/94, s. 7; 69/95, s. 19]

Tomlinson v. Tomlinson (1992), 12 C.P.C. (3d) 8 (Ont. Gen. Div.).

The court refused to grant a consent motion for summary judgment in a family law matter where the court was not satisfied that reasonable arrangements had been made for support of the children of the marriage.

Darling v. Darling (1987), 21 C.P.C. (2d) 80 (Ont. H.C.).

Motions for summary judgment are available in divorce actions, even where there is a counterpetition for corollary relief. Rule [69.19] does not exclude summary judgment motions.

ADJOURNMENT OF TRIAL

Resumption after Adjournment

69.20(1) Where a judgment grants an adjournment of the trial under subsection 10(2) of the Act before hearing any evidence, a motion for resumption of the trial under subsection 10(3) of the Act may be made to any judge.

(2) Where a judge grants an adjournment of the trial under subsection 10(2) of the Act after commencing the hearing of evidence, a motion for resumption of the trial under subsection 10(3) of the Act may be made only to the same judge.

Notice to Attorney General

(3) The judge trying a divorce action may adjourn the trial for any reason to such time and place as are just and, in a proper case, may direct that the registrar forthwith give notice to the Attorney General of the proceeding, its state and the reasons of the judge for directing that notice be given.

(4) Where notice is given, the Attorney General may appear by counsel on the adjourned trial and make submissions and otherwise participate in the proceeding to the extent that the judge allows.

REFERENCE TO A FAMILY LAW COMMISSIONER

69.21(1) A judge sitting at Toronto may, on consent of the parties, refer any question or issue arising in the action relating to custody, support or access to a family law commissioner for inquiry and report.

(2) Where a reference is directed under subrule (1), the commissioner shall inquire into the question or issue referred and shall make a report.

(3) The report may be confirmed on a motion to a judge, or to the referring judge if the order of reference so directs.

(4) The judge may require the commissioner to give reasons for his or her findings or conclusions and may confirm the report in whole or in part or make such other order as is just.

Tam v. Tam (1982), 38 O.R. (2d) 418, 29 C.P.C. 278, 29 R.F.L. (2d) 162, 138 D.L.R. (3d) 302 (C.A.).

The report of a family law commissioner should not be interfered with unless the commissioner has either (a) exceeded his jurisdiction, (b) come to a conclusion that is inconsistent with the evidence adduced on the references, (c) made a patent mathematical error or (d) departed from the proper principles which ought to be applied in the facts of the matter before him.

Parry v. Parry (1978), 6 C.P.C. 20, 3 R.F.L. (2d) 180, affirmed 8 C.P.C. 56 (Ont. C.A.).

The report of a family law commissioner should be complete in its assessment of the witnesses and factual bases for the conclusions and recommendations so that the judge may be in a position to exercise his judgment.

CERTIFICATE OF DIVORCE

69.22 The registrar in the office where a divorce action was commenced shall issue a certificate of divorce (Form 69V) when,

(a) the divorce has taken effect;

(b) a requisition has been filed with the registrar, accompanied by an affidavit sworn after the divorce took effect and stating that,

    (i) no appeal from the divorce is pending, or any such appeal has been abandoned or dismissed, and

    (ii) no order has been made extending the time for appealing from the divorce, or if any such order has been made, the extended time has expired without an appeal being taken; and

(c) the registrar has searched the court records and ascertained that there is no indication that the affidavit is incorrect.

REGISTRAR TO NOTIFY LOCAL REGISTRAR OF APPEAL

69.23 On the filing of a notice of appeal from a divorce or the making of an order extending the time for such an appeal, the Registrar of the Court of Appeal shall forthwith notify the registrar in the office where the action was commenced.

VARIATION OF FINAL ORDER FOR COROLLARY RELIEF

By Application

69.24(1) A person who wishes to vary, suspend or rescind a final order for support, custody or access under section 17 of the Act or to obtain such an order after a divorce shall do so by notice of application.

Filing of Financial Statement

(2) If an application under subrule (1) is in respect of support, the applicant shall file and serve a financial statement (short form) (Form 69M) and a notice to file financial statement (Form 69W) with the notice of application, and the respondent shall deliver a financial statement (short form) (Form 69M) with the notice of appearance.

(3) A respondent who does not intend to defend the application shall nevertheless deliver a financial statement (short form) (Form 69M) within the time prescribed for delivery of a notice of appearance, but a respondent's failure to do so does not prevent the applicant from bringing the application on for hearing.

(4) Where a respondent fails to comply with a notice to file financial statement, the applicant may move without notice for an order requiring the delivery of a financial statement within a specified time.

(5) Where a financial statement is required to be filed or delivered under subrule (2) or (3), the registrar shall not accept the notice of application or notice of appearance for issuing or filing without the financial statement.

(6) In an application in which a claim is made in relation to custody of a child, the court may order the parties to deliver financial statements within a specified time.

Contents of Affidavit in Support

(7) An affidavit in support of the application shall set out,

(a) the place or ordinary residence of the parties and the children of the marriage;

(b) the current marital status of the parties;

(c) particulars of the change in circumstances relied on;

(d) particulars of current custody and access arrangements and of any proposed change;

(e) particulars of current support arrangements and any proposed change;

(f) particulars of any arrears of support under an order or agreement; and

(g) particulars of any efforts made to mediate the matters in issue or of any assessment made in relation to custody or access.

Interprovincial Variation

(8) Evidence given by a person in Ontario in an application referred to in subsection 18(2) of the Act (provisional order) shall be given by affidavit, unless the court orders otherwise.

(9) The registrar shall serve a notice of confirmation hearing (Form 69X) under subsection 19(2) of the Act and the other documents referred to in that subsection,

(a) on the respondent, in the same manner as an originating process; and

(b) on the applicant, by mail.

(10) A respondent in an application referred to in subsection 18(2) of the Act shall serve and file a financial statement (short form) (Form 69M) within ten days after service of the notice of confirmation hearing.

(11) Where a court outside Ontario remits a variation proceeding to a court in Ontario for further evidence, the registrar shall serve a notice requiring further evidence (Form 69Y) on the parties by mail.

(12) Where a court in Ontario receives further evidence from a court outside Ontario under subsection 18(6) or 19(6) of the Act, the registrar shall serve a notice of resumption of hearing (Form 69Z) on the parties by mail.

(13) The registrar shall perform the duties imposed on the court or an officer of the court by subsections 18(3) and (6) and 19(3) and (12) of the Act (transmission and filing of documents).

Englar v. Englar (1978), 19 O.R. (2d) 561, 2 R.F.L. (2d) 237, 85 D.L.R. (3d) 609 (C.A.).

The court has jurisdiction to reduce or cancel arrears for maintenance ordered to be paid by a decree *nisi* for divorce.

Lipman v. Lipman (1978), 19 O.R. (2d) 486, 3 R.F.L. (2d) 49, 85 D.L.R. (3d) 558 (H.C.).

The court has jurisdiction to make an order for maintenance of children at a time after the granting of a decree absolute where there is evidence of an intention to claim such maintenance and notwithstanding that the decree *nisi* is silent on the point.

Brouillard v. Brouillard (1978), 19 O.R. (2d) 464, 85 D.L.R. (3d) 314 (H.C.).

The court has jurisdiction to make an order for maintenance of a spouse after a decree absolute notwithstanding that the decree *nisi* is silent on the point.

Blane v. Blane (1975), 7 O.R. (2d) 5, 17 R.F.L. 238, 54 D.L.R. (3d) 169, affirmed 13 O.R. (2d) 466, 23 R.F.L. 195, 71 D.L.R. (3d) 351 (C.A.).

The court has no jurisdiction to vary an award of maintenance made in another province.

Soo v. Martineau (1974), 6 O.R. (2d) 593, 17 R.F.L. 349, 53 D.L.R. (3d) 481 (Prov. Ct.).

A family court has no jurisdiction to vary maintenance awarded in a decree *nisi* even where the decree purports to authorize it.

REGISTRATION OF ORDERS FOR COROLLARY RELIEF FROM OTHER PROVINCES

69.25(1) An order under section 15, 16 or 17 of the Act that was made by a court outside Ontario may be registered under paragraph 20(3)(a) of the Act by filing a certified copy with the local registrar at Toronto, and the order shall then be entered as an order of the court.

(2) The certified copy of the order may be filed with the local registrar at Toronto by forwarding it to him or her by ordinary mail, accompanied by a written request that it be registered under paragraph 20(3)(a) of the Act. [am. O. Reg. 73/92, s. 3]

COSTS

69.26 The costs of a divorce action shall be assessed in accordance with Tariff B, unless a judge orders otherwise.

Wilson v. Wilson (1978), 21 O.R. (2d) 703, 8 C.P.C. 305, 7 R.F.L. (2d) 159, 91 D.L.R. (3d) 566 (Div. Ct.).

Discussion of the principles surrounding the awarding of costs in matrimonial matters. It is wrong to adopt as settled practice that no costs should generally be awarded in matrimonial matters.

Royal v. Royal (1975), 8 O.R. (2d) 241, 21 R.F.L. 389, 57 D.L.R. (3d) 529 (H.C.).

Where material in support of an application for interim disbursements lacks sufficient detail, some allowance can still be made by reference to the Tariff.

Sorensen v. Sorensen (1978), 7 C.P.C. 306, 8 R.F.L. (2d) 185 (Ont. Div. Ct.).

Where the petitioner failed to obtain custody but succeeded in her unopposed divorce claim, the court awarded her 75 per cent of her costs on a contested basis.

Chester v. Chester (1977), 2 C.P.C. 121 (Ont. H.C.).

Where a co-respondent has engaged in conduct undermining the marriage relationship during a period when he knew reconciliation was being attempted, he may be penalized in costs.

Boerop v. Boerop, [1970] 3 O.R. 289, 2 R.F.L. 85 (Master).

The court may award interim disbursements in a divorce action.

Woodbeck v. Woodbeck, [1970] 1 O.R. 662, 2 R.F.L. 83, 9 D.L.R. (3d) 244 (H.C.).

Where the ground for a divorce is separation for more than three years, costs should generally not be awarded.

SUPPORT ORDER ENFORCEMENT

　　69.27　Rule 70.10.1 (support order enforcement) applies, with necessary modifications, to a divorce action and to a support order made in a divorce action. [re-en. O. Reg. 73/92, s. 4].

RULE 70　FAMILY LAW PROCEEDINGS

Highlights

Rule 70 is largely based on Rule 69 (Divorce Actions) and incorporates portions of it by reference. There are no major innovations in Rule 70 other than those made by Rule 69 for financial statements (but note under Rule 70 they cannot be waived — see ss. 8 and 41 of the *Family Law Act*) and references to family law commissioners. See the discussion of Rule 69.

One important provision is the place of hearing rule (rule 70.05) for custody and access cases which must be heard where the child in question ordinarily resides.

Technical changes have been made in rule 70.10 to standardize the procedure in appeals to the Ontario Court (General Division) under the *Family Law Act* and *Children's Law Reform Act* with those under the *Child and Family Services Act* in Rule 71.

Support enforcement. Rule 70.10.1, added on March 1, 1992, by O. Reg. 73/92, created important new procedures and remedies in support proceedings, primarily to fit with the *Family Support Plan Act*, which was extensively revised as of that date (it was formerly known as the *Support and Custody Orders Enforcement Act*). The Act created the "support deduction order", which is to be made to accompany virtually every support order and provides for automatic, at source deduction of support payments (even though no default has occurred) and remittance of the support to the Director of the Family Support Plan. The rules provide for completion of the information form necessary for the making of the support deduction order (and required by O. Reg. 765/91 made under the Act). The form of the support deduction order (and any order suspending it) is also prescribed by the regulation, and these orders are drawn by court staff, so these orders are exempt from the usual requirement (rule 59.03) for approval as to form. The terminology in support enforcement orders and other process (such as execution and garnishment) is changed, with "payor" replacing "debtor" and "recipient" replacing "creditor" (but note there is a saving provision for documents generated during 1992 using the old terms). The rule takes a major departure from the normal rule (37.03) governing where motions are heard: support enforcement matters are usually to be heard in the recipient's county (but see rule 70.10.1(6) for important exceptions). Garnishments issued by the Director of the Family Support Plan now provide for all payments to be made to the Director (not the court or sheriff), just like support deduction orders. The rule also allows for periodic orders that are indexed for inflation to be enforced by garnishment without issuing a new garnishment every time the payments increase; instead, the recipient or Director can serve a statutory declaration setting out the new payment amount. Three new forms (70A.1, 70A.2 and 70A.3) are created to go with the new provisions.

Former Rules: Rules 775a-775lb.

APPLICATION OF THE RULE

70.01　Rules 70.02 to 70.14 apply to proceedings under,
(a)　Parts I, II and III of the *Family Law Act*;
(b)　Part III of the *Children's Law Reform Act*;
(c)　the *Reciprocal Enforcement of Maintenance Orders Act*;
(d)　section 11 of the *Change of Name Act*; and
(e)　the *Family Support Plan Act*. [am. O. Reg. 73/92, s. 5]

DEFINITIONS

70.02 In rules 70.03 to 70.14,
"applicant" includes a plaintiff;
"respondent" includes a defendant; and
"responding document" means a statement of defence, defence to counterclaim or affidavit in opposition to an application.

ORIGINATING PROCESS

Claim for Relief
70.03(1) An originating process that contains a claim for support or division of property shall set out the nature and amount of relief claimed and, if support is claimed, the amount for each dependant.

Application by Government Agency
(2) Where the Ministry of Community and Social Services, a municipality, a district welfare administration board or a band is an applicant for an order for the support of a dependant under subsection 33(3) of the *Family Law Act*, it shall serve the originating process on the dependant.

Re Tong and Perisiol (1984), 46 O.R. (2d) 761 (Dist. Ct.).
In an application by a mother for support of a child born outside of marriage, although no declaration of paternity had been made by the High Court under the *Children's Law Reform Act*, the District Court ruled it had jurisdiction to determine parentage as a material part of the dispute (the obligation to support the child) was within its jurisdiction.

Sayer v. Rollin (1980), 16 R.F.L. (2d) 289 (Ont. C.A.).
In a proceeding for the support of a child born outside marriage, it is not necessary to obtain a formal declaration of paternity from the Supreme Court first. Any court that has jurisdiction to make a support order under the *Family Law Reform Act* may determine the issue of paternity.

FINANCIAL STATEMENTS

Applicant's Financial Statement
70.04(1) Where an order is sought under section 7 (division of property), 33 (support) or 37 (variation of support) of the *Family Law Act*, a financial statement (Form 69K) shall be filed and served with the originating process, together with a notice to file financial statement (Form 69W).

(2) Where the originating process is a notice of action, the financial statement shall be delivered with the statement of claim.

Respondent's Financial Statement
(3) A respondent served with the applicant's financial statement shall deliver a financial statement with his or her responding document.

(4) A respondent who does not intend to defend the proceeding shall nevertheless deliver a financial statement within the time prescribed for the delivery of his or her responding document, but a respondent's failure to do so does not prevent the applicant from bringing the proceeding on for hearing or moving for judgment.

Registrar to Refuse Documents Unless Accompanied by Financial Statements

(5) Where a financial statement is required to be filed or delivered with an originating process, statement of claim or responding document, the registrar shall not accept the originating process, statement of claim or responding document for issuing or filing without the financial statement.

Order for Delivery

(6) Where a respondent fails to comply with a notice to file financial statement, the applicant may move without notice for an order requiring the delivery of a financial statement within a specified time.

(7) In a proceeding in which a claim is made for custody of a child, the court may order the parties to deliver financial statements (short form) (Form 69M) within a specified time.

Subrules 69.14(8) to (14) Apply

(8) Subrules 69.14(8) to (14) (particulars, failure to deliver, cross-examination, duty to correct) apply, with necessary modifications, to financial statements referred to in subrules (1) to (7).

Net Family Property Statement

(9) In a proceeding in which a claim is made for a division of property, each spouse shall deliver a net family property statement (Form 69N) at least seven days before each of the following:

1. A pre-trial conference.
2. A motion for judgment.
3. The hearing.

Divorce Action

(10) Where a claim under the *Family Law Act* or the *Children's Law Reform Act* is made in a divorce action, the obligations of the spouses respecting financial statements are governed by rule 69.14.

Cross-Reference: See cases under rule 69.14.

Ferwerda v. Ferwerda (1985), 48 C.P.C. 285 (Ont. Dist. Ct.).

Rule [70.04(6)] does not apply to an action commenced by notice of action. In that case the financial statement is required with the statement of claim.

PLACE OF HEARING

70.05(1) An applicant who makes a claim for custody of or access to a child who ordinarily resides in Ontario shall name in the originating process as the place of hearing a place where the court normally sits in the county in which the child ordinarily resides.

(2) Where a claim referred to in subrule (1) is made in a divorce action, the place of trial is governed by rule 69.17.

(3) The hearing shall be held at the place named in the originating process unless an order is made under rule 46.03 to change the place of hearing, and for the purpose of changing the place of hearing an application shall be treated as an action.

Rodrigues v. Rodrigues, [1996] W.D.F.L. 661 (Ont. Gen. Div.).

The court held that Ontario courts had jurisdiction in this custody dispute notwithstanding custody proceedings had been initiated in Portugal.

Kerr v. Irvine (1989), 70 O.R. (2d) 275, 22 R.F.L. (3d) 462 (Div. Ct.).

Applications to vary orders for custody are to be brought in the place where the court normally sits in the county in which the child ordinarily resides.

CHILDREN'S LAWYER'S REPORT

70.06 Subrules 69.16(1) to (8) (Children's Lawyer's report) apply, with necessary modifications, to proceedings under Part III of the *Children's Law Reform Act*. [am. O. Reg. 69/95, s. 19]

REFERENCE TO A FAMILY LAW COMMISSIONER

70.07 Rule 69.21 (reference to family law commissioner) applies, with necessary modifications, to any question or issue arising under the *Family Law Act* or the *Children's Law Reform Act*.

INTERIM RELIEF

70.08 Rule 69.15 (interim relief) applies, with necessary modifications, to a motion for interim relief in a proceeding under the *Family Law Act* or the *Children's Law Reform Act*.

PROCEEDING TRANSFERRED FROM ONTARIO COURT (PROVINCIAL DIVISION)

70.09(1) Where a proceeding is transferred from the Ontario Court (Provincial Division) to the Ontario Court (General Division) under subsection 2(2) of the *Family Law Act* or section 66 of the *Children's Law Reform Act*, the proceeding shall continue without duplication of any steps taken before the transfer unless the court to which the proceeding is transferred directs otherwise.

(2) The court to which a proceeding is transferred may, on motion, give directions for the conduct of the proceeding.

APPEAL FROM ONTARIO COURT (PROVINCIAL DIVISION)

Commencement of Appeal

70.10(1) An appeal from the Ontario Court (Provincial Division) to the Ontario Court (General Division) under section 48 of the *Family Law Act*, section 73 of the *Children's Law Reform Act* or section 11 of the *Change of Name Act* shall be commenced by serving a notice of appeal (Form 70A) on all parties whose interests are affected by the appeal, within thirty days after the date of the order appealed from.

Filing Notice of Appeal

(2) The notice of appeal, with proof of service, shall be filed in the office of the local registrar within five days after service.

Grounds to be Stated

(3) The notice of appeal (Form 70A) shall state the relief sought and shall set out the grounds of appeal, and no other grounds may be argued except by leave of the court.

Appeal Record

(4) The appellant shall, at least ten days before the hearing of the appeal, file with the local registrar and serve on each respondent an appeal record containing, in the following order,

(a) a table of contents describing each document, including each exhibit, by its nature and date and, in the case of an exhibit, by exhibit number or letter;

(b) a copy of the notice of appeal;

(c) a copy of the order appealed from, as signed, and the reasons, if any, as well as a further typed or printed copy of the reasons if they are handwritten;

(d) a transcript of the evidence; and

(e) such other material that was before the court appealed from as is necessary for the hearing of the appeal,

and a factum consisting of a concise statement, without argument, of the facts and law relied on by the appellant.

(5) Each respondent shall, at least three days before the hearing of the appeal, file with the local registrar and serve on every other party,

(a) any further material that was before the court appealed from and is necessary for the hearing of the appeal; and

(b) a factum consisting of a concise statement, without argument, of the facts and law relied on by the respondent.

Dispensing with Compliance

(6) A judge may, before or at the hearing of the appeal, dispense with compliance with subrule (4) or (5) in whole or in part.

SUPPORT ORDER ENFORCEMENT

Support deduction information form

70.10.1(1) In a proceeding where support or a variation of support is claimed, the parties shall file with the court, with the material for the hearing of a motion for judgment or for interim support and with the material for the trial or the hearing of the application, the support deduction order information form prescribed by the regulations under the *Family Support Plan Act* (Form 70A.1).

(2) The court may proceed in the absence of complete information on the information form about the payor's address or income sources.

Form of support deduction order or suspension order

(3) Subrule 59.03(1) (approval of draft order) does not apply to a support deduction order or suspension order under the *Family Support Plan Act.*

Terminology in enforcement

(4) In any document in relation to the enforcement of a support order, "recipient" shall be used instead of "creditor" and "payor" shall be used instead of "debtor".

(5) Despite subrule (4), a document served, filed or issued before the 1st day of January, 1993 is not incorrect for the reason that it uses "creditor" or "debtor".

Place of hearing

(6) A hearing in relation to the enforcement of a support order, including the hearing of a motion for a suspension order, shall be held, despite subrule 37.03(2) (place of hearing of motion made on notice),

(a) in the county where the recipient under the order resides;

(b) where the recipient does not reside in Ontario, in the county where the support order is filed for enforcement with a sheriff or with the Director of the Family Support Plan;

(c) on consent of the person enforcing the order, in the county where the payor under the order resides; or

(d) in the case of a motion made under subsection 3.3(18) of the *Family Support Plan Act*, in the county where the income source resides.

Garnishment by Director of Family Support Plan

(7) A notice of garnishment issued on requisition by the Director of the Family Support Plan shall be in Form 70A.2, and subrules 60.08(11) to (19) (liability, payment, dispute, enforcement) apply, with necessary modifications, as if the Director were a sheriff.

Statutory declaration indexing garnishment

(8) Subrules (9) and (10) apply where a notice of garnishment is issued to enforce a support order, domestic contract or paternity agreement that provides for indexation of periodic payments to account for inflation.

(9) The person enforcing the order, contract or agreement may serve on the garnishee and the payor, by ordinary mail, personal service or an alternative to personal service under rule 16.03, a statutory declaration (Form 70A.3) setting out the new amount to be paid under the order, contract or agreement as a result of indexation, and may file the declaration with the court with proof of service.

(10) The garnishee is liable from the date of service on the garnishee to pay the new amount set out in the declaration as if that amount were set out in the notice of garnishment, and subrules 60.08(15) to (19) (dispute, enforcement, payment) apply, with necessary modifications. [en. O. Reg. 73/92, s. 6]

WARRANT FOR ARREST

70.11 A warrant for the arrest of a debtor or respondent referred to in section 43 of the *Family Law Act* or section 13 of the *Family Support Plan Act* shall be in (Form 70B). [am O. Reg. 351/94, s. 8]

RECOGNIZANCE

70.12 A recognizance required by an order made under subsection 46(1) of the *Family Law Act* or section 35 of the *Children's Law Reform Act* shall be in (Form 70C) and shall be entered into before the registrar or such other officer as a judge directs.

RECIPROCAL ENFORCEMENT OF MAINTENANCE ORDERS

70.13 On receipt by the registrar of a written request under subsection 2(3) of the *Reciprocal Enforcement of Support Orders Act*, the registrar shall deem a final order of the court within the meaning of section 1 of that Act that is referred to in the request to be a registered order under subsection 2(3) of that Act and shall issue a certificate accordingly.

REQUEST BY EXTRA-PROVINCIAL TRIBUNAL FOR EVIDENCE IN CUSTODY CASES

Issuing Summons to Give Evidence

70.14(1) Where the Attorney General refers a request of an extra-provincial tribunal to the court under section 33 of the *Children's Law Reform Act*, the registrar shall issue a summons in (Form 70D) requiring the person named in the request to produce or give evidence in accordance with the request.

Service of Summons

(2) The summons and a copy of the request of the extra-provincial tribunal and any supporting material that accompanied the request shall be served on the person named in the request, personally and not by an alternative to personal service, at least five days before he or she is required to produce or give evidence.

(3) Where the person named in the request is not a party to the proceeding before the extra-provincial tribunal and the summons requires the person to give oral evidence, attendance money calculated in accordance with Tariff A shall be paid or tendered to the person when the summons is served.

(4) A copy of the summons shall be served on the Attorney General within the time prescribed by subrule (2).

Affidavit Evidence

(5) Where the summons does not require the person to give oral evidence, the person may file with the registrar the evidence required, verified by the person's affidavit.

Oral Evidence

(6) Where the summons requires the person to give oral evidence, the person shall attend before a judge or officer of the court, as set out in the summons, to be examined in accordance with the summons.

Evidence to be Sent to Extra-Provincial Tribunal

(7) The registrar shall send to the extra-provincial tribunal a certified copy of evidence produced or given under this rule.

Sanctions for Disobeying Summons

(8) Subrules 53.04(7) and (8) apply, with necessary modifications, to a person who after having been served in accordance with subrules (2) and (3) fails to comply with the summons.

RULE 71   CHILD AND FAMILY SERVICES ACT APPEALS

Highlights

    General.   Technical changes have been made in rule 71.02 to standardize the appeal provisions here with those in rule 70.10 for appeals to the Ontario Court (General Division) under the *Family Law Act* and *Children's Law Reform Act.* Rule 71.03 provides expressly for the procedure in rule 71.02 to apply to appeals from the Unified Family Court to the Divisional Court.

    Former Rule: Rule 775m.

DEFINITION

    71.01   In rules 71.02 and 71.03 "Act" means the *Child and Family Services Act.*

APPEAL FROM ONTARIO COURT (PROVINCIAL DIVISION)

Commencement of Appeal

    71.02(1)   An appeal from the Ontario Court (Provincial Division) to the Ontario Court (General Division) under section 69 or 156 of the Act shall be commenced by serving a notice of appeal (Form 70A), within thirty days after the date of the decision appealed from,

    (a)   on the clerk of the Ontario Court (Provincial Division) in the county in which the proceeding was heard;

    (b)   on all other persons entitled to appeal the decision; and

    (c)   in the case of an appeal under section 69 of the Act, on all other persons entitled to notice of the proceeding under subsection 39(3) of the Act who appeared at the hearing.

Service of Notice of Appeal

    (2)   Service under subrule (1) may be made by any method authorized by Rule 16 or by mailing a copy of the notice of appeal to the person to be served, at the person's last known address.

Filing Notice of Appeal

    (3)   The notice of appeal, with proof of service, shall be filed in the office of the local registrar within five days after service.

Grounds to be Stated

    (4)   The notice of appeal (Form 70A) shall state the relief sought and shall set out the grounds of appeal, and no other grounds may be argued except by leave of the court.

Appeal Record

    (5)   The record on the appeal shall be the record prepared for the purpose of the appeal under the rules of the Ontario Court (Provincial Division) by the clerk of the court and sent by him or her for filing with the local registrar and shall contain, in the following order,

(a) a table of contents;

(b) a copy of the notice of appeal;

(c) a copy of the decision appealed from, as signed, and the reasons for the decision, if any, as well as a further typed or printed copy of the reasons if they are handwritten;

(d) a transcript of the evidence, obtained and filed by the appellant; and

(e) such other material that was before the court appealed from as is necessary for the hearing of the appeal.

Hearing Date

(6) The appeal shall be heard within thirty days after the filing of the appeal record with the local registrar.

Dispensing with Compliance

(7) Subject to subsections [69(5)] and [156(4)] (extension of time for appeal) of the Act, a judge may, before or at the hearing of the appeal, dispense with compliance with this rule in whole or in part.

Cook v. Mounce (1979), 26 O.R. (2d) 129, 12 C.P.C. 5, 104 D.L.R. (3d) 635 (Div. Ct.).

Consideration of whether new evidence would be heard on an appeal under the *Child Welfare Act.*

APPEAL FROM UNIFIED FAMILY COURT

71.03 Rules 71.01 and 71.02 apply, with necessary modifications, to an appeal under section 69 or 156 of the Act from the Unified Family Court to the Divisional Court as provided in subsection 61(3) of the *Courts of Justice Act.*

RULE 72 PAYMENT INTO AND OUT OF COURT

Highlights

The scope of this Rule is somewhat broader than its title might at first suggest. It deals not only with payment into court (rule 72.02) and payment out of court (rule 72.03), but also with the discharge of a mortgage held by the accountant (rule 72.04) and the obtaining of a stop order in respect of money or securities held by the accountant (rule 72.05).

Payment into court. Rule 72.02 provides the procedure to be followed in making a payment into court. This rule does not itself specify when money is to be paid into court: that obligation will arise from a statute, a court order or a rule, see *e.g.*, rule 7.09 (order for payment of money to a party under disability); rule 55.06(12) (proceeds of the sale of land on a reference); rule 56.04 (security for costs); rule 49.07(3) and (4) (payment into court as a term of an offer to settle or the acceptance of an offer to settle). With introduction of a general offer to settle procedure, the latter provision is the only remnant of the former procedure for payment into court in satisfaction.

Payment out of court. Rule 72.03 provides the mechanics of payment of money out of court. In particular it defines the circumstances in which money may be paid directly to a solicitor, rather than to a party, without a court order to that effect (rule 72.03(8)), to an insurer (rule 72.03(6)), to a personal representative (rule 72.03(9)) and to a party under disability (rule 72.03(10)).

Rule amendment of 1990. Prior to the merger of the courts, payment into and out of the Supreme Court was handled by the accountant, but the payment of money into and out of the District Court was handled by the local registrar. With the introduction of court reform, it was decided to move towards centralized management of money paid into court by having it paid to the accountant since the accountant is able to obtain higher rates of interest because of the large sums of money he has on deposit at all times. However, within this overall centralized scheme, it was perceived that there was a need to provide for local payment in and out of court to avoid delays in payments out in respect of cases where small sums are held for only a short time. The resulting scheme is that, in general, moneys that are to be paid into court are to be paid to the accountant, but in proceedings under the *Landlord and Tenant Act* or the *Repair and Storage Liens Act* commenced outside Toronto, payment is to be made to the registrar. In respect of any proceeding commenced in Toronto, payment is to be made directly to the accountant, but in any proceeding commenced outside Toronto, payment in and out of court may be made either through the accountant or the local registrar. Provision is also made for transfer to the accountant after one year of all moneys paid to the local registrar under the *Landlord and Tenant Act* or the *Repair and Storage Liens Act.*

Regulations. A regulation concerning money paid into court is reproduced following rule 72.02.

Former Rules: Rules 226, 306-318a, 382, 726-741, 772-775.

DEFINITIONS

72.01 In rules 72.02 to 72.05,
"accountant" means the Accountant of the Ontario Court;

"registrar" means the registrar in the location where the proceeding was commenced.

PAYMENT INTO COURT

General Procedure
72.02(1) A person who seeks to pay money into court shall file with the accountant or, if the proceeding was commenced outside Toronto, with the accountant or registrar,
(a) a requisition for payment into court that refers to any statutory provision or rule that authorizes the payment into court; and
(b) a copy of any order, report, offer to settle or acceptance of offer under which the money is payable.
(2) Despite subrule (1), in a proceeding under the *Landlord and Tenant Act* or the *Repair and Storage Liens Act* commenced outside Toronto, the material referred to in subrule (1) shall be filed with the registrar.
(3) On receiving the material referred to in subrule (1), the accountant shall provide the party with a direction to receive the money addressed to the bank into which the money is to be paid.
(4) Where the direction is obtained from a registrar, the registrar shall forthwith send to the accountant the material filed under subrule (1).
(5) Subrule (3) does not apply to payments into court in the proceedings referred to in subrule (2).
(6) The party paying the money into court shall pay it into an account in the name of the accountant in a bank listed in Schedule I or II to the *Bank Act* (Canada), in accordance with the direction.
(7) On receiving the money, the bank shall give a receipt to the party paying the money in and shall forthwith send a copy of the receipt to the accountant.
(8) A party paying into court under an offer to settle or an acceptance of offer shall forthwith serve a notice of payment into court (Form 72A) on every interested party, but the notice shall not be filed.

Transfer to Accountant
(9) If money paid into court in a proceeding referred to in subrule (2) is not paid out after one year, it shall be transferred to the accountant unless the court orders otherwise.

Regulations
The following regulation was made pursuant to the *Courts of Justice Act.*

R.R.O. 1990, Regulation 190
[am. O. Regs. 391/91; 619/91; 176/92; 213/93; 599/94; 187/95]

MONEY PAID INTO COURT

1.—(1) Subject to subsection (2), money paid into the Ontario Court (General Division) shall be paid to the Accountant of the Ontario Court unless it is paid into the Small Claims Court.

(2) Money paid into the Ontario Court (General Division) in a proceeding under the *Landlord and Tenant Act* or the *Repair and Storage Liens Act* shall be paid to the local registrar of the Ontario Court (General Division) for the location where the proceeding was commenced, if the proceeding was commenced outside The Municipality of Metropolitan Toronto.

(3) Money paid into court in a proceeding referred to in subsection (2) that is not paid out after one year shall be transferred forthwith to the Accountant.

(4) Money paid or transferred to the Accountant shall bear interest on the minimum monthly balance,

(a) in the case of money held for a minor, at the rate of 8 per cent per year compounded semi-annually;

(b) in the case of all other money, at the rate of 5 per cent per year compounded semi-annually.

(5) Mortgages and other securities taken under an order of the Ontario Court (General Division) shall be taken in the name of the Accountant of the Ontario Court and shall be deposited in the Accountant's office, unless an order provides otherwise.

(6) The Accountant has no duty or obligation in respect of the instruments deposited under subsection (5) except as custodian of the instruments, unless an order provides otherwise.

2.—(1) The Deputy Attorney General or the person or persons designated by the Deputy Attorney General has control and management of the money in the Ontario Court (General Division), the investment of the money and the securities in which it is invested unless the money is paid into the Small Claims Court.

(2) Money that is available for investment shall be invested in investments in which the Treasurer of Ontario may invest public money under section 3 of the *Financial Administration Act.*

(3) The person who has control and management of money paid into court may employ a trust company to make the investments, or act as custodian of the securities purchased as investments.

(4) Money paid or transferred to the Accountant shall bear interest on the minimum monthly balance,

(a) in the case of money held for a minor, at the rate of 8 per cent per year compounded semi-annually;

(b) in the case of all other money, at the rate of 5 per cent per year compounded semi-annually.

Cases

Repo v. Michael Jay Real Estate Ltd. (1982), 26 C.P.C. 153 (Ont. Master).

A master does not have jurisdiction to order that funds paid into court as security for costs be invested in a particular way.

PAYMENT OUT OF COURT

Authority for Payment Out

72.03(1) Money may be paid out of court only in accordance with an order or report, or on consent under subrule (4).

Payment Out under Order or Report

(2) A person who seeks payment of money out of court in accordance with an order or report shall file with the accountant or registrar,

(a) a requisition for payment out;

(b) a certified copy of the order or report, unless one has already been filed with the accountant or registrar; and

(c) an affidavit stating,

(i) in the case of a report, that the report has been confirmed and the manner of confirmation, or

(ii) in the case of an order, that the time prescribed for an appeal has expired and no appeal is pending,

unless such an affidavit has already been filed with the accountant or registrar,

and the accountant or registrar shall then pay the money to the person to whom the order or report directs that it be paid.

(3) Where the Children's Lawyer or the Public Guardian and Trustee seeks payment out in accordance with an order or report, he or she may file one requisition dealing with more than one proceeding and need not file the affidavit referred to in clause (2)(c).

Payment Out on Consent

(4) A party who seeks payment out of court, on consent, of money paid in under an offer to settle or an acceptance of offer or as security for costs shall file with the accountant or registrar,

(a) a requisition for payment out;

(b) the consent of all parties or their solicitors; and

(c) an affidavit stating that all parties have consented to the payment and that neither the party who paid the money into court nor the party to whom it is to be paid is under disability,

and the accountant or registrar shall then pay the money out to the party in accordance with the consent.

Payment Out of Interest

(5) Money paid out of court under subrule (2) or (4) shall be paid out with accrued interest, if any, unless the order, report or consent provides otherwise.

Consent by Insurer on Behalf of Party

(6) Where the insurer of a party has paid money into court on behalf of the party and an affidavit setting out the relevant facts is filed with the accountant or registrar, the consent required by clause (4)(b) may be given by the insurer on behalf of the party and, where the party is entitled to payment out, the money may be paid out to the insurer.

Minor Attaining Age of Majority

(7) Money in court to which a party is entitled under an order or report when the party attains the age of majority may be paid out to the party on filing with the accountant or registrar,

(a) a requisition for payment out; and

(b) an affidavit proving the identity of the party and that the party has attained the age of majority.

Payment Directly to Solicitor

(8) Where money has been paid into court as security for costs or an order has been made for payment of costs out of money in court and the order does not provide for payment out directly to a solicitor, the money may

be paid out to the solicitor for the party entitled, on filing with the accountant or registrar the material required by subrule (2) or (4) and the affidavit of the party stating that the party consents to payment of the money directly to the solicitor rather than to the party.

Payment to Personal Representative

(9) Where money or securities in court are to be paid out or transferred to a person named in an order or report who has died, the money or securities may be paid or transferred to the deceased person's personal representative on proof to the satisfaction of the accountant of the person's death and of the personal representative's authority.

Party under Disability

(10) An order for payment out of court of money in court to the credit of a person under disability may be obtained on motion to a judge by or on notice to the Children's Lawyer, unless the Public Guardian and Trustee is the person's litigation guardian, in which case the motion shall be made by or on notice to the Public Guardian and Trustee.

(11) A motion under subrule (10), other than a motion made by the Children's Lawyer or the Public Guardian and Trustee, shall be supported by an affidavit in (Form 72B).

(12) A motion under subrule (10) by the Children's Lawyer or the Public Guardian and Trustee may be made without notice unless the court orders otherwise.

(13) In an order under subrule (10), the judge may fix the costs of the moving party and direct that they be paid out of the money in court directly to the moving party's solicitor.

(14) Where an order is made under subrule (10) for maintenance of a minor, the Children's Lawyer shall, on request of the moving party, obtain the cheque from the accountant and send it without charge to the moving party. [am. O. Reg. 69/95, ss. 9, 19, 20]

Larrow v. Larrow (1986), 14 C.P.C. (2d) 101 (Ont. Dist. Ct.).

Unless money standing in court is in respect of an offer to settle or was paid as security for costs, a party seeking payment out must proceed under rule [72.03(2)].

Longoz v. Mantle (1985), 57 O.R. (2d) 254 (Dist. Ct.).

The court held that an order for payment out of court to solicitors is not permitted in an interpleader matter.

Brohman v. Good (1979), 27 O.R. (2d) 702 (H.C.).

Where a plaintiff paid money into court as a term of an order discharging a mortgage, interest on the money was held to belong to the defendant.

DISCHARGE OF A MORTGAGE

72.04(1) A person entitled to the discharge of a mortgage held by the accountant may leave with the accountant or registrar the required discharge with a request that it be executed.

(2) **Where the accountant is satisfied that the money secured by the mortgage has been paid in full and that the discharge is in proper form, the accountant shall execute the discharge.**

(3) **After executing the discharge, the accountant shall hand over all documents that relate to the mortgage in return for a receipt for the documents and shall assign any policy of insurance in respect of the mortgaged property to the person entitled to the discharge or as the person directs in writing.**

STOP ORDER

72.05(1) On motion without notice in a proceeding or, where there is no proceeding pending, on application without notice by a person who claims to be entitled to money or securities held or to be held in the future by the accountant for the benefit of another person, the court may make a stop order (Form 72C) directing that the money or securities shall not be dealt with except on notice to the moving party or applicant.

(2) **On a motion or application for a stop order, the moving party or applicant shall, unless the court orders otherwise, undertake to abide by any order concerning damages that the court may make if it ultimately appears that the granting of the order has caused damage to any person for which the moving party or applicant ought to compensate the person.**

(3) **A person who has obtained an order under subrule (1) may make a motion on notice to all interested parties for an order for payment out.**

Burford Textiles Ltd. v. Allendale Mutual Ins. Co. (1982), 39 O.R. (2d) 417, 31 C.P.C. 56, 140 D.L.R. (3d) 114 (H.C.).

A plaintiff in an action to set aside a fraudulent conveyance may apply for a stop order with respect to moneys paid into court in another action in which the defendant transferee is a plaintiff.

RULE 73   RECIPROCAL ENFORCEMENT OF UNITED KINGDOM JUDGMENTS

Highlights

This rule regulates the registration of United Kingdom judgments under reciprocal enforcement of judgments legislation.

United Kingdom judgments may be registered on application in Form 73A supported by affidavit material which may include statements on information and belief (rule 73.02(4)) and must include original or certified copies of the U.K. judgment and U.K. proof of service.

DEFINITIONS

73.01 In rules 73.01 to 73.03,
"Act" means the *Reciprocal Enforcement of Judgments (U.K.) Act*;
"Convention" means the convention appearing as a schedule to the Act;
"judgment" means a judgment to which the Convention applies.

APPLICATION FOR REGISTRATION OF JUDGMENT

Notice of Application

73.02(1) Notice of an application under the Act for registration of a judgment granted by a court in the United Kingdom shall be in (Form 73A).

Supporting Material

(2) The application shall be supported by an affidavit that confirms the statements contained in the notice of application and sets out any additional facts necessary to establish that the applicant is entitled to register and enforce the judgment.

(3) The judgment and the original proof of service of the originating process of the United Kingdom court, or certified copies of them, shall accompany the affidavit as exhibits.

(4) The affidavit may contain statements of the deponent's information and belief, if the source of the information and the fact of the belief are specified in the affidavit.

Evans Dodd v. Gambin Associates (1994), 17 O.R. (3d) 803, 26 C.P.C. (3d) 189 (Gen. Div.).

The court refused to register a U.K. default judgment where none of the traditional common law jurisdictional tests were met. The extension of the common law principles in *Morguard Investments Ltd. v. de Savoye* (1990), 52 B.C.L.R. (2d) 160, [1991] 2 W.W.R. 217, 76 D.L.R. (4th) 256, 122 N.R. 81 (S.C.C.), may not apply to judgments originating outside Canada.

Fabrelle Wallcoverings & Textiles Ltd. v. North American Decorative Products Inc. (1992), 6 C.P.C. (3d) 170 (Ont. Gen. Div.).

The court permitted registration of a U.K. judgment notwithstanding the defendant had not attorned to the jurisdiction of the U.K. court.

ENFORCEMENT OF JUDGMENT

73.03 A judgment registered under the Act may be enforced as if it had been granted by the court.

RULE 74   ESTATES — NON-CONTENTIOUS PROCEEDINGS

Highlights

General. Rule 74 is based on the work of the Haley Committee and came into force on January 1, 1995. It and Rule 75, which deals with contentious proceedings, replaced the Estate Rules, R.R.O. 1990, Reg. 197. Rule 74 regulates the overwhelming majority of cases in which there is no dispute of any sort.

Terminology. The rule changes the terminology used in estate cases. "Executor" and "administrator" become "estate trustee"; "probate" and "letters of administration" are now "certificate of appointment"; "certificate of appointment of succeeding estate trustee without a will" replaces "letters of administration *de bonis non administratis*"; and "caveat" is now "objection to issuing certificate of appointment". Note that as a matter of substantive law there are some differences between executors and administrators which may be important notwithstanding the new term "estate trustee".

Deposit of wills. Wills and codicils may be deposited with a registrar for safekeeping (rule 74.02) in which case the registrar will notify the Estate Registrar for Ontario. The Estate Registrar for Ontario maintains a computer database which may be searched to locate deposited wills and codicils.

Interventions. A person with a financial interest in an estate may file a request for notice under rule 74.03 and receive notice of the commencement of any proceeding in the estate.

Appointment of estate trustee. Applications for appointment of an estate trustee with a will are governed by rule 74.04. Applications for appointment of an estate trustee without a will are governed by rule 74.05. In either case notice of the application must be given to all persons entitled to share in the distribution of the estate (*e.g.* the beneficiaries): rules 74.04(2) and 74.05(2).

Applications to appoint a succeeding estate trustee to replace the original estate trustee are regulated by rule 74.06 (with a will) and rule 74.07 (without a will). As to applications to confirm the appointment of an estate trustee made outside Ontario see rule 74.08 (Canada, U.K. and British possessions) and rule 74.09 (elsewhere). Rule 74.10 deals with applications to appoint estate trustees during litigation.

Rule 74.12(1) requires certain material from the Estate Registrar before an estate trustee is appointed.

The fees required by the *Estates Act* must be paid, with stated exceptions, when the application to appoint the estate trustee is made: rule 74.13.

If the application to appoint the estate trustee is considered complete, the registrar may issue the certificate of appointment: rule 74.14(1). The registrar may refer the application to a judge if it appears to be incomplete or doubtful: rule 74.14(2).

Orders for assistance. Orders for assistance (formerly "citations") may be issued under rule 74.15 for various purposes. These may generally be obtained by motion made without notice except an order for further particulars which requires 10 days' notice to the estate trustee: rule 74.15(2).

Passing of accounts. Applications to pass accounts are governed by rule 74.18. The notice of application to pass accounts must be issued by the court (rule 74.18(2)) and served on each person who has a contingent or vested interest in the estate (rule 74.18(3)). (As to service on the Public Guardian and Trustee or the Children's Lawyer, see rule 74.18(3.1)). A person who objects to the accounts may deliver a notice of objection at least 20 days before the hearing: rule 74.18(7). If there is no objection the court may grant judgment on passing accounts without a hearing: rule 74.18(9).

The form of accounts to be filed with the court is set out in rule 74.17.

By rule 74.16 the procedures for passing accounts of estate trustees apply, with necessary modifications, to other persons required to pass accounts including trustees other than estate trustees, persons acting under power of attorney, committees of mentally incompetent persons and of persons who are incapable of managing their affairs, persons acting as guardians of the property of a minor, and persons having similar duties who are directed by the court to prepare accounts.

Practice directions. See practice direction, below.

Related former Rules. Estate Rules, R.R.O. 1990, Reg. 197, Rules 1, 3-5, 9, 12-17, 20-39, 49-56, 60-68.

PRACTICE DIRECTION

Ontario Court (General Division)

Re: NEW RULES FOR ESTATE PROCEEDINGS

To: The Legal Profession and to
     Registrars of the Court:

New rules and forms for estate proceedings come into effect January 1, 1995. They are contained in new rules 74 and 75 of the Rules of Civil Procedure, added by Ontario Regulation 484/94. The old estate rules and forms are revoked effective the same date by Ontario Regulation 485/94.

Members of the profession are advised that effective January 1, 1995 they are required to submit, where appropriate, the following draft documents for the use of the court office:

1. Order leading to issuance of confirmation by resealing of appointment of estate trustee with or without a will.

2. Certificate of appointment in the appropriate form (Form 74.13, Form 74.20, Form 74.23, Form 74.26, Form 74.29 and Form 74.31).

The certificates of appointment which replace the letters probate etc. granted by the court must be on a form printed by a law stationer, or comparable reproduction. A backsheet is required for each certificate. Members of the profession should pay particular attention to rule 4.01(1) (legibility, typesize, paper quality) and to rule 4.02(3) (backsheet). Computer-generated forms will not be acceptable unless they meet this standard.

With the exception of certificates of appointment, to facilitate the change-over to the new estate forms, all registrars of the Ontario Court (General Division) dealing with estate matters are directed that they shall continue to accept old forms authorized by regulation 197, R.R.O. 1990, containing the comparable information required under the new rules, for a period of one year from January 1, 1995. After the expiry of the one-year period, the registrar will require the new forms with the exception that any document in the old form containing comparable information required under the new rules and executed before January 1, 1996, shall be accepted by the registrar.

This direction shall not be interpreted as waiving compliance with the new rules regarding the content of any document unless such compliance is waived by the judge.

Dated at Toronto this 16th day of November, 1994.

R. Roy McMurtry
Chief Justice of the Ontario Court

DEFINITIONS

74.01 In this Rule and in Rule 75,

"certificate of appointment of estate trustee" means letters probate, letters of administration or letters of administration with the will annexed;

"estate trustee" means an executor, administrator or administrator with the will annexed;

"estate trustee during litigation" means an administrator appointed pending an action;

"estate trustee with a will" means an executor or an administrator with the will annexed;

"estate trustee without a will" means an administrator;

"objection to issuing of certificate of appointment" means a caveat;

"will" includes any testamentary instrument of which probate or administration may be granted. [en. O. Reg. 484/94, s. 12]

DEPOSIT OF WILLS AND CODICILS FOR SAFEKEEPING

74.02(1) A registrar shall not receive and keep a will or codicil under section 2 of the *Estates Act* unless the deposit is made by,

    (a) the testator;

    (b) a person authorized by the testator in writing;

    (c) a solicitor who held the will or codicil at the time of retirement from practice;

    (d) the estate trustee of a solicitor who held the will or codicil at the time of the solicitor's death;

    (e) the representative of a trust corporation that held the will or codicil when it ceased to do business in Ontario; or

    (f) a person authorized by the court to deposit the will or codicil.

(2) An affidavit of execution of the will or codicil (Form 74.8) may be deposited at the same time as the will or codicil.

(3) The registrar shall cause every will or codicil that is deposited for safekeeping to be enclosed in an envelope that is securely sealed in the presence of the depositor, and shall cause to be endorsed on the envelope the date of the deposit, the name and address of the depositor and of the testator and estate trustee or trustees named in the will, the date of birth of the testator and the date of the will or codicil.

Notice to Estate Registrar

(4) When a will or codicil is deposited with the registrar, the registrar shall send a notice of the deposit (Form 74.1) to the Estate Registrar for Ontario within seven days after the deposit is made.

Access to Deposited Will or Codicil

(5) No person, except the testator in person or a committee of the estate of the testator, or except by order of the court, shall remove, copy or inspect a will or codicil on deposit during the testator's lifetime.

(6) After the death of the testator, any person may copy or inspect a will or codicil of the testator on deposit, on filing a written request stating the testator's date of birth and a death certificate issued by the Registrar General or a funeral director.

Delivery of Will or Codicil to Estate Trustee

(7) After the death of the testator, the registrar shall, on the filing of a written request stating the testator's date of birth and of a death certificate issued by the Registrar General or a funeral director, deliver the will or codicil of the testator that is on deposit to the estate trustee named in the will, or to such other person as the court directs, and the registrar shall,

(a) retain a copy of the will and any codicil, certified to be a true copy by the registrar, and the receipt of the person to whom the will or codicil is delivered; and

(b) send a notice of the withdrawal (Form 74.2) to the Estate Registrar for Ontario.

Archivist of Ontario

(8) The registrar shall deposit with the Archivist of Ontario wills and codicils that have been held for safekeeping for 125 years or more. [en. O. Reg. 484/94, s. 12]

REQUEST FOR NOTICE OF COMMENCEMENT OF PROCEEDING

74.03(1) At any time before a certificate of appointment of an estate trustee has been issued, a person who has a financial interest in the estate and who desires to be informed of the commencement of a proceeding in the estate may file with the registrar a request for notice (Form 74.3), and thereafter is entitled to receive notice of the commencement of any proceeding in the estate until a certificate of appointment of an estate trustee is issued, unless the court orders otherwise.

(2) Notice by the registrar under subrule (1) may be sent by regular lettermail to the address shown in the request for notice.

(3) A request for notice expires three years after it is filed but a further request may be filed at any time before a certificate of appointment of an estate trustee for the estate is issued. [en. O. Reg. 484/94, s. 12]

CERTIFICATE OF APPOINTMENT OF ESTATE TRUSTEE WITH A WILL

Material to Accompany Application

74.04(1) An application for a certificate of appointment of estate trustee with a will (Form 74.4 or 74.5) shall be accompanied by,

(a) the original of the will and of every codicil;

(b) an affidavit (Form 74.6) attesting that notice of the application (Form 74.7) has been served in accordance with subrules (2) to (7);

(c) an affidavit of execution (Form 74.8) of the will and of every codicil, or if neither of the witnesses to the will or the codicil can be found, or both have died, such other evidence of due execution as the court may require;

(d) if the will or a codicil is in holograph form, an affidavit (Form 74.9) attesting that the handwriting and signature in the will or codicil are those of the deceased;

(e) if the will or a codicil is not in holograph form but contains an alteration, erasure. obliteration or interlineation that has not been attested, an affidavit as to the condition of the will or codicil at the time of execution (Form 74.10);

(f) a renunciation (Form 74.11) from every living person who is named in the will or codicil as estate trustee who has not joined in the application and is entitled to do so;

(g) if the applicant is not named as an estate trustee in the will or codicil, a consent to the applicant's appointment (Form 74.12) by persons who are entitled to share in the distribution of the estate and who together have a majority interest in the value of the assets of the estate at the date of death;

(h) the security required by the *Estates Act*; and

(i) such additional or other material as the court directs.

Notice to Interested Persons

(2) Notice of the application shall be served on all persons entitled to share in the distribution of the estate, including charities and contingent beneficiaries.

Notice — Charity

(3) If a charity is entitled to share in the distribution of the estate, notice of the application shall also be served on the Public Guardian and Trustee.

Notice — Minor

(4) If a person who is entitled to share in the distribution of the estate is less than 18 years of age, notice of the application shall not be served on the person, despite subrule (2), but shall be served on a parent or guardian and on the Children's Lawyer.

Notice — Unborn or Unascertained Persons

(5) If there may be unborn or unascertained beneficiaries, notice of the application shall be served on the Children's Lawyer.

Notice — Mentally Incapable Person

(6) If a person who is entitled to share in the distribution of the estate is mentally incapable within the meaning of section 6 of the *Substitute Decisions Act, 1992* in respect of an issue in the proceeding, notice of the application shall also be served,

(a) if there is a guardian with authority to act in the proceeding, on the guardian;

(b) if there is no guardian with authority to act in the proceeding but there is an attorney under a power of attorney with authority to act in the proceeding, on the attorney;

(c) if there is neither a guardian nor an attorney with authority to act in the proceeding, on the Public Guardian and Trustee.

Regular Lettermail

(7) Notice under this rule shall be served on all persons, including charities, the Children's Lawyer and the Public Guardian and Trustee, by regular lettermail sent to the person's last known address.

Certificate

(8) The certificate of appointment of estate trustee with a will shall be in Form 74.13. [en. O. Reg. 484/94, s. 12; am. O. Regs. 740/94, s. 1; 69/95, ss. 11, 19, 20]

CERTIFICATE OF APPOINTMENT OF ESTATE TRUSTEE WITHOUT A WILL

Material to Accompany Application

74.05(1) An application for a certificate of appointment of estate trustee without a will (Form 74.14 or 74.15) shall be accompanied by,

(a) an affidavit (Form 74.16) attesting that notice of the application (Form 74.17) has been served in accordance with subrules (2) to (5);

(b) a renunciation (Form 74.18) from every person who is entitled in priority to be named as estate trustee and who has not joined in the application;

(c) a consent to the applicant's appointment (Form 74.19) by persons who are entitled to share in the distribution of the estate and who together have a majority interest in the value of the assets of the estate at the date of death;

(d) the security required by the *Estates Act*; and

(e) such additional or other material as the court directs.

Notice to Interested Persons

(2) Notice of the application shall be served on all persons entitled to share in the distribution of the estate.

Notice — Minor

(3) If a person who is entitled to share in the distribution of the estate is less than 18 years of age, notice of the application shall not be served on the person, despite subrule (2), but shall be served on a parent or guardian and on the Children's Lawyer.

Notice — Mentally Incapable Person

(4) If a person who is entitled to share in the distribution of the estate is mentally incapable within the meaning of section 6 of the *Substitute Decisions Act, 1992* in respect of an issue in the proceeding, notice of the application shall also be served,

(a) if there is a guardian with authority to act in the proceeding, on the guardian;

(b) if there is no guardian with authority to act in the proceeding but there is an attorney under a power of attorney with authority to act in the proceeding, on the attorney;

(c) if there is neither a guardian nor an attorney with authority to act in the proceeding, on the Public Guardian and Trustee.

Regular Lettermail

(5) Notice under this rule shall be served on all persons, including the Children's Lawyer and the Public Guardian and Trustee, by regular letter-mail sent to the person's last known address.

Certificate

(6) The certificate of appointment of estate trustee without a will shall be in Form 74.20. [en. O. Reg. 484/94, s. 12; am. O. Regs. 740/94, s. 1; 69/95, ss. 12, 19, 20]

CERTIFICATE OF APPOINTMENT OF SUCCEEDING ESTATE TRUSTEE WITH A WILL

74.06(1) An application for a certificate of appointment of estate trustee to succeed an estate trustee with a will (Form 74.21) shall be accompanied by,

(a) the original certificate of appointment or, if the original certificate has been lost, a copy of it certified by the court;

(b) a renunciation (Form 74.11) from every living person who is named in the will or codicil as an estate trustee and who has not joined in the application and is entitled to do so;

(c) if the applicant is not named as an estate trustee in the will or codicil, a consent (Form 74.22) to the application by persons who are entitled to share in the distribution of the remaining estate and who together have a majority interest in the value of the assets remaining in the estate at the date of the application;

(d) the security required by the *Estates Act*; and

(e) such additional or other material as the court directs.

(2) The certificate of appointment of a succeeding estate trustee with a will shall be in Form 74.23. [en. O. Reg. 484/94, s. 12]

CERTIFICATE OF APPOINTMENT OF SUCCEEDING ESTATE TRUSTEE WITHOUT A WILL

74.07(1) An application for a certificate of appointment of estate trustee to succeed an estate trustee without a will (Form 74.24) shall be accompanied by,

(a) the original certificate of appointment or, if the original certificate has been lost, a copy of it certified by the court;

(b) a consent (Form 74.25) to the application by persons who are entitled to share in the distribution of the remaining estate and who together have a majority interest in the value of the assets remaining in the estate at the date of the application;

(c) the security required by the *Estates Act*; and

(d) such additional or other material as the court directs.

(2) The certificate of appointment of a succeeding estate trustee without a will shall be in Form 74.26. [en. O. Reg. 484/94, s. 12]

CONFIRMATION BY RESEALING OF APPOINTMENT OF ESTATE TRUSTEE WITH OR WITHOUT A WILL

74.08(1) An application for confirmation by resealing of the appointment of an estate trustee with or without a will that was granted by a court of competent jurisdiction in the United Kingdom, in a province or territory of Canada or in any British possession (Form 74.27) shall be accompanied by,

(a) a certified copy of the document under the seal of the court that granted it, and a certificate under the seal of that court, stating that the grant is still effective;

(b) the security required by the *Estates Act*; and

(c) such additional or other material as the court directs.

(2) A confirmation by resealing of the appointment of an estate trustee with or without a will shall be in Form 74.28. [en. O. Reg. 484/94, s. 12; am. O. Reg. 740/94, s. 2]

CERTIFICATE OF ANCILLARY APPOINTMENT OF ESTATE TRUSTEE WITH A WILL

74.09(1) An application for a certificate of ancillary appointment of an estate trustee with a will where the applicant has been appointed by a court having jurisdiction outside Ontario, other than a jurisdiction referred to in rule 74.08, (Form 74.27) shall be accompanied by,

(a) two certified copies of the document under the seal of the court that granted it, and a certificate under the seal of that court, stating that the grant is still effective;

(b) the security required by the *Estates Act*; and

(c) such additional or other material as the court directs.

(2) A certificate of ancillary appointment of an estate trustee with a will shall be in Form 74.29. [en. O. Reg. 484/94, s. 12; am. O. Reg. 740/94, s. 3]

CERTIFICATE OF APPOINTMENT OF ESTATE TRUSTEE DURING LITIGATION

74.10(1) An application for a certificate of appointment of en estate trustee during litigation (Form 74.30) shall be accompanied by,

(a) a copy of the order appointing the applicant as estate trustee during litigation;

(b) the security required by the *Estates Act*; and

(c) such additional or other material as the court directs.

(2) A certificate of appointment of an estate trustee during litigation shall be in Form 74.31. [en. O. Reg. 484/94, s. 12]

BONDS

74.11(1) Unless the court orders otherwise,

(a) the bond required by section 35 of the *Estates Act* shall be the bond of an insurance or guarantee company licensed to carry on business in Ontario (Form 74.32) or of one or more personal sureties (Form 74.33);

(b) a registrar of the court or a solicitor shall not be a personal surety;

(c) a personal surety must be a resident of Ontario who is not a minor;

(d) one personal surety is sufficient where the value of the assets of the estate does not exceed $100,000;

(e) the security required for a succeeding estate trustee shall be based on the value of the assets of the estate remaining to be administered at the time the application for a certificate of appointment as succeeding estate trustee is made; and

(f) the security required for confirmation by resealing of the appointment of an estate trustee, or for an ancillary appointment of an estate trustee, shall be based on the value of the assets of the estate over which the estate trustee seeks jurisdiction in Ontario.

(2) Any person, including a creditor, who has a contingent or vested interest in an estate may at any time, on notice to the estate trustee or applicant for appointment, move for an order to have a bond filed or the amount of an existing bond increased or reduced. [en. O. Reg. 484/94, s. 12]

GENERAL PROCEDURE ON APPLICATIONS FOR CERTIFICATES OF APPOINTMENT OF ESTATE TRUSTEES

Material Required from Estate Registrar

74.12(1) A certificate of appointment of estate trustee shall not be issued until the court has received from the Estate Registrar,

(a) the certificate required by section 17 of the *Estates Act* that no other application has been filed in respect of the estate;

(b) a certificate that there is no notice of objection under rule 75.03 in effect;

(c) on an application where there is a will, a certificate that no will or codicil of a later date than that for which the certificate of appointment is sought has been deposited in the Ontario Court (General Division);

(d) on an application where there is no will, a certificate that no will or codicil has been deposited in the Ontario Court (General Division).

Where Certificate Shows Deposited Will or Codicil

(2) Where the application is for a certificate of appointment of an estate trustee with a will and the certificate of the Estate Registrar shows that a

later will or codicil has been deposited, the registrar shall send to the applicant a copy of the certificate of the Estate Registrar by regular lettermail and shall send a notice (Form 74.34) to the estate trustee named in the deposited will or codicil by regular lettermail at the last address on record with the court.

(3) Where the application is for a certificate of appointment of an estate trustee without a will and the certificate of the Estate Registrar shows that a will or codicil has been deposited, the registrar shall send the applicant a copy of the certificate by regular lettermail and shall send a notice (Form 74.35) to the estate trustee named in the deposited will or codicil by regular lettermail at the last address on record with the court.

Establishing Date of Execution
(4) If a will is not dated or is dated imperfectly, the date of execution may be established by the evidence of an attesting witness or, where the evidence as to the date of execution cannot be obtained, evidence that the execution took place between two specific dates or that a search has been made and no will that could be of a later date has been found.

Registrar's Notes
(5) If a beneficiary or spouse of a beneficiary under a will or codicil has attested the will or codicil or has signed the will or codicil for the testator, and the provision for the beneficiary appears to the registrar to be void by reason of section 12 of the *Succession Law Reform Act*, the registrar shall note the fact on the will or codicil and the note shall be reproduced on the copy attached to the certificate of appointment.

(6) Where a devise or bequest of a beneficial interest in property to a former spouse of the testator, or an appointment of a former spouse as estate trustee, or the conferring of a general or special power of appointment on a former spouse, is revoked by reason of section 17 of the *Succession Law Reform Act*, the registrar shall note the fact on the will or codicil and the note shall be reproduced on the copy of the will that is attached to the certificate of appointment. [en. O. Reg. 484/94, s. 12]

FEES

Fees Payable at Time of Application
74.13(1) The fees referred to in the *Estates Act* shall be paid at the time an application for a certificate of appointment as an estate trustee is made.

Exception
(2) The court may issue the certificate of appointment where the applicant,
    (a) files with the court an affidavit as to the estimated value of the estate at the time of the application and pays the prescribed fees calculated on the estimated value; and

(b) provides an undertaking to the court to file a sworn statement of the total value of the estate and to pay the balance of the fees owing within six months of the filing of the undertaking.

(3) Where an undertaking given under subrule (2) is not fulfilled, the court may, on the request of the registrar, make an order for compliance. [en. O. Reg. 484/94, s. 12]

ISSUING CERTIFICATE OF APPOINTMENT OF ESTATE TRUSTEE

74.14(1) Where an application for a certificate of appointment as an estate trustee and the material required to accompany the application are complete, the registrar may issue the certificate.

(2) Where, in the opinion of the registrar, the application and accompanying material are not complete or contain information on which the registrar has a doubt, the application shall be referred to a judge for determination. [en. O. Reg. 484/94, s. 12; am. O. Reg. 740/94, s. 4]

ORDERS FOR ASSISTANCE

Kinds of Orders
74.15(1) In addition to a motion under section 9 of the *Estates Act,* any person who appears to have a financial interest in an estate may move,

Order to Accept or Refuse Appointment
(a) for an order (Form 74.36) requiring any person to accept or refuse an appointment as an estate trustee with a will;
(b) for an order (Form 74.37) requiring any person to accept or refuse an appointment as an estate trustee without a will;

Order to Consent or Object to Proposed Appointment
(c) for an order (Form 74.38) requiring any person to consent or object to a proposed appointment of an estate trustee with or without a will;

Order to File Statement of Assets of the Estate
(d) for an order (Form 74.39) requiring an estate trustee to file with the court a statement of the nature and value, at the date of death, of each of the assets of the estate to be administered by the estate trustee;

Order for Further Particulars
(e) after receiving the statement described in clause (d), for an order for further particulars by supplementary affidavit or otherwise as the court directs;

Order to Beneficiary Witness
(f) for an order (Form 74.40) requiring a beneficiary or the spouse of a beneficiary who witnessed the will or codicil, or who signed the will or codicil for the testator, to satisfy the court that the beneficiary or spouse did not exercise improper or undue influence on the testator;

Order to Former Spouse
(g) for an order (Form 74.41) requiring a former spouse of the deceased to take part in a determination under subsection 17(2) of the *Succession Law Reform Act* of the validity of the appointment of the former spouse as estate trustee, a devise or bequest of a beneficial interest to the former spouse or the conferring of a general or special power of appointment on him or her;

Order to Pass Accounts
(h) for an order (Form 74.42) requiring an estate trustee to pass accounts; and

Order for Other Matters
(i) for an order providing for any other matter that the court directs.

Notice of Motion
(2) A motion under subrule (1) may be made without notice, except a motion under clause (1)(e), which requires 10 days notice to the estate trustee.

Service
(3) An order referred to in subrule (1) and an order for production under section 9 of the *Estates Act* shall be served by personal service, by an alternative to personal service or as the court directs.

Examination
(4) The court may require any person to be examined under oath for the purpose of deciding a motion under subrule (1). [en. O. Reg. 484/94, s. 12]

PASSING OF ESTATE ACCOUNTS

74.16 Rules 74.17 and 74.18 apply to accounts of estate trustees and, with necessary modifications, to accounts of trustees other than estate trustees, persons acting under a power of attorney, guardians of the property of mentally incapable persons, guardians of the property of a minor and persons having similar duties who are directed by the court to prepare accounts relating to their management of assets or money. [en. O. Reg. 484/94, s. 12; am. O. Reg. 69/95, s. 13]

FORMS OF ACCOUNTS

74.17(1) Estate trustees shall keep accurate records of the assets and transactions in the estate and accounts filed with the court shall include,
(a) on a first passing of accounts, a statement of the assets at the date of death, cross-referenced to entries in the accounts that show the disposition or partial disposition of the assets;
(b) on any subsequent passing of accounts, a statement of the assets on the date the accounts for the period were opened, cross-referenced to entries in the accounts that show the disposition or partial disposition

of the assets, and a statement of the investments, if any, on the date the accounts for the period were opened;

(c) an account of all money received, but excluding investment transactions recorded under clause (e);

(d) an account of all money disbursed, including payments for trustee's compensation and payments made under a court order, but excluding investment transactions recorded under clause (e);

(e) where the estate trustee has made investments, an account setting out,

    (i) all money paid out to purchase investments,

    (ii) all money received by way of repayments or realization on the investments in whole or in part, and

    (iii) the balance of all the investments in the estate at the closing date of the accounts;

(f) a statement of all the assets in the estate that are unrealized at the closing date of the accounts;

(g) a statement of all money and investments in the estate at the closing date of the accounts;

(h) a statement of all the liabilities of the estate, contingent or otherwise, at the closing date of the accounts;

(i) a statement of the compensation claimed by the estate trustee and, where the statement of compensation includes a management fee based on the value of the assets of the estate, a statement setting out the method of determining the value of the assets; and

(j) such other statements and information as the court requires.

(2) The accounts required by clauses (1)(c), (d) and (e) shall show the balance forward for each account.

(3) Where a will or trust deals separately with capital and income, the accounts shall be divided to show separately receipts and disbursements in respect of capital and income. [en. O. Reg. 484/94, s. 12]

APPLICATION TO PASS ACCOUNTS

Material to be Filed

74.18(1) On the application of an estate trustee to pass accounts, the estate trustee shall file,

(a) the estate accounts for the relevant period verified by affidavit of the estate trustee (Form 74.43);

(b) a copy of the certificate of appointment of the applicant as estate trustee;

(c) a copy of the latest judgment, if any, of the court relating to the passing of accounts.

Notice of Application

(2) On receiving the material referred to in subrule (1), the court shall issue a notice of the application to pass accounts (Form 74.44).

Service

(3) The applicant shall serve the notice of application and a copy of a draft of the judgment sought on each person who has a contingent or vested interest in the estate by regular lettermail.

(3.1) Where the Public Guardian and Trustee or the Children's Lawyer represents a person who has a contingent or vested interest in the estate, the Public Guardian and Trustee or the Children's Lawyer shall be served with the documents referred to in subrules (1) and (3).

(4) Where the person is served in Ontario, the documents shall be served at least 45 days before the hearing date of the application.

(5) Where the person is served outside Ontario, the documents shall be served at least 60 days before the hearing date of the application.

Appointment of Person to Represent Interest

(6) Where a person who has a financial interest in an estate is under a disability or is unknown and the Public Guardian and Trustee or Children's Lawyer is not authorized to represent the interest under any Act and there is no guardian or other person to represent the interest on the passing of the accounts, the court may appoint a person for the purpose.

Notice of Objection to Accounts

(7) Subject to subrule (8), a person who is served with documents under subrule (4) or (5) and who wishes to object to the accounts shall do so by serving on the estate trustee and filing with proof of service a notice of objection to accounts (Form 74.45), at least 20 days before the hearing date of the application.

(8) Where a person who has a contingent or vested interest in the estate is represented by the Public Guardian and Trustee or Children's Lawyer, the Public Guardian and Trustee or Children's Lawyer, as the case may be, shall serve on the estate trustee and file with proof of service, at least 20 days before the hearing date of the application, a notice of objection to accounts (Form 74.45) or a notice of no objection to accounts (Form 74.46).

Judgment on Passing of Accounts Granted Without Hearing

(9) The court may grant a judgment on passing accounts without a hearing if the estate trustee files with the court, at least 10 days before the hearing date of the application,

(a) a record containing,

(i) an affidavit of service of the documents referred to in subrules (4) and (5),

(ii) the notices of no objection of the Children's Lawyer and Public Guardian and Trustee, if served,

(iii) an affidavit (Form 74.47) of the applicant or applicant's solicitor stating that a copy of the accounts was provided to each person who was served with the notice of application and requested a copy, that the time for filing notices of objection to accounts has expired and that no notice of objection to accounts was received from any person served, or that, if a notice of objection was received, it was withdrawn as evidenced by a notice of withdrawal of objection (Form 74.48) attached to the affidavit,

(iv) requests (Form 74.49), if any, for costs of the persons served, and

(v) the certificate of a solicitor stating that all documents required by subclauses (i) to (iv) are included in the record; and

(b) a draft of the judgment sought, in duplicate.

(10) Where the court grants an unopposed judgment on passing accounts, the costs awarded shall be assessed in accordance with Tariff C, unless the court orders otherwise.

Hearing

(11) Where the court declines to grant an unopposed judgment, the hearing shall proceed on the date specified in the notice of application.

(12) No objection shall be raised at the hearing that was not raised in a notice of objection to accounts, unless the court orders otherwise.

(13) At the hearing the court may assess, or refer to an assessment officer, any bill of costs, account or charge of solicitors employed by the estate trustee.

Form of Judgment

(14) The judgment on a passing of accounts shall be in Form 74.50 or 74.51. [en. O. Reg. 484/94, s. 12; am. O. Regs. 69/95, ss. 18, 19, 20; 377/95, s. 6]

RULE 75   ESTATES — CONTENTIOUS PROCEEDINGS

Highlights

General. Rule 75 is based on the work of the Haley Committee and came into force on January 1, 1995. It and Rule 74, which deals with non-nontentious proceedings, replaced the Estate Rules, R.R.O. 1990, Reg. 197. Rule 75 regulates the minority of cases in which there is a dispute.

Objections. A notice of objection (formerly "citation") may be filed at any time before a certificate of appointment of estate trustee has been issued (rule 75.03(1)) and is effective for three years (rule 75.03(2)). The registrar notifies the applicant who must deliver a notice to objector: rule 75.03(3) and (4). The objector must then deliver a notice of appearance within 20 days failing which the application proceeds without regard to the objection: rule 75.03(5).

Motion for directions. A person who has a financial interest in the estate may apply for directions to bring a matter before the court (rule 75.06(1)) and the court may give directions regarding the issues to be decided, the parties and the procedures to be used (rule 75.06(3)). The "citation to see" or "citation to parties concerned" has been abolished.

Submission of rights to court. Where a statement of claim has been issued a defendant may elect to deliver a statement of submission of rights to the court or a statement of defence (with or without counterclaim): rule 75.07(1). A defendant who delivers a statement of submission of rights to the court is not considered to be a party to the proceeding and is not entitled to or liable for costs: rule 75.07.1. He or she is entitled to notice of the hearing and copy of the judgment and can object to any settlement: rule 75.07.1.

Revocation of appointment. By rule 75.04 the court may revoke a certificate of appointment of an estate trustee. The court may require the return of a certificate of appointment under rule 75.05.

Claims against an estate. Rule 75.08 prescribes forms for a notice of contestation (Form 75.13) and a claim against an estate (Form 75.14) under s. 44 or 45 of the *Estates Act.* The trial is to proceed in a summary manner unless a judge orders otherwise: rule 75.08(5).

Solicitor of record. A solicitor who files a notice of objection under rule 75.03, moves for return of a certificate under rule 75.05, or moves for directions under rule 75.06 is deemed to be the solicitor of record: rule 75.09(1).

Practice directions. See practice direction following highlights to Rule 74.

Related former Rules. Estate Rules, R.R.O. 1990, Reg. 197, Rules 19, 40-48, 57, and 83.

FORMAL PROOF OF TESTAMENTARY INSTRUMENT

75.01 An estate trustee or any person having a financial interest in an estate may make an application under rule 75.06 to have a testamentary instrument that is being put forward as the last will of the deceased proved in such manner as the court directs. [en. O. Reg. 484/94, s. 12]

PROOF OF LOST OR DESTROYED WILL

75.02 The validity and contents of a will that has been lost or destroyed may be proved on an application,

(a) by affidavit evidence without appearance, where all persons who have a financial interest in the estate consent to the proof; or

(b) in the manner provided by the court in an order giving directions made under rule 75.06. [en. O. Reg. 484/94, s. 12]

OBJECTION TO ISSUING CERTIFICATE OF APPOINTMENT

Notice of Objection

75.03(1) At any time before a certificate of appointment of estate trustee has been issued, any person who has a financial interest in the estate may give notice of an objection by filing with the registrar or the Estate Registrar for Ontario a notice of objection (Form 75.1), signed by the person or the person's solicitor, stating the nature of the interest and of the objection.

Expiry, Withdrawal and Removal of Notice of Objection

(2) A notice of objection expires three years after it is filed and may be withdrawn by the person who filed it at any time before a hearing for directions under rule 75.06 in an application for the certificate or may be removed by order of the court.

Notice to Applicant

(3) Where an application for a certificate of appointment of estate trustee has been made and a notice of objection is filed, the registrar shall send notice of the filing (Form 75.2) by regular lettermail to the applicant or the applicant's solicitor at the mailing address shown in the application.

Notice to Objector

(4) An applicant who receives a notice under subrule (3) shall serve on the objector a notice to objector (Form 75.3) and file a copy of the notice and proof of service with the court.

(5) Where the objector does not serve and file a notice of appearance (Form 75.4) within 20 days after service of the notice to objector, the application shall proceed as if the notice of objection had not been filed.

Motion For Directions

(6) If the applicant does not move for directions within 30 days after service of the notice of appearance, the objector may move for directions. [en. O. Reg. 484/94, s. 12]

REVOCATION OF CERTIFICATE OF APPOINTMENT

75.04 On the application of any person having a financial interest in an estate, the court may revoke the certificate of appointment of the estate trustee where the court is satisfied that,

(a) the certificate was issued in error or as a result of a fraud on the court;

(b) the appointment is no longer effective; or

(c) the certificate should be revoked for any other reason. [en. O. Reg. 484/94, s. 12]

RETURN OF CERTIFICATE

Motion for Return of Certificate
75.05(1) The court may, on motion, order that a certificate of appointment be returned to the court where,
    (a) the moving party seeks a determination of the validity of the testamentary instrument for which the certificate was issued or of the entitlement of the estate trustee to the certificate; or
    (b) an application has been made under rule 75.04.

Notice
(2) The motion may be made without notice unless the court orders otherwise.

Effect of Order
(3) On service of the order to return the certificate of appointment, the estate trustee shall forthwith deposit the original certificate with the registrar, and the appointment has no further effect and shall not be acted on until,
    (a) the issues referred to in clause (1)(a) or the application referred to in clause (1)(b), as the case may be, have been determined by the court; or
    (b) the release of the certificate is ordered under subrule (6).

Motion for Directions
(4) A party who obtains an order under clause (1)(a) shall move for directions under rule 75.06 within 30 days after the making of the order.
(5) The estate trustee may at any time move for directions under rule 75.06 for determination by the court of the matters referred to in clause (3)(a).

Release of Certificate
(6) If a motion for directions referred to in subrule (4) or (5) is not made, the court may, on motion of the estate trustee without notice, order the release to the estate trustee of the certificate of appointment. [en. O. Reg. 484/94, s. 12]

APPLICATION OR MOTION FOR DIRECTIONS

75.06(1) Any person who has a financial interest in an estate may apply for directions, or move for directions in another proceeding under this rule, as to the procedure for bringing any matter before the court.

Service
(2) An application for directions (Form 75.5) or motion for directions (Form 75.6) shall be served on all persons having a financial interest in the estate, or as the court directs, at least 10 days before the hearing of the application or motion.

Order
(3) On an application or motion for directions, the court may direct,
(a) the issues to be decided;
(b) who are parties, who is plaintiff and defendant and who is submitting rights to the court;
(c) who shall be served with the order for directions, and the method and times of service;
(d) procedures for bringing the matter before the court in a summary fashion, where appropriate;
(e) that the plaintiff file and serve a statement of claim (Form 75.7);
(f) that an estate trustee be appointed during litigation, and file such security as the court directs;
(g) such other procedures as are just.
(4) An order giving directions shall be in Form 75.8 or 75.9. [en. O. Reg. 484/94, s. 12]

PROCEDURE WHERE STATEMENT OF CLAIM SERVED

Defendant: Statement of Defence, Statement of Defence and Counterclaim or Submission of Rights to Court
75.07(1) Where a statement of claim is delivered as directed under subrule 75.06(3), each defendant served may serve on each party and file with proof of service,
(a) a statement of defence or a statement of defence and counterclaim; or
(b) a statement of submission of rights to the court (Form 75.10).

Plaintiff: Reply or Reply and Defence to Counterclaim
(2) A plaintiff may deliver a reply or a reply and defence to counterclaim.
(3) [Revoked O. Reg. 740/94, s. 5]

Effect of Failure to File Pleadings
(4) A person who is served with a statement of claim and who does not file a statement of defence, a statement of defence and counterclaim or a statement of submission of rights to the court is not a party to the proceeding and his or her consent to any settlement, agreement or consent judgment is not required. [en. O. Reg. 484/94, s. 12; am. O. Reg. 740/94, s. 5]

SUBMISSION OF RIGHTS TO COURT

75.07.1 Where a person files a statement of submission of rights to the court in response to service of a statement of claim or on a motion or application for directions,
(a) the person is not a party to the proceeding and is entitled only to service by the plaintiff of written notice of the time and place of the trial and a copy of the judgment disposing of the matter;

(b) the person is not entitled to costs in the proceeding and is not liable for costs, except indirectly to the extent that costs are ordered to be paid out of the estate; and

(c) a judgment on consent following settlement shall not be given without,

(i) the written consent of the person, or

(ii) an affidavit of a solicitor of record in the proceeding attesting that a notice of settlement (Form 75.11), appended as an exhibit to the affidavit, has been personally served on the person and no rejection of settlement (Form 75.12) has been filed with the court within 10 days after service of the notice. [en. O. Reg. 740/94, s. 6]

CLAIMS AGAINST AN ESTATE

Notice of Contestation of Claim

75.08(1) A notice of contestation of a claim under section 44 or 45 of the *Estates Act* shall be in Form 75.13.

Claims

(2) A claim made against an estate under section 44 or 45 of the *Estates Act* shall be in Form 75.14.

Service

(3) The claimant shall serve the claim on the estate trustee and file the claim and the notice of contestation, with proof of service, within 30 days after service of the notice of contestation on the claimant.

Date of Trial

(4) When the claim and notice of contestation are filed, the registrar shall fix a date for trial.

Manner of Trial

(5) The trial shall proceed in a summary manner unless the judge considers it appropriate to give directions as to the issues, parties and pleadings. [en. O. Reg. 484/94, s. 12]

SOLICITOR OF RECORD

75.09(1) The solicitor who takes any of the following steps on a party's behalf is the party's solicitor of record:

1. Filing a notice of objection under rule 75.03.

2. Moving for return of a certificate under rule 75.05.

3. Moving for directions under rule 75.06.

(2) Rule 15.02 applies, with necessary modifications, as if the notice or motion were an originating process. [en. O. Reg. 484/94, s. 12]

RULE 76   SIMPLIFIED PROCEDURE

Highlights

Policy and purpose. The policy behind the rule is to attempt to reduce the cost of litigating claims of modest amounts *i.e.*, claims for up to $25,000, by reducing the amount of procedure available in such cases.

Major features

No examination for discovery or cross-examination on affidavits filed on motions. The major change under the simplified procedure is the unavailability of certain out-of-court examinations: examination for discovery, cross-examination of a deponent on an affidavit filed on a motion or the examination of a witness on a pending motion are not permitted in actions under the simplified procedure: rule 76.05. To make up for part of what will be missed through the absence of examination for discovery, the affidavit of documents under the simplified procedure must include (in addition to what is normally required) "a list of the names and addresses of persons who might reasonably be expected to have knowledge of transactions or occurrences in issue in the action", unless the court orders otherwise: rule 76.04(1) (compare rule 31.06(2) (obligation on examination for discovery to reveal identity of persons having knowledge)).

Summary trial. Under the simplified procedure either party may opt for a summary trial but if the opposing party objects this will not occur (see below): rule 76.06.

Summary judgment. The test for summary judgment under the simplified procedure has potentially a much lower threshold than the applicable test under rule 20.04. Notwithstanding that there may be a genuine issue for trial, summary judgment is to be granted unless the judge is unable to decide the issues in the action in the absence of cross-examination, or it would be otherwise unjust to decide the issues on the motion: rule 76.06(14).

Costs sanctions. The enforcement mechanism is that if at trial the plaintiff recovers $25,000 or less and at the time of trial the action is not under the simplified procedure, the plaintiff will recover no costs, unless the court is satisfied that it was reasonable for the plaintiff to have commenced and continued the action under the ordinary procedure: rule 76.10(1) and (2).

Unless otherwise provided all other rules apply. The rules that apply to an action apply to an action under the simplified procedure, except where Rule 76 provides otherwise: rule 76.01(3).

Availability

The simplified procedure applies to actions commenced on or after March 11, 1996, but does not apply to actions under the *Class Proceedings Act*, the *Construction Lien Act*, to divorce actions or to family law proceedings: rule 76.01(1). The simplified procedure also applies to actions commenced before March 11, 1996 if the parties file a consent: rule 76.01(2).

As spelled out below, the use of the simplified procedure is mandatory in some cases, but a plaintiff may opt to use the procedure in any case, subject to the defendant objecting. Provision is made for the application of the simplified procedure where counterclaims, crossclaims or third party claims are asserted.

Where use of the simplified procedure is mandatory. A plaintiff is required to use the simplified procedure where the claim being made is for $25,000 or less: rule 14.03.1 and rule 76.02(1). Rule 76.02(1) states this requirement in detail: the simplified procedure is to be used where the plaintiff's claim is exclusively for:

(a)   an amount of $25,000 or less, exclusive of interest and costs;

(b)   real or personal property whose fair market value at the date of the commencement of the action is $25,000 or less; or

(c)   both an amount of money and real or personal property whose total value at the date of the commencement of the action is $25,000 or less, exclusive of interest and costs, having regard for the fair market value of the property at that date.

Where there are multiple plaintiffs the use of the simplified procedure is required, except in the case of joint claims, if each plaintiff's claim, considered separately, meets the $25,000 or less requirement of rule 76.02(1): rule 76.02(8).

Optional use of simplified procedure. The plaintiff has the option of using the simplified procedure in actions beyond $25,000 (rules 14.03.1 and 76.02(2)), but where this is done the defendant may object to the simplified procedure in the statement of defence: rule 76.02(4). In this case the plaintiff may, in the reply, abandon claims that are not within the $25,000 requirement of rule 76.02(1) and if the plaintiff does so the action stays under the simplified procedure: rule 76.02(5). (Abandoned claims may not be pursued in any other proceeding: rule 76.02(6).) If the defendant objects and the plaintiff does not so abandon the excess claims, the action proceeds under the ordinary procedure: rule 76.02(7).

> *Example.* Plaintiff commences an action for $40,000 under the simplified procedure. If the defendant does not object to the use of the simplified procedure in the statement of defence, the case will remain in the simplified procedure: rule 76.02(2). However, if the defendant objects, by so stating in the statement of defence, and the plaintiff abandons in the reply the claim in excess of $25,000 the case remains under the simplified procedure: rule 76.02(5). If the defendant objects and the plaintiff does not reduce the claim in the reply, the action proceeds under the ordinary procedure: rule 76.02(7).

Availability where there is a counterclaim, crossclaim or third party claim: rule 76.02(9)-(11). If the main action is under the simplified procedure and the defendant makes a counterclaim, crossclaim or third party claim, the proceeding remains under the simplified procedure if any one of three conditions is met (rule 76.02(9)) *i.e.*,

- the defendant's claim meets the $25,000 or less requirement of rule 76.02(1);
- the defendant to the counterclaim, crossclaim or third party claim does not object to proceeding under the simplified procedure; or
- the defendant making the claim abandons in the reply any claim that does not meet the $25,000 or less requirement of rule 76.02(1).

If none of the above conditions apply, the main action and the counterclaim, crossclaim and third party claim all proceed under the ordinary procedure: rule 76.02(10).

> *Example.* Plaintiff commences an action for $20,000 under the simplified procedure and the defendant counterclaims. If the counterclaim is for $25,000 or less the action remains under the simplified procedure: rule 76.02(9)(a). If the counterclaim is for $35,000 the action and the counterclaim remain under the simplified procedure, unless the plaintiff objects in the statement of defence to the counterclaim: rule 76.02(9)(b). If the plaintiff objects to the simplified procedure applying, the case moves into the ordinary procedure (rule 76.02(10)), unless the defendant in the reply to the counterclaim abandons the claim in excess of $25,000: rule 76.02(9)(c). [Note that here, if the defendant does not reduce the counterclaim to $25,000 and fails to recover more than $25,000 on the counterclaim at trial, by reason of rule 76.10 (cost sanctions) the defendant will not recover any costs unless the court is satisfied that it is reasonable to have continued the action under the ordinary procedure: rule 76.10(2) and see below.]

Amending Into or Out of the Simplified Procedure

Provision is also made for the parties, by amending their claims to bring the action within the $25,000 limit, to move from the ordinary procedure to the simplified procedure. Similarly, the parties may move from the simplified procedure to the ordinary procedure by amending their claims to exceed the $25,000 threshold.

Plaintiff amending to simplified procedure. A plaintiff who commences an action by the ordinary procedure may amend the statement of claim to meet the $25,000 or less requirements of rule 76.02(1) and then the action continues under the simplified procedure: rule 76.03(1). (Where this is done the amended statement of claim is to state that the action was commenced under the ordinary procedure and has been continued under the simplified procedure: rule 76.03(2).)

Defendant amending to simplified procedure. Similarly a defendant, where the action was originally under the simplified procedure but was removed to the ordinary procedure because of a counterclaim, crossclaim or third party claim that was beyond the $25,000 requirement of rule 76.02(1), can amend the counterclaim, crossclaim or third party claim to meet the requirements of rule 76.02(1) and then the case comes into the simplified procedure: rule 76.03(3). (Where this occurs the amended pleading must so state: rule 76.03(4)).

But there is a cost penalty for "amending into" the simplified procedure: the amending party (regardless of the outcome of the action) shall pay on a solicitor and client basis any costs incurred by the opposing party up to the date of the amendment that would not have been incurred in the action had it been commenced under the simplified procedure, unless the court orders otherwise: rule 76.03(5). The major purpose of this provision is to prevent a party choosing or insisting on the ordinary procedure, in order to obtain examination for discovery, and then amending "down" into the simplified procedure.

Amending from simplified procedure to the ordinary procedure. Where the action is commenced under the simplified procedure and a claim is increased by amendment (and this would include a counterclaim, crossclaim or third party claim) so that it no longer comes within the $25,000 requirement of rule 76.02(1), the simplified procedure ceases to apply unless the parties consent: rule 76.03(6). (Where this occurs and the parties do not file a consent, the amended pleading must state that the action was commenced under the simplified procedure and is being continued under the ordinary procedure: rule 76.03(7).)

> *Example.* After commencing an action under the simplified procedure asserting a claim for $20,000, the plaintiff decides to amend to increase the damage claim to $35,000. Now the amended claim does not meet the requirements of rule 76.02(1) and the ordinary procedure, not the simplified procedure, now governs (unless the parties consent to the continued application of the simplified procedure: rule 76.03(6)).

Costs Consequences

This is the device that drives the whole system. If the plaintiff obtains a judgment that falls within the claims described in rule 76.02(1) *i.e.*, $25,000 etc. or less, the plaintiff shall recover no costs unless

- the action was under the simplified procedure at the commencement of the trial, or
- the court is satisfied that it was reasonable for the plaintiff to have commenced and continued the action under the ordinary procedure: rule 76.10(1) and (2).

Moreover, where the action should have been under the simplified procedure at the commencement of the trial but was not, the trial judge has a discretion to order the plaintiff to pay all or part of the defendant's costs, including solicitor and client costs, in addition to any costs the plaintiff may be required to pay under subrule 49.10(2) (defendant's offer): rule 76.10(5). However, these costs sanctions do not apply if the simplified procedure was not available because the defendant made a counterclaim, crossclaim or third party claim which took the case out of the simplified procedure: rule 76.10(4). But the adverse costs sanctions for the plaintiff apply despite any offer to settle which might have given the plaintiff costs advantages under rule 49.10: rule 76.10(3).

> *Examples.*
>
> (1) *Paradigm case.* A plaintiff commences an action claiming $40,000 using the ordinary procedure, but at trial the plaintiff recovers only $20,000. The plaintiff will recover no costs (rule 76.10(2)(a)) unless the court grants relief on the grounds of reasonableness (rule 76.10(2)(b)). Moreover, the trial judge has a discretion to order the plaintiff to pay all or part of the defendant's costs, including solicitor and client costs: rule 76.10(5).

(2) *Offer to settle.* There is no different result in (1) if the plaintiff had offered to settle (under Rule 49) for $18,000: rule 76.10(3).

(3) *Plaintiff abandoning excess to come under simplified procedure.* What if the plaintiff commenced an action for $40,000 under the simplified procedure? Here the defendant can object to the simplified procedure by so stating in the statement of defence: rule 76.02(4). When this happens if the plaintiff wants to stay within the simplified procedure the plaintiff has to abandon any non-rule 76.02(1) claim in the reply *i.e.*, abandon the claims beyond $25,000. Note that if the defendant does not object in the statement of defence to the simplified procedure in these circumstances, the claim remains one for $40,000 and continues under the simplified procedure and if the plaintiff recovers $20,000 at trial there is no costs sanction against the plaintiff because at the commencement of the trial the action was under the simplified procedure: see rule 76.10(2)(a).

(4) *Action not under simplified procedure because of "excessive" counterclaim.* A plaintiff sues for $25,000 under the simplified procedure and the defendant counterclaims for $30,000, the plaintiff objects to the use of the simplified procedure and defendant does not abandon the excess of the counterclaim over $25,000. The case now proceeds under the ordinary procedure: rule 76.02(10). If the plaintiff recovers $25,000 or less at trial costs sanctions under rule 76.10 do not apply because the simplified procedure was unavailable because of rule 76.02(10); see rule 76.10(4).

(5) *Defendant who recovers $25,000 or less on a counterclaim, etc. and who forced the use of ordinary procedure may also be subject to costs sanctions.* Assume the plaintiff commences the action under the simplified procedure and the defendant counterclaims for more than $25,000, the plaintiff objects to the use of the simplified procedure because of the amount of the counterclaim, the defendant does not abandon the amount of the claim beyond $25,000 (so that the action is under the ordinary procedure: see rule 76.02(10)) and at trial the defendant recovers only $15,000 on the counterclaim. In these circumstances it would seem that the defendant is subject to the same costs sanctions as a plaintiff who recovers $25,000 or less and the case was, at the time of the trial, not under the simplified procedure: see rule 76.10(8) (which provides that rule 76.10(1)-(7) apply, with necessary modifications, to counterclaims, crossclaims or third party claims). Note also that by rule 1.03 "plaintiff" means a "person who commences an action" and "action" is defined to include a proceeding commenced by a counterclaim, crossclaim or third party or subsequent party claim. Hence, it would seem, that "plaintiff" as used in rule 76.10(1) and (2) includes a defendant by counterclaim, etc.

(6) *Application of costs sanctions where the action (or counterclaim, etc.) is dismissed.* The operation of the costs sanction rule, rule 76.10, is triggered by the plaintiff *obtaining a judgment* for $25,000 or less and does not purport to apply where the plaintiff's action is dismissed, *i.e.*, there is no judgment in the plaintiff's favour: rule 76.10(1). Consequently, if the plaintiff sues for $40,000 using the ordinary procedure and the plaintiff's damages are assessed at $15,000, but the action is dismissed, the costs sanctions provided in the rule (and in particular the power given by rule 76.10(5) for the judge to award the defendant solicitor and client costs) do not apply, despite the fact that, logically, the rule could have given the defendant a costs advantage in these circumstances since the plaintiff, who really had a simplified procedure claim, used the ordinary procedure).

Summary Trial

Under the simplified procedure either party may request a summary trial by making a motion for a summary trial: rule 76.06(1). The procedure on a summary trial (rule 76.06(16)) is that

- evidence-in-chief is to be adduced by affidavit, not orally
- the opposing party may cross-examine the witness orally, which can be followed by oral re-examination for not more than 10 minutes
- all of a party's cross-examinations may not exceed 50 minutes
- after the evidence is complete, each party may make an oral argument for not more than 45 minutes.

However, a summary trial, if requested, will not take place if the opposing (responding) party objects. The responding party, after being served with the moving party's material, may serve and file a notice refusing summary trial, in which case the motion for summary trial is converted into and proceeds as a motion for summary judgment (rule 76.06(4)), unless the moving party (*i.e.*, the party who requested the summary trial) delivers a notice of abandonment: rule 76.06(5). It is further provided that whether "the notice of abandonment is delivered before or after service of the responding party's affidavit material" the costs of the motion payable to that party shall not exceed $200, unless the court orders otherwise, and the court may order that no costs of the motion are payable. The reasons for these somewhat convoluted provisions are as follows. The making of a motion for summary trial requires the moving party to serve on the responding party the supporting affidavit material, which will amount to all of the evidence-in-chief of the moving party, *i.e.*, the party requesting the summary trial. If the responding party was simply entitled to refuse the request for a summary trial at this stage, the responding party would be in the position of having seen all of the moving party's evidence without having to provide similar disclosure to the moving party. It is for this reason that rule 76.06(4) somewhat strangely provides that where the responding party delivers a notice refusing a summary trial the motion is automatically converted into a motion for summary judgment. As a consequence, the responding party comes under an obligation (rule 76.06(8)), within 30 days after being served with the moving party's material, to serve any affidavit material for use on the motion for summary judgment. It is the intent of the rule that the moving party should be entitled to insist that the responding party serve this affidavit material. On receipt of the responding party's affidavit material, rule 76.06(5) and (6) give the moving party the right to abort the enforced motion for summary judgment by delivering a notice of abandonment and where this is done the costs payable to the responding party (as a result of the abandonment of the moving party's motion) shall not exceed $200, unless the court orders otherwise, and the court may order that no costs of the motion are payable: rule 76.06(6). Of course, the moving party, who initially requested a summary trial, may permit the motion for summary judgment to proceed, but in many circumstances, this may be quite inappropriate, *i.e.*, the moving party may have been happy to have a summary trial but may be well aware that the case is one that is inappropriate for the awarding of a summary judgment (*e.g.*, cross-examination may be essential to the moving party's case). To recapitulate, the enforced conversion of a motion for summary trial into a motion for summary judgment is not designed to actually force a summary judgment hearing in such circumstances, but rather to ensure that the party who requested summary trial is not exposed to having made unilateral disclosure of its case without receiving similar disclosure from the responding party. It needs to be kept in mind that such disclosure is significant under the simplified procedure since examination for discovery is prohibited.

Summary Judgment

The summary judgment procedure under the simplified procedure (see rule 76.06) is in many respects similar to the procedure under Rule 20, but there are several important differences. The first difference arises from the general principle embodied in rule 76.05, *i.e.*, cross-examination of a deponent on an affidavit filed for use on a motion is not permitted under the simplified procedure, *i.e.*, motions for summary judgment will be heard on un-cross-examined affidavit material. Second, the test to be applied by the judge hearing the motion for summary judgment is different to (and less demanding than) that under rule 20.04 which requires a decision as to whether or not there is a "genuine issue for trial". Instead, under rule 76.06(14) the power given to the presiding judge is much broader. The presiding judge shall grant judgment unless

- the judge is unable to decide the issues in the action in the absence of cross-examination, or
- it would be otherwise unjust to decide the issues on the motion.

These provisions are modelled after British Columbia Rule 18A and Manitoba Rule 20.03(4) which in effect give the judge power to grant summary judgment, notwithstanding that there may be a genuine issue for trial (in the sense that the term is used in Ontario rule 20.04) where the judge is satisfied that on the material before the court, that genuine issue can be resolved on the motion for summary judgment.

Settlement, Pre-trial Conference and Setting Down For Trial

Settlement conference. Within 60 days after the close of pleadings, the solicitors for the parties shall consider the possibility of settlement of any or all of the issues in the action, either by way of a meeting or by telephone call: rule 76.07(1). In any event, when an action is set down for trial, the solicitor for the party setting the action down must certify in the notice of readiness for pre-trial conference that there was a settlement conference: rule 76.08(2).

Pre-trial conference. Prior to the pre-trial conference the parties are to provide to the pre-trial judge or officer a copy of the party's affidavit of documents, a copy of any medical report and any other material necessary for the conference, but a pre-trial conference memorandum shall not be provided unless the parties consent: rule 76.07(2).

Setting down for trial. Rather than the rule 48.02 procedure applying, a party who wishes to set a defended action down for trial under the simplified procedure does so by delivering a notice of readiness for pre-trial conference (rule 76.08(1)) and the pre-trial conference judge or official shall fix a date for trial (subject to the direction of the regional senior judge): rule 76.07(3).

Summaries of Procedure

See Procedural Charts (CHARTS).

Application of Rule

76.01(1) The simplified procedure set out in this Rule applies to actions commenced on or after March 11, 1996, but it does not apply to actions under,

(a) the *Class Proceedings Act, 1992*;

(b) the *Construction Lien Act*;

(c) Rule 69 or 70.

(2) The simplified procedure also applies to actions commenced before March 11, 1996 if the parties file a consent.

Application of Other Rules

(3) The rules that apply to an action apply to an action under the simplified procedure, except where this Rule provides otherwise.

AVAILABILITY OF SIMPLIFIED PROCEDURE

When Mandatory

76.02(1) The simplified procedure shall be used in an action where the plaintiff's claim is exclusively for,

(a) an amount of $25,000 or less, exclusive of interest and costs;

(b) real or personal property whose fair market value at the date of commencement of the action is $25,000 or less; or

(c) both an amount of money and real or personal property whose total value at the date of commencement of the action is $25,000 or less, exclusive of interest and costs, having regard to the fair market value of the property at that date.

When Optional
(2) The simplified procedure may be used in any other action at the option of the plaintiff, subject to subrules (4) to (11).

Originating Process
(3) The statement of claim (Form 14A, 14B or 14D) or notice of action (Form 14C) shall indicate that the action is being brought under the simplified procedure.

Where Defendant may Object to Simplified Procedure
(4) Where the plaintiff makes a claim other than those referred to in subrule (1) or in excess of the monetary limit set out in that subrule, the defendant may object to proceeding under the simplified procedure by so stating in the statement of defence.

Abandonment of Claims by Plaintiff
(5) Where the defendant objects under subrule (4), the action shall nevertheless proceed under the simplified procedure if the plaintiff abandons in the reply the claims that are other than or in excess of the claims referred to in subrule (1).
(6) A plaintiff who abandons claims under subrule (5) may not bring them in any other proceeding.

Ordinary Procedure if Plaintiff does not Abandon
(7) Where the defendant objects under subrule (4) and the plaintiff does not abandon all the claims referred to in subrule (5), the action shall proceed under the ordinary procedure rather than the simplified procedure.

Multiple Plaintiffs
(8) Except for a joint claim, where there is more than one plaintiff, the simplified procedure shall be used if each plaintiff's claim, considered separately, meets the requirements of subrule (1).

Counterclaim, Crossclaim or Third Party Claim
(9) Where a defendant in an action under the simplified procedure makes a counterclaim, crossclaim or third party claim, the main action and the counterclaim, crossclaim or third party claim remain under the simplified procedure if,
(a) the defendant's claim meets the requirements of subrule (1);
(b) the defendant to the counterclaim or crossclaim, or the third party, as the case may be, does not object to proceeding under the simplified procedure in the defence to the defendant's claim; or
(c) the defendant making the claim abandons in the reply any claim that does not meet the requirements of subrule (1).

(10) Where a defendant in an action under the simplified procedure makes a counterclaim, crossclaim or third party claim and none of clauses (9)(a), (b) and (c) apply, the main action and the counterclaim, crossclaim or third party claim shall proceed under the ordinary procedure.

(11) Subrules (2) to (10) apply, with necessary modifications, where a third party delivers a statement of defence in the main action and the main action is under the simplified procedure.

CHANGE TO OR FROM SIMPLIFIED PROCEDURE

Change to Simplified Procedure — Action
76.03(1) Where an action was not commenced under the simplified procedure, the plaintiff may amend the statement of claim to continue the action under the simplified procedure if the claim, as amended, meets the requirements of subrule 76.02(1).

(2) The amended statement of claim shall state that the action was commenced under the ordinary procedure and has been continued under the simplified procedure.

Change to Simplified Procedure — Counterclaim, etc.
(3) Where an action that was under the simplified procedure comes under the ordinary procedure because of the application of subrule 76.02(10), the defendant making the counterclaim, crossclaim or third party claim may amend it to meet the requirements of subrule 76.02(1); in that case, the action shall proceed under the simplified procedure.

(4) The amended counterclaim, crossclaim or third party claim, as the case may be, shall,

   (a) state that the action was previously under the simplified procedure but then came under the ordinary procedure because of the application of subrule 76.02(10);
   (b) refer to the amendment; and
   (c) state that the action shall proceed under the simplified procedure.

Liability for Costs
(5) Regardless of the outcome of the action, the party whose pleading has been amended to continue the action under the simplified procedure shall pay on a solicitor and client basis those costs incurred by the opposing party to the date of the amendment that would not have been incurred if the action had been commenced under the simplified procedure, unless the court orders otherwise.

Change from Simplified Procedure
(6) Where an action was commenced under the simplified procedure and an amended claim does not meet the requirements of subrule 76.02(1), the simplified procedure is not available in the action unless the parties file a consent.

(7) If no consent is filed under subrule (6), the amended pleading shall state that the action was commenced under the simplified procedure and has been continued under the ordinary procedure.

AFFIDAVIT OF DOCUMENTS

List of Potential Witnesses

76.04(1) A party to an action under the simplified procedure shall include in the party's affidavit of documents (Form 30A or 30B) a list of the names and addresses of persons who might reasonably be expected to have knowledge of transactions or occurrences in issue in the action, unless the court orders otherwise.

Effect of Failure to Disclose

(2) A party may not call as a witness at the trial of the action a person whose name has not been disclosed in the affidavit of documents under subrule (1), or any supplementary affidavit of documents, except with leave of the trial judge.

Solicitor's Certificate

(3) The solicitor's certificate under subrule 30.03(4) (full disclosure in affidavit) shall include a statement that the solicitor has explained to the deponent the necessity of complying with subrule (1).

DISCOVERY, CROSS-EXAMINATION ON AN AFFIDAVIT AND EXAMINATION OF A WITNESS

76.05 An examination for discovery under rule 31.03 or 31.10, a cross-examination of a deponent on an affidavit under rule 39.02 and an examination of a witness on a motion under rule 39.03 are not permitted in an action under the simplified procedure.

SUMMARY JUDGMENT AND SUMMARY TRIAL

Where Available

76.06(1) After the close of pleadings, a party may move before a judge with supporting affidavit material for summary judgment or for a summary trial of the action and any counterclaim, crossclaim or third party claim.

Notice of Motion

(2) A notice of motion for summary judgment or for a summary trial shall state that the motion is to be heard or the trial held on a date to be fixed by the registrar not earlier than 50 days after service of the notice of motion.

(3) Immediately after serving the notice of motion and supporting material, the moving party shall file, with proof of service, in the court office where the motion is to be heard, the notice of motion, but not the supporting material.

Summary Trial Converted to Summary Judgment

(4) Where the motion is for a summary trial, the responding party may, within 30 days after being served with the moving party's material, serve on every other party and file, with proof of service, in the court office where the motion is to be heard, a notice refusing a summary trial, in which case the motion shall, subject to subrule (5), proceed as a motion for summary judgment in accordance with subrules (8) to (15).

Abandoning Motion for Summary Judgment

(5) Where the responding party serves a notice refusing summary trial under subrule (4), the moving party may avoid having the motion proceed as a motion for summary judgment by delivering a notice of abandonment.

(6) Whether the notice of abandonment is delivered before or after service of the responding party's affidavit material, the costs of the motion payable to that party shall not exceed $200, unless the court orders otherwise, and the court may order that no costs of the motion are payable.

Application of Summary Judgment Procedure

(7) Rules 20.05, 20.07, 20.08 and 20.09 (summary judgment procedure) apply to a motion for summary judgment and to a motion converted to a motion for summary judgment under subrule (4), but rules 20.01 to 20.04 (availability, affidavits, factums, disposition of motion) and rule 20.06 (costs) do not apply.

Responding Party's Material

(8) Within 30 days after being served with the moving party's material, the responding party shall serve, but not file, any affidavit material for use on the motion for summary judgment or for a summary trial.

(9) In response to affidavit material supporting a motion for summary judgment, the responding party may not rest on the mere allegations or denials of the party's pleadings, but must set out, in affidavit material, specific facts to show that judgment ought not to be granted.

(10) In response to affidavit material supporting a motion for a summary trial, a responding party may not rest on the mere allegations or denials of the party's pleadings, but must set out, in affidavit material, specific facts to prove the party's claim or defence.

Affidavit's Contents

(11) An affidavit for use on a motion for summary judgment or for a summary trial may be made on information and belief as permitted by subrule 39.01(4), but on the hearing of the motion or at the summary trial an adverse inference may be drawn, if appropriate, from the failure of a party to provide the evidence of persons having personal knowledge of contested facts.

Motion Record Required

(12) The moving party shall serve a motion record on every other party to the motion and file it, with proof of service, in the court office where the

motion is to be heard or the trial is to be held, as the case may be, at least five days before the date fixed by the registrar for the hearing of the motion for summary judgment or for the summary trial.

Contents of Motion Record

(13) The motion record shall contain, in consecutively numbered pages arranged in the following order,

(a) a table of contents describing each document, including each exhibit, by its nature and date and, in the case of an exhibit, by exhibit number or letter;

(b) a copy of the notice of motion;

(c) a copy of all affidavits served by any party for use on the motion or at the summary trial; and

(d) a copy of the pleadings, including those relating to any counterclaim, crossclaim or third party claim.

Test for Summary Judgment

(14) On a motion for summary judgment under this rule, the presiding judge shall grant judgment unless,

(a) the judge is unable to decide the issues in the action in the absence of cross-examination; or

(b) it would be otherwise unjust to decide the issues on the motion.

Place of Hearing

(15) Unless the parties agree otherwise, the hearing of a motion for nmary judgment or a summary trial, as the case may be, shall be held,

(a) where a responding party resides in Ontario, in the county where the solicitor's office of any responding party is located or where a responding party who acts in person resides; or

(b) where no responding party resides in Ontario, in the county where the proceeding was commenced or where the solicitor's office of the solicitor of record for any party is located or where any party who acts in person resides.

Summary Trial Procedure

(16) At a summary trial, the order of presentation shall be regulated as follows, unless the trial judge directs otherwise:

1. The moving party shall adduce evidence by affidavit.

2. A party who is adverse in interest may cross-examine the deponent of any affidavit served by the moving party.

3. The moving party may re-examine any deponent who is cross-examined under this subrule for not more than 10 minutes.

4. When any cross-examination and re-examination of the moving party's deponents are concluded, the responding party shall adduce evidence by affidavit.

5. A party who is adverse in interest may cross-examine the deponent of any affidavit served by a responding party.

6. A party shall complete all of the party's cross-examinations within 50 minutes.

7. A responding party may re-examine any deponent who is cross-examined under this subrule for not more than 10 minutes.

8. When any cross-examinations and re-examinations of the responding party's deponents are concluded, the moving party may, with leave of the trial judge, adduce any proper reply evidence.

9. After the presentation of evidence, each party may make oral argument for not more than 45 minutes.

(17) A party who intends to cross-examine the deponent of an affidavit at the summary trial shall, at least 10 days before the date of the trial, give notice of that intention to the party who filed the affidavit, who shall arrange for the deponent's attendance at the trial.

Judgment after Summary Trial
(18) The judge shall grant judgment after the conclusion of the summary trial.

SETTLEMENT AND PRE-TRIAL CONFERENCES

Settlement Conference
76.07(1) Within 60 days after the close of pleadings, the solicitors for the parties shall consider the possibility of settlement of any or all issues in the action either by way of a meeting or by telephone call.

Pre-trial Conference — Documents to be Available
(2) At least five days before the pre-trial conference, a party shall provide to the pre-trial conference judge or officer a copy of the party's affidavit of documents, a copy of any medical report and any other material necessary for the conference, but a pre-trial conference memorandum shall not be provided unless the parties consent.

Date for Trial
(3) Subject to the direction of the regional senior judge, the pre-trial conference judge or officer shall fix a date for trial.

HOW DEFENDED ACTION SET DOWN FOR TRIAL

Defended Action
76.08(1) Despite rule 48.02 (how action set down for trial), a party who wishes to set a defended action under the simplified procedure down for trial shall do so by serving a notice of readiness for pre-trial conference (Form 76A) on every party to the action and any counterclaim, crossclaim or third party claim and forthwith filing the notice with proof of service.

Solicitor's Certificate
(2) Where the party who sets the action down for trial is represented by a solicitor, the solicitor shall certify in the notice of readiness for pre-trial conference that there was a settlement conference.

Trial Record
(3) Not less than 10 days before the commencement of the trial, the party who set the action down for trial shall serve a trial record in accordance with rule 48.03 on every party to the action and any counterclaim, crossclaim or third party claim and shall forthwith file the trial record with proof of service.

PLACING DEFENDED ACTION ON TRIAL LIST

76.09 Despite rule 48.06 (placing on trial list), a defended action under the simplified procedure shall be placed on the appropriate trial list by the registrar immediately after a notice of readiness for pre-trial conference has been filed.

COSTS WHERE JUDGMENT DOES NOT EXCEED $25,000

Where Rule Applies
76.10(1) This rule applies to a plaintiff who obtains a judgment awarding exclusively,
(a) an amount of $25,000 or less, exclusive of interest and costs;
(b) real or personal property whose fair market value at the date of commencement of the action was $25,000 or less; or
(c) both an amount of money and real or personal property whose total value is $25,000 or less, exclusive of interest and costs, having regard to the fair market value of the property at the date of commencement of the action.

Plaintiff Denied Costs
(2) The plaintiff shall not recover any costs unless,
(a) the action was under the simplified procedure at the commencement of the trial; or
(b) the court is satisfied that it was reasonable for the plaintiff to have commenced and continued the action under the ordinary procedure.
(3) Subrule (2) applies despite subrule 49.10(1) (plaintiff's offer to settle).
(4) Subrule (2) does not apply if the simplified procedure was unavailable because subrule 76.02(10) applied (counterclaim, etc.).

Plaintiff may be Ordered to Pay Defendant's Costs
(5) The plaintiff may, in the trial judge's discretion, be ordered to pay all or part of the defendant's costs, including solicitor and client costs, in addition to any costs the plaintiff is required to pay under subrule 49.10(2) (defendant's offer).

Defendant Objecting to Simplified Procedure
(6) In an action in which the claim is for real or personal property, if the defendant objected to proceeding under the simplified procedure on the

ground that the property's fair market value exceeded $25,000 at the date the action was commenced and the court finds the value did not exceed that amount at that date, the defendant shall pay on a solicitor and client basis the costs incurred by the plaintiff that would not have been incurred if the action had remained under the simplified procedure, unless the court orders otherwise.

Burden of Proof

(7) The burden of proving that the fair market value of the real or personal property at the date of commencement of the action was $25,000 or less is on the plaintiff.

Counterclaims, Crossclaims and Third Party Claims

(8) Subrules (1) to (7) apply, with necessary modifications, to counter-claims, crossclaims or third party claims.

REVOCATION

76.11 This Rule is revoked on March 11, 2000. [en. O. Reg. 533/95, s. 6; am. O. Reg. 60/96, s. 1]

FORMS

TABLE OF FORMS

This is merely a list of the forms.
The full text of the forms is contained in the companion volume,
Forms, Case Management Guide and Special Materials.

FORMS

TARIFFS

Authors' Comment: Fees and disbursements incurred prior to the new Rules coming in force (January 1, 1985) are governed by the former tariffs unless the court otherwise orders: rule 1.02(4). The former tariffs are reproduced at p. 788 of the 1985 edition and p. 853 of the 1986 edition of Watson and McGowan, *Ontario Supreme and District Court Practice.* Digests of cases related to the tariffs are collected under rule 58.05.

TARIFF A

Solicitors' Fees and Disbursements
Allowable Under Rule 58.05

PART I — SOLICITORS' FEES

Item	Amount
1. Pleadings, up to	$100

This item includes all services, except motions, up to and including delivery of pleadings.

An increased fee may be allowed in the discretion of the assessment officer.

2. Financial statements, up to	$100

An increased fee may be allowed in the discretion of the assessment officer.

3. Discovery of documents, up to	$100

This item includes affidavits of documents, requests to inspect, production for inspection and inspection.

An increased fee may be allowed in the discretion of the assessment officer.

4. Drawing and settling issues on a special case	$ 75
Subject to increase, in the discretion of the assessment officer, up to	$350
5. Setting down for trial	$ 30
6. Pre-motion conference	$ 75

This item includes preparation and counsel fee.

An increased fee and a fee to junior counsel may be allowed in the discretion of the assessment officer.

7. Motion, up to	$ 75

This item includes notice of motion, affidavits, motion record, factum, preparation, counsel fee, and settling, signing and entering the order.

An increased fee and a fee to junior counsel may be allowed in the discretion of the assessment officer.

Item	Amount

8. Application

This item includes all preliminary steps, notice of application, affidavits, correspondence, application record, factum, preparation, counsel fee on hearing or settlement and attendance to hear judgment.

The fee to be allowed is in the discretion of the assessment officer. A fee to junior counsel may be allowed in the discretion of the assessment officer.

9. Examination, up to $100

This item applies to each oral or written examination out of court, including preliminary steps, preparation and counsel fee, except an examination in aid of execution (item 18).

An increased fee may be allowed in the discretion of the assessment officer.

10. Pre-trial conference .... $ 75

This item includes preparation, counsel fee and preparation of memorandum and order.

An increased fee and a fee to junior counsel may be allowed in the discretion of the assessment officer.

10.1 Settlement conference under rule 76.07 .... $100

This item includes preparation and counsel fee.

11. Notice or offer .... $ 35

This item applies to each notice, including offer to settle, offer to contribute, notice of acceptance, notice of withdrawal of offer, request to admit, response to request to admit and notice of payment into court.

An increased fee may be allowed in the discretion of the assessment officer.

12. Preparation for trial, up to $350

This item includes correspondence, brief at trial, summoning witnesses and counsel fee on settlement.

An increased fee may be allowed in the discretion of the assessment officer.

13. Assignment court, up to $50

This item applies to each attendance at a sitting of the court convened for the purpose of managing the list of cases to be tried.

TAR.

Item	Amount

14. Trial

This item includes counsel fee, written argument and attendance to hear judgment.

The fee to be allowed is in the discretion of the assessment officer. A fee to junior counsel may be allowed in the discretion of the assessment officer.

15. Order

To the party having carriage .... $ 35

To other parties .... $ 15

This item includes settling, signing and entering an order, whether obtained on default or otherwise, where not included in item 7 or 10.

Subject to increase, in the discretion of the assessment officer, up to $100

16. (a) Appeal to an appellate court

This item includes all preliminary steps, notices, appeal book, factum, preparation, counsel fee on a motion for leave to appeal, counsel fee on appeal and attendance to hear judgment.

The fee to be allowed is in the discretion of the assessment officer. A fee to junior counsel may be allowed in the discretion of the assessment officer.

(b) Appeal to a judge .... $ 75

This item includes all preliminary steps, notices, appeal record, factum, preparation, counsel fee and attendance to hear judgment.

An increased fee may be allowed in the discretion of the assessment officer.

17. Reference

This item includes all preliminary steps, notices, affidavits, appointments, attendances, correspondence, preparation, counsel fee on reference and preparing, settling, signing and confirming the report. The fee to be allowed is in the discretion of the assessment officer.

In a sale action, additional fees may be allowed in the discretion of the assessment officer for arranging for a private sale or a sale by tender or for preparation of conditions of sale and the advertisement, arranging for advertising and for an auctioneer, conducting the sale, arranging for payment of the purchase price and for the preparation of a transfer where one is executed.

Item	Amount
18. Issuing or renewing a writ of execution or notice of garnishment	$ 15
19. Examination in aid of execution	$ 50
An increased fee may be allowed in the discretion of the assessment officer.	
20. Seizure or seizure and sale under a writ of execution or notice of garnishment	$ 25
An increased fee may be allowed in the discretion of the assessment officer.	

NOTES:

1. Where for any reason the services covered by an item were not completed, the fee may be reduced by the assessment officer.

2. Any item of a counterclaim, crossclaim or third party claim may be assessed as in a separate action and items common to the main action and a counterclaim, crossclaim or third party claim may be apportioned where appropriate.

PART II — DISBURSEMENTS

Item	Amount
21. Attendance money actually paid to a witness who is entitled to attendance money, to be calculated as follows:	
1. Attendance allowance for each day of necessary attendance	$ 50
2. Travel allowance, where the hearing or examination is held,	
(a) in a city or town in which the witness resides, $3.00 for each day of necessary attendance;	
(b) within 300 kilometres of where the witness resides, 24¢ a kilometre each way between his or her residence and the place of hearing or examination;	
(c) more than 300 kilometres from where the witness resides, the minimum return air fare plus 24¢ a kilometre each way from his or her residence to the airport and from the airport to the place of hearing or examination.	
3. Overnight accommodation and meal allowance, where the witness resides elsewhere than the place of hearing or examination and is required to remain overnight, for each overnight stay	$ 75

Item	Amount

22. Fees or expenses actually paid to a court, court reporter, official examiner or sheriff under the regulations under the *Administration of Justice Act.*

23. For service or attempted service of a document,
    (a) in Ontario, the amount actually paid, not exceeding the fee payable to a sheriff under the regulations under the *Administration of Justice Act;*
    (b) outside Ontario, a reasonable amount;
    (c) that was ordered to be served by publication, a reasonable amount.

24. For an examination and transcript of evidence taken on the examination, the amount actually paid, not exceeding the fee payable to an official examiner under the regulations under the *Administration of Justice Act.*

25. For the preparation of a plan, model, videotape, film or photograph reasonably necessary for the conduct of the proceeding, a reasonable amount.

26. For experts' reports that were supplied to the other parties as required by the *Evidence Act* or these rules and that were reasonably necessary for the conduct of the proceeding, a reasonable amount.

27. The cost of the investigation and report of the Official Guardian.

28. For an expert who gives opinion evidence at the hearing or whose attendance was reasonably necessary at the hearing, a reasonable amount not exceeding $350 a day, subject to increase in the discretion of the assessment officer.

29. For an interpreter for services at the hearing or on an examination, a reasonable amount not exceeding $100 a day, subject to increase in the discretion of the assessment officer.

29a. Where ordered by the presiding judge or officer, for translation into English or French of a document that has been filed, a reasonable amount.

30. Where ordered by the presiding judge or officer, such travelling and accommodation expenses incurred by a party as, in the discretion of the assessment officer, appear reasonable.

31. For copies of any documents or authorities prepared for or by a party for the use of the court and supplied to the opposite party, a reasonable amount.

32. For copies of records, appeal books and factums, a reasonable amount.

Item	Amount

33. The cost of certified copies of documents such as orders, birth, marriage, and death certificates, abstracts of title, deeds, mortgages and other registered documents where reasonably necessary for the conduct of the proceeding.

34. The cost of transcripts of proceedings of courts or tribunals,
    (a) where required by the court or the rules; or
    (b) where reasonably necessary for the conduct of the proceeding.

35. Where ordered by the presiding judge or officer, for any other disbursement reasonably necessary for the conduct of the proceeding, a reasonable amount in the discretion of the assessment officer.

36. Goods and services tax actually paid or payable on the solicitor's fees and disbursements allowable under rule 58.05.

[am. O. Regs. 219/91, s. 16; 351/94, s. 19; 533/95, s. 12 (amendment revoked March 11, 2000)]

TARIFF B

Solicitors' Fees in Divorce Actions allowed under Rule 69.26

For all services in a divorce action up to obtaining a certificate of divorce $400

TARIFF C

Solicitor's Costs Allowed on an Unopposed Judgment on Passing of Accounts

(1) ESTATE TRUSTEE

If receipts are less than $50,000	$ 600.00
If receipts are $50,000 or more but less than $100,000	800.00
If receipts are $100,000 or more but less than $500,000 ..	1,500.00
If receipts are $500,000 or more but less than $1,000,000	2,000.00
If receipts are $1,000,000 or more but less than $1,500,000	2,500.00
If receipts are $1,500,000 or more	3,000.00

(2) PERSON HAVING A FINANCIAL INTEREST IN THE ESTATE

A person having a financial interest in an estate who approves the accounts and files a request for costs is entitled to one-half of the amount payable to the estate trustee.

Note: Where two or more persons are represented by the same solicitor, they are entitled to receive only one person's costs.

Note: Any person entitled to costs under this Tariff is also entitled to the amount of G.S.T. on those costs.

[en. O. Reg. 484/94, s. 14]

COURT AND SHERIFFS' FEES

O. Reg. 293/92
[am. O. Regs. 272/94; 359/94; 802/94]

ONTARIO COURT (GENERAL DIVISION) AND COURT OF APPEAL — FEES

REGULATION MADE UNDER THE ADMINISTRATION OF JUSTICE ACT

1. The following fees are payable:

1. On the issue of,

    i.   a statement of claim or notice of action $132.00

    ii.   a petition for divorce 125.00

    iii.   a notice of application,

        A.   under Part IV of the *Landlord and Tenant Act* 45.00

        B.   other than under Part IV of the *Landlord and Tenant Act* 132.00

    iv.   a third or subsequent party claim 132.00

    v.   a statement of defence and counterclaim adding a party or an answer and counterpetition adding a party 132.00

    vi.   a summons to a witness 18.00

    vii.   a certificate, other than a certificate of a search by the registrar required on an application for a grant of probate, and not more than five pages of copies of the Court document annexed 18.00

        for each additional page 1.00

    viii.   a commission 37.00

    ix.   a writ of execution 48.00

    x.   a notice of garnishment (including the filing of the notice with the sheriff) 89.00

2. On the signing of,

    i.   an order directing a reference, except an order on requisition directing the assessment of a solicitor and client bill of costs ... 179.00

    ii.   an order on requisition directing the assessment of a solicitor and client bill of costs 53.00

     iii.   an appointment for the assessment of party and party costs 26.00

3.   On the filing of,

     i.   a notice of intent to defend 74.00

     ii.   a statement of defence or an answer where no notice of intent to defend has been filed by the same party 74.00

     iii.   a notice of appearance 74.00

     iv.   a notice of motion served on another party or a notice of motion for leave to appeal, except a motion for a consent order 48.00

     v.   a notice of motion for judgment in a divorce action 170.00

     vi.   a notice of appeal from an interlocutory order 132.00

     vii.   a notice of appeal to an appellate court of a final order of a small claims court 48.00

     viii.   a notice of appeal to an appellate court of a final order of any court or tribunal other than a small claims court 132.00

     ix.   a request to redeem or request for sale 18.00

4.   On the filing of a trial record, for the first time only 268.00

5.   For making up and forwarding of papers, documents and exhibits 26.00

                                                    and the transportation costs

6.   For making copies of documents,

     i.   not requiring certification, per page 1.00

     ii.   requiring certification, per page 2.50

7.   For the inspection of a court file,

     i.   by a solicitor or party in the proceeding ....no charge

     ii.   by a person who has entered into an agreement with the Attorney General for the bulk inspection of court files, per file 1.30

     iii.   by any other person, per file 8.50

    1.1—(1) If a minor or other person under disability is entitled to receive a payment or payments under a multi-provincial/territorial assistance program agreement between Ontario and a person who has been infected with the human immunodeficiency virus through the receipt by transfusion of blood or a blood product, no fee is payable for the issue of a notice of application under Rule 7.08 of the Rules of

Civil Procedure on behalf of the minor or other person under disability, and sub-subparagraph B of subparagraph iii of paragraph 1 of section 1 does not apply.

(2) Where before the coming into force of this Regulation an applicant on behalf of a minor or other person under disability has paid a fee for the issue of a notice of application referred to in subsection (1), the fee shall be refunded to the applicant.

2.—(1) The following fees are payable in estate matters:

1. For a certificate of appointment of estate trustee, other than a certificate of succeeding estate trustee or a certificate of estate trustee during litigation,

    i.   on the first $50,000 of the value of the estate being administered, per thousand dollars or part thereof .... $ 5.00

    ii.   on the portion of the value of the estate being administered that exceeds $50,000, per thousand dollars or part thereof 15.00

2. For a certificate of succeeding estate trustee or a certificate of estate trustee during litigation 50.00

3. For an application of an estate trustee to pass accounts, including all services in connection with it 255.00

4. For a notice of objection to accounts 45.00

5. For an application other than an application to pass accounts, including an application for proof of lost or destroyed will, a revocation of a certificate of appointment, an application for directions or the filing of a claim under notice of contestation 125.00

6. For a notice of objection other than a notice of objection to accounts, including the filing of a notice of appearance 45.00

7. For a request for notice of commencement of proceeding 45.00

8. For the deposit of a will or codicil for safekeeping 17.00

9. For an assessment of costs, including the certificate 25.00

(2) The fees set out in section 1 are payable in estate matters in addition to the fees set out in subsection (1).

3.—(1) The following fees are payable on the filing of a statement of claim, crossclaim, counterclaim or third party claim in an action under the *Construction Lien Act*:

1. For a claim, crossclaim, counterclaim or third party claim exceeding $1000 .... 35.00

2. For a claim, crossclaim, counterclaim or third party claim exceeding $1000 but not exceeding $6000 .... 50.00

3.   For a claim, crossclaim, counterclaim or third party claim exceeding
      $6000 .... 132.00

(2) The fees set out in section 1, except those in paragraphs 1, 2, 3 and 4, are payable in an action under the *Construction Lien Act* in addition to the fees set out in subsection (1).

4.—(1) The following fees are payable in respect of an application under the *Repair and Storage Liens Act*:

1.   To file an application 48.00

2.   To issue an initial certificate 18.00

3.   To file a notice of objection 21.00

4.   To issue a final certificate 18.00

5.   To issue a writ of seizure 48.00

6.   To file a waiver of further claim and a receipt ....no
                                                                                                    charge

(2) The fees set out in section 1, except those in paragraphs 1, 2, 3 and 4, are payable in an application under the *Repair and Storage Liens Act* in addition to the fees set out in subsection (1).

5.—(1) The following fees are payable to an official examiner:

i.   for the appointment, for each person examined 9.50

ii.   for the provision of facilities per hour or part 16.00

iii.   for a reporter's attendance, per hour or part 19.50

iv.   for the transcript of an examination, per page, regardless of the party
       ordering,

       A.   for one copy of the first transcript ordered 4.00

       B.   for one copy of each transcript ordered after the reporter has
             satisfied the order for a transcript described in subparagraph A
             .... 3.40

       C.   for each additional copy ordered before the reporter has satisfied
             the order for a transcript described in subparagraph A or B 0.80

v.   for handling costs, per invoice 5.50

vi.   for cancellation of or failure to keep an appointment, with less than
       three working days notice,

A.   for the cancellation or failure to attend 11.50

B.   for each hour or part reserved for the appointment 36.00

(2) The official examiner shall be paid, in addition to the fees set out in subsection (1), a travelling allowance in accordance with [R.R.O. 1990, Reg. 11], for attendance out of the office.

(3) If a party requires a transcript within five working days of placing the order for the transcript, the party shall pay the official examiner 75 cents per page, in addition to the fee set out in paragraph iv of subsection (1).

(4) If a party requires a transcript within two working days of placing the order for the transcript, the party shall pay the official examiner $1.50 per page, in addition to the fee set out in paragraph iv of subsection (1).

(5) If more than one party requires a transcript as described in subsection (3) or (4), only the first party to place the order shall be required to pay the additional fee.

Note: A solicitor who is charged more than the amounts provided in section 5 of this Regulation or who receives a transcript that does not substantially conform with Rule 4.09 of the Rules of Civil Procedure should notify the Assistant Deputy Minister, Courts Administration Division, Ministry of the Attorney General, in writing.

6. Ontario Regulations 158/83, 405/84, 605/85, 171/90 and 393/90 are revoked.

O. Reg. 294/92
[am. O. Regs. 431/93; 358/94]

SHERIFFS — FEES

REGULATION MADE UNDER THE
ADMINISTRATION OF JUSTICE ACT

1.—(1) The following fees are payable to a sheriff:

1. For up to three attempts, whether or not successful, to serve a document, for each person to be served $41.00

2. For filing or renewing a writ of execution or order which a sheriff is liable or required to enforce 32.00

3. For delivering a copy of a writ of execution or a renewal of it to the land registrar of a land titles division 9.00

4. For filing a writ of seizure or a direction to seize under the *Repair and Storage Liens Act* 48.00

5. For each attempt, whether or not successful, to enforce,

   i.   a writ of delivery,

   ii. a writ of sequestration,

   iii. an order for interim recovery of personal property,

   iv. an order for interim preservation of personal property, or

   v.   a writ of seizure or direction to seize under the *Repair and Storage Liens Act* 163.00

6. For each attempt, whether or not successful, to enforce a writ of seizure and sale or an order directing a sale 90.00

7. For each attempt, whether or not successful, to enforce any other writ of execution or order 74.00

8. For a search for writs, per name searched 11.00

9. For each writ listed on an abstract obtained on a search for writs 11.00

to a maximum of
$110 for each
requisition for
a search

10.   For preparing a schedule of distribution under the *Creditors' Relief Act*, per writ or notice of garnishment listed on the schedule 18.00

                                                                                        to a maximum
                                                                                        of an amount
                                                                                        equal to 20%
                                                                                        of the money
                                                                                        received

11.   For a calculation for satisfaction of writs and garnishments, per writ or notice of garnishment 18.00

12.   For any service or act ordered by a court for which no fee is provided, for each hour or part of an hour spent performing the service or doing the act 23.00

13.   For making copies of documents,

      i.   not requiring certification, per page 1.00

      ii.   requiring certification, per page 2.50

(2) In addition to the fees set out in paragraphs 5, 6, 7 and 12 of subsection (1), the person who requests the service shall pay the sheriff his or her reasonable and necessary disbursements in carrying out the services described in those paragraphs.

2. In addition to the fees and disbursements set out in section 1, the person who requests the service shall pay the sheriff a travel allowance as set out in [R.R.O. 1990, Reg. 11] for the distance he or she necessarily travels, both ways, between the court house and the place where the sheriff,

      (a)   serves or attempts to serve a document;

      (b)   enforces or attempts to enforce a writ or order; or

      (c)   performs or attempts to perform any other service directed by a court.

3. Ontario Regulation 392/90 is revoked.

INDEX

All references in this Index are to the Rules of Civil Procedure and Forms, unless preceded by "s." which indicates sections of the Courts of Justice Act, or "p." which indicates pages of the text. Forms are located in Companion Volume.

ABANDONMENT. *See* APPEALS;
APPLICATIONS; MOTIONS

ABRIDGMENT OF TIME
appeals, 3.02(3)
consent in writing, 3.02(4)
generally, 3.02
two proceedings in court, placing on trial list,
6.01(2)

ABSENTEES
personal service, 16.02(1)(i)
persons under disability, 1.03
representation in court proceedings, 7.02(1.1),
7.03(2.1)

ABUSE OF PROCESS
determination of issue before trial, 21.01(3)
documents, 25.11
motions, 37.16
pleadings, 25.11

ACCEPTANCE OF OFFER. *See* OFFERS TO
SETTLE

ACCESS. *See* CHILDREN; DIVORCE
ACTIONS; FAMILY LAW
PROCEEDINGS

ACCOUNTANT
definition, payment into or out of court, 72.01
discharge of mortgage, 72.04
payment into court
  account in chartered bank, 72.02(6)
  bank receipt, 72.02(7)
  direction, 72.02(3)
  material to be filed, 72.02(1)
payment out of court
  consent by insurer on behalf of party,
    72.03(6)
  maintenance of a minor, 72.03(14)
  minor attaining age of majority, 72.03(7)
  payment directly to solicitor, 72.03(8)
  payment out on consent, 72.03(4)

payment out under order or report,
    72.03(2), (3)
  payment to personal representative 72.03(9)
  stop order, 72.05
references, 55.05(1), (3)

ACCOUNTING
summary judgments, 20.04(5)

ACCOUNTS
change of account
  after day fixed for payment, 64.06(25)
  before day fixed for payment, 64.06(24)
  final order fixing new day for payment,
    64.06(22)
  mortgage references, 64.06(21)
  motions, by dissatisfied party, 64.06(23)
  notice of change, 64.06(21)
estates. *See* ESTATE ACCOUNTS
interest, administration proceedings, 65.02(2)
mortgage references
  change of account, 64.06(21)
  time for taking of new account, 64.06(18)
notice of change
  defendant noted in default, 19.02(3)
passing, costs, 58.08
proceedings for administration, 65.01(3)
proof, where mortgage assigned, 64.06(15)
references, 55.04
  books of account, 55.04(4)
  failure to pass accounts when required,
    55.07(2)
  powers of referee, 55.04(1)
  preparation, 55.04(2), (3)
  production and inspection of vouchers,
    55.04(5)
  questioning accounts, 55.04(6)
taking of accounts
  action, s.122
  directing reference, 54.02(2)
  foreclosure actions, 64.03(8), (10), (11)
  mortgage reference, duties and powers of
    referee, 64.06(3)
  sale action, notice to defendant, 64.04(7)

BOOKS
accounts, proof on reference, 55.04(4)
assessment of costs, production, 58.05(4)
disclosure and production. *See* DISCOVERY
referee's procedure book, 55.02(11)

BY-LAWS
application for interpretation, 14.05(3)(d)
proceeding for interpretation, representation
  orders, 10.01(1)

CAPACITY
parties under disability. *See* PARTIES UNDER
  DISABILITY
plaintiff or defendant lacking, 21.01(3)(b)
suing or being sued, 5.01(2)

CARRIAGE OF REFERENCE. *See*
  REFERENCES

CASE MANAGEMENT RULES. *See*
  Companion Volume

CERTIFICATES
appeal from interlocutory order
  contents of appellant's record, 62.01(7), (9)
appellant's, respecting evidence, 61.04(1),
  61.05(1), 62.02(8)
  contents of appeal book, 61.10(1)
  modifying order for transcript, 61.05(6)
appointment of estate trustee. See ESTATE
  TRUSTEES
assessment of costs, 58.09, 58C
  appeals, 58.11, 62.01(1)
  enforcement of costs where no order
    awarding, 60.02(3)
  withholding, objections, 58.10(1)
completeness of appeal book, 61.10(1), 61H
divorce, of, 69.22
forms
  appellant's certificate respecting evidence,
    61C
  certificate of completeness of appeal books,
    61H
  certificate of divorce, 69V
  certificate of stay, 63A
  Registrar's certificate (divorce), 69U
  respondent's certificate respecting
    evidence, 61D
marriage or registration of marriage, 69.03(2),
  69.18(a), 69.19(c), (d)
pending litigation
  claim must be in originating process,
    42.01(2)
  discharge, s. 103(6); 42.02
  effect, s. 103(1)

form, 42A
generally, 42
leave to issue required, 42.01
liability for registering, s. 103(4)
motion without notice, 42.01(3)
registration, s. 103(2)
service of order, 42.01(4)
perfection, 61.09(3), (5)
  judicial review proceeding, 68.05, 68.06
prior pending petitions, 69.18(b)
reciprocal enforcement of maintenance orders,
  70.13
registrar's, motion for judgment, 69.19(9)
respondent's, respecting evidence, 61.05(2), (3)
  contents of appeal book, 61.10(1)
  modifying order for transcript, 61.05(6)
solicitor's
  affidavit of documents, 30.03(4)
  setting down action, 48.03(1)
stay pending appeal, 63.03(4), 63A
Supreme Court of Canada
  entry, 59.05(6)

CERTIFIED COPIES
court documents, 4.03
discovery, 30.10(4)

CHAMBERS. *See* MOTIONS

CHANGE OF VENUE. *See* PLACE OF
  TRIAL; TRIALS

CHARGES. *See* ENCUMBRANCES

CHILD AND FAMILY SERVICES ACT
  APPEALS
appeal record, 71.02(5)
commencement, 71.02(1)
dispensing with compliance, 71.02(7)
filing notice of appeal, 71.02(3)
form, notice of appeal to Ontario Court
  (General Division), 70A
generally, 71
grounds to be stated in notice, 71.02(4)
hearing date, 71.02(6)
service of notice of appeal, 71.02(1), (2)

CHILDREN
See also DIVORCE ACTIONS; FAMILY
  LAW PROCEEDINGS; MINORS
access
  interim, 69.15
  reference to family law commissioner,
    69.21, 70.07
  variation application, 69.24(1)

CLASS ACTIONS. *See* CLASS
  PROCEEDINGS

CLASS PROCEEDINGS
See also Companion Volume
costs, 12.04
definitions, 12.01
discovery of class members, 12.03
judgments, contents, 12.05(1)
leave to appeal, 12.06
orders, contents, 12.05(1), (2)
representative defendant, 12.07
simplified procedure does not apply, 76.01(1)
title of proceeding, 12.02

COMMENCEMENT OF PROCEEDINGS
See also ORIGINATING PROCESS
administration proceedings, 65.01(1)
appeals
  persons to be served, 61.04(1)
  time for appeal, 61.04(1)
application for certificate of appointment of
  estate trustee, 74.04
applications for judicial review, 68.01
approval of sale, mortgage, lease concerning
  minor, 67.01
demand for declaration of authority, 15.02(1)
divorce actions, 69.03(1)
family law proceedings, 70.03
generally, 14
minor's estates, proceedings concerning, 67.01
motions before, 37.17
partition or sale of land, 66.01
proceedings for judicial review, 68.01
request for notice of, estates, 74.03
stay of proceeding commenced without
  authority, 15.02(4)
without client's authority, 15.02(3)
without solicitor's authority, 15.02(2)

COMMISSIONERS
examination out of Ontario, 36.03
taking evidence before trial, persons out of
  Ontario, 34.07, 34C

COMMITTAL
contempt motions, imprisonment, 60.11(7),
  60L

COMMITTEES. *See* LITIGATION
  GUARDIANS

COMPROMISE. *See* OFFERS TO SETTLE;
  SETTLEMENTS

COMPUTATION OF TIME. *See* TIME

CONDUCT MONEY. *See* ATTENDANCE
  MONEY

CONFIRMATION
appellant's certificate respecting evidence,
  61.05(3)
report of family law commissioner, 69.21(3)
reports on references, 54.07-54.09
  defendants noted in default, 19.02(3)

CONSENT
adding party as plaintiff or applicant, 5.04(3)
amendment of pleadings, 26.02
applications, delivery of affidavit after cross-
  examining, 39.02(2)
defendant noted in default, 19.02(2)
  consent of plaintiff to step by defendant,
    19.02(1)(b), 19.03(2)
determination of question before trial,
  admission of evidence, 21.01(2)(a)
directing reference, 54.02
discontinuance, 23.01(1)(c)
  effect on subsequent action, 23.04(1)
examinations out of court, 34.06
  taking evidence before trial, 36.01
extending or abridging time, 3.02(4)
joinder of necessary parties, 5.03(5)
judgment in main action
  notice to third party, 29.06(b)
  parties under disability, 7.08(2)
litigation guardian agreeing to act, 7.02(2)
medical examinations, 33.08
minor over sixteen, approval of settlement,
  7.08(4)
minor's estates, consent of minor, 67.03
motions
  absence of the public, 37.11(1)
  conference telephone, 37.12
  delivering affidavit after cross-examining,
    39.02(2)
  reference, consent of referee for motion to
    judge or master, 54.05(1)
payment out of court, 72.03(1), (4)
  insurer on behalf of party, 72.03(6)
  payment directly to solicitor, 72.03(8)
pleading subsequent to reply, 25.01(5)
reference to family law commissioner, 69.21(1)
references, payment out of court, 55.05(3),
  55.06(14)
trials
  appointment of experts, 52.03(1)
  from December 24-January 6, 3.03(1)
  return of exhibits, 52.04(2)
withdrawal of admissions, 51.05
withdrawal of statement of defence,
  23.06(1)(a), 51.05

JUDGMENTS — *continued*
fact or document yet to be proved, 52.10
failure to testify, adverse party called as
  witness, 53.07(4)
foreclosure actions. *See* FORECLOSURE,
  SALE AND REDEMPTION
foreign currency obligations, s. 121
form and contents, 59.03(3), (4), 59B
forms
  application for registration of U.K.
    judgment, 73A
  default judgment (debt or liquidated
    demand), 19A
  default judgment (recovery of possession of
    personal property), 19C
  default judgment (recovery of possession of
    land), 19B
  default judgments, mortgage actions. *See*
    FORECLOSURE, SALE AND
    REDEMPTION
  divorce actions. *See* DIVORCE ACTIONS
  general form of judgment, 59B
  judgment for administration of estate, 65A
  judgment for partition or sale, 66A
incorporating terms of offer to settle, 49.07(6)
joint liability not affected, s. 139
offer to settle, accepted, 49.09
partition or sale of land, 66.02
reciprocal enforcement of U.K. judgments
  definitions, 73.01
  effect of registration, 73.03
  notice of application for registration of,
    73.02(1)
  supporting material on application,
    73.02(2), (3), (4)
redemption actions, 64.05(4), (5)
references. *See* REFERENCES
sale actions. *See* FORECLOSURE, SALE
  AND REDEMPTION
set aside, party failing to attend, 52.01(3)
set-off of mutual debts, s. 111
special case, 22.05(2)
summary. *See* SUMMARY JUDGMENTS
third party
  default, 29.07
  effect of defence, 29.06
variation, party failing to attend, 52.01(3)
without prejudice to persons not parties,
  5.04(1)

JUDICIAL REVIEW
application records
  applicant's, 68.04(1), (2)
  copies for use of the court, 68.04(7)
  failure of applicant to deliver, 68.06
  material served on application, 68.04(8)

  respondent's, 68.04(4), (5)
  transcript of evidence, 68.04(9)
applications to Divisional Court, 38.01(2)
certificate of perfection
  failure to file, 68.06
  general, 68.05(1)
commencement of proceeding
  application commenced outside regional
    centre, 68.01(2)
  notice of application, 68.01(1)
dismissal for delay, 68.06
factums
  applicant's, 68.04(1), (3)
  copies for use of the court, 68.04(7)
  failure of applicant to deliver, 68.06
  respondent's, 68.04(4), (6)
forms
  notice of application to Divisional Court for
    judicial review, 68A
  notice of listing for hearing, 68B
  order dismissing application for judicial
    review for delay, 68C
generally, 68
hearing date in Divisional Court, 68.03
procedure
  Divisional Court, 68.02(1)
  General Division, 68.02(2)
  jurisdiction, 38.02
  listing for hearing, 68.05(2)

JUDICIAL REVIEW PROCEDURE ACT. See
  Companion Volume

JURIES
addresses, order of presentation, 52.07
answering only some questions, 52.08(1)
bilingual jury, s. 126(2)
composition, s. 108(4)
conflicting answers, 52.08(1)
continuation with five jurors, s. 108(8)
damages, guidance and submissions, s. 118
disagreement, 52.08(1)
discharge of juror, s. 108(7)
inspection of property or location, 52.05
judgment only on some claims, 52.08(2)
jury notice
  availability, s. 108; 47.01
  form, 47A
  striking out, 47.02
  time for delivery, 47.01
  trial record to contain, 48.03(1)
no finding, 52.08(1)
recording verdicts, 52.09
request for jury trial, s. 108(1)
trial lists, 48.08(1), (2)
trials without jury, s. 108(2)
verdicts or questions, s. 108(5)

OFFICIAL GUARDIAN. *See* CHILDREN'S
LAWYER

OFFICERS. *See* ASSESSMENT OFFICERS;
CORPORATIONS; JUDGES AND
OFFICERS

OMISSIONS. *See* ERRORS AND
OMISSIONS

ONTARIO COURT (GENERAL DIVISION).
See also DIVISIONAL COURT; SMALL
CLAIMS COURT; FAMILY COURT
appeal from interlocutory orders, 62.01
appeal from Ontario Court (Provincial
Division)
   appeal record and factum, 70.10(4),
     71.02(5)
   commencement, 70.10(1), 71.02(1)
   filing notice of appeal, 70.10(2), 71.02(3)
   generally, s. 40
appeals to General Division, s. 17
application of rules of court, 1.02(1)
applications
   date of hearing, 38.03(2), (3), (3.1)
   proceeding for administration, 65.01(1)
   to whom made, 38.02
   under rule, 14.05(3)
   under statute, 14.05(2)
Chief Justice of Ontario Court
   absence, s. 14(4)
   meetings with regional senior judges, s.
     14(6)
   powers and duties, s. 14(1)
Commercial List, 37, 38
composition
   generally, s. 12(1)
   hearings, s. 16
default judgment with reference, mortgage
   action, 64.02
directing reference, 54.03(1)
interpleader motions by sheriff, 43.05(6), (7)
judges
   additional judges, s. 12(2)
   assignment of Court of Appeal judges to
     General Division, s. 13
   assignment of General Division judges to
     Court of Appeal, s. 4
   former High Court and District Court
     judges, s. 15(3)
   regional assignment, s. 15
   regional senior judges, s. 14(2), (3), (5), (6)
   supernumerary judges, s. 12(3)
jurisdiction, s. 11(2)
jury trials, s. 108(1)

motions
   jurisdiction, 37.02
   obtaining hearing date, 37.05(1), (2), (3)
   record, 37.10(1)
   to whom made, 37.04
payment into court, 72.02
practice directions, 1.07. *See also* INDEX TO
   PRACTICE DIRECTIONS
proceedings concerning estates of minors,
   67.01
seal, s. 147
sittings outside Toronto, trial list, 48.08
stop orders, 72.05
superior court of record, s. 11(1)
transfer of family law proceedings from
   Provincial Division, 70.09

ONTARIO COURT (PROVINCIAL
DIVISION). *See also* PROVINCIAL
JUDGES
appeals from, generally, s. 40
appeals of family law matters
   appeal record and factum, 70.10(4), (6)
   commencement, 70.10(1)
   filing notice of appeal, 70.10(2)
appeals to General Division generally
   appeal record and factum, 71.02(5)
   commencement, 71.02(1)
   filing notice of appeal, 71.02(3)
   hearing date, 71.02(6)
Chief Judge of Provincial Division
   absence, s. 36(4)
   meetings with regional senior judges, s.
     36(6)
   powers and duties, s. 36(1)
   regional assignment of judges, s. 37
composition, s. 35
criminal jurisdiction, s. 38(1)
disturbance outside courtroom, s. 41
documents filed in French, s. 126(4)
family law, appeals from Provincial Division,
   70.10
presiding officials, s. 39
process in French, s. 126(5)
provincial offences and family jurisdiction, s.
   38(2)
regional senior judges, s. 36(2), (3), (5)
transfer of family law proceedings to General
   Division, 70.09
translation of documents or process into
   French, s. 126(6)
youth court jurisdiction, s. 38(3)

ONTARIO JUDICIAL COUNCIL. *See*
PROVINCIAL JUDGES

ORDERS IN COUNCIL
application for interpretation, 14.05(3)
proceedings for interpretation, representation
    orders, 10.01(1)

ORIGINATING PROCESS
See also ACTIONS; APPLICATIONS;
    COUNTERCLAIMS;
    COUNTERPETITIONS; PETITIONS;
    STATEMENT OF CLAIM; THIRD
    PARTIES
amendment, 14.09
claim for certificate of pending litigation to be
    included, 42.01(2)
commencement of proceeding, 14.01(1)
    exceptions, 14.01(2)
    leave required, 14.01(3)
counterclaim against non-party, 14.03(1), 27.03
counterpetition, 14.04, 69.09(6)
court seal, application, s. 147(2)
definition, s. 1; 1.03
divorce action, 14.04, 69.03(1)
family law proceedings, 70.03
    applicant's financial statements, 70.04(1),
        (2), (5)
filing, 14.07(2)
forms
    counterpetition (against petitoner and
        another person), 69G
    notice of action, 14C
    notice of application, 14E
    notice of application for registration of
        United Kingdom judgment, 73A
    notice of application to Divisional Court for
        judicial review, 68A
    petition for divorce, 69A, 69B
    statement of claim (action commenced by
        notice of action), 14D
    statement of claim (general), 14A
    statement of claim (mortgage action), 14B
generally, 14
inspection of documents mentioned therein,
    30.04(2)
issuance, 4.05(1), 14.07(1)
notice of action, 14.03(2)
notice of application, 14.05(1)
petition for divorce, 14.04, 69.03(1)
reliance on subsequent fact, 14.01(4)
service, 16.01(1)
    impractical, 16.04(1)
    where amended pleading, 26.04(3)
service not required, 16.01(2)
service outside Ontario. *See* SERVICE
    OUTSIDE ONTARIO
statement of claim, 14.03(1)
    simplified procedure, 76.02(3)

striking out or amending, 14.09
third or subsequent party claim, 29.02(1), 29.11
title of proceeding, 14.06(1), (2), (3)
    exception, 14.06(4)
transfer of proceedings from wrong forum, s.
    110

PARTICULARS
demand, 25.10
    trial record, 48.03(1)
financial statement, 69.14(8), 70.04(7)
    sanctions for failure to give, 69.14(9),
        70.04(8)
notice of change of account, 64.06(21)
pleadings, 25.06(8)
    claim for special damages, 25.06(9)
request for sale by subsequent encumbrancers,
    64.03(18), (19)
requested to redeem by subsequent
    encumbrancer, foreclosure action, 64.03(7)
requisition for certificate of stay, 63.03(5)
taking of accounts on references, 55.04(6)

PARTIES
acting in bad faith, motion for summary
    judgment, 20.06(2)
acting in person, service of Children's
    Lawyer's report, 69.16(5)
addition, deletion, substitution amendment of
    pleadings, 26.02
    estate or trust proceedings, 9.01(4)
    intervention by persons not parties, 13.01
administration proceedings, 65.01(1), (2)
adverse
    cross-examination on affidavit, 39.02
    examination for discovery, 31
assignee of chose in action, 5.03(3), 11
bankrupt, 11
conduct during proceeding, consideration in
    awarding costs, 57.01(1)
consent of insurer, payment out of court,
    72.03(6)
corporations, solicitor required, 15.01(2)
correcting name in proceeding, 5.04(2)
costs against successful parties, 57.01(2)
counterclaim, 27.01
    against non-party, 27.03
    against persons already parties, 14.01(2)
    amending defence to add counterclaim,
        27.07
counterpetition
    against non-party, 69.09(6), 69.10(2)
    against person involved in adultery,
        69.09(3)
    against persons already parties, 14.01(2),
        69.09(1), (2), 69.10(1)

PAYMENT INTO COURT — *continued*
receipt from bank, 72.02(7)
references
  deposit for purchase of property, 55.06(9)
  failure to comply when required, 55.07(2)
  purchase money from sale, 55.06(12)
representative proceedings, 12.02
security, motion for interim recovery of
  personal property, 44.03
security for costs, 56.04, 64.03(18)-(21), (25)
specific fund, interim preservation of property,
  45.02
summary judgment, term of order to proceed to
  trial, 20.05(3), (4)
transfer to accountant, 72.02(9)
writ of seizure and sale, 60.07(4)

PAYMENT OUT OF COURT
accountant, definition, 72.01
authority for payment out, 72.03(1)
consent by insurer on behalf of party, 72.03(6)
discharge of a mortgage, 72.04
forms
  affidavit (motion for payment out of court),
    72B
  stop order, 72C
generally, 72.03, 72.04, 72.05
minor attaining age of majority, 72.03(7)
motion by person obtaining stop order,
  72.05(3)
party under disability
  affidavit in support of motion, 72.03(11)
  costs, 72.03(13)
  motion by Children's Lawyer or Public
    Guardian and Trustee, 72.03(12)
  motion for order for payment out, 72.03(10)
  order for maintenance of a minor, 72.03(14)
payment
  directly to solicitor, 72.03(8)
  foreign payee, s. 145
  interest, 72.03(5)
  on consent, 72.03(4)
  personal representative, 72.03(9)
  references, 55.05(2)-(5), 55.06(14)
  stop order, 72.05
  under order or report, 72.03(2), (3)

PENDING LITIGATION. *See*
CERTIFICATES, pending litigation

PERSONAL PROPERTY. *See* PROPERTY

PERSONS
not parties
  approval of settlements affecting, 10.01(3),
    (4)

enforcement of orders against, 60.06(2)
  enforcement of orders by, 60.06(1)
  interim preservation of property, 45.01
  intervention as friend of the court, 13.02
representation orders, 10.01(1)
under disability,
  definition, 1.03
  examination for discovery, 31.03(5),
    31.11(5)
  representation, 7.04

PETITIONERS
See also DIVORCE ACTIONS
affidavit on motion for judgment form, 69R
answer to counterpetition, 69.12(1), (2), (5)
counterpetition for divorce, 69.09
definition, 69.03(3)
financial statements, divorce actions, 69.15(1),
  (2), 69.24
naming place of trial, 69.17(1), (2), (3)
not to effect service of divorce petition,
  69.04(3)

PETITIONS
See also DIVORCE ACTIONS
certificate of marriage or of registration,
  69.03(2), 69.18(a), 69.19(2)(c), (d)
certificate respecting prior pending petitions,
  69.18(b)
counterpetition. *See* COUNTERPETITIONS
defined as originating process, 1.03
financial statement must accompany, 69.14(4)
form, 69A, 69B, 69.03(1)
joinder of person involved in adultery, 69.03(4)
joint petition, 69.03(5)
naming place of trial, 69.17
originating process, 69.03(1)
service
  acknowledgment of service, 69.04(2)
  Children's Lawyer, 69.16(3)
  person alleged involved in adultery,
    69.04(3)
  petitioner not to effect service, 69.04(4)
  respondent, 69.04(1)
  substituted service, 69.04(1)
  substituted service by advertisement,
    69.04(6)
service outside Ontario, 69.04(5)
time for service, 69.05

PLACE OF HEARING
See also APPLICATIONS; MOTIONS
applications
  Landlord and Tenant Act, 38.03(1.1)
  motion to set aside or vary judgment,
    38.11(2)

INDEX TO PRACTICE DIRECTIONS

All references are to the Courts of Justice Act or Rules of Civil Procedure.